Lecture Notes in Computer Science 665

Edited by G. Goos and J. Hartmanis

Advisory Board: W. Brauer   D. Gries   J. Stoer

P. Enjalbert   A. Finkel   K.W. Wagner   (Eds.)

STACS 93

10th Annual Symposium
on Theoretical Aspects of Computer Science
Würzburg, Germany, February 25-27, 1993
Proceedings

Springer-Verlag

Berlin Heidelberg New York
London Paris Tokyo
Hong Kong Barcelona
Budapest

Series Editors

Gerhard Goos
Universität Karlsruhe
Postfach 69 80
Vincenz-Priessnitz-Straße 1
W-7500 Karlsruhe, FRG

Juris Hartmanis
Cornell University
Department of Computer Science
4130 Upson Hall
Ithaca, NY 14853, USA

Volume Editors

Patrice Enjalbert
Université de Caen, Laboratoire d'Informatique
F-14032 Caen Cedex, France

Alain Finkel
ENS Cachan, LIFAC, 61, Avenue du President Wilson
F-94235 Cachan, France

Klaus W. Wagner
Lehrstuhl für Theoretische Informatik, Universität Würzburg
Am Exerzierplatz 3, W-8700 Würzburg, Germany

CR Subject Classification (1991): F, B.2, B.6, D.1, D.4, G.1-2, I.3.5

ISBN 3-540-56503-5 Springer-Verlag Berlin Heidelberg New York
ISBN 0-387-56503-5 Springer-Verlag New York Berlin Heidelberg

© Springer-Verlag Berlin Heidelberg 1993
Printed in Germany

Typesetting: Camera ready by author/editor
Printing and binding: Druckhaus Beltz, Hemsbach/Bergstr.
45/3140-543210 - Printed on acid-free paper

Foreword

The annual Symposium on Theoretical Aspects of Computer Science (STACS) is held each year, alternatively in Germany and France. STACS is organized jointly by the Special Interest Group for Theoretical Computer Science of the Gesellschaft für Informatik (GI) and the Special Interest Group for Applied Mathematics of the Association Française des Sciences et Technologies de l'Information et des Systèmes (afcet).

STACS '93, the tenth in this series, was held in Würzburg, February 25-27, 1993. It was preceded by symposia in Cachan (1992), Hamburg (1991), Rouen (1990), Paderborn (1989), Bordeaux (1988), Passau (1987), Orsay (1986), Saarbrücken (1985), and Paris (1984); the proceedings of all these symposia are published in this Lecture Notes series.

The dramatic increase of the number of submitted papers to 256 and their high scientific quality proves again the great importance of STACS for the Theoretical Computer Science community. The Program Committee decided to keep the ratio of accepted papers at 25%. This, on the one side, has led to the rejection of many good papers. On the other side, the number of 64 short presentations within $2\frac{1}{2}$ days forced us to run them completely in parallel sessions.

We would like to express our gratitude to all members of the Program Committee consisting of H. Bodlaender (Utrecht), M. Crochemore (Paris), P. Enjalbert (Caen, co-chair), A. Finkel (Cachan, co-chair), D. Gouyou-Beauchamps (Paris), J. Karhumäki (Turku), A. de Luca (Roma), M. Rusinowitch (Nancy), A. Salwicki (Pau), E. Shamir (Jerusalem), P. Starke (Berlin), K.W. Wagner (Würzburg, chair), E. Welzl (Berlin), P. Widmayer (Zürich), M. Wirsing (München). The Program Committee selected the papers on the base of over one thousand referee reports. We would like to thank the many referees and all those who submitted papers to this symposium.

STACS '93 offered three invited talks which opened each day of the symposium: Ilaria Castellani (Valbonne): Causal and distributed semantics for concurrent processes; Burkhard Monien (Paderborn): Parallel architecture: design and efficient use; Laszlo Babai (Chicago): Transparent proofs. A number of software systems were presented which showed the possibilities of applying theoretical results to software construction as well as providing a help for doing research.

We acknowledge the help of the following sponsoring institutions and corporations: Deutsche Forschungsgemeinschaft, Bayerische Julius-Maximilians-Universität Würzburg, Vogel Verlag, IBM Deutschland, Fremdenverkehrsamt Würzburg, Castell Bank Würzburg, Keupp, Faber-Castell, and Staedtler-Mars.

Finally we would like to thank the Organizing Committee consisting of J. Albert, G. Buntrock, D. Emme, S. Frank, U. Hertrampf, H. Vollmer, K.W. Wagner, J. Wolff v. Gudenberg (chair) and G. Hoppe (secretary).

Würzburg, January 1993

Patrice Enjalbert
Alain Finkel
Klaus W. Wagner

Referees

S. Abiteboul (Paris), A. Aiello (Napoli), D. Alberts (Berlin), J. P. Allouche (Bordeaux), L. Alonso (Nancy), H. Alt (Berlin), R. Amadio (Nancy), K. Ambos-Spies (Heidelberg), S. Anantharaman (Orleans), K. R. Apt (Amsterdam), A. Arnold (Bordeaux), J.-M. Autebert (Paris), J. Avenhaus (Kaiserslautern), F. Baader (Saarbrücken), P. Balbiani (Toulouse), J. L. Balcázar (Barcelona), G. Baliga (Newark), M. Bauer (Saarbrücken), H. Baumeister (Saarbrücken), M. Beaudoin-Lafon (Orsay), D. Beauquier (Paris), G. Becher (Caen), C. Beeri (Jerusalem), C. Beierle (Stuttgart), R. Beigel (New Haven), M. Ben Or (Jerusalem), U. Berger (München), R. Berghammer (München), C. Berline (Paris), L. Bernardinello (Milano), G. Bernot (Evry), J. Berstel (Paris), D. Bert (Grenoble), E. Bevers (Louvain), N. Bidoit (Villetaneuse), G. Blanc (Marseille), J. Blömer (Berlin), L. Boasson (Paris), M. P. Bonacina (Stony Brook), M. A. Bonuccelli (Roma), R. Book (Santa Barbara), K. Bothe (Berlin), A. Bouajjani (Grenoble), S. Boucheron (Orsay), A. Bouchet (Le Mans), V. Bouchitté (Lyon), G. Boudol (Nice), F. Bouladoux (Paris), P. Bourgine (Antony), F. Boussinot (Nice), Z. Bouziane (Cachan), F.-J. Brandenburg (Passau), A. Brandstädt (Duisburg), S. Brlek (Montréal), C. Brzoska (Karlsruhe), H. Buhrman (Amsterdam), G. Buntrock (Würzburg), E. Burattini (Napoli), H.-D. Burkhard (Berlin), M. Cadoli (Roma), R. Caferra (Grenoble), A. Carpi (Napoli), F. Carrez (Strasbourg), J. Case (Newark), Y. Caseau (Morristown), G. Castagna (Paris), M. Cengarle (München), E. Chang (Stanford), B. Charron-Bost (Paris), J. Chazarain (Nice), C. Choffrut (Paris), E. Clarke (Pittsburgh), F. Clerin-Debart (Caen), L. Colson (Paris), H. Comon (Orsay), M. Coppo (Torino), T. Coquand (Roquencourt), R. Cori (Bordeaux), A. Corradini (Pisa), J.-F. Costa (Lisboa), A. Coste (Toulouse), B. Courcelle (Bordeaux), G. Cousineau (Paris), C. Crépeau (Paris), P.-L. Curien (Paris), I. Dahn (Berlin), W. Damm (Oldenburg), P. Darondeau (Rennes), A. Datta (Saarbrücken), M. T. de Berg (Utrecht), L. De Floriani (Genova), P. de Groote (Nancy), W. F. De La Vega (Orsay), R. De Nicola (Roma), M. de Rougemont (Orsay), A. De Santis (Salerno), R. De Simone (Nice), F. Dederichs (München), P. Degano (Pisa), F. Dehne (Ottawa), P. Dehornoy (Caen), M. Delest (Bordeaux), C. Delorme (Orsay), J. Denzinger (Kaiserslautern), N. Dershowitz (Jerusalem), D. Deschreye (Louvain), P. Devienne (Lille), O. Devillers (Valbonne), J. Devolder (Lille), M. Dezani-Ciancaglini (Torino), G. Di Battista (Roma), J. Díaz (Barcelona), M. Dietzfelbinger (Paderborn), E. Domenjoud (Nancy), W. Dosch (Augsburg), G. Dowek (Austin), D. Dranidis (München), D. Dubois (Toulouse), G. Duchamp (Paris), S. Dulucq (Bordeaux), J. P. Duval (Rouen), H. Edelsbrunner (Champaign), H. Ehler (München), P. van Emde Boas (Amsterdam), J. Engelfriet (Leiden), M. Eytan (Strasbourg), A. Fabri (Valbonne), E. Fachini (Roma), F. Fages (Paris), D. Fayard (Orsay), S. Fei (Zürich), S. Felsner (Berlin), G. Ferrand (Orleans), A. Ferreira (Lyon), R. Fessler (Zürich), P. Fiorini (Arcueil), P. Flajolet (Rocquencourt), W.-J. Fokkink (Amsterdam), M. Formann (Berlin), P. Fraigniaud (Lyon), Y. Freund (Santa Cruz), L. Fribourg (Paris), C. Froidevaux (Orsay), C. Frougny (Paris), U. Furbach (Koblenz), J. Gabarró (Barcelona),

B. Gärtner (Berlin), Z. Galil (New York), D. Galmiche (Nancy), L. Gang (Montréal), D. Gardy (Orsay), L. Gasiennec (Warszawa), P. Gastin (Paris), F. Gecseg (Turku), M. Gelfond (El Paso), C. Germain (Orsay), A. Geser (Ulm), R. Ghavamizadeh (Cachan), G. Ghelli (Pisa), E.-G. Giessmann (Berlin), S. Gnesi (Pisa), A. Gomolinska (Warszawa), P. Goralcik (Rouen), R. Gore (Manchester), G. Gottlob (Wien), E. Gradel (Basel), A. Grazon (Rennes), S. Grigorieff (Paris), V. Grolmusz (Saarbrücken), I. Guessarian (Paris), J. Gustedt (Berlin), P. J. M. van Haaften (Utrecht), S. Haber (Bellcore), T. Hagerup (Barcelona), A. Hallmann (Dortmund), T. Harju (Turku), J.-J. Hebrard (Caen), A. Hefner (Passau), W. Heinle (München), L. Hemachandra (Rochester), R. Hennicker (München), T. Herman (Utrecht), H. Herre (Leipzig), U. Hertrampf (Trier), D. Hofbauer (Berlin), F. Hoffmann (Berlin), J. Honkala (Turku), P. Hoogers (Leiden), P. Horster (Karlsruhe), J. Hromkovič (Paderborn), F. Huber (Zürich), G. Huet (Roquencourt), C. Huizing (Eindhoven), H. Hussman (München), E. Ihrer (Zürich), C. Iliopoulos (London), N. Immerman (New Haven), P. Inverardi (Pisa), M. Jantzen (Hamburg), B. Josko (Oldenburg), M. Jünger (Köln), V. Kann (Stockholm), G. Kant (Utrecht), J. Kari (Turku), L. Kari (Turku), J. Karkzmarczuk (Caen), M. Karpinski (Bonn), J. Katajainen (Turku), M. Kaufmann (Passau), C. Kenyon (Lyon), H. Kirchner (Nancy), L. M. Kirousis (Patras), R. Klasing (Paderborn), J. Kleijn (Leiden), R. Klein (Hagen), P. Kleinschmidt (Passau), T. Kloks (Utrecht), T. Knapik (Paris), J. Köbler (Ulm), J. N. Kok (Utrecht), J.-C. Konig (Orsay), K. Kriegel (Berlin), J.-L. Krivine (Paris), D. Krob (Paris), F. Kröger (München), G. Kucherov (Nancy), A. Labella (Roma), J.-L. Lambert (Caen), J. Lang (Toulouse), S. Lange (Leipzig), K.-J. Lange (München), R. Langerak (Enschede), E. Laporte (Paris), C. Lavault (Rennes), U. Lechner (Passau), T. Lecroq (Paris), C. Lengauer (Passau), M. Lenzerini (Roma), A. Lepistö (Turku), C. Lerman (Rennes), P. Lescanne (Nancy), L. Lestrée (Paris), J. Lilius (Helsinki), N. Lindenstraus (Jerusalem), N. Linial (Jerusalem), I. Litovsky (Bordeaux), M. Löwe (Berlin), S. Loffreda (Cachan), S. Loiseau (Orsay), E. Lozinski (Jerusalem), F. Luccio (Pisa), D. Lugiez (Nancy), J. Madelaine (Caen), J. A. Makowsky (Haifa), L. Mandel (München), I. Manoussakis (Orsay), A. Marchetti-Spaccamela (Roma), J.-Y. Marion (Paris), P. Marquis (Nancy), B. Martens (Louvain), A. Mateescu (Turku), J. Matoušek (Praha), E. Mayordomo (Barcelona), E. Mayr (Frankfurt), J. Mazoyer (Lyon), K. Mehlhorn (Saarbrücken), D. Mery (Nancy), S. Merz (München), Y. Métivier (Bordeaux), J. J. C. Meyer (Amsterdam), F. Meyer auf der Heide (Paderborn), P. Michel (Paris), P. Miglioli (Milano), P. B. Miltersen (Aarhus), E. Minicozzi (Napoli), G. Mirkowska (Pau), D. A. Mix Barrington (Amherst), R. Möhring (Berlin), B. Möller (Augsburg), Y. Moinard (Rennes), C. Montagero (Pisa), T. Mora (Genova), A. Morgana (Roma), M. Morvan (Montpellier), Y. Moses (Rehovot), A. Mück (München), W. Müller (Berlin), D. Mundici (Milano), A. Munier (Orsay), J. F. Myoupo (Orsay), A. Napoli (Nancy), K.-P. Neuendorf (Berlin), V. H. Nguyen (Zürich), F. Nickl (München), X. Nicollin (Grenoble), R. Niedermeier (München), M. Nielsen (Aarhus), V. Niemi (Turku), O. Nurmi (Helsinki), W. Nutt (Saarbrücken), C. O'D'unlaing (Dublin), S. Öhring (Würzburg), H. J. Ohlbach (Saarbrücken), T. Ohler (Zürich), L. Ojala (Helsinki), J. Opatrny (Montréal), F. Orejas

(Barcelona), P. Orponen (Helsinki), L. Pacholski (Wrocław), P. Padawitz (Dortmund), M. Parigot (Paris), F. Parisi-Presice (L'Aquila), K. Park (London), V. T. Paschos (Paris), D. Pastre (Paris), C. Paulin-Mohring (Lyon), P. Péladeau (Paris), F. Pellegrini (Bordeaux), E. Pelz (Orsay), G. Penaud (Bordeaux), G. R. Perrin (Besançon), D. Perrin (Paris), J.-F. Perrot (Paris), G. Persiano (Salerno), U. Petermann (Leipzig), H. Peterreins (München), A. Petit (Orsay), M. Penttonen (Joensuu), C. Peyrat (Nice), M. Pezzè (Milano), G. Pighizzini (Milano), J. E. Pin (Paris), G. Plateau (Villetaneuse), M. Pocchiola (Paris), L. Popova-Zeugmann (Berlin), A. Preller (Montpellier), V. Prince (Cachan), M. Protasi (Roma), C. Puech (Paris), A. Quéré (Nancy), H. Rahbar (Caen), L. Ramshaw (Palo Alto), D. Ranjan (Saarbrücken), C. Rank (Passau), J.-C. Raoult (Beaulieu), A. Raspaud (Bordeaux), M. Rauhamaa (Helsinki), M. Régnier (Rocquencourt), R. Reischuk (Darmstadt), W. Reisig (München), A. Renvall (Turku), A. Restivo (Palermo), B. Reus (München), J.-M. Rifflet (Paris), C. Ringeissen (Nancy), J. Roman (Bordeaux), S. Ronchi Della Rocca (Torino), T. Roos (Zürich), P. Rossmanith (München), V. Royer (Toulouse), B. Rozoy (Orsay), L. Rudolph (Jerusalem), N. Saheb (Bordeaux), A. Salibra (Pisa), A. Salomaa (Turku), Y. Sami (Orsay), M. Santha (Orsay), A. Saoudi (Villetaneuse), J. Saquet (Caen), J. Sauloy (Toulouse), M. Schäffter (Berlin), R. Schapire (Cambridge), K.-D. Schewe (Hamburg), G. Schmidt (Saarbrücken), P. H. Schmitt (Karlsruhe), P.-Y. Schobbens (Nancy), U. Schöning (Ulm), O. Schoett (München), K. Schulz (München), J. Schulze (Paderborn), J. Schumann (München), A. Schuster (Haifa), O. Schwarzkopf (Utrecht), P. Séébold (Paris), R. Seidel (Berkeley), G. Sénizergues (Bordeaux), O. Serra (Barcelona), A. Sgarro (Trieste), J. Sibeyn (Saarbrücken), D. Siefkes (Berlin), B. Simeone (Roma), L. Škarvada (Brno), G. Smolka (Saarbrücken), W. Snyder (Boston), P. Sole (Nice), M. Soria (Paris), P. Spirakis (Patras), R. Stabl (München), B. Steffen (Aachen), M. Steinby (Turku), B. von Stengel (München) J. Stern (Paris), J.-M. Steyaert (Palaiseau), C. Stirling (Edinburgh), H. Straubing (Boston), T. Streicher (München), V. S. Subramanian (Maryland), G. Tel (Utrecht), I. Tellier (Cachan), J. Thibon (Paris), C. Thiel (Saarbrücken), L. Thimonier (Amiens), W. Thomas (Kiel), M. Tiusanen (Helsinki), H. Tolba (Nancy), J. Torán (Barcelona), L. Torenvliet (Amsterdam), R. Treinen (Saarbrücken), E. Ukkonen (Helsinki), J. Ullman (Stanford), B. Vallée (Caen), P. Valtr (Berlin), M. Vardi (Almaden), S. Varicchio (L'Aquila), J. Vauzeilles (Villetaneuse), M. Veldhorst (Utrecht), F. Ventriglia (Napoli), B. Victorri (Caen), G. Vidal-Naquet (Marcoussis), P. Vitanyi (Amsterdam), J. S. Vitter (Providence), H. Vogler (Ulm), W. Vogler (München), H. Volger (Passau), H. Vollmer (Würzburg), S. Vorobyov (Nancy), S. Waack (Dortmund), P. A. Wacrenier (Lille), D. Wagner (Berlin), F. Wagner (Berlin), E. Wanke (Paderborn), M. Warmuth (Santa Cruz), R. Weber (Heidelberg), I. Wegener (Dortmund), P. Weil (Paris), V. Weispfenning (Heidelberg), M. Werman (Jerusalem), L. Wernisch (Berlin), R. Wiehagen (Berlin), A. Wigderson (Jerusalem), P. Winter (København), B. Wolfers (Berlin), P. Wolper (Liège), M. Yvinec (Valbonne), W. Zielonka (Bordeaux), M. Zipstein (Paris), V. Zissimopoulos (Orsay).

Table of Contents

Friday, February 26, 1993

Saturday, February 27, 1993

Invited Talk:

Session 7A: Circuit Complexity
Chair: Andrzej Salwicki (Pau)

Session 7B: ω-Automata
Chair: Aldo de Luca (Roma)

Causal and Distributed Semantics
for
Concurrent Processes

Ilaria Castellani

INRIA Sophia-Antipolis
2004, Route des Lucioles
F-06565 Valbonne Cedex – France

Distributed semantics for concurrent systems, accounting for the spatial distribution of processes, focus on different aspects of behaviour than causal semantics, although both fall in the general class of non-interleaving or "true-concurrency" descriptions of systems. Roughly speaking, a distributed semantics keeps track of the locality of different parts of behaviour and thus is appropriate for describing phenomena like a local deadlock in some component; on the other hand a causal semantics is concerned with the flow of causality among activities and thus is better suited to model the interaction of processes and the global control structure of a system.

In this talk I shall concentrate on a distributed semantics for CCS, which is based on a static notion of location. The idea is that the actions of a system are observed together with the location at which they occur. This semantics, and the notion of equivalence it induces, will be compared with earlier distributed semantics and with a well known causality-based equivalence, the history preserving bisimulation.

The Alternation Hierarchy for Sublogarithmic Space: An Exciting Race to STACS'93

Klaus W. Wagner

In 1988 Szelepcsényi [Sze88] and Immerman [Imm88] proved that nondeterministic space classes are closed under complementation (and therefore the alternation hierarchy for space classes collapses to the Σ_1-level, i.e. to nondeterministic space).

However, this result was proved only for space bounds $s(n) \geq \log n$, and it was not clear at this time how the alternation hierarchy for sublogarithmic space behaves. In the sequel, several authors or groups of authors attacked this problem completely independently and without knowing about the efforts of the others. In summer 1992, there existed three independent partial solutions to this problem with several stages of improvements, and now, at the end of 1992 there are three announcements about the complete solution to the problem of whether the alternation hierarchy for sublogarithmic space is infinite. This note tries to give a chronology of the events in this exciting race.

By strong-Σ_kSPACE(s) and strong-Π_kSPACE(s) we denote the Σ_k-level and Π_k-level, resp., of the alternation hierarchy for two-way machines with strong space bound s, where by weak-Σ_kSPACE(s) and weak-Π_kSPACE(s), we denote the Σ_k-level and Π_k-level, resp., of the alternation hierarchy for weak space bound s. For exact definitions, see the two subsequent papers [Bra93, LiRe93]. We only give an idea about the difference between strong space bounds and weak space bounds (which is irrelevant for constructible bounds $s(n) \geq \log n$). Strong space bound s: for every input of length n, every configuration reached for this input has worktape bound $s(n)$. Weak space bound s: for all accepted inputs of length n, there exists an accepting computation tree in which every configuration has worktape bound $s(n)$. It is evident that strong-Σ_kSPACE$(s) \subseteq$ weak-Σ_kSPACE(s) and strong-Π_kSPACE$(s) \subseteq$ weak-Π_kSPACE(s) for every k.

For better understanding of the following results let us mention two points in which the world below $\log n$ might differ from the world above (there are even more such points; the world below $\log n$ seems to be the Hades of complexity theory): it is not known whether strong-Σ_kSPACE(s) is the class of complements of the sets from strong-Π_kSPACE(s), and it is not known whether strong-Σ_kSPACE$(s) =$ strong-Π_kSPACE(s) implies the collapse of the alternation hierarchy to the class strong-Σ_kSPACE(s). (The same is not known for the weak classes.)

Here is the chronology of events:

(1) K. Iwama [Iwa86] proves

$$\text{strong-}\Pi_4\text{SPACE}(\log\log n) \setminus \text{weak-}\Sigma_1\text{SPACE}(o(\log n)) \neq \emptyset.$$

Thus the alternation hierarchy for every strong space bound s cannot collapse to the first level.

(2) J.H. Chang, O.H. Ibarra, B. Ravikumar, and L. Berman [CIRB87] show

$$\text{strong-}\Pi_2\text{SPACE}(\log\log n) \setminus \text{weak-}\Sigma_1\text{SPACE}(o(\log n)) \neq \emptyset,$$

whereas A. Ito, K. Inoue, and I. Takanami [IIT87] prove

$$\text{strong-}\Sigma_2\text{SPACE}(\log\log n) \setminus \text{weak-}\Pi_1\text{SPACE}(o(\log n)) \neq \emptyset.$$

(3) In summer 1991, B. von Braunmühl proves in his habilitation thesis [Bra91] that

$$\text{strong-}\Sigma_k\text{SPACE}(\log\log n) \setminus \text{weak-}\Pi_k\text{SPACE}(o(\log n)) \neq \emptyset \quad \text{for } k = 2, 3, \text{ and}$$
$$\text{strong-}\Pi_k\text{SPACE}(\log\log n) \setminus \text{weak-}\Sigma_k\text{SPACE}(o(\log n)) \neq \emptyset \quad \text{for } k = 2, 3, 4.$$

Thus, the alternation hierarchy for strong bound s as well as for weak bound s cannot collapse to a level lower than the fifth. These results have been submitted to STACS'93 and appear in this volume [Bra93]. (In [Bra91] it is also proved that the alternation hierarchy for one-way machines with weak bounds between $\log\log n$ and $o(\log n)$ is infinite. I concentrate on the two-way model which I consider to be more natural.)

(4) In spring 1992, V. Geffert [Gef92] proves independently of [Bra91] that

$$\text{strong-}\Sigma_2\text{SPACE}(\log\log n) \setminus \text{strong-}\Pi_2\text{SPACE}(o(\log n)) \neq \emptyset, \quad \text{and}$$
$$\text{strong-}\Pi_2\text{SPACE}(\log\log n) \setminus \text{strong-}\Sigma_2\text{SPACE}(o(\log n)) \neq \emptyset.$$

This paper was not submitted to STACS'93, and it is not clear to me whether it appeared in another conference proceedings or journal. Geffert uses a method which he has developed in [Gef91].

(5) In summer 1992, M. Liśkiewicz and R. Reischuk [LiRe92a] prove the result mentioned under (4) independently of [Bra91] and [Gef92], but also using the method of [Gef91]. The paper [LiRe92a] was submitted to STACS'93. (By the way, it also includes the results

$$\text{weak-}\Sigma_k\text{SPACE}(\log\log n) \setminus \text{strong-}\Sigma_k\text{SPACE}(o(\log n)) \neq \emptyset \quad \text{for } k \geq 0, \text{ and}$$
$$\text{weak-}\Pi_k\text{SPACE}(\log\log n) \setminus \text{strong-}\Pi_k\text{SPACE}(o(\log n)) \neq \emptyset \quad \text{for } k \geq 0.)$$

(6) In autumn 1992, M. Liśkiewicz and R. Reischuk extend their results and show (still not knowing about [Bra91] and [Gef92]) that

$$\text{strong-}\Sigma_3\text{SPACE}(\log\log n) \setminus \text{strong-}\Pi_3\text{SPACE}(o(\log n)) \neq \emptyset, \quad \text{and}$$
$$\text{strong-}\Pi_3\text{SPACE}(\log\log n) \setminus \text{strong-}\Sigma_3\text{SPACE}(o(\log n)) \neq \emptyset.$$

This theorem has been included in the paper which appears in this volume [LiRe93]. At this point I informed von Braunmühl and Reischuk of the existence of the other papers and results. This seemingly has sped up the race.

(7) On December 18, 1992, von Braunmühl sends me an abstract [BGR92] in which it is announced that

$$\text{strong-}\Sigma_k\text{SPACE}(\log\log n) \setminus \text{weak-}\Pi_k\text{SPACE}(s) \neq \emptyset \quad \text{for } k \geq 2, \text{ and}$$
$$\text{strong-}\Pi_k\text{SPACE}(\log\log n) \setminus \text{weak-}\Sigma_k\text{SPACE}(s) \neq \emptyset \quad \text{for } k \geq 2.$$

Thus the alternation hierarchy for strong bound s as well as for weak bound s is infinite. The witness languages and methods are those used in [Bra91, Bra93].

(8) On December 30, 1992, Reischuk tells me on the phone that he and Liśkiewicz proved that

$$\text{strong-}\Sigma_k\text{SPACE}(\log\log n) \setminus \text{strong-}\Pi_k\text{SPACE}(s) \neq \emptyset \quad \text{for } k \geq 2, \text{ and}$$
$$\text{strong-}\Pi_k\text{SPACE}(\log\log n) \setminus \text{strong-}\Sigma_k\text{SPACE}(s) \neq \emptyset \quad \text{for } k \geq 2.$$

(9) On December 31, 1992, on my request, von Braunmühl faxes me the handwritten manuscript with full proofs, and, 90 minutes later, Reischuk faxes me a 6 page extended abstract [LiRe92b] with outlines of the proofs.

(10) On January 6, 1993, an e-mail from V. Geffert (bearing the date of October 17, 1992) came to my knowledge, in which he already announced the results mentioned under (9) and where he wrote that he had sent the proofs for checking to B. Rovan and R. Szelepcsényi (Bratislava).

It is interesting to note that the method used in [Bra91, Bra93, BGR92] differs considerably from the method used in [Gef91, Gef92, LiRe92a, LiRe93, LiRe92b]. One main difference is the following: The first method uses witness languages which are even in the corresponding one-way classes (and thus automatically yield the corresponding one-way results), which is at least not obviously possible with the second method. This method, on the other side, uses witness languages having a simple block structure which seems to be closer to tally languages.

What remains still open? It is quite a curiosity that we know strong-Σ_kSPACE(s) $\neq$ strong-Π_kSPACE(s) and weak-Σ_kSPACE(s) $\neq$ weak-Π_kSPACE(s) for every $k \geq$ 2, but we do not know whether this is true for $k = 1$. Furthermore, it is not clear whether the hierarchies remain infinite if we consider only tally languages.

Acknowledgement. I am grateful to Heribert Vollmer, Würzburg, for stimulating discussions and technical help during the preparation of this note.

References

[Bra91]   Braunmühl, B. von, Alternationshierarchien von Turingmaschinen mit kleinem Speicher, habilitation thesis, Bonn, Juni 1991.

[Bra93]   Braunmühl, B. von, Alternation for two-way machines with sublogarithmic space, this volume.

[BGR92]   Braunmühl, B. von, Gengler, R., Rettinger, R., The alternation hierarchy for two-way machines with sublogarithmic space is infinite, abstract, December 1992.

[CIRB87]   Chang, J.H., Ibarra, O.H., Ravikumar, B., Berman, L., Some observations concerning alternating Turing machines using small space, IPL 25 (1987), 1–9; Erratum 27 (1988), 53.

[Gef91]   Geffert, V., Nondeterministic computations in sublogarithmic space and space constructibility, SIAM J. Comput. 20 (1991), 484–498.

[Gef92]   Geffert, V., Sublogarithmic Σ_2-space is not closed under complementation and other separation results, technical report, Šafárik University, Košice 1992.

[Imm88]   Immerman, N., Nondeterministic space ic closed under complementation, SIAM J. Comput. 7 (1988), 935–938.

[IIT87]   Ito, A., Inoue, K., Takanami, I., A note on alternating Turing machines using small space. The Transactions of the IEICE E 70 no. 10, (1987), 990–996.

[Iwa86]   Iwama, K., ASPACE($o(loglog)$) is regular, research report, KSU/ICS Kyoto Sangyo University, Kyoto 1986.

[LiRe92a] Liśkiewicz, M., Reischuk, R., Separating the lower levels of the sublogarithmic space hierarchy, manuscript, summer 92 (submitted to STACS'93).

[LiRe92b] Liśkiewicz, M., Reischuk, R., The sublogarithmic space hierarchy is infinite, extended abstract, December 1992.

[LiRe93]   Liśkiewicz, M., Reischuk, R., Separating the lower levels of the sublogarithmic space hierarchy, this volume.

[Sze88]   Szelepcsényi, R., The method of forced enumeration for nondeterministic automata, Acta Informatica 26 (1988), 279–284.

Alternation for Two-way Machines with Sublogarithmic Space

Burchard von Braunmühl

Institut für Informatik I, Universität Bonn
Römerstrasse 164, D-5300 Bonn 1

Abstract. The alternation hierarchy for two-way Turing machines with a space bound in o(log) does not collapse below level five.

1 Introduction

In structural complexity theory many hierarchies have been considered but only seldom results have about their extension been found. Of course some negative results are well known. E.g. all oracle hierarchies and, therefore, all alternation hierarchies related to space-bounded machines collapse, provided that we consider strong space complexity and space-bounds in $\Omega(\log)$ [Imm88],[Sze88]. The strong exponential time hierarchy SEH collapses in P^{NE} [Hem87],[SW88] and so does the hierarchy $IP(k)$ $(k \in \mathbb{N})$ of interactive proof systems [BM88].

Positive answers are even more rare, although some interrelations between hierarchies have been detected. A separation has been achieved for the circuit classes AC^0 and AC^1 [Yao85],[Has86], whereas within AC^0 there is a proper hierarchy related to circuit depth. This corresponds to the hierarchy of logarithmic time-bounded alternating Turing machines with random access input tape. The nondeterministic space hierarchy of Turing machines leads to a proper alternation hierarchy which is related to reversal-bounded one-tape Turing machines without input tape [LL89].

Although we know that the alternation hierarchies for Turing machines with space-bound log or greater collapse, the question remains whether a hierarchy for space-bounds less than log exists. For one-way Turing machines with an arbitrary space-bound in o(log) an infinite alternation hierarchy has been established [Bra91].

This paper deals with the corresponding issue concerning two-way Turing machines. We shall show that the alternation hierarchy for two-way Turing machines with a space-bound in o(log) does not collapse below level five.

2 Notations

In this section we collect the bulk of notations and introduce several expressions. We would ask the reader to refer to this part of the paper if need be.

Let $Q^\forall, Q^\exists, \Gamma$ be disjoint finite sets not containing the symbol $\square$ (blank). Let $Q := Q^\forall \cup Q^\exists$, $\Sigma \subseteq \Gamma$, $\delta \subseteq Q \times \Sigma \cup \{\square\} \times \Gamma \cup \{\square\} \times Q \times \Gamma \times \{-1, 0, 1\} \times \{-1, 0, 1\}$

and q^0, q^e elements of Q. Then we call the relational structure
$$M := (Q^\forall, Q^\exists, \Gamma, \Sigma, \delta, q^0, q^e, \square, -1, 0, 1)$$
an *alternating (two-way) Turing machine* (2ATM). We call the elements of Q *states*, those of $Q^\forall$ $\forall$-*states*, those of $Q^\exists$ $\exists$-*states*, those of Σ *input symbols*, those of Γ *work symbols* and those of δ *instructions*. We call q^0 the *start state* and q^e the *accepting state*. M is an alternating *one-way* Turing machine (1ATM) if every instruction $(q, a, A, q', d_1, d_2) \in \delta$ satisfies $d_1 \in \{0, 1\}$. We call
$$C_M := \{(q, W, \mu) \mid q \in Q, W \in \Gamma^*, \mu \in [0, |W|+1]\}$$
the set of *configurations* of M.

We call $s = (c, p)$ a situation of M if $c \in C_M$ and $p \in \mathbb{N}$. p is the input position of s and is noted by $pos(s)$. A configuration c (situation s) is of *type* $\forall$ if its state is a $\forall$-state, and of *type* $\exists$ if its state is a $\exists$-state. $s_0 = (q^0, \varepsilon, 0, 1)$ is the *start situation* of M.

For $w \in \Sigma^*$ and situations s and s' we employ $s \vdash_{M}^{w} s'$ in the usual way. s is called *stop situation* for input w if there is no situation s' with $s \vdash_{M}^{w} s'$. s is an *accepting* or *rejecting* situation for input w if s is a stop situation for w with state q^e or $\neq q^e$) respectively. π is a *(computation) path* for input w if π is a sequence $s_1, s_2, s_3, \ldots$ of situations of M with $s_i \vdash_{M}^{w} s_{i+1}$ $(i = 1, 2, 3, \ldots)$. π *leads from* situation s_1 *to* situation s_n if π finite and s_n is the last situation in π. A *success path* is a maximal path which terminates with an accepting situation. T is a *success tree* of M for input w rooted in situation s if T is a finite tree with nodes labelled by situations such that the following holds true:

(1) The root is labelled by s and every leaf is labelled by an accepting situation.
(2) If a node r is labelled by a $\forall$-situation s_0 and $s_1, \ldots, s_k$ are the immediate successors of s_0 with respect to $\vdash_{M}^{w}$ then r has exactly k sons $r_1, \ldots, r_k$ labelled by $s_1, \ldots, s_k$.
(3) If a node r is labelled by an $\exists$-situation s_0 other than a stop situation for w then r has one son exactly which is labelled by an immediate $\vdash_{M}^{w}$-successor of s_0.

M *accepts* the input w if there is a success tree of M for w rooted in the start situation s^0. The *language* of M is $L(M) := \{w \in \Sigma^* \mid M \text{ accepts } w\}$. An *alternation* in a path π or in a success tree T is a node, with a predecessor of the other type and with at least one successor. *Alter*(π) is the number of the alternations in the path π. The path π is *alternation-free* if the alternation number is zero. The *alternation depth alter*(T) of a success tree T is the maximal number of alternations of a path in T. The space cost *cost*(c) of a configuration c (*cost*(s) of a situation s) is the length of its working tape. The cost of a computation π (*cost*(π)) is the maximal cost of any of its situations. *cost*(T) is defined analogously. C_M^b is the set of the configurations of M with cost b.

We use a machine constant c_M of M defined by $c_M := 2 \log |\Gamma| + |Q| + 1$. Note that $|C_M^b| \leq 2^{c_M b}$. A configuration c (situation s) is *b-bounded* if $cost(c) \leq b$ ($cost(s) \leq b$). A path π is *b,k-bounded* if $cost(\pi) \leq b$ and $alter(\pi) \leq k$. T is a *b, k-success tree* if $cost(T) \leq b$ and $alter(T) \leq k$. k is omitted if it is clear from the context. T is a *b, k-bounded success tree* of M for w. The situation s is *b, k-successful for input* w if there is a *b, k*-success tree for w rooted in s.

Let f be an arithmetic function and $r \in \mathbb{N}$. M is an f, r–bounded alternating Turing machine if the start situation s^0 is $f(|w|), r$–successful for all $w \in L(M)$. If all paths starting at s^0 are $f(|w|), r$–bounded for all inputs $w \in \Sigma^*$, we call M a *strongly* f, r–bounded Turing machine. M is a $2\Sigma_r[f]$–TM ($2\Pi_r[f]$–TM) if M is an f, r–bounded 2ATM and the start situation s^0 is of type $\exists$ (of type $\forall$). $2\Sigma_r[f]$ and $2\Pi_r[f]$ are the classes of languages recognized by $2\Sigma_r[f]$–Turing machines and $2\Pi_r[f]$–Turing machines respectively.

M is a *normal* $2\Sigma_r[f]$–TM ($2\Pi_r[f]$–TM) if

(i) every stop situation for input w has position $|w| + 1$ (a path terminates only on the blank right of w), if

(ii) there is no infinite alternation-free path with all situations on the same position, and if

(iii) all maximal paths starting in the start situation of M contain $r - 1$ alternations exactly.

Note: For each $2\Sigma_r[f]$–TM ($2\Pi_r[f]$–TM) there is a normal version which recognizes the same language. These notions also apply to $1\Sigma_r$ and $1\Pi_r$.

Finally we lay down the following notations:

$b_i :=$ mirror of the binary representation of i ($|b_i| = \lfloor \log i \rfloor + 1$)

$\mathrm{Bin}(n) = b_1 \overset{1}{\#} b_2 \overset{1}{\#} \ldots \overset{1}{\#} b_n$

($|\mathrm{Bin}(n)| := \lfloor \log 1 \rfloor + \cdots + \lfloor \log n \rfloor + 2n - 1 < n \log n + 2n + 1 < 2n \log n$ if $n > 8$)

For arithmetic functions f, g we write:

$$f \prec g \quad \text{iff} \quad f \in o(g) \quad \text{iff} \quad \lim_{n \to \infty} (f(n)/g(n)) = 0$$

$$f \underset{\sim}{\prec} g \quad \text{iff} \quad g \notin O(f) \quad \text{iff} \quad \liminf_{n \to \infty} (f(n)/g(n)) = 0$$

3 Summary and the upper bounds

We begin with the definition of our witness languages. We have (infinitely many) special symbols $\overset{i}{\#}$ ($i \in \mathbb{N}$). Let $\Sigma := \{0, 1\}$ and $\Sigma_r := \Sigma \cup \{\#\} \cup \{\overset{i}{\#} \mid i \in \mathbb{N}, \ i \leq r\}$.

Let $\quad D_1 := \Sigma^*$ and

$\quad D_i := (D_{i-1}\{\overset{i}{\#}\})^* \cdot D_{i-1} \quad (i \geq 2)$,

$\exists D_1(u) := \forall D_1(u) := \{u\}, \quad$ and, for $i \geq 2$,

$\exists D_i(u) := \{W_1 \overset{i}{\#} \ldots \overset{i}{\#} W_m \in D_i \mid \exists i \ \ W_i \in \forall D_{i-1}(u), \ m \in \mathbb{N}\}$ and

$\forall D_i(u) := \{W_1 \overset{i}{\#} \ldots \overset{i}{\#} W_m \in D_i \mid \forall i \ \ W_i \in \exists D_{i-1}(u), \ m \in \mathbb{N}\}$.

Now we define the following languages:

$L_i^{\exists} := \bigcup \{\exists D_i(u) \cdot \{\overset{1}{\#} u \overset{1}{\#} \mathrm{Bin}(n)\}\{\#\}^* \mid u \in \Sigma^{\log n - 1}, \ n \in \mathbb{N}\} \quad (i \geq 2)$

$L_i^{\forall} := \bigcup \{\forall D_i(u) \cdot \{\overset{1}{\#} u \overset{1}{\#} \mathrm{Bin}(n)\}\{\#\}^* \mid u \in \Sigma^{\log n - 1}, \ n \in \mathbb{N}\} \quad (i \geq 2)$

Example:

$L_2^{\exists} = \{w_1 \overset{2}{\#} \ldots \overset{2}{\#} w_m \overset{1}{\#} u \overset{1}{\#} \mathrm{Bin}(n)\#^* \mid u \in \Sigma^{\log n - 1}; \ n, m \in \mathbb{N}; \ \forall i \ w_i \in \Sigma^*, \ \exists i \ w_i = u\}$

We shall show

$L_2^{\exists} \in 1\Sigma_2[\log \log]$ but $\notin 2\Pi_2[\underset{\sim}{\prec} \log]$, $\quad L_2^{\forall} \in 1\Pi_2[\log \log]$ but $\notin 2\Sigma_2[\underset{\sim}{\prec} \log]$,

$L_3^{\exists} \in 1\Sigma_3[\log \log]$ but $\notin 2\Pi_3[\underset{\sim}{\prec} \log]$, $\quad L_3^{\forall} \in 1\Pi_3[\log \log]$ but $\notin 2\Sigma_3[\underset{\sim}{\prec} \log]$,

$L_4^{\forall} \in 1\Pi_4[\log \log]$ but $\notin 2\Sigma_4[\underset{\sim}{\prec} \log]$

Hence the classes $2\Sigma_k[f]$ and $2\Pi_k[f]$, and even $2\Sigma_k[f]$ and $1\Pi_k[f]$, as well as $1\Sigma_k[f]$ and $2\Pi_k[f]$ ($k = 2, 3$) are incomparable and the class $2\Pi_4[f]$ and all the classes above are not contained in $2\Sigma_4[f]$. Thus it follows from $2\Sigma_2[f] \not\subseteq 1A[f]$ [IIT87] that the classes $2\Sigma_4[f]$ and $1\Pi_4[f]$ are incomparable, too. This holds for weak space complexity as well as for strong space complexity (see the note at the end of this section).

First we shall consider the upper bounds. The following is more general than actually needed.

Theorem 1. $\quad L_i^{\exists} \in 1\Sigma_i[\log\log]$ *and* $L_i^{\forall} \in 1\Pi_i[\log\log]$ $(i \geq 2)$

The proof is by induction. It is straightforward and left to the reader. For $L_2^{\exists}$ and $L_2^{\forall}$ we find analogous assertions in [IIT87].

Note that a two-way strongly $\log\log$–space bounded Turing machine can decide the language $\{\text{Bin}(n) \mid n \in \mathbb{N}\}$ deterministically [LSH65]. Therefore the languages $L_k^{\exists}$ and $L_k^{\forall}$ $(k \in \mathbb{N})$ can be accepted by strongly $\log\log$–bounded $2\Sigma_k$–Turing machines, too.

4 The second level of the hierarchy

Definition 2 table. Let M be a 2ATM and C_M^b the set of its configurations with cost b. For any $w \in (\Sigma \cup \frac{2}{\#})^*$ and any cost $b \in \mathbb{N}$ we can define the *table*
$$T_M^b(w) \subseteq (C_M^b \times \{l,r\}) \times (C_M^b \times \{l,r\} \cup \{\infty, >, \bot\}),$$
of w with respect to b and M:
(let $p(s) = 1$ if $s = l$, $p(s) = |w|$ otherwise; $p'(s) = 0$ if $s = l$, $p'(s) = |w|+1$ otherwise)

- $((c,s),(c',s')) \in T_M^b(w)$ if there is an alternation-free path (for w) leading from $(c,p(s))$ to $(c',p'(s'))$ which has cost $\leq b$ and does not leave w.
- $((c,s),\infty) \in T_M^b(w)$ if there is an alternation-free infinite path starting at $(c,p(s))$ which has cost $\leq b$ and does not leave w.
- $((c,s),>) \in T_M^b(w)$ if there is an alternation-free path starting at $(c,p(s))$ which has cost $> b$ and does not leave w.
- $((c,s),\bot) \in T_M^b(w)$ if there is a path starting at $(c,p(s))$ which has an alternation, has cost $\leq b$ and does not leave w.

Note that for $c_M = 2\log|\Gamma| + |Q| + 1$ there are at most 2^{bc_M} configurations in C_M^b and at most $2^{(2 \cdot 2^{bc_M})(2 \cdot 2^{bc_M}+3)} \leq 2^{2^{3bc_M}}$ different tables $T_M^b(w)$ $(w \in \Sigma_2^*)$. Given a word $W = w_1 \# \ldots \# w_n$, we call $\{w_1, \ldots, w_n\}$ the *content* of W. In $G_n = (\Sigma^{\log n-1} \{\frac{2}{\#}\})^{n-1} \Sigma^{\log n-1}$ there are $2^{2^{\log n-1}} - 1$ equivalence classes of words with the same content. Thus if $3bc_M < \log n - 1$ there are two words in G_n with the same table but different contents. For given M, b, n we fix two of these words, say $U(n,b,M)$, and $V(n,b,M)$, together with a distinguishing subword $u(n,b,M)$ in such a way that $u(n,b,M)$ is in the content of $U(n,b,M)$ but not in the content of $V(n,b,M)$. Note that $|U(n,b,M)| = |V(n,b,M)| = n\log(n)-1$ and $|u(n,b,M)| = \log(n) - 1$.

Lemma 3 table lemma. *Let M be a 2ATM (input alphabet Σ_M), U and V words in Σ_M^* with $|U| = |V|$ und $T_M^b(U) = T_M^b(V)$. Let $W = X_1 W_1 \ldots X_n W_n X_{n+1}$*

and $W' = X_1 W'_1 \ldots X_n W'_n X_{n+1}$ *be words in* Σ^*_M *with the subwords* $W_i, W'_i \in \{U, V\}$ *beginning at the positions* $p_i := |X_1 W_1 \cdots X_i| + 1$ $(i = 1, \ldots, n)$. *Then for all situations* s, s' *with* $pos(s) \notin \bigcup^n_{k=1}[p_k + 1 , p_k + |W_k| - 2]$ *and* $pos(s') \notin \bigcup^n_{k=1}[p_k , p_k + |W_k| - 1]$ *the following holds true:*

1. *if there is an alternation-free path for* W *leading from* s *to* s' *with cost* $\leq b$ *then also for* W',
2. *if there is an alternation-free path for* W *starting at* s *with cost* $> b$ *then also for* W',
3. *if there is an infinite alternation-free path for* W *starting at* s *with cost* $\leq b$ *then also for* W',
4. *if there is an path for* W *starting at* s *with cost* $\leq b$ *and with alternations then also for* W'.

The proof is essentially straight forward although several cases have to be considered.

Theorem 4. $L^3_2 \notin 2\Pi_2[f]$ *for any* $f \gtrsim \log$

Proof. Recall that
$L^3_2 = \{w_1 \overset{2}{\#} \cdots \overset{2}{\#} w_m \overset{1}{\#} u \overset{1}{\#} \mathrm{Bin}(n) \#^t \mid m, n, t \in \mathbb{N}, \forall i \; w_i \in \Sigma^*, u \in \Sigma^{\log n - 1}, \exists j \; w_j = u\}$.
Assume that M is a normal $2\Pi_2[f]$–TM ($f \gtrsim \log$) recognizing L^3_2. Let $N > 4^3$ be such that $f(N) < \frac{1}{18c_M} \log N$ and let n be a natural number satisfying $n^2 \leq N \leq n^3$. Then $n > 4$ and $3c_M f(N) < \log n - 1$. Hence the words $U = U(n, f(N), M)$, $V = V(n, f(N), M)$, $u = u(n, f(N), M)$ exist. We choose $t = N - (2n + 1) \log n - |\mathrm{Bin}(n)|$ and $S = \overset{1}{\#} u \overset{1}{\#} \mathrm{Bin}(n) \#^t$. The words in the subset $H = \{U \overset{2}{\#} US, \; U \overset{2}{\#} VS, \; V \overset{2}{\#} US\}$ of L^3_2 have exactly length N. We will show that M also accepts the word $W = V \overset{2}{\#} VS \notin L^3_2$, i.e. we will show that every maximal alternation-free path starting at the start situation s^0 terminates in a situation s which is $f(N), 1$–successful for W.

Let π be a maximal alternation-free path for W starting at s^0. π is finite and of cost $\leq f(N)$, for otherwise, according to the table lemma, there would also be an alternation-free path for $U \overset{2}{\#} VS$ which starts at s^0 and has cost $> f(N)$ or is infinite (which is impossible since $U \overset{2}{\#} VS \in L^3_2$). As M is normal, π ends in an alternation s. Assume $pos(s) < n \log n$ (the other case is handled analogously). According to the table lemma, there is also an alternation-free path for $V \overset{2}{\#} US$ from s^0 to s with cost $< b$. Therefore, there is an alternation-free successful path for $V \overset{2}{\#} US$ from s to some accepting situation s^e. Hence, according to the table lemma, even in the case of $V \overset{2}{\#} VS$ there is an alternation-free path from s to s^e with cost $< b$. $\square$

Theorem 5. $L^\vee_2 \notin 2\Sigma_2[f]$ *for any* $f \gtrsim \log$

Proof. Recall that
$L^\vee_2 = \{w_1 \overset{2}{\#} \cdots \overset{2}{\#} w_m \overset{1}{\#} u \overset{1}{\#} \mathrm{Bin}(n) \#^t \mid m, n, t \in \mathbb{N}, \forall i \; w_i \in \Sigma^* - \{u\}, u \in \Sigma^{\log n - 1}\}$.
Assume that M is a normal $2\Sigma_2[f]$–TM ($f \gtrsim \log$) recognizing $L^\vee_2$. We choose N, n, U, V, u and H just as in the proof of theorem 4. We will show that M accepts a word in H although $H \cap L^\vee_2 = \emptyset$. M accepts $W = V \overset{2}{\#} VS \in L^\vee_2$, i.e.

there is an $f(N), 1$–success tree T for W rooted in the start situation s^0. Let s be the first alternation in T. Moreover, assume $pos(s) < n \log n$ (the other case is handled analogously). Then there is also an alternation-free path for $V \#^2 US$ which leads from s^0 to s and has cost $\leq b$. We will show that every maximal path π for $V \#^2 US$ starting at s is alternation-free and $f(N)$–bounded and leads to an accepting stop situation.

π is finite, alternation-free, and $f(N)$–bounded, for otherwise, according to the the table lemma, there would also be a path for W which starts at s and either is infinite or has an alternation or cost $> f(N)$ which is impossible. Let π lead to situation s'. Again, according to the table lemma, there is also a maximal alternation-free path for W from s to s' with cost $\leq b$. Hence s' is an accepting stop situation. □

5 The third level of the hierarchy

Consider the language

$$L_3^3 = \{W_1 \#^3 \cdots \#^3 W_m \#^{\frac{1}{2}} u \#^{\frac{1}{2}} \mathrm{Bin}(n) \#^t \mid m, n, t \in \mathbb{N} \wedge u \in \Sigma^{\log n - 1} \wedge$$
$$\forall i \ W_i \in (\Sigma^* \#)^* \Sigma^* \wedge \exists j \ u \notin content(W_j)\}.$$

Theorem 6. $\qquad L_3^3 \notin 2\Pi_3[f] \quad$ for any $f \gtrsim \log$

Proof. Assume that M is a normal $2\Pi_3[f]$–Turing machine ($f \gtrsim \log$) recognizing L_3^3. We choose n, N, t, ε such that $n > 9$, $\varepsilon < \frac{1}{2}$, $3c_M f(N) < \varepsilon \log n$, $2n^2 \log n + \log n + |\mathrm{Bin}(n)| + t = N$. Then $|C_M^{f(N)}| < n^\varepsilon$ and the words $U = U(n, f(N), M)$, $V = V(n, f(N), M)$, $u = u(n, f(N), M)$ exist. Consider the word $W \#^3 WS$ where $W = (V \#^2)^{n-1} V$ and $S = \#^{\frac{1}{2}} u \#^{\frac{1}{2}} \mathrm{Bin}(n) \#^t$, i.e.

$$W \#^3 WS = \underbrace{V \#^2 \cdots \#^2 V}_{n-times} \#^3 \underbrace{V \#^2 \cdots \#^2 V}_{n-times} \#^{\frac{1}{2}} u \#^{\frac{1}{2}} \mathrm{Bin}(n) \#^t .$$

This word is in L_3^3, has length N and two $\#^3$–blocks with the borders 0, $n^2 \log n$, and $2n^2 \log n$. We call a situation s a *border situation* of the first $\#^3$–block if $pos(s)$ is 1 or $n^2 \log n - 1$, and of the second $\#^3$–block if $pos(s)$ is $n^2 \log n + 1$ or $2n^2 \log n - 1$. Both $\#^3$–blocks have at most $2n^\varepsilon$ border situations. Let s be an existential border situation of a $\#^3$–block B and let s have at least one $f(N), 2$–success tree for $W \#^3 WS$ whose alternation and earlier situations have their respective positions in B. Then we relate one of these trees to the situation s and mark the position of its alternation in B. In this way we get at most $2n^\varepsilon$ marked positions in both $\#^3$–blocks. Because of $n > 2n^\varepsilon$ every $\#^3$–block contains a V without a mark. We note one of these particular V's in both $\#^3$–blocks and exchange it for U. We then get a word $W_i \#^3 W_j S$ where $W_k = V \#^2 \cdots \#^2 U \#^2 \cdots \#^2 V$ with U in the k-th position. Let us now call an area with the inscription V a V–block.

Claim: *If the $\exists$–situation s with $pos(s) \leq n^2 \log n$ ($\geq n^2 \log n$) is $f(N), 2$–successful for $W_i \#^3 WS$ ($W \#^3 W_j S$) then s has an $f(N), 2$–success tree with no alternation in the fixed V–block right (left) of $\#^3$.*

Proof of the claim: Assume that T is an $f(N), 2$–success tree for $W_i \# WS$ rooted in s with the alternation s_a in the fixed $(j$–th$)$ V–block of W. Let π be the path from s to s_a in T and let s_b be the last border situation of the right $\#$–block in π. s_b decomposes π into $\pi_1\pi_2$. The situation s_b has an $f(N), 2$–success tree beginning with π_2 for $W \# WS$,too. For π_2 is a path for $W \# WS$, too, and every maximal path for $W \# WS$ starting at s_a is $f(N), 1$–successful (otherwise according to the table lemma there would also be a path for $W_i \# WS$ starting at s_a which is rejecting or infinite or with cost $> f(N)$ or with alternations contrary to the fact that s_a is $f(N), 1$–successful). Therefore there is an $f(N), 2$–success tree for $W \# WS$ related to s_b which has an alternation right of $\#$ before it leaves the right side but no alternation in the fixed $(j$–th$)$ V–block. According to the table lemma, s_b has an $f(N), 2$–success tree not alternating in the fixed V–block for $W_i \# WS$, too, and thus s as well. The case in parentheses is proved analogously. ◇

M accepts the words $W \# WS$, $W_i \# WS$, $W \# W_j S$, all in L_3^3. We will show that M accepts the word $W_i \# W_j S$, too, though it is not in L_3^3. In this respect, we will show that all maximal alternation-free paths for $W_i \# W_j S$ which begin at the start situation s^0 terminate in $f(N), 2$–successful situations. Let π be a maximal alternation-free path for $W_i \# W_j S$ starting at s^0. π is finite and $f(N)$–bounded for otherwise there would be a maximal alternation-free path for $W \# WS$ which is infinite or of cost $> f(N)$. Thus π terminates in an alternation s_1. Assume that s_1 is on the left of $\#$ ($pos(s_1) < n^2 \log n$) (the other case is proved analogously). Then, according to the table lemma, there is a maximal alternation-free $f(N)$–bounded path from s^0 to s_1 for $W_i \# WS$, too. Therefore, s_1 is $f(N), 2$–successful for $W_i \# WS$. According to the claim, the situation s_1 has an $f(N), 2$–success tree for $W_i \# WS$ whose alternation s_2 is not in the fixed $(j$–th$)$ V–block on the left of $\#$. Then s_1 is $f(N), 2$–successful for $W_i \# W_j S$, too. For there is an alternation-free $f(N)$–bounded path from s_1 to s_2 for $W_i \# W_j S$ and every maximal path for $W_i \# W_j S$ starting at s_2 is $f(N), 1$–successful. Otherwise, according to the table lemma, there would be a path for $W_i \# WS$ which starts at s_2 and is either rejecting or infinite or has cost $> f(N)$ or is alternating contrary to the fact that s_2 is $f(N), 1$–successful for $W_i \# WS$. □

The language $L_3^\vee$ is defined by:

$$L_3^\vee = \left\{ W_1 \# \cdots \# W_m \# u \# \mathrm{Bin}(n) \#^t \mid m, n, t \in \mathbb{N} \wedge u \in \Sigma^{\log n - 1} \wedge \right.$$
$$\left. \forall i \; [\, W_i = w_1 \# \cdots \# w_k \text{ with } \forall j \; w_j \in \Sigma^* \wedge \exists j \; w_j = u \,] \right\}.$$

Theorem 7. $L_3^\vee \notin 2\Sigma_3[f]$ *for any* $f \gtrsim \log$

Proof. Assume that M is a normal $2\Sigma_3[f]$–TM recognizing $L_3^\vee$. We choose n, N, t, ε just as in the proof of theorem 6. Hence there are at most n^ε configurations with cost $< f(N)$ and the words $U = U(n, f(N), M)$, $V = V(n, f(N), M)$, and $u = u(n, f(N), M)$ exist. Let $W = (V \#)^{n-1} V$ and $W_k = (V \#)^{k-1} U \#(V \#)^{n-k-1} V$. We will now consider the n^2 words of the set $\{W_i \# W_j S | i, j \in [1, n]\} \subseteq L_3^\vee$ where $S = \# u \# \mathrm{Bin}(n) \#^t$. All these words have length N. For any of these words we fix one of its $f(N), 3$–success trees. In half of the cases these success trees have their first alternation on the same side of $\overset{3}{\#}$. Assume the left side (the other case is proved analogously). Among these $\frac{n^2}{2}$ words there are at least $\frac{n}{2}$ which do not differ on the left side; let $H = \{W_{i_0}\overset{3}{\#}W_{j_k}S \mid k=1,\ldots,\frac{n}{2}\}$ be a set of $\frac{n}{2}$ of these latter words.

A $\forall$–situation s with input position $pos(s) = n^2\log n$ (the position of $\overset{3}{\#}$) is called *bad* if s is $f(N),2$–successful for $W_{i_0}\overset{3}{\#}WS$ (note that $W_{i_0}\overset{3}{\#}WS \notin L_3^{\vee}$). Otherwise it is called *good*.

Claim: *If a $\forall$–situation s with $pos(s) = n^2\log n$ is $f(N),2$–successful for two words of H then s is bad.*

Proof of the claim: we assume that s is $f(N),2$–successful for $W_{i_0}\overset{3}{\#}W_{j_1}S$ and $W_{i_0}\overset{3}{\#}W_{j_2}S$. Let π be a maximal alternation-free path for $W_{i_0}\overset{3}{\#}WS$ starting at s. π ist finite, $f(N)$–bounded and not rejecting for otherwise there would also be an alternation-free path for $W_{i_0}\overset{3}{\#}W_{j_1}S$ starting at s which is infinite or not $f(N)$–bounded or rejecting (table lemma); but this is impossible. Therefore π terminates in an alternation s_a (observe that M is normal).

Assume that the alternation s_a is in the j_1-th V–block of the right side of W. Then there is an alternation-free $f(N)$–bounded path for $W_{i_0}\overset{3}{\#}W_{j_2}S$ from s to s_a (table lemma). Therefore there is an $f(N),1$–successful path for $W_{i_0}\overset{3}{\#}W_{j_2}S$ starting at s_a. Now there is an $f(N),1$–successful path starting at s_a for $W_{i_0}\overset{3}{\#}WS$, too (table lemma). Assume that s_a is in the j_2-th V–block of the right side of W. Then we proceed analogously using the word $W_{i_0}\overset{3}{\#}W_{j_1}S$ instead of $W_{i_0}\overset{3}{\#}W_{j_2}S$. If s_a is neither in the j_1-th nor in the j_2-th V–block we arrive at a similar conclusion. Thus s_a is $f(N),1$–successful for $W_{i_0}\overset{3}{\#}WS$ in all cases. Hence s is bad. $\diamond$

Every good $\forall$–situation with input position $p = n^2\log n$ (position of $\overset{3}{\#}$) is $f(N),2$–successful for at most one word in H. Since there are $\frac{n}{2}$ words in H but at most n^ε $f(N)$–bounded situations with position p there are words in H for which no good $\forall$–situation with position p is $f(N),2$–successful or to put it another way: there are words in H such that all their $f(N),2$–successful $\forall$–situations with position p are bad, i.e. successful for $W_{i_0}\overset{3}{\#}WS$.

Let $W_{i_0}\overset{3}{\#}W_{j_k}S$ be such a word and T the $f(N),3$–success tree fixed for it. Let s_1 be the first alternation of T (it is left of $\overset{3}{\#}$). According to the table lemma, there is an alternation-free $f(N)$–bounded path for $W_{i_0}\overset{3}{\#}WS$ from s^0 to s_1. We will show that M also accepts the word $W_{i_0}\overset{3}{\#}WS$ which does not belong to $L_3^{\vee}$. For this purpose we will prove that s_1 is $f(N),2$–successful for this input, i.e. all maximal alternation-free paths starting at s_1 lead to $f(N),1$–successful situations.

Let π be a maximal alternation-free path for $W_{i_0}\overset{3}{\#}WS$ starting at s_1. The path π is finite and $f(N)$–bounded since otherwise there would be a path for $W_{i_0}\overset{3}{\#}W_{j_k}S$ starting at s_1 which is infinite or not $f(N)$–bounded. Thus π terminates in an alternation s_a (M is normal).

Assume s_a is on the left of $\overset{3}{\#}$. For $W_{i_0}\overset{3}{\#}W_{j_k}$, too, the situation s_a is reached from s_1 without alternation and with cost $\leq f(N)$. Now s_a is $f(N),1$–successful for $W_{i_0}\overset{3}{\#}WS$ since it is for $W_{i_0}\overset{3}{\#}W_{j_k}S$. Assume that s_a is on the right of $\overset{3}{\#}$.

Let s_2 be the last situation in π before s_a which has input position p (position of $\frac{3}{\#}$). Thus for $W_{i_0}\frac{3}{\#}W_{j_k}S$ the situation s_2 is reached from s_1 without alternation and with cost $\leq f(N)$ (table lemma). Therefore s_2 is $f(N), 2$-successful for $W_{i_0}\frac{3}{\#}W_{j_k}S$. Thus, according to the choice of $W_{i_0}\frac{3}{\#}W_{j_k}S$, the situation s_2 is bad, i.e. $f(N), 2$-successful for $W_{i_0}\frac{3}{\#}WS$. Hence s_a is $f(N), 1$-successful for $W_{i_0}\frac{3}{\#}WS$.

This holds for all maximal alternation-free paths starting at s_1. It follows that s_1 is $f(N), 2$-successful for $W_{i_0}\frac{3}{\#}WS$. □

6 The fourth level of the hierarchy

The language $L_4^{\vee}$ is defined as follows:

$$\exists D_3(u) = \{W_1\frac{3}{\#}\cdots\frac{3}{\#}W_m \mid m \in \mathbb{N}; \forall i\ W_i \in (\Sigma^*\frac{2}{\#})\Sigma^* \quad \text{and}$$
$$\exists j\ W_j = w_1\frac{2}{\#}\cdots\frac{2}{\#}w_r \text{ with } \forall k\ w_k \neq u \text{ for some } r\},$$
$$L_4^{\vee} = \{X_1\frac{4}{\#}\cdots\frac{4}{\#}X_m\frac{1}{\#}u\frac{1}{\#}\mathrm{Bin}(n)\frac{4}{\#}{}^t \mid m, n, t \in \mathbb{N}, u \in \Sigma^{\log n-1}, \forall i\ X_i \in \exists D_3(u)\}.$$

An area separated by $\frac{3}{\#}$ is called a $\frac{3}{\#}$-block.

Theorem 8. $\qquad L_4^{\vee} \notin 2\Sigma_4[f] \quad \text{for any} \quad f \precsim \log$

Proof. Assume that M is a normal $2\Sigma_4[f]$-TM ($f \precsim \log$) recognizing $L_4^{\vee}$. We choose n, N, t, ε such that $n > 9$, $\varepsilon < \frac{1}{2}$, $3c_M f(N) < \varepsilon \log n$, and $2n^3 \log n + \log n + |\mathrm{Bin}(n)| + t = N$. Hence there are at most n^ε configurations with cost $\leq f(n)$ and the words $U = U(n, f(N), M)$, $V = V(n, f(N), M)$, $u = u(n, f(N), M)$ exist. Let

$$\mathcal{V} = (V\frac{2}{\#})^{n-1}V = \underbrace{V\frac{2}{\#}\cdots\frac{2}{\#}V}_{n-times} \quad \text{and} \quad X = \underbrace{\mathcal{V}\frac{3}{\#}\cdots\frac{3}{\#}\mathcal{V}}_{n-times}\frac{4}{\#}\underbrace{\mathcal{V}\frac{3}{\#}\cdots\frac{3}{\#}\mathcal{V}}_{n-times}S$$

where $S = \frac{1}{\#}u\frac{1}{\#}\mathrm{Bin}(n)\frac{4}{\#}{}^t$. X has length N and is in $L_4^{\vee}$. Let B be an $\frac{3}{\#}$-block in X beginning at position p_a and ending at position p_e. In analogy to the proof of theorem 6 we call a situation s a *border situation* of B if $pos(s)$ is p_a or p_e. B has at most $2n^\varepsilon$ border situations. Again we allocate to every existential border situation of B an $f(N), 2$-success tree for X which is alternating in B before leaving B, provided that such a tree exists, and we mark the position of the first alternation of this tree. In this way we get at most $2n^\varepsilon$ markings in B. Because of $n > 2n^\varepsilon$, B has a V-block without any marking. We fix such a V-block and exchange its content for U. If we do so for every $\frac{3}{\#}$-block of X, we get the word $X^l\frac{4}{\#}X^r$ where $X^l = \mathcal{V}_1^l\frac{3}{\#}\cdots\frac{3}{\#}\mathcal{V}_n^l$ and $X^r = \mathcal{V}_1^r\frac{3}{\#}\cdots\frac{3}{\#}\mathcal{V}_n^r$, with $\mathcal{V}_i^l$ ($\mathcal{V}_i^r$) as the content of the i-th $\frac{3}{\#}$-block on the left (right) of $\frac{4}{\#}$ after the exchange of the content of the fixed V-block. We get the word $X_i^l = \mathcal{V}_1^l\frac{3}{\#}\cdots\frac{3}{\#}\mathcal{V}_{i-1}^l\frac{3}{\#}\mathcal{V}\frac{3}{\#}\mathcal{V}_{i+1}^l\frac{3}{\#}\cdots\frac{3}{\#}\mathcal{V}_n^l$ if we undo the exchange in the i-th $\frac{3}{\#}$-block on the left of $\frac{4}{\#}$ in X^l, i.e. if we again replace the U by the V. Analogously we obtain the word X_i^r. The n^2 words of length N in the set $H := \{X_i^l\frac{4}{\#}X_j^r S \mid i, j \in [1, n]\}$ are all in $L_4^{\vee}$ and are all accepted by M.

Claim 1: *Let B be a $\frac{3}{\#}$-block in $X_i^l\frac{4}{\#}X_j^r S$ and s an $\exists$-situation not lying in B (pos(s) not in B) and $f(N), 2$-successful for $X_i^l\frac{4}{\#}X_j^r S$. Then s has a $f(N), 2$-*

success tree for $X_i^l \# X_j^r S$ with no alternation in the fixed V–block of B.
The proof is analogous to that of the claim in theorem 6.

For each of the n^2 words in H we fix one of its $f(N)$, 4–success trees. In half of the cases the fixed success trees have their first alternation on the same side of $\#$, say on the left (the other case is proven analogously). Among these there are again at least $\frac{n}{2}$ words with the same content on their left side, say $X_{i_0}^l$. Let $H' = \{X_{i_0}^l \# X_{j_k}^r \mid k = 1, \ldots, \frac{n}{2}\}$ be a set of $\frac{n}{2}$ of these words.

A $\forall$–situation s with input position $n^3 \log n$ (the position of $\#$) is called *bad* if s is $f(N)$, 3–successful for $X_{i_0}^l \# X^r S$. Otherwise it is called *good*.

Claim 2: *If a $\forall$–situation s with input position $n^3 \log n$ is $f(N)$, 3–successful for two words in H' then it is bad.*

Proof of claim 2: we assume that s is $f(N)$, 3–successful for $X_{i_0}^l \# X_{j_1}^r S$ and for $X_{i_0}^l \# X_{j_2}^r S$. We will show that s is $f(N)$, 3–successful for $X_{i_0}^l \# X^r S$, too, by showing that every maximal alternation-free path for this input starting at s leads to an $f(N)$, 2–successful situation.

Let π be a maximal alternation-free path starting at s for $X_{i_0}^l \# X^r S$. π is finite, $f(N)$–bounded and not rejecting (otherwise, according to the table lemma, there would be a maximal alternation-free path starting at s for $X_{i_0}^l \# X_{j_1}^r S$ which is infinite or not $f(N)$–bounded or rejecting), i.e. π is a path from s to s_1 (for some s_1). If s_1 is an accepting stop situation then s_1 is $f(N)$, 2–successful. Hence we assume that s_1 is an alternation.

Assume that s_1 is in the j_1-th $\#$-block of $X_{i_0}^l \# X^r$ on the right of $\#$. Then there is an alternation-free, $f(N)$–bounded path π' from s to s_1 for $X_{i_0}^l \# X_{j_2}^r S$, too. Since s is $f(N)$, 3–successful for this word by assumption, s_1 has an $f(N)$, 2–success tree for this word the first alternation of which, s_2, is not in the fixed V–block of the j_2-th $\#$-block on the right of $\#$ (claim 1). Then there is an alternation-free, $f(N)$–bounded path π for $X_{i_0}^l \# X^r$ from s_1 to s_2 (table lemma). s_2 is also $f(N)$, 2–successful for $X_{i_0}^l \# X^r$ since every maximal path starting at s_2 is $f(N)$, 1–successful (otherwise the table lemma would imply that there is a path for $X_{i_0}^l \# X_{j_2}^r$ starting at s_2 which is infinite or not $f(N)$–bounded or rejecting). If s_1 is not in the j_1-th $\#$-block, we argue in an analogous way using the word $X_{i_0}^l \# X_{j_1}^r$. $\diamond$

As in the proof of theorem 7 we draw our conclusions from claim 2: since there are $\frac{n}{2}$ words in H' but only n^ε border situations with cost $< f(N)$, there is a word in H', say $X_{i_0}^l \# X_{j_0}^r S$, for which all $f(N)$, 3–successful situations with the position $p = n^3 \log n$ (position of $\#$) are bad, i.e. $f(N)$, 3–successful for $X_{i_0}^l \# X^r S$. Let T be the $f(N)$, 4–success tree fixed for $X_{i_0}^l \# X_{j_0}^r S$ and s_1 its first alternation (s_1 is on the left of $\#$). We will show that s_1 is reached from s^0 by an alternation-free path for $X_{i_0}^l \# X^r S$, too, and that s_1 is $f(N)$, 3–successful, which means that M accepts this word although it is not in $L_4^\forall$. The former holds according to the the table lemma. Thus it remains to be shown that every maximal alternation-free path for $X_{i_0}^l \# X^r S$ starting at s_1 leads to an $f(N)$, 2–successful situation.

So let π be a maximal alternation-free path for $X_{i_0}^l \, \sharp X^r S$ starting at s_1. π is finite and $f(N)$-bounded (otherwise there would be a infinite or not $f(N)$-bounded path for $X_{i_0}^l \, \sharp X_{j_0}^r S$ starting at s_1 – the table lemma). Let π end in s_2. Since M is normal, s_2 is not a stop situation but an alternation.

1) Assume that s_2 lies on the right of $\sharp$. Let s_b be the last situation in π before s_2 with position $p = n^3 \log n$ (position of $\sharp$). Then there is an alternation-free $f(N)$-bounded path for $X_{i_0}^l \, \sharp X_{j_0}^r S$ from s_1 to s_b and s_b is $f(N)$, 3–successful for this input. Thus, according to the choice of $X_{i_0}^l \, \sharp X_{j_0}^r S$, the situation s_b is bad, i.e. $f(N)$, 3–successful for $X_{i_0}^l \, \sharp X^r S$ (and thus s_2 is $f(N)$, 2–successful).

2) Assume that s_2 lies on the left of $\sharp$. Then there is an alternation-free $f(N)$-bounded path for $X_{i_0}^l \, \sharp X_{j_0}^r S$ from s_1 to s_2, too, and s_2 is $f(N)$, 2–successful for this input. Hence according to the claim 1, s_2 has an $f(N)$, 2–success tree for this input whose first alternation s_3 is not in the fixed V–block of the j_0-th $\sharp$–block on the right of $\sharp$. Thus there is an alternation-free, $f(N)$-bounded path for $X_{i_0}^l \, \sharp X^r S$ from s_2 to s_3 (table lemma). s_3 is $f(N)$, 1–successful for this input, since every maximal path starting at s_3 is accepting (otherwise there would be an alternation-free path for $X_{i_0}^l \, \sharp X_{j_0}^r S$ starting at s_3 which is not accepting – see table lemma). □

References

[BM88] L. Babai and S. Moran. Arthur–Merlin games: a randomized proof–system, and a hierarchy of complexity classes. *Journal of Computer and System Sciences 36 (1988) 254–276*, 36:254–276, 1988.

[Bra91] B. v. Braunmühl. Alternationshierarchien von Turingmaschinen mit kleinem Speicher. Informatik Berichte 83, Inst. für Informatik, Universität Bonn, 1991.

[Has86] J. Hastad. Almost optimal lower bounds for small depth circuits. In *Proc. 18. STOC*, pages 6–20, 1986.

[Hem87] L. A. Hemachandra. The strong exponential hierarchy collapses. In *Proc. 19th. STOC Conference*, pages 110–122, 1987.

[IIT87] A. Ito, K. Inoue, and I. Takanami. A note on alternating Turing machines using small space. *The Transactions of the IEICE*, E 70 no. 10:990–996, 1987.

[Imm88] N. Immerman. NSPACE is closed under complement. *SIAM J. Comput.*, 17:935–938, 1988.

[LL89] M. Liśkiewicz and K. Loryś. On reversal complexity for alternating Turing machines. In *Proc. 30st Ann. Symp. on Foundations of Computer Science*, pages 618–623, 1989.

[LSH65] P. M. Lewis, R. E. Stearns, and J. Hartmanis. Memory bounds for recognition of context–free and context–sensitive languages. In *IEEE Conf. Switch. Circuit Theory and Logic Design*, pages 191–202, 1965.

[SW88] U. Schöning and K. W. Wagner. Collapsing oracle hierarchies, census functions and logarithmically many queries. In *Proc. 5th. STACS 88, LNCS 294*, pages 91–97, 1988.

[Sze88] R. Szelepcsényi. The method of forced enumeration for nondeterministic automata. *Acta Informatica*, 26:279–284, 1988.

[Yao85] A. Yao. Separating the polynomial time hierarchy by oracles. In *Proc. 26th. FoCS*, pages 1–10, 1985.

Separating the Lower Levels of the Sublogarithmic Space Hierarchy

Maciej Liśkiewicz[*]   and   Rüdiger Reischuk

Technische Hochschule Darmstadt[†]

Abstract. For $S(n) \geq \log n$ it is well known that the complexity classes $NSPACE(S)$ are closed under complementation. Furthermore, the corresponding alternating space hierarchy collapses to the first level. Till now, it is an open problem if these results hold for space complexity bounds between $\log \log n$ and $\log n$, too. In this paper we give some partial answer to this question. We show that for each S between $\log \log n$ and $\log n$, $\Sigma_2 SPACE(S)$ and $\Sigma_3 SPACE(S)$ are not closed under complement. This implies the hierarchy

$$\Sigma_1 SPACE(S) \subset \Sigma_2 SPACE(S) \subset \Sigma_3 SPACE(S) \subset \Sigma_4 SPACE(S).$$

We also compare the power of weak and strong sublogarithmic space bounded ATMs.

1   Introduction

It is well known that if a Turing machine – deterministic or nondeterministic – uses less than $\log \log n$ space then it can recognize only regular languages. On the other hand, one can construct a non-regular language that belongs to $DSPACE(\log \log n)$. These results show that one can restrict attention to space bounds $S(n) \geq \log \log n$. The function $\log n$ seems to be the most dramatic bound for space complexity. Most techniques used in space complexity investigations only work for bounds above $\log n$. There are several important results for such space classes known, and it is an open question whether they hold also for space bounds below $\log n$. One of the most exciting problem of this type is whether the closure under complement remains valid for sublogarithmic classes.

Theorem A (Immerman [6] and Szelépcsenyi [10])
For arbitrary S with $S(n) \geq \log n$ holds $NSPACE(S) = co\text{-}NSPACE(S)$.

---

[*] On leave of Institute of Computer Science, University of Wrocław supported by the Alexander-von-Humboldt-Stiftung

[†] Institut für Theoretische Informatik, Alexanderstraße 10, 6100 Darmstadt, Germany
e-mail: liskiewi/reischuk @ iti.informatik.th-darmstadt.de

Problem 1 *Is the same equality valid for space bounds between* $\log\log n$ *and* $\log n$ *?*

This question is related to another classical open problem in complexity theory:

Problem 2 *Is* $DSPACE(S) = NSPACE(S)$ *for* $S(n) \geq \log\log n$ *?* [1]

If the Immerman-Szelépcsenyi's theorem does not hold for sublogarithmic space bounds then $DSPACE(S) \subset NSPACE(S)$ for any function $S \in \Omega(\log\log n) \cap o(\log n)$. Let us denote this class of bounds by $\textbf{\textit{SUBLOG}}$. The fact above follows from

Theorem B (Sipser [8]) *For any* S $DSPACE(S) = co\text{-}DSPACE(S)$.

Recently, Alt, Geffert, and Mehlhorn ([1]) and independently Szepietowski ([11]) have proved the following result that gives a partial positive answer to Problem 1.

Theorem C ([1], [11]) *Let* S *be any function, let* $\{a_1, a_2, \ldots a_k\}$ *be a finite set of symbols, and let* $L \subseteq a_1^* a_2^* \ldots a_k^*$ *be a bounded language. Then* $L \in NSPACE(S)$ *implies* $\bar{L} \in NSPACE(S)$.

Still, we conjecture that Problem 1 has a negative answer. Towards this direction we will prove

Theorem 1 $\Sigma_2 SPACE(S)$ *and* $\Sigma_3 SPACE(S)$ *are not closed under complementation for any* $S \in SUBLOG$.

Recall that for $k \geq 1$ the class $\Sigma_k SPACE(S)$ is defined as the set of languages accepted by alternating S space-bounded TMs that make at most $k-1$ alternations and begin in an existential state (by definition $\Sigma_1 SPACE(S) = NSPACE(S)$). $\Pi_k SPACE(S)$ are the languages accepted in space S by alternating TMs that make also at most $k-1$ alternations, but start in a universal state. By standard techniques it follows from Immerman-Szelépcsenyi's theorem that

Corollary D *For* S *with* $S(n) \geq \log n$ *and for all* $k \geq 1$
$$\Sigma_1 SPACE(S) = \Sigma_k SPACE(S) = \Pi_k SPACE(S).$$

Note that these techniques do not work for sublogarithmic space bounds. Thus, there is no proof yet excluding the possibility that some levels of this hierarchy for sublogarithmic bounds are identical while others higher up are distinct. Recently, Chang et al. ([3]) have shown that there is a language in $\Pi_2 SPACE(\log\log n)$ that does not belong to $NSPACE(o(\log n))$. Clearly, this proves that for space bounds S between $\log\log n$ and $\log n$, the alternating S space hierarchy does not collapse to the first level and that $\Sigma_1 SPACE(S) \subset \Pi_2 SPACE(S)$. It is an open problem whether the whole alternating hierarchy for sublogarithmic space is strict:

Problem 3 $\Sigma_k SPACE(S) \subset \Sigma_{k+1} SPACE(S)$ *for* $k \geq 1$ *and* $S \in SUBLOG$ *?*

Here we will prove that the first four levels of this hierarchy are distinct.

---

[1] In [12, p.419] it is incorrectly cited that $DSPACE(S) \subset NSPACE(S)$, for $S(n) \geq \log\log n$ and $S(n) = o(\log n)$, thus Problem 2 is still open for any $S(n) \geq \log\log n$ (see Remark 6.1 in [7]).

Theorem 2 *For each* $S \in SUBLOG$,

$$\Sigma_1 SPACE(S) \subset \Sigma_2 SPACE(S) \subset \Sigma_3 SPACE(S) \subset \Sigma_4 SPACE(S).$$

We also obtain the same separation for the first four levels of the $\Pi_k SPACE$ classes.

For space bounded computations different definitions of acceptance have been used. It is well known that for space bounds greater or equal to $\log n$ they are basically equivalent. For sublogarithmic bounds we have a quite different situation.

Definition 1 *Let* M *be an alternating Turing machine (ATM). We say that* M *is (strongly)* S *space-bounded if it can only enter configurations using at most* $S(|x|)$ *space on every input* x. *M is weakly S space-bounded if, for every input* x *that is accepted, it has an accepting computation tree all of which configurations use at most* $S(|x|)$ *space. DSPACE(S) and weakDSPACE(S) denote the class of languages accepted by* S *space-bounded (resp. weakly S space-bounded) deterministic TMs (DTMs). A corresponding notation is used for nondeterministic machines (NTMs) and ATMs.*

So far we have measured the space complexity in the usual strong sense. One can show that for weakly sublogarithmic space bounded computations Sipser's theorem as well as Immerman-Szelépcsenyi's theorem do not hold. The language $L = \{1^n 01^n : n \in \mathbb{N}\}$ is not in $weakNSPACE(o(\log n))$ but $\bar{L}$, the complement of L, belongs to $weakDSPACE(\log \log n)$ [2]. As an immediate consequence we obtain that, for any function $S \in SUBLOG$

$$DSPACE(S) \subset weakDSPACE(S).$$

In [3] Chang et al. stated as an open problem whether weak and strong sublogarithmic space-bounded NTMs, resp. ATMs have the same power. Recently, Geffert ([4]) has proved that for $S \in SUBLOG$ weakly S space-bounded nondeterministic TMs accept more languages than strongly-bounded ones. This paper solves the problem of Chang et al. for ATMs.

Theorem 3 $weakDSPACE(\log \log n) \setminus ASPACE(o(\log n)) \neq \emptyset$.

As consequences one obtains

Corollary 1 *For any* $k \geq 1$ *and each* $S \in SUBLOG$

$$\begin{aligned}\Sigma_k SPACE(S) &\quad\subset\quad weak\Sigma_k SPACE(S) \text{ and} \\ \Pi_k SPACE(S) &\quad\subset\quad weak\Pi_k SPACE(S).\end{aligned}$$

Corollary 2 *For each* $S \in SUBLOG$

$$ASPACE(S) \subset weakASPACE(S).$$

The paper is organised as follows: In section 2 we show some basic properties of sublogarithmic space bounded computations. Section 3 contains proofs of our main results (Theorems 1, 2, and 3). We define languages that separate the first four levels of the alternating space hierarchy, $\Sigma_k SPACE$ and co-$\Sigma_k SPACE$, for $k = 2, 3$, as well as strong and weak alternating space complexity classes. In section 4 we consider some further consequences of these results.

2 Preliminaries

In [4] Geffert has shown that for sublogarithmic space bounded computations, the behavior of a nondeterministic TM on inputs 1^n and $1^{n+kn!}$, for any $k \geq 0$, is exactly the same. The proof is based on the so called $n \rightarrow n + n!$ technique developed by Stearns, Hartmanis, and Lewis [9]. It is easy to check that the same fact holds for TMs on inputs $1^n 0 1^n$ and $1^{n+kn!} 0 1^{n+ln!}$. Below we state this fact formally.

The Turing machine model we consider has a two-way read-only input tape and a single two-way read-write work tape. It is assumed that an input word is placed on the input tape between the left end-marker $\cent$ and the right end-marker $\$ $.

Definition 2 *Let M be a Turing machine. A memory state of M is an orderd triple $\alpha = (q, u, i)$, where q is a state of M, u is a string written on its work tape, and i is a position of the work tape head. A configuration of M on an input x is a pair (α, j) consisting of a memory state α and a position j with $0 \leq j \leq |x| + 1$ of the input head. $j = 0$ or $j = |x| + 1$ means that this head scans the left, resp. the right end-marker. For a memory state $\alpha = (q, u, i)$, let $|\alpha|$ denote the length of the word u.*

Lemma 1 *Let $L(m) \leq o(\log m)$ and let M be an ATM. Then there exists a constant $\hat{m}$ such that for all $m \geq \hat{m}$, for all words u, v, and for all memory states α_1, α_2, with $|\alpha_1| \leq |\alpha_2| \leq L(m)$, and for any $k \geq 0$, holds:*

1. *There is a computation path for the input $x := u 1^m v$ that starts in the memory state α_1 with the input head on string $\cent u$ or $v\$$ and ends in memory state α_2 with the input head on $\cent u$ or $v\$$ if and only if there is a computation path on input $x' := u 1^{m+km!} v$ that also starts in α_1 and ends in α_2 with the input head on the corresponding symbols of $\cent u$, resp. $v\$$.*

2. *There is a computation path for x that starts in the memory state α_1 with the input head on string $\cent u$ or $v\$$ and ends in memory state α_2 with the input head on the string of 1's of x if and only if there is a computation on input x' that also starts in α_1 (with the input head on the same symbol of string $\cent u$ or $v\$$) and ends in α_2 (with the input head somewhere on the string of 1's of x').*

The proof given in [4] easily generalizes to these situations.

Definition 3 *Let M be an off-line Turing machine and let x be an input. We define $Space_M(x)$ as the maximum of the space used in configurations that are reachable by M from the initial configuration on input x.*

Lemma 2 *Let $S(n) \leq o(\log n)$ and let M be an S space-bounded alternating TM. Then there exists a constant $\hat{n}$ such that for all $n \geq \hat{n}$, and $k, l \geq 0$*

$$Space_M(1^n 0 1^n) = Space_M(1^{n+kn!} 0 1^{n+ln!}).$$

The next four lemmata describe important properties of computations of Σ_2, Π_2, Σ_3, and Π_3 Turing machines on inputs of the form $1^n 0 1^m$.

Lemma 3 (Σ_2 machines) *Let $S(n) \leq o(\log n)$ and let M be an S space-bounded alternating $\Sigma_2 TM$. Then there exists a constant n_0 such that for all $n \geq n_0$ and for all $k, l \geq 0$ the following properties are fulfilled:*

1. *For each __existential__ configuration (α, j), with $0 \leq j \leq n + kn! + 1$, that is reachable on input $x := 1^{n+kn!}01^n$ from $M's$ initial configuration holds: if M started in (α, j) with x on its input tape accepts then M started in configuration (α, j) with $y := 1^{n+kn!}01^{n+ln!}$ on its input tape accepts, too.*

2. *For each __existential__ configuration (α, j), with $n+1 \leq j \leq n+1+n+ln!+1$, that is reachable on input $x := 1^n01^{n+ln!}$ from $M's$ initial configuration holds: if M started in (α, j) with x on its input tape accepts then M started in configuration $(\alpha, j + kn!)$ with y on its input tape accepts, too.*

Proof. We will only give a proof for case 1. Let n_0 be larger than $2\hat{m}$ and $\hat{n}$, where $\hat{m}$ is the constant from Lemma 1 and $\hat{n}$ is the constant from Lemma 2. Let $n \geq n_0$, and let k, l be nonnegative integers. Let n_k denote the number $n + kn!$ and n_l the number $n + ln!$. Now let us assume that for a position j with $0 \leq j \leq n_k + 1$

1. the existential configuration (α, j) is reachable on input $x = 1^{n_k}01^n$ from an initial configuration, and
2. M started in configuration (α, j) with x on its input tape accepts.

We will show that M started in configuration (α, j) with $y = 1^{n_k}01^{n_l}$ on its input tape accepts, too. Let us note first that M started in (α, j) with x on its input tape uses no more space than $Space_M(x)$. By Lemma 2 this quantity is bounded by $Space_M(1^n01^n) \leq S(2n + 1)$. By assumption 1 and Lemma 1(1) the configuration (α, j) is reachable on input y from the initial configuration of M, too. Therefore, started in (α, j) with y on the input tape, M uses no more space than $Space_M(y)$, which by Lemma 2 also is bounded by $S(2n+1)$. Hence

($1'$) For any memory state β M can reach starting in (α, j) with input x or y holds $|\beta| \leq S(2n + 1)$.

Since M is a Σ_2 TM, from 2. it follows that there exists a __universal__ configuration (or if M does not alternate a final accepting configuration) (β_0, h) with $0 \leq h \leq |x| + 1 = n_k + n + 2$, such that

($2'$) There is an existential computation path of M on input x that starts in (α, j) and ends in (β_0, h) and

($2''$) Each computation path C on input x that starts in (β_0, h) is finite. In addition, the final configuration of each such C is accepting.

We divide the string x according to h into three parts. Let $m := \lfloor n/2 \rfloor$. Define $h_1 := n_k + 1 + m$ if $h \leq n_k + 1 + m$, and $h_1 := n_k + 1$, otherwise. Let $h_2 := h_1 + m + 1$. Now let u denote the prefix of x of length h_1, i.e. $u := 1^{n_k}01^{h_1-n_k-1}$. Moreover let v denote the suffix of x of length $|x| + 1 - h_2$, i.e. $v := 1^{n_k+n+2-h_2}$ (note that v can be an empty word), hence $x = u1^m v$. For such a partition of x, the head of M in memory state (β_0, h) is located on string

ϕu, if $h \leq n_k + 1 + m$ and on string $v\$$, otherwise. Let $a := (m+1)(m+2)\dots n$ and let $l' := la$. We will show that M started in (α, j) with

$$x' := u1^{m+l'm!}v$$

on its input tape accepts. This proves the lemma since

$$x' = u1^{m+l'm!}v = 1^{n_k}01^{h_1-n_k-1}1^{m+lam!}1^{n_k+n+2-(h_1+m+1)} = 1^{n_k}01^{n_l} = y \,.$$

Let $L(s) := S(4s+1)$ if n is even and let $L(s) := S(4s+2+1)$ otherwise. Note that in both cases $L(s) \leq o(\log s)$ and that $L(m) = S(2n+1)$. From Lemma 1(1) and by $(1')$ and $(2')$ it follows that there exists an existential computation of M with x' on the input tape that starts in (α, j) and ends in (β_0, h'), where $h' := h$ if $h \leq n_k + 1 + m$, and $h' := h + l'm!$, otherwise. Our lemma follows from this property and from the following claim.

Claim M *started in configuration* (β_0, h') *with* x' *on its input tape accepts.*

Proof: Assume, to the contrary, that M starting in (β_0, h') does not accept x'. We can distinguish two cases:
(a) M starting in (β_0, h') stops in a final configuration (β, t) and rejects, or
(b) M starting in (β_0, h') performs an infinite computation on x'.
From Lemma 1, it follows that the memory state β is reachable on x, too. We get a contradiction since by condition $(2'')$ it must hold: if M reaches a final memory state on x then it should be accepting. Therefore case (a) cannot occur. Below we will prove that case (b) cannot occur, too. More precisely, we will show that if (b) holds then there exists an infinite computation path for input x which starts in (β_0, h'), also yielding a contradiction to $(2'')$.

Let C be an infinite computation path for input x' that starts in (β_0, h'). From C we will construct an infinite computation path for input x that also starts in (β_0, h'). Let h'_2 denote the index of the first symbol of the string $v\$$ on the input tape with input x', i.e. let $h'_2 := h_2 + l'm!$. Three cases have to be distinguished.

Case 1: *The boundary between the prefix u and the string $1^{m+l'm!}$ or the boundary between the string $1^{m+l'm!}$ and the suffix v is crossed infinitely often in C (see the figure below).*

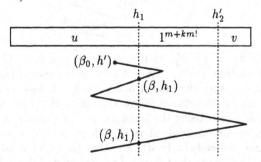

Let the boundary between the prefix u and the string $1^{m+l'm!}$ be crossed infinitely many times. Then there exists a memory state β such that the configuration

(β, h_1) occurs in C at least twice. From Lemma 1(1) one can conclude that when M starts in (β_0, h'), the configuration (β, h_1) is reachable with input x, too, and that there is a computation path of M on x which starts and ends in (β, h_1). So, we obtain that M starting in (β_0, h') makes an infinite loop on x. The subcase when the boundary between the string $1^{m+l'm!}$ and the suffix v is crossed infinitely many times in C is similar to this one.

Case 2: *There is an initial part C_1 of C and an infinite rest C_2 of C such that in C_2 M scans only the input to the left of h_1 or to the right of h'_2 (see the figure below).*

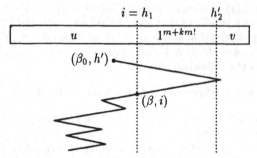

Let (β, i), for $i = h_1$ or $i = h'_2$, be the last configuration of C_1. From the Lemma 1(1) we have that (β, i) is reachable from (β_0, h') on x, too. Let C'_1 denote a computation path from (β_0, h') to (β, i) for input x. Then $C'_1 C_2$ is an infinite computation path for x.

Case 3: *There is an initial part C_1 of C and an infinite rest C_2 of C such that in C_2 M scans only the string $1^{m+l'm!}$ (see the figure below).*

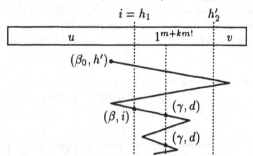

Let (β, i), for $i = h_1$ or $i = h'_2$, be the last configuration of C_1. Without loos of generality, assume that $i = h_1$. Since C_2 is infinite there exsists $h_1 < d < h'_2$ and a memory state γ such that (γ, d) occurs on C_2 at least twice. All memory states on computation path between the two instances of (γ, d) use at most $L(m)$ space (by condition (1')). Using the standard counting argument on the number of crossing sequences one can easily show that there exists a computation path D such that D starts and ends in (γ, d), and that the input head is never moved farther than $\frac{1}{3}m$ positions to the left and $\frac{1}{3}m$ positions to the right of d. Let C_2^1 denote the part of C_2 between (β, i) and the first (γ, d) on C_2. Using once again the counting argument on the number of crossing sequences and the condition (1')

that all memory states use less space than $L(m)$ from C_2^1 one can easily construct a computation path D^1 such that
- D^1 starts in (β, i),
- the input head is never moved farther than $\frac{2}{3}m$ positions to the right of i,
- D^1 ends in (γ, d'), for some d' with $\min(d, i + \frac{1}{3}m) \leq d' < i + \frac{2}{3}m$.

Finally, let C_1' denote a computation path for input x starting in (β_0, h') and ending in (β, i). By Lemma 1(1) such a path exists. The computation path $C_1' D^1 DDD...$ is an infinite computation on x. ∎

Let us now consider Π_2 TMs of sublogarithmic space complexity. Assume that for sufficiently large n and an integer $k \geq 0$ a Π_2 TM M started in a universal configuration (α, j) with $x := 1^{n+kn!}01^n$ on its input tape rejects. Then there exists an existential configuration (β_0, h) such that: M starting in (α, j) and working in universal states reaches (β_0, h) and each computation of M on x started in (β_0, h) is rejecting. Using the methods from the above proof one can show that for any integer $l \geq 0$ there exists an existential configuration (β_0, h') such that M starting in (α, j) on the input $y := 1^{n+kn!}01^{n+ln!}$ and working in universal states reaches (β_0, h'), and that each computation of M on y that starts in (β_0, h') is rejecting. For $x := 1^n 01^{n+kn!}$ the analog property holds, too. Hence we obtain

Lemma 4 (Π_2 machines) *Let $S(n) \leq o(\log n)$ and let M be an S space-bounded alternating Π_2 TM. Then there exists a constant n_0 such that for each $n \geq n_0$ and for each $k, l \geq 0$ the following holds:*

1. *For each __universal__ configuration (α, j), with $0 \leq j \leq n + kn! + 1$, that is reachable on input $x := 1^{n+kn!}01^n$ from M's initial configuration holds: if M started in (α, j) with x on its input tape rejects then M started in configuration (α, j) with $y := 1^{n+kn!}01^{n+ln!}$ on its input tape also rejects.*

2. *For each __universal__ configuration (α, j), with $n+1 \leq j \leq n+1+n+ln!+1$, that is reachable on input $x := 1^n 01^{n+ln!}$ from M's initial configuration holds: if M started in (α, j) with x on its input tape rejects then M started in configuration $(\alpha, j + kn!)$ with y on its input tape rejects, too.*

We use the above properties of Σ_2 and Π_2 TM computations to prove the following properties of Σ_3 and Π_3 machines.

Lemma 5 (Σ_3 machines) *Let $S(n) \leq o(\log n)$ and let M be an S space-bounded alternating $\Sigma_3 TM$. Then there exists a constant n_0 such that for each $n \geq n_0$ and for each $k, l \geq 0$ holds: if M accepts the input $y := 1^{n+kn!}01^{n+ln!}$ then M also accepts the input $x_1 := 1^{n+kn!}01^n$ or the input $x_2 := 1^n 01^{n+ln!}$.*

Proof. Let M be an S space-bounded $\Sigma_3 TM$, where $S(n) \leq o(\log n)$. Let us assume that the set of existential states of M is divided into two disjoint sets E_1 and E_2 such that until the first alternation M, enters only states in E_1 and after the second alternation only states in E_2. It is obvious that for $\Sigma_3 TM$ of space complexity S, one can construct an equivalent $\Sigma_3 TM$ of the same space complexity S that fulfils the above property. Let M' denote the ATM obtained from M by declaring all states in E_1 universal. Note that M' is a Π_2 TM and that it is still S space-bounded. Of course, $L(M)$ and $L(M')$ may be different.

However, for any universal configuration of M, (α, j), and any input z, M started in (α, j) with z on its input tape accepts if and only if M' started in (α, j) on the same input z accepts. Let n_0 be the constant from Lemma 4 for machine M'. Let $n \geq n_0$, and let k, l be nonnegative integers. Assume that M accepts the input $y = 1^{n+kn!}01^{n+ln!}$, i.e. that for M with y on the input tape holds:

(1)' There exists an existential computation path from an initial configuration of M to a <u>universal</u> configuration (α, j), with $0 \leq j \leq |y| + 1 = n + kn! + 1 + n + ln! + 1$, such that M started in (α, j) accepts.

Note that the last condition of (1) is equivalent to

(2) The machine M' started in (α, j) with y on the input tape accepts.

Let us first consider the case $0 \leq j \leq n + kn! + 1$. From (1) and from Lemma 1(1) we have that for M with $x_1 = 1^{n+kn!}01^n$ on the input tape holds:

(1') there exists an existential computation path from an initial configuration of M to the configuration (α, j).

This means that (α, j) is reachable on input x_1 from an initial configuration of M', too. Now we use Lemma 4(1). Since the assumptions of the lemma are fulfilled, (2) implies that M' started in (α, j) with x_1 on the input tape accepts. Hence M started in (α, j) with the input x_1 also accepts. This property together with (1') proves that M accepts x_1.

If $n + kn! + 2 \leq j \leq |y| + 1$ then similarly one can show that $x_2 = 1^n 01^{n+ln!} \in L(M)$. ∎

Using the property of Σ_2 TM computations from Lemma 3, one can symmetrically prove the following result for Π_3 machines.

Lemma 6 (Π_3 machines) *Let $S(n) \leq o(\log n)$ and let M be an S space-bounded alternating $\Pi_3 TM$. Then there exists a constant n_0 such that for each $n \geq n_0$, and for each $k, l \geq 0$ holds: if M rejects the input $y := 1^{n+kn!}01^{n+ln!}$ then M also rejects the input $x_1 := 1^{n+kn!}01^n$ or the input $x_2 := 1^n 01^{n+ln!}$.*

3 Lower Space Bounds for Recognizing Specific Languages

In this section we will give proofs for the main results. Let $L := \{1^n 01^m : n \neq m\}$. First it will be shown that $L \notin ASPACE(o(\log n))$. This proves Theorem 3 since from [2] we know that $L \in weakDSPACE(\log \log n)$. Then we will define languages C_1, C_2 and U such that

1. $\bar{C}_1, \bar{C}_2 \in \Sigma_2 SPACE(\log \log n) \setminus \Pi_2 SPACE(o(\log n))$
2. $C_1, C_2 \in \Pi_2 SPACE(\log \log n) \setminus \Sigma_2 SPACE(o(\log n))$
3. $\bar{U} \in \Pi_3 SPACE(\log \log n) \setminus \Sigma_3 SPACE(o(\log n))$
4. $U \in \Sigma_3 SPACE(\log \log n) \setminus \Pi_3 SPACE(o(\log n))$

Theorem 1 follows from (1) - (4), Theorem 2 is a consequence of (1), (2) and (3).

Proposition 1 $L = \{1^n 01^m : n \neq m\} \notin ASPACE(o(\log n))$.

Proof. Let us assume, to the contrary, that L is recognized by an S space-bounded ATM A for some $S(n) \leq o(\log n)$. From Lemma 2 it follows that there exists $\hat{n}$ such that for all $k, l \geq 0$

$$Space_A(1^{\hat{n}} 01^{\hat{n}}) = Space_A(1^{\hat{n}+k\hat{n}!} 01^{\hat{n}+l\hat{n}!}). \tag{1}$$

For this fixed $\hat{n}$ we define the language $\hat{L} = \{1^{\hat{n}+k\hat{n}!} 01^{\hat{n}+l\hat{n}!} : k, l \in \mathbb{N} \text{ and } k \neq l\}$ and construct an automaton $\hat{A}$ that recognizes $\hat{L}$. $\hat{A}$ performs the following algorithm:

1. Check deterministically if the input x has the form $1^{\hat{n}+k\hat{n}!} 01^{\hat{n}+l\hat{n}!}$ for some integers k and l; reject and stop if this condition does not hold;
2. Move the head to the first symbol of the input and start to simulate A.

It is obvious that $\hat{A}$ accepts an input $x = 1^{\hat{n}+k\hat{n}!} 01^{\hat{n}+l\hat{n}!}$ if and only if A accepts x. Hence we have $L(\hat{A}) = \hat{L}$. It is easy to see that step 1 can be performed within space $O(\log \hat{n}!)$, which is a constant. Moreover from (1) it follows that step 2 also requires only constant space $\hat{s} := Space_A(1^{\hat{n}} 01^{\hat{n}})$. Hence $\hat{A}$ recognizes $\hat{L}$ within constant space. We get a contradiction since $\hat{L}$ is non-regular. ∎

Definition 4 *Let $F(n)$ be the smallest positive integer that does not divide n and*

$$
\begin{aligned}
\mathcal{F} &:= \{n \in \mathbb{N} : \forall_{(1 \leq k < n)} F(k) < F(n)\}, \\
C_1 &:= \{1^{n_1} 01^{n_2} : n_1 \in \mathcal{F}\}, \quad C_2 := \{1^{n_1} 01^{n_2} : n_2 \in \mathcal{F}\}, \\
U &:= C_1 \cup C_2.
\end{aligned}
$$

Lemma 7 *For any integer $n \geq 1$, $f(n) \notin \mathcal{F}$, where*

$$
f(n) := \begin{cases} n + n! & \text{if } n + n! \notin \mathcal{F}, \\ n + 2n! & \text{otherwise.} \end{cases}
$$

Proposition 2 $U \notin \Pi_3 SPACE(o(\log n))$ *and* $\bar{U} \notin \Sigma_3 SPACE(o(\log n))$.

Proof. Let us assume, to the contrary, that $U \in \Pi_3 SPACE(S)$, for some $S(n) \leq o(\log n)$. Let M be an S space-bounded $\Pi_3 TM$ for U. Choose $n \in \mathcal{F}$ sufficiently large. By Lemma 7 $y := 1^{f(n)} 01^{f(n)} \notin U$, hence M has to reject y. From Lemma 6 we conclude that M rejects also input $x_1 := 1^{f(n)} 01^n$ or $x_2 := 1^n 01^{f(n)}$, which both belong to U – a contradiction!

Assume now that a $\Sigma_3 TM$ M recognizes $\bar{U}$ in space $S(n) \leq o(\log n)$. Let $n \in \mathcal{F}$ be sufficiently large. Since $y := 1^{f(n)} 01^{f(n)} \in \bar{U}$, M has to accept y. From Lemma 5 we obtain that M accepts also input $x_1 := 1^{f(n)} 01^n$ or $x_2 := 1^n 01^{f(n)}$. This yields a contradiction since $x_1 \notin \bar{U}$ and $x_2 \notin \bar{U}$. ∎

Fact 1 *For any S and for all $k \geq 1$ $\Sigma_k SPACE(S)$ is closed under union and $\Pi_k SPACE(S)$ is closed under intersection.*

This closure properties of alternating space classes have straightforward proofs. Using this fact together with Proposition 2 one can easily show

Proposition 3 $C_1, C_2 \notin \Sigma_2 SPACE(o(\log n))$ and $\bar{C}_1, \bar{C}_2 \notin \Pi_2 SPACE(o(\log n))$.

We close this section with the following upper space bounds for recognizing the languages C_1, C_2, U, and their complements.

Proposition 4 For the languages C_1, C_2 and U holds:

1. $C_1, C_2 \in \Pi_2 SPACE(\log\log n)$ and $\bar{C}_1, \bar{C}_2 \in \Sigma_2 SPACE(\log\log n)$,
2. $U \in \Sigma_3 SPACE(\log\log n)$ and $\bar{U} \in \Pi_3 SPACE(\log\log n)$.

4 Conclusions

It is well known that for any function S, $NSPACE(S)$ ($= \Sigma_1 SPACE(S)$) is closed under union and intersection (see e.g. [12]) however it is still an open problem whether for $S \in SUBLOG$, $NSPACE(S)$ is closed under complementation. For $k > 1$ any class $\Sigma_k SPACE(S)$ is closed under union, and symmetrically, $\Pi_k SPACE(S)$ is closed under intersection (Fact 1). In this paper we have shown that for $S \in SUBLOG$, $\Sigma_2 SPACE(S)$ and $\Sigma_3 SPACE(S)$ are not closed under complementation. Our results imply that

Theorem 4 For any $S \in SUBLOG$, $\Sigma_2 SPACE(S)$ and $\Sigma_3 SPACE(S)$ are not closed under intersection. Moreover, $\Pi_2 SPACE(S)$ and $\Pi_3 SPACE(S)$ are not closed under union and complementation.

Furthermore, we have shown also that for $S \in SUBLOG$ the first four levels of the S space-bounded alternating hierarchy are distinct. Considering the separating languages one notices that the necessary counters, which are not available to sublogarithmic space-bounded TM, can be replaced by alternations.

From Propositions 2 - 4 it follows that, for $k = 2, 3$ $\Sigma_k SPACE(\log\log n) \setminus \Pi_k SPACE(o(\log n)) \neq \emptyset$ and $\Pi_k SPACE(\log\log n) \setminus \Sigma_k SPACE(o(\log n)) \neq \emptyset$. Hence one obtains

Corollary 3 For any $S \in SUBLOG$, $\Sigma_2 SPACE(S) \neq \Pi_2 SPACE(S)$ and $\Sigma_3 SPACE(S) \neq \Pi_3 SPACE(S)$.

Note that the above corollary is not trivially equivalent to Theorem 1, which said that sublogarithmic $\Sigma_2 SPACE$ and $\Sigma_3 SPACE$ are not closed under complementation. Sublogarithmic space-bounded machines do not have a counter which could detect an infinite path of computation. It is an interesting open problem whether $\Pi_k SPACE(S) = co\text{-}\Sigma_k SPACE(S)$, for $k = 1, 2, \ldots$. Using a similar proof technique as in [1] and [11] one can show the following partial answer to this question.

Proposition 5 Let S be any function, let $\{a_1, a_2, \ldots a_k\}$ be a finite set of symbols, and let $L \subseteq a_1^* a_2^* \ldots a_k^*$ be a bounded language. Then $L \in co\text{-}\Sigma_1 SPACE(S)$ if and only if $L \in \Pi_1 SPACE(S)$.

As further consequences of the separation of $\Sigma_k SPACE$ and $\Pi_k SPACE$ one obtains

Theorem 5 *For* $S \in SUBLOG$ *and* $k \leq 3$: $\Pi_k SPACE(S) \subset \Pi_{k+1} SPACE(S)$.

Theorem 6 *For each* $S \in SUBLOG$, *and for* $k = 1, 2, 3$:

$$\Pi_k SPACE(S) \subset \Sigma_{k+1} SPACE(S) \quad and \quad \Sigma_k SPACE(S) \subset \Pi_{k+1} SPACE(S).$$

The following diagram summarizes these results: | means inclusion, ↑ means proper inclusion, and - - - means that two classes are incomparable. S is an arbitrary function from $SUBLOG$.

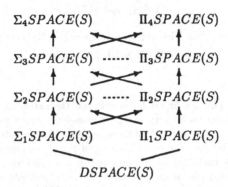

Similar separation results using different languages and techniques have independently been obtained by Viliam Geffert (see [5]) and Burchard von Braunmühl (see this proceedings).

References

1. H. Alt, V. Geffert, and K. Mehlhorn, *A lower bound for the nondeterministic space complexity of context-free recognition*, IPL 42, 1992, 25-27.

2. H. Alt, and K. Mehlhorn, *Lower bounds for the space complexity of context free recognition*, Proc. 3. ICALP, 1976, 339-354.

3. J. Chang, O. Ibarra, B. Ravikumar, and L. Berman, *Some observations concerning alternating Turing machines using small space*, IPL 25, 1987, 1-9.

4. V. Geffert, *Nondeterministic computations in sublogarithmic space and space constructability*, SIAM J. Comput., 20, 1991, 484-498.

5. V. Geffert, *Sublogarithmic Σ_2 -space is not closed under complement and other separation results*, Technical Report, University of Safarik, 1992.

6. J. Hartmanis, and D. Ranjan, *Space bounded computations: review and new separation results*, Proc. 14. MFCS, 1989, 46-66 (also TCS 80, 1991, 289-302).

7. N. Immerman, *Nondeterministic space is closed under complementation*, SIAM J. Comput., 17, 1988, 935-938.

8. P. Michel, *A survey of space complexity*, TCS 101, 1992, 99-132.

9. M. Sipser, *Halting space-bounded computations*, TCS 10, 1980, 335-338.

10. R. Stearns, J. Hartmanis, and P. Lewis, *Hierarchies of memory limited computations*, Proc. IEEE Conf. on Switching Circuit Theory and Logical Design, 1965, 179-190.

11. R. Szelépcsenyi, *The method of forced enumeration for nondeterministic automata*, Acta Informatica, 26, 1988, 279-284.

12. A. Szepietowski, *Turing machines with sublogarithmic space*, unpubl. manuscript.

13. K. Wagner, and G. Wechsung, *Computational Complexity*, Reidel, 1986.

Locating P/poly Optimally in the Extended Low Hierarchy

Johannes Köbler

Abteilung für Theoretische Informatik, Universität Ulm
D-W-7900 Ulm, Germany

Abstract. The low hierarchy in NP and the extended low hierarchy have turned out to be very useful in classifying many interesting language classes, and almost all of them could be located optimally therein. However, until now, the exact location of P/poly remained open.

We show that P/poly is contained in the third theta level $EL_3^{P,\Theta}$ of the extended low hierarchy. Since Allender and Hemachandra have shown that there exist sparse sets outside of $EL_2^{P,\Sigma}$, this is optimal.

1 Introduction

The low and high hierarchies inside NP were introduced by Schöning [19] and have turned out to be an important structural tool for classifying decision problems in NP not known to be NP-complete or in P. This idea was extended by Balcázar, Book, and Schöning [4] who defined the extended low and high hierarchies in order to classify decision problems and language classes not contained in NP. The low hierarchies, originally based only on the Σ-levels of the polynomial hierarchy, were subsequently refined on the base of the Δ and Θ-levels [20, 2, 15]. The Θ-levels of the polynomial hierarchy were introduced by Wagner [25] who demonstrated their robustness and importance by establishing a variety of very different characterizations for them.

All sets that could be located within the low hierarchies roughly fall into two categories. Either they have *low complexity*, i.e., they are "close" to the class P, like the primality [18] or graph isomorphism [21] problems, or they are of *low information content* like sparse sets or sets reducible to (or equivalent to) sparse or tally sets via different kinds of reducibilities. Various classes of sets reducible to sparse and tally sets have been shown to be included in the extended low hierarchy (for an overview see for example [20, 2, 15, 9, 3]). Allender and Hemachandra [2] and Long and Sheu [15] proved the optimality of the location of almost all the classes known to be in the extended low hierarchy, and they showed that also the location of most of the classes within the low hierarchy is optimal in some relativized world.

However, until now, the exact location of P/poly remained an open problem. The class P/poly is well studied and coincides with the class of languages that can be computed by polynomially size bounded circuits [17], and with the class of sets Turing reducible to some sparse set (attributed to A. Meyer in [6]). Ko and Schöning [11] showed that all NP sets in P/poly are contained in the third Σ-level of the low hierarchy. This result was extended by Balcázar, Book, and Schöning [4] who located all of P/poly in the $\mathrm{EL}_3^{p,\Sigma}$ level of the extended low hierarchy.

In this paper we show that P/poly is contained in the third Θ-level of the extended low hierarchy. Since there exist sparse sets that are not contained in $\mathrm{EL}_2^{p,\Sigma}$ [2], P/poly is not included in the next lower level of the extended low hierarchy. The $\mathrm{EL}_2^{p,\Sigma}$ lower bound for P/poly was improved by Long and Sheu [15] who showed that for every function f with the property that for some constant c, $f(n) < c \log n$ infinitely often, there exists a sparse set S such that $\Theta_2^p(S) \not\subseteq \mathrm{P}^{\mathrm{NP}(\mathrm{SAT} \oplus S)}[f(n)]$.[1] These lower bounds indicate that the location of P/poly in $\mathrm{EL}_3^{p,\Theta}$ is optimal.

As a consequence of our result, all NP sets in P/poly are located in the third Θ-level of the low hierarchy. Furthermore, it turns out that the proof showing that P/poly is contained in $\mathrm{EL}_3^{p,\Theta}$ actually reveals that even the class $(\mathrm{NP} \cap \mathrm{co}\text{-}\mathrm{NP})/\mathrm{poly}$ is $\mathrm{EL}_3^{p,\Theta}$-low, and therefore every NP set in the class $(\mathrm{NP} \cap \mathrm{co}\text{-}\mathrm{NP})/\mathrm{poly}$ is contained in the third Θ-level of the low hierarchy.

The paper is organized as follows. Section 2 introduces notation and gives basic definitions. In Section 3 we show that for every set $A \in \mathrm{P}/\mathrm{poly}$ correct advice can be computed in $\mathrm{FP}(\mathrm{NP}(A) \oplus \Sigma_2^p)$. The previous upper bound for the complexity of advice functions for a set A in P/poly was $\mathrm{FP}(\Sigma_2^p(A))$ [11, 20]. Very recently, Gavalda [8] obtained an $\mathrm{FP}(\mathrm{NP}(A) \oplus \Sigma_3^p)$ upper bound which is incomparable to the $\mathrm{FP}(\Sigma_2^p(A))$ bound. By combining the ideas developed by Gavalda with the method of Stockmeyer [24] to increase the accuracy of $\mathrm{FP}(\Sigma_2^p(A))$ approximations for #P functions, we are able to subsume the $\mathrm{FP}(\Sigma_2^p(A))$ as well as Gavalda's upper bound.

In Section 4 we refine the techniques used to prove the new $\mathrm{FP}(\mathrm{NP}(A) \oplus \Sigma_2^p)$ upper bound of Section 3 and apply a census argument to show that for every set A in P/poly a given advice string can be tested for correctness by an $\mathrm{NP}(\mathrm{NP} \oplus A)$ machine that takes the advice of an $\mathrm{F}\Theta_2^p(\mathrm{NP} \oplus A)$ function. Based on this result, the $\mathrm{EL}_3^{p,\Theta}$-lowness of P/poly is easily obtained.

2 Preliminaries and Notation

For a set A let $A^{=n}$ ($A^{\leq n}$) denote all strings in A of length n (up to length n, respectively). The cardinality of A is denoted by $|A|$. A set T is called a tally set if $T \subseteq 0^*$. A set S is called sparse if the cardinality of $S^{\leq n}$ is bounded above by a polynomial in n.

The join $A \oplus B$ of two sets A and B is defined as $\{0x \mid x \in A\} \cup \{1x \mid x \in B\}$. For set classes $\mathcal{C}_1, \mathcal{C}_2$, $\mathcal{C}_1 \oplus \mathcal{C}_2$ is the class $\{A \oplus B \mid A \in \mathcal{C}_1, B \in \mathcal{C}_2\}$.

A deterministic polynomial-time oracle machine [oracle transducer] that asks on inputs of length n at most $O(\log n)$ queries to A is called a Θ machine [resp., Θ transducer]. For a set A, the class $\Theta(A)$ [15] contains all languages $L(M, A)$ accepted by some Θ machine M using oracle A. The Θ-levels of the (relativized)

---

[1] $f(n)$ bounds the number of oracle queries of the base P machine to the $\mathrm{NP}(\mathrm{SAT} \oplus S)$ oracle.

polynomial time hierarchy are defined as $\Theta_k^p(A) = \Theta(\Sigma_{k-1}^p(A)), k \geq 1$ [15, 25]. Similarly, the class $F\Theta(A)$ contains all functions computable by some Θ transducer T using oracle A, and $F\Theta_k^p(A) = F\Theta(\Sigma_{k-1}^p(A)), k \geq 1$.

Schöning [19, 20] defined the Σ and Δ-levels of the low hierarchy inside NP. Recently, the low hierarchy was refined by Long and Sheu [15] on the base of the Θ-levels of the polynomial hierarchy [23, 25].

The low hierarchy was extended by Balcázar, Book, and Schöning [4] who defined the Σ-levels of the extended low hierarchy in order to classify language classes not contained in NP. Allender and Hemachandra [2], and Long and Sheu [15] refined the extended low hierarchy by introducing intermediate levels based on the Δ and Θ-levels of the polynomial hierarchy, respectively.

Definition 2.1 [4, 2, 15] *The Σ, Δ, and Θ-levels of the extended low hierarchy (denoted $\mathrm{EL}_k^{p,\Sigma}$, $\mathrm{EL}_k^{p,\Delta}$, and $\mathrm{EL}_k^{p,\Theta}$, respectively) are defined as below.*

a) $\mathrm{EL}_k^{p,\Sigma} = \{A \mid \Sigma_k^p(A) \subseteq \Sigma_{k-1}^p(\mathrm{SAT} \oplus A)\}$, $k \geq 1$,

b) $\mathrm{EL}_k^{p,\Delta} = \{A \mid \Delta_k^p(A) \subseteq \Delta_{k-1}^p(\mathrm{SAT} \oplus A)\}$, $k \geq 2$,

c) $\mathrm{EL}_k^{p,\Theta} = \{A \mid \Theta_k^p(A) \subseteq \Theta_{k-1}^p(\mathrm{SAT} \oplus A)\}$, $k \geq 2$.

Proposition 2.2 [4, 2, 15]

i) $\mathrm{EL}_1^{p,\Sigma} = \mathrm{EL}_2^{p,\Theta} = \mathrm{EL}_2^{p,\Delta}$,

ii) *For each* $k \geq 2$, $\mathrm{EL}_{k-1}^{p,\Sigma} \subseteq \mathrm{EL}_k^{p,\Theta} \subseteq \mathrm{EL}_k^{p,\Delta} \subseteq \mathrm{EL}_k^{p,\Sigma}$.

Karp and Lipton [10] introduced the notion of advice functions in order to define nonuniform complexity classes. For a class $\mathcal{C}$ of sets and a class $\mathcal{F}$ of functions from 0^* to Σ^* let $\mathcal{C}/\mathcal{F}$ be the class of sets A such that there is a set $B \in \mathcal{C}$ and a function $h \in \mathcal{F}$ such that for all $x \in \Sigma^*$, $\chi_A(x) = \chi_B(x, h(0^{|x|}))$. The functions in $\mathcal{F}$ are called advice functions. Note that the value $h(0^{|x|})$ of the advice function depends only on the length of x. The best studied nonuniform complexity class is P/poly where poly is the advice function class $\{h \mid$ there exists a polynomial p such that for all $n, |h(0^n)| \leq p(n)\}$.

For further definitions used in this paper see some standard textbook on structural complexity theory (e.g. [20, 5]).

3 A new Upper Bound for the Complexity of Computing Correct Advice

Sipser [22] used universal hashing, originally invented by Carter and Wegman [7], to decide (probabilistically) whether a finite set X is large or small. A linear hash function h from Σ^p to Σ^m is given by a Boolean (m, p)-matrix (a_{ij}) and maps a given string $x = x_1 \ldots x_p \in \Sigma^p$ to the string $y = y_1 \ldots y_m$ where $y_i = \oplus_{j=1}^p (a_{ij} \wedge x_j)$. A family $H = h_1, \ldots, h_s$ of linear hash functions from Σ^p to Σ^m hashes a set $X \subseteq \Sigma^p$ if

$$\forall x \in X \, \exists k \, (1 \leq k \leq s) \, \forall y \in X : x \neq y \Rightarrow h_k(x) \neq h_k(y)$$

We denote the set of all families $H = h_1, \ldots, h_s$ of s linear hash functions from Σ^p to Σ^m by $\mathcal{H}(s, p, m)$ and say that a set $X \subseteq \Sigma^p$ is hashable in $\mathcal{H}(s, p, m)$ if there exists an $H \in \mathcal{H}(s, p, m)$ that hashes X. In the case that the size s coincides with the dimension m of the range of the hash families we simply write $\mathcal{H}(s, p)$ instead of $\mathcal{H}(s, p, s)$. The following theorem follows by a pigeon-hole argument.

Theorem 3.1 [22] *If a set $X \subseteq \Sigma^p$ is hashable in $\mathcal{H}(s, p, m)$ then $|X| \leq s \cdot 2^m$.*

The next theorem (called Coding Lemma in [22]) states that every set X is hashed with high probability by a random hash family of suitable size.

Theorem 3.2 [22] *Let $X \subseteq \Sigma^p$ be a set of cardinality at most 2^{m-1}. Then the probability that a uniformly at random chosen hash family $H \in \mathcal{H}(m, p)$ hashes X is at least $1/2$.*

The above two theorems allow already a rough estimation of the cardinality of a given set $X \subseteq \Sigma^p$ depending on the minimum hash family size m for which X is hashable in $\mathcal{H}(m, p)$: $2^{m-2} < |X| \leq m2^m$. By estimating the size of the set X^r (for some large enough integer r) one can obtain a much sharper estimation for the size of the set X (cf. [24, 13, 12]).

Corollary 3.3 *For every polynomial $t > 0$ there is a polynomial $r > 0$ such that for every set $X \subseteq \Sigma^p$ and every j, $0 < j \leq 2^p$,*

$$|X| \leq j \quad \Rightarrow \quad X^{r(p)} \text{ is hashable in } \mathcal{H}(\lceil r(p) \log j \rceil + 1, p \cdot r(p))$$
$$\Rightarrow \quad |X| \leq j + j/t(p).$$

Gavalda extended Sipser's Coding Lemma (Theorem 3.2) to the case of collections $\mathcal{X}$ of sets and showed that all sets in $\mathcal{X}$ can be hashed simultaneously by relatively small hash families.

Theorem 3.4 [8] *Let $\mathcal{X}$ be a collection of sets $X_1, \ldots, X_{2^n} \subseteq \Sigma^p$ each of cardinality at most 2^{m-1}. Then the probability that a uniformly at random chosen hash family $H \in \mathcal{H}(m(n + 1), p, m)$ hashes every X_i, $1 \leq i \leq 2^n$, is at least $1/2$.*

Theorem 3.5 *Every set $A \in P/poly$ has an advice function in $FP(NP(A) \oplus \Sigma_2^p)$.*

Proof Sketch Let A be in P/poly witnessed by a set $B \in P$ and an advice function $h \in$ poly. Without limitation of generality (by a padding argument) we can assume that there is a polynomial $p > 0$ such that for all n it holds that $|h(0^n)| = p(n)$ and $|\{w \in \Sigma^{p(n)} \mid \forall x \in \Sigma^n : \chi_A(x) = \chi_B(x, w)\}| \geq 4(n+1)p(n)$, i.e., the number of advice strings in $\Sigma^{p(n)}$ that are correct for all inputs of length n is at least $4(n + 1)p(n)$. We show that a function g satisfying for all x,

$$\chi_A(x) = \chi_B(x, g(0^{|x|}))$$

can be computed in polynomial time by an oracle transducer M using an oracle set in $NP(A) \oplus \Sigma_2^p$. The intuitive idea behind the algorithm performed by M is the following: M on input 0^n first computes a *sample* S of pairs $\langle x_1, \chi_A(x_1) \rangle, \ldots, \langle x_k, \chi_A(x_k) \rangle$ such that the set

$$Consistent(S) = \{w \in \Sigma^{p(n)} \mid \forall i, 1 \leq i \leq k : \chi_A(x_i) = \chi_B(x_i, w)\}$$

of all advice strings w *consistent* with S has the property that for every string x of length n the majority of the advice strings in $Consistent(S)$ decides x correctly, i.e.,

$$x \in A \iff |Accept(x, S)| > |Reject(x, S)|$$

where $Accept(x, S)$ is the set $\{w \in Consistent(S) \mid \chi_B(x, w) = 1\}$ of all consistent advice strings that accept x, and $Reject(x, S)$ is defined accordingly. Moreover, S is constructed in such a way that the two sets $Accept(x, S)$ and $Reject(x, S)$ are very different in size, i.e., for every $x \in \Sigma^n$ a large majority of strings in $Consistent(S)$ is in the set

$$Correct(x, S) = \{w \in Consistent(S) \mid \chi_B(x, w) = \chi_A(x)\}$$

of consistent advice strings that decide x correctly, and only a small minority is in the set $Incorrect(x, S)$ of consistent advice strings that decide x incorrectly. In addition to S machine M constructs a hash family H that hashes simultaneously all the sets $Incorrect(x, S)$, $x \in \Sigma^n$, but none of the sets $Correct(x, S)$, $x \in \Sigma^n$. Having constructed S and H, machine M can determine by prefix search the lexicographically smallest correct advice string w_{min} using the following Σ_2^p oracle set U,

$\langle 0^n, S, H, u \rangle \in U \iff$

there is a v such that $|uv| = p(n)$ and for all $x \in \Sigma^n$, either $\chi_B(x, uv) = 1$ and H hashes $Reject(x, S)$ or $\chi_B(x, uv) = 0$ and H hashes $Accept(x, S)$.

We now describe the algorithm in more detail. Since the function $c(S) = |Consistent(S)|$ is in $\#P$ it can be approximated by $F\Delta_3^p$ functions within an arbitrarily small inverse polynomial relative error [24, 13, 12], i.e., for every polynomial $q > 0$ (which we will fix later) there is a $F\Delta_3^p$ function c'' such that

$$0 \leq \frac{c''(S) - c(S)}{c(S)} < 1/q(n).$$

Note that c'' never underestimates c, i.e., c'' actually is an upper bound for c. To obtain a lower bound for c we define the function

$$c'(S) = \frac{q(n)}{q(n)+1} c''(S). \tag{1}$$

Since $4(n+1)p(n) \leq c(S) \leq 2^{p(n)}$ we can without limitation of generality assume that

$$4(n+1)p(n) \leq c'(S) \leq c(S) \leq c''(S) \leq 2^{p(n)}. \tag{2}$$

Next we choose a suitable function m which is small enough to make sure that no hash family $H \in \mathcal{H}((n+1) \cdot m(S), p(n), m(S))$ is able to hash for some $x \in \Sigma^n$ simultaneously the two sets $Accept(x, S)$ and $Reject(x, S)$. Define

$$m(S) = \left\lfloor \log \frac{c'(S)}{2(n+1)p(n)} \right\rfloor. \tag{3}$$

Claim 1 *For every sample S and every $x \in \Sigma^n$, if one of the two sets $Accept(x, S)$ and $Reject(x, S)$ is hashable in $\mathcal{H}((n + 1) \cdot m(S), p(n), m(S))$ then the other one is not, and the size of the other set is at least $c(S)/2$.*

Now we describe how the algorithm constructs a sample S and a hash family $H \in \mathcal{H}((n+1) \cdot m(S), p(n), m(S))$ that simultaneously hashes all the sets $Incorrect(x, S)$, $x \in \Sigma^n$. The algorithm starts with the empty sample $S = \emptyset$. By Theorem 3.4 the existence of H is guaranteed if all the sets $Incorrect(x, S)$, $x \in \Sigma^n$ are sufficiently small. As long as there are input strings $x \in \Sigma^n$ for which the set $Incorrect(x, S)$ is large, the algorithm computes such an input string, say x', and extends the sample S to S' by including the pair $\langle x', \chi_A(x') \rangle$ into S. Since $c(S') = c(S) - |Incorrect(x', S)|$, it suffices to guarantee that for some polynomial t,

$$|Incorrect(x', S)| \geq \frac{c(S)}{t(n)}$$

in order to bound the number of such extentions by a polynomial (this procedure is similar to the so-called "logarithmic strategy" due to D. Angluin [1]). Machine M first tries to expand S by an $x' \in \Sigma^n$ such that both the sets $Accept(x', S)$ and $Reject(x', S)$ (and therefore also $Incorrect(x', S)$) are large. If such an input string does not exist, then M constructs a hash family $H \in \mathcal{H}((n+1) \cdot m(S), p(n), m(S))$ that hashes for every $x \in \Sigma^n$ (exactly) one of the two sets $Accept(x, S)$ and $Reject(x, S)$. If for some $x' \in \Sigma^n$ the set $Correct(x', S)$ is hashed by H then $Incorrect(x', S)$ must be large, and thus M can expand S by x'. Otherwise H is the desired hash family and M can determine the lexicographically smallest correct advice string w_{min}. We give now a formal description of M (r is a polynomial and l is a function that will be fixed later).

> **input** 0^n
> $S := \emptyset$
> **loop**
>   **if** there exists an $x \in \Sigma^n$ such that
>   there exist $H_1, H_2 \in \mathcal{H}(l(S), r(n) \cdot p(n))$ such that
> H_1 hashes $Accept(x, S)^{r(n)}$ and H_2 hashes $Reject(x, S)^{r(n)}$
>   **then**
>   construct by prefix search the lexicographically first such x
> $S := S \cup \{\langle x, \chi_A(x) \rangle\}$
>   **else**
>   construct by prefix search the lexicographically first hash family
> $H \in \mathcal{H}((n+1) \cdot m(S), p(n), m(S))$ such that for all $x \in \Sigma^n$,
> H either hashes $Accept(x, S)$ or $Reject(x, S)$
>   **if** for some $x \in \Sigma^n$, H does not hash $Incorrect(x, S)$ **then**
>   construct by prefix search the lexicographically first such x
> $S := S \cup \{\langle x, \chi_A(x) \rangle\}$
>   **else** exit(loop) **end**
>   **end**
> **end loop**
> compute the smallest correct advice string w_{min} by asking oracle U
> **output** w_{min}

Note that in order to increase the accuracy of our knowledge about the sizes of $Accept(x, S)$ and $Reject(x, S)$, we test the hashability of the sets $Accept(x, S)^{r(n)}$ and $Reject(x, S)^{r(n)}$ instead of $Accept(x, S)$ and $Reject(x, S)$, respectively. To make sure that one of the two sets $Accept(x, S)$ and $Reject(x, S)$ has cardinality less than $2^{m(S)-1}$ if not both sets $Accept(x, S)^{r(n)}$ and $Reject(x, S)^{r(n)}$ are hashable in $\mathcal{H}(l(S), r(n) \cdot p(n))$, we choose parameter $l(S)$ as

$$l(S) = \lceil r(n) \log(c''(S) - 2^{m(S)-1}) \rceil + 1. \tag{4}$$

Claim 2 Let $r > 0$ be any polynomial. If both $Accept(x, S)$ and $Reject(x, S)$ are of cardinality at least $2^{m(S)-1}$, then each of the two sets $Accept(x, S)^{r(n)}$ and $Reject(x, S)^{r(n)}$ is hashable in $\mathcal{H}(l(S), r(n) \cdot p(n))$.

What remains to show is that the polynomials q and r can be chosen so that if there is an $x \in \Sigma^n$ such that $Accept(x, S)^{r(n)}$ and $Reject(x, S)^{r(n)}$ are hashable in $\mathcal{H}(l(S), r(n) \cdot p(n))$ then $Accept(x, S)$ and $Reject(x, S)$ are smaller in size than $c(S) - c(S)/t(n)$, for some polynomial t. The following claim shows that it is possible to choose the polynomials q and r in such a way that this holds for $t = 2q$.

Claim 3 The polynomials q and r can be chosen so that if each of the two sets $Accept(x, S)^{r(n)}$ and $Reject(x, S)^{r(n)}$ is hashable in $\mathcal{H}(l(S), r(n) \cdot p(n))$, then $Accept(x, S)$ and $Reject(x, S)$ are of cardinality at least $c(S)/2q(n)$.

The proof of the theorem is completed by the following claim.

Claim 4 Transducer M on input 0^n outputs the lexicographically smallest correct advice string, and this computation can be performed in $FP(NP(A) \oplus \Sigma_2^p)$.
□

We notice that it follows already from Theorem 3.5 that P/poly is contained in the $EL_3^{p,\Delta}$ level of the extended low hierarchy. The proof of Theorem 3.5 can be adjusted to prove the following result.

Theorem 3.6 Every set A in $(NP \cap co\text{-}NP)/poly$ has an advice function computable in $FP(NP(A) \oplus \Sigma_2^p)$.

4 Lowness

In this section we refine the techniques used to prove Theorem 3.5 and apply a census argument to show that for every set A in P/poly a given advice string can be tested for correctness by an $NP(NP \oplus A)$ machine that takes the advice of an $F\Theta_2^p(NP \oplus A)$ function. Note that in order to obtain the Σ_3^p-lowness of all NP sets in P/poly, Ko and Schöning [11] showed that the correctness of a given advice string is decidable in co-NP(A). As a consequence of our $NP(NP \oplus A)/F\Theta_2^p(NP \oplus A)$ bound we are able to locate P/poly in the $EL_3^{p,\Theta}$ level of the extended low hierarchy, thus proving the Θ_3^p-lowness of $NP \cap P/poly$.

Theorem 4.1 Let A be a set in P/poly witnessed by a set B in P and an advice function $h \in$ poly, and let $p(n)$ be a polynomial bounding the length of $h(0^n)$. Then the set of all correct advice strings for A w.r.t. B,

$$\{\langle 0^n, w \rangle \mid |w| \le p(n) \land \forall x \in \Sigma^n : \chi_A(x) = \chi_B(x, w)\}$$

can be decided in $NP(NP \oplus A)/F\Theta_2^p(NP \oplus A)$.

Proof Sketch Let $\langle 0^n, w \rangle$ be the given input. By padding the advice strings we can assume, without limitation of generality, that $|w| = p(n)$ and

$$|\{w' \in \Sigma^{p(n)} \mid \forall x \in \Sigma^n : \chi_A(x) = \chi_B(x, w')\}| \geq 4(n+1)p(n).$$

We first specify which kind of advice we use and show that it can be provided by an $\mathrm{F}\Theta_2^p(\mathrm{NP} \oplus A)$ computation (see [14] for a discussion of complexity-restricted advice functions).

Claim 5 *For every polynomial $t > 0$ there is a polynomial $r > 0$ and an $\mathrm{F}\Theta_2^p(\mathrm{NP} \oplus A)$ function g computing a triple $g(0^n) = \langle c', k, l \rangle$ such that*

i) *there exists a sample S of size at most k such that the set $\mathit{Consistent}(S)^{r(n)}$ is hashable in $\mathcal{H}(l, r(n) \cdot p(n))$,*

ii) *for every such sample S and every $x \in \Sigma^n$, $c(S) \geq c'$ and the set $\mathit{Incorrect}(x, S)$ is of cardinality at most $c'/t(n)$.*

Now we are ready to give the $\mathrm{NP}(\mathrm{NP} \oplus A)$ algorithm that, given the advice of function g, decides the correctness of the advice string w (t, r are polynomials, and m is a function that will be fixed later).

> **input** $\langle 0^n, w, c', k, l \rangle$
> $(\star \ \langle c', k, l \rangle = g(0^n)$ is the advice provided by $g \ \star)$
> **guess** $x_1, \ldots, x_k \in \Sigma^n$
> $S := \{\langle x_1, \chi_A(x_1) \rangle, \ldots, \langle x_k, \chi_A(x_k) \rangle\}$
> **guess** $H \in \mathcal{H}(l, r(n) \cdot p(n))$
> **if** H hashes $\mathit{Consistent}(S)^{r(n)}$ **then**
>   **guess** $H' \in \mathcal{H}((n+1)m(c'), p(n), m(c'))$
>   **if** for all $x \in \Sigma^n$ either $\chi_B(x, w) = 1$ and H' hashes $\mathit{Reject}(x, S)$,
>   or $\chi_B(x, w) = 0$ and H' hashes $\mathit{Accept}(x, S)\}$
>   **then** *accept* **else** *reject* **end**
> **else** *reject* **end**

Clearly, the above procedure can be performed in $\mathrm{NP}(\mathrm{NP} \oplus A)$. By Claim 5, there exists a sample S of size (at most) k such that $\mathit{Consistent}(S)^{r(n)}$ is hashable in $\mathcal{H}(l, r(n) \cdot p(n))$, provided we choose r accordingly. Furthermore, if we define the function m as

$$m(c') = \left\lfloor \log \tfrac{c'}{2(n+1)p(n)} \right\rfloor$$

and the polynomial t as $t(n) = 8(n+1)p(n)$, then it follows by Claim 5 that for all $x \in \Sigma^n$,

$$|\mathit{Incorrect}(x, S)| \leq c'/t(n) \leq 2^{m(c')-1}.$$

Thus, by Theorem 3.4, there is a hash family $H' \in \mathcal{H}((n+1)m(c'), p(n), m(c'))$ that simultaneously hashes all the sets $\mathit{Incorrect}(x, S)$, $x \in \Sigma^n$. Since c' is a lower bound for $c(S)$, it follows from Claim 1 that H' hashes for every $x \in \Sigma^n$ only one of the two sets $\mathit{Accept}(x, S)$ and $\mathit{Reject}(x, S)$, i.e., H' does not hash any of the sets $\mathit{Correct}(x, S)$, $x \in \Sigma^n$. Therefore it holds for every $x \in \Sigma^n$ that

$x \in A$ if and only if H' hashes the set $Reject(x, S)$, and $x \notin A$ if and only if H' hashes the set $Accept(x, S)$. This shows that exactly the advice strings $w \in \Sigma^{p(n)}$ that are correct for all inputs of length n are accepted by the above procedure provided that the right advice $g(0^n) = \langle c', k, l \rangle$ is given along with the input $\langle 0^n, w \rangle$. $\quad\square$

Using standard techniques it is now not hard to proof our main result.

Theorem 4.2 P/poly *is contained in* $\mathrm{EL}_3^{p,\Theta}$.

A careful inspection of the proof reveals that in fact also the class $(\mathrm{NP} \cap \mathrm{co\text{-}NP})/\mathrm{poly}$ is contained in $\mathrm{EL}_3^{p,\Theta}$.

Theorem 4.3 $(\mathrm{NP} \cap \mathrm{co\text{-}NP})/\mathrm{poly}$ *is contained in* $\mathrm{EL}_3^{p,\Theta}$.

As a direct consequence of Theorems 4.2 and 4.3 we get an improvement of Ko's and Schöning's result that $\mathrm{NP} \cap \mathrm{P/poly}$ is low for Σ_3^p [11].

Corollary 4.4 *Every set* $A \in \mathrm{NP} \cap (\mathrm{NP} \cap \mathrm{co\text{-}NP})/\mathrm{poly}$ *is low for* Θ_3^p, *that is,* $\Theta_3^p(A) = \Theta_3^p$.

Acknowledgments. For helpful conversations and suggestions regarding this work the author is very grateful to V. Arvind, M. Mundhenk, U. Schöning and R. Schuler.

References

[1] D. ANGLUIN. Queries and concept learning. *Machine Learning*, 2:319-342, 1988.

[2] E. ALLENDER AND L. HEMACHANDRA. Lower bounds for the low hierarchy. *Journal of the ACM*, 39(1):234-250, 1992.

[3] V. ARVIND, J. KÖBLER, M. MUNDHENK. Lowness and the complexity of sparse and tally descriptions. To appear in *Proceedings 3rd Symposium on Algorithms and Computation*, Springer-Verlag, 1992.

[4] J.L. BALCÁZAR, R. BOOK, AND U. SCHÖNING. Sparse sets, lowness and highness. *SIAM J. Comput.*, 23:679-688, 1986.

[5] J.L. BALCÁZAR, J. DÍAZ, J. GABARRÓ. *Structural Complexity Theory I + II.* Springer-Verlag, 1988 and 1990.

[6] L. BERMAN, J. HARTMANIS. On isomorphism and density of NP and other complexity classes. *SIAM J. Comput.*, 6:305-327, 1977.

[7] J.L. CARTER AND M.N. WEGMAN. Universal classes of hash functions. *Journal of Computer and System Sciences* 18:143-154, 1979.

[8] R. GAVALDA. Bounding the complexity of advice functions. In *Proceedings of the 7th Structure in Complexity Theory Conference*, 249-254. IEEE Computer Society Press, June 1992.

[9] L. HEMACHANDRA, M. OGIWARA, AND O. WATANABE. How hard are sparse sets. In *Proceedings of the 7th Structure in Complexity Theory Conference*, 222-238. IEEE Computer Society Press, June 1992.

[10] R.M. KARP AND R.J. LIPTON. Some connections between nonuniform and uniform complexity classes. *Proc. 12th ACM Symp. Theory of Comput. Science*, 302-309, 1980.

[11] K. KO AND U. SCHÖNING. On circuit-size complexity and the low hierarchy in NP. *SIAM Journ. Comput.* 14:41-51, 1985.

[12] J. KÖBLER. *Strukturelle Komplexität von Anzahlproblemen*. Doctoral Dissertation. University of Stuttgart, 1989.

[13] J. KÖBLER, U. SCHÖNING, J. TORÁN. On counting and approximation. *Acta Informatica*, 26:363–379, 1989.

[14] J. KÖBLER AND T. THIERAUF. Complexity classes with advice. *Proceedings 5th Structure in Complexity Theory Conference*, 305-315, IEEE Computer Society, 1990.

[15] T.J. LONG AND M.-J. SHEU. A refinement of the low and high hierarchies. Technical Report OSU-CISRC-2/91-TR6, The Ohio State University, 1991.

[16] M.-J. SHEU AND T.J. LONG. The extended low hierarchy is an infinite hierarchy. *Proceedings of 9th Symposium on Theoretical Aspects of Computer Science*, Lecture Notes in Computer Science, #577:187-189, Springer-Verlag 1992.

[17] N. PIPPENGER. On simultaneous resource bounds. In *Proceedings 20th Symposium on Foundations of Computer Science*, 307-311, IEEE Computer Society, 1979.

[18] V. PRATT. Every prime has a succinct certificate. *SIAM Journal on Computing* 4 (1975), 214-220.

[19] U. SCHÖNING. A low hierarchy within NP. *Journal of Computer and System Sciences*, 27:14-28, 1983.

[20] U. SCHÖNING. *Complexity and Structure*. Springer-Verlag *Lecture Notes in Computer Science* 211, 1986.

[21] U. SCHÖNING. Graph isomorphism is in the low hierarchy. *Journal of Computer and System Sciences*, 37:312-323, 1988.

[22] M. SIPSER. A complexity theoretic approach to randomness. *Proc. 15th ACM Symp. Theory of Comput. Science*, 330-335, 1983.

[23] L.J. STOCKMEYER. The polynomial-time hierarchy. *Theor. Comput. Science*, 3:1-22, 1977.

[24] L.J. STOCKMEYER. On approximation algorithms for #P. *SIAM Journ. Comput.* 14:849-861, 1985.

[25] K.W. WAGNER. Bounded query classes. *SIAM Journ. Comput.* 19(5):833-846, 1990.

[26] C. WRATHALL. Complete sets and the polynomial-time hierarchy. *Theor. Comput. Science* 3:23–33, 1977.

Measure, Stochasticity, and the
Density of Hard Languages

Jack H. Lutz*
Dept. of Computer Science
Iowa State University
Ames, Iowa 50011
U.S.A.

Elvira Mayordomo†
Dept. LSI
Univ. Politècnica de Catalunya
Pau Gargallo 5
08028 Barcelona, Spain

Abstract

The main theorem of this paper is that, for every real number $\alpha < 1$ (e.g., $\alpha = 0.99$), only a measure 0 subset of the languages decidable in exponential time are $\leq^P_{n^\alpha-tt}$-reducible to languages that are not exponentially dense. *Thus every $\leq^P_{n^\alpha-tt}$-hard language for E is exponentially dense.* This strengthens Watanabe's 1987 result, that every $\leq^P_{O(\log n)-tt}$-hard language for E is exponentially dense. The combinatorial technique used here, the *sequentially most frequent query selection*, also gives a new, simpler proof of Watanabe's result.

The main theorem also has implications for the structure of NP under strong hypotheses. Ogiwara and Watanabe (1991) have shown that the hypothesis P $\neq$ NP implies that every $\leq^P_{btt}$-hard language for NP is non-sparse (i.e., not polynomially sparse). Their technique does not appear to allow significant relaxation of either the query bound or the sparseness criterion. It is shown here that a stronger hypothesis—namely, that NP does not have measure 0 in exponential time—implies the stronger conclusion that, for every real $\alpha < 1$, every $\leq^P_{n^\alpha-tt}$-hard language for NP is exponentially dense. Evidence is presented that this stronger hypothesis is reasonable.

Also presented here (and used in proving the main theorem) is a *weak stochasticity theorem*, ensuring that almost every language in E is statistically unpredictable by feasible deterministic algorithms, even with linear nonuniform advice.

1 Introduction

How dense must a language $A \subseteq \{0,1\}^*$ be in order to be hard for a complexity class $\mathcal{C}$? The ongoing investigation of this question, especially important when $\mathcal{C} = $ NP, has yielded several significant results [3, 10, 18, 20, 21, 28, 29] over the past 15 years.

---

*This author's research was supported in part by National Science Foundation Grant CCR-9157382, with matching funds from Rockwell International, and in part by DIMACS, where he was a visitor during the first phase of this work.

†This author's research, performed while visiting Iowa State University, was supported in part by the ESPRIT EC project 3075 (ALCOM), in part by National Science Foundation Grant CCR-9157382, and in part by Spanish Government grant FPI PN90.

Any formalization of this question must specify the class C and give precise meanings to "hard" and "how dense." The results of this paper concern the classes $E = \text{DTIME}(2^{\text{linear}})$, $E_2 = \text{DTIME}(2^{\text{polynomial}})$, and all subclasses C of these classes, though we are particularly interested in the case $C = \text{NP}$.

We will consider the polynomial-time reducibilities $\leq_m^P$ (*many-one* reducibility), $\leq_T^P$ (*Turing* reducibility), $\leq_{btt}^P$ (*bounded truth-table* reducibility), and $\leq_{q-tt}^P$ (truth-table reducibility with $q(n)$ queries on inputs of length n, where $q : \mathbf{N} \to \mathbf{Z}^+$). If $\leq_r^P$ is any of these reducibilities, we say that a language A is $\leq_r^P$-*hard* for a class C of languages if $C \subseteq P_r(A)$, where $P_r(A) = \{ B \subseteq \{0,1\}^* \mid B \leq_r^P A \}$.

Two criteria for "how dense" a language A is have been widely used. A language A is (*polynomially*) *sparse*, and we write $A \in \text{SPARSE}$, if there is a polynomial p such that $|A_{\leq n}| \leq p(n)$ for all $n \in \mathbf{N}$, where $A_{\leq n} = A \cap \{0,1\}^{\leq n}$. A language A is (*exponentially*) *dense*, and we write $A \in \text{DENSE}$, if there is a real number $\epsilon > 0$ such that $|A_{\leq n}| \geq 2^{n^\epsilon}$ for all sufficiently large $n \in \mathbf{N}$. It is clear that no sparse language is dense.

For any of the above choices of the reducibility $\leq_r^P$, *all known* $\leq_r^P$-*hard languages for NP are dense*. Efforts to explain this observation (and similar observations for other classes and reducibilities) have yielded many results. (See [7]) for a thorough survey). We mention four such results that are particularly relevant to the work presented here.

Let DENSE^c denote the complement of DENSE, i.e., the set of all languages A such that, for all $\epsilon > 0$, there exist infinitely many n such that $|A_{\leq n}| < 2^{n^\epsilon}$. For each reducibility $\leq_r^P$ and set S of languages, we write $P_r(S) = \bigcup_{A \in S} P_r(A)$.

The first result on the density of hard languages was the following.

Theorem 1.1. (Meyer [20]). Every $\leq_m^P$-hard language for E (or any larger class) is dense. That is, $\text{E} \not\subseteq P_m(\text{DENSE}^c)$.

Theorem 1.1 was subsequently improved to truth-table reducibility with $O(\log n)$ queries:

Theorem 1.2. (Watanabe [29, 28]). Every $\leq_{O(\log n)-tt}^P$-hard language for E is dense. That is, $\text{E} \not\subseteq P_{O(\log n)-tt}(\text{DENSE}^c)$.

Regarding NP, Berman and Hartmanis [3] conjectured that no sparse language is $\leq_m^P$-hard for NP, unless $P = \text{NP}$. This conjecture was subsequently proven correct:

Theorem 1.3. (Mahaney [18]). If $P \neq \text{NP}$, then no sparse language is $\leq_m^P$-hard for NP. That is, $P \neq \text{NP} \implies \text{NP} \not\subseteq P_m(\text{SPARSE})$.

Theorem 1.3 has recently been extended to truth-table reducibility with a bounded number of queries:

Theorem 1.4. (Ogiwara and Watanabe [21]). If $P \neq \text{NP}$, then no sparse language is $\leq_{btt}^P$-hard for NP. That is, $P \neq \text{NP} \implies \text{NP} \not\subseteq P_{btt}(\text{SPARSE})$.

The Main Theorem of this paper, Theorem 3.2, extends Theorems 1.1 and 1.2 above by showing that, for every real $\alpha < 1$ (e.g., $\alpha = 0.99$), only a measure 0 subset of the languages in E are $\leq^{P}_{n^{\alpha}-tt}$-reducible to non-dense languages. "Measure 0 subset" here refers to the resource-bounded measure theory of Lutz [15, 13]. In the notation of this theory, our Main Theorem says that, for every real $\alpha < 1$,

$$\mu(P_{n^{\alpha}-tt}(\text{DENSE}^{c})|E) = 0. \qquad (1.1)$$

This means that $P_{n^{\alpha}-tt}(\text{DENSE}^{c}) \cap E$ is a *negligibly small* subset of E [15, 13].

In particular, this implies that

$$E \not\subseteq P_{n^{\alpha}-tt}(\text{DENSE}^{c}), \qquad (1.2)$$

i.e., that every $\leq^{P}_{n^{\alpha}-tt}$-hard language for E is dense. This strengthens Theorem 1.2 above by extending the truth table reducibility from $O(\log n)$ queries to n^{α} queries ($\alpha < 1$). It is also worth noting that the combinatorial technique used to prove (1.1) and (1.2)—the *sequentially most frequent query selection*—is simpler than Watanabe's direct proof of Theorem 1.2. This is not surprising, once one considers that our proof of (1.2) via (1.1) is a resource-bounded instance of the *probabilistic method* [4, 23, 24, 5, 25, 1], which exploits the fact that it is often easier to prove the *abundance* of objects of a given type than to construct a *specific* object of that type.

Our proof of (1.1) also shows that, for every real $\alpha < 1$,

$$\mu(P_{n^{\alpha}-tt}(\text{DENSE}^{c}) \mid E_2) = 0. \qquad (1.3)$$

Much of our interest in the Main Theorem concerns the class NP and Theorems 1.3 and 1.4 above. As already noted, for all reducibilities $\leq^{P}_{r}$ discussed in this paper, all known $\leq^{P}_{r}$-hard languages for NP are dense. One is thus led to ask whether there is a reasonable hypothesis θ such that we can prove results of the form

$$\theta \implies NP \not\subseteq P_r(\text{DENSE}^{c}), \qquad (1.4)$$

for various choices of the reducibility $\leq^{P}_{r}$. (Such a result is much stronger than the corresponding result $\theta \implies NP \not\subseteq P_r(\text{SPARSE})$, because there is an enormous gap between polynomial and 2^{n^t} growth rates.)

Ogiwara and Watanabe's proof of Theorem 1.4 does not appear to allow significant relaxation of either the query bound or the sparseness criterion. In fact, it appears to be beyond current understanding to prove results of the form (1.4) if θ is "P $\neq$ NP." Karp and Lipton [10] have proven that $\Sigma^{p}_{2} \neq \Pi^{p}_{2}$ implies NP $\not\subseteq$ P(SPARSE). That is, the stronger hypothesis $\Sigma^{p}_{2} \neq \Pi^{p}_{2}$ gives a stronger conclusion than those of Theorems 1.3 and 1.4. However, Karp and Lipton's proof does not appear to allow relaxation of the sparseness criterion, and results of the form (1.4) do not appear to be achievable at this time if θ is taken to be "$\Sigma^{p}_{2} \neq \Pi^{p}_{2}$."

To make progress on matters of this type, Lutz has proposed investigation of the measure-theoretic hypotheses $\mu(NP \mid E_2) \neq 0$ and $\mu(NP \mid E) \neq 0$. These expressions say that NP does not have measure 0 in E_2 ("NP is not a negligible subset of E_2") and that NP does not have measure 0 in E ("NP $\cap$ E is not a negligible subset of E"), respectively. We now explain the meaning of these hypotheses. Both are best understood in terms of their negations.

The condition $\mu(\text{NP} \mid E_2) = 0$ means that there exist a *fixed* polynomial q, a *fixed* positive quantity c_0 of capital (money), and a *fixed* betting strategy (algorithm) σ with the following properties: Given any language A, the strategy σ *bets* on the membership or nonmembership of the successive strings $\lambda, 0, 1, 00, 01, 10, \cdots$ in A. Before the betting begins, σ has capital (money) c_0. When betting on a string $w \in \{0,1\}^*$, the strategy σ is given as input the string consisting of the successive bits $[\![v \in A]\!]$ for all strings v that precede w in the standard ordering of $\{0,1\}^*$. On this input, the strategy σ computes, in $\leq 2^{q(|w|)}$ steps, a fraction $r \in [-1, 1]$ of its current capital to bet that $w \in A$. If σ's capital prior to this bet is c, then σ's capital after the bet is $c(1 + r)$ if $w \in A$, and $c(1 - r)$ if $w \notin A$. (That is, the betting is fair.) Finally, the strategy σ is *successful*, in the sense that, for all $A \in$ NP, σ's capital diverges to $+\infty$ as the betting progresses through the successive strings $w \in \{0,1\}^*$.

Thus, *the condition $\mu(\text{NP} \mid E_2) = 0$ asserts the existence of a fixed $2^{q(n)}$-time-bounded algorithm* for betting successfully on membership of strings in languages in NP. If NP $\subseteq$ DTIME$(2^{r(n)})$ for some fixed polynomial r, it is easy to devise such a strategy, so $\mu(\text{NP} \mid E_2) = 0$. Conversely, if $\mu(\text{NP} \mid E_2) = 0$, then NP is "nearly contained in some fixed DTIME$(2^{q(n)})$," in the sense that there is a fixed $2^{q(n)}$-time-bounded algorithm σ for successfully betting on all languages in NP.

There does not appear to be any *a priori* reason for believing that such a strategy σ exists, i.e., there does not appear to be any *a priori* reason for believing that $\mu(\text{NP} \mid E_2) = 0$. Similarly, there does not appear to be any *a priori* reason for believing that $\mu(\text{NP} \mid E) = 0$. The hypotheses $\mu(\text{NP} \mid E_2) \neq 0$ and $\mu(\text{NP} \mid E) \neq 0$ are thus *reasonable relative to our current knowledge*. (The hypothesis that the polynomial-time hierarchy separates into infinitely many levels enjoys a similar status: it *may* be false, but if it *is* false, then a very remarkable algorithm exists.) In fact, Lutz has conjectured that $\mu(\text{NP} \mid E_2) \neq 0$ and $\mu(\text{NP} \mid E) \neq 0$.

We are interested in the conditions $\mu(\text{NP} \mid E_2) \neq 0$ and $\mu(\text{NP} \mid E) \neq 0$, not as conjectures (which cannot be proven or disproven at this time), but rather as *scientific hypotheses*, which may have more *explanatory power* than traditional complexity-theoretic hypotheses such as P $\neq$ NP or the separation of the polynomial-time hierarchy. Until such time as a mathematical proof or refutation is available, the reasonableness (or unreasonableness) of such hypotheses can be illuminated only by investigation of their *consequences*. Such investigation may indicate, for example, that the consequences of $\mu(\text{NP} \mid E_2) \neq 0$ form, *en masse*, a credible state of affairs, thereby increasing the reasonableness of this hypothesis. On the other hand, such investigation may uncover implausible consequences of $\mu(\text{NP} \mid E_2) \neq 0$, or even a proof that $\mu(\text{NP} \mid E_2) = 0$. Either outcome would contribute to our understanding of NP.

Our Main Theorem implies that, for all $\alpha < 1$, each of the hypotheses

$\mu(\text{NP} \mid E_2) \neq 0$ and $\mu(\text{NP} \mid E) \neq 0$ implies that every $\leq^{P}_{n^{\alpha}-tt}$-hard language for NP is dense. (This is Theorem 3.4 below.) This conclusion, which is credible and consistent with all observations to date, is not known to follow from $P \neq NP$ or other traditional complexity-theoretic hypotheses.

Recent investigation has also shown that the hypotheses $\mu(\text{NP} \mid E_2) \neq 0$ and $\mu(\text{NP} \mid E) \neq 0$ imply that NP contains P-bi-immune languages [19] and that every $\leq^{P}_{m}$-hard language for NP has an exponentially dense, exponentially hard complexity core [8]. Taken together, such results appear to indicate that these are reasonable hypotheses which may have considerable explanatory power.

When proving results of the form $\mu(X|\mathcal{C}) = 0$, where $\mathcal{C}$ is a complexity class, it often simplifies matters to have available some general-purpose randomness properties of languages in $\mathcal{C}$. The term "general-purpose randomness property" here is heuristic, meaning a set Z of languages with the following two properties.

(i) Almost every language in $\mathcal{C}$ has the property (of membership in) Z. (This condition, written $\mu(Z|\mathcal{C}) = 1$, means that $\mu(Z^c|\mathcal{C}) = 0$, where Z^c is the complement of Z.)

(ii) It is often the case that, when one wants to prove a result of the form $\mu(X|\mathcal{C}) = 0$, it is easier to prove that $X \cap Z = \emptyset$.

For example, in ESPACE=DSPACE(2^{linear}), it is known [15, 9] that almost every language has very high space-bounded Kolmogorov complexity. A variety of sets X have been shown to have measure 0 in ESPACE, simply by proving that every element of X has low space-bounded Kolmogorov complexity [15, 9, 17, 14]. Thus high space-bounded Kolmogorov complexity is a "general-purpose randomness property" of languages in ESPACE.

In §2 below, we present a Weak Stochasticity Theorem, stating that almost every language in E, and almost every language in E_2, is "weakly stochastic," i.e., is statistically unpredictable by feasible deterministic algorithms, even with linear nonuniform advice. (See §2 for precise definitions.) This is used to prove our Main Theorem and appears to be, in the above sense, a general-purpose randomness property of languages in E and E_2 that will be useful in future investigations.

2 Measure and Weak Stochasticity

In this section, we state the Weak Stochasticity Theorem. This theorem is used in the proof of our main result in §3. We also expect it to be useful in future investigations of the measure structure of E and E_2.

In this paper, we do not include fundamentals of Resource-bounded measure, which can be found in [15, 13].

We first formulate our notion of weak stochasticity. For this we need a few definitions. Our notion of advice classes is standard [10]. An *advice function* is a function $h : \mathbf{N} \to \{0, 1\}^*$. Given a function $q : \mathbf{N} \to \mathbf{N}$, we write ADV($q$) for the set of all advice functions h such that $|h(n)| \leq q(n)$ for all $n \in \mathbf{N}$. Given a language $A \subseteq \{0,1\}^*$ and an advice function h, we define the language A/h ("A with advice h") by $A/h = \{x \in \{0,1\}^* \mid \langle x, h(|x|)\rangle \in A\}$. Given functions $t, q : \mathbf{N} \to \mathbf{N}$, we define the *advice class*

$$\text{DTIME}(t)/\text{ADV}(q) = \{A/h \mid A \in \text{DTIME}(t), h \in \text{ADV}(q)\}.$$

Definition. Let $t, q, \nu : \mathbf{N} \to \mathbf{N}$ and let $A \subseteq \{0,1\}^*$. Then A is *weakly (t, q, ν)-stochastic* if, for all $B \in \text{DTIME}(t)/\text{ADV}(q)$ and all $C \in \text{DTIME}(t)$ such that $|C_{=n}| \geq \nu(n)$ for all sufficiently large n,

$$\lim_{n \to \infty} \frac{|(A \triangle B) \cap C_{=n}|}{|C_{=n}|} = \frac{1}{2}.$$

Intuitively, B and C together form a "prediction scheme" in which B tries to guess the behavior of A on the set C. A is weakly (t, q, ν)-stochastic if no such scheme is better in the limit than guessing by random tosses of a fair coin.

Our use of the term "stochastic" follows Kolmogorov's terminology [11, 27] for properties defined in terms of limiting frequencies of failure of prediction schemes. The adverb "weakly" distinguishes our notion from a stronger stochasticity considered in [12], but weak stochasticity is a powerful and convenient tool.

Theorem 2.1 (Weak Stochasticity Theorem).

(1) For all $c \in \mathbf{N}$ and $\gamma > 0$, almost every language $A \in \mathrm{E}$ is weakly $(2^{cn}, cn, 2^{\gamma n})$-stochastic.

(2) Almost every language $A \in \mathrm{E}_2$ is, for all $c \in \mathbf{N}$ and $\gamma > 0$, weakly $(2^{cn}, cn, 2^{\gamma n})$-stochastic.

3 The Density of Hard Languages

In this section we present our main result, that for every real $\alpha < 1$, the set $\mathrm{P}_{n^\alpha - tt}(\text{DENSE}^c)$ has measure 0 in E and in E_2. We then derive some consequences of this result.

Our main results follow from the following lemma. Recall that $WS_{c,\gamma}$ is the set of all weakly $(2^{cn}, cn, 2^{\gamma n})$-stochastic languages.

Lemma 3.1. For every real $\alpha < 1$, $\mathrm{P}_{n^\alpha - tt}(\text{DENSE}^c) \cap WS_{3, \frac{1}{2}} = \emptyset$.

The proof, based on the combinatorial technique of the *sequentially most frequent query*, appears in [16].

Our main results are now easily derived. We start with the fact that most languages decidable in exponential time are not $\leq^{\mathrm{P}}_{n^\alpha - tt}$-reducible to non-dense languages.

Theorem 3.2 (Main Theorem). For every real number $\alpha < 1$,

$$\mu(\mathrm{P}_{n^\alpha - tt}(\text{DENSE}^c) \mid \mathrm{E}) = \mu(\mathrm{P}_{n^\alpha - tt}(\text{DENSE}^c) \mid \mathrm{E}_2) = 0.$$

The Main Theorem yields the following separation result.

Theorem 3.3. For every real $\alpha < 1$, $E \nsubseteq P_{n^\alpha - tt}(\text{DENSE}^c)$. That is, every $\leq_{n^\alpha - tt}^P$-hard language for E is dense.

Note that Theorem 3.3 strengthens Theorem 1.2 by extending the number of queries from $O(\log n)$ to n^α, where $\alpha < 1$ (e.g., $\alpha = 0.99$).

It is worthwhile to examine the roles played by various methods. Theorem 3.2, a measure-theoretic result concerning the *quantitative* structure of E and E_2, yields the *qualitative* separation result Theorem 3.3. From a technical standpoint, this proof of Theorem 3.3 has the following three components.

(i) The sequentially most frequent query selection (Lemma 3.1). This is used to prove that every language in $P_{n^\alpha - tt}(\text{DENSE}^c)$ is predictable, i.e., fails to be weakly stochastic (with suitable parameters).

(ii) The Weak Stochasticity Theorem (Theorem 2.1). This shows that only a measure 0 subset of the languages in E are predictable.

(iii) The Measure Conservation Theorem [15]. This shows that E is not a measure 0 subset of itself.

Of these three components, (ii) and (iii) are general theorems concerning measure in E. Only component (i) is specific to the issue of the densities of $\leq_{n^\alpha - tt}^P$-hard languages. That is, *given the general principles* (ii) and (iii), the proof of Theorem 3.3 is just the sequentially most frequent query selection, i.e., the proof of Lemma 3.1. The latter proof is combinatorially much simpler than Watanabe's direct proof of Theorem 1.2. This is not surprising, once it is noted that our proof of Theorem 3.3 is an application of (a resource-bounded generalization of) the *probabilistic method* [4, 23, 24, 5, 25, 1], which exploits the fact that it is often easier to establish the *abundance* of objects of a given type than to construct a *specific* object of that type. Much of our proof of Theorem 3.3 is "hidden" in the power of this method (i.e., in the proofs of the Measure Conservation and Weak Stochasticity Theorems), freeing us to apply the sequentially most frequent query selection to the problem at hand.

An important feature of this general method is that it is *uniformly constructive* in the following sense: Taken together, the proofs of the Measure Conservation and Weak Stochasticity Theorems give a straightforward, "automatic" construction of a language $A \in E \cap WS_{3,\frac{1}{2}}$. By Lemma 3.1, it follows immediately that $A \in E \backslash P_{n^\alpha - tt}(\text{DENSE}^c)$. Thus one can apply this complexity-theoretic version of the probabilistic method with complete assurance that the resulting existence proof will automatically translate into a construction.

The primary objective of resource-bounded measure theory is to give a detailed account of the *quantitative structure* of E, E_2, and other complexity classes. The derivation of *qualitative* separation results, such as Theorems 3.3 and 1.2, is only a by-product of this quantitative objective. (By analogy, the value of classical Lebesgue measure and probability far surpasses their role as tools for existence proofs.) In the case of E, for example, the quantitative content of Theorem 3.2 is that the set $P_{n^\alpha - tt}(\text{DENSE}^c) \cap E$ is a *negligibly small* subset of E.

As noted in the introduction to this paper, we are interested in the consequences of the hypothesis that NP is *not* a negligibly small subset of exponential time. In this regard, our main theorem yields the following result.

Theorem 3.4. If $\mu(\text{NP}|E) \neq 0$ or $\mu(\text{NP}|E_2) \neq 0$, then for all $\alpha < 1$, every $\leq_{n^\alpha - tt}^P$-hard language for NP is dense, i.e., NP $\not\subseteq P_{n^\alpha - tt}(\text{DENSE}^c)$.

Note that the hypothesis and conclusion of Theorem 3.4 are both stronger than their counterparts in Ogiwara and Watanabe's result that $P \neq NP$ implies NP $\not\subseteq P_{btt}(\text{SPARSE})$. Note also that our proof of Theorem 3.4 actually shows that NP $\cap WS_{3,\frac{1}{2}} \neq \emptyset$ implies NP $\not\subseteq P_{n^\alpha - tt}(\text{DENSE}^c)$. In fact, this implication and Theorem 3.4 both hold with NP replaced by PH, PP, PSPACE, or any other class.

4 Conclusion

The density criterion in Theorem 3.2 cannot be improved, since for every $\epsilon > 0$ there is a language $A \in E$ that is $\leq_m^P$-hard for E_2 and satisfies $|A_{\leq n}| < 2^{n^\epsilon}$ for all n. It is an open question whether the query bound n^α can be significantly relaxed. A construction of Wilson [30] shows that there is an oracle B such that $E^B \subseteq P_{O(n)-tt}^B(\text{SPARSE})$, so progress in this direction will require nonrelativizable techniques.

There are several open questions involving special reducibilities. We mention just one example. Very recently, Arvind, Köbler, and Mundhenk [2] have proven that $P \neq NP$ implies NP $\not\subseteq P_{btt}(P_{ctt}(\text{SPARSE}))$, where P_{ctt} refers to polynomial-time *conjunctive* reducibility. (This strengthens Theorem 1.4.) Does the class $P_{btt}(P_{ctt}(\text{DENSE}^c))$ have measure 0 in E?

As noted in the introduction, all known $\leq_T^P$-hard languages for NP are dense, i.e., our experience suggests that NP $\not\subseteq P(\text{DENSE}^c)$. This suggests two open questions. (See Figure 1.) Karp and Lipton [10] have shown that $\Sigma_2^p \neq \Pi_2^p$ implies NP $\not\subseteq P(\text{SPARSE})$. Theorem 3.4 of the present paper shows that, for $\alpha < 1$, $\mu(\text{NP} \mid E_2) \neq 0$ implies NP $\not\subseteq P_{n^\alpha - tt}(\text{DENSE}^c)$. The first question, posed by Selman [22], is whether the strong hypothesis $\mu(\Sigma_2^p \backslash \Pi_2^p \mid E_2) \neq 0$ can be used to combine these ideas to get a conclusion that NP $\not\subseteq P(\text{DENSE}^c)$. The second, more fundamental, question is suggested by the first. A well-known downward separation principle [26] says that, if the polynomial time hierarchy separates at some level, then it separates at all lower levels. Thus, for example, $\Sigma_2^p \neq \Pi_2^p$ implies that $P \neq NP$. Is there a "downward measure separation principle," stating that $\mu(\Sigma_{k+1}^p \backslash \Pi_{k+1}^p \mid E_2) \neq 0 \Longrightarrow \mu(\Sigma_k^p \backslash \Pi_k^p \mid E_2) \neq 0$? In particular, does $\mu(\Sigma_2^p \backslash \Pi_2^p \mid E_2) \neq 0$ imply that $\mu(\text{NP} \mid E_2) \neq 0$?

The hypothesis that $\mu(\text{NP}|E_2) \neq 0$, i.e., that NP is not a negligibly small subset of E_2, has recently been shown to have a number of credible consequences:

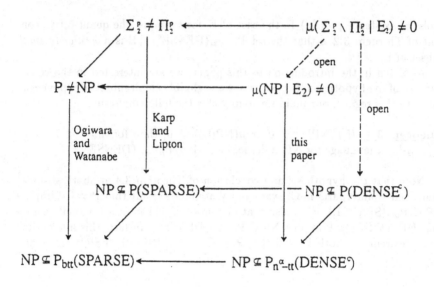

Figure 1: Two open questions

If $\mu(\mathrm{NP}|\mathrm{E}_2) \neq 0$, then NP contains p-random languages [12]; NP contains E-bi-immune languages [19]; every $\leq^P_m$-hard language for NP has an exponentially dense, exponentially hard complexity core [8]; and now, by Theorem 3.3 above, every $\leq^P_{n^\alpha-tt}$-hard language for NP $(\alpha < 1)$ is exponentially dense. Further investigation of the consequences and reasonableness of $\mu(\mathrm{NP}|\mathrm{E}_2) \neq 0$ and related strong, measure-theoretic hypotheses is clearly indicated.

NOTE ADDED IN PROOF: Very recently, and independently, Fu [6] has used resource-bounded Kolmogorov complexity to prove results similar to Theorem 3.3, but for Turing reducibilities instead of truth-table reducibilities.

Acknowledgements

The first author thanks Bill Gasarch and Alan Selman for helpful discussions.

References

[1] N. Alon and J. H. Spencer, *The Probabilistic Method*, Wiley, 1992.

[2] V. Arvind, J. Köbler, and M. Mundhenk, Bounded truth-table and conjunctive reductions to sparse and tally sets, Technical report, University of Ulm, 1992, Technical Report Ulmer Informatik-Berichte 92–01.

[3] L. Berman and J. Hartmanis, On isomorphism and density of NP and other complete sets, *SIAM Journal on Computing* 6 (1977), pp. 305–322.

[4] P. Erdös, Some remarks on the theory of graphs, *Bulletin of the American Mathematical Society* 53 (1947), pp. 292–294.

[5] P. Erdös and J. Spencer, *Probabilistic Methods in Combinatorics*, Academic Press, New York, 1974.

[6] B. Fu, With quasi-linear queries EXP is not polynomial time Turing reducible to sparse sets, manuscript, August 1992.

[7] L. A. Hemachandra, M. Ogiwara, and O. Watanabe, How hard are sparse sets?, *Proceedings of the Seventh Annual Structure in Complexity Theory Conference*, 1992, pp. 222–238. IEEE Press.

[8] D. W. Juedes and J. H. Lutz, The complexity and distribution of hard problems, Technical Report 92-23, Department of Computer Science, Iowa State University, 1992. Submitted.

[9] D. W. Juedes and J. H. Lutz, Kolmogorov complexity, complexity cores, and the distribution of hardness, In O. Watanabe, editor, *Kolmogorov Complexity and Computational Complexity*. Springer-Verlag, 1992, pp. 43–65.

[10] R. M. Karp and R. J. Lipton, Some connections between nonuniform and uniform complexity classes, *Proceedings of the 12th ACM Symposium on Theory of Computing*, 1980, pp. 302–309, also published as Turing machines that take advice, *L'Enseignement Mathematique* **28** (1982), pp. 191–209.

[11] A. N. Kolmogorov and V. A. Uspenskii, Algorithms and randomness, translated in *Theory of Probability and its Applications* **32** (1987), pp. 389–412.

[12] J. H. Lutz, Intrinsically pseudorandom sequences, in preparation.

[13] J. H. Lutz, Resource-bounded measure, in preparation.

[14] J. H. Lutz, An upward measure separation theorem, *Theoretical Computer Science* **81** (1991), pp. 127–135.

[15] J. H. Lutz, Almost everywhere high nonuniform complexity, *Journal of Computer and System Sciences* **44** (1992), pp. 220–258.

[16] J. H. Lutz and E. Mayordomo. Measure, stochasticity, and the density of hard languages. Technical Report 92-11, Department of Computer Science, Iowa State University, 1992. Submitted.

[17] J. H. Lutz and W. J. Schmidt, Circuit size relative to pseudorandom oracles. *Theoretical Computer Science A* **107** (1993), to appear.

[18] S. R. Mahaney, Sparse complete sets for NP: Solution of a conjecture of Berman and Hartmanis, *Journal of Computer and System Sciences* **25** (1982), pp. 130–143.

[19] E. Mayordomo, Almost every set in exponential time is P-bi-immune, *Seventeenth International Symposium on Mathematical Foundations of Computer Science*, 1992. Springer-Verlag, to appear.

[20] A. R. Meyer, 1977, reported in [3].

[21] M. Ogiwara and O. Watanabe, On polynomial bounded truth-table reducibility of NP sets to sparse sets, *SIAM Journal on Computing* **20** (1991), pp. 471–483.

[22] A. L. Selman, 1992, personal communication.

[23] C. E. Shannon, A mathematical theory of communication, *Bell System Technical Journal* **27** (1948), pp. 379–423, 623–656.

[24] C. E. Shannon, The synthesis of two-terminal switching circuits, *Bell System Technical Journal* **28** (1949), pp. 59–98.

[25] J. H. Spencer, *Ten Lectures on the Probabilistic Method*, SIAM, 1987.

[26] L. J. Stockmeyer, The polynomial-time hierarchy, *Theoretical Computer Science* **3** (1977), pp. 1–22.

[27] V. A. Uspenskii, A. L. Semenov, and A. Kh. Shen', Can an individual sequence of zeros and ones be random?, *Russian Mathematical Surveys* **45** (1990), pp. 121–189.

[28] O. Watanabe, *On the Structure of Intractable Complexity Classes*, PhD thesis, Tokyo Institute of Technology, 1987.

[29] O. Watanabe, Polynomial time reducibility to a set of small density, *Proceedings of the Second Structure in Complexity Theory Conference*, 1987, pp. 138–146.

[30] C. B. Wilson, Relativized circuit complexity, *Journal of Computer and System Sciences* **31** (1985), pp. 169–181.

Halting Problem of One Binary Horn Clause is Undecidable.*

Philippe Devienne, Patrick Lebègue, Jean–Christophe Routier

Laboratoire d'Informatique Fondamentale de Lille – CNRS U.A. 369
Université des Sciences et Technologies de Lille
59655 Villeneuve d'Ascq Cedex, FRANCE
tel : [33] 20.43.47.18 – fax : [33] 20.43.65.66
{devienne, lebegue, routier} @ lifl.fr

Abstract. This paper proposes a codification of the halting problem of any Turing machine in the form of only <u>one</u> right–linear binary Horn clause as follows :

$$p(t) \;\leftarrow\; p(tt) \;.$$

where t (resp. tt) is any (resp. linear) term. Recursivity is well–known to be a crucial and fundamental concept in programming theory. This result proves that in Horn clause languages there is no hope to control it without additional hypotheses even for the simplest recursive schemes.

Some direct consequences are presented here. For instance, there exists an explicitly constructible right–linear binary Horn clause for which no decision algorithm, given a goal, always decides in a finite number of steps whether or not the resolution using this clause is finite. The halting problem of derivations w.r.t. one binary Horn clause had been shown decidable if the goal is ground [SS88] or if the goal is linear [Dev88, Dev90, DLD90]. The undecidability in the non–linear case is an unexpected extension.

The proof of the main result is based on the unpredictable iterations of periodically linear functions defined by J.H. Conway within number theory. Let us note that these new undecidability results are proved w.r.t. any type of resolution (bottom–up or top–down, depth–first or breadth–first, unification with or without occur–check).

1   Introduction

For imperative languages, C. Böhm and G. Jacopini [BJ66] proved that all programming can be done with at most one while loop. A corollary was that the control structures *goto* and *while* have the same expressive power. For term rewriting system (using pattern–matching), Max Dauchet [Dau92] proved that it is possible with only one left–linear rewriting rule to simulate any Turing machine. In comparison to Horn clauses languages, the rewriting of the (supposed ground) goal w.r.t. one rule is non–deterministic because the rule is applied to any sub–term of the goal or not only to the whole goal.

Within number theory, other numerous examples can be found, in particular the Hilbert's tenth problem (1900) which was solved by Matijasevits in 1970 and

---

* This work has been partially supported by GRECO de Programmation of CNRS.

there exists an explicitly constructable universal diophantine equation with degree 4. Another remarkable codification was proposed by J.H. Conway in 1972 by using only periodically linear functions from $I\!N$ to $I\!N$. The iterations of these integer functions are generalizations of the famous "$3x + 1$" conjecture that we will recall later.

Closer to our study domain, for Horn clauses without function symbols as Datalog languages, a similar codification has been obtained using quasi-iterative programs (that is, each clause contains at most one occurrence of a recursive predicate) [GM87]. For Horn Clause languages, it has been established that all programming can be done with one recursive clause and three facts [PDL91]. The proof, like that of [BJ66], is simple and direct, that is, by an immediate translation of any Horn clause program directly into such a Horn clause program verifying the above form.

The right–linear binary clauses, $p(t) \leftarrow p(tt)$, may induce infinite computation that W. Bibel, S. Hölldobler and J. Würtz [BHW92] call *"cycle unification "*. Within dynamic analysis, some works were done for controlling recursivity [ABK89]. In Section 2, we introduce binary Horn clauses and their resolution, then a codification of the famous "$3x + 1$" conjecture is given. In Section 3, a generalization of this conjecture is presented and based on the works of J.H. Conway. In Section 4, we show how the unpredictable iterations of [Con72] can be simulated by binary clauses and we use it to prove the undecidability of halting problem of binary clauses.

2 Binary Clauses

Let F be a set of function symbols (which contains at least one constant and one symbol whose arity is greater than 1) and Var be an infinite countable set of variables, we denote $M(F, Var)$ the set of terms built from F and Var.

Definition 1. The binary (recursive) Horn clauses have the following form :

$$p(t^1, ..., t^n) \leftarrow p(tt^1, ..., tt^n) \ .$$

where t^i and tt^i are any terms of $M(F, Var)$.

A binary clause is said to be right–linear (resp. left–linear) if all variable occurs at most once in the body part (resp. the head part).

For example, "append($[X \mid L], LL, [X \mid LLL]) \leftarrow$ append(L, LL, LLL)." is a right–linear binary clause.

It is well known that during the resolution, before applying any clause, the formal variables of the clause have been renamed to fresh variables which do not appear anywhere else. The simplest way to do it is to put an additional index on all formal variables, which corresponds, for instance, to the number of the inference.

i^{th} inference : append($[X_i \mid L_i], LL_i, [X_i \mid LLL_i]) \leftarrow$ append(L_i, LL_i, LLL_i) .

The sequence of inferences using the clause, left $\leftarrow$ right, can be drawn in the form of a series of dominoes :

$$\cdots \boxed{\text{left}_1 \leftarrow \text{right}_1} \boxed{\text{left}_2 \leftarrow \text{right}_2} \cdots \boxed{\text{left}_{n-1} \leftarrow \text{right}_{n-1}} \boxed{\text{left}_n \leftarrow \text{right}_n} \cdots$$

Like in the domino series, the ith domino can be followed by an $i+1^{th}$ one, if terms $left_{i+1}$ and $right_i$ can be unifiable and this constraint is compatible with those of the other iterations. Hence, applying n times this binary clause is equivalent to solve the following system :

$$\{ \ left_{i+1} = right_i \mid \forall i \in [1, n-1]\} \ .$$

For example applying n times "append" clause is equivalent to solve the following system :

$$\{append([X_{i+1} \mid L_{i+1}], LL_{i+1}, [X_{i+1} \mid LLL_{i+1}]) = append(L_i, LL_i, LLL_i) \mid \forall i \in [1, n-1]\},$$

that is in a solved form :

$$\forall i \in [1, n-1] \begin{cases} L_i = [X_{i+1} \mid L_{i+1}] \\ LL_i = LL_{i+1} \\ LLL_i = [X_{i+1} \mid LLL_{i+1}] \end{cases} .$$

If good intuition is possible about simple binary clauses such as the above one, the non–linearity of the terms, the existence of some variables on one side of the clause, and the permutation of variables during inference generally make intuitive comprehension of behaviour impossible.

The following example shows how difficult the problem of proving termination can be. The exact origin of the Collatz conjecture – also called "Syracuse conjecture" or "$3x + 1$ problem" [Lag85] is not clearly known. It had circulated by word of mouth among the mathematical community for many years. This problem is credited to Lothar Collatz at the University of Hamburg. This conjecture asserts that the following program, given any integer n, always terminates.

> While $n > 1$ <u>Do</u>
>> <u>If</u> n is even
>>> <u>Then</u> $n \leftarrow \frac{n}{2}$
>>> <u>Else</u> $n \leftarrow 3n + 1$
>> <u>EndIf</u>
> <u>EndWhile</u>

Nabuo Yoneda at the University of Tokyo has checked it for all $n < 2^{40}$. The behaviour of the Collatz's series seems to be structureless and "random". For instance, from $(2^{500} - 1)$, integers greater than $(2^{500} \times 10^{88})$ are reached.

The Collatz's program can be translated into equivalence relations on $Var \times \mathbb{N}$:

$$\forall k \in \mathbb{N} \ \underline{If} \ k \text{ is even } \underline{Then} \ X_k = X_{\frac{k}{2}} \quad \underline{Else} \ X_k = X_{3k+1} \ .$$

Let f be the function such that $\forall i > 0$, $f(2i) = i$ and $f(2i - 1) = 6i - 2$. Since there does not exist some $k \in \mathbb{N}$ such that $f^k(1) = n$ $(\forall n > 4)$, we may assert that we may extend the previous relation to the following system of equations :

$$\begin{cases} X_i = X_{2i} \\ X_{2i-1} = X_{3(2i-1)+1} \end{cases}$$

The following binary clause and goal generate such equations :

$$\begin{cases} p([X \mid U], [Y, X \mid V], [\_, \_, \_, Y, \_, \_ \mid W]) \leftarrow p(U, V, W). \\ \leftarrow p(Z, Z, Z). \end{cases}$$

From the general goal $\leftarrow p(L, LL, LLL)$, through the inferences the solved systems of equations increases as :

1.	$L = [X_1 \mid U_1]$	$LL = [Y_1, X_1 \mid V_1]$
2.	$L = [X_1, X_2 \mid U_2]$	$LL = [Y_1, X_1, Y_2, X_2 \mid V_2]$
$\vdots$	$\vdots$	$\vdots$
$n.$	$L = [X_1, X_2, \cdots, X_n \mid U_n]$	$LL = [Y_1, X_1, Y_2, X_2 \cdots, Y_n, X_n \mid V_n]$

1. $LLL = [\_, \_, \_, Y_1, \_, \_ \mid W_1]$
2. $LLL = [\_, \_, \_, Y_1, \_, \_, \_, \_, \_, Y_2, \_, \_ \mid W_2]$
   $\vdots \quad \vdots$
$n.$ $LLL = [\_, \_, \_, Y_1, \_, \_, \cdots, \_, \_, \_, Y_n, \_, \_ \mid W_n]$

Then, from the goal $\leftarrow p(Z, Z, Z)$, we force the equalities :

1. $L = LL \implies X_{2i-1} = Y_i$ and $X_{2i} = X_i$
2. $L = LLL \implies X_{6i-2} = Y_i$.

With a goal of the form :

$$\leftarrow p(\underbrace{[a, \_, \cdots, \bar{a} \mid L]}_{n}, \underbrace{[a, \_, \cdots, \bar{a} \mid L]}_{n}, \underbrace{[a, \_, \cdots, \bar{a} \mid L]}_{n}) \ .$$

we force $X_1 = a$ and $X_n = \bar{a}$. Therefore, the resolution is finite iff a unification fails because of $X_n \neq X_1$, that is, if the "$3x + 1$" program is finite from the input n. In other words, the "$3x + 1$" conjecture is equivalent to prove that, given any goal $p(L, L, L)$ where L is a list of the form $[a, \_, \cdots, \bar{a} \mid \_]$, the resolution is finite.

3 A Generalization of the "3x+1" Problem

J.H. Conway [Con72] considers the class of periodically piecewise linear functions $g : \mathbb{N} \to \mathbb{N}$ having the structure :

$$\forall \, 0 \leq k \leq d - 1, \text{ if } n \, (\bmod \, d) = k \, , \quad g(n) = a_k n \ .$$

where $a_0, \cdots, a_{d-1}$ are rational numbers such that $g(n) \in \mathbb{N}$. These are exactly the functions $g : \mathbb{N} \to \mathbb{N}$ such that $\frac{g(n)}{n}$ is periodic. Conway studies the behaviour of the iterates $g^k(n)$ and he states the following theorem :

Theorem 2. (Conway). *If f is any partial recursive function, there is a function g such that :*

1. $\frac{g(n)}{n}$ is periodic $(\bmod \, d)$ for some d and takes rational values.

2. $g^{(k)}(2^n) = 2^{f(n)}$ for the minimal $k \geq 1$ such that $g^{(k)}(2^n)$ is a power of 2.

Principle of proof. Conway's proof uses Minsky machines[Min67], which have the same computational power as Turing machines. He shows that to every Minsky machine, it is possible to associate such a function g which simulates the behaviour of this machine. In fact, he explains how to construct this function g from the Minsky machines.

Since it is undecidable whether or not a given partial recursive function is everywhere defined and identically zero, we obtain the corollary :

Corollary 3. (Conway). *There is no algorithm, which, given a function g with $\frac{g(n)}{n}$ periodic, and given a number n, determines whether or not there is k with $g^k(n) = 1$.*

We are now going to establish some variant of this corollary. To every partial recursive function f, we associate a function f' such that :

$$\begin{cases} f'(0) = 0 \\ f'(x) = f(x-1), & \text{if } x-1 \text{ is in the domain of } f \end{cases}$$

It is clear that f' is identically zero iff f is. Since 0 is in the domain of the function f', if we consider the function g', defined as previously, associated to f', there is some $p \in \mathbb{N}^*$ such that :

$$g'^p(2^0) = g'^p(1) = 2^{f'(0)} = 1 \ .$$

Therefore, we can naturally extend the Corollary 3 :

Corollary 4. *There is no algorithm, which, given a function g with $\frac{g(n)}{n}$ periodic such that $\exists\, p \in \mathbb{N}^*$, $g^p(1) = 1$, and given a number n, determines whether or not there is k with $g^k(n) = 1$.*

4 Partial Recursive Functions and Binary Clauses

In this section, we codify the Conway's generalization from which we deduce the undecidability of the halting problem for one right–linear binary Horn clause.

4.1 Codification of the Conway's Unpredictable Iterations

Proposition 5. *For every periodically piecewise linear function g, there exist a right–linear binary clause $p(t) \leftarrow p(tt)$, a variable X and a goal $\leftarrow p(\gamma)$ such that :*

$$(\{\gamma = t_1\} \cup \{tt_i = t_{i+1} \mid \forall i > 0\})\!\uparrow_{\{X\}} \equiv \{X_n = X_{g(n)} \mid \forall n > 0\} \ .$$

($S\!\uparrow_{\{X\}}$ is the projection onto the variables X_i of the equations expressed in S.)

Lemma 6. *For every natural integers a, a', b, b', there exist two variables X and Y, a right–linear binary clause $p(t) \leftarrow p(tt)$ and a goal $\leftarrow p(\gamma)$ such that :*

$$(\{\gamma = t_1\} \cup \{tt_i = t_{i+1} \mid \forall i > 0\})\!\uparrow_{\{X,Y\}} \equiv \{X_{ai+b} = Y_{a'i+b'} \mid i > 0\} \ .$$

Proof. The following program :

$$\begin{cases} p([\underbrace{\_,\cdots,\_,}^{a}\overbrace{Z}^{},\underbrace{\_,\cdots,\_}_{b}|L],[X|LL]) \leftarrow p(L,LL). \\ \leftarrow p(L,L). \end{cases}$$

because of the equality of the two arguments in the goal generates : $Z_i = X_{ai+b}$.

By composition of two programs like this one, we obtain :

$$\begin{cases} p([\underbrace{\_,\cdots,}^{a}Z,\underbrace{\_,\cdots}_{b}|L1],[X|L2],[\underbrace{\_,\cdots,}^{a'}Z,\underbrace{\_,\cdots}_{b'}|L3],[Y|L4]) \leftarrow p(L1,L2,L3,L4). \\ \leftarrow p(L,L,LL,LL). \end{cases}$$

It involves the equalities :

$$X_{ai+b} = Z_i \quad \text{and} \quad Y_{a'i+b'} = Z_i \ .$$

By adding a function symbol it is quite easy to transform a any–arity predicate in a unary predicate. □

Proof of proposition. Let g be a periodically piecewise linear function characterized by $d, a_0, \cdots, a_{d-1}$. g can be decomposed into a finite number of equivalence relations in the form $(X_{ai+b} = Y_{a'i+b'})_{i>0}$. All the right–linear binary clauses and goals which characterized these relations (see Lemma 6) can be merged in one right–linear binary clause and one goal by merging the arguments of these right–linear clauses. □

4.2 The Undecidability Theorems

Notation 7. *We denote* $\forall k \in \mathbb{N}$, $g^{-k}(n) = \{m \in \mathbb{N} \mid g^k(m) = n\}$.
In order to simplify the proofs, $g^{-k}(n)$ will represent any integer, if it exists, of this set.

Theorem 8. *There is no algorithm that, when given a right–linear binary Horn clause and given a goal, always decides in a finite number of steps whether or not the resolution (with or without occur–check) stops.*

Proof. Let us choose a function g such that $\frac{g(n)}{n}$ is periodic and such that there exists $p \in \mathbb{N}^*$, $g^p(1) = 1$ and consider the following systems of equations :

$$\forall i \in \mathbb{N}^*, \ X_i = X_{g(i)} \ ; \ X_1 = \bar{a} \ ; \ X_n = a \ . \tag{1}$$

It involves that $\forall k \in \mathbb{Z}$, $X_{g^k(n)} = a$. Therefore, if – and only if – there exists some $k \in \mathbb{Z}$ such that $g^k(n) = 1$, there is a contradiction between :

$$X_1 = \bar{a} \quad \text{and} \quad X_{g^k(n)} = a \ .$$

Furthermore, since there exists $p \in \mathbb{N}^*$ such that $g^p(1) = 1$ and $k \in \mathbb{Z}$ such that $g^k(n) = 1$ we can claim that there exists $k' \in \mathbb{N}^*$ such that $g^{k'}(n) = 1$. Then

Corollary 4 asserts that there is no algorithm that, when given $n \in \mathbb{N}$, decides in a finite number of steps whether or not the above systems of equations (1) produces a contradiction.

According to Proposition 5 and its lemma, we are able to construct a right–linear binary clause $p(t) \leftarrow p(tt)$ such that for some variable X and a goal $\leftarrow p(\gamma)$:

$$(\{\gamma = t_1\} \cup \{tt_i = t_{i+1} \mid \forall i > 0\}) \uparrow_{\{X\}} \equiv \{X_n = X_{g(n)} \mid \forall n > 0\} .$$

In the same way as in the Collatz codification, we can easily add the equations : $X_n = a$ and $X_1 = \bar{a}$ in the goal. Then we construct the following systems of equations :

$$X_i = X_{g(i)} , \ X_1 = \bar{a} , \ X_n = a .$$

Hence, we can conclude that there is no algorithm that decides in a finite number of steps whether or not the resolution stops. It is easy to verify that the occur–check will not play any role. $\square$

As an immediate consequence, we can state the following corollary :

Corollary 9. *There is no algorithm that when given a program in the following form :*

$$\begin{cases} p(f) \leftarrow . \\ p(t) \leftarrow p(tt). \end{cases}$$

where f, t, tt are terms and a goal, "$\leftarrow p(g)$.", decides in a finite number of steps whether or not there exists a finite number of answer–substitutions.

Proof. If we consider the program built with :

- the binary Horn clause and the goal defined in the previous proof,
- a fact, "$p(X) \leftarrow .$", where X is a variable.

Through a reasoning similar to the previous one, we can conclude that this problem is undecidable. Indeed, if n is such that there exists $k \in \mathbb{N}$ such that $g^k(n) = 1$ then the program will have a finite number of solutions else an infinite number. $\square$

But it is possible to establish a more stronger form of the previous theorem and corollary :

Theorem 10. *There exists an explicitly constructible, right–linear binary Horn clause for which there is no Turing machine that, when given a goal, always decides in a finite number of steps whether or not the resolution (with or without occur–check) stops.*

Proof. Let us consider one of the partial recursive function ϕ associated to the following program :

> input f, n ;where f is any partial recursive function.
> compute $f(n)$
> write 0

In fact this program answers 0 if and only if n is in the domain of f (i.e. iff f halts with input n). It is possible to characterized the function f by its Gödel number [Rog87]. (In the following, f represents equally the function or the associated Gödel number. The context should clear the ambiguity if any.) Consequently, it is possible to characterized the input of ϕ by the number $2^f 3^n$ and then to consider that ϕ has just one argument. It is obvious that we may impose $\phi(0) = 0$ without change.

In summary, we have a function ϕ such that $\phi(0) = 0$ and such that for every input of the form $2^f 3^n$, ϕ gives 0 iff n is in the domain of f. Then $2^f 3^n$ is in the domain of ϕ iff n is in the domain of f.

Let g be the Conway function associated to ϕ (from the Minsky machine which codes ϕ, we are able to construct g). According to the Conway's theorem, $2^f 3^n$ is in the domain of ϕ iff there exists some $k \in \mathbb{N}^*$ such that $g^k(2^{2^f 3^n}) = 2^{\phi(2^f 3^n)} = 2^0 = 1$. Since it is undecidable to know whether or not n is in the domain of f, it is undecidable to know whether or not $2^f 3^n$ is in the domain of ϕ (i.e. if ϕ halts with the input $2^f 3^n$). Therefore, it is undecidable to know whether or not, for a given n, there exists $k \in \mathbb{N}$ such that $g^k(n) = 1$. Let us note that since $\phi(0) = 0$, we have some $p \in \mathbb{N}^*$ such that $g^p(1) = 1$.

Therefore, as in the proof of Theorem 8, it is possible to construct a right-linear binary clause $p(t) \leftarrow p(tt)$ such that for some variable X and a goal $\leftarrow p(\gamma)$:

$$(\{\gamma = t_1\} \cup \{tt_i = t_{i+1} \mid \forall i > 0\})\!\uparrow_{\{X\}} \equiv \{X_n = X_{g(n)} \mid \forall n > 0\} \ .$$

Then by adding the equalities $X_n = a$ and $X_1 = \bar{a}$ in the goal, we construct the following systems of equations :

$$X_i = X_{g(i)} \ , \ X_1 = \bar{a} \ , \ X_n = a \ .$$

Hence, we can conclude that for this particular right-linear Horn clause, there is no algorithm that decides in a finite number of steps whether or not the resolution stops. It is easy to verify that the occur-check will not play any role. □

Corollary 11. *There is a particular explicitly constructible program in the following form :*

$$\begin{cases} p(f) \leftarrow . \\ p(t) \leftarrow p(tt). \end{cases}$$

where f, t, tt are terms, such that it is undecidable to know whether or not, given a goal, "$\leftarrow p(g)$.", there exists a finite number of answer-substitutions.

Proof. The proof is similar to the one of Corollary 9. □

4.3 Some Immediate Consequences

The next result follows directly from the previous corollary :

Corollary 12. *There exists a particular explicitly constructible program, built from a right-linear binary Horn clause, a goal and a fact, for which there is no Turing machine which decides in a finite number of steps whether or not this program is bounded[1] .*

---

[1] A program is said to be bounded if there exists an equivalent program written only with a finite number of unary clauses.

Proof. Let us consider the program used in the proof of Corollary 11, since it is undecidable to know whether or not this program has a finite number of solutions (answer–substitutions), the boundedness of this program is undecidable. □

Through a minor modification of the proof of Theorem 10, it is possible to establish the following theorem :

Theorem 13. *There exists an explicitly constructible right–linear binary Horn clause for which it is undecidable to know whether or not, when given a goal, the occur–check will be necessary during the resolution.*

Proof. In the proof of Theorem 10, if we replace the equalities :
$$X_1 = \bar{a} \text{ and } X_n = a$$
by the equalities :
$$X_1 = h(Y, s(Y)) \text{ and } X_n = h(Z, Z) .$$

It is undecidable to know whether or not the program will stop because of the equalities $Z = Y$ and $Z = s(Y)$, that is because of the occur–check. □

Remark. Any right–linear binary Horn clause can be simulated by a right–linear binary Horn clause $p(t) \leftarrow p(tt)$ such that $Var(t) = Var(tt)$, that is without local variable.

Proof. By adding a trash–argument to the predicate ([PDL91]) :
$$p(X, Y) \leftarrow p(X, Z) \equiv p(X, Y, trash([Z \mid L], LL)) \leftarrow p(X, Z, trash(L, [Y \mid LL])) .$$
□

5 Conclusion

In this paper we have proved the undecidability of the halting problem for programs with one binary recursive Horn clause and one goal. As an immediate consequence, the undecidability of the existence of a finite or infinite number of solutions for programs built with one binary and two unary clauses, has been proved. The next sensible question is to consider the problem (called cycle unification problem in [BHW92]) of the existence of at least one solution for this class of programs. We recently proved that *cycle unification is undecidable* [DLR92].

The proof ot this last result is based on the same principle using the codification of the Conway functions which are associated to Minsky machines. Roughly speaking, we synchronise two processes in one binary recursive Horn clause,

- the one put a mark at the $(2^n)^{th}$ element of a list, in less that 2^n iterations steps, iff n is in the domain of Minsky machine $\mathcal{M}$,
- the other put a distinct mark at the $(2^n)^{th}$ element of another list at the $(2^n)^{th}$ iterations step

The fact is chosen such that at the pth iteration :

- if $p \neq 2^n$ there is no solution,
- if $p = 2^n$ we unify the $(2^n)^{th}$ elements of the two lists.

Consequently, we will have solutions iff there exists n such that n is not in the domain of $\mathcal{M}$. Hence, this program will have solutions iff $\mathcal{M}$ is not total, this is of course undecidable.

Acknowledgements : We would like to thank Prof. Max Dauchet and Prof. Jean–Paul Delahaye for their illuminating discussion and their helpful collaboration, Eric Wegrzynowski and Benham Bani–Eqbal for their attentive and clever readinds. We would like as well to thank anonymous referees for their helpful comments.

References

[ABK89]   Apt K.R., Bol R.N., Klop J.W. "On the safe termination of PROLOG programs." *ICLP'89, Lisbon, pp. 353–368.* 1989.

[BHW92]   Bibel W., Hölldobler S., Würtz J. "Cycle Unification." *CADE pp. 94–108.* June 1992.

[BJ66]   Böhm C., Jacopini G. "Flow diagrams, Turing machines and languages with only two formation rules." *Communications of the Association for Computing Machinery, Vol.9, pp. 366–371.* 1966.

[Con72]   Conway J.H. "Unpredictable Iterations." *Proc. 1972 Number Theory Conference. University of Colorado, pp 49–52.* 1972.

[Dau92]   Dauchet M. "Simulation of Turing Machines by a regular rewrite rule." *Journal of Theoretical Computer Science. n° 103. pp. 409–420* 1992.

[Dev88]   Devienne P. "Weighted graphs – tool for studying the halting problem and time complexity in term rewriting systems and logic programming (extended abstract)." *Fifth Generation Computer Systems 88, Tokyo, Japan.* 1988.

[Dev90]   Devienne P. "Weighted graphs – tool for studying the halting problem and time complexity in term rewriting systems and logic programming." *Journal of Theoretical Computer Science, n° 75, pp. 157–215.* 1990.

[DLD90]   Devienne P., Lebègue P., Dauchet M. "Weighted Systems of Equations." *Informatika 91, Grenoble, Special issue of TCS.* 1991.

[DLR92]   Devienne P., Lebègue P., Routier J.C. "Cycle Unification is Undecidable." *LIFL Technical Report n° IT 241, Lille.* 1992.

[GM87]   Gaiman, Mairson "Undecidable optimisation problems for database logic programs." *Symposium on Logic in Computer Science, New-York, pp. 106–115.* 1987.

[Lag85]   Lagarias J.C. "The $3x+1$ problem and its generalizations." *Amer. Math Monthly 92, pp. 3–23.* 1985.

[Min67]   Minsky M. *"Computation : Finite and Infinite Machines."* Prentice–Hall. 1967.

[PDL91]   Parrain A., Devienne P., Lebègue P. "Prolog programs transformations and Meta–Interpreters." *Logic program synthesis and transformation, Springer–Verlag, LOPSTR'91, Manchester.* 1991.

[Rog87]   Rogers H. *"Theory of Recursive Functions and Effective Computability."* The MIT Press. 1987.

[SS88]   Schmidt–Schauss M. "Implication of clauses is undecidable." *Journal of Theoretical Computer Science, n° 59, pp. 287–296.* 1988.

Decidability and Undecidability Results
for Duration Calculus[1]

Zhou Chaochen[2], Michael R. Hansen[3], and Peter Sestoft[4]

1 Introduction

Duration calculus [5] extends interval temporal logic [6] with assertions about the duration of states, without mention of absolute time. It is used for specification and verification of real-time systems [8, 10].

This paper identifies decidable and undecidable subsets of duration calculus.

We show that for the subset whose only primitive formula is $\lceil P \rceil$, which means "P holds almost everywhere", satisfiability is decidable for discrete and dense time. It is still decidable for discrete time when the primitive formula $\ell = k$, which means "the interval has length k", is allowed, but becomes undecidable for dense time. Adding the integral equation $\int P = \int Q$, which means "P and Q hold for the same duration", or adding universal quantification ($\forall x. \ldots \ell = x \ldots$) over durations, makes satisfiability undecidable for discrete as well as dense time.

2 Duration Calculus

2.1 The Syntax Used in This Paper

A *state* is either a *constant* 0 or 1, a *state variable* X, a *negation* $\neg P$, or a *disjunction* $P \vee Q$ (where P and Q are states).

A *term* r is either a *constant* k_i, a *duration* $\int P$ (where P is a state), or a *global variable* x.

A *formula* is either an *atomic formula* $r_1 = r_2$ (where r_1 and r_2 are terms), *true*, a *negation* $\neg \mathcal{D}_1$, a *disjunction* $\mathcal{D}_1 \vee \mathcal{D}_2$, a "chop" $\mathcal{D}_1 \frown \mathcal{D}_2$, or a *quantification* $(\forall x)\mathcal{D}_1$, (where $\mathcal{D}_1$ and $\mathcal{D}_2$ are formulas and x is a global variable). The connectives $\neg$ and $\vee$ on formulas are semantically different from those on states.

2.2 Semantics

We consider three possible time domains: $\mathbb{N}$, $\mathbb{Q}^+$ (non-negative rationals), and $\mathbb{R}^+$ (non-negative reals) for discrete, rational, and continuous time. We denote the time domain under consideration by *Time*. Rational and continuous time are considered collectively under the name *dense* time.

When $b, e \in Time$ and $b \leq e$, then the *Time-interval* $[b, e]$ is the real interval $\{t \in \mathbb{R}^+ \mid b \leq t \leq e\}$. Thus an $\mathbb{N}$-interval is a (bounded, closed) real interval whose endpoints b and e are natural numbers.

[1] Partially funded by ProCoS ESPRIT BRA 7071, by the Danish Technical Research Council project **RapID**, and by the Danish Natural Science Research Council.
[2] UNU/IIST, Apartado 3058, Macau
[3] Fachbereich Informatik, Universität Oldenburg, Germany. On leave from:
[4] Department of Computer Science, Technical University of Denmark, DK-2800 Lyngby

For each constant k_i, there is an associated value $\underline{k}_i \in Time$.

An *interpretation* I associates a total function $X_I : \mathbf{R}^+ \to \{0, 1\}$ with each state variable X. The number of discontinuity points for X_I in any $Time$-interval must be finite, and the discontinuity points must belong to $Time$. An interpretation I can be extended to a function $I[P] : \mathbf{R}^+ \to \{0, 1\}$ with each state P.

A *valuation* is a pair $(\mathcal{V}, [b, e])$ where the *value assignment* $\mathcal{V}$ associates a value $\mathcal{V}(z) \in Time$ with each global variable z, and $[b, e]$ is a $Time$-interval. Let Val be the set of all valuations. Two value assignments $\mathcal{V}$ and $\mathcal{V}'$ are *z-equivalent* if $\mathcal{V}(y) = \mathcal{V}'(y)$ for every y different from z.

The semantics of a term r in an interpretation I is a function $I[r] : Val \to \mathbf{R}$ defined by:

$$I[k_i](\mathcal{V}, [b, e]) = \underline{k}_i$$
$$I[\int P](\mathcal{V}, [b, e]) = \int_b^e I[P](t)\, dt$$
$$I[z](\mathcal{V}, [b, e]) = \mathcal{V}(z)$$

The semantics of a formula $\mathcal{D}$ in an interpretation I is a function
$I[\mathcal{D}] : Val \to \{tt, ff\}$ defined by:

$$
\begin{aligned}
&I[true](\mathcal{V}, [b, e]) = tt \\
&I[r_1 = r_2] = tt && \text{iff } I[r_1](\mathcal{V}, [b, e]) = I[r_2](\mathcal{V}, [b, e]) \\
&I[(\neg \mathcal{D})](\mathcal{V}, [b, e]) = tt && \text{iff } I[\mathcal{D}](\mathcal{V}, [b, e]) = ff \\
&I[(\mathcal{D}_1 \vee \mathcal{D}_2)](\mathcal{V}, [b, e]) = tt && \text{iff } I[\mathcal{D}_1](\mathcal{V}, [b, e]) = tt \text{ or } I[\mathcal{D}_2](\mathcal{V}, [b, e]) = tt \\
&I[(\mathcal{D}_1 \frown \mathcal{D}_2)](\mathcal{V}, [b, e]) = tt && \text{iff } I[\mathcal{D}_1](\mathcal{V}, [b, m]) = tt \text{ and } I[\mathcal{D}_2](\mathcal{V}, [m, e]) = tt, \\
&&& \text{for some } m \in Time \text{ where } m \in [b, e] \\
&I[(\forall z)\mathcal{D}](\mathcal{V}, [b, e]) = tt && \text{iff } I[\mathcal{D}](\mathcal{V}', [b, e]) = tt \\
&&& \text{for all } \mathcal{V}' \text{ z-equivalent with } \mathcal{V}
\end{aligned}
$$

For continuous time the above semantics is equivalent to that in [7].

A formula $\mathcal{D}$ is *true* in the interpretation I (written $I \models \mathcal{D}$) iff $I[\mathcal{D}](\mathcal{V}, [b, e]) = tt$ for every valuation $(\mathcal{V}, [b, e])$. Furthermore, $\mathcal{D}$ is *valid* (written $\models \mathcal{D}$) iff $I \models \mathcal{D}$ for every interpretation I. A formula $\mathcal{D}$ is *satisfiable* iff there exists an interpretation I and a valuation $(\mathcal{V}, [b, e])$ such that $I[\mathcal{D}](\mathcal{V}, [b, e]) = tt$. It is easy to see that $\mathcal{D}$ is satisfiable iff $\not\models \neg \mathcal{D}$, where $\not\models \neg \mathcal{D}$ reads: $\neg \mathcal{D}$ is not valid.

When $\mathcal{D}$ is a propositional formula (that is, without quantifiers and global variables z), only the interval component of the valuation $(\mathcal{V}, [b, e])$ matters. Then we say that $\mathcal{D}$ *holds on* $[b, e]$ for interpretation I if there is some valuation $(\mathcal{V}, [b, e])$ such that $I[\mathcal{D}](\mathcal{V}, [b, e]) = tt$.

We use the standard abbreviations for $\wedge$, $\Rightarrow$, and $\Leftrightarrow$ in both state and formulas. Furthermore, the "length of an interval" symbol ℓ is defined by: $\ell \cong \int 1$. Many frequently occurring duration formulas are abbreviations. Here and below a.e. means "almost everywhere":

$$
\begin{aligned}
&\lceil P \rceil \cong (\int P = \int 1) \wedge \neg(\int 1 = \int 0) && \text{reads "}P\text{ a.e. on a non-point interval"} \\
&\lceil \, \rceil \cong \neg\lceil 1 \rceil && \text{reads "point interval"} \\
&\Diamond \mathcal{D} \cong true \frown \mathcal{D} \frown true && \text{reads "for some subinterval"} \\
&\Box \mathcal{D} \cong \neg \Diamond(\neg \mathcal{D}) && \text{reads "for every subinterval"} \\
&\Diamond_p \mathcal{D} \cong \mathcal{D} \frown true && \text{reads "for some prefix interval"} \\
&\Box_p \mathcal{D} \cong \neg \Diamond_p(\neg \mathcal{D}) && \text{reads "for every prefix interval"}
\end{aligned}
$$

2.3 Subsets of Duration Calculus

We define subsets of duration calculus by restricting the formulas. For example, a $\lceil P \rceil$-restricted formula is built from primitive formulas of form $\lceil P \rceil$, using the connectives ($\neg$, $\vee$, and $\frown$) of propositional duration calculus.

The ($\lceil P \rceil, \ell = k$)-restricted formulas and the ($\int P = \int Q$)-restricted formulas are defined similarly, as subsets of propositional duration calculus. Note that $\lceil P \rceil$ is definable in the ($\int P = \int Q$)-restricted duration calculus as $\int P = \int 1$.

A ($\forall x, \lceil P \rceil, \ell = x$)-restricted formula is built from primitive formulas $\lceil P \rceil$ and $\ell = x$, using the connectives ($\neg, \vee, \frown$, and $\forall x$) of duration calculus.

The results on decidability of satisfiability are summarized in the table below:

Subset	$\lceil P \rceil$	$\lceil P \rceil, \ell = k$	$\int P = \int Q$	$\lceil P \rceil, \forall x, \ell = x$
Discrete time	Decidable	Decidable	Undecidable	Undecidable
Dense time	Decidable	Undecidable	Undecidable	Undecidable
Theorems	3, 10	4, 11	12	13

3 Decidability of the $\lceil P \rceil$-subset

We show that satisfiability of a $\lceil P \rceil$-restricted formula $\mathcal{D}$ is decidable by defining a regular language $\mathcal{R}(\mathcal{D})$, such that $\mathcal{D}$ is satisfiable if and only if $\mathcal{R}(\mathcal{D})$ is non-empty.

Let S be the (finite) set of state variables occurring in $\mathcal{D}$. Then the *alphabet* A of the language $\mathcal{R}(\mathcal{D})$ is the set $A = \mathsf{P}(S)$ of subsets of S. A letter $a \in A$ is called a *basic conjunct* and is interpreted as the state $\bigwedge\{X | X \in a\} \wedge \neg \bigwedge\{X | X \in (S \setminus a)\}$, which asserts that all state variables in a are true, and those not in a are false.

The disjunctive normal form of a state P is a disjunction $\bigvee_{i=1}^{n} a_i$ of basic conjuncts, $n \geq 0$. We let $\mathrm{DNF}(P) = \{a_1, \ldots, a_n\} \subseteq A$ denote the set of basic conjuncts of P. This set is uniquely determined.

3.1 Decidability for Discrete Time

We represent a formula $\mathcal{D}$ by a regular language $\mathcal{R}(\mathcal{D}) \subseteq A^*$, such that $\mathcal{D}$ holds on interval $[b, e]$ for a given interpretation $\mathcal{I}$ if and only if there is a string v in $\mathcal{R}(\mathcal{D})$ which corresponds to the interpretation $\mathcal{I}$. A letter $a \in A$ corresponds to the unit interval. The formula $\mathcal{D}$ is satisfiable if and only if the language $\mathcal{R}(\mathcal{D})$ is non-empty. Since emptiness of a regular language is decidable [9], we obtain a procedure for deciding satisfiability of $\mathcal{D}$.

The definition of $\mathcal{R}(\mathcal{D})$ is quite straightforward. An "almost everywhere" formula $\lceil P \rceil$ is represented by the positive closure B^+, where $B = \mathrm{DNF}(P)$ is the set of basic conjuncts of P. Disjunction $\mathcal{D}_1 \vee \mathcal{D}_2$ is represented by union, negation $\neg \mathcal{D}_1$ by complement, and chop $\mathcal{D}_1 \frown \mathcal{D}_2$ by concatenation. Since B^+ is a regular language, and the family of regular languages is closed under union, complement, and concatenation, every formula is represented by a regular language. More precisely,

$$
\begin{aligned}
\mathcal{R}(\lceil P \rceil) &= (DNF(P))^+ \\
\mathcal{R}(\mathcal{D}_1 \vee \mathcal{D}_2) &= \mathcal{R}(\mathcal{D}_1) \cup \mathcal{R}(\mathcal{D}_2) \\
\mathcal{R}(\neg \mathcal{D}_1) &= A^* \setminus \mathcal{R}(\mathcal{D}_1) \\
\mathcal{R}(\mathcal{D}_1 \frown \mathcal{D}_2) &= \mathcal{R}(\mathcal{D}_1) \mathcal{R}(\mathcal{D}_2)
\end{aligned}
$$

The last line uses the concatenation $L_1 L_2 = \{vu \mid v \in L_1, u \in L_2\}$ of two regular languages L_1 and L_2. Positive closure, union, complement, and concatenation of regular languages can be realized by operations on finite state automata [9].

Definition 1. String $v = a_1 \ldots a_N \in A^*$ *corresponds to interpretation* $\mathcal{I}$ *on interval* $[0, N]$ *if* $\mathcal{I}[\![a_i]\!](t) = 1$ *a.e. for* $t \in [i-1, i]$, $i \in \{1, \ldots, N\}$. *(If* $N = 0$ *then* $v = \epsilon$ *is the empty string).*

Lemma 2. *Let a* $\lceil P \rceil$-*restricted duration formula* $\mathcal{D}$, *an interpretation* $\mathcal{I}$, *and a corresponding string* $v = a_1 \ldots a_N$ *be given. Then* $\mathcal{D}$ *holds in discrete time on* $[0, N]$ *for* $\mathcal{I}$ *if and only if* v *belongs to* $\mathcal{R}(\mathcal{D})$.

Proof. By induction on the structure of $\mathcal{D}$. The "if" and "only if" directions must be proven jointly because of the complement $(\neg \mathcal{D})$ case. $\qquad\qquad\square$

Now for every string v in A^* there is an interpretation $\mathcal{I}$ such that v corresponds to $\mathcal{I}$, and conversely: for every interpretation $\mathcal{I}$ and interval $[0, N]$ there is a string $v = a_1 \ldots a_N$ in A^* which corresponds to $\mathcal{I}$. Thus by Lemma 2, a $\lceil P \rceil$-restricted duration formula $\mathcal{D}$ is satisfiable in discrete time if and only if the regular language $\mathcal{R}(\mathcal{D})$ is non-empty, and we have:

Theorem 3. *The satisfiability in discrete time of duration formulas built from* $\lceil P \rceil$ *is decidable.*

Observe that in the $\lceil P \rceil$-restricted *discrete time* calculus (only), $\ell = 1$ can be expressed as $\lceil 1 \rceil \wedge \neg(\lceil 1 \rceil \frown \lceil 1 \rceil)$. Also, for any natural number $k > 0$, and any time domain,

$$\ell = k \Leftrightarrow \underbrace{\ell = 1 \frown \ldots \frown \ell = 1}_{k \text{ occurrences}}$$

and $\ell > k \Leftrightarrow \ell = k \frown \neg \lceil \ \rceil$, and obviously $\ell \geq k$, $\ell < k$ and $\ell \leq k$ can be expressed in terms of these. Thus:

Theorem 4. *The satisfiability in discrete time of duration formulas built from* $\lceil \ \rceil$, *true,* $\lceil P \rceil$, $\ell = k$, $\ell > k$, $\ell \geq k$, $\ell \leq k$, *and* $\ell < k$, *is decidable.*

3.2 Decidability for Dense Time

For dense time the encoding of a formula $\mathcal{D}$ by a regular language $\mathcal{R}(\mathcal{D}) \subseteq A^*$ is rather similar to that for discrete time. However, in the dense time encoding a letter $a \in A$ corresponds to an arbitrary non-point interval and no longer to a unit interval.

The only change in the encoding is the representation of a chop $\mathcal{D}_1 \frown \mathcal{D}_2$. It is still based on the concatenation $L_1 L_2$ of regular languages, but because of the (dense time) equivalence $\lceil P \rceil \frown \lceil P \rceil \Leftrightarrow \lceil P \rceil$, the resulting language must be extended to include the string vau whenever it contains the string $vaau$ where $v, u \in A^*$ and $a \in A$. The extended language $\downarrow(L_1 L_2) \supseteq L_1 L_2$ is here called the *contraction closure* of $L_1 L_2$.

$$\begin{aligned}
\mathcal{R}(\lceil P \rceil) &= (DNF(P))^+ \\
\mathcal{R}(\mathcal{D}_1 \vee \mathcal{D}_2) &= \mathcal{R}(\mathcal{D}_1) \cup \mathcal{R}(\mathcal{D}_2) \\
\mathcal{R}(\neg \mathcal{D}_1) &= A^* \setminus \mathcal{R}(\mathcal{D}_1) \\
\mathcal{R}(\mathcal{D}_1 \frown \mathcal{D}_2) &= \downarrow (\mathcal{R}(\mathcal{D}_1)\mathcal{R}(\mathcal{D}_2))
\end{aligned}$$

To formalize the contraction closure we introduce some auxiliary concepts.

Definition 5. Let $L \subseteq A^*$. Then L is *c-closed* if $vaau \in L \Rightarrow vau \in L$ for all $v, u \in A^*$ and $a \in A$. Also, L is *e-closed* if $vau \in L \Rightarrow vaau \in L$ for all $v, u \in A^*$ and $a \in A$.

The positive closure B^+ is trivially c- and e-closed. When L_1 and L_2 are c- and e-closed, then the union $L_1 \cup L_2$ and the complement $A^* \setminus L_1$ are c- and e-closed; and the concatenation $L_1 L_2$ is e-closed but in general not c-closed. The contraction closure $\downarrow L$ is c-closed for any L, and is e-closed if L is e-closed. Thus $\mathcal{R}(\mathcal{D})$ is c-closed and e-closed for all $\mathcal{D}$.

From an automaton $\mathcal{A}$ recognizing L we construct another automaton $\downarrow\mathcal{A}$ which recognizes $\downarrow L$, as follows:

Definition 6. Let the automaton $\mathcal{A} = (Q, A, \delta, q_0, F)$ be given. The automaton $\downarrow\mathcal{A} = (Q, A, \downarrow\delta, q_0, F)$ has the same states Q, alphabet A, starting state q_0, and accepting states F as $\mathcal{A}$. Its transition relation $\downarrow\delta$ is defined as follows

$$q \xrightarrow{a} q' \text{ in } \downarrow\mathcal{A} \text{ if and only if } \exists n \geq 0, q_1, \ldots, q_n. \ q \xrightarrow{a} q_1 \xrightarrow{a} \ldots \xrightarrow{a} q_n \xrightarrow{a} q' \text{ in } \mathcal{A}.$$

for states $q, q' \in Q$ and letter $a \in A$.

Clearly $\downarrow\mathcal{A}$ is a finite automaton, and it is not hard to see that it recognizes $\downarrow L$ when $\mathcal{A}$ recognizes L. Thus if L is a regular language, then $\downarrow L$ is a regular language. Moreover, from an automaton $\mathcal{A}$ recognizing L we can effectively construct the automaton $\downarrow\mathcal{A}$ recognizing $\downarrow L$.

The proof of the dense time encoding relies on the following lemma:

Lemma 7. *Let L_1 and L_2 be c-closed languages over alphabet A and let $v \in \downarrow(L_1 L_2)$. Then either there are $v_1 \in L_1$ and $v_2 \in L_2$ such that $v = v_1 v_2$, or there are $v_1 \in L_1$, $v_2 \in L_2$ and $a \in A$ such that $v = v_1' a v_2'$ with $v_1 = v_1' a$ and $v_2 = a v_2'$.*

Since a letter of v no longer represents a fixed amount of time, the correspondence between an interpretation $\mathcal{I}$ and a string v now depends on a partition of the interval considered. A *partition* of an interpretation $\mathcal{I}$ is a list of reals $0 = b_0 < b_1 < \ldots < b_N = e$ such that $\mathcal{I}[X](t)$ is constant a.e. on $[b_{i-1}, b_i]$ for every state variable X and $i \in \{1, \ldots, N\}$.

Definition 8. String $v = a_1 \ldots a_N \in A^*$ *corresponds* to interpretation $\mathcal{I}$ on $[0, e]$ with partition $0 = b_0 < b_1 < \ldots < b_N = e$ if $\mathcal{I}[a_i](t) = 1$ a.e. for $t \in [b_{i-1}, b_i]$, $i \in \{1, \ldots, N\}$. (If $N = 0$ then $v = \epsilon$ and $e = 0$).

For any given string v and interval $[0, e]$ with some partition there is an (almost everywhere uniquely determined) interpretation $\mathcal{I}$ such that v corresponds to $\mathcal{I}$. Conversely, for any given interpretation $\mathcal{I}$ and interval $[0, e]$ with some partition there is a unique corresponding string $v \in A^*$.

When $b_i = i$ for all i, we have the special case of discrete time from Section 3.1.

Lemma 9. *Let a $\lceil P \rceil$-restricted duration formula $\mathcal{D}$, an interval $[0, e]$, an interpretation $\mathcal{I}$ with partition $0 = b_0 < b_1 < \ldots < b_N = e$, and a corresponding string $v = a_1 \ldots a_N$ be given. Then $\mathcal{D}$ holds in dense time on $[0, e]$ for $\mathcal{I}$ if and only if v belongs to $\mathcal{R}(\mathcal{D})$.*

Proof. By induction on the structure of $\mathcal{D}$, much as in Lemma 2. Only the "chop" case, where $\mathcal{D}$ is $\mathcal{D}_1 \frown \mathcal{D}_2$, is more complicated. It uses the definition of contraction closure in the "only if" direction, and Lemma 7 in the "if" direction. □

Now for every string v in A^* there is an interpretation $\mathcal{I}$ and a partition such that v corresponds to $\mathcal{I}$ with that partition, and conversely: for every interpretation $\mathcal{I}$ and partition there is a corresponding string v in A^*. Thus by Lemma 9:

Theorem 10. *The satisfiability in dense time of duration formulas built from $\lceil P \rceil$ is decidable.*

4 Undecidability of the ($\lceil P \rceil$, $\ell = k$)-subset (dense time)

We now show that adding the primitive formula $\ell = k$ makes satisfiability in dense time undecidable. We reduce the (undecidable) halting problem for a two-counter machine M to satisfiability of a formula built from $\lceil P \rceil$ and $\ell = k$, where $k \in \mathit{Time}$ is positive.

4.1 Counter Machines

A *two-counter machine* has a current *label* Q and two *counters* C_1 and C_2 which can hold arbitrary non-negative integers. The set of labels is finite. A *program* for such a machine is a finite set of labelled *instructions* m_i.

The only instructions are "increment C_1 by one" (C_1^+) and "test C_1 and decrement by one" (C_1^-), and similarly for C_2. For example $Q_i : C_1^+ \to Q_j$ is the instruction at label Q_i; it increments C_1 by one and continues with instruction Q_j.

A *configuration* s of a counter machine is a triple $s = (Q, c_1, c_2)$ of the current label Q and the values $c_1, c_2 \in \mathbb{N}$ of the two counters C_1 and C_2. The configuration (Q, c_1, c_2) is *final* if there is no instruction labelled Q in the program.

A *computation step* $s \Longrightarrow s'$ transforms a non-final configuration s into a configuration s'. The configuration s' is determined as follows (and similarly for C_2):

Instruction	s	$\Longrightarrow s'$
$Q : C_1^+ \to Q_j$	(Q, c_1, c_2)	$\Longrightarrow (Q_j, c_1 + 1, c_2)$
$Q : C_1^- \to Q_j, Q_k$	$(Q, 0, c_2)$	$\Longrightarrow (Q_j, 0, c_2)$
$Q : C_1^- \to Q_j, Q_k$	$(Q, c_1 + 1, c_2)$	$\Longrightarrow (Q_k, c_1, c_2)$

A *computation* is a (finite or infinite) sequence $\sigma = s_0, s_1, s_2, \ldots$ of configurations, such that $s_n \Longrightarrow s_{n+1}$.

We call s_0 the *initial configuration*. In the applications below we will usually have $s_0 = (Q_0, 0, 0)$, where Q_0 is a designated *initial label*. We shall exploit that the halting problem for two-counter machines with initial counter values $c_1 = c_2 = 0$ is undecidable [3, p. 78].

4.2 The Encoding of a Counter Machine

The encoding of a two-counter machine M uses the following state variables: one state variable Q_i for each machine label q_i, two state variables C_1 and C_2 to represent the counter values, and two auxiliary state variables B and L, used as delimiters. We assume there is a designated starting label Q_0 and a designated final label Q_{fin}. A machine configuration (Q, c_1, c_2) is encoded on an interval of length $4k$ as follows:

$$| \underbrace{Q}_{k} | \underbrace{Val_1}_{k} | \underbrace{L}_{k} | \underbrace{Val_2}_{k} | \text{ where } Val_j \text{ represents the value of counter } C_j$$

The transition from one configuration to the next is described by a duration formula. Let the value of counter C_1 be $c_1 \geq 0$. Since the time domain is dense, the counter value can be represented on an interval of fixed length $k > 0$ using the formula:

$$(\lceil B \rceil \frown \lceil C_1 \rceil \frown \lceil B \rceil \frown \ldots \frown \lceil B \rceil \frown \lceil C_1 \rceil \frown \lceil B \rceil) \wedge \ell = k$$

with c_1 occurrences of $\lceil C_1 \rceil$. This representation was inspired by [2].

The initial configuration is $(Q_0, 0, 0)$, which is represented by the formula:

$$Init \hat{=} \lceil Q_0 \rceil^k \frown \lceil B \rceil^k \frown \lceil L \rceil^k \frown \lceil B \rceil^k \frown true$$

Here $\lceil P \rceil^k$ abbreviates $(\lceil \rceil \vee \lceil P \rceil) \wedge \ell = k$, which means "$P$ holds for duration k". State variables must be mutually exclusive: $Mutex(Q_0, \ldots, Q_n, C_1, C_2, B, L) \hat{=}$

$$\bigwedge_{X \neq Y} \Box \neg \lceil X \wedge Y \rceil \text{ where } X \text{ and } Y \text{ range over } Q_i, C_1, C_2, B, \text{ and } L$$

Certain states will appear periodically with $4k$ as period. If formula $\mathcal{D}$ is true only on intervals of length k ($\mathcal{D} \Rightarrow \ell = k$), periodic behaviour of $\mathcal{D}$ is described by:

$$Per(\mathcal{D}) \hat{=} \Box((\mathcal{D} \frown \ell = 4k) \Rightarrow (\ell = 4k \frown \mathcal{D}))$$

where $\ell = 4k$ abbreviates $\ell = k \frown \ell = k \frown \ell = k \frown \ell = k$. Machine labels, counter values, and the separator L have periodic behaviour: $Periodic \hat{=}$

$$Per(\bigvee \lceil Q_i \rceil^k) \wedge Per(\lceil C_1 \vee B \rceil^k) \wedge Per(\lceil L \rceil^k) \wedge Per(\lceil C_2 \vee B \rceil^k)$$

For each instruction m_i of M we give a formula $F(m_i)$ encoding the computation step performed by the instruction. This is done such that the n-th configuration appears in the interval $[4nk, 4(n+1)k]$, $n \geq 0$. The initial (0-th) configuration is described by $Init$ above.

Consider the machine instruction $m = Q_i : C_1^+ \rightarrow Q_j$. To encode it, we use formulas of the form: $\neg(\mathcal{D}_1 \frown \neg \mathcal{D}_2)$, which can be read: "if the interval starts with $\mathcal{D}_1$, it must end with $\mathcal{D}_2$". Here $\mathcal{D}_1$ characterizes certain configurations whose label is Q_i, and $\mathcal{D}_2$ fixes part of the next configuration.

Formula F_1 copies C_1's to the same place in the next configuration:

$$F_1 \hat{=} \neg(\lceil Q_i \rceil^k \frown \ell < k \frown \lceil C_1 \rceil \frown ((\lceil C_1 \rceil \frown true) \wedge \ell = 4k) \frown \neg(\lceil \rceil \vee (\lceil C_1 \rceil \frown true)))$$

where $\ell < k$ abbreviates $\neg(\ell = k \frown true)$.

One can copy the B's occurring before C_1 to the same place in the next configuration by a similar formula. The formulas F_2 and F_3 increment the value of C_1 by replacing the last $\lceil B \rceil$ section of C_1's value with $\lceil B \rceil \frown \lceil C_1 \rceil \frown \lceil B \rceil$ in the next configuration. (F_2 handles the case $c_1 = 0$, and F_3 handles the case $c_1 > 0$.)

$$F_2 \hat{=} (\lceil Q_i \rceil^k \frown \lceil B \rceil^k \frown \ell = 4k) \Rightarrow (true \frown (l = k \wedge (\lceil B \rceil \frown \lceil C_1 \rceil \frown \lceil B \rceil)))$$

$$F_3 \hat{=} (\lceil Q_i \rceil^k \frown \ell < k \frown \lceil C_1 \rceil \frown (\begin{smallmatrix} \lceil B \rceil \frown \lceil L \rceil \frown true \\ \wedge \ell = 5k \end{smallmatrix}))$$
$$\Rightarrow (true \frown (\ell = k \wedge (\lceil B \rceil \frown \lceil C_1 \rceil \frown \lceil B \rceil \frown \lceil L \rceil)))$$

Note that the beginnings of succeeding L sections are exactly $4k$ apart, and therefore in F_3 the length of the $\lceil B \rceil \frown \lceil C_1 \rceil \frown \lceil B \rceil$ section in the consequent is precisely as long as the last $\lceil B \rceil$ section in the antecedent. Thus the "effect" of $F_2 \wedge F_3$ is to increase the number of $\lceil C_1 \rceil$ sections by one, as desired.

The remaining instructions m_i can be encoded as formulas $F(m_i)$ by techniques similar to those already used. Then the entire machine is encoded by:

$$Machine \hat{=} Mutex(Q_0, \ldots, Q_n, C_1, C_2, B, L) \wedge Init \wedge Periodic \wedge \bigwedge_{m_i} \Box F(m_i)$$

By the construction of formula *Machine* we know that the machine terminates if and only if the formula $(Machine \wedge \Diamond \lceil Q_{fin} \rceil)$ is satisfiable.

Theorem 11. *The satisfiability in dense time of duration formulas built from $\lceil P \rceil$ and $\ell = k$ is undecidable.*

5 Undecidability of the $(\int P = \int Q)$-subset

We reduce the halting problem for two-counter machines to satisfiability of formulas built from atomic formulas $\int P = \int Q$. The reduction applies for both discrete and dense time and shows that satisfiability for this subset is undecidable. The encoding of a given two-counter machine M uses the following state variables: one state variable Q_i for each machine label, two state variables C_j^+ and C_j^- for each of the two counters ($j = 1, 2$), and a state variable L used as delimiter. We assume there is a designated starting label Q_0 and a designated final label Q_{fin}.

We use the abbreviations $C^\vee \hat{=} C_1^+ \vee C_1^- \vee C_2^+ \vee C_2^-$ and $C^\wedge \hat{=} C_1^+ \wedge C_1^- \wedge C_2^+ \wedge C_2^-$ for the states which express that at least one of the counter state variables holds, and that all the counter state variables holds, respectively. We require that the states Q_i, L, and $C^\vee$ are mutually exclusive; this assumption is easily formalized as a formula $Mutex(Q_0, \ldots, Q_n, L, C^\vee)$. In the encoding of the machine a *period* is a non-empty interval $|Q|L|C|$ divided into three *sections* of equal length, where Q is one of the Q_j, L is the delimiter, and C either is one of C_1^+, C_1^-, C_2^+, or C_2^-, or is their conjunction $C^\wedge$. All periods must have the same length. A configuration (and a computation) is represented by a sequence of periods:

$$|Q_0|L|C^\wedge|Q_1|L|C|Q_2|L|C|\ldots|Q_n|L|C|$$

such that $\int C_i^+ = \int C_i^-$ holds for this sequence iff the counter C_i has the value 0 after n computation steps. The conjunction $C^\wedge$ is used to keep the counter values unchanged from one period to the next (by increasing $\int C_i^+$ as much as $\int C_i^-$).

The initial configuration $(Q_0, 0, 0)$ is described by:

$$Init \hat{=} ((\lceil Q_0 \rceil \frown \lceil L \rceil \frown \lceil C^\wedge \rceil) \wedge \int Q_0 = \int L = \int C^\wedge) \frown true$$

In any section following $\lceil C^\vee \rceil$, one of the state variables Q_i must hold initially, and it must last as long as the preceding $\lceil C^\vee \rceil$ section and no longer:

$$Constraint \stackrel{\wedge}{=} \bigwedge \begin{array}{l} \Box(\lceil L\rceil \frown \lceil C^\vee\rceil \frown \lceil Q^\vee\rceil \Rightarrow \int C^\vee \geq \int Q^\vee) \\ \\ \Box(\lceil L\rceil \frown \lceil C^\vee\rceil \frown \lceil Q^\vee\rceil \frown \lceil L\rceil \Rightarrow \int C^\vee = \int Q^\vee) \end{array}$$

where $Q^\vee$ abbreviates $Q_0 \vee Q_1 \vee \cdots \vee Q_n$. Note that although the present subset does not include $\int P \geq \int Q$, the formula $(\lceil L\rceil \frown \lceil C^\vee\rceil \frown \lceil Q^\vee\rceil) \wedge \int C^\vee \geq \int Q^\vee$ can be represented as $(\lceil L\rceil \frown \lceil\ \rceil \vee \lceil C^\vee\rceil) \frown ((\lceil C^\vee\rceil \frown \lceil Q^\vee\rceil) \wedge \int C^\vee = \int Q^\vee)$ because of the mutual exclusion requirement.

The entire machine is encoded by the formula

$$Machine \stackrel{\wedge}{=} Mutex(Q_0, \ldots, Q_n, L, C^\vee) \wedge Init \wedge Constraint \wedge \bigwedge_{m_i} \Box_p \neg G(m_i)$$

where $G(m_i)$ encodes instruction m_i of the counter machine M. The encoding of each machine instruction is defined as follows:

The formula $G(Q_i : C_1^- \rightarrow Q_j, Q_k)$ is defined for the case $C_1 = 0$ by:

$$\left(\begin{array}{l} true \frown \lceil Q_i\rceil \frown ((\lceil L\rceil \frown \lceil C^\vee\rceil) \wedge \int L = \int C^\vee) \\ \wedge \quad \int C_1^+ = \int C_1^- \end{array} \right) \frown \neg R(Q_j, C^\wedge)$$

where $R(Q, C) \stackrel{\wedge}{=}$

$$\begin{array}{l} (\lceil Q\rceil \vee \lceil\ \rceil) \\ \vee (\lceil Q\rceil \vee \lceil\ \rceil) \frown ((\lceil Q\rceil \frown \lceil L\rceil) \wedge \int Q = \int L) \\ \vee (\lceil Q\rceil \frown (\lceil L\rceil \vee \lceil\ \rceil) \frown ((\lceil L\rceil \frown \lceil C\rceil) \wedge \int L = \int C)) \wedge \int Q = \int L \\ \vee ((\lceil Q\rceil \frown \lceil L\rceil \frown \lceil C\rceil) \wedge \int Q = \int L = \int C) \frown true \end{array}$$

Note that $Constraint$ guarantees that the Q section has the right length. The case where $C_1 > 0$ can be defined using the same technique, and the formulas $G(m_i)$ for the other instructions are defined similarly. Then the formula $(Machine \wedge \Diamond \lceil Q_{fin}\rceil)$ is satisfiable if and only if the machine terminates.

Theorem 12. *The satisfiability (in discrete and dense time) of duration formulas built from $(\int P = \int Q)$ is undecidable.*

6 Undecidability of the $(\forall x, \lceil P\rceil, \ell = x)$-subset

We reduce the halting problem for a two-counter machine M to satisfiability of a formula built from $\lceil P\rceil$, $\forall x$ and $\ell = x$, thereby showing satisfiability of such formulas to be undecidable (in discrete as well as dense time).

The encoding of M uses state variables L_1, L_2, C, and $Q_0, \ldots Q_n$, where L_1 and L_2 delimit machine configurations, C is used to represent the counter values, and the Q_i are labels of the counter machine. All these state variables must be mutually exclusive. This is easily expressed by a formula $Mutex(Q_0, \ldots, Q_n, L_1, L_2, C)$. We assume there is a designated initial label Q_0 and a designated final label Q_{fin}.

A configuration (Q_i, c_1, c_2) is represented by a sequence of sections:

$$|Q_i| \underbrace{C|\dots|C}_{c_1} |L_1| \underbrace{C|\dots|C}_{c_2} |L_2|$$

All sections $|Q_i|$, $|C|$, $|L_1|$ and $|L_2|$ must have the same length (u, say).

We let $\lceil P \rceil^x$ abbreviate $(\lceil \ \rceil \vee \lceil P \rceil) \wedge \ell = x$, meaning P holds for duration x.

Initially, the machine label is Q_0 and both counters c_1 and c_2 are zero. This is the configuration $|Q_0|L_1|L_2|$, which is prescribed by the requirement:

$$Init \ \widehat{=} \ \exists u.(\lceil Q_0 \rceil \wedge \ell = u) ^\frown (\lceil L_1 \rceil \wedge \ell = u) ^\frown (\lceil L_2 \rceil \wedge \ell = u) ^\frown true$$

Since $\exists u.\mathcal{D}$ is equivalent to $\neg\forall u.\neg\mathcal{D}$, this requirement can in fact be expressed in the present subcalculus. Note that $u > 0$ and that u is the "time unit": the length of every section.

Each instruction m_i of the counter machine is encoded as a duration formula $H(m_i)$, defined below, which relates one configuration of the machine to the next one. The encoding of the entire machine is:

$$Machine \ \widehat{=} \ Mutex(Q_0, \dots, Q_n, L_1, L_2, C) \wedge \ Init \wedge \bigwedge_{m_i} \Box H(m_i)$$

The instruction $Q_i : C_1^+ \to Q_j$ transforms the configuration as follows:

$$|Q_i| \underbrace{C|\dots|C}_{c_1} |L_1| \underbrace{C|\dots|C}_{c_2} |L_2| \implies |Q_j| \underbrace{C|C|\dots|C}_{c_1+1} |L_1| \underbrace{C|\dots|C}_{c_2} |L_2|$$

This computation step is encoded by the formula $H(Q_i : C_1^+ \to Q_j)$:

$$\forall u, c_1, c_2. \ \lceil Q_i \rceil^u {}^\frown \lceil C \rceil^{c_1} {}^\frown \lceil L_1 \rceil^u {}^\frown \lceil C \rceil^{c_2} {}^\frown \lceil L_2 \rceil^u {}^\frown \ell = c_1 + c_2 + 4u$$
$$\Rightarrow \ell = c_1 + c_2 + 3u {}^\frown \lceil Q_j \rceil^u {}^\frown \lceil C \rceil^u {}^\frown \lceil C \rceil^{c_1} {}^\frown \lceil L_1 \rceil^u {}^\frown \lceil C \rceil^{c_2} {}^\frown \lceil L_2 \rceil^u$$

The formula $H(Q_i : C_2^+ \to Q_j)$ is similar. Note that the formula $\ell = c_1 + c_2 + 3u$ can be thought of as an abbreviation for $\ell = c_1 {}^\frown \ell = c_2 {}^\frown \ell = u {}^\frown \ell = u {}^\frown \ell = u$.

The instructions $Q_i : C_1^- \to Q_j, Q_k$ and $Q_i : C_2^- \to Q_j, Q_k$ are encoded similarly.

Encoding each machine instruction m_i this way, the formula $Machine \wedge \Diamond \lceil Q_{fin} \rceil$ is satisfiable if and only if the machine terminates.

Theorem 13. *The satisfiability (in discrete and dense time) of duration formulas built from $\lceil P \rceil$ and $\forall x. \ \dots \ell = x \dots$ is undecidable.*

7 Discussion

We have presented decidable and undecidable subsets of duration calculus. The circuit specifications given in [8] uses the $(\lceil P \rceil, \ell = k)$-subset, and so can be automatically verified for a discrete time domain.

The literature already gives some results on decidability and undecidability of real-time logics.

For example, the real-time propositional temporal logic TPTL is decidable for discrete time but undecidable for dense time [1]. Furthermore, an extension towards

TPTL with Presburger arithmetics is undecidable when general addition is allowed. However, whereas the real time temporal logic makes assertions about points in time, duration calculus makes assertions about intervals of time and about durations (integrals over time). Thus the results for real time temporal logic do not apply to duration calculus.

It is stated without proof in [6] that interval temporal logic is undecidable. This we now can prove as follows: The validity of duration formulas can be reduced to the validity of interval temporal logic formulas [7]. Since satisfiability in duration calculus is undecidable, so is validity, and so is validity in interval temporal logic.

The practical and theoretical complexity of the decision procedures given in this paper is currently being studied.

Acknowledgements Thanks to Ernst-Rüdiger Olderog, Anders P. Ravn, and Jens Ulrik Skakkebæk for comments on a draft.

References

1. R. Alur and T.A. Henzinger: A Really Temporal Logic. In *30th Annual IEEE Symp. on Foundations of Computer Science*, October 1989, pp. 164-169.
2. R. Alur, C. Courcoubetis, and D. Dill: Model-Checking for Real-Time Systems. In *Fifth Annual IEEE Symp. on Logic in Computer Science*, 1990, pp. 414-425.
3. R. Bird. *Programs and Machines*. John Wiley & Sons, 1976.
4. N.S. Bjørner: *On Formally Undecidable Propositions of Duration Calculus*, Personal note, Dept. of Comp. Science, Technical University of Denmark, April 15, 1992.
5. Zhou Chaochen, C.A.R. Hoare, and A.P. Ravn: A Calculus of Durations. In *Information Processing Letters* 40(5), 1991, pp. 269-276.
6. J. Halpern, B. Moszkowski, and Z. Manna: A Hardware Semantics Based on Temporal Intervals. In *ICALP'83*, LNCS 154, Springer-Verlag 1983, pp. 278-291.
7. M.R. Hansen and Zhou Chaochen: Semantics and Completeness of Duration Calculus. In J.W. deBakker, K. Huizing, W.P. de Roever, and G. Rozenberg (eds.): *Real-Time: Theory in Practice, 1991*, LNCS 600, Springer-Verlag 1992, pp. 209-225.
8. M.R. Hansen, Zhou Chaochen, and J. Staunstrup: A Real-Time Duration Semantics for Circuits. In *TAU 1992 ACM/SIGDA Workshop on Timing Issues in the Specification and Synthesis of Digital Systems*, Princeton Univ., NJ, March 1992.
9. J.E. Hopcroft and J.D. Ullman. *Introduction to Automata Theory, Languages, and Computation*. Addison-Wesley, 1979.
10. A.P. Ravn, H. Rischel, and K.M. Hansen: Specifying and Verifying Requirements of Real-Time Systems. IEEE Transactions on Software Engineering. (To appear).

Defining λ-Typed λ-Calculi
by Axiomatizing the Typing Relation

Philippe de Groote

INRIA-Lorraine – CRIN – CNRS
Campus Scientifique – B.P. 239
54506 Vandœvre-lès-Nancy Cedex – FRANCE

Paper received late. Please refer to page 712.

The Complexity of Logic-Based Abduction*

Thomas Eiter and Georg Gottlob

Christian Doppler Laboratory for Expert Systems
Institut für Informationssysteme
Technische Universität Wien
Paniglgasse 16, A-1040 Wien, Austria
{eiter,gottlob}@vexpert.dbai.tuwien.ac.at

Abstract. Abduction is an important form of nonmonotonic reasoning allowing one to find explanations for certain symptoms or manifestations. When the application domain is described by a logical theory, we speak about *logic-based abduction*. Candidates for abductive explanations are usually subjected to minimality criteria such as subset-minimality, minimal cardinality, minimal weight, or minimality under prioritization of individual hypotheses. This paper presents a comprehensive complexity analysis of relevant problems related to abduction on propositional theories. They show that the different variations of abduction provide a rich collection of natural problems populating all major complexity classes between P and Σ_3^P, Π_3^P in the refined polynomial hierarchy. More precisely, besides polynomial, NP-complete and co-NP-complete abduction problems, abduction tasks that are complete for the classes Δ_i^P, $\Delta_i^P[O(\log n)]$, Σ_i^P, and Π_i^P, for $i = 2, 3$, are identified.

1 Introduction

This paper is on the computational complexity of abduction, which is a powerful formalization of relevant principles of commonsense reasoning. Abductive reasoning is used to generate explanations for observed symptoms or manifestations.

Several formalizations of abductive reasoning have been introduced. A prominent class is that of the *set-cover based approaches* (cf. [24]) where explicit causal links between hypotheses and sets of manifestations are represented by functional mappings. This paper considers *logic-based abduction*, where such links are implicitly contained in a logical domain theory.

Logic-based abduction is more general than most other formal approaches to abduction and has attracted a great deal of interest, especially in recent years due, to progress in logic programming and logic-based knowledge representation [18, 21]. It can be described as follows. Given a logical theory T formalizing a particular application domain, a set M of atomic formulas describing some manifestations, and a set H of (usually atomic) formulas containing possible individual hypotheses, find an *explanation* for M, i.e., a suitable set $S \subseteq H$ such that $T \cup S$ is consistent and logically entails M.

---

* This paper is an overview of [10], which contains detailed proofs of all results.

Usually, some minimality criteria are imposed on a solution S. Often S is required to be parsimonious, i.e., $T \cup S'$ should not imply M for any proper subset $S' \subset S$. Other authors require minimum cardinality of S, i.e., no solution S' with $|S'| < |S|$ may exist. This criterion is useful if the hypotheses in H represent statistically independent rather unlikely events but may be inadequate in some other cases [26].

More refined minimality criteria are the methods of priorities (*prioritization*) and penalties (*penalization*). By the method of priorities, the set H of hypotheses is partitioned into groups of different priority and solutions containing higher priority atoms are preferred over solutions consisting of atoms of lower priority. The method of penalties is a refinement of the method of priorities combined with the minimum cardinality measure. It allows to attach a weight (penalty) to each hypothesis from H and looks for solutions with minimum total weight. These weights may be subjective values (similar to certainty factors) or the outcome of a statistical analysis.

In the context of logic-based abduction, the main decision problems are:

(i) to determine whether an explanation for the given manifestations exists;
(ii) to determine whether an individual hypothesis $h \in H$ is *relevant*, i.e., whether it is part of at least one acceptable explanation;
(iii) to determine whether an individual hypothesis is *necessary*, i.e., whether it occurs in all acceptable explanations.

Due to the results in [1, 4], the complexity of these problems in the context of set-covering abduction is quite well understood. The complexity of logic based abduction, however, was only partially investigated. The work in [29, 3, 12] studies the particular case where T is a propositional Horn theory and $\subseteq$-based minimality is used. The complexity of abductive reasoning in the general propositional case was left open, and it was also unclear how different minimality criteria affect the complexity in the general and in the Horn case.

This paper sheds light on these questions by providing completeness results for several complexity classes at lower levels of the refined polynomial hierarchy [33]. They show that different variations of abduction provide a rich collection of natural problems populating all major complexity classes between P and Σ_3^P, Π_3^P. Abduction appears to be one of the few natural practical problems with this characteristic, and to our knowledge the first such problem in AI.

The rest of this abstract is organized as follows. Section 2 introduces some basic notation, and Section 3 contains the formalization of logical abduction. Section 4 gives a detailed overview of the main results, which are discussed in Section 5. Section 6 provides as an appendix proof sketches for some results.

2 Preliminaries

Let $\mathcal{L}_V$ be the language of propositional logic over an alphabet V of propositional variables, with syntactic operators $\wedge$, $\vee$, $\neg$, $\rightarrow$, $\leftrightarrow$, $\top$ (a constant for truth), and $\perp$ (falsity). A theory is a finite set $T \subseteq \mathcal{L}_V$. We refer to a theory T also as the conjunction of its formulae. Each variable is an atom, and a literal is an atom or a negated atom. A clause is a disjunction $x_1 \vee \cdots \vee x_k \vee \neg x_{k+1} \vee \cdots \vee \neg x_n$ of (pairwise distinct) literals. We refer to a clause also as the set of its literals. A clause is Horn (definite Horn) iff $k \leq 1$ ($k = 1$); a theory is in clausal form iff all its formulae are clauses. Classical logical consequence is denoted by $\models$.

Recall that the classes Δ_k^P, Σ_k^P, and Π_k^P of the polynomial time hierarchy (PH) are defined as follows, cf. [14]: $\Delta_0^P = \Sigma_0^P = \Pi_0^P = P$, and for all $k \geq 0$, $\Delta_{k+1}^P = P^{\Sigma_k^P}$, $\Sigma_{k+1}^P = NP^{\Sigma_k^P}$, and $\Pi_{k+1}^P = \text{co-}\Sigma_{k+1}^P$. We say that a problem is at the k-th level of PH if it is complete for Δ_{k+1}^P under Turing reductions.

Δ_k^P was refined to account for the required number of oracle calls to solve a problem [31, 19, 16, 32, 33]. $\Delta_{k+1}^P[O(\log n)]$ (also denoted by $P^{\Sigma_k^P[O(\log n)]}$, or by Θ_{k+1}^P) is the class of problems decidable in deterministic polynomial time with $O(\log n)$ queries to a Σ_k^P oracle, where n is the input size (see [33] for details).

3 Abduction model

Definition 1. A propositional abduction problem (*PAP*) $\mathcal{P}$ is a tuple $\langle V, H, M, T \rangle$, where V is a finite set of propositional variables, $H \subseteq V$ is the set of hypotheses, $M \subseteq V$ is the set of manifestations, and $T \subseteq \mathcal{L}_V$ is a consistent theory.

Definition 2. $S \subseteq H$ is a solution (or explanation) to PAP $\mathcal{P} = \langle V, H, M, T \rangle$ iff $T \cup S$ is consistent and $T \cup S \models M$. *Sol*($\mathcal{P}$) is the set of all solutions to $\mathcal{P}$.

A hypothesis plays here the role of what in other models is called an abducible proposition [6]. Note that only positive atoms are allowed in solutions (cf. [17] for a similar model). This is no restriction of generality, since we may add to T a formula $x' \leftrightarrow F$ where x' is a new variable added to the hypotheses H.

We consider several restrictions of *Sol*($\mathcal{P}$) to a subset of "acceptable" solutions, which are formalized by suitable preference relations between solutions. We model such relations by preorders, since reflexivity and transitivity are natural axioms. $\preceq$ denotes a preorder on the powerset 2^H of the hypotheses H. $a \prec b$ stands for $a \preceq b \wedge b \not\preceq a$. The preferred (or acceptable) solutions *Sol*$_\preceq$($\mathcal{P}$) of a PAP $\mathcal{P}$ under order $\preceq$ are defined as follows.

Definition 3. *Sol*$_\preceq$($\mathcal{P}$) $= \{S \in \textit{Sol}(\mathcal{P}) : \not\exists S' \in \textit{Sol}(\mathcal{P}) : S' \prec S\}$.

An important property for preference relations is *irredundancy* of solutions [24, 29, 4, 17]: $\preceq$ is *irredundant* iff $\forall S, S' \in \textit{Sol}(\mathcal{P}) : S \subset S' \Rightarrow S \prec S'$.

Two well-known orders of this kind are irredundancy itself, that is, $S \preceq S'$ iff $S \subseteq S'$, which we denote by $\subseteq$, and *minimum solution size* (e.g. [24]), that is, $S_1 \preceq S_2$ iff $|S_1| \leq |S_2|$, which we denote by $\leq$. Further preference orders we consider are prioritization and penalties.

Definition 4. Let H be a finite set and $\preceq$ be a preorder defined on 2^H, and let $P = \langle P_1, \ldots, P_k \rangle$, $k \geq 1$, such that $H = P_1 \cup \cdots \cup P_k$, , where $P_i \cap P_j = \emptyset$, $1 \leq i < j \leq k$. Then, define the relation $\preceq_P$ on 2^H by $A \preceq_P B$ iff $A = B$ or there exists $i \in \{1, \ldots, k\}$ such that $A \cap P_j \preceq B \cap P_j$, $B \cap P_j \preceq A \cap P_j$, for all $1 \le j < i$, and $A \cap P_i \preceq B \cap P_i$, $B \cap P_i \not\preceq A \cap P_i$.

Intuitively, $A \preceq_P B$ iff A, B are of equal preference on $P_1, \ldots, P_{i-1}$ and A is preferred over B on P_i. The same method of prioritization appears in [11] in the context of theory update, in prioritized circumscription [22], and in the preferred subtheories approach for default reasoning [2]. Note that $\preceq_P$ is irredundant if $\preceq$ is irredundant, and $\preceq_P$ is polynomially decidable if $\preceq$ is.

Definition 5. Let $\mathcal{P} = \langle V, H, M, T \rangle$ be a *PAP*, and let $p : H \to \{1, 2, 3 \ldots\}$ be a penalty attachment, which is extended to 2^H by $p(H') = \sum_{h \in H'} p(h)$, for all $H' \subseteq H$. The preference relation $\le^p$ on *Sol*$(\mathcal{P})$ is defined by $S \le^p S'$ iff $p(S) \le p(S')$.

Notice that $\le^p$ generalizes $\le$ (let $p(h) = p(h')$, $\forall h, h' \in H$); it also generalizes $\le_P$ (see full paper).

Definition 6. Let $\mathcal{P} = \langle V, H, M, T \rangle$ be a *PAP*, and let $h \in H$. h is $\preceq$-relevant for $\mathcal{P}$ iff there exists $S \in Sol_{\preceq}(\mathcal{P})$ such that $h \in S$, and h is $\preceq$-necessary for $\mathcal{P}$ iff for all $S \in Sol_{\preceq}(\mathcal{P})$, $h \in S$.

We say that h is $\preceq$-dispensable for $\mathcal{P}$ iff h is not $\preceq$-necessary for $\mathcal{P}$ (in [15], necessity is termed indispensability).

4 Overview of Results

The main results of our analysis, together with previously known results, are compactly presented in Tables 1–3. Besides the general case (resp. clausal form), the restriction of T to Horn theories, and definite Horn theories is distinguished. Most results are shown under the additional restriction $H \cup M = V$. Each entry NP, co-NP, etc. means completeness for the respective complexity class.

Notice that all classes of the polynomial hierarchy PH, refined by adopting $\Delta_k^P[O(\log n)]$ classes, from P up to Σ_3^P and Π_3^P are covered, and that except for one case (definite Horn, $\subseteq$), deciding $\preceq$-necessity is as complex as the complementary problem to deciding $\preceq$-relevance. Intuitively, $\preceq$-necessity is easier because the structure of the set of solutions (see Section 5) allows to decide the problem after checking a single candidate for a solution that does not contain h. The results of main interest are Σ_2^P-completeness of deciding whether a propositional abduction problem has any solution and that deciding $\preceq$-relevance or $\preceq$-necessity of a hypothesis is complete for any class at the second level of PH in case of no preference ($=$), preference of irredundant solutions ($\subseteq$), and preference of minimum-sized solutions ($\le$). Prioritization ($\subseteq_P, \le_P$) leads to a complexity increase, which reaches for $\subseteq_P$ the third level of PH. Under $\le_P$-preference, which is "easier" than $\subseteq_P$-preference, the problems are still at the second level, and are as hard as under preference by penalty attachments ($\le^p$).

It is not surprising that abduction for clausal theories is not easier than for arbitrary theories, since generally decision problems for arbitrary logical formulas are no more difficult than in the clausal case. If the underlying theory is

Table 1. Complexity results for propositional abduction ($\leq_m^p$-completeness)

$\mathcal{P} = \langle V, H, M, T \rangle$	general case, clausal form	T is Horn	T is definite Horn
Deciding $Sol(\mathcal{P}) \neq \emptyset$	Σ_2^P	NP [29]	in P [3]

Table 2. Complexity results for propositional abduction, contd.

Propositional Abduction	Deciding whether $h \in H$ is $\preceq$-relevant for $\mathcal{P}$					
$\mathcal{P} = \langle V, H, M, T \rangle$	$=$	$\subseteq$	$\leq$	$\subseteq_P$	$\leq_P$	$\leq^P$
general case, clausal form	Σ_2^P	Σ_2^P	$\Delta_3^P[O(\log n)]$	Σ_3^P	Δ_3^P	Δ_3^P
T is Horn	NP [29]	NP [29]	$\Delta_2^P[O(\log n)]$	Σ_2^P	Δ_2^P	Δ_2^P
T is definite Horn	in P [12, 3]	NP [12]	$\Delta_2^P[O(\log n)]$	NP	Δ_2^P	Δ_2^P

Table 3. Complexity results for propositional abduction, contd.

Propositional Abduction	Deciding whether $h \in H$ is $\preceq$-necessary for $\mathcal{P}$					
$\mathcal{P} = \langle V, H, M, T \rangle$	$=$	$\subseteq$	$\leq$	$\subseteq_P$	$\leq_P$	$\leq^P$
general case, clausal form	Π_2^P	Π_2^P	$\Delta_3^P[O(\log n)]$	Π_3^P	Δ_3^P	Δ_3^P
T is Horn	co-NP	co-NP	$\Delta_2^P[O(\log n)]$	Π_2^P	Δ_2^P	Δ_2^P
T is definite Horn	in P [12, 3]	in P [12, 3]	$\Delta_2^P[O(\log n)]$	co-NP	Δ_2^P	Δ_2^P

Horn, then the complexity of the problems is always lowered by one level of PH. Further restriction to definite Horn theories only affects the complexity of the set-inclusion based preference methods ($\subseteq, \subseteq_P$), and lowers the complexity of the problems, except for one case, by another level of PH.

5 Conclusion

Problems at the second level of the polynomial hierarchy PH are considered much harder than problems at the first level, since – unless PH collapses, what we assume to be false for the rest of this section – they cannot be solved in deterministic polynomial time even if an oracle for any problem in NP is available.

Thus, abduction is much harder than classical consequence $\models$, which is co-NP-complete. Besides $\models$, the choice of candidates $S \subseteq H$ for a solution S is a second source of complexity that lifts abduction to the second level of PH.

Similarly, problems at the third level of PH are considered much harder than problems at the second level, and hence prioritized abduction with $\subseteq$-minimality is not polynomial even if an oracle for $\subseteq$-minimal abduction without prioritization is available. Prioritization adds a third source of complexity, since for each $\subseteq$-solution S, which is a potential candidate for a $\subseteq_P$-solution, still exponentially many other such candidates S' such that $S' \subset_P S$ may exist. In the case of $\leq$-solutions, the method of priorities is a "weaker" source of complexity since it does not scale abduction up to the third level of PH, but moves it still from $\Delta_3^P[O(\log n)]$ to the class of Δ_3^P-complete problems, which are considered more difficult than the problems in $\Delta_3^P[O(\log n)]$.

In the Horn case, the first source of complexity ($\models$) is eliminated, which effects the one-level decrease of complexity. Under the further restriction to definite Horn theories, the structure of the set of solutions ($S \in Sol(\mathcal{P})$ implies $S' \in Sol(\mathcal{P})$, for $S \subset S' \subseteq H$) reduces the search space such that in some cases polynomial time algorithms are known.

Our results explain how the syntactic form of theories interacts with various minimality criteria and may support a designer of an abductive expert system in choosing the right settings. For instance, our results suggest that – if permitted by the application – using penalties is preferable to using prioritization together with the usual $\subseteq$-minimality criterion, except in the definite Horn case.

More recently, complexity results at the second level of PH have been derived for other forms of non-classical reasoning, e.g. [23, 27, 13, 8, 9, 28] (see [5] for a survey of the field). For example, it is known that relevant reasoning tasks in Reiter's default logic or in Moore's autoepistemic logic are Π_2^P-complete [13]. Thus, one can polynomially translate abduction problems to default or autoepistemic reasoning tasks and take advantage of existing algorithms and proof procedures. Vice-versa, any abductive reasoning engine can be used to solve problems in other nonmonotonic logics. Polynomial translations extracted from complexity proofs may not be very appealing; however, knowing that such translations exist, one can search for (and usually finds) more intuitive and useful ones.

6 Appendix: Proof sketches

In this section, we give proof sketches for some of the results in Tables 1–3. Proofs for all results can be found in the full paper [10].

Theorem 7. *Deciding $Sol(\mathcal{P}) \neq \emptyset$ for a given PAP $\mathcal{P} = \langle V, H, M, T \rangle$ is Σ_2^P-complete, even if $H \cup M = V$ and T is in clausal form.*

Proof. (Sketch) It is easy to see that For a PAP $\mathcal{P} = \langle V, H, M, T \rangle$ and $S \subseteq H$, deciding $S \in Sol(\mathcal{P})$ is in Δ_2^P. Thus verifying a guess for $S \in Sol(\mathcal{P})$ is in Δ_2^P; membership in Σ_2^P follows.

Σ_2^P-hardness of this problem is shown by a transformation from deciding the validity of a quantified Boolean formula (QBF) $\Phi = \exists x_1 \cdots \exists x_n \forall y_1 \cdots \forall y_m E$, the canonical Σ_2^P-complete problem [14]. Let $X = \{x_1, \ldots, x_n\}$, $Y = \{y_1, \ldots, y_m\}$, $X' = \{x_1', \ldots, x_n'\}$, and let further s be a new variable. Define a PAP $\mathcal{P} = \langle V, H, M, T \rangle$ as follows.

$$V = X \cup Y \cup X' \cup \{s\}, \quad H = X \cup X', \quad M = Y \cup \{s\}$$
$$T = \{x_i \leftrightarrow \neg x_i' : 1 \le i \le n\} \cup \{(\neg E \wedge \neg s) \vee (s \wedge y_1 \wedge \cdots \wedge y_m)\}$$

Note that T is consistent and that $\mathcal{P}$ is constructible in polynomial time. It can be shown that Φ is valid iff $Sol(\mathcal{P}) \neq \emptyset$.

It remains to show that deciding $Sol(\mathcal{P}) \neq \emptyset$ is Σ_2^P-hard even if $H \cup M = V$ and T is in clausal form. The former already holds. By the results in [30] we may assume that E is in DNF. Hence a CNF formula $\overline{E} = C_1 \wedge C_2 \wedge \cdots \wedge C_r$ with $\overline{E} \equiv \neg E$ can efficiently be constructed. It is not difficult to verify that $(\neg E \wedge \neg s) \vee (s \wedge y_1 \wedge \cdots \wedge y_m)$ is logically equivalent to the clausal theory

$$C = \{C_i \cup \{s\}, C_i \cup \{y_j\} : 1 \le i \le r, 1 \le j \le m\} \cup \{\{\neg s, y_i\} : 1 \le i \le m\}$$

Clearly, C can be easily constructed from E as well as the clausal theory $T' = C \cup \{\neg x_i \vee \neg x_i', x_i \vee x_i' : 1 \le i \le n\}$. Since $T' \equiv T$, the theorem follows. $\square$

Lemma 8. *Let $\mathcal{P} = \langle V, H, M, T \rangle$ be a PAP and assume deciding $\preceq$ is polynomial. Then, deciding whether h is $\preceq$-relevant ($\preceq$-dispensable) for $\mathcal{P}$ is in Σ_3^P.*

Theorem 9. *Deciding $\subseteq_P$-relevance and $\subseteq_P$-dispensability of a hypothesis h for a $\mathcal{P} = \langle V, H, M, T \rangle$ is Σ_3^P-complete, even if $P = \langle P_1, P_2 \rangle$. The same holds if T is in clausal form.*

Proof. (Sketch) By Lemma 8, it suffices to show Σ_3^P-hardness by a $\le_m^p$-reduction of deciding validity of a QBF $\Phi = \exists x_1 \cdots \exists x_{n_x} \forall y_1 \cdots \forall y_{n_y} \exists z_1 \cdots \exists z_{n_z} E$.

Let $H_x = \{x_1, x_1', \ldots, x_{n_x}, x_{n_x}'\}$, $H_y = \{y_1, y_1', \ldots, y_{n_y}, y_{n_y}'\}$, $H_z = \{z_1, \ldots, z_{n_z}\}$, $M_x = \{r_1, \ldots, r_{n_x}\}$, $M_y = \{w_1, \ldots, w_{n_y}\}$, and let p, s, t be new variables. Define a PAP $\mathcal{P} = \langle V, H, M, T \rangle$ as follows.

$$V = H_x \cup H_y \cup H_z \cup M_x \cup M_y \cup \{p, s, t\}, \qquad M = M_x \cup M_y \cup \{t\}$$
$$H = H_x \cup H_y \cup \{p, s\}$$
$$T = \{\neg x_i \vee \neg x_i', x_i \to r_i, x_i' \to r_i : 1 \le i \le n_x\} \cup \{\neg s \wedge p \to t, \neg E \wedge s \to t\} \cup$$
$$\{y_i \wedge y_i' \leftrightarrow \neg s, y_i \wedge y_i' \to w_i, s \to w_i : 1 \le i \le n_y\}.$$

Note that T is consistent and constructible in polynomial time. Define two priority levels $P = \langle P_1, P_2 \rangle$, where $P_1 = H - \{s\}$ and $P_2 = \{s\}$.

It can be shown that p is $\subseteq_P$-relevant for $\mathcal{P}$ iff Φ is valid, which shows Σ_3^P-hardness of deciding $\subseteq_P$-relevance. Furthermore, it can be shown that for each $S \in Sol_{\subseteq_P}(\mathcal{P})$, $s \in S$ iff $p \notin S$. Hence, p is $\subseteq_P$-relevant for $\mathcal{P}$ iff s is $\subseteq_P$-dispensable for $\mathcal{P}$, and Σ_3^P-hardness of $\subseteq_P$-dispensability checking follows.

Since without loss of generality it can be assumed that E is in CNF [30], T can be efficiently rewritten in clausal form, from which the result follows. $\square$

Theorem 10. *Let $\mathcal{P}$ be a PAP and let $P = \langle P_1, \ldots, P_k \rangle$ be a prioritization. Deciding $\leq_P$-relevance and $\leq_P$-dispensability of a hypothesis h for $\mathcal{P}$ is Δ_3^P-complete. This holds if $H \cup M = V$ and T is in clausal form.*

Proof. (Sketch) Membership in Δ_3^P is shown as follows. For all $S, S' \in Sol_{\leq_P}(\mathcal{P})$ we have $|S \cap P_i| = |S' \cap P_i|$, $1 \leq i \leq k$. Let $s_i = |S \cap P_i|$ for such an S, $1 \leq i \leq k$. First, $s_1, \ldots, s_i, \ldots, s_k$ are determined in that order, where s_i is computed by queries to the Σ_2^P oracle (e.g. in a binary search) whether there exists $S \in Sol(\mathcal{P})$ such that $|S \cap P_j| = s_j$, for $1 \leq j < i$, and $|S \cap P_i| \leq r$. This can be done with polynomially many Σ_2^P oracle calls. Then, the Σ_2^P oracle is queried whether there exists $S \in Sol(\mathcal{P})$ such that $|S \cap P_i| = s_i$, $1 \leq i \leq k$ and $h \in S$ ($h \notin S$).

Δ_3^P-hardness is shown by a reduction from the following Δ_3^P-complete problem (cf. [20]). Decide if the w.r.t. $\langle x_1, \ldots, x_{n_x} \rangle$ lexicographically maximum truth assignment[2] ϕ to $x_1, \ldots, x_{n_x}$ that makes the QBF $\Phi_\phi = \forall y_1 \cdots \forall y_{n_y} E_\phi$ valid satisfies $\phi(x_{n_x}) = true$. (E_ϕ is obtained from E by replacing every x_i with $\phi(x_i)$.) Let $X = \{x_1, \ldots, x_{n_x}\}$, $X' = \{x'_1, \ldots, x'_{n_x}\}$, $Y = \{y_1, \ldots, y_{n_y}\}$, $U = \{u_1, \ldots, u_{n_x}\}$, and let s be an additional variable. Define a PAP $\mathcal{P} = \langle V, H, M, T \rangle$ as follows.

$$V = X \cup X' \cup Y \cup U \cup \{s\}, \quad H = X \cup X', \quad M = U \cup Y \cup \{s\},$$
$$T = \{\neg x_i \vee \neg x'_i, \, x_i \rightarrow u_i, \, x'_i \rightarrow u_i : 1 \leq i \leq n_x\} \cup \{(\neg E \wedge \neg s) \vee (s \wedge \bigwedge_{i=1}^{n_y} y_i)\}$$

Note that $H \cup M = V$. Define a prioritization $P = \langle P_1, \ldots, P_{2n_x} \rangle$ as follows: $P_{2i-1} = \{x'_i\}$, $P_{2i} = \{x_i\}$, for $1 \leq i \leq n_x$. It can be shown that

$$Sol_{\leq_P}(\mathcal{P}) = \{\{x_i : \phi_m(x_i) = true, 1 \leq i \leq n_x\} \cup \{x'_i : \phi_m(x_i) = false, 1 \leq i \leq n_x\}\},$$

where ϕ_m is w.r.t. $\langle x_1, \ldots, x_{n_x} \rangle$ the lexicographically maximum ϕ such that $\forall y_1 \cdots \forall y_{n_y} E_\phi$ is valid. Therefore, x_n is $\leq_P$-relevant (and x'_n is $\leq_P$-dispensable) for $\mathcal{P}$ iff $\phi_m(x_n) = true$. Assuming without loss of generality that E is in DNF [20], T can be efficiently rewritten in clausal form. The result follows. $\square$

Proposition 11. *If $\mathcal{P} = \langle V, H, M, T \rangle$ is a Horn PAP, checking $S \in Sol(\mathcal{P})$ for $S \subseteq H$ is polynomial.*

Proof. Follows from the polynomiality of Horn satisfiability, cf. [7]. $\square$

Theorem 12. *Deciding if h is $\leq$-dispensable ($\leq$-relevant) for a Horn PAP $\mathcal{P} = \langle V, H, M, T \rangle$ is $\Delta_2^P[O(\log n)]$-complete, even if $\mathcal{P}$ is definite Horn and $H \cup M = V$.*

Proof. (Sketch) Membership in $\Delta_2^P[O(\log n)]$ is shown for both problems as follows: compute $s = \min\{|S| : S \in Sol(\mathcal{P})\}$ by binary search, querying an NP oracle whether $S \in Sol(\mathcal{P})$ exists such that $|S| \leq k$, where k is in the input. Then, query the oracle whether there exists $S \in Sol(\mathcal{P})$ such that $|S| = k$ and $h \notin S$ ($h \in S$). The oracle answers yes iff h is $\leq$-dispensable (h is $\leq$-relevant).

---

[2] ϕ is w.r.t. $\langle x_1, \ldots, x_{n_x} \rangle$ lexicographically greater than ψ iff $\phi(x_i) = true$, $\psi(x_i) = false$ for the least i such that $\phi(x_i) \neq \psi(x_i)$.

Hardness for is shown by a $\leq_m^p$-reduction from the following problem, which is shown $\Delta_2^P[O(\log n)]$-complete in the full paper. Call a truth assignment ϕ to variables X csat-maximum for a clause set $C = \{C_1, \ldots, C_m\}$ on X iff ϕ satisfies a maximum number of clauses in C. Given $k \in \{1, \ldots, m\}$, decide if every csat-maximum ϕ for C satisfies C_k.

Let $X^i = \{x_1^i, \ldots, x_m^i\}$, $X'^i = \{x_1'^i, \ldots, x_m'^i\}$, $1 \leq i \leq n$, $W = \{w_1, \ldots, w_n\}$, $G = \{g_1, \ldots, g_{m+1}\}$, $F = \{f_1, \ldots, f_{m+1}\}$ be sets of new variables. Define a definite Horn PAP $\mathcal{P} = \langle V, H, M, T \rangle$ as follows.

$$V = X^1 \cup X'^1 \cdots \cup X^n \cup X'^n \cup W \cup G \cup F, \qquad M = W \cup G$$

$$H = X^1 \cup X'^1 \cdots \cup X^n \cup X'^n \cup F$$

$$T = \{x_1^i \wedge \cdots \wedge x_m^i \to w_i,\ x_1'^i \wedge \cdots \wedge x_m'^i \to w_i : 1 \leq i \leq n\} \cup$$
$$\{f_i \to g_i : 1 \leq i \leq m+1\} \cup \{f_k \to g_{m+1}\} \cup$$
$$\bigcup_{j=1}^m \{x_1^i \wedge \cdots \wedge x_m^i \to g_j,\ x_1'^r \wedge \cdots \wedge x_m'^r \to g_j : x_i, \neg x_r \in C_j, 1 \leq i, r \leq n\}.$$

It can be shown that f_{m+1} is $\leq$-relevant for $\mathcal{P}$ iff all csat-maximum ϕ for C satisfy C_k, and that f_{m+1} is $\leq$-relevant for $\mathcal{P}$ iff f_k is $\leq$-dispensable for $\mathcal{P}$. $\quad\square$

Acknowledgment. The authors would like to thank L. Console, D. Theseider Dupré, E. Köhler and the reviewers for their constructive comments and K. W. Wagner for sending papers.

References

1. D. Allemang, M.C.Tanner, T. Bylander, and J. Josephson. Computational Complexity of Hypothesis Assembly. In *Proc. IJCAI-87*, 112–117, 1987.
2. G. Brewka. *Nonmonotonic Reasoning: Logical Foundations of Commonsense.* Cambridge Univ. Press, 1991.
3. T. Bylander. The Monotonic Abduction Problem: A Functional Characterization on the Edge of Tractability. In *Proc. KR-91*, 70–77, 1991.
4. T. Bylander, D. Allemang, M. Tanner, and J. Josephson. The computational complexity of abduction. *Artificial Intelligence*, 49:25–60, 1991.
5. M. Cadoli and M. Schaerf. A Survey on Complexity Results for Non-monotonic Logics. Technical report, Dipartimento di Informatica e Sistemistica, Università di Roma "La Sapienza", 1992.
6. L. Console, D. Theseider Dupré, and P. Torasso. On the Relationship Between Abduction and Deduction. *Journal of Logic and Computation*, 1(5):661–690, 1991.
7. W. Dowling and J. H. Gallier. Linear-time Algorithms for Testing the Satisfiability of Propositional Horn Theories. *Journal of Logic Programming*, 3:267–284, 1984.
8. T. Eiter and G. Gottlob. Propositional Circumscription and Extended Closed World Reasoning are Π_2^P-complete. *Theoretical Computer Science*, to appear.
9. T. Eiter and G. Gottlob. On the Complexity of Propositional Knowledge Base Revision, Updates, and Counterfactuals. *Artificial Intelligence*, 57:227–270, 1992.
10. T. Eiter and G. Gottlob. The Complexity of Logic-Based Abduction. Technical Report CD-TR 92/35, Christian Doppler Laboratory for Expert Systems, TU Vienna, 1992.

11. R. Fagin, J. D. Ullman, and M. Y. Vardi. On the Semantics of Updates in Databases. In *Proc. PODS-83*, 352–365, 1983.
12. G. Friedrich, G. Gottlob, and W. Nejdl. Hypothesis Classification, Abductive Diagnosis, and Therapy. In *Proc. International Workshop on Expert Systems in Engineering*, number 462 in LNAI, 69–78, September, 1990.
13. G. Gottlob. Complexity Results for Nonmonotonic Logics. *Journal of Logic and Computation*, 2(3):397–425, June 1992.
14. D. S. Johnson. A Catalog of Complexity Classes. volume A of *Handbook of Theoretical Computer Science*, chapter 2. 1990.
15. J. Josephson, B. Chandrasekaran, J. J. W. Smith, and M. Tanner. A Mechanism for Forming Composite Explanatory Hypotheses. *IEEE Transactions on Systems, Man, and Cybernetics*, SMC-17:445–454, 1987.
16. J. Kadin. $P^{NP[O(\log n)]}$ and Sparse Turing-Complete Sets for NP. *Journal of Computer and System Sciences*, 39:282–298, 1989.
17. K. Konolige. Abduction versus closure in causal theories. *Artificial Intelligence*, 53:255–272, 1992.
18. R. Kowalski. Logic Programs in Artificial Intelligence. In *Proc. IJCAI-91*, 596–601, 1991.
19. M. Krentel. The Complexity of Optimization Problems. *Journal of Computer and System Sciences*, 36:490–509, 1988.
20. M. Krentel. Generalizations of OptP to the Polynomial Hierarchy. *Theoretical Computer Science*, 1992.
21. H. Levesque. A knowledge-level account for abduction. In *Proc. IJCAI-89*, 1061–1067, 1989.
22. V. Lifschitz. Computing Circumscription. In *Proc. IJCAI-85*, 121–127, 1985.
23. B. Nebel. Belief Revision and Default Reasoning: Syntax-Based Approaches. In *Proc. KR-91*, 417–428, 1991.
24. Y. Peng and J. Reggia. *Abductive Inference Models for Diagnostic Problem Solving*. Symbolic Computation – Artificial Intelligence. Springer, 1990.
25. D. Poole. A Logical Framework for Default Reasoning. *Artificial Intelligence*, 36:27–47, 1988.
26. R. Reiter. A Theory of Diagnosis From First Principles. *Artificial Intelligence*, 32:57–95, 1987.
27. V. Rutenburg. Complexity Classification in Truth Maintenance Systems. In *Proc. STACS-91*, 373–383, 1991.
28. G. Schwarz and M. Truszczyński. Nonmonotonic reasoning is sometimes easier. manuscript, August. 1992.
29. B. Selman and H. J. Levesque. Abductive and Default Reasoning: A Computational Core. In *Proc. AAAI-90*, 343–348, July 1990.
30. L. Stockmeyer and A. Meyer. Word Problems Requiring Exponential Time. In *Proc. of the Fifth ACM STOC*, 1–9, 1973.
31. K. Wagner. More Complicated Questions about Maxima and Minima, and Some Closures of NP. *Theoretical Computer Science*, 51:53–80, 1987.
32. K. Wagner. Bounded Query Computations. Technical Report 172, Universität Augsburg, March 1988.
33. K. Wagner. Bounded query classes. *SIAM J. Comp.*, 19(5):833–846, 1990.

Treewidth of Chordal Bipartite Graphs

T. Kloks[1]* and D. Kratsch[2]**

[1] Department of Computer Science, Utrecht University
P.O.Box 80.089, 3508 TB Utrecht, The Netherlands
[2] Fakultät Mathematik, Friedrich-Schiller-Universität
Universitätshochhaus, O-6900 Jena, Germany

Abstract. Chordal bipartite graphs are exactly those bipartite graphs in which every cycle of length at least six has a chord. The treewidth of a graph G is the smallest maximum cliquesize among all chordal supergraphs of G decreased by one. We present a polynomial time algorithm for the exact computation of the treewidth of all chordal bipartite graphs.

1 Introduction

In many recent investigations of computer science the notions of treewidth and pathwidth play an increasingly important role. One reason for this is that many NP-complete problems become solvable in polynomial and usually even linear time, when restricted to the class of partial k-trees for some *constant* k [2]. Of crucial importance for these algorithms is that an embedding in a k-tree is given in advance. The treewidth of a graph is the minimum k for which the graph is the subgraph of a k-tree. Much research has been done in finding embeddings in k-trees with a reasonably small k.

There are very few classes of graphs for which the treewidth can be computed in polynomial time. This can be done for example for chordal graphs (trivially), cographs, circular arc graphs and permutation graphs [5, 12, 4]. Treewidth is NP-complete for bipartite graphs and for cobipartite graphs [1]. We present a polynomial time algorithm to compute the treewidth of chordal bipartite graphs. Since so many NP-complete problems remain NP-complete when restricted to chordal bipartite graphs, it is of great importance to be able to use the partial k-tree algorithms for these problems.

We do not claim that our algorithm is a very practical one, however we feel that it is one of the first non-trivial polynomial time algorithms for computing the treewidth of a relatively large class of graphs. Note that it narrows the gap between classes where treewidth is computable in polynomial time and classes where the corresponding decision problem is NP-complete significantly. Indeed, the gap between chordal bipartite graphs and the class of all bipartite graphs is relatively small.

---

* This author is supported by the foundation for Computer Science (S.I.O.N) of the Netherlands Organization for Scientific Research (N.W.O.), Email: ton@cs.ruu.nl

** Email: DIETER.KRATSCH@mathematik.uni-jena.dbp.de

2 Preliminaries

2.1 Preliminaries on chordal bipartite graphs

In this section we start with some definitions and easy lemmas. For more information the reader is referred to [10] or [6].

Definition 1. A graph is called *chordal bipartite* (or weakly chordal bipartite) if it is bipartite and each cycle of length at least six has a chord.

Definition 2. Let $G = (X, Y, E)$ be a bipartite graph. Then $(u, v) \in E$ is called a *bisimplicial edge* if $N(u) \cup N(v)$ induces a complete bipartite subgraph of G.

Definition 3. Let $G = (X, Y, E)$ be a bipartite graph. Let $(e_1, \ldots, e_k)$ be an ordering of the edges of G. For $i = 0, \ldots, k$ define the subgraph $G_i = (X_i, Y_i, E_i)$ as follows. $G_0 = G$ and for $i \geq 1$ G_i is the subgraph of G_{i-1} with $X_i = X_{i-1}, Y_i = Y_{i-1}$ and $E_i = E_{i-1} \setminus \{e_i\}$ (i.e. the edge e_i is removed but not the endvertices). The ordering $(e_1, \ldots, e_k)$ is a *perfect edge without vertex elimination ordering* for G if each edge e_i is bisimplicial in G_{i-1}, and G_k has no edge.

The following lemma appears for example in [6].

Lemma 4. *G is chordal bipartite if and only if there is a perfect edge without vertex elimination ordering.*

It is easy to see that we can start a perfect edge without vertex elimination ordering with *any* bisimplicial edge. In [9] it is shown that a bisimplicial edge in a chordal bipartite graph with n vertices can be found in $O(n^2)$ time. This proves the following.

Lemma 5. *We can find a perfect edge without vertex elimination scheme in time $O(n^2 m)$, where n is the number of vertices and m is the number of edges.*

A chord (x, y) in a cycle C of even length is *odd* if the distance between x and y in the cycle is odd.

Definition 6. A graph is called *strongly chordal* if it is chordal and each cycle of even length at least six has an odd chord.

Definition 7. For a bipartite graph $G = (X, Y, E)$ let $split(G) = (X, Y, \hat{E})$ with $\hat{E} = E \cup \{(x, x') \mid x, x' \in X \wedge x \neq x'\}$.

The following characterization of chordal bipartite graphs appeared in [7].

Lemma 8. *$G = (X, Y, E)$ is chordal bipartite if and only if $split(G)$ is strongly chordal.*

If x is a vertex of a graph $G = (V, E)$, we denote by $N[x]$ the *closed neighborhood* of x, i.e. $N[x] = \{y \mid (x, y) \in E\} \cup \{x\}$.

Definition 9. A vertex v is *simple* if for all $x, y \in N[v]$, $N[x] \subseteq N[y]$ or $N[y] \subseteq N[x]$.

Notice that a simple vertex is simplicial (i.e. the neighborhood is complete). We shall use the following property of strongly chordal graphs [8].

Lemma 10. *A graph G is strongly chordal if and only if every induced subgraph has a simple vertex.*

2.2 Preliminaries on treewidth

In this paper we show how to compute the *treewidth* of chordal bipartite graphs. For more general information on treewidth the reader is referred to the survey paper [3].

Definition 11. A k-tree is defined recursively as follows: A clique with $k+1$ vertices is a k-tree. Given a k-tree T_n with n vertices, a k-tree with $n+1$ vertices is constructed by making a new vertex x_{n+1} adjacent to a k-clique of T_n and nonadjacent to the $n - k$ other vertices of T_n. A *partial k-tree* is a subgraph of a k-tree. The treewidth of a graph G is the minimum k for which G is a partial k-tree.

There are other equivalent definitions of the notion treewidth [3]. Notice that k-trees are triangulated (i.e. they do not contain a chordless cycle of length ≥ 4), and have maximum clique size $k + 1$.

Definition 12. A *triangulation* of a graph G is a chordal graph H with the same vertex set as G such that G is a subgraph of H.

We make extensive use of the following (well known) result.

Lemma 13. *A graph G is a partial k-tree if and only if there is a triangulation of G with maximum cliquesize at most $k + 1$.*

3 Triangulations

In this section, let $G = (X, Y, E)$ be chordal bipartite. We denote complete bipartite graphs as $M = (A, B)$, i.e. the vertex set of this graph M is $A \cup B$ and the edge set $E = \{(a, b) \mid a \in A \wedge b \in B\}$. In this paper, by definition, a complete bipartite graph (A, B) is such that $|A| \geq 2$ and $|B| \geq 2$. If $G = (X, Y, E)$ is a bipartite graph, then we call the sets X and Y the color classes of G.

Lemma 14. *If $G = (X, Y, E)$ is chordal bipartite, then it contains at most $|E|$ maximal complete bipartite subgraphs.*

Proof. G is chordal bipartite, hence there is a perfect edge without vertex elimination ordering $(e_1, \ldots, e_k)$. Consider a maximal complete bipartite subgraph, (A, B). Let e_i be the first edge in the ordering which is an edge of (A, B). Let $e_i = (x, y)$ with $x \in A$ and $y \in B$. Since e_i is bisimplicial and (A, B) is maximal we have $A = N(y)$ and $B = N(x)$. This proves the lemma. □

Remark. It is not difficult to see that there exist chordal bipartite graphs for which the number of maximal complete bipartite subgraphs is $\Omega(n^2)$.

If (A, B) is a complete bipartite graph, and H is a triangulation of (A, B), then either $H[A]$ (i.e. the subgraph of H induced by A) or $H[B]$ is a complete subgraph of H (otherwise there would be a chordless C_4). Now let G be chordal bipartite, and let $\mathcal{M}$ be the set of maximal complete bipartite subgraphs (A, B) of G (with $|A| \geq 2$ and $|B| \geq 2$). If H is a triangulation of G, then for each $(A, B) \in \mathcal{M}$, either $H[A]$ or $H[B]$ is a complete subgraph of H. Consider the following process. For *each* $(A, B) \in \mathcal{M}$, choose one color class $C \in \{A, B\}$, and add all edges between vertices of C. We say the color class C is completed. Unfortunately, the resulting graph need not be chordal. We restrict the choices of the colorclasses to be completed.

Definition 15. Let $M_1 = (A_1, B_1)$ and $M_2 = (A_2, B_2)$ be two maximal complete bipartite subgraphs. We say that M_1 and M_2 *cross* if either $A_2 \subseteq A_1$ and $B_1 \subseteq B_2$, or $A_1 \subseteq A_2$ and $B_2 \subseteq B_1$.

Definition 16. For each $M \in \mathcal{M}$ choose one color class $C(M)$. The set $\mathcal{C} = \{C(M) \mid M \in \mathcal{M}\}$ is called *feasible*, if for each pair $(A_1, B_1), (A_2, B_2) \in \mathcal{M}$ that cross with $A_2 \subseteq A_1$ and $B_1 \subseteq B_2$, *not both* A_1 and B_2 are in $\mathcal{C}$.

We want to proof in this section that if $\mathcal{C}$ is feasible and we complete each $C \in \mathcal{C}$, then the resulting graph is triangulated.

Theorem 17. *Let $\mathcal{C}$ be a feasible set of color classes of a chordal bipartite graph G. Let H be the graph obtained by making each $C \in \mathcal{C}$ complete. Then H is chordal.*

Proof. Assume G is a *minimal* counterexample; i.e. for every induced subgraph the theorem is true. Assume H is not chordal and let S be a chordless cycle of length greater than three in H. Let $G = (X, Y, E)$. We call the vertices of X red and the vertices of Y black. An edge of S is called red (black), if *both* its endvertices are red (black). The red and black edges of S are called colored edges. Notice that there must exist at least one colored edge. Let $\mathcal{R}$ be the set of all red edges of S and $\mathcal{B}$ be the set of all black edges of S. Without loss of generality we may assume that $\mathcal{R} \neq \emptyset$.

Consider a red vertex $x \notin S$, and let $e \in \mathcal{B}$ be a black edge of S. We say that x *creates* e, if there is a maximal complete bipartite subgraph (A, B) with $e \subseteq B$, $x \in A$, and $B \in \mathcal{C}$. A red vertex r is called *redundant*, if $r \notin S$ and it does not create any black edge. A black vertex $b \notin S$ is called redundant, if it does not create a red edge.

Lemma 18. *There are no redundant vertices.*

Proof. Suppose there is a redundant red vertex x. Consider the induced subgraph $G' = G[V \setminus \{x\}]$. Clearly, also G' is chordal bipartite. We create a feasible set of color classes $\mathcal{C}'$ as follows. Consider a maximal complete bipartite subgraph $M = (A, B)$ of G'. If M is also maximal in G, we put $C(M)$ in $\mathcal{C}'$. If M is not maximal in G then $N = (A \cup \{x\}, B)$ must be a maximal complete bipartite subgraph of G. In this case we put $C(N) \setminus \{x\}$ in $\mathcal{C}'$. It is easy to see that $\mathcal{C}'$ is a feasible set of color classes for G'.

Let H' be the graph obtained from G' by completing each set of $\mathcal{C}'$. We claim that S is also a chordless cycle in H'.

Let e be a colored red edge of S. There is a maximal complete bipartite subgraph (A, B), with $e \subseteq A$ and $A \in \mathcal{C}$. If $x \notin A$, then (A, B) is a maximal complete bipartite subgraph of G'. Hence $A \in \mathcal{C}'$. Now assume $x \in A$. Then $|A| \geq 3$. Take B' such that $B \subseteq B'$ and $(A \setminus \{x\}, B')$ is a maximal complete bipartite subgraph of G' (i.e. B' is the set of common neighbors of $A \setminus \{x\}$). If (A, B') is maximal in G, then $B' = B$ and $A \setminus \{x\} \in \mathcal{C}'$. Otherwise $(A \setminus \{x\}, B')$ is maximal in G. Notice that (A, B) and $(A \setminus \{x\}, B')$ cross. Hence $A \setminus \{x\}$ is in $\mathcal{C}$ and hence also in $\mathcal{C}'$.

Now let e be a black edge, and let (A, B) be a maximal complete bipartite subgraph with $e \subseteq B$ and $B \in \mathcal{C}$. Notice that since x is redundant, $x \notin A$. Hence (A, B) is also maximal in G' and $B \in \mathcal{C}'$. This shows that S is also a cycle in G'.

Since G was a minimal counterexample, there must be a chord in G' between two vertices p and q of S. Without loss of generality assume p and q are both red (the case where they are both black is similar). There exists a maximal complete bipartite subgraph (A, B) in G' such that $p, q \in A$ and $A \in C'$. By definition either $A \cup \{x\} \in C$ or $A \in C$. Hence (p, q) is also an edge in G. This proves that there are no redundant red vertices. A similar argument shows that there are no redundant black vertices either. □

Consider the graph $G^* = split(G)$ obtained by making Y complete. Since G is chordal bipartite, we know that G^* is strongly chordal. Hence we know that G^* has a simple vertex. Let s be the simple vertex. The next lemma shows that s must be a red vertex.

Lemma 19. *A simple vertex s of G^* is red.*

Proof. Assume $s \in Y$ is simple. If s is not an element of the cycle, it must be in some maximal complete bipartite subgraph (A, B) creating some edge, otherwise s would be redundant. But then it has at least two nonadjacent neighbors, which is a contradiction. Assume s is a black vertex of the cycle S. Clearly s can not have two red neighbors, because red vertices are not adjacent in G. Hence s is incident with at least one edge of B. Consider a maximal path of S, which contains only black vertices, and which contains s. Let p and q, be the endvertices of this path. We know that $p \neq q$. Since s is simple, and p and q are neighbors of s in G^*, either $N[p] \subseteq N[q]$ or $N[q] \subseteq N[p]$. Since p and q are both incident with a red vertex in S, it follows that S contains only one red vertex. This is a contradiction, because we assumed that $\mathcal{R} \neq \emptyset$. □

Lemma 20. *A simple vertex s is an element of S.*

Proof. We know s is red. Assume s is not in S. Then we know that s creates some black edge $e = (p, q)$. Without loss of generality assume $N[p] \subseteq N[q]$. If p has a red neighbor in S, then this would also be a neighbor of q, and there would be a chord in S. Hence p has another black neighbor r in S. Consider the maximal complete bipartite subgraph (K, L) with $p, r \in L$ and $L \in C$. Then p is adjacent to every vertex of K. Hence also q is adjacent to every vertex of K. It follows that $q \in L$. But $L \in C$. Hence q and r are adjacent in H. This is a chord in S. □

We have to consider three more cases. First we show that s is incident with at least one edge of $\mathcal{R}$.

Lemma 21. *A simple vertex s is incident with at least one red edge of S.*

Proof. We know s is a red vertex of S. Assume it has two black neighbors in S, x and y. We may assume $N[x] \subseteq N[y]$. If in the cycle x has two red neighbors, then also y is adjacent to both red neighbors, which is a contradiction. Hence x is adjacent to a black vertex z in S. Consider a maximal complete bipartite subgraph (K, L) creating the edge (x, z). Then x is adjacent to every vertex of K, and hence this also holds for y. But then $y \in L$. $L \in C$ hence x and y are adjacent in H. This is a chord in S. □

Lemma 22. *A simple vertex s is incident with exactly one red edge of S.*

Proof. We know that $s \in S$ and s has at least one red neighbor in S. Asume s has *two* red neighbors x and y in S. Consider the maximal complete bipartite subgraphs (K_x, L_x) creating the edge (s, x) and (K_y, L_y) creating (s, y). Now there must exist $p \in L_x \setminus L_y$ which is not adjacent to y, otherwise $(K_x \cup \{y\}, L_x)$ is complete bipartite. Also there must exist $q \in L_y \setminus L_x$ which is not adjacent to x. Without loss of generality we may assume $N[p] \subseteq N[q]$. But then we have a contradiction since $x \in N[p] \subseteq N[q]$. $\square$

Hence we know that a simple vertex s is a red vertex of the cycle S with one red neighbor x and one black neighbor y. Let (K_x, L_x) be the maximal complete bipartite subgraph that creates (s, x). Since s is simple and y is not adjacent to x, we must have $N[y] \cap X \subseteq K_x$. Now assume that in the cycle y is adjacent to another red vertex u. Then $u \in N[y] \cap X \subseteq K_x$. But then u, x and s would form a triangle, which is a contradiction. Hence y is adjacent to a black vertex v in the cycle. Let (K_v, L_v) be the maximal complete bipartite subgraph creating (y, v). Notice that $K_v \subseteq N[y] \cap X \subseteq K_x$. It follows that $L_x \subseteq L_v$, and hence (K_x, L_x) and (K_v, L_v) cross. But L_v and K_x are completed, hence $\mathcal{C}$ is not feasible. This completes the proof of Theorem 17. $\square$

In the next section we show that there exists a feasible set of color classes of G such that the triangulated graph H is optimal, i.e. has the smallest possible maximum cliquesize.

4 Treewidth

Let $G = (X, Y, E)$ be a chordal bipartite graph. If $\mathcal{C}$ is a feasible set of color classes, we denote by $H_\mathcal{C}$ the chordal graph obtained from G, by completing each $C \in \mathcal{C}$. In this section we show the following.

Theorem 23. *Let G be a chordal bipartite graph with treewidth $\leq k$. Then there exists a feasible set of color classes $\mathcal{C}$ such that $H_\mathcal{C}$ has cliquesize $\leq k + 1$.*

Proof. Let H be any triangulation of G. We show that there is a feasible set of color classes $\mathcal{C}$ such that $H_\mathcal{C}$ is a subgraph of H. Let $\mathcal{M}$ denote again the set of all maximal complete bipartite subgraphs of G. Suppose we list the elements of $\mathcal{M}$ one by one, creating a feasible set of color classes $\mathcal{C}$ as follows. Start with $\mathcal{C} = \emptyset$. For each $M \in \mathcal{M}$ at least one of the color classes is a complete subgraph in H. Let $M = (A, B)$ and assume A is complete in H. Check the list $\mathcal{C}$ created thus far, if there is a maximal complete subgraph (C, D) which crosses with (A, B), such that $C \subseteq A$ and $D \in \mathcal{C}$. If not, then put A in $\mathcal{C}$. Otherwise put B in $\mathcal{C}$. Notice that there cannot be a maximal complete bipartite subgraph (K, L) crossing with (A, B), such that $L \subseteq B$ and $K \in \mathcal{C}$. Otherwise (K, L) and (C, D) would also cross with $C \subseteq K$ and $K, D \in \mathcal{C}$. This shows that in this way we create a feasible set of color classes. Now notice that $H_\mathcal{C}$ is a subgraph of H, hence the cliquesize of $H_\mathcal{C}$ does not exceed the cliquesize of H. $\square$

5 Cliques

Let $G = (X, Y, E)$ be a chordal bipartite graph and let C be a feasible set of color classes. In this section we analyse the structure of the maximal cliques in H_C. We first look at a clique B with vertices only in one color class.

Definition 24. Let B be a clique with all vertices in Y. We say that a set A of maximal complete bipartite subgraphs is a *cover* for B, if the following two conditions are satisfied:

1. For each $(A', B') \in A : B' \in C$.
2. for every pair $x, y \in B$ there is a maximal complete bipartite subgraph $(A', B') \in A$ such that $x, y \in B'$.

Theorem 25. *Let B be a clique of H_C with all vertices in Y. Assume $|B| \geq 2$. A minimal cover for B has only one element.*

Proof. Let $A = \{(A_1, B_1), \ldots (A_t, B_t)\}$ be a minimal cover for B. Assume $t \geq 2$. Let $A = \bigcup_i A_i$.

Lemma 26. *Every vertex of A has at least two neighbors in B.*

Proof. Assume there is a vertex $a \in A$ with only one neighbor b in B. There is a complete bipartite subgraph (A_i, B_i) containing a. We claim that B is covered by $A \setminus \{(A_i, B_i)\}$. For every other vertex $b' \in B$ the pair (b, b') must be in some (A_j, B_j) with $j \neq i$. This proves the lemma. □

Lemma 27. *Every vertex of B has at least two neighbors in A.*

Proof. Let $b \in B$. Take another vertex $b' \in B$. The pair (b, b') must be in some maximal complete bipartite subgraph (A_i, B_i). Since $|A_i| \geq 2$ the lemma follows. □

Take the subgraph H of G induced by $A \cup B$. Let $W = split(H)$ obtained by making A a complete graph. W is strongly chordal. Each vertex of A has two nonadjacent neighbors, hence A can not contain a simple vertex. Let $b \in B$ be a simple vertex. Let $a_1, \ldots, a_k$ be the neighbors of b in A, and let $N[a_1] \subseteq N[a_2] \subseteq \ldots \subseteq N[a_k]$. Notice that $k \geq 2$. Since A is a clique in W, we have that $N[a_1] \cap B \subseteq \ldots \subseteq N[a_k] \cap B$. We claim that not all a_i's can be contained in one color class A_i.

Lemma 28. $\forall_i \exists_j [a_j \notin A_i]$

Proof. Assume that $\{a_1, \ldots, a_k\} \subseteq A_i$ for some color class A_i. Take $b' \notin B_i$. There exists a maximal complete bipartite subgraph (A_j, B_j) such that $\{b, b'\} \subseteq B_j$. Clearly $A_j \subseteq \{a_1, \ldots, a_k\} \subseteq A_i$. This implies $B_i \subseteq B_j$. This is a contradiction since A is minimal. □

Now we can finish the proof of Theorem 25. Let (A_1, B_1) be a maximal complete bipartite subgraph containing a_1. Let $i > 1$. Notice $B_1 \subseteq N[a_1] \cap B \subseteq N[a_i] \cap B$. Hence $(A_1 \cup \{a_i\}, B_1)$ is a complete bipartite subgraph. This implies that $a_i \in A_1$ for all $1 \leq i \leq k$, which is a contradiction. This proves Theorem 25. □

The following theorem shows that the structure of the maximal cliques in H_C is very simple.

Theorem 29. *Let K be a maximal clique in H_C with $|K| > 2$. Let $K_x = K \cap X$ and $K_y = K \cap Y$. Assume $|K_x| \geq 2$. Then one of the following two cases holds:*

1. *$|K_y| = 1$ and there exists a maximal complete bipartite subgraph (A, B) so that $K_x = A$, $y \in B$ and $A \in C$.*
2. *$|K_y| > 1$ and there exist maximal complete bipartite subgraphs (A_1, B_1) and (A_2, B_2), with $A_1 \in C$ and $B_2 \in C$ such that $K_x \subseteq A_1$ and $K_y \subseteq B_2$.*

Proof. By Theorem 25 there exists a maximal complete bipartite subgraph (A_1, B_1) such that $K_x \subseteq A_1$ and $A_1 \in C$. Assume $K_y = \emptyset$. Then clearly, K cannot be maximal, since for any vertex $y \in B_1$, $A_1 \cup \{y\}$ is a clique. Assume $|K_y| = 1$. Let $K_y = \{y\}$. Notice that $(K_x, \{y\})$ is contained in a complete bipartite subgraph $(K_x, B_1 \cup \{y\})$ in G. Hence $(K_x, B_1 \cup \{y\})$ is contained in a maximal complete bipartite subgraph (A_2, B_2) in G. Since $B_1 \subseteq B_2$, we have $A_2 \subseteq A_1$. Since C is feasible, and $A_1 \in C$, we must have $A_2 \in C$. Hence the first case holds. Now assume $|K_y| \geq 2$. By Theorem 25 there exists a maximal complete bipartite subgraph (A_2, B_2) with $K_y \subseteq B_2$ and $B_2 \in C$. $\qquad\square$

6 The algorithm

Let $G = (X, Y, E)$ be a chordal bipartite graph. In this section we show a polynomial time algorithm which determines whether the treewidth of G is at most some given integer k, and if so triangulates G such that the maximum cliquesize does not exceed $k + 1$. In the method we use, we construct a digraph with vertex set $\mathcal{M}$. We direct an edge from $M_1 = (A_1, B_1)$ to $M_2 = (A_2, B_2)$, with $A_1, A_2 \in X$, if $A_1 \in C$ implies that also $A_2 \in C$. Next we color some of the vertices of this graph red or black. A vertex (A, B) is colored red if necessarily $A \in C$ and black if necessarily $B \in C$. In the next step we try to extend this coloring to the whole graph.

step 1 If $k \leq 3$ then use the algorithm described in [11] to decide whether the treewidth of G is at most k and if so find a suitable triangulation. If $k > 3$ perform the following steps.

step 2 First make a list $\mathcal{M}$ of all maximal complete bipartite subgraphs of G.

step 3 Make a directed graph W with vertex set $\mathcal{M}$ as follows. Let $M_1 = (A_1, B_1)$ and $M_2 = (A_2, B_2)$ be two distinct elements of $\mathcal{M}$. We direct an edge from M_1 to M_2 if one of the following cases holds:
   - Compute the maximum number of vertices of a maximal complete bipartite subgraph in the induced subgraph $G[A_1 \cup B_2]$. (M_1, M_2) is a directed edge if this size exceeds $k + 1$.
   - If M_1 and M_2 cross, with $A_2 \subseteq A_1$ then (M_1, M_2) is a directed edge.

step 4 Color some of the vertices of W as follows. If $M = (A, B)$ is a maximal complete bipartite subgraph with $|A| > k$ and $|B| > k$ then output that the treewidth of G exceeds k. Otherwise, if $|B| > k$, then we color M red and if $|A| > k$, then we color M black. In case $|A| \leq k$ and $|B| \leq k$, then we do not color M yet.

step 5 While there is some arc (M_1, M_2) with M_1 colored red and M_2 not colored red then consider the following cases:
- If M_2 is black then output that the treewidth of G exceeds k
- If M_2 is not colored, then color M_2 red.

step 6 All vertices which do not yet have a color, are colored black.

step 7 For all elements $M = (A, B)$ of $\mathcal{M}$: If the color of M is red, then complete A, and if the color of M is black then complete B.

Theorem 30. *Let G be chordal bipartite. If the treewidth of $G \leq k$ then the algorithm produces a triangulation with maximum cliquesize at most $k + 1$.*

Proof. Clearly, the theorem is true when $k \leq 3$. Assume $k > 3$. It is easy to see that each $M \in \mathcal{M}$ is colored, since the algorithm only fails to do so is some necessary condition is not satisfied. Consider the set $\mathcal{C}$ of color classes, defined as follows. If $M = (A, B)$ is red, then $A \in \mathcal{C}$, otherwise $B \in \mathcal{C}$. It is easily checked that $\mathcal{C}$ is a feasible set of color classes. It follows from Theorem 17 that the algorithm produces a triangulation H. Assume H has a maximal clique K with more than $k + 1$ vertices. By Theorem 29 there are two cases to consider. First consider the case $|K_y| = 1$, let $K_y = \{y\}$. Then $|K_x| > k$. There is a maximal complete bipartite subgraph $M = (A, B)$, with $K_x \subseteq A \in \mathcal{C}$, and $y \in B$. However, the algorithm can not color M red (step 4) hence A cannot be in $\mathcal{C}$. A similar argument shows that $|K_x| = 1$ is also not possible. Now assume $|K_x| \geq 2$ and $|K_y| \geq 2$. By Theorem 29, there exist complete maximal bipartite subgraphs, $M_1 = (A_1, B_1)$ and $M_2 = (A_2, B_2)$, such that $K_x \subseteq A_1$ and $K_y \subseteq B_2$, with $A_1 \in \mathcal{C}$ and $B_2 \in \mathcal{C}$. This means that M_1 is colored red and M_2 is colored black. But (K_x, K_y) is a complete bipartite subgraph in the induced subgraph $G[A_1 \cup B_2]$, hence there is an arc (M_1, M_2) (step 3). This is a contradiction. $\square$

In the last part of this section we discuss the running time of the algorithm and we show it is polynomial. Consider the time it takes to find all maximal complete bipartite subgraphs. Lemma 5 shows we can find a perfect edge without vertex elimination ordering in time $O(n^4)$. Each bisimplicial edge gives a complete bipartite subgraph. It follows that we can find a list with at most e complete bipartite subgraph in time $O(e^2)$. From this list we can get the maximal complete bipartite subgraphs in time $O(e^2 n)$. It follows that step 2 can be performed in $O(e^2 n)$. Now clearly, the time complexity is dominated by step 3 of the algorithm. For each pair $M_1 = (A_1, B_1)$ and $M_2 = (A_2, B_2)$ we have to find the maximum size of a complete bipartite subgraph in $G[A_1 \cup B_2]$. We can do this as follows. First we compute for each pair (A_1, B_1) and (A_2, B_2) the number of vertices in $A_1 \cap A_2$ and in $B_1 \cap B_2$. Then for each $M \in \mathcal{M}$ we can compute the number of vertices in $A_1 \cup B_2$ in time $O(n \log n)$. It follows that for each pair M_1, M_2 we can decide if there is an arc (M_1, M_2) in time $O(e)$ (checking whether they cross can be done in $O(n \log n)$). It follows that step 3 of the algorithm can be performed in $O(e^3)$. This is also the total time complexity of the algorithm which can be easily checked. This proves the following theorem.

Theorem 31. *Let G be chordal bipartite and let k be an integer. Then there is a polynomial time algorithm to decide whether the treewidth of G is at most k. If so, the algorithm returns a chordal embedding of G with cliquesize at most $k + 1$.*

7 Conclusions

In this paper we showed that computing the treewidth of a chordal bipartite graph can be done in polynomial time. There are other classes of graphs for which the treewidth can be computed in polynomial time. For example chordal graphs, cographs [5], permutation graphs [4] and circular arc graphs [12]. It would be of interest to know if there are other large classes of graphs for which the treewidth can be computed in polynomial time, for example complements of chordal graphs. Another interesting question is of course whether the time bound of this algorithm can be improved. Computing the pathwidth is usually a more complicated matter. For example, for chordal graphs, computing the pathwidth is already NP-complete. Is the pathwidth problem NP-complete for chordal bipartite graphs?

8 Acknowledgements

We like to thank H. Bodlaender, A. Brandstädt, H. Müller and D. Seese for valuable discussions.

References

1. S. Arnborg, D.G. Corneil and A. Proskurowski, Complexity of finding embeddings in a k-tree, *SIAM J. Alg. Disc. Meth.* **8**, 277 – 284, 1987.
2. S. Arnborg, J. Lagergren and D. Seese, Easy problems for tree-decomposable graphs, *J. Algorithms* **12**, 308 – 340, 1991.
3. H.L. Bodlaender, A tourist guide through treewidth, Technical report RUU-CS-92-12, Department of computer science, Utrecht University, Utrecht, The Netherlands, 1992. To appear in: *Proceedings 7th International Meeting of Young Computer Scientists*, Springer Verlag, Lecture Notes in Computer Science.
4. H. Bodlaender, T. Kloks and D. Kratsch, Treewidth and pathwidth of permutation graphs, Technical report RUU-CS-92-30, Department of computer science, Utrecht University, Utrecht, The Netherlands, 1992.
5. H. Bodlaender and R.H. Möhring, The pathwidth and treewidth of cographs, In *Proceedings 2nd Scandinavian Workshop on Algorithm Theory*, 301 – 309, Springer Verlag, Lecture Notes in Computer Science vol. 447, 1990.
6. A. Brandstädt, Special Graph Classes—A Survey, Schriftenreihe des Fachbereichs Mathematik, SM-DU-199 1991, Universität Duisburg Gesamthochschule.
7. E. Dahlhaus, Chordale Graphen im besonderen Hinblick auf parallele Algorithmen, Habilitationsschrift , Bonn, 1989.
8. M. Farber, Characterizations of strongly chordal graphs, *Discrete Mathematics* **43** 173 – 189, 1983.
9. L. Goh and D. Rotem, Recognition of perfect elimination bipartite graphs, *Information Processing Letters*, **15**, No. 4, 179 – 182, 1982.
10. M.C. Golumbic, *Algorithmic Graph Theory and Perfect Graphs*, Academic Press, New York, 1980.
11. J. Matoušek and R. Thomas, Algorithms Finding Tree-Decompositions of Graphs, *Journal of Algorithms* **12**, 1 – 22, 1991.
12. R. Sundaram, K. Sher Singh and C. Pandu Rangan, Treewidth of circular arc graphs, Manuscript 1991.

On Paths in Networks with Valves

Ulrich Huckenbeck, Universität Würzburg, Am Hubland, W-8700 Würzburg, GERMANY, Email: hu@informatik.uni-wuerzburg.de

Abstract: We consider networks $\mathcal{G}$ with the property that valves are installed in some of the nodes v. Entering v by an arc (u, v) and leaving it by another arc (v, w) is only possible if (u, v) and (v, w) are connected by a valve adjustment. A path $[x_1, \ldots, x_k]$ is *admissible* if a valve adjustment exists which connects each arc $(x_\kappa, x_{\kappa+1})$ with $(x_{\kappa+1}, x_{\kappa+2})$.

We investigate the complexity of deciding whether there exists an admissible path from a node s to another node t of $\mathcal{G}$.

1. Introduction

This paper is about digraphs $\mathcal{G}$ which represent a network of pipes with valves; we investigate the complexity of deciding the existence of a path from a node s to another node t in $\mathcal{G}$. A heuristic solution of a similar problem was presented by U.Braun in [1]. He developed a program system for the numeric control of the "SIMATIC S5". This device is produced by the Siemens AG and automatically adjusts valves in pipe sytems of breweries and refineries according to a route P planned before.

U.Braun mainly considered *directed* graphs $\mathcal{G}$. They describe the situation that pumps are installed in every tube so that the stream of liquid can only run in one direction.

A further example for the great practical relevance of our decision problem is the situation of a computer network. Here the switches connecting particular pairs of ports can be interpreted as valves. In often occurs that the interconnections can only be used in one direction; therefore they should be represented by arcs in a digraph.

At the first sight, the desired path P can be found with several well-known strategies like Depth-First-Search or Dijkstra's algorithm. But unlike the usual situation, *not* all arcs meeting at a node v can be used arbitrarily if a valve is installed in v. An example is *Figure 1* where three possible valve adjustments of v are shown; if ϑ_2 is given then v may only be entered via $\tilde{r}_2$; after this, v must be left via r'_1, r'_3 or r'_4 while r'_2 is forbidden.

So the question about the existence of P is very difficult because the possible positions of all valves in the network must be considered.

Here we present a thorough investigation about the complexity of this decision. If $\mathcal{G}$ is a digraph the problem can be solved in polynomial time as long as all valves belong to a particular class T_0; otherwise the problem is NP-complete.

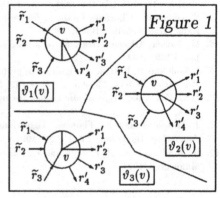

Figure 1

2. Notations and Definitions

Definition 2.1.

The set of all *natural numbers* is $\mathbf{N} := \{1,2,3,\ldots\}$; we write $\mathbf{N}_0 := \mathbf{N} \cup \{0\}$. — If X, Y are two arbitrary sets then $X \times Y$ is their *cartesian product*. Moreover, $|X|$ is the *cardinality* of X. At last, the set 2^X consists of all subsets of X. ∎

Definition 2.2.

A *digraph (without parallels and loops)* is a pair $\mathcal{G} = (\mathcal{V}, \mathcal{R})$ of sets where $\mathcal{V}$ is the set of *nodes* and $\mathcal{R} \subseteq (\mathcal{V} \times \mathcal{V}) \setminus \{(v,v) \mid v \in \mathcal{V}\}$ is the set of *arcs*.

For any arc $r = (u,v) \in \mathcal{R}$ we write $\alpha(r) := u$ and $\omega(r) := v$. Moreover, u and v are called *incident with* r.

If $\mathcal{G} = (\mathcal{V}, \mathcal{R})$ is directed and $v \in \mathcal{V}$ then we define the sets $\mathcal{R}^-(v)$, $\mathcal{R}^+(v) \subseteq \mathcal{R}$ as $\mathcal{R}^-(v) := \{(x,y) \in \mathcal{R} \mid y = v\}$ and $\mathcal{R}^+(v) := \{(x,y) \in \mathcal{R} \mid x = v\}$. The quantities $g^-(v) := |\mathcal{R}^-(v)|$ and $g^+(v) := |\mathcal{R}^+(v)|$ are the *in-degree* and the *out-degree* of v, resp.

Moreover, $S^-(\mathcal{V}) := \{v \in \mathcal{V} \mid g^-(v) = 0\}$ is the set of all *sources*, and $S^+(\mathcal{V}) := \{v \in \mathcal{V} \mid g^+(v) = 0\}$ is the set of all *sinks*. ∎

Remark 2.3. Throughout our paper we only consider *finite* graphs. ∎

Definition 2.4. *(Paths in Graphs)*

Given a digraph $\mathcal{G}$.

A *path* in $\mathcal{G}$ is a sequence $P = [x_0, \ldots, x_l]$ with $(x_\lambda, x_{\lambda+1}) \in \mathcal{R}$ for all $\lambda = 0, \ldots, l-1$. We write $\alpha(P) := x_0$ and $\omega(P) := x_l$.

If $x_0 = x_l$ then P is called a *cycle*. We say that P is *elementary* iff all nodes $x_0, \ldots, x_{l-1}$ are pairwise distinct and $x_l \notin \{x_1, \ldots, x_{l-1}\}$; in particular, elementary cycles with $x_0 = x_l$ are possible.

If $P = [v_0, \ldots, v_l]$ is given then any path $Q = [v_0, \ldots, v_\lambda]$ with $\lambda \leq l$ is called a *prefix* of P ("$Q \leq P$"). If $Q = [v_{\lambda'}, v_{\lambda'+1}, \ldots, v_{\lambda''}]$ with $0 \leq \lambda' \leq \lambda'' \leq \lambda$ then Q is a *subpath* of P; this is written as $Q \subseteq P$. In particular, P is a prefix and a subpath of itself.

Given two paths Q and Q' with $\alpha(Q') = \omega(Q)$. Then the *concatenation* $P := Q \oplus Q'$ is the path that first uses Q and then traverses Q'. The operation '$\oplus$' is also defined for arcs; e.g., the path $P = Q \oplus r \oplus r' \oplus Q'$ uses the path Q, the arcs r, r' and the path Q' in this order.

The set of all paths in $\mathcal{G}$ is written as $\mathcal{P}(\mathcal{G})$. Moreover, if $v, w \in \mathcal{V}$ then $\mathcal{P}(v)$ is the set of all paths starting from v, and $\mathcal{P}(v, w)$ contains all paths from v to w; every element of $\mathcal{P}(v, w)$ is called a *v-w-path*. ∎

3. The Complexity of Valve Problems

We consider the following situation: A valve is installed in some nodes v of a digraph $\mathcal{G}$; each valve adjustment connects exactly one incoming arc $r^- \in \mathcal{R}^-(v)$ with some outgoing arcs $r^+ \in \mathcal{R}^+(v)$. This corresponds to the requirement that a stream of liquid may enter a valve only by one incoming pipe.

Definition 3.1. A *(directed) valve graph* is a triple $(\mathcal{G}, \widehat{\mathcal{V}}, \gamma)$ with the following properties:

$\mathcal{G} = (\mathcal{V}, \mathcal{R})$ is a directed graph. The set $\widehat{\mathcal{V}} \subseteq \mathcal{V} \setminus (S^-(\mathcal{G}) \cup S^+(\mathcal{G}))$ contains all *valve nodes* of $\mathcal{G}$. The third component is the *valve function* γ; for every arc (u,v) with $v \in \widehat{\mathcal{V}}$, the set $\gamma(u,v)$ consists of all arcs (v,w) which can be used after (u,v). E.g., $\gamma(\widetilde{r}_1) = \{r'_2, r'_4\}$ in *Fig. 1*.

More formally, $\gamma : \bigcup_{v \in \widehat{V}} \mathcal{R}^-(v) \longrightarrow 2^{\mathcal{R}}$ with the following properties:

($) $\gamma(u,v) \subseteq \mathcal{R}^+(v)$ for all $v \in \widehat{V}$ and $(u,v) \in \mathcal{R}$.

($$) For every node $v \in \widehat{V}$ and every arc $(v,w) \in \mathcal{R}$ there exists an arc $(u,v) \in \mathcal{R}$ such that $(v,w) \in \gamma(u,v)$.

The last condition means that every outgoing arc (v,w) can be reached from at least one incoming arc (u,v).

Given a valve graph $(\mathcal{G}, \widehat{V}, \gamma)$. A *valve adjustment* is a function $\vartheta : \widehat{V} \to \mathcal{R}$ such that $\vartheta(v) \in \mathcal{R}^-(v)$ for all $v \in \widehat{V}$. This means that the arc $\vartheta(v)$ is connected with all arcs $r^+ \in \gamma(\vartheta(v))$; moreover, each connection between any further incoming arc $r^- \neq \vartheta(v)$ and any outgoing arc $r \in \mathcal{R}^+(v) \backslash \gamma(\vartheta(v))$ is interrupted.

Given a valve adjustment ϑ and a path $P \in \mathcal{P}(\mathcal{G})$. Then P is called ϑ-*admissible* or ϑ-*legal* iff P can be realized by ϑ; this means that every valve node v visited by P is entered via $\vartheta(v)$ and left by an arc $r^+ \in \gamma(\vartheta(v))$.

A path P is called *admissible* or *legal* iff there exists a valve adjustment ϑ such that P is ϑ-admissible. ∎

The next definition is to classify valve nodes which have an equal structure.

Definition 3.2.

a) A *valve type* or *normalized valve node* is a triple $\langle k^-, k^+, f \rangle$ where $k^-, k^+ \in \mathbf{N}$. The function f says which of the outgoing arcs $1, \ldots, k^+$ are connected with a given incoming arc $\kappa \in \{1, \ldots, k^-\}$. More precisely, f is defined as $f : \{1, \ldots, k^-\} \to 2^{\{1, \ldots, k^+\}} \backslash \emptyset$

such that

(++) $\quad \bigcup_{\kappa^- = 1}^{k^-} f(\kappa^-) = \{1, \ldots, k^+\}$.

This condition is analogous to ($$) in *Definition 3.1* and means that each outgoing arc κ^+ can be reached by an incoming arc κ^-.

An example can be seen in *Figure 2* where $\tau = \langle 2, 2, f \rangle$ with $f(1) = \{1\}$ and $f(2) = \{2\}$.

The set of all valve types $\tau = \langle k^-, k^+, f \rangle$ is defined as **T**.

b) A normalized valve $\tau = \langle k^-, k^+, f \rangle$ is *complete* if $f(\kappa^-) = \{1, \ldots, k^+\}$ for all $\kappa^- = 1, \ldots, k^-$. This means that each outgoing arc can be reached from any given incoming one. The set of these valve types is $\mathbf{T_0}$. All further valve types are called *incomplete* and form the set $\mathbf{T_1} := \mathbf{T} \backslash \mathbf{T_0}$.

c) Given a valve graph $(\mathcal{G}, \widehat{V}, \gamma)$ and $v \in \widehat{V}$. Then we say that v is of type $\tau = \langle g^-(v), g^+(v), f \rangle$ if there exist bijections $\eta : \mathcal{R}^-(v) \to \{1, \ldots, g^-(v)\}$ and $\chi : \mathcal{R}^+(v) \to \{1, \ldots, g^+(v)\}$ with the following property: The fact that some arc $r^- \in \mathcal{R}^-(v)$ is connected with $r^+ \in \mathcal{R}^+(v)$ is equivalent to a connection from $\eta(r^-)$ to $\chi(r^+)$ in the normalized valve nodes. More formally,

(*) $\quad \left(\forall \; r^- \in \mathcal{R}^-(v), \, r^+ \in \mathcal{R}^+(v) \right.$
$r^+ \in \gamma(r^-) \iff \chi(r^+) \in f(\eta(r^-$

$\left(\begin{array}{l} \text{Another formulation of (*) is :} \\ \gamma(r^-) = \{\chi^{-1}(\kappa^+) \,|\, \kappa^+ \in f(\eta(r^-)) \\ \text{for all } r^- \in \mathcal{R}^-(v). \end{array} \right.$

For example, recall *Figure 1* and let

$\eta(\tilde{r}_i) := i$ $(i = 1, 2, 3)$ and $\chi(r'_j) :=$ j $(j = 1, 2, 3, 4)$. Then v is of type $\langle 3, 4, f \rangle$ where $f(1) = \{2, 4\}$, $f(2) = \{1, 3, 4\}$ and $f(3) = \{1, 2\}$.

The fact that v is of type τ is abbreviated as $v \leadsto \tau$. Note that v can be of different types $\langle g^-(v), g^+(v), f_1 \rangle \neq \langle g^-(v), g^+(v), f_2 \rangle$ because the enumerations η and χ can be changed.

d) Let $T \subseteq \mathbf{T}$. Then $(\mathcal{G}, \widehat{\mathcal{V}}, \gamma)$ is called a T-graph iff for every $v \in \mathcal{V}$ there exists a $\tau \in T$ such that v is of type T. In this case we write $(\mathcal{G}, \widehat{\mathcal{V}}, \gamma) \leadsto T$ or $\mathcal{G} \leadsto T$. ∎

We now formulate the <u>V</u>alve <u>P</u>roblem for digraphs $(\mathbf{VP}_d(T))$ where $T \subseteq \mathbf{T}$ is fixed set of valve types:

Given a valve graph $(\mathcal{G}, \widehat{\mathcal{V}}, \gamma) \leadsto T$ and two nodes $s \in S^-(\mathcal{V})$, $t \in S^+(\mathcal{V})$. Does there exist an admissible s-t-path P?

Here we investigate the complexity of this problem for all sets $T \supseteq \mathbf{T}_0$. In the case of $T = \mathbf{T}_0$, a polynomial solution can be found, but the problem is NP-complete if $T \supsetneq \mathbf{T}_0$.

Let us start with the case $T = \mathbf{T}_0$.

Theorem 3.3. If $(\mathcal{G}, \widehat{\mathcal{V}}, \gamma)$ is a $\mathbf{T}_0$-graph then the existence of an admissible path can be decided in polynomial time.

Proof: The assumption $\mathcal{G} \leadsto \mathbf{T}_0$ implies that $\gamma(r^-) = \mathcal{R}^+(v)$ for all valve nodes v and all incoming arcs r^-. This yields the following solution of the problem:

Ignore that some vertices of $\mathcal{G}$ are valve nodes and try to construct an elementary s-t-path P (e.g. by Depth-First-Search).

IF such a path P does not exist then

there is not any <u>admissible</u> path, too.

ELSE the elementary path P is even admissible.

To see the admissibility of P we consider a valve node v which is entered by P via $r^- \in \mathcal{R}^-(v)$ and left via $r^+ \in \mathcal{R}^+(v)$. Then we define $\vartheta(v) := r^-$. As mentioned above, the arc r^+ is indeed an element of $\gamma(\vartheta(v)) = \mathcal{R}^+(v)$. Note that it cannot happen that P visits v again via another arc $r_2^- \neq r^-$; the reason is that P is elementary. ∎

We next consider a further special case. For this we define the normalized valve node $\tau^* := \langle 2, 2, f^* \rangle$ with $f^*(i) := \{i\}$ $(i = 1, 2)$ (see *Figure 2*).

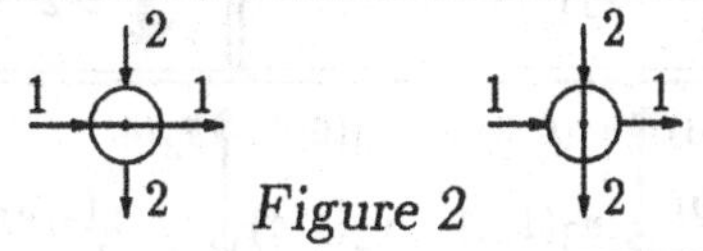

Figure 2

Then the following complexity theoretical result is true:

Theorem 3.4. Let $T^* := \mathbf{T}_0 \cup \{\tau^*\}$. Then $\mathbf{VP}_d(T^*)$ is NP-complete.

Proof: It is easy to see that the problem can be solved by a nondeterministic Turing Machine M working in polynomial time. If a T^*-graph $(\mathcal{G}, \widehat{\mathcal{V}}, \gamma)$ is given, the automaton M guesses a path $P \in \mathcal{P}(s)$ and a valve adjustment ϑ. Then M tests whether P ends with t and whether P is not in conflict with ϑ.

To show that $\mathbf{VP}_d(T^*)$ is NP-hard we reduce 3SAT to this problem; our idea is similar to that of [2], but we have to construct a more complicated graph.

Given the Boolean formula $C = C_1 \cdot \ldots \cdot C_k$ where $C_i = (u_{i1} + u_{i2} + u_{i3})$, $i = 1, \ldots, k$ and $u_{11}, u_{12}, u_{13}, \ldots, u_{k1}, u_{k2}, u_{k3} \in$

$\{x_1, \ldots, x_n, \overline{x}_1, \ldots, \overline{x}_n\}$. Then the T^*-graph $(\mathcal{G}, \widehat{\mathcal{V}}, \gamma)$ is constructed as follows:

For every $\nu = 1, \ldots, n$ we generate a T^*-graph $(\mathcal{G}_\nu, \widehat{\mathcal{V}}_\nu, \gamma_\nu)$. It is structured like a grid representing each occurence of x_ν (of $\overline{x}_\nu$) in some clause C_κ by a horizontal (vertical, resp.) line (see Fig. 3(a)).

Figure 3 (a)

$C' := (x_1 + x_2 + \overline{x}_4)(x_2 + x_3 + x_4) \cdot (\overline{x}_2 + \overline{x}_3 + \overline{x}_4)(\overline{x}_1 + \overline{x}_2 + \overline{x}_3)$

The precise definition of $\mathcal{G}_\nu$, $\mathcal{V}_\nu$ and γ_ν is the following: Let

$X_\nu := \{\kappa \mid x_\nu \text{ occurs in } C_\kappa\}$ and
$\overline{X}_\nu := \{\overline{\kappa} \mid \overline{x}_\nu \text{ occurs in } C_{\overline{\kappa}}\}$.

We assume that

$X_\nu = \{\kappa_\nu(1), \ldots, \kappa_\nu(q_\nu)\}$ and
$\overline{X}_\nu = \{\overline{\kappa}_\nu(1), \ldots, \overline{\kappa}_\nu(\overline{q}_\nu)\}$ where

$\kappa_\nu(0) := 0 < \kappa_\nu(1) < \ldots < \kappa_\nu(q_\nu) < k + 1 =: \kappa_\nu(q_\nu + 1)$ and $\overline{\kappa}_\nu(0) := 0 < \overline{\kappa}_\nu(1) < \ldots < \overline{\kappa}_\nu(\overline{q}_\nu) < k + 1 =: \overline{\kappa}_\nu(\overline{q}_\nu + 1)$.

Then the set of nodes is defined as $\mathcal{V}_\nu = \mathcal{S}_\nu \cup \overline{\mathcal{S}}_\nu \cup \widehat{\mathcal{V}}_\nu \cup \mathcal{T}_\nu \cup \overline{\mathcal{T}}_\nu$ with

$\mathcal{S}_\nu := \left\{ s_\nu(\kappa_\nu(i)) \mid i = 1, \ldots, q_\nu \right\}$,

$\overline{\mathcal{S}}_\nu := \left\{ \overline{s}_\nu(\overline{\kappa}_\nu(j)) \mid j = 1, \ldots, \overline{q}_\nu \right\}$,

$\widehat{\mathcal{V}}_\nu :=$
$\left\{ v_\nu(\kappa_\nu(i), \overline{\kappa}_\nu(j)) \mid \begin{matrix} 1 \le i \le q_\nu, \\ 1 \le j \le \overline{q}_\nu \end{matrix} \right\}$,

$\mathcal{T}_\nu := \left\{ t_\nu(\kappa_\nu(i)) \mid i = 1, \ldots, q_\nu \right\}$,

$\overline{\mathcal{T}}_\nu := \left\{ \overline{t}_\nu(\overline{\kappa}_\nu(j)) \mid j = 1, \ldots, \overline{q}_\nu \right\}$.

Moreover, we introduce the following notations:

For $i = 1, \ldots, q_\nu$:

$v_\nu(\kappa_\nu(i), \overline{\kappa}_\nu(0)) = v_\nu(\kappa_\nu(i), 0) := s_\nu(\kappa_\nu(i))$,

$v_\nu(\kappa_\nu(i), \overline{\kappa}_\nu(\overline{q}_\nu + 1)) = v_\nu(\kappa_\nu(i), k + 1) := t_\nu(\kappa_\nu(i))$;

for $j = 1, \ldots, \overline{q}_\nu$:

$v_\nu(\kappa_\nu(0), \overline{\kappa}_\nu(j)) = v_\nu(0, \overline{\kappa}_\nu(j)) := \overline{s}_\nu(\kappa_\nu(j))$,

$v_\nu(\kappa_\nu(q_\nu + 1), \overline{\kappa}_\nu(j)) = v_\nu(k + 1, \overline{\kappa}_\nu(j)) := \overline{t}_\nu(\kappa_\nu(j))$.

Then the set of arcs of $\mathcal{G}_\nu$ is $\mathcal{R}_\nu := \mathcal{R}_\nu^{(1)} \cup \mathcal{R}_\nu^{(2)}$ where $\mathcal{R}_\nu^{(1)}$ contains all horizontal arcs and $\mathcal{R}_\nu^{(2)}$ consists of all vertical ones. More precisely, $\mathcal{R}_\nu^{(1)}$ consists of all arcs $\left(v_\nu(\kappa_\nu(i), \overline{\kappa}_\nu(j)), v_\nu(\kappa_\nu(i), \overline{\kappa}_\nu(j + 1)) \right)$ with $i = 1, 2, \ldots, q_\nu$ and $j =$

$0, 1, \ldots, \overline{q}_\nu$; the set $\mathcal{R}_\nu^{(2)}$ contains all arcs $\left(v_\nu(\kappa_\nu(i), \overline{\kappa}_\nu(j)), v_\nu(\kappa_\nu(i+1), \overline{\kappa}_\nu(j)) \right)$ for which $i = 0, 1, \ldots, q_\nu$ and $j = 1, 2, \ldots, \overline{q}_\nu$.

For every $v \in \widehat{\mathcal{V}}_\nu$ and all $\mu = 1, 2$, we define $r^-(v, \mu)$ and $r^+(v, \mu)$ as the only element of $\mathcal{R}^-(v) \cup \mathcal{R}_\nu^{(\mu)}$ (of $\mathcal{R}^+(v) \cup \mathcal{R}_\nu^{(\mu)}$, resp.); e.g., $r^+(v, 2)$ is the vertical arc leaving v.

The valve function γ_ν is defined such that either the horizontal or the vertical direction is opened, i.e.

$$\left(\forall \, v \in \widehat{\mathcal{V}}_\nu, \ \mu = 1, 2 \right)$$
$$\gamma_\nu(r^-(v, \mu)) := \{ r^+(v, \mu) \}.$$

In addition, for $i = 1, \ldots, q_\nu$ and $j = 1, \ldots, \overline{q}_\nu$ we define the horizontal path $P_\nu(\kappa_\nu(i))$ and the vertical path $\overline{P}_\nu(\overline{\kappa}_\nu(j))$ as follows:

The path $P_\nu(\kappa_\nu(i))$ visits the nodes $v_\nu(\kappa_\nu(i), \overline{\kappa}_\nu(\overline{\varrho}))$, $\overline{\varrho} = 0, \ldots, \overline{q}_\nu + 1$; in particular, $P_\nu(\kappa_\nu(i))$ starts at $v_\nu(\kappa_\nu(i), \overline{\kappa}_\nu(0)) = s_\nu(\kappa_\nu(i))$ and ends with $v_\nu(\kappa_\nu(i), \overline{\kappa}_\nu(\overline{q}_\nu + 1)) = t_\nu(\kappa_\nu(i))$.

The path $\overline{P}_\nu(\overline{\kappa}_\nu(j))$ visits the nodes $v_\nu(\kappa_\nu(\varrho), \overline{\kappa}_\nu(j))$, $\varrho = 0, \ldots, q_\nu + 1$; this implies that $\overline{P}_\nu(\overline{\kappa}_\nu(j))$ is a path from $\overline{s}_\nu(\overline{\kappa}_\nu(j))$ to $\overline{t}_\nu(\overline{\kappa}_\nu(j))$.

We next complete the con-struction of $\left(\mathcal{G}, \widehat{\mathcal{V}}, \gamma \right)$. (This is illustrated in *Figure 3 (b)*.)

We introduce new vertices $m(1) =: s, m(2), \ldots, m(k), m(k+1) := t$. Then the vertices of $\mathcal{G}$ are given by

$$\mathcal{V} := \bigcup_{\kappa=1}^{k+1} \{ m(\kappa) \} \cup \bigcup_{\nu=1}^{n} \mathcal{V}_\nu.$$

The set $\mathcal{R}$ of arcs is defined as

$$\mathcal{R} :=$$
$$\left\{ \left(m(\kappa), s_\nu(\kappa) \right) \, \middle| \, \begin{array}{c} 1 \leq \kappa \leq k, \\ 1 \leq \nu \leq n, \\ \kappa \in X_\nu \end{array} \right\} \cup$$
$$\left\{ \left(m(\overline{\kappa}), \overline{s}_\nu(\overline{\kappa}) \right) \, \middle| \, \begin{array}{c} 1 \leq \overline{\kappa} \leq k, \\ 1 \leq \nu \leq n, \\ \overline{\kappa} \in \overline{X}_\nu \end{array} \right\} \cup$$
$$\mathcal{R}_1 \cup \mathcal{R}_2 \cup \ldots \cup \mathcal{R}_n \cup$$
$$\left\{ \left(t_\nu(\kappa), m(\kappa+1) \right) \, \middle| \, \begin{array}{c} 1 \leq \kappa \leq k, \\ 1 \leq \nu \leq n, \\ \kappa \in X_\nu \end{array} \right\} \cup$$
$$\left\{ \left(\overline{t}_\nu(\overline{\kappa}), m(\overline{\kappa}+1) \right) \, \middle| \, \begin{array}{c} 1 \leq \overline{\kappa} \leq k, \\ 1 \leq \nu \leq n, \\ \overline{\kappa} \in \overline{X}_\nu \end{array} \right\}.$$

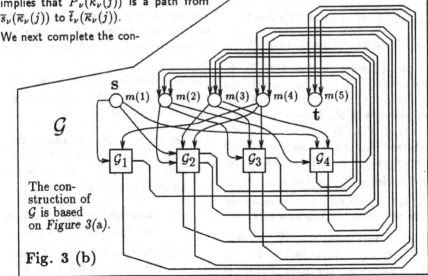

The construction of $\mathcal{G}$ is based on *Figure 3(a)*.

Fig. 3 (b)

Moreover, let $\widehat{\mathcal{V}} := \bigcup_{\nu=1}^{n} \widehat{\mathcal{V}}_{\nu}$.

At last, γ is defined such that $\gamma(r) = \gamma_{\nu}(r)$ if r occurs in $\mathcal{G}_{\nu}$ ($\nu = 1, \ldots, n$)

To show that this valve graph $(\mathcal{G}, \widehat{\mathcal{V}}, \gamma)$ yields an appropriate reduction of the given instance of 3SAT we prove the following fact:

(1) C can be satisfied $\Longleftrightarrow$
There is an admissible s-t-path P in $(\mathcal{G}, \widehat{\mathcal{V}})$.

Proof of "$\Longrightarrow$": Then for every ν a Boolean value $b(x_{\nu}) \in \{0,1\}$ can be found such that C becomes true. We define the valve adjustment $\vartheta : \widehat{\mathcal{V}} \to \mathcal{R}$ the horizontal (vertical, resp.) direction is opened within $\mathcal{G}_{\nu}$ if $b(x_{\nu}) = 1$ ($b(x_{\nu}) = 0$, resp.). More precisely,

$(\forall \nu = 1, \ldots, n)$ $(\forall v \in \widehat{\mathcal{V}}_{\nu})$

$$\vartheta(v) := \begin{cases} r^{-}(v,1) & \text{if } b(x_{\nu}) = 1, \\ r^{-}(v,2) & \text{if } b(x_{\nu}) = 0. \end{cases}$$

We next show that for all $\lambda = 1, \ldots, k$ there exists an admissible path Q_{λ} from $m(\lambda)$ to $m(\lambda+1)$. For this we note that for every λ there exists a ν such that one of the following assertions is true:

(i) x_{ν} occurs in C_{λ} and $b(x_{\nu}) = 1$,

(ii) $\overline{x}_{\nu}$ occurs in C_{λ} and $b(x_{\nu}) = 0$.

In case (i) we note that $\lambda \in X_{\nu}$ by the definition of X_{ν}. Consequently, the arcs $(m(\lambda), s_{\nu}(\lambda))$ and $(t_{\nu}(\lambda), m(\lambda+1))$ are elements of $\mathcal{R}$. Moreover, the path $P_{\nu}(\lambda) \in \mathcal{P}(s_{\nu}(\lambda), t_{\nu}(\lambda))$ exists in the subgraph $\mathcal{G}_{\nu}$, and it is even admissible since $\vartheta(v) = r^{+}(v,1)$ for all valve nodes in $\mathcal{G}_{\nu}$. Hence $Q_{\lambda} := \big(m(\lambda), s_{\nu}(\lambda)\big) \oplus P_{\nu}(\lambda) \oplus \big(t_{\nu}(\lambda), m(\lambda+1)\big)$ is an admissible path from $m(\lambda)$ to $m(\lambda+1)$.

If (ii) is true then $\lambda \in \overline{X}_{\nu}$ so that $(m(\lambda), \overline{s}_{\nu}(\lambda))$, $(\overline{t}_{\nu}(\lambda), m(\lambda+1)) \in \mathcal{R}$. Moreover, the path $\overline{P}_{\nu}(\lambda) \in$

$\mathcal{P}(\overline{s}_{\nu}(\lambda), \overline{t}_{\nu}(\lambda))$ exists in the subgraph $\mathcal{G}_{\nu}$, and it is even admissible because of $\vartheta(v) = r^{+}(v,2)$ for all valve nodes in $\mathcal{G}_{\nu}$. Hence $Q_{\lambda} := \big(m(\lambda), \overline{s}_{\nu}(\lambda)\big) \oplus \overline{P}_{\nu}(\lambda) \oplus \big(\overline{t}_{\nu}(\lambda), m(\lambda+1)\big)$ is an admissible path from $m(\lambda)$ to $m(\lambda+1)$.

So the valve adjustment ϑ opens the path $P := Q_1 \oplus \ldots \oplus Q_k$, which connects $m(1) = s$ with $m(k+1) = t$.

Proof of "$\Longleftarrow$": Given a valve adjustment ϑ and a ϑ-admissible s-t-path P. To show that this yields a verification of the formula C we consider the behaviour of P within the graphs $\mathcal{G}_{\nu}$.

(2) Let $\nu \in \{1, \ldots, n\}$ and let P' be a subpath of P starting from a node $x \in S_{\nu} \cup \overline{S}_{\nu}$ and ending with a vertex $y \in T_{\nu} \cup \overline{T}_{\nu}$. Then there exists

(i) either a $\kappa \in X_{\nu}$ such that $x = s_{\nu}(\kappa)$, $P' = P_{\nu}(\kappa)$ and $y = t_{\nu}(\kappa)$.

(ii) or a $\overline{\kappa} \in \overline{X}_{\nu}$ such that $x = \overline{s}_{\nu}(\overline{\kappa})$, $P' = \overline{P}_{\nu}(\overline{\kappa})$ and $y = \overline{t}_{\nu}(\overline{\kappa})$.

The reason is that also $P' \subseteq P$ must be admissible; therefore it must use exclusively horizontal or exclusively vertical arcs.

The next assertion says that two subpaths $P_1', P_2' \subseteq P$ within the same graph $\mathcal{G}_{\nu}$ must be parallel:

(3) Let $P_1', P_2' \subseteq P$. We assume that each of them starts in $S_{\nu} \cup \overline{S}_{\nu}$ and ends in $T_{\nu} \cup \overline{T}_{\nu}$. Then one of the following assertions is true:

(i) There exist $\kappa_1, \kappa_2 \in X_{\nu}$ such that $P_i' = P_{\nu}(\kappa_i)$, $i = 1, 2$.

(ii) There exist $\overline{\kappa}_1, \overline{\kappa}_2 \in \overline{X}_{\nu}$ such that $P_i' = \overline{P}_{\nu}(\overline{\kappa}_i)$, $i = 1, 2$.

To see this we consider the remaining cases following from (2):

$$\Big(P_1' = P_\nu(\kappa_1) \text{ and } P_2' = \overline{P}_\nu(\overline{\kappa}_2) \Big) \text{ or}$$

$$\Big(P_1' = \overline{P}_\nu(\overline{\kappa}_1) \text{ and } P_2' = P_\nu(\kappa_2) \Big).$$

But then P_1' and P_2' would cross each other at $v_\nu(\kappa_1, \overline{\kappa}_2)$ or at $v_\nu(\overline{\kappa}_1, \kappa_2)$, resp., and these crossings are forbidden because $v_\nu(\kappa_1, \overline{\kappa}_2)$ and $v_\nu(\overline{\kappa}_1, \kappa_2)$ are valve nodes of type τ^*.

We next consider the structure of P itself and obtain:

(4) P visits each vertex $m(\lambda)$, $\lambda = 1, \ldots, k+1$.

The proof is a simple induction on λ: First, the assertion is true for $\lambda = 1$ because P starts at $s = m(1)$.

We now assume that P visits $m(\lambda)$, $\lambda < k$. The only arcs emanating from $m(\lambda)$ are of the form $\Big(m(\lambda), s_\nu(\lambda) \Big)$ or $\Big(m(\lambda), \overline{s}_\nu(\lambda) \Big)$ where $\lambda \in X_\nu$ ($\lambda \in \overline{X}_\nu$, resp.). According to (2), the only admissible continuations of this arcs are $Q_\nu(\lambda) := \Big(m(\lambda), s_\nu(\lambda) \Big) \oplus P_\nu(\lambda) \oplus \Big(t_\nu(\lambda), m(\lambda+1) \Big)$ or $\overline{Q}_\nu(\lambda) := \Big(m(\lambda), \overline{s}_\nu(\lambda) \Big) \oplus \overline{P}_\nu(\lambda) \oplus \Big(\overline{t}_\nu(\lambda), m(\lambda+1) \Big)$ so that in any case $m(\lambda+1)$ is visited.

In addition to (4), the following is true for all $\lambda = 1, \ldots k$ and for all $\nu = 1, \ldots, n$:

(5) If $Q_\nu(\lambda)$ is a subpath of P then the clause C_λ can be made true by putting $b(x_\nu) := 1$.

If $\overline{Q}_\nu(\lambda)$ is a subpath of P then the clause C_λ becomes true by putting $b(x_\nu) := 0$.

This fact follows from the definition of the set $\mathcal{R}$; note that

$\Big(m(\lambda), s_\nu(\lambda) \Big) \in \mathcal{R}$ in the first case and $\Big(m(\lambda), \overline{s}_\nu(\lambda) \Big) \in \mathcal{R}$ in the second case. This implies that $\lambda \in X_\nu$ ($\lambda \in \overline{X}_\nu$, resp.). Hence x_ν ($\overline{x}_\nu$, resp.) occurs in the clause C_λ so that it can indeed made true by the above definition of $b(x_\nu)$.

We now can complete the proof that C is satisfiable. For this we define the following Boolean values (for all $\nu = 1, \ldots, n$):

$$b(x_\nu) := \begin{cases} 1 & \text{if } (\exists \lambda \in \{1, \ldots, k\}) \\ & P_\nu(\lambda) \subseteq P, \\ 0 & \text{if } (\exists \lambda \in \{1, \ldots, k\}) \\ & \overline{P}_\nu(\lambda) \subseteq P, \\ 1 & \text{else.} \end{cases}$$

Then b is well-defined; the only critical case arises if there are λ and λ' such that $b(x_\nu) = 1$ because of $P_\nu(\lambda) \subseteq P$ and $b(x_\nu) = 0$ because of $\overline{P}_\nu(\lambda') \subseteq P$; but this situation is in conflict with (3).

It follows from (4) that for every clause C_λ there exists a subpath $P_\nu(\lambda)$ or $\overline{P}_\nu(\lambda)$, and fact (5) says that the definition of $b(x_\nu)$ makes C_λ true. Hence *every* clause C_λ becomes true by the Boolean function b defined above, and C is indeed satisfiable. ∎

After considering type-τ^*-valves we next investigate a further special case: Let $\tau^{**} := \langle 2, 2, f^{**} \rangle$ with $f^{**}(1) := \{1\}$ and $f^{**}(2) := \{1, 2\}$ (see *Figure 4*).

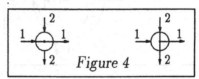

Figure 4

Then the following is true:

Theorem 3.5. Let $T^{**} := T_0 \cup \{\tau^{**}\}$. Then the problem $\mathbf{VP}_d(T^{**})$ is NP-complete.

Proof: We show that the NP-complete problem $\mathbf{VP}_d(T^*)$ can be reduced to $\mathbf{VP}_d(T^{**})$.

For this we consider the T^{**}-graph $(\mathcal{G}_0, \widehat{V}_0, \gamma_0)$ in *Figure 5*; all incoming and outgoing arcs of valve nodes are labeled with numbers $\kappa^- \in \{1, \ldots, k^-\} = \{1, 2\}$ and or $\kappa^+ \in \{1, \ldots, k^+\} = \{1, 2\}$. The four possible valve adjustments are $\vartheta_1, \ldots, \vartheta_4$.

Obviously, ϑ_i allows a path from r_i^- to r_i^+ $(i = 1, 2)$ while all other connections are closed. ϑ_3 and ϑ_4 interrupt all paths from any r_i^- to any r_j^+. This means that $\mathcal{G}_0$ behaves like a valve of type τ^*.
So the following reduction is possible: Given a T^*-graph $(\mathcal{G}, \widehat{V}, \gamma)$. Then replace every $v \in \widehat{V}$ with $v \leadsto \tau^*$ by a copy of $\mathcal{G}_0$. ∎

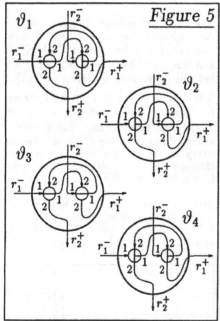

Figure 5

The next case is more general: Let $\tau = \langle k^-, k^+, f \rangle \in T \backslash T_0$. Then the following result is true:

Theorem 3.6. If $T = T_0 \cup \{\tau\}$ then $\mathbf{VP}_d(T)$ is NP-complete .

Proof: Recall the terminology of *Theorem 3.4 and 3.5*. We show that every

instance of $\mathbf{VP}_d(T^*)$ or every instance of $\mathbf{VP}_d(T^{**})$ can be reduced to a search of an admissible s-t-path in a T-graph. For this we consider τ:

As $\tau \notin T_0$ there exists an i_1 such that $\emptyset \subsetneq f(i_1) \subsetneq \{1, \ldots, k^+\}$; hence there exist j_1, j_2 such that $j_1 \in f(i_1)$ and $j_2 \notin f(i_1)$. Moreover, $j_2 \in \bigcup_{\kappa=1}^{k^-} f(\kappa)$ by $(++)$ of *Definition 3.2*. Consequently, there exists an $i_2 \neq i_1$ such that $j_2 \in f(i_2)$. Then the following cases are possible:

CASE 1: $j_1 \notin f(i_2)$. Then consider the T-graph $(\mathcal{G}_0, \widehat{V}_0, \gamma_0^*)$ in *Figure 6*. Its only valve node is v_0, i.e. $\widehat{V}_0 = \{v_0\}$. We assume that $\eta(r_1) = i_1$, $\eta(r_2) = i_2$, $\chi(r_3) = j_1$ and $\chi(r_4) = j_2$; if $k^- > 2$ we add $(k^- - 2)$ arcs of the form (u, v_0), and if $k^+ > 2$ we generate $(k^+ - 2)$ further arcs of the form (v_0, w). In *Figure 6*, these nodes u and w are symbolized by a $'o'$.

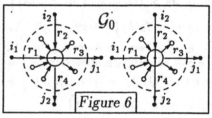

Figure 6

The function γ_0^* is defined as $\gamma_0^*(r_1) = \{r_3\}$ and $\gamma_0^*(r_2) = \{r_4\}$. Then $\mathcal{G}_0$ behaves like a valve of type τ^* since alternatively the connection from r_1 to r_3 and from r_3 to r_4 is generated.

This means that every T^*-graph $(\mathcal{G}, \widehat{V}, \gamma)$ can be transformed into an equivalent T-graph by replacing each $\mathcal{G}$-node $v \leadsto \tau^*$ by a copy of $\mathcal{G}_0$; in particular, all arcs incident with v are identified with the corresponding arcs r_1, r_2, r_3, r_4.

CASE 2: $j_1 \in f(i_2)$. Then consider the valve graph $(\mathcal{G}_0, \widehat{V}_0, \gamma_0^{**})$ in *Figure 7*; $\mathcal{G}_0$ and $\widehat{V}_0$ are defined as in the previous case, and $\gamma_0^{**}(r_1) := \{r_3\}$, $\gamma_0^{**}(r_2) := \{r_3, r_4\}$.

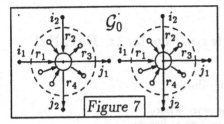

Figure 7

Obviously, this graph behaves like a valve of type τ^{**}. So the following reduction process is possible: If $(\mathcal{G}, \widehat{\mathcal{V}}, \gamma)$ is a T^{**}-graph then replace every valve node $v \rightsquigarrow \tau^{**}$ by a copy of $\mathcal{G}_0$. ∎

With the help of these assertions we can easily prove our main result:

Theorem 3.7. Let $T \supseteq T_0$. Then $\mathbf{VP}_d(T)$ can be solved in polynomial time if $T = T_0$. If however $T \supsetneq T_0$ then the problem is NP-complete.

Proof: The first part of our assertion was shown in *Theorem 3.3*. Let now $T \supsetneq T_0$, then there exists a $\tau \in T_1$ with $T \supseteq T' := T_0 \cup \{\tau\}$. The NP-completeness of $\mathbf{VP}_d(T')$ was shown in *Theorem 3.6*, and $\mathbf{VP}_d(T)$ is at least as hard as $\mathbf{VP}_d(T')$. Therefore this problem is NP-hard.

On the other hand, $\mathbf{VP}_d(T)$ can be solved in nondeterministic polynomial time by guessing a path and testing its admissibility. ∎

4. Concluding Remarks

In this section we consider several modifications of the previous problems and situations.

Modified types of valves: The definitions *3.1* and *3.2* were based on the assumption that every adjustment $\vartheta(v)$ of the valve v opens exactly one incoming arc. If some valves of a graph $\mathcal{G}$ do *not* satisfy this condition then the complexity of finding an admissible s-t-path is still unknown.

Undirected Graphs: If all pipes in a network can be used in both directions then an *undirected* graph is a realistic model

of this situation. A similar argumentation as in *Theorem 3.4* yields the NP-complexity of finding s-t-paths in undirected graphs if all valves of $\mathcal{G}$ are of type τ^*. (Of course, the arcs incident with the valve nodes must be replaced by *edges*.) But if the valves of $\mathcal{G}$ are *not* of type τ^*, the complexity of our path problem is *not* known. It is not even clear how define general types of valves in the undirected case; this seems to be more vomplicated than replacing arcs by edges in *Definition 3.2.a*).

Cost Bounded s-t-Paths: Given a function $h : \mathcal{R} \rightarrow \mathbf{N}$ and a cost measure $H(P) := \sum_{i=1}^{k-1} h(x_i, x_{i+1})$ for all paths $P = [x_1, \ldots, x_k]$. Let $B > 0$. The problem is to decide whether there exists an admissible s-t-path P^+ in a valve graph such that $H(P^+) \le B$.

This problem was already treated in [3], but it can be easily solved with the results proven above:

In the situation of *Theorem 3.3*, the existence of P^+ can be decided in in polynomial time by searching an s-t-path P^* with *minimal* H-value (and later adjusting all valves according to P^*). In all other cases, however, our problem is NP-complete: Let $B := 1 + \sum_{r \in \mathcal{R}} h(r)$; then *every* admissible elementary s-t-path is bounded by B. Consequently, the NP-complete problem $\mathbf{VP}_d(T)$ is reduced to the search of a legal path with $H(P) \le B$.

References

[1] U.BRAUN, *Graphentheoretische Modellierung und Lösungsverfahren bei der rechnergestützten Wegeplanung in der Prozeßautomatisierung.* Diploma Thesis, University at Würzburg, Würzburg (1990).

[2] H.N.GABOW, S.N.MAHESWARI, L.J.OSTERWEIL, *On two problems in the generation of program test paths.* IEEE Trans. Software Engrg. SE-2 (1976), page 227 – 231.

[3] U.HUCKENBECK, *Cost-Bounded Paths in Networks of Pipes with Valves.* Technical Report No. 42, University at Würzburg, Institute of Computer Science (May 1992).

Scheduling Interval Ordered Tasks in Parallel

S. Sunder and Xin He*

Department of Computer Science,
State University of New York at Buffalo,
Buffalo, NY 14260, USA

Abstract. We present the first NC algorithm for scheduling n unit length tasks on m identical processors for the case where the precedence constraint is an interval order. Our algorithm runs on a priority CRCW PRAM in $O(\log^2 n)$ time with $O(n^5)$ processors, or in $O(\log^3 n)$ time with $O(n^4)$ processors. The algorithm constructs the same schedule as the one produced by the sequential algorithm (list scheduling). On the other hand, we show that when the precedence constraints are allowed to be arbitrary, the construction of the list schedule is P-complete.

1 Introduction

The problem of scheduling unit execution time tasks on m identical processors under arbitrary precedence constraints has been studied extensively in the past. The problem is known to be NP-hard when m, the number of processors, is part of the input [1]. Polynomial time algorithms are known when $m = 2$ [2, 3, 4]. The problem with $m = 3$ is an outstanding open problem in scheduling theory and has motivated considerable research [5]. Polynomial time algorithms for solving this problem are known when m is part of the input and the precedence constraints are trees [6] or interval orders [7]. (see [8] for a survey of results on other special cases of the problem)

The main algorithmic tool employed in obtaining polynomial time sequential algorithms for solving this problem is known as *list scheduling*. Briefly the method works as follows: Form a priority list of tasks and construct a schedule iteratively by choosing a maximal set of $r \leq m$ independent tasks (tasks with no precedence constraints within them) of highest priority in each iteration. The sequential algorithms for 2-processor scheduling [2], for scheduling interval orders [7], and for scheduling trees [6] are based on the list scheduling method. Helmbold and Mayr [9] showed that the construction of the list schedule (with $m = 2$, *arbitrary* execution times for tasks and empty precedence constraints) is P-complete, and hence unlikely to be parallelizable. However, NC algorithms based on completely different ideas are known for 2-processor scheduling [10, 11] and for scheduling trees [9, 12].

In this paper, we present the first NC algorithm for solving the m-processor scheduling problem for interval orders. This problem was posed as an open problem in [9]. Our algorithm makes use of structural properties of interval orders and some techniques developed by Bartusch et al [5]. We also strengthen the P-complete result

* Research supported in part by NSF grant CCR-9011214

in [9] by showing that the construction of the list schedule for general precedence constraint graphs is P-complete, even when all tasks have unit execution time. Surprisingly, our parallel algorithm for scheduling interval orders constructs the same list schedule produced by the sequential algorithm in [7].

The parallel computation model we use is a *parallel random access machine* (PRAM). The model consists of a number of identical processors and a common memory. In each time unit, a processor can read a memory cell, perform an arithmetic or logic operation and write into a memory cell. Both concurrent read and concurrent write are allowed. In case of a write conflict, the processor with the highest priority succeeds. The present paper is organized as follows. In section 2, we introduce basic definitions and prove our P-complete result. Section 3 presents an algorithm for computing the optimal schedule length for interval orders. Section 4 presents our NC algorithm for scheduling interval orders.

2 Basic Definitions and List Scheduling

Let $G = (V, A)$ be a partial order (or equivalently a transitive acyclic directed graph) consisting of $n = |V|$ nodes. We sometimes refer to G as a *precedence constraint graph* and the elements of V as *tasks*. A node u is a *successor* of a node v if there is a directed path from v to u in G. The set of successors of v is denoted by $N_G(v)$ (or simply $N(v)$ if the context is clear). v is a *maximal* node if $N(v) = \emptyset$.

A *schedule* of *length* t for G on m processors is an $m \times t$ matrix S, where the columns are indexed by $1, \ldots, t$ and the rows are indexed by $1, \ldots, m$. Each task x is assigned to an unique entry $(p(x), t(x))$ in S such that $(x, y) \in A$ implies $t(x) < t(y)$. For any task $x \in V$, the entry $(p(x), t(x))$ denotes that x is scheduled on processor $p(x)$ at time instant $t(x)$. No two tasks are assigned to the same entry in S. The length of S is denoted by $\|S\|$. An entry in S is also called a *slot*. An entry of S to which no task is assigned is said to be *empty*. Two schedules S_1 and S_2 for G are considered to be the same if for every task x in G, the column assigned to x in S_1 is the same as the column assigned to x in S_2. (Since the processors are identical, it is irrelevant which processor is assigned to the task.) We denote the *sub-schedule* of S consisting of columns $i, i + 1, \ldots, j$ $(1 \leq i \leq j \leq t)$ by $S[i, j]$. Let S', S'' be two schedules of size $m \times t_1$ and $m \times t_2$ for two partial orders G_1 and G_2. The *concatenation* of S' and S'', denoted by $S' \circ S''$, is the schedule of size $m \times (t_1 + t_2)$ obtained by concatenating the two matrices S' and S''.

The following *list scheduling* algorithm is frequently used in sequential scheduling algorithms. The inputs to the algorithm are: an arbitrary precedence constraint graph $G = (V, A)$, a *precedence-preserving* list L of the tasks in V (namely if u is a successor of v in G then v precedes u in L), and the number of processors m.

Algorithm List-Schedule $(G = (V, A), L, m)$

1. $t = 1$.
2. While $L \neq \emptyset$ Do
   (a) Initialize an empty set L'.
   (b) Put the first node v of L into L'. Scan L from left to right. When a node w is scanned, if w is independent with every node in L' (namely, for any $u \in L'$,

$(u, w) \notin A$ and $(w, u) \notin A)$, then include w into L'. Repeat this process until either L' contains m nodes, or all nodes of L have been considered.

(c) Schedule the nodes in L' in column t.

(d) $L = L - L', t = t + 1$.

3. Output the schedule constructed.

The following property of the algorithm List-Schedule can be easily seen:

Lemma 1: Let $G = (V, A)$ be a precedence constraint graph and L a precedence-preserving list of the tasks in V. Let $S = $ List-Schedule(G, L, m) and the length of S be t. Then for each $i \leq n$, the first i tasks in L are assigned to columns $1, \ldots, p$ (for some $p \leq t$) of S and every column j $(1 \leq j \leq p)$ of S contains at least one of the first i tasks in L.

The *list scheduling problem* is defined as follows: Given an arbitrary precedence constraint graph $G = (V, A)$, a precedence-preserving list L of V and the number of processors m, compute List-Schedule(G, L, m). Next we show that the list scheduling problem is P-complete. First, we need the following definitions.

An *outforest* is a directed graph F in which the indegree of every node is at most one. The *height* of a node u in an outforest F is the length of the longest path from u to some leaf node (outdegree is zero) of F. A *height priority schedule* for an outforest F is obtained by sorting the nodes of F into a list L by nonincreasing order of their height, and then computing the list schedule of F associated with the list L. A *processor profile* is a function μ from natural numbers to natural numbers such that $\mu(t)$ is the number of processors available at time instant t. μ is *nondecreasing* iff $t_1 < t_2$ implies $\mu(t_1) \leq \mu(t_2)$.

Theorem 1: The list scheduling problem is P-complete under NC reduction.

Proof : Dolev et al [12] have shown that constructing a height priority schedule, for an outforest with nondecreasing profile μ, is P-complete. We reduce this problem to the list scheduling problem using an NC reduction.

Given an outforest $F = (V_T, A_T)$ and a processor profile μ, define a new precedence constraint graph $G = (V_G, A_G)$ as follows. For each time instant t $(1 \leq t \leq n)$, let V_t be a set consisting of $\mu(n) - \mu(t)$ new nodes. For every pair $1 \leq t < t' \leq n$, add directed edges from each node in V_t to every node in $V_{t'}$. Let A' be the set of added edges. Define $V_G = V_T \cup (\cup_{t=1}^n V_t)$ and $A_G = A_T \cup A'$. Next construct a list L of the nodes in V_G as follows: Find the height of each node in F and form a list L' of the nodes in F by nonincreasing order of height. For each $1 \leq t \leq n$, let L_t be an arbitrary list of the nodes in V_t. Form a list L by concatenating the lists $L_1, \ldots, L_n, L'$. Finally, define $m = \mu(n)$. This construction can be easily done by an NC algorithm. Let $S = $ List-Schedule(G, L, m). Clearly, the restriction of S to the nodes of V_F is a height priority schedule of F. $\square$

An *interval order* is a partial order $G = (V, A)$ where V is a set of intervals on the real line and $(u, v) \in A$ (u *precedes* v) iff $x \in u, y \in v$ implies $x < y$. We sometimes refer to the elements of V as *intervals*. The left and the right endpoint of an interval $u \in V$ is denoted by $l(u)$ and $r(u)$, respectively. We assume that, without loss of generality, all endpoints are distinct. For each $v \in V$, clearly $N_G(v) = \{u \in V | l(u) > r(v)\}$. In the following discussion, we denote the interval order corresponding to a list L of intervals by $G(L)$. For any two lists L_1 and L_2, let $L_1.L_2$ denote the *concatenation* of the two lists. The cardinality of a list L is denoted by $|L|$. For

$1 \leq i \leq j \leq |L|$, $L(i)$ denotes the ith element in L and $L(i, \ldots, j)$ denotes the sublist of L consisting of the elements $L(i), L(i + 1), \ldots, L(j)$.

Let L be a list of intervals and $u \notin L$ be an arbitrary interval. Let $S = $ List-Schedule$(G(L), L, m)$. A column in S is *incomplete* if less than m tasks are scheduled in it. We say an incomplete column c in S is *feasible* for u if the column c does not contain any interval which precedes u. An empty slot in an incomplete column that is feasible for u is said to be *available* for u.

Next we describe an algorithm which is equivalent to the list scheduling algorithm. This description is useful in understanding our parallel algorithm in section 4. The inputs to the algorithm are two precedence preserving lists of intervals L_1, L_2 and the number of processors m.

Algorithm Alternate(L_1, L_2, m)

1. Compute $R = $ List-Schedule$(G(L_1), L_1, m)$. Let $|L_2| = k$ and the length of R be l.
2. For $i = 1$ to k Do
   If there is an incomplete column in R which is feasible for $L_2(i)$ then schedule $L_2(i)$ in the smallest such feasible column.
   Else: (a) $l = l + 1$.
         (b) Add a new column (with column number l) to R and schedule $L_2(i)$
   in it.

Lemma 2: Let L_1, L_2 be two lists of intervals such that $L_1.L_2$ is precedence preserving. Then Alternate$(L_1, L_2, m) = $ List-Schedule$(G(L_1.L_2), L_1.L_2, m)$.

Proof: Follows from the way the list scheduling algorithm works. □

The sequential algorithm in [7] for solving the m-processor scheduling problem for an interval order $G = (V, A)$ is a list scheduling algorithm. Let L be a list of intervals representing G.

Algorithm Sequential-Schedule (L, m)

1. Sort the list L of intervals by increasing order of right endpoints.
2. Compute $S = $ List-Schedule$(G(L), L, m)$.

In [7], Papadimitriou and Yannakakis gave an implementation of the above algorithm which runs in sequential time $O(n)$. In the next two sections, we present an NC algorithm for scheduling interval orders. Our algorithm reduces the problem of constructing the optimal schedule to the problem of computing the optimal schedule length, which is discussed in the next section.

3 Computing the Optimal Schedule Length

Consider the following decision problem: Given an interval order $G = (V, A)$, is there a schedule for G on m processors of length t? The method we use to solve this decision problem is based on a representation theorem of Bartusch et. al. [5] which holds for the m-processor scheduling problem with arbitrary precedence constraint graphs. However, the theorem in its general form does not yield polynomial time algorithms when the precedence constraint graphs are arbitrary. We briefly review the results in [5] tailored to the special case of interval orders.

Bartusch et al. defined the following *bounding function* b on the node set V: For all maximal nodes x of G, let $b(x) = t$. For non-maximal nodes x, define:

$$b(x) = \min_{i \in C}\{i - \lceil |\{y \in N(x)|b(y) \leq i\}|/m \rceil\}$$

where $j \in C$ iff there is a successor u of x such that $b(u) \leq j$.

For each $v \in V$, $b(v)$ is an upper bound on the column number by which the node v must be scheduled in any schedule for G of length t. The representation theorem of Bartusch et al. is as follows:

Theorem 2 [5]: There exists a schedule for the interval order G on m processors with length t iff for every i with $1 \leq i \leq t$, $|\{u|b(u) \leq i\}| \leq mi$.

It is shown in [5] that if there is a schedule for G on m processors of length at most t, it can be constructed by forming a list L of the nodes sorted by nondecreasing order of bounds and then computing the list schedule associated with L. The main difficulty in parallelizing this approach is that the computation of the bounding function b is inherently sequential. We introduce another bounding function b' such that Theorem 2 holds with respect to b', and b' can be computed in parallel. Our bounding function b' is computed by the following algorithm:

Algorithm Bound $(G = (V_G, E_G), m, t)$

1. Define a directed acyclic graph $D = (V_D, E_D, w)$ with integral edge weights w as follows:
   (a) $V_D = V_G \cup \{s\}$ where s is a new sink node.
   (b) $E_D = E_G \cup \{(v, s)|v \in V_G\}$.
   (c) Define $w(v, s) = 0$ for all $v \in V_D$. For every $(v, u) \in E_D$ such that $u \neq s$ compute:
   $$S(v, u) = \{x \in N_G(v)|r(x) \leq r(u)\}$$
   $$w(v, u) = \lceil |S(v, u)|/m \rceil$$
2. For all $v \in V_D$, find $d(v)$, the length of the longest path in D from v to the sink s (by matrix squaring).
3. For every $v \in V_G$, compute $b'(v) = t - d(v)$.

The complexity of above algorithm is dominated by step 2 which involves $\log n$ matrix multiplications. The matrix multiplication is over the semiring $(\aleph, (\max, +))$, where $\aleph$ denotes the set of non-negative integers. Evaluating each entry of the product matrix involves finding the maximum of n numbers. Since the numbers involved are all bounded by n, this can be done on a priority CRCW PRAM in $O(1)$ time using $O(n)$ processors. Thus a single matrix multiplication can be implemented on a priority CRCW PRAM in $O(1)$ time using $O(n^3)$ processors. Hence step 2 takes $O(\log n)$ time with $O(n^3)$ processors. Next we prove that Theorem 2 remains true when $b(v)$ is replaced by $b'(v)$.

Lemma 3 : Let x and y be two nodes in an interval order G. (1) If $r(x) < r(y)$ then $b(x) \leq b(y)$. (2) If $b(x) < b(y)$ then $r(x) < r(y)$.

Proof: (1) $r(x) < r(y)$ implies $N_G(y) \subseteq N_G(x)$. The claim follows from the definition of $b(x)$ and $b(y)$. (2) follows from (1) immediately. $\square$

Lemma 4: Let S be a schedule for an interval order $G = (V_G, A_G)$ on m processors with length t. Then for any $v \in V_G$, v must be scheduled in one of the columns $1, \ldots, b'(v)$ in S. (In other words, $b'(v)$ is a *valid upper bound* on the column number by which v must be scheduled in S).

Proof: If v is a maximal node of G, then $d(v) = 0$ and $b'(v) = t$. Hence the bound is valid for maximal nodes.

Suppose v is a non-maximal node of G. Let $(u_0, u_1, \ldots, u_p)$ (for some $p \geq 2$) be the longest path in D from $v = u_0$ to the sink $s = u_p$. Consider the sets $S(u_0, u_1), S(u_1, u_2), \ldots, S(u_{p-1}, u_p)$. For any $x \in S(u_i, u_{i+1})$ and $y \in S(u_{i+1}, u_{i+2})$, we have $r(x) \leq r(u_{i+1}) < l(y)$. Hence x precedes y in G and x must be scheduled in a column before the column for y in S. Thus the nodes in $\bigcup_{i=0}^{p-1} S(u_i, u_{i+1})$ must occupy at least $\sum_{i=0}^{p-1} \lceil |S(u_i, u_{i+1})|/m \rceil = d(v)$ columns in S. Since $v = u_0$ precedes every node in $S(u_0, u_1)$, v must be scheduled in a column c in S with $c \leq t - d(v) = b'(v)$. □

Lemma 5: $b'(v) \leq b(v)$.

Proof: Consider the definition of $b(v)$. Suppose $b(v) = i_1 - \lceil |S_1'|/m \rceil$ where $S_1' = \{y \in N_G(v) | b(y) \leq i_1\}$. Let $u_1 \in S_1'$ such that $b(u_1) = i_1$ and $r(u_1) = \max \{r(x) | x \in N_G(v) \text{ and } b(x) = i_1\}$. By Lemma 3 (1), $S(v, u_1) \subseteq S_1'$. Consider any $y \in S_1'$. By Lemma 3 (2) and the choice of u_1, $r(y) \leq r(u_1)$. Hence $S_1' \subseteq S(v, u_1)$. We can iterate this process to obtain a path $P = (v = u_0, u_1, \ldots, u_q)$ such that $S(u_i, u_{i+1}) = S_{i+1}'$ and u_q is some maximal node of G and $b(v) = t - length(P)$ where $length(P) = \sum_{i=1}^{q} \lceil |S_i'|/m \rceil$ is the length of P in D. Let P' be the longest path from v to the sink s in D. Then $length(P') \geq length(P)$. By definition, $b'(v) = t - length(P')$. Therefore, $b'(v) \leq b(v)$. □

Lemma 6: We can replace $b(v)$ by $b'(v)$ in Theorem 2.

Proof: Suppose there is a schedule for G on m processors with length t. Since b' is a valid upper bound, it must satisfy the constraints in Theorem 2. Suppose b' satisfies the constraints in Theorem 2. By Lemma 5, for any i ($1 \leq i \leq t$), $\{u | b(u) \leq i\} \subseteq \{u | b'(u) \leq i\}$. Hence b also satisfies these constraints. By Theorem 2, there exists a schedule for G with length t. □

The following procedure finds the optimal schedule length for an interval order G. The input to the procedure is a list L of intervals representing G.

Algorithm Length (L, m)

1. As in the algorithm Bound, construct the edge weighted graph $D = (V_D, A_D, w)$ from $G(L)$ and compute, for each node u of $G(L)$, the longest distance $d(u)$ in D.
2. In parallel, for every $1 \leq t \leq n$, check if the following conditions are true:
   For every $1 \leq i \leq t$, $|\{u | b'(u) = t - d(u) \leq i\}| \leq mi$.
3. Output the smallest t such that the above conditions are true.

The correctness of this algorithm follows from Lemma 6. The complexity of the algorithm Length is dominated by step 1 which takes $O(\log n)$ time on $O(n^3)$ processors. The steps 2 and 3 take at most $O(\log n)$ time with $O(n^2)$ processors.

4 Constructing an Optimal Schedule

In this section, we describe a parallel algorithm which constructs the same list schedule for an interval order $G = (V, A)$ as the sequential algorithm. Let L be the list of the tasks of V in increasing order of right endpoints. Let $SeqS$ = Sequential-Schedule(L, m) = List-Schedule$(G(L), L, m)$. Suppose $\|SeqS\| = t$ and $t_1 = \lfloor t/2 \rfloor$. Let $S' = SeqS[1, t_1]$ and $S'' = SeqS[t_1 + 1, t]$. We will construct S' and S'' in parallel. By Lemma 1, there exists an integer $i \leq n$ such that all tasks in $L(1, \ldots, i)$ (and possibly some other tasks) are scheduled in the columns of S' and each column of S' contains at least one task from $L(1, \ldots, i)$. The difficult part in this approach is to determine which tasks, in addition to the tasks in $L(1, \ldots, i)$, are scheduled in the columns of S'. We use our optimal schedule length finding algorithm from the previous section to accomplish this goal. The input to our algorithm is a list L of intervals of G sorted by increasing order of right endpoints and the number of processors m.

Algorithm Parallel-Schedule (L, m)

1. For each i $(1 \leq i \leq n)$, compute Length$(L(1, \ldots, i), m)$. Suppose t = Length $(L(1, \ldots, n), m)$.
   If $t = 1$, then schedule all tasks of L in one column and return.
   Otherwise, let s be the integer such that Length$(L(1, \ldots, s), m) \leq \frac{t}{2}$ and Length $(L(1, \ldots, s + 1), m) > \frac{t}{2}$. Let $L_1 = L(1, \ldots, s)$ and $L_2 = L(s + 1, \ldots, n)$.
2. Let u be the last interval in L_1. Define $L_3 = \{x \in L_2 | l(x) < r(u)\}$.
   Note: L_3 is the set of intervals in L_2 that might be scheduled with the intervals in L_1.
3. Compute $X = \text{Jump}(L_1, L_3, m)$.
   Note: Jump(L_1, L_3, m) is a function (to be defined later) which returns a subset X of L_3 with the following property: $x \in X$ iff x is scheduled in a column containing a node in L_1 by the Sequential-Schedule algorithm.
4. Let $L' = L_1.X$ and $L'' = L_2 - X$.
5. Recursively find $S' = \text{Parallel-Schedule}(L', m)$ and $S'' = \text{Parallel-Schedule}(L'', m)$.
6. Output $S' \circ S''$.

Before describing the procedure Jump (L_1, L_3, m), we need some notations. Let $SeqS_1$ = Sequential-Schedule(L_1, m) and $\|SeqS_1\| = t_1$. Consider a node $x \in L_3$. Let $c(x)$ denote the column number of the smallest feasible column for x in $SeqS_1$. (Note that every incomplete column c' in $SeqS_1$ such that $c(x) \leq c' \leq t_1$ is feasible for x.) Suppose that x is the kth element in L. The nodes in $L(s + 1, \ldots, k - 1)$ (recall that $u = L(s)$ is the last element of L_1) can be partitioned into three lists:
$$A(x) = \{y \in L(s + 1, \ldots, k - 1) \mid l(y) < l(x) \text{ and } r(y) < r(x)\},$$
$$B(x) = \{y \in L(s + 1, \ldots, k - 1) \mid l(x) < l(y) < r(u) \text{ and } r(y) < r(x)\},$$
$$C(x) = \{y \in L(s + 1, \ldots, k - 1) \mid r(u) < l(y) \text{ and } r(y) < r(x)\}.$$
$A(x)$, $B(x)$ and $C(x)$ are sorted by increasing order of right endpoints. Note that $A(x) \subseteq L_3$, $B(x) \subseteq L_3$ and $C(x) \cap L_3 = \emptyset$. Suppose that x is scheduled in a column c in $SeqS$. Then every node in $A(x)$ must be scheduled in $SeqS$ in a column $c' \leq c$. A node in $B(x)$ may be scheduled in any column of $SeqS$. A node in $C(x)$ must

be scheduled in $SeqS$ in a column $c' > t_1$. For each node $x \in L_3$, let $SeqS_1(x) =$ Sequential-Schedule($L_1.A(x), m$).

The function Jump is computed by the following algorithm. Roughly speaking, the question of whether a node $x \in L_3$ should belong to X is decided by counting the number of empty slots that are available for x in $SeqS_1$ and $SeqS_1(x)$.

Algorithm Jump (L_1, L_3, m)

1. For every $x \in L_3$ compute $A(x)$ and $B(x)$.
2. For every $x \in L_3$ compute:
    $S_1(x) = $ the number of empty slots available for x in $SeqS_1[c(x), t_1]$.
    $S_2(x) = $ the number of empty slots available for x in $SeqS_1(x)[c(x), t_1]$.
3. For every $x \in L_3$, let $B(x) = \{b_1^x, \ldots, b_{k_x}^x\}$ sorted by increasing order of *left* endpoints. Output: $X = \{x | (\exists j : 1 \leq j \leq k_x : S_2(x) - S_1(b_j^x) \geq j) \text{ or } (S_2(x) > k_x)\}$.

We now describe how step 2 of Jump can be computed. For $1 \leq i \leq n$, define the list $C(x, i) = \{c_1, \ldots, c_i\}$ where c_j $(1 \leq j \leq i)$ is a copy of the interval x. Since $S_1(x)$ is the number of empty slots in $SeqS_1[c(x), t_1]$, evaluating $S_1(x)$ is equivalent to finding the largest $i \leq n$ such that the intervals in $C(x, i)$ can be scheduled in empty slots of $SeqS_1[c(x), t_1]$. Hence, Length($L_1.C(x, i), m$) $> t_1$ iff $S_1(x) < i$. Similarly, since $S_2(x)$ is the number of empty slots in $SeqS_1(x)[c(x), t_1]$, evaluating $S_2(x)$ is equivalent to finding the largest $i \leq n$ such that the intervals in $C(x, i)$ can be scheduled in empty slots in $SeqS_1(x)[c(x), t_1]$. There are two cases.

Case 1: Suppose $\|SeqS_1(x)\| > t_1$. Then at least one node in $A(x)$ is scheduled in $SeqS_1(x)$ in a column $c' > t_1$. Since every node in $A(x)$ must be scheduled before the node x, there are no empty slots available for x in $SeqS_1(x)[c(x), t_1]$. Hence $S_2(x) = 0$.

Case 2: Suppose $\|SeqS_1(x)\| = t_1$. We can evaluate $S_2(x)$ using the following condition: Length($L_1.A(x).C(x, i), m$) $> t_1$ iff $S_2(x) < i$.

Thus for each $x \in L_3$, $S_1(x)$ and $S_2(x)$ can be computed by either making $O(n)$ calls in parallel to algorithm Length or $O(\log n)$ calls in sequence by doing a binary search. Hence, the complexity of step 2 is $O(\log^2 n)$ time with $O(n^4)$ processors or $O(\log n)$ time with $O(n^5)$ processors. The complexity of other steps of the algorithm Jump is dominated by step 2. Next we show the condition in step 3 for deciding the membership of X is correct.

Lemma 7: Let $x \in L_3$ and $y \in A(x)$. Suppose y is scheduled in column c' in $SeqS_1(x)$.

1. If $c' \leq c(x) - 1$, then y is scheduled in the same column c' in $SeqS$.
2. If $c' \geq c(x)$, then y is scheduled in some column $c'' \geq c(x)$ in $SeqS$.

Proof : Suppose that $|L_1| = s$, y is the jth element in L and the kth element in $A(x)$. First observe that the column assigned to y in $SeqS$ depends on only the elements in $L(1, \ldots, j)$ and the column assigned to y in $SeqS_1(x)$ depends only on the elements in $L(1, \ldots, s).A(x)(1, \ldots, k)$. By Lemma 2:
Sequential-Schedule($L(1, \ldots, s).A(x)(1, \ldots, k), m$) = **Alternate** $(L(1, \ldots, s), A(x)$ $(1, \ldots, k), m)$ and Sequential-Schedule($L(1, \ldots, j), m$) = Alternate($L(1, \ldots, s), L(s+ 1, \ldots, j), m$).

By the definition of $A(x)$, we have $A(x)(1,\ldots,k) \subseteq L(s+1,\ldots,j)$. If $L(s+1,\ldots,j) = A(x)(1,\ldots,k)$, the claims of the lemma follow immediately. So suppose there exists $z \in L(s+1,\ldots,j) - A(x)(1,\ldots,k)$. Note that either $z \notin L_3$ or $z \in B(x)$.

Suppose $c' \leq c(x) - 1$. Consider the computation of the algorithm Alternate on input $(L(1,\ldots,s), L(s+1,\ldots,j), m)$. Let $z \in L(s+1,\ldots,j) - A(x)$. If $z \notin L_3$, then z is scheduled in some column $\bar{c} > t_1$. If $z \in B(x)$, then $c(z) \geq c(x)$ and hence z can not be scheduled in the first $c(x) - 1$ columns. Hence when the algorithm Alternate is run on input $(L(1,\ldots,s), L(s+1,\ldots,j), m)$, the first $c(x)-1$ columns is exactly the same as the first $c(x) - 1$ columns when it is run on the input $(L(1,\ldots,s), A(x)(1,\ldots,k), m)$. Therefore y is scheduled in column c' in $SeqS$ also.

Suppose $c' \geq c(x)$. Then in the computation of the algorithm Alternate on input $(L(1,\ldots,s), A(x)(1,\ldots,k), m)$, there are no available empty slots for y in the first $c(x) - 1$ columns. Since $A(x)(1,\ldots,k) \subseteq L(s+1,\ldots,j)$, when the algorithm Alternate is run on the input $(L(1,\ldots,s), L(s+1,\ldots,j), m)$ there are no available empty slots for y in the first $c(x) - 1$ columns. Hence, the algorithm Alternate assigns y to some column $c'' \geq c(x)$. $\square$

For each $x \in L_3$, define $\bar{A}(x) = \{y \in A(x) | y$ is scheduled in a column $c' \geq c(x)$ in $SeqS\}$.

Lemma 8: For each $x \in L_3$, if $\|SeqS_1(x)\| = t_1$, then $|\bar{A}(x)| = S_1(x) - S_2(x)$.

Proof: Let $A_1(x) = \{y \in A(x) | y$ is scheduled in a column $c' \leq c(x) - 1$ in $SeqS_1(x)\}$ and $A_2(x) = \{y \in A(x) | y$ is scheduled in a column $c' \geq c(x)$ in $SeqS_1(x)\}$. Since $S_1(x)$ is the number of empty slots in $SeqS_1[c(x), t_1] =$ Alternate $(L_1, \emptyset, m)[c(x), t_1]$ and $S_2(x)$ is the number of empty slots in $SeqS_1(x)[c(x), t_1] =$ Alternate$(L_1, A(x), m)[c(x), t_1]$, it follows that $S_1(x) - S_2(x)$ is the number of elements from $A(x)$ that are scheduled in $SeqS_1(x)[c(x), t_1]$. Since $\|SeqS_1(x)\| = t_1$, $|A_2(x)| = S_1(x) - S_2(x)$. Hence by Lemma 7, $|\bar{A}(x)| = |A_2(x)| = S_1(x) - S_2(x)$. $\square$

The following lemma establishes the correctness of the algorithm Jump.

Lemma 9: Let $x \in L_3$ and $B(x) = \{b_1,\ldots,b_k\}$ ($k = 0$ when $B(x) = \emptyset$) sorted by increasing order of *left* endpoints. Then x is scheduled in a column $\hat{c}$ in $SeqS$ such that $1 \leq \hat{c} \leq t_1$ iff ($\exists j$ ($1 \leq j \leq k$) such that $S_2(x) - S_1(b_j) \geq j$) or $S_2(x) > k$.

Proof: Only If: Suppose that x is scheduled in a column $\hat{c}$ of $SeqS$ with $1 \leq \hat{c} \leq t_1$. Since each element in $A(x)$ must be scheduled in some column $c' \leq \hat{c} \leq t_1$ in $SeqS$, there are enough empty slots in $SeqS_1[1, \hat{c}]$ to schedule all the elements from $A(x)$. Hence, $\|SeqS_1(x)\| = t_1$. By Lemma 8, $(S_1(x) - S_2(x))$ tasks from $A(x)$ are scheduled in $SeqS[c(x), \hat{c}]$. Let $j \leq k$ be the minimal integer (if it exists) such that $c(b_j) > \hat{c}$. Since each task in $\{b_1,\ldots,b_{j-1}\}$ is feasible for column $\hat{c}$ and occurs before x in L, it must be scheduled in some column c' such that $c(x) \leq c' \leq \hat{c}$. Hence the number of empty slots in $SeqS_1[c(x), \hat{c}]$ should be at least $S_1(x) - S_2(x) + j$. But the number of empty slots in $SeqS_1[c(x), \hat{c}]$ is at most $S_1(x) - S_1(b_j)$. Hence, $S_1(x) - S_1(b_j) \geq S_1(x) - S_2(x) + j$. Therefore, $S_2(x) - S_1(b_j) \geq j$. If there is no $j \leq k$ such that $c(b_j) > \hat{c}$, a similar argument gives $S_2(x) > k$.

If: Suppose $S_2(x) > k$. Note that $S_2(x)$ is the number of empty slots in $SeqS_1(x)$ $[c(x), t_1]$. Observe that $b_1,\ldots,b_k$ are the only tasks that occur before x in L and are potentially feasible for these empty slots. Hence, even if all of the tasks $b_1,\ldots,b_k$ are feasible for empty slots in $SeqS_1(x)[c(x), t_1]$, there is still an empty slot available for x in some column $\hat{c}$ such that $c(x) \leq \hat{c} \leq t_1$. Hence x will be scheduled in the column $\hat{c}$ in $SeqS$.

Suppose there exists j with $1 \leq j \leq k$ such that $S_2(x) - S_1(b_j) \geq j$. Then $S_2(x) > 0$. By the remarks after the algorithm Jump, $S_2(x) > 0$ implies $\|SeqS_1(x)\| = t_1$. Note that $S_2(x) - S_1(b_j) \geq j$ is equivalent to $S_1(x) - S_1(b_j) \geq S_1(x) - S_2(x) + j$. This means that the number of empty slots in $SeqS_1[c(x), c(b_j) - 1]$ is at least $S_1(x) - S_2(x) + j$. Observe that $A(x) \cup \{b_1, \ldots, b_{j-1}\}$ are the only tasks that occur before x in L and are potentially feasible for these empty slots. By Lemma 8, the number of tasks from $A(x)$ that are scheduled in $SeqS[c(x), t_1]$ is equal to $S_1(x) - S_2(x)$. Hence even if all the tasks in $\{b_1, \ldots, b_{j-1}\}$ are scheduled in $SeqS[c(x), t_1]$, there is still an empty slot available for x in some column $\hat{c}$ such that $c(x) \leq \hat{c} \leq t_1$. Hence x will be scheduled in the column $\hat{c}$ in $SeqS$. $\square$

Theorem 3: The list scheduling problem for interval order can be solved on a priority CRCW PRAM either in $O(\log^2 n)$ time with $O(n^5)$ processors, or in $O(\log^3 n)$ time with $O(n^4)$ processors.

Proof: The correctness of the algorithm Parallel-Schedule follows from the discussion above. Step 1 ensures that the recursion depth of Parallel-Schedule is $O(\log n)$ since each recursive call reduces the schedule length by a factor of 2. It is easily seen that Step 1 can be implemented in $O(\log n)$ time with $O(n^4)$ processors. We have seen that the complexity of procedure Jump is $O(\log n)$ time with $O(n^5)$ processors, or $O(\log^2 n)$ time with $O(n^4)$ processors. Hence, the algorithm Parallel-Schedule can be implemented within the claimed time and processor bounds.

References

1. J. D. Ullman. Complexity of sequencing problems. In E. G. Coffman, editor, *Computer and Job Scheduling Theory*. John Wiley and sons, 1976.
2. E. G. Coffman and R. L. Graham. Optimal scheduling for two processor systems. *Acta Informatica*, 1:200–213, 1971.
3. M. R. Garey and D. S. Johnson. Scheduling tasks with nonuniform deadlines on two processors. *Journal of the ACM*, 23:461–467, 1976.
4. H. N. Gabow. An almost linear time algorithm for two processor scheduling. *J. Assoc. Comput. Mach.*, 29:766–780, 1982.
5. M. Bartusch, R. H. Mohring, and F. J. Radermacher. *M-machine unit time scheduling : a report of ongoing research*, volume 304 of *Lecture Notes in Economics and Mathematical Systems*, pages 165–212. Springer-Berlin, 1988.
6. T. C. Hu. Parallel sequencing and assembly line problems. *Operations Research*, 9:841–848, 1961.
7. C. H. Papadimitriou and M. Yannakakis. Scheduling interval-ordered tasks. *SIAM J. on Computing*, 8:405–409, 1979.
8. E. L. Lawler, J. K. Lenstra, A. H. G. Rinnooy Kan, and D. B. Shmoys. Sequencing and scheduling : Algorithms and complexity. Technical report, Centrum voor Wiskunde en Informatica, 1989.
9. D. Helmbold and E. Mayr. *Fast Scheduling Algorithms on Parallel Computers*. Advances in Computing Research. Jai press inc., London, 1987.
10. D. HelmBold and E. Mayr. Two processor scheduling is in NC. *SIAM J. on Computing*, 16:747–759, August 1987.
11. H. Jung, P. Spirakis, and M. Serna. A parallel algorithm for two processors precedence constrained scheduling. In *Proceedings of ICALP*, 1991.
12. D. Dolev, E. Upfal, and M. Warmuth. Scheduling trees in parallel. In P. Bertolazzi and F. Luccio, editors, *VLSI: Algorithms and Architectures*, 1985.

An $O(\sqrt{n})$-Worst-Case-Time Solution to the Granularity Problem*

A. Pietracaprina ** ***   and   F.P. Preparata***

Abstract. In this paper we deal with the granularity problem, that is, the problem of implementing a shared memory in a distributed system where n processors are connected to n memory modules through a complete network (Module Parallel Computer). We present a memory organization scheme where $m \in \Theta(n^2)$ variables, each replicated into a $2c - 1$ copies (for constant c), are evenly distributed among the n modules, so that a suitable access protocol allows any set of at most n distinct read/write operations to be performed by the processors in $O(\sqrt{n})$ parallel steps in the worst case. The well known strategy based on multiple copies is needed to avoid the worst-case $O(n)$-time, since only a majority of the copies of each variable need be accessed for any operation. The memory organization scheme can be extended to deal with $m \in \Theta(n^3)$ variables attaining an $O(n^{2/3})$-time complexity in the worst case.

Key Words. Algorithms and Data Structures, Theory of Parallel and Distributed Computing, P-RAM Simulation.

1 Introduction

A central problem in the design and implementation of a parallel computer is represented by the organization of data that must be available to the system's processors. More specifically, given n processors, n memory modules and $m \gg n$ data items (*variables*), a memory organization scheme is sought to distribute the data among the modules so that any subset of $n' \leq n$ variables can be efficiently accessed by the processors. The problem, often referred to as the *granularity problem*, has received considerable attention in the literature. The survey by [Kuc77] cites a number of works dealing with particular instances of the problem. More recently, the granularity problem has become a major obstacle in the development of efficient P-RAM simulation schemes [MV84, UW87, AHMP87, KU88, LPP88, Her89, LPP90, Her90, Ran91].

In order to focus on the essence of the problem, most authors assume that processors and memory modules are connected by a complete bipartite graph, and that, in a synchronous mode of operations, each memory module can fulfill at most one access (read/write) request per time unit (*Module Parallel Computer* (MPC)). With this strategy, the time to complete a parallel access to a set of variables is proportional to the maximum number of requests addressed to a single module. Mehlhorn

---

* This paper was partially supported by NFS Grant CCR-91-96152.

** Department of Computer Science, University of Illinois at Urbana-Champaign, Urbana, IL 61801

*** Department of Computer Science, Brown University, Providence, RI 02912

and Vishkin [MV84] first pointed out the difficulty of finding a deterministic memory organization that allows a parallel access to n variables in time significantly less than the trivial $O(n)$ bound. They introduced the idea of replicating each variable into several copies so that a read operation needs to access only one (the most convenient) copy. For $m \in O(n^c)$, they present a memory organization scheme that uses c copies per variable and allows a set of read requests to be satisfied in time $O(cn^{1-1/c})$. However, to execute write operations all the copies of the variables must be accessed, so requiring $O(cn)$ time.

Later, Upfal and Widgerson [UW87] refined the strategy based on multiple copies introducing to the realm of P-RAM simulation the majority concept previously developed for data bases [Gif79]: given $2c-1$ copies per variable, only c of them need to be accessed by any (read or write) operation. They also proposed a new memory organization scheme, based on a bipartite graph with particular expansion properties, which, when m is polynomial in n, attains an $O(\log n(\log \log n)^2)$ time bound. Unfortunately, no explicit construction for such a graph is known. With a probabilistic argument, the authors prove its existence, and prove that a random graph will have the desired expansion properties, with high probability. However, as we will show in this paper, no efficient way is known to test a graph for these properties.

All deterministic schemes subsequently developed for solving the granularity problem [AHMP87, Her89, LPP90, Her90] follow the ideas in [UW87] and are non-constructively based on the existence of similar expander graphs. (It must be pointed out that most of the cited works also considered the distribution of shared data on more realistic models where processors and memory modules are interconnected by bounded degree networks.) Using randomization, the granularity problem appears to be of easier solution as the results in [MV84, KU88, LPP88, Ran91] show. A common feature of these works is the use of a class of universal hash functions to distribute the variables among the memory modules. Moreover, randomized schemes do not need to replicate the variables since the worst case is avoided in the probabilistic sense.

In this paper we present a simple deterministic memory organization scheme for the MPC that distributes $m \in \Theta(n^2)$ variables among the n memory modules so that any n read/write operations can be performed in parallel in $O(\sqrt{n})$ worst-case-time. As in [UW87], each variable is represented by $2c-1$ copies only c of which need to be accessed in a read/write operation. The assignment of the copies to the memory modules is governed by the structure of Balanced Incomplete Block Design, a well known incidence structure, which guarantees that for any two variables there exists at most one module containing copies of both. The construction of such a graph is possible by using simple group theory; moreover, the physical addresses of the copies can be efficiently determined by the processors. This scheme can be extended to accommodate $m \in \Theta(n^3)$ variables. In this case, a set of n memory requests can be satisfied in $O(n^{2/3})$ worst-case-time.

It is important to underscore that in all the previous works a major problem was represented not only by the explicit construction of the memory organizations, but also by the storage of an adequate description of the memory map, these two aspects being closely interdependent. In fact, with the exception of [Her89, Her90], where the author is explicitly concerned with implementation issues, all other works assume that each processor has, in some form of local storage, a complete description of the memory map, a solution that is highly space inefficient.

The next section presents the memory organization scheme and the protocol to access a set of variables, and analyzes its worst case time complexity. In Section 3, we present a direct construction that can be easily implemented and allows to efficiently determine the physical addresses of the copies of any variable. Finally, in Section 4 we point out the difficulty inherent in proving expansion properties for graphs used for the memory organizations.

2 The Memory Organization Scheme

Suppose we want to store $q = 2c - 1$ copies of each of m variables into n memory modules, so that any module receives at most one copy of each variable. This can be conveniently described by a regular bipartite graph $G = (V, U; E)$ where V represents the set of variables, U the set of modules and for any variable $v \in V$ there are q edges $\{(v, u_1), \ldots, (v, u_q)\} \subset E$ whose second components represent the modules storing the copies of v. The particular graph we intend to use is conveniently described in terms of a combinatorial structure known as *Balanced Incomplete Block Design* [Hal86].

Definition 1. A *Balanced Incomplete Block Design* with parameters v, k and λ ((v, k, λ)-*BIBD*) is a pair $(X, \mathcal{L})$ where X is a finite set of v objects (*varieties*) and $\mathcal{L}$ is a family of k-subsets of X (*blocks*) such that any pair of varieties is contained in exactly λ blocks.

We choose G to be a subgraph of an $(n, q, 1)$-BIBD (i.e., $\lambda = 1$), where the varieties are interpreted as memory modules and each variable is associated with a block of q modules, which are the modules storing its copies. It is well known that the number of blocks in a (v, k, λ)-BIBD is $b = \lambda(v(v-1))/(k(k-1))$, [Hal86]; therefore, the number of variables that can be accommodated using a $(v, k, 1)$-BIBD structure is

$$m \leq \frac{n(n-1)}{q(q-1)},$$

that is, $m \in \Theta(n^2)$, for constant q. In the next section we present an explicit construction for such a BIBD where q is an odd prime power and $n = q^d$, for any integer d.

To complete the description of the memory organization scheme, we must specify how a set of memory requests issued by the processors can be satisfied. The access protocol we propose is similar to the one used by [UW87]. Suppose each processor issues a request (read or write) for a distinct variable[1]. The n processors are subdivided into n/q *clusters*, with q processors per cluster. Let $P(i, j)$ denote the jth processor in cluster i, $1 \leq i \leq n/q$ and $1 \leq j \leq q$, and let $v(i, j)$ denote the variable requested by $P(i, j)$. The protocol consists of q phases: each phase has an initialization step and l iterations. In the jth phase, the processors in each cluster cooperate to access the copies of the variable requested by their jth companion (i.e.,

---

[1] The case of less than n memory requests requires only minor modifications, which we omit for brevity.

processor $P(i, l)$ will be in charge of the lth copy of $v(i, j)$, $1 \leq i \leq n/q$. This is done in t consecutive iterations (the parameter t will be determined later), where in each iteration the processors request the copies they have been assigned to, and every module satisfies one request (if any). A processor stops sending its request as soon as it succeeds or at least c copies of the same variable have been accessed. At the end of each iteration each cluster counts the copies accessed so far.

At any time, a variable is *alive* if less than c of its copies have been accessed; a copy is *alive* if it has not been accessed yet. The code for Phase j is shown in Figure 1. For each variable, a flag is used to indicate whether the variable is alive or not.

Phase j

```
begin
  for i := 1 to n/q do in parallel
    P(i, j) broadcasts v(i, j) to the processors in cluster i;
    for l := 1 to q do in parallel
      P(i, l) determines the address of the lth copy of v(i, j)
    endfor;
    set flag(i, j) 'alive';
    while flag(i, j) = 'alive' do
      for l := 1 to q do in parallel
        P(i, l) tries to access the lth copy of v(i, j), if not yet accessed
      endfor;
      \* Each memory module accepts one request (if any) *\
      count the number of copies of v(i, j) accessed so far;
      if count ≥ c then set flag(i, j) 'dead' endif
    endwhile
  endfor
end.
```

Fig. 1. Code for Phase j

Let t be the maximum number of iterations required by the while loop in any phase. Since the processors communicate through a complete network, it is easy to see that each phase takes $O(t \log q)$ time. Therefore, all the variables will be accessed in time $O(tq \log q)$.

In order to estimate the parameter t, we first need a technical lemma. Consider a set of variables S and suppose that for each variable some of its copies, fewer than c, have already been accessed; that is, the variables are alive. Let $\Gamma(S)$ denote the set of modules storing the copies of the variables in S which have not been accessed yet.

Lemma 2. *Let τ be the maximum number of live copies of variables in S stored in the same module. Then*

$$|\Gamma(S)| \geq \frac{q-1}{2}\tau + 1$$

Proof. Let u be a module storing τ live copies of variables in S. Since a variable has its copies assigned to distinct modules, these τ copies belong to τ distinct variables, say $v_1, \ldots, v_\tau$. Each v_i has at least other $c - 1 = (q - 1)/2$ live copies, and, by the definition of $(n, q, 1)$-BIBD, for $1 \le i \ne j \le \tau$, v_i and v_j cannot share any module other than u. Therefore, $\Gamma(S)$ includes u and at least other $((q - 1)/2)\tau$ modules.

Theorem 3. $t \in O(\sqrt{n/q})$ *iterations of the while loop are sufficient to access all the variables requested in any phase.*

Proof. For a given phase, let L_k denote the number of copies accessed in the kth iteration of the while loop. Let $\alpha = (q - 1)/2$. Define k_0 to be such that $L_k \ge \sqrt{n\alpha}$, for $k \le k_0$, and $L_k < \sqrt{n\alpha}$, for $k > k_0$. Note that

$$k_0 \le \sqrt{n/\alpha}$$

otherwise after k_0 iterations more than n copies would be accessed, which is impossible since the n/q variables requested in the phase account only for n copies. Consider the $(k_0 + 1)$st iteration. The number of modules receiving requests in this iteration are $L_{k_0+1} < \sqrt{n\alpha}$. By Lemma 2 each module receives less than $\sqrt{n\alpha}/\alpha = \sqrt{n/\alpha}$ requests. Therefore, at most other $\sqrt{n/\alpha}$ iterations are sufficient to access all the remaining live copies. Hence,

$$t \le k_0 + \sqrt{n/\alpha} \le 2\sqrt{n/\alpha} \in O(\sqrt{n/q})$$

iterations are sufficient to satisfy all the memory requests of the phase.

Therefore, the entire access protocol is completed in $O(\sqrt{nq}\log q)$ time. If $q \in \Theta(1)$, we get

Corollary 4. *A set of $m \in \Theta(n^2)$ variables can be distributed with constant redundancy among n memory modules of an MPC, so that n distinct read/write operations can be performed in $O(\sqrt{n})$ parallel steps.*

The above scheme can be generalized to accommodate $m \in \Theta(n^3)$ variables as follows. The variables are allocated within the n modules, using a 3-$(n, q + 1, 1)$-*design*, a generalization of the BIBD that guarantees that any three modules are shared by exactly one variable. In this case we have $m \le \frac{(q^d+1)q^d(q^d-1)}{(q+1)q(q-1)}$ variables, and $n = q^d + 1$ memory modules, for any prime power $q > 2$ and integer d. Note that q has to be even to make $q + 1 = 2c - 1$ odd. Consider a set of variables S, each with at least c live copies. Let $\Gamma(S)$ denote the set of modules spanned by the live copies of S. We can prove

Lemma 5. *Let τ be the maximum number of live copies of variables in S stored in the same module. Then*

$$|\Gamma(S)| \ge \left(\frac{q}{2} - 1\right)\sqrt{\tau} + 1$$

Using the access protocol described before we get

Theorem 6. $t \in O((n/q)^{2/3})$ *iterations of the while loop are sufficient to access all the variables requested in any phase.*

Corollary 7. *A set of* $m \in \Theta(n^3)$ *variables can be distributed with constant redundancy among* n *memory modules of an MPC, so that* n *distinct read/write operations can be performed in* $O(n^{2/3})$ *parallel steps.*

The details of this Memory Organization Scheme and its explicit construction will be given in the full version of the paper.

3 Explicit Construction of an $(n, q, 1)$- BIBD

In this section, we present a direct method for constructing an $(n, q, 1)$-BIBD using elementary field theory. In fact, we will describe an explicit mapping to assign the copies of the m variables to the n memory modules and prove that it satisfies the properties of a BIBD. The construction can be shown to be equivalent to the one known in the literature based on affine spaces [Hal86]. For simplicity, we will assume that the number of variables is maximum, that is $m = n(n - 1)/(q(q - 1))$; trivial modifications yield a memory map for smaller m. As mentioned before, the construction requires that q, the number of copies per variable, be an odd prime power, and that $n = q^d$, for some integer d; therefore, $m = q^{d-1}(q^d - 1)/(q - 1)$.

Suppose that an arbitrary ordering has been fixed for the variables and the memory modules. Let v_i denote the ith variable, $0 \le i < m$, and u_j the jth module, $0 \le j < n$. Let $\mathbf{F}_q$, denote the field with q elements, with its elements represented by the integers $0, \ldots, q - 1$. Consider the set of d-dimensional vectors over $\mathbf{F}_q$

$$S(q, d) = \{(a_{d-1}, \ldots, a_1, a_0) : a_i \in \mathbf{F}_q\}.$$

These vectors can be regarded as the base q representation of the integers $\{0 \ldots n-1\}$.

The module u_j will be associated with the vector of $S(q, d)$ representing the integer j, $0 \le j < n$. The variable v_i will be associated with the pair $\langle s_1(i), s_2(i) \rangle$, where $s_1(i), s_2(i) \in S(q, d)$ are defined as follows. Let

$$i = \alpha_i \frac{q^d - 1}{q - 1} + \beta_i$$

with $0 \le \alpha_i < q^{d-1}$ and $0 \le \beta_i < (q^d - 1)/(q - 1)$. Let $(a_{d-2} \ldots a_1 a_0)$ be the representation of α_i in base q and k the unique integer such that

$$\frac{q^k - 1}{q - 1} \le \beta_i < \frac{q^{k+1} - 1}{q - 1},$$

$0 \le k < d - 1$. (Observe that $k = 0 \Leftrightarrow \beta_i = 0$.) For $k \ge 1$ we set

$$s_1(i) \stackrel{\Delta}{=} (a_{d-2}, \ldots, a_k, 0, a_{k-1}, \ldots, a_1, a_0) \in S(q, d)$$

and

$$s_2(i) \stackrel{\Delta}{=} (0, \ldots, 0, 1, b_{k-1}, \ldots, b_1, b_0) \in S(q, d)$$

where $(b_{k-1} \ldots b_1 b_0)$ is the representation of $\beta_i - (q^k - 1)/(q - 1)$ in base q. For $k = 0$, we consistently have $s_1(i) = (a_{d-2}, \ldots, a_0, 0)$ and $s_2(i) = (0, \ldots, 0, 1)$.

The assignment of the copies of v_i to q distinct memory modules and their location within each module can be established as follows. The jth copy of v_i will be assigned to module

$$(a_{d-2}, \ldots, a_k, j, a_{k-1} + jb_{k-1}, \ldots, a_1 + jb_1, a_0 + jb_0)$$

where all the operations are in $\mathbf{F}_q$. Also, each copy of v_i will be stored in the β_ith cell of its module. In the following lemma, we show that the above scheme is well defined.

Lemma 8.

1. The mappings $U \to S(q,d)$ and $V \to S(q,d) \times S(q,d)$ are one-to-one.
2. No two copies in the same module are assigned to the same location within the module.
3. Each modules receives $(q^d - 1)/(q - 1)$ copies of distinct variables.

Proof.

1. The mapping $U \to S(q,d)$ is clearly one-to-one. To show that the mapping $V \to S(q,d) \times S(q,d)$ is also one-to-one, consider two distinct variables $v_i, v_j \in V$. If $\beta_i \neq \beta_j$ then $s_2(i) \neq s_2(j)$ and we are done. Now suppose $\beta_i = \beta_j$. The value k will be the same for v_i and v_j; however, $i \neq j$ and $\beta_i = \beta_j$ imply $\alpha_i \neq \alpha_j$, hence $s_1(i) \neq s_1(j)$.
2. Suppose that for $i \neq j$ a copy of v_i and a copy of v_j are assigned to the same location in a given module. This implies that $\beta_i = \beta_j$, $s_2(i) = s_2(j)$ and that the value k is the same for v_i and v_j. Since the copies are in the same module, it is easy to see that also $\alpha_i = \alpha_j$. Therefore, $i = j$, which contradicts the hypothesis
3. This is easily implied by the previous property.

Note that the initial ordering of the variables is not necessarily maintained within each memory module; however, the scheme is consistent in the sense that each processor is able to determine the exact location of any copy.

Theorem 9. *The assignment of the copies to the memory modules described above has the structure of an $(n, q, 1)$-BIBD.*

Proof. We must only show that for any pair of modules there is exactly one variable with copies in both modules. In fact, it is sufficient to prove that no two variables share the same pair of modules. Let $u_1, u_2 \in U$ be two distinct modules storing copies of a variable $v \in V$. Let v be represented by the pair

$$\langle (a_{d-2}, \ldots, a_k, 0, a_{k-1}, \ldots, a_0), (0, \ldots, 0, 1, b_{k-1}, \ldots, b_0) \rangle$$

and let

$$u_1 = (a_{d-2}, \ldots, a_k, \delta, a_{k-1} + \delta b_{k-1}, \ldots, a_0 + \delta b_0)$$
$$u_2 = (a_{d-2}, \ldots, a_k, \gamma, a_{k-1} + \gamma b_{k-1}, \ldots, a_0 + \gamma b_0)$$

for $\delta, \gamma \in \mathbf{F}_q$, $\delta \neq \gamma$. Suppose another variable v' has copies assigned to both u_1 and u_2 and let v' be represented by the pair

$$\langle (a'_{d-2}, \ldots, a'_h, 0, a'_{h-1}, \ldots, a'_0), (0, \ldots, 0, 1, b'_{h-1}, \ldots, b'_0) \rangle$$

Then we must have

$$u_1 = (a'_{d-2}, \ldots, a'_h, \delta', a'_{h-1} + \delta' b'_{h-1}, \ldots, a'_0 + \delta' b'_0)$$
$$u_2 = (a'_{d-2}, \ldots, a'_h, \gamma', a'_{h-1} + \gamma' b'_{h-1}, \ldots, a'_0 + \gamma' b'_0)$$

for some $\delta' \neq \gamma'$. Observing the two representations for u_1 and u_2, we note that the first component from the left where they differ is the $(d-k)$th, in one case, and the $(d-h)$th in the other. This obviously implies $h = k$ and, therefore, $\gamma' = \gamma$, $\delta' = \delta$ and $a'_i = a_i$, for $k \leq i \leq d-2$. Also, for $0 \leq i \leq k-1$,

$$a_i + \delta b_i = a'_i + \delta b'_i$$
$$a_i + \gamma b_i = a'_i + \gamma b'_i$$

which, since $\delta \neq \gamma$, implies $a_i = a'_i$ and $b_i = b'_i$, $0 \leq i \leq k-1$; that is, $v = v'$.

The above scheme can be efficiently implemented. A processor is able to determine the physical location of any copy of a given variable by performing $O(d) = O(\log n)$ operations in $\mathbf{F}_q$. More importantly, only $O(1)$-size storage is required to represent the memory map, which makes the scheme very attractive from a practical standpoint.

4 The difficulty of testing good memory organization schemes

In order to study the performance of a Memory Organization Scheme that allocates m variables, each represented by q copies, within n memory modules, it is often necessary to answer the following question: given a set of at most n variables, what is the minimum number of modules spanned by their copies? One might think to resort to the bound proved independently by Tanner [Tan84] and Alon and Milman [AM85], which is the only known method to test such expansion properties. However, we show below that when $m \gg n$ this bound does not provide an accurate estimate. Therefore, most of the Memory Organization Schemes in the literature, based on existential proofs of bipartite graphs with certain expansion properties result impractical in the sense that, although randomly generated graphs are likely to have the desired properties, based on available knowledge, there seems to be no ways (except for an impractical enumeration) of testing such graphs.

Let the graph $G = (V, U; E)$ represent, as before, the distribution of the copies of m variables among the n memory modules, and assume that each node in V have degree $d_v = q$ (i.e., the number of copies per variable) and each node in U have degree $d_u = q(m/n)$ (i.e., the number of copies stored in each module). Let M be the $m \times n$ adjacency matrix of G and let $d_v d_u = \lambda_1 > \lambda_2 > \ldots > \lambda_d$ be the set of distinct eigenvalues of MM^T. Given a set S of at most n variables, the size of the set $\Gamma(S)$ of modules occupied by the copies of S is bound from below as follows [Tan84, AM85]

$$|\Gamma(S)| \geq |S| \frac{q^2}{\frac{|S|}{m}(\lambda_1 - \lambda_2) + \lambda_2} \tag{1}$$

The proof of (1) is based on two inequalities. Let A_S be the characteristic vector of S and let $C = A_S M$. We have

I1: $|\Gamma(S)| \geq \frac{(|S|q)^2}{\|C\|^2}$.

I2: $\|C\|^2 \leq |S|[(|S|/m)(\lambda_1 - \lambda_2) + \lambda_2]$

We show that, when $m \gg n$, either inequality can be grossly inaccurate. We first observe this fact on the BIBD analyzed in the previous sections, and then point to its generality. We need a technical fact (see [Hal86]).

Lemma 10. *Let G be an $(n, q, 1)$-BIBD. Then*

$$\lambda_2 = d_u - 1 = q(m/n) - 1$$

Let S be the all the variables storing one copy in a chosen memory module. Using the definition of an $(n, q, 1)$-BIBD, it can be shown that $|S| = q(m/n)$, $|\Gamma(S)| = n$ and that the vector C defined before has one entry equal to $q(m/n)$ and $n - 1$ entries equal to 1. Therefore

$$\|C\|^2 = (q(m/n))^2 + n - 1$$

For this case, Inequality I1 shows

$$|\Gamma(S)| \geq \frac{(q(m/n))^2 q^2}{(q(m/n))^2 + n - 1}$$

where the RHS is $\Theta(q^2)$ (i.e., $\Theta(1)$ if q is a constant). Instead, Inequality I2 shows

$$\|C\|^2 \leq q\frac{m}{n}\left(\frac{q}{n}(q^2(m/n) - q(m/n) + 1) + q(m/n)\right)$$

where the RHS is $\Theta((q(m/n))^2)$ if $q \in O(\sqrt{(n)})$ is a constant. Thus, in this example we note that I1 is very loose whereas I2 provides a tight bound. On the other hand, if we take $|S| = 1$ it is easily seen that I1 is tight (it actually becomes an equality), whereas I2 is loose.

Consider now any bipartite graph G describing the memory organization. Note that for a set of variables S, the entry c_j of the vector C represents the number of copies of variables in S stored in the jth module, $1 \leq j \leq n$. So c_j may take any value between 0 and d_u, which is a large range. It is not difficult to see that the accuracy of I1 (which is proven by using the Jensen's inequality) depends on the uniformity of C and, therefore, it might turn out very inaccurate when the entries of C take values within a large range, as the previous example showed. As for I2, we note that in the previous example the problem was created by λ_2 being large. Unfortunately, this is the case for any bipartite graph G with m inputs, $n \ll m$ outputs, input degree q and output degree $q(m/n)$. Let M be the adjacency matrix of such a graph. Basic linear algebra shows that 0 is an eigenvalue of MM^T with multiplicity at least $m - n$, so that there are at most n nonzero eigenvalue. Since the trace of MM^T is mq and, by the regularity of G, the largest eigenvalue is $q^2(m/n)$, the second largest eigenvalue λ_2 is such that

$$\lambda_2 \geq \frac{mq - q^2(m/n)}{n - 1}$$

Thus if $q \ll n$, $\lambda_2 \in \Theta(q(m/n))$. Since, the RHS of I2 is at least $|S|\lambda_2$, the fact that λ_2 is large weakens, in many cases, the upper bound to $\|C\|^2$. Also we have that the best estimate to $|\Gamma(s)|$ that (1) provides is of order $O(|S|q(n/m))$, whereas a probabilistic counting shows that there exist graphs where any set S of at most n/q variables is connected to $|\Gamma(S)| \geq |S|(q/b)$ modules for a suitable constant b [UW87] and $q \in O(\log m)$.

References

[AHMP87] H. Alt, T. Hagerup, K. Mehlhorn, and F.P. Preparata. Deterministic simulation of idealized parallel computers on more realistic ones. *SIAM J. on Computing*, 16(5):808–835, 1987.

[AM85] N. Alon and V. D. Milman. λ_1, isoperimetric inequalities for graphs and superconcentrators. *Journal of Combinatorial Theory Series* B, 38:73–88, 1985.

[Gif79] D.K. Gifford. Weighted voting for replicated data. *Proc. of the 7th ACM Symp. on Operating System Principles*, pages 150–159, 1979.

[Hal86] M. Hall Jr. *Combinatorial Theory*. John Wiley & Sons, New York NY, second edition, 1986.

[Her89] K.T. Herley. Efficient simulations of small shared memories on bounded degree networks. *Proc. of the 30th IEEE Symp. on Foundations of Comp. Sc.*, pages 390–395, 1989.

[Her90] K.T. Herley. Space-efficient representations of shared data for parallel computers. *Proc. of the 2nd ACM Symp. on Parallel Algorithms and Architectures*, pages 407–416, 1990.

[KU88] A.R. Karlin and E. Upfal. Parallel hashing: An efficient implementation of shared memory. *J. ACM*, 35(4):876–892, 1988.

[Kuc77] D.J. Kuck. A survey of parallel machine organization and programming. *ACM Computing Surveys*, 21:339–374, 1977.

[LPP88] F. Luccio, A. Pietracaprina, and G. Pucci. A probabilistic simulation of PRAMs in VLSI. *Information Processing Lett.*, 28(3):141–147, 1988.

[LPP90] F. Luccio, A. Pietracaprina, and G. Pucci. A new scheme for the deterministic simulation of PRAMs in VLSI. *Algorithmica*, 5:529–544, 1990.

[MV84] K. Mehlhorn and U. Vishkin. Randomized and deterministic simulations of prams by parallel machines with restricted granularity of parallel memories. *Acta Informatica*, 9(1):29–59, 1984.

[Ran91] A.G. Ranade. How to emulate shared memory. *J. on Computers and System Sci.*, 42:307–326, 1991.

[Tan84] R.M. Tanner. Explicit concentrators from generalized n-gons. *SIAM J. on Algebraic Discrete Methods*, 5(3):287–293, 1984.

[UW87] E. Upfal and A. Widgerson. How to share memory in a distributed system. *J. ACM*, 34(1):116–127, 1987.

The Synthesis Problem of Petri Nets [1]

Jörg Desel and Wolfgang Reisig

Institut für Informatik, Technische Universität München, Arcisstr.21, D-8000 München 2

Abstract. The problem of deriving concurrent operational models from sequentially observed behaviour is solved for elementary Petri nets. Labelled directed graphs are used to represent behaviour. A new characterization of graphs representing the behaviour of some elementary Petri net is given. It is shown how the set of all nets exhibiting the behaviour given by a graph can be constructed and that, if this set is not empty, it contains a net with a polynomial number of elements in the size of the graph.

1 Introduction

The synthesis problem of concurrent systems is the problem of synthesizing a concurrent system from sequential observations. This problem has been attacked for various different system models, including parallel programs [5], COSY-expressions [3], and Petri Nets [4,2,6].

In this paper, we consider a very general representation of sequential observations, i.e. transition systems (finite, directed, arc labelled graphs), and a "fitting" system model, i.e. elementary Petri nets. For this setting, a basic solution of the synthesis problem has been suggested in [2], employing the theory of 2-structures. To be more specific, necessary and sufficient conditions are given to decide whether, to a given transition system, there exists an elementary Petri net, such that the graph constructed from this net's states and state transitions is isomorphic to the transition system. For each accepted transition system, a corresponding Petri net is constructed.

We adopt the core idea of "regions" from [2]. But we hope to have found more convenient proofs and results. Particularly it turns out that, in [2], the decision criteria for graphs to represent abstract state spaces of Petri nets are partly redundant. More important, the obtained nets are in general large (exponential in the size of the transition system) and not too intuitive. Therefore, we strive at constructing "smaller" solutions. It turns out that there exists, if any solution, then a solution which is polynomial in the size of the transition system. We show how to obtain directly *all* solutions. Finally, all results can adequately be proven without the machinery of 2-structures. This paper nevertheless strongly bases on [2] and may be considered as an extension of their work.

The problem to decide if a graph is isomorphic to some transition system generated by a Petri net was first solved in [4] for place/transition Petri nets (a generalization of elementary Petri nets). In [6], the results of [2] are generalized to place/transition Petri nets. Using concepts of category theory, it is particularly investigated in [6] whether a given (infinite) graph represents the behaviour of some finite Petri net.

Sections 2 and 3 provide the (few) standard notations on graphs and elementary net systems, to be employed in the sequel. Section 4 gives the basic solution of the synthesis problem. The systems considered in Section 4 are in general large and unhandy. On our way to avoid their construction, we consider *all* solutions of the synthesis problem in Section 5. The paper ends with concluding remarks in Section 6.

---
[1] Work supported by SFB 342 WG A3: SEMAFOR and ESPRIT WG 6067: CALIBAN

2 Directed, Arc Labelled, Initialized Graphs

Sequential system observation, consisting in global state occurrences and state transitions is conveniently described by help of *transition systems*. A transition system can formally be represented as a directed graph with labelled arcs. As different state transitions may be caused by equal events, different arcs may be labelled by equal symbols. The initial state is identified by a distinguished "initial" node.

2.1 Definition Let K and L be finite disjoint sets, let $G \subseteq K \times L \times K$, and let $k_0 \in K$. Then $\mathcal{G} = (K, L, G, k_0)$ is a *finite, directed, arc labelled, initialized graph*. K and L are the sets of *nodes* and *labels* of $\mathcal{G}$, respectively. Each $(h, l, k) \in G$ is an *arc of* $\mathcal{G}$. The node k_0 is the *initial node* of $\mathcal{G}$. A node k is *reachable* iff there exists a sequence $(k_0, l_1, k_1), (k_1, l_2, k_2) \ldots (k_{n-1}, l_n, k_n)$ of arcs such that $k_n = k$.

In this paper, the term "graph" always denotes a finite, directed, arc labelled, initialized graph with every node being reachable. We employ the usual graphical conventions for graphs, indicating the initial node by an extra arc without source.

2.2 Example

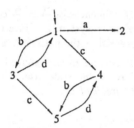

This graph has nodes $1, \ldots, 5$ and labels $a, \ldots, d$. Its initial node is 1.

2.3 Definition Let $\mathcal{G} = (K, L, G, k_0)$ and $\mathcal{G}' = (K', L', G', k_0')$ be graphs. A bijection $f : K \to K'$ is an *isomorphism* from $\mathcal{G}$ to $\mathcal{G}'$ (written $f : \mathcal{G} \to \mathcal{G}'$) iff $f(k_0) = k_0'$ and $(h, l, k) \in G$ iff $(f(h), l, f(k)) \in G'$. We call two graphs $\mathcal{G}$ and $\mathcal{G}'$ *isomorphic* (written $\mathcal{G} \simeq \mathcal{G}'$) iff there exists an isomorphism $f : \mathcal{G} \to \mathcal{G}'$.

2.4 Proposition $\simeq$ *is an equivalence relation on graphs.*

3 Elementary Net Systems

We recall the basic definition of the fundamental class of Petri nets, usually called *elementary net systems* [7]. We only consider elementary net systems with finitely many conditions and events.

3.1 Definition Let B and E be finite disjoint sets, let $F \subseteq (B \times E) \cup (E \times B)$, and let $c_0 \subseteq B$. Then $\Sigma = (B, E, F, c_0)$ is called *elementary net system* (en-system, for short). The elements of B and E are called *conditions* and *events*, respectively. F is the *flow relation* and c_0 is the *initial state*. For $x \in B \cup E$, we denote the *pre-set* $\{y \mid (y, x) \in F\}$ of x by ${}^\bullet x$ and the *post-set* $\{y \mid (x, y) \in F\}$ of x by $x^\bullet$.

We employ the usual graphical representation for en-systems: Circles and squares denote conditions and events. The flow relation is denoted by arrows. The elements of the initial state are distinguished by a *token* (a dot) in the corresponding circle.

3.2 Example

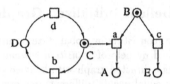

This en-system has conditions $A,\ldots,E$ and events $a,\ldots,d$. Its initial state is $\{B,C\}$.

3.3 Definition Let $\Sigma = (B, E, F, c_0)$ be an en-system, let $c, d \subseteq B$, and let $e \in E$.

    i. c *enables* e iff $\,^{\bullet}e \subseteq c$ and $e^{\bullet} \cap c = \emptyset$.

    ii. (c, e, d) is a *state transition* (written $c \xrightarrow{e} d$) iff c enables e and $d = (c \setminus {}^{\bullet}e) \cup e^{\bullet}$.

    iii. A set $c \subseteq B$ is a *reachable state* iff either $c = c_0$ or there exist state transitions $c_0 \xrightarrow{e_1} c_1 \xrightarrow{e_2} \cdots \xrightarrow{e_r} c_r$ such that $c_r = c$.

    iv. A state transition $c \xrightarrow{e} d$ is called *reachable* iff c is a reachable state.

3.4 Example The initial state in 3.2 enables the events a, b and c. The corresponding state transitions are: $\{B,C\} \xrightarrow{a} \{A\}$, $\{B,C\} \xrightarrow{b} \{B,D\}$ and $\{B,C\} \xrightarrow{c} \{C,E\}$. $\{D, E\}$ is a reachable state and $\{D, E\} \xrightarrow{d} \{C, E\}$ is a reachable state transition.

Starting with the initial state c_0, sequences $c_0 \xrightarrow{e_1} c_1 \xrightarrow{e_2} c_2 \xrightarrow{e_3} \cdots$ of state transitions form the sequential behaviour of an en-system Σ. Since the set of conditions of Σ is finite, they can finitely be represented as the paths in a graph, the *state graph* of Σ.

3.5 Definition Let $\Sigma = (B, E, F, c_0)$ be an en-system, let C be the set of reachable states and let G be the set of reachable state transitions of Σ. Then the graph $sg(\Sigma) = (C, E, G, c_0)$ is the *state graph of* Σ.

3.6 Example

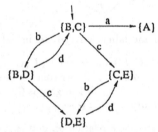

The state graph of the en-system in 3.2

3.7 Definition A graph $\mathcal{G}$ is an *abstract state graph* iff there exists an en-system Σ such that $\mathcal{G} \simeq sg(\Sigma)$.

3.8 Examples

    i. The state graph of the en-system in 3.2, shown in 3.6, is isomorphic to the graph in 2.2. Hence, the graph in 2.2 is an abstract state graph.

    ii. There is no en-system with a state graph isomorphic to

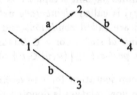

(this will later be proven). Hence, this graph is not an abstract state graph.

The central issue of this paper can now be stated as follows:

The Synthesis Problem: *Is a given graph G an abstract state graph?*
If yes, construct some ("small") en-system Σ satisfying $G \simeq sg(\Sigma)$.

3.9 Definition An en-system is called *reduced* iff every event occurs in a reachable state transition and, for each two distinct conditions b and b', there exists a reachable state c satisfying either $b \in c$ and $b' \notin c$, or $b' \in c$ and $b \notin c$.

All en-systems used in examples of this paper are reduced.

Events which do not occur in any state transition do no affect the behaviour of an en-system and can hence be removed without changing the state graph. In an en-system without such "useless events", two conditions which agree on all reachable states have identical pre-sets, post-sets and initial tokens. Therefore, removing one of it yields an en-system with an isomorphic state graph. Since this transformation can be done for each pair of "equivalent conditions", and since there are only finitely many conditions, we get

3.10 Proposition *For every en-system Σ, there exists a reduced en-system Σ' such that $sg(\Sigma) \simeq sg(\Sigma')$.*

4 The Basic Solution of the Synthesis Problem

In this section, we develop a procedure to decide whether or not a given graph G is an abstract state graph. In the positive case, the procedure provides an en-system with a state graph isomorphic to G.

First, we motivate the notion of "regions", which is one of the essential concepts of this paper. Consider an abstract state graph G. Then G is isomorphic to the state graph of some en-system Σ. So assume w.l.o.g. that the nodes of G are the reachable states of Σ and that every label of G is an event of Σ. Let b be a condition of Σ and let R_b the set of reachable states of Σ which contain b. Every event e of Σ is related to b in exactly one of four manners: 1. $b \in {}^\bullet e$ and $b \notin e^\bullet$, 2. $b \notin {}^\bullet e$ and $b \in e^\bullet$, 3. $b \notin {}^\bullet e$ and $b \notin e^\bullet$ or 4. $b \in {}^\bullet e$ and $b \in e^\bullet$. According to 3.3(i), this implies, for the set of nodes R_b of G, one of the following alternatives: In case 1, all source nodes and no target node of e-labelled arcs belong to R_b. In case 2, no source node, but all target nodes of e-labelled arcs belong to R_b. In case 3, each e-labelled arc has either both its source- and target-node in R_b, or none of them. Finally, in the 4th case, e belongs to no state transition of Σ and, hence, there exists no e-labelled arc. A set R of nodes enjoying these properties for every event e is called a *region* of G.

4.1 Definition Let G be a graph. A set R of nodes of G is a *region* of G iff for equally labelled arcs (h, l, k) and (h', l, k'):

If $h \in R$ and $k \notin R$ then $h' \in R$ and $k' \notin R$, and
if $h \notin R$ and $k \in R$ then $h' \notin R$ and $k' \in R$.

$\emptyset$ and K are called *trivial regions* of G. $reg(G)$ denotes the set of all regions of G.

4.2 Examples

i. The graph in 2.2 has 10 nontrivial regions: A = {2}, B = {1,3}, C = {1,4}, D = {3,5}, E = {4,5}, F = {1,3,4,5}, G = {2,4,5}, H = {2,3,5}, I = {1,2,4} and J = {1,2,3}. Some of them are outlined in the following figure:

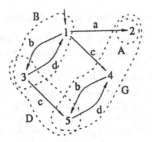

ii. The graph in 3.8(ii) has 4 nontrivial regions: $A = \{1,2\}, B = \{1,3\}, C = \{2,4\}$ and $D = \{3,4\}$.

The essential of a region is the uniform treatment of equally labelled arcs: Given a region R and an arc label l, either all l-labelled arcs "enter" R or all l-labelled arcs "leave" R, or l does not touch R. This motivates the following definition.

4.3 Definition Let l be a label of a graph $\mathcal{G}$. The *pre-set* $^{\rightharpoonup}l$ and the *post-set* $l^{\rightharpoonup}$ of l are the sets of regions of $\mathcal{G}$ satisfying

$$R \in {}^{\rightharpoonup}l \text{ iff for all arcs } (h,l,k) \text{ of } \mathcal{G}, h \in R \text{ and } k \notin R, \text{ and}$$
$$R \in l^{\rightharpoonup} \text{ iff for all arcs } (h,l,k) \text{ of } \mathcal{G}, h \notin R \text{ and } k \in R.$$

4.4 Example For the graph in 2.2 and the notions of 4.2(i) we have $^{\rightharpoonup}c = \{B,J\}$ and $c^{\rightharpoonup} = \{E,G\}$.

The following propositions state that there is a close relation between conditions of en-systems and regions of their state graphs. The proofs are straightforward and therefore omited.

4.5 Proposition *Let Σ be an en-system and let b be a condition of Σ. Let R_b be the set of reachable states c of Σ satisfying $b \in c$. Then R_b is a region of $sg(\Sigma)$.*

Conversely, a region does not necessarily correspond to an existing condition, but to a "potential" condition. Adding this condition to the en-system preserves the behaviour, i.e. the augmented en-system has an isomorphic state graph.

4.6 Definition Let $\Sigma = (B,E,F,c_0)$ be an en-system and let R be a region of $sg(\Sigma)$. Let b_R be a new condition, $b_R \notin B \cup E$. Define the en-system $\Sigma^{+R} = (B',E',F',c_0')$ by $B' = B \cup \{b_R\}$, $E' = E$, $F' = F \cup \{(b_R,e) \mid R \in {}^{\rightharpoonup}e\} \cup \{(e,b_R) \mid R \in e^{\rightharpoonup}\}$, $c_0' = c_0 \cup \{b_R\}$ if $c_0 \in R$ and $c_0' = c_0$ if $c_0 \notin R$.

4.7 Proposition *Let Σ be an en-system and let R be a region of $sg(\Sigma)$. Then $sg(\Sigma) \simeq sg(\Sigma^{+R})$.*

Since every condition corresponds to a region, and every region generates a potential condition, we can construct en-systems from graphs, using only generated conditions.

4.8 Definition Let $\mathcal{G} = (K,L,G,k_0)$ be a graph and let m be a set of regions of $\mathcal{G}$. Then the *m-generated en-system* is $sy(\mathcal{G},m) = (m,L,F,c_0)$, where, for each $R \in m$ and each $l \in L$, $(R,l) \in F$ iff $R \in {}^{\rightharpoonup}l$, $(l,R) \in F$ iff $R \in l^{\rightharpoonup}$, and $R \in c_0$ iff $k_0 \in R$.

4.9 Examples

i. The graph in 2.2 with the regions A,...,J mentioned in 4.2(i) generates the en-system

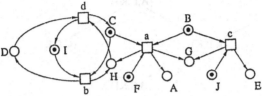

ii. The graph in 3.8(ii) with the regions A,...,D mentioned in 4.2(ii), generates the en-system

$$B \odot\!\!-\!\!\!\!\raisebox{0pt}{$\square$}\!\!-\!\!\!\rightarrow\!\! \bigcirc C$$

$$A \odot\!\!-\!\!\!\!\raisebox{0pt}{$\square$}\!\!-\!\!\!\rightarrow\!\! \bigcirc D$$
$$b$$

In the rest of this section, we consider en-systems generated by *all* regions of a graph. The basic solution of the synthesis problem can now be stated as follows:

4.10 Theorem *A graph $\mathcal{G}$ is an abstract state graph iff $\mathcal{G} \simeq sg(sy(\mathcal{G}, reg(\mathcal{G})))$.*

Proof: If $\mathcal{G} \simeq sg(sy(\mathcal{G}, reg(\mathcal{G})))$ then $\mathcal{G}$ is an abstract state graph by definition.

Let, conversely, $\mathcal{G}$ be an abstract state graph. By 3.10, $\mathcal{G} \simeq sg(\Sigma)$ for some reduced en-system Σ. Since Σ is reduced, there exists for each region R of $sg(\Sigma)$ at most one condition b which belongs exactly to the states of R. If there is a region R of $sg(\Sigma)$ with no corresponding condition, then the addition of such a condition to Σ yields the system Σ^{+R}. By 4.7, Σ and Σ^{+R} have isomorphic state graphs. Let Σ' be an en-system which is obtained by exhaustive repetition of this transformation. Then $sg(\Sigma) \simeq sg(\Sigma')$ and, for every region of $sg(\Sigma)$, there is exactly one corresponding condition of Σ' and vice versa. Hence, Σ' equals the en-system $sy(\mathcal{G}, reg(\mathcal{G}))$, up to the names of conditions. In particular, both en-systems have isomorphic state graphs. Hence $\mathcal{G} \simeq sg(\Sigma) \simeq sg(\Sigma') \simeq sg(sy(\mathcal{G}, reg(\mathcal{G})))$.

4.11 Examples

i. The graph $\mathcal{G}$ in 2.2 is an abstract state graph. The state graph of $sy(\mathcal{G}, reg(\mathcal{G}))$ is shown below (using the notions of 4.2(i) and $K = \{1, 2, 3, 4, 5\}$). It is isomorphic to $\mathcal{G}$.

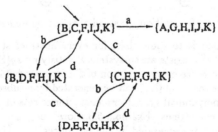

ii. The graph $\mathcal{G}$ in 3.8(ii) is not an abstract state graph. The state graph of $sy(\mathcal{G}, reg(\mathcal{G}))$ is shown below (using the notions of 4.2(ii) and $K = \{1,2,3,4\}$). It is not isomorphic to $\mathcal{G}$.

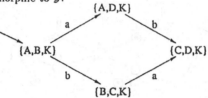

5 The General Solution of the Synthesis Problem

Theorem 4.10 provides a decision procedure as well as (together with Definition 4.8) a constructive solution of the synthesis problem. This way, a distinguished system $sy(\mathcal{G}, reg(\mathcal{G}))$ is assigned to each abstract state graph $\mathcal{G}$. This system is reduced in the sense of Definition 3.9. However, the number of its conditions can grow exponentially with the number of nodes of $\mathcal{G}$. Consider the following example:

5.1 Example

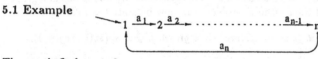

The graph $\mathcal{G}_n$ for $n \geq 2$

Since, in 5.1, no label occurs more than once, every subset of nodes is a region of the graph. Hence, the number of regions grows exponentially with the number of nodes. The same holds for the number of conditions of the system generated by all regions:

5.2 Example

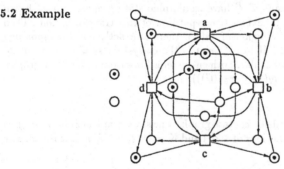

$sy(\mathcal{G}_4, reg(\mathcal{G}_4))$ has $2^4 = 16$ conditions (instead of $a_1, \ldots, a_4$ we use the labels $a, \ldots, d$).

The aim of this section is to show that, for every abstract state graph $\mathcal{G}$ with n nodes and m labels, there exists an en-system Σ satisfying $sg(\Sigma) \simeq \mathcal{G}$ with at most $n \cdot (n + m)$ conditions. Since every condition of Σ corresponds to a region of its state graph and, hence, to a region of $\mathcal{G}$, Σ can be generated by a subset of regions of $\mathcal{G}$. In order to achieve the polynomial growth, we characterize sets of regions which suffice to construct suitable en-systems. Example 5.3 shows such en-systems for the graph $\mathcal{G}_4$, defined in 5.1. They are generated by the sets of regions $\{\{1\}, \{2\}, \{3\}, \{4\}\}$ and $\{\{1,3\}, \{2,3\}, \{3,4\}\}$, respectively.

5.3 Example

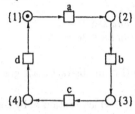 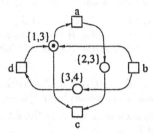

Somewhat surprising, a set m of three (of the sixteen) regions suffices to construct an en-system $sy(\mathcal{G}_4, m)$ satisfying $sg(sy(\mathcal{G}_4, m)) \simeq sg(sy(\mathcal{G}_4, reg(\mathcal{G})))$ (where, in this case, by Theorem 4.10, $sg(sy(\mathcal{G}_4, reg(\mathcal{G}))) \simeq \mathcal{G}$ since $\mathcal{G}$ is an abstract state graph). Of course, not every subset of regions has this property. So, we distinguish:

5.4 Definition Let $\mathcal{G}$ be a graph and let $m \subseteq reg(\mathcal{G})$. m is called *admissible* iff $sy(\mathcal{G}, reg(\mathcal{G}))$ and $sy(\mathcal{G}, m)$ have isomorphic state graphs.

5.5 Example Let $\mathcal{G}_4$ be as in 5.1. The sets $m_1 = \{\{1\}, \{2\}, \{3\}, \{4\}\}$ and $m_2 = \{\{1,3\}, \{2,3\}, \{3,4\}\}$ are admissible. No proper subsets of these sets are admissible.

The set of conditions of an en-system corresponds to an admissible set of regions of its state graph. Conversely, for each reduced en-system, its conditions are generated by an admissible set of regions:

5.6 Theorem *Let $\mathcal{G}$ be an abstract state graph. A reduced en-system Σ satisfies $\mathcal{G} \simeq sg(\Sigma)$ iff there exists an admissible set $m \subseteq reg(\Sigma)$ such that Σ equals $sy(\mathcal{G}, m)$ up to renaming of places.*

Proof:
($\Rightarrow$): Every condition of Σ corresponds to a region of $sg(\Sigma)$ and, hence, to a region of $\mathcal{G}$, by 4.5. Let m be the set of regions which correspond to conditions of Σ. Then, for every $R \in m$, there exists at least one condition b corresponding to R. There exists at most one such condition b, since Σ is reduced. Again since Σ is reduced, every event of Σ occurs in some reachable state transition. Therefore, and by construction of $sy(\mathcal{G}, m)$, $^\bullet b$ in Σ equals $^\bullet R$ in $sy(\mathcal{G}, m)$ and the same holds for the post-sets. b belongs to the initial state of Σ iff the initial state is in the corresponding region R_b iff R_b belongs to the initial state of $sy(\mathcal{G}, m)$. Hence, Σ and $sy(\mathcal{G}, m)$ coincide up to renaming of places.

 m is admissible since $sg(\Sigma) \simeq sg(sy(\mathcal{G}, reg(\mathcal{G})))$ by 4.10 and $sg(\Sigma) \simeq sg(sy(\mathcal{G}, m))$ by the above.
($\Leftarrow$) follows from 5.4 and 4.10.

This result gives a "complete" picture of all solutions of the synthesis problem. It implies that each reduced en-system is entirely (up to renaming of places) characterized by an admissible set of regions of an abstract state graph.

 Now let us return to our original task: How can we find "small solutions" of the synthesis problem? The key to that problem is the following characterization of admissible sets:

5.7 Theorem *Let $\mathcal{G}$ be an abstract state graph. A set $m \subseteq reg(\mathcal{G})$ is admissible iff for each two different nodes h, k of $\mathcal{G}$, there exists a region $R \in m$ satisfying*
 (a) $h \in R$ *and* $k \notin R$ *or* (b) $h \notin R$ *and* $k \in R$,

and, for every node k and every label l, at least one of the following conditions is true:

(c) *there exists an arc (k, l, k') of $\mathcal{G}$ for some node k',*
(d) *there exists a region $R \in m$ satisfying $R \in {}^{-\!}l$ and $k \notin R$,*
(e) *there exists a region $R \in m$ satisfying $R \in l^{-}$ and $k \in R$.*

Proof:

Define $\Sigma = sy(\mathcal{G}, reg(\mathcal{G}))$ and $\Sigma' = sy(\mathcal{G}, m)$. Since $\mathcal{G}$ is an abstract state graph, and by 4.10, there is an isomorphism $f: \mathcal{G} \to sg(\Sigma)$.

(i) f maps each node k of $\mathcal{G}$ to the set of regions of $\mathcal{G}$ which contain k, by construction of Σ.

(ii) Let c_0 be the initial state of Σ. Then $c_0 \cap m$ is the initial state of Σ', by construction of Σ and Σ'.

(iii) Let $c \xrightarrow{e} d$ be a state transition of Σ. We show that $(c \cap m) \xrightarrow{e} (d \cap m)$ is a state transition of Σ'.
The pre-set of e in Σ' equals the intersection of m and the pre-set of e in Σ. For the post-set of e we get the corresponding property. Hence, $c \cap m$ enables e in Σ' and the occurrence of e yields $d \cap m$.

(iv) Let $c \xrightarrow{e} d$ be a reachable state transition of Σ. Then $(c \cap m) \xrightarrow{e} (d \cap m)$ is a reachable state transition of Σ'.
This follows inductively from (ii) and (iii).

($\Rightarrow$): Since m is admissible, there is an isomorphism $g: sg(\Sigma) \to sg(\Sigma')$. By (ii) and (iv), each node c of $sg(\Sigma)$ is mapped to $c \cap m$. Let h and k be two different nodes of $\mathcal{G}$. Since f is bijective, $f(h) \neq f(k)$. Since g is bijective, $g(f(h)) \neq g(f(k))$ and, hence, $(f(h) \cap m) \neq (f(k) \cap m)$. Therefore, by definition of f, at least one region of m contains h but not k or k but not h. So either (a) or (b) holds.
Let k be a node and let l be a label of $\mathcal{G}$ such that (d) and (e) do not hold for k and l. Then $g(f(k))$ is a reachable state of Σ', l is an event of Σ', every condition in ${}^\bullet l$ belongs to $g(f(k))$ (since (d) does not hold) and no condition in $l^\bullet$ belongs to $g(f(k))$ (since (e) does not hold). Hence, $g(f(k))$ enables l in Σ'. As $\mathcal{G}$ is an abstract state graph and m is admissible, we have $\mathcal{G} \simeq sg(\Sigma')$. Thus (c) does hold.
($\Leftarrow$): We prove that $g: sg(\Sigma) \to sg(\Sigma')$, defined by $f(c) = c \cap m$ for every reachable state c of Σ, is an isomorphism.
By (ii) and (iv), g is surjective. g is injective since, by (a) or (b), for each two different nodes $f(h)$ and $f(k)$ of $sg(\Sigma)$, there is a region of m which is contained in exactly one of these nodes and, hence, $g(f(h)) \neq g(f(k))$. By (ii), g maps the initial node of $sg(\Sigma)$ to the initial node of $sg(\Sigma')$.
Let (c, e, d) be an arc of $sg(\Sigma)$. By (iv), $(g(c), e, g(d))$ is an arc of $sg(\Sigma')$.
Let conversely $(g(c), e, g(d))$ be an arc of $sg(\Sigma')$. Let $c = f(k)$. Neither (d) nor (e) holds for k and e since $g(c)$ enables e in Σ'. Hence, (c) holds for k and e. So, there exists an e-labelled arc leaving k in $\mathcal{G}$ and, by $\mathcal{G} \simeq sg(\Sigma)$, there exists an arc (c, e, d') in $sg(\Sigma)$. By (iv), there exists an arc $(g(c), e, g(d'))$ in $sg(\Sigma')$. Thus $g(c) \xrightarrow{e} g(d)$ and $g(c) \xrightarrow{e} g(d')$ are state transitions of Σ'. Since the resulting state of a state transition is uniquely determined by the current state and the occurring event, we obtain $g(d) = g(d')$. Since g is bijective, $d = d'$. Hence, (c, e, d) is an arc of $sg(\Sigma)$.

5.8 Corollary *For every abstract state graph $\mathcal{G} = (K, L, G, k_0)$, there exists an en-system Σ satisfying $\mathcal{G} \simeq sg(\Sigma)$ with at most $|K| \cdot (|K| - 1) + |K| \cdot |L| - |G|$ conditions. An upper bound of this value is $|K| \cdot (|K| + |L|)$.*

6 Conclusion

The synthesis problem of concurrent systems has been completely solved in this paper, for the case of taking elementary net systems as concurrent system model. We have given a necessary and sufficient condition for the existence of a solution. We proved that, in the positive case, their exists a *small* solution, which is polynomial in the size of the given graph.

Sequential observations have been described in a very general form, i.e. as transition systems. Among concurrent system models corresponding to transition systems, elementary net systems appear a canonical candidate: No other model solves the synthesis problem likewise neatly.

The concept of regions of graphs has been introduced in [2], and the synthesis problem has been taken there as one application for regions. Abstract state graphs (there called "abstract sequential case graphs") are characterized by a number of requirements, including (in our terminology) isomorphism of $\mathcal{G}$ and $sg(sy(\mathcal{G}, reg(\mathcal{G})))$. Theorem 4.10 shows that this condition is sufficient. It is suggested in [2] first to decide whether or not a graph $\mathcal{G}$ is an abstract state graph, and (in case $\mathcal{G}$ is) then to construct $sy(\mathcal{G}, reg(\mathcal{G}))$. The given procedure to decide whether or not $\mathcal{G}$ is an abstract state graph includes already (up to technicalities) the construction of $sg(sy(\mathcal{G}, reg(\mathcal{G})))$. Therefore, we suggest first to construct $sy(\mathcal{G}, reg(\mathcal{G}))$ and then to decide, by constructing an isomorphism $f : \mathcal{G} \rightarrow sg(sy(\mathcal{G}, reg(\mathcal{G})))$, whether or not $\mathcal{G}$ is an abstract state graph. The construction of this isomorphism is simple, because there exists at most one (which assigns each node k of $\mathcal{G}$ to the set of regions which contain k). 2-structures, employed in [2], have their own merits. But we consider it advantageous to avoid them in handling the synthesis problem. Furthermore, it is not necessary to exclude different events with equal pre- and post-sets, as done in [2].

The present paper is a short version of [1]. There, we consider moreover the construction of small en-systems for a given graph. For that purpose, *redundant* conditions of elementary net systems are defined, which can be removed without affecting the state graph (up to isomorphism). Using the characterization of admissible sets of regions given by Theorem 5.7, we prove a series of sufficient conditions for redundancy.

References

[1] J. Desel, W. Reisig: *The Synthesis Problem of Petri Nets.* Technische Universität München, SFB-Bericht 342/20/92 A (1992)

[2] A. Ehrenfeucht, G. Rozenberg: *Partial (Set) 2-Structures. Part I, II.* Acta Informatica 27, pp. 315–368 (1990)

[3] R. Janicki: *Transforming Sequential Systems into Concurrent Systems.* Theoretical Computer Science 36, pp. 27–58 (1985)

[4] B. Krieg: *Petrinetze und Zustandsgraphen.* Institut für Informatik, Universität Hamburg, IFI-Bericht B-29/77 (1977)

[5] C. Lengauer, E.C.R. Hehner: *A methodology for programming with concurrency: An informal presentation.* Science of Computer Programming 2, pp. 1–18 (1982)

[6] M. Mukund: *A transition system characterization of Petri nets.* SPIC science foundation, school of mathematics, Madras, internal report TCS-91-2 (1991)

[7] P.S. Thiagarajan: *Elementary Net Systems.* Advances in Petri Nets 1986, Part I, Lecture Notes in Computer Science 254, Springer-Verlag, pp. 26–59 (1987)

General Refinement and Recursion Operators for the Petri Box Calculus[1]

Eike Best[2], Raymond Devillers[3] and Javier Esparza[2]

Abstract

New generalised definitions are given for the refinement and recursion operators in the calculus of Petri Boxes. It is shown that not only recursion, but also other operators such as sequence, choice and iteration can be viewed as based on refinement. Various structural properties of these operators can be deduced from a general property of (simultaneous) refinement. A partial order based denotational approach for recursion is presented, which yields a unique fixpoint even in unguarded cases. The construction is based on a judicious naming discipline for places and transitions and yields a closed form for the fixpoint.

1 Introduction

This work is pertinent to a large body of recent work on giving Petri net semantics of existing process calculi such as CCS [12], CSP [11] or ACP [1] (to wit, for instance, [5, 6, 7, 8, 13, 14]). The Petri Box Calculus PBC [3], which has been developed in the Esprit Basic Research Action DEMON (Design Methods Based on Nets), is a blend which is partially derived from the existing calculi and is partially novel. The PBC was designed to satisfy two requirements. Firstly, it should be firmly based on a Petri net semantics, and secondly, it should be oriented towards easing the compositional definition of the semantics of various concurrent programming languages such as occam (including all data aspects, as has been discussed and shown in [10]). The process calculus which the PBC resembles most closely is Milner's CCS. However, there are some essential differences: the PBC features a different synchronisation operator and a refinement operator not present in CCS; the PBC is not prefix-driven but, on the contrary, treats entry and exit point of processes symmetrically; as a consequence, the sequence operator is basic and the recursion operator is more general and not limited to tail-end recursion.

The aim of the work presented in this paper is to consolidate, generalise and unify the definition of some of the operators of the calculus. In particular, we define refinement and recursion in general, while there have been limitations in [3] and in other previous work on refinement such as [9]. We introduce (informally) the notions of the PBC we need, as we go along.

---

[1]Work done within the Esprit Basic Research Working Group 6067 **CALIBAN** (CAusal calcuLI BAsed on Nets).

[2]Institut für Informatik, Universität Hildesheim, Germany.

[3]Laboratoire d'Informatique Théorique, Université Libre de Bruxelles, Belgium.

Petri Boxes, or Boxes for short, with the generic names B, are based on the notion of labelled Petri nets, with the generic names $\Sigma = (S, T, W, \lambda)$, where S, T and W are places, transitions and arc weights (as usual) and λ is a labelling of both places and transitions. The labels for the places may be: e (entry places, where tokens may enter the net), x (exit places, from where tokens may leave the net) and $\emptyset$ (internal places); the transition labels may be *action* labels (finite multisets of elementary actions, although the multiset aspect is not relevant for this paper) or *hierarchical* labels (of the form X, where X is a variable name). The nets are unmarked but the e-places define a natural initial marking (one token on each e-place and no tokens elsewhere), and the x-places a natural terminating marking (one token on each x-place and no tokens elsewhere), thus allowing to speak about the behaviour of a net. Labelled nets must fulfill some contraints:

- each transition has input and output places;

- there are entry and exit places;

- there are no arcs to entry places or from exit places.

Boxes are equivalence classes of labelled nets. The equivalence allows to change the names or identities of the nodes (and to add/drop duplicate places and action-transitions, but this feature is not relevant for the present paper). We will mainly be concerned with definitions of operations on Boxes. All these definitions follow the same general scheme: Suitable representatives of the operands are chosen; the operation is defined on these representatives; and the resulting equivalence class is formed (showing also that it does not depend on the initial choice of representatives[4]). The two Box operations we are concerned with in this paper are, in their simplest form, *refinement*: $B[X \leftarrow B']$, meaning "B, where all X-labelled transitions are refined into B'", and *recursion*: $\mu X.B$, meaning "B, where each X-labelled transition t leads to a recursive execution of B".

The proofs of all propositions, including those of representative independence, can be found in the long version [2] of this paper.

2 A general refinement operator

The difficulty in defining a refinement operator arises from the generality we want, in particular from the possible distributed input (many e's) and output (many x's) of the refining nets, from the possible complexity of the connections between the transitions to be refined and their surrounding places (allowing for instance side loops), and from the possible multitude of X-labelled transitions (including the case of there being infinitely many).

---

[4]This representative independence allows us to be somewhat imprecise in the following, for instance referring to the transitions of a Box but meaning the transitions of an arbitrary representative.

The construction we present generalises the ones of [3, 9] and gives an explicit closed form of the result. It works in the presence of side loops, and also if there are infinitely many transitions to be refined (we do not want to exclude this case since some operators - in particular, recursion - may generate infinite nets). Moreover, the new construction allows simultaneous refinements: $B[X_i \leftarrow B_i | i \in I]$, meaning "refine all X_i-labelled transitions by their respective B_i's". It is a feature of the construction that the result does not depend on the order of the individual refinements.

If X is a variable name and $\mathcal{X} = \{X_i \mid i \in I\}$ is a set of such names, we use the notation $T^X = \{t \in T \mid \lambda(t) = X\}$ and $T^{\mathcal{X}} = \bigcup_{X \in \mathcal{X}} T^X$.

Definition 2.1 *Simultaneous Refinements*

Let B and B_i ($i \in I$) be Boxes and let $\Sigma = (S, T, W, \lambda)$, $\Sigma_i = (S_i, T_i, W_i, \lambda_i)$ be representatives of them (for $i \in I$). ${}^{\bullet}\Sigma_i$ and $\Sigma_i^{\bullet}$ will denote the entry place set (the exit place set) of the system Σ_i.

$\Sigma[X_i \leftarrow \Sigma_i \mid i \in I]$ is defined as the labelled system $\tilde{\Sigma} = (\tilde{S}, \tilde{T}, \tilde{W}, \tilde{\lambda})$ where

$$\tilde{T} = (T \backslash T^{\mathcal{X}}) \cup \bigcup_{i \in I} T^i \quad \text{with } T^i = \{t.t_i \mid t \in T^{X_i}, t_i \in T_i\}$$

$$\tilde{S} = \bigcup_{i \in I} S^i \cup \bigcup_{s \in S} S^s \quad \text{with } S^i = \{t.s_i \mid t \in T^{X_i}, s_i \in S_i \backslash ({}^{\bullet}\Sigma_i \cup \Sigma_i^{\bullet})\}$$

and S^s is the set of all labelled trees[5] of the following form:

i.e., there is an arc labelled t for each (if any) $t \in s^{\bullet}$ with a label of the form X_i, going to some entry place e_t of Σ_i, and there is an arc labelled t' for each $t' \in {}^{\bullet}s$ (if any) with a label of the form X_i, coming from some exit place $x_{t'}$ of Σ_i. We view this tree primarily as undirected, its root being s. The direction of its arcs is secondary, pertaining to the entry/exit place distinction.

$$\tilde{W}(\tilde{t}, \tilde{s}) = \begin{cases} w & \text{if } \tilde{t} = t \in (T \backslash T^{\mathcal{X}}), \tilde{s} \in S^s, W(t, s) = w \\ w \cdot w_i & \text{if } \tilde{t} = t.t_i \in T^i, \tilde{s} \in S^s, s \xleftarrow{t} s_i, W(t, s) = w, W_i(t_i, s_i) = w_i \\ w_i & \text{if } \tilde{t} = t.t_i \in T^i, \tilde{s} = t.s_i \in S^i, W_i(t_i, s_i) = w_i \\ 0 & \text{otherwise} \end{cases}$$

$$\tilde{W}(\tilde{s}, \tilde{t}) = \begin{cases} w & \text{if } \tilde{t} = t \in (T \backslash T^{\mathcal{X}}), \tilde{s} \in S^s, W(s, t) = w \\ w \cdot w_i & \text{if } \tilde{t} = t.t_i \in T^i, \tilde{s} \in S^s, s \xrightarrow{t} s_i, W(s, t) = w, W_i(s_i, t_i) = w_i \\ w_i & \text{if } \tilde{t} = t.t_i \in T^i, \tilde{s} = t.s_i \in S^i, W_i(s_i, t_i) = w_i \\ 0 & \text{otherwise} \end{cases}$$

---

[5] As usual, when we consider labelled trees, we will only be interested in their labels, not in the identity of the various nodes, i.e., we will consider isomorphism classes of such trees.

$$\tilde{\lambda}(\tilde{t}) = \begin{cases} \lambda(t) & \text{if } \tilde{t} = t \in (T \backslash T^{\mathcal{X}}) \\ \lambda_i(t_i) & \text{if } \tilde{t} = t.t_i, t_i \in T_i \text{ and } \lambda(t) = X_i \end{cases}$$

$$\tilde{\lambda}(\tilde{s}) = \begin{cases} \lambda(s) & \text{if } \tilde{s} \in S^s \\ \emptyset & \text{otherwise} \end{cases}$$

By definition, $B[X_i \leftarrow B_i \mid i \in I]$ is the equivalence class of $\tilde{\Sigma}$. ∎ 2.1

Let us note that S^s may be a single tree reduced to its root (if s has no input or output transition labelled by one of the variables X_i). In order to get a more uniform description, one may also consider the components of S^i as trees reduced to their roots. S^i and T^i give the fragments of the refined net corresponding to disjoint copies of the interior of Σ_i, one for each transition in Σ with a label X_i. $T \backslash T^{\mathcal{X}}$ gives the transitions of Σ which do not have to be refined. S^s gives the interface-places originating from s; this may be s itself (i.e., a single root) if s is not connected to any X_i-labelled transition; this may be a true tree-set, as shown above, if s is connected in any way to some X_i-labelled transitions; they all have the same label as s. A transition t is connected to a place in S^s like it is connected to s in Σ; a transition $t \cdot t_i$ is connected to a place $t \cdot s_i$ like t_i is connected to s_i in Σ_i; it is connected to a place $\tilde{s}$ in S^s like t_i is connected to e_t or x_t in Σ_i (and like t is connected to s in Σ). Finally, we may notice that if s is an entry (exit) place of Σ, all the children (if any) of the tree-places in S^s are entry (exit) places of the Σ_i's.

We may also represent a tree in S^s by a set of sequences $\{s, t.e_t, \cdots, t'.x_{t'}, \cdots\}$, describing the root and all the children together with the arc label. With this convention, the definition is illustrated in Figure 1; labels of the elements are written in their insides, while their names are written next to them.

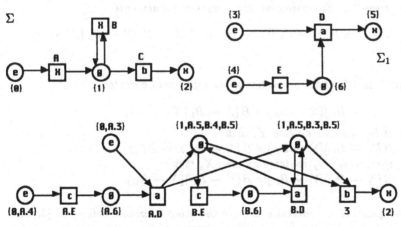

Figure 1: A refinement with a side loop

The place $\{1\}$ of Σ has two input transitions with hierarchical labels X, namely the transitions **A** and **B**, and one output transition with hierarchical label, namely

B again. Hence, the trees corresponding to this place have {1} as root, two arcs entering {1} labelled by **A** and **B**, and one arc leaving {1} labelled by **B**. The arcs entering {1} must come from an exit place of Σ_1. Since {5} is the only exit place of Σ_1, both arcs must come from {5}. The arc leaving {1} must lead to an entry place of Σ_1. Since Σ_1 has two entry places, namely {3} and {4}, there are two possibilities, which correspond to two different trees. In sequence notation, the two trees are {1, **A**.5, **B**.4, **B**.5} and {1, **A**.5, **B**.3, **B**.5}.

It may be verified that, with the natural initial marking, the behaviour of the refined net corresponds to what may be expected (see [4] for a more detailed analysis). Also, by using more general trees or sequence sets, it is possible to 'expand' the names of a refined net. For instance, if a two-level tree as exhibited in Definition 2.1 has leaves whose labels are themselves labelled trees, it is possible to replace those leaves by the corresponding (sub)trees; and if an internal copied place $t.s_i$ is such that s_i is itself a labelled tree, we may simply incorporate t as a prefix to the label of the root. The sequence set which equivalently describes such trees is the set of all the node labels prefixed by the transition paths going from the root to them.

It is then possible to prove many properties of this operator, often directly at the net level. The following basic proposition, which is here given for a special case, concerns two successive refinements; its general form [2] states that the second refinement simply has to be applied to the refining Boxes of the first refinement and to the transitions of the original Box which have not been removed by the first refinement. The general result is very powerful and allows to merge or split refinements; amongst its many corollaries are parts (i) and (ii) of the following proposition.

Proposition 2.2 *Expansion law for successive refinements*

If $X \neq Y$ then $B[X \leftarrow B_1][Y \leftarrow B_2] = B[X \leftarrow B_1[Y \leftarrow B_2], Y \leftarrow B_2]$.

Proposition 2.3 *Other properties of the refinement operator*

(i) $B[X \leftarrow B_1][X \leftarrow B_2] = B[X \leftarrow B_1[X \leftarrow B_2]]$.

(ii) *If B_1 contains no label Y, then*
$B[X \leftarrow B_1][Y \leftarrow B_2] = B[X \leftarrow B_1, Y \leftarrow B_2]$;
if moreover B_2 contains no label X, then
$B[X \leftarrow B_1][Y \leftarrow B_2] = B[Y \leftarrow B_2][X \leftarrow B_1]$.

It is now possible to synthesise most of the other operators defined in [3], and to derive their properties (associativity, commutativity, distributivity, ...). To this end, let $B_;$, $B_{\square}$, $B_{\parallel}$ and B_* be the Boxes shown in Figure 2. We may, for instance, define:

(i) $B_1; B_2 = B_;[X \leftarrow B_1, Y \leftarrow B_2]$ (sequence)

(ii) $B_1 \,\Box\, B_2 = B_{\,\Box}[X \leftarrow B_1, Y \leftarrow B_2]$ (choice)

(iii) $B_1 \| B_2 = B_\|[X \leftarrow B_1, Y \leftarrow B_2]$ (concurrent composition)

(iv) $[B_1 * B_2 * B_3] = B_*[X \leftarrow B_1, Y \leftarrow B_2, Z \leftarrow B_3]$ (iteration)

Note the essential use of simultaneous refinement in this definition. Properties of the derived operations follow from properties of refinement. For instance, the associativity of sequential composition follows as a direct consequence of the refinement expansion law (and the special result for $B_;$).

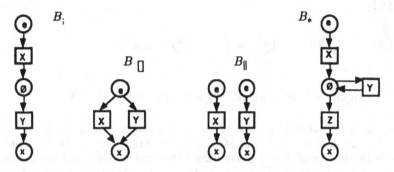

Figure 2: Basic Boxes for sequence, choice, composition and iteration

3   A general recursion operator

In this section, we define a recursion operator $\mu X.B$. This definition can be smoothly generalised to a simultaneous recursion operator, as shown in [2].

Let X and B be fixed in the sequel. $\mu X.B$ is defined along the following lines:

> Choose a representative Σ of B (and let Σ be fixed from now on as well).
>
> Let Σ_0 be a (carefully chosen) representative of the **stop** Box (i.e., by definition, the Box having neither transitions nor internal places) with as many entry/exit places as Σ. We shall discuss this 'careful choice'.
>
> Let $\Sigma_i = \Sigma[X \leftarrow \Sigma_{i-1}]$; due to the careful choice of Σ_0, we have $\Sigma_i \subseteq \Sigma_{i+1}$ (where the inclusion is defined componentwise on places and transitions, preserving arcs and labels).
>
> Define $\mu X.\Sigma$ as $\bigcup_{i \geq 0} \Sigma_i$ (where the union of labelled nets is defined componentwise), and $\mu X.B$ as the equivalence class of $\mu X.\Sigma$.

In the guarded case (no entry/exit place is connected to an X-labelled transition), the inclusion property can be obtained by just letting Σ_0 inherit the place names of Σ. To illustrate that this may no longer be true for non-guarded recursion, let us consider the simplest unguardedly recursive expression $\mu X.X$ (where X represents the Box with a single transition labelled X, connected to all the entry/exit places), which should lead to a **stop** Box; the corresponding series of nets is shown in Figure 3.

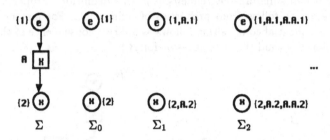

Figure 3: The simplest unguarded recursion $\mu X.X$

We have $\Sigma_0 \subseteq \Sigma$, but not the desired series of inclusions $\Sigma_0 \subseteq \Sigma_1 \subseteq \Sigma_2\ldots$, because, for instance, the place $\{1\}$ of Σ_0 is not contained in Σ_1. At this point we exploit the liberty of choosing the names of representatives and start with the names $A^\star.1$ and $A^\star.2$ instead, corresponding to the infinite linear trees where all the nodes are labelled 1 (or 2) and all the arcs are labelled A; then the entry and exit places are stable, because $\{i\} \cup A.A^\star.i = A^\star.i$ ($i = 1, 2$). This naming technique may be extended to the general case, but sequences are not enough because an entry (exit) place may be connected to more than one X-labelled transition. The principle is to choose for Σ_0 the **stop** Box with, as entry/exit places, all the (possibly infinite) trees of the form depicted in Figure 4.

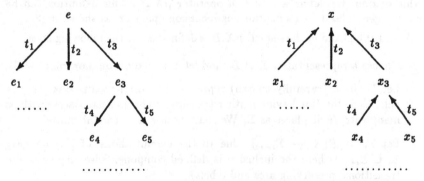

Figure 4: Entry and exit names

The next two definitions (Definitions 3.1 where the names of the places of the limit are defined and 3.2 where the limit net itself is defined) formalise this idea. We may assume that the places and transitions of Σ are 'elementary': only singleton sets (i.e., single roots) and sequences.

Definition 3.1 *A gallery of trees*

Entry trees: Let τ^e be the set of labelled trees where the nodes have a label s in $^\bullet\Sigma$, and for each $t \in s^\bullet \cap T^X$ (if any) there is an arc from s labelled by t.
Exit trees: Let τ^x be the set of labelled trees where the nodes have a label s in $\Sigma^\bullet$, and for each $t \in {}^\bullet s \cap T^X$ (if any) there is an arc from s (but graphically it will be represented as an arc leading to s) labelled by t.
Internal trees: Let $\tau^\bullet$ be the set of labelled trees whose roots have a label of the form $\sigma.s$ where σ is a finite, possibly empty sequence of transitions of T^X; $s \in \Sigma\backslash(\Sigma^\bullet \cup {}^\bullet\Sigma)$; for each $t \in s^\bullet \cap T^X$ (if any) there is an arc from s labelled by t going to the root of a τ^e-tree, and for each $t \in {}^\bullet s \cap T^X$ (if any) there is an arc from s labelled by t going to (but graphically it will be represented as an arc leading to s) the root of a τ^x-tree. ■ 3.1

These definitions are shown schematically in the subsequent Figure; it may happen that $\tau^\bullet$ is empty, while this may not be the case for τ^e or τ^x. In the more general case - simultaneous recursion - this definition has to be significantly extended [2].

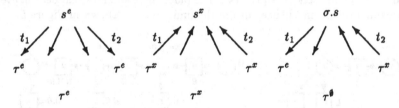

We shall now introduce an operator whose intuitive idea is to replace in B all X's by B's 'ad infinitum'; using the naming just introduced, it yields an explicit closed form of the result.

Definition 3.2 *The recursion operator*

With the notations introduced above, let us define $\mu X.B$ as the equivalence class of $\tilde{\Sigma}$, where $\tilde{\Sigma} = (\tilde{S}, \tilde{T}, \tilde{W}, \tilde{\lambda})$ is the labelled system defined in the following way:

$\tilde{S} = \tau^e \cup \tau^x \cup \tau^\bullet$.

$\tilde{T}$ is the set of all the finite non-empty transition sequences $\sigma \in T^\star$ such that all transitions of σ but the last are labelled by X.

For any $\tilde{t} \in \tilde{T}$ and $\tilde{s} \in \tilde{S}$, $\tilde{W}(\tilde{s}, \tilde{t})$ and $\tilde{W}(\tilde{t}, \tilde{s})$ are inductively defined:
if $\tilde{t} = t \in T$ and $\tilde{s}$ has a root labelled s then $\tilde{W}(\tilde{s}, \tilde{t}) = W(s, t)$ and $\tilde{W}(\tilde{t}, \tilde{s}) = W(t, s)$;
if $\tilde{t} = \sigma.\sigma'$ and $\tilde{s} \in \tau^\bullet$ with a root labelled $\sigma.s$ then $\tilde{W}(\tilde{s}, \tilde{t}) = \tilde{W}(\tilde{s}', \sigma')$

and $\tilde{W}(\tilde{t},\tilde{s}) = \tilde{W}(\sigma',\tilde{s}')$, where $\tilde{s}'$ is $\tilde{s}$ with its root relabelled s;
if $\tilde{t} = t.\sigma$ and in $\tilde{s}$ there is an arc labelled t from the root labelled s to
a node ν labelled s', then $\tilde{W}(\tilde{s},\tilde{t}) = W(s,t) \cdot \tilde{W}(\tilde{s}',\sigma)$ and $\tilde{W}(\tilde{t},\tilde{s}) = W(t,s) \cdot \tilde{W}(\sigma,\tilde{s}')$, where $\tilde{s}'$ is the subtree of $\tilde{s}$ starting with the root ν;
if none of these rules applies, then $\tilde{W} = 0$.

For any $\tilde{s} \in \tau^{\bullet}$, $\tilde{\lambda}(\tilde{s}) = \emptyset$;
for any $\tilde{s} \in \tau^e \cup \tau^x$, $\tilde{\lambda}(\tilde{s})$ is the label of the root (e or x);
for any $\tilde{t} \in \tilde{T}$, $\tilde{\lambda}(\tilde{t})$ is the label of its last component.   ■ 3.2

In the sequel, let Σ_0 denote the **stop** net whose entry places are the trees of τ^e and whose exit places are the trees of τ^x. For $k \geq 1$ define inductively Σ_k as $\Sigma[X \leftarrow \Sigma_{k-1}]$; to make the subsequent Proposition 3.3 true in general, Σ_k must be in expanded form (cf. just before Proposition 2.2).

In the guarded case, the trees in τ^e and τ^x are reduced to their roots (i.e., in Σ_0 the entry and exit places are named exactly as in Σ), and the trees in $\tau^{\bullet}$ have a depth of at most two (nodes). The first line of Figure 5 shows an example; on the left, the body Σ is shown while on the right, the net for $\mu X.\Sigma$ is shown. The second line of Figure 5 shows an example for non-guarded recursion; as Σ contains an X-labelled transition named B which borders both on place $\{2\}$ and on place $\{4\}$, Σ_0 (not shown) contains places named B*.2 and B*.4, respectively, as well as infinitely many other places corresponding to finite trees (and thus to finite sets of sequences). The places B*.2 and B*.4 reappear in every approximation Σ_k and hence, also in the limit which is shown in Figure 5.

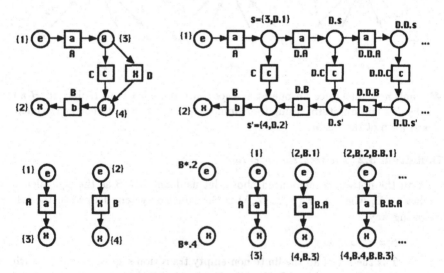

Figure 5: Two examples of recursion

Part (ii) of the next proposition provides the connection between the closed form defined in Definition 3.2 and its denotational fixpoint aspect; it shows that recursion is a fixpoint of refinement.

Proposition 3.3 *Properties of the recursion operator*

(i) $\Sigma_k \subseteq \Sigma_{k+1}$, and $\mu X.B$ is the equivalence class of $\bigcup_{k \geq 0} \Sigma_k$.

(ii) $\mu X.B = B[X \leftarrow \mu X.B]$.

Given a set $\mathcal{X} = \{X_i \mid i \in I\}$ of variable names and a Box B, the simultaneous recursion operator $\mu\{X_i.B_i \mid i \in I\}B$ defined in [2] is the result of replacing in B every occurrence of X_i by the Box B_i 'ad infinitum'. In particular, $\mu X.B = \mu\{X.B\}X$. The fixpoint equation of simultaneous recursion is

$$\mu\{X_i.B_i \mid i \in I\}B = B[X_i \leftarrow \mu\{X_j.B_j \mid j \in I\}B_i \mid i \in I]$$

i.e., simultaneous recursion is a fixpoint of simultaneous refinement. This equation can be derived from a powerful unfolding law that permits to split simultaneous recursions and unroll cross-recursions. For instance, we have the property

$$\mu\{X_j.B_j[X_i \leftarrow \mu X_i.B_i] \mid j \in I \setminus \{i\}\}\mu X_i.B_i = \mu\{X_j.B_j \mid j \in I\}B_i$$

which allows us to unfold the i-th recursive equation.

4 Conclusions

The main contribution of this paper can be seen as providing general definitions of (simultaneous) refinement and (based thereon) recursion in the context of basic (i.e., non-high level) Petri nets. It solves some previously open problems, such as the commutativity of refinement (conjectured without proof in [9] for a restricted case) and the denotational Petri net semantics of recursion (mentioned in [13] as an open problem).

We have shown, in particular, how a good naming policy for the interface-places allows to define the two operators without any of the applicability restrictions needed previously. We also derived many properties of these operators, including various expansion laws. As a pleasant by-product, we were able to use the first of them to synthesise more classical operators together with their main rules.

While our main definitions for recursion may appear complex at first sight, they specialise nicely - and yield limits that stay within countable infinity - for the practically important cases; moreover, they provide closed forms of the result. One of the main directions in which this work needs to be extended is to define more liberal equivalence relations on labelled nets and to investigate the resulting equivalence classes in view of there being 'more' finite representatives, while still staying in the denotational framework.

Acknowledgements

We are indebted to Richard P. Hopkins for inspiring discussions; he first suggested to use the stop Box as the starting point in the recursions. Glynn Winskel suggested a set theoretical solution for the denotational semantics of recursion. We thank the anonymous referees for their comments.

References

[1] J.C.M.Baeten and W.P.Weijland: *Process Algebra*. Cambridge Tracts in Theoretical Computer Science (1990).

[2] E.Best, R.Devillers and J.Esparza: General Refinement and Recursion Operators for the Box Calculus. Hildesheimer Informatikbericht (December 1992).

[3] E.Best, R.Devillers and J.Hall: The Box Calculus: a New Causal Algebra with Multi-label Communication. Advances in Petri Nets 1992. Springer-Verlag Lecture Notes in Computer Science Vol. 609, 21-69 (1992).

[4] E.Best and H.G.Linde-Göers: Compositional Process Semantics of Petri Boxes. Hildesheimer Informatikbericht (December 1992).

[5] G.Boudol and I.Castellani: Flow Models of Distributed Computations: Event Structures and Nets. Rapport de Recherche, INRIA, Sophia Antipolis (July 1991).

[6] P.Degano, R. De Nicola and U.Montanari: A Distributed Operational Semantics for CCS Based on C/E Systems. Acta Informatica 26 (1988).

[7] R.J.van Glabbeek and F.V.Vaandrager: Petri Net Models for Algebraic Theories of Concurrency. Proc. PARLE 89, Springer-Verlag Lecture Notes in Computer Science Vol.259, 224-242 (1987).

[8] U.Goltz: *Über die Darstellung von CCS-Programmen durch Petrinetze.* (In German.) R.Oldenbourg Verlag, GMD-Bericht Nr.172 (1988).

[9] U.Goltz and R.J.van Glabbeek: Refinement of Actions in Causality Based Models. Proc. of REX Workshop on Stepwise Refinement of Distributed Systems, Springer-Verlag Lecture Notes in Computer Science, 267-300 (1989).

[10] R.P.Hopkins, J.Hall and O.Botti: A Basic-Net Algebra for Program Semantics and its Application to occam. Advances in Petri Nets 1992. Springer-Verlag Lecture Notes in Computer Science Vol. 609, 179-214 (1992).

[11] C.A.R.Hoare: *Communicating Sequential Processes*. Prentice Hall (1985).

[12] R.Milner: *Communication and Concurrency*. Prentice Hall (1989).

[13] E.R.Olderog: *Nets, Terms and Formulas*. Habilitation (1989). Cambridge Tracts in Theoretical Computer Science (1991).

[14] D.Taubner: *Finite Representation of CCS and TCSP Programs by Automata and Petri Nets*. Springer-Verlag Lecture Notes in Computer Science Vol. 369 (1989).

On fairness in distributed automated deduction [*]

Maria Paola Bonacina   **Jieh Hsiang**
Department of Computer Science
SUNY at Stony Brook
Stony Brook, NY 11794-4400, USA
{bonacina,hsiang}@sbcs.sunysb.edu

1 Introduction

In this paper we present a new approach to distributed automated deduction called *Clause-Diffusion*; in this context we describe the associated notion of *distributed fairness* of a derivation and propose solutions to the problems involved.

A theorem proving strategy consists of an *inference mechanism* (a set of inference rules) and a *search plan*. We further refine the inference mechanism into *expansion* inference rules, e.g. resolution and paramodulation, and *contraction* inference rules, e.g. subsumption and simplification via rewrite rules. The motivation for studying distributed theorem proving is to improve the efficiency of theorem proving strategies by exploiting parallelism. The Clause-Diffusion approach is concerned mainly with *parallelism at the search level*, by partitioning the search space among concurrent, asynchronous theorem proving processes. These processes traverse their portions of the search space of the given problem, looking for a solution. As soon as one of them succeeds, the entire process succeeds and terminates. Since each process is assigned only a segment of the data, the processes need to communicate so that a proof involving data at different processes can be found. The processes send their clauses to other processes in form of messages, termed *inference messages*. Here we encounter the problem of *fairness*, as a requirement that the policies which control the handling of inference messages need to satisfy.

Fairness is a property of the search plan of a theorem proving strategy [5]. Intuitively, a fair search strategy ensures that no inference step which is necessary to find a proof will be postponed forever. Fairness is guaranteeed by a stronger condition, *uniform fairness*, which requires that expansion steps between persistent clauses, those that are not deleted by contraction, are considered. Since two persistent clauses may be stored at two different nodes in a distributed environment, distributed uniform fairness requires that any two such clauses meet eventually at some site. Thus, it poses an additional fairness requirement on the communication part of a distributed

---
[*] Research supported in part by grant CCR-8901322, funded by the National Science Foundation. The first author is also supported by a scholarship of Università degli Studi di Milano, Italy.

theorem strategy, i.e. the part of the search plan which establishes when to send messages and when and how to process received messages.

The first result concerning fairness in the paper is to turn these intuitions into formal requirements, to be realizable by actual procedures. We start by giving a definition of *distributed derivations* and extend the definition of uniform fairness of a sequential derivation to a distributed derivation. If only one theorem proving process is active, then distributed derivation and distributed uniform fairness reduce to their sequential counterparts. We then present a set of more concrete conditions and prove that they are *sufficient* for the uniform fairness of a distributed derivation. To our knowledge, this is the first analysis of fairness in distributed deduction. Several techniques for implementing these sufficient conditions for uniform fairness in different architectures are described. These techniques introduce a certain amount of additional *redundancy*. We present a new contraction inference rule to delete redundant messages. These techniques and inference rule are implemented in our distributed theorem prover *Aquarius* [7].

Our Clause-Diffusion methodology for distributed theorem proving and study of distributed uniform fairness apply to theorem proving in general. However, we shall emphasize on *contraction-based strategies*. The distinguishing features of these strategies are a well-founded ordering $\succ$ on terms, equations and clauses, powerful contraction rules, strong restrictions to the application of expansion rules and a *simplification-first* search plan [12], i.e. a search plan which gives priority to contraction steps. The motivation for emphasizing simplification-based strategies is two-fold. First, there are both experimental evidence and theoretical understanding that they are more effective than expansion-oriented methods. Second, the issues of parallelism and fairness are more difficult and more interesting for contraction-based strategies than for other strategies, due to the dynamic behaviour of the data base caused by contraction. In this sense, strategies without contraction can be regarded as a special case of the study of strategies with contraction.

The rest of the paper is organized as follows. We first recall the basic definitions in theorem proving, including the definition of uniform fairness of a sequential derivation. We then outline the Clause-Diffusion methodology for distributed deduction. The treatment of fairness follows: formal definition, reduction to concrete requirements and techniques to implement them. We conclude the paper with some discussion on the relationships between our work and the general issue of fairness in applications of distributed data bases.

2   Basic concepts in contraction-based deduction

A *theorem proving problem* consists in deciding, given a set of clauses S and a clause φ, whether φ is a theorem of S. A theorem proving strategy $\mathcal{C}$ is specified by a set of *inference rules* I and a *search plan* Σ. *Expansion* inference rules derive new clauses from existing ones, and add them to the data base. Resolution, hyperresolution and paramodulation are examples of expansion rules. *Contraction* inference rules delete existing clauses or replace them by logically equivalent but smaller ones. Examples of contraction rules are (proper) subsumption [17], simplification [20], tautology elimination, conditional simplification and normalization.

The search plan Σ chooses the inference rule and the premises for the next step. By iterating the application of I and Σ, a *derivation*

$$S_0 \vdash_C S_1 \vdash_C \ldots S_i \vdash_C \ldots,$$

is constructed. A derivation is *successful* if it reaches a solution. A theorem proving strategy C is *complete*, if, whenever the input target is indeed a theorem, the derivation constructed by C halts successfully. Completeness involves both the inference rules I and the search plan Σ. First, it requires that if the input target is a theorem, there exist successful derivations by I (*completeness of the inference mechanism*). Second, it requires that whenever successful derivations exist, the search plan Σ selects a successful derivation among the possible derivations by I from the given input (*fairness of the search plan [1]*).

Fairness for theorem proving is implied by a stronger fairness property, which we call *uniform fairness* (e.g. [2, 3, 4, 13, 20]). We adopt here the definition given in [4]. This definition uses two additional concepts: *redundant* clauses and *persistent* clauses. Intuitively, a clause is *redundant* in a derivation if it is not necessary to prove the given target theorem [4, 6, 20]. Approaches to capture the notion of redundancy usually assume the existence of a *well-founded ordering on the proof structure* [2, 3, 4, 6, 12, 20, 22]. Given such an ordering, redundant data are identified as those whose deletion does not increase the complexity of proofs. Contraction inference rules are designed as concrete mechanisms to delete redundant data.

The notion of persistent clauses appeared first in [3, 13]: a clause is *persistent* in a derivation if it is generated at some stage of the derivation and never deleted afterwards. Given a derivation starting from a presentation S_0, the possibly infinite set $S_\infty = \bigcup_{j \geq 0} \bigcap_{i \geq j} S_i$ of all the persistent clauses is called the *limit* of the derivation. Given a strategy $C = \langle I; \Sigma \rangle$ and a set of clauses S, we denote by $I_e(S)$ the set of clauses which can be generated from S in one step by an expansion rule of I. We denote by R the *redundancy criterion* associated to C [4]. For a set of clauses S, $R(S)$ is the set of all the clauses which are redundant in S based on R. The redundancy criterion R is associated to C in the sense that whenever a contraction rule of I deletes or replaces a clause ψ in S, ψ is in $R(S)$. A redundancy criterion is required to be *monotonic*, i.e. if $S_1 \subseteq S_2$, then $R(S_1) \subseteq R(S_2)$. Other requirements may be found in [4]. Finally, uniform fairness says that *all clauses that can be derived from persistent, non-redundant clauses should be generated eventually*:

Definition 2.1 (Bachmair and Ganzinger 1992) [4] *A derivation*

$$S_0 \vdash_C S_1 \vdash_C \ldots S_i \vdash_C \ldots$$

by a strategy C is uniformly fair *if $I_e(S_\infty - R(S_\infty)) \subseteq \bigcup_{j \geq 0} S_j$.*

Studies of contraction and redundancy are motivated by the observation that contraction inference rules are an indispensable part of many successful theorem provers, e.g. [1, 15, 19]. From the theoretical side, however, their inclusion had posed a great challenge to the completeness proofs of theorem proving strategies, because in the

---

[1] The use of the word "fairness" rather than "completeness" for the search plan has been inspired by its use for Knuth-Bendix type completion procedures.

presence of contraction steps the data base of clauses is not monotonically increasing during a derivation. It is only until recently that formal techniques for dealing with the completeness issues of contraction rules have been discovered [2, 6, 20, 4].

3 Distributed deduction

Given a complete theorem proving strategy $C = <I; \Sigma>$, we address the problem of how to execute C in a distributed environment. By a *distributed environment* we mean a network of computers or a loosely coupled, asynchronous multiprocessor with distributed memory. The latter may be endowed with a shared memory component. Our "Clause-Diffusion" methodology does not depend on a specific architecture; it can be realized on different ones. Parameters such as the amount of *memory at each processor*, the availability of *shared memory* and the *topology* of the interconnection of the processors or *nodes*, are variable.

The basic idea in our approach is *to partition the search space* among the nodes. The search space is determined by the input clauses and the inference rules. At the clauses level, the input and the generated clauses are distributed among the nodes. For this purpose we need an *allocation algorithm*, which decides where to allocate a clause. Once a clause ψ is assigned to processor p_i, ψ becomes a *resident* of p_i. In this way each node p_i is allotted a subset S^i of the global data base. The union of all the S^i's, which are not necessarily disjoint, forms the current *global data base* S. Each processor is responsible for applying the inference rules in I to its residents, according to the search plan Σ. Since the global data base is partitioned among the nodes, no node is guaranteed to find a proof using only its own residents. To ensure that a solution will be found when one exists, the nodes need to exchange information, by sending each other their residents in form of messages, called *inference messages*. The inference messages issued by p_i let the other processors know which clauses belong to p_i, so that they can use them to perform inferences with their own residents. In a purely distributed system, the inference messages may be sent via routing or broadcasting. If a mixed environment, i.e. with distributed memory and a shared memory component, they may be communicated through the shared memory.

The separation of residents and inference messages can also be used to partition the search space at the inference level. Using the paramodulation inference rule as an example, one may establish that the inference messages are paramodulated *into* the residents, but not vice versa. This restriction has two purposes. First, it distributes the expansion inference steps among the nodes. Second, it prevents a systematic duplication of steps: if this restriction were not in place, then paramodulation steps between two residents ψ_1 of p_1 and ψ_2 of of p_2 would be performed twice, once when ψ_1 visits p_2 and once when ψ_2 visits p_1. Other expansion inference rules can be treated in a similar way. While subdividing the expansion steps serves its purpose, it is not productive to subdivide the contraction steps, since the motivation behind contraction is to keep the data base always at the minimal. In a *contraction-based strategy*, an expansion step should be performed only if all the premises are fully reduced, at least with respect to the local data base. To ensure this, we require that each processor keep both its residents and received inference messages fully contracted.

Let us call the clause newly generated from an expansion step a *raw clause*. In the presence of contraction rules, a raw clause does not become a resident until it has been fully contracted. Thus, our method also features a number of *distributed contraction schemes* [7] to reduce a raw clause with respect to the global data base. After contraction, a raw clause becomes a *new settler*. New settlers are given to the allocation algorithm to be assigned to some node. Remark that we do not assume a central control process devoted to execute the allocation algorithm. Every process executes the allocation algorithm for its new settlers: it may decide either to retain a new settler or to send it to another node. The purpose of the allocation algorithm is to partition the search space and keep the work-load balanced as much as possible.

This is the basic working of the "Clause-Diffusion" approach to distributed automated deduction: inter-contraction and local expansion inferences at the nodes among residents and inference messages, distributed contraction of raw clauses, allocation of new settlers, and mechanisms for passing inference messages. By specifying the inference mechanism I, the search plan Σ to schedule inference steps and communication steps, the allocation algorithm, the distributed contraction scheme and the algorithms for routing and broadcasting of messages, one obtains a specific strategy. We refer to [7] for full detail of the methodology and its implementation.

The above elements are summarized in the following notion of *distributed derivation*: every processor p_k, $1 \le k \le n$, computes a derivation

$$(S; M; CP; NS)_0^k \vdash_c (S; M; CP; NS)_1^k \vdash_c \ldots (S; M; CP; NS)_i^k \vdash_c \ldots$$

where S_i^k is the set of *residents*, M_i^k is the set of *inference messages*, CP_i^k is the set of *raw clauses* and NS_i^k is the set of *new settlers* at p_k at stage i.

A distributed derivation is the collection of the asynchronous derivations computed by the nodes. The *state* of the derivations at processor p_k and stage i is represented by the tuple $(S; M; CP; NS)_i^k$. More components may be added if indicated by a specific strategy. A distributed derivation succeeds as soon as the derivation at one node finds a proof. A step in a distributed derivation can be either an *expansion* step or a *contraction* step or a *communication* step. For instance, sending an inference message for $\psi \in S^k$ from node p_k to an adjacent node p_j can be written as $(S^k \cup \{\psi\}, M^j) \vdash (S^k \cup \{\psi\}, M^j \cup \{\psi\})$. Settling a new settler at node p_k can be written as $(S^k, NS^k \cup \{\psi\}) \vdash (S^k \cup \{\psi\}, NS^k)$. This representation assumes that communication between any two adjacent nodes is instantaneous. It does *not* assume, however, that communication between *any* two nodes is instantaneous. If an inference message sent by p_i reaches p_j through $p_{x_1} \ldots p_{x_m}$, it appears first in M^{x_1}, then in M^{x_2} and so on. The time elapsed in going from the source to the destination is captured in our description, by showing the message stored, at successive stages, in the appropriate component of all the nodes on the path.

4 Uniform fairness of distributed derivations

In order to extend Definition 2.1 to the distributed case, we need to define the limit of a distributed derivation. First, we define the *local data base* at node p_k at stage i as the union $G_i^k = S_i^k \cup M_i^k \cup CP_i^k \cup NS_i^k$. Then, the *local limit* at processor p_k is $G_\infty^k = \bigcup_{i \ge 0} \bigcap_{j \ge i} G_j^k$. The *global data base* at stage i is the union of the local data bases, i.e. $G_i = \bigcup_{k=1}^{n} G_i^k$, and the *global limit* is $G_\infty = \bigcup_{k=1}^{n} G_\infty^k$. Local and global limits may be defined similarly for each component of the states in a distributed derivation, e.g. S_∞^k and S_∞, M_∞^k and M_∞. Then, the definition of uniform fairness is extended to a distributed derivation as follows:

Definition 4.1 *A distributed derivation*

$$(S; M; CP; NS)_0^k \vdash_C (S; M; CP; NS)_1^k \vdash_C \ldots (S; M; CP; NS)_i^k \vdash_C \ldots,$$

for all k, $1 \le k \le n$, *is uniformly fair if* $I_e(G_\infty - R(G_\infty)) \subseteq \bigcup_{k=1}^{n} \bigcup_{j \ge 0} G_j^k$.

The following three conditions form a more concrete specification of uniform fairness of distributed derivations.

1. All messages should be processed eventually and thus there are *no persistent messages*:

   $$\forall k, 1 \le k \le n, M_\infty^k = CP_\infty^k = NS_\infty^k = \emptyset.$$

2. Given k and $\psi \in S_\infty^k$, we define the *abstract birth-time* of ψ in k to be the smallest index $i \ge 0$ such that $\psi \in \bigcap_{j \ge i} S_j^k$.[2] Then for every node p_k and for every persistent, non-redundant resident φ at p_k, *all persistent, non-redundant residents at the other nodes will eventually appear as inference messages at p_k, after the birth of φ*:

   $$\forall k, 1 \le k \le n, \forall \varphi \in (S_\infty^k - R(S_\infty^k)), \text{ if } i \text{ is the abstract birth-time of } \varphi, \text{ then } \forall h,$$
   $1 \le h \ne k \le n, \forall \psi \in (S_\infty^h - R(S_\infty^h))$, there exists an $l > i$ such that $\psi \in M_l^k$.

   Notice that i and l are stages of the same derivation, i.e. the derivation at p_k.

3. The derivation is uniformly fair with respect to the local inferences at each node. That is, every clause that can be generated from persistent, non-redundant clauses at p_k will be generated: $\forall k, 1 \le k \le n, I_e(S_\infty^k - R(S_\infty^k)) \subseteq \bigcup_{i \ge 0} CP_i^k$.

While Condition 3 paraphrases the requirement that the sequential strategy to begin with is fair, Conditions 1 and 2 take care of the distributed part of the derivation. Intuitively, Conditions 1 and 2 guarantee that a clause which can be generated from two persistent non-redundant clauses φ_1 and φ_2 residing at two different nodes, will be considered. Condition 2 ensures that φ_1 and φ_2 will eventually meet each other through inference messages. Condition 1 makes sure that all inference messages be processed ($M_\infty = \emptyset$), all raw clauses (those that, in the presence of contraction rules, remain non-trivial after having been fully contracted) become new settlers ($CP_\infty = \emptyset$) and all new settlers become residents at some place ($NS_\infty = \emptyset$). Because the definition of uniform fairness, and consequently our three conditions, focus only on persistent, non-redundant clauses, it is fairly simple to show that these three conditions imply Definition 4.1:

Theorem 4.1 *If a distributed derivation satisfies Conditions 1, 2 and 3, then it is uniformly fair, i.e.* $I_e(G_\infty - R(G_\infty)) \subseteq \bigcup_{k=1}^{n} \bigcup_{i \ge 0} G_i^k$.

---

[2] The adjective *abstract* indicates that i is an index in the abstract view of the derivation, and not a time of any processor's clock.

Proof: let φ be any clause in $I_e(G_\infty - R(G_\infty))$ with parents ψ_1 and ψ_2. Since $M_\infty^- = CP_\infty = NS_\infty = \emptyset$, $G_\infty = S_\infty$, i.e. $\psi_1, \psi_2 \in S_\infty$. It follows that $\psi_1 \in (S_\infty^k - R(S_\infty))$ and $\psi_2 \in (S_\infty^h - R(S_\infty))$ for some $1 \leq k, h \leq p$.

If $k = h$, then $\varphi \in I_e(S_\infty^k - R(S_\infty))$. Since $S_\infty^k \subseteq S_\infty$, by the monotonicity of the redundancy criterion, $R(S_\infty^k) \subseteq R(S_\infty)$ and thus $I_e(S_\infty^k - R(S_\infty)) \subseteq I_e(S_\infty^k - R(S_\infty^k))$. By Condition 3, there exists an i such that $\varphi \in CP_i^k \subseteq G_i^k \subseteq \bigcup_{k=1}^n \bigcup_{i \geq 0} G_i^k$.

If $k \neq h$, let i_1 and i_2 be the abstract birth-times of ψ_1 and ψ_2 respectively. By Condition 2, we have $\psi_1 \in M_{l_1}^h$ for some $l_1 > i_2$ and $\psi_2 \in M_{l_2}^k$ for some $l_2 > i_1$. Since $M_\infty = \emptyset$ by Condition 1, we know that the inference message ψ_1 does not persist at p_h and the inference message ψ_2 does not persist at p_k. An inference message may be deleted before performing expansion steps, by a contraction step. Since ψ_1 and ψ_2 are in $G_\infty - R(G_\infty)$, i.e. they are globally persistent and non-redundant, this is impossible. It follows that the inference messages $\psi_1 \in M_{l_1}^h$ and $\psi_2 \in M_{l_2}^k$ are deleted only after having been processed. Thus, paramodulation of ψ_1 into ψ_2 is tried at p_h and paramodulation of ψ_2 into ψ_1 is tried at p_k. Either one of these two steps generates φ, i.e. either $\varphi \in CP_i^h$ or $\varphi \in CP_i^k$ at some stage i, i.e. $\varphi \in \bigcup_{k=1}^n \bigcup_{i \geq 0} G_i^k$. $\square$

By this theorem, the abstract definition of uniform fairness is reduced to three more concrete requirements:

Corollary 4.1 *Let $C = <I; \Sigma >$ be a complete (sequential) theorem proving strategy and $\mathcal{D}$ be its distributed version. If the algorithms and policies handling messages satisfy Conditions 1 and 2, then $\mathcal{D}$ is a complete distributed theorem proving strategy.*

5 Techniques to satisfy the conditions for uniform fairness

5.1 Inference messages and localized image sets

The second of the sufficient conditions for uniform fairness requires that for every persistent resident φ at node p_k, all persistent residents of other nodes appear eventually at p_k as inference messages after the abstract birth-time of φ. In the following we describe some techniques to ensure this condition. In addition to giving a general method, we also provide techniques for fine-tuning according to the parameters of different architectures.

The basic idea is that a new resident ψ, once settled, should emit a message of itself, so that inferences between residents at other nodes and ψ can be performed. We assign, to each resident, an *identifier* and a *birth-time*. When a new settler ψ becomes a resident at p_i, it is given an identifier a never used before at p_i, and the current time at p_i's clock as its birth-time. We remark that this birth-time has no relationship with the abstract birth-time of persistent residents mentioned in previous sections; the latter is only for conceptual simplicity of the formalism. Thus, the format of a resident is $< \psi, a, x >$, where a is the identifier and x is the birth-time, and the pair $< i, a >$ represents a unique *global identifier* for ψ.

An inference message may need to be emitted when a new settler becomes a resident and when a resident is updated due to contraction. In addition to the clause, an inference message also carries its global identifier and birth-time. Thus, an inference message for $< \psi, a, x > \in S^i$ has the form $m = < \psi, i, a, x >$. If a resident ψ is contracted to ψ', its birth-time is updated: $< \psi, a, x >$ is replaced by $< \psi', a, y >$, where y is the current time at the node's clock. Intuitively, this means that ψ' is "new" and therefore should be re-scheduled to be sent as message. When node p_j receives $m = < \psi, i, a, x >$, p_j stores it in a *queue of messages*. This queue may be sorted according to different criteria, which are part of the search plan executed at the node. When the message m is selected from the queue, it is used for contraction inferences and expansion inferences (such as paramodulate *into* the residents of p_j) according to the local search plan.

One question which needs to be addressed is what p_j should do with m after p_j has used m to perform all possible inferences within its current local data base. A natural solution is to simply delete m, since the content of m already exists at node p_i and, thus, its presence (or absence) at p_j does not have any effect on the global data base. A complication arises, however, because new residents may be created at p_j *after* m has been deleted. Then, in order to ensure fairness, the content of the identifier $< i, a >$ should be known at p_j again, so that inferences between the new residents and the content of $< i, a >$ can be performed. This can be done by using "control messages" to stir the re-edition of inference messages. That is, node p_j sends a *wake-up call* to p_i requesting the content of $< i, a >$. Upon receiving the wake-up call, p_i will send the relevant information to p_j. The disadvantage of this approach is that it may generate a large amount of communication. Although by carefully analyzing the routing algorithms one can eliminate some messages [7], it may still worsen the computation/communication ratio quite significantly. On the other hand, if the architecture under consideration has very limited amount of local memory for each node and has low latency and high throughput in communication, then this scheme may be considered.

Assuming that each node has sufficient local memory, one can then choose to have each node saving the used messages in its memory. In this way, each node p_k progressively builds a *localized image set* SH^k, i.e. a local, approximate image of the global data base. Each SH^k can be implemented as a *hash table* with the global identifier of the incoming messages as the *key*: message $m = < \psi, i, a, x >$ is inserted in the hash table under key $< i, a >$. If the architecture supports an additional shared memory component, then a single *global image set* SH can be built in the shared memory, so that it can be used by all nodes, thus saving the duplication of building different hash tables. Under this scheme, there is no need for wake-up calls and replies. If a new resident is produced, it can simply go through the hash table to find the needed data to perform necessary expansion inferences. This cuts down the amount of communication significantly.

In summary, the diffusion of clauses as inference messages allows expansion steps between clauses at remote sites. Each node p_i is responsible for sending its residents. Birth-times are used to ensure local fairness in the emission of messages. Because the data bases at the nodes are dynamic, inference messages need to be saved by the receiver or re-issued by the sender upon the receipt of wake-up calls.

5.2 Deletion of redundant inference messages

The above techniques, however, do introduce some redundancy. The reason is that during a derivation it is not known which residents are persistent. Thus, inference messages may carry residents for which the messages are not necessary, because these residents are contracted after the generation of the message. For instance, assume that ψ is a resident at p_i and that a message $m_1 =< \psi, i, a, x >$ has been emitted for ψ. Suppose later p_i has additional data enabling it to contract ψ to ψ'. Then, another message $m_2 =< \psi', i, a, y >$ for ψ' is sent. A node p_j, which receives both m_1 and m_2, does not know that m_1 is redundant and may use both messages for inferences, thus producing redundancy. Furthermore, a contraction-based distributed strategy may prescribe to forward inference messages only after having tried to contract their content. If message m_1 from p_i reaches p_j by going through intermediate nodes, node p_j will receive in general a message $< \psi'', i, a, x >$, where ψ'' is a contracted form of ψ. Clause ψ'' may actually render ψ' redundant. One needs to design a way to take full advantage of the results of these contractions.

A solution to these problems lies in the utilization of the global identifier and birth-time which come with the messages. Suppose node p_j has received two messages $m_1 =< \psi_1, i, a, x >$ and $m_2 =< \psi_2, i, a, y >$, with the same global identifier $< i, a >$. Then, we know that ψ_1 and ψ_2 are *logically equivalent* since they are (contracted) forms of the same resident. We term such messages *generalized duplicates*. If $\psi_1 = \psi_2$ and $x = y$, the two messages are just two plain duplicates. If $\psi_1 \neq \psi_2$, but $x = y$, then the two messages were originally plain duplicates, whose clauses have been contracted to two different forms during their traversal through the network. If $x < y$, then the original clause of the message m_2 is a contracted form of the original clause of m_1, since m_2 is emitted later. The case for $x > y$ is symmetric.

Let $m_1 =< \psi_1, i, a, x >$ and $m_2 =< \psi_2, i, a, y >$ be two generalized duplicates such that $y \geq x$. If they carry the same clause, i.e. $\psi_1 = \psi_2$, then we discard m_1, the message carrying an earlier time-stamp. Otherwise, we discard m_1 if $\psi_1 \succ \psi_2$ and discard m_2 if $\psi_2 \succ \psi_1$. If ψ_1 and ψ_2 are not comparable, then we discard m_1 since it was emitted earlier. The following inference rule captures the above ideas:

Discard Message: Let i and k be two nodes, and $y \geq x$.

$$\bullet \quad \frac{M^k \cup \{< \psi_1, i, a, x >, < \psi_2, i, a, y >\}}{M^k \cup \{< \psi_2, i, a, y >\}} \quad \text{if } \psi_2 \not\succ \psi_1$$

$$\bullet \quad \frac{M^k \cup \{< \psi_1, i, a, x >, < \psi_2, i, a, y >\}}{M^k \cup \{< \psi_1, i, a, x >\}} \quad \text{if } \psi_2 \succ \psi_1$$

These inference rules formalize a mechanism which discards redundant inference messages at the receiver. By the nature of the theorem proving applications, it is not possible to discard generalized duplicates at the sender. In fact, it is never the case that two generalized duplicates $< \psi_1, i, a, x >$ and $< \psi_2, i, a, y >$ be present at the same time at the sender, i.e. node p_i, because the content of $< i, a >$ is only one clause at any given time. The issue may be addressed at the sender in terms of the delay between contraction and communication. On one hand, when a resident is contracted, we would like to send it as inference message as soon as possible to let the other processes see the reduced form. On the other hand, we may prefer to wait for a longer interval, in case the resident will be reduced again shortly. A suitable trade-off may be determined empirically. The infererence rule of Discard Message may be applied to other aspects of the Clause diffusion methodology, such as for updating the contents of the image sets [7].

6 Discussion

In this paper we outlined a general approach to distribued automated deduction terms "clause-diffusion", and we described the related problem of fairness in a distributed derivation, and how to ensure it in our methodology. Although our work applies to distributed theorem proving methods in general, we have concentrated on contraction-based strategies, since they pose the most challenging problems both in theory and in implementation. The Clause-Diffusion methodology is a general method which can be implemented on a variety of architectures and yields a high degree of parallelism by tolerating extra global redundancy, as the same clauses may be generated in different ways by different processes. Our view is that it is better to let the processes proceed eagerly in parallel, generating extra redundant clauses and deleting them afterwards, rather than synchronize the processes, thus forcing them to wait, in order to prevent redundancies. Next, we applied the notion of uniform fairness from [4] to the distributed framework. We pointed out the new problem on fairness represented by the additional component of communication and presented a set of sufficient conditions to ensure fairness. Our conditions are fairly general and the correctness is proved.

We then discussed how these sufficient conditions can be realized on various architectures. The problem of redundancy resulting from the inference messages is also discussed in detail and technical solutions are described.

Not much work has been done in distributed theorem proving. The DARES system [9] and the team-work method [10] apply to theorem proving artificial intelligence techniques for distributed problem solving. Theoretical treatments were not given in the papers. DARES has been designed for strategies without backward contraction. The team-work method relies on a central control to synchronize periodically the processes and evaluate their work, whereas our approach is intrinsically distributed and asynchronous. Therefore, most of the results presented here appear to be new. They include the Clause-Diffusion methodology for distributed deduction, the sufficient conditions and techniques for ensuring fairness, the observation of the backward contraction bottleneck problem and the schemes for implementing distributed global contraction.

We also feel that part of our study may be applicable to distributed data bases. One of the important problems in distributed data bases is to maintain the global consistency of data in the presence of updates. The same problem also appears in our study although in a weaker form. Contraction inferences are in fact a form of update, since they replace data by others. Our counterpart to the notion of consistency, on the other hand, is not as rigid. The main difference is that once a datum is modified through contraction, it is not necessary to require that all of its copies (in the form of inference messages) be updated immediately into identical form. This is because a contracted datum is still *logically equivalent* to the original one, which is all that is required in automated deduction. What is lost by not keeping copies of the same datum identical is not consistency, but minimality: there is a possible temporary increase of redundancy which, although undesirable, does not disturb the global integrity of the system. This is why it is relatively easier to come up with a reasonable solution for our problem than for the similar problem for distributed data bases. Some of our work may be useful to distributed data bases applications with less stringent requirements of consistency.

References

[1] S.Anantharaman, J.Hsiang, Automated Proofs of the Moufang Identities in Alternative Rings, *JAR*, Vol. 6, No. 1, 76–109, 1990.

[2] L.Bachmair, N.Dershowitz and J.Hsiang, Orderings for Equational Proofs, in *Proc. of LICS-86*, 346–357, 1986.

[3] L.Bachmair, Proofs Methods for Equational Theories, Ph.D. Thesis, Dept. of Computer Science, Univ. of Illinois at Urbana, 1987.

[4] L.Bachmair, H.Ganzinger, Non-Clausal Resolution and Superposition with Selection and Redundancy Criteria, in *Proc. of LPAR-92*, LNAI 624, 273–284, 1992.

[5] M.P.Bonacina, J.Hsiang, On fairness of completion-based theorem proving strategies, in R.V. Book (ed.), *Proc. of RTA-91*, LNCS 488, 348–360, 1991.

[6] M.P.Bonacina, J.Hsiang, Towards a Foundation of Completion Procedures as Semidecision Procedures, submitted and Tech. Rep. Dept. of Computer Science, SUNY at Stony Brook, Aug. 1991.

[7] M.P.Bonacina, Distributed Automated Deduction, Ph.D. Thesis, Dept. of Computer Science, SUNY at Stony Brook, Dec. 1992.

[8] J.D.Christian, High-Performance Permutative Completion, Ph.D. Thesis, Univ. of Texas at Austin, and MCC Tech. Rep. ACT-AI-303-89, Aug. 1989.

[9] S.E.Conry, D.J.MacIntosh and R.A.Meyer, DARES: A Distributed Automated REasoning System, in *Proc. of AAAI-90*, 78–85, 1990.

[10] J.Denzinger, Distributed knowledge-based deduction using the team work method, Tech. Rep., Univ. of Kaiserslautern, 1991.

[11] D.J.Hawley, A Buchberger Algorithm for Distributed Memory Multi-Processors, in *Proc. of the Int. Conf. of the Austrian Center for Parallel Computation*, Linz, Oct. 1991.

[12] J.Hsiang, M.Rusinowitch, On word problems in equational theories, in Th.Ottman (ed.), *Proc. of ICALP-87*, LNCS 267, 54–71, 1987.

[13] G.Huet, A Complete Proof of Correctness of the Knuth-Bendix Completion Algorithm, *JCSS*, Vol. 23, 11–21, 1981.

[14] A.Jindal, R.Overbeek and W.Kabat, Exploitation of parallel processing for implementing high-performance deduction systems, *JAR*, Vol. 8, 23–38, 1992.

[15] D.Kapur. H.Zhang, RRL: a Rewrite Rule Laboratory, in E.Lusk, R.Overbeek (eds.), *Proc. of CADE-9*, LNCS 310, 768–770, 1988.

[16] C.Kirchner. P.Viry, Implementing Parallel Rewriting, in B.Fronhöfer and G.Wrightson (eds.), *Parallelization in Inference Systems*, LNAI 590, 123–138, 1992.

[17] D.W.Loveland, *Automated Theorem Proving: A Logical Basis*, North-Holland, Amsterdam, 1978.

[18] E.L.Lusk, W.W.McCune, Experiments with ROO: a Parallel Automated Deduction System, in B.Fronhöfer and G.Wrightson (eds.), *Parallelization in Inference Systems*, LNAI 590, 139–162, 1992.

[19] W.W.McCune, OTTER 2.0 Users Guide, Tech. Rep. ANL-90/9, Argonne National Lab., Mar. 1990.

[20] M.Rusinowitch, Theorem-proving with Resolution and Superposition, *JSC*, Vol. 11, No. 1 & 2, 21–50, Jan./Feb. 1991.

[21] K.Siegl, Gröbner Bases Computation in STRAND: A Case Study for Concurrent Symbolic Computation in Logic Programming Languages, M.S. Thesis and Tech. Rep. 90-54.0, RISC-LINZ, Nov. 1990.

[22] R.Socher-Ambrosius, How to Avoid the Derivation of Redundant Clauses in Reasoning Systems, in *JAR*, Vol. 9, No. 1, Aug. 1992.

[23] M.E.Stickel, The Path-Indexing Method for Indexing Terms, Tech. Note 473, SRI Int., Oct. 1989.

[24] J.-P.Vidal, The Computation of Gröbner Bases on A Shared Memory Multiprocessor, in A.Miola (ed.), *Proc. of DISCO-90*, LNCS 429, 81–90, 1990 and Tech. Rep. CMU-CS-90-163, Aug. 1990.

[25] K.A.Yelick, S.J.Garland, A Parallel Completion Procedure for Term Rewriting Systems, in D.Kapur (ed.), *Proc. of CADE-11*, LNAI 607, 109–123, 1992.

Divide-and-Conquer Algorithms on the Hypercube

Ernst W. Mayr   Ralph Werchner

Fachbereich Informatik
J.W. Goethe-University
Frankfurt am Main
Germany

Abstract. We show how to implement divide-and-conquer algorithms without undue overhead on a wide class of networks. We give an optimal generic divide-and-conquer implementation on hypercubes for the class of divide-and-conquer algorithms for which the total size of the subproblems on any level of the recursion does not exceed the parent problem size. For this implementation, appropriately sized subcubes have to be allocated to the subproblems generated by the divide-steps. We take care that these allocation steps do not cause any unbalanced distribution of work, and that, asymptotically, they do not increase the running time. Variants of our generic algorithm also work for the butterfly network and, by a general simulation, for the class of hypercubic networks, including the shuffle-exchange and the cube-connected-cycles network. Our results can also be applied to optimally solve various types of routing problems.

Topics: *Theory of Parallel and Distributed Computation, Algorithms and Data Structures*

1   Introduction

The divide-and-conquer approach is one of the most successful programming paradigms. Especially in the field of parallel processing one of the most natural methods to solve problems is to divide them into subproblems, solve these in parallel and then recombine the solutions to a solution of the given problem instance.

The complete execution of a divide-and-conquer algorithm can be visualized as a tree, with the root representing the given instance of the problem and the other nodes representing subproblems. In this tree, we can associate with each node (subproblem) the set of processors dealing with the corresponding subproblem. From this point of view, the problem of efficiently allocating sets of processors to the subproblems (nodes of the tree) becomes evident. Our goal in this paper is to solve this problem in a way causing minimal overhead in addition to the running time needed by the divide- and conquer-steps themselves. Unlike for PRAM's [FW78] which provide complete processor interconnection and hence simple processor allocation mechanisms (but see also [vG89]), this problem is much more difficult on network architectures. Two major hurdles are (i) allocating appropriately sized subnetworks to subproblems and (ii) routing the subproblems to their subnetworks.

These two objectives are conflicting with each other. If we want to find appropriately sized subnetworks leaving only very few processors idle, the subproblems might have to be routed over long distances. On the other hand, keeping routes short may imply that not enough suitably sized subnetworks are available. We show that a compromise between these two extremes of the trade-off yields asymptotically optimal results for a wide class of divide-and-conquer algorithms.

Results concerning closely related allocation problems on the hypercube can be found in [CL90], [CS87], and [KDL89]. These papers consider the problem of allocating appropriately sized subcubes to incoming tasks in an on-line fashion on a hypercube that is already partially allocated. Our approach differs since we allocate subcubes to all subproblems on the same level of recursion simultaneously.

In [ZRL91] an implementation of divide-and-conquer is considered where each divide or conquer step is executed by a single processor. Thus, if a divide step always creates two subproblems, the resulting dependency structure between processors is a binomial tree, whose embeddings into de Bruijn and other networks are discussed.

2 Fundamental Concepts and Notation

2.1 Networks

Consider networks consisting of p processors interconnected by bidirectional communication channels capable of transmitting $\Theta(\log p)$ bits per step. In particular, we consider the family of boolean hypercubes and the family of butterfly networks. Our main results also hold for the so called *hypercubic networks*, such as the shuffle-exchange network, the de-Bruijn network, and the cube-connected-cycles network, by a general simulation given in [S90].

A *d-dimensional hypercube* contains 2^d processors. Their id's are the strings in $\{0,1\}^d$. Two processors are connected iff their id's differ in exactly one bit. If we associate with each processor the integer represented by its id, the set of processors can be ordered according to this numbering. Let an interval $[a, b)$ of processors in a hypercube denote the set of processors with numbers $a, a+1, \ldots, b-1$. This interval is an i-dimensional subcube iff $2^i \mid a$ and $a + 2^i = b$. In this paper we consider only subcubes which are intervals in this sense (though there are many more subcubes).

A *d-dimensional butterfly* contains $(d + 1) 2^d$ processors named by tupels from $[0, d] \times \{0, 1\}^d$. Connections are between processors (i, a) and $(i + 1, b)$ iff $a = b$ or a and b differ only in position $i+1$. The set of processors $[0, i] \times [a, b)$ is an i-dimensional subbutterfly iff $2^i \mid a$ and $a + 2^i = b$. By cutting all edges between the nodes of level i and level $i + 1$ the d-dimensional butterfly is disconnected into 2^{d-i} i-dimensional butterflies and 2^{i+1} $(d - i - 1)$-dimensional butterflies. These subbutterflies will be used in our construction. We assume that the nodes in the butterfly network are ordered lexicographically, with the second component more significant than the first. An extensive collection of results concerning hypercubes and hypercubic networks can be found in [L92].

In the following sections we will focus on hypercube algorithms. In section 6 we then show how to modify our results for the butterfly network.

2.2 Restrictions on the Divide and the Conquer-Implementations

We consider divide-and-conquer algorithms with the following properties:

- in the divide-step, each problem is split into subproblems with sizes adding up to no more than the size of the problem itself; size is measured in processor words;
- the solution to each subproblem is no longer than the subproblem itself;
- each subproblem is treated in a subcube at least its size. The input of the divide-step is assumed to be stored contiguously in a subcube (interval) starting at the first processor, and the output of a divide step is a sequence of subproblems each stored in an interval of processors. The conquer-step works in an analogous manner. Note, however, that the intervals of subproblems are generally not subcubes.

Let the running time of the divide-step and the conquer-step for inputs of size n be bounded by $T(n)$, let the sizes of the generated subproblems be bounded by $s(n)$, and let c be the size of problems solved without any more recursive steps. Then an obvious lower bound for the running time of the divide-and-conquer algorithm is

$$\bar{T}(n) = T(n) + T(s(n)) + T(s(s(n))) + \ldots + T(c).$$

In the sequel we show how to reach this bound asymptotically for hypercubes and hypercubic networks.

From the properties we agreed on for the divide-step and the conquer-step, the following algorithmic problems become apparent:

- the generated subproblems in general don't match the sizes of subcubes (resp. subbutterflies);
- in general, subproblems are stored in intervals which are not subcubes; rather, the intervals have to be routed to subcubes.

We define the *subcube allocation problem with expansion* x as follows:

Suppose we are given a sequence of intervals of total length $\leq n$ where each interval length is a power of 2. Then the intervals have to be aligned with subcubes in the interval $[0, xn)$. The algorithm has to be executed on a hypercube with a size of the next power of 2 greater than or equal xn.

3 The Subcube Allocation Problem

In this section we consider several subcube allocation algorithms for the hypercube. In the algorithms we use the following primitive operations for which logarithmic time algorithms are well-known:

- parallel-prefix (for a sequence $a_1, a_2, \ldots, a_p$ and an associative operator $\circ$, have, for all i, the i-th processor compute the value of $\bigcirc_{1 \leq j \leq i} a_j$) [S80];
- pipelined parallel-prefix ($\log p$ independent parallel-prefix operations) [PM89];

– concentration routing, inverse concentration routing, monotone routing (each processor is the source and the destination of at most one data item, the order of the data items is preserved by the routing, and, in concentration routings, the data items are concentrated to the leftmost processors, one item per processor) [NS81].

Lemma 1. *There is an $O(\log \log n \log n)$ time algorithm for the subcube allocation problem with expansion 1.*

Proof. As the length of each interval is a power of 2, it is sufficient to sort the given intervals according to their size in descending order, and to concentrate the resulting sequence to the left. There are at most $\log n$ distinct lengths. The intervals are divided into groups according to their lengths. Using parallel-prefix operations and concentration routings, the upper half of groups is concentrated to the left and the lower half to their right. This process is repeated recursively within the two halves until the intervals are sorted according to their lengths. The depth of the recursion is bounded by $\log \log n$.   □

If the running time of the given divide-step and conquer-step is only logarithmic in n the above method leads to a suboptimal algorithm due to the $\log \log n$ factor. Our next lemma shows how to achieve an optimal running time at the cost of a somewhat larger expansion.

Lemma 2. *There is an $O(\log n)$ time algorithm for the subcube allocation problem with expansion 2.*

Proof. Assume that the sequence of intervals (each with length a power of 2) with a total length of n is stored in the leftmost processors of a hypercube of size at least $2n$. We first route the intervals to the right so that immediately to the left of each interval there is empty space equal to the size of the interval. Then each interval is shifted to the left until it is aligned with an appropriately sized subcube. In this shift operation no two intervals interfere with each other.

It is obvious that the final destinations of the intervals can be computed in advance and only one inverse concentration route has to be carried out.   □

The following result shows that the two previous lemmata can be viewed as the extreme points of a trade-off between the expansion and the time required for the routing. For notational convenience let $\log x$ be 1 for $x \le 2$.

Theorem 3. *The subcube allocation problem with expansion $1 + \varepsilon$ can be solved in $O(\log \log 1/\varepsilon \log n)$ steps, for $\frac{1}{n} \le \varepsilon \le 1$.*

It turns out that it is also possible to embed intervals into subcubes with expansion 1 using only logarithmic time. For this algorithm we use our generic divide-and-conquer method presented in the following section as a bootstrap.

4 A Generic Divide-and-Conquer Algorithm

4.1 A Suboptimal Solution

As already noted in the introduction a divide-and-conquer algorithm can be viewed as a tree with the root corresponding to the given problem, the other nodes corresponding to the subproblems, and the leaves corresponding to subproblems solved directly. Our first implementation of the divide-and-conquer paradigm proceeds in phases corresponding to the levels of the tree. Each phase consists of the following steps:

A1. All subproblems at the current level of the tree are padded in size to the next larger power of 2 and are stored contiguously from the left of the hypercube. Using the algorithm of Lemma 2 each subproblem is routed to its own subcube;

A2. for each subproblem the divide-step is executed within its associated subcube.

When all subproblems are of some constant size, they are solved directly. In the ascending ("conquer") part of the algorithm we recombine these solutions to the subproblems. To guarantee correct combination of the computed results we have to remember the data movements made in the subcube allocation routines of the descending part, and reverse them. Suitable techniques to remember moves with just a small amount of additional memory are proposed in (the full version of) [MW92]. We only need a constant number of bits per processor for each phase to store the moves.

Note that for the algorithm to work correctly the size of the hypercube must be at least $4n$ for inputs of size n.

Each of the subcube allocation steps in the above algorithm takes $O(\log n)$ steps. Thus, the total running time is

$$T(n) + O(\log n) + T(s(n)) + O(\log n) + T(s(s(n))) + \ldots + O(\log n) + T(c)$$

where again $T(n)$ is a bound on the running time of the divide-step and the conquer-step, $s(n)$ is the maximum size of a subproblem, and c is the size of problems solved directly.

Since the time required for the subcube allocation steps does not decrease on deeper levels of the recursion, this running time may be significantly larger than the lower bound $\bar{T}(n)$. In our next algorithm we manage to resolve this deficiency by restricting the subproblem allocation routings to smaller subcubes.

4.2 An Optimal Solution

We describe the descending part of our optimal algorithm. For an i-dimensional cube C, which is initially the whole cube, the algorithm consists of the following steps:

1. Execute steps A1 and A2 on C until all subproblems are smaller than $2^{\lfloor i/4 \rfloor}$.
2. Divide the subproblems in C into $2^{\lceil i/2 \rceil}$ roughly equally sized groups as follows: Concentrate all intervals comprising the subproblems to the first processors in C, say $[a, a + n')$. For all j with $0 \leq j < 2^{\lceil i/2 \rceil}$, assign to group j all intervals beginning in

$$\left[a + \left\lfloor j \frac{n'}{2^{\lceil i/2 \rceil}} \right\rfloor , a + \left\lfloor (j+1) \frac{n'}{2^{\lceil i/2 \rceil}} \right\rfloor \right).$$

Route the intervals of group j into the j-th $\lfloor i/2 \rfloor$-dimensional subcube of C, i.e. the subcube starting at processor $a + j \, 2^{\lfloor i/2 \rfloor}$. Call this algorithm recursively for each of these subcubes provided that their dimension $\lfloor i/2 \rfloor$ is not below some appropriately chosen constant d_0. Otherwise, all subproblems are of constant size and are solved directly.

To guarantee that the subcube allocation steps in the phases can be executed correctly, we had to assume in the previous subsection that the cube was at least 4 times as large as the input size, or, as we shall say subsequently, the initial load of the cube was at most 1/4.

Lemma 4. *With an initial load ≤ 0.183 and $d_0 = 8$, the above algorithm is never invoked on a subcube with a load $> 1/4$.*

Proof. Consider an i-dimensional subcube C invoking, in step 2, the algorithm recursively for an i'-dimensional subcube C'. Let $l(C)$ and $l(C')$ denote the load of C and C', then we have

$$l(C') < \left(\frac{l(C) \, 2^i}{2^{i-i'}} + 2^{\lfloor i/4 \rfloor} \right) \frac{1}{2^{i'}}$$
$$= l(C) + 2^{\lfloor i/4 \rfloor - i'}$$
$$= l(C) + 2^{\lfloor i/4 \rfloor - \lfloor i/2 \rfloor}$$
$$\leq l(C) + 2^{-i'/2}$$

Thus, for an i-dimensional subcube, for which the algorithm is invoked recursively starting from a d-dimensional hypercube, the load is bounded by

$$0.183 + 2^{-\lfloor d/2 \rfloor/2} + 2^{-\lfloor \lfloor d/2 \rfloor/2 \rfloor/2} + \ldots + 2^{-i/2}$$
$$\leq 0.183 + \sum_{j \geq 0} \left(2^{-i/2} \right)^{\left(2^j \right)}$$

An easy computation shows that this sum is less than 1/4 for $i \geq 8$. □

To analyze the running time of this divide-and-conquer algorithm, we only have to consider the descending part, because the ascending part is symmetrical.

Let us at first estimate the running time of step 2, the grouping and routing of subproblems. These operations need $O(i)$ steps in an i-dimensional subcube. But as the dimension of the subcubes is halved on each level of recursive calls, the sum of these running times is $O(\log n)$.

Secondly, the time needed for the subcube allocation algorithm (step A1) executed in an i-dimensional subcube is also $O(i)$. We want to compare this time with the time needed for the immediately following divide-step (step A2) in the largest allocated subcube, which must be at least of size $2^{\lfloor i/4 \rfloor}$ by our termination criterion for the loop of step 1. Provided that the running time of the divide-step or conquer-step is $T(n) = \Omega(\log n)$, we spend $\Omega(i)$ steps for this divide-step or the corresponding conquer-step. Therefore, the subcube allocation steps cause only a constant factor overhead in the running time.

We should note here that the authors could hardly think of a divide-step and conquer-step for any nontrivial problem running in $o(\log n)$ time on the hypercube.

Theorem 5. *Given a divide-step and a conquer-step satisfying the assumptions listed in section 2, with running times $T(n) = \Omega(\log n)$ on the hypercube, there is an algorithm solving problems of size n on a $\lceil \log n \rceil$-dimensional hypercube in time $O(\bar{T}(n))$, with*

$$\bar{T}(n) = T(n) + T(s(n)) + T(s(s(n))) + \ldots + T(c),$$

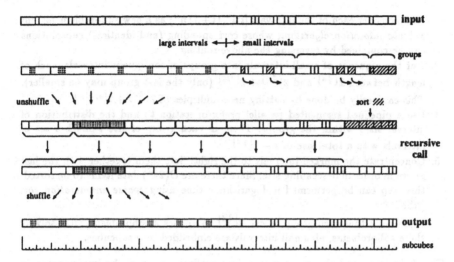

Fig. 1. Recursive subcube allocation algorithm

for some constant c and a bound s(n) on the size of subproblems.

Proof. We have given an algorithm achieving the time bound on a hypercube with an initial load of at most 0.183. This larger hypercube can be simulated by a $\lceil \log n \rceil$-dimensional hypercube with a slowdown of at most 8.   □

5   Applications

In [MW92] a divide-and-conquer algorithm is given that performs a special class of partial permutations called *parentheses-structured routings* in logarithmic time on hypercubes. In a well-formed string of parentheses, these partial permutations map each opening parenthesis to its matching closing parenthesis. The method used in [MW92] employs specific properties of this problem in order to obtain an efficient algorithm. The generic approach presented in this paper gives an alternative algorithm with the same running time.

As another application of Theorem 5, we present a subcube allocation algorithm with expansion 1 for hypercubes which runs in logarithmic time.

Let d be the dimension of the cube. We execute the following steps (see Figure 1):

1. Separate the *small* intervals of size $< 2^{\lceil d/3 \rceil}$ from the *large* intervals concentrating the large intervals to the left and the small intervals to their right.

2. Let n' denote the total size of the large intervals, and set $n'' = n'/2^{\lceil d/3 \rceil}$. Redistribute the large intervals by performing an *unshuffle permutation*, i.e. route the data item stored in processor $i + j\,2^{\lceil d/3 \rceil}$ (for $0 \le i < 2^{\lceil d/3 \rceil}$ and $0 \le j < n''$) to processor $j + i\,n''$, using a bit-permute-permutation [NS82a] and a concentration routing.

Now consider each of the intervals $[i\,n'', (i+1)\,n'')$ as a new subproblem *for our subcube allocation algorithm*, whose corresponding (and identical) subsolutions can be combined by reversing the above routing.

3. Cut the sequence of small intervals into groups of contiguous intervals, each of length between $2^{\lfloor \frac{2}{3}d \rfloor}$ and $2^{\lfloor \frac{2}{3}d \rfloor} + 2^{\lceil d/3 \rceil}$ (only the last group may be smaller). This can easily be done by cutting near multiples of $2^{\lfloor \frac{2}{3}d \rfloor} + 2^{\lceil d/3 \rceil - 1}$.

4. Use a pipelined segmented parallel prefix operation to find the distribution of interval sizes within the groups. Then, in each group of size s mark a set of intervals with a total size of $s - 2^{\lfloor \frac{2}{3}d \rfloor}$.

5. Concentrate the marked intervals to the right. Sort them together with the last group in order of descending size. Since there are $O(2^{\frac{2}{3}d})$ data items to be sorted, this step can be performed in logarithmic time using *sparse enumeration sort* [NS82b].

Again note that each group of size $2^{\lfloor \frac{2}{3}d \rfloor}$ comprises a subproblem; after solving these subproblems, all small intervals are embedded into subcubes.

The divide-step and the conquer-step just outlined can both be implemented in logarithmic time on a d-dimensional hypercube. All generated subproblems are of size $\leq 2^{\lfloor \frac{2}{3}d \rfloor}$. Thus we can apply Theorem 5 with

$$T(n) = O(\log n), \quad s(n) \leq n^{2/3}, \quad \text{and hence} \quad \bar{T}(n) = O(\log n),$$

and obtain:

Theorem 6. *There exists an $O(\log n)$ time algorithm for the subcube allocation problem with expansion 1.*

6 The Butterfly

For the butterfly network we require two modifications of the method presented in section 4.

The first modification is due to the fact that butterflies cannot easily be divided into subbutterflies. As noted in section 2, a butterfly of dimension $2\,i+1$ can be divided into 2^{i+2} i-dimensional butterflies whereas a butterfly of dimension $2\,i$ has to be divided into 2^i i-dimensional and 2^{i+1} $(i-1)$-dimensional butterflies. Thus step 2 (grouping of subproblems) has to be adjusted appropriately so as to distribute the load roughly equally to the subbutterflies.

The second problem is that the subnetwork allocation for the butterfly is slightly more complicated than for the hypercube.

For the following lemma assume that the intervals to be embedded have lengths matching the sizes of butterflies.

Lemma 7. *The subnetwork allocation problem with expansion 8 for butterflies can be solved in $O(\log n)$ steps if each of the intervals given in a d-dimensional butterfly is at least of size $(\lfloor d/4 \rfloor + 1)\, 2^{\lfloor d/4 \rfloor}$.*

Proof. Let a sequence of intervals be given, and let the length of the j-th interval be $(d_j + 1) 2^{d_j}$. Since the expansion is at least 8, we have

$$\sum_j (d_j + 1) 2^{d_j} \leq \frac{1}{8}(d + 1) 2^d$$

$$\implies \quad \sum_j 2^{d_j} \leq \frac{1}{2} 2^d$$

Using the simple technique of Lemma 1, we can embed a sequence of intervals with lengths 2^{d_j} into subcubes of a d-dimensional hypercube without changing the order of the intervals. If, instead, in the hypercube the j-th interval is embedded in $[a_j, a_j + 2^{d_j})$, then we solve our problem for the butterfly by routing the j-th interval to the set of processors $[0, d_j] \times [a_j, a_j + 2^{d_j})$. This routing is monotone in our lexicographic ordering of the d-dimensional butterfly. □

For the i-dimensional butterfly we substitute the upper bound for the subproblem sizes that we could guarantee after step 1 by $(\lfloor i/4 \rfloor + 1) 2^{\lfloor i/4 \rfloor}$. We can also achieve this bound by collecting, after each execution of steps A1 and A2, those subproblems that are already smaller than $(\lfloor i/4 \rfloor + 1) 2^{\lfloor i/4 \rfloor}$ to one end of the butterfly and subdividing further only those subproblems that are still too large. In this way we can guarantee the condition of Lemma 7.

A proof very similar to that of Theorem 5 (and therefore omitted) yields:

Theorem 8. *We are given a divide-step and a conquer-step for a problem P satisfying the assumptions given in section 2 with running times $T(n) = \Omega(\log n)$ on a butterfly of size $b(n)$, where $b(n)$ is the smallest size $\geq n$ of a butterfly. Then P can be solved for instances of size n on a butterfly of size $b(n)$ in time $O(\bar{T}(n))$.*

There are many networks with a structure very similar to the butterfly. These *hypercubic networks* include the cube-connected-cycles network, the Benes network, the shuffle-exchange network, and the de Bruijn network. The analogue of Theorem 8 is valid for each of these networks. This follows from a result shown by Schwabe in [S90] stating that a network of one of these types can be simulated by a similar size network of any other type with a constant factor slowdown. To obtain Theorem 8 for some family F, we have to simulate the divide-step and the conquer-step by a butterfly, apply Theorem 8, and simulate the complete butterfly divide-and-conquer algorithm on the given network of type F.

A direct proof of Theorem 8 for each of the hypercubic networks seems to be difficult because the subnetwork allocation problem can become quite complicated. Indeed, for the cube-connected-cycles network, it is unsolvable since no connected regular network can contain a regular subnetwork of the same degree.

7 Conclusion and Open Problems

In this paper we have implemented divide-and-conquer on the hypercube and the hypercubic networks with an asymptotically optimal running time. If the goal is minimizing the constant factor in the overhead caused by our method, there is a number of design decisions that can be made, depending on the parameters $T(n)$ and $s(n)$. We have presented a number of different subcube allocation algorithms, and one could use different subcube sizes for the recursive calls and different parameters for allocating subcubes. The choices given in this paper work relatively well in all cases. Indeed, it is not even necessary to know the bounds $T(n)$ and $s(n)$.

A more general (and, of course, more complicated) approach to the problems considered in this paper would be to allow the total size of subproblems generated on any one level to exceed the original problem size and/or to allow the number of processors performing a divide-step or conquer-step to depend non-linearly on the problem size.

Another interesting open question is to find a direct optimal algorithm for the subcube allocation problem with expansion 1.

References

[CL90]   M.Y. Chan and S.-J. Lee. Subcube recognition, allocation/deallocation and relocation in hypercubes. *Proceedings of the 2nd IEEE Symposium on Parallel and Distributed Processing*, 87–93, 1990.

[CS87]   M.-S. Chen and K.G. Shin. Processor allocation in an N-cube multiprocessor using Gray codes. *IEEE Transactions on Computers*, C-36:1396–1407, 1987.

[FW78]   S. Fortune and J. Wyllie. Parallelism in random access machines. *Proceedings of the 10th ACM Symposium on Theory of Computing*, 114–118, 1978.

[vG89]   A. van Gelder. PRAM processor allocation: A hidden bottleneck in sublogarithmic algorithms *IEEE Transactions on Computers*, C-38:289–292, 1989.

[KDL89] J. Kim and C.R. Das and W. Lin. A processor allocation scheme for hypercube computers. *Proceedings of the 1989 International Conference on Parallel Processing*. Vol. 2 Software, 231–238, 1989.

[L92]   F.T. Leighton. *Introduction to Parallel Algorithms and Architectures*. Morgan Kaufmann Publishers, 1992.

[MW92]   E.W. Mayr and R. Werchner. Optimal routing of parentheses on the hypercube. *Proceedings of the 4th Annual ACM Symposium on Parallel Algorithms and Architectures*, 109–117, 1992.

[NS81]   D. Nassimi and S. Sahni. Data broadcasting in SIMD computers. *IEEE Transactions on Computers*, C-30:101–107, 1981.

[NS82a] D. Nassimi and S. Sahni. A self-routing Benes network and parallel permutation algorithms. *IEEE Transactions on Computers*, C-31:148–154, 1982.

[NS82b] D. Nassimi and S. Sahni. Parallel permutation and sorting algorithms and a new generalized connection network. *JACM*, 29:642–667, 1982.

[PM89]   C.G. Plaxton and E.W. Mayr. Pipelined parallel prefix computations and sorting on a pipelined hypercube. Technical Report STAN-CS-89-1269, Stanford University, 1989. To appear in J. Parallel Distrib. Comput..

[S90]   E.J. Schwabe. On the computational equivalence of hypercube-derived networks. *Proceedings of the 2nd Annual ACM Symposium on Parallel Algorithms and Architectures*, 388–397, 1990.

[S80]   J.T. Schwartz. Ultracomputers. *ACM Transactions on Programming Languages and Systems*, 2:484–521, 1980.

[ZRL91] X. Zhong, S. Rajopadhye and V.M. Lo. Parallel implementations of divide-and-conquer algorithms on binary de Bruijn networks. Technical Report CIS-TR-91-21 University of Oregon, 1991.

A First-Order Isomorphism Theorem

Eric Allender*[1], Jose Balcázar**[2], and Neil Immerman***[3]

[1] Department of Computer Science, Princeton University
35 Olden St., Princeton, NJ, USA 08903
allender@cs.princeton.edu
[2] U. Politècnica de Catalunya, Departamento L.S.I.
Pau Gargallo 5, E-08071 Barcelona, Spain
balqui@lsi.upc.es
[3] Computer Science Department, University of Massachusetts
Amherst, MA, USA 01003
immerman@cs.umass.edu

Abstract. We show that for most complexity classes of interest, all sets complete under first-order projections are isomorphic under first-order isomorphisms. That is, a very restricted version of the Berman-Hartmanis Conjecture holds.

1 Introduction

In 1977 Berman and Hartmanis noticed that all NP complete sets that they knew of were polynomial-time isomorphic, [BH77]. They made their now-famous isomorphism conjecture: namely that all NP complete sets are polynomial-time isomorphic. This conjecture has engendered a large amount of work (cf. [KMR, You] for surveys).

The isomorphism conjecture was made using the notion of NP completeness via polynomial-time, many-one reductions because that was the standard definition at the time. In [Coo71], Cook proved that the Boolean satisfiability problem (SAT) is NP complete via polynomial-time Turing reductions. Over the years SAT has been shown complete via weaker and weaker reductions, e.g. polynomial-time many-one [Kar], logspace many-one [Jon], one-way logspace many-one [HIM], and first-order projections (fops) [Dah]. These last reductions, defined in Section 3, are provably weaker than logspace reductions. It has been observed that *natural* complete problems for various complexity classes remain complete via fops, cf. [Imm87, IL, Ste].

On the other hand, Joseph and Young, [JY] have pointed out that polynomial-time, many-one reductions are so powerful as to allow *unnatural* NP-complete sets. Most researchers now believe that the isomorphism conjecture as originally stated by Berman and Hartmanis is false.[4]

* On leave from Rutgers University; supported in part by National Science Foundation grant CCR-9204874.
** Supported in part by ESPRIT-II BRA EC project 3075 (ALCOM) and by Acción Integrada Hispano-Alemana 131 B
*** Supported by NSF grants CCR-9008416 and CCR-9207797.
[4] One way of quantifying this observation is that since Joseph and Young produced their unnatural NP-complete sets, Hartmanis has been referring to the isomorphism conjecture as the "Berman" conjecture.

We feel on the other hand, that the problem is simply that the choice of reduction at the time was made for historical rather than scientific reasons. Since natural complete problems turn out to be complete via very low-level reductions such as fops, it is natural to modify the isomorphism conjecture to consider NP-complete reductions via fops. Motivating this in another way, one could propose as a slightly more general form of the isomorphism conjecture the question: is completeness a structural sufficient condition for isomorphism? Our work answers this question by presenting a notion of completeness for which the answer is yes. Namely for every nice complexity class including P, NP, etc, any two sets complete via fops are not only polynomial-time isomorphic, they are first-order isomorphic.

There are additional reasons to be interested in first-order computation. It was shown in [BIS] that first-order computation corresponds exactly to computation by uniform AC^0 circuits under a natural notion of uniformity. Although it is known that AC^0 is properly contained in NP, knowing that a set A is complete for NP under polynomial-time (or logspace) reductions does not currently allow us to conclude that A is not in AC^0; however, knowing that A is complete for NP under first-order reductions does allow us to make that conclusion.

First-order reducibility is a uniform version of the constant-depth reducibility studied in [FSS, CSV]; sometimes this uniformity is important. For a concrete example where first-order reducibility is used to provide a circuit lower bound, see [AG].

Preliminary results and background on isomorphisms follow in Section 2. Definitions and background on descriptive complexity are found in Section 3. The main result is stated and proved in Section 4, and then we conclude with some related results and remarks about the structure of NP under first-order reducibilities.

2   Short History of the Isomorphism Conjecture

Definition 1. For $A, B \subseteq \Sigma^*$, we say that A and B are *p-isomorphic* $(A \overset{p}{\cong} B)$ iff there exists a bijection $f \in$ FP with inverse $f^{-1} \in$ FP such that $A \leq_m B$ via f (and therefore $B \leq_m A$ via f^{-1}).

Observation 2 [BH77]. *All the NP complete sets in [GJ] are p-isomorphic.*

How did Berman and Hartmanis make their observation? They did it by proving a polynomial-time version of the Schröder-Bernstein Theorem. Recall:

Theorem 3 (Schröder-Bernstein Theorem). *Let A and B be any two sets. Suppose that there are 1:1 maps from A to B and from B to A. Then there is a 1:1 and onto map from A to B.*

Proof Let $f : A \to B$ and $g : B \to A$ be the given 1:1 maps. For simplicity assume that A and B are disjoint. For $a, c \in A \cup B$, we say that c is an *ancestor* of a iff we can reach a by a finite (non-zero) number of applications of the functions f and/or g. Now we can define a bijection $h : A \to B$ which applies either f or g^{-1} according as whether a point has an odd number of ancestors or not:

$$h(a) = \begin{cases} g^{-1}(a) & \text{if } a \text{ has an odd number of ancestors} \\ f(a) & \text{if } a \text{ has an even or infinite number of ancestors} \end{cases}$$

The feasible version of the Schröder-Bernstein theorem is as follows:

Theorem 4 [BH77]. *Let* $f : A \leq_m B$ *and* $g : B \leq_m A$, *where* f *and* g *are 1:1, length-increasing functions. Assume that* $f, f^{-1}, g, g^{-1} \in$ FP *where* f^{-1}, g^{-1} *are inverses of* f, g. *Then* $A \cong^p B$.

Proof This follows from the proof of Theorem 3 because in this case all ancestor chains are at most linear in length. ∎

Consider the following definition:

Definition 5 [BH77]. We say that the language $A \subseteq \Sigma^*$ has *p-time padding functions* iff there exist $e, d \in$ FP such that

1. For all $w, x \in \Sigma^*$, $w \in A \Leftrightarrow e(w, x) \in A$
2. For all $w, x \in \Sigma^*$, $d(e(w, x)) = x$
3. For all $w, x \in \Sigma^*$, $|e(w, x)| \geq |w| + |x|$

As a simple example, the following is a padding function for SAT,

$$e(w, x) = (w) \wedge c_1 \wedge c_2 \wedge \cdots \wedge c_{|x|}$$

where c_i is $(y \vee \bar{y})$ if the ith bit of x is 1 and $(\bar{z} \vee z)$ otherwise, where y and z are Boolean variables numbered higher than all the Boolean variables occurring in w.

Then the following theorem follows from Theorem 4:

Theorem 6 [BH77]. *If* A *and* B *are NP complete and have p-time padding functions, then* $A \cong^p B$.

Finally, Observation 2 now follows from the following:

Observation 7 [BH77]. *All the NP complete problems in [GJ] have p-time padding functions.*

Berman and Hartmanis also extended the above work as follows: Say that A has *logspace-padding functions* if there are logspace computable functions as in Definition 5.

Theorem 8 [BH77]. *If* A *and* B *are NP complete via logspace reductions and have logspace padding functions, then* A *and* B *are logspace isomorphic.*

Proof Since A and B have logspace padding functions, we can create functions f and g as in Theorem 4 that are length squaring and computable in logspace. Then, the whole ancestor chain can be computed in logspace because each successive iteration requires half of the previous space. ∎

Here, we show that sets complete under a very restrictive notion of reducibility are isomorphic under a very restricted class of isomorphisms. This result is incomparable to a very recent result of [AB], showing that all sets complete under one-way logspace reductions (1-L reductions) are isomorphic under polynomial-time computable isomorphisms. (This work of [AB] improves an earlier result of [All88].) Note that it is easy to prove that the class of 1-L reductions is incomparable with the class of first-order projections. Other interesting results concerning 1-L reductions may be found in [BH90, HH].

3 Descriptive Complexity

In this section we recall the notation of Descriptive Complexity which we will need to state and prove our main results. See [Imm89] for a survey and [IL] for an extensive discussion of the reductions we use here including first-order projections.

We will code all inputs as finite logical structures. The most basic example is a binary string, w of length $n = |w|$. We will represent w as a logical structure:

$$\mathcal{A}(w) = \langle \{0, 1, \ldots, n-1\}, R \rangle$$

where the unary relation $R(x)$ holds in $\mathcal{A}(w)$ (in symbols, $\mathcal{A}(w) \models R(x)$) just if bit x of w is a 1. As is customary, the notation $|\mathcal{A}|$ will be used to denote the universe $\{0, 1, \ldots, n-1\}$ of the structure $\mathcal{A}$. We will write $\|\mathcal{A}\|$ to denote n, the cardinality of $|\mathcal{A}|$.

A *vocabulary* $\tau = \langle R_1^{a_1} \ldots R_s^{a_s}, c_1, \ldots, c_s \rangle$ is a tuple of input relation and constant symbols. Let STRUC[τ] denote the set of all finite structures of vocabulary τ. We define a complexity theoretic *problem* to be any subset of STRUC[τ] for some τ.

For any vocabulary τ there is a corresponding first-order language $\mathcal{L}(\tau)$ built up from the symbols of τ and the logical relation symbols and constant symbols[5]: $=, \leq$, s, BIT, 0, m, using logical connectives: $\wedge, \vee, \neg$, variables: $x, y, z, \ldots$, and quantifiers: $\forall, \exists$.

First-Order Interpretations and Projections

In [Val], Valiant defined the *projection,* an extremely low-level many-one reduction.

Definition 9. A k-ary *projection* from S to T is a sequence of maps $\{p_n\}$, $n = 1, 2, \ldots$, such that for all n and for all binary strings s of length n, $p_n(s)$ is a binary string of length n^k and,

$$s \in S \quad \Leftrightarrow \quad p_n(s) \in T.$$

Let $s = s_0 s_1 \ldots s_{n-1}$. Then each map p_n is defined by a sequence of n^k literals: $\langle l_0, l_1, \ldots, l_{n^k-1} \rangle$ where

$$l_i \in \{0, 1\} \cup \{s_j, \bar{s}_j \mid 0 \leq j \leq n-1\} .$$

Thus as s ranges over strings of length n, each bit of $p_n(s)$ depends on at most one bit of s,

$$p_n(s)[[i]] \quad = \quad l_i(s)$$

---

[5] Here $\leq$ refers to the usual ordering on $\{0, \ldots, n-1\}$, s is the successor relation, "BIT(i, j)" means that the ith bit of the binary representation of j is 1, and 0 and m refer to 0 and $n - 1$, respectively. Some of these are redundant, but useful for quantifier-free interpretations. For simplicity we will assume throughout that $n > 1$ and thus $0 \neq$ m. Sometimes the logical relations are called "numeric" relations. For example, "BIT(i, j)" and "$i \leq j$" depend only on the numeric values of i and j and do not refer to the input.

Projections were originally defined as a non-uniform sequence of reductions – one for each value of n. That is, a projection can be viewed as a many-one reduction produced by a family $\{C_n\}$ of circuits with depth one and *no gates*. That is, the circuits consist entirely of wires connecting inputs to outputs. If the circuit family $\{C_n\}$ is sufficiently *uniform*, we arrive a the class of *first-order projections*. (Recall that first-order corresponds to uniform AC^0 [BIS].) We find it useful to work in the framework of first-order logic rather than in the circuit model. The rest of this section presents the necessary definitions of first-order reductions.

The idea of our definition is that the choice of the literals $\langle l_0, l_1, \ldots, l_{n^k-1} \rangle$ in Definition 9 is given by a first-order formula in which no input relation occurs. Thus the formula can only talk about bit positions, and not bit values. The choice of literals depends only on n. In order to make this definition, we must first define first-order interpretations. These are a standard notion from logic for translating one theory into another, cf. [End], modified so that the transformation is also a many-one reduction, [Imm87]. (For readers familiar with databases, a first-order interpretation is exactly a many-one reduction that is definable as a first-order query.)

Definition 10 First-Order Interpretations. Let σ and τ be two vocabularies, with $\tau = \langle R_1^{a_1}, \ldots, R_r^{a_r}, c_1, \ldots, c_s \rangle$. Let $S \subseteq \text{STRUC}[\sigma]$, $T \subseteq \text{STRUC}[\tau]$ be two problems. Let k be a positive integer. Suppose we are given an r-tuple of formulas $\varphi_i \in \mathcal{L}(\sigma)$, $i = 1, \ldots, r$, where the free variables of φ_i are a subset of $\{x_1, \ldots, x_{k \cdot a_i}\}$. Finally, suppose we are given an s-tuple of closed terms[6] $t_1, \ldots, t_s$ from $\mathcal{L}(\sigma)$. Let $I = \lambda_{x_1 \ldots x_d} \langle \varphi_1, \ldots, \varphi_r, t_1, \ldots, t_s \rangle$ be a tuple of these formulas and closed terms. (Here $d = \max_i (ka_i)$.)

Then I induces a mapping $\hat{I}$ from $\text{STRUC}[\sigma]$ to $\text{STRUC}[\tau]$ as follows. Let $\mathcal{A} \in \text{STRUC}[\sigma]$ be any structure of vocabulary σ, and let $n = \|\mathcal{A}\|$. Then the structure $\hat{I}(\mathcal{A})$ is defined as follows:

$$\hat{I}(\mathcal{A}) = \langle \{0, \ldots, n^k - 1\}, R_1, \ldots, R_r \rangle$$

where the relation R_i is determined by the formula φ_i, for $i = 1, \ldots, r$. More precisely, let the function $\langle \cdot, \cdots, \cdot \rangle : |\mathcal{A}|^k \to |\hat{I}(\mathcal{A})|$ be given by

$$\langle u_1, u_2, \ldots, u_k \rangle = u_k + u_{k-1}n + \cdots + u_1 n^{k-1}$$

Then,

$$R_i = \{((u_1, \ldots, u_k), \ldots, (u_{1+k(a_i-1)}, \ldots, u_{ka_i})) \mid \mathcal{A} \models \varphi_i(u_1, \ldots u_{ka_i})\}$$

If the structure $\mathcal{A}$ interprets some variables $\bar{u}$ then these may appear freely in the the φ_i's and t_j's of I, and the definition of $\hat{I}(\mathcal{A})$ still makes sense.

Suppose that $\hat{I}$ is a many-one reduction from S to T, i.e. for all $\mathcal{A}$ in $\text{STRUC}[\sigma]$,

$$\mathcal{A} \in S \quad \Leftrightarrow \quad \hat{I}(\mathcal{A}) \in T$$

---

[6] A closed term is an expression involving constants and function symbols. This is as opposed to an open term which also has free variables. In this paper, since we do not have function symbols, closed terms are synonymous with constant symbols. Note that a more general way to interpret constants and functions is via a formula φ such that $\vdash (\forall \bar{x})(\exists! y)\varphi(\bar{x}, y)$. However, in this paper the simpler definition using closed terms suffices.

Then we say that $\hat{I}$ is a k-ary *first-order interpretation* of S to T.

Note that I induces a map which we will also call I from $\mathcal{L}(\tau)$ to $\mathcal{L}(\sigma)$. For $\varphi \in \mathcal{L}(\tau)$, $I(\varphi)$ is the result of replacing all relation and constant symbols in φ by the corresponding formulas and closed terms in I. Note that if I is a k-ary interpretation then each variable in φ is replaced by a k-tuple of variables. Furthermore, the logical relations $s, \leq, =$ are replaced by the corresponding quantifier-free formulas on k-tuples ordered lexicographically. For example, with $k = 2$, an occurrence of the successor relation, $s(x, y)$, would be replaced by

$$I(s(x, y)) = (x_1 = y_1 \wedge s(x_2, y_2)) \vee (x_2 = m \wedge y_2 = 0 \wedge s(x_1, y_1))$$

The logical constants, $0, m$, are replaced by k-tuples of the same constants.

Note that the logical relation BIT when mapped to k-tuples cannot be easily replaced by a quantifier-free formula. However, BIT on tuples is definable in FO (with BIT), cf. [Lin].

It follows immediately from the definitions that:

Proposition 11. *Let σ, τ, and I be as in Definition 10. Then for all sentences $\varphi \in \mathcal{L}(\tau)$ and all structures $\mathcal{A} \in \mathrm{STRUC}[\sigma]$,*

$$\mathcal{A} \models I(\varphi) \quad \Leftrightarrow \quad \hat{I}(\mathcal{A}) \models \varphi$$

We are now ready to define first-order projections, a syntactic restriction of first-order interpretations. If each formula in the first-order interpretation $\hat{I}$ satisfies this syntactic condition then it follows that $\hat{I}$ is also a projection in the sense of Valiant. In this case we call $\hat{I}$ a first-order projection.

Definition 12 (First-Order Projections). Let $\hat{I}$ be a k-ary first-order interpretation from S to T as in Definition 10. Let $I = \langle \varphi_1, \ldots, \varphi_r, t_1, \ldots, t_s \rangle$. Suppose further that the φ_i's all satisfy the following *projection condition:*

$$\varphi_i \equiv \alpha_1 \vee (\alpha_2 \wedge \lambda_2) \vee \cdots \vee (\alpha_s \wedge \lambda_s) \tag{13}$$

where the α_j's are mutually exclusive formulas in which no input relations occur, and each λ_j is a literal, i.e. an atomic formula $P(x_{j_1}, \ldots x_{j_a})$ or its negation.

In this case the predicate $R_i(\langle u_1, \ldots, u_k \rangle, \ldots, \langle \ldots, u_{k a_i} \rangle)$ holds in $\hat{I}(\mathcal{A})$ if $\alpha_1(\bar{u})$ is true, or if $\alpha_j(\bar{u})$ is true for some $1 < j \leq t$ and the corresponding literal $\lambda_j(\bar{u})$ holds in $\mathcal{A}$. Thus each bit in the binary representation of $\hat{I}(\mathcal{A})$ is determined by at most one bit in the binary representation of $\mathcal{A}$. We say that $\hat{I}$ is a *first-order projection.* Write $S \leq_{\mathrm{fop}} T$ to mean that S is reducible to T via a first-order projection.

Example 14. To help the reader grasp an intuition of the way an fop reduction behaves, let us describe an example. We present here the reduction from 3-SAT, satisfiability of CNF Boolean expressions with exactly three literals per clause, to 3-COL, the problem of coloring the vertices of a graph with 3 colors under the constraint that the endpoints of all edges get different colors. We use the same reduction as described in section 11.4.5 of [M89], so that the reader in need of additional help can consult it there.

The respective vocabularies for the input and output structures are as follows. To describe instances of 3-SAT, clauses and Boolean variables are each numbered from 0 through $n-1$. There are six predicates: $P_i(x,c)$, $N_i(x,c)$, $i=1,2,3$, indicating that variable x occurs positively or negatively in the ith position of the clause c. The vocabulary for the output structures is simply a binary predicate E standing for the Boolean adjacency matrix of the output graph. Thus $E(u,v)$ is true exactly when the edge (u,v) is present in the output graph.

The output graph consists of 6 vertices per clause and two vertices per Boolean variable, plus three additional vertices usually named T, F, and R (standing for true, false, and red). Let an arbitrary 3CNF formula be coded by an input structure,

$$\mathcal{A} = \langle \{0,1,\ldots,n-1\}, P_1, P_2, P_3, N_1, N_2, N_3\rangle$$

The output structure will be a graph with $8n+3$ relevant vertices. The easiest way for us to code this is to use an fop of arity 2. We will assume for simplicity that n is always greater than or equal to 9.

$$\hat{I}(\mathcal{A}) = \langle\{\langle a,b\rangle : 0 \le a, b < n\}, E\rangle = \langle\{0, \ldots n^2-1\}, E\rangle$$

where, $\quad E = \{(\langle x_1, x_2\rangle, \langle y_1, y_2\rangle) \mid \mathcal{A} \models \varphi(x_1, x_2, y_1, y_2)\}$

It remains to write down the first-order projection, φ. To do this, we need some nitty gritty coding. We will let the vertices T, F, and R be the elements $\langle 0,0\rangle$, $\langle 1,0\rangle$, and $\langle 2,0\rangle$ of $\hat{I}(\mathcal{A})$ respectively. The formula φ will have three pieces:

$$\varphi(x_1, x_2, y_1, y_2) = \alpha(x_1, x_2, y_1, y_2) \vee \beta(x_1, x_2, y_1, y_2) \vee \beta(y_1, y_2, x_1, x_2) \vee$$

$$\gamma(x_1, x_2, y_1, y_2) \vee \gamma(y_1, y_2, x_1, x_2)$$

Where α says that there are edges between T, F, and R; β says that vertices $\langle x, 1\rangle$ and $\langle x, 2\rangle$ representing variable x and its negation are connected to each other and to R; and; γ says that for clause $C = (a \vee b \vee d)$, vertices $\langle C, 6\rangle$, $\langle C, 7\rangle$, $\langle C, 8\rangle$ are connected to each other, and the following edges exist: $(\langle C, 3\rangle, \langle C, 6\rangle)$, $(\langle C, 4\rangle, \langle C, 7\rangle)$, $(\langle C, 5\rangle, \langle C, 8\rangle)$, as well as the edges $(a, \langle C, 3\rangle), (T, \langle C, 3\rangle), (b, \langle C, 4\rangle), (T, \langle C, 4\rangle)$, and $(d, \langle C, 5\rangle), (T, \langle C, 5\rangle)$.

In case anyone really wants to see them, here are the formulas written out:

$\alpha(x_1, x_2, y_1, y_2) \equiv (x_2 = y_2 = 0) \wedge (x_1 \ne y_1) \wedge (x_1 = 0 \vee x_1 = 1 \vee x_1 = 2)$
$\wedge (y_1 = 0 \vee y_1 = 1 \vee y_1 = 2)$

$\beta(x_1, x_2, y_1, y_2) \equiv (x_2 = 1 \wedge y_2 = 2 \wedge x_1 = y_1)$
$\vee (x_1 = 2 \wedge x_2 = 0 \wedge (y_2 = 1 \vee y_2 = 2))$

$\gamma(x_1, x_2, y_1, y_2) \equiv (x_1 = x_2 = 0 \wedge (y_2 = 3 \vee y_2 = 4 \vee y_2 = 5))$
$\vee\quad (x_1 = y_1 \wedge [(x_2 = 3 \wedge y_2 = 6) \vee (x_2 = 4 \wedge y_2 = 7) \vee (x_2 = 5 \wedge y_2 = 8)])$
$\vee\quad [(x_2 = 1 \wedge y_2 = 3) \wedge P_1(x_1, y_1)] \vee [(x_2 = 2 \wedge y_2 = 3) \wedge N_1(x_1, y_1)]$
$\vee\quad [(x_2 = 1 \wedge y_2 = 4) \wedge P_2(x_1, y_1)] \vee [(x_2 = 2 \wedge y_2 = 4) \wedge N_2(x_1, y_1)]$
$\vee\quad [(x_2 = 1 \wedge y_2 = 5) \wedge P_3(x_1, y_1)] \vee [(x_2 = 2 \wedge y_2 = 5) \wedge N_3(x_1, y_1)] \quad \vee$
$(x_1 = y_1 \wedge x_2 \ne y_2 \wedge (x_2 = 6 \vee x_2 = 7 \vee x_2 = 8) \wedge (y_2 = 6 \vee y_2 = 7 \vee y_2 = 8))$

4 Main Theorem and Proof

Theorem 15. *Let C be a nice complexity class, e.g., L, NL, P, NP, etc. Let S and T be complete for C via first-order projections. Then S and T are isomorphic via a first-order isomorphism.*

To prove Theorem 15 we begin with the following

Lemma 16. *Let I be an fop that is 1:1 and of arity greater than or equal to two (i.e. it at least squares the size). Then the following are expressible concerning a structure $\mathcal{A}$:*

a. $IE(\mathcal{A})$, i.e., $\hat{I}^{-1}(\mathcal{A})$ exists.

b. $\#Ancestors(\mathcal{A}, r)$, i.e., the length of $\mathcal{A}$'s maximal ancestor chain is r.

Proof Let $I = \lambda_{x_1...x_d}\langle \varphi_1, \ldots, \varphi_r, t_1, \ldots, t_s \rangle$, where each φ_i is in the form of Equation 13. To prove (a) just observe that each bit of the relation R_i of $\mathcal{A}$ either (1) depends on exactly one bit of some pre-image $\mathcal{B}$ (specified by an occurrence of a literal λ_{ij} in φ_i), or (2) it doesn't depend on any bit of a pre-image. In case (2) a given bit of $\mathcal{A}$ is either "right" or "wrong." Thus, $\mathcal{A}$ has an inverse iff no bit of $\mathcal{A}$ is wrong, and no pair of bits from $\mathcal{A}$ are determined by the same bit of $\mathcal{A}$'s preimage in conflicting ways. We can check this in a first-order way by checking that for all pairs of bits from $\mathcal{A}$: $R_i(\bar{a})$ and $R_{i'}(\bar{b})$, either they do not depend on the same bit from $\mathcal{B}$, or the same value of that bit gives the correct answer for $R_i(\bar{a})$ and $R_{i'}(\bar{b})$. Furthermore, the preimage $\mathcal{B}$ if it exists can be described uniquely by a first-order formula that chooses the correct bits determined by entries of $\mathcal{A}$. Since we have assumed that $\hat{I}$ is 1:1 every bit of the preimage is determined. This observation is important enough that it should be repeated: every bit of $\hat{I}^{-1}(\mathcal{A})$ is determined by some bit of $\mathcal{A}$.

(b) In order to define $\#Ancestors(\mathcal{A}, r)$, we will first define the related predicate $\#Anc.induct(\mathcal{A}, r)$ which will evaluate to true iff the implication

$\mathcal{A}$ has at least r ancestors implies $\mathcal{A}$ has at least $r + 1$ ancestors.

is true. Note that $\#Ancestors(\mathcal{A}, r)$ is equivalent to

$$(r = 0 \wedge \neg IE(\mathcal{A})) \vee$$

$$(r > 0 \wedge IE(\mathcal{A}) \wedge (\forall (t \leq r - 1)\#Anc.induct(\mathcal{A}, t)) \wedge \neg\#Anc.induct(\mathcal{A}, r)).$$

Let us use the notation $\mathcal{A}_t(\bar{b})$ to denote the $\bar{b}$-th bit of the string encoding the structure $\mathcal{A}_t$. If the assumption that the number of ancestors of $\mathcal{A}$ is at least r is true, this means that there is a chain:

$$\mathcal{A}_r \xrightarrow{I} \mathcal{A}_{r-1} \xrightarrow{I} \cdots \xrightarrow{I} \mathcal{A}_1 \xrightarrow{I} \mathcal{A}_0 = \mathcal{A}$$

where each $\mathcal{A}_t$ is a structure over a domain of size n^{1/k^t}. If this chain exists, that means that for each bit $\bar{b}_r$ of $\mathcal{A}_r$ there is a *certificate* of the form

$$C = \langle (\mathcal{A}_r(\bar{b}_r), \bar{b}_r), (\mathcal{A}_{r-1}(\bar{b}_{r-1}), \bar{b}_{r-1}), \ldots, (\mathcal{A}_0(\bar{b}_0), \bar{b}_0) \rangle$$

where this certificate has the meaning that for each t, bit $\bar{b}_t$ of $\mathcal{A}_t$ is determined by bit $\bar{b}_{t-1}$ of $\mathcal{A}_{t-1}$, and furthermore bit $\mathcal{A}_0(\bar{b}_0)$ agrees with bit $\bar{b}_0$ of the input structure $\mathcal{A}$.

The predicate $\#Anc.induct(\mathcal{A}, r)$ is equivalent to saying that if this sequence exists, then $IE(\mathcal{A}_r)$. Just as in part (a), this is equivalent to saying that for all $b_r \leq$ the number of bits in the description of $\mathcal{A}_r$, either (1) there exists a certificate for bit b_r showing that it is "right", or (2) there exists a certificate of the form

$$C = \langle (\mathcal{A}_{r+1}(\bar{b}_{r+1}), \bar{b}_{r+1}), (\mathcal{A}_r(\bar{b}_r), \bar{b}_r), \ldots, (\mathcal{A}_0(\bar{b}_0), \bar{b}_0) \rangle$$

such that $\hat{I}$ defines bit b_r of $\mathcal{A}_r$ in terms of bit $\bar{b}_{r+1}$ of $\mathcal{A}_{r+1}$, and for all pairs of bits $\bar{b}_r$, $\bar{b}_{r'}$, there do not exist certificates showing that bits $\mathcal{A}_r(\bar{b}_r)$ and $\mathcal{A}_r(\bar{b}_{r'})$ depend on $\mathcal{A}_{r+1}(\bar{b}_{r+1})$ in contradictory ways.

The fact that $\hat{I}$ squares the size of structures implies that the size of the certificate C, fits in $O(\log n)$ bits, i.e., a bounded number of first-order variables. Furthermore, it is easy to see that the problem of determining if C is a legal certificate for $\mathcal{A}$ is first-order expressible. (All that is required is to check that for all $j \leq |C|$, if j is the start of a field of C, then the information in this field is locally consistent with $\hat{I}$. It is clear that this can be done by an alternating Turing machine running in logarithmic time and making $O(1)$ alternations; first-order expressibility follows by [BIS].) It now follows that $\#Anc.induct(\mathcal{A}, r)$ is expressible in first-order. ∎

Lemma 17. *If S and T are interreducible via 1:1 fops I and J each of arity at least two, then S and T are isomorphic via first-order isomorphisms.*

Proof Let $\mathcal{A}$ be a structure in the vocabulary of S, and, as in the proof of 3 define the length of the ancestor chain of $\mathcal{A}$ to be the length of the longest sequence of the form $\hat{J}^{-1}(\mathcal{A}), \hat{I}^{-1}(\hat{J}^{-1}(\mathcal{A})), \hat{J}^{-1}(\hat{I}^{-1}(\hat{J}^{-1}(\mathcal{A}))), \ldots$ The argument given in Lemma 16 shows that there is a formula $\#Ancestors(\mathcal{A}, r)$ that evaluates to true iff $\mathcal{A}$'s ancestor chain has length r. Lemma 16 also shows that there is a formula computing $\hat{J}^{-1}$. The desired isomorphism is now the function b such that the i-th bit of $b(\mathcal{A})$ is one iff the following first-order formula evaluates to 1:

$$\exists r \#Ancestors(\mathcal{A}, r) \wedge (BIT(0, r) \wedge \hat{I}(i)) \vee (\neg BIT(0, r) \wedge \hat{J}^{-1}(i))$$

(Note that this first-order isomorphism b is not, strictly speaking, a first-order interpretation, since it maps some inputs to strictly shorter outputs, which is impossible for an interpretation.) ∎

It now remains to show,

Lemma 18. *Suppose that a problem S is complete via fops for a nice complexity class, C. Then S is complete via 1:1 length squaring fops for C.*

Proof Of course it remains to define "nice", but here is the proof. Every nice complexity class has a universal complete problem:

$$U_C = \left\{ M\$w\#^r \mid M(w) \downarrow \text{ using resources } f_C(r) \right\}.$$

Here $f_C(r)$ defines the appropriate complexity measure, e.g. r nondeterministic steps for NP, deterministic space $\log r$, for L, etc. (Note that we can always take r to be at least $|w|^2$.)

We claim that U_C is complete via 1:1 length squaring fops for C. In order to make this claim, we need to agree on an encoding of inputs to U_C that allows us to interpret them as structures over some vocabulary. Since all of our structures are encoded in binary, we will encode \$ and # by 10 and 11 respectively, and the binary bits 0 and 1 constituting M and w will be encoded by 00 and 01 respectively. Now, as in, for example, [Imm87], we consider a binary string of length n to be a structure with a single unary predicate over a universe of size n. Now for any given problem $T \in C$ accepted by machine M, the fop simply checks that if $i \leq 2|M|$ then the odd-numbered bits are 0 and bit number $i = 2j$ is the j-th bit of M, and if $2|M| + 2 < i \leq 2(|M| + |w| + 1)$ then the odd-numbered bits are 0 and the even numbered bits are the corresponding bit of w, etc.

To complete the proof of the lemma, let T be any problem in C and let S be as above. Then we reduce T to S via a 1:1, length squaring fop as follows. First reduce T to U_C as per the claim. Next reduce U_C to S via the fop promised in the statement of the lemma. It is easy to verify that, using the encoding we have chosen for U_C, it holds that for every length n, for all $i \leq n$, there are two strings x and y of length n, differing only in position i, such that $x \in U_C$ and $y \notin U_C$. Thus the fop from U_C cannot possibly ignore any of the bits in its input. It follows that the composition of these two fops is the 1:1 length squaring fop that we desire. (Note that an fop by definition must have arity at least one and thus cannot be length decreasing on Boolean strings.) ∎

From the above three lemmas we have a first-order version of Theorem 3 and thus Theorem 15 follows.

5 More on the Relationship between Isomorphisms and Projections

There are several questions about isomorphisms among complete sets that can be answered in the setting of first-order computation but are open for general polynomial-time computation. For example, given a one-way function f, it is an open question if $f(SAT)$ can be poly-time isomorphic to SAT. In part, this remains open because there is no function f that can be proven to be one-way at this time. On the other hand, the bijection $f(x) = 3x \pmod{2^{|x|}}$ was shown in [BL] to be one-way for first-order computation, in the sense that f is first-order expressible, but f^{-1} is not. (See also [Há] for other examples.) However, it is not too hard to show that for this choice of f, $f(SAT)$ is complete for NP under first-order projections, and thus it is first-order isomorphic to SAT.

The next result shows that the class of sets complete under first-order projections is not closed under first-order isomorphisms. (This also seems to be the first construction of a set that is complete for NP under first-order (or even poly-time) many-one reductions, that is not complete under first-order projections.)

Theorem 19. *There is a set first-order isomorphic to SAT that is not complete for NP under first-order projections.*

Proof Let $g(x)$ be a string of $|x|^2$ bits, with bit $z_{i,j}$ representing the logical AND of bits i and j of x. Let $A = \{\langle x, g(x) \rangle : x \in \text{SAT}\}$. By an extension of the techniques used in proving Theorem 15, it can be shown that A is first-order isomorphic to SAT. However a direct argument shows that there cannot be any projection (even a nonuniform projection) from SAT to A. ∎

A natural question that remains open is the question of whether every set complete for NP under first-order many-one reductions is first-order isomorphic to SAT. A related question is whether one can construct a set complete for NP under poly-time many-one reductions that is not first-order isomorphic to SAT. Since so many tools are available for proving the limitations of first-order computation, we are optimistic that this and related questions about sets complete under first-order reductions should be tractable. Furthermore, we hope that insights gleaned in answering these questions will be useful in guiding investigations of the polynomial-time degrees.

Acknowledgments The authors wish to thank the organizers of the 1992 Seminar on Structure and Complexity Theory at Schloß Dagstuhl, where this work was initiated. We also thank Richard Beigel for comments on an earlier draft.

References

[AB]   Manindra Agrawal and Somenath Biswas, "Polynomial Isomorphism of 1-L-Complete Sets," manuscript, 1992.

[All88] Eric Allender, "Isomorphisms and 1-L Reductions," *J. Computer Sys. Sci.* **36** (1988), 336-350.

[All89] Eric Allender, "P-Uniform Circuit Complexity," *JACM* **36** (1989), 912-928.

[AG]   Eric Allender and Vivek Gore, "A Uniform Circuit Lower Bound for the Permanent," DIMACS Tech Report 92-30. A preliminary version appeared as "On Strong Separations from AC^0," *Proc. FCT '91*, Lecture Notes in Computer Science 529, Springer-Verlag, 1991, 1-15.

[BIS]   D. Barrington, N. Immerman, H. Straubing, "On Uniformity Within NC^1," *J. Computer Sys. Sci.* 41 (1990), 274-306.

[BH77] Len Berman and Juris Hartmanis, "On Isomorphism and Density of NP and Other Complete Sets," *SIAM J. Comput.* **6** (1977), 305-322.

[BL]   Ravi Boppana and Jeff Lagarias, "One-Way Functions and Circuit Complexity," *Information and Computation* 74, (1987), 226-240.

[BH90] Hans-Jörg Burtschick and Albrecht Hoene, "The degree structure of 1-L reductions," *Proc. Math. Foundations of Computer Science*, Lecture Notes in Computer Science 629, Springer-Verlag, 1992, 153-161.

[CSV]   Ashok Chandra, Larry Stockmeyer, and Uzi Vishkin, "Constant Depth Reducibility," *SIAM J. Comput.* **13**, (1984), 423-439.

[Coo71] Stephen Cook, "The Complexity of Theorem Proving Procedures," *Proc. Third Annual ACM STOC Symp.* (1971), 151-158.

[Dah]   Elias Dahlhaus, "Reduction to NP-Complete Problems by Interpretations," in *Logic and Machines: Decision Problems and Complexity*, Börger, Rödding, and Hasenjaeger eds., Lecture Notes In Computer Science 171, Springer-Verlag, 1984, 357-365.

[End]   Herbert Enderton, *A Mathematical Introduction to Logic*, Academic Press, 1972.

[FSS]   Merrick Furst, James Saxe, and Michael Sipser, "Parity, Circuits, and the Polynomial-Time Hierarchy," *Math. Systems Theory* 17 (1984), 13-27.

174

[GJ]   M. R. Garey and D. S. Johnson, *Computers and Intractability*, Freeman, 1979.

[Hå]   Johan Håstad, "One-Way Permutations in NC^0," *Information Processing Letters* 26 (1987), 153-155.

[HIM]   Juris Hartmanis, Neil Immerman, and Stephen Mahaney, "One-Way Log Tape Reductions," *19th IEEE FOCS Symp.* (1978), 65-72.

[HH]   L. Hemachandra and A. Hoene, "Collapsing Degrees Via Strong Computation," to appear in *J. of Computer Sys. Sci.*.

[Imm87] Neil Immerman, "Languages That Capture Complexity Classes," *SIAM J. Comput.* 16, (1987), 760-778.

[Imm89] Neil Immerman, "Descriptive and Computational Complexity," *Computational Complexity Theory*, ed. J. Hartmanis, *Proc. Symp. in Applied Math.*, 38, American Mathematical Society (1989), 75-91.

[IL]   N. Immerman, S. Landau, "The Complexity of Iterated Multiplication," *Fourth Annual Structure in Complexity Theory Symp.* (1989), 104-111. Revised version submitted to *Information and Computation*.

[Jon]   Neil Jones, "Space-Bounded Reducibility among Combinatorial Problems," *J. Computer Sys. Sci.* 11 (1975), 68–85.

[JY]   Deborah Joseph and Paul Young, "Some Remarks on Witness Functions for Non-polynomial and Non-complete sets in NP," *Theoretical Computer Science* 39 (1985), 225-237.

[Kar]   Richard Karp, "Reducibility Among Combinatorial Problems," in *Complexity of Computations*, R.E.Miller and J.W.Thatcher, eds. (1972), Plenum Press, 85-104.

[KMR]   Stuart Kurtz, Stephen Mahaney, James Royer, "The Structure of Complete Degrees," in *Complexity Theory Retrospective* (Alan Selman, Ed.), Springer-Verlag, 1990, pp. 108-146.

[Lin]   Stephen Lindell, "A Purely Logical Characterization of Circuit Uniformity," *Seventh IEEE Structure in Complexity Theory Symp.* (1992), 185-192.

[M89]   Udi Manber, *Introduction to Algorithms: A Creative Approach*, Addison-Wesley, 1989.

[Ste]   Iain Stewart, "Using the Hamiltonian Operator to Capture NP," to appear in *J. Comput. Sys. Sci.* (1992).

[Val]   L.G. Valiant, "Reducibility By Algebraic Projections," *L'Enseignement mathématique*, 28, 3-4 (1982), 253-68.

[You]   Paul Young, "Juris Hartmanis: Fundamental Contributions to Isomorphism Problems," in *Complexity Theory Retrospective*, Alan Selman, ed., Springer-Verlag (1990), 28-58.

Splittings, Robustness and Structure of Complete Sets

Harry Buhrman[1], Albrecht Hoene[2], Leen Torenvliet[1]

[1] Departments of Mathematics and Computer Science, University of Amsterdam, Plantage Muidergracht 24, 1018 TV Amsterdam, The Netherlands
[2] Department of Computer Science, Technische Universität Berlin, D-1000 Berlin 10, Germany. Partially sponsored by Deutsche Forschungsgemeinshaft, Postdoktorandenstipendium

Abstract. We investigate the structure of EXP and $NEXP$ complete and hard sets under various kinds of reductions. In particular, we are interested in the way in which information that makes the set complete is stored in te set. To address this question for a given set A, we construct a sparse set S, and ask whether $A - S$ is still hard. It turns out, that for most of the reductions considered and for an arbitrary given sparseness condition, there is a single subexponential time computable set S that meets this condition, such that $A - S$ is not hard for any A. On the other hand we show that for any *polynomial time computable* sparse set S, the set $A - S$ *remains* hard.
In the second part of the paper we address the question whether the information that is evidently abundantly present can be used to produce two disjoint complete sets from a single complete set A, i.e. the question whether exponential-time complete sets are *mitotic*. It turns out that the many-one complete sets are, yet there is strong evidence that other complete sets may not be. In particular we show the existence of a 3-tt complete set that can not be split into two many-one complete sets. Finally we show a complexity theoretic counterpart to Sacks' splitting theorem, i.e. we show that any many-one complete set for EXP can be split into two incomplete sets.

1 Introduction

The structure of complete sets under various notions of the reducibility concept is a well-studied subject in structural complexity theory. In [AS84b, AS84a, BHT91, BST91, Ber76, BH77, GH89, Har78, Jon75, Kar72, LLS75, Wag86, Wat87] and *many* other papers results on this subject can be found. Questions like which reducibility notions differ and which are the same on what kind of complete sets, and what kind of subsets can be found in which type of complete sets have been extensively researched. Yet many open problems remain. On the most interesting complexity class, NP, almost every question is open. Even in surroundings where theorems are more easily proved, like exponential time, many questions remain. For instance, the question whether all (non)deterministic exponential time $\leq_m^P$-complete set are p-isomorphic is still a very hard open problem.

In this paper we put another, albeit small, step forward on the dark path. We investigate the question whether, and if so which, harm can be done to exponential time complete sets when taking out or putting in sparse sets. This type of question was studied by Schöning [Sch86] and in [TFL91]. In [TFL91], it was shown that for an arbitrary sparseness condition, there exists a single sub-exponential time computable set S such that for any $\leq_m^P$-complete set A, the set $A - S$ is incomplete. This instable behavior seems to vanish when the set S is sparse and polynomial time computable, i.e. for any complete set A and sparse polynomial time computable set S, the set $A - S$ is still complete. Note here that it is not interesting to look at dense polynomial time computable sets, because then we could take out Σ^* and certainly destroy the completeness.

We study this question for complete sets under different types of reductions. For conjunctive, disjunctive, and general bounded truth-table complete sets we can derive more or less the same theorems as for many-one complete sets. For Turing reductions the situation seems completely different. A problem here is that not much is known about the structure of $\leq_T^P$-complete sets for EXP. In particular it is not known whether $\leq_T^P$-complete sets are dense. In the—unexpected—case that there exist sparse $\leq_T^P$-complete sets, it might be possible to remove the entire set by a polynomial time computable superset. This intuition is made precise at the end of Sect. 3. Theorems of this kind suggest that the complete sets have regions where they possess information that is "crucial" for their completeness. Our theorems show that this information can be traced in subexponential (superpolynomial) time, but is evasive to polynomial time.

In the second part of the paper we study "redundancy" of complete sets. Can we divide a complete set into two parts that are itself again complete? We show–if this is possible–that the information that makes a set complete was in a way redundantly present. These kind of questions have been studied in recursion theory, where those sets that possess this property are called *mitotic*. We follow the line of Ambos-Spies [AS84a] and prove that $\leq_m^P$-complete sets for EXP indeed are (weakly-p-m-) mitotic.

In the remaining part of the paper we show that there exists a $\leq_{3tt}^P$-complete set that is not weakly-p-m-mitotic. Furthermore, we have a counterpart of Ladner's splitting theorems [Lad75], i.e. we construct a set that can be split into two parts that are strictly below the degree of complete sets, but are $\equiv_m^P$, instead of incomparable.

2 Definitions and Notations

We assume the reader familiar with standard notions in structural complexity theory, as are defined e.g. in [BDG88]. All kinds of *polynomial time bounded* reductions—many-one, (disjunctive and conjunctive) truth table and Turing—are frequently used without explanation. Various definitions for these concepts can be found, e.g. in [LLS75, BHT91, BST91]. We think of polynomial time bounded reductions as being modeled by adaptive and non-adaptive oracle machines, and use enumerations $\{M_i\}_i$ of these reductions. Without loss of generality we always assume machine M_i in such an enumeration to be time-bounded by $n^i + i$, where n is the length of the input. Usually we denote the set of strings queried on input x by machine i with oracle A by $Q_i^A(x)$, or by $Q_i(x)$ if M_i is non-adaptive. The result of the computation (accept/reject or the value computed) of machine M_i on input x (relative to oracle A) is sometimes denoted as $M_i(x)$ ($M_i^A(x)$).

Sets are denoted by capital letters and are subsets of Σ^*, where $\Sigma = \{0, 1\}$. The cardinality of a set A is denoted as $\|A\|$. Strings are denoted as small letters

$x, y, u, v, \ldots.$ The value of the *characteristic function* of a set A on a string x is denoted by $\chi_A(x)$, i.e. $\chi_A(x) = 1$ if $x \in A$ and 0 otherwise. We assume easy to compute *pairing and projection functions*. For strings, the pairing of $x_1, \ldots, x_n$ is denoted by $<x_1, \ldots, x_n>$, and $\pi_i(y)$ is the projection of y onto its ith coordinate.

The length of a string x is denoted by $|x|$. For a set A:

- for $n \in \omega$, we let the notation $A^{\leq n}$ stand for the set consisting of all strings in A of length $\leq n$ and
- for a string x, we let $A^{[x]}$ stand for the x *section of* A, i.e. the set $\{<y, z> : y = x$ and $<y, z> \in A\}$. In this case z may also be $<z_1, \ldots, z_n>$, so that we get the set $\{<y, z_1, \ldots, z_n> : y = x$ and $<y, z_1, \ldots, z_n>$ in $A\}$.
- In order to measure the density of A, we say that A is $g(n)$-sparse for some nondecreasing function $g : \mathbb{N} \to \mathbb{N}$, if $|A^{\leq n}| < g(n)$.

The main complexity classes considered in this paper are P—polynomial time, EXP—exponential time, and $NEXP$—nondeterministic exponential time. For the latter classes, we allow polynomials to act as exponents in the time bounds, e.g. $EXP = \bigcup_{i \in \omega} DTIME(2^{n^i})$. For EXP, the set K is the universal complete set. $K = \{<i, x, l> : M_i$ accepts x in $\leq l$ steps $\}$.

3 The Robustness of Exponential Time Completeness Notions

In this section we study the question which sparse sets can be removed from exponential time complete sets of different types without disturbing their completeness. The question originates from work of Schöning [Sch86], who showed that for all complete sets A in EXP and every set D in P the set $A \Delta D$ is of exponential density. In [TFL91], Tang, Fu and Liu showed that even for subexponential time computable D, the difference $A \Delta D$ remains exponential time complete.

They further show that for an arbitrary sparseness condition, there exists a single subexponential time computable set S, such that for *any* exponential time complete set A, the set $A - S$ is no longer exponential time hard. Their proof hinges on the fact that for any exponential time computable set B and any exponential time complete set A, there exists a *length increasing* reduction from B to A. Subsequently, the subexponential time computable set is constructed by chosing a sufficiently sparse polynomial time computable subset of $\{0\}^*$, and defining S as the image of this set varying over all polynomial time computable functions, i.e. $S = \{0^{b_i} : |f_i(0^{b_i})| > b_i\}$, where the b_i are chosen sufficiently far apart.

A closer look at the proof learns that, though the theorem just states that S is subexponential time computable, there are various ways of making S come arbitrarily close to polynomial time. It therefore seems reasonable to ask, whether we can also chose S to be polynomial time computable. The answer to this question is negative, as observed in [TFL91]. From the $\leq_1^P$-reduction of $K' = K \times \Sigma^*$ to the EXP complete set A, we can easily construct a $\leq_m^P$-reduction to $A - S$ for any polynomial time computable sparse set S.

The set K' itself is, of course, $\leq_m^P$-complete for EXP. In fact it is $\leq_{dtt}^P$-complete for EXP in a special way. For a given string x either all strings $<x, y>$ are in this set, or all are out depending on $x \in K$. Therefore, as long as S is $p(n)$-sparse, the set $K' - S$ remains $\leq_{dtt}^{P}$-complete for EXP. The reduction from K to K' on input x just queries the set $\{<x,y>|0 \leq y \leq p(2n)+1\}$. Since all these strings have length $\leq 2|x|$, at least one of them is not in S and it is in K' iff $x \in K$. This explains why a theorem like "*There exists a sparse set S, such that for any $\leq_{dtt}^{P}$-complete set A for EXP, the set $A - S$ is not $\leq_{dtt}^{P}$-complete for EXP*" cannot exist. The number of strings in S must at least be as large as the number of strings that can be queried. Therefore, if we wish to obtain a theorem for sets for which the density comes close to being constant, the best possible theorem involves bounded truth table reductions.

Theorem 1. *Given a recursive non-decreasing function $g(n)$ with $\lim_{n \to \infty} g(n) = \infty$. There exists a $g(n)$-sparse subexponential time computable set S, such that for any $\leq_{btt}^{P}$-complete set A for EXP, the set $A - S$ is no longer $\leq_{btt}^{P}$-complete.*

Proof. Without loss of generality we assume that $|Q_i(x)| \leq i$ for any x. We define a set of numbers $\{b_i\}_i$ sufficiently far apart and sufficiently easy to recognize, i.e. we want that for each n the question "$\exists i[n = b_i]$?" can be answered in time $O(n)$, and furthermore we want for each i that $g(b_i) > i^2$. Next we let $S = \bigcup_{i \in \omega} Q_i(0^{b_i})^{>b_i}$, and claim that S is the set searched for.

First, $|S^{\leq n}| \leq g(n)$ for each n by definition of b_i. Second, for any $\leq_{btt}^{P}$-complete set A, the set $A - S$ is not $\leq_{btt}^{P}$-hard. Consider the set $L_A = \{0^{b_i} : M_i^{(A-S)^{\leq b_i}}(0^{b_i}) = \text{reject}\}$. $L_A \in EXP$, so if $A - S$ were $\leq_{btt}^{P}$ complete, then one of the M_i, say M_w is the reduction from L_A to $A - S$. However, $0^{b_w} \in L_A$ iff $M_w^{(A-S)^{\leq b_w}}(0^{b_w}) = M_w^{A-S}(0^{b_w}) = \text{reject}$, a contradiction. $\square$

We observe that for *conjunctive* truth table reductions the statement of the theorem is stronger.

Corollary 2. *Given a recursive non-decreasing function $g(n)$ with $\lim_{n \to \infty} g(n) = \infty$. There exists a $g(n)$-sparse subexponential time computable set S such that for any $\leq_{ctt}^{P}$-complete set A for EXP the set $A - S$ is no longer $\leq_{ctt}^{P}$-complete.*

Conjunctive truth table reducibilities form an exception in yet another way. For these reductions the statement of the theorem can be generalized to EXP-hard sets. We use the fact that for conjunctive truth table reductions (or for any truth table reduction that computes a fixed type of truth table on any input) we can get a kind of 1-1 behavior for the query sets. A similar result for $\leq_m^{P}$-hard sets that uses the fact that these sets are also hard under $\leq_1^{P}$-reductions appears in [TFL91]. We can force the query sets belonging to two distinct inputs to differ on at least one string.

Lemma 3. *If A is EXP-hard under any reduction that computes a fixed type of truth table for each input, then for any set B in EXP there exists a reduction M_B of the same type such that $Q_B(x) \neq Q_B(y)$ whenever $x \neq y$.*

From this lemma we get:

Theorem 4. *Given a recursive non-decreasing function $g(n)$ with $\lim_{n \to \infty} g(n) = \infty$. There exists a $g(n)$-sparse set S in EXP such that for any $\leq_{ctt}^{P}$-hard set A for EXP the set $A - S$ is no longer $\leq_{ctt}^{P}$-hard.*

Proof. Again, we let the numbers b_i be sufficiently far apart to guarantee sparseness of S if we put one string in S for each b_i, and such that 0^{b_i} is again easy to recognize. Furthermore we let $2 \times (b_{i-1})^{i-1} < b_i$ to avoid confusion later on. Then we put the least string in $\bigcup_{|y| \le b_i} Q_i(<0^{b_i}, y>)$ of length $\ge b_i/2 - 1$ in S. (If no such string exists we do nothing.)

S is exponential time computable and $A - S$ is not $\le_{ctt}^P$-complete, since there can be no "Lemma 3" type *conjunctive* reduction from $\{0^{b_i} | i \in \omega\} \times \Sigma^*$ to $A - S$. $\quad\square$

Conjunctive and disjunctive truth table reducibilities are kind of each others complement on *EXP*. If a set is conjunctive truth table reducible to a set A then it is disjunctive truth table reducible to $\overline{A}$. So we find.

Corollary 5. *Given a recursive non-decreasing function $g(n)$ with $\lim_{n\to\infty} g(n) = \infty$. There exists a $g(n)$-sparse set S in EXP such that for any $\le_{dtt}^P$-hard set A for EXP the set $A \cup S$ is no longer $\le_{dtt}^P$-complete.*

As in the case of $\le_m^P$-reductions in the case of complete sets, we can let S come arbitrarily close to being polynomial time computable, and as in the case of $\le_m^P$-reductions, polynomial time computability is exactly the cut-off point.

Theorem 6. *For any set A that is $\le_{ctt}^P$-hard for EXP and any $p(n)$-sparse polynomial time computable set S, the set $A - S$ remains $\le_{ctt}^P$-hard for EXP.*

Proof. We construct an *EXP* computable set W consisting of pairs $<i, x>$ such that there exists an i for which K reduces $\le_m^P$ to $W^{[i]}$, and $W^{[i]}$ reduces $\le_{ctt}^P$ to $A - S$. Then $A - S$ is $\le_{ctt}^P$-hard. As before, $\{M_i\}_i$ is an enumeration of polynomial time $\le_{ctt}^P$-reductions. W is constructed according to the following rules:
If $z > p(|<i, x, z>|^i + i) + 1$ then $<i, x, z> \notin W$. For $<i, x, z>$ with $0 \le z \le p(|<i, x, z>|^i + i) + 1$, let $U_i(i, x, z) = \bigcup_{z' < z} (Q_i(<i, x, z'>) \cap S)$. If $Q_i(<i, x, z> \cap S) \subseteq U_i(i, x, z)$ then $<i, x, z> \in W$ iff $x \in K$ else $<i, x, z> \in W$.

First W is exponential time computable and hence one of the machines, say M_w is a polynomial time $\le_{ctt}^P$-reduction from W to A. Next there is a $\le_{ctt}^P$-reduction from $W^{[w]} = \{<y, x, z> | y = w$ and $<y, x, z> \in W\}$ to $A - S$. Finally, there is a many-one reduction from K to $W^{[w]}$. $\quad\square$

A proof along the same lines, but with different rules for building W, yields:

Theorem 7. *For any set A that is $\le_{dtt}^P$-hard for EXP and any $p(n)$-sparse polynomial time computable set S, the set $A - S$ remains $\le_{dtt}^P$-hard for EXP.*

The next logical step would be to prove that the same statement holds for $\le_{btt}^P$-reductions. This however seems to require more involved techniques. As things stand, we only have a proof for $\le_{2tt}^P$-reductions.

Theorem 8. *Let A be $\le_{2tt}^P$-hard for EXP and S a polynomial time computable $p(n)$-sparse set. The set $A - S$ is still $\le_{2tt}^P$-hard for EXP.*

Proof. (Sketch) Again, we construct an exponential time computable set W. Let $\{M_i\}_i$ be an enumeration of all $\leq_{2tt}^P$-reductions. This time we have the following goal in mind for the reduction M_w from W to A. For some fixed polynomial q depending only on p we want for each x that there exists a pair of strings $(<w, x, z>, <w, x, z'>)$ for $0 \leq z \leq q(n) + 1$ such that $|Q_w(w, x, z) \cap S| + |Q_w(w, x, z') \cap S| < 2$. That is, *either* for one of the sets both queried strings are outside S, or they have at most one (common) string in S. Then we will construct W such that one of the two strings $<w, x, z>, <w, x, z'>$ is in W iff $x \in K$ and its membership in W can be decided on the basis of two strings in $(Q_w(<w, x, z>) \cup Q_w(<w, x, z'>)) - S$. So $A - S$ remains $\leq_{2tt}^P$-hard. The rest of the proof requires some rather involved diagonalizations and case analysis, and will appear in the final version of this paper.

□

For $\leq_{3tt}^P$-reductions the case analysis quickly blows up. We would have to find a more general property behind the reductions before we could attack the problem for $\leq_{btt}^P$-reductions. For general truth table reductions, such an attack would not even work. The proof method above relativizes, and we can show that there exists an oracle set A relative to which EXP has a $\leq_{tt}^P$-complete tally set T. Then $T - \{0\}^* = \emptyset$, which cannot be complete.

Lemma 9. *If $EXP \subseteq P/poly$ then there exists a tally set T that is $\leq_{tt}^P$-complete for EXP.*

Wilson [Wil85] showed the existence of an oracle A where $EXP^A \subseteq P^A/poly$. Using this oracle together with Lemma 9 we get that there exists a tally set T that is complete for EXP^A. Setting $B = T$ and $S = \{0\}^*$, we get that $B - S = \emptyset$ and $\emptyset$ is not $\leq_{tt}^{P^A}$-complete for EXP^A.

Theorem 10. *There exists an oracle A, such that there exists a $\leq_{tt}^{P^A}$-complete set B for EXP^A and a polynomial time computable, sparse set S, such that $B - S$ is not $\leq_{tt}^{P^A}$-hard for EXP^A.*

4 Splittings of EXP Complete Sets

In this section we want to investigate to what extent one can *split* EXP-complete sets. A splitting of an r.e. (EXP) set is the construction of two r.e. (EXP) sets $A_0, A_1 \subseteq A$, such that $A_0 \cap A_1 = \emptyset$ and $A_0 \cup A_1 = A$. One of the things to look at is, can this splitting be done so that the subsets both have the same information as A? For complete sets this would mean that the complete set can be split into subsets, that is itself again complete. This type of question has been studied in a recursion theoretical setting by Ladner [Lad73]. He observed that there exist sets that are non-splittable, or non-*mitotic* as he called them. The recursion theoretical definition is as follows:

Definition 11. An r.e. set A is called (m-)mitotic iff there exist r.e. sets A_1 and A_0 such that $A_1 \cup A_0 = A$, $A_1 \cap A_0 = \emptyset$, and $A \equiv_{(m)T} A_1 \equiv_{(m)T} A_0$.

Note here that in the case of $\leq_T$-reductions we only need $A_1 \equiv_T A_0$. To see this note that $A \leq_T A_1 \oplus A_0$ and $A_1 \oplus A_0 \leq_T A_1$. To reduce A_1 to A, the reduction queries on input x whether x is in A. If this is not the case it rejects straight out, otherwise it starts enumerating A_1 and A_0, since x must be in one of them.

Later, Ambos-Spies [AS84a] studied the complexity theoretical variant of mitotic sets and introduced the term p-*mitotic* sets. Ambos-Spies introduced four definitions; two for the Turing reductions and two for the many-one reductions. One option is demanding $A \equiv_T^P A_1 \equiv_T^P A_0$. Since we are interested in complete sets for complexity classes, we could demand that A_0 and A_1 should be in the complexity class under consideration. A problem is, that this definition can not be weakened to $A_1 \equiv_T^P A_0$. Ambos-Spies chose a Breidbart/Owings [Bre78, Owi75] type of splitting (*by another set*):

Definition 12. A recursive set A is p-m(T)-mitotic if there is a set $B \in P$ such that $A \equiv_{m(T)}^P A \bigcap B \equiv_{m(T)}^P A \bigcap \overline{B}$.

When using this definition, the problem of reducing A_1 to A is settled for the Turing case. Namely, x is in A_1 iff x is in B and x is in A. A disadvantage of this definition however, is that the requirement that the splitting has to be polynomial time computable seems too strong. In order to capture this feeling, we also want to look at the definition discussed above. Note here also that since our main interest is in complete sets, we will not have the trouble that A_0 (or A_1) does not reduce to A (This because A is complete)

Definition 13. An r.e. set A is called weakly-p-m(T) mitotic iff there exist r.e. sets A_1 and A_0, such that $A_1 \bigcup A_0 = A$, $A_1 \bigcap A_0 = \emptyset$, and $A \equiv_{m(T)}^P A_1 \equiv_{m(T)}^P A_0$.

One of the questions that arise is, are $\leq_m^P$-complete sets for EXP (weakly) p-m mitotic? In order to answer this question, we first take a look at the r.e. complete sets. There it is known, due to Myhill, that the $\leq_m$-complete sets are all isomorphic. Now using the fact that K, the standard r.e. $\leq_m$-complete set, is m-mitotic and that this property is preserved under isomorphisms, it follows that all $\leq_m$-complete sets are m-mitotic. Unfortunately it is not known whether the $\leq_m^P$-complete sets for EXP are p-isomorphic, but it is known that they are all 1-1, length increasing equivalent [Ber77, GH89, Wat87]. This now is sufficient to prove that they are weakly-p-m-mitotic.

Theorem 14. *All $\leq_m^P$-complete sets for EXP are weakly-p-m-mitotic.*

Proof. Let A be a $\leq_m^P$-complete set for EXP. Let $A \oplus A \leq_m^P A$ via f that is 1-1 and length increasing. Set $A_0 = \{y : \exists 0x [x \in A \wedge y = f(0x)]\}$. Since f is 1-1 and length increasing A_0 is in EXP. It is also $\leq_m^P$-complete, because $x \in A$ iff $f(0x) \in A_0$. Now set $A_1 = A - A_0$. Then $A_0 \bigcup A_1 = A$ and $A_0 \bigcap A_1 = \emptyset$. It remains to show that A_1 is also $\leq_m^P$-complete. Let $A^1 = \{1x : x \in A\}$. Note that $A^1 \subseteq A \oplus A$, and is $\leq_m^P$-complete. Because f is 1-1 : $1x \in A^1 \Rightarrow f(1x) \in A - A_0$, and $1x \notin A^1 \Rightarrow 1x \notin A \oplus A \Rightarrow f(1x) \notin A \Rightarrow f(1x) \notin A - A_0$. $\qquad\square$

For EXP, the 1-1 length increasing property seems to be enough to get weak p-m-mitoticity. For $NEXP$ the situation is somewhat different, because we do not know whether we have the length increasing property for complete sets. We do however have the 1-1 property and the fact that the reductions are not more than exponential length decreasing, i.e. $2^{|f(x)|} > |x|$ [GH89]. The main problem however is that when applying the same proof as above, the set difference used to define $A_1 = A - A_0$ is not known to be in $NEXP$, because it is not known whether $NEXP$ is closed under complementation (and thus under set difference). We can prove:

Theorem 15. *Every $\leq^P_m$-complete set A for $NEXP$ can be split into infinitely many disjoint subsets $A_1, A_2 \ldots$ such that $\bigcup_{i=0}^\infty A_i = A$, such that for all i, $A_i \subseteq A$ and A_i is complete for $NEXP$.*

Proof. We start the same way as in the EXP case. Let $A \oplus A \leq^P_m A$ via f that is 1-1 and exponentially honest. Set $A_0 = \{y : \exists\, 0x[y = f(0x) \wedge y \in A]\}$. We define A_1 in a similar way. $A_1 = \{y : \exists\, 1x[y = f(1x) \wedge y \in A]\}$. We now have two complete sets A_0 and A_1 and some leftover of A, namely $T_0 = A - (A_0 \bigcup A_1)$. At this point we repeat this procedure with A_0 resulting in A_{00} and A_{01} and again some leftover T_1. Repeating this we get an infinite sequence of sets A_{0^i1} and a set $T = \bigcup_{i=0}^\infty T_i$ so that $(\bigcup_{i=0}^\infty A_{0^i1}) \bigcup T = A$. Since T is countable (it is a subset of $\mathbb{N}$), we can add the ith element of T to A_{0^i1} resulting in a sequence A'_{0^i1} satisfying the properties of the theorem. □

Although this looks hopeful, the following example shows that the infinite version of mitoticity can be independent of mitoticity. Ladner [Lad73] showed the existence of *non-mitotic* sets. Together with the following observation this yields the somewhat bizarre existence of a set that cannot be split into two parts, but can be split in infinitely many parts of the same complexity.

Observation 16. *every r.e. set A can be split into infinitely many disjoint r.e. subsets $A_1, A_2, \ldots$ of A such that they remain in the same Turing degree as A.*

We try to follow the same line now as Ladner [Lad73], and try to proof that there exist non (weakly-p-m) mitotic sets in EXP. We succeed in this and can also proof that those sets can be $\leq^P_{3tt}$-complete. (Note that this also proves that the same result is true for p-m mitoticity.)

Theorem 17. *There exists a set A in EXP that is not weakly-p-m-mitotic and $\leq^P_{3tt}$-complete.*

Proof. (Sketch) We prove the following: There exists a set A, so that for all sets $A_0, A_1 \in EXP$ that split A, $A_0 \neq^P_m A_1$. It is enough to prove this for EXP computable splittings (i.e. A_i is in EXP) to avoid weak p-m-mitoticity. This is because for a weakly-p-m-mitotic set B in EXP, the parts B_0 and B_1 are in EXP, because they are $\equiv^P_m B$. Let $M_{i'}$ be an enumeration of exponential time machines that run in time $2^{n^i} + i$, and let f_j be an enumeration of polynomial time many one reductions.

To construct A, we have requirements for all $i0', i1', i0, i1$: If $L(M_{i0'})$ and $L(M_{i1'})$ split A, then either $L(M_{i1'}) \not\leq^P_m L(M_{i0'})$ via f_{i1} or $L(M_{i0'}) \not\leq^P_m L(M_{i1'})$ via f_{i0}.

We introduce a function b to have a set of strings to diagonalize over. Let $b(0) = 1$ and $b(i) = (b(i-1)^{i-1})^i + i + 1$. The idea is then, to put three copies of K into A. At each stage n of the diagonalization, we compute $f_{i0}(0^{b(n)})$ and $f_{i1}(0^{b(n)})$. It turns out, after some involved case analysis, that we can remove again at most two of the pairs $<i, x>$ from A to discombobulate mitoticity. As consequently one of the three pairs always remains in A, the set A remains $\leq_{3tt}^P$ (in fact $\leq_{3-d}^P$)-complete. □

The next logical step would be to prove this result for Turing complete sets. We are not yet able to do this but suspect that there exist Turing complete sets that are not weakly-p-T-mitotic.

Another line of splittings in recursion theory is the existence of a splitting of an r.e. set A in A_0 and A_1 that are incomparable. Examples of this are the splitting theorem of Sacks [Sac63] and the time bounded versions by Ladner [Lad75]. The next theorem is in a way a counterpart to this. In this theorem the sets A_0 and A_1 are strictly below A, but are in the same many one degree. Seen in another light, this theorem can be seen as a generalization of the fact that there exists $\leq_{2-d}^P$-complete sets for EXP that are not $\leq_m^P$-complete [Wat87, GH89].

Theorem 18. *If A is $\leq_m^P$-complete for EXP, then A can be split into A_0 and A_1, such that $A_0 \equiv_m^P A_1$, and both A_0 and A_1 are $\leq_{2-d}^P$-complete for EXP but not $\leq_m^P$-complete.*

Proof. (Sketch) Let A be $\leq_m^P$-complete and K be the standard $\leq_m^P$-complete set. Since the $\leq_m^P$-complete sets for EXP are 1-1 length increasing equivalent, we can construct the following length increasing 1-1 function h from A to A. Let f be the 1-1, l.i. reduction from A to K and g the one from K to A. Let $h(x) = f(g(x))$. We say that x is a *root* if $h^{-1}(x)$ is undefined and x is *on a chain* if $h^{-1}(x)$ is defined. We construct W, A_0, and A_1 in stages, such that elements of A_0 and A_1 are either roots or sequential elements on a chain, and W is exponential time computable, but reducible to neither A_0 nor A_1. □

Acknowledgements. We would like to thank Peter van Emde Boas for discussions about the results. Furthermore we would like to thank Steven Homer, Dick de Jongh and Jan van Neerven for discussions and ideas. Finally we would like to thank Stephen Wilcox for pointing out an error that we thought was grammatical, but that turned out to be mathematical.

References

[AS84a] K. Ambos-Spies. On the structure of polynomial time degrees. In M. Fontet and K. Mehlhorn, editors, *STACS 84, Lecture Notes in Computer Science 166*, pages 198–208. Springer-Verlag, 1984.

[AS84b] K. Ambos-Spies. P-mitotic sets. In E. Börger, G. Hasenjäger, and D. Roding, editors, *Logic and Machines, Lecture Notes in Computer Science 177*, pages 1–23. Springer-Verlag, 1984.

[BDG88] J. Balcázar, J. Díaz, and J. Gabarró. *Structural Complexity I*. Springer-Verlag, 1988.

[Ber76] L. Berman. On the structure of complete sets: Almost everywhere complexity and infinitely often speedup. *Proc. 17th IEEE Symp. on Foundations of Computing*, pages 76–80, 1976.

[Ber77] L. Berman. *Polynomial Reducibilities and Complete Sets.* PhD thesis, Cornell University, 1977.

[BH77] L. Berman and H. Hartmanis. On isomorphisms and density of NP and other complete sets. *SIAM J. Comput.*, 6:305–322, 1977.

[BHT91] H. Buhrman, S. Homer, and L. Torenvliet. On complete sets for nondeterministic classes. *Math. Systems Theory*, 24:179–200, 1991.

[Bre78] S. Breidbart. On splitting recursive sets. *J. Comput. System Sci.*, 17:56–64, 1978.

[BST91] H. Buhrman, E. Spaan, and L. Torenvliet. Bounded reductions. In C. Chofrut and M. Jantzen, editors, *STACS 1991, Lecture Notes in Computer Science 480*, pages 410–421, 1991.

[GH89] K. Ganesan and S. Homer. Complete problems and strong polynomial reducibilities. In B. Monien and R. Cori, editors, *STACS 89, Lecture Notes in Computer Science 349*, pages 240–250, 1989.

[Har78] J. Hartmanis. On the logtape isomorphism of complete sets. *Theoretical Computer Science*, 7:273–286, 1978.

[Jon75] N. Jones. Space bounded reducibilities among combinatorial problems. *J. Comput. System Sci.*, 11:68–85, 1975.

[Kar72] R. Karp. Reducibility among combinatorial problems. In R. Miller and J. Thatcher, editors, *Complexity of Computer Computations*, pages 85–103. Plenum Press, New York, 1972.

[Lad73] R.E. Ladner. Mitotic recursively enumerable sets. *J. Symbolic Logic*, 38(2):199–211, 1973.

[Lad75] R. Ladner. On the structure of polynomial time reducibility. *J. Assoc. Comput. Mach.*, 22:155–171, 1975.

[LLS75] R. Ladner, N. Lynch, and A. Selman. A comparison of polynomial time reducibilities. *Theor. Comput. Sci.*, 1:103–123, 1975.

[Owi75] J.C. Owings. Splitting a context-sensitive set. *J. Computer and System Sciences*, 10:83–87, 1975.

[Sac63] G.E. Sacks. On degrees less than 0'. *Ann. of Math.*, 2(77):211–231, 1963.

[Sch86] U. Schöning. Complete sets and closeness to complexity classes. *Math. Systems Theory*, 19:24–41, 1986.

[TFL91] S. Tang, B. Fu, and T. Liu. Exponential time and subexponential time sets. In *Proc. Structure in Complexity Theory sixth annual conference*, pages 230–237, 1991.

[Wag86] K. Wagner. More complicated questions about maxima and minima and some closures of NP. In *13th ICALP, Lecture Notes in Computer Science 226*, pages 434–443, 1986.

[Wat87] O. Watanabe. A comparison of polynomial time completeness notions. *Theoret. Comput. Sci.*, 54:249–265, 1987.

[Wil85] C.B. Wilson. Relativized circuit complexity. *J. Computer and System Sciences*, 31:169–181, 1985.

Defying Upward and Downward Separation*

*Lane A. Hemachandra*** and *Sudhir K. Jha****
Department of Computer Science
University of Rochester
Rochester, NY 14627

Abstract

Upward and downward separation results link the collapse of small and large classes, and are a standard tool in complexity theory. We study the limitations of upward and downward separation.

We show that the exponential-time limited nondeterminism hierarchy does not robustly possess downward separation. We show that probabilistic classes do not robustly possess upward separation. Though NP is known [19] to robustly possess upward separation, we show that NP does not robustly possess upward separation with respect to strong (immunity) separation. On the other hand, we provide a structural sufficient condition for upward separation.

1 Introduction

Downward separation (equivalently, upwards collapse) refers to the gravitational effect on large classes of the collapse of small classes; for example, if P = NP, then the entire polynomial hierarchy collapses to P [31,37]. The upward separation technique refers to a technique of Hartmanis, Immerman, and Sewelson ([19], see also [7]) showing that the separation (via sets of low density) of small classes implies the separation of larger classes; for example, it is known that NP − P contains a sparse set if and only if NE ≠ E [19]. In this paper, we discuss the range of application of upward and downward separation.

Section 3 studies the exponential-time analog of the limited nondeterminism hierarchy of Kintala and Fischer [27], and shows that it does not robustly possess downward separation. For each $k > 1$, there are relativized worlds in which all the hierarchy's levels are closed under complementation and the first k levels collapse to E, yet levels $k + 1, k + 2, \cdots$, form an infinite non-collapsing hierarchy. We prove our result indirectly, exploiting an upward separation property of the limited nondeterminism hierarchy, and using the substantial power of Kolmogorov complexity [28].

As to earlier results about other hierarchies, it is known that the polynomial hierarchy possesses strong downward separation properties [31,37], as does the strong exponential hierarchy except at its lowest levels (though the collapse of that hierarchy

---

* Research supported in part by the National Science Foundation under grant CCR-8957604. A full version is available upon request to lane@cs.rochester.edu.

** Work done in part while visiting Friedrich Schiller Universität Jena and Universität Ulm.

*** Current address: Intel Corporation, Design Technology, SC3-38, 2880 Northwestern Parkway, Santa Clara, CA 95052.

makes the issue moot) [21,20] and in the (weak) exponential hierarchy a specific counterexample is known at a low level but it remains open whether this reflects a more general behavior (we conjecture that it does) [19,25].

Turning to upward separation, Section 4 shows that upward separation does not robustly apply either to probabilistic classes or to strong separations. We prove the latter via a novel approach we call the "hedging the bet" technique. Among the results we obtain are that none of the following holds robustly:

- NP contains a P-immune sparse set if and only if NE is E-immune.

- BPP − P contains a sparse set if and only if BPE $\neq$ E.

- VPP − P (that is, R − P) contains a sparse set if and only if VPE $\neq$ E.

- ZPP − P contains a sparse set if and only if ZPE $\neq$ E.

Allender and Wilson [1,3] have shown failings of the upward separation technique for huge *run times*. We show the first failings based on mode of computation (probabilistic) or strength of separation (immunity). The failure of ZPP − P, R − P, and BPP − P to robustly display upward separation is proven via exploiting the fact that these are "promise classes [23]"; there is a "promise"—the error bound—built into the definition that is hard to capture in a presentation of machines purportedly covering the class [17,32]. Promise classes are the bad boys of complexity theory; various ones[4] do not robustly possess: nice presentations (of machines) [17,32], constructive programming systems [32], many-one or Turing complete sets [36,15,29,4,17,32,9,22], or positive relativization theorems [23]. Given the naughty nature of BPP, and thus the failure of BPP − P to robustly yield to the upward separation technique, one might suspect that NP − BPP would also defy robust upward separation. However, we note that NP − BPP *does* robustly possess upward separation, and we identify a general property of classes C sufficient to ensure that NP − C possesses upward separation.

2 Definitions

It is assumed that the reader is familiar with the basic concepts of complexity theory, such as Turing machines, oracle Turing machines, and complexity classes such as P, NP, the polynomial hierarchy, and so on. For background, see [24,11,26].

For any string x, $|x|$ denotes the length of the string x. $[n]$ denotes the set consisting of the integers 1 through n. A set is of *density* $d(n)$ if and only if it has less than $d(n)$ number of strings of length n, for all values of n. A set is said to be *sparse* if it is of density $p(n)$ for some polynomial p. We'll say that a set T is a *tally set* if $T \subseteq 0^*$ (see, e.g., [7]). TALLY denotes the class of all tally sets. For any set A, $A^{=n}$ denotes all length n strings in A, and $A^{\leq n}$ denotes all strings in A of length at most n. $\mathcal{N} = \{0, 1, \cdots\}$ and $\mathcal{Z}^+ = \{1, 2, \cdots\}$.

An infinite language L is called C-immune if L has no infinite subset that is in the complexity class C. A complexity class $\mathcal{D}$ is called C-immune if some language

---

[4] And probably essentially all, though trivialized promises—e.g., the threshold class corresponding to R [16]—provide exceptions.

in $\mathcal{D}$ is $\mathcal{C}$-immune [33]. Immunity is often studied in a complexity-theoretic setting (see, e.g., [6,12,13]).

In this paper, E and NE are used to refer to $\bigcup_{c>0} \text{DTIME}[2^{cn}]$ and $\bigcup_{c>0} \text{NTIME}[2^{cn}]$ respectively.

The limited nondeterminism hierarchy (or "beta" hierarchy [10]) of Kintala and Fisher [27] is defined as those languages in NP that can be accepted using at most poly-logarithmically many bits of nondeterminism.

Definition 1. [27] For every $k \in \mathcal{N}$, define

$$\beta_k = \bigcup_{c>0} \text{NONDET-TIME}[c \log^k n, \, n^c + c],$$

where $\text{NONDET-TIME}[f(n), \, g(n)]$ is the class of languages accepted by nondeterministic Turing machines that on inputs of size n are $f(n)$ nondeterminism-bounded and $g(n)$ time-bounded.

Clearly $\beta_0 = \beta_1 = P$ [27].

We'll also be interested in exponential-time classes of limited nondeterminism.

Definition 2. For every $k \in \mathcal{N}$, define

$$\beta\text{E}_k = \bigcup_{c>0} \text{NONDET-TIME}[cn^k, \, 2^{cn}].$$

Clearly $\beta\text{E}_0 = \beta\text{E}_1 = E$.

It is easy to see that one standard type of downward separation result that links the polynomial-time hierarchy to the exponential-time hierarchy [18,7] also links the two beta hierarchies.

Proposition 3. *1.* $(\forall k \in \mathcal{N}) \, [\beta_k = \beta_{k+1} \Rightarrow \beta\text{E}_k = \beta\text{E}_{k+1}]$,

2. $(\forall k \in \mathcal{N}) \, [\beta_k = \text{co}\beta_k \Rightarrow \beta\text{E}_k = \text{co}\beta\text{E}_k]$,

The probabilistic classes BPP, R, and ZPP were introduced by Gill [14]. While defining these classes here, we will require that all the computation trees of the nondeterministic machines of the definitions are depth-normalized complete binary trees with the depth is independent of the particular oracle (so each path is of the same length and has the same number of nondeterministic choices). (For any such machine given, the bounded error requirement may hold for some oracles and fail for some oracles, and of course only for the oracles for which the appropriate bounded error requirement is met will the machine define a language in BPP or R relative to the oracle.)

BPP is the class of sets probabilistically accepted by some nondeterministic polynomial-time machine with bounded error probability. Given our normalization requirement, this is equivalent to saying that for each string x either more than half of the computations of the machine accept x (and the string is said to be accepted), or less than one fourth of the computations accept x (and the string is said to be rejected). BPE is the exponential-time analog of BPP.

R is the class of sets probabilistically accepted by some nondeterministic polynomial-time machine with one-sided error (due to our normalization requirement, this can be expressed as: for each string x either more than half of the computations of the machine accept or none of the computations accept). VPE is the exponential analog of R. coR is the class of complements of sets in R. ZPP, the class of sets that can be recognized in expected polynomial time, is R ∩ coR. ZPE is the exponential analog of ZPP, VPE ∩ coVPE.

Let $\{P_1, P_2, \cdots\}$ be a standard enumeration of deterministic polynomial-time Turing machines such that machine P_i^A takes at most $p_i(x) = |x|^i + i$ steps on input x, regardless of its oracle A. Similarly, let $\{NE_1, NE_2, \cdots\}$ be a standard enumeration of nondeterministic exponential-time Turing machines such that—independent of oracle A—machine NE_i^A takes at most $h_i(x) = 2^{i|x|}$ steps on input x and on any given input all computation paths have the same number of steps.

3 The Exponential-Time Beta Hierarchy: Downward Separations?

In this section, we show that the exponential-time beta hierarchy does not robustly possess the downward separation properties of the polynomial hierarchy. For example, there are relativized worlds in which each level of the exponential-time beta hierarchy is closed under complement, and yet the hierarchy separates completely. Also, there are relativized worlds in which the first k levels of the hierarchy collapse to E, and yet the rest of the hierarchy separates completely.

Often, the structure of tally sets in small classes controls the overall structure of larger classes. For example, Book [7] showed that E ≠ NE ⟺ NP − P contains tally sets. Below, we note that the same holds for the beta hierarchies; this connection will allow us to prove results about the exponential-time beta hierarchy via results about the structure of tally sets in the beta hierarchy. One can view the following as a strengthened version of Proposition 3.

Theorem 4. *1. $(\forall k, k' \in \mathcal{N} : k \geq k' \geq 0)\, [\beta E_k - \beta E_{k'} \neq \emptyset \iff \beta_k - \beta_{k'}$ contains a tally set].*

2. $(\forall k \in \mathcal{N})\, [\beta E_k \neq co\beta E_k \iff (\beta_k \cap \mathrm{TALLY}) \neq (co\beta_k \cap \mathrm{TALLY})].$

3. Each of the above claims relativizes.

The proof of Theorem 4 is an analog of the corresponding results for the polynomial-time and exponential-time hierarchies [7,19,35].

Now, we would like to ask whether the exponential-time beta hierarchy robustly (i.e., with respect to every oracle) has the downward separation and inclusion properties that the polynomial hierarchy robustly has. Recall the following standard results.

Theorem 5. [31,37]

1. $(\forall k \in \mathcal{N})\, [\Sigma_k^p \subseteq \Sigma_{k+1}^p \cap \Pi_{k+1}^p].$

2. $(\forall k \in \mathcal{N})\, [\Sigma_k^p = \Pi_k^p \Rightarrow \Sigma_k^p = \Sigma_{k+1}^p].$

3. $(\forall k \in \mathcal{N})\, [\Sigma_k^p = \Sigma_{k+1}^p \Rightarrow \Sigma_{k+1}^p = \Sigma_{k+2}^p].$

Each of the three parts of the above theorem holds robustly. Except at the lowest levels, very similar results can be proven in the strong exponential hierarchy, though such claims are an academic exercise given that the hierarchy outright collapses [21]; on the other hand, for the weak exponential hierarchy, such results do not hold robustly [19,25]. We'll now show that all three of the above properties do not hold robustly for the exponential-time beta hierarchy. Clearly, the exponential-time beta hierarchy analog of Part 1 of Theorem 5 fails to hold robustly.

Proposition 6. $(\forall k \in \mathcal{N} : k \geq 2)(\exists A) [\beta E_k^A \not\subseteq \bigcup_{\ell \geq 0} \mathrm{co} \beta E_\ell^A]$.

Corollary 7. $(\forall k \in \mathcal{N} : k \geq 2)(\exists A) [\beta_k^A \not\subseteq \bigcup_{\ell \geq 0} \mathrm{co} \beta_\ell^A]$.

Corollary 8. [27, Theorem 4.1] $(\forall k \in \mathcal{N} : k \geq 2)(\exists A) [\beta_k^A \neq \mathrm{co} \beta_k^A]$.

Proposition 6 is immediate from the techniques of Baker, Gill, and Solovay ([5], see also [39]), which, in this setting, clearly yield a world in which βE_k^A is not even contained, for any $\epsilon > 0$, in $\bigcup_{c>0} \mathrm{coNTIME}^A[2^{cn^{k-\epsilon}}]$. Corollary 7 follows from Proposition 6 via a standard padding (i.e., downward separation) argument.

We now turn to the unfortunately more challenging task of tainting Parts 2 and 3 of the exponential-time beta hierarchy analogs of Theorem 5.

Theorem 9. For any $k \in \mathcal{Z}^+$, there is an oracle W for which

1. $(\forall i \in \mathcal{N}) [\beta E_i^W = \mathrm{co} \beta E_i^W]$,

2. $(\forall i \in \mathcal{N} : i \geq k) [\beta E_i^W \neq \beta E_{i+1}^W]$, and

3. $(\forall i \in \mathcal{N} : i \leq k) [\beta E_i^W = E^W]$.

That is, the exponential-time beta hierarchy is unlike the polynomial-time hierarchy, which robustly has downward separation. In particular, it follows immediately that the analogs of Parts 2 and 3 of Theorem 5 do not hold robustly.

Corollary 10. $(\forall k \in \mathcal{Z}^+)(\exists A) [\beta E_k^A = \mathrm{co} \beta E_k^A \text{ yet } \beta E_k^A \neq \beta E_{k+1}^A]$.

Corollary 11. $(\forall k \in \mathcal{Z}^+)(\exists A) [E^A = \beta E_k^A \text{ yet } \beta E_k^A \neq \beta E_{k+1}^A]$.

Note also that there is a relativized world in which the exponential-time beta hierarchy separates completely, yet each of its levels is closed under complement.

Corollary 12. $(\exists A) [\beta E_1^A = \mathrm{co} \beta E_1^A \subsetneq \beta E_2^A = \mathrm{co} \beta E_2^A \subsetneq \cdots]$.

It is not currently know whether beta hierarchy analogs of Theorem 9 and Corollaries 10, 11, and 12 hold—an interesting question we'll return to at the end of the paper.

Rather than prove Theorem 9, we establish the following lemma that, by Theorem 4 (in its relativized form), is equivalent.

Lemma 13. For any $\varrho \in \mathcal{Z}^+$, there is an oracle W for which

1. $(\forall i \in \mathcal{Z}^+) [(\beta_i^W \cap \mathrm{TALLY}) = (\mathrm{co} \beta_i^W \cap \mathrm{TALLY})]$,

2. $(\forall i \in \mathcal{Z}^+ : i \geq \varrho) [(\beta_i^W \cap \mathrm{TALLY}) \neq (\beta_{i+1}^W \cap \mathrm{TALLY})]$, and

3. $(\forall i \in \mathcal{N} : i \leq \varrho) [(\beta_i^W \cap \mathrm{TALLY}) = (\mathrm{P}^W \cap \mathrm{TALLY})]$.

Like many oracle constructions (dating as far back as the $P^A = NP^A \cap coNP^A \neq NP^A$ construction of Baker, Gill, and Solovay [5]), ours will be built upon a PSPACE "platform." Suppose, for purposes of illustration, that our goal were merely to separate the tally sets in β_{17}^W from the tally sets in β_{18}^W. Informally speaking, putting a string with $\log^{18} \alpha_n$ Kolmogorov hard bits as its suffix (and a tally prefix) at length α_n, for a widely spaced set α_n, in such a way as to diagonalize against β_{17}^W machines, would work fine. But now, consider the relation between the tally sets in β_{16}^W and the tally sets in β_{17}^W. Of course, each machine from either of these classes can, on input 0^{α_n}, access the α_n length string in the oracle for only a finite number of α_n's (as the α_n's have too much randomness to be named, on input 0^{α_n}, by such machines). However, crucially, note that on inputs of the form $0^{m+\alpha_n}$, as m increases from 0 upwards, the length α_n string will potentially slip into the sights of (i.e., potentially could be queried by) a β_{17}^W machine earlier than it will potentially slip into the slights of any β_{16}^W machine (ignoring for each β_{16}^W machine a finite number of possibly exceptional α_n). This blocks our hope of collapsing $\beta_{16}^W \cap$ TALLY and $\beta_{17}^W \cap$ TALLY.

Can we get around this roadblock? Our proof presents a scheme that allows the problem to be avoided. Speaking very informally (and the proof formally implements this idea), we allow an α_n to remain mysterious for only enough lengths for the diagonalization to be performed. Then, long before the α_n can fall into this "slipping into the sights" spoiler behavior, the oracle loudly proclaims to the world the value of α_n. That is, we code α_n explicitly into the oracle at some well-known place. If the location of the revelation is sufficiently small, this makes accessing α_n, for machines whose nondeterminism is less than $\log^{18} n$, a matter of run-time rather than a matter of degree of nondeterminism. Thus, we regain the possibility of separating large classes while collapsing smaller classes. Of course, if the location of the revelation is too close to α_n, this would ruin our diagonalization. Furthermore, the lemma will require an infinite set of separations at different Kolmogorov complexity levels (not just at the 18th level), and will require corresponding revelations. The proof does just that: it obscures via Kolmogorov complexity, and then via coding judiciously reveals that which was obscured—all at appropriately chosen lengths.

As a technical note, the proof of the above result actually shows a bit more than claimed. In fact, the first part of the statement of Lemma 13 in fact can be strengthened to $(\forall i \in \mathcal{Z}^+) [(\beta_i^W \cap \text{TALLY}) = (co\beta_i^W \cap \text{TALLY}) = (U\beta_i^W \cap \text{TALLY}) = (coU\beta_i^W \cap \text{TALLY})]$ and similarly the first part of the statement of Theorem 9 can be strengthened to $(\forall i \in \mathcal{N}) [\beta E_i^W = co\beta E_i^W = U\beta E_i^W = coU\beta E_i^W]$, where the U classes indicate that the machines are required to have at most one accepting path on each input (the unique version of NP has been studied by Valiant [38] and many others, and is usually referred to as UP, rather than the more natural, uniform, and flexible UNP), and the coU classes indicate the complements of such classes.

4 Upward Separation

4.1 Defying Strong Separation

Theorem 14. *There exists a recursive oracle A such that NP^A has P^A-immune sparse sets yet NE^A is not E^A-immune.*

In order to prove this theorem, we have to construct an oracle that separates a pair of classes yet collapses another pair of classes. In oracle constructions of this nature, each stage can usually be divided into two major steps, a diagonalizing step and an encoding step. In the diagonalizing step we try to separate two classes, while in the encoding step we try to collapse the other two classes.

These two steps are contradictory in their nature, which may result into difficulties of various kinds. These are handled in many ways depending on the circumstances. In most oracle constructions in the literature, these problems are resolved by performing the encoding step first, and in such a way that there is enough "room" left for the diagonalizing step to succeed. However this was not possible in our case. The main obstacle is to maintain the sparseness of the diagonalizing set when doing the encoding (which is an additional requirement in our case).

In order to handle the conflict between the encoding step and the diagonalizing step, we introduce a new technique, called "hedging the bet." Instead of doing one diagonalization, we do many diagonalizations, one for each possible outcome of the encoding step. This is done in order to ensure that the result of the diagonalization step is consistent with any possible outcome of the encoding step yet to be done. The technique exploits the fact that we have to do a very small amount of encoding at every stage.

4.2 Probabilistic Classes and Upward Separation

Theorem 15. *There exists an oracle A such that $BPP^A - P^A$ has sparse sets and yet $BPE^A = E^A$.*

In the proof of the above theorem, the set $L(A)$ is also in R^A. Together with the fact that $VPE^A \subseteq BPE^A$ for any oracle A, the following corollary is immediate.

Corollary 16. (to the proof of previous theorem) *There exists an oracle A such that $R^A - P^A$ has sparse sets and yet $VPE^A = E^A$.*

In fact we can prove a stronger theorem than Theorem 15 above, by choosing a language in ZPP^A and then showing the diagonalization. Since $ZPP^A \subseteq R^A \subseteq BPP^A$ and $ZPE^A \subseteq VPE^A \subseteq BPE^A$ for any oracle A, both Theorem 15 and Corollary 16 will be a corollaries to the following theorem.

Theorem 17. *There exists an oracle A such that $ZPP^A - P^A$ has sparse sets and yet $BPE^A = E^A$.*

Corollary 18. *There exists an oracle A such that $ZPP^A - P^A$ has sparse sets and yet $ZPE^A = E^A$.*

4.3 A Sufficient Condition for Upward Separation

The previous section asked whether one could change the "NP" of Hartmanis, Immerman, Sewelson's "NP − P" result, and the answer was that for probabilistic classes, one can not robustly make this change. However, we note here that one can change the "P" to certain probabilistic classes, and to certain other classes. In fact, one can state a simple sufficient condition.

Adopting the notation of [2,8], for any class C and any r and t for which $\leq_r^t$ is defined, define $R_r^t(C) = \{L \mid (\exists C \in C)\,[L \leq_r^t C]\}$. $A \leq_m^e B$ if A exponential-time (i.e., $\bigcup_{c>0} \mathrm{DTIME}[2^{cn}]$) many-one reduces to B, and $A \leq_{m,\,eld}^p B$ if $A \leq_m^p B$ via a reduction f that is exponentially length-decreasing (i.e., $(\exists c > 0)(\forall x)[2^{c|f(x)|} \leq |x|]$).

Definition 19. We say that a pair of classes (A, B) is an *associated pair* if $R_m^e(A) \subseteq B$ and $R_{m,\,eld}^p(B) \subseteq A$.

For example,

Proposition 20. *The following are associated pairs:*

1. (P, E),

2. (NP, NE),

3. (R, VPE),

4. (BPP, BPE),

5. (ZPP, ZPE),

6. (NP $\cap$ coNP, NE $\cap$ CONE),

7. (UP $\cap$ coUP, UE $\cap$ coUE), *where* UP *and* UE *are the unambiguous [38] analogs of NP and NE.*

The Hartmanis-Immerman-Sewelson technique [19] in fact naturally establishes (keeping in mind Selman's observations that allow one to change a Turing reduction into a truth-table reduction [34]) the following result.

Theorem 21. *If A is closed downwards under polynomial-time truth-table reductions (that is, $R_{tt}^p(A) \subseteq A$),[5] and (A, B) is an associated pair then:*

$$\mathrm{NE} \subseteq B \iff \mathrm{NP} - A \text{ contains no sparse sets.}$$

We state below just a few of the many possible applications (note that it is well-known or clear that BPP, ZPP, NP $\cap$ coNP, and UP $\cap$ coUP are closed downwards under polynomial-time truth-table reductions).

Corollary 22. *1.* NP $-$ BPP *contains sparse sets if and only if* NE $\not\subseteq$ BPE.

2. NP $-$ ZPP *contains sparse sets if and only if* NE $\neq$ ZPE.

3. NP $-$ (NP $\cap$ coNP) *contains sparse sets if and only if* NE $\neq$ NE $\cap$ CONE.

4. [19] NP $-$ P *contains sparse sets if and only if* NE $\neq$ P.

5. NP $-$ (UP $\cap$ coUP) *contains sparse sets if and only if* NE $\neq$ UE $\cap$ coUE.

---

[5] Or even if A merely satisfies $R_{tt}^p(A \cap \mathrm{TALLY}) \subseteq A$.

5 Open Questions and Conclusions

In Section 3, we established results about the exponential-time beta hierarchy; do such results also apply to the beta hierarchy? We did show that they apply to the tally sets in the beta hierarchy. A first step beyond this might be to see whether they apply to the sparse sets in the beta hierarchy. One possible obstacle (related to Section 4 of this paper) to such a step is the fact that the upward separation results of Hartmanis, Immerman, and Sewelson [19] seem to break down for the beta hierarchy. For example, it seems unlikely that one can prove: $(\forall k \in \mathcal{N})\,[\beta_k - P$ has sparse sets $\iff \beta\!E_k - E \neq \emptyset]$. We note here, however, that a weaker version of that result does hold.

Definition 23. For any sparse set S let the *Hartmanis-Immerman-Sewelson [19] encoding of S, $HIS(S)$*, be defined as $HIS(S) = \{\langle n, cen, j, k, b\rangle \,|\,(\exists x_1 <_{lex} \cdots <_{lex} x_{cen})\,[\text{bit } j \text{ of } x_k \text{ is } b \wedge (\forall i : 1 \leq i \leq cen)\,[|x_i| = n \wedge x_i \in S]]\}$.

Hartmanis, Immerman, and Sewelson [19] showed that if S is a sparse set in NP, then $HIS(S)$ is in NE. It would be nice if one could show: if S is a sparse set in β_k, then $HIS(S)$ is in $\beta\!E_k$. However, we can show only the weaker result below. Let K[*short-name-size*(n), *time-bound*(n)] represent generalized (i.e., time-bounded) Kolmogorov complexity (see [30]).

Theorem 24. *Let k, j, and ℓ be elements of $\mathcal{N}$. If $S \in \beta_k - P$ and $\|S^{=n}\| = \mathcal{O}(\log^j n)$ and $S \subseteq K[\log^\ell n, n^{\mathcal{O}(1)}]$, then $HIS(S) \in \beta\!E_{j+\max(\ell,k)} - E$.*

Relatedly, can one prove results like those of Section 4.2 for the non-promise class PP?

Acknowledgments

We are grateful to S. Jain, R. Szelepcsényi, Y. Han, A. Hoene, V. Arvind, and an anonymous referee for helpful suggestions, corrections, conversations, and comments, and to U. Schöning and G. Wechsung for hosting visits during which this work was done in part.

References

1. E. Allender. Limitations of the upward separation technique. *Mathematical Systems Theory*, 24(1):53–67, 1991.

2. E. Allender, L. Hemachandra, M. Ogiwara, and O. Watanabe. Relating equivalence and reducibility to sparse sets. *SIAM Journal on Computing*, 21(3):521–539, 1992.

3. E. Allender and C. Wilson. Downward translations of equality. *Theoretical Computer Science*, 75(3):335–346, 1990.

4. K. Ambos-Spies. A note on complete problems for complexity classes. *Information Processing Letters*, 23:227–230, 1986.

5. T. Baker, J. Gill, and R. Solovay. Relativizations of the P=?NP question. *SIAM Journal on Computing*, 4(4):431–442, 1975.

6. J. Balcázar and D. Russo. Immunity and simplicity in relativizations of probabilistic complexity classes. *Theoretical Informatics and Applications (RAIRO)*, 22(2):227–244, 1988.

7. R. Book. Tally languages and complexity classes. *Information and Control*, 26:186–193, 1974.

8. R. Book and K. Ko. On sets truth-table reducible to sparse sets. *SIAM Journal on Computing*, 17(5):903–919, 1988.

9. D. Bovet, P. Crescenzi, and R. Silvestri. A uniform approach to define complexity classes. Technical Report CS-017/91, Università di Roma "La Sapienza," Dipartimento di Matematica, Rome, Italy, Feb. 1991.

10. J. Díaz and J. Torán. Classes of bounded nondeterminism. *Mathematical Systems Theory*, 23(1):21–32, 1990.

11. M. Garey and D. Johnson. *Computers and Intractability: A Guide to the Theory of NP-Completeness*. W. H. Freeman and Company, 1979.

12. W. Gasarch. Oracles for deterministic versus alternating classes. *SIAM Journal on Computing*, 16(4):613–627, 1987.

13. J. Geske. A note on almost-everywhere complexity, bi-immunity and nondeterministic space. In *Advances in Computing and Information: Proceedings of the 1990 International Conference on Computing and Information*, pages 112–116. Canadian Scholars' Press, May 1990.

14. J. Gill. Computational complexity of probabilistic Turing machines. *SIAM Journal on Computing*, 6(4):675–695, 1977.

15. Y. Gurevich. Algebras of feasible functions. In *Proceedings of the 24th IEEE Symposium on Foundations of Computer Science*, pages 210–214. IEEE Computer Society Press, Nov. 1983.

16. Y. Han, L. Hemachandra, and T. Thierauf. Threshold computation and cryptographic security. Technical Report TR-443, University of Rochester, Department of Computer Science, Rochester, NY, Nov. 1992.

17. J. Hartmanis and L. Hemachandra. Complexity classes without machines: On complete languages for UP. *Theoretical Computer Science*, 58:129–142, 1988.

18. J. Hartmanis and H. Hunt. The LBA problem and its importance in the theory of computing. *SIAM-AMS Proceedings*, 7:1–26, 1974.

19. J. Hartmanis, N. Immerman, and V. Sewelson. Sparse sets in NP−P: EXPTIME versus NEXPTIME. *Information and Control*, 65(2/3):159–181, 1985.

20. L. Hemachandra. *Counting in Structural Complexity Theory*. PhD thesis, Cornell University, Ithaca, NY, May 1987. Available as Cornell Department of Computer Science Technical Report TR87-840.

21. L. Hemachandra. The strong exponential hierarchy collapses. *Journal of Computer and System Sciences*, 39(3):299–322, 1989.

22. L. Hemachandra, S. Jain, and N. Vereshchagin. Banishing robust Turing completeness. In *Proceedings of Logic at Tver '92: Symposium on Logical Foundations of Computer Science*, pages 168–197. Springer-Verlag *Lecture Notes in Computer Science #620*, July 1992.

23. L. Hemachandra and R. Rubinstein. Separating complexity classes with tally oracles. *Theoretical Computer Science*, 92(2):309–318, 1992.

24. J. Hopcroft and J. Ullman. *Introduction to Automata Theory, Languages, and Computation*. Addison-Wesley, 1979.

25. R. Impagliazzo and G. Tardos. Decision versus search problems in super-polynomial time. In *Proceedings of the 30th IEEE Symposium on Foundations of Computer Science*, pages 222–227. IEEE Computer Society Press, October/November 1989.

26. D. Johnson. A catalog of complexity classes. In J. V. Leeuwen, editor, *Handbook of Theoretical Computer Science*, chapter 2, pages 67–161. MIT Press/Elsevier, 1990.

27. C. Kintala and P. Fisher. Refining nondeterminism in relativized polynomial-time bounded computations. *SIAM Journal on Computing*, 9(1):46–53, 1980.

28. A. Kolmogorov. Three approaches for defining the concept of information quantity. *Prob. Inform. Trans.*, 1:1–7, 1965.

29. W. Kowalczyk. Some connections between representability of complexity classes and the power of formal reasoning systems. In *Proceedings of the 11th Symposium on Mathematical Foundations of Computer Science*, pages 364–369. Springer-Verlag Lecture Notes in Computer Science #176, 1984.

30. M. Li and P. Vitanyi. Applications of Kolmogorov complexity in the theory of computation. In A. Selman, editor, *Complexity Theory Retrospective*, pages 147–203. Springer-Verlag, 1990.

31. A. Meyer and L. Stockmeyer. The equivalence problem for regular expressions with squaring requires exponential space. In *Proceedings of the 13th IEEE Symposium on Switching and Automata Theory*, pages 125–129, 1972.

32. K. Regan. Provable complexity properties and constructive reasoning. Manuscript, Apr. 1989.

33. H. Rogers, Jr. *The Theory of Recursive Functions and Effective Computability*. McGraw-Hill, 1967.

34. A. Selman. A note on adaptive vs. nonadaptive reductions to NP. Technical Report 90-20, State University of New York at Buffalo Department of Computer Science, Buffalo, NY, Sept. 1990.

35. V. Sewelson. *A Study of the Structure of NP*. PhD thesis, Cornell University, Ithaca, NY, Aug. 1983. Available as Cornell Department of Computer Science Technical Report #83-575.

36. M. Sipser. On relativization and the existence of complete sets. In *Proceedings of the 9th International Colloquium on Automata, Languages, and Programming*. Springer-Verlag Lecture Notes in Computer Science #140, 1982.

37. L. Stockmeyer. The polynomial-time hierarchy. *Theoretical Computer Science*, 3:1–22, 1977.

38. L. Valiant. The relative complexity of checking and evaluating. *Information Processing Letters*, 5:20–23, 1976.

39. M. Zimand. On relativizations with a restricted number of accesses to the oracle set. *Mathematical Systems Theory*, 20:1–11, 1987.

Counting, Selecting, and Sorting by Query-Bounded Machines

Albrecht Hoene* and *Arfst Nickelsen*

Technische Universität Berlin, Fachbereich Informatik, FR 6–2
Franklinstr. 28–29, 1000 Berlin 10, Germany

Abstract. We study the query-complexity of counting, selecting, and sorting functions. That is, for a given set A and a positive integer k, we ask, how many queries to an arbitrary oracle does a polynomial-time machine on input $(x_1, x_2, \ldots, x_k)$ need to determine how many strings of the input are in A. We also ask how many queries are necessary to select a string in A from the input $(x_1, x_2, \ldots, x_k)$ if such a string exists and to sort the input $(x_1, x_2, \ldots, x_k)$ with respect to the ordering $x \preceq y$ if and only if $x \in A \Rightarrow y \in A$. We obtain optimal query-bounds for these problems, and show that sets for which these functions have a low query-complexity must be easy in some sense. For such sets we obtain optimal placements in the extended low hierarchy. We also show that in the case of NP-complete sets the lower bounds for counting and selecting hold unless P=NP. Finally, we relate these notions to cheatability and p-superterseness. Our results yield as corollaries extensions of previously know results.

1 Introduction

The number of queries a polynomial-time oracle machine makes to solve certain problems has turned out to be a useful complexity measure. In [Kre88] optimization problems such as Clique and Travelling Salesperson were classified. Query-bounded oracle machines yield characterizations of other complexity classes such as the Boolean hierarchy over NP [PZ83, CGH+88, Bei91]. Results on query bounds also yield corollaries about other questions in complexity theory [Kad89, Wag90, Bei91, Bei87, Cha89, GHH].

For the general approach started in [AG88, Bei87] the principal question is: Given a set A, how many queries to an oracle must a polynomial-time machine make to solve the k-fold membership problem. That is, how hard is it in terms of number of queries to compute on input $(x_1, x_2, \ldots, x_k)$ which strings are in A and which strings are not.

In this paper we study counting, selecting, and sorting functions with regard to their query-complexity. The counting problem was introduced by Gasarch in [Gas91]: for a set A and a positive integer k one has to determine from a given input $(x_1, x_2, \ldots, x_k)$ the number of strings that are in A. Counting strings with a special property plays an important role in a variety of proofs (see, e.g., [Mah82, Imm88, Sze88, Kad89, Hem89]). The selecting problem for a set A and

---

* Research supported by a Deutsche Forschungsgesellschaft Postdoktorandenstipendium.

a positive integer k is to find a string in an input $(x_1, x_2, \ldots, x_k)$ that is in A (if such a string exists). Sets with polynomial-time computable selector functions for $k = 2$ (without querying an oracle) were introduced in [Sel82]. These sets are called p-selective. Their most prominent members are left-cuts of real numbers [Sel81]. Finally, the sorting problem for a set A and a positive integer k is to sort an input $(x_1, x_2, \ldots, x_k)$ with respect to the ordering defined by $x \preceq y$ if and only if $x \in A \Rightarrow y \in A$. Thus, sorting provides another generalization of p-selectivity. For each of these problems we ask: How many times must a polynomial-time oracle machine query an arbitrary oracle to solve the problem? If solving the problem requires less queries than in the standard case, what can be said about the underlying set A?

2 Preliminaries

IN is the set of positive integers including zero. Each polynomial appearing in the paper will implicitly be strictly monotonically increasing. For a string w we will denote its length by $|w|$. If A is a finite set then $\|A\|$ denotes its cardinality. For any set A the characteristic function of A is χ_A, that is, $\chi_A(x) = 1$ if $x \in A$ and $\chi_A(x) = 0$ otherwise. For complexity classes such as P, PSPACE, EXPTIME, and so on we use standard notation (see, e.g., [BDG88]).

A set A is self-reducible if there is a polynomial-time oracle machine M that accepts A with oracle A, and on any input x, M is only allowed to query strings that are strictly shorter than x. A is disjunctively self-reducible if A is self-reducible via a machine M satisfying that, on input x, if M queries the strings $x_1, \ldots, x_k$ then $x \in A \iff \exists i : x_i \in A$.

A set A is p-selective [Sel82] if there is a polynomial-time computable function $f : (\Sigma^*)^2 \rightarrow \Sigma^*$ that has the properties (1) $f(x, y) \in \{x, y\}$ and (2) $[x \in A$ or $y \in A] \Rightarrow f(x, y) \in A$ for all $x, y \in \Sigma^*$.

Throughout the paper we will employ an enumeration $(M_i)_{i \in \mathbb{N}}$ of polynomial-time oracle machines. We will assume that, for every $i \in \mathbb{N}$, the machine M_i runs in time $n^i + i$ on each input of size n.

FP^A is the class of functions computable by a polynomial-time bounded oracle machine with oracle $A \subseteq \Sigma^*$. We write FP for $\text{FP}^\emptyset$. For a function $f : \Sigma^* \rightarrow \mathbb{N}$ the class $\text{FP}^A[f(x)]$ consists of all functions that are in FP^A and the corresponding oracle machine queries the oracle A on input x at most $f(x)$ times. For an oracle machine M let

$Psb_M(x, k) = \{y \in \Sigma^* : \text{there is an oracle } A \subseteq \Sigma^* \text{ such that } M^A \text{ on input}$

x outputs y after having made at most k queries to $A\}$.

The elements of $Psb_M(x, k)$ we will call the possible strings (of M on input x) after k queries. Clearly, if M is a polynomial-time machine then, for each $k \in \mathbb{N}$, we can compute the set $Psb_M(x, k)$ in polynomial time, too.

Let $A \subseteq \Sigma^*$ and $k \in \mathbb{N}$. The function F_k^A is defined by $F_k^A(x_1, \ldots, x_k) = (\chi_A(x_1), \ldots, \chi_A(x_k))$. A set A is k-p-superterse [AG88] if $F_k^A \notin \text{FP}^X[k-1]$ for all $X \subseteq \Sigma^*$. A is p-superterse if A is k-p-superterse for all $k \geq 1$. A is k-cheatable [Bei91] if there exists an oracle $X \subseteq \Sigma^*$ such that $F_{2^k}^A \in \text{FP}^A[k]$. Finally, A is cheatable if A is k-cheatable for some $k \geq 1$.

We will refer various times to the following useful fact.

Proposition 1. *Let $A \subseteq \Sigma^*$ and $k \in \mathbb{N}$. If there is a polynomial-time computable function $f : (\Sigma^*)^k \to \{0,1\}^k$ such that $f(x_1, x_2, \ldots, x_k) \neq F_k^A(x_1, x_2, \ldots, x_k)$ for all $x_1, \ldots, x_k \in \Sigma^*$ then A is not $(2k-1)$-p-superterse.*

Proof. Let A, k, and f be given as above. Let X be the following set $\{(b_1, \ldots, b_{2k-1}, x_1, \ldots, x_{2k-1}) : b_i \in \{0,1\}, x_i \in \Sigma^* \text{ for } 1 \leq i \leq 2k-1, \text{ and } F_{2k-1}^A(x_1, \ldots, x_{2k-1}) \text{ is lexicographically smaller than } (b_1, \ldots, b_{2k-1})\}$.

By a result of Beigel [Bei87, Corollary 5.2] there are only $\Sigma_{i=0}^{k-1} \binom{n}{i}$ bitstrings $(b_1, \ldots, b_n)$ such that $f(x_{i_1}, \ldots, x_{i_k}) \neq (b_{i_1}, \ldots, b_{i_k})$ for every k-element subset $\{x_{i_1}, \ldots, x_{i_k}\}$ of $\{x_1, \ldots, x_n\}$. Thus, on input $(x_1, \ldots, x_{2k-1})$ we can compute in polynomial time a set of $\Sigma_{i=0}^{k-1} \binom{2k-1}{i} = 2^{2k-2}$ possible outputs of $F_{2k-1}^A(x_1, \ldots, x_{2k-1})$. Now a polynomial-time algorithm can find the correct output via binary search by making at most $2k-2$ queries to the oracle X. $\square$

A set A is in EL_k (is extended low k) for $k \geq 1$ [Sch83] if it holds that $\Sigma_k^{p,A} \subseteq \Sigma_{k-1}^{p,SAT \oplus A}$, where $\Sigma_k^{p,A}$ denotes the kth level of the polynomial-time hierarchy relative to the oracle A ($SAT \oplus A$ stands for the disjoint union of SAT and A).

3 Counting

In this section we study counting functions and their query complexity. The following definition is due to Gasarch.

Definition 2. [Gas91] Let $A \subseteq \Sigma^*$ and $k \in \mathbb{N}$. The function Cnt_k^A is defined by $Cnt_k^A(x_1, x_2, \ldots, x_k) = \|\{i : 1 \leq i \leq k, x_i \in A\}\|$.

We start with the general upper and lower bounds on the number of queries to compute Cnt_k^A.

Proposition 3. *1. [Gas91] For all $A \subseteq \Sigma^*$ and $k \in \mathbb{N}$ there exists an oracle $X \subseteq \Sigma^*$ such that $Cnt_k^A \in \mathrm{FP}^X[\lceil \log(k+1) \rceil]$.*

2. There exists an $A \subseteq \Sigma^*$ such that for all $k \in \mathbb{N}$ and oracles $X \subseteq \Sigma^*$, $Cnt_k^A \notin \mathrm{FP}^X[\lceil \log(k+1) \rceil - 1]$.

Proof. 2: A will be constructed in stages. Let $A_0 = \emptyset$ and let $n_0 = 0$. For each $i \in \mathbb{N}$, $i = \langle j, k \rangle$, let $n_i = \min\{m \in \mathbb{N} : 2^m > k \text{ and } m > 2^{n_{i-1}}\}$. In stage i we construct A_i, which will be a finite extension of A_{i-1} by at most k strings of length n_i. In this stage it will be made sure that the machine M_j does not compute Cnt_k^A with less than $\lceil \log(k+1) \rceil$ queries. Finally, we let $A = \cup_{i \geq 0} A_i$.
Stage $i = \langle j, k \rangle$:
Let $x_1, \ldots, x_k$ be the first k strings of length n_i in lexicographical order.
Let $Psb_{M_j}((x_1, x_2, \ldots, x_k), \lceil \log(k+1) \rceil - 1) = \{m_1, \ldots, m_r\}$.
(⋆) Choose the smallest $t \in \{0, 1, \ldots, k\} \setminus \{m_1, \ldots, m_r\}$.
Let $A_i = A_{i-1} \cup \{x_1, \ldots, x_t\}$.
End of stage i.
Note that, since M_j has made at most $\lceil \log(k+1) \rceil - 1$ queries, in line (⋆) the set $\{0, 1, \ldots, k\} \setminus \{m_1, \ldots, m_r\}$ is never empty. Now it follows by standard arguments

that there cannot be an oracle machine M_j, an oracle $X \subseteq \Sigma^*$, and a $k \in \mathbb{N}$ such that M_j^X computes Cnt_k^A correctly with less than $\lceil \log(k+1) \rceil$ queries. $\qquad \square$

In the following we will call a set $A \subseteq \Sigma^*$ *easily k-countable* if there exists an oracle X such that $Cnt_k^A \in \text{FP}^X[\lceil \log(k+1) \rceil - 1]$. A is *easily countable* if A is easily k-countable for some $k \geq 1$.

Theorem 4. *Let $A \subseteq \Sigma^*$ and $k \in \mathbb{N}$.*

1. *If A is k-cheatable then A is easily 2^k-countable.*
2. *If A is easily k-countable then A is not $(2k-1)$-p-superterse.*

Proof. 1: Immediate, since if $F_{2^k}^A \in \text{FP}^X[k]$ for some $X \subseteq \Sigma^*$ then $Cnt_{2^k}^A \in \text{FP}^X[k]$.
2: If A is easily k-countable then there is a polynomial-time computable function $g : (\Sigma^*)^k \rightarrow \mathbb{N}$ such that $g(x_1, x_2, \ldots, x_k) \neq Cnt_k^A(x_1, x_2, \ldots, x_k)$ for all $x_1, \ldots, x_k \in \Sigma^*$. It follows that the function $f(x_1, x_2, \ldots, x_k) = (1, \ldots, 1, 0, \ldots, 0)$ ($g(x_1, x_2, \ldots, x_k)$ times 1) fulfills the requirements in Proposition 1. Hence A is not $(2k-1)$-p-superterse. $\qquad \square$

We obtain the following corollary from [ABG90, Theorem 10] and the fact that sets in P/poly are extended low 3 [BBS86].

Corollary 5. *Let $A \subseteq \Sigma^*$ and $k \in \mathbb{N}$. If A is easily countable then $A \in$ P/poly and $A \in \text{EL}_3$.*

Note that this solves a conjecture by Gasarch [Gas91, page 73, 4]. Next we show that EL_3 cannot be improved to EL_2.

Theorem 6. *There exists a set $A \subseteq \Sigma^*$ such that A is easily 3-countable and $A \in \text{EL}_3 \setminus \text{EL}_2$.*

Proof. The construction of A has to make sure that $\Sigma_2^{p,A} \not\subseteq \text{NP}^{SAT \oplus A}$. Let $L_B = \{0^n : \forall x \ |x| = n \Rightarrow x \in B\}$. Clearly, for all B it holds that $L_B \in \text{coNP}^B$, and thus, in particular, $L_B \in \Sigma_2^{p,B}$. We construct A such that $L_A \notin \text{NP}^{SAT \oplus A}$ and A is easily 3-countable.

Let $(N_i)_{i \in \mathbb{N}}$ be an enumeration of polynomial-time bounded nondeterministic oracle machines. W. l. o. g. we assume that N_i runs in time $n^i + i$. A will be defined in stages. Initially, let $A_0 = \emptyset$. In stage i the set A_i is defined as a finite extension of A_{i-1} to make sure that $N_i^{SAT \oplus A}$ does not accept L_A. Finally, $A = \cup_{i \geq 0} A_i$.

Let $n_0 = 0$ and for all $i \geq 1$ let $n_i = \min\{j \in \mathbb{N} : j \geq 2^{n_{i-1}} \text{ and } 2^j > j^i + i\}$. Then the construction in stage i with $i > 0$ is as follows:

Run $N_i(0^{n_i})$ with oracle $SAT \oplus (A_{i-1} \cup \{x \in \Sigma^* : |x| = n_i\})$.

1. There is an accepting computation. Fix some accepting computation path and let y be the smallest string of length n_i that is not queried along this path ($\star$). Let $A_i = A_{i-1} \cup \{x : |x| = n_i \text{ and } x \neq y\}$.
2. There is no accepting computation path. Let $A_i = A_{i-1} \cup \{x : |x| = n_i\}$.

This ends the construction of stage i.

Note that in ($\star$) a string of the required form always exists, since n_i was chosen such that $2^{n_i} > (n_i)^i + i$. To prove that $L_A \notin \text{NP}^{SAT \oplus A}$ assume to the contrary that N_i with oracle $SAT \oplus A$ accepts L_A. By the choice of n_i, $N_i^{SAT \oplus A}$ accepts 0^{n_i} if and only if $N_i^{SAT \oplus A_i}$ accepts 0^{n_i}. If there is a string y of length n_i that is not in A_i then, by construction, N_i accepts 0^{n_i} with oracle $SAT \oplus A_i$ but $0^{n_i} \notin L_A$. If N_i does not accept 0^{n_i} with oracle $SAT \oplus A_i$ then all strings of length n_i are in A and thus $0^{n_i} \in L_A$. Hence, N_i with oracle $SAT \oplus A$ does not accept L_A.

It remains to prove that A is easily 3-countable, that is, $Cnt_3^A \in \mathrm{FP}^X[1]$ for some oracle X. On input (x_1, x_2, x_3) a polynomial-time oracle machine first checks[2] that $|x_1| = |x_2| = |x_3| = n_i$ for some i. If this is the case then $Cnt_3^A(x_1, x_2, x_3)$ can only have the values 2 or 3. This holds, since in each stage i we either put all strings of length n_i into A_i (case 2) or we put all strings but one into A_i (case 1). It follows that one query to the oracle $X = \{(j, x_1, x_2, x_3) :$ there are at least j strings in $\{x_1, x_2, x_3\} \cap A\}$ suffices to determine $Cnt_3^A(x_1, x_2, x_3)$. Hence, A is easily 3-countable.

$\square$

By Theorem 4, the set A is also not p-superterse. Thus, we obtain the solution to an open problem posed in [ABG90].

Corollary 7. *There exists a set $A \subseteq \Sigma^*$ such that A is not p-superterse and $A \in$ $\mathrm{EL}_3 \setminus \mathrm{EL}_2$.*

In fact, a closer look to the set A constructed in the proof of Theorem 6 reveals that $\lceil \log(k+1) \rceil$ queries suffice to compute F_k^A. Thus, the result that cheatable sets are extended low 2 is optimal in some sense.

Next we ask what happens if an NP-complete set is easily countable.

Theorem 8. *If a set $A \subseteq \Sigma^*$ is disjunctively self-reducible and A is easily countable then $A \in \mathrm{P}$.*

Proof. Let A be easily k-countable. Then there is a polynomial-time computable function $f : (\Sigma^*)^k \to \mathbb{N}$ such that $f(x_1, x_2, \ldots, x_k) \neq Cnt_k^A(x_1, x_2, \ldots, x_k)$ for all $x_1, \ldots, x_k \in \Sigma^*$. Let M be the oracle machine that accepts A in a disjunctive self-reducing fashion. Assume that M is time-bounded by the polynomial p. The query tree of $M(x)$ is the tree, in which the root is marked with the string x; for each node in the tree that is marked with a string y its children are marked with the strings queried by M on input y.

We will give a breadth-first pruning algorithm for the query tree of $M(x)$. While searching the query tree we maintain a subtree T, which is of size polynomial in $|x|$. We will maintain the following invariants for T:

1. each leaf of T has height $\leq k$ in T,
2. the number of nodes in T is at most $p(|x|)^{k+1}$, and
3. if $x \in A$ then there is a leaf in T that is marked with a string in A.

Initially, T is the query tree up to depth k and the first leaf to be considered is the leftmost leaf of T that has height k in T. Since every node in the query tree has

---

[2] Strings v such that $\forall i : |v| \neq n_i$ are not in A. If $|x_k| = n_{i_1}$, $|x_l| = n_{i_2}$ for some $i_1 > i_2$ then we can compute membership of x_l in A in time polynomial in $|x_k|$, since $\log n_{i_1} \geq n_{i_1-1} \geq n_{i_2}$.

at most $p(|x|)$ children, the number of nodes up to level k is bounded by $p(|x|)^{k+1}$. We perform in a breadth-first way the following pruning steps until all leaves of T are marked with strings for which M computes membership in A without further querying the oracle. Then we can determine whether $x \in A$ or not.

Let x_k be the next leaf to be considered that has height k in T. Let $x_1, \ldots, x_{k-1}$ be all ancestors of x_k in T in descending order. Note that it holds that $(\forall i, j : 1 \leq i < j \leq k)\ x_j \in A \Rightarrow x_i \in A$. Compute $f(x_1, x_2, \ldots, x_k) = m$.

If $m = 0$ then $Cnt_k^A(x_1, x_2, \ldots, x_k) \neq 0$, and hence $x \in A$. In this case the algorithm stops.

If $m = k$ then $x_k \notin A$. Thus we can prune the node marked with x_k from T (if this makes x_{k-1} a leaf we mark x_{k-1} not to be considered again). The next leaf to be considered is the leftmost leaf in T that is marked with a string of maximal length of all leaves in T.

If $0 \neq m \neq k$ then $x_m \in A \Rightarrow x_{m+1} \in A$ (since otherwise it would hold that $Cnt_k^A(x_1, x_2, \ldots, x_k) = m$). In this case we append x_{m+1} with its subtree in T as a new child to x_{m-1} in T. We also add one new level of children in the subtree rooted at x_{m+1} to T and remove x_m and its entire subtree from T. The next leaf to be considered is the leftmost leaf in T that is marked with a string of maximal length of all leaves in T.

This ends one pruning step.

Note that if there is a leaf of T in A then after a pruning step there still is a leaf of T in A. Thus if $x \in A$ it follows that we finally end up with a leaf y of T for which we can detect $y \in A$ in polynomial time. It is also not hard to see that after each pruning step the conditions 1 and 2 of the invariant hold and that the procedure runs in time polynomial in $|x|$. □

Using the fact that the class of easily countable sets is closed downwards under polynomial-time many-one reductions we obtain the following corollary.

Corollary 9. *There exists a set $A \subseteq \Sigma^*$ that is hard for NP under polynomial-time many-one reductions and easily countable if and only if P=NP.*

4 Selecting

In this section we study selecting functions and their query complexity. The results and proofs are similar to those in the previous section. Therefore the proofs are omitted.

Definition 10. Let $A \subseteq \Sigma^*$ and $k \in \mathbb{N}$. A function $g : (\Sigma^*)^k \to \Sigma^*$ is an (A, k)-selector function if it satisfies

1. $g(x_1, x_2, \ldots, x_k) \in \{x_1, x_2, \ldots, x_k\}$ and
2. $(\exists i : i \in \{1 \ldots, k\}\ \&\ x_i \in A) \Rightarrow g(x_1, x_2, \ldots, x_k) \in A$.

Thus, a set A is p-selective if and only if there is a polynomial-time computable $(A, 2)$-selector function.

Proposition 11. *1. For all $A \subseteq \Sigma^*$ and $k \in \mathbb{N}$ there exists a set $X \subseteq \Sigma^*$ and an (A, k)-selector function g such that $g \in \mathrm{FP}^X[\lceil \log k \rceil]$.*

2. *There exists an $A \subseteq \Sigma^*$ such that for all $k \in \mathbb{N}$ and $X \subseteq \Sigma^*$ there does not exist an (A, k)-selector function $g \in \mathrm{FP}^X[\lceil \log k \rceil - 1]$.*

We say that a set $A \subseteq \Sigma^*$ is *easily k-selectable* if there is an (A, k)-selector function $g \in \mathrm{FP}^X[\lceil \log k \rceil - 1]$ for some oracle $X \subseteq \Sigma^*$. We call A *easily selectable* if A is easily k-selectable for some $k \geq 1$.

Theorem 12. *Let $A \subseteq \Sigma^*$ and $k \in \mathbb{N}$.*

1. *If A is k-cheatable then A is easily 2^{k+1}-selectable.*
2. *If A is easily k-selectable then A is not $(2k - 1)$-p-superterse.*

Corollary 13. *If $A \subseteq \Sigma^*$ is easily selectable then $A \in \mathrm{P/poly}$ and $A \in \mathrm{EL}_3$.*

Theorem 14. *There exists a set $A \subseteq \Sigma^*$ such that A is easily 3-selectable and $A \in \mathrm{EL}_3 \setminus \mathrm{EL}_2$.*

Proof. One can show that for the set A constructed in the proof of Theorem 6 there exists an $(A, 3)$-selector function in $\mathrm{FP}^A[1]$. □

Next, we consider the question what happens if an NP-complete set has an easy selector function. By a similar pruning technique as in the proof of Theorem 8 one can prove the following result.

Theorem 15. *Let $A \subseteq \Sigma^*$. If A is easily selectable and A is disjunctively self-reducible then $A \in \mathrm{P}$.*

Since the class of easily selectable sets is closed downwards under polynomial-time many-one reductions we get the following corollary.

Corollary 16. *There is a set $A \subseteq \Sigma^*$ that is hard for NP with respect to polynomial-time many-one reductions and is easily selectable if and only if P=NP.*

5 Sorting

In this section we study sorting functions and their query complexity.

Definition 17. *Let $A \subseteq \Sigma^*$ and $k \in \mathbb{N}$. A function $f : (\Sigma^*)^k \to (\Sigma^*)^k$ is an (A, k)-sorting function if for all $x_1, x_2, \ldots, x_k, y_1, y_2, \ldots, y_k \in \Sigma^*$*

1. $f(x_1, x_2, \ldots, x_k) = (y_1, y_2, \ldots, y_k) \Rightarrow \{x_1, x_2, \ldots, x_k\} = \{y_1, y_2, \ldots, y_k\}$ *and*
2. $(\forall i, j : 1 \leq i < j \leq k)\, [y_i \in A \Rightarrow y_j \in A]$.

It is easy to see that the notion of sorting generalizes the one of p-selectivity. First we show upper and lower bounds on the number of queries needed to compute sorting functions in polynomial time.

Theorem 18. *1. For every $A \subseteq \Sigma^*$ and $k \in \mathbb{N}$ there exists an $X \subseteq \Sigma^*$ such that there exists a polynomial-time sorting function $g \in \mathrm{FP}^X[\lceil \log \binom{k}{\lceil \frac{k}{2} \rceil} \rceil]$.*

2. *There exists an $A \subseteq \Sigma^*$ such that for all $k \in \mathbb{N}$ and $X \subseteq \Sigma^*$ there does not exist a polynomial-time sorting function $g \in \mathrm{FP}^X[\lceil \log \binom{k}{\lceil \frac{k}{2} \rceil} \rceil - 1]$.*

Proof. 1: The proof is based on the fact that one permutation covers more than one membership situation for a given input. It follows from Dilworth's Theorem [Dil50] that one can find a fixed set T_k of $\lceil \frac{k}{2} \rceil$ permutations such that for every input $(x_1, x_2, \ldots, x_k)$ there is a permutation in T_k that sorts the input according to membership in A. Thus one can find a correct sorting via binary search with $\lceil \log(\binom{k}{\lceil \frac{k}{2} \rceil}) \rceil$ queries.

2: A will be constructed in stages. Let $A_0 = \emptyset$ and let $n_0 = 0$. For each $i \in \mathbb{N}$, $i = \langle j, k \rangle$, let $n_i = \min\{m \in \mathbb{N} : 2^m > k \text{ and } m > 2^{n_{i-1}}\}$. In stage $i = \langle j, k \rangle$ we construct A_i, which will be a finite extension of A_{i-1} by $\lceil \frac{k}{2} \rceil$ strings of length n_i. In this stage it will be made sure that the machine M_j does not compute an (A, k)-sorting function with less than $\lceil \log \binom{k}{\lceil \frac{k}{2} \rceil} \rceil$ queries. Finally, we let $A = \cup_{i \geq 0} A_i$.

Stage $i = \langle j, k \rangle$:

Let $x_1, \ldots, x_k$ be the first k strings in lexicographical order of length n_i.

Define T to be the set of permutations $(y_1, \ldots, y_k)$ of $(x_1, \ldots, x_k)$ that are contained in $Psb_{M_j}((x_1, \ldots, x_k), \lceil \log \binom{k}{\lceil \frac{k}{2} \rceil} \rceil - 1)$.

Choose the lexicographically first permutation $(z_1, \ldots, z_k)$ of $(x_1, \ldots, x_k)$ such that for all $t = (y_1, \ldots, y_k) \in T$ it holds that $\{y_1, \ldots, y_{\lceil \frac{k}{2} \rceil}\} \neq \{z_1, \ldots, z_{\lceil \frac{k}{2} \rceil}\}$.

Let $A_i = A_{i-1} \cup \{z_1, \ldots, z_{\lceil \frac{k}{2} \rceil}\}$.

End of stage i.

Now it is easy to see that there doesn't exist a polynomial-time oracle machine M_j that computes an (A, k)-sorting function with $\lceil \log \binom{k}{\lceil \frac{k}{2} \rceil} \rceil - 1$ queries to some oracle X. □

We say that a set $A \subseteq \Sigma^*$ is *easily k-sortable* if there is an (A, k)-sorting function $g \in \mathrm{FP}^X[\lceil \log \binom{k}{\lceil \frac{k}{2} \rceil} \rceil - 1]$ for some some oracle $X \subseteq \Sigma^*$. A is *easily sortable* if A is easily k-sortable for some $k \geq 1$.

Theorem 19. *Let $A \subseteq \Sigma^*$ and $k \in \mathbb{N}$.*

1. *If A is easily k-sortable then A is not $(2k-1)$-p-superterse.*
2. *If A is not k-p-superterse then A is easily $3k$-sortable.*

Proof. 1: One can show that if A is easily k-sortable there is a polynomial-time computable function $f : (\Sigma^*)^k \to \{0, 1\}^k$ that fulfills the requirements of Proposition 1, i.e., $f(x_1, \ldots, x_k) \neq F_k^A(x_1, \ldots, x_k)$ for all $x_1, \ldots, x_k \in \Sigma^*$. It follows that A is not $(2k-1)$-p-superterse.

2: Instead of Proposition 1 this proof makes use of Lemma 20. Let A be not k-p-superterse and M the machine that computes F_k^A in polynomial time with less than k queries to an oracle X. On input $(x_1, \ldots, x_k)$ we compute $Psb_M((x_1, \ldots, x_k), k-1)$. Thus we get a set of less than 2^k possible values of $F_k^A(x_1, \ldots, x_k)$. $f(x_1, \ldots, x_k)$ is chosen as an (e.g., the lexicographically smallest) element of $\{0, 1\}^k$ that is not in this set. Thus f fulfills the reqirements of Lemma 20 and A is easily $3k$-sortable. □

We now give the Lemma that is needed to complete the proof of Theorem 19.

Lemma 20. *Let $A \subseteq \Sigma^*$ and $k \in \mathbb{N}$. If there is a polynomial-time computable function $f : (\Sigma^*)^k \to \{0,1\}^k$ such that $f(x_1, x_2, \ldots, x_k) \neq F_k^A(x_1, x_2, \ldots, x_k)$ for all $x_1, \ldots, x_k \in \Sigma^*$ then A is easily $3k$-sortable.*

Proof. Let A, k and f be given as above. By the result of Beigel [Bei87, Corollary 5.2] also employed in the proof of Proposition 1 there are only $\Sigma_{i=0}^{k-1} \binom{n}{i}$ bitstrings $(b_1, \ldots, b_n)$ such that $f(x_{i_1}, \ldots, x_{i_k}) \neq (b_{i_1}, \ldots, b_{i_k})$ for every k-element subset $\{x_{i_1}, \ldots, x_{i_k}\}$ of $\{x_1, \ldots, x_n\}$. If $\Sigma_{i=0}^{k-1} \binom{n}{i} \leq \frac{1}{2} \binom{n}{\lceil \frac{n}{2} \rceil}$ on a given input $(x_1, \ldots, x_n)$ we can compute in polynomial time a set of $\Sigma_{i=0}^{k-1} \binom{n}{i}$ possible values of $F_n^A(x_1, \ldots, x_n)$ and then find the correct value by binary search making at most $\lceil \log \frac{1}{2} \binom{k}{\lceil \frac{k}{2} \rceil} \rceil = \lceil \log \binom{k}{\lceil \frac{k}{2} \rceil} \rceil - 1$ queries to an appropriate oracle X. Knowing the value of $F_k^A(x_1, \ldots, x_n)$ it is easy to compute a correct sorting of $(x_1, \ldots, x_n)$.

It remains to show that $2\Sigma_{i=0}^{k-1} \binom{3k}{i} \leq \binom{3k}{\lceil \frac{3k}{2} \rceil}$. To prove this we use the fact that for all $n, r \in \mathbb{N}$ holds $\Sigma_{i=0}^n \binom{r+i}{i} = \binom{r+n+1}{n}$ $(\star)$ (see, e.g., [Knu73]).

First case: k is even. If $k = 2$ the inequality holds. Now let $k \geq 4$. Applying $(\star)$ to $n = \frac{3k}{2}$ and $r = \frac{3k}{2} - 1$ we get $\Sigma_{i=0}^{\frac{3k}{2}} \binom{\frac{3k}{2}+i-1}{i} = \binom{3k}{\frac{3k}{2}}$. Hence $\binom{3k}{\frac{3k}{2}} \geq \Sigma_{i=\frac{k}{2}+1}^{\frac{3k}{2}} \binom{\frac{3k}{2}+i-1}{i} = \Sigma_{i=0}^{k-1} \binom{2k+i}{\frac{k}{2}+i+1}$. Letting $2\binom{3k}{i} = \lambda_i$ and $\binom{2k+i}{\frac{k}{2}+i+1} = \rho_i$ it suffices to show that $\lambda_i \leq \rho_i$ for $i \in \{0, \ldots, k-1\}$. Elementary calculations show that $\frac{\rho_i}{\lambda_i} \geq \frac{\rho_{i+1}}{\lambda_{i+1}}$ for $i \leq k-2$. Therefore it remains to show that $\lambda_{k-1} \leq \rho_{k-1}$. This means we have to show $2\binom{3k}{k-1} \leq \binom{3k-1}{\frac{3k}{2}} = \frac{1}{2}\binom{3k}{\frac{3k}{2}}$. This is equivalent to $4 \cdot k \cdots \binom{3k}{2} \leq (\frac{3k}{2} + 1) \cdots (2k+1)$. This inequality certainly holds if $4 \cdot k \cdot (k+1) \cdot (k+2) \leq (2k-1) \cdot 2k \cdot (2k+1)$ (there are at least three factors on each side since $k \geq 4$). But this is equivalent to $2k^2 - 6k + 3 \geq 0$ which holds for all $k \in \mathbb{N}$.

Second case: k is odd. We apply $(\star)$ to $n = \frac{3k-1}{2}$ and $r = \frac{3k-1}{2}$ and can do an analogous calculation as in the first case. $\quad\square$

As an immediate corollary of this theorem we get

Corollary 21. *1. Let $A \subseteq \Sigma^*$. A is easily sortable if and only if A is not p-superterse.*

2. If A is easily sortable then $A \in$ P/poly and $A \in$ EL$_3$.

Corollary 21, part 1 also implicitly answers the question under which conditions NP-hard sets can be easily sortable. In [Bei88] it was shown that sets that are hard for NP under polynomial-time truth-table reductions must be p-superterse unless P=UP and RP=NP.

Acknowledgments

We wish to thank Hubert Wagener and Hans-Jörg Burtschick for stimulating conversations and Richard Beigel and Bill Gasarch for providing helpful references. We are also grateful to Martin Kummer for various helpful comments.

References

[ABG90] A. Amir, R. Beigel, and W. Gasarch. Some connections between bounded query classes and non-uniform complexity. In *Proceedings 5th Structure in Complexity Theory Conference*, pages 232–243. IEEE Computer Society Press, 1990.

[AG88]   A. Amir and W. Gasarch. Polynomial terse sets. *Information and Computation*, 77:37–55, 1988.

[BBS86]   J. Balcázar, R. Book, and U. Schöning. Sparse sets, lowness, and highness. *SIAM Journal on Computing*, 15:739–747, 1986.

[BDG88]   J. Balcázar, J. Díaz, and J. Gabarró. *Structural Complexity I*. Springer Verlag, 1988.

[Bei87]   R. Beigel. A structural theorem that depends quantitavely on the complexity of SAT. In *Proceedings 2nd Structure in Complexity Theory Conference*, pages 28–32. IEEE Computer Society Press, 1987.

[Bei88]   R. Beigel. NP-hard sets are p-superterse unless R=NP. Technical Report 88–04, Johns Hopkins University, Baltimore, MD, USA, 1988.

[Bei91]   R. Beigel. Bounded queries to SAT and the boolean hierachy. *Theoretical Computer Science*, 84(2):199–224, 1991.

[CGH⁺88]   J. Cai, T. Gundermann, J. Hartmanis, L. Hemachandra, V. Sewelson, K. Wagner, and G. Wechsung. The boolean hierarchy I: Structural properties. *SIAM Journal on Computing*, 17(6):1232–1252, 1988.

[Cha89]   R. Chang. On the structure of bounded queries to arbitrary NP sets. In *Proceedings 4th Structure in Complexity Theory Conference*, pages 250–258. IEEE Computer Society Press, 1989.

[Dil50]   R. P. Dilworth. A decomposition theorem for partially ordered sets. *Ann. of Math.*, 51:161–166, 1950.

[Gas91]   W. Gasarch. Bounded queries in recursion theory: A survey. In *Proceedings 6th Structure in Complexity Theory Conference*, pages 62–78. IEEE Computer Society Press, 1991.

[GHH]   W. Gasarch, L. Hemachandra, and A. Hoene. On checking versus evaluating multiple queries. *Information and Computation*. To appear.

[Hem89]   L. Hemachandra. The strong exponential hierarchy collapses. *Journal of Computer and System Sciences*, 39(3):299–322, 1989.

[Imm88]   N. Immerman. Nondeterministic space is closed under complementation. *SIAM Journal on Computing*, 17:935–938, 1988.

[Kad89]   J. Kadin. $P^{NP[\log n]}$ and sparse Turing complete sets for NP. *Journal of Computer and System Sciences*, 39:282–298, 1989.

[Knu73]   D. Knuth. *The Art of Computer Programming III*. Addison Wesley, second edition, 1973.

[Kre88]   M. Krentel. The complexity of optimization problems. *Journal of Computer and System Sciences*, 36:490–509, 1988.

[Mah82]   S. Mahaney. Sparse complete sets for NP: solution to a conjecture of Berman and Hartmanis. *Journal of Computer and System Sciences*, 25:130–143, 1982.

[PZ83]   C. Papadimitriou and S. Zachos. Two remarks on the power of counting. In *Proceedings 6th GI Conference on Theoretical Computer Science*, pages 269–276. Springer-Verlag Lecture Notes in Computer Science #145, 1983.

[Sch83]   U. Schöning. A low and a high hierarchy in NP. *Journal of Computer and system sciences*, 27:14–28, 1983.

[Sel81]   A. Selman. Some observations on NP real numbers and P-selective sets. *Journal of Computer and System Sciences*, 23:326–332, 1981.

[Sel82]   A. Selman. Analogues of semirecursive sets and effective reducibilities to the study of NP complexity. *Information and Control*, 1:36–51, 1982.

[Sze88]   R. Szelepcsényi. The method of forced enumeration for nondeterministic automata. *Acta Informatica*, 26:279–284, 1988.

[Wag90]   K. Wagner. Bounded query classes. *SIAM Journal on Computing*, 19(5):833–846, 1990.

Cancellation in Context-Free Languages: Enrichment by Reduction

M. Jantzen   H. Petersen

Fachbereich Informatik, Universität Hamburg

Abstract

The following problem is shown to be decidable: Given a context-free grammar G and a string $w \in X^*$, does there exist a string $u \in L(G)$ such that w is obtained from u by deleting all substrings u_i that are elements of the symmetric Dyck set D_1^* ?

The intersection of any two context-free languages can be obtained from only one context-free language by cancellation either with the smaller semi-Dyck set $D_1'^* \subset D_1^*$ or with D_1^* itself.

Also, the following is shown here for the first time: If the set $EQ := \{x^n \bar{x}^n \mid n \in I\!N\} \subset D_1'^*$ is used for this cancellation, then each recursively enumerable set can be obtained from linear context-free languages.

1 Introduction

Adding a further control mechanism to the somewhat limited power of context-free grammars is a rich source of new insights into the field of formal language theory. Let us only mention matrix grammars, indexed grammars and programmed grammars. In this paper we will investigate another approach: a context-free language is modified by a reduction $x\bar{x} \to \lambda$. In fact, the iterated application of this reduction reduces the well known semi-Dyck set $D_1'^*$ over one pair of parentheses to the empty word λ. Likewise, the two-sided reduction $x\bar{x} \to \lambda$, $\bar{x}x \to \lambda$ yields the symmetric Dyck set D_1^*.

Dyck reductions were studied in [1, 2, 3, 4, 5, 8, 10, 17, 18, 19] mostly by considering general Dyck sets having more than one type of parentheses for the cancellation which then yields the full class of recursively enumerable sets. This result is very famous and can be found in several places, see [8, 19, 16]. It has been shown in [5], that even linear context-free languages are sufficient, a result recently rediscovered in [3]. In the case of only one pair of parentheses it is not yet clear whether the generated class of languages is equally large. The authors extended the results of Savitch on cancellation grammars in [11, 12] and showed that the cancellation of complete substrings from the semi-Dyck language $D_1'^*$ in context-free languages not only yielded the full class $\underline{L}$ of terminal Petri net languages, see [9], but moreover their elementwise intersection with the context-free languages, i.e. the family $\underline{L} \wedge \underline{Cf}$. The simulations used are even strong enough for generating the closure with respect to nested iterated substitution and non-erasing homomorphisms of the above language class. Kimura uses the cancellation of two symbols as a means for describing restricted communication between systems [14].

Since it is known [1, 2, 10], that regular sets are closed with respect to Dyck-reductions, the question arose which class of languages would be obtained by applying the cancellation with the semi-Dyck set $D_1'^*$ to the slightly larger class of linear context-free sets. As a first step in this direction we showed in [13], how the class of terminal Petri net languages can be obtained from the linear context-free languages, (abb. *Lin*), by complete cancellation of substrings from any of the sets EQ, $D_1'^*$, or D_1^*.

The new result presented here will show, that even the intersections of two context-free languages form a subclass of $\underline{Cf}\%D_1^*$ and moreover their closure with respect to non-erasing homomorphisms and nested iterated substitution, see [7].

2 Definitions and Results

Definition 1 *Let Reg (resp. Lin, Cf, $Cf^\triangle$, Rec, RE) denote the family of regular sets (linear context-free, context-free, λ-free context-free, recursive, and recursively enumerable sets, respectively).* □

Definition 2 *Let $X := \{x_i, \bar{x}_i \mid 1 \leq i \leq k\}$ be an alphabet of k pairs of matching parentheses, where x_i is the opening and $\bar{x}_i$ the closing bracket. Cancelling a matching pair $x_i\bar{x}_i$ ($1 \leq i < k$), within a string $ux_i\bar{x}_iv \in V^*$, where V is any alphabet containing X_k , yields the word uv. This one-step reduction is denoted by $\triangle_k(ux_i\bar{x}_iv) := uv$. $D_k'^*$ denotes the one-sided (or semi-) Dyck set of all strings $w \in X_k^*$ which can be reduced to the empty string λ by finitely many cancellations of typ $\triangle_k$. Instead of using the reduction based on $\triangle_k$ as in [2, 12] we follow Kimura[14] and use the cancellation of subwords on a language $K \subseteq V_1^*$ with any set $L \subseteq V_2^*$ defined by:*

$$K\%L :=$$
$$\{w \in (V_1 \setminus V_2)^* \mid \exists w_1 \in K \; \exists n \in I\!N \; \forall 0 \leq i \leq n \; \exists u_i \in V_1^* \; \exists v_i \in L :$$
$$w_1 = u_0v_1u_1 \ldots v_nu_n \text{ and } w = u_0u_1 \ldots u_n\}$$

$K\%L$ is called a $Dyck_k$-reduction if L equals the Dyck set $D_k'^*$. Whenever we use the Dyck sets D_1^*, $D_1'^*$, or $EQ := \{x^n\bar{x}^n \mid n \in I\!N\}$ we use the brackets x and $\bar{x}$ from the alphabet $X := \{x, \bar{x}\}$ and omit the index 1 in X_k that is used only for the sets $D_k'^*$ where $k \geq 2$.

The canonical extension to families $\mathcal{K}$ and $\mathcal{L}$ is defined by

$$\mathcal{K}\%\mathcal{L} := \{K\%L \mid K \in \mathcal{K} \text{ and } L \in \mathcal{L}\}$$

and we will write $\mathcal{K}\%L$ as a shorthand for $\mathcal{K}\%\{L\}$.

For a class of languages $\mathcal{C}$ we denote by $H(\mathcal{C})$ the closure of $\mathcal{C}$ with respect to non-erasing homomorphisms. If τ is a substitution such that $a \in \tau(a)$ for any *symbol a, then we denote by $\tau^{\infty}(L)$ the operation of nested iterated substitution of the language L, the union of all languages obtained by finitely often applying τ to L. A more detailed definition of this operation may be found in [7]. For a language class C we define the closure of C with respect to nested iterated substitution $\tau^{\infty}(C)$ to be the smallest language class containing C and being closed under nested iterated substitution.*

For any family C let $C^{\triangle} := \{L \setminus \{\lambda\} \mid L \in C\}$ be a class of λ-free languages. Often, but not always we find $C^{\triangle} \subseteq C$.

□

It has been shown in [12, Theorem 7] that the emptiness problem for the family $\underline{Lin}\%D_1'^*$ is undecidable. That proof at the same time shows that undecidability result for the families $\underline{Lin}\%D_1^*$ and $\underline{Lin}\%EQ$, because only subwords from the set $EQ \subseteq D_1'^* \subseteq D_1^*$ were used for cancellation. The problem, as to whether the family $\underline{Cf}\%D_1'^*$ only contains recursive sets is approached, though not solved, by the following result:

Theorem 1 $\mathcal{L}\%D_1^* \subseteq \underline{Rec}$, for any family $\mathcal{L}$ of languages closed w.r.t. inverse homomorphisms, intersection with regular sets and for which we can effectively compute the Parikh image of every language.

Proof: The proof of the first result uses the decidability of the emptiness of semilinear vector sets, is fairly straight forward, and is only sketched. For any language $K \subseteq \mathcal{L}$, $K \subseteq (V \cup X)^*$ and each string $w = w_1 w_2 \ldots w_n$, where $w_i \in V \setminus X$, an algorithm will be given which decides, whether $w \in K\%D_1^*$.

For each i, $1 \leq i \leq n+1$, define $Y_i := \{x_i, \bar{x}_i\}$ and $h : Y_n \to X$ by $h(x_i) := x$ and $h(\bar{x}_i) := (\bar{x})$. Then $L_w := h^{-1}(K) \cap Y_1^* \{w_1\} Y_2^* \{w_2\} Y_3^* \cdots Y_n^* \{w_n\} Y_{n+1}^*$ is a set of which one can decide emptiness. Now, $w \in K\%D_1^*$ only if $L_w \neq \emptyset$. Finally we have to decide whether there exists a string $u_1 w_1 u_2 w_2 u_3 \ldots u_n w_n u_{n+1} \in L_w$ such that $u_i \in Y_i^*$ is indeed an element of the symmetric Dyck set and has the same number of opening and closing brackets. To do this we look at the Parikh image $P := \psi(L_w) \subseteq \mathbb{N}^{2n+|V|}$ which forms a semilinear vector set. If $Q \subseteq \mathbb{N}^{2n+|V|}$ denotes the semilinear set which satisfies $m(x_i) = m(\bar{x}_i)$ for each $1 \leq i \leq n$ and each element $m \in Q$ and is arbitrary in the remaining coordinates, then $Q \cap P \neq \emptyset$ if and only if $w \in K\%D_1^*$.

□

Corollary 1 $\underline{Cf}\%D_1^* \subset \underline{Rec}$

Obviously the family $\underline{Cf}$ fulfills the desired closure properties, moreover a simple diagonalization by enumerating strings and context-free grammars shows proper containment: the language $\{w_i \mid w_i \notin L(G_i)\%D_1^*\}$ is recursive but not equal to $L(G_k)\%D_1^*$ for any index k.

□

Theorem 2 $\underline{Lin}\%EQ = \underline{RE}$

This proof is more involved and the result should be compared with similar results by Frougny et al. [5] and Brandenburg, Dassow [3] who showed $\underline{Lin}\%D_2^* = \underline{RE}$.

Proof of Theorem 2: Let $E \subseteq (V \setminus X)^*$ be any recursively enumerable set which is accepted by $M = (\Sigma, Z, Z_{\text{start}}, Z_{\text{end}}, K)$, a nondeterministic one-way two counter automaton. Here $\Sigma := V \setminus X$ is the input alphabet, Z is the finite set of states with subsets Z_{start} and Z_{end} of initial and final states, respectively.

The two counters are named A (resp. B) and can each be altered by operations c_A (resp. c_B), where c_A and c_b are elements of $\{+1, -1, \text{test}\}$ with the following meaning:

$$c_A, c_B := \begin{cases} +1 & \text{add 1 to the respective counter} \\ -1 & \text{subtract 1 from the respective counter} \\ test & \text{this move only if the respective counter stores zero} \end{cases}$$

$K \subseteq Z \times (\Sigma \cup \lambda) \times \{+1, -1, \text{test}\} \times \{+1, -1, \text{test}\} \times Z$ is the set of transitions of M and an element $(z_i, y, c_A, c_B, z_j) \in K$ has the obvious meaning: move from state z_i into state z_j, read the element y from the one-way input tape, and perform the operation c_A or c_B on the respective counter. M begins with an initial state and accepts $w \in \Sigma^*$ if the transitions lead M to a final state while reading w and both counters are empty. The contents of the two counters, $(m_1, m_2) \in I\!N^2$, is encoded unary by $p := 2^{m_1} \cdot 3^{m_2} \in I\!N$ and will be encoded by strings of the form x^p or $\bar{x}^p$. As in [13] , the change of counter A by c_A will be done by multiplying p by 2, if c_A is $+1$, by dividing by 2, if c_A is -1, or by checking whether division leaves a remainder of 1, if c_A is 'test'. Division will be done by successively subtracting 2 from p, which can be encoded by using 2 closing brackets $\bar{x}$ as often as possible. If counter B is used, the same is done with the prime 3 instead of 2.

In order to design a linear context-free grammar G_M we will need the following sets of nonterminals: $\Sigma_Z := \{H_i \mid z_i \in Z\}$, $\Sigma_A := \{A_k \mid k \in K\}$, $\Sigma_B := \{B_k \mid k \in K\}$ and S as the starting symbol of G_M.

The rules of G_M are collected in the following sets:

$\{S \rightarrow H_j \bar{x} \mid z_j \in Z_{\text{start}}\}$ start M in an initial state with empty counters.

For each transition $k := (z_i, y, c_A, c_B, z_j) \in K$ the following sets of rules are defined :

$\{H_i \rightarrow y A_k\}$ M reads y and starts to try the operation c_A on counter A, which means that the encoding of p by the string $\bar{x}^p$ appears to the right of the nonterminal A_k.

$\{A_k \rightarrow x A_k x^2 \mid \text{if } c_A = -1\}$ the successive subtraction is done by opening 2 brackets until there are as many as there are closing brackets, which will finally be checked by cancelling with the set EQ.

$\{A_k \rightarrow x^2 A_k x \mid \text{if } c_A = +1\}$ twice as many brackets x are opened at the left of A_k as there appear closing brackets at the right.

$\{A_k \rightarrow x^2 A_k x^2 \mid \text{if } c = \text{test}\}$ the number p at the right of A_k is divided by 2, hopefully with a remainder and recovered at the left of A_k.

$\{A_k \rightarrow B_k x \bar{x} \mid \text{if } c_A = +1 \text{ or } c_A = -1\}$ the additional pair $x\bar{x}$ leads to a string in EQ only if the string immediately to the right of these two symbols is already an element of EQ^*, remember: $L\%EQ = L\%EQ^*$. The symbol B_k means that, still with transition number k, counter B will now be altered according c_B.

$\{A_k \rightarrow x B_k x \bar{x} x \mid \text{if } c_A = \text{test}\}$ the remainder 1 is subtracted, $x\bar{x}$ marks the empty counter A and the former counter content is correctly restored at the left hand side of the new symbol B_k.

$\{B_k \rightarrow \bar{x}^3 B_k \bar{x} \mid \text{if } c_B = -1\}$

$\{B_k \rightarrow \bar{x} B_k \bar{x}^3 \mid \text{if } c_B = +1\}$

$\{B_k \rightarrow \bar{x}^3 B_k \bar{x}^3 \mid \text{if } c_B = \text{test}\}$

$\{B_k \rightarrow x\bar{x}H_j \mid \text{if } c_B = +1 \text{ or } c_B = -1\}$

$\{B_k \rightarrow xx\bar{x}H_j\bar{x} \mid \text{if } c_B = \text{test}\}$

$\{B_k \rightarrow \bar{x}^2 x\bar{x}H_j\bar{x}^2 \mid \text{if } c_B = \text{test}\}$ these rules yield the altering of counter B by similar rules as before. If the next state z_j is a final state, and both counters are empty, then we can accept the string produced so far by the symbols in $V \setminus X$ and the nonterminal H_j may disappear through the last rule in the set:

$\{H_j \rightarrow x\bar{x} \mid z_j \in Z_{\text{end}}\}$ □

$L(G_M)\%EQ = E$ is thus proved, since G_M is linear context-free, the cancellation with the set EQ checks the contents of the counters and in addition tests that the moves of the counter automaton were performed properly.

Corollary 2 *The following holds:* $\underline{Cf}\%D_1'^* \subseteq \underline{Lin}\%EQ$, $\underline{Cf}\%D_1^* \subset \underline{Lin}\%EQ$, *and* $\underline{Lin}\%D_1'^* \subset \underline{Lin}\%EQ$

Proof: The inclusions follow directly from Theorem 2. Theorem 1 proves the second inclusion to be proper, and the inclusion $\underline{Lin}\%D_1'^* \subset \underline{Rec}$ has been shown in [12]. □

Definition 3 *The operation twist :* $V^* \rightarrow V^*$ *is defined recursively for any* $w \in V^*$, *and symbols* $a, b \in V$, *by:* $twist(awb) := ab \cdot twist(w)$, $twist(a) := a$, *and* $twist(\lambda) := \lambda$. *The operator TWIST is defined on families of languages* $\mathcal{L}$ *in the usual way by:* $TWIST(\mathcal{L}) := \{twist(L) \mid L \in \mathcal{L}\}$.

It is not hard to see that the family of context-free languages $\underline{Cf}$ is *not* closed under TWIST: Consider the language $K := \{a^{2n}b^m c^m d^n \mid n, m \in \mathbb{N}\} \in \underline{Lin} \subseteq \underline{Cf}$, then twist($K$) is not context-free, since

$$twist(K) \cap \{ad\}^* \{ac\}^* \{b\}^* = \{(ad)^n (ac)^n b^n \mid n \geq 0\}$$

Note also, that with COPY := $\{ww \mid w \in V^*\}$ and PAL := $\{ww^{\mathrm{rev}} \mid w \in V^*\}$ one has twist(COPY) = PAL, and twist(PAL) = $\{yy \mid y \in V\}^* \in \underline{Reg}$.

It is not surprising that regular sets are closed under twist: $\mathrm{twist}(\overline{R})$ is regular for any regular set $R \in \underline{Reg}$.. The easy proof is left for the reader.

We were able to establish the same closure property for terminal Petri net languages in [13]. This class can also be characterized as the smallest trio closed under intersection and containing the language $D_1'^*$, denoted by $\mathcal{M}_\cap(D_1'^*)$. For further details cf. [9]. The result is thus rephrased:

Theorem 3 $TWIST(\mathcal{M}_\cap(D_1'^*)) \subseteq \mathcal{M}_\cap(D_1'^*)$, i.e. , twist(L) is a terminal Petri net language for any Petri net language $L \in \mathcal{M}_\cap(D_1'^*)$.

In [11] it was shown that $\mathcal{M}_\cap(D_1'^*) \subset Cf\%D_1'^*$, and we have generalized this result by using the smaller family $\underline{Lin}$ of linear context-free languages in [13] showing $\mathcal{M}_\cap(D_1'^*) \subset \underline{Lin}\%D_1'^*$.

Theorem 2 showed that the class $\underline{Lin}\%EQ$ contains each recursively enumerable set. This characterization presumably is not valid for the class $Cf\%D_1'^*$. The following results were proved in [12]: The emptiness problem is undecidable for the class $\underline{Lin}\%D_1'^*$ and the word problem is decidable for the class $\underline{Lin}\%D_1'^*$.

Still unknown, however, is the question, whether the word problem is decidable for the class $Cf\%D_1'^*$.

In [12] a deterministic context-free grammar G is given that yields an *NP*-complete language as $L(G)\%D_1'^*$. This establishes a lower bound for the hardness of the word-problem.

Our second important result relies on the encoding of sentential forms and of counters using strings from the set $D_1'^*$ and will also work with D_1^*. The following lemma is only used for a simpler proof of Theorem 4 and shows, that under certain restrictions the leftmost derivations of a context-free grammar that lead to a terminal word, in which every subword from $\{x, \bar{x}\}^*$ belongs to a (possibly longer) word from $D_1'^*$, are uniquely determined by the so far generated substring from $\{x, \bar{x}\}^*$.

Lemma 1 Let $G = (N, T, P, S)$ be a context-free grammar, $\{x, \bar{x}\} \subseteq T$, $V := N \cup T$. If for a nonterminal $A \in N$ there is a $k \in N$ such that 1. through 3. below hold, then for any sentential form $wuAv$, $w \in (T \setminus \{x, \bar{x}\})^*$, $u \in \{x, \bar{x}\}^*$, $v \in V^*$, there is at most one sentential form $wuu'av'v$ derivable from $wuAv$ such that $uu' \in D_1'^*$:

1. $P \cap \{A \to v_1 A v_2 \mid v_1, v_2 \in V^*\}$ contains exactly one element, namely $A \to \bar{x}^k A w$, $w \in \{x\}^*$

2. for each n, $0 \le n \le k$, there is at most one production $A \to \bar{x}^n aw$, $a \in T \setminus \{x, \bar{x}\}$, $w \in V^*$

3. there are no productions other than those mentioned in 1. or 2. with a lefthand side A.

Proof: Suppose to the contrary, that there are two distinct sentential forms that could be derived from $wuAv$, say wuu_1av_1v and wuu_2bv_2v, such that uu_1 and uu_2 are in $D_1'^*$. Then $u_1 = u_2$ since all productions of G with left-hand side A derive $\bar{x}$ to the left of A. All terminating productions derive less than k symbols $\bar{x}$, so $A \to \bar{x}^k Aw$ has to be applied $|u_1|$div k times, and then only one production may be used. Thus the leftmost derivation of $wuAv$ is uniquely determined. $\square$

The following theorem shows the relation between the class $\underline{Cf}^\triangle \% D_1^*$ and the closure of intersections of λ-free context-free languages with respect to nested iterated substitution denoted by τ^∞, see [7]. The symbol $\wedge$ denotes the wedge operation of elementwise intersection.

Theorem 4 $\tau^\infty(\mathcal{H}(\underline{Cf}^\triangle \wedge \underline{Cf}^\triangle)) \subseteq \underline{Cf}\% D_1^*$

Proof: As a simplification we omit the non-erasing homomorphism, but it will become clear that we could by introducing more productions include it into the construction. We will now prove by induction a slightly stronger version of the above theorem: for every language $L \in \tau^\infty(\underline{Cf}^\triangle \wedge \underline{Cf}^\triangle)$ there is a context-free grammar G with $L(G)\% D_1^* = L$ and G derives no terminal string that ends or begins with a parenthesis symbol. To this end we will use induction on the generation of languages by application of nested iterated substitution starting with the intersections of context-free languages. For the basis of the induction let $L_1 = L(G_1)$ and $L_2 = L(G_2)$ be context-free languages, G_1 and G_2 are context-free grammars. Without loss of generality be $G_1 = (N_1, T_1, P_1, S_1)$ in Chomsky normal form and $G_2 = (N_2, T_2, P_2, S_2)$ in the following version of the super normal form from [15]:

$$P \subseteq \{A \to aBC \mid A, B, C \in N_2, a \in T_2\} \cup \{A \to w \mid A \in N_2, w \in T_2^+\}$$

where we may suppose further that $(T_1 \cup T_2) \cap \{x, \bar{x}\} = \emptyset$ and $\lambda \notin L_1 \cup L_2$.

In the sequel we will step by step construct a context-free grammar $G :=$ (N, T, P, S), that generates $L = L_1 \cap L_2 = L(G)\% D_1^*$. For every string $w \in L$ with less than 3 characters P will contain a production $S \to w$. For every sentential form $ABC \in N^*$ that is derivable from S_1 and contains exactly 3 nonterminal symbols there is a rule $S \to L_A BR_C$ in P. The symbols L_A and R_C serve as end markers that prevent G from generating x's and $\bar{x}$'s at the end or beginning of a sentential form. The terminating productions of L and R symbols will generate encodings of initial and final pushdown contents resp., according to the encoding described below. The remaining productions are divided into two groups: the first simulate productions of G_1 and do not generate terminal symbols directly but derive an H, J or K symbol whenever G_1 would yield a terminal symbol. The nondeterministic choice of H, J or K depends on how G_2 yields a terminal symbol, let us call it a, at this point. $K_{B \to aw}$ means a production $B \to aw$ of G_2 is applied, $J_{B \to aCD}$ means a production $B \to aCD$ is applied and H_a means that the symbol a is generated by an application of a production $A \to vaw$ to the left of a.

The remaining productions of G make sure, that the choices of the above symbols were made correctly by keeping a pushdown stack of yet unprocessed symbols encoded by parentheses. We set $k := |N_2| + |T_2| + 1$ and define a mapping $f : (T_2 \cup N_2)^* \to I\!N$ by:

$$f(\lambda) := 0$$
$$f(t_i w) := |N_2| + i + k \cdot f(w) \text{ for } t_i \in T_2, 1 \le i \le |T_2|$$
$$f(A_j w) := j + k \cdot f(w) \text{ for } A_j \in N_2, 1 \le j \le |N_2|$$

We are now prepared for the set of productions of P:

$$
\begin{aligned}
P \quad := \quad & \{S \to w \mid |w| \le 2\} \\
\cup \quad & \{S \to L_A B R_C \mid ABC \text{ is derivable from } S_1\} \\
\cup \quad & \{A \to BC \mid A \to BC \in P_1\} \\
\cup \quad & \{A \to H_a \mid A \to a \in P_1\} \\
\cup \quad & \{A \to J_{B \to aCD} \mid A \to a \in P_1, B \to aCD \in P_2\} \\
\cup \quad & \{A \to K_{B \to aw} \mid A \to a \in P_1, B \to aw \in P_2\} \\
\cup \quad & \{L_A \to L_B C \mid A \to BC \in P_1\} \\
\cup \quad & \{R_A \to B R_C \mid A \to BC \in P_1\} \\
\cup \quad & \{L_A \to ax^{f(BC)} \mid A \to a \in P_1, S_2 \to aBC \in P_2\} \\
\cup \quad & \{R_A \to \bar{x}^{f(E)}a \mid A \to a \in P_1, E \to a \in P_2\} \\
\cup \quad & \{R_A \to \bar{x}^{f(a)}a \mid A \to a \in P_1\} \\
\cup \quad & \{J_{B \to aCD} \to \bar{x} J_{B \to aCD} x^{k^2} \mid B \to aCD \in P_2\} \\
\cup \quad & \{J_{B \to aCD} \to \bar{x}^{f(B)} ax^{f(CD)} \mid B \to aCD \in P_2\} \\
\cup \quad & \{H_a \to \bar{x}^k H_a x \mid a \in T_1\} \\
\cup \quad & \{H_a \to \bar{x}^{f(a)}a \mid a \in T_1\} \\
\cup \quad & \{K_{B \to aw} \to \bar{x}^k K_{B \to aw} x^{k^{|w|}} \mid B \to aw \in P_2\} \\
\cup \quad & \{K_{B \to aw} \to \bar{x}^{f(B)} ax^{f(w)} \mid B \to aw \in P_2\}
\end{aligned}
$$

Inspection of P shows, that the first part indeed simulates G_1 and the productions with a left-hand side J, H or K conform with the premise of Lemma 1. Taking into account, that each L symbol generates encodings of initial sentential forms only, and R symbols yield encodings of final sentential forms, it is thus inductively guaranteed by Lemma 1, that the leftmost derivation of a string consisting entirely of J, H and K symbols is uniquely determined if it is to derive complete Dyck subwords. It will yield a terminal string if and only if the choice of productions is correct.

Obviously no parentheses are ever generated at the edges of sentential forms. This concludes the basis of the proof. For the inductive step suppose, that a language L on an n element alphabet and n languages $L_1, L_2, \ldots, L_n$ are given, $a_i \in L_i$ for all terminal symbols a_i of L, $1 \le i \le n$. Further $\{L, L_1, \cdots, L_n\} \subset \tau^\infty(Cf\%D_1^*)$ and there are grammars of the above type for all $n+1$ languages by the inductive hypothesis, $L = L(G)\%D_1^*$, $G = (N, T, P, S)$, $L_i = L(G_i)\%D_1^*$.

For the nested iterated substitution τ given by : $\tau(a_i) := L_i$ for every terminal symbol a_i of L we will describe a grammar for $\tau^\infty(L)$. Without loss of generality we suppose, that the nonterminal symbols of the grammars generating the above languages L_i are disjoint. Now, omitting further details, the grammar $G_\tau := (N_\tau, T_\tau, P_\tau, S)$ for $\tau^\infty(L)$ is given by: $N_\tau := N \cup N_1 \cup N_2 \cdots N_n$,

$T_r := T_1 \cup \cdots \cup T_n$, and $P_r := P' \cup P_1 \cup P_2 \cdots \cup P_n$, where P' consists of the productions P, modified in such a way, that on the right side of each production terminal symbols are replaced by starting symbols of the appropriate grammar for $L_1, \ldots, L_n$. Finally we observe that terminal symbols may be replaced by nonempty strings without disturbing the simulations. This proof equally works for the one-sided reduction with $D_1'^*$. □

Corollary 3 $\mathcal{H}(\underline{Cf} \wedge \underline{Cf}) \subseteq \underline{Cf\%D_1'^*}$ and $\mathcal{H}(\underline{Cf} \wedge \underline{Cf}) \subseteq \underline{Cf\%D_1^*}$

Proof: By Theorem 4 we have $\underline{Cf}^\triangle \wedge \underline{Cf}^\triangle \subseteq \underline{Cf\%D_1^*}$ for the trivial substitution of a terminal symbol with itself. Should the intersection of two languages contain λ, then we include the production $S \to \lambda$ into the context-free grammar in which the Dyck strings are to be cancelled. It should be noticed, that the second inclusion can not be generalized to nested iterated substitution. Substitution of a language containing the empty word means unlimited erasing. This would yield non-recursive sets if applied to intersections of context-free languges. But due to Theorem 1 that is not possible. □

Note, that the inclusion $\underline{Cf}^\triangle \wedge \underline{Cf}^\triangle \subset \underline{Cf\%D_1^*}$ is proper. To see this consider the language
$$E := \{a^m \mid m = 2^n, n \in \mathbb{N}\} \in \underline{Cf\%D_1^*}$$
which cannot be the intersection of two context-free, 1-bounded languages, that are always regular.

3 Acknowledgements

We are indebted to the anonymous referees of the 12th Intern. Colloquium on Petri Nets for their proposals for improvements. We would like to thank Manfred Kudlek and also all other members of the working group TGI for their vivid discussions on the presented subject.

References

[1] M. Benois: *Parties rationelles du groupe libre.* C. R. Acad. Sc. Paris, Ser. A t. 269 (1969) 1188–1190.

[2] R.V. Book, M. Jantzen, C. Wrathall: *Monadic Thue systems.* Theoret. Comput. Sci. 19 (1982) 231–251.

[3] F.J. Brandenburg: *Cancellations in linear context-free languages.* Techn. report MIP-8904, Univ. Passau (1989).

[4] F.J. Brandenburg, J. Dassow: *Reductions of picture words.* Techn. report MIP-8905, Univ. Passau (1989).

[5] Ch. Frougny, J. Sakarovitch, P. Schupp: *Finiteness conditions on subgroups and formal language theory.* Proc. London Math. Soc. 58 (1989) 74–88.

[6] V. Geffert: *Grammars with context dependency restricted to synchronization.* LNCS vol. 233, Springer-Verlag (1986) 370–378.

[7] S.A. Greibach: *Full AFLs and nested iterated substitution.* Inf. Contr. 16 (1970) 7–35.

[8] T.V. Griffiths: *Some remarks on derivations in general rewriting systems.* Inform. Control 12 (1968) 27–45.

[9] M. Hack: *Petri net languages.* C.S.G. Memo 124, Project MAC, MIT (1975).

[10] M. Jantzen: *Confluent string rewriting.* EATCS Monographs 14, Springer-Verlag (1988).

[11] M. Jantzen, H. Petersen: *Petri net languages and one-sided $Dyck_1$-reductions of context-free sets.* in K. Voss, H. Genrich, G. Rozenberg (eds.): Concurrency and nets. Springer-Verlag (1987) 245–252.

[12] M. Jantzen, M. Kudlek, K.-J. Lange, H. Petersen: *$Dyck_1$-reductions of context-free languages.* Comp. and Artificial Intelligence, 9 (1990) 3–18.

[13] M. Jantzen, H. Petersen: *Twisting Petri net languages and how to obtain them by reducing linear context-free sets.* In: Proc. 12th Intern. Conf. on Petri nets, Gjern (1991) 228–236.

[14] T. Kimura: *Formal description of communication behaviour.* Proc. Johns Hopkins Conf. on Information Sciences and Systems (1979).

[15] H.A. Maurer, A. Salomaa, D. Wood: *A Supernormal-Form Theorem for Context-Free Grammars.* JACM 30 (1983) 95-102.

[16] W.J. Savitch: *How to make arbitrary grammars look like context-free grammars.* SIAM J. Comput. 2 (1973) 174–182.

[17] W.J. Savitch: *Some characterizations of Lindenmayer systems in terms of Chomsky-type grammars and stack machines.* Inf. Contr. 27 (1975) 37–60.

[18] W.J. Savitch: *Parenthesis grammars and Lindenmayer sytems.* In: G. Rozenberg, A. Salomaa (eds.): The Book of L, Springer-Verlag (1986) 403–411.

[19] D. Stanat: *Formal languages and power series.* 3rd ACM Sympos. Theory of Computing (1971) 1–11.

Counting Overlap-Free Binary Words

Julien Cassaigne

L.I.T.P., Institut Blaise Pascal,
4 place Jussieu, F-75252 Paris Cedex 05, France

Abstract. A word on a finite alphabet A is said to be overlap-free if it contains no factor of the form $xuxux$, where x is a letter and u a (possibly empty) word. In this paper we study the number u_n of overlap-free binary words of length n, which is known to be bounded by a polynomial in n. First, we describe a bijection between the set of overlap-free words and a rational language. This yields recurrence relations for u_n, which allow to compute u_n in logarithmic time. Then, we prove that the numbers $\alpha = \sup \{\, r \mid n^r = \mathcal{O}(u_n) \,\}$ and $\beta = \inf \{\, r \mid u_n = \mathcal{O}(n^r) \,\}$ are distinct, and we give an upper bound for α and a lower bound for β. Finally, we compute an asymptotically tight bound to the number of overlap-free words of length less than n.

1 Introduction

In general, the problem of evaluating the number u_n of words of length n in the language U consisting of words on some finite alphabet A with no factors in a certain set F is not easy. If F is finite, it amounts to counting words in the rational language U and there are well-known techniques for this, e.g. computing the generating function. But if for instance F is the set of images of a pattern p by non-erasing morphisms, it is not even known how to decide whether U is finite or infinite (i.e. whether p is unavoidable or avoidable on A). However, Brandenburg [2] proved that u_n grows exponentially for the pattern $p = \alpha^2$ on a ternary alphabet A (then U is the set of square-free ternary words), and Goralcik and Vanicek [7] proved the same for any 2-avoidable binary pattern p on a binary alphabet A (also proved by Brandenburg for $p = \alpha^3$).

Here we shall study the growth of u_n in the case where F is the set

$$F = \{\, xuxux \mid x \in A \text{ and } u \in A^* \,\}$$

with $A = \{a, b\}$; the elements of U are then called *overlap-free binary words*. After recalling what is known about u_n (end of this section), we describe (Section 2) a bijection between U and a rational language. From the automaton recognizing this language we construct (Section 3) explicit recurrence relations verified by u_n (showing that u_n can be computed in logarithmic time). In Section 4, we study the consequences of these relations on the asymptotic behaviour of u_n. In particular we prove that, although u_n is bounded from below and from above by polynomial quantities, it is not itself equivalent to a polynomial.

1.1 Overlap-Free Binary Words

We consider words on the alphabet $A = \{a, b\}$, i.e. elements of the monoid A^*. The letter ε denotes the empty word. We shall use the notation $\bar{a} = b$ and $\bar{b} = a$.

A word w contains an *overlap* if some factor v appears at two overlapping positions. It is equivalent to say that w contains a factor of the form $xuxux$ with $x \in A$ and $u \in A^*$.

A word w is called *overlap-free* if it contains no overlap.

In the language of *patterns* an overlap-free word is a word which simultaneously *avoids* the patterns $\alpha\beta\alpha\beta\alpha$ and α^3.

1.2 Previous Results

In 1906, Axel Thue [11, 12] proved that there are infinitely many overlap-free binary words, (or, equivalently: there are arbitrarily long overlap-free binary words). To do this, he constructed an infinite overlap-free word, $\theta^\omega(a)$, where θ is the morphism:

$$\theta: A^* \longrightarrow A^*$$
$$a \longmapsto ab$$
$$b \longmapsto ba$$

and $\theta^\omega(a)$ means the limit of the sequence $\left(\theta^k(a)\right)$:

$$\theta^\omega(a) = abbabaabbaababbabaabababbaabbabaabba\ldots .$$

This infinite word $\theta^\omega(a)$ is overlap-free because the morphism θ is itself overlap-free, which means that if w is an overlap-free word, then $\theta(w)$ is overlap-free too.

The problem arising naturally is the following: let u_n be the number of overlap-free binary words of length n. Is it possible to find a bound to u_n? An equivalent? Recurrence relations? Here are some results about this problem.

A linear lower bound to u_n is given by the number of factors of length n in $\theta^\omega(a)$ (see [3, 5]):

$$\begin{cases} \text{If } 2.2^k \leq n \leq 3.2^k, \ \theta^\omega(a) \text{ has } 4n - 2.2^k \text{ factors of length } n+1 \\ \text{If } 3.2^k \leq n \leq 4.2^k, \ \theta^\omega(a) \text{ has } 2n + 4.2^k \text{ factors of length } n+1 \end{cases}$$

(this holds for all $k \geq 0$).

Restivo and Salemi [10] gave a polynomial upper bound to u_n: $u_n \leq Cn^r$ with $C > 0$ and $r = \log_2 15 \simeq 3.906$.

Kobayashi [9] improved these bounds:

$$C_1 n^{1.155} \leq u_n \leq C_2 n^{1.587} .$$

The lower bound is obtained by counting the overlap-free words that are infinitely extensible on the right.

Carpi [4] proved that a finite automaton can be used to compute u_n, and gave a way to find upper bounds Cn^r with r arbitrarily near of the optimal value. However he didn't publish any numerical result.

2 A Bijection Between the Language of Overlap-Free Binary Words and a Rational Language

2.1 A Decomposition of Overlap-Free Binary Words

As we shall see later, we need to consider not only overlap-free words, but also words that contain only one overlap, which covers them entirely. We call them *simple overlaps*.

Definition 1. A word $w \in A^*$ is called a *simple overlap* if it can be written $w = xuxux$ with $x \in A$ and $u \in A^+$ such that $xuxu$ and $uxux$ are overlap-free.

Moreover, to avoid special cases as much as possible, we shall restrict ourselves to words of length at least 4. We define three sets U, V and S as follows:

U is the set of overlap-free words of length greater than 3 (13 words are excluded);

V is the set of simple overlaps of length greater than 3 (only aaa and bbb are excluded);

S is the finite set containing the elements of $U \cup V$ of length less than 8. This set has 76 elements.

Kfoury [8], Kobayashi [9] and Carpi [4] use results similar to the following lemma:

Lemma 2. *A word $w \in (U \cup V) \setminus S$ can be written $w = r_1 \theta(u) r_2$ with u overlap-free and $r_i \in \{\varepsilon, a, b, aa, bb\}$. This decomposition is unique.* $\square$

Using this lemma, they construct overlap-free words by starting with a small word and alternatively applying θ and adding letters to the left or to the right of the current word. We shall use a similar approach, but instead of adding new letters we shall remove or modify existing letters.

Definition 3. Let $E = \{\delta, \iota, \kappa\}$, and G be the monoid $(E \times E)^*$. The unit of G is denoted by 1. We define an action of G on A^* in the following way:

For all $g \in G$, let $\varepsilon.g = \varepsilon$.

Given $\gamma = (\gamma_1, \gamma_2) \in E \times E$ and $w \in A^+$, we write the image of w by θ as $\theta(w) = x_1 u x_2$ with $u \in A^*$, $x_1 \in A$ and $x_2 \in A$, and $w.\gamma$ is given by the table:

	$\gamma_2 = \delta$	$\gamma_2 = \iota$	$\gamma_2 = \kappa$
$\gamma_1 = \delta$	u	$u\overline{x_2}$	ux_2
$\gamma_1 = \iota$	$\overline{x_1}u$	$\overline{x_1}u\overline{x_2}$	$\overline{x_1}ux_2$
$\gamma_1 = \kappa$	$x_1 u$	$x_1 u\overline{x_2}$	$x_1 u x_2$

(recall that $\overline{a} = b$ and $\overline{b} = a$). For instance, if $w = aabb$ and $\gamma = (\delta, \iota)$, to compute $w.\gamma$ we take $\theta(w) = ababbaba$, we delete the first letter and invert the last one: $w.\gamma = babbabb$.

For all $w \in A^*$, let $w.1 = w$.

Finally, for $g \in G$, $\gamma \in E \times E$ and $w \in A^*$, let $w.(\gamma g) = (w.\gamma).g$.

Lemma 4. *A word $w \in (U \cup V) \setminus S$ can be uniquely written $w = v.\gamma$ with $\gamma \in E \times E$ and $v \in (U \cup V)$. Moreover, $|v| < |w|$.*

Proof. Lemma 2 gives a unique decomposition $w = r_1\theta(u)r_2$. We define $v = x_1ux_2$ and $\gamma = (\gamma_1, \gamma 2)$ as follows:

	$r_1 = \varepsilon$	$r_1 = a$	$r_1 = b$	$r_1 = aa$	$r_1 = bb$
x_1	ε	b	a	b	a
γ_1	κ	δ	δ	ι	ι

	$r_2 = \varepsilon$	$r_2 = a$	$r_2 = b$	$r_2 = aa$	$r_2 = bb$
x_2	ε	a	b	a	b
γ_2	κ	δ	δ	ι	ι

and it is easy to check that $w = v.\gamma$ and $3 < |v| < |w|$ (in fact $\frac{|w|}{2} \leq |v| \leq \frac{|w|}{2}+1$).

The word u is overlap-free. If x_1ux_2 were not in $U \cup V$, x_1u would begin with an overlap, or ux_2 would end with one. Suppose that x_1u begins with an overlap: then $\overline{x_1}\theta(u)$ begins with an overlap too; this is only possible if $w = \overline{x_1}\theta(u) \in V$, and then $x_2 = \varepsilon$, hence $x_1ux_2 = x_1u \in V$. The other case is symmetric. Note that v can be in V even if w is in U, for instance $aabbaabb = babab.(\delta, \delta)$. That's why we have to consider $U \cup V$ instead of simply U.

The unicity of (v, γ) is a consequence of the unicity of (u, r_1, r_2). □

Let Z be the subset of $S \times G$ containing all elements except those of the form $(s, \gamma g)$ with $|s.\gamma| < 8$. To any $z = (s, g) \in Z$, we associate the word $[z] = s.g \in A^*$. Conversely, we can represent certain words by elements of Z:

Theorem 5. *Every word $w \in U \cup V$ has a unique decomposition $w = s.g$ with $(s, g) \in Z$.*

Proof. Let's prove this theorem by induction on the length of w. If $|w| < 8$, $w \in S$ and $(s, g) = (w, 1)$ is the only possibility according to the definition of Z. Now suppose that the theorem has been proved for words of length less than n; then if w is a word of length n, by Lemma 4 this word can be uniquely written $w = v.\gamma$ with $\gamma \in E \times E$, and $|v| < n$. By the inductive hypothesis, v has a unique decomposition $v = s.g$ hence w also has a unique decomposition $w = s.(g\gamma)$. □

Elements of Z should be viewed as words on the alphabet $S \cup (E \times E)$, with only their first letter in S. The set Z is clearly a rational language on this alphabet: the restriction $(s, \gamma g) \notin Z$ if $|s.\gamma| < 8$ (needed for the unicity in Theorem 5) amounts to defining Z as

$$Z = (S \times G) \setminus (S_4 \times \{(\delta, \delta), (\delta, \iota), (\delta, \kappa), (\iota, \delta), (\kappa, \delta)\}G)$$

where $S_4 = \{aaba, aabb, abaa, abab, abba, baab, baba, babb, bbaa, bbab\}$ is the set of the elements of length 4 in S.

2.2 The Rational Languages Representing U and V

Let $L = \{\, z \in Z \mid [z] \in U \,\}$ and $M = \{\, z \in Z \mid [z] \in V \,\}$. We shall prove that L and M are rational languages. To do this we have to answer the question: under which conditions (on z) is the word $[z]$ an element of U or of V?

First, let's see what can be said about $[z\gamma] = [z].\gamma$ when the status of $[z]$ is known, and $\gamma = (\gamma_1, \gamma_2) \in E \times E$.

- If $[z]$ is not in $U \cup V$, then $[z\gamma]$ cannot be in $U \cup V$ either.
- If $[z] \in U$, $\gamma_1 \in \{\delta, \kappa\}$ and $\gamma_2 \in \{\delta, \kappa\}$, then $[z\gamma] \in U$.
- If $[z] \in V$, then $[z(\iota, \kappa)]$, $[z(\kappa, \iota)]$ and $[z(\kappa, \kappa)]$ are not in $U \cup V$, $[z(\delta, \kappa)]$ and $[z(\kappa, \delta)]$ are in V, and $[z(\delta, \delta)]$ is in U.
- If $[z]$ does not begin with $aaba$ or $bbab$, then $[z(\iota, \gamma_2)] \notin U \cup V$.
- If $[z]$ does not end with $abaa$ or $babb$, then $[z(\gamma_1, \iota)] \notin U \cup V$.
- If $[z]$ begins with $aaba$ and either $\gamma_2 \in \{\delta, \kappa\}$ and $[z] \in U$, or $\gamma_2 = \delta$ and $[z] \in V$, then $[z(\iota, \gamma_2)] \in U$: it begins with $bbabbaa$, and if there were an overlap, $bbabba$ would appear somewhere else in this word, which is impossible. This result holds also if $[z]$ begins with $bbab$.
- If $[z]$ ends with $abaa$ or $babb$ and either $\gamma_1 \in \{\delta, \kappa\}$ and $[z] \in U$, or $\gamma_1 = \delta$ and $[z] \in V$, then by a similar argument $[z(\gamma_1, \iota)] \in U$.
- If $[z]$ begins with $aaba$ or $bbab$, ends with $abaa$ or $babb$, and is in $U \cup V$, then $[z(\iota, \iota)] \in U$.

We can see that we need to know a small prefix (at most four letters) and a small suffix of $[z]$ to conclude.

Definition 6. We define the *type* of a word $w \in U \cup V$ as the couple (i, j) where

$$
\begin{cases}
i = 1 \text{ if } w \text{ begins with } aba \text{ or } bab \\
i = 2 \text{ if } w \text{ begins with } abb \text{ or } baa \\
i = 3 \text{ if } w \text{ begins with } aaba \text{ or } bbab \\
i = 4 \text{ if } w \text{ begins with } aabb \text{ or } bbaa
\end{cases}
\text{ and }
\begin{cases}
j = 1 \text{ if } w \text{ ends with } aba \text{ or } bab \\
j = 2 \text{ if } w \text{ ends with } bba \text{ or } aab \\
j = 3 \text{ if } w \text{ ends with } abaa \text{ or } babb \\
j = 4 \text{ if } w \text{ ends with } bbaa \text{ or } aabb
\end{cases}
$$

(as w contains neither aaa nor bbb, this is always defined). We call i the *prefix type* and j the *suffix type* of w.

Knowing the type (i, j) of $[z]$, one can compute the type (i', j') of $[z(\gamma_1, \gamma_2)]$ (when this word is in $U \cup V$) using the formula

$$(i', j') = (\varphi(i, \gamma_1), \varphi(j, \gamma_2))$$

where φ is the function defined by the following table:

	1	2	3	4
δ	4	3	1	1
ι			3	
κ	2	2	1	1

where an empty box means that $[z(\gamma_1, \gamma_2)]$ cannot be in $U \cup V$.

Note that φ is nothing else than the transition function of a 4-state automaton that computes the prefix type or the suffix type of $[z]$. Taking the direct product of this automaton by itself, we get a 16-state automaton computing the type of $[z]$: as far as type is concerned, there is no interaction between the beginning and the end of $[z]$.

If now we take two copies of this automaton (one for L and one for M), and we place arrows between these two copies according to the rules given at the beginning of the present section, we get an automaton that recognizes L or M depending on what final states we choose. This automaton as 32 states, plus a few states to initialize the process, minus a few states that can be suppressed because they are not reached.

3   Using Matrices to Compute u_n

We consider two sequences of 4 by 4 matrices, U_n and V_n:

$U_n(i,j)$ is the number of words in U of length n and of type (i,j),
$V_n(i,j)$ is the number of words in V of length n and of type (i,j).

Let δ, ι, κ be the matrices associated with the transformations δ, ι, κ, so that for example $(\kappa U_n{}^t\iota)(i,j)$ is the number of words $u.(\kappa,\iota)$ of type (i,j) for any $u \in U$ of length n:

$$\delta = \begin{pmatrix} 0 & 0 & 1 & 1 \\ 0 & 0 & 0 & 0 \\ 0 & 1 & 0 & 0 \\ 1 & 0 & 0 & 0 \end{pmatrix}, \quad \iota = \begin{pmatrix} 0 & 0 & 0 & 0 \\ 0 & 0 & 0 & 0 \\ 0 & 0 & 1 & 0 \\ 0 & 0 & 0 & 0 \end{pmatrix}, \quad \kappa = \begin{pmatrix} 0 & 0 & 1 & 1 \\ 1 & 1 & 0 & 0 \\ 0 & 0 & 0 & 0 \\ 0 & 0 & 0 & 0 \end{pmatrix}.$$

Taking into account the conditions given in Section 2, we can establish the

Theorem 7. *The matrices U_n and V_n defined above verify the following recurrence formulas:*

$$\begin{cases} V_{2n} & = & 0 \\ V_{2n+1} & = & \kappa V_{n+1}{}^t\delta + \delta V_{n+1}{}^t\kappa \\ U_{2n} & = & \iota V_n{}^t\iota \; + \delta V_{n+1}{}^t\delta + (\kappa + \iota)U_n{}^t(\kappa + \iota) + \; \delta U_{n+1}{}^t\delta \\ U_{2n+1} & = & \iota V_{n+1}{}^t\delta + \delta V_{n+1}{}^t\iota + \; (\kappa + \iota)U_{n+1}{}^t\delta \; + \delta U_{n+1}{}^t(\kappa + \iota) \end{cases}$$

for any integer n greater than 3. □

Given the first few values:

$$V_4 = 0, \qquad V_5 = \begin{pmatrix} 2 & 0 & 0 & 0 \\ 0 & 0 & 0 & 0 \\ 0 & 0 & 0 & 0 \\ 0 & 0 & 0 & 0 \end{pmatrix}, \; V_6 = 0, \qquad V_7 = \begin{pmatrix} 0 & 0 & 2 & 0 \\ 0 & 2 & 0 & 0 \\ 2 & 0 & 0 & 0 \\ 0 & 0 & 0 & 0 \end{pmatrix},$$

$$U_4 = \begin{pmatrix} 2 & 0 & 2 & 0 \\ 0 & 2 & 0 & 0 \\ 2 & 0 & 0 & 0 \\ 0 & 0 & 0 & 2 \end{pmatrix}, \; U_5 = \begin{pmatrix} 0 & 2 & 2 & 0 \\ 2 & 0 & 0 & 2 \\ 2 & 0 & 2 & 0 \\ 0 & 2 & 0 & 0 \end{pmatrix}, \; U_6 = \begin{pmatrix} 2 & 2 & 0 & 2 \\ 2 & 2 & 2 & 0 \\ 0 & 2 & 2 & 0 \\ 2 & 0 & 0 & 2 \end{pmatrix}, \; U_7 = \begin{pmatrix} 4 & 2 & 0 & 2 \\ 2 & 0 & 2 & 2 \\ 0 & 2 & 0 & 2 \\ 2 & 2 & 2 & 0 \end{pmatrix}$$

it is therefore possible to compute U_n and V_n in logarithmic time, and hence u_n:

Theorem 8. *The number u_n of overlap-free binary words can be computed with the recurrence formulas of Theorem 7 and the relation*

$$u_n = \sum_{i,j} U_n(i,j)$$

which holds for $n > 3$ ($u_0 = 1$, $u_1 = 2$, $u_2 = 4$, $u_3 = 6$).

The sequence u_n is therefore a 2-regular sequence in the sense of [1]. □

Remark. The recurrence for V_n can be solved:

$$V_5, V_7 \text{ as above}, V_9 = \begin{pmatrix} 0 & 0 & 0 & 0 \\ 0 & 0 & 0 & 2 \\ 0 & 0 & 0 & 0 \\ 0 & 2 & 0 & 0 \end{pmatrix}, V_{13} = \begin{pmatrix} 0 & 2 & 0 & 2 \\ 2 & 0 & 2 & 0 \\ 0 & 2 & 0 & 0 \\ 2 & 0 & 0 & 0 \end{pmatrix},$$

$$V_{2^k+1} = \frac{2^{k-3}}{3} \begin{pmatrix} 0 & 2 & 1 & 1 \\ 2 & 0 & 1 & 1 \\ 1 & 1 & 0 & 0 \\ 1 & 1 & 0 & 0 \end{pmatrix} + \frac{2(-1)^k}{3} \begin{pmatrix} 0 & 1 & 2 & -1 \\ 1 & 0 & -1 & -1 \\ 2 & -1 & 0 & 0 \\ -1 & -1 & 0 & 0 \end{pmatrix},$$

$$V_{3.2^{k-1}+1} = 2^{k-3} \begin{pmatrix} 0 & 2 & 1 & 1 \\ 2 & 0 & 1 & 1 \\ 1 & 1 & 0 & 0 \\ 1 & 1 & 0 & 0 \end{pmatrix} \text{ for } k > 3; V_n = 0 \text{ otherwise.}$$

Summing the coefficients we get the value of the number of simple overlaps, $v_n = \sum_{i,j} V_n(i,j)$ for $n > 3$: the only nonzero values are $v_{2^k+1} = 2^{k-1}$ and $v_{3.2^k+1} = 3.2^k$ for $k \geq 1$. Hence $v_n < n$.

4 Asymptotic Study of u_n

4.1 Simpler Recurrence Relations

It is easier to deal with vector sequences than matrix sequences: taking into account the fact that U_n and V_n are symmetric, and eliminating the components of V_n which are always zero, we can code both matrices by a 15-dimensional vector:

$$X_n = \big(U_n(1,1), U_n(1,2), U_n(1,3), U_n(1,4), U_n(2,2), U_n(2,3), U_n(2,4),$$
$$U_n(3,3), U_n(3,4), U_n(4,4), V_n(1,2), V_n(1,3), V_n(1,4), V_n(2,3), V_n(2,4)\big) \ .$$

The recurrence relations become, for $n > 6$:

$$\begin{cases} X_{2n} = AX_n + BX_{n+1} \\ X_{2n+1} = CX_{n+1} \end{cases}$$

where A, B and C are 15 by 15 matrices:

$$A = \begin{pmatrix}
0 & 0 & 0 & 0 & 0 & 0 & 0 & 1 & 2 & 1 & 0 & 0 & 0 & 0 & 0 \\
0 & 0 & 1 & 1 & 0 & 1 & 1 & 0 & 0 & 0 & 0 & 0 & 0 & 0 & 0 \\
0 & 0 & 0 & 0 & 0 & 0 & 0 & 1 & 1 & 0 & 0 & 0 & 0 & 0 & 0 \\
0 & 0 & 0 & 0 & 0 & 0 & 0 & 0 & 0 & 0 & 0 & 0 & 0 & 0 & 0 \\
1 & 2 & 0 & 0 & 1 & 0 & 0 & 0 & 0 & 0 & 0 & 0 & 0 & 0 & 0 \\
0 & 0 & 1 & 0 & 0 & 1 & 0 & 0 & 0 & 0 & 0 & 0 & 0 & 0 & 0 \\
0 & 0 & 0 & 0 & 0 & 0 & 0 & 0 & 0 & 0 & 0 & 0 & 0 & 0 & 0 \\
0 & 0 & 0 & 0 & 0 & 0 & 1 & 0 & 0 & 0 & 0 & 0 & 0 & 0 & 0 \\
0 & 0 & 0 & 0 & 0 & 0 & 0 & 0 & 0 & 0 & 0 & 0 & 0 & 0 & 0 \\
0 & 0 & 0 & 0 & 0 & 0 & 0 & 0 & 0 & 0 & 0 & 0 & 0 & 0 & 0 \\
0 & 0 & 0 & 0 & 0 & 0 & 0 & 0 & 0 & 0 & 0 & 0 & 0 & 0 & 0 \\
0 & 0 & 0 & 0 & 0 & 0 & 0 & 0 & 0 & 0 & 0 & 0 & 0 & 0 & 0 \\
0 & 0 & 0 & 0 & 0 & 0 & 0 & 0 & 0 & 0 & 0 & 0 & 0 & 0 & 0 \\
0 & 0 & 0 & 0 & 0 & 0 & 0 & 0 & 0 & 0 & 0 & 0 & 0 & 0 & 0 \\
0 & 0 & 0 & 0 & 0 & 0 & 0 & 0 & 0 & 0 & 0 & 0 & 0 & 0 & 0
\end{pmatrix}, $$

$$B = \begin{pmatrix}
0 & 0 & 0 & 0 & 0 & 0 & 0 & 1 & 2 & 1 & 0 & 0 & 0 & 0 & 0 \\
0 & 0 & 0 & 0 & 0 & 0 & 0 & 0 & 0 & 0 & 0 & 0 & 0 & 0 & 0 \\
0 & 0 & 0 & 0 & 0 & 1 & 1 & 0 & 0 & 0 & 0 & 0 & 0 & 1 & 1 \\
0 & 0 & 1 & 1 & 0 & 0 & 0 & 0 & 0 & 0 & 0 & 1 & 1 & 0 & 0 \\
0 & 0 & 0 & 0 & 0 & 0 & 0 & 0 & 0 & 0 & 0 & 0 & 0 & 0 & 0 \\
0 & 0 & 0 & 0 & 0 & 0 & 0 & 0 & 0 & 0 & 0 & 0 & 0 & 0 & 0 \\
0 & 0 & 0 & 0 & 0 & 0 & 0 & 0 & 0 & 0 & 0 & 0 & 0 & 0 & 0 \\
0 & 0 & 0 & 0 & 1 & 0 & 0 & 0 & 0 & 0 & 0 & 0 & 0 & 0 & 0 \\
0 & 1 & 0 & 0 & 0 & 0 & 0 & 0 & 0 & 0 & 1 & 0 & 0 & 0 & 0 \\
1 & 0 & 0 & 0 & 0 & 0 & 0 & 0 & 0 & 0 & 0 & 0 & 0 & 0 & 0 \\
0 & 0 & 0 & 0 & 0 & 0 & 0 & 0 & 0 & 0 & 0 & 0 & 0 & 0 & 0 \\
0 & 0 & 0 & 0 & 0 & 0 & 0 & 0 & 0 & 0 & 0 & 0 & 0 & 0 & 0 \\
0 & 0 & 0 & 0 & 0 & 0 & 0 & 0 & 0 & 0 & 0 & 0 & 0 & 0 & 0 \\
0 & 0 & 0 & 0 & 0 & 0 & 0 & 0 & 0 & 0 & 0 & 0 & 0 & 0 & 0 \\
0 & 0 & 0 & 0 & 0 & 0 & 0 & 0 & 0 & 0 & 0 & 0 & 0 & 0 & 0
\end{pmatrix}, $$

$$C = \begin{pmatrix}
0 & 0 & 0 & 0 & 0 & 0 & 2 & 4 & 2 & 0 & 0 & 0 & 0 & 0 & 0 \\
0 & 0 & 1 & 1 & 0 & 1 & 1 & 0 & 0 & 0 & 0 & 0 & 0 & 0 & 0 \\
0 & 0 & 0 & 0 & 0 & 1 & 1 & 1 & 1 & 0 & 0 & 0 & 0 & 0 & 0 \\
0 & 0 & 1 & 1 & 0 & 0 & 0 & 0 & 0 & 0 & 0 & 0 & 0 & 0 & 0 \\
0 & 0 & 0 & 0 & 0 & 0 & 0 & 0 & 0 & 0 & 0 & 0 & 0 & 0 & 0 \\
0 & 1 & 0 & 0 & 1 & 0 & 0 & 0 & 0 & 0 & 0 & 0 & 0 & 0 & 0 \\
1 & 1 & 0 & 0 & 0 & 0 & 0 & 0 & 0 & 0 & 0 & 0 & 0 & 0 & 0 \\
0 & 0 & 0 & 0 & 0 & 2 & 0 & 0 & 0 & 0 & 0 & 0 & 0 & 2 & 0 \\
0 & 0 & 1 & 0 & 0 & 0 & 0 & 0 & 0 & 0 & 0 & 1 & 0 & 0 & 0 \\
0 & 0 & 0 & 0 & 0 & 0 & 0 & 0 & 0 & 0 & 0 & 0 & 0 & 0 & 0 \\
0 & 0 & 0 & 0 & 0 & 0 & 0 & 0 & 0 & 0 & 0 & 1 & 1 & 1 & 1 \\
0 & 0 & 0 & 0 & 0 & 0 & 0 & 0 & 0 & 0 & 0 & 0 & 0 & 1 & 1 \\
0 & 0 & 0 & 0 & 0 & 0 & 0 & 0 & 0 & 0 & 0 & 1 & 1 & 0 & 0 \\
0 & 0 & 0 & 0 & 0 & 0 & 0 & 0 & 0 & 0 & 1 & 0 & 0 & 0 & 0 \\
0 & 0 & 0 & 0 & 0 & 0 & 0 & 0 & 0 & 0 & 1 & 0 & 0 & 0 & 0
\end{pmatrix}. $$

We can also write $Y_n = \begin{pmatrix} X_{n+1} \\ X_{n+2} \end{pmatrix}$, $F = \begin{pmatrix} C & 0 \\ A & B \end{pmatrix}$ and $G = \begin{pmatrix} A & B \\ 0 & C \end{pmatrix}$. Then $Y_{2n} = FY_n$ and $Y_{2n+1} = GY_n$ for $n > 6$.

Remark. These recurrence relations may seem much simpler than those given in Theorem 7; however the complexity of the problem is hidden in the huge matrices F and G.

4.2 The Exponents α and β

As the growth of u_n is polynomial, it is natural to study the numbers

$$\alpha = \sup \{ r \mid \exists C > 0, \forall n, u_n \geq Cn^r \}$$

and

$$\beta = \inf \{ r \mid \exists C > 0, \forall n, u_n \leq Cn^r \} \ .$$

Theorem 9. $\alpha < \beta$.

Note 10. We say that a sequence f_n *grows as* another sequence g_n if there are two positive constants C_1 and C_2 such that $C_1 g_n \leq f_n \leq C_2 g_n$ for n large enough (i.e. $f_n = \Theta(g_n)$).

Proof. First consider the subsequence $Y_{7.2^k} = F^k Y_7$. The matrix F has one simple eigenvalue of maximal modulus $\rho(F)$, (the spectral radius of F, which is approximately 2.421), and it is easy to check that Y_7 is not in the sum of the characteristic spaces corresponding to the other eigenvalues. Hence at least one element of $Y_{7.2^k}$ grows as $\rho(F)^k$. As $u_{7.2^k+1} + v_{7.2^k+1} + u_{7.2^k+2} + v_{7.2^k+2}$ is a combination with positive coefficients of these elements, it also grows as $\rho(F)^k$, therefore either $u_{7.2^k+1}$ or $u_{7.2^k+2}$ grows as $\rho(F)^k$ (we have seen that v_n has a linear upper bound). We have found a subsequence of u_n growing as n^r with $r = \log_2 \rho(F) \simeq 1.275$, therefore $\alpha < 1.276$.

Then consider the subsequence $Y_{22.4^k-1} = (GF)^k Y_7$. It grows, by similar arguments, as $\rho(GF)^k$ with $\rho(GF) \simeq 6.340$. Hence there is a subsequence of u_n growing as n^r with $r = \log_4 \rho(GF) \simeq 1.3322$, therefore $\beta > 1.332$. $\quad\square$

Remark. These results, together with Kobayashi's, yield the following bounds:

$$1.155 < \alpha < 1.276 < 1.332 < \beta < 1.587 \ .$$

4.3 Partial Sums

Let

$$s_n = \sum_{k=0}^{n-1} u_k$$

be the number of overlap-free words of length less than n. We can precisely describe the asymptotic behaviour of this sequence:

Theorem 11. *The sequence s_n grows as n^r, with $r = \log_2 \zeta \simeq 2.310$, where*

$$\zeta = \rho(F + G) = \frac{3}{2} + \sqrt{3} + \sqrt{\frac{5}{4} + \sqrt{3}}$$

is the largest root of the polynomial $X^4 - 6X^3 + 5X^2 + 4$.

Proof. Let $S_n = \sum_{k=7}^{n-1} Y_k$, for $n > 6$. Then

$$S_{2n} = \sum_{k=7}^{13} Y_k + \sum_{k=7}^{n-1} Y_{2k} + \sum_{k=7}^{n-1} Y_{2k+1} = S_{14} + (F + G)S_n \ .$$

One can check that $F + G - 1$ is a regular matrix, so let $T = (F + G - 1)^{-1}S_{14}$: then $S_{2n} + T = (F + G)(S_n + T)$, and $S_{7.2^k} = (F + G)^k T - T$, therefore at least one element of $S_{7.2^k}$ grows as ζ^k. As before, we deduce that $s_{7.2^k}$ also grows as ζ^k.

If $7.2^k \le n \le 7.2^{k+1}$, then $s_{7.2^k} \le s_n \le s_{7.2^{k+1}}$, so s_n grows as $\zeta^{\log_2 n}$, i.e. $n^{\log_2 \zeta}$. $\qquad\square$

References

1. J.-P. ALLOUCHE AND J. SHALLIT, The ring of k-regular sequences, *Theoret. Comput. Sci.* **98** (1992), 163–197.
2. F.-J. BRANDENBURG, Uniformly growing k-th power-free homomorphisms, *Theoret. Comput. Sci.* **23** (1983), 69–82.
3. S. BRLEK, Enumeration of factors in the Thue-Morse word, *Discr. Appl. Math.* **24** (1989), 83–96.
4. A. CARPI, Overlap-free words and finite automata. Preprint, 1990.
5. A. DE LUCA AND S. VARRICCHIO, Some combinatorial properties of the Thue-Morse sequence and a problem in semigroups, *Theoret. Comput. Sci.* **63** (1989), 333–348.
6. F. DEJEAN, Sur un théorème de Thue, *J. Combin. Th. A* **13** (1972), 90–99.
7. P. GORALCIK AND T. VANICEK, Binary patterns in binary words, *Inter. J. Algebra Comput.* **1,3** (1991), 387–391.
8. R. KFOURY, A linear time algorithm to decide whether a binary word contains an overlap, *Theoret. Inform. Appl.* **22** (1988), 135–145.
9. Y. KOBAYASHI, Enumeration of irreducible binary words, *Discr. Appl. Math.* **20** (1988), 221–232.
10. A. RESTIVO AND S. SALEMI, Overlap-free words on two symbols, in *Automata on Infinite Words*, M. Nivat and Perrin, eds, pp. 198–206, no. 192 in *Lect. Notes Comp. Sci.*, Springer-Verlag, 1985.
11. A. THUE, Über unendliche Zeichenreihen, *Norske Vid. Selsk. Skr., I. Mat. Nat. Kl., Christiana* **7** (1906), 1–22.
12. A. THUE, Über die gegenseitige Lage gleicher Teile gewisser Zeichenreihen, *Norske Vid. Selsk. Skr., I. Mat. Nat. Kl., Christiana* **10** (1912), 1–67.

The Limit Set
of Recognizable Substitution Systems

Philippe Narbel

L.I.T.P, Institut Blaise Pascal, Paris 7

e-mail: narbel@litp.ibp.fr

Abstract. *This paper introduces the global limit set of a morphism language. This set is generated by a process called "reversed morphism" which is a systematic way to embed words in each other. If the morphism is recognizable, i.e. locally invertible, then the limit set is shown in bijection with a rational language. This allows us to deduce that the limit set can be uncountable, can be structured by a natural dynamics and can contain only strictly quasiperiodic words.*

Introduction

The limit sets of a word language have become a familiar concept in formal language theory of rational languages and this, even for bi-infinite words (see for instance [NP82, Bea86]). The limit idea appeared also for L systems, mostly as fixed points of $D0L$ systems [Sal81, CIS82, Que87], i.e. for deterministic context-free systems. Another case where asymptotic sets were used was in the understanding of some unbounded tilings of the plane [GS87, LP87, DB90]. There were evidences from some results of J. Conway for Penrose tilings that the three approaches could be conciliated. This was initiated by N.G. De Bruijn [DB89] who paved the way for a generalization.

The aim of this paper is thus to link the limit of formal languages to the fixed points of $D0L$ systems and to Conway's method of tiling investigation. It leads to the definition of the *global limit set* of a language generated by some iterated morphism, i.e. by a substitution system. This set consists of the limits of sequences of successively embedded words. Its explicit construction can rely on a process called *reversed morphism* which seems to be a new way to generate infinite words as compared for instance to the recent paper [CIK92]. One of the advantages of the method is that it allows the generation of bi-infinite words together with one-way infinite ones and sometimes uncountably many. Also, it is directly linked to topological concepts since the considered sequences of words can be seen as Cauchy sequences when the language has been structured by some metrics.

The main result is that, if the morphism is recognizable, i.e. locally invertible, then there is a bijection between the limit set and its relative Cauchy sequences which can be coded into a rational language of one-way infinite words. Moreover, the shift function applied on the coding language induces a dynamical system on the limit set. It can be seen as a generalization of what happens when one speaks of a fixed point of a $D0L$ system. Also, the bijection allows us to exhibit conditions such that the global limit set is uncountable and contains only strictly quasiperiodic words.

The first part of this paper defines the global limit set, the on-focus substitution system language, and the metric structure used on words. The second one introduces the reversed morphism, and presents the bijection between the limit set and a rational language. The third section is dedicated to presenting some of the consequences of the bijection.

1 Definitions

Let Σ be a finite alphabet of symbols, and Σ^* be the set of all finite words plus the empty word λ, that is the free monoid generated by Σ using the concatenation product. The set Σ^+ is just equal to $\Sigma^* \setminus \{\lambda\}$. A right (respect. left, bi) infinite word is intuitively a word that has symbols to infinity to the right (respect. to the left, to both) directions. To be preciser, let the sets N and Z denote respectively the positive numbers and the integers, and let the set $\tilde{N}$ be equal to $(Z \setminus N) \cup 0$. A *right infinite word* (respect. *left infinite word*) may be seen as a map $w : N \to \Sigma$ (respect. $w : \tilde{N} \to \Sigma$). The bi-infinite words are more difficult to define since they do not have any default distinct point. So, consider first a map $\hat{w} : Z \to \Sigma$, and an equivalence relation based on the *shift* function $\sigma(\hat{w}(n))_{n \in Z} = \hat{w}(n+1)_{n \in Z}$ so that $\hat{w} \sim \sigma^m(\hat{w})$ for all $m \in Z$. Then, a *bi-infinite word* consists of a full $\sim_\sigma$-class of maps. The set Σ^ω denotes the set of all the right-infinite words, the set $^\omega\Sigma$ of all the left-infinite ones, the set $^\omega\Sigma^\omega$ of all the bi-infinite ones, the set Σ^Ω of all the infinite ones and the infinitary set $^\infty\Sigma^\infty$ of all finite and infinite ones. Any subset of $^\infty\Sigma^\infty$ is called a *language* on Σ.

However, the difficulty in handling bi-infinite words in their original definition leads to the preferable use of *pointed words*, i.e. words with a fixed indexing. So, a *pointed bi-infinite word* is just a map $\hat{w} : Z \to \Sigma$. For one-way infinite words, define for all $m > 0$ the sets $N_m = N \cup \{-m, .., -1\}$ and $\tilde{N}_m = \tilde{N} \cup \{1, .., m-1\}$, so that the *right* (respect. *left*) *infinite pointed words* are maps $\hat{w} : N_m \to \Sigma$ (respect. $\hat{w} : \tilde{N}_m \to \Sigma$). In general, a hat will be added over the symbols representing pointed words or pointed languages. The image of $\hat{w}(n)$ is abbreviated w_n and the symbol w_0 is called *the origin*. In the pointed infinitary set $^\infty\hat{\Sigma}^\infty$, the *finite words* are maps on finite intervals of Z including zero. We stress that in $^\infty\hat{\Sigma}^\infty$, for example, the finite pointed word $\hat{w} = aaa\mathbf{b}babbb$ is not equal to $\hat{v} = aaabb\mathbf{a}bbb$, where the bold characters indicate the respective origins. The length of a word $\hat{w}$, which is equal to the cardinality of its source set, is denoted by $|w|$. A *factor* of a word $\hat{w}$ is just a submap of $\hat{w}$. It is denoted by $[w_k..w_l]$, where $[k, l]$ is a subinterval of the source set of $\hat{w}$.

In order to homogenize the infinitary set $^\infty\hat{\Sigma}^\infty$, it can be supposed that all its words which are not yet bi-infinite have been padded to both infinities with some dummy symbol not already in Σ. This allows us to say that for any pointed language $\hat{L}$ included in $^\infty\hat{\Sigma}^\infty$, its non-pointed counterpart can be recovered by quotienting it: $L = \hat{L}/\sim_\sigma$.

The infinitary set $^\infty\widehat\Sigma^\infty$ can be made into a metric space. The distance relies on the longest common factor around the origin: let $\widehat u, \widehat v \in {}^\infty\widehat\Sigma^\infty$ and $p > 1$,

$$d_p(\widehat u, \widehat v) = \left\{ \begin{array}{ll} 0 & \text{iff } \widehat u = \widehat v \\ p^{-|\widehat u, \widehat v|} & \text{otherwise} \end{array} \right. \quad \text{where} \quad |\widehat u, \widehat v| = \left\{ \begin{array}{ll} 0 & \text{iff } u_0 \ne v_0 \\ 1 + max\{k \in N \mid [u_{-k}, u_k] = [v_{-k}, v_k]\} \end{array} \right. \tag{1}$$

The considered metric space is then the pair $({}^\infty\widehat\Sigma^\infty, d_p)$. Recall then that a *Cauchy sequence* in $({}^\infty\widehat\Sigma^\infty, d_p)$ is a sequence (α_n) of words in $^\infty\widehat\Sigma^\infty$ such that

$$\forall \epsilon > 0 , \ \exists k \ \text{such that} \ d_p(\alpha_n, \alpha_m) < \epsilon, \quad \forall n, m > k$$

Since $({}^\infty\widehat\Sigma^\infty, d_p)$ can be shown compact (see [MH38]), the Cauchy sequences are convergent sequences. Asymptotic sets of a language $\widehat L$ can be then described by a set of Cauchy sequences whose limits are not yet in $\widehat L$.

In this paper, we shall restrict our attention to languages included in $\widehat\Sigma^*$ and containing Σ. This means that the considered Cauchy sequences (α_n) must lead to limit words which are included in $\widehat\Sigma^\Omega$, i.e. they must be infinite. Since only the limit words are used, their relative sequences can be assumed monotonic, i.e. $d_p(\alpha_{n+1}, \alpha_n) \le d_p(\alpha_n, \alpha_{n-1})$ for all n, and their first element α_0 can be a single symbol in Σ. The *global pointed limit set* $Lim\widehat L$ of a language $\widehat L \subset \widehat\Sigma^*$ consists of the set of the limits of the Cauchy sequences (α_n) which satisfy the following recursive definition: let $\alpha_n \in \widehat L$ for all n, then:

$$\begin{aligned} &\alpha_0 \in \Sigma, \\ &\alpha_{n+1} = \gamma_n \alpha_n \beta_n \ \text{where} \ \ \gamma_n, \beta_n \in \Sigma^*, \end{aligned} \tag{2}$$

Therefore, such a sequence (α_n) is associated to two sequences $(\beta_n), (\gamma_n)$ of growing factors indexed by their embeddings in (α_n). Note that the origin of the limit word is given naturally by α_0. Also, since the global limit set consists only of infinite words, it can be figured out that the limit words are of three different types:

  left-infinite words in $^\omega\widehat\Sigma$ if $\exists n_0 \in N$ such that $\beta_n = \lambda, \forall n > n_0$,
  right-infinite words in $\widehat\Sigma^\omega$ if $\exists n_0 \in N$ such that $\gamma_n = \lambda, \forall n > n_0$,
  bi-infinite words in $^\omega\widehat\Sigma^\omega$ otherwise.

Hence, $Lim\widehat L$ decomposes itself in three sets respectively denoted by $LLim\widehat L$, $RLim\widehat L$ and $BiLim\widehat L$. They can be shown to be identical to their usual counterparts [NP82, DL91].

Up to now, the discussion has been about pointed languages only. The global non-pointed limit set $LimL$ of a non-pointed language $L \subset \Sigma^*$ can be defined as $(Lim\widehat L/\sim_e)$, where $\widehat L$ is the pointing of L consisting of all possible indexings of the words in L. Note however that this is only a practical definition since the quotient space can be metrically non-separated.

A map $\theta : \Sigma \to \Sigma^+$ is said to be a *morphism* when it is extended to $^\infty\Sigma^\infty$ by the following rule:

$$\theta(w) = \theta(...s_i s_{i+1} s_{i+2}...) = ...\theta(s_i)\theta(s_{i+1})\theta(s_{i+2})..., \quad s_i \in \Sigma.$$

The nth iteration of a morphism is just the nth power of its composition. A *substitution system* is given by a pair (Σ, θ) whose language is given by

$$L_\theta = \{w \in \Sigma^* \mid \theta^n(s_j) = w, \ \forall n \geq 0, \forall s_j \in \Sigma\}.$$

Note that θ^0 is considered to be the identity function. The *order* of a word $w \in L_\theta$ is the minimum number of iterations of θ to obtain it. The sublanguage L^n consists of all words of order n. Also, the *father symbol* of a word $w = \theta^n(s_i)$ is just the symbol s_i. The *growth functions* of L_θ are given by $g_j(n) = |\theta^n(s_j)|$ with $s_j \in \Sigma$. If $lim_{n \to \infty}|g_j(n)| = \infty$ for all j, then the morphism is said *progressive*.

The aim of the following sections is to describe the limit set $Lim\widehat{L}_\theta$. It will be done by generating explicitly and systematically the Cauchy sequences verifying definition 2.

2   The Pointed Limit Set

A word of $Lim\widehat{L}_\theta$ is given by the limit of a Cauchy sequence. Therefore, if there was a systematic way to define all these sequences, it would result in an explicit description of the entire set $Lim\widehat{L}_\theta$. The first idea is to take the symbols of Σ, try all possibilities to embed them in the other words of $\widehat{L}_\theta$, take these words, try again the possibilities of embedding and so on. However, a great deal of effort can be spared by using a constrained way to embed words in each other. This is implemented by what is called here the reversed morphism. It defines the set of the shortest words in $\widehat{L}_\theta$ which embed a specific word. Here is what we mean by "shortest": since $\widehat{w} \in \widehat{L}_\theta$, there exists a symbol $s_i \in \Sigma$ such that $\theta^n(s_i) = w$ (recall that w is the associated $\sim_\theta$-class of $\widehat{w}$); so, the shortest words which contain $\widehat{w}$ are given, first, by determining all the possible choices to embed the symbol s_i in the elements of $\{\theta_i\}$, and then, by applying θ^n to these θ_i replacing $\widehat{w}$ at its original location. The *reversed morphism* of a morphism defined on Σ is then a correspondence $\rho_\theta : \widehat{L}_\theta \to 2^{\widehat{L}_\theta}$ defined for each $w \in \widehat{L}_\theta$ by,

$$\rho_\theta(\widehat{w}) = \{\widehat{v} \in \widehat{L}_\theta \mid \ \widehat{v} = \theta^n(u)\widehat{w}\,\theta^n(u') \quad \text{where}$$
$$u, u' \in \Sigma^* \text{ are such that } ut_iu' \in \{\theta_i\} \text{ with } \theta^n(t_i) = w, \ t_i \in \Sigma, \ n \geq 0\} \tag{3}$$

As an example, take the morphism defined by $\theta(p) = ppq$, $\theta(q) = pq$ and recall that the bold characters indicate the origins of the words. Then $\rho_\theta(\mathbf{p}) = \{\mathbf{p}pq, p\mathbf{p}q, p\mathbf{q}\}$ and $\rho_\theta(\mathbf{q}) = \{pp\mathbf{q}, p\mathbf{q}\}$. Next, consider $\widehat{w} = p\mathbf{p}q$: since $w = \theta(p)$, take all possibilities to embed p in θ_i (which is exactly $\rho_\theta(\mathbf{p})$) and apply θ^2 to obtain $\rho_\theta(\widehat{w}) = \{p\mathbf{p}qppqpq, ppqp\mathbf{p}qpq, pp\mathbf{q}pq\}$.

Thus, the reversed morphism can be recursively iterated since each word of $\rho_\theta^{n-1}(\widehat{w})$ defines its own subset in $2^{\widehat{L}_\theta}$ and their union yields $\rho_\theta^n(\widehat{w})$, i.e

$$\rho_\theta^n(\widehat{w}) = \{\widehat{v} \in \widehat{L}_\theta \mid \ \widehat{v} \in \rho_\theta(\widehat{u}), \ \widehat{u} \in \rho_\theta^{n-1}(\widehat{w})\}, \quad \forall n > 1. \tag{4}$$

Its associated language is then defined by:

$$\widehat{L}\rho_\theta = \{w \in \rho_\theta^n(s_j), \ n \geq 0, s_j \in \Sigma\}. \tag{5}$$

(i)

$(p,p,0) \rightarrow$ ...

```
                              1 ↗ (ppqppqpq,p,2) ...
              (ppq,p,1) →2→ (ppqPpqppq,p,2)...
           1↗        4↘ (ppqpq,q,2) ...
          /      1↗ (ppqppqpq,p,2) ...
     /2  (ppq,p,1) →2→ (ppqPpqpq,p,2) ...
(p,p,0) →          4↘ (ppqpq,q,2) ...
      4↘        3↗ (ppqppqPq,p,2) ...
        (pq,q,1) 5↗ (ppqPq,q,2) ...
```

```
                           1↗ (ppqppqpq,p,2) ...
            (ppq,p,1) →2→ (ppqppqPpq,p,2) ...
         3↗        4↘ (ppqpq,q,2) ...
(q,q,0)
      5↘        3↗ (ppqppqpq,p,2) ...
        (pq,q,1) 5↗ (ppqpq,q,2) ...
```

(ii)

```
                      3↗ (bab,b,2) ...
(a,a,0) →2→ (ab,b,1)
                      1↗ (ab,a,2) ...
```

```
                    3↗ (ab,b,1) →3↗ (bab,b,2) ...
                             1↘ (ab,a,2) ...
(b,b,0)
                    1↘ (b,a,1) →2→ (bab,b,2) ...
```

(iii)

$(a,a,0) \xrightarrow{1} (ab,a,2) \xrightarrow{1} (abc,a,2)$ ...

```
            4↗ (b,c,1) →3→ (b,b,2) ...
(b,b,0)
            2↘ (ab,a,1) →1→ (abc,a,2) ...
```

```
                         4↗ (c,c,2) ...
(c,c,0) →3↗ (c,b,1)
                         2↘ (abc,a,2) ...
```

Figure 1: *The beginnings of the reversed morphism trees when the morphisms are defined by $\theta(p) = ppq$, $\theta(q) = pq$ in (i), by $\theta(a) = b$, $\theta(b) = ab$ in (ii), and by $\theta(a) = ab$, $\theta(b) = c$, $\theta(c) = b$ in (iii). The bold characters indicate the origins of the words. The label map f_θ for (i) $f_\theta(p, ppq) = 1$, $f_\theta(p, ppq) = 2$, $f_\theta(q, ppq) = 3$, $f_\theta(p, pq) = 4$, $f_\theta(q, pq) = 5$, for (ii) it is defined by $f_\theta(b, b) = 1$, $f_\theta(a, ab) = 2$, $f_\theta(b, ab) = 3$, and (iii) by $f_\theta(a, ab) = 1$, $f_\theta(b, ab) = 2$, $f_\theta(c, c) = 3$, $f_\theta(b, b) = 4$.*

The iterations of ρ_θ can be represented by a directed graph. Its nodes consist of 3-tuples $(\hat{w}, s_i, n)$ where $w = \theta^n(s_i)$, i.e. s_i is the father symbol of $\hat{w}$ which is of order n. Its edges are defined such that $(\hat{w}, s_i, n)$ is linked to $(\hat{v}, s_j, n+1)$, whenever $\hat{v} \in \rho_\theta(\hat{w})$. Thus, the full language $\hat{L}\rho_\theta$ can be represented as a forest of directed trees whose roots are the individual symbols of Σ. Figure 1 shows the beginnings of the trees for some morphisms (the meaning of the labels will be given later on).

By definition of the reversed morphism, the words of successive nodes in any path of the trees define a sequence which satisfies the conditions to be a Cauchy sequence in $(^\infty\hat{\Sigma}^\infty, d_p)$. However, some paths converge to finite words so that the sequences are ultimately constant (see example (iii) in figure 1). Let us denote by R_θ the set of all limits such that their paths go through an infinite number of nodes where the length of the word increases. According to the definition of the global limit set (see equation 2), the following holds:

$$R_\theta \subseteq Lim\widehat{L}_\theta. \tag{6}$$

In order to justify the use of the reversed morphism, the next step is to show the converse, that is for any word in the global limit set, there is a corresponding path in the reversed morphism trees. In order to formally obtain this result, the paths of R_θ are coded: each time the word to "reverse" has s_i as father symbol, then the given choices are exactly all the ways to embed s_j in $\{\theta_i\}$. Thus, each branch in the trees may be labeled by using a bijective map, denoted by f_θ and defined as

$$f_\theta : \quad \Sigma \times \theta_i \quad \to \quad \Gamma$$
$$(s_i, (us_iu')) \quad \mapsto \quad g$$

where Γ is the set of labels which are called *connectors* in [DB89]. For a node $(\widehat{w}, s_i, n)$, the arc going to $(\widehat{v}, s_j, n+1)$ is labeled by $f_\theta(s_i, us_iu')$ where us_iu' is the specific embedding of s_i in $\{\theta_i\}$ to get $\widehat{v}$. Look at figure 1 to see the application of f_θ on some morphisms. Every node can be then mapped to the label of its corresponding path, which consists in the labels of its successive edges. This leads to the existence of the following coding map:

$$\psi : \quad (\widehat{L}_\theta \setminus \Sigma, \Sigma, N) \quad \to \quad \Gamma^+$$
$$(\widehat{w}, s_i, n) \quad \mapsto \quad g_1 ... g_n$$

where $\psi(s_i, \Sigma, 0) = \lambda$ for all $s_i \in \Sigma$. This map can be extended for the set of the limit paths of R_θ. We set that,

$$\psi(R_\theta, \Sigma, \infty) = \Gamma_\theta^\omega \subseteq \Gamma^\omega$$

Therefore, the set Γ_θ^ω consists of all paths which lead to words in the limit set. In order to study the relationship between $Lim\widehat{L}_\theta$ and R_θ, the map ψ must be explicitly constructed. Let us define the inverse correspondence θ^{-1}: if $\widehat{w} \in \widehat{L}_\theta$, then there is at least one way to *factorize* $\widehat{w}$ with the set $\{\theta_i\}$, i.e.

$$\widehat{w} = ...x_ix_{i+1}..., \quad \text{with} \quad x_i \in \{\theta_i\}. \tag{7}$$

If x_0 is assumed to contain the origin, then the *inversion* of the morphism θ is defined by

$$\theta^{-1}(\widehat{w}) = ...s_is_{i+1}... \in \widehat{L}_\theta \quad \text{with} \quad \theta(s_i) = x_i, \ s_i \in \Sigma. \tag{8}$$

It can be also iterated in $\widehat{L}_\theta$ by setting $\theta^{-m}(\widehat{w}) = ...s_is_{i+1}...$, with $s_i \in \Sigma$, $\theta^m(s_i) = x_i$. If $\widehat{w} \in \Sigma$, we set that $\theta^{-m}(\widehat{w}) = \widehat{w}$, for all m. The coding of a node in the reversed morphism trees can be recovered by iterating the factorization of the corresponding word $\widehat{w}$ by $\{\theta_i\}$, and by applying at each step the connector map f_θ on the factor containing the origin of $\widehat{w}$. This can be recursively defined as follows: let w_0 denote the origin and x_0 the factor which contains it:

$$\begin{aligned}
\psi(\widehat{w}, s_i, n) &= f_\bullet(w_0, x_0)\psi(\theta^{-1}(\widehat{w}), s_i, n-1) = \\
&\quad f_\bullet(w_0, uw_0u')\psi(\theta^{-1}(\widehat{w}), s_i, n-1) = \\
&\quad g_1\psi(\theta^{-1}(\widehat{w}), s_i, n-1) = \\
&\quad g_1...g_n\psi(\theta^{-n}(\widehat{w}), s_i, 0) = \\
&\quad g_1...g_n.
\end{aligned} \qquad (9)$$

For instance, take again the morphism $\theta(p) = ppq$, $\theta(q) = pq$ with the connector map defined as in figure (1). Consider the word $\widehat{w} = ...qpqppqppqpqpqppqp....$ Its factorization in $\{\theta_i\}$ can be shown to be $..q/pq/ppq/ppq/pq/ppq/p....$ Hence $g_1 = f_\bullet(q, ppq) = 3$, and $\theta^{-1}(\widehat{w}) = ..qppqp...$ The map ψ must be then reapplied on $\theta^{-1}(\widehat{w})$. Its factorization in $\{\theta_i\}$ is $..q/ppq/p..$, so that $g_2 = f_\bullet(p, ppq) = 1$ and $\theta^{-2} = ...p....$ Note that if $\widehat{w}$ was restricted to be $ppqppqpq$, the coding would be reduced to $g_1g_2 = 31$.

The extension of the explicit definition of ψ for $(R_\bullet, \Sigma, \infty)$ is readily obtained: the process just described is just applied infinitely often. Now, since the words of $Lim\widehat{L}_\bullet$ are given by limits of words in $\widehat{L}$ the same process can be applied. This gives an infinite word which represents an infinite path included in $\Gamma_\bullet^\omega$. This means that $Lim\widehat{L}_\bullet \subseteq R_\bullet$ holds, and thus we can conclude with equation (6) that the reversed morphism is powerful enough to generate the limit set, i.e.:

Lemma 2.1 *Let θ be a morphism. Then $Lim\widehat{L}_\bullet = R_\bullet$.*

Henceforth, the coding map will be abbreviated for infinite sets by being applied only on words rather than entire nodes. The situation can be then summed up by saying that $\psi(R_\bullet) = \psi(Lim\widehat{L}_\bullet) = \Gamma_\bullet^\omega$. Thus, the goal now is to explicit the conditions so that ψ is a bijection.

The problem is just to show that ψ is one-to-one, that is a single path in the trees leads to a single word in $Lim\widehat{L}_\bullet$. The contrary can occur: let θ be defined by $\theta(a) = aba$, $\theta(b) = bab$. It can be checked that the periodic words $^\omega(ab)ab(ab)^\omega$ and $^\omega(ab)ab(ab)^\omega$ are the only words in $Bilim\widehat{L}_\bullet$, though an infinite number of different paths leads to them.

In fact, the map ψ is injective whenever θ^{-1} is a uniquely defined function (see equation (9)), i.e. the factorization in $\{\theta_i\}$ is unique, and this at each iteration. For the last example, note that $^\omega(ab)ab(ab)^\omega$ can be factorized so that either $x_0 = bab$ or $x_0 = aba$.

The correspondence θ^{-1} is uniquely defined on an infinite word if the factorization is uniquely and locally determined. This is ensured by the *recognizability* property [Que87, Mos90]. For our case, a language $\widehat{L}$ is said to be k-*recognizable* if the following occurs: for all $\widehat{w}$ in $\widehat{L}$, its centered factors $u_i = [w_{i-l}, w_{i+l}]$ with $l > k$ satisfy:

$$u_i = yx_0..x_ny' = zx_0'..x_m'z', \quad \forall\, i,j,\; x_i, x_j' \in \{\theta_i\} \quad \text{and} \quad y, y', z, z' \in \Sigma^*,$$

where the words y, y', z, z' are minimum in size; then, denoting the respective factors $\{x_i\}$, $\{x_j'\}$ containing w_i as x_{i_0} and x_{j_0}',

$$x_{i_0} = x_{j_0}' \,,\quad yx_0..x_{i_0-1} = zx_0'..x_{j_0-1}' \quad \text{and} \quad x_{i_0+1}..x_ny' = x_{j_0+1}'..x_m'z'.$$

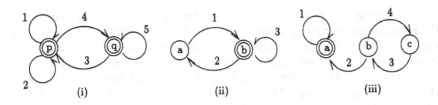

Figure 2: *The respective automata of the limit sets of the morphisms of figure (1). The final states have a double surrounding circle.*

By extension, a morphism which leads to a k-recognizable limit language is said to be k-recognizable. It can be checked that if $\widehat{L}_\theta$ is k-recognizable, then $Lim\widehat{L}_\theta$ is k-recognizable. So, we have the following result:

Theorem 2.1 *Let θ be a k-recognizable morphism. Then, $\psi : Lim\widehat{L}_\theta \leftrightarrow \Gamma_\theta^\omega$ is bijective.*

Let us now prove that Γ_θ^ω is in fact a rational language. First, recall that a symbol $g_k \in \Gamma$ means a specific embedding in some θ_j as well as a corresponding symbol s_j to be embedded again to obtain the next symbol $g_{k+1} \in \Gamma$. Hence, a pair of symbols $g_k g_{k+1}$ can occur by ψ, iff

$$f_\theta(t_i, \theta_j) = g_k, \quad \theta_j = \theta(s_j), \text{ and } f_\theta(s_j, \theta_h) = g_{k+1}.$$

Since a specific g_k corresponds uniquely to some $s_j \in \Sigma$, all symbols g_{k+1} are possible after it if $g_k g_{k+1}$ is an allowed pair. This means that the set of the infinite paths in the reversed morphism trees is *language of finite type* included in Γ^ω. Now, a path leads to a limit in R_θ if it passes through an infinite number of nodes which expand their words. These are exactly the conditions to build a Büchi automaton A_θ for infinite words (see for instance[PP92]) which recognize Γ_θ^ω. It is defined so that its states are the symbols of Σ, the labels are the connectors Γ^∞, and an edge exists between two states s_i and s_j, if s_i is included in θ_j and its labels are given by $f_\theta(s_i, \theta_j)$. Every state is initial and the final states are all the symbols s_i such that $|\theta(s_i)| > 1$. The corresponding automata of the morphisms of figure 1 are shown in figure 2. Therefore, we can restate the theorem 2.1 to be:

Theorem 2.1 (bis) *Let θ be a k-recognizable morphism. Then, the global limit set $Lim\widehat{L}_\theta$ is bijectively sent to the rational language Γ_θ^ω.*

Note that the sublanguages $\psi(Llim\widehat{L}_\theta)$, $\psi(Rlim\widehat{L}_\theta)$ and $\psi(Bilim\widehat{L}_\theta)$ can be checked to be also rational. They can be recognized by a Müller automaton with the same topology as A_θ.

Before going for the next section, let us discuss the decidability question of the recognizability property. First, it is at least semi-decidable. This is so since the set of factors of a fixed length in $\widehat{L}_\theta$ must appear after a finite number of iterations. A sufficient condition is given if the set $\{\theta_i\}$ is a *synchronous, limited* or *circular* code [BP85]. For instance, $\{ppq, pq\}$, $\{ab, b\}$ and $\{ab, b, c\}$ can be checked to be such codes. Also, a morphism θ has been shown recognizable when it is *primitive* and *aperiodic* [Mos90], i.e. respectively, it exists an index $n < \infty$ such that all symbols of Σ are included in $\theta^n(s_i)$, for all $s_i \in \Sigma$; and, there is no word in $Lim\widehat{L}_\theta$ such that there exists an index p such that $w_i = w_{i+p}$ for all i. Note that being primitive is easily seen decidable. Also, the decidability of the aperiodicity property for $Lim\widehat{L}_\theta$ can be shown by using two results: one from [HL86] saying that the ultimate periodicity of the limit of a *D0L* system is decidable, a second one from [Mos90] saying that a primitive aperiodic morphism generates only words which are n-power free for n big enough, i.e. they contain no factors u^n.

3 The Structure of the Limit Set

In this section, we shall investigate some consequences of the preceding coding theorem. First, from the definitions of the limit set and the reversed morphism, it can be deduced that applying θ^{-1} on some word in $Lim\widehat{L}_\theta$ is the same as applying it to all elements of the corresponding sequence (α_n). Therefore,

Proposition 3.1 *Let θ be k-recognizable. Then $\theta^{-1}(Lim\widehat{L}_\theta) \subseteq Lim\widehat{L}_\theta$.*

A dynamical system is a pair (X, h) where X is a metric space and h is a continuous map from X to X. A point $x \in X$ is said p-*periodic* if it exists p such that $h^p(x) = x$. A 1-periodic point x is said to be *fixed*. If the morphism θ is k-recognizable, then θ^{-1} can be seen continuous. With the last proposition, the pair $(Lim\widehat{L}_\theta, \theta^{-1})$ is thus a dynamical system. In fact, it can be seen as a generalization of the usual theory of the infinitely iterated *D0L* systems [Sal81] where only the fixed points with the origin fixed on the left extremity of the word are taken in consideration.

Let the shift function on one-way infinite words be $\tau(w_n)_{n \in N} = (w_{n+1})_{n \in N}$. Then, $(\Gamma_\theta^\omega, \tau)$ is also a dynamical system. Note that if the morphism is progressive, i.e. every path leads to an infinite word, and therefore the language Γ_θ^ω is of finite type. In that case, the resulting dynamical system is a very well-known one called a *subshift of finite type* (see [DGS76], chapter 17). Moreover, for any $\widehat{w} \in Lim\widehat{L}_\theta$, then $\psi(\theta^{-1}(w)) = \tau(\psi(w))$ holds. Moreover, since ψ is a bijection, it means that the following diagram is commutative:

$$
\begin{array}{ccc}
Lim\widehat{L}_\theta & \xrightarrow{\psi_\theta} & \Gamma_\theta^\omega \\
\theta^{-1} \downarrow & & \downarrow \tau \\
Lim\widehat{L}_\theta & \xrightarrow{\psi_\theta} & \Gamma_\theta^\omega
\end{array}
$$

It can be then readily checked that:

Proposition 3.2 *The periodic points of* $(Lim\widehat{L}_\theta, \theta^{-1})$ *are in bijection with the periodic words of* Γ^ω_θ.

Note that in order to have a *topological conjugacy*, the bijection ψ is required to be an homeomorphism. In fact, ψ is continuous only from $Lim\widehat{L}_\theta$ to Γ^ω_θ. The other way is not. But if one uses the induced metric from Γ^ω_θ for $Lim\widehat{L}_\theta$, so that the compared factors for the distance are obtained by the successive factorizations given by θ^{-1}, then ψ is bicontinuous.

The automaton A_θ is a good mean to obtain the cardinality of the global limit set $Lim\widehat{L}_\theta$. A *cycle* in an automaton is just a path which goes from a state to itself; this state is called the *base* of the cycle. Then, for instance, it can be proved that:

Proposition 3.3 *Let* θ *be a k-recognizable morphism. If its automaton A_θ has no final state which is the base of a cycle, then* $|Lim\widehat{L}_\theta| = \emptyset$.

Proposition 3.4 *Let* θ *be a k-recognizable morphism. If its automaton A_θ has a state which is the base of two distinct cycles which contain at least one final state, then* $|Lim\widehat{L}_\theta|$ *is uncountable.*

In particular, any progressive k-recognizable morphism leads to an uncountable global limit set. Note that being primitive means to be progressive. Recall that the non-pointed set $LimL_\theta$ was defined as $(Lim\widehat{L}_\theta / \sim_\sigma)$. Since the $\sim_\sigma$-classes contain a countable number of elements, $LimL_\theta$ is uncountable if $Lim\widehat{L}_\theta$ is also.

Finally, we shall prove a special property of the words in the limit set whenever the morphism is progressive. A word $\widehat{w}$ is said to be *p-periodic* if $w_i = w_{i+p}$ for all i and p, and *aperiodic* on the contrary.

Proposition 3.5 *Let* θ *be a progressive k-recognizable morphism. Then, all words in* $Lim\widehat{L}_\theta$ *are aperiodic.*

Proof. Suppose that $\widehat{w} \in Lim\widehat{L}_\theta$ is p-periodic, with $p > 1$, and k-recognizable in $\{\theta_i\}$. Notice that k must be less than $2p$. This is so since getting over more than one period is not informative for applying θ^{-1}. Now, $\theta^{-1}(\widehat{w})$ is also periodic, since for a symbol $w_i \subset w$ and its periodic counterpart w_{i+np} with $n \in Z$, the unique factorization must be applied equivalently because of the k-recognizability. Using the fact that $\theta^{-1}(Lim\widehat{L}_\theta) \subseteq Lim\widehat{L}_\theta$, the last reasoning can be iterated. But, since θ was supposed progressive, it exists $n \in N$ such that $\theta^{-n}(\widehat{w})$ is q-periodic, with $q < p$. Hence, there exists an index $m \in N$ such that $\theta^{-n}(\widehat{w})$ is 1-periodic. Therefore, there is a word in $LimL_\theta$ which has the form $^\omega s_j^\omega$ or s_j^ω or $^\omega s_j$ with $s_j \in \Sigma$. However, from the sequence-based definition of $Lim\widehat{L}_\theta$, this word can occur only if the morphism θ is such that $\exists\, p, q > 0$ such that $\theta^q(s_j) = s_j^p$, with $s_j \in \Sigma$. This implies that $^\omega s_j s_j s_j^\omega$ must be a word in $Lim\widehat{L}_\theta$. But, it cannot be k-recognizable and this is a contradiction. $\Diamond$

A word is said to be *quasiperiodic* if all of its factors occur in bounded gaps. From ([Que87], chapter 5), it can be deduced that if the morphism θ is primitive

236

then every word in $\widehat{LimL}_\theta$ is quasiperiodic. With proposition 3.5, it means that every word in $\widehat{LimL}_\theta$ is strictly quasiperiodic when the morphism is primitive and k-recognizable.

Acknowledgment. The author is grateful to D. Beauquier for her numerous comments on a preliminary version of this paper.

References

[Bea86] Beauquier (D.). - *Automates de mots bi-infinis.* - Paris, 1986. Thèse d'Etat.

[BP85] Berstel (J.) and Perrin (D.). - *Theory of Codes.* - Academic Press, 1985.

[CIK92] Culik II (K.) and Karhumäki (J.). - Iterative devices generating infinite words. In: *Proceedings of STACS'92*, pp. 531–543.

[CIS82] Culik II (K.) and Salomaa (A.). - On infinite words obtained by iterating morphisms. *Theoretical Computer Science*, vol. 19, 1982, pp. 29–38.

[DB89] De Bruijn (N.G.). - Updown generation of Beatty sequences. *Indag. Math.*, vol. 51, 1989, pp. 385–407.

[DB90] De Bruijn (N.G.). - Updown generation of Penrose patterns. *Indag. Mathem., New Series.*, vol. 1, 1990, pp. 201–219.

[DGS76] Denker (M.), Grillenberger (C.) and Sigmund (K.). - *Ergodic theory on compact spaces.* - Springer-Verlag, 1976, *Lecture Notes in Mathematics*, volume 527.

[DL91] Devolder (J.) and Litovsky (I.). - Finitely generated biω−languages. *Theoretical Computer Science*, vol. 85, 1991, pp. 33–52.

[GS87] Grunbaum (B.) and Shephard (G.C.). - *Tilings and Patterns.* - Freeman and co., 1987.

[HL86] Harju (T.) and Linna (T.). - On the periodicity of morphisms on free monoids. *RAIRO, Theoretical Informatics and Applications*, vol. 20, number 1, 1986, pp. 47–54.

[LP87] Lunnon (W.F.) and Pleasants (P.A.B.). - Quasicrystallographic tilings. *J. Math. Pures et Appl.*, vol. 66, 1987, pp. 217–263.

[MH38] Morse (M.) and Hedlund (G.A.). - Symbolic dynamics. *American Journal of Mathematics*, vol. 60, 1938, pp. 815–866.

[Mos90] Mossé (B.). - *Puissances de mots et reconnaissabilité des points fixes d'une substitution.* - Technical report, PRC Mathématique Informatique, Université Aix-Marseille, 1990.

[NP82] Nivat (N.) and Perrin (D.). - Ensembles reconnaissables de mots bi-infinis. In: *14th ACM Symp. on Theory of Computing*, pp. 47–59.

[PP92] Perrin (D.) and Pin (J.P.). - *Mots infinis.* - Technical Report number 92.17, LITP, april 1992.

[Que87] Queffelec (M.). - *Substitution Dynamical Systems - Spectral Analysis.* - Springer-Verlag, 1987, *Lecture Notes in Mathematics*, volume 1294.

[Sal81] Salomaa (A.). - *Jewels of Formal Language Theory.* - Rockville, MD, Computer Science Press, 1981.

Partially Commutative Lyndon Words

D. Krob [1] - P. Lalonde [2]

1 Introduction

In a famous paper of 1958, Chen, Fox and Lyndon defined the lexicographically standard words, now known as Lyndon words (see [2]). These words play an important role in several contexts : free Lie algebras, fast pattern matching, ... (cf [4,5,19,20] for instance) and their theory is now a classical part of combinatorics on words.

Free partially commutative monoids were introduced by Cartier and Foata in [1]. They were intensively studied, especially due to the fact that they were used as a model for parallel computing. On the other hand, they can be seen as a natural generalization of free monoids. Indeed, several classical results of the free monoid theory can be extended to the partially commutative framework. This research direction was followed by a lot of people (see [3], [6], [7] or [18] for good surveys of this kind of results) and this paper takes also place in the same movement.

In particular, a natural question was to see if one can propose a good notion of partially commutative Lyndon word that generalizes the usual definition. A positive answer was found by Lalonde (see [14,15]) who obtained the first important results in this direction. Here, the partially commutative Lyndon words are exactly the primitive words which are minimal in their conjugacy classes for a given order on the underlying free partially commutative monoid. Another attempt was also done by Duchamp and Krob who introduced colored Lyndon words that satisfy the complete factorization property (see [9]).

However Lalonde obtained all its results in the framework of heaps monoids initiated by Viennot (cf [21]). Therefore the problem remained to translate Lalonde's results in the usual framework of partially commutative words or traces and to unify explicitly Lalonde's and Duchamp-Krob's definitions. This is exactly the purpose of this short paper. It should be noticed that the results given here are not new since they appeared already in [14,15]. The originality of this note resides in our proofs which are indeed completely different from the original ones. In fact, we wanted to give here a short and simple presentation of the main results concerning partially commutative Lyndon words.

---

[1] LACIM and CNRS(LITP; Institut Blaise Pascal) Mailing adress : Université de Rouen - Laboratoire d'Informatique de Rouen - 76134 Mont Saint-Aignan Cedex - France

[2] M.I.T. - Department of Mathematics - Cambridge - Massachusets - USA - 02139

Let us finally end this introduction by giving the structure of our paper. After some preliminaries, we present Lalonde's definition of partially commutative Lyndon words. Our first important result shows the relation between this definition and another one based on elimination ideas. Then we prove other characterizations of Lyndon words that generalize several classical properties of usual Lyndon words. We end finally this paper by showing how the standard factorization property can be extended in the partially commutative framework.

2 Preliminaries

In the sequel, A always denotes a *finite* alphabet.

2.1 Generalities

A *commutation alphabet* is a pair (A, ϑ) that consists in an alphabet A equipped with a *partial commutation* ϑ, i.e. with a symmetric and non-reflexive relation on $A \times A$. We associate with such a commutation alphabet the congruence of A^* denoted $\equiv_\vartheta$ which is generated by the relations :

$$\forall\, (a, b) \in \vartheta, \quad ab \equiv_\vartheta ba.$$

The corresponding free partially commutative monoid is then the monoid denoted $M(A, \vartheta)$ which is equal to $A^* / \equiv_\vartheta$. We denote by π_ϑ the canonical projection of A^* onto $M(A, \vartheta)$. For every subset B of A, $M(B, \vartheta)$ denotes the submonoid of $M(A, \vartheta)$ which is generated by B.

Let $w \in M(A, \vartheta)$. Then the *initial alphabet* of w is the subset of A denoted $IA(w)$ and defined by $IA(w) = \{\, a \in A \mid \exists\, u \in M(A, \vartheta),\ w = au \,\}$.

Example : Let us consider the commutation alphabet defined by $A = \{\, a, b, c, d \,\}$ and by $\vartheta = \{\, (a, b), (b, a), (b, c), (c, b), (c, d), (d, c) \,\}$. Then the congruence class of the word $w = cdab$ is for instance $\{\, cdba, dcab, cdba, dcba \,\}$ and its initial alphabet is $IA(w) = \{\, d, c \,\}$.

2.2 Conjugacy

Let us now recall some definitions coming from [7]. A partially commutative word $w \in M(A, \vartheta)$ is said to be *primitive* iff we have $w = uv = vu \implies u = 1$ or $v = 1$ for every $u, v \in M(A, \vartheta)$. Two partially commutative words $u, v \in M(A, \vartheta)$ are said to be *independent* iff $(a, b) \in \vartheta$ for every letter a of u and b of v. Such a situation is denoted $u \, I \, v$. Observe that two independent partially commutative words have in particular disjoint alphabets. Two elements $u, v \in M(A, \vartheta)$ are said to be *transposed* iff there exists $x, y \in M(A, \vartheta)$ such that $u = xy$ and $v = yx$. Finally two elements u, v of $M(A, \vartheta)$ are said to be *conjugated* iff there exists a sequence of transpositions that allows to go from u to v.

Examples : All the examples that follow are given with the commutation alphabet defined by $A = \{\, a, b, c, d \,\}$ and by $\vartheta = \{\, (a, c), (c, a), (a, d), (d, a), (b, d), (d, b) \,\}$.

1) The partially commutative word $cdab$ is primitive, while $cada \equiv_\vartheta cdaa \equiv_\vartheta aacd$ and $cbcaba \equiv_\vartheta (cba)^2$ are not.

2) The conjugacy class of abc consists in the set $\{\, abc, cab \equiv_\vartheta acb, bca \equiv_\vartheta bac, cba \,\}$. Observe that abc and cba are not transposed.

We will need the following result of C. Duboc (cf [7] th. 3.3.3 or [8] th. 3.12).

THEOREM 2.1 : Let $u, v \in M(A, \vartheta)$. Then u and v are conjugated iff there exists a sequence $(z_i)_{i \in [0,k]}$ of partially commutative words such that

1) $u = z_0 z_1 \ldots z_k$ and $v = z_k z_{k-1} \ldots z_0$;
2) for every $i, j \in [0, k]$ with $|i - j| > 1$, we have $z_i\, I\, z_j$.

2.3   A total order on $M(A, \vartheta)$

Let us suppose now that A is totally ordered by some total order $<$. With every $w \in M(A, \vartheta)$, we associate the word $std(w) \in A^*$ which is the maximal word (for the lexicographic order on A^*) in the class $\pi_\vartheta^{-1}(w)$. This allows us to equip $M(A, \vartheta)$ with the total order defined by

$$\forall\, u, v \in M(A, \vartheta),\ u < v \ \text{iff}\ std(u) < std(v).$$

In the sequel, we always consider that $M(A, \vartheta)$ is equipped with this order.

Note that if $u, v \in M(A, \vartheta)$, then we clearly have $std(u)std(v) \in \pi_\vartheta^{-1}(uv)$. It follows immediately that $std(uv) \geq std(u)std(v) \geq std(u)$. Therefore, any proper prefix of a partially commutative word w is less than w. We will often use in the sequel this basic property of our order.

Example : Let us consider again the commutation alphabet used in the examples of the previous section. We order A by $a < b < c < d$. Then we have for instance :

$$\pi_\vartheta^{-1}(acbd) = \{\, acbd, acdb, cabd, cadb, cdab \,\} \quad \text{with } acbd < acdb < cabd < cadb < cdab.$$

Hence, $std(acbd) = cdab$. In the same way, we have :

$$\pi_\vartheta^{-1}(bacd) = \{\, bacd, bcad, bcda \,\} \quad \text{with } bacd < bcad < bcda$$

and therefore $std(bacd) = bcda$. Observe that $bacd \equiv_\vartheta bcda < cdab \equiv_\vartheta acbd$.

2.4   Elimination

Let us suppose again that A is totally ordered by some total order $<$. We can then write $A = \{\, a_1, a_2, \ldots, a_n \,\}$ with $a_1 < a_2 < \ldots < a_n$. Following [9], we define for every $i \in [1, n]$ the Z-code C_i by

$$C_i = \{\, w \in M(A, \vartheta) \mid w = a_i u,\ IA(w) = \{a_i\},\ u \in M(\{a_{i+1}, \ldots, a_n\}, \vartheta) \,\}.$$

According to [9], the submonoid C_i^* of $M(A, \vartheta)$ which is generated by C_i is free of basis C_i for every $i \in [1, n]$. Moreover the monoid $M(A, \vartheta)$ can be factorized in a unique way as follows

$$M(A, \vartheta) = C_n^* \ \ldots \ C_2^* \, C_1^* \qquad \text{(Fact)}.$$

Hence we can identify the free monoid C_i^* with its image in $M(A, \vartheta)$. We also equip C_i^* with the total order induced by the total order of $M(A, \vartheta)$ defined in the previous subsection.

The above factorization respects the *std* operation previously defined. In fact, let w be a partially commutative word of $M(A, \vartheta)$ decomposed according to (Fact) as

$$ w = c_i^1 \ldots c_i^{k_i} \; c_{i-1}^1 \ldots c_{i-1}^{k_{i-1}} \; \ldots \; c_j^1 \ldots c_j^{k_j} $$

where $i \geq j$ and $c_l^k \in C_l$ for every $l \in [j, i]$ and $k \in [1, k_l]$. It is then easy to prove that the following relation holds

$$ std(w) = std(c_i^1) \ldots std(c_i^{k_i}) \; std(c_{i-1}^1) \ldots std(c_{i-1}^{k_{i-1}}) \; \ldots \; std(c_j^1) \ldots std(c_j^{k_j}). $$

Moreover it can also easily be shown that we have $std(c_i) = a_i \, std(u)$ for every element $c_i = a_i u$ of the Z-code C_i.

Note : The definition of a Z-code that we used here is not formally the same than in [9] but is obviously equivalent to it by a mirror symmetry.

3 Partially commutative Lyndon words

In this section, (A, ϑ) denotes always a commutation alphabet equipped with some total order $<$.

3.1 Definition

Let us first recall Lalonde's definition of a partially commutative Lyndon word which generalizes obviously the classical definition of usual Lyndon words.

DEFINITION 3.1 : A *partially commutative Lyndon word* is a non-empty, primitive (partially commutative) word which is minimal in its conjugacy class.

Examples : 1) Let us consider again the commutation alphabet used in the examples of section 2.2. It is then easy to see that abc is a partially commutative Lyndon word. Note that this is not the case for $acb \equiv_\vartheta cab$, even if the word acb is a usual Lyndon word in A^*.

2) Any element of a Z-code C_i is clearly a partially commutative Lyndon word.

3.2 The main characterization result

This section is devoted to the proof of the main characterization of partially commutative Lyndon words. We will need the following lemma.

LEMMA 3.1 : Let l be a partially commutative word which is strictly less than all its proper transposes. Then l is a usual Lyndon word over some Z-code C_i for some $i \in [1, n]$.

Proof : Let l be a partially commutative word which is strictly less than all its proper transposes. According to (Fact), we can write

$$ l = c_i \, c_{i-1} \, \ldots \, c_j $$

where $i \geq j$ and where $c_k \in C_k^*$ for every $k \in [j, i]$. Let us suppose now that $i > j$. Let us then consider

$$l' = c_{i-1} \ \ldots \ c_j \ c_i$$

which is therefore a proper transpose of l. Hence we have $l < l'$. But the first letter of $std(l)$ is clearly a_i. Observe that $a_{i-1} \in IA(l') \subseteq \{ a_{i-1}, \ldots, a_j, a_i \}$. Hence, the first letter of $std(l')$ is either a_{i-1} or a_i. Since $l < l'$, it must be a_i. Thus l' and c_i have a common non-empty prefix. Thus, the decomposition of l' according to (Fact) must be of the form

$$l' = c_i' \ c_{i-1}' \ldots c_j'$$

where $c_k' \in C_k^*$ for every $k \in [j, i]$ and where c_i' is in particular a non-empty prefix of c_i. Since $l \neq l'$, we necessarily have $c_i' \neq c_i$. Hence $c_i' < c_i$. It follows easily from this relation that $l' < l$, which is not the case. This contradiction ends our proof. ∎

The following corollary is an immediate consequence of the previous lemma.

COROLLARY 3.2 : Every partially commutative Lyndon word l has always an initial alphabet reduced to a single letter which is also the minimal letter of l.

Note : The above corollary says that every partially commutative Lyndon word is an admissible pyramid (in the terminology of [14]).

We can now prove our main theorem which was first obtained by Lalonde in [14] using difficult combinatorical constructions involving heaps. It is important to notice that this result unifies in fact the two viewpoints of [14,15] and [9].

THEOREM 3.3 : The two following assertions are equivalent :

1) l is a partially commutative Lyndon word;

2) l is a usual Lyndon word over the Z-code C_i for some $i \in [1, n]$.

Proof : The fact that 1) $\Longrightarrow$ 2) is an obvious consequence of the previous lemma. Let us now prove that 2) $\Longrightarrow$ 1). Let then l be a usual Lyndon word over the Z-code C_i for some $i \in [1, n]$. Using the argument involved in the proof of the previous lemma, it is easy to see that l is strictly less than all its proper transposes. Hence l is primitive and so is any conjugate of l. Therefore we can consider the unique partially commutative Lyndon word l' which is conjugate of l. Note first that l and l' can not be properly transposed since it would follow from definition 3.1 and from the above property that $l < l' \leq l$ which is not possible. According to theorem 2.1, we can write

$$l = z_0 z_1 \ldots z_k \quad \text{and} \quad l' = z_k z_{k-1} \ldots z_0$$

where $z_0, \ldots, z_k$ are non-empty partially commutative words such that $z_i \, I \, z_j$ for every $i, j \in [0, k]$ such that $|i - j| > 1$. But according to the previous corollary, the initial alphabet of l and l' is reduced to the same single letter a_i which is the minimal letter of l. Hence a_i must belong both to the alphabet of z_0 and of z_k, but this is not possible if $k > 2$. On the other hand, the case $k = 2$ is also not possible since l and l' would then be properly transposed. It follows that $k = 1$ and hence that $l = l'$. Thus, l is a partially commutative Lyndon word. This ends therefore our proof. ∎

Notes : 1) When $i > j$, every Lyndon word on the Z-code C_i is strictly greater than every Lyndon word on the Z-code C_j by an obvious first letter comparison. It follows easily that the partially commutative Lyndon words form a complete factorization of $M(A, \vartheta)$ (see also [9,10]).

2) From the above result, $l\,l'$ is clearly a partially commutative Lyndon word when $l < l'$ are two partially commutative Lyndon words with the same first unique letter. Moreover this property can be extended. In fact, if l, l' are partially commutative Lyndon words, then $l\,l'$ is a partially commutative Lyndon if and only if $l < l'$ and the first letter of l' does not commute with l (cf [14] for more details).

As an immediate corollary of the two previous results, we get the following characterization of partially commutative Lyndon words which was first proved in [14].

COROLLARY 3.4 : The two following assertions are equivalent :

1) l is a partially commutative Lyndon word,

2) l is strictly less than any of its proper transposes.

3.3 Other characterizations

This section is devoted to the proof of other characterizations of Lyndon words that were first obtained in [14]. Here our main tool is again the elimination theory.

PROPOSITION 3.5 : The two following assertions are equivalent :

1) l is a partially commutative Lyndon word,

2) l is strictly less that all its non-empty proper right factors.

Proof : Let us first prove that 2) $\implies$ 1). Let $l = uv$ be a non-trivial decomposition of l with $u, v \in M(A, \vartheta) - \{1\}$. Since 2) holds, we can clearly write $l = uv < v < vu$. Using corollary 3.4, we can now conclude that l is a partially commutative Lyndon word.

Now, we prove that 1) $\implies$ 2). Let l be a partially commutative Lyndon word. According to theorem 3.3, there exists $i \in [1, n]$ such that l is a usual Lyndon over the Z-code C_i. Hence we can write $l = c_i^1 \ldots c_i^k$ with $c_i^j \in C_i$ for every $j \in [1, k]$ and l is a usual Lyndon word in the letters c_i^j. Let us now consider a non-empty proper right factor v of l. Two cases can then occur.

a) $IA(v) \neq \{a_i\}$: the initial alphabet of v contains then a letter a_j with some $j > i$. But the first letter of $std(l)$ is a_i. Hence it follows immediately that $std(v) > std(l)$, i.e. that $v > l$.

b) $IA(v) = \{a_i\}$: in this case, v is necessarily equal to a product $c_i^j c_i^{j+1} \ldots c_i^k$ for some $j > 1$. Hence $v > l$ by a classical property of usual Lyndon words.

This ends theorefore the proof of our proposition. ∎

We also have the following characterization that connects directly partially commutative Lyndon words with usual Lyndon words on A.

PROPOSITION 3.6 : The two following assertions are equivalent :

1) l is a partially commutative Lyndon word,

2) $std(l)$ is a usual Lyndon word in A^*.

Proof : Let us first prove that 1) $\Longrightarrow$ 2). Let then l be a partially commutative Lyndon word. Hence there exists some $i \in [1,n]$ such that $l = c_i^1 \ldots c_i^k$ with $c_i^j \in C_i$ for every $j \in [1,k]$ and l is a usual Lyndon word on the letters c_i. It follows immediately that

$$std(l) = std(c_i^1) \ldots std(c_i^k) \qquad (1).$$

Let now u be a proper right factor of $std(l)$. Two cases are now to be considered as in the proof of proposition 3.5.

a) If u respects factorization (1), we have $u = std(c_i^j) \ldots std(c_i^k) = std(c_i^j \ldots c_i^k)$ for some $j > 1$. It follows then immediately from proposition 3.5 that $std(l) < u$.

b) If u does not respect factorization (1), the first letter of u is necessarily a_j with $j > i$. Since the first letter of $std(l)$ is a_i, we have $std(l) < u$.

Hence, we proved that $std(l)$ is always strictly less than all its proper right factors. That turns $std(l)$ into a usual Lyndon word of A^*.

On the other hand, let us prove that 2) $\Longrightarrow$ 1). Let l be a partially commutative word such that $std(l)$ is a usual Lyndon word. According to (Fact), we can write

$$l = c_i \, c_{i-1} \ldots c_j$$

where $i \geq j$ and where $c_k \in C_k^*$ for every $k \in [j,i]$. Suppose now that $i > j$. Since $std(l)$ is a usual Lyndon word, we have

$$std(l) = std(c_i)\, std(c_{i-1}) \ldots std(c_j) \; < \; std(c_j).$$

But the first letter of $std(l)$ is a_i and the first letter of $std(c_j)$ is a_j. Hence the above inequality is not possible. Thus, l belongs to C_i^* for some $i \in [1,n]$. Using theorem 3.3 and relation (1), it is now easy to conclude that l is a partially commutative Lyndon word. This ends therefore our proof. ∎

3.4 Standard factorization

The purpose of this last section is to present the notion of standard factorization in the partially commutative framework. This generalization was first done by Lalonde (see [14]) who proposed the following definition.

DEFINITION 3.2 : Let w be a partially commutative word of $M(A, \vartheta)$ of length ≥ 2. Then w can be factorized in a unique way as a product $w = fn$ (SF) such that :

1) $f \neq 1$,

2) n is a partially commutative Lyndon word,

3) n is minimal among all possible partially commutative Lyndon words such that relation (SF) holds.

The unique pair (f,n) defined by these conditions is then denoted $\Sigma(w)$ and called the *standard factorization* (or *standard decomposition*) of w.

Notes : 1) This definition generalizes clearly the usual definition in the free monoid case (cf [17]).

2) The usual standard factorization is one of the main tool in the construction of the Lyndon basis of the free Lie algebra (see [17]). Again the above result can also

be used for the same purposes in the context of the free partially commutative Lie algebra (see [11,14,16] for more details).

Example : Let us consider again the commutation alphabet which is defined by $A = \{a, b, c, d\}$ and by $\vartheta = \{(a, c), (c, a), (a, d), (d, a), (b, d), (d, b)\}$. We order A as in section 2.3 by $a < b < c < d$. Let now w be the partially commutative word equal to $w = ababcdb$. Then we can find three factorizations for w that respect rules 1) and 2) of definition 3.2 :

$$w = (ababcd)(b) = (ababcb)(d) = (ab)(abcdb).$$

The one with the minimal right factor is the last. Hence we have $\Sigma(w) = (ab, abcdb)$. In the same way, it can be shown for instance that $\Sigma(abcdb) = (abcd, b)$.

We can now give the following proposition that generalizes a classical basic property of usual Lyndon factorization.

PROPOSITION 3.7 : Let l be a partially commutative Lyndon word of length ≥ 2 with a_i as unique initial letter and let $\Sigma(l) = (f, n)$ be its standard factorization. Then f is also a partially commutative Lyndon word with a_i as unique initial letter. Moreover, we have $f < l < n$.

Proof : Let l be a partially commutative Lyndon word with a_i as unique initial letter. Then according to theorem 3.3, we can write

$$l = c_i^1 c_i^2 \ldots c_i^k \qquad (1)$$

where $c_i^j \in C_i$ for every $j \in [1, k]$ and l is a usual Lyndon word in the letters c_i^j. Two cases can now occur :

a) $k = 1$. In this case, $l = c_i^1 = a_i u \in C_i$. Let us consider the standard decomposition $l = fn$ of l. Since $f \neq 1$, f has necessarily a unique initial letter which is a_i. Hence f belongs to C_i and is a partially commutative Lyndon word according to theorem 3.3. Moreover we clearly have $f < l$ since f is a proper prefix of l and $l < n$ by an immediate first letter argument.

b) $k > 1$. We can then consider the usual standard decomposition $l = FN$ of l considered as a word over C_i^* where we have

$$F = c_i^1 c_i^2 \ldots c_i^j \qquad \text{and} \qquad N = c_i^{j+1} \ldots c_i^k$$

for some $j \in [1, k-1]$. Let now u be a proper right factor of l which is a partially commutative Lyndon word. If the initial alphabet of u is not equal to $\{a_i\}$, we clearly have $N < u$ by an obvious first letter argument. On the other hand, if $IA(u) = \{a_i\}$, this means that $u = c_i^r \ldots c_i^k$ for some $r \in [2, k]$. It follows that $N \leq u$ by a classical property of the usual Lyndon factorization. Hence, we proved that (N, F) is in fact the standard decomposition of l. It follows again from a classical property of the usual standard factorization that $F < l < N$. This ends therefore our proof. ∎

Note : The above proof connects also the partially commutative standard factorization with the usual one for words of length ≥ 2 over the alphabet C_i.

4 Conclusion

As a way of concluding this paper, let us present some natural interesting connected problems. A *chromatic partition* of a commutation alphabet (A, ϑ) is a partition $(A_i)_{i=1,n}$ of A such that every subalphabet A_i is totally non-commutative. Then a colored Lyndon word is just a usual Lyndon word on some alphabet

$$C_i = \{\, w = a.u \mid IA(w) = \{a\},\ a \in A_i,\ u \in M(B_i, \vartheta) \,\} \qquad \text{where } B_i = \bigcup_{j=i+1,n} A_j$$

(see [9] for all the details). Hence our paper gives essentially a good word combinatorical definition for colored Lyndon words associated with trivial chromatic partitions where every A_i is reduced to a single letter. In a previous version of this paper, we asked if it was possible to find a "good" characterization of the general family of colored Lyndon words. This problem was solved very recently by Kobayashi (cf [13]) who obtained results for the general case very similar to the one presented here.

An interesting problem would be therefore to generalize Duval's algorithm (see [12]) in the general partially commutative context (without going back to the free case by using theorem 3.3 or proposition 3.6, or Kobayashi's corresponding results) and to see if such results can be used for obtaining new partially commutative pattern matching algorithms.

References

[1] CARTIER P., FOATA D., *Problèmes combinatoires de commutation et de réarrangements*, Lect. Notes in Math., **85**, Springer, 1969

[2] CHEN K.T., FOX R.H., LYNDON R.C., *Free differential calculus IV : The quotient groups of the lower central series*, Ann. Math., **68**, pp. 81-95, 1958

[3] CHOFFRUT C., *Monoïdes partiellement commutatifs libres*, LITP Report 86-20, Paris, 1986

[4] CROCHEMORE M., *String-matching on ordered alphabets*, Theor. Comput. Sci., **92**, pp. 33-47, 1992

[5] CROCHEMORE M., PERRIN D., *Two-way string matching*, J. of the Assoc. of Comput. Machin., **38**(3), pp. 651-675, 1991

[6] DIEKERT V., *Combinatorics on traces*, Lect. Notes in Cpmut. Sci., **454**, Springer, 1990

[7] DUBOC C., *Commutations dans les monoïdes libres : un cadre théorique pour l'étude du parallélisme*, Thèse d'Université, Université de Rouen, 1986

[8] DUBOC C., *On some equations in free partially commutative monoids*, Theor. Comput. Sci., **46**, pp. 159-174, 1986

[9] DUCHAMP G., KROB D., *Lazard's factorizations of free partially commutative monoids*, [in "Proceedings of 18th ICALP"], Lect. Notes in Comput. Sci, **510**, pp. 242-253, Springer, 1991

[10] DUCHAMP G., KROB D., *Factorisations du monoïde partiellement commutatif libre*, C.R.A.S., Série I, **312**(1), pp. 189-192, 1991

[11] DUCHAMP G., KROB D., *The Free Partially Commutative Lie Algebra: Bases and Ranks*, to appear in Adv. in Math..

[12] DUVAL J.P., *Factorizing words over an ordered alphabet*, Journ. of Algorithms, **4**, pp. 363-381, 1983

[13] KOBAYASHI Y., *Lyndon traces and shuffle algebras*, preprint, 1992

[14] LALONDE P., *Contribution à l'étude des empilements*, Thèse, Publications du LACIM, **4**, Montréal, 1991

[15] LALONDE P., *Lyndon Heaps: an Analogue of Lyndon Words in Free Partially Commutative Monoids*, submitted.

[16] LALONDE P., *Bases de Lyndon des algèbres de Lie libres partiellement commutatives*, submitted.

[17] LOTHAIRE M., *Combinatorics on words*, Encyclopedia of Maths., **17**, Addison Wesley, Reading, 1983

[18] PERRIN D., *Partial commutations*, [in "Proceedings of 16th ICALP"], Lect. Notes in Comput. Sci., **372**, pp. 637-651, Springer, 1989

[19] REUTENAUER C., *Free Lie algebras*, To appear

[20] VIENNOT G., *Algèbres de Lie libres et monoïdes libres*, Lecture Notes in Maths., **691**, Springer, 1978

[21] VIENNOT X.G., *Heaps of pieces, I : Basic definitions and combinatorial lemmas*, [in "Combinatoire Enumérative", G. Labelle, P. Leroux, eds.], Lect. Notes in Maths., **1234**, pp. 321-350, Springer, 1986

Parallel Architectures: Design and Efficient Use *

B. Monien, R. Feldmann, R. Klasing, R. Lüling

Department of Computer Science, University of Paderborn, Germany

Abstract. In this paper we want to demonstrate the large impact of theoretical considerations on the design and efficient use of parallel machines. We describe interconnection networks for parallel computers, tools for their efficient use (mapping, load balancing) and the parallelization of a problem which is hard to parallelize (chess programming).

1 Introduction

Over the last years parallel computing has received considerable attention of researchers in science and engineering. Among others, the main reasons for the growing interest are the difficulties to increase the performance of sequential computers due to technical and physical limitations. Furthermore, the availability of cheap mass fabricated microprocessors and communication switches makes it more economical to connect hundreds and thousands of these components than to build highly specialized sequential computers.

Theoretically, such a collection of processors working in parallel can achieve unbounded performance and is therefore suitable to solve problems of all areas of science and engineering. Among these are, for example, computationally intensive problems like weather forecasting and computational fluid dynamics or real time problems like vision and speech recognition.

A number of different architectures for the construction of parallel computers have been proposed. Flynn [18] has given a classification based on the way data and instructions are processed. Conventional von Neumann architectures perform a single operation on one data set per computation step (SISD architecture). The architecture is called SIMD if in each step one instruction is performed on a number of data sets in parallel. This architecture has been realized in a number of *massively parallel computers* like the DAP, Connection Machine and MasPar MP-1 systems. All these systems consist of many very small processing elements (up to 65536 in the case of the Connection Machine) providing large performance for suitable applications.

MIMD-type architectures, which are at present most popular for the design of parallel computer systems, perform a number of different instructions on multiple data streams in one step. In comparison with the existing SIMD systems, the processors used for this architecture are usually much more powerful. In most cases, conventional microprocessors are used. Popular systems of this kind are Intel's Paragon and iWarp systems, NCubes, Alliant FX, the CM-5 of Thinking Machines Corp., the KSR1 of Kendall Square Research and Transputer networks.

* This work was partly supported by the German Federal Department of Science and Technology (BMFT), PARAWAN project 413-5839-ITR 9007 BO

The processors in a MIMD system communicate with each other either via one global memory, as in the case of the Alliant FX computer, or via message passing using an interconnection network. In the case of a message passing parallel system (distributed memory system), the structure of the underlying network decisively effects the efficiency of any algorithm performed on such a system. A number of different network topologies are suggested.

One of the most important networks is the hypercube. It is used in the Intel iPSC, the NCube and also for the Connection Machine CM-2. Other important networks are meshes, used for the Intel Paragon machine and multistage networks used for the Transputer System SC 320, the CM-5 and the Meiko CS-2 machine. At present, most of the realized systems contain less than 1000 processors, but there is an ongoing effort to build MIMD systems performing 1 TFlop per second. It is a well-accepted fact that these large scale parallel computer systems based on today's and shortly forthcoming technologies can only be realized as asynchronous processor networks, working in MIMD fashion, connected by a point-to-point interconnection network.

In this paper we want to demonstrate the large impact of theoretical consideration for the design and efficient use of parallel machines. We describe interconnection networks for parallel computers, tools for their efficient use (mapping, load balancing) and the parallelization of a problem which is hard to parallelize (chess programming).

In section 2 we describe several interconnection networks and their properties. We introduce the "hypercube family" and multistage interconnection networks and focus our attention on measures like diameter, bisection width, network performance, latency time and realizability.

Most application problems have a well defined communication structure and for achieving good efficiency it is necessary to find a good mapping of this communication structure onto the network of the physical machine. In section 3 we discuss the mapping problem, give an overview over some of the results and describe in detail mappings of complete binary trees into grids using different optimization criteria. In section 4 we discuss the load balancing problem. Dynamic load balancing is necessary in the case that load packets are created dynamically and consumed during runtime in an unpredictable way. We give an overview of some theoretical results and describe a load balancing algorithms which was applied successfully on distributed branch and bound algorithms.

The $\alpha\beta$-algorithm is the algorithmic backbone of nearly all game playing programs. Finding a good parallelization was a research topic for many years. This is not surprising since game playing is $PSPACE$ hard in general. In section 5 we describe a parallelization of game tree evaluation which achieved a very good speedup. Our algorithm was used in the distributed chess program Zugzwang which finished 2nd place at the World Computer Chess Championship 1992.

2 Interconnection Networks

An interconnection network should fulfill the following properties:
efficient routing algorithms, no bottlenecks, small diameter, small node degree,

good simulation properties, good fault tolerance properties, large bisection width and good layout into three-dimensional space.

Networks are evaluated also according to network capacity and latency time. These measures are defined as follows : If every processor sends a packet to a random destination at each time step with probability λ, the network capacity is the maximum number λ such that the system is still stable. The latency time is the average delay of a packet in a network running with its full capacity.

The most popular interconnection networks are hypercubes and meshes.

The *d-dimensional mesh* of dimensions $a_1, a_2, \ldots, a_d$, denoted by $[a_1 \times a_2 \times \ldots \times a_d]$, is the graph whose nodes are all d-tuples of positive integers $(z_1, z_2, \ldots, z_d)$, where $1 \leq z_i \leq a_i$, for all i $(0 \leq i \leq d)$, and whose edges connect d-tuples which differ in exactly one coordinate by 1.

Clearly, $[a_1 \times a_2 \times \ldots \times a_d]$ has $a_1 \cdot a_2 \cdot \ldots \cdot a_d$ nodes. Its diameter is $(a_1 - 1) + (a_2 - 1) + \ldots + (a_d - 1)$ and its maximum node degree is $2 \cdot d$, if each a_i is at least three. The *binary hypercube* of dimension n, denoted by $Q(n)$, is the graph whose nodes are all binary strings of length n and whose edges connect those binary strings which differ in exactly one position.

Clearly, a binary hypercube $Q(n)$ has 2^n nodes and, as each node is connected to n edges, a total of $n2^{n-1}$ edges. It is also easy to see that the diameter of the hypercube $Q(n)$ is n, which is the logarithm of the number of its nodes. An illustration of $Q(4)$ is shown in Figure 1.

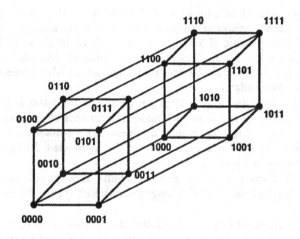

Fig. 1. The binary hypercube of dimension 4

The hypercube fulfills nearly all the properties which we have listed above and which a good interconnection network should have. Its main handicap is its non constant node degree. Cube-connected cycles, butterflies, shuffle-exchange networks and DeBruijn networks are networks of bounded degree sharing many of the hypercube's good properties.

The *butterfly network* of dimension n, denoted by $BF(n)$, is the graph whose nodes are all pairs (i, x), where i is a nonnegative integer $(0 \leq i < n)$ and x is a binary string of length n and whose edges connect (i, x) with both $((i+1)mod\ n, x)$ and with $((i+1)mod\ n, x|i+1)$, where $x|i+1$ denotes the binary string which is identical to x except in the $((i+1)mod\ n)$-th bit.

$BF(n)$ has $n2^n$ nodes and $n2^{n+1}$ edges, for all $n > 2$. Its diameter is $n + \lfloor(n/2)\rfloor$ and it has maximum node degree 4. An illustration of $BF(3)$ is shown in Figure 2.

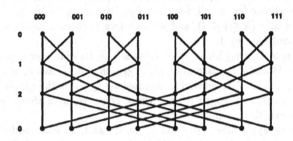

Fig. 2. The butterfly network of dimension 3

The *DeBruijn network* of dimension n, denoted by $DB(n)$, is the graph whose nodes are all binary strings of length n and whose edges connect each string xa, where x is a binary string of length $n - 1$ and a is in $\{0, 1\}$, with the string bx, where $b \neq a$ is a symbol in $\{0, 1\}$, and with the string ax. (An edge connecting xa with $bx, a \neq b$, is called a *shuffle-exchange* edge and an edge connecting xa with ax is called a *shuffle* edge.)

$DB(n)$ has 2^n nodes and $2(2^n - 1)$ edges. (Actually, the latter is a count of the directed edges, namely two from each node. The number of undirected edges will be smaller, as some of the connections are identical). Its diameter is n and it has maximum node degree 4. An illustration of the undirected $DB(3)$ without any self-loops is shown in Figure 3.

Because of lack of space we do not give the definitions of the cube-connected cycle network $CCC(n)$ and the shuffle-exchange network $SE(n)$ here. These can be found in [35].

This whole family of networks is often called the "hypercube family". Their structural similarities can be described best by using the notion of Cayley graphs (see [2]). It is easy to see that by collapsing the columns (these are cycles of length n) the n-dimensional cube-connected cycles and butterfly networks are transformed into a hypercube of dimension n. Thus $Q(n)$ is a factor-graph of $CCC(n)$ and of $BF(n)$. A study of the group representing the Cayley graphs $CCC(n)$ and $SE(n)$ shows, that $SE(n)$ is a coset-graph of $CCC(n)$ and $DB(n)$ is a coset-graph of $BF(n)$ [2]. Furthermore, as it was shown in [15], $CCC(n)$ is a subgraph of $BF(n)$ and $SE(n)$ is a subgraph of $DB(n)$.

These structural similarities allow to transform a large class of synchronous algo-

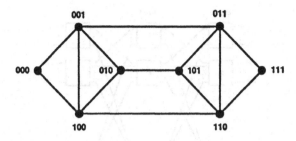

Fig. 3. The DeBruijn network of dimension 3

rithms (the so-called normal algorithms, [29, 45]) from the hypercube to any member of the hypercube family with only a constant time delay. $CCCs, BNs, SEs$ and DBs have constant degree, small diameter ($O(logN)$, N=number of nodes) and high bisection width ($O(N/logN)$) indicating high network performance and low latency time. This makes them well-suited as interconnection networks for parallel computers. Especially the DeBruijn network is an excellent candidate (see also sections 4, 5 of this paper).

A different approach are the multistage interconnection networks. A typical example is the FFT network. The drawing of figure 2 can also be viewed as a FFT network by not identifying the nodes on the first and on the last level. The FFT network of dimension n has two external levels and $n - 1$ internal levels. The nodes on level 0 and level n can be viewed as senders and receivers, respectively. The nodes on the internal levels are switches controlling the traffic from level 0 to n. Networks of this kind have been studied extensively in telephone switching theory [4, 8].

The most important contribution to this field was the theorem of Petersen from 1891 [43], stating that every regular graph of degree $2 \cdot k$ can be decomposed into k regular graphs of degree 2. As a consequence, every bipartite regular graph of degree $2 \cdot k$ can be decomposed into $2 \cdot k$ regular graphs of degree 1 (i.e. into $2 \cdot k$ complete matchings). Using this result, for every $N = m \cdot k$, a $N \times N$ permutation network can be built in three stages consisting of k $m \times m$ switches [2] in the first and third stage and of $k \times k$ switches in the middle stage. Such a network is called Clos network and is shown in figure 4.

Special members of the family of Clos networks are the Beneš and complementary Beneš networks. These networks use only equal-sized switches. The Beneš network is constructed from a Clos network by setting $m = 2$ and $k = \frac{n}{2}$ and recursively decomposing the center stage until the complete network consists of 2×2 switches. The complementary Beneš network results from the recursive decomposition of a Clos network with $m = \frac{n}{2}$ and $k = 2$.

By using Clos networks, efficient reconfigurable architectures for Transputer Sys-

---

[2] We distinguish double sided switches having different input and output links and one sided switches wherein all communication channels are bidirectional and therefore equally treated.

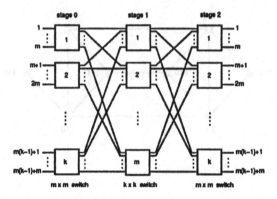

Fig. 4. Construction of Clos networks

tems can be built. The Transputer T800, introduced in 1986, is a microprocessor which integrates a 1.75 MFLOP floating point unit, a 10 MIPS processor, 4 KByte on-chip-memory and 4 serial communication links. These processors can be connected to build a network of any size and a maximal degree of four.

The objective was to design an architecture which allows to configure every graph of degree 4. Two solutions were found and realized [19, 39]. The companies Meiko and Telmat built their systems according to the architecture designed within the ESPRIT project P1085 [39] and the company Parsytec Computer used the approach developed by joint research between Parsytec and the University of Paderborn [19]. The latter approach also uses clustering techniques and minimizes thereby the number of switches and the communication time. A description of this architecture is shown in Figure 5.

The system consists of 20 clusters each containing 16 processors and one single sided switch of 96 links. In a second stage of the network, 8 switches connect the 32 external edges of each cluster.

We use a distributed simulated annealing algorithm to partition the network [11]. This algorithm is able to separate all given graphs arising in practice very quickly, since these graphs consisting of up to 320 nodes have a huge number of short cycles.

To map the 32 external edges onto the switches of the top stage we treat the clusters of the bottom stage as a regular network of degree 32. The graph is partitioned into 8 graphs of degree 4. J. Petersen [43] showed that such a partition exists. The algorithm he presented is based on the construction of an eulerian circle and an alternating coloring of the edges. This algorithm works in linear time for networks whose degree is a power of two, as in our case.

In order to prove that our architecture is able to realize every graph of degree 4 we have to find an appropriate partition into clusters. It is easy to show that every n node graph of degree 4 can be partitioned into clusters of size l with at most $2 \cdot l + 4$ external edges each. In general it is not true that such a partition can be found also with only $2 \cdot l$ external edges per cluster. Note that if a cluster of size l has at

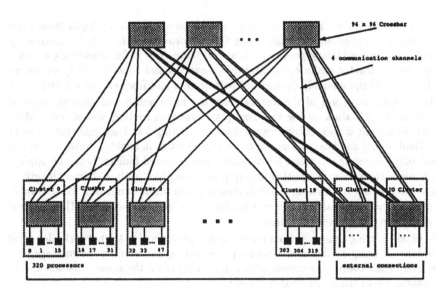

Fig. 5. The parallel computer SC 320

most $2 \cdot l$ external edges, then it contains at least l internal edges and therefore it contains a cycle of length at most l. It is known [6] that for every $l \geq 0$ there exists some $n = n_l$ and some graph of degree four with n_l nodes whose longest cycle has length larger than l. These numbers n_l which arise from the construction are very large. In our system we have to partition graphs of 320 nodes into clusters of size 16 and it is easy to see [6] that a regular graph of degree four has a cycle of length smaller than 12. We conjecture that every graph of degree four with 320 nodes can be partitioned into clusters of size 16 such that every cluster has at most 32 external edges. Whoever can help to prove or disprove this conjecture can be sure to get a reward.

Also in the case of dynamic switches the multistage interconnection networks form a very attractive model. This is due to their low diameter and their large number of distinct paths of shortest length connecting any pair of processor.

Let the switches have $2 \cdot p$ entries. Then the network $Clos(p, n)$ is defined in a similar way as the FFT network of dimension $n - 1$ with the exception that to each switch on level 0 p processors are connected and that the connection structure is not defined by a binary alphabet but by an alphabet with p letters.

The network $Clos(p, n)$ connects $N = p^n$ processors and has n levels. The processors are connected to the switches on level 0.

Each level consists of N/p switches. The longest path has length $2n$ and between any two nodes of distance $2n$ there exist N/p distinct paths of length $2n$. As an example consider the FFT network shown in Figure 2 and let 2 processors be connected to each switch at level 0. Then $p = 2, n = 4, N = 16$ and for any two processors which are not connected by a subnetwork of smaller depth there exist 8 distinct paths of length 8 connecting the two processors. In fact, for arbitrary p and n and for arbitrary processors a and b, these N/p paths connecting a and b can be constructed easily by computing for every a and b and for every switch on the top level the uniquely determined path from a and from b to this switch.

The regular structure of the network and the large number of disjoint paths of shortest length allow to use the concepts of random routing and of local adaptive routing in a very efficient way. Random routing has been introduced by L. Valiant in [54] and has been shown to be very effective in avoiding bottlenecks. Local adaptive routing is useful for networks with bounded buffers. It can be applied whenever there exists more than one link belonging to a path of shortest length to the destination. In this case a link is chosen whose buffer is not full. The improvements gained by local adaptive routing have been demonstrated in [21] for several networks by extensive simulations.

In detail, routing a message from processor a to processor b in the network Clos (p, k) is done by using randomized local adaptive routing and sending the message to a random least common successor of a and b. Afterwards the message is sent deterministically to the destination processor.

There exist several papers concerning analytic estimations of network performance (see [16, 29]) and a lot of experimental work (see [9, 10, 21]). In the following we describe some experiments we carried out in Paderborn.

Table 1 shows the network capacity λ and the latency time for two-dimensional meshes and for Clos networks with switches of size 8. The number of processors varies between 64 and 4096. In order to use the 8 links of each switch 4 processors are connected to each switching node of the mesh. The bisection width leads to a trivial upper bound on the network capacity (see [29]). Table 1 shows up to which percentage this upper bound was reached.

Clos networks have a much better performance than meshes. This remains true even if their large number of switches is taken into account by measuring capacity per switch. However, due to the long wires and to the large number of crossings these networks are hard to realize for larger processor numbers. Extremely advanced technology is needed (leading to high costs) in order to guarantee reliability. In our table we model this behavior by measuring capacity per VLSI-area. According to this measure the mesh is a clear winner. In a more realistic cost model the radio λ/cost would be even smaller for Clos networks since the cost of wires is increasing superlinearly with the length.

For reasons of realizability and reliability, we defined in [37] the so-called *Fat Mesh of Clos network*. A Fat Mesh of $Clos(p, n, r)$ is defined by substituting the r top stages of a complete $Clos(p, n)$ network of height n by a mesh structure. The deletion of the r top stages partitions the Clos network into p^r clusters, each consisting of a Clos network of height $n - r$. Such network has p^{n-r-1} switches in its top stage with p external links each. For $1 \leq i \leq p^{n-r-1}$ the i-th switch of all clusters' top stages are connected by a mesh of dimension $\frac{p}{2}$ resulting in p^{n-r-1} independent meshes.

Then $Clos(p, n, 0)$ is equal to the network $Clos(p, n)$ and $Clos(p, n, n-1)$ is the mesh of dimension $\frac{p}{2}$ with p processors per switching node as defined above. Table

n	r	proc.	latency	λ	λ/bisec	λ/switch·10^4	λ/area·10^7
3	0	64	10.91	0.50782	0.50782	126.955	619.897
3	1	64	11.28	0.34427	0.68854	107.584	896.536
3	2	64	11.70	0.16539	0.66156	103.368	1722.812
4	0	256	11.48	0.43618	0.43618	19.472	33.277
4	1	256	11.97	0.33307	0.66614	17.347	54.211
4	2	256	13.09	0.17228	0.68912	13.459	112.161
4	3	256	13.77	0.06997	0.55976	10.932	182.213
5	0	1024	14.79	0.38770	0.38770	3.365	1.848
5	1	1024	15.41	0.31665	0.63330	3.092	3.221
5	2	1024	15.57	0.17264	0.69056	2.248	7.025
5	3	1024	16.29	0.07889	0.63112	1.540	12.840
5	4	1024	18.28	0.03285	0.52560	1.283	21.386
6	0	4096	19.26	0.34384	0.34384	0.611	0.102
6	1	4096	23.58	0.25006	0.50012	0.488	0.158
6	2	4096	25.23	0.16408	0.65632	0.400	0.417
6	3	4096	27.40	0.08048	0.64384	0.261	0.818
6	4	4096	28.59	0.03659	0.59040	0.178	1.488
6	5	4096	32.32	0.01753	0.56096	0.171	2.853

Table 1. Results for packet routing, $p = 4$

1 shows that Fat Mesh of Clos networks Clos(p, n, r) with some r between 0 and n-1 are attractive network structures if capacity and costs both have to be taken into account. We think that these networks are of even more importance if instead of network capacity a distribution of destinations is considered which favors local communication (see [37]).

3 Mapping

In this section, we will show how to use a distributed system effectively from an applications point of view. Two problems which are important for the performance of the system are first, the mapping of an application onto a distributed system and second, the effective communication within a distributed system. In this context, we want to emphasize how theoretical results can be successfully transferred into practice. Because of lack of space, we concentrate on the *mapping problem*. An overview of common communication strategies is contained in [22]. Two typical problems which arise in this context are *broadcasting* and *gossiping*. In broadcasting, one node has a piece of information which it wants to disseminate to all other nodes in the network. In gossiping, all nodes have a piece of information which they wish to disseminate to all other nodes. The complexity of these problems depends heavily on the available communication mode. This is very important for practical applications, because with changing technology the model must be altered.

But let us take a look now at the *mapping problem*. This problem arises when some application program has to be executed on a distributed system. In order to do this, the process graph of the application must be mapped onto the interconnection structure of the physical computer network. Here, the nodes of the process graph correspond to processes of the application and the edges of the process graph correspond to the communication between the processes, while the nodes in the processor graph correspond to nodes/computing units in the network and the edges in the processor graph correspond to communication links/wires in the network. (In this section, we will assume that the process graph is fixed and known in advance. Then the mapping is static and can be precomputed. If processes are generated dynamically, other methods have to be applied which will be described in Section 4.) Now, the algorithm of the application can be executed on the network by routing communication between the processes via a path between the two processors which the two processes are mapped to. If this mapping is done automatically, the user is provided with a *virtual topology* corresponding to his process graph. As messages must be routed via paths in the network, the maximum length of these paths is crucial for the efficiency of the simulation. Other important issues are the maximum amount of work to be done by a processor, and the number of messages which have to be routed through a single edge in the network. All these notions are captured by the following commonly used, so-called *graph embedding* model for the mapping problem.

Let G and H be finite undirected graphs. An *embedding* of G into H is a mapping f from the nodes of G to the nodes of H. G is called the *guest* graph and H is called the *host* graph of the embedding f. The *dilation* of the embedding f is the maximum distance in the host between the images of adjacent guest nodes. Its *load* factor is the maximum number of vertices of the guest graph G that are mapped to the same host graph vertex. (The *optimum load* achievable is the ratio $\left\lceil \frac{|G|}{|H|} \right\rceil$ of the number of nodes in G and H.) Its *expansion* is the ratio of the number of nodes in the host graph to the number of nodes in the guest, i.e. $|\text{nodes}(H)|/|\text{nodes}(G)|$. When hosts are chosen from a collection C and no graph K in C satisfies $|\text{nodes}(G)| \leq |\text{nodes}(K)| \leq |\text{nodes}(H)|$, then H is called an *optimal* host in C for G. The *edge congestion* of the embedding f is the maximum number of edges that are routed through a single edge of H. (A *routing* is a mapping r of G's edges to paths in H, $r(v_1, v_2) = $ a path from $f(v_1)$ to $f(v_2)$ in H.) When embedding graphs into simple paths, dilation is customarily called *bandwidth*. The bandwidth of a graph is the minimum bandwidth of all such embeddings.

A whole wealth of results is known in the area of graph embeddings, for a survey see e.g. [29, 35, 48]. Many excellent embedding results have been derived for the hypercube which show that the hypercube can simulate many other network structures very efficiently. This is part of the reason why the hypercube is regarded as such a versatile interconnection network and has become so popular. An overview of important results in the area of graph embeddings is displayed in Table 2, for references see [35].

To illustrate some of the techniques which are used in graph embeddings, we concentrate on a very instructive example which is of high practical importance,

Embedding	Cost
X-tree(n) → Q(n+1)	load 1, dilation 2
tree → X-tree [36]	load 16, dilation 3
CCC(l) → CCC(k), l>k [26]	dilation 2 and optimal load
	dilation 1 and almost optimal load
BF(l) → BF(k), l>k	same results as for CCC
CCC(n) → BF(n) [15]	CCC is a subgraph of BF
BF(n) → hypercube	dilation 1 for even n, 2 else
tree → hypercube	load 1, dilation 5
SE(n) → DB(n)	SE is a subgraph of DB
DB(n) → Q(n)	dilation $\lceil \frac{1}{3} n \rceil$
torus → grid	dilation 2
complete binary tree → grid [20]	$\left\lceil \frac{2^{\frac{(k+1)}{2}} - 2}{k-1} \right\rceil + x$, x=2 for even k, 5 else
complete binary tree → hypercube	load 1, dilation 2
d-dim. grid → hypercube	is a subgraph under certain conditions
2-dim. grid → hypercube	dilation 2

Table 2. Embedding results

namely the embedding of complete binary trees into grids. The importance of tree-like structures arises from their use as data and algorithm structures. Although meshes/grids have a small bisection width, they are often used as interconnection networks because of the scalability/extendability of the network and because many numerical algorithms are supported by a mesh structure. Finally, embeddings of graphs into meshes are of special interest in VLSI layout (see e.g. [53]).

First, we want to minimize the dilation of the embedding. To do this, we will construct the embedding in two steps. First, the whole tree is divided into complete binary subtrees each of which is embedded with optimal bandwidth into the line. Then, the collection of these lines is embedded in a suitable way into the grid. This technique was described in detail in [20].

We illustrate the embedding technique for the case of odd k. In this case, $T(k)$ which is defined to be the complete binary tree of height k, has to be embedded into an $(m \times m)$-mesh M where $m = 2^{(k+1)/2}$. We partition $T(k)$ into subtrees $T_0, T_1, \ldots, T_m$ as shown in Figure 6.

The embedding of $T(k)$ into M is now described as follows:

1. First, the tree T_0 is embedded into the $(m/2)$-th row of M, leaving the last node in that row empty.
2. Then, for each i, $1 \leq i \leq m$, the i-th node of level $(k+1)/2$ of $T(k)$, i.e. the root of T_i, is mapped to the i-th node of the $(m/2 + 1)$-st row of M.
3. Finally, for each i, $1 \leq i \leq m$, the tree T_i is embedded into the i-th column of the mesh M, leaving the $(m/2)$-th row of M empty.

The overall embedding scheme is displayed in Figure 7.

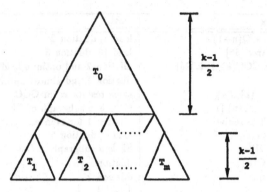

Fig. 6. Partitioning of $T(k)$, k odd

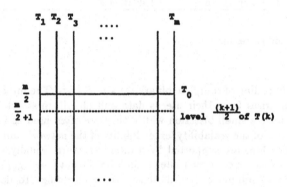

Fig. 7. Embedding of $T(k)$, k odd

We can see from the construction that we do not even need the whole mesh structure, but only a substructure shaped like a "twofold comb".

The dilation of the whole embedding depends largely on the bandwidth of the embeddings of the subtrees, supposing that the leaves of T_0 are (almost) evenly distributed in the line. A straightforward embedding of the complete binary tree $T(\ell)$ into the line, which can also be directly implemented, is the well-known inorder embedding, $f(\alpha) = \alpha 10^{\ell-|\alpha|}$, where the number on the right side is interpreted as a binary number. Using the inorder embedding for the subtrees leads to dilation $2^{(k-3)/2}$ (and edge congestion $(k-1)/2$) for the whole embedding into the grid. This differs significantly from the trivial lower bound

$$\left\lceil \frac{\text{diameter of the mesh}}{\text{diameter of the tree}} \right\rceil = \left\lceil \frac{2 \cdot (\lceil \sqrt{2^{k+1} - 1}\rceil - 1)}{2k} \right\rceil \geq \left\lceil \frac{2^{(k+1)/2} - 2}{k} \right\rceil .$$

The dilation can be improved by using an optimal bandwidth algorithm for embedding the complete binary subtrees in the line as presented in [20]. Basically, the algorithm proceeds by laying out the nodes of the tree roughly from left to right into "blocks" of a certain size. The algorithm also has the required property that it distributes the leaves of the tree almost evenly into the line. Using this embedding for the subtrees in the grid embedding leads to the general result that the complete binary tree $T(k)$ can be embedded into its optimal square mesh with dilation at most

$$\left\lceil \frac{2^{(k+1)/2} - 2}{k-1} \right\rceil + 2 \text{ if } k \text{ is odd,} \qquad \left\lceil \frac{2^{(k+1)/2} - 2}{k-2} \right\rceil + 5 \text{ if } k \text{ is even.}$$

This yields a near optimal embedding in terms of dilation, because the dilation differs only by a factor of $(1+\epsilon)$ from the trivial lower bound stated above. However, the edge congestion is quite enormous.

Now, let us try to minimize the edge congestion of the embedding of the complete binary tree $T(k)$ into the grid. The following recursive construction, due to [56], achieves edge congestion 2 (and dilation $1/3 \cdot 2^{(k+3)/2} + O(1)$) for odd k.

Let $M(k)$ denote the $(m \times m)$-mesh with $m = 2^{(k+1)/2}$. First, embed $T(1)$ into the (2×2)-mesh $M(1)$ such that the two leaves of $T(1)$ are in the same column. In order to embed $T(k + 2)$ into $M(k + 2)$, the embedding f_k of $T(k)$ into $M(k)$ is used. The four subtrees at level 2 of $T(k + 2)$ are embedded as follows. Take $M(k)$ and embed $T(k)$. Then reflect this embedding on its right margin. After that reflect both $M(k)$'s on their lower margin. Thus, an almost complete embedding of $T(k + 2)$ is obtained. Now, levels 0 and 1 of $T(k + 2)$ are embedded into the remaining free four positions such that the nodes at level 1 are again in the same column. It can easily be verified that this embedding of $T(k)$ into $M(k)$ has edge congestion 2 [56].

We have presented above three embeddings of the complete binary tree into the grid, the first one achieving (almost) optimal dilation, the second one achieving (almost) optimal edge congestion, and the third one achieving average dilation and edge congestion. But none of the constructions was able to minimize both of the two cost measures at the same time. So, obviously there is some kind of trade-off between these two measures, but there is no proof so far for this trade-off. For practical purposes, it would be desirable to obtain embeddings which trade off dilation d and edge congestion e over the whole range of values for d and e. Then, the parameters d and e can be chosen such that the overall performance of the distributed system can be minimized.

Another important consideration for practical purposes, which has been largely neglected so far, is that it should be possible to calculate the embedding very quickly on the distributed system itself. Setting up the virtual topology for the user should take as little time as possible. Such an approach has been taken in [7] for embeddings of grids into hypercubes, but many questions of practical interest remain open in this area.

4 Dynamic Load Balancing

To map the computational and communication load of a distributed algorithm onto a processor network, we distinguish between the mapping problem for static workload as described in the previous section and the problem of dynamic load balancing. The dynamic load balancing problem addresses the mapping problem in the case when load packets are dynamically generated and consumed during runtime in an unpredictable way. Depending on the requirements of the application we distinguish two variations of this problem :

- For some applications it is sufficient to balance the workload in a way such that every processor has some load at any time. If this is guaranteed, the relative workload difference between any two processors is negligible. A huge number of load balancing algorithms have been presented for this type of applications. Typical representatives are presented in [30, 31, 38, 52]. Applications requiring such load balancing algorithms are distributed algorithms for game tree evaluation described in the next section, backtracking, distributed operating systems and many others.

- Other applications need a balancing of load that does not only minimize processor idle times, but also keeps the workload of all processors on a nearly equal level according to some measure. Applications for this type of distributed load balancing are distributed best first branch & bound algorithms. Throughout this section we will focus on this type of load balancing problems.

Up to now distributed load balancing algorithms were mostly investigated by direct applications or simulations. Only a small number of theoretical results have been presented in the past. Most of these results concern the so-called packet distribution problem. Solving the packet distribution problem a number of load packets are statically assigned to each processor. The task is to find efficient algorithms distributing these packets equally throughout the network while minimizing load balancing operations. First results were found by Peleg and Upfal [42] for expander graphs and by Plaxton for the hypercube network [44]. In [24] results for the shuffle-exchange, cube-connected-cycles and butterfly network are presented using this model.

A model which is closely related to the dynamic nature of most applications was first used by Rudolph et.al. in [49]. They made no special assumptions about the workload pattern of the underlying distributed computation, but assumed an arbitrary generation and consumption of workload on each processor.

Rudolph et.al. analyzed an algorithm where every processor balances its load with a randomly chosen processor in each time step with a probability inversely proportional to its own load. The algorithm is adaptive to the local load situation but not to local load changes leading to unnecessary activities in case of an already completely balanced network.

It was shown that the expected load of a processor differs from the average load only by a constant factor independent from the network size. Further questions to be studied are the number of migration activities and the exact balancing quality of the algorithm.

Further theoretical results have been gained for the dynamic embedding of trees into different networks. The model assumes a dynamic growing tree as it occurs in backtrack search. This tree is embedded into the network by placing new generated nodes onto neighboring processors in the network. First results for the embedding of dynamically growing binary trees into the hypercube were proved in [5]. They showed that an embedding with optimal load can be reached with high probability. These results were generalized in [28] by embedding arbitrary trees into butterflies and hypercubes. In this paper an embedding strategy with constant dilation was presented. Furthermore questions of edge congestion were taken into account. Both papers use randomization techniques for the placement of newly spanned child nodes. The embedding policy of [28] was also used in [46] for the embedding of backtrack search trees into the butterfly network.

Practical experience with dynamic load balancing algorithms used in many applications have shown that the following principles are useful for the design of effective and efficient algorithms:

- distributed organization
- adaptive behavior to local load changes
- migration activity adaptive to the overall system load

In the following we will present a distributed dynamic load balancing algorithm applied to the solution of combinatorial optimization problems using best first branch & bound methods fulfilling the above requirements. We will also discuss the impact of the network architecture on the efficiency of this load balancing algorithm.

Best first branch & bound algorithms perform a systematic search through the solution space of a combinatorial optimization problem, using heuristic knowledge to cut off parts of the search tree. The sequential algorithm explores in each step a subproblem which may lead to the best solution according to the available knowledge (bound on the cost function). The parallel algorithm performs this search by exploring several nodes of the tree in parallel. As the search tree is in general unpredictable in size and structure, the subtrees have to be mapped dynamically onto the processor network.

The minimal bound of the complete tree is not available to all processors of a processor network. Therefore it is likely that the parallel algorithm explores more nodes than the sequential one does (search overhead). This overhead can be reduced by balancing the subtrees in a way that all processors work on problems having nearly the same bound. Therefore the aim of the load balancing algorithm is to balance the load of all processors according to the value of a weight function w : local load $\rightarrow$ IN. As an example, the quality of a subproblem can be measured according to its distance from the actual upper bound of the solution.

The load balancing algorithm is based on the local balancing between neighboring processors such that the weights of these processors differ at most by δ percent. This leads to a balancing throughout the network in a way that the load between any two processors differ at most by a factor of $(1 + \delta)^d$ if d is the network diameter. Thus, the network architecture plays an important role for the efficiency of our strategy making a very low parameter δ necessary. The average distance in a processor network was already found to be important for the efficiency of most available strategies [31].

To minimize the overhead caused by this algorithm, load balancing is only performed if the local load increases by a constant factor. In case of a load decrease the neighboring processors are informed about this and initiate a load balancing activity if the difference between both processors is larger than a fixed percentual threshold.

As low parameters δ can cause very large migration activities between neighboring processors in case of large load differences, we use a feedback strategy to control δ. This algorithm increases δ in case of increasing migration activities and lowers it otherwise. The parameters of the control process are only dependent on the data size of a load unit and the communication capabilities of the used hardware, thus leading to a simple and effective load balancing algorithm.

We have used this algorithm for the solution of the Traveling Salesman [33] and the Vertex Cover problem [32]. The results presented for the Vertex Cover problem in the table below show that nearly linear speedups could be reached also for very short computation times.

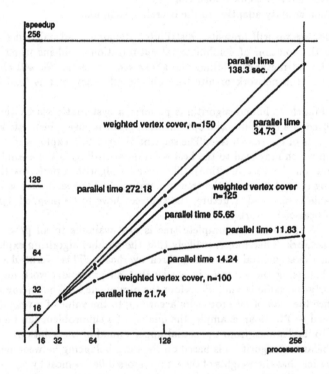

Table 3. Results for the Vertex Cover problem

The used control strategy makes it possible to achieve high speedups also on networks with very large diameter. As an example we could achieve a speedup of

115.98 on a 128 processor ring network for a computation time of 280 seconds. This shows that the presented strategy is also suitable for load balancing on even larger networks if enough parallelism is provided by the problem instance. As this is the case for most branch & bond applications these algorithms can be parallelized in a very effective way using the described strategy.

5 Distributed Game Tree Search

Making decisions based on heuristic information is a common problem in Artificial Intelligence, especially in the area of computers playing games. To calculate its next move computers usually use some lookahead and estimate the consequences of a move, i.e. given a position with the computer to move it generates all successor positions, all successors of these successor positions and so on. In this way a tree, the so called game tree is built up. This game tree may be infinite, however. In order to avoid infinite sequences of moves the computer stops generating successor positions after a certain depth has been reached. At a leave node of the resulting finite game tree the computer estimates the value of that leaf by computing a static evaluation function f that maps the set of legal positions onto the integers. With the help of this function f a function F can easily be defined assigning an integer to every node of the game tree:

$$F(v) := \begin{cases} f(v) & \text{if } v \text{ is a leave} \\ max\{F(w)\} & w \text{ is a successor of } v \\ & \text{and the computer is to move at } v \\ min\{F(w)\} & w \text{ is a successor of } v \\ & \text{and the computer is not to move at } v \end{cases}$$

This corresponds to the fact that whenever the computer is to move it wants to move to the successor position with the highest value and whenever the opponent is to move the computer expects him to choose the successor position that is worst for the computer, therefore choosing the successor with the minimum value.

The $\alpha\beta$-algorithm [51] determines the F - value of the root position and thus determines the best move for the computer, which is the move to one of the successor positions of the root node that has the same F - value as the root. It uses cutoffs to skip the search of large parts of the tree which will not change the value of the root. The $\alpha\beta$-algorithm and a lot of its variations are described in [47]. Figure 8 gives an example how it works. Note that the right successors of the right successors of the root need not be evaluated because the F - value of the successors of the root is guaranteed to be less or equal to 0. A cutoff occurred. Similarly the evaluation of the right successors of the nodes at depth three can be avoided because their F - values cannot have any influence on the F - value of the root. Their evaluation is skipped by a deep cutoff. Thus the $\alpha\beta$-algorithm does not compute the exact F - value for every node of the game tree but instead computes upper or lower bounds whenever these bounds are sufficient to guarantee that the real F - values of these nodes will not have any influence on the F - value of the root.

Knuth and Moore [27] analyzed the $\alpha\beta$-algorithm and showed that in the best case the $\alpha\beta$-algorithm searching a b/d - uniform game tree, i.e. a tree of uniform breadth

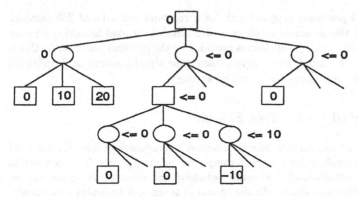

Fig. 8. Searching a Game Tree Sequentially

b and depth d, visits exactly

$$b^{\lceil \frac{d}{2} \rceil} + b^{\lfloor \frac{d}{2} \rfloor} - 1$$

leaves of the tree, whereas all b^d leaves have to be searched in the worst case. Moreover, they showed that the best case arises if for any inner node v the first successor w of v is the best one, i.e. $F(v) = F(w)$. Baudet [3] showed that the $\alpha\beta$-algorithm visits $O((\frac{b}{\ln b})^d)$ leaves, if searching random trees with continuous leaf values, Pearl showed in [41] that random trees with discrete values can be searched by visiting an average of $O(\sqrt{b}^d)$ leaves. In most practical applications heuristics help to keep the number of visited leaves close to $c \cdot (b^{\lceil \frac{d}{2} \rceil} + b^{\lfloor \frac{d}{2} \rfloor})$ for a constant c close to 1.

Therefore a lot of heuristics have been developed to guarantee a good ordering of the successor positions speeding up the search. The most important one is the Transposition Table combined with the Iterative Deepening method. The Transposition Table is a hash table for positions. Whenever some results are computed for a position, these results are stored in the table. Before the search of a subtree with root v is started, the results, if any, stored for v in the Transposition Table are looked up. If v has been searched before, the results obtained from the Transposition Table can be used to speed up the search below v:

1. If v has been searched sufficiently deep before and an exact value has been determined for v, then the search below v may be skipped. This happens if a transposition of moves leads to the same position.
2. If v has been searched sufficiently deep before and a bound has been determined, this bound may speed up the search below v by allowing more cutoffs.
3. If v has been searched before but not to sufficient depth, the best move found for v should be tried first in the new search below v. The move that has been found best during a search to smaller depth is likely to be the best move in the deeper search. Thus it should be searched first in order to come closer to the best case for the $\alpha\beta$-algorithm.

The use of a Transposition Table turns out to be even more successful in combination with a method called Iterative Deepening. For Iterative Deepening one evaluates the game tree to depths 1, 2, 3, ... , $d - 1$ and d instead of directly evaluating the game tree to depth d. Results found during the shallower searches are used to speed up the depth d search. The combination of the two methods is the main reason that today's state of the art game playing programs do not search significantly more than the minimal game tree on the average.

Parallelizations of the $\alpha\beta$-algorithm have to deal with three problems:

1. **Search Overhead:** In parallel $\alpha\beta$-search processors may often search parts of the game tree that would not be searched by the sequential $\alpha\beta$-algorithm. For example processors may start the evaluation of a subtree that is cut off by a left brother evaluated in parallel. In this case the bound necessary to perform the cutoff may not be available on time.

2. **Load:** Iterative Deepening is a crucial point for getting well-ordered game trees. However, for parallel $\alpha\beta$-search, searching many small game trees one after another causes load balancing problems. The game trees are too small to distribute them efficiently over large networks. Our algorithm achieves very good load balancing by using a randomized work stealing method to keep idle times short.

3. **Communication Overhead:** The Transposition Table combined with Iterative Deepening is the most important $\alpha\beta$-enhancement to get the game trees well ordered. Former research in [34] showed that local tables as well as one global table on one processor did not perform well. In order to implement a Transposition Table in our parallel $\alpha\beta$-algorithm we distributed the hash table over the whole network. This leads to the problem of emulating shared memory in a distributed system. Processors that want to access the hash table have to route messages to other processors. We show that in our application access to the distributed hash table can be done very efficiently as long as communication networks with low diameter and large network capacity are used. Another advantage of the distributed hash table compared to the local tables is that the size of the table grows with the size of the system, i.e. the more processors you use, the faster you search, the more entries are provided by your hash table.

Many parallel $\alpha\beta$-algorithms have been implemented until now [17, 34, 40, 50, 23]. More or less they did not cover all of the above three problems at the same time. Several techniques to avoid search overhead and still to keep the processor work load balanced are described in [12, 13, 55]. Results in [14] indicate that our implementation of the distributed hash table works well as long as suitable communication networks are chosen. For the experiments presented in table 4 we used a 256 processor system. The processors were interconnected as a DeBruijn network.

Theoretical analysis of parallel $\alpha\beta$-algorithms turned out to be difficult. Even a load balancing analysis of a work stealing algorithm like our distributed $\alpha\beta$-algorithm has not yet been done. Karp and Zhang [25] and Althöfer [1] presented parallel algorithms that achieve linear speedup. However their results are not of any practical interest, because they assume the depth of the trees to be at least equal to the number of processors.

Table 4 contains the main results from the following experiment: 256 processors ran a set of test positions using hash tables that are available in a distributed system of

	Size of the Hash table						
	1	2	4	8	16	32	64	256
Speedup	119.41	127.38	134.23	135.98	139.58	141.08	144.72	146.13
Search Overhead (%)	45.05	33.96	25.79	23.56	20.81	17.95	14.51	13.03
Load (%)	76.92	76.00	75.71	75.31	75.53	74.68	74.39	73.62
Performance Loss (%)	15.41	15.78	16.33	16.33	16.15	16.33	16.51	16.96

Table 4. 256 Processors Using Hash Tables of Different Sizes

at least $1, 2, 4, \ldots, 64, 256$ processors. The speedup compared to a sequential version is measured as well as the search overhead (the percentage of nodes searched by the parallel algorithm but not by the sequential one), the average processor work load, and the performance loss of a processor in the 256 processor system. The loss of performance of about 16% is caused by message routing. Most of this loss of performance is due to messages used for Transposition Table access. Two effects can be oberserved from table 4: First the parallel $\alpha\beta$-algorithm benefits from the use of larger distributed hash tables. The use of a larger hash table improves the move ordering in the tree and reduces search overhead. Second, the performance is almost constant no matter what hash table size is used. This is due to the fact, that the elements of the hash table are distributed uniformly among all processors for every table size. It can be observed that the processor load is roughly 75%.

	Debruijn	16x16 Torus	16x16 Grid
Speedup	146.13	121.79	107.93
Search Overhead (%)	13.03	19.57	21.39
Load (%)	73.62	72.09	70.59
Performance Loss (%)	15.96	24.22	30.46

Table 5. Parallel game tree search using different networks

Table 5 compares the 256 processor DeBruijn network with the grid and the torus. The main result one can read from table 5 is that message routing in the torus is much more expensive than message routing in the DeBruijn network and message routing in the grid is again much more expensive than in the torus. In the DeBruijn network roughly $\frac{1}{6}$ of the CPU time was necessary to route the messages produced by our parallel $\alpha\beta$-algorithm, in the grid roughly $\frac{1}{3}$ of the CPU time is wasted for this job. This decrease in performance is not due to the smaller network capacity of the gridlike networks. Our experiments have shown that for 256 processors the network capacity of the grid is sufficient for our purposes. The loss of performance is caused only by the time processors have to spend to route the messages. The smaller search overhead of the DeBruijn network version is due to some minor changes in the algorithm exploiting locality. These methods cannot be applied to the gridlike networks since they need networks of smaller diameter. Without these methods the search overhead of the DeBruijn network version is roughly 17%. Therefore the search overhead can be considered almost the same for all of the three networks.

We developed an efficient distributed game tree search algorithm. Our algorithm was used in the distributed chess program Zugzwang which finished 2nd place at the World Computer Chess Championships 1992 showing its usefulness in practice. A theoretical analysis of our distributed game tree search algorithm searching random trees similar to those arising in practice would be of great interest.

References

1. I. Althöfer, *A Parallel Game Tree Search Algorithm with linear Speedup*, to appear in Journal of Algorithms

2. F. Annexstein, M. Baumslag, A.L. Rosenberg, *Group Action Graphs And Parallel Architectures*, SIAM J. Comput. Vol. 19, No. 3, pp. 544-569, June 1990

3. G.M. Baudet, *On the Branching Factor of the Alpha-Beta Pruning Algorithm*, Artificial Intelligence, No. 10, 1978, pp 173-199

4. V.E. Benes, *Mathematical Theory of Connecting Networks and Telephone Traffic*, New York, Acadamy Press, 1965

5. S. Bhatt, J. Y. Cai, *Take a Walk, Grow a Tree*, Proc. of 27th Symposium on Foundations of Computer Science, 1988, pp. 469-478

6. B. Bollobás, *Extremal Graph Theory*, Academic Press 1978

7. M.Y. Chan, F.Y.L. Chin, *Parallelized Simulation of Grids by Hypercubes*, Technical Report TR-90-11, Department of Computer Science, University of Hong Kong, Hong Kong.

8. C. Clos, *A study of non blocking switching networks*, Bell System Technical Journal, March 1953, pp. 407-424

9. W.J. Dally, C.L. Seitz, *The Torus Routing Chip*, Distributed Computing, 1986, no 1, pp. 187-196

10. W.J. Dally, C.L. Seitz, *Deadlock-Free Message Routing in Multiprocessor Interconnection Networks*, IEEE Transactions on Computers, vol. c-36 1987, no. 5, pp. 547-553

11. R. Diekmann, R. Lüling, J. Simon, *Distributed Simulated Annealing and its Applications*, Springer Lecture Notes in Economic Sciences, 1992

12. R. Feldmann, B. Monien, P. Mysliwietz, O. Vornberger *Distributed Game Tree Seach*, Parallel Algorithms for Machine Intelligence and Pattern Recognition, V. Kumar, L.N. Kanal, P.S. Gopalakrishnan (Editors), 1990, Springer Verlag

13. R. Feldmann, B. Monien, P. Mysliwietz *A Fully Distributed Chess Program*, Advances in Computer Chess VI, D.F. Beal (Editor), 1990, pp 1-27

14. R. Feldmann, P. Mysliwietz, B. Monien *Experiments with a Fully Distributed Chess Program*, Heuristic Programming in Artificial Intelligence, 3, J. van den Herik, V. Allis (Editors), 1991, pp 72-87

15. R. Feldmann, W. Unger, *The Cube-Connected Cycles Network is a Subgraph of the Butterfly Network*, Parallel Processing Letters, Vol. 2, No. 1, 1992, pp. 13-19.

16. S. Felperin, P. Raghavan, E. Upfal, *A Theory of Wormhole Routing in Parallel Computers*, ACM Symposium on Foundations of Computer Science, 1992, pp. 563-572

17. Ch. Ferguson, R.E. Korf *Distributed Tree Search and its Application to Alpha-Beta Pruning*, Proceedings AAAI-88, Seventh National Conference on Artificial Intelligence, Vol. 2, 1988, pp 128-132

18. M.J. Flynn, *Very high-speed computing systems*, Proceedings of the IEEE 54, 12, Dec. 1966, pp. 1901-1909

19. R. Funke, R. Lüling, B. Monien, F. Lücking, H. Blanke-Bohne, *An optimized reconfigurable architectre for transputer networks*, Proc. of the 25th Hawaii Int. Conf. on System Science, 1992, col. 1, pp. 237-245

20. R. Heckmann, R. Klasing, B. Monien, W. Unger, *Optimal Embedding of Complete Binary Trees into Lines and Grids*, Proc. of the 17th Int. Workshop on Graph-Theoretic Concepts in Computer Science (WG '91), Lecture Notes in Computer Science 570, Springer Verlag, pp. 25-35

21. H. Hofestädt, A. Klein, E. Reyzl, *Performance Benefits from Locally Adaptive Interval Routing in Dynamically Switched Interconnection Networks*, Proc. of 2nd European Distributed Memory Computing Conference, Lecture Notes in Computer Science 487, Springer Verlag, pp. 193-202

22. J. Hromkovič, R. Klasing, B. Monien, R. Peine, *Dissemination of Information in Interconnection Networks (Broadcasting and Gossiping)*, manuscript, University of Paderborn, 1992, to appear as a book chapter.

23. F.H. Hsu, *Large Scale Parallelization of Alpha-Beta Search: An Algorithmic Architectural Study with Computer Chess*, PhD Thesis, Carnegie Mellon University, Pittsburgh, USA, 1990

24. J. JáJá, K. W. Ryo, *Load Balancing and Routing on the Hypercube and Related Networks*, Journal of Parallel and Distributed Computing, 14, 1992, pp. 431-435

25. R. M. Karp, Y. Zhang, *On Parallel Evaluation of Game Trees*, ACM Symposium on Parallel Algorithms and Architectures 1989, pp 409-420

26. R. Klasing, R. Lüling, B. Monien, *Compressing Cube-Connected Cycles and Butterfly Networks*, Proceedings of the 2nd IEEE Symposium on Parallel and Distributed Processing, 1990, pp. 858-865.

27. D.E. Knuth, R.W. Moore, *An Analysis of Alpha - Beta Pruning*, Artificial Intelligence, No. 6, pp 293-326, 1975

28. T. Leighton, M. Newman, A. Ranade, E. Schwabe, *Dynamic Tree Embedding in Butterflies and Hypercubes*, ACM Symposium on Parallel Algorithms and Architectures, 1989, pp. 224-234

29. F.T. Leighton, *Introduction to Parallel Algorithms and Architectures, Arrays, Trees, Hypercubes*, Morgan Kaufmann Publishers, 1992

30. F. C. H. Lin, R. M. Keller, *The Gradient Model Load Balancing Method*, IEEE Transactions on Software Engineering, Vol. 13, No. 1 January 1987

31. R. Lüling, B. Monien, F. Ramme, *Load Balancing in Large Networks : A Comparative Study*, Proc. of 3rd IEEE Symposium on Parallel and Distributed Processing, Dallas, 1991, pp. 686-689

32. R. Lüling, B. Monien, *Load Balancing for Distributed Branch & Bound Algorithms*, Proceedings of Int. Parallel Processing Symposium 1992, pp. 543-549

33. R. Lüling, B. Monien, M. Räcke, S. Tschöke, *Efficient Parallelization of a Branch & Bound Algorithm for the Symmetric Traveling Salesman Problem*, European Workshop on Parallel Computing (EWPC) 1992, Barcelona

34. T.A. Marsland, M. Olafsson, J. Schaeffer, *Multiprocessor Tree-Search Experiments*, Advances in Computer Chess IV, D.F. Beal (Editor), Pergamon Press, 1986, pp. 37-51

35. B. Monien, I.H. Sudborough, *Embedding one Interconnection Network in Another*, Computing Suppl. 7 1990, pp. 257-282.

36. B. Monien, *Simulating binary trees on X-trees*, Proc. of the 3rd ACM Symposium on Parallel Algorithms and Architectures (SPAA '91), pp. 147-158.

37. B. Monien, R. Lüling, F. Langhammer, *A realizable efficient parallel architecture*, Proc. of 1st Int. Heinz Nixdorf Symposium : Parallel Architectures and Their Efficient Use, Paderborn, 1992

38. L. M. Ni, C. W. Xu, T. B. Gendreau, *Drafting Algorithm - A Dynamic Process Migration Protocoll for Distributed Systems*, Proc. of 5 th Int. Conf. on Distr. Comp. Systems 1985, pp. 539-546

39. D.A. Nicole, E.K. Loyds, J.S. Ward, *Switching Networks for Transputer Links*, Proceedings of the 8th Occam User Group Technical Meeting, 1988, pp. 147-166

40. S.W. Otto, E.W. Felten, *Chess on a Hypercube*, The Third Conference on Hypercube Concurrent Computers and Applications, Vol. 2, 1988, pp 1329-1341

41. J. Pearl *Asymptotic Properties of Minmax Trees and Game Searching Procedures*, Artificial Intelligence, No. 14, 1980, pp 113-139

42. D. Peleg, E. Upfal, *The Token Distribution Problem*, SIAM Journal of Computing, vol. 18, no. 2, April 1989, pp. 229-243

43. J. Petersen, *Die Theorie der regulfen Graphen*, Acta Math. 15 1891, pp. 193-220

44. C. G. Plaxton *Load Balancing, Selection and Sorting on the Hypercube*, ACM Symposium on Parallel Algorithms and Architectures, 1989, pp. 64-73

45. F. Preparata, J. Vuillemin, *The Cube-Connected Cycles : A versatile Network for Parallel Computation*, Communications of the ACM, 24 (5), May 1981, pp. 300-309

46. A. Ranade, *Optimal Speedup for Backtrack Search on a Butterfly Network*, ACM Symposium on Parallel Algorithms and Architectures, 1991, pp. 40-48

47. A. Reinefeld, *Spielbaum-Suchverfahren*, Informatik Fachberichte 200, Springer-Verlag, 1989

48. A.L. Rosenberg, *Graph embeddings 1988: Recent breakthroughs, new directions*, Proceedings of the 3rd Aegean Workshop on Computing (AWOC): VLSI Algorithms and Architectures, 1988, LNCS 319, pp. 160-169.

49. L. Rudolph, M. Slivkin-Allalouf, E. Upfal, *A Simple Load Balancing Scheme for Task Allocation in Parallel Machines*, ACM Symposium on Parallel Algorithms and Architectures 1991, pp. 237-245

50. J. Schaeffer, *Distributed Game-Tree Searching*, Journal of Parallel and Distributed Computing, Vol. 6 No. 2, 1989, pp 90-114

51. J.R. Slagle, J.K. Dixon, *Experiments with some Programs that Search Game Trees*, Journal of the ACM, 16, 1969, pp 189-207

52. J. A. Stankovic, I. S. Sidhu, *An Adaptive Bidding Algorithm for Processes, Clusters and Distributed Groups*, Proc. of 4 th Int. Conf. on Distributed Computing Systems 1984, pp 49-59

53. J.D. Ullman, *Computational Aspects of VLSI*, Computer Science Press, 1984.

54. L.G. Valiant, G.J. Brebner, *Universal Schemes for parallel communication*, Proc. of ACM STOC 1981, pp. 263-277

55. O. Vornberger, B. Monien, *Parallel Alpha-Beta versus Parallel SSS**, Proceedings IFIP Conference on Distributed Processing, North Holland, 1987, pp 613-625

56. P. Zienicke, *Embedding of Treelike Graphs into 2-dimensional Meshes*, Proceedings of the 16th International Workshop on Graph-Theoretic Concepts in Computer Science, Lecture Notes in Computer Science 484, pp. 182-190.

Weighted Closest Pairs*

Michael Formann

Institut für Informatik, Fachbereich Mathematik, Freie Universität Berlin
Arnimallee 2-6, D-1000 Berlin 33, Germany

Abstract. In this paper we study the following *scaling problem*: Given a set of planar starshaped objects with centerpoints (in the kernel), determine the *maximal scaling factor* δ_{max}, such that the objects scaled by δ_{max} about their centerpoints are pairwise disjoint.

We describe a method to compute the maximal scaling factor for n disks with different radii in optimal $\mathcal{O}(n \log n)$ time. In this case the problem can be viewed as computing the *closest pair* of a set of *weighted* points.

We indicate how to extend the method to a broader class of objects, including disks generated by L_p-norms ($1 \leq p \leq \infty$).

A different approach, using the *parametric search technique* is taken to solve the scaling problem for an even wider class, namely starshaped, x-monotone objects. This method runs in $\mathcal{O}(n \log^2 n)$ time. As a corollary of this result we can compute the maximal scaling factor of a set of starshaped polygons (not necessarily x-monotone) with a total number of n edges in $\mathcal{O}(n \log^2 n)$ time.

1 Introduction

In this paper we study the following *scaling problem*: Given a set of n planar starshaped objects with centerpoints (in the kernel), determine the *maximal scaling factor* δ_{max}, such that the objects scaled by δ_{max} about their centerpoints are pairwise disjoint. Note, that the objects do not have to be disjoint initially, and if they are not disjoint, then the scaling factor would be less than 1. Note further, that for non-starshaped objects there may be more than one (local) maximum and therefore we restrict our studies to starshaped objects.

Clearly δ_{max} can be computed in $\mathcal{O}(n^2)$ time, by taking the minimum of all $\binom{n}{2}$ pairwise maximal scaling factors. (It is assumed, that the computation of the maximal scaling factor of two objects is a primitive operation that can be done in $\mathcal{O}(1)$ time.) The goal of this paper is to beat the $\mathcal{O}(n^2)$ time bound.

If all the objects considered are unit-disks, to be scaled around their centers, then we are faced with the so-called *closest pair problem*, that is, to determine the closest distance between any pair of points (here between pairs of centers of the disks). This is a well-studied fundamental problem of computational geometry (cf. [HNS90], [SH75], [BS76]). In our case, where the disks may have different radii, we can view the problem as a *(multiplicatively) weighted closest pair problem*. Furthermore different object shapes allow for different *distance functions*. Another related problem is finding the closest pair among a set of objects (cf. [BH92], [For87], [Sha85], [Yap87]).

* This work was partially supported by the ESPRIT Basic Research Action of the European Community under contract No. 7141 (project ALCOM II).

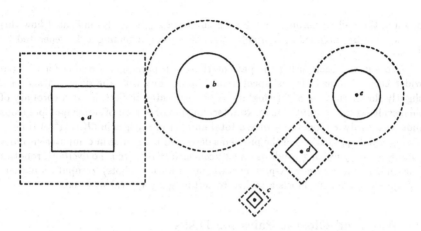

Fig. 1. Five objects (solid) scaled by $\delta_{\max}$ (dashed)

Figure 1 illustrates the aforementioned closeness concepts. Five objects are drawn in solid lines in their original size. The $\delta_{\max}$-scaled objects are shown in dashed lines (here $\delta_{\max} = 2$). The square around a and the disk around b are the weighted closest pair, points c and d are the closest pair of points (in the Euclidean metric) and the shortest distance between any pair of objects occurs between the square around d and the disk around e.

In principle, we could determine the maximal scaling factor via a Voronoi diagram approach. For example we are given a set of disks with different radii. From the center p of a disk we measure the weighted distance from p as

$$d_p(x) := \frac{\| p - x \|}{r_p},$$

where r_p denotes the radius of the disk around p. The type of Voronoi diagram induced by these distance functions, called the *(multiplicatively) weighted Voronoi diagram*, is discussed in full detail in [AE84]. The bisector of two disks with centers p, q and weights r_p, r_q will be the set of points in the plane that have equal weighted distance to p and to q. We define a pair p, q as *closest pair*, if it minimizes the shortest weighted distance to its bisector among all pairs. Exactly the closest pairs of $\delta_{\max}$-scaled disks will touch and can be extracted from the Voronoi diagram. This approach does not lead to an efficient solution, because the Voronoi diagram might have quadratic complexity (cf. [AE84]).

In Sect. 2 we will describe a method to compute the maximal scaling factor in optimal $\mathcal{O}(n \log n)$ time for disks with different radii. The basic idea is as follows: In a preprocessing step we compute an over-estimate $\delta \geq \delta_{\max}$ for $\delta_{\max}$. Clearly, if $\delta > \delta_{\max}$ then there are intersections in the set of δ-scaled objects. We ensure, that after the preprocessing step only a linear number of pairs of the δ-scaled objects will intersect. We detect these intersections in $\mathcal{O}(n \log n)$ time by a standard sweep-technique and compute the related pairwise maximal scaling factors. The minimum of δ and these $\mathcal{O}(n)$ numbers will be the number $\delta_{\max}$. It is also indicated how this method can be extended to a broader class of objects, including disks generated by L_p-norms ($1 \leq p \leq \infty$).

Another approach, using the parametric search paradigm, working for an even wider class of objects (starshaped, x-monotone), but with the disadvantage of a slightly slower runtime of $\mathcal{O}(n \log^2 n)$ will be presented in Sect. 3. As a corollary of this result we can compute the maximal scaling factor of a set of starshaped polygons (not necessarily x-monotone) with a total number of n edges in $\mathcal{O}(n \log^2 n)$ time.

Potential applications of the problems described here, arise in computer graphics (simultaneously resizing windows on a screen such that there is no overlap), robotics (maximizing the secure workspace of stationary rotating robots), computational cartography (maximizing labels attached to certain geographical sites) etc.

2 Weighted Closest Pairs for Disks

In this section we will describe how to compute the maximal scaling factor for a set of (topologically open) disks with (possibly) different radii. We always assume that the all the disks will be scaled around their centers. Firstly we define a certain property, the *halfmoon property* for disks. Then we show that if that property holds for a set of disks, then the number of intersecting pairs of disks is only linear. We will then present an algorithm to preprocess a set of disks — we scale them — such that the halfmoon property is fulfilled. On the way we describe how we glue everything together to an algorithm for computing the maximal scaling factor.

Let us now start with a definition.

Definition 1. Let $\mathcal{D} = \{D_1, D_2, \ldots, D_n\}$ be a set of disks in $\mathbb{R}^2$. We say, that $\mathcal{D}$ fulfills the *halfmoon-property* if no disk in $\mathcal{D}$ cuts the vertical diameter of another disk of $\mathcal{D}$. For a disk $D_i \in \mathcal{D}$ we will call the two parts of D_i to the left and to the right of the vertical diameter *left* and *right halfmoon* of D_i and denote them by D_i^- and D_i^+ resp.

We sum up some simple facts about a set of disks that fulfills the halfmoon-property.

Observation 2. *Let $\mathcal{D} = \{D_1, D_2, \ldots, D_n\}$ be a set of disks with the halfmoon property:*

(1) No two left and no two right halfmoons intersect.
(2) No disk is completely contained in another one.
(3) No point in the plane is covered by more than 2 disks of $\mathcal{D}$.

Proof. (1) and (2) are immediately clear. Note, that Fact (1) is equivalent to the halfmoon property. If (3) is violated, then we have a point in two left halfmoons or in two right halfmoons — a contradiction to (1). □

Note, that by Fact (2) all intersections are proper. We are now ready to present our main lemma:

Lemma 3. *The number of intersecting pairs in a set of n disks that fulfills the halfmoon property is at most $3n - 6$.*

Proof. Let $\mathcal{D} = \{D_1, D_2, \ldots, D_n\}$ be a set of disks with the halfmoon property. We will show, that the graph G formed by putting vertices at the centers of the disks and drawing edges by straight line segments between centers of intersecting disks is plane. Then the claim follows.

Look at two embedded edges $\overline{ab}$ and $\overline{rs}$ with disjoint endpoints. There must be a point c on $\overline{ab}$ that is contained in the disk around a and also in the disk around b by definition of the edges. Similarly, there is a point t on $\overline{rs}$ that is contained in the disks around r and s. The points c and t must be distinct, otherwise we have found a point $c = t$ that is contained in four disks, a contradiction to Observation 2(3). Now draw the perpendicular bisector g between c and t. s and c must lie on different sides of g, otherwise the disk around s contains c and therefore c is contained in three disks. Similarly r and c must lie on different sides of g. Therefore s, t and r lie on the same side of g. By mirrorsymmetric arguments a, b and c lie on the other side of g. Therefore the segments $\overline{ab}$ and $\overline{rs}$ do not cross. □

In the proof of the Lemma above, we have shown that the "intersection graph" of a set of disks with the halfmoon property is planar. The converse implication is also true, Koebe [Koe36] showed that any planar graph can be realized as the "contact graph" of a set of nonoverlapping disks in the plane.

An alternative proof of Lemma 3 may be obtained via power diagrams (see [Aur87] for the apparatus of power diagrams). Here the distance functions $d_p(x) := \|\, p - x \,\| - r_p^2$, the so-called *power* of a point x with respect to a site p, define the Voronoi diagram. Note, that the regions of two intersecting disks are neighbours in the power diagram because of Observation 2(3), only for the centers of the two intersecting disks the power of the points in the intersection is negative. Therefore the edges of G are a subgraph of the dual graph of the power diagram, which is planar.

Let us now turn our attention to the description of our main algorithm. Similarly to the halfmoon property we could define two properties as follows.

Definition 4. Let $\mathcal{D} = \{D_1, D_2, \ldots, D_n\}$ be a set of disks in $\mathbb{R}^2$. We say, that $\mathcal{D}$ fulfills the *left (right) halfmoon-property* if no two left (right) halfmoons in the set $D_1^-, D_2^-, \ldots, D_n^-$ ($D_1^+, D_2^+, \ldots, D_n^+$) intersect.

Similarly to the definition of the maximal scaling factor $\delta_{\max}$ we define the *maximal left scaling factor* $\delta_{\max}^-$ of a set of disks as the maximal number such that in the set of $\delta_{\max}^-$-scaled disks no two left halfmoons intersect, $\delta_{\max}^+$ is analogously defined as the *maximal right scaling factor*. Clearly $\delta_{\max} \leq \min\{\delta_{\max}^-, \delta_{\max}^+\}$ and if we scale the disks by $\min\{\delta_{\max}^-, \delta_{\max}^+\}$ then the left and the right halfmoon properties and therefore also the halfmoon property itself hold for the scaled disks. After that scaling process we can run a standard intersection reporting algorithm (cf. [BO79]) that will output at most $3n - 6$ intersecting pairs of disks, since the intersection graph G is planar as proven in Lemma 3. Then we take the minimum of those pairwise scaling factors and of $\min\{\delta_{\max}^-, \delta_{\max}^+\}$. This number clearly is $\delta_{\max}$ the desired output of our algorithm.

So far we have reduced our original problem to that of computing the maximal left and right scaling factors. Without loss of generality we describe only the algorithm for computing the maximal right scaling factor δ^+_{max}. The basic idea of that algorithm is as follows: We start with an initial assumption about δ^+_{max}, say we set $\delta := +\infty$. Then we sweep in the plane with a vertical line from left to right. Whenever we meet a centerpoint of a disk D_i, we insert that disk into the vertical structure. In the following we always assume that all the disks are scaled by the current δ of the algorithm. If the right halfmoon of the newly inserted disk has intersections with right halfmoons of disks inserted before, we decrease δ so that the intersections disappear. When all disks have been processed the algorithm stops and outputs $\delta^+_{max} = \delta$.

In order to work correctly our algorithm will maintain the following two invariants:

Invariant 1: All δ-scaled disks, whose right halfmoon intersect the sweepline, are stored in the vertical structure (sweepline-status), ordered by the y-coordinates of their centerpoints. All δ-scaled disks, whose right halfmoon is to the right of the sweepline, are not stored in the vertical structure.

Invariant 2: δ always equals the maximal right scaling factor of the subset of disks, whose centers lie to the left of the sweepline.

It is clear, that we have to insert a disk into the vertical structure exactly when the sweepline passes over the centerpoint of that disk. Invariant 1 allows, that disks whose right halfmoon does no longer cut the sweepline, remain in the sweepline. Note that Invariant 1 is not destroyed, if we decrease δ.

The only problem appears, when a new disk D_i is inserted into the sweepline. Its right halfmoon may intersect other right halfmoons already processed and we have to decrease δ, since Invariant 2 is violated. Note, that the intersections of the already inserted right halfmoons with the sweepline are disjoint, and that therefore their ordering along the sweepline is well-defined and is clearly the same as the vertical order of the centerpoints of the disks. We detect intersections of the new right halfmoon during its insertion and handle them as follows:

Look at the upper neighbour D_j of D_i in the vertical structure, three cases may appear:

1. D_j lies completely behind the sweepline. Then it is clear that $D_j^+ \cap D_i^+ = \emptyset$ and we may delete D_j from the vertical structure.
2. $D_j^+ \cap D_i^+ = \emptyset$. Then it is clear, that D_i also does not cut any right halfmoon which is in the vertical structure and whose centerpoint is above the centerpoint of D_i.
3. $D_j^+ \cap D_i^+ \neq \emptyset$. Then we compute the pairwise maximal right scaling factor of D_j^+ and D_i^+. This number δ_{ij} must be lower than the current δ and we set $\delta := \delta_{ij}$ and rescale all disks.

   Two subcases may appear:

   (a) D_j^+ now lies completely behind the sweepline. We proceed as in Case 1.
   (b) D_j^+ still cuts the sweepline. We proceed as in Case 2.

After the process, D_i might have a new upper neighbour (in Cases 1 and 3a) and we have to repeat the process until either Case 2 occurs, or D_i does no longer have an upper neighbour. Then a similar processing is done for the lower neighbour of D_i. Finally we will have established Invariant 2 again.

As already said, we start the sweeping process with $\delta := +\infty$. If the sweepline is to the left of the leftmost centerpoint, then the vertical structure is empty and if we scale the disks by $+\infty$ Invariant 2 holds. During the algorithm δ will only be decreased when required (Case 3) and only so much, that all intersections of right halfmoons disappear and still two right halfmoons will touch and therefore Invariant 2 holds. By Invariant 2 it is clear that the final value of δ equals $\delta^+_{\max}$. Note, that for our purpose it is not necessary to compute the pairwise maximal right scaling factor in Case 3. In an actual implementation we could compute the pairwise maximal scaling factor instead, since finally we are interested in the maximal scaling factor and not in the maximal right scaling factor. Clearly, Invariant 2 has then to be modified appropriately.

Lemma 5. *The maximal right scaling factor $\delta^+_{\max}$ of a set of n disks in the plane can be computed in $\mathcal{O}(n \log n)$ time.*

Proof. By the discussion above, our algorithm computes $\delta^+_{\max}$. We only have to analyze the runtime. If we use some appropriate balanced tree scheme for the vertical structure then an insertion or deletion of a disk can be done in $\mathcal{O}(\log n)$ time. But when we process an inserted disk in order to maintain the invariants, we may have to look at many other disks.

The amount of work done for one of these disks is $\mathcal{O}(\log n)$ (neighbour-finding and computing the pairwise maximal right scaling factor). If the disk is deleted we charge that work to the deletion. At most two disks — the topmost and bottommost processed — are not deleted. That work is charged to the insertion.

Now insertions and deletions cost at most $\mathcal{O}(\log n)$ time. Note, that every disk is inserted exactly once and deleted at most once. Therefore the total runtime of our algorithm is $\mathcal{O}(n \log n)$. □

We have now described all ingredients to solve the weighted closest pair problem and sum up in the following Theorem.

Theorem 6. *The maximal scaling factor of a set of n disks can be computed in $\mathcal{O}(n \log n)$ time and $\mathcal{O}(n)$ space.*

Since our problem is a generalization of the closest pair problem, the $\Omega(n \log n)$ lower bound for this problem in the algebraic computation tree model (see [PS85]) also applies in our more general setting. It is easy to see, that the space requirement of our algorithm is $\mathcal{O}(n)$.

Another $\mathcal{O}(n \log n)$ time solution for the weighted closest pair problem is (implicitly) given in [ERW89]. This approach is not extendible to other object shapes as we will do it in the following for our solution.

Weighted Closest Pairs for Generalized Disks. The method developed above for disks can be used for other objects shapes. In the following we demonstrate this for unit-disks generated by L_p-norms ($1 \leq p \leq \infty$) to be scaled around their centers.

So our setting is as follows: Given a set of n convex planar objects, each of them being a disk of some L_p-norm ($1 \leq p \leq \infty$) scaled by some positive number (weight) — henceforth called *bodies* — determine the *maximal scaling factor* δ_{max}, such that the bodies scaled by δ_{max} are pairwise disjoint.

Note that different bodies are allowed to be disks from different L_p-norms and to have different weights. In a typical robot environment for example, some robots could be abstracted as ordinary disks (L_2), others could be squares (L_1, L_∞) etc. (see Fig. 1).

As in the case of disks, we again define a halfmoon property, where each body is divided into a left and a right halfmoon by a vertical line through the centerpoint of the body. Unfortunately it is no longer true, that the straight line embedding of the "intersection graph" for a set of bodies with the halfmoon property is plane, but it is still planar, i.e. there is some other embedding of the graph which is crossing-free, but the straight line embedding has crossings. So again, the number of intersecting pairs of bodies is only linear. These intersections can be determined by a plane-sweep algorithm, the minimum of only linearly many pairwise scaling factors could be computed etc. similarly as demonstrated for disks.

In the remainder of this section we show only the planarity result. Note that analogous facts as in Observation 2 hold also for bodies.

Lemma 7. *Let* $\mathcal{B} = \{B_1, B_2, \ldots, B_n\}$ *be a set of bodies with the halfmoon property. The graph G with vertex set $\mathcal{B}$ and edges between any pair of intersecting bodies is planar.*

Proof. We place the vertices at the centerpoints of the bodies. Let us now take a look at some right (w.l.o.g.) halfmoon B_i^+ of some body B_i. By the fact that no two left and no two right halfmoons intersect and that all bodies are convex, it follows that the intersections of B_i^+ with left halfmoons of other bodies all lie in disjoint open horizontal stripes and to the right of the vertical diameter. A similar argument holds for the left halfmoon B_i^-. If we now look at the relative complement of $\{B_j \mid 1 \leq j \leq n, i \neq j\}$ with respect to B_i

$$\text{residue}(B_i) := B_i \setminus \{B_j \mid 1 \leq j \leq n, j \neq i\}$$

we observe that this is a simply connected area containing the vertical diameter.

As already stated, the straight-line embedding of the edges of G is not plane, i.e. there may be intersections. So we will give another layout for the edges. Any edge will be laid out completely in the two bodies, whose intersection defines it. So we split an edge going from B_i to B_j into three parts, the part which will be laid out in residue(B_i), the part in $B_i \cap B_j$ and the part in residue(B_j). The first parts of all edges with one endpoint in B_i can now be easily laid out star-like in residue(B_i) since this is a simply connected area and no intersections with other edges will appear. By symmetry, the third part of an edge can be laid out like its first part. The second part of an edge going from B_i to B_j is the only edge that must be laid out in $B_i \cap B_j$ and is therefore crossing-free. It can easily be laid out to link the two other parts. $\qquad\square$

At the end of this section we remark, that the methods introduced in this section can be extended further. This is demonstrated in the forthcoming thesis of the author [For93].

3 Applying the Parametric Search Technique

In this section we apply the parametric search paradigm invented in [Meg83] to solve the weighted closest pair problem in $\mathcal{O}(n \log^2 n)$ time for objects that are starshaped and x-monotone. Firstly we use the basic technique invented by [Meg83] which enables us to solve the weighted closest pair problem in $\mathcal{O}(n \log^3 n)$ time and then we refine the method using improvements of [Col87] and we trim down one log-factor resulting in $\mathcal{O}(n \log^2 n)$ time. We assume that the scaling center is some point in the *kernel* of the object and that object intersections for some fixed scaling factor can be found by standard intersection techniques as invented by [SH76] and extended to x-monotone objects by [Sha85]. Furthermore we require that the computation of the pairwise maximal scaling factor of two objects is a $\mathcal{O}(1)$ time operation.

Basic Technique. Suppose we have identified an interval $[\delta_l, \delta_r)$ such that (1) the maximal scaling factor falls into that interval, i.e. $\delta_{max} \in [\delta_l, \delta_r)$, and (2) for any $\delta \in [\delta_l, \delta_r)$ the sorted sequence of the leftmost and rightmost points (x-extreme points) of the set of δ-scaled objects is the same. In that case, we can easily find the maximal scaling factor δ_{max} by a slight modification of the intersection detection algorithm in [SH76] as follows:

We start with $\delta := \delta_r$ and whenever the intersection detection algorithm reports an intersection, instead of stopping, we remove the intersection by computing the pairwise maximal scaling δ_{AB} factor of the two objects A and B that intersect, decrease δ to δ_{AB} and continue the algorithm. Since intersections are only detected, when an object is inserted into or deleted from the sweepline only $2n$ such corrections of δ happen and the whole algorithm runs in $\mathcal{O}(n \log n)$ time. If an intersection is found during an insertion, this can be interpreted as an advancing of the sweepline and in case of a deletion as a withdraw. The crucial point is that the intersection algorithm still works because the insertion/deletion order of the objects does not change.

So our goal is to identify an interval with the desired properties (1) and (2). This is done with the help of the parametric search paradigm. We will try to find the sorted sequence of the leftmost and rightmost points of the δ_{max}-scaled objects for the yet unknown maximal scaling factor δ_{max}.

For an object A denote by $\mathrm{left}(A)$ the absolute difference in x-coordinates of the center of A and its leftmost point. Let A and B be a pair of objects. If A is to the left of B and $\mathrm{left}(A) \geq \mathrm{left}(B)$ then for any scaling factor $\delta \in (0, +\infty)$ the ordering of the leftmost points of the two δ-scaled objects is "A before B". By $\mathrm{dx}(A, B)$ denote the difference in x-coordinates of the centers of A and B. If A is to the left of B and $\mathrm{left}(A) < \mathrm{left}(B)$ then for any scaling factor

$$\delta \in \left(0, \frac{\mathrm{dx}(A, B)}{\mathrm{left}(B) - \mathrm{left}(A)}\right)$$

the ordering of the leftmost points of the two δ-scaled objects is "A before B" and for any

$$\delta \in \left(\frac{\mathrm{dx}(A, B)}{\mathrm{left}(B) - \mathrm{left}(A)}, +\infty\right)$$

the ordering is "B before A". The value

$$\frac{dx(A, B)}{\text{left}(B) - \text{left}(A)}$$

is called the *critical point (value)* of the leftmost point of A and the leftmost point of B. Analogously, we define critical values for the other combinations of x-extreme points, i.e. leftmost/rightmost, and rightmost/rightmost.

For any critical point δ we can decide in $\mathcal{O}(n \log n)$ time, whether the maximal scaling factor δ_{max} is smaller or greater than δ by running the intersection detection algorithm for the critical value δ. Namely, if there is an intersection in the set of δ-scaled objects then $\delta_{max} < \delta$ and if there are no intersections then $\delta_{max} \geq \delta$. We then also know the order of the leftmost points for the two δ_{max}-scaled objects, since we know on which side of the critical value of A and B the maximal scaling factor δ_{max} lies.

Let us run a parallel sorting algorithm on $2n$ processors in $\mathcal{O}(\log n)$ parallel time (cf. [Col88]), to find the sequence of the x-extreme points of the δ_{max}-scaled objects. Initially set $\delta_l := 0$ and $\delta_r := +\infty$. After one step of the parallel algorithm, the $2n$ processors want to know the result of $\mathcal{O}(n)$ comparisons between x-extreme points of pairs of objects, or with other words they want to know whether δ_{max} is to the left, or to the right of the corresponding critical points. We compute sequentially these $\mathcal{O}(n)$ corresponding critical points, sort them, and filter out those that fall into the interval $[\delta_l, \delta_r)$. (For the others we already know the outcome of the comparison.) On that subset of critical values we do a binary search for the value δ_{max} by intersection tests as described above. In that way the interval $[\delta_l, \delta_r)$ is successively diminished. Once we have finished the binary search, we know the result of all $\mathcal{O}(n)$ comparisons and continue the parallel sorting algorithm. The next parallel step will give us again $\mathcal{O}(n)$ comparisons (critical values resp.) and again we do a binary search and so on. Finally the algorithm will stop with an interval $[\delta_l, \delta_r)$, fulfilling (1) and (2).

The parallel sorting algorithm is simulated sequentially, since the reason for using it is simply to batch blocks of $\mathcal{O}(n)$ comparisons to be answered later, and therefore runs in $\mathcal{O}(n \log n)$ sequential time. In each of the $\mathcal{O}(\log n)$ parallel steps we sort n elements in $\mathcal{O}(n \log n)$ time, then we do a binary search with $\mathcal{O}(\log n)$ steps. In each of this binary steps we run an intersection detection algorithm with $\mathcal{O}(n \log n)$ runtime. Thus we have the following Lemma:

Lemma 8. *The maximal scaling factor δ_{max}, such that a set of n starshaped, x-monotone objects, scaled by δ_{max}, does not intersect, can be computed in $\mathcal{O}(n \log^3 n)$ time.*

Using Cole's Improvement of Parametric Search. Let us now show how the time-bound in Lemma 8 can be improved by one log-factor to $\mathcal{O}(n \log^2 n)$. The tools to reach this target have been developed by [Col87]. We briefly review his ideas and show how they apply in our case.

The basic idea is, that not all of the comparisons to be made in the sorting network, have to be evaluated immediately at that stage when they appear, but they can be postponed to a later stage. This is done by assigning exponentially decreasing (according to the stage) weights to the comparisons. The rule, which we have to follow, is, that at every stage at least one weighted half of the comparisons not yet evaluated, has to be evaluated.

It is shown in [Col87], that for a sorting network with *width* (also called *degree of parallelism*) $n/2$ and *depth* $f(n)$ such a "delayed" sorting algorithm sorts n numbers in $\mathcal{O}(f(n) + \log n)$ stages.

Recall the basic idea of parametric search: Essentially we run a parallel sorting algorithm which, at every stage, wants to know the outcome of $\mathcal{O}(n)$ comparisons. We compute the $\mathcal{O}(n)$ related critical points, sort them and by binary search we find one critical value δ, where the transition between intersecting and non-intersecting happens. The binary search forces $\mathcal{O}(\log n)$ intersection tests, each at the a cost of $\mathcal{O}(n \log n)$, which results in a runtime of $\mathcal{O}(n \log^2 n)$ at each of the $\mathcal{O}(\log n)$ stages and a total runtime of $\mathcal{O}(n \log^3 n)$.

Now, the modification of this algorithm, based on [Col87], is done as follows: At every stage the algorithm wants to know the outcome of $\mathcal{O}(n)$ weighted comparisons. We now don't have to supply the algorithm with the outcome of all comparisons, because the algorithm is satisfied with at least a weighted half of the answers. We provide him with these answers in the following way. We sort the $\mathcal{O}(n)$ comparisons according to the related critical values. We find the "middle one" critical value δ, where the sum of the weights to the left and to the right of that middle one critical value are both approximately one half of the total sum of the weights. We make an intersection test for δ. If the set of objects scaled by δ does not intersect, then for the weighted half of critical values to the left, we immediately know the outcome of all their related comparisons. And if the set of δ-scaled objects does intersect, then for the weighted half of critical values to the right we immediately know the outcome of all their related comparisons.

To be precise, let $\delta_1, \delta_2, \ldots, \delta_k$, $1 \leq k \in \mathcal{O}(n)$ the sorted of critical values and let $w_1, w_2, \ldots, w_k$ be the set of weights assigned to the comparisons by Cole's algorithm. Let

$$W := \sum_{l=1}^{k} w_l$$

be the total sum of the weights and

$$m := min\left\{ j \,\middle|\, 1 \leq j \leq k, \ \sum_{l=1}^{j} w_l \geq \frac{W}{2} \right\}$$

be the index of the "middle one" critical value. If the set of objects scaled by δ_m does not intersect, then this holds for $\delta_1, \delta_2, \ldots, \delta_m$ and the sum of the weights of this subset is not less than $W/2$. If the set of objects scaled by δ_m does intersect, then this also holds for $\delta_m, \delta_{m+1}, \ldots, \delta_k$ and again the sum of the weights of this subset is not less than $W/2$. In any case our main sorting algorithm can be satisfactory supplied with at least a weighted half of the comparisons.

If we now use the sorting network of [AKS83] which has width $n/2$ and depth $\mathcal{O}(\log n)$, delay it as described in the previous paragraphs, then we have a parallel sorting algorithm with $\mathcal{O}(\log n)$ stages. At each of these stages, we have to sort $\mathcal{O}(n)$ numbers in $\mathcal{O}(n \log n)$ time and then we have to do *only one* intersection test at the cost of $\mathcal{O}(n \log n)$, instead of $\mathcal{O}(\log n)$ such tests, as before. Again the algorithm is simulated sequentially and thus we have the following Theorem:

Theorem 9. *The maximal scaling factor $\delta_{\max}$, such that a set of n starshaped, x-monotone objects, scaled by $\delta_{\max}$, does not intersect, can be computed in $\mathcal{O}(n \log^2 n)$ time.*

Note, that instead of using the complicated and highly inefficient (with respect to the constants involved) sorting network of [AKS83], it is also possible to use the simpler parallel merge sort algorithm of [Col88], where the improvement of parametric search also works.

We shall remark here, that the technique of *randomized halving* by Matoušek and Welzl (cf. [MW89] and [Mat91]) can also be applied to achieve an $\mathcal{O}(n \log^2 n)$ expected time algorithm for computing the maximal scaling factor of a set of n starshaped, x-monotone objects. (See the forthcoming thesis of the author [For93] on this subject.)

The Maximal Scaling Factor of Starshaped Polygons. In the remainder of this section we show how to compute efficiently the maximal scaling factor of a set of starshaped polygons. Note, that Theorem 9 does not apply immediately, since the computation of the pairwise maximal scaling factor of two starshaped polygons is not a constant time operation. Nevertheless we can reach the same total time bounds, as the following corollary shows.

Corollary 10. *Given a set of starshaped polygons with a total number of n edges, the maximal scaling factor can be found in $\mathcal{O}(n \log^2 n)$ time.*

Proof. We use a very simple trick to reduce our problem to a simpler one: Triangulate each starshaped polygon by introducing additional edges from the scaling center to each vertex of the polygon. Now we have transformed the starshaped polygons into a set of n triangles. Clearly the maximal scaling factor of this set of triangles equals the maximal scaling factor of the original set of starshaped polygons. (The scaling factor of a single starshaped polygon is not affected by the triangulation, i.e. the maximal scaling factor of the triangles of a single polygon is $+\infty$. Two maximally scaled starshaped polygons touch with two triangles.)

We therefore compute the maximal scaling factor of these triangles with the improved parametric search algorithm in $\mathcal{O}(n \log^2 n)$ time. □

References

[AE84] Franz Aurenhammer and Herbert Edelsbrunner. An optimal algorithm for constructing the weighted Voronoi diagram in the plane. *Pattern Recognition*, 17:251–257, 1984.

[AKS83] Miklos Ajtai, János Komlós, and Endre Szemerèdi. An $O(n \log n)$ sorting network. *Combinatorica*, 3:1–19, 1983.

[Aur87] Franz Aurenhammer. Power diagrams: properties, algorithms, and applications. *SIAM J. Comput.*, pages 78–96, 1987.

[BH92] Frank Bartling and Klaus Hinrichs. A plane-sweep algorithm for finding a closest pair among convex planar objects. In *Proc. 9th Annual Symposium on Theoretical Aspects of Computer Science*, pages 221–232, 1992.

[BO79] Jon Bentley and Thomas Ottmann. Algorithms for reporting and counting geometric intersections. *IEEE Trans. Comput.*, 28:643–647, 1979.

[BS76] Jon Bentley and Michael I. Shamos. Divide and conquer in multidimensional space. In *Proceedings 8th Annual Symp. Theory Comput.*, pages 220–230, 1976.

[Col87] Richard Cole. Slowing down sorting networks to obtain faster sorting algorithms. *J. Assoc. Comput. Mach.*, 34:200–208, 1987.

[Col88] Richard Cole. Parallel merge sort. *SIAM J. Comput.*, 17:770–785, 1988.

[ERW89] Herbert Edelsbrunner, Günter Rote, and Emo Welzl. Testing the necklace condition for shortest tours and optimal factors in the plane. *Theoret. Comput. Sci.*, 66:157–180, 1989.

[For87] Steven Fortune. A sweepline algorithm for Voronoi diagrams. *Algorithmica 2*, pages 153–174, 1987.

[For93] Michael Formann. *Algorithms for Geometric Packing and Scaling Problems*. PhD thesis, Freie Universität Berlin, Fachbereich Mathematik, 1993.

[HNS90] Klaus Hinrichs, Jurg Nievergelt, and Peter Shorn. Plane-sweep solves the closest pair problem elegantly. *Information Processing Letters*, pages 337–342, 1990.

[Koe36] Paul Koebe. Kontaktprobleme der konformen Abbildung. *Berichte der Verhandlungen der Sächsischen Akademie der Wissenschaften zu Leipzig*, pages 141–164, 1936. Math.-Phys. Klasse 88.

[Mat91] Jiří Matoušek. Randomized optimal algorithm for slope selection. *Inform. Process. Lett.*, 39:183–187, 1991.

[Meg83] Nimrod Megiddo. Linear-time algorithms for linear programming in R^3 and related problems. *SIAM J. Comput.*, 12:759–776, 1983.

[MW89] Jiří Matoušek and Emo Welzl. Good splitters for counting points in triangles. In *Proc. 5th Annual ACM Symposium on Computational Geometry*, pages 124–130, 1989.

[PS85] Franco Preparata and Michael I. Shamos. *Computational Geometry: An introduction*. Springer-Verlag, New York, 1985.

[SH75] Michael I. Shamos and Dan J. Hoey. Closest-point problems. In *Proc. 16th Annual IEEE Symposium on Foundations of Computer Science*, pages 151–162, 1975.

[SH76] Michael I. Shamos and Dan J. Hoey. Geometric intersection problems. In *Proc. 17th Annual IEEE Symposium on Foundations of Computer Science*, pages 208–215, 1976.

[Sha85] Micha Sharir. Intersection and closest pair problems for a set of planar discs. *SIAM J. Comput.*, 14:448–468, 1985.

[Yap87] Chee Yap. An $O(n \log n)$ algorithm for the Voronoi diagram of a set of simple curve segments. *Discrete Comput. Geom.*, 2:365–393, 1987.

Rectilinear Path Queries in a Simple Rectilinear Polygon[*]

Sven Schuierer[†]

Abstract

We present a data structure that allows to preprocess a rectilinear polygon such that shortest path queries in the rectilinear link or L_1 metric for any two points can be answered in time $O(\log n + k)$ where k is the length of the shortest path. If only the distance is of interest, the query time reduces to $O(\log n)$. Furthermore, if the query points are two vertices the distance can be reported in time $O(1)$ and a shortest path can be constructed in time $\acute{O}(1+k)$. The data structure can be computed in time $O(n)$ and needs $O(n)$ storage.

1 Introduction

In many applications such as VLSI-design rectilinear paths play an important role. Usually one is interested in minimizing the length of a path between two points; see [CKV87]. A natural metric to measure the length of a rectilinear path is the L_1-metric but sometimes it is also useful to take the number of turns on the path into account. This gives rise to the so called (*rectilinear*) *link metric* which is defined as follows. If we are given a rectilinear path $\mathcal{P}$ consisting of n line segments or *links*, its (*rectilinear*) *link length*, denoted by $\lambda_{rl}(\mathcal{P})$, is defined to be n. The *link distance* between two points is then the link length of a path between the points with the least number of links.

A variety of problems have been considered in this context. Das and Narasimhman [DN91] give an $O(n \log n)$ algorithm to compute the shortest rectilinear link path among a set of disjoint rectilinear polygons. As a byproduct they also obtain a linear space data structure to answer shortest path queries in time $O(\log n)$ if one of the query points is fixed. de Berg et al. [dvNO90] consider a linear combination of the L_1 and the link metric to construct a data structure that answers shortest path queries according to the combined metric among rectilinear line segments that are allowed to intersect. Again one of the query points is fixed. The time needed for the construction of the data structure is $O(n^2)$ while queries can be answered in $O(\log n)$ time. The storage requirement is $O(n \log n)$.

If we restrict ourselves to simple rectilinear polygons, the situation gets considerably simpler since it can be shown that there is always a rectilinear path between two points that is shortest w.r.t. both the L_1 and the link metric [dB91,HS91]. In

---

[*]This work was supported by the Deutsche Forschungsgemeinschaft under Grant No. Ot 64/5–4.

[†]Institut für Informatik, Universität Freiburg, Rheinstr. 10–12, D-7800 Freiburg, Fed. Rep. of Germany; email: schuierer@informatik.uni-freiburg.de

this setting de Berg presents a data structure that allows to answer the following types of queries. If we are given two arbitrary points inside a polygon, the rectilinear link distance and the L_1 distance between the two points can be reported in time $O(\log n)$. If we are given two vertices of the polygon, both distances can be reported in constant time. His data structure needs $O(n \log n)$ space and preprocessing. We summarize the results in the following table (k is used to denote the link length of the shortest path).

	Distance (L_1 or link length)	Path (L_1 and link length)
vertices	$O(1)$	$O(1 + k)$
points	$O(\log n)$	$O(\log n + k)$

In this paper we present a data structure that achieves the same time complexities as shown in the above table but improves both the space and preprocessing requirements to linear in the number of vertices of the polygon. This should also be contrasted with the Euclidean world where there exists a data structure to answer shortest L_2-path queries in a simple polygon in $O(\log n)$ time with linear preprocessing and space [GH87] but to achieve the same query time for the link distance $O(n^3)$ preprocessing time and space are needed [AMS92].

The paper is organized as follows. After introducing some of the definitions and notation in Section 2, we deal with constructing the data structure for shortest path queries in simple rectilinear polygons. We concentrate on the rectilinear link metric in Section 3. In Section 4 we show how to adapt the results to queries in the L_1-metric.

2 Definitions

In the following we will only consider rectilinear polygons and rectilinear paths. In particular, we assume that we are given a rectilinear polygon P with n vertices. Whenever we talk of polygons, we mean simple rectilinear polygons and whenever we talk of paths, we mean rectilinear paths in P.

Let e and e' be two axis parallel line segments in P. We say a polygonal path $\mathcal{P}$ from line segment e to line segment e' is *admissible* if it is rectilinear and the first link of $\mathcal{P}$ is orthogonal to e and the last link is orthogonal to e'. We define the link distance of e and e', denoted by $rl(e, e')$, to be the length of the shortest admissible path from a point of e to a point of e'. A point p is considered a degenerate line segment and, hence, all directions are admissible. If $\mathbf{P}_1$ and $\mathbf{P}_2$ are two disjoint rectilinear subpolygons of P, then we define $rl(\mathbf{P}_1, \mathbf{P}_2)$ to be the shortest admissible path from an edge of $\mathbf{P}_1$ to an edge of $\mathbf{P}_2$.

If e is an axis-parallel line segment in P and p is a point in P, we define the *d-interval of p on e* to be the set of points p can reach with an admissible path of length d or less on e and denote it by $e(p, d)$. It is easy to show that $e(p, d)$ is either empty or a connected subsegment of e (see Figure 1a).

A *histogram* is a monotone rectilinear polygon with one of the monotone chains forming a single straight line segment which is called the *base* of the histogram. A

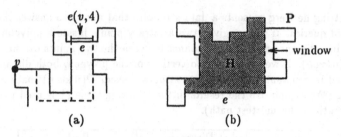

Figure 1: The definition of an interval and a maximal histogram.

horizontal (vertical) histogram is a histogram with a horizontal (vertical) base. An *upper* histogram is a horizontal histogram with its interior above the base. *Lower*, *left*, and *right* histograms are defined similarly. We define a *maximal histogram* **H** inside a rectilinear polygon **P** having an axis parallel chord b in **P** as its base to be the maximum area histogram interior to **P** with b as its base (see Figure 1b).

A *window* is a maximal segment on the boundary of a histogram which is not also part of the boundary of **P**. Note that every window splits **P** into two parts.

Since we will be dealing with trees quite a bit, we give short definitions of the standard terminology in connection with trees. A rooted tree T is a connected, planar, acyclic graph with one designated node, called the *root*, r of T such that there is only one path from r to any node in T. The *depth* of a node n is the length of the path from r to n in T. We denote it by $\delta(n)$. The node n' immediately before n on the unique path $\mathcal{P}$ from r to n is called the *parent* of n and n is called a *child* of n'. The nodes on $\mathcal{P}$ are called the ancestors of n and n is called a *descendant* of a node on $\mathcal{P}$. If n and n' are two nodes, then the *nearest common ancestor* (*nca*) denoted by $nca(n, n')$ is the node of T with the highest depth that is ancestor of both n and n'.

3 A Data Structure for Shortest Link Path Queries

We first address the question of how to compute shortest paths if we measure the path length with the rectilinear link metric. The main structure that allows us to answer queries efficiently is given by the *histogram tree* which is defined below.

3.1 The Histogram Tree

Let **P** be a simple rectilinear polygon and e some edge of **P**. We define the *histogram partition* $\mathcal{H}(\mathbf{P}, e)$ of **P** w.r.t. e inductively as follows [Lev87]. If **P** is a histogram with base e, then $\mathcal{H}(\mathbf{P}, e) = \{\mathbf{P}\}$. Otherwise, let **H** be the maximal histogram of e in **P** and $w_1, \dots, w_k$ the windows of **H**. Each window w_i is a chord in **P** that splits **P** into two subpolygons one of which does not contain **H**. We denote this subpolygon by $\mathbf{P}_{w_i}$. The histogram partition is now given by $\mathcal{H}(\mathbf{P}, e) = \bigcup_{1 \leq i \leq k} \mathcal{H}(\mathbf{P}_{w_i}, w_i) \cup$

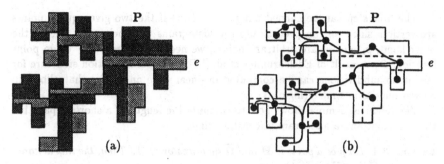

Figure 2: The tree associated to the histogram partition of **P**.

{H}. For illustration see Figure 2a. If a triangulation of the polygon is given (see [Cha90]), a histogram partition can be computed in linear time [Lev87].

Note that each window of a histogram in $\mathcal{H}(\mathbf{P}, e)$ is the base of some other histogram and vice versa with the only exception of the histogram with base e. Since a window splits **P** into two subpolygons and every base b is a window, we can speak of the *subpolygon* $\mathbf{P}_b$ *of* b which is meant to denote the part of **P** that contains the histogram of $\mathcal{H}(\mathbf{P}, e)$ with base b. We also say that b *cuts off* $\mathbf{P}_b$ in this case.

If we are given a point p in **P**, we define the *histogram of* p to be the histogram of $\mathcal{H}(\mathbf{P}, e)$ that contains p and denote it by $\mathbf{H}(p)$.

With the histogram partition there is a natural tree structure associated to it. We call it the *histogram tree of* **P** *and* e and denote it by $\mathcal{T}(\mathbf{P}, e)$ (see Figure 2). It is defined as follows. The nodes of $\mathcal{T}(\mathbf{P}, e)$ are the histograms of $\mathcal{H}(\mathbf{P}, e)$. There is an edge between histogram $\mathbf{H}_1$ and $\mathbf{H}_2$ in $\mathcal{H}(\mathbf{P}, e)$ if the base of $\mathbf{H}_1$ is a window of $\mathbf{H}_2$. The root of $\mathcal{T}(\mathbf{P}, e)$ is the histogram with base e. If we use the terminology of trees in connection with histograms, it is implied that we refer to the tree structure of $\mathcal{T}(\mathbf{P}, e)$. From now on we will assume that any histogram we refer to is an element of $\mathcal{H}(\mathbf{P}, e)$ if not explicitly stated otherwise.

The first observation we make is that a subtree of $\mathcal{H}(\mathbf{P}, e)$ that is rooted at histogram **H** with base b contains all and only those histograms that form the subpolygon $\mathbf{P}_b$ of b. Hence, if we are given two query points p_1 and p_2 in the histograms $\mathbf{H}_1$ and $\mathbf{H}_2$, respectively, we conclude that a shortest path from p_1 to p_2 has to pass through the nearest common ancestor $\overline{\mathbf{H}}$ of $\mathbf{H}_1$ and $\mathbf{H}_2$. This leads to a three step procedure to answer a shortest path query.

(i) Find $\mathbf{H}_1$ and $\mathbf{H}_2$.

(ii) Compute the part of the shortest path from p_1 to $\overline{\mathbf{H}}$ and the part from p_2 to $\overline{\mathbf{H}}$.

(iii) Connect the two parts in $\overline{\mathbf{H}}$.

The first step can be carried out in time $O(1)$ if the two given query points are vertices since we can precompute the histograms they belong to. If, on the other hand, p_1 and p_2 are arbitrary points, we need to preprocess P to do point location. By a result of Edelsbrunner et al. [EGS86] a point location structure for monotone subdivisions can be computed in linear time and space that allows to answer queries in time $O(\log n)$.

The following lemma shows how to compute the length of a shortest path between a point and a histogram in constant time.

Lemma 3.1 *Let p be a point in H and $\overline{H}$ an ancestor of H. Then, the link distance from p_1 to $\overline{H}$ is $\delta(H) - \delta(\overline{H})$.*

Note that this in particular implies that the distance from p_1 to $nca(H_1, H_2)$ can be computed in constant time since nearest common ancestor queries in an arbitrary tree can be answered in $O(1)$ time [HT84].

3.2 Connecting the Paths

As we pointed out above the third step of the query is to connect the two shortest paths from p_1 to $\overline{H}$ and from p_2 to $\overline{H}$ so that they yield a shortest path from p_1 to p_2. In order to do so we make use of the definition of a d-interval. Recall that the d-interval $w(p, d)$ of a point p on a window w is the set of points on w such that there is an admissible path of d links or less from p to w. The only interesting values for d are the distance $rl(p, w)$ of p to w and $rl(p, w) + 1$ since we have $w(p, d) = \emptyset$ if $d < rl(p, w)$ and it is also easy to see that $w(p, d) = w$ if $d > rl(p, w) + 1$.

In the following we only treat the case that H_1 and H_2 are two histograms of $\mathcal{H}(P, e)$ such that neither H_1 is an ancestor of H_2 nor vice versa. If one of the histograms turns out to be an ancestor of the other, the results presented here can be easily adapted. Let $\overline{H}$ be their nearest common ancestor. For the ease of discussion we assume that $\overline{H}$ is an upper histogram. We denote the window of $\overline{H}$ that cuts off the subpolygon containing histogram H_i by w_i, $i = 1, 2$ and let $d_i = rl(p_i, \overline{H})$. With this notation we obtain the following lemma as a consequence of the above observation on the intervals $w_i(p_i, d_i)$.

Lemma 3.2 *There is a shortest path $\mathcal{P}$ from p_1 to p_2 such that the first link of $\mathcal{P}$ that intersects w_1 orthogonally is either the d_1^{st} or the $(d_1 + 1)^{st}$ link of $\mathcal{P}$.*

In the following we assume that we are given the intervals $I_i = w_i(p_i, d_i)$ and $J_i = w_i(p_i, d_i + 1)$. The problem of how to compute these efficiently will be addressed later.

We first show that given the intervals of p_1 and p_2 on w_1 and w_2 there is a "short" path from p_1 to p_2. Recall that the distance between two intervals is the shortest *admissible* path between them.

Lemma 3.3 *If p_i is a point in H_i and d_i' an integer such that $I_i' = w_i(p_i, d_i')$ is non-empty (i.e., $d_i' \geq d_i$), for $i = 1, 2$, then $rl(p_1, p_2) \leq d_1' + d_2' + rl(I_1', I_2') - 2$.*

The above lemma establishes an upper bound on the length of a shortest path from p_1 to p_2. With the help of this inequality and Lemma 3.2 we are in a position to prove the main result about shortest paths in rectilinear polygons.

Lemma 3.4 *If k is defined as* $\min\{rl(I_1, I_2), rl(I_1, J_2)+1, rl(J_1, I_2)+1, rl(J_1, J_2)+2\}$, *then* $rl(p_1, p_2) = d_1 + d_2 - 2 + k$.

The intuitive meaning behind Lemma 3.4 is that it might pay off to spend one more link on the path from p_1 to w_1 or from p_2 to w_2 than necessary if it is then easier to connect the two paths. The above lemma leaves us with the following two problems.

(i) Find the intervals I_1, J_1 and I_2, J_2.

(ii) Compute the distance $rl(I', I'')$ between two intervals in a histogram.

3.3 The Distance Between Two Intervals

In this section we describe how to compute a data structure in an upper histogram H such that if we are given two vertical line segments we can compute their distance in time $O(1)$ if we know the end points of the line segments in advance and $O(\log n)$ otherwise.

Our approach is to first reduce the distance problem between two intervals to a geometric problem and then to reduce the geometric problem again to a nearest common ancestor query in an appropriately defined tree. In the next lemma we give the first reduction. Here a *pyramid* is defined as a histogram that is monotone w.r.t. to both the x- and y-axis.

Lemma 3.5 *If* H *is a histogram and I_1 and I_2 are two vertical line segments on the boundary of* H*, then*

$$
rl(I_1, I_2) = \begin{cases} 1 & \text{if there is an axis-parallel line segment in H that connects} \\ & \quad I_1 \text{ and } I_2; \\ 3 & \text{if there is a pyramid in H that intersects both } I_1 \text{ and } I_2; \\ 5 & \text{otherwise.} \end{cases}
$$

With the above result the task of finding the distance between two intervals essentially reduces to determining whether there is a common pyramid that intersects them. We now introduce a data structure that allows to make efficient queries of exactly this type.

Definition 3.1 *Let* H *be a horizontal (upper) histogram. We define the following subdivision $S(H)$ of* H*. For each reflex vertex v of* H*, we extend the horizontal edge incident to v to the left or right. Thus,* H *is divided into a number of rectangles or cells.*

There is a natural tree structure T_H associated to $S(H)$. The nodes of T_H are the cells of $S(H)$. There is an edge between two nodes if the two cells are adjacent in the subdivision. The root of the tree is the cell adjacent to the base of H*.*

For a point p in H*, we denote the cell of $S(H)$ (= node of T_H) p belongs to by $C(p)$.*

$S(H)$ can be computed in time proportional to the size of H by a left to right scan of the boundary of H to compute all extensions to the right and then a right to left scan to compute all extensions to the left of the reflex vertices.

It is easy to see that if a cell C_1 of $S(H)$ is directly above a cell C_2 of $S(H)$, then the x-interval spanned by C_1 is contained in the x-interval spanned by C_2. An easy induction yields that this is true even if C_2 is not a parent but just an ancestor of C_1. The next lemma shows that the ancestor relation of T_H and the question if there is common pyramid that contains two points are closely connected.

Lemma 3.6 *Let p_1 and p_2 be two points in H. There exists a pyramid that contains p_1 and p_2 if and only if $C(p_1)$ is an ancestor of $C(p_2)$ or vice versa.*

If we are given a vertical interval I on the boundary of H and a point q in I, then any pyramid that contains q also contains all points of I below q since a pyramid gets wider at the bottom. With this observation we have the following corollary of Lemma 3.6.

Corollary 3.7 *If I_1 and I_2 are two vertical intervals on the boundary of H, then there exists a pyramid that intersects I_1 and I_2 if and only if the cell of the lower end point of I_1 is an ancestor of the cell of the lower end point of I_2 or vice versa.*

Thus, we have reduced the problem of determining if there is a common pyramid that intersects two intervals to ancestor queries in T_H. It turns out that we can treat the problem if there is a horizontal line segment that connects two intervals in the same way.

Lemma 3.8 *Let $I_1 = [p_1, q_1]$ and $I_2 = [p_2, q_2]$ be two intervals on differently oriented vertical edges of H where p_i is above q_i. There is a horizontal line segment in H that connects I_1 and I_2 if and only if $C(p_2)$ is a descendant of $C(q_1)$ and $C(p_1)$ is a descendant of $C(q_2)$.*

Combining the results of Corollary 3.7 and Lemma 3.8 we obtain the following algorithm to compute $rl(I_1, I_2)$ for two intervals I_1 and I_2 in H.

> **Algorithm Interval Distance**
> let p_i be the upper and q_i be the lower end point of I_i, $i = 1, 2$;
> compute $C(p_i)$ and $C(q_i)$ of $S(H)$;
> if $nca(C(q_1), C(q_2)) = C(q_1)$ or $= C(q_2)$
>   then if $nca(C(p_1), C(q_2)) = C(q_2)$ and $nca(C(q_1), C(p_2)) = C(q_1)$
>   then $rl(I_1, I_2) = 1$
>   else $rl(I_1, I_2) = 3$
>   end if
>   else $rl(I_1, I_2) = 5$
> end if

The proof of correctness follows immediately from the above results. The time needed for the algorithm is $O(\log n)$ if the interval end points are not known in

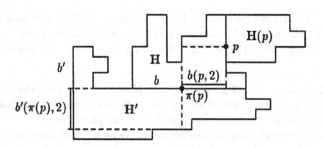

Figure 3: The definition of the parent $\pi(p)$ of p.

advance since then we have to do a point location to find the cells $C(p_i)$ and $C(q_i)$, $i = 1, 2$ [EGS86]. Otherwise, if the interval end points are taken from a given set, we can precompute $C(p_i)$ and $C(q_i)$, $i = 1, 2$, and the algorithm takes constant time since nearest common ancestor queries can be answered in time $O(1)$.

3.4 A Data Structure for Intervals

We now turn to the problem of computing the intervals I_1, J_1 and I_2, J_2. So the query problem we are concerned with is of the following type. Given a point p and an ancestor H of $H(p)$ such that window w of H cuts off $H(p)$, report $w(p, rl(p, w))$ and $w(p, rl(p, w) + 1)$. We will again reduce this problem to a tree problem.

The first observation that allows for the efficient computation of intervals is that though there is a quadratic number of possible intervals, there are only a linear number of *interval end points*. In the next lemma we show that, indeed, the interval end points are given by the orthogonal projection of the vertices of the histograms onto their bases.

Lemma 3.9 *Let p be a point in P and H an ancestor of $H(p)$ with base b. If $d \geq rl(p, b) \geq 2$, then the end points of $b(p, d)$ are orthogonal projections of two vertices of H onto b.*

Since the total complexity of the histogram decomposition is linear [Lev87], there is only a linear number of possible interval end points in P. We denote this set by $\mathcal{I}$.

The second observation we need is that, for each interval, there is one end point that "dominates" all other points in the interval. This is stated more precisely in the next lemma.

Lemma 3.10 *Let H be an upper horizontal histogram with base b and I a vertical interval on the boundary of H with lower end point p'. Then, $b(p, 2) \subseteq b(p', 2)$, for all $p \in I$.*

This leads to the following definition which is illustrated in Figure 3.

Definition 3.2 *Let p be a point in $\mathbf{P}$, $\mathbf{H}$ the parent of $\mathbf{H}(p)$ with base b, and $\mathbf{H}'$ the parent of $\mathbf{H}$ with base b'. According to Lemma 3.10 there is one end point p' of $I = b(p, 2)$ with $b'(p', 2) = b'(I, 2)$. We call p' the parent of p and denote it by $\pi(p)$.*

Note that the parent of p can be easily identified once the interval $b(p, 2)$ is known if we associate a direction with b that indicates which way the base b' of $\mathbf{H}'$ is. The end point of $b(p, 2)$ that is closer to b' is the parent of p.

With this parent relation we immediately have an induced tree structure on the points of $\mathcal{I}$. Of course, we do not obtain one tree but a forest of rooted trees. The roots of the trees are the points in $\mathcal{I}$ that are on the windows of the root histogram of $\mathcal{H}(\mathbf{P}, e)$.

In order to compute this forest in linear time we proceed as follows. Let $\mathbf{H}$ be an horizontal histogram with windows $w_1, \ldots, w_k$ and base b. For each point p of $\mathcal{I}$ on w_i, $1 \leq i \leq k$, we compute the opposite vertical edge e. This clearly can be done in linear time. Note that the x-coordinate of w_i determines one end point of $b(p, 2)$ and the x-coordinate of the e the other end point. Once we are given $b(p, 2)$, the computation of $\pi(p)$ can be done in constant time by make use of the direction associated to b. Hence, we can compute $\pi(p)$, for all $p \in \mathcal{I} \cap \mathbf{H}$, in one scan of the upper boundary of $\mathbf{H}$ in time $O(|\mathcal{I} \cap \mathbf{H}| + |\mathbf{H}|)$ where $|\cdot|$ denotes the cardinality of a set. So the total time used to perform this computation for all histograms $\mathbf{H} \in \mathcal{H}(\mathbf{P}, e)$ is still linear.

The following lemma shows how this tree structure can employed to find intervals.

Lemma 3.11 *Let p be a point and $\mathbf{H}$ an ancestor of $\mathbf{H}(p)$ with base b and $rl(p, b) \geq 3$. If $d = rl(p, b)$, then $b(p, d) = b(\pi^{d-2}(p), 2)$.*

A similar statement also holds if $d = rl(p, b) + 1$. So in order to find the d-interval of p on b we have to

1. locate $\pi(p)$,

2. find the ancestor p' of $\pi(p)$ at depth $\delta(\pi(p)) - (d - 3)$, and

3. compute $b(p', 2)$.

Finding the parent $\pi(p)$ of p and computing $b(p', 2)$ can be easily achieved in constant resp. logarithmic time with the help of $\mathcal{S}(\mathbf{H})$ depending on the fact if p is a vertex or not. Step 2 needs only constant time by a result on computing level ancestors in trees; see [BV89]. There it is shown that if we are given a node n in arbitrary tree T, then we can find the kth ancestor of n in constant time— independent of k—given linear time to preprocess T appropriately.

We are now able to put the results together and obtain the following algorithm to compute the distance between two points.

Algorithm Rectilinear Link Distance Query
1. compute $\mathbf{H}_1$ and $\mathbf{H}_2$;

2. let $\overline{H} = nca(H_1, H_2)$;
3. let $d_i = \delta(H_i) - \delta(\overline{H})$;
4. compute I_i and J_i;
5. compute $rl(I_1, I_2)$, $rl(I_1, J_2)$, $rl(J_1, I_1)$, $rl(J_1, J_2)$;
6. let $k = \min\{rl(I_1, I_2), rl(I_1, J_2) + 1, rl(J_1, I_1) + 1, rl(J_1, J_2) + 2\}$;
7. let $rl(p_1, p_2) = d_1 + d_2 + k - 2$;

The analysis of the algorithm can be summarized as follows. Steps 2, 3, 5, 6, and 7 take only constant time while point location has to be done in Steps 1 and 4. Since we can preprocess the polygon and each histogram in linear time in order to do point location in time $O(\log n)$ [EGS86] we immediately obtain that link distance queries for two arbitrary points can be answered within this time bound. If, on the other hand, we take vertices, point location can be avoided by a linear time preprocessing phase that computes, for each vertex, the histogram it belongs to and its parent in the interval tree structure. Hence, Steps 1 and 4 also take only constant time and this is then the time needed to answer a query.

From the information provided by the interval tree an explicit description of a shortest path can be easily obtained. We just have to successively connect p_1 and p_2 to their parent by the two link path that is contained in **P**. The only freedom in choice is at the very beginning depending on the fact if we want to reach the I- or J-intervals which depends on Step 6 in the above algorithm. Computing the path in $\overline{H}$ can be achieved in constant time by making use of $S(\overline{H})$.

4   Distance Queries in the L_1-Metric

In this section we address the problem of computing the distance between two points in the L_1 metric and indicate how to obtain a shortest path w.r.t. the rectilinear link metric and the L_1-metric. The approach is very similar to one presented in Section 3 for the rectilinear link metric and, therefore, we give only a brief sketch of it. Again we can show that the shortest path between two points p_1 and p_2 has to pass through the nearest common ancestor $\overline{H}$ of $H(p_1)$ and $H(p_2)$. As in the previous section let w_i be the window of $\overline{H}$ that cuts off the subpolygon containing p_i.

Lemma 4.1 *There is one point q_i on w_i such that $L_1(p_i, q_i) = L_1(p_i, w_i)$ and $L_1(p_i, q) = L_1(p_i, q_i) + L_1(q_i, q)$, for all points q on w_i, for $i = 1, 2$.*

The claim of the previous lemma can be strengthened in the following way. If we denote the distance $L_1(p_i, w_i)$ by d_i, for $i = 1, 2$, it can be shown that q_i is one of the end points of the interval $I_i = w_i(p_i, d_i)$. Hence, the basic steps of the algorithm are as follows.

1. Locate p_1 and p_2 in $T(\mathbf{P}, e)$ and let H_1 and H_2 be the two histograms that contain them.

2. Compute the nearest common ancestor $\overline{H}$ of H_1 and H_2. Let w_1 and w_2 be the windows that cut off the subpolygons that contain H_1 and H_2.

3. Compute q_1 and q_2 and their distance to p_1 and p_2.

4. Compute the distance between q_1 and q_2 in $\overline{H}$.

The main problem arises in the computation of q_1 and q_2. In order to show how this can be achieved efficiently, we consider again the situation as illustrated in Figure 3. We want to impose a tree structure on the set $\mathcal{I}$ of interval end points. We define the L_1-*parent* of a point p to be the closest point to p on the base b of the parent of $H(p)$ and denote it by $\pi_{L_1}(p_i)$. It is easy to see that $\pi_{L_1}(p)$ is an end point of $b(p,2)$. In Figure 3 $\pi_{L_1}(p)$ is the end point of $b(p,2)$ that is different from $\pi(p)$, i.e., the orthogonal projection of p onto b. Thus, we obtain a forest of rooted trees whose nodes are the points in $\mathcal{I}$. Some minor adaptions of the technique described in Section 3.4 allow us to build this structure in linear time. If $\delta(H(p_i)) - \delta(\overline{H}) = k_i$, this structure allows to compute q_1 and q_2 in the following way.

1. Compute $\pi_{L_1}(p_1)$ and $\pi_{L_1}(p_2)$.

2. Let $q_i = \pi_{L_1}^{k_i-1}(p_i)$, for $i = 1,2$.

In order to compute the distance $L_1(p_i,q_i)$, we store additional *weight information* $w(p)$ at a point p in $\mathcal{I}$. We show inductively how the weights are assigned. The roots all store a weight that is larger than the greatest distance between two points in P, say the perimeter of P. Assume we have already assigned weights to all the points at depth d. If p is a point at depth $d+1$, we store the weight $w(\pi_{L_1}(p)) - L_1(p,\pi_{L_1}(p))$ at p. An easy induction yields that $L_1(p,\pi_{L_1}^k(p)) = w(\pi_{L_1}^k(p)) - w(p)$, for all $k \leq \delta(p)$. Hence, $L_1(p_i,q_i) = w(q_i) - w(p_i)$.

The only remaining task is to compute the distance between q_1 and q_2 which is only problematic if q_1 and q_2 do not belong to a pyramid in $\overline{H}$ since any two points in a pyramid can be connected by a staircase, i.e., a shortest path in the L_1-metric without obstacles. So our main tool is again the subdivision $S(\overline{H})$ which allows us to if q_1 and q_2 are contained in a pyramid. If, on the other hand, there is no pyramid that contains both points, it is easy to show that the L_1-distance between q_1 and q_2 is given by the L_1-distance between q_1 and q_2 without obstacles and plus twice the distance from the lower one of the two points to the cell that is the nearest common ancestor of $C(q_1)$ and $C(q_2)$.

The analysis of the steps involved to answer a shortest path query in the L_1-metric is pretty much the same as in Section 3 and, therefore, omitted.

5 Conclusions

In this paper we presented a data structure to answer rectilinear link and L_1-distance queries between two points in a simple rectilinear polygon. The achieved query time as well as the preprocessing time and the space requirements are optimal. If we leave the setting of a simple polygon, the query problem becomes considerably harder. There is no known algorithm to solve the one shot problem among polygonal obstacles in subquadratic time if the metric used is a linear combination of the L_1- and rectilinear link metric.

Another natural generalization of the considered problem is to allow the paths to follow more than two orientations. It is not clear whether the presented technique can be extended to handle this problem as well. Very little is known about shortest paths with a fixed number of orientations.

References

[AMS92] E. Arkin, J. Mitchell, and S. Suri. Optimal link path queries in a simple polygon. In *Proc. 3rd Symposium on Discrete Algorithms*, 1992.

[BV89] O. Berkman and U. Vishkin. Recursive*-tree parallel data-structure. In *Proc. 30th Symposium on Foundations of Computer Science*, pages 196–202, 1989.

[Cha90] Bernard Chazelle. Triangulating a simple polygon in linear time. In *Proceedings of the 31th Symposium on Foundations of Computer Science*, pages 220–230,, IEEE, 1990.

[CKV87] K.L. Clarkson, S. Kapoor, and P.M. Vaidya. Rectilinear shortest paths through polygonal obstacles in $O(n \log^2 n)$ time. In *Proc. 3rd Annual Conference on Computational Geometry*, pages 251–257, 1987.

[dB91] M. de Berg. On rectilinear link distance. *Computational Geometry: Theory and Applications*, 1(1):13–34, 1991.

[DN91] G. Das and G. Narasimhan. Geometric searching and link distance. In F. Santoro F. Dehne, J.-R. Sack, editor, *Proc. 2nd Workshop on Algorithms and Data Structures*, pages 261–272, LNCS 519, 1991.

[dRLW89] P.J. de Rezende, D.T. Lee, and Y.F. Wu. Rectilinear shortest paths with rectangular barriers. *Journal of Discrete and Computational Geometry*, 4:41–53, 1989.

[dvNO90] M.T. de Berg, M.J. van Kreveld, B.J. Nilsson, and M.H. Overmars. Finding shortest paths in the presence of orthogonal obstacles using a combined l_1 and link metric. In *Proc. 2nd Scandinavian Workshop on Algorithm Theory*, pages 213–224, LNCS 447, Springer Verlag, 1990.

[EGS86] H. Edelsbrunner, L.J. Guibas, and J. Stolfi. Optimal point location in a monotone subdivision. *SIAM Journal of Computing*, 15(2):317–340, 1986.

[GH87] L. Guibas and J. Hershberger. Optimal shortest path queries in a simple polygon. In *Proc. 3rd Symposium on Computational Geometry*, pages 50–63, Waterloo, Ontario, 1987.

[HS91] J. Hershberger and J. Snoeyink. Computing minimum length paths of a given homotopy class. In F. Santoro F. Dehne, J.-R. Sack, editor, *Proc. 2nd Workshop on Algorithms and Data Structures*, pages 331–342, LNCS 519, Springer Verlag, 1991.

[HT84] D. Harel and R. E. Tarjan. Fast algorithms for finding nearest common ancestors. *SIAM Journal on Computing*, 13:338–355, 1984.

[Lev87] Christos Levcopoulos. *Heuristics for Minimum Decompositions of Polygons*. PhD thesis, University of Linköping, Linköping, Sweden, 1987.

Parallel Algorithm for the Matrix Chain Product and the Optimal Triangulation Problems[*] (Extended abstract)

Artur Czumaj
Warsaw University[†]

Abstract

This paper considers the problem of finding an optimal order of the multiplication chain of matrices and the problem of finding an optimal triangulation of a convex polygon. For both these problems the best sequential algorithms run in $\Theta(n \log n)$ time. All parallel algorithms known use the dynamic programming paradigm and run in a polylogarithmic time using, in the best case, $O(n^6/\log^k n)$ processors for a constant k. We give a new algorithm which uses a different approach and reduces the problem to computing certain recurrence in a tree. We show that this recurrence can be optimally solved which enables us to improve the parallel bound by a few factors. Our algorithm runs in $O(\log^3 n)$ time using $n^2/\log^3 n$ processors on a CREW PRAM.

We also consider the problem of finding an optimal triangulation in a monotone polygon. An $O(\log^2 n)$ time and n processors algorithm on a CREW PRAM is given.

Key words : parallel algorithms, computational geometry, dynamic programming

1 Introduction

The problem of computing an *optimal order of matrix multiplication* (*the matrix chain product problem*) is defined as follows. Consider the evaluation of the product of n matrices $M = M_1 \times M_2 \times \cdots \times M_n$, where M_i is a $d_{i-1} \times d_i$ ($d_i \geq 1$) matrix. Since matrix multiplication satisfies the associative law, the final result is the same for all orders of multiplying. However, the order of multiplication greatly affects the total number of operations to evaluate M. The problem is to find an optimal order of multiplying the matrices, such that the total number of operations is minimized. Here we assume that the number of operations to multiply a $p \times q$ matrix by a $q \times r$ matrix is pqr.

---

[*]Supported in part by the EC Cooperative Action IC 1000 Algorithms for Future Technologies "ALTEC" and by the grant KBN 2–1190–91–01.

[†]Author's address — Institute of Informatics, Warsaw University, ul. Banacha 2, 02-097 Warszawa, Poland. E-mail : aczumaj@mimuw.edu.pl.

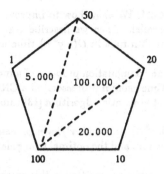 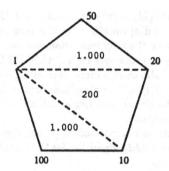

Figure 1: Geometric representation of the evaluation of a matrix chain. Above triangles correspond to the chain $M_1 \times M_2 \times M_3 \times M_4$, where dimensions are as follows $50 \times 20 \times 10 \times 100 \times 1$. The left triangualtion corresponds to the order $(M_1 \times (M_2 \times M_3)) \times M_4$ while the right one to $M_1 \times (M_2 \times ((M_3 \times M_4))$. The second order is optimal.

One can show that this problem is equivalent to the problem of finding an *optimal triangulation of a convex polygon* (see [13]). Given a convex polygon $(v_0, v_1, \ldots, v_n)$ with positive weights at vertices. Divide it into triangles, such that the total cost of partitioning is the smallest possible. The total cost of a triangulation is defined to be the sum of costs of all triangles in this partition. The cost of a triangle is the product of weights at each vertex of the triangle (see also figure 1).

Transformation from one problem to another can be done in a linear sequential time [13] and also in $O(1)$ parallel time using n processors on a CREW PRAM [8]. Therefore we will consider only the latter problem.

The first polynomial time algorithm for the matrix chain product problem was discovered by Godbole [9] and run in $O(n^3)$ time. Then Hu and Shing [13] gave an $O(n \log n)$ sequential time algorithm which was recently proved to be optimal [17]. All these algorithms seem to be highly sequential. The only previous known approach to design parallel algorithms for these problems is based on the dynamic programming. Using this technique Valiant et. al. [19] showed that these problems are in $\mathcal{NC}$. Their algorithm runs in $O(\log^2 n)$ time using n^9 processors. This result was improved by Rytter [18] to $n^6/\log n$ processors on a CREW PRAM. Then Huang et. al. [12] and Galil and Park [10] modified Rytter's algorithm and reduced the number of processors to respectively $n^6/\log^5 n$ and $n^6/\log^6 n$.

So there was a big gap between the best sequential and parallel algorithms. Recently only approximate parallel algorithms have discovered. Czumaj [8] and Bradford [3] gave one which runs in $O(\log n)$ time on a CREW PRAM and in $O(\log \log n)$ time on a CRCW PRAM, in both cases with a linear number of operations. It approximates an optimal solution with an error ratio at most 15%.

In the paper we show a new algorithm for the matrix chain product and for the optimal triangulation problems. It reduces the triangulation problem to the problem of solving certain recurrence in a tree which enables us to find an optimal partition. The recurrence can be easily computed by a sequential dynamic programming algorithm in $\Theta(n^2)$ time. Using the same approach we can get an $\mathcal{NC}$ parallel algorithm with roughly $O(n^6)$ processors on a CREW PRAM. We show how to improve this result and optimally solve the recurrence in parallel. Then we describe a reconstruction of an optimal triangulation. Our algorithm runs in $O(\log^3 n)$ time using $n^2/\log^3 n$ processors on a CREW PRAM.

We also show a more efficient algorithm for the triangulation problem of a monotone polygon. Our algorithm runs in $O(\log^2 n)$ time using n processors on a CREW PRAM. Notice that this result is close to the best sequential algorithm [13] running in linear time.

Very recently Bradford [4] has shown an $O(\log^3 n)$ time and $n^3/\log n$ processors CRCW PRAM algorithm for the matrix chain product and the optimal triangulation problems.

Due to the space limitation some proofs and details are omitted in this extended abstract and will appear in the full version of the paper.

2 Basic definitions

2.1 The convex least weight subsequence problem

The least weight subsequence problem may be defined as follows [10]. Given $d(n)$ and a real-valued weight function $w(i, j)$. Compute $d(i) = \min_{i < j \le n}\{w(i, j) + d(j)\}$, for all $1 \le i < n$. The weight function w is said to be *convex* if it satisfies the inverse quadrangle inequality

$$w(i, j) + w(i + 1, j + 1) \ge w(i, j + 1) + w(i + 1, j), \quad \text{for all } 1 \le i < j - 1 < n.$$

In the general case the least weight subsequence problem can sequentialy be solved in $\Theta(n^2)$ time and in $O(\log^2 n)$ parallel time using $O(n^3/\log^4 n)$ processors on a CREW PRAM [10]. For the convex weight function the best sequential algorithm runs in $O(n\alpha(n))$ time [15], while the best parallel in $O(\log^2 n)$ time using n processors on a CREW PRAM[1][6].

2.2 Notation concerning the triangulation problem

Throughout this paper we will use $v_0, v_1, \ldots, v_n$ to denote vertices as well as their weights in a convex polygon. For simplicity we assume that all weights are distinct.

We will use notation an *arc* to denote any diagonal of a polygon and a *side* to denote a boundary connecting two successive vertices (*neighbours*) in a polygon. Define a vertex v_i to be the *smallest* one if for each other vertex v_j we have $v_i < v_j$. Similarly we define the kth *smallest* vertex to be v_i if there are exactly $k-1$ vertices smaller than v_i.

Define a *basic polygon* to be a polygon where the second and the third smallest vertices are adjacent by sides to the smallest vertex. The following fact reduces our problem to the triangulation of basic polygons.

---

[1] In [6] was shown an algorithm which runs in $O(\log^2 n \log \log n)$ time with $O(n \log^2 n)$ total work on a CREW PRAM. But we can simply improve it to the presented form using the result for finding the all row minima in a totally monotone 2-dimensional array given in [2].

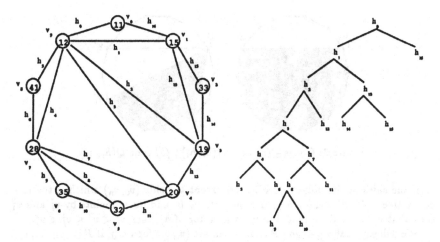

Figure 2: Candidates in a polygon and corresponding tree of candidates.

Fact 2.1 *[13] There exists an optimal triangulation of a convex polygon containing arcs or sides connecting the smallest vertex and both the second smallest and third smallest vertices.*

Hence in finding an optimal triangulation of a polygon we can divide it into subpolygons by joining the smallest vertex with the second smallest and third smallest vertices respectively, until each subpolygon has the smallest vertex adjacent to the second smallest and third smallest vertices. In [8] was shown that such a partitioning can be found in $O(\log n)$ time using $n/\log n$ processors on a CREW PRAM.

From now on, we shall find an optimal triangulation in each basic subpolygon independently. We will consider only basic polygons of the form $(v_0, v_1, \ldots, v_n)$, where $v_0 < v_n < v_1 < v_i$, for each $1 < i < n$.

We will use also the following fact.

Fact 2.2 *[13] There exists an optimal triangulation of a basic polygon containing either the arc connecting the smallest vertex to the fourth smallest vertex or the arc connecting the second smallest vertex to the third smallest one.*

2.3 Sequential $O(n^2)$ time algorithm

Yao uses tabulation method (dynamic programming) to find an optimal triangulation in $O(n^2)$ time [20]. We briefly describe a modified version of that algorithm.

Define a *candidate* to be an arc or side (v_i, v_j) such that for each k, $i < k < j$, the inequalities $v_i < v_k$, $v_j < v_k$ hold (see figure 2). Define a *tree of candidates* (see figure 2). A candidate (v_i, v_j) is an ancestor of a candidate (v_k, v_l) if and only if $i \leq k < l \leq j$ and $(v_i, v_j) \neq (v_k, v_l)$. It is easy to see that the tree of candidates defined by the ancestor relation is binary. In [8] was shown how to find the tree of candidates[2] in $O(\log n)$ time using $n/\log n$ processors on a CREW PRAM. In this

---

[2]In that paper was shown how to find all internal vertices of this tree and one can easily modified

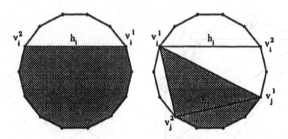

Figure 3: Cones - *(a)* cone $Q(h_i, h_i)$; *(b)* cone $Q(h_i, h_j)$

tree, the sides of the polygon are leaves, except the side (v_0, v_n) which is the root of the tree. We will denote an i-th candidate by h_i and its endpoints by v_i^1 and v_i^2 such that $v_i^1 < v_i^2$. Note that if h_i is an ancestor of h_j, then $v_i^1 < v_i^2 \leq v_j^1 < v_j^2$.

We will say that a polygon P is *below* an arc (v_i, v_j) for $i < j$, if $P = (v_i, \ldots, v_j)$. Define a *cone* (see figure 3) to be a subpolygon Q of the input polygon which is the sum of the polygon below some candidate $h_j = (v_j^1, v_j^2)$ and of the triangle (v_i^1, v_j^1, v_j^2), where $h_i = (v_i^1, v_i^2)$ is an ancestor of h_j or $h_i = h_j$. We will denote such a cone by $Q(h_i, h_j)$ or $Q(i, j)$. Note that if $h_i = h_j$, then Q is the polygon below h_i.

Define $l(i)$ (and $r(i)$) to be the left (respectively the right) son of a candidate h_i in the tree of candidates. Define also $s(i)$ (respectively $g(i)$) to be the son of h_i in the tree of candidates which is joined to the smaller (greater) vertex of candidate h_i, that is to v_i^1 (respectively v_i^2). Denote by $\Delta(v_i^1, h_j)$ the cost of the triangle (v_i^1, v_j^1, v_j^2). That is $\Delta(v_i^1, h_j) = v_i^1 v_j^1 v_j^2$. Define also by $c(h_i, h_j)$ or $c(i, j)$ the cost of an optimal triangulation of the cone $Q(i, j)$.

Assume we want to compute value $c(i, i)$ (see figure 4 (a)). Since $c(i, i)$ is the cost of the polygon below h_i where v_i^1 is the smallest vertex, v_i^2 is the second smallest one and $v_{l(i)}^2$ is the third smallest one, we can join vertex v_i^1 to $v_{l(i)}^2$ using Fact 2.1.

Let us assume that we want to compute value $c(i, j)$ where h_i is an ancestor of h_j (see figure 4 (b)(c)). In $Q(i, j)$, v_i^1 is the smallest vertex, v_j^1, v_j^2 are the second smallest and the third smallest vertices and $v_{l(j)}^2$ is the fourth smallest vertex. Thus using Fact 2.2 we have to choose the smallest of the partitions either after connecting v_i^1 to $v_{l(j)}^2$, or after connecting v_i^1 to v_j^2.

These observations reduce the triangulation problem to the problem of solving the following recurrence in the tree of candidates.

$$c(i, i) = \begin{cases} 0 & \text{if } h_i \text{ is a leaf} \\ c(i, g(i)) + c(s(i), s(i)) & \text{if } h_i \text{ is not a leaf} \end{cases}$$

and when h_i is an ancestor of h_j

$$c(i, j) = \begin{cases} \Delta(v_i^1, h_j) & \text{if } h_j \text{ is a leaf} \\ \min \begin{cases} \Delta(v_i^1, h_j) + c(j, j) \\ c(i, r(j)) + c(i, l(j)) \end{cases} & \text{if } h_j \text{ is not a leaf} \end{cases}$$

that construction to obtain the complete tree.

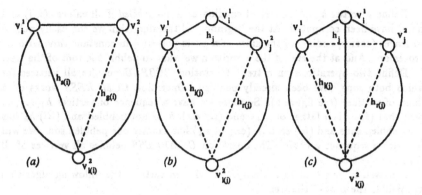

Figure 4: Possible partitioning of a cone and possible computations of values c.

$$(a) \qquad c(i,i) = c(i,g(i)) + c(s(i),s(i))$$
$$(b) \qquad c(i,j) = \Delta(i,j) + c(j,j)$$
$$(c) \qquad c(i,j) = c(i,l(j)) + c(i,r(j))$$

Our goal is to compute value $c((v_0, v_n), (v_0, v_n))$, i.e., $c(\text{ROOT}, \text{ROOT})$. And the reconstruction of an optimal triangulation from computed values $c(i, j)$ can be easily done in a linear sequential time.

Fact 2.3 *There exists an algorithm for computing an optimal triangulation of a convex polygon which runs in $O(n^2)$ time.* □

3 Outline of the parallel algorithm

In Section 2 we showed how to reduce the triangulation problem to the problem of computing certain recurrence in a tree. Using standard methods for solving recurrence equations ([11] or [16]) we can solve it in $O(\log^2 n)$ time using n^6 processors. In this section we show how to reduce the number of processors needed.

Our algorithm runs in the following four steps:

1. Divides the polygon into basic polygons.

2. Computes the tree of candidates for basic polygon.

3. Computes $c(i, j)$ for all pairs i, j.

4. Finds an optimal triangulation using the values c.

Steps (1) and (2) can be done in $O(\log n)$ time using $n/\log n$ processors on a CREW PRAM as was shown in [8]. So we only present how to implement steps (3) and (4) efficiently. In this section we give an outline of step (3) which will be analysed in details in the following section. Section 5 describes an algorithm for the reconstruction of an optimal polygon using the recurrence for the array c.

Define a vertex h_j in the tree of candidates to be *pebbled* if all values $c(i,j)$ and $c(j,i)$ have been computed. At the beginning of the algorithm we can easily pebble all leaves (corresponding to the sides of a basic polygon) in constant time with n^2 processors. And at the end of the algorithm we want to pebble the root of the tree.

Define two operations on a tree. Operation *PEBBLE* pebbles all vertices for which both sons have been already pebbled. Operation *COMPRESS* works on a chain of vertices (see figure 5). Suppose we have a sequence of vertices $h_1, \ldots, h_k$ such that (*i*) h_i is a father of h_{i+1} and (*ii*) each h_i is not pebbled and (*iii*) h_k has two pebbled sons and (*iv*) each h_i (except h_k) has exactly one pebbled son. We will call such a sequence a *chain*. The operation *COMPRESS* pebbles all vertices of all chains of the tree.

It is well known that in a binary tree with m vertices the following algorithm will pebble the root of the tree

    repeat $\lceil \log_2 m \rceil$ times
        PEBBLE; COMPRESS;

Thus it is enough to show how the operations *PEBBLE* and *COMPRESS* can be performed efficiently. We will also ensure the following invariant after each operation. If a vertex h_i is pebbled then all its descendants are also pebbled.

4 Computing the cost of an optimal triangualtion

Since the operation *PEBBLE* can be easily done in a constant time with $O(n^2)$ number of processors, we have only to show how to perform the operation *COMPRESS* with the same bound. We start by computing values $c(i,i)$ for all h_i on chains and then we compute values $c(i,j)$ for h_j on chains.

4.1 Computing values $c(i,i)$

Throughout this section we will consider a chain of candidates $h_1, h_2, \ldots, h_k$ (see figure 5), where h_i is the father of h_{i+1} and p_{i+1}, and where p_{i+1} has been already pebbled. Both sons of h_k (p_{k+1} and p_{k+2}) have been already pebbled. One property of a chain is that $v_i^1 < v_i^2 < v_{i+1}^2$ and that either $v_i^1 = v_{i+1}^1$, or $v_i^2 = v_{i+1}^1$.

Let $bottom(i)$ denotes the cost of an optimal triangulation of the polygon below candidate h_i with no candidate from the chain. Let also $fan(i,j)$ denotes the cost of an optimal triangulation of the polygon between two candidates from the chain h_i and h_j with no other candidate from the chain. We will always assume that h_i is an ancestor of h_j.

In an optimal triangulation of the polygon below h_i we have two cases - either there exists at least one candidate from the chain $h_1, h_2, \ldots, h_k$ below h_i, or there does not. If there is no candidate from the chain in an optimal triangulation below h_i, then $c(i,i) = bottom(i)$. Otherwise let h_j be the highest candidate from this partition (i.e., with the smallest index). In this case we get $c(i,i) = fan(i,j) + c(j,j)$. Since we are interested in the best partitioning, we obtain the following formula for computing $c(i,i)$.

$$c(i,i) = \min \left\{ \begin{array}{l} bottom(i) \\ \min_{i < j \le k}\{fan(i,j) + c(j,j)\} \end{array} \right.$$

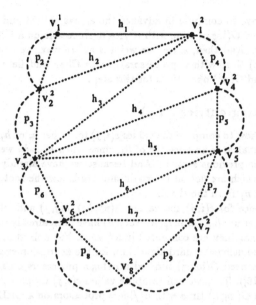

Figure 5: Chain $h_1, h_2, \ldots, h_7$. Candidates $p_2, \ldots, p_9$ are pebbled and h_i is a father of h_{i+1}. Note also that $v_1^2 \equiv v_2^1 \equiv v_4^1$, $v_3^2 \equiv v_4^1 \equiv v_5^1$, $v_5^2 \equiv v_6^1$ and $v_6^2 \equiv v_7^1$.

This recurrence is equivalent to the least weight subsequence problem. In this case, for $1 \le i \le k$, $d(i) = c(i, i)$, $d(k+1) = 0$, and for $1 \le i < j \le k+1$

$$w(i,j) = \begin{cases} bottom(i) & \text{if } j = k+1 \\ fan(i,j) & \text{if } i < j < k+1 \end{cases} \tag{1}$$

To reduce our problem to the above one we have to compute in advance values $bottom(i)$ and $fan(i, j)$. We can do it using the following lemma.

Lemma 4.1 *Let h_i and h_j be two candidates such that h_i is an ancestor of h_j. If there is no candidates from the chain between h_i and h_j in an optimal triangulation of the polygon below h_i, then v_i^1 is joined to both v_j^1 and v_j^2.* □

Using this lemma we can compute the functions *bottom* and *fan*.

$$bottom(i) = \sum_{r=i+1}^{k+2} c(h_i, p_r), \qquad fan(i,j) = \Delta(v_i^1, h_j) + \sum_{r=i+1}^{j} c(h_i, p_r)$$

Since all candidates p_r have been pebbled, all values $c(h_i, p_r)$ are already computed. Hence we can compute the functions *bottom* and *fan* in $O(\log n)$ time using $n^2/\log n$ processors on a CREW PRAM. Thus we can compute all values $c(i, i)$ with $O(n^3/\log^2 n)$ work, but we can improve this bound because the following lemma holds.

Lemma 4.2 *Function w defined by equation (1) is convex.* □

Because we have to compute in advance the arrays *bottom* and *fan* with $O(n^2)$ total work, we need $O(\log n)$ time with $n^2/\log n$ processors on a CREW PRAM for the preprocessing. And then, since our weights are convex, we compute all values $c(i,i)$ in $O(\log^2 n)$ time with n processors due to Chan and Lam [6]. This gives $O(\log^2 n)$ time and $O(n^2)$ operations for this step.

4.2 Computing entries $c(i,j)$

Now we describe how to compute the values $c(i,j)$ for either h_i or h_j from the chain. We may assume that h_i is an ancestor of h_j, since when $h_i = h_j$ we have computed these values in the previous section. And because we have already computed such values for all h_j which are not on the chain and are below the root of the chain, we will only consider h_j from the chain.

In the recurrence for $c(i,j)$ the values $\Delta(v_i^1, h_j)$, $c(j,j)$ and either $c(i, r(j))$ or $c(i, l(j))$ (because either $h_{l(j)}$ or $h_{r(j)}$ is pebbled) have been already computed. Hence we may assume that they are computed in advance. For a fixed index i this recurrence can be solved using standard algorithms for the expression evaluation problem which is known to need $O(\log n)$ time with $n/\log n$ processors on a EREW PRAM (see e.g. [11] or [16]). Thus we can compute values $c(i,j)$ for all $i \neq j$, such that h_j lies on a chain, in $O(\log n)$ time with $n^2/\log n$ processors on a CREW PRAM.

4.3 Computing all entries of the array c

Now we can count the total work of the algorithm. The operation *PEBBLE* can be done in $O(1)$ time with n^2 processors on a CREW PRAM. We need $O(\log^2 n)$ time with $n^2/\log^2 n$ processors to perform the operation *COMPRESS*. Hence we obtain the algorithm for solving the recurrence for the array c, running in $O(\log^3 n)$ time with $n^2/\log^2 n$ processors on a CREW PRAM.

But let us look more carefully at the needed number of operations. Let m_t be the number of vertices which are pebbled in the t-th step of the main loop. The operation *PEBBLE* can be done in a constant time with $O(m_t^2)$ operations. The operation *COMPRESS* need $O(\log^2 n)$ time and only $O(nm_t)$ operations on a CREW PRAM. Hence in the t-th step both the operations *PEBBLE* and *COMPRESS* can be performed in $O(\log^2 n)$ time with $O(nm_t)$ total work. Since $\sum_t m_t = O(n)$, we get $O(n^2)$ number of operations in the whole algorithm. Using Brent's theorem [5] we can decrease the number of needed processors to $n^2/\log^3 n$ for a CREW PRAM. Hence we obtain the following lemma.

Lemma 4.3 *We can compute the array c in $O(\log^3 n)$ time using $n^2/\log^3 n$ processors on a CREW PRAM.*

5 Reconstruction of an optimal triangulation

Now the array c is correctly computed. Thus to solve the triangulation problem we must only show how to find an optimal partition of a basic convex polygon using the array c. There exists a simple sequential linear time algorithm for the reconstruction but is much harder to find an $O(n^2)$ work $\mathcal{NC}$ parallel algorithm for this problem.

Our algorithm runs in three steps. First, it finds *ceil* of every candidate. Then for each candidate, it computes the set of descendants which are in an optimal triangulation of the polygon below this candidate. In the last step the algorithm finds all arcs which are in an optimal triangulation.

5.1 Finding ceils

For each candidate h_i which is an arc, define its *ceil* to be a maximal set of candidates $\{h_{j_1}, \ldots, h_{j_{t_i}}\}$ such that

1. every h_{j_s} is a descendant of h_i

2. every h_{j_s} exists in an optimal triangulation of the polygon below h_i

3. all candidates from the ceil are the highest ones satisfying (1) and (2), that is, if h_k lies between h_i and h_{j_s}, then h_k does not belong to the ceil of h_i

Such defined set is denoted by $Ceil(h_i)$. We compute the sets $Ceil(h_i)$ for each h_i independently. One can show that the problem of finding $Ceil(h_i)$ can be reduced to the following one. Given a binary tree T with $h_{g(i)}$ as the root. There are some marked vertices in the tree (h_j is marked iff $c(h_i, h_j) = \Delta(v_i^1, h_j) + c(h_j, h_j)$ or h_j is a leaf). For each marked vertex check whether all its ancestors are not marked. This problem can be solved in $O(\log n)$ time using $n/\log n$ processors on a CREW PRAM using e.g. the Euler tour technique. Hence we can find $Ceil(h_i)$ for all candidates h_i in $O(\log n)$ time with $O(n^2)$ total work on a CREW PRAM.

5.2 Finding all candidates existing in an optimal triangulation of the polygon below h_i

For each two candidates h_i, h_j, where h_i is an ancestor of h_j, define $D(i, j) = 1$ iff candidate h_j exists in an optimal triangulation of the polygon below h_i. Otherwise $D(i, j) = 0$. The array D denotes the transitive closure of the function $Ceil$.

Initialy we set $D(i, j) := 0$ for all i, j. We will fill entries of the array D during performing the operations *PEBBLE* and *COMPRESS* of the algorithm. We will ensure the following invariant after each operation. If a candidate h_i is pebbled, then for all j, values $D(i, j)$ are correctly computed.

When we perform the operation *PEBBLE* on some vertex h_i, we can compute values $D(i, j)$ as follows. We start with setting $D(i, k) := 1$ for all $h_k \in Ceil(h_i)$. All other candidates existing in an optimal triangulation of the polygon below h_i are descendants of candidates from $Ceil(h_i)$ which have been already pebbled. Thus we can find them in $O(1)$ time using n processors for each pebbling vertex h_i. Hence we can execute all *PEBBLE* steps in $O(\log n)$ time with $O(n^2)$ total work on a CREW PRAM.

When we perform the operation *COMPRESS* on the chain, we compute values $D(i, j)$ in a similar way. Thus we can compute all values $D(i, j)$ for h_i on the chain in $O(\log n)$ time with $O(n)$ total work on a CREW PRAM. Summarizing the discussion above, one can compute the array D in $O(\log^2 n)$ time using $n^2/\log^2 n$ processors on a CREW PRAM.

5.3 Reconstruction of an optimal triangulation

Now we can easily reconstruct an optimal triangulation from the arrays D and $Ceil$. Values $D(0, j)$, where h_0 denotes the root of the tree of candidates, give all candidates existing in an optimal triangulation of the whole polygon. Let h_j be one of them. We know that between h_j and its ceil does not exist any candidate. Thus we may triangulate the polygon between h_j and its ceil using Lemma 4.1. We must only join v_j to all vertices from $Ceil(h_j)$. Hence we can perform this step in a constant time with $O(n)$ work on a CREW PRAM.

Summarizing all discussions so far, we get the following lemma[3].

Lemma 5.1 *We can reconstruct an optimal triangulation of the convex polygon in $O(\log^2 n)$ time using $n^2/\log^2 n$ processors on a CREW PRAM.*

This lemma implies the main theorem.

Theorem 1
The matrix chain product problem and the problem of finding an optimal triangulation of a convex polygon can be solved in $O(\log^3 n)$ time using $n^2/\log^3 n$ processors on a CREW PRAM.

6 The triangulation of a monotone polygon

Define a *monotone polygon* to be a convex basic polygon with weights $(v_0, v_1, \ldots, v_n)$, such that for some k, $v_0 < v_1 < \ldots < v_k$ and $v_k > v_{k+1} > \ldots > v_n$. Hu and Shing [13] described an $O(n)$ sequential time algorithm for finding an optimal triangulation of such polygons. But there is not known any parallel $\mathcal{NC}$ algorithm which solves this problem more efficiently than for general polygons. We show how to find an optimal triangulation with $O(n \log^2 n)$ total work on a CREW PRAM.

In the monotone polygon the tree of candidates is almost a chain. Each vertex is either a leaf or has at least one son which is a leaf. Thus after pebbling all leaves we obtain exactly one chain. So all non-chained candidates correspond to sides of a polygon. and our problem reduces to finding an optimal triangulation below h_0 (the root of the tree). We can solve it in a similar way as in Section 4 to get an $O(n^2)$ total work algorithm. But since we are interested only in the value $c(h_0, h_0)$, we can reduce our problem to the convex least weight subsequence problem. It gives us an $O(\log^2 n)$ time and n processors CREW PRAM algorithm. Unfortunately the preprocessing for this problem (i.e., computing the function w) seems to need $O(n^2)$ work. But one can show that since all p_i (i.e., all pebbles sons) are sides, each value *bottom* and *fan* can be computed in constant time with a single processor after an $O(\log n)$ time preprocessing which uses $n/\log n$ processors on a CREW PRAM.

Hence we can compute the cost of an optimal triangulation of a monotone polygon in $O(\log^2 n)$ time using n processors on a CREW PRAM. And it is easy to see that we can rebuild this partition in $O(\log n)$ time using $n/\log n$ processors on a CREW PRAM. This gives the following theorem.

Theorem 2
The problem of finding an optimal triangulation of a monotone polygon can be

---

[3] One can improve this result to $O(\log n)$ time with $O(n^2)$ total work on a CREW PRAM.

solved in $O(\log^2 n)$ time using n processors on a CREW PRAM. □

References

[1] M.J. ATALLAH, S.R. KOSAJARU, L.L. LARMORE, G.L. MILLER, S-H. TENG, *Constructing trees in parallel*, SPAA 1989, pp. 421–431.

[2] M.J. ATALLAH, S.R. KOSAJARU, *An efficient algorithm for the row minima of a totally monotone matrix*, SODA 1991, pp. 394–403.

[3] P.G. BRADFORD, *A parallel approximation algorithm for matrix chain ordering*, manuscript, 1992.

[4] P.G. BRADFORD, *Efficient parallel dynamic programming*, manuscript, 1992.

[5] R.P. BRENT, *The parallel evaluation of general arithmetic expressions*, J. Assoc. Comput. Mach., 21 (1974), pp. 201–206.

[6] K.F. CHAN, T.W. LAM, *Finding least-weight subsequences with fewer processors*, SIGAL 1990, LNCS 450, pp. 318–327, also to appear in *Algorithmica*.

[7] R. COLE, U. VISHKIN, *Approximate and exact parallel scheduling with applications to list, tree and graph problems*, FOCS 1986, pp. 478–491.

[8] A. CZUMAJ, *An optimal parallel algorithm for computing a near-optimal order of matrix multiplications*, SWAT 1992, LNCS 621, pp. 62–72.

[9] S.S. GODBOLE, *On efficient computation of matrix chain products*, IEEE Trans. Comput., C-22, 9 (1973), pp. 864–866.

[10] Z. GALIL, K. PARK, *Parallel dynamic programming*, manuscript, 1992, submitted to J. Parallel Distrib. Comput.

[11] A.M. GIBBONS, W. RYTTER, *Efficient parallel algorithms*, Cambridge University Press, 1988.

[12] S-H.S. HUANG, H. LIU, V. VISWANATHAN, *Parallel dynamic programming*, IEEE Symposium on Parallel and Distributed Processing, 1990, pp. 497–500.

[13] T.C. HU, M.T. SHING, *Some theorems about matrix multiplications*, FOCS 1980, pp. 28–35.

[14] T.C. HU, M.T. SHING, *Computation of matrix chain products. Part I*, SIAM J. Comput., 11(1982), pp. 362–373.

[15] M.M. KLAWE, D.J. KLEITMAN, *An almost linear time algorithm for generalized matrix searching*, SIAM J. Discrete Math., 3 (1990), pp. 81–97.

[16] R.M. KARP, V. RAMACHANDRAN, *A survey of parallel algorithms for shared-memory machines*, in *Handbook of Theoretical Computer Science*, North-Holland, 1990, pp. 869–941.

[17] P. RAMANAN, *A new lower bound technique and its application: tight lower bound for a polygon triangulation problem*, SODA 1991, pp. 281–290.

[18] W. RYTTER, *On efficient parallel computations for some dynamic programming problems*, Theoret. Comput. Sci., 59 (1988), pp. 297–307.

[19] L. VALIANT, S. SKYUM, S. BERKOWITZ, C. RACKOFF, *Fast parallel computation of polynomials using few processors*, SIAM J. Comput., 12 (1983), pp. 641–644.

[20] F.F. YAO, *Speed-up in dynamic programming*, SIAM J. Algebraic and Discrete Methods, 3 (1982), pp. 532–540.

Multi-list ranking: complexity and applications

Anders Dessmark[*]   Andrzej Lingas[†]   Anil Maheshwari[‡]

Abstract

A natural combinatorial generalization of the convex layer problem, termed *multi-list ranking*, is introduced. It is proved to be P-complete in the general case. When the number of lists or layer size are bounded by $s(n)$, multi-list ranking is shown to be log-space hard for the class of problems solvable simultaneously in polynomial time and space $s(n)$. On the other hand, simultaneous polynomial-time and $O(s(n) \log n)$-space solutions in the above cases are provided. Also, NC algorithms for multi-list ranking when the number of lists or layer size are constantly bounded are given. In result, the first NC solutions (SC solutions, respectively) for the convex layer problem where the number of orientations or the layer size are constantly bounded (poly-log bounded, respectively) are derived.

1 Introduction

The *convex layer problem* is to partition the input set S of n points in the Euclidean plane into the set of convex polygons defined iteratively as follows : compute the convex hull of S and remove its vertices from S. This problem is a natural extension of the convex hull problem. Chazelle [2] presented an optimal $O(n \log n)$ time sequential algorithm for computing the convex layers. For applications of this problem, see Chazelle [2].

The convex hull of the given n points can be computed optimally in parallel in $O(\log n)$ time using $O(n)$ processors in EREW PRAM model of computation (combine [3] with [4]). Several researchers have attempted to either present an NC algorithm for the convex layer problem or to show it to be $P - complete$ [1]. Still this problem remains one of the most important unresolved problems in parallel computational geometry. Also, the question of its space complexity (related by the parallel computation thesis [9]) is interesting.

In this paper we consider a natural combinatorial generalization of the convex layer problem which we term multi-list ranking. It is defined on the input lists $l_1, l_2, ..., l_q$ iteratively (with $i = 1$ initially) as follows: Pick the first element from each list and assign the rank i to each of them. Remove all elements of rank i

---

[*]Department of Computer Science, Lund University, Box 118, S-22100, Lund, Sweden
[†]Department of Computer Science, Lund University, Box 118, S-22100, Lund, Sweden
[‡]Computer Systems and Communications Group, Tata Institute of Fundamental Research, Homi Bhabha Road, Bombay 400 005, India, E-mail : manil@tifrvax.bitnet

from all the lists, set i to $i + 1$ and if there is at least one non-empty list left iterate. The multi-list ranking problem (MLRP) is to compute the sets (called *layers*) of elements of rank i, $i = 1, 2, ...$.

We show a natural log-space (and thus, also NC) reduction of the convex layer problem to MLRP (section 2). Unfortunately, the reduction cannot help us in solving the convex layer problem as we prove (the decision version of) MLRP to be *P-complete* (section 3). In section 4, we show that MLRP with $O(s(n))$ lists is log-space hard for the class of problems solvable simultaneously in polynomial time and space $s(n)$, i.e. for the class $TS[n^{O(1)}, s(n)]$ (see [10]). On the other hand, we provide simultaneous polynomial-time and $O(s(n) \log n)$-space solutions to MLRP with $O(s(n))$ lists or with $O(s(n))$ layer size. In this way, the first natural, almost complete problems for Steve's classes $SC^i = TS[n^{O(1)}, log^i n]$, $i = 1, 2, ...$ (in honour of Steven Cook [10]) are in particular obtained.

In section 5, we prove that the multi-list ranking problem is solvable in $O(\log n \log \log n)$-time using $O(n^k)$ processors if the number of lists is bounded by k. We also show that if the layer size is bounded by a constant c, MLRP can be solved in logarithmic time using $O(n^{c+3})$ processors.

As corollary, the first SC algorithm (NC algorithm, respectively) for the problem of computing convex layers with $O(\log^{O(1)} n)$ layer size (constantly bounded layer size, respectively) is obtained (section 6). We can also compute the convex layers in SC (NC, respectively) if each convex polygon is oriented in c specified directions where $c = O(\log^{O(1)} n)$ (c is a constant, respectively). In particular, if we consider two opposite vertical directions and two opposite horizontal directions then we obtain an NC and SC solution to a rectangular layer problem which can be interpreted as the convex layer problem in L_1!

2 Multi-List Ranking Problem

The multi-list ranking problem (MLRP) is a problem on the multi-list $L = \{l_1, l_2, ..., l_q\}$, where each list l_i contains one or more integers. Let $|L| = |l_1| + |l_2| + ... + |l_q|$ be the total size of the multi-list L. The *rank* of an element of L is defined as follows. The first elements on the lists l_1 through l_q form the set R_1 of rank 1 elements. Remove all elements of rank 1 from each list in L. Now the first elements on the reduced lists comprise the set R_2 of rank 2 elements. Iteratively, we define the sets R_i of rank i elements, $i = 3, 4....$ The multi-list ranking problem (MLRP) is to compute the sets $R_1, R_2, ..., R_m$, $m \leq |L|$, which we shall call *layers* of L. The multi-list ranking problem with layer size $s(n)$ is to compute the initial sequence $R_1, ..., R_l$ of $R_1, R_2, ..., R_m$ where each of the layers $R_1, ..., R_l$ has no more than $s(n)$ elements. The decision version of MLRP is to decide for an element e of L and an integer i whether the rank of e is not greater than i. The decision version of MLRP with layer size $s(n)$ is to decide for e and i whether the rank r of e is not greater i and each of the layers $R_1, ..., R_r$ has no more than $s(n)$ elements.

If an element in the list l_i occurs more than once, then it can be seen that only its first occurrence in the list will decide its rank. So from now on we assume that each element in a list occurs at most once.

Now we present a log-space (and thus also NC) reduction of the convex layer problem to MLRP. Observe that it is enough to solve an analogous decision version of the convex layer problem, i.e., for each point to compute the number of the convex layer it lies in. This is because, once we know all points in a convex layer, we can compute the order of these points along the boundary of the convex polygon by sorting the points with respect to their polar coordinates.

Let us see what the list l_i corresponds to in the convex layer problem. We sweep the given set S of n points by a line in $O(n^2)$ directions. A direction is determined by the perpendicular direction to a line passing through a pair of points. In each direction we sweep a line and make a list of the points as they appear on the line. It may happen that a few of the points are collinear in some direction. Let us assume that k points are collinear in some particular direction. Without loss of generality assume that the points are $p_{i+1}, p_{i+2},..., p_{i+k}$. Also assume that $p_1, p_2, ..., p_i$ be the points which appear on this list before p_{i+1}. Create the following k lists.

$p_1, p_2, ..., p_i, p_{i+1}, p_{i+2}, ...$

$p_1, p_2, ..., p_i, p_{i+2}$

$p_1, p_2, ..., p_i, p_{i+3}$

$\vdots$

$p_1, p_2, ..., p_i, p_{i+k}$

Only the first list, the main list, will contain all the points in a total order which is an extension of the partial order resulting from the sweep. All occurrences of collinear points in a direction will be handled by seperate sets of auxiliary prefix lists of the main list containing all the points strictly before the respective collinearity.

The set of at most $O(n^3)$ lists obtained as above forms the multi-list L. Let CL_i denote the set of points on the ith convex layer, i.e. the ith convex polygon. We show that $CL_i = R_i$ by induction on i.

Consider the base case, $i = 1$. Let $p_i p_j$ be a convex hull edge of the point set S. Observe that p_i (or p_j) will be the first element in the list determined by sweeping the line in the direction corresponding to the pair of points p_i and p_j. So, $CL_1 \subset R_1$. Sweeping a line in any direction will result in encountering first a point of the convex hull of S. This implies that the first element in each list l_i is a point on the convex hull of S. So, $R_1 \subset CL_1$. Hence $CL_1 = R_1$.

Assume that $CL_i = R_i, \forall i \leq k$. Now we show that $CL_{k+1} = R_{k+1}$. Remove all points from S which belongs to CL_i, where $i \leq k$. Similarly, remove all elements from each list l_j of L which belongs to R_i, where $i \leq k$. Now it is sufficient to show a 1-1 correspondence between the points on the convex hull of the remaining points of S and the first element of each reduced list l_i. The proof is analogous to the base case. We conclude the above observations in the following theorem.

Theorem 2.1 *The convex layer problem is log-space reducible to the multi-list ranking problem.*

3 Time complexity of MLRP

We will first present a sequential algorithm for MLRP and then analyze its complexity. After that we show that MLRP is $P - complete$.

To each list l_i of L, assign a pointer which will traverse the list from left to right during the course of the algorithm. In beginning each pointer points to the first element of its list. The set R_1 of L contains the elements pointed by the pointers initially. Assume that we have computed the sets $R_1, R_2, ..., R_{j-1}$ and we wish to compute the set R_j. In each list l_i perform the following operations. Keep moving the pointer to the element on the right till either the end of the list is encountered or an element has been found whose rank is $\nleq j - 1$. Now in each list the element pointed by the pointer is an element of R_j. So the time complexity of the above algorithm is of the order of the size of the multi-list times the time required to find the rank of the next element in the list. Since we know that the elements of multi-list are integers, we sort $|L|$ elements and store them in the sorted order in an array. During the above mentioned procedure for computing $R_j's$, we assign the rank of each element found so far in this array. So it requires a binary search in this array to find out the rank of any element in any list. We summarize the above results in the following theorem.

Theorem 3.1 *Multi-list ranking problem can be solved in $O(|L|\log|L|)$ time, where $|L|$ is the size of the multi-list. Moreover, if the elements in the multi-list are bounded by an integer z then MLRP can be solved in $O(|L|)$ time using $O(z)$ space.*

Now we show that MLRP is $P - complete$.

Theorem 3.2 *The decision version of MLRP is log-space P-complete.*

Proof: Let x be an instance of a problem L that can be solved by a one-tape deterministic TM M in polynomial time $t(n)$. Note that M uses no more than $t(n)$ space. Let A be the tape alphabet of M, and let Q be the set of states of M. The configuration of M, achieved after its first i steps, can be described with a word in $(A \cup A \times Q)^+$, describing the contents of consecutive cells of the tape, and marking the cell under the head with the symbol in $A \times Q$, giving its contents and the current state of M. We will use $a_{i,j}$, where $a \in A \cup A \times Q$, i is the time ($i \in \{0..t(n)\}$), and j is the number of the tape cell ($i \in \{1..t(n)\}$) as the elements in MLRP. We will also use $t_1, .., t_{t(n)}$ as dummy elements with layer numbers corresponding to their index. Let the input word $x = x_1...x_n$, let $B \in A$ be the blank tape symbol and q_0 the initial state. The initial configuration will be represented by $t(n)$ lists, each with one element:

$$\{(x_1 \times q_0)_{0,1}\}, \{(x_2)_{0,2}\}, ..., \{(x_n)_{0,n}\}, \{B_{0,n+1}\}, ..., \{B_{0,t(n)}\}.$$

Also for each step i, each cell j, and for each combination of $a, b, c \in A \cup A \times Q$ where at most one element is in $A \times Q$, create the list
$$\{t_1, t_2, ..., t_i, a_{i-1,j-1}, b_{i-1,j}, c_{i-1,j+1}, d_{i,j}\}$$
where d is the description of the cell j uniquely determined by the descriptions a, b, c of the cells $j - 1, j, j + 1$ respectively (if $j - 1 = 0$ or $j + 1 > t(n)$ we use only two cells).

If the j-th cell after step i is described by $a \in A \cup A \times Q$, the corresponding element $a_{i,j}$ will be in layer $i + 1$, otherwise it will belong to layer i+2 (since there is a list beginning with $t_1, ..., t_{1+1}, a_{i,j}$) When the instance of MLRP is solved, it will be easy to see if an accepting state has been reached in time $t(n)$, by looking at the layer number of the elements corresponding to the Turing machine configuration in the last step.

It can be easily seen that the above lists can be constructed in log-space. Hence we can construct the instance of MLRP in log-space and MLRP is $P -$ *complete*.

□

4 Space complexity of restricted MLRP

In this section we show that MLRP with $s(n)$ lists or layer size $s(n)$ can be computed by a TM operating simultaneously in polynomial time and $O(s(n) \log n)$ space. Thus these both restrictions of MLRP belong to the class $TS[n^{O(1)}, s(n) \log n]$ (see [10]). On the other hand, we prove that MLRP with $s(n)$ lists or layer size $s(n)$ is log-space hard for $TS[n^{O(1)}, s(n)]$.

4.1 Number of lists is bounded

When the number of lists is bounded from above by $s(n)$ we need only $O(s(n) \log n)$ cells of a working tape of a Turing machine to encode the current pointer configuration. Also, given such an encoding, a Turing machine with $O(s(n) \log n)$ working tape can test whether a given list element occurs before the pointer on any other input list in total linear time. As the total number of tests is $O(n)$ we obtain the following theorem.

Theorem 4.1 *Let $s(n)$ be a positive integer function. MLRP with $O(s(n))$ lists is in $TS[n^2, s(n) \log n]$.*

Corollary 4.2 *MLRP with $O(\log^k n)$ lists is in SC^{k+1}.*

Having in mind the parallel computation thesis [9] it is natural to ask whether MLRP with poly-log bounded number of list is in NC? In the following we show in particular that the above question is equivalent to the unresolved SC⊂NC? question. In fact we obtain a much more general result which exhibits MLRP with $s(n)$ lists as the first natural log-space hard problem for $TS[n^{O(1)}, s(n)]$. To start with we need the following technical lemma.

Lemma 4.3 *For any language P in $TS(n^{0(1)}, s(n))$, where $s(n) = \Omega(\log n)$, there exists a TM which recognizes P in polynomial time and $s(n)$ working space regularly sweeping the input word with its input head from the left to the right and vice versa.*

Proof: Let M be a TM which operates in working space $s(n)$ and polynomial time. We can simulate M with such an input sweeping TM M' as follows. We equip M' with few additional working tapes of logarithmic size. To simulate a single step of M the TM M' updates the current position of the input head of M in binary on an additional working tape. Next, it computes the number of moves of its input head necessary to reach the next position of the input head of M. Observe that M' needs logarithmic time for the above operations. Simultaneously its head on the input tape continues its regular sweep of the input tape. Using another additional working tape as an unary counter M' updates the number of remaining moves of its input head after every $O(\log n)$ of own moves in this way leaving enough time for the updates. When the input head M' is within logarithmic distance from the new position of the input head of M the TM M' uses unary logarithmic counter to not overlook the sought new position. □

Theorem 4.4 *Let $s(n)$ be a function satisfying $s(n) = \Omega(\log n)$ and computable in logarithmic space. MLRP with $s(n)$ lists is log-space hard for $TS[n^{O(1)}, s(n)]$.*

Proof: Let x be the input to a Turing machine M operating in working space $s(n)$ and polynomial time $t(n)$. By Lemma 4.3 we may assume without loss of generality that M sweeps the input tape. We shall modify the construction of the instance of MLRP for x and M from the proof of the P-completeness of MLRP. First of all we restrict the description of the current configuration to the $s(n)$ bounded working space. The missing position of the input head of M after i moves and the input symbol under it can be easily computed in logarithmic space from the time index i. Therefore the range of the second index j for the list elements in the constructed instance of MLRP can be decreased to $1, 2, ..., s(n)$. To decrease the number of necessary lists we use only the lists for the initial tape configuration, one list with the dummy elements $\{t_1, t_2, ..., t_{t(n)}\}$ and two lists for every combination of $a, b, c \in A \cup A \times Q$ and tape cell j. The $t(n)$ lists

$$\{t_1, a_{0,j-1}, b_{0,j}, c_{0,j+1}, d_{1,j}\}$$
$$\{t_1, t_2, a_{1,j-1}, b_{1,j}, c_{1,j+1}, d_{2,j}\}$$
$$\vdots$$
$$\{t_1, t_2, ..., t_{t(n)}, a_{t(n)-1,j-1}, b_{t(n)-1,j}, c_{t(n)-1,j+1}, d_{t(n),j}\}$$

are replaced by two following lists

$$\{t_1, a_{0,j-1}, b_{0,j}, c_{0,j+1}, d_{1,j}, t_3, a_{2,j-1}, b_{2,j}, c_{2,j+1}, d_{3,j}, t_5...\}$$
$$\{t_1, t_2, a_{1,j-1}, b_{1,j}, c_{1,j+1}, d_{2,j}, t_4, a_{3,j-1}, b_{3,j}, c_{3,j+1}, d_{4,j}, t_6...\}$$

with the first taking care of the odd steps and the second taking care of the even steps. The dummy elements between the transitions make sure that the latter do not effect the layer numbers within the lists. The layer number of $d_{i,j}$ will be $i+1$ or $i+2$ and it will have no effect on the layer number of t_{i+2} which will remain $i+2$ so $d_{i+2,j}$ will get the correct layer number. As there is one list containing only dummy elements (this list can actually be avoided), $s(n)$ lists with the initial configuration and $O(s(n))$ list pairs for the transitions, the total number of lists is $O(s(n))$.

$\square$

Corollary 4.5 *MLRP with $O(\log^k n)$ lists is log-space hard for SC^k and belongs to SC^{k+1}.*

4.2 Layer size is bounded

When the layer size is bounded from above by $s(n)$ we need only $O(s(n)\log n)$ cells of a working tape of a Turing machine to encode the current layer R_i. Given such an encoding, a Turing machine with $O(s(n)\log n)$ working space can find the current position of the pointer on a given input list in time $O(s(n)n)$. To find the next position of the pointer it can test the consecutive elements of the list following the pointer for occurrence before the current pointers on the other lists. Each such test takes time $O(s(n)nk)$ where k is the number of lists. The next position of the pointer on the list gives us an element of the next layer R_{i+1} corresponding to the list. By repeating the operation of pointer moving for the remaining lists the whole R_{i+1} can be produced. The total number of the tests during the whole computation is bounded by the total length of lists, i.e. it is $O(n)$. Since also $k = O(n)$, we obtain the following theorem.

Theorem 4.6 *Let $s(n)$ be a positive integer function. MLRP with layer size $s(n)$ is in $TS[s(n)n^3, s(n)\log n]$.*

Corollary 4.7 *MLRP with layer size $O(\log^k n)$ is in SC^{k+1}.*

Since MLRP with $\leq s(n)$ lists is a special case of MLRP with layer size $s(n)$, by Theorem 4.4 we obtain the following hardness result for the former.

Corollary 4.8 *Let $s(n)$ be a function satisfying $s(n) = \Omega(\log n)$ and computable in logarithmic space. MLRP with layer size $s(n)$ is log-space hard for $TS[n^{O(1)}, s(n)]$.*

Corollary 4.9 *MLRP with layer size $O(\log^k n)$ is log-space hard for SC^k and belongs to SC^{k+1}.*

5 NC algorithms for special cases of MLRP

5.1 Number of lists is constant

We are given a constant number of lists, say k, where the number of elements in each list is at most n. It follows that the total number of elements in the multi-lists in $O(n)$. By sorting the lists in time $O(\log n)$ using $O(n)$ processors, we can enumerate the elements to be able to assume further that they are in the range $\{1..O(n)\}$. Our objective is to compute the layers R_i, where $1 \leq i \leq n$.

Before we present our parallel algorithm we describe a preprocessing step which is required in the algorithm. For each element z in the multi-list L, where $z = O(n)$, we compute the position of the occurrence of z in each list and store it in an array of size k. So i^{th} location in the array corresponding to z is the position of z in the ith list l_i. This can be achieved by sorting all elements of L and it requires $O(\log n)$ time using $O(n)$ processors. Recall that each element appears at most once in each list.

Recall the sequential algorithm from section 3 for solving MLRP on the k lists. Let us assume that we have computed sets $R_1, R_2, ..., R_{j-1}$, and we wish to compute R_j. We have k pointers, one for each list, which will traverse the list from the left to the right. Currently the pointers are pointing at the element in its list which belongs to R_{j-1}. In the next step each pointer moves to the right in order to locate an element which has not appeared in any of the sets computed so far. At the end of this step each pointer points to an element of R_j. So the sequential algorithm computes the *next pointer configuration* from the *present configuration*. The algorithm starts with the first pointer configuration which is the first element in each list.

The sequential algorithm can be easily parallelized. Notice that there are only $O(n^k)$ possible pointer configurations. For each pointer configuration we can compute the next configuration in $O(\log n)$ time using $O(n)$ processors as follows. Let $x(i)$ be the pointer position in the list l_i for the given configuration, where $1 \leq i \leq k$. The pointer position in l_i for the next configuration can be computed by first finding out all elements after $x(i)$ in l_i which haven't appeared between the first and the $x(j)^{th}$ element in any of the lists l_j where $j \neq i$. Once we know all such elements after $x(i)$ in l_i, the element with the least index among the remaining ones is the desired element. Using the preprocessing information we can compute the required element in $O(\log n)$ time. Now we know how to compute next pointer configuration from the given one. So the remaining task is to compute the pointer configurations corresponding to the sets R_i. By performing parallel list ranking we can trace the pointer configurations starting from the first one.

Now we analyze the complexity of the above naive parallel algorithm. For each configuration the next configuration can be computed in $O(\log n)$ time using $O(n)$ processors. Since there are in all $O(n^k)$ configurations, this step requires $O(\log n)$ time using $O(n^{k+1})$ processors. Parallel list ranking on the list of size $O(n^k)$ can be done in $O(\log n)$ time using $O(n^k)$ processors [9]. Hence the overall complexity of the parallel algorithm for computing sets R_i is $O(\log n)$ time using $O(n^{k+1})$ processors in CREW PRAM model of computation. We summarize the above results in the following theorem.

Theorem 5.1 *The multi-list ranking problem for k lists, each of size at most n, can be solved in $O(\log n)$ time using $O(n^{k+1})$ processors in CREW PRAM model of computation.*

In the above algorithm we require $O(n)$ processors for each pointer configuration to compute its next configuration. In place of carrying out the computation for all configurations simultaneously we can carry out the computations in a certain number of steps. This will allow us to use the same set of processors which have been used in the earlier steps. In result we obtain the following theorem where a 2 page proof is omited because of space considerations (see [5]).

Theorem 5.2 *The multi-list ranking problem for k lists, each of size at most n, can be solved in $O(\log n \log \log n)$ time using $O(n^k)$ processors in CREW PRAM model of computation.*

5.2 Layer size is bounded by a constant

Assume that the number of lists is k, and that each element on the lists is in $\{1..m\}$. Also assume that it is known that the number of elements in each rank is bounded by a constant c. In this section we present NC algorithm for computing the layers R_i.

We will use parallel list ranking on the limited number of pointer configurations which arises in this case. Since each $|R_i|$ is bounded by c, only $O(m^c)$ combinations are possible for each rank. Given one such combination of elements, the corresponding pointer configuration in the multi-list can be computed as follows. The pointer in each list should point to the leftmost element among the elements in the list which belong to the combination. Assign one processor to each element in each of the lists. The leftmost element which belongs to the combination can be found in $O(\log m)$ time by parallel list ranking. In fact we can avoid repeating here parallel list ranking for different combinations by applying it in a preprocessing stage to rank the list elements. Then the leftmost element can be found even in a constant time. If a list doesn't contain any of the elements, place the pointer at the end of the list. Hence given a combination, the corresponding configuration in the multi-list can be computed in $O(1)$ time using $O(mk)$ processors.

For each of the pointer configurations computed above, find the next configuration as follows. Use an array of length m and mark ith location in the array if i appears before the pointer in any of the lists. This can be done in $O(\log k)$ time using $O(mk)$ processors. The $O(\log k)$ factor is because in our model of computation we do not allow common write. Then find the first unmarked element after the pointer in each list. This requires $O(\log m)$ time using $O(mk)$ processors. These unmarked elements correspond to the next pointer configuration. Hence we require $O(m^{c+1}k)$ processors to compute the next configuration for all possible configurations. Note that if the next configuration of a configuration X has more than c elements, then the next configuration of X is assigned empty.

We can find the configurations corresponding to the sets R_i by tracing the configurations starting from the first one. This can be achieved by performing parallel list ranking on the list of size $O(m^c)$ and it requires $O(\log m)$ time using

$O(m^c)$ processors. The above observations can be summarized in the following theorem.

Theorem 5.3 *The multi-list ranking problem with layer size c can be solved in time $O(\log k + \log m)$ with $O(m^{c+1}k)$ processors on a CREW PRAM model of computation.*

6 Applications of MLRP

In this section we present SC and NC algorithms for special cases of the convex layer problem.

Given a set of c orientations in the plane, a polygon is *c-oriented* if each its edge has an orientation in this set. The problem is to partition the given set S of n points into the set of c-oriented convex polygons defined iteratively as follows. Compute the smallest c-oriented convex polygon (layer) enclosing S and remove the set of points in S on its perimeter from S. The case when there are exactly two isothetic orientations corresponds to that of computing axis-parallel rectangular layers. Here we present an SC algorithm (NC algorithm, respectively) for computing c-oriented layers by reducing it to an equivalent multi-list ranking problem where the number of lists is poly-logarithmic (a constant, respectively). In order to perform the reduction we preprocess the input points by enumerating them.

Since we are interested in computing c-oriented layers, we need to do line sweep of the the given point set in only $2c$ directions in order to obtain the equivalent MLRP. Note that for each of the c-orientations we need to do line sweep of S in exactly two opposite directions. It can easily be seen that collinearity will not increase the complexity since the actual number of possible pointer configurations will not increase. The computation of the next configuration in the cases where a pointer points to a collinear point can easily be done without adding the prefix lists discussed earlier. By Theorem 4.2 we obtain the following result.

Theorem 6.1 *For $c = \log^k n$, the problem of computing c-oriented layers of a n point set is in SC^{k+1}.*

Analogously, using Theorem 5.2 we obtain the following result.

Theorem 6.2 *For a constant c, the c-oriented layers of a n point set in plane can be computed in $O(\log n \log \log n)$ time using $O(n^{2c})$ processors in CREW PRAM model of computation.*

In this section we also present an SC algorithm (NC algorithm, respectively) for computing convex layers where each layer has a poly-log number (constant number, respectively) of points by reducing it to an equivalent MLRP with poly-log (constant, respectively) layer size.

Sweep the given point set S of n elements in $O(n^2)$ directions and obtain the lists as in Section 2. It can be done by a Turing machine in log-space or by

CREW PRAM in $O(\log n)$ time using linear number of processors. Now we use Corollary 4.7 with $s(n) = \log^k n$ (as in c-oriented layers, collinear points will not add complexity) to obtain the following theorem.

Theorem 6.3 *The convex layer problem where each layer has $O(\log^k n)$ points is in SC^{k+1}.*

Analogously we can use Theorem 5.3 where $k = O(n^2)$, $m = n$ and c is the maximum constant layer size to obtain the following theorem.

Theorem 6.4 *The convex layer problem where each layer has no more than c points can be solved in $O(\log n)$ time using $O(n^{c+3})$ processors in CREW PRAM model of computation.*

Final remarks: The obtained hardness results suggest that a combinatorial approach to the convex layer problem is not sufficient to derive NC algorithms for the geometric problem but for restricted cases.

Is it possible to overcome the logarithmic gap in space bounds between our hardness results for MLRP with $O(s(n))$ lists or $O(s(n))$ layer size and our solutions to these problems?

Acknowledgements: Thanks go to Subhash Suri for interesting comments.

References

[1] M. J. Atallah, P. Callahan and M. T. Goodrich, $P-$ *complete geometric problems*, 2nd Annual ACM Symposium on Parallel Algorithms and Architectures, 1990, pp. 317-326.

[2] B. Chazelle, *On the convex layers of the planar set*, IEEE Transactions on Information Theory, Vol. IT-31, 1985, pp. 509-517.

[3] Chen D.Z. "An EREW PRAM algorithm for the convex hull of a sorted point set". Technical Report TR 89-928, Dept. of Computer Science, Purdue University, Nov. 1989.

[4] R. Cole, Parallel Merge Sort, SIAM J. Comput., 17:770-785, 1988.

[5] A. Dessmark, A. Lingas and A. Maheshwari, *Multi-list ranking: complexity and applications*, LU-CS-TR.:92-107, Lund University, 1992.

[6] M. T. Goodrich, *Efficient parallel techniques for computational geometry*, Ph.D. Thesis, Department of Computer Science, Purdue University, 1987.

[7] A. Gibbons and W. Rytter, *Efficient parallel algorithms*, Cambridge University Press, 1988, pp. 236-240.

[8] J. Hershberger, *Upper envelope onion peeling*, 2nd Scandinavian Workshop on Algorithm Theory, 1990, LNCS 447, 1990, pp. 368-379.

[9] R. M. Karp and V. Ramachandran, *Parallel algorithms for shared memory machines*, Handbook of Theoretical Computer Science, Ed. J. van Leeuwen, Elsevier Science Publishers, 1990, pp. 869-941.

[10] D. S. Johnson, *A Catalog of Complexity classes*, Handbook of Theoretical Computer Science, Ed. J. van Leeuwen, Elsevier Science Publishers, 1990, pp. 67-161.

Exact Algorithms for a Geometric Packing Problem (Extended Abstract)

L. Kučera, K. Mehlhorn, B. Preis, and E. Schwarzenecker

Max-Planck-Institut für Informatik and Fachbereich Informatik, Universität des Saarlandes, Im Stadtwald, 66 Saarbrücken, Germany.
e-mail: mehlhorn@mpi-sb.mpg.de

Abstract. We investigate the following packing problem: given n points $p_1, \ldots, p_n$ in the plane determine the supremum σ_{opt} of all reals σ, for which there are n pairwise disjoint, axis-parallel squares $Q_1, \ldots, Q_n$ of side length σ, where for each i, $1 \leq i \leq n$, p_i is a corner of Q_i. The problem arises in the connection with lettering of maps, and its decision version is NP-complete. We present two *exact* algorithms for the decision problem with time complexities $4^{O(\sqrt{n})}$ and $4^{O(\sqrt{n \log n})}$, resp. While the first one is of only theoretical interest because of a large multiplicative factor in the exponent, the other is suitable for practical computation.

1 Introduction

The following packing problem arises in the connection with lettering of maps: given n points $p_1, \ldots, p_n$ in the plane determine the supremum σ_{opt} of all reals σ, for which there are n pairwise disjoint, axis-parallel squares $Q_1, \ldots, Q_n$ of side length σ, where for each i, $1 \leq i \leq n$, p_i is a corner of Q_i. In [FW91] Formann and Wagner showed that the related decision problem is NP-complete, that there is an $O(n \log n)$ approximation algorithm which finds a packing with side length $\sigma \geq \sigma_{opt}/2$, and that there is no better approximation algorithm unless P equals NP.

In this paper we discuss *exact* algorithms for the decision problem: Given a set X of n points $p_1, \ldots, p_n$ in the plane, decide whether there are unit-size, pairwise disjoint, axis-parallel squares $Q_1, \ldots, Q_n$ where for each i, $1 \leq i \leq n$, p_i is a corner of Q_i. It is easy to see that the optimization problem can be reduced to $O(n^2)$ decision problems; one only has to observe that σ_{opt} is the x-distance or y-distance of two points in X or half of such a distance.

The goal of our research is to develop algorithms which can solve packing problems with up to one hundred points exactly. Applying such an algorithm to subproblems of larger packing problems would allow to compute *upper* bounds for σ_{opt}. Combined with the *lower* bound given by the approximation algorithm of Formann and Wagner, we hope to obtain very good (within a few percent) estimates of σ_{opt}. Our experiments substantiate this hope.

Let X denote our set of points. In [FW91] it was shown that if the placement problem for X has a solution then no square with side length 3 can contain more than 25 points of X. In view of this observation we make (for this extended abstract but not for the full paper) the simplifying assumption that X is sparse, where a set X of points is called *sparse* if any two points of X have distance at least one.

A naive algorithm checks all 4^n placements of the n squares and thus has running time $O(4^n poly(n))$. It can be used to solve problems with at most 10 points in a few seconds on a SUN SPARC. In section 2 we give an asymptotically much faster algorithm.

Theorem 1. *The decision problem can be solved in time $4^{O(\sqrt{n})}$.*

The algorithm is based on a variant of the planar separator theorem [LT79] given in [LM84]. Unfortunately, this algorithm is of only theoretical interest and does not extend the range of problems which can be solved in realistic amounts of time.

In section 3 we give a simple sweep line algorithm. It sweeps the plane orthogonally to a carefully chosen direction d. Call an element of $[0, \pi)$ a *direction* and call

$$C_X(d) = \max_{y \in \mathbb{R}^2} |\{x \in X \; ; \; |(x_1 - y_1) \cos d + (x_2 - y_2) \sin d| \le \sqrt{2}\}|$$

the *complexity* of X in direction d. Note that $C_X(d)$ is the largest number of elements of X contained in any stripe of width $2\sqrt{2}$ orthogonal to vector $(\cos d, \sin d)$. Let C_X be the minimal value of $C_X(d)$ where d ranges over all directions, and let $C(n)$ be the maximal value of C_X for any set X of n points. We show

Theorem 2. *Let X be a sparse set of cardinality n.*

1. *The sweep algorithm, when used in direction d, solves the decision problem in time $O(4^{C_X(d)} poly(n))$.*
2. *A direction d minimizing $C_X(d)$ can be found in polynomial time.*
3. *$C(n) \le 16\sqrt{(n \ln n)/\pi}$.*
4. *$C(n) = \Omega(\sqrt{n \log n})$.*

The proof of part 4 was given by J. Matoušek [Mat92].

The picture at the end of the article shows a labeling constructed by the sweep algorithm.

We close this introduction with some definitions. Identify the four possible placements of a single square with the symbols in the set $A = \{$SW,SE,NE,NW$\}$ and identify the possible placements of the squares for a set X of points with the functions from X to A. Call a placement ρ *legal* if the squares are disjoint when placed as given by ρ. Let X' be a subset of X. Call a placement ρ' for X' *extendible* if there is a legal placement ρ for X which extends ρ', i.e., $\rho(x) = \rho'(x)$ for all $x \in X'$.

2 A Proof of Theorem 1

We sketch a proof of Theorem 1. This following Lemma is essential.

Lemma 3. *Let X be a sparse set of n points. Then X can be partitioned into sets X_1, S, and X_2 such that*

1. *$|S| = O(\sqrt{n})$,*

2. $|X_1|, |X_2| \leq 2n/3$,
3. *any point in X_1 has distance at least two from any point in X_2,*
4. *the partition can be determined in polynomial time.*

Proof. The proof is a modification of the proof of [LM84, Theorem 3].

The algorithm is now as follows. Partition X into sets X_1, S, and X_2. Cycle through all placements π_S for S and use the algorithm recursively to check whether π_S can be extended to placements π_1 for $S \cup X_1$ and π_2 for $S \cup X_2$. If there is such a placement π_S then declare the problem solvable, if not declare it unsolvable. The correctness of this algorithm follows from the observation that the squares for the points in X_1 and X_2 can be placed independently since points in X_1 have distance at least two from points in X_2.

Let $T(n)$ be the maximal running time of the algorithm on an input of n points. Then T obeys the recurrence

$$T(n) = 4^{O(\sqrt{n})}(poly(n) + max\{T(n_1) + T(n_2) ; n_i \leq 2n/3 + O(\sqrt{n}) \text{ for } i = 1, 2$$
$$\text{and } n_1 + n_2 = n + O(\sqrt{n})\})$$

This recurrence has solution $T(n) = O(4^{O(\sqrt{n})}poly(n))$.

3 A Proof of Theorem 2

We first describe the algorithm and prove parts 1 and 2 of the theorem. We then turn to parts 3 and 4.

3.1 The Sweep Algorithm

Let d be a direction. The algorithm sweeps a line orthogonal to d across the plane. For a position p of the sweep line, let $B(p)$ be the set of points in X behind the sweep line and let $X(p)$ be the set of points in $B(p)$ which are within distance $2\sqrt{2}$ of the sweep line. The algorithm maintains all placements for $X(p)$ which can be extended to a legal placement of $B(p)$. The set $X(p)$ changes $2n$ times as each point enters and leaves $X(p)$ exactly once. When $X(p)$ changes the set of placements needs to be updated. We will show in the full paper that this can be done in time $O(4^{|X(p)|}poly(n))$. Since $|X(p)| \leq C(d)$ this implies part 1.

Part 2 follows from the observation that the search for an optimal d can be restricted to a set of polynomially many candidate directions and that $C(d)$ for a fixed direction d can be determined in linear time.

3.2 An Upper Bound for $C(n)$

We prove part 3. Let $m = 16\sqrt{(n \ln n)/\pi}$ (= our claimed upper bound on $C(n)$), let $k = 2n/m = \sqrt{\pi n/(64 \ln n)}$, and for i, $1 \leq i \leq k$, let $d_i = i\pi/k$. Let $\epsilon = 2\sqrt{2}$ and suppose that for each $i \in [1..k]$ there is a stripe Q_i of width ϵ, containing at least m elements of X.

Given two stripes of width $1 + \varepsilon$, the area of the intersection of the stripes is at most $(1 + \varepsilon)^2 \sin^{-1} \gamma \leq 16 \sin^{-1} \gamma \leq 8\pi/\gamma$, where γ is the angle between the stripes.

Note that if a stripe of width ε around a given line contains a point x, then a stripe of width $1 + \varepsilon$ contains x together with the $1/2$-ball centered at x, and if x, y are two different elements of X, then the $1/2$-balls around them are disjoint. Hence the intersection of any two stripes of width ε contains at most $(8\pi/\gamma)/(\pi/4) = 32/\gamma$ elements of X.

We say that a point $x \in X$ is *ambiguous*, if it is contained in at least two different stripes Q_i, $i = 1, \ldots, k$. Since for any i and any $s \leq k$ there are at most $2s$ elements $j \in [1..k]$, such that $|d_i - d_j| \leq \alpha s/k$ it follows that, for any fixed i, the total number of points in X in

$$Q_i \cap \bigcup_{j \neq i} Q_j$$

is at most

$$2\frac{32}{\pi/k} + 2\frac{32}{2\pi/k} + 2\frac{32}{3\pi/k} + \cdots + 2\frac{32}{(k/2)\pi/k} =$$

$$= \frac{64k}{\pi}\left(1 + \frac{1}{2} + \cdots + \frac{1}{k/2}\right) <$$

$$< \frac{64k \ln k}{\pi} \leq \frac{64k \ln n}{\pi} = \frac{m}{2}$$

for large n. Therefore each stripe Q_i, $i = 1, \ldots, k$, contains more than $\frac{m}{2}$ unambiguous points, which implies that the number of points of X should be more than $mk/2 = n$, which is a contradiction.

3.3 A Lower Bound for $C(n)$

We show that $C(n) = \Omega(\sqrt{n \ln n})$.

In [Bes63] the following result was shown: Let $p \geq 2$ be an integer and let $m = 2^{p-2}$. Consider a two by two square which is partitioned into $4m$ triangles; each triangle has a base of length $2/m$ aligned with one of the sides of the square and has the center of the square as its third vertex. Then it is possible to rearrange the triangles (by translating them individually) such that the resulting figure, call it B, has area less than or equal to $4/p$.

Let $C = 100mp$, let B' be the figure B scaled up by factor C and let B'' be the set of grid points contained in B'.

Claim 1 B' *contains at most* $5 \cdot 10^4 m^2 p$ *grid points.*

Proof. B' is the union of $4m$ triangles each with perimeter less than $400mp$. Such a triangle can contain at most $500mp$ grid points such that the unit square centered at the grid point intersects the boundary of the triangle.

For every grid point contained in B' the unit square centered at the grid point is either completely contained in B' or intersects the boundary of one of the triangles forming B'. There are at most $4C^2/p$ grid points of the former kind and at most $4m \cdot 500mp$ grid points of the latter kind.

Claim 2 $C_{B''} \geq 20mp$.

Proof. The figure B contains for each direction d a $1/4$ by $1/m$ rectangle with its longer side aligned with direction d. Thus B' contains a $25mp$ by $100p$ rectangle for each direction. Consider any such rectangle. It contains at least $2000mp^2$ grid points (since its area is $2500mp^2$ and its perimeter is less than $60mp$). Thus, if one partitions the rectangle into $100p$ rectangles with sides $25mp$ and 1 then one of the resulting rectangles contains at least $20mp$ grid points. This shows $C_{B''} = 20mp$.

Lemma 4. $C(n) = \Omega(\sqrt{n \log n})$.

Proof. Choose p maximal such that $5 \cdot 10^4 \cdot m^2 p \leq n$ where $m = 2^p/4$. Then $C(n) \geq 20mp$ by Claims 1 and 2.

References

[Bes63] A.S. Besicovitch. The Kakeya problem. *The American Mathematical Monthly*, 70:697–706, 1963.

[FW91] M. Formann and F. Wagner. A packing problem with applications to lettering of maps. Technical Report B 91-04, Institut für Informatik, FU Berlin, 1991.

[LM84] T. Lengauer and K. Mehlhorn. Four results on the complexity of VLSI computations. In *Advances in Computing Research, Vol 2*, pages 1–22. JAI Press Inc., 1984.

[LT79] R. Lipton and R.E. Tarjan. A separator theorem for planar graphs. *SIAM Journal on Applied Mathematics*, 3, 1979.

[Mat92] J. Matoušek. Personal communication. 1992.

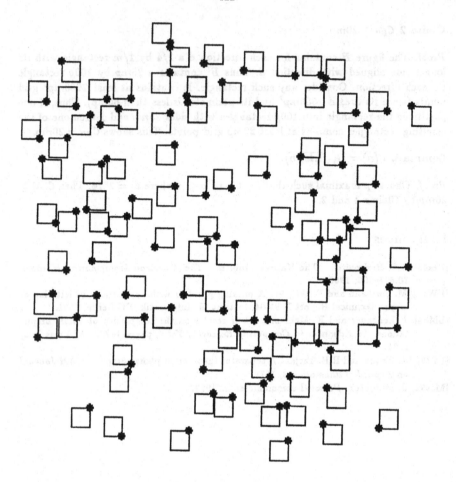

A Decomposition Theorem for Probabilistic Transition Systems

Oded Maler*

LGI-IMAG (Campus)

B.P. 53x

38041 Grenoble

France

maler@vercors.imag.fr

Abstract. In this paper we prove that every finite Markov chain can be decomposed into a cascade product of a Bernoulli process and several simple permutation-reset *deterministic* automata. The original chain is a state-homomorphic image of the product. By doing so we give a positive answer to an open question stated in [Paz71] concerning the decomposability of probabilistic systems. Our result is based on the surprisingly-original observation that in probabilistic transition systems, "randomness" and "memory" can be separated in such a way that allows the non-random part to be treated using common deterministic automata-theoretic techniques. The same separation technique can be applied as well to other kinds of non-determinism.

---

* The results presented in this paper have been obtained while the author was with IN-RIA/IRISA, Rennes, France.

1 Preliminaries

The object of our study is the probabilistic input-output state-transition system. Its definition is not new and has appeared under various titles in the past (e.g., [Arb68, Paz71, Sta72]).

Definition 1 (Probabilistic Transition Systems) *A probabilistic transition system (PTS) is $\mathcal{A} = (X, Q, Y, p)$ where X is the input alphabet, Q is the state-space, Y is the output alphabet and $p : Q \times X \times Q \times Y \rightarrow [0,1]$ is the input-transition-output probability function satisfying for every $q \in Q, x \in X$:*

$$\sum_{(q',y) \in Q \times Y} p(q, x, q', y) = 1 \tag{1}$$

The intuitive meaning of this definition is that whenever $\mathcal{A}$ is in a state q and reads the input x it will move to state q' and emit y with probability $p(q, x, q', y)$. Throughout this paper we will consider only finite Q, X, and Y. Several well-known models can be considered as degenerate variants of PTSs where either X or Q are singletons, $|Y| \leq |Q|$ or some additional constraints are imposed upon p. We will mention few of these:

- A *Markov process*: X is a singleton, $Y = Q$ and $p(q, x, q', y) > 0$ only if $q' = y$. The intuitive meaning is that the behavior of the chain depends only on the passage of time, and the observable output coincides with the internal state. In this case we will refer to the transition probability (also known as transition matrix) as $p(q, q')$.
- A *probabilistic automaton*: a Markov chain with a non-singleton input alphabet. In the Markovian terminology this is a controlled process where the input letter determines which of the several transition matrices will be applied at each step.
- A *deterministic input-output automaton*: for every $q \in Q$, $x \in X$ there exists exactly one $q' \in Q$, $y \in Y$ such that $p(q, x, q', y) = 1$. In this case we can express p using a transition function $\delta : Q \times X \rightarrow Q$ and an output function $\gamma : Q \times X \rightarrow Y$. When the output is suppressed, i.e., $\gamma(q, x) = q$, it is probabilistic automaton with a $0 - 1$ transition matrix.
- An *acceptor*: $Y = \{0, 1\}$. In the deterministic case it is said to accept all input sequences that produce output sequences ending with 1. In the probabilistic case it can accept all the input sequences such that the expected value of their corresponding last output is above some threshold. If we suppress the input we can get what is also known as a partially-observable Markov chain.
- A *Bernoulli process*: both X and Q are singletons. In this case the system has no memory and no input and it produces its output according to a fixed probability.

2 Homomorphisms between PTSs

One of the most important notions concerning transition systems is the notion of homomorphism. One system is homomorphic to another if, in some sense, it approximates it. This notion is very well developed and studied in the context of deterministic systems but its application to probabilistic systems is a bit more subtle. We will consider here only *state* homomorphism, that is, homomorphism between two PTSs having *the same* input and output alphabets. These definitions can be extended to mapping between the input and the output alphabets of the two systems.

Definition 2 (PTS Homomorphism) *Given two PTSs $A_1 = (X, Q, Y, p_1)$ and $A_2 = (X, R, Y, p_2)$, a (state) homomorphism from A_1 to A_2 is a surjective function $\varphi : Q \to R$ such that for every $(r, x, r', y) \in R \times X \times R \times Y$ and every $q \in \varphi^{-1}(r)$ we have*

$$p_2(r, x, r', y) = \sum_{q' \in \varphi^{-1}(r')} p_1(q, x, q', y) \tag{2}$$

We denote this fact by $A_2 \leq_\varphi A_1$. Two systems are isomorphic if φ is a bijection.

Intuitively it means that A_2 can be constructed by partitioning Q into blocks in such a way that the transition probabilities between the blocks are consistent with the transition probabilities between their elements (this is also termed as the *lumpability condition* in the Markovian terminology). It can be seen that in the case of $0-1$ probabilities this notion coincides the commonly-used automaton homomorphism, namely $\varphi(\delta(q, x)) = \delta'(\varphi(q), x)$.

An essential property of homomorphisms is their transitivity, that is, if A_2 approximates A_1 and A_3 approximates A_2 then A_3 approximates A_1.

Claim 1 (Transitivity of Homomorphism) *If $A_2 \leq_\varphi A_1$ and $A_3 \leq_\psi A_2$ then $A_3 \leq_\theta A_1$ where $\theta = \psi\varphi$.*

Proof: We will give the proof on Markov chains for reasons of clarity – the generalization to input-output PTSs can be done. Let $A_1 = (Q, p_1)$, $A_2 = (R, p_2)$ and $A_3 = (S, p_3)$ be three chains satisfying the premise of the claim. We want to show that for every $s, s' \in S$ and every $q \in \theta^{-1}(s)$ we have

$$p_3(s, s') = \sum_{q' \in \theta^{-1}(s')} p_1(q, q') \tag{3}$$

But $\theta(q) = s$ if for some $r \in R$, $\varphi(q) = r$ and $\psi(r) = s$. Thus for every $s \in S$

$$\theta^{-1}(s) = \bigcup_{r \in \psi^{-1}(s)} \varphi^{-1}(r) \tag{4}$$

Thus we have to prove that for every $r \in \psi^{-1}(s)$ and $q \in \varphi^{-1}(r)$

$$p_3(s, s') = \sum_{r' \in \psi^{-1}(s')} \left(\sum_{q' \in \varphi^{-1}(r')} p_1(q, q') \right) \tag{5}$$

But since $A_2 \leq_\varphi A_1$ we can replace, for every $q \in \varphi^{-1}(r)$, the expression in the parentheses by $p_2(r, r')$ and obtain

$$p_3(s, s') = \sum_{r' \in \psi^{-1}(s')} p_2(r, r') \tag{6}$$

which, in turn, follows from $A_3 \leq_\psi A_2$. $\qquad\qquad\square$

3 Composition of PTSs

Two PTSs can be connected together such that the output of the first is the input of the second, or formally:

Definition 3 (Cascade Product) *Given two PTSs* $A_1 = (X, Q_1, Z, p_1)$ *and* $A_2 = (Z, Q_2, Y, p_2)$, *their cascade product is* $A_1 \circ A_2 = (X, Q, Y, p)$ *where* $Q = Q_1 \times Q_2$ *and for every* $(q_1, q_2), (q_1', q_2') \in Q$, $x \in X$ *and* $y \in Y$:

$$p((q_1, q_2), x, (q_1', q_2'), y) = \sum_{z \in Z} p_1(q_1, x, q_1', z) \cdot p_2(q_2, z, q_2', y) \qquad (7)$$

This definition can be extended to a family $A_1, \ldots, A_k$ of PTSs such that the input alphabet of A_{i+1} is the output alphabet of A_i. The product defined this way is associative and we can interpret (i.e., put the parentheses on) $A_1 \circ A_2 \circ \ldots \circ A_k$ as we like. One can see that this definition reduces to the common notion of cascade product when both systems are deterministic, $Z = X \times Q_1$ and $Y = Q_2$. In that case we have the following well-known result ([KR65]), stating that every finite automaton can be constructed from simple building blocks:

Theorem 2 (Krohn-Rhodes Decomposition) *Every deterministic automaton A is inverse-homomorphic to a cascade product of simple permutation automata and reset automata.*

This theorem is beyond the scope of this paper, so we will only mention that:

1. The permutations groups of the components divide the subgroups of the transformation semigroup of A (which implies that counter-free automata can be decomposed into a cascade of reset automata).
2. The number of automata in the cascade is bounded by $|Q|$.
3. The number of states in the decomposition can be exponential in $|Q|$.

Additional details can be found in [Eil72, Gin68, MP90]. With respect to this theorem, the following question has been asked in [Paz71, p. 115]: *Can every Markov system be "embedded" in a nontrivial way into a cascade type interconnection of systems which have a specific simple form? In other words, is there any theorem which can be proved for Markov systems and which parallels in some way the Krohn-Rhodes theorem for the deterministic case?* In this paper we give an affirmative answer, although one may argue about the non-triviality.

4 Our Result

First we will show how to decompose a finite-state PTS into an isomorphic cascade product of a Bernoulli process and a deterministic automaton. For simplicity we will consider the degenerate case of a Markov chain, and show that every such chain can be simulated by a product of two systems, the first one taking care of the randomness and the other behaving deterministically according to the outcome of the former. In other words, instead of throwing a different coin at every state, we throw each time *the same* (but much larger) coin, whose outcome tells us which transition to take from each of the states we might be in. The probabilities of all the possible trajectories of the original chain and those of its associated decomposition are the same.

Definition 4 (Probability of Transformations) *For a set $Q = \{q_1, \ldots, q_n\}$, we let $M = Q^Q$ denote the set of all n^n transformation on Q. Equipped with the composition operation, M is a semigroup. With every Markov chain[2] $\mathcal{A} = (\{x^*\}, Q, Q, p)$ we associate a function $\pi : M \to [0,1]$ by letting*

$$\pi(m) = \prod_{i=1}^{n} p(q_i, m(q_i)) \tag{8}$$

Claim 3 $\sum_{m \in M} \pi(m) = 1$.

Proof: Follows from

$$\sum_{m \in M} \pi(m) = \sum_{i_1=1}^{n} \sum_{i_2=1}^{n} \cdots \sum_{i_n=1}^{n} p(q_1, q_{i_1}) \cdot p(q_2, q_{i_2}) \ldots p(q_n, q_{i_n}) \tag{9}$$

$$= \prod_{i=1}^{n} \sum_{j=1}^{n} p(q_i, q_j) = \prod_{i=1}^{n} 1 \tag{10}$$

Claim 4 (New Decomposition I) *Every Markov chain $\mathcal{A} = (\{x^*\}, Q, Q, p)$ with $|Q| = n$ is isomorphic to a cascade product of a Bernoulli generator with at most n^n outcomes and a deterministic n-state automaton.*

Proof: We define a Bernoulli process $\mathcal{B} = (\{x^*\}, \{q^*\}, M, \pi)$ and a deterministic automaton $\mathcal{A}' = (M, Q, p')$ where for all $m \in M, q \in Q$, $p'(q, m, m(q)) = 1$. Their product $\mathcal{C} = \mathcal{B} \circ \mathcal{A}'$ is a Markov chain $\mathcal{C} = (\{x^*\}, \{q^*\} \times Q, Q, \bar{p})$ where $\bar{p}$ is defined as

$$\bar{p}((q^*, q), (q^*, q')) = \sum_{m \in M} \pi(m) \cdot p'(q, m, q') = p(q, q') \tag{11}$$

and the straightforward state bijection $\varphi((q^*, q)) = q$ is indeed a PTS isomorphism between $\mathcal{A}$ and $\mathcal{C}$. $\qquad \Box$

Note that $\mathcal{B}$ can be further decomposed into a direct product of n independent Bernoulli trials, each having at most n outcomes. This result extends easily to input-output PTSs: instead of an input-less Bernoulli process we will have a one-state PTS with input; from the output we can get rid by state splitting.[3] Note also that in order to generalize this construction to countable Markov chains, we will need a non-countable Bernoulli process, unless all but finitely many rows are deterministic.

In order to take advantage of this decomposition result and combine it with the Krohn-Rhodes decomposition we need (a weak version of) the following:

Claim 5 *Let $\mathcal{B} = (X, Q, Z, p)$, $\mathcal{A}_1 = (Z, R, Y, p_1)$ and $\mathcal{A}_2 = (Z, S, Y, p_2)$ be PTSs. If $\mathcal{A}_2 \leq \mathcal{A}_1$ then $\mathcal{B} \circ \mathcal{A}_2 \leq \mathcal{B} \circ \mathcal{A}_1$.*

---

[2] We omit singleton input, state and output sets from the definition of p.

[3] As is done in the proof of equivalence of Moore and Mealy machines.

Proof: Without loss of generality we let $Y = Q \times S$ and thus $\mathcal{B} \circ \mathcal{A}_1 = (X, Q \times R, Q \times S, \bar{p}_1)$ and $\mathcal{B} \circ \mathcal{A}_2 = (X, Q \times S, Q \times S, \bar{p}_2)$. Based on the assumed homomorphism $\varphi : R \to S$ we construct a surjective mapping $\bar{\varphi} : Q \times R \to Q \times S$ by letting $\bar{\varphi}(q, r) = (q, \varphi(r))$. According to our definition, $\bar{\varphi}$ is a homomorphism if for every $x \in X$, $y \in Y$, $(q, s), (q', s') \in Q \times S$ and for every $(q, r) \in \bar{\varphi}^{-1}(q, s)$:

$$\bar{p}_2((q, s), x, (q', s'), y) = \sum_{(q', r') \in \bar{\varphi}^{-1}(q', s')} p_1((q, r), x, (q', r'), y) \tag{12}$$

Using the definition of the product we get:

$$\sum_{z \in Z} p(q, x, q', z) \cdot p_2(s, z, s', y) = \sum_{r' \in \varphi^{-1}(s')} \sum_{z \in Z} p(q, x, q', z) \cdot p_1(r, z, r', y) \tag{13}$$

Since $p(q, x, q', z)$ does not depend on r we can rearrange the right hand side and get

$$\sum_{z \in Z} p(q, x, q', z) \cdot p_2(s, z, s', y) = \sum_{z \in Z} p(q, x, q', z) \cdot \sum_{r' \in \varphi^{-1}(s')} p_1(r, z, r', y) \tag{14}$$

which follows from the fact that φ is a homomorphism. $\quad\square$

Corollary 6 (New Decomposition II) *Every finite Markov chain is inverse homomorphic to a cascade product of a Bernoulli process and a chain of deterministic permutation-reset automata.*

Proof: Follows from the above and the Krohn-Rhodes primary decomposition theorem. $\quad\square$

An example appears in the appendix. In the full paper we show how a similar result holds for non-deterministic input-output automata, where the original automaton is decomposed into a non-deterministic input-output one-state automaton, and a deterministic automaton using the same technique.

5 Discussion

We have shown how the automata-theoretic framework, emphasizing the notions of communication between processes, can be used in order to decompose arbitrary probabilistic transition matrices into products of several "communicating" simple zero-one matrices.

In addition to the solution we give to an open problem, the connection we establish between every finite Markov chain and its "characteristic" deterministic automaton might be used in order to transfer various results between automata theory and the theory of stochastic processes. For example, the algebraic theory of deterministic automata and their associated semigroups is well-developed (see [Eil76], [Lal79], [Pin86]) and it will be interesting to investigate the relation between the detailed classification results concerning automata, and various properties of stochastic processes discussed in the Markovian literature ([KS60]).

Finally, it is worth mentioning that this technique works as well for other types of non-determinism. For example, it is possible to decompose any non-deterministic automaton with input into an inverse-homomorphic (in the appropriate sense of homomorphism) cascade of a non-deterministic one-state input-output automaton and a deterministic automaton.

Acknowledgement

I would like to thank A. Benveniste for commenting on previous drafts of this paper.

References

[Arb68] M.A. Arbib, *Theories of Abstract Automata*, Prentice-Hall, Englewood Cliffs, 1968.

[Eil76] S. Eilenberg, *Automata, Languages and Machines, Vol. B*, Academic Press, New York, 1976.

[Gin68] A. Ginzburg, *Algebraic Theory of Automata*, Academic Press, New York, 1968.

[KS60] J.G. Kemeny and J.L. Snell, *Finite Markov Chains*, Van Nostrand, New York, 1960.

[KR65] K. Krohn and J.L. Rhodes, Algebraic Theory of Machines, I Principles of Finite Semigroups and Machines, *Transactions of the American Mathematical Society* 116, 450-464, 1965.

[Lal79] G. Lallement, *Semigroups and Combinatorial Applications*, Wiley, New York, 1979.

[MP90] O. Maler and A. Pnueli, Tight Bounds on the Complexity of Cascaded Decomposition of Automata, *Proc. 31st FOCS*, 672-682, 1990.

[Paz70] A. Paz, *Introduction to Probabilistic Automata*, Academic Press, New York, 1970.

[Pin86] J.-E. Pin, *Varieties of Formal Languages*, Plenum, New York, 1986.

[Sta72] P.H. Starke, *Abstract Automata*, North-Holland, Amsterdam, 1972.

Appendix: An Example

Consider the chain $A = (\{x^*\}, Q, Q, p)$ with $Q = \{1,2,3\}$ depicted in figure 1. It is first decomposed into an isomorphic product $B \circ A'$ of a Bernoulli process $B = (\{x^*\}, \{q^*\}, Z, \pi)$ with $Z = \{a, b, c, d\}$ and a deterministic automaton $A' = (Z, Q, Q, \delta)$ where $\delta : Z \times Q \to Q$ is a deterministic transition function (see figure 2). Note that we have considered only those transformations $m \in Q^Q$ for which $\pi(m) > 0$.

By applying the Krohn-Rhodes decomposition theorem, we decompose A into a inverse homomorphic product $A_1 \circ A_2$ where $A_1 = (Z, Q_1, Z \times Q_1, \delta_1)$ and $A_2 = (Z \times Q_1, Q_2, Q_1 \times Q_2, \delta_2)$ with $Q_1 = \{4,5,6\}$ and $Q_2 = \{7,8\}$ – see figure 3. Note that all input symbols in both automata induce either a reset or a permutations.

Their product yields the automaton $C' = (Z, Q_1 \times Q_2, Q_1 \times Q_2, \bar{\delta})$ of figure 4, which when multiplied from the left by B yields the chain $C = (\{x^*\}, Q_1 \times Q_2, Q_1 \times Q_2, \bar{p})$ of figure 5. One can verify that the mapping $\varphi : Q_1 \times Q_2 \to Q$ defined in figure 6 which is a deterministic state-homomorphism from C' to A' is also a PTS homomorphism from C to A.

Note also that the projection $\psi : Q_1 \times Q_2 \to Q_1$ is a state-homomorphism from $A_1 \circ A_2$ to A_1. It is also a PTS homomorphism form $B \circ A_1 \circ A_2$ to $B \circ A_1$ (see figures 7 and 8).

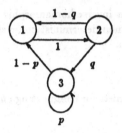

Fig. 1. A Markov chain $\mathcal{A}$.

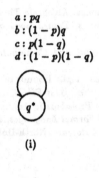

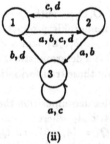

Fig. 2. (i) The Bernoulli process $\mathcal{B}$ and (ii) the deterministic automaton $\mathcal{A}'$ such that $\mathcal{B} \circ \mathcal{A}'$ is isomorphic to the original Markov chain $\mathcal{A}$.

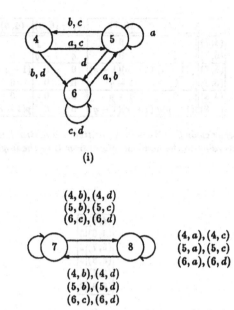

(i)

(ii)

Fig. 3. The decomposition of the automaton $\mathcal{A}'$ into a cascade of deterministic permutation-reset automata (i) $\mathcal{A}_1$ and (ii) $\mathcal{A}_2$.

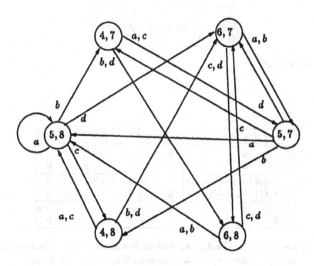

Fig. 4. The automaton $\mathcal{C}' = \mathcal{A}_1 \circ \mathcal{A}_2$.

	(4,7)	(6,7)	(5,7)	(6,8)	(4,8)	(5,8)
(4,7)	0	0	p	$1-p$	0	0
(6,7)	0	0	q	$1-q$	0	0
(5,7)	$p(1-q)$	$(1-p)(1-q)$	0	0	$(1-p)q$	pq
(6,8)	0	$1-q$	0	0	0	q
(4,8)	0	$1-p$	0	0	0	p
(5,8)	$(1-p)q$	$(1-p)(1-q)$	0	0	$p(1-q)$	pq

Fig. 5. The markov chain $C = B \circ A_1 \circ A_2$ written in a matrix form. The rows and columns are arranged according to the homomorphism from C to the original chain A.

(4,7)	1
(4,8)	3
(5,7)	2
(5,8)	3
(6,7)	1
(6,8)	2

Fig. 6. The homomorphism $\varphi : Q_1 \times Q_2 \to Q$.

p	4	5	6
4	0	p	$1-p$
5	$q+p-2pq$	pq	$(1-p)(1-q)$
6	0	q	$1-q$

Fig. 7. The chain $B \circ A_1$.

	(4,7)	(4,8)	(5,7)	(5,8)	(6,7)	(6,8)
(4,7)	0	0	p	0	0	$1-p$
(4,8)	0	0	0	p	$1-p$	0
(5,7)	$p(1-q)$	$(1-p)q$	0	pq	$(1-p)(1-q)$	0
(5,8)	$(1-p)q$	$p(1-q)$	0	pq	$(1-p)(1-q)$	0
(6,7)	0	0	q	0	0	$1-q$
(6,8)	0	0	0	q	$1-q$	0

Fig. 8. The markov chain $C = B \circ A_1 \circ A_2$ written in a matrix form. The rows and columns are arranged according to the projection homomorphism from C to $B \circ A_1$.

Local Automata and Completion

Rosa Montalbano

Dipartimento di Matematica e Applicazioni, Università di Palermo, via Archirafi,34
I-90123 Palermo Italy

Abstract. The problem of completing a finite automata preserving its properties is here investigated in the case of deterministic local automata. We show a decision procedure and give an algorithm which complete a deterministic local automaton (if the completion exists) with another one, having the same number of states.

1 Introduction

Finite automata are extensively used as an efficient and simple tool for representing rational languages and codes and investigating about them.

A finite automaton is complete if any word of a given alphabet is label of at least a path of the automaton. For deterministic automata this means that the transition function is defined for all states and letters. The completion of a finite automaton $\mathcal{A}$ is a complete automaton which, in some sense, preserves $\mathcal{A}$ and its properties. An intensively investigated problem about automata and their completions is the following:

Given a finite automaton which satisfies a property $\mathcal{P}$, does it admit a completion with respect to $\mathcal{P}$?

The problem is that of deciding whether a completion exists, and eventually to construct it. For any automaton a trivial completion is obtained adding a sink state, but this generally does not solve the problem. What is fundamental is to add to the automaton new edges and new states in such a way that it becomes complete, but preserving its properties. This problem is strictly related with the embedding one in theory of codes: to find a maximal code which includes a given one and satisfies the same properties (for a survey on this problem see [3]).

The question not always has a positive answer, since there exist finite automata which do not admit any completion with respect to some properties: this is the case of deterministic local automata. This class of automata was first introduced in [6], with the notation of definite automata. Deterministic local automata are such that $\delta(Q, v)$ is at most a singleton for any long enough word v, where δ denotes a transition function and Q a finite set of states.

Local automata are a subclass of the class of permutation–free automata, for which the problem is still unsolved. A fundamental result due to Schützenberger [7] states that the class of the languages recognized by permutation–free automata is just the one of star–free languages. The link between local automata and formal languages is that the stabilizer of a state of a local automaton is generated by a circular code. These codes are related with those with bounded synchronization delay [8, 9], and both of them are of interest for the problem of coding a message when the transmission channel has to satisfy a system of constraints. For these families the embedding problem is open too.

In this paper the completion problem is solved for deterministic local automata. Some properties on local automata are given and two transformations are defined, state–merging and state–splitting, which allow to construct complete and local automata starting from a given one. By means of mergings and splittings it is possible to decide whether a local automaton $\mathcal{A}$ admits a local completion or not. If yes, it is possible to construct a completion. Let us point out that the cardinality of the set of states in the completion is just the same as in the given automaton (while, in general, we have to increase the order, which is defined as the least integer k such that $\delta(Q, v)$ is at most a singleton for any word v of length k). Moreover, if $\mathcal{A}$ is a completable strongly connected automaton, we prove that it admits a strongly connected local completion.

2 The completion problem and local automata

Let A be a finite alphabet. We denote by A^* the free monoid generated by A. The elements of A are called *letters*, the ones of A^* *words*. λ denotes the null word.

A *finite automaton* over A is a pair $\mathcal{A} = (Q, \delta)$, where Q is a finite set of states and δ is a transition function from the set $Q \times A$ in Q.

$\mathcal{A}$ is called *deterministic* if and only if $card(\delta(q, a)) \leq 1, \forall q \in Q, a \in A$.

$\mathcal{A}$ is called *strongly connected (s.c.)* if and only if $\forall p, q \in Q \ \exists v \in A^*$ such that $\delta(p, v) = q$.

$\mathcal{A}$ is called *complete* if and only if for any $v \in A^*$ a path in $\mathcal{A}$ exists of label v.

Let us now define the notion of completion for a finite automaton $\mathcal{A} = (Q, \delta)$. Let the property $\mathcal{P}$ hold for $\mathcal{A}$. We say that $\mathcal{A}$ admits a *completion* with respect to $\mathcal{P}$ if an automaton $\mathcal{A}' = (Q', \delta')$ exists such that:

- $Q \subseteq Q'$.
- $\delta'_{/I} = \delta$, where $\delta'_{/I}$ is the restriction of δ' to the set $I = \{(p, a) \in Q \times A \mid \delta(p, a) \text{ is defined} \}$.
- $\mathcal{A}'$ is complete and $\mathcal{P}$ holds for $\mathcal{A}'$.

Given an automaton $\mathcal{A}$ which satisfies a property $\mathcal{P}$, a natural question arises: there exists a completion of $\mathcal{A}$ with respect to $\mathcal{P}$? We deal with this problem in the case of deterministic local automata.

Let $\mathcal{A}$ be a deterministic automaton. $\mathcal{A}$ is called *local automaton* if there exists an integer $k \geq 1$ such that: $\forall v \in A^k$: $card(\delta(Q, v)) \leq 1$.

We say that $\mathcal{A}$ is *k-local* if k is the least integer that satisfies the previous condition.

Remark. If $\mathcal{A}$ is not a local automaton, then there exists at least a word v in A^* that is label of two different cycles in $\mathcal{A}$ (see also [1]).

Example 1. Let $\mathcal{A}$ be defined by the following state graph:

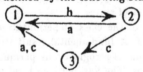

$\mathcal{A}$ is not 1-local because $\delta(Q, c) = \{1, 3\}$, but it is a 2-local automaton. In fact

$\delta(Q, a^2) = \delta(Q, ac) = \delta(Q, b^2) = \emptyset$, $\delta(Q, ba) = \delta(Q, ca) = \delta(Q, c^2) = \{1\}$, $\delta(Q, ab) =$
$\delta(Q, cb) = \{2\}$, and finally $\delta(Q, bc) = \{3\}$.

Let us now give a characterization of local and complete automata by means of the stabilizers of their states (see [4] for a similar result for locally testable automata). If $A = (Q, \delta)$ is a deterministic automaton, the *stabilizer* of a state $p \in Q$ is the set:

$$stab(p) = \{v \in A^* \mid \delta(p, v) = p\}.$$

Theorem 1. *Let* $A = (Q, \delta)$ *be a deterministic and complete automaton.*

$$A \text{ is a local automaton} \iff \forall p, q \in Q : stab(p) \cap stab(q) = \{\lambda\}. \qquad (1)$$

Example 2. For the local automaton of the example 1, it is easy to verify that: $stab(\{1\}) = (ba + bc(a + c))^*$, $stab(\{2\}) = (ab + c(a + c)b)^*$, $stab(\{3\}) = ((a + c)(ba)^*bc)^*$, so that the condition 1 is satisfied.

However, there exist local automata which do not admit any local completion. The following result gives a class of such automata.

Theorem 2. *If* $A = (Q, \delta)$ *is a s.c., complete, local automaton, then* $\cap_{a \in A} \delta(Q, a) = \emptyset$.

If A is a s. c. and local automaton in which a state p exists such that the set of labels of the edges entering in p is just the alphabet A, then $p \in \cap_{a \in A} \delta(Q, a)$ and A admits no local completion.

Example 3. Let A be the local automaton defined by the following graph:

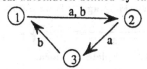

Since $\delta(Q, a) \cap \delta(Q, b) = \{2\}$, this automaton does not admit any local completion.

3 State–merging

The transformation called state-merging, or briefly merging, allows to construct local and complete automata, starting from a given one.

The following lemma gives an interesting property of local automata, from which the notion of confluent states is deduced.

Lemma 3. *Let* $A = (Q, \delta)$ *be a complete and local automaton, such that* $card(Q) \geq 2$. *Then there exist two states* q, q' *such that:*

$$\delta(q, a) = \delta(q', a), \quad \text{for all } a \in A.$$

A pair (q, q') that satisfies the condition of lemma 3 is called pair of *confluent states*.

Let A, q, q' be as in lemma 3, and let $[q]$ denote a new state. Let us consider the automaton $A' = (Q', \delta')$ defined by:

- $Q' = Q \setminus \{q, q'\} \cup \{[q]\}$,

- $\forall p \in Q \setminus \{q, q'\}, \forall a \in A$: $\delta'(p, a) = \begin{cases} \delta(p, a) & \text{if } \delta(p, a) \neq q, q' \\ [q] & \text{otherwise} \end{cases}$

- $\forall a \in A$: $\delta'([q], a) = \begin{cases} \delta(q, a) & \text{if } \delta(q, a) \neq q, q' \\ [q] & \text{otherwise} \end{cases}$

We say that A' is obtained from A by the *state-merging* of q and q'.

Theorem 4. A' *is a complete and local automaton.*

Theorem 4 is based on the following results:

Lemma 5. *For any $p, p' \in Q' \setminus \{[q]\}, v \in A^*$: $\delta(p, v) = p' \Longleftrightarrow \delta'(p, v) = p'$.*

Remark. *Following lemma 5, it is easy to verify that for any state $p \in Q$:*

$$\delta(p, v) = q \text{ or } \delta(p, v) = q' \Longleftrightarrow \delta'(p, v) = [q]$$

In particular, for $p = q$ (or $p = q'$), we have $\delta(q, v) = q$ ($\delta(q', v) = q$) or $\delta(q, v) = q'$ ($\delta(q', v) = q'$) if and only if $\delta'([q], v) = [q]$.

Lemma 6. *For any $p \in Q' \setminus [q]$: $stab_{A'}(p) = stab_A(p)$. Furthermore:*

$$stab_{A'}([q]) = stab_A(q') \cup stab_A(q).$$

Example 4. Let us consider the following automaton A:

A is a s. c., complete and local automaton. Since for any $a \in A$, $\delta(2, a) = \delta(3, a)$, (2, 3) is a pair of confluent states. Merging (2, 3) we obtain A':

a ⟲ 1 ⟷ [2] ⟲ b

Observe that A' is again s. c., complete and local.

4 State-splitting

Let A be a complete and local automaton, q a state of A and q' a new state.

Let us consider the automaton $A' = (Q', \delta')$ defined by:

- $Q' = Q \cup \{q'\}$,

- $\forall p \in Q \setminus \{q\}, \forall a \in A$: $\delta'(p, a) = \begin{cases} \delta(p, a) & \text{if } \delta(p, a) \neq q \\ q \text{ or } q' & \text{otherwise} \end{cases}$

- $\forall a \in A$: $\delta'(q, a) = \delta'(q', a) = \begin{cases} \delta(q, a) & \text{if } \delta(q, a) \neq q \\ q \text{ or } q' & \text{otherwise} \end{cases}$

We say that A' is obtained from A by the *state-splitting* of q.

Remark. (q, q') *is a pair of confluent states. Moreover, splitting q we can obtain more than one automaton, depending from the choice between q and q' in defining δ'.*

Theorem 7. $\mathcal{A}'$ *is a complete and local automaton.*

The completeness and locality of $\mathcal{A}'$ immediately follows from the next lemmas.

Lemma 8. *For any $p \in Q$ and for any $v \in A^*$:*
- *If $\delta(p, v) = q$: $\delta(p, v) = q \iff \delta'(p, v) = q$ or $\delta'(p, v) = q'$.*
- *If $\delta(p, v) = p' \neq q$: $\delta(p, v) = p' \iff \delta'(p, v) = p'$.*

Lemma 9. *For any $p \neq q$: $stab_{\mathcal{A}}(p) = stab_{\mathcal{A}'}(p)$. Furthermore:*

$$stab_{\mathcal{A}}(q) = stab_{\mathcal{A}'}(q) \cup stab_{\mathcal{A}'}(q').$$

5   How to complete a local automaton

The idea for deciding whether $\mathcal{A}$ is completable is that at least one of its completions (if they exist) can be obtained from $\mathcal{A}$ without adding states. Then there should exist in $\mathcal{A}$ itself pairs of states which in this completion would be confluent states. We have to find such pairs and to force δ, so that they really become confluent.

Lemma 3 states that if $\mathcal{A}' = (Q \cup Q', \delta')$ is a completion of $\mathcal{A} = (Q, \delta)$, then a pair (q, q') in $\mathcal{A}'$ exists of confluent states. We say that at least a completion exists in which q, q' are states of Q. We have to consider two cases:

If $q, q' \in Q'$, merging $\mathcal{A}'$ with respect to (q, q') we obtain a completion of $\mathcal{A}$ (since the states and the transitions of $\mathcal{A}$ are not involved in the merging). We can repeat this operation until a pair of confluent states exists, one of which is in Q.

At this point, it is possible that $q \in Q$, and $q' \in Q'$. Merging q, q' we obtain a completion of $\mathcal{A}$ (identifying the state $[q]$ with q, we can note that the transitions of $\mathcal{A}$ are not involved in the merging). Again we can repeat this operation until there exists at least a pair of confluent states, both of which is in Q.

Given a local automaton $\mathcal{A} = (Q, \delta)$, we say that a pair of states of $\mathcal{A}$ is *compatible* if there exists a completion of $\mathcal{A}$ in which this is a pair of confluent states.

Remark. *A first obvious condition for a pair (q, q') of states to be compatible is that for any $a \in A$ either $\delta(q, a) = \delta(q', a)$, or one of these transitions is not defined.*

Let (q, q') be a pair of compatible states. The *completion of $\mathcal{A}$ with respect to q and q'* is the automaton obtained adding in $\mathcal{A}$ the transitions $\delta(q, a) = \delta(q', a)$, for those letters a for which only one between $\delta(q, a)$, $\delta(q', a)$ is defined.

Example 5. Let $\mathcal{A}$ be defined by the following state graph:

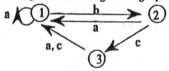

Since $\delta(2, c) = 3$, and $\delta(3, c) = 1$, the states $(2, 3)$ are not compatible . $(1, 3)$ are compatible, as we will see later, and the completion of $\mathcal{A}$ with respect this pair is

$\mathcal{A}'$:

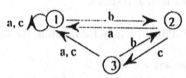

where we have forced $\delta(3,b)$ to be equal to 2, and $\delta(1,c)$ to be equal to 1.

Let $\mathcal{A} = (Q, \delta)$ be a completable local automaton and let $q, q' \in Q$ be compatible states with respect to some completion $\mathcal{A}'$ of $\mathcal{A}$. If $\mathcal{A}_1$ is obtained completing $\mathcal{A}$ with respect to (q, q') and merging q and q', then it is a completable local automaton, one of its completions being that obtained from $\mathcal{A}'$, merging q and q'. Furthermore, if $\mathcal{A}_1$, obtained completing $\mathcal{A}$ with respect to q and q' and then merging q, q', admits a completion $\mathcal{A}'_1$, then $\mathcal{A}$ is also completable, one of its completions being that obtained from $\mathcal{A}'_1$ splitting the state $[q]$ in q and q'.

The algorithm to decide whether $\mathcal{A}$ is completable, based on the previous consideration, consists in reducing $\mathcal{A}$ k times ($k \leq card(Q) - 2$) by means of mergings, until either $\mathcal{A}_k$ is complete or in $\mathcal{A}_k$ there are no compatible states. In the first case $\mathcal{A}$ will be completable and by means of a sequence of splittings we will complete it.

Algorithm 1
INPUT:$\mathcal{A}$;
$i = 0$;
$\mathcal{A}_0 = \mathcal{A}$;
$S = \emptyset$; { S is the sequence of the pairs with respect to which we complete and merge the automata $\mathcal{A}_i$ }
$c = 0$; { c is a constant of control. If $c = 1$ then $\mathcal{A}$ is not completable }
WHILE ($\mathcal{A}_i$ is not complete or $c = 1$) DO
 Order the pairs of $Q_i \times Q_i$: $\{p_{i,1}, \ldots, p_{i,m_i}\}$;
 $j_i = 1$;
 $S = S \cup \{p_{i,j_i}\}$;
 Complete $\mathcal{A}_i$ with respect to p_{i,j_i}, and merge with respect to the same pair. Denote with $\mathcal{A}'_i$ this new automaton;
 IF $\mathcal{A}'_i$ is not a local automaton THEN
  CHANGESEQUENCE(S, i, j_i, c)
 ELSE
  $\mathcal{A}_{i+1} = \mathcal{A}'_i$;
  $i = i + 1$.
OUTPUT: $\mathcal{A}_0, \ldots, \mathcal{A}_i$.

The procedure Changesequence searchs for the first pair in S that causes $\mathcal{A}_i$ not to be local and changes it. If all the possible pairs have been considered, then $\mathcal{A}$ is not completable and Changesequence returns the value $c = 1$.

Changesequence(S, i, j_i, c)
IF $j_i < m_i$ THEN
 $S = S \setminus \{p_{i,j_i}\}$;
 $j_i = j_i + 1$;
 $S = S \cup \{p_{i,j_i}\}$
ELSE

```
IF i > 0 THEN
    S = S \ {p_{i,j_i}};
    i = i - 1;
    IF j_i < m_i THEN
        j_i = j_i + 1;
        S = S ∪ {p_{i,j_i}}
    ELSE
        c = 1
ELSE
    c = 1.
```

At the end of the While in Algorithm 1, if $c = 0$ then A_i is complete and then A is completable. Algorithm 2 construct one of its completions, starting from A_i. A pair of states p_{k,j_k} of S will be denoted in Algorithm 2 by (q_k, q'_k).

Algorithm 2

INPUT: $A_0, \ldots, A_i$;

FOR $k = i - 1$ DOWNTO 0 DO

Add to A_k the following transitions:

For any $p \in Q_k \setminus \{q_k, q'_k\}$ and for any $a \in A$ such that $\delta_k(p, a)$ is not

defined: $\delta_k(p, a) = \begin{cases} \delta_{k+1}(p, a) & \text{if } \delta_{k+1}(p, a) \neq [q_k] \\ q_k & \text{otherwise} \end{cases}$

For any $a \in A$ such that $\delta_k(q_k, a)$ and $\delta_k(q'_k, a)$ are not defined: $\delta_k(q_k, a) =$

$\delta_k(q'_k, a) = \begin{cases} \delta_{k+1}([q_k], a) & \text{if } \delta_{k+1}([q_k], a) \neq [q_k] \\ q_k & \text{otherwise} \end{cases}$

$A = A_0$;

OUTPUT: A.

Since A_i is a complete and local automaton and in the Algorithm 2 we split A_{k+1} with respect to $[q_k]$, from theorem 7 it follows that the automaton obtained at the end of any step will be complete and local. Then A_0 will be a completion of A.

Remark. *If, at the k-th step, $\delta_k(p, a) = q_k$, we can change q_k with q'_k, obtaining a complete, local automaton. Then we can construct more than one local completion.*

Remark. *The pairs of states merged in Algorithm 1 are the same obtained from the splittings in Algorithm 2. Then the set of states in the completion of A is Q itself.*

Example 6. In the example 5, A' is the completion of A with respect to $(1, 3)$. Merging $(1, 3)$ we obtain A_1:

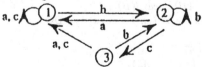

$([1], 2)$ is a pair of compatible states, so that we can put $\delta_1(2, b) = 2$. The automaton A'_1 is a complete and local automaton and we can conclude that A admits a local completion, which is the following:

6 Strongly connected local automata

State–merging and state–splitting preserve strongly connectivity, so that if A is a completable s.c. local automaton, then its completion is s.c. too.

Theorem 10. *Let $A = (Q, \delta)$ be a s. c. local automaton, and let A' the automaton defined by the state–merging transformation. Then A' is a s. c. automaton.*

Theorem 11. *Let $A = (Q, \delta)$ be a s. c. local automaton and A' the automaton defined by the state-splitting transformation, where q is a state in which enters at least two edges and in defining δ', between q and q', we have to choose at least one time q, and one time q'. A' is a s. c. automaton.*

Let us give a necessary condition for s.c. complete local automata. It allows to reduce the number of attempts to find (if there exists) a "good" sequence S in the Algorithm 1.

Theorem 12. *Let $A = (Q, \delta)$ be a s. c., complete and local automaton. There exists a partition $\mathcal{P}_A = (A_1, \ldots, A_n)$ of the alphabet A such that $\mathcal{P}_Q = (\delta(Q, A_1), \ldots, \delta(Q, A_n))$ is a partition of Q.*

The set $\mathcal{P}_A$ is constructed by the following algorithm:

```
Algorithm 3
INPUT: A;
l = 0;          { l denotes the cardinality of P_A }
i = 1;          { i denotes the i-th letter of A }
REPEAT
    B = ∅;
    card(B) = 0;
    l = l + 1;
    A_l = {a_i};
    Mark a_i;
    FOR j = i + 1 TO card(A) DO
        IF a_j is not marked THEN
            IF δ(Q, A_l) ∩ δ(Q, a_j) ≠ ∅ THEN
                A_l = A_l ∪ {a_j};
                Mark a_j;
                FOR k = 1 TO card(B) DO
                    IF δ(Q, a_j) ∩ δ(Q, b_k) ≠ ∅ THEN
                        A_l = A_l ∪ {b_k};
                        Mark the letter of A corresponding to b_k;
                        B = B \ {b_k};
                        card(B) = card(B) − 1
            ELSE
                B = B ∪ {a_j};
                card(B) = card(B) + 1
    WHILE ( a_i is marked or i < card(A) ) DO
        i = i + 1
UNTIL i > card(A);
OUTPUT: P_A = (A_1, ..., A_n).
```

Example 7. Let $\mathcal{A}$ be the s. c. local automaton defined by the following state graph:

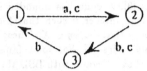

Since $\delta(Q,a) = \{2\}$, $\delta(Q,b) = \{1,3\}$ and $\delta(Q,c) = \{2,3\}$ then there exists no partition of Λ that induces a partition of Q. We can conclude that $\mathcal{A}$ is not completable.

Remark. A corollary of theorem 12 is theorem 2 that we have just seen.

The next theorem gives a necessary condition for a pair of states to be compatible.

Theorem 13. *Let $\mathcal{A}$ be a s. c. local automaton, $\mathcal{P}_A, \mathcal{P}_Q$ be as in theorem 12. If (q, q') is a pair of compatible states, $q \in \delta(Q, \Lambda_i), q' \in \delta(Q, \Lambda_j)$, then*

$$\mathcal{P}_A \setminus \{\Lambda_i, \Lambda_j\} \cup (\Lambda_i \cup \Lambda_j)$$

is a partition of Λ that induces a partition in Q.

Example 8. In the automaton of example 5 , $\mathcal{P}_A = \{\{a,c\}, \{b\}\}, \mathcal{P}_Q = \{\{1,3\}, \{2\}\}$ and then the only possible compatible states are $(1, 3)$, as we have previously seen.

If $\mathcal{A}$ is a s. c. and local automaton, in order to decide whether $\mathcal{A}$ admits a completion or not, we can proceed in the following way:

Apply Algorithm 1, constructing at each step the partitions $\mathcal{P}_{A_i}$ of Λ_i and $\mathcal{P}_{Q_i}$ of Q_i. Before inserting $p_{i,j}$ in S, control that it satisfies the condition of theorem 13.

7 Open problems

Let us consider the general definition of local automaton: a finite automaton $\mathcal{A}$ is local if and only if there exist two constants n, k such that for any word $v \in \Lambda^n$, if there exist two paths of label v then they pass through the same k-th state. For deterministic automata this definition correspond to that given in section 2 . In this general case the completion problem is still unsolved. The same is for the class of permutation-free automata, of which the one of local automata is a subclass. These automata are such that for any subset of the set of states does not exist a word which induces a not trivial permutation in it.

Example 9. The following automaton is permutation-free, but it is not local, since $a \in stab(1) \cap stab(2)$:

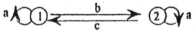

Local automata are related with circular codes, which are such that for any two words u, v the condition $uv, vu \in X^*$ implies that $u, v \in X^*$.

Theorem 14. *The stabilizer of a state of a local automaton is a regular language X^*, where X is a circular code. Moreover, if X is a finite circular code, then its flower automaton is a local automaton.*

342

The notion of circularity is equivalent to that of bounded synchronization delay in the case of finite codes [8]. A code has bounded synchronization delay (BSD) if and only if there exists an integer k such that for any $(u,v) \in X^k \times X^k$ the condition $xuvy \in X^*$ implies that $xu, vy \in X^*$. These notions are also related, but not equivalent, for rational codes [9]. For some families of codes the embedding problem is solved (see [3]), but for codes with BSD the problem is still open. Infact, given a code with BSD, if the language that it generates is the stabilizer of a state of a deterministic local automaton which admits a completion, then we obtain a completion for the code too, but the converse in general is not true:

Example 10. The local automaton of example 3 does not admit a local completion, even if the code $X = \{uab, bab\}$, which generates $stab(1)$, admits a completion with BSD: $Y = \{aa^*b, bb^*aa^*b\}$.

ACKNOWLEDGEMENT

I wish to thank Professor A. Restivo for having me proposed the problem and for his suggestions.

References

[1] M.P. Beal, Codes circulaire, automates locaux et entropie, *Theoret.Comput. Sci.*, **57** (1988), 283-302.

[2] J. Berstel and D. Perrin, *Theory of Codes*, Academic Press, New York, London, 1985.

[3] V. Bruyere, Completion of codes,*Proc. Colloquium on Words, Languages and Combinatorics*, World Scientific Publishing Singapore, M. Ito , ed., 1992, 30-44.

[4] S. Kim, R. McNaghton and R. McCloskey, A polynomial time algorithm for the local testability problem of deterministic finite automata, *Proc. Workshop on Algorithms and Data Structures 89. Lecture Notes in Computer Science*, **382** (1989), 420-436.

[5] R. McNaughton and S. Papert, *Counter Free Automata*, MIT Press, Cambridge, Mass., 1971.

[6] M. Perles, M.O. Rabin and E. Shamir, The theory of definite automata, *IEEE Trans. Electron. Comput.*, EC-12 (1963), 233-243.

[7] M.P. Schützenberger, On finite monoids having only trivial subgroups, *Information and Control*, 8 (1965), 190-194.

[8] A. Restivo, On a question of McNaughton and Papert, *Information and Control,*25 (1974), 93-101.

[9] A. Restivo, A combinatorial property of codes having finite synchronization delay, *Theoret. Comput. Sci.*, 1 (1975), 95-101.

Extended Abstract

Efficient Compression of Wavelet Coefficients for Smooth and Fractal-like Data

Karel Culik II[1] and Simant Dube[2]

[1] Dept. of Computer Science, University of South Carolina, Columbia, SC 29208, USA

[2] Dept. of Math., Stat. and Comp. Sci., University of New England, Armidale, NSW 2351, Australia

Abstract. We show how to integrate wavelet-based and fractal-based approaches for data compression. If the data is self-similar or smooth then one can efficiently store its wavelet coefficients using fractal compression techniques resulting in high compression ratios.

1   Introduction

In recent years, two lossy techniques to compress data and images have emerged. The first is based on fractals and here the basic idea is to capture explicit structure of an image implicitly in terms of relationships between different parts of the image across all scales of magnification [1, 3, 7, 11]. The other is based on wavelet theory and here the basic idea is to perform a multiresolution decomposition of the given image at different frequencies and store only high magnitude frequency components (specified by wavelet coefficients) [12, 9].

Since wavelet functions are defined in a recursive manner, it is not surprising to notice a relationship between the two. In [4], it is shown that Daubechies basic wavelet functions and wavelet transform [8] can be implemented by Weighted Finite Automata (WFA). WFA have been introduced in [6] and studied as devices computing real functions including many smooth and fractal-like functions. The image definition powers of WFA and that of Iterated Function Systems (IFS) [1] are incomparable. Each of these systems is a special case of Mutually Recursive Function Systems considered in [3].

In this paper, we show how these two techniques can be naturally integrated. The idea is to implement wavelet transform with WFA and then simplify this WFA using fractal-based approach. If the original image happens to be smooth or fractal-like then in general this integrated method gives results better than those obtained by using either pure fractal-based method or pure wavelet-based method. The decoding is done by a WFA-decoder that is the same as in [7], i.e. it does not know that wavelets have been used in the encoding process.

We have implemented this integrated compression method for 1-dimensional and also for 2-dimensional functions (images). We will show examples of results for both, however, we explain the technique only for the 1-dimensional case, the generalization to two dimensions is straightforward.

2 Weighted Finite Automata

Let Σ be a finite alphabet and Σ^* the set of words over Σ. The empty word is denoted by ε. The length of a word w is denoted by $|w|$. We will also consider (one-way) infinite words, called ω-words, over Σ. Formally, an infinite word σ over Σ is a sequence $a_1 a_2 \ldots$ with $a_i \in \Sigma$. The prefix $a_1 a_2 \ldots a_n$ of the length n of σ is denoted by $\text{pref}_n(\sigma)$. Set of all ω-words over Σ is denoted by Σ^ω.

As it is well known each ω-word can be interpreted as a real number in the interval $[0, 1]$. Here we will use solely the binary alphabet $\Sigma = \{0, 1\}$ and the binary representation of numbers. The only real numbers in $[0, 1]$ which do not have unique representation are numbers represented by $w10^\omega$ and $w01^\omega$ for some $w \in \Sigma^*$. We refer to the first one as the *standard* representation of the considered number and may write simply $w1$ instead of $w10^\omega$. Clearly, the standard representation gives a one-to-one mapping $\Lambda : \Sigma^\omega \to [0, 1]$. For d-dimensional space $[0, 1]^d$ we would use the alphabet Σ^d. Using the inclusion $(\Sigma^d)^\omega \subseteq (\Sigma^\omega)^d$, we can then interpret every word in $(\Sigma^d)^\omega$ as an n-tuple of coordinates in d-dimensional space, i.e. a point in $[0, 1]^d$. So for functions of two variables (images) we use $\Sigma = \{00, 01, 10, 11\}$ or abbreviated $\Sigma = \{0, 1, 2, 3\}$.

Now we introduce our tool to define real functions.

A *weighted finite automaton* (WFA) is a 5-tuple $A = (Q, \Sigma, W, I, F)$ where

(i) Q is a finite set of *states*.
(ii) Σ is a *finite alphabet* (here $\Sigma = \{0, 1\}$).
(iii) $W : Q \times \Sigma \times Q \to \mathbb{R}$ is a *weight function*.
(iv) $I : Q \to \mathbb{R}$ is an *initial (weight) distribution*.
(v) $F : Q \to \mathbb{R}$ is a *final (weight) distribution*.

Let $|Q| = t$. Then, clearly the weight function W specifies a $t \times t$ matrix W_a for each $a \in \Sigma$.

A WFA A specifies a function $F_A : \Sigma^* \to \mathbb{R}$, called $\mathbb{R}$-rational function, see [10, 2, 13]. First, we define recursively *distributions* $P_A : \Sigma^* \to \mathbb{R}^t$ by:

$$P_A(\varepsilon) = I \ ,$$

$$P_A(wa) = P_A(w) \cdot W_a \text{ for } w \in \Sigma^*.$$

Then $F_A : \Sigma^* \to \mathbb{R}$ is defined by

$$F_A(w) = P_A(w) \cdot F \text{ for } w \in \Sigma^*.$$

The products are, of course, matrix products. Informally, $F_A(w)$ is the sum of all products of the form $I(p).R.F(q)$ where R is the product of weights on a path from state p to q and labeled with w.

We extend the function F_A to a partial function on ω-words $F_A : \Sigma^\omega \to \mathbb{R}$ by

$$F_A(\sigma) = \lim_{n \to \infty} F_A(\text{pref}_n(\sigma))$$

if the limit exists.

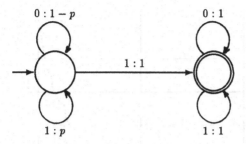

Fig. 1. An average preserving WFA A_p

Finally, we use our assumption $\Sigma = \{0, 1\}$ and define the (partial) real function $f_A : [0, 1] \to \mathbb{R}$ specified by WFA A as $f_A(x) = F_A(w)$ where w is the standard binary representation of $x \in [0, 1]$.

By the underlying automaton of a WFA A we mean the nondeterministic automaton whose transitions consist of those triples (p, a, q) for which $W(p, a, q) \neq 0$ and the initial and final states are those which get nonzero value under I and F, respectively. If $I, F \in \{0, 1\}^t$, i.e. all the nonzeros values are 1, we talk about the initial and final states of a WFA as well, and such a WFA is fully specified by a usual diagram of a nondeterministic automaton with weights labeling the edges (besides inputs). As it is common the initial states will be shown by incoming "half-edges" and the final states by double circles. Note that the function F_A can be viewed as the *multiresolution* representation of a function (image) f_A. The values $F_A(w)$ for all $w \in \Sigma^k$ give an equidistant table of 2^k values of the real function f_A. In the case of 2-dimensional images it specifies the pixel values for the resolution $2^k \times 2^k$.

We say that a function $f : \{0, 1\}^\star \to \mathbb{R}$ is *average preserving* if $f(w) = \frac{1}{2}(f(w0)) + f(w1))$ for each $w \in \Sigma^\star$.

A WFA $A = (Q, \{0, 1\}, W, I, F)$ is *average preserving* if for each $q \in Q$

$$\sum_{a \in \{0,1\}, p \in Q} W(q, a, p) F(p) = 2F(q).$$

It can be easily shown that an average preserving WFA computes an average preserving function.

Example 1. For $0 < p < 1$ an average preserving WFA A_p is shown in Fig. 1. The graphs of the function f_{A_p} for $p = \frac{1}{4}, \frac{3}{4}$ and $\frac{1}{2}$ are shown in Fig. 2. The first two are continuous fractal-like functions, $f_{A_{1/2}}$ is a linear function.

Automata with a few states and simple structure generate an enormous variety of smooth, continuous or everywhere discontinuous functions. It was shown in [7] that the only perfectly smooth functions, that is the functions that have all the derivatives everywhere in $(0, 1)$, definable by WFA are the polynomials.

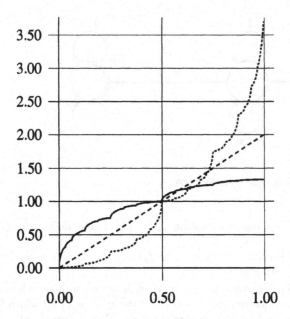

Fig. 2. The graphs of the functions generated by $A_{\frac{1}{4}}$, $A_{\frac{3}{4}}$, and $A_{\frac{1}{2}}$

That contrasts with the fact that we will demonstrate here, that all the smooth functions can be closely approximated by WFA, and that such approximations can be computed efficiently.

3 Wavelets

In transform-based data compression we try to express a given function f : $[0,1]^n \to \mathbb{R}$ in the form $f = \sum_{i=0}^{\infty} a_i \psi_i$ and then disregard the coefficients at the "high frequencies". Wavelets [9, 14] give base function $\psi_0, \psi_1, \ldots$ for which the coefficients $a_0, a_1, \ldots$ can be computed easily. Wavelets $\psi_1, \psi_2, \ldots$ are obtained by dilations and translations of the basic wavelet $\psi_0 = \psi$. Using double indexing we have

$$\psi_{j,k} = 2^{\frac{1}{2}}\, \psi(2^j x - k) \text{ for } j = 1, 2, \ldots \text{ and } k = 0, \ldots, 2^j - 1. \tag{1}$$

Daubechies [8] found good basic wavelets of the form

$$W_{2n} = \sum_{k=2-N}^{1} (-1)^k c_{1-k}\, \phi^{2n}(2x - k) \tag{2}$$

where ϕ_{2n} is the solution of the dilation equation [14]

$$\phi_{2n} = \sum_{k=0}^{N-1} c_k\, \phi_{2n}(2x - k) \tag{3}$$

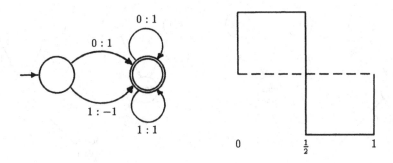

Fig. 3. WFA A_2 and Haar's wavelet W_2 generated by A_2

and $c_0, c_1, \ldots$ are chosen so that the wavelets are orthonormal. For details see [4, 14].

For $n = 1, c_0 = c_1 = 1$, ϕ_2 is the constant 1 and W_2 (Haar's wavelet) is the step function shown in Fig. 3 together with a WFA generating it. Because of of the recursive specification (3) ϕ_{2n} for all $n = 1, 2, \ldots$ can be generated by a WFA. Using (2) every W_{2n} is generated by a WFA. For details see [4]. It should be pointed out that the WFA generating ϕ_{2n} are the first natural examples of WFA with strongly connected diagrams. In [6] has been shown that all polynomials and many other functions are generated by level-WFA in which all cycles are of the length 1 (selfloops).

We choose the Haar wavelet as our basic wavelet function $\psi = \psi_{00}$ and for a 1-D image of resolution d (i.e. 2^d pixels), construct a WFA with 2^d states that can generate any linear combination of the constant function and $2^d - 1$ wavelets of the form (1) i.e. function expressed as

$$f = a + \sum_{j=0}^{d-1} \sum_{k=0}^{2^j-1} a_{j,k} \psi_{j,k} \tag{4}$$

where $\psi_{j,k}$ is given by (1).

In Fig. 4 we show WFA H with 2^d states for d=4. Its initial distribution is shown inside the circles representing the states. It is easy to verify that H generates f from (4) for any values of a and $a_{j,k}$ that specify its initial distribution. The WFA is very economical, it has one state for every wavelet in the base.

4 Compression Algorithm

The data compression method based on the Wavelet Transform method is simple. One chooses a particular wavelet W_N (normally W_6), computes the wavelet

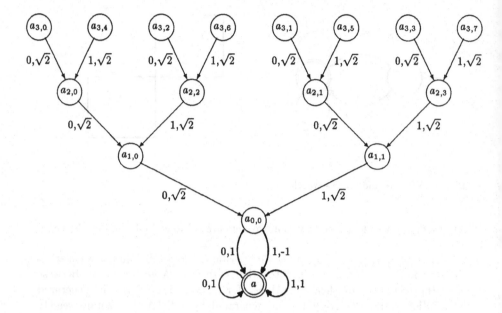

Fig. 4. WFA H

coefficients for the given function f and retains only the coefficients with highest magnitude according to the specified compression ratio [9].

In this section, we describe how the implementation of the Wavelet Transform with WFA results in an altogether different technique to compress data.

We will describe the algorithm in reference to 1-D Haar wavelets (Fig. 4) though it can be generalized to higher wavelets in a straightforward manner.

Consider Fig. 4. Denote the subtree with h many levels and rooted at node v by Subtree(v, h). With each subtree we associate a vector whose elements are the initial weights of the states (nodes) of the subtree represented as an array in the standard manner. For example, denoting for convenience a state by its initial weight on the L.H.S of the following:

$$\text{Subtree}(a_{0,0}, 1) = [a_{0,0}]$$
$$\text{Subtree}(a_{0,0}, 4) = [a_{0,0}\ a_{1,0}\ a_{1,1}\ a_{2,0}\ \cdots\ a_{3,3}\ a_{3,7}]$$
$$\text{Subtree}(a_{2,1}, 2) = [a_{2,1}\ a_{3,1}\ a_{3,5}]$$

Therefore these subtrees can be viewed as *vectors* and one talk about their linear combinations. For example, if subtrees $T_1 = [a \; b \; c]$, $T_2 = [d \; e \; f]$ and

$$T_3 = [ra + sd \quad rb + se \quad rc + sf]$$

then we may write $T_3 = rT_1 + sT_2$.

In our description of the algorithm, the subtrees can have different sizes. If we say that Subtree(v, h) is expressed in terms of a bigger subtree Subtree(u, h') where v and u are two states and $h' > h$, then it means that we are actually expressing Subtree(v, h) in terms of Subtree(u, h) (which is Subtree(u, h') being considered upto only h levels, the other remaining levels being ignored).

Now we are ready to describe the algorithm.

Input: A function f on unit interval specified up to resolution p i.e. M data values where $M = 2^p$ for some $p > 0$.

Output: A WFA computing f.

Algorithm:

Step 1: Compute the wavelet coefficients of f and construct the WFA H shown in Fig. 4 with M states and p levels. Let $N \leftarrow 1$ (the index of the last state created so far in the optimized WFA) and $i \leftarrow 1$ (the index of the next state to be processed). Denote the state with initial weight $a_{0,0}$ as v_1. Let $\mathcal{T} = \{\text{Subtree}(v_1, p)\}$ and denote Subtree(v_1, p) by T_1.

Step 2: Process state v_i: Let $a_{r,s}$ be the initial weight of v_i. Let $h = p - r$ (i.e. h is the height of v_i in the tree).

Step 3: For each label $a \in \{0, 1\}$ consider the corresponding child u of v_i (u has a transition labeled with a to v_i) and do the following.

If $T = \text{Subtree}(u, h-1)$ can be expressed as a linear combination of subtrees in $\mathcal{T} = \{T_1, T_2, \ldots, T_N\}$ as

$$T = k_1 T_1 + k_2 T_2 + \ldots + k_N T_N$$

and the number of nonzero constants among k_j's is less than the size of T i.e. $\sum_{k_j \neq 0} 1 < 2^{h-1} - 1$, *then* replace T by the above linear combination as follows:

1. Delete the entire subtree T.
2. Let k_j be nonzero. Let T_j be rooted at state v_j. Then add an edge (transition) from v_j to v_i with label a and weight $\sqrt{2}k_j$.

Else let $\mathcal{T} \leftarrow \mathcal{T} \cup \{T\}$, $N \leftarrow N + 1$ and denote u by v_N, T by T_N.

Step 4: Let $i \leftarrow i + 1$. If $i \leq N$ then go to Step 2.

Step 5: Output the optimized WFA.

To carry out Step 3, one keeps an orthogonal basis for the linear space generated by the vectors (subtrees) in $\mathcal{T}$. Note that at every step, each of these vectors consists of $2^{h-1} - 1$ elements where h is the height of the state v_i currently being processed. Therefore, when the value of h gets decremented or when a new vector is added to $\mathcal{T}$ then one needs to recompute this orthogonal basis.

In Step 3, we first try to express T as a linear combination of subtrees in $\mathcal{T}$ and if it can be done then we check if it really results in some saving of space by comparing the number of new potential edges with the size of T. Only if fewer edges need to be introduced, we delete T.

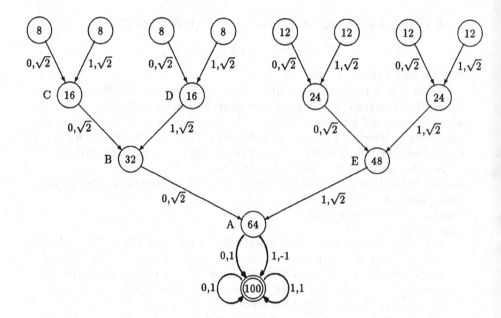

(a) Original WFA with 16 states

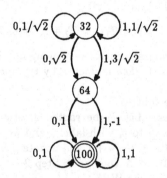

(b) Optimized WFA with 3 states

Fig. 5. Illustration of the Algorithm

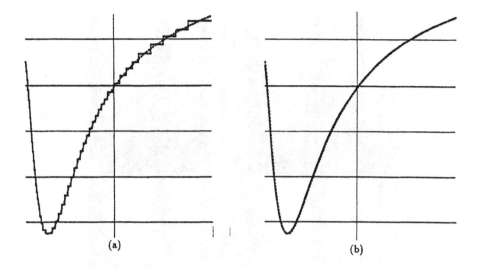

Fig. 6. Compression of a smooth function

Example 2. Suppose the input to the algorithm is a set of 16 data values which results in the WFA shown in Fig. 5 (a) after executing Step 1. At this point $T = \{T_1\}$ where $T_1 = \text{Subtree}(A, 4)$. We first consider the left child B of state A and the subtree rooted at B. This subtree $T_2 = \text{Subtree}(B, 3)$ is linearly independent of T_1, therefore we add it to T and proceed to the right child E of A. Now since $\text{Subtree}(E, 3) = 3/2T_2$ we delete this subtree and add an edge from B to A with label 1 and weight $3/\sqrt{2}$. We then process state B and find that $\text{Subtree}(C, 2)$ can be expressed in terms of T_2 as $\text{Subtree}(C, 2) = 1/2T_2$. Thus we add a self-loop at B with label 0 and weight $1/\sqrt{2}$. A similar optimization is done for $\text{Subtree}(D, 2)$. The resulting optimized WFA is shown in Fig. 5 (b).

Example 3. In this example we show the performance of our data compression algorithm on some actual data and images. In Fig. 6(a), there is a graph of a smooth 1-D function plotted in dotted lines at 8192 points. Also shown is the output of the pure wavelet transform based compression method (using Haar wavelets) in solid lines with 400 times compression. In Fig. 6(b), we have compressed the same function with our algorithm for the same compression ratio. Note that in this case the regenerated function is almost identical with the original one.

In Fig. 7, we compare the results of three different compression methods for two images. In both cases we show the original (top left) and the regenerated images using compression by pure Haar wavelets (top right), pure WFA compression algorithm from [7] (bottom left) and the algorithm described here (bottom right). The compression for the smooth and fractal-like image is 100 (for all three

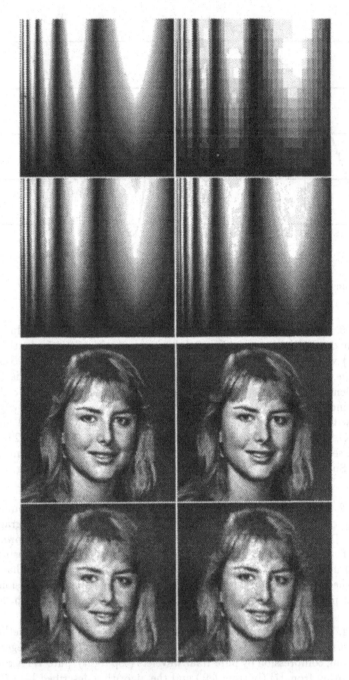

Fig. 7. Comparison of compression methods

methods) and for the girl's face it is 10. For the smooth and fractal-like image the new algorithm gives a far better result, that is the regenerated result is much closer to the original for the same compression ratio.

5 Conclusions

We investigated how the Haar wavelet based and fractal based compression methods can be integrated. This integrated method works better for "smooth" and "fractal-like" data and images. The extension of this approach to higher Debauchies wavelets is studied in [5].

References

1. Barnsley, M. F.: Fractals Everywhere. Academic Press (1988)
2. Berstel, J., Reutenauer, Ch.: Rational Series and Their Languages. Springer-Verlag, Berlin (1988)
3. Culik II, K., and Dube S.: Encoding Images as Words and Languages. International Journal of Algebra and Computation (to appear)
4. Culik II, K., and Dube S.: Implementing Wavelet Transform with Automata and Applications to Data Compression. Manuscript (submitted to Graphical Models & Image Processing)
5. Culik II, K., Dube S., Rajcany, P.: Efficient Compression of Wavelet Coefficients for Smooth and Fractal-like Data. Manuscript (submitted to CDD'93)
6. Culik II, K., Karhumäki, J.: Finite Automata Computing Real Functions. TR 9105, Univ. of South Carolina (1991) (submitted to SIAM J. on Computing)
7. Culik II, K., Kari, J.: Image Compression Using Weighted Finite Automata. (1992) (submitted to Computer & Graphics)
8. Daubechies, I.: Orthonormal Basis of Compactly Supported Wavelets. Communications on Pure and Applied Math. **41** (1988) 909–996
9. DeVore, R. A., Jawerth, B., Lucier, B.J.: Image Compression through Wavelet Transform Coding. IEEE Transactions on Information Theory **38** (1991) 719–746
10. Eilenberg, S.: Automata, Languages and Machines. Vol. A, Academic Press, New York (1974)
11. Fisher, Y.: Fractal Image Compression. Course Notes, SIGGRAPH'92.
12. Mallat, S. G.: A Theory of Multiresolution Signal Decomposition: The Wavelet Representation, IEEE Transactions on Pattern Analysis and Machine Intelligence. **11** (1989) 674–693
13. Salomaa, A., Soittola, M.: Automata-Theoretic Aspects of Formal Power Series. Springer-Verlag, Berlin (1978)
14. Strang, G.: Wavelets and Dilation Equations: A Brief Introduction. SIAM Review **31** 4 (1989) 614–627

On the Equivalence of Two-way Pushdown Automata and Counter Machines over Bounded Languages

Oscar H. Ibarra*, Tao Jiang**, Nicholas Tran*, Hui Wang***

Abstract. It is known that two-way pushdown automata are more powerful than two-way counter machines. The result is also true for the case when the pushdown store and counter are reversal-bounded. In contrast, we show that two-way reversal-bounded pushdown automata over bounded languages (i.e., subsets of $w_1^* \ldots w_k^*$ for some nonnull words $w_1, \ldots, w_k$) are equivalent to two-way reversal-bounded counter machines. We also show that, unlike the unbounded input case, two-way reversal-bounded pushdown automata over bounded languages have decidable emptiness, equivalence and containment problems.

1 Introduction

A two-way reversal-bounded multicounter machine is a two-way deterministic finite automaton augmented with a finite number of counters which can reverse (i.e., alternate between increasing and decreasing modes) at most a fixed number of times. It is known that the emptiness problem for such machines (i.e., deciding if a given machine accepts the empty language) is undecidable even when the machines have only two counters and accept only strictly bounded languages (i.e., subsets of $a_1^* \ldots a_k^*$, for distinguished symbols $a_1, \ldots, a_k$) [Iba78]. On the other hand, two-way reversal-bounded multicounter machines over a unary alphabet accept only regular sets, and the emptiness problem is decidable [GI79]. It is also known that for machines with only one reversal-bounded counter over strictly bounded languages, the emptiness problem is decidable [GI82]. In contrast, machines over a unary alphabet with one unrestricted counter have an undecidable emptiness problem [Min61].

For pushdown automata, it was shown in [Chr84] that every two-way reversal-bounded pushdown automaton over a unary alphabet can effectively be converted to a two-way reversal-bounded multicounter machine. Hence such a pushdown automaton accepts only a regular set, and the emptiness problem is decidable. Here we improve this result. We show that every two-way reversal-bounded pushdown automaton over a strictly bounded language can effectively be converted to a two-way reversal-bounded one-counter machine. The result generalizes to machines over bounded languages (i.e., subsets of $w_1^* \ldots w_k^*$, for nonnull words $w_1, \ldots, w_k$). The

* Department of Computer Science, University of California, Santa Barbara, CA 93106. Research supported in part by NSF Grant CCR89-18409.

** Department of Computer Science and Systems, McMaster University, Hamilton, Ontario L8S 4K1, Canada. Research supported in part by NSERC Operating Grant OGP 0046613.

*** Department of Computer Science, University of Alabama in Huntsville, AL 35899.

construction is rather interesting in that we show that two-way reversal-bounded one-counter machines can compute fairly complicated functions. As a consequence, we obtain that the emptiness, equivalence and containment problems for two-way reversal-bounded pushdown automata over bounded languages are decidable. This can be viewed as a generalization over bounded languages of the well-known result [Val74] that the equivalence problem for one-way reversal-bounded pushdown automata is decidable.

In [DG82], it was shown that two-way pushdown automata are more powerful than two-way one-counter machines. The result also holds for the case when the pushdown store and counter are reversal bounded. Our result above shows that the restricted machines are equivalent over bounded languages. It remains an interesting question whether two-way one-counter machines and two-way pushdown machines over bounded languages are equivalent. We conjecture that the two classes are different, even over unary alphabet. One possible way to prove this is to use the fact that the unary encoding of every language in P (= the class of languages accepted by polynomial time-bounded deterministic Turing machines) can be accepted by a two-way pushdown automaton [Mon84] and show that the unary encoding of a most complicated language in P (i.e., complete for P) cannot be accepted by a two-way one-counter machine.

The rest of the paper is organized as follows. The basic definitions and notations are given in Section 2. In Section 3, we show that reversal-bounded two-way one-counter machines can compute a fairly complicated class of functions. These functions are useful in obtaining the main result of the paper, which is proved in Section 4. In Section 5, we look at some decision problems concerning pushdown automata and give new decidability results.

2 Preliminaries

Definition 1. A language is *strictly bounded* if it is a subset of $a_1^* a_2^* \ldots a_k^*$ for some distinct letters $a_1, a_2, \ldots, a_k$. A language is *bounded* if it is a subset of $w_1^* w_2^* \ldots w_k^*$ for some nonnull words $w_1, w_2, \ldots, w_k$.

Definition 2. The class of r-reversal deterministic counter machines, denoted by *2DCM(r)*, are deterministic automata having a two-way input head and a counter that makes at most r reversals in any computation. $\cup_{r>0} 2DCM(r)$ is the class of reversal-bounded counter machines.

Definition 3. The class of r-reversal two-way deterministic pushdown automata, denoted by *2DPDA(r)*, are deterministic pushdown automata having a two-way input and a stack that makes at most r reversals in any computation. $\cup_{r>0} 2DPDA(r)$ is the class of reversal-bounded deterministic two-way pushdown automata.

Suppose that M is an r-reversal 2DPDA and $x = a_1^{x_1} a_2^{x_2} \ldots a_k^{x_k}$ is an input to it, where $a_1, a_2, \ldots, a_k$ are distinct letters. Each $a_i^{x_i}$ is called an *input segment*. In the following definition, the term *boundary* refers to the boundary between adjacent input segments. Since the input to M is of bounded form, it is not difficult to see that the contents of M's stack during the computation is also bounded, i.e., it is always of the form $w_1^{j_1} w_2^{j_2} \ldots w_n^{j_n}$ for some words $w_1, w_2, \ldots, w_n$ depending only on M. Each such word w_i is called a *stack word* and each $w_i^{j_i}$ is called a *stack segment* with length j_i. Furthermore, the segment that appears on top of the stack at some instant is called *top segment* at that moment. The computation of M on x can be decomposed into bounded number of phases based on its input head and stack operations. A phase is said to be a *pushing* (or *popping*) phase if the stack operations in the phase are just *pushing* (or *popping*). The stack grows during a pushing phase and shrinks during a popping phase. Moreover, a popping phase is viewed as either *looping* or *nonlooping*. A popping phase is said to be *looping* if it begins with the M's input head being at some boundary and during the phase, the head will return to the same boundary with M's being in the same state.

Definition 4. Let M be a 2DPDA and $x = a_1^{x_1} a_2^{x_2} \ldots a_k^{x_k}$ be an input to M. Denote by *turn points* the moments in the computation of M on x when the input head of M hits a boundary during a pushing phase or a nonlooping popping phase, or the current top stack segment is completely erased during a looping popping phase.

Clearly, there can be a bounded number of such turn points during an accepting computation of M on input x if M is a reversal-bounded 2DPDA.

3 Computing Functions by Reversal-Bounded 2DCM's

Here we explore the capability of reversal-bounded 2DCM's as a device that computes functions. We show that a fairly complicated class of functions is computable by reversal-bounded 2DCM's. These functions will be used in the simulation of a reversal-bounded 2DPDA. In the following, we assume that $a_1, \ldots, a_k$ are k distinct letters.

Definition 5. A 2DCM is said to compute a (non-negative) function $f(x_1, \ldots, x_k)$ if, when given input $a_1^{x_1} \ldots a_k^{x_k}$, the machine halts with its counter value being $f(x_1, \ldots, x_k)$.

Observe that a 2DCM can also be used to compute a general function whose value is not necessarily non-negative. The sign is then recorded in the machine's finite control while the absolute value of the function is stored in the counter. Now we formally define the class of the so called *combined modulo functions*. In the following, $x_1, \ldots, x_k$ denote the independent variables, and by a function, we always mean a function of $x_1, \ldots, x_k$. Thus, whenever there is no confusion, a function $f(x_1, \ldots, x_k)$ is simply written as f.

Definition 6. We inductively define the functions.

Each linear function (i.e., $c_1 * x_1 + \ldots + c_k * x_k + d$, for some constants $c_1, \ldots, c_k, d$) is a combined modulo function.

Suppose that $f_1, \ldots, f_m$ are some combined modulo functions and g is a linear function with positive coefficients. Then both $h_1 = c_1 * f_1 + \ldots + c_m * f_m$ and $h_2 = (c_1 * f_1 + \ldots + c_m * f_m) \bmod g$ are also combined modulo functions, where $c_1, \ldots c_m$ are some constants.

We show, starting from simpler functions, how a reversal-bounded 2DCM computes combined modulo functions. From now on, we assume that the input is $a_1^{x_1} \ldots a_k^{x_k}$.

Lemma 7. *Let* $h(x_1, x_2, \ldots, x_k) = f(x_1, x_2, \ldots, x_k) \bmod g(x_1, x_2, \ldots, x_k)$, *where both* f *and* g *are linear functions and the coefficients in* g *are positive. Then* h *can be computed by a reversal-bounded 2DCM.*

Proof. Suppose $f = c_1 * x_1 + c_2 * x_2 + \ldots + c_k * x_k + d$ and $g = c_1' * x_1 + c_2' * x_2 + \ldots + c_k' * x_k + d'$. We construct a 2DCM to compute h. M first computes $f(x_1, \ldots, x_k)$ as follows. Its input head sweeps the a_1 segment c_1 times while increasing its counter for each step of head movement. If c_1 is negative, M records the negative sign (as the sign for counter) in its finite control. M then works with $c_2 * x_2$ of f. Now suppose that c_2's sign is different from the counter's. Then the counter is decreased while the input head sweeps the a_2 segment. If the counter reaches 0 before the input head finishes making c_2 sweeps, M changes counter's sign and increases the counter thereafter. In case both c_2 and counter have the same sign, M increases the counter while its head sweeps a_2 segment c_2 times. The same process is repeated for all other terms of f. Since f has only $k + 1$ terms (including the constant d), the counter makes at most $2k + 1$ reversals.

After f is computed and recorded in the counter, M computes $f \bmod g$ by repeatedly subtracting $g(x_1, \ldots, x_k)$ from the counter. Note that, it is essential that the coefficients of g are all positive. Since otherwise the counter has to reverse unboundedly many times. Once again we need to distinguish the cases when the counter sign is positive or negative. If the counter value is positive, then M repeatedly computes g and subtracts the value of g from the counter. Once the counter reaches 0, M reverses its computation of g until its input head has made c_1' sweeps on the a_1 segment. the value in the counter is then $f \bmod g$. If the counter value is negative, $f \bmod g$ is computed similarly except when the counter reaches 0, M continues the computation of g while increasing the counter.

Let "$/$" denote the binary operation of integer division. Using the technique of computing $f \bmod g$, a 2DCM is able to obtain the parity of f/g with a bounded number of counter reversals. Furthermore, a reversal-bounded 2DCM can calculate the parity of f/g while it computes $f \bmod g$. This is needed in proving the following lemma.

Lemma 8. *Let* $h = f_1 \bmod g_1 + f_2 \bmod g_2$ *be a function, where* f_1, f_2, g_1, g_2 *are linear functions and the coefficients in* g_1 *and* g_2 *are all positive. Then* h *can be computed by a reversal-bounded 2DCM.*

Proof. By Lemma 7, a reversal-bounded 2DCM is able to compute either $f_1 \bmod g_1$ or $f_2 \bmod g_2$. But a difficulty arises that once $f_1 \bmod g_1$ is computed and stored in the counter, f_2 cannot be computed without losing the value that is already in the counter. This problem can be solved with the help of the following proposition.

Proposition 9. *If* $g_1 \le g_2$, *then*

$$f_1 \bmod g_1 + f_2 \bmod g_2 = (f_1 \bmod g_1 + f_2) \bmod g_2 + p * g_2$$

where $p = 0$ *if* f_2/g_2 *and* $(f_1 \bmod g_1 + f_2)/g_2$ *have the same parity,* $p = 1$ *otherwise.*

Proof. Since $g_1 \leq g_2$, $f_1 \bmod g_1 < g_2$. Suppose that f_2/g_2 and $(f_1 \bmod g_1 + f_2)/g_2$ have the same parity. Then $f_1 \bmod g_1 + f_2 \bmod g_2 < g_2$ and thus $f_1 \bmod g_1 + f_2 \bmod g_2 = (f_1 \bmod g_1 + f_2) \bmod g_2$. If f_2/g_2 and $(f_1 \bmod g_1 + f_2)/g_2$ have different parities, then $f_1 \bmod g_1 + f_2 \bmod g_2 \geq g_2$. It is easy to see that in this case, $f_1 \bmod g_1 + f_2 \bmod g_2 - (f_1 \bmod g_1 + f_2) \bmod g_2 = g_2$.

(Proof of Lemma 8 continues.) We construct a 2DCM M to compute h. With the counter reversing twice, M can check which of g_1 and g_2 is larger. Suppose $g_1 \leq g_2$. In what follows, M first determines the parity of f_2/g_2 by computing $f_2 \bmod g_2$ and stores the parity in its finite control. M proceeds to compute $f_1 \bmod g_1$ and store it in the counter. Then M computes $(f_1 \bmod g_1 + f_2) \bmod g_2$ and records the parity of $(f_1 \bmod g_1 + f_2)/g_2$. The counter remains unchanged if the two parities are the same. Otherwise, M simply adds g_1 to the counter.

The above lemma can be extended to more general cases, e.g, when $h = f_1 \bmod g_1 + \ldots + f_m \bmod g_m$, for some constant m. To compute such a function, the 2DCM first sorts all g_i's. Since a 2DCM whose counter reverses once can compare two functions g_i and g_j, the sorting process would require no more than a constant number of counter reversals. Assume that the order is $g_1 \leq g_2 \leq \ldots \leq g_m$. For each i, let B_i denote the last $\lceil log_2 i \rceil$ (binary) bits of f_i/g_i. The machine then computes successively, for each $1 < i \leq m$, $f_i \bmod g_i$, and records B_i in its finite control. Then for each i, the 2DCM computes $h_i = f_1 \bmod g_1 + \ldots + f_i \bmod g_i$, starting from $i = 1$. Suppose that it has just finishing computing h_{i-1}. Then to compute h_i, the machine first computes $(h_{i-1} + f_i) \bmod g_i$ and records, B_i', the last $\lceil log_2 i \rceil$ bits of $(h_{i-1} + f_i)/g_i$. Then,

$$h_i = (h_{i-1} + f_i) \bmod g_i + |B_i' - B_i| * g_i$$

This can be seen from Proposition 9 and the fact that $g_1 \leq \ldots \leq g_m$, which guarantees that $h_i < i * g_i$.

Definition 10. A *simple modulo* function h is $t_1 + \ldots + t_m$, where each term t_i is of the form

$$(\ldots(f \bmod g_1)\ldots) \bmod g_m$$

where $f, g_1, \ldots, g_m$ are some linear functions and the coefficients in $g_1, \ldots, g_m$ are positive.

Lemma 11. *Each simple modulo function can be computed by a reversal-bounded 2DCM.*

Proof. We show how a 2DCM M computes a simple modulo functions of just two terms, $t_1 + t_2$. The extension to more general case is similar to the above discussion.
Let $t_1 = (\ldots(f_1 \bmod g_1)\ldots) \bmod g_m$ and $t_2 = (\ldots(f_2 \bmod h_1)\ldots) \bmod h_n$. First, we can assume that $g_1 > \ldots > g_m$ and $h_1 > \ldots > h_n$. For otherwise, e.g., if $g_1 \leq g_2$, we can simply remove $\bmod\ g_2$ from t_1, without affecting the final result. The 2DCM M first compares g_m with h_n to see which is smaller. Suppose $g_m \leq h_n$. Then M computes the parities of f_2/h_1, $(f_2 \bmod h_1)/h_2$, $\ldots$, $(\ldots((f_2 \bmod h_1) \bmod h_2)\ldots)/h_n$, and records them in its finite control. M can easily compute t_1 with a bounded number of counter reversals. Let the value of t_1 be v_1.

After obtaining v_1, M computes $(v_1 + f_2) \bmod h_1$ and and the parity of $(v_1 + f_2)/h_1$. By comparing the parities of f_2/h_1 and $(v_1 + f_2)/h_1$, M can obtain $v_1 + f_2 \bmod h_1$ adding either 0 or h_1 to $(v_1 + f_2) \bmod h_1$. Note that, here $h_1 > h_n \geq g_m$. Similarly, M can obtain $v_1 + (f_2 \bmod h_1) \bmod h_2$, ..., $v_1 + ((f_2 \bmod h_1) \ldots) \bmod h_n$, one by one.

Now we are ready to show how a bounded-reversal 2DCM can compute combined modulo functions. The idea is to show that each combined modulo function can be easily converted to a simple modulo function.

Theorem 12. *Combined modulo functions can be computed by a reversal-bounded 2DCM.*

Proof. (Sketch) We show that a combined modulo function can be transformed to a simple modulo function. The theorem then follows from Lemma 11. Note that a 2DCM can record the "form" (i.e., the definition) of a function in the finite control. So, really, the transformation of a function means that the 2DCM modifies the function in its finite control. Observe that the essential difference between a combined modulo function form and a simple modulo function form is that the former allows terms of the form $c * ((f_1 + \ldots + f_m) \bmod g)$. It suffices to show how to convert this form to a form allowed by simple modulo function.

First, assuming that c is positive, then

$$c * ((f_1 + \ldots + f_m) \bmod g) = (c * f_1 + \ldots + c * f_m) \bmod (c * g)$$

Thus we just consider conversion of $(f_1 + \ldots + f_m) \bmod g$. In particular, terms of form $(f_1 + f_2) \bmod g$ can be rewritten as $f_1 \bmod g + f_2 \bmod g + p * g$, where p is 0 if $f_1 \bmod g + f_2 \bmod g < g$, or -1 otherwise. If f_1 and f_2 are some linear functions, then a 2DCM can check if $f_1 \bmod g + f_2 \bmod g < g$ by computing $g - (f_1 \bmod g + f_2 \bmod g)$. The same idea can easily be extended to $(f_1 + \ldots + f_m) \bmod g$. In the general case when $f_1, \ldots, f_m$ are combined modulo functions, the conversion should be performed starting from the innermost level.

4 Simulating a Reversal-bounded 2DPDA by a Reversal-bounded 2DCM

It was shown in [Chr84] that every reversal-bounded 2DPDA over a unary alphabet can effectively be converted to a two-way reversal-bounded multicounter machine. Here we prove a stronger result. We show that every reversal-bounded 2DPDA over a strictly bounded language can effectively be converted to a reversal-bounded 2DCM. Our construction is much more involved than the one in [Chr84], since the stack contents of a 2DPDA on a strictly bounded input can be very complicated.

Let M be a reversal-bounded 2DPDA and $x = a_1^{x_1} \ldots a_k^{x_k}$ an input. Recall that since the input is of bounded form, M's stack should also be bounded, i.e., it is always of the form $w_1^{j_1} \ldots w_n^{j_n}$ for some small words $w_1, \ldots, w_n$ depending only on M. Observe that M may operate quite differently in a pushing phase and in a popping phase during an accepting computation: it can make repeated moves (i.e., it loops) only in a popping phase. Further, M has only a bounded number of turn points in an accepting computation and the stack reverses only at a turn point. Also, the input head sweeps during each phase.

Lemma 13. *Every reversal-bounded 2DPDA over strictly bounded languages can be simulated by a reversal-bounded 2DCM.*

Proof. We construct a reversal-bounded 2DCM N that simulates the 2DPDA M on input $x = a_1^{x_1} \ldots a_k^{x_k}$. We assume, without loss of generality, that M accepts x iff it is in a final state with empty stack and its input head being at the rightmost boundary. Denote by *surface configuration* of M at a turn point its state, head position, top stack segment length, and top stack word w_j. The basic idea of the simulation is to construct N which simulates M by sequentially constructing M's surface configurations at each turn point. More precisely, we show that the input head position and top stack segment length of M at each turn point can be represented as combined modulo functions of $x_1, \ldots, x_k$, defined in the previous section. Since these functions are computable by a 2DCM, N just needs to construct the function forms of M's head position and top stack segment length at each turn point.

Suppose that N has just constructed function forms of M's input head position and top stack segment length at turn point i. Then it determines the function forms at turn point $i + 1$, and records these function forms (including all the constants/coefficients) in its finite control, by computing the input head position and top stack segment length of M at turn point i. The details are given below.

Now N needs to determine first what will cause M to make turn $i + 1$. From the definition of turn points, we know that N has to decide which of the following will occur next:

1. *The next phase is pushing;*
2. *The next phase is a nonlooping popping phase and and the input head will hit a boundary before the top stack segment is erased;*
3. *The next phase is a nonlooping popping phase and the top stack segment will be erased before the input head hits a boundary;*
4. *The next phase is a looping popping phase.*

We show how N determines the correct case and constructs corresponding function forms for it. Let the function forms of M's top stack segment length and input head position at turn point i be t and h, respectively. N can easily determine whether M is in a pushing or popping phase. It can also determine whether a popping phase is looping by checking if the current top segment of M will be "long" enough for the input head to visit the same boundary twice with M being in the same state. This requires N to compute the top segment length at turn point i, and compare it with relevant input segment lengths. Suppose that a loop is detected. Then the next turn point is when the top stack segment is erased. Suppose that the period of the loop is $g = c_1 * x_1 + \ldots + c_k * x_k$. (Note that here the constants $c_1, \ldots, c_k$ are all positive.) Then the function form for the next input head position is $t \bmod g$ and the function form for the next top segment length is simply the function form for the stack segment underneath the current top stack segment, which should be stored in N's finite control.

Now suppose that next phase is a nonlooping popping phase. N has to decide whether the input head hits a boundary first by comparing h with t. Consider the situation when the head is in a left-to-right sweep over some input segment $a_i^{x_i}$. N checks whether $c_1 * (\sum_{j=1}^{i} x_j - h) - c_2 * t$ is non-negative, where c_1, c_2 are some constants depending on M's operation, e.g., $c_1 = 2$, $c_2 = 1$ if M pops one stack word when the input head moves two steps to the right. N can compute $c_1 * (\sum_{j=1}^{i} x_j - h) - c_2 * t$ since $c_1 * (\sum_{j=1}^{i} x_j - h) - c_2 * t$ is really in combined modulo form. If $c_1 * (\sum_{j=1}^{i} x_j - h) - c_2 * t \geq 0$, the the top stack segment is erased before the input head hits a boundary, then the next input head position should be $h - c_1 * t / c_2$ and the next top stack segment should be the stack segment underneath the current top stack segment. Otherwise the input head hits a boundary first and the function forms at the next turn point should be: $\sum_{j=1}^{i} x_j$ for input head position and $t - c_2 * (\sum_{j=1}^{i} x_j - h) / c_1$ for top stack segment length.

The case when the next phase is pushing is handled similarly. Now along with the construction of the function forms, N also has to compute M's state and the top stack word at each turn point. Suppose that the next phase is a looping popping phase. To compute M's state at next turn point, N first computes and stores in its counter the length of M's top stack segment at current turn point, moves its head to appropriate input segment boundary, and then simulates M until the counter becomes empty. The other cases are even simpler, and can be worked out easily. The computation of the top stack follows the same idea.

It is clear that N's counter reverses a bounded number of times in the above simulation since the total number of turn points is bounded and each computation of a function takes a bounded number of reversals.

Thus we have the following theorem.

Theorem 14. $\cup_{r>0} 2DCM(r)$ and $\cup_{r>0} 2DPDA(r)$ are equivalent over strictly bounded languages.

The same proof technique can be extended to the machines over bounded languages, i.e., languages that are subsets of $w_1^* \ldots w_k^*$ for some nonnull words $w_1, \ldots, w_k$. Here we need to adopt some parsing scheme to distinguish the boundaries between input segment, since now the boundaries are not clearly marked. The details are omitted here.

Theorem 15. $\cup_{r>0} 2DCM(r)$ and $\cup_{r>0} 2DPDA(r)$ are equivalent over bounded languages.

It is known that the set of palindromes $L = \{x \# x^R \mid x \in \{0,1\}^* \}$, cannot be accepted by any reversal-bounded 2DCM [DG82]. On the other hand, L can easily be accepted by a 2DPDA (in fact, a one-way DPDA) whose stack reverses once, and by a 2DCM with an unrestricted counter. It follows that reversal-bounded 2DCM's are weaker than 2DCM's and weaker than reversal-bounded 2DPDA, over general (i.e., unbounded) languages. These contrast with the above result.

So far we have considered pushdown automata and counter machines with restrictions on the number of stack/counter reversals. Another way of restricting the power of these machines is to limit the number of *input head* reversals. Denote these machines as *finite-head-turn* 2DPDA's (2DCM's). It is interesting to note that finite-head-turn 2DPDA's are equivalent to finite-head-turn 2DCM's over strictly bounded languages. (They all accept semi-linear sets.) In fact the finite-head-turn 2DCM's can be further restricted to have a bounded number of counter reversals. Also it can be shown that over strictly bounded languages reversal-bounded 2DCM's are more powerful than finite-head-turn reversal-bounded 2DCM's.

The language L of palindromes cannot be accepted by a finite-head-turn 2DCM [DG82]. It follows that over unbounded languages, finite-head-turn 2DCM's are weaker than finite-head-turn 2DPDA's. Thus the restriction of being "over bounded languages" in Theorem 15 cannot be removed.

5 Some Decision Problems Concerning 2PDA's

The results above can be used to show that several decision problems concerning 2DPDA's are decidable. The *emptiness problem* for a class of machines is defined as the problem of deciding for an arbitrary machine M in the class whether or not M accepts any input. The *containment* (respectively, *equivalence*) *problem* for a class of machines is the problem of deciding for arbitrary machines M_1 and M_2 in the class whether or not $L(M_1) \subseteq L(M_2)$ (respectively, $L(M_1) = L(M_2)$).

It was shown in [GI82] that the emptiness, equivalence and containment problems for reversal-bounded 2DCM's over strictly bounded languages are decidable. Extension of this result to bounded languages is trivial. Hence we have

Theorem 16. *The emptiness, equivalence and containment problems for reversal-bounded 2DPDA's over bounded languages are decidable.*

The above theorem is best possible in view of the following:

1. *The emptiness problem for 2DCM's (and hence also for 2DPDA's) over unary alphabet is undecidable.* (This follows from the result in [Min61].)
2. *The emptiness problem for 2DPDA's over unbounded inputs whose input head and stack make at most 1 reversal each is undecidable (Theorem 21).*

The emptiness, equivalence and containment problems for finite-head-turn 2DPDA's (with unrestricted stack) over bounded languages are decidable. In fact there is a stronger result. One can augment the pushdown automata with counters. Interestingly, the following result was shown in [Iba78] ("N" stands for nondeterministic).

Theorem 17. *The following problems are decidable*

1. *The emptiness problem for one-way NPDA's (1NPDA's) augmented with reversal-bounded counters (whose stack is unrestricted).*
2. *The emptiness, equivalence and containment problems for finite-head-turn 2NPDA's augmented with reversal-bounded counters over bounded languages.*

The proof of this theorem consists of showing that the Parikh maps of the languages defined by the machines are effectively computable semilinear sets. Theorem 17 has some nice applications. An example is concerned with checking PCP (Post Correspondence Problem) - like properties. Given two n-tuples of nonnull words $(u_1, \ldots, u_n)$ and $(v_1, \ldots, v_n)$ define the following languages:

$$L = \{\ x \mid x = u_{f(1)} \ldots u_{f(k)} = v_{g(1)} \ldots v_{g(k)} \text{ for some } k \text{ and functions } f \text{ and } g\ \},$$
$$L' = \{\ x \mid x = u_{f(1)} \ldots u_{f(k)} = v_{g(1)} \ldots v_{g(k)} \text{ for some } k \text{ and functions } f \text{ and } g,$$
$$\text{where } g(1), \ldots, g(k) \text{ is a permutation of } f(1), \ldots, f(k)\ \},$$

Let C be a context-free language specified by a 1NPDA or a CFG. Then one can effectively construct 1NPDA's augmented with reversal bounded counters to accept L, L', and $L' \cap C$. It follows that the properties defined by L, L', and $L' \cap C$ for arbitrary $\{u_1, \ldots, u_n\}$ and $\{v_1, \ldots, v_n\}$ and C are decidable. Note that these properties are almost like the PCP property which is undecidable.

In part 1 of Theorem 17, the one-way machine has one unrestricted pushdown and several reversal-bounded counters. If instead there is only one unrestricted counter and one reversal-bounded pushdown, the problem becomes undecidable:

Theorem 18. *The emptiness problem is undecidable for one-way deterministic one-counter machines augmented with 1-reversal pushdown (the counter is unrestricted).*

Proof. This follows from the fact that the emptiness problem is undecidable for 1-input reversal two-way deterministic counter machines [Iba78].

We now consider reversal-bounded 2NPDA over bounded languages. We shall show that the emptiness problem for this class is undecidable even when restricted to unary alphabets.

We first make the following observation:

Observation 19. *Given a single-tape TM M, we can effectively construct a two-counter machine (without input tape) M' which simulates M on blank tape. M' is normalized in that its computation can be organized in phases starting with both counters zero. Each phase starts with one counter $C1$ decreasing it's value until it becomes zero, while the other counter $C2$ increases its value (from zero). In the next phase, $C2$ decreases to zero while $C1$ increases from zero, etc.*

The construction of M' is a simple modification of Minsky's construction (see, e.g., [IJ91]).

In contrast to Theorem 16, we have

Theorem 20. *The emptiness problem is undecidable for sweeping 1-reversal 2NPDA over unary languages.*

Proof. Let M be a normalized 2-counter machine as described in Observation 19. We construct a 1-reversal 2NPDA M' which simulates M as follows. Given an input a^n, M' first writes $(\#a^n)^i$ on the pushdown for some nondeterministically chosen i. Then M uses the input to simulate one counter and the pushdown to simulate the other counter. The simulation of a counter by the pushdown can be made by just popping the stack. When the simulation of a phase of the 2-counter machine M has been completed, M' continues moving its input head (in the same direction) and popping its stack (thus preserving the difference between the counter values) until the input head reaches an endmarker. By exchanging the roles of the input head and pushdown stack (with respect to the counters they are simulating), the simulation can then be continued. Clearly, M' is sweeping, almost deterministic, and makes exactly one reversal on the stack.

One can prove a theorem similar to the one above if we make the input unbounded.

Theorem 21. *The emptiness problem is undecidable for 1-reversal 2DPDA's over the language* $(0^+\#)^+$ *which makes at most one reversal on the input.*

Proof. Again we use the fact that a 2-counter machine (without input) normalized as described in Observation 19 can simulate a TM on blank tape. So let M be such a 2-counter machine. We construct a 2DPDA M' which simulates M as follows. Given an input, M' copies the input on the pushdown and checks that it's of the form $\%0^{i_1}\#0^{i_2}\#\ldots\#0^{i_k}\#$. (% is the left endmarker.) At the end of this process, the input and pushdown heads are on \$. The simulation of M is done while M' moves its input head to the left and pops it stack towards %. M' simulates the 2-counter machine but when a phase of M is completed, M' continues moving its head and popping its stack simultaneously until the input head reaches a $\#$ or the top of the stack is a $\#$, whichever comes first. Then it simulates the next phase, etc. Note that the simulation can be carried out correctly if the i_j's are large enough and it is not necessary that they are the same.

References

[Chr84] M. Chrobak. A note on bounded-reversal multipushdown machines. *Info. Proc. Letters*, 19:179–180, 1984.

[DG82] P. Duris and Z. Galil. Fooling a two way automaton or one pushdown store is better than one counter for two way machines. *Theoretical Computer Science*, 21:39–53, 1982.

[GI79] E. M. Gurari and O. H. Ibarra. Simple counter machines and number-theoretic problems. *J. Comput. System Sci.*, 19:145–162, 1979.

[GI82] E. M. Gurari and O. H. Ibarra. Two-way counter machines and diophantine equations. *J. Assoc. Comput. Mach.*, 29:863–873, 1982.

[Iba78] O. H. Ibarra. Reversal-bounded multicounter machines and their decision problems. *J. Assoc. Comput. Mach.*, 25:116–133, 1978.

[IJ91] O. Ibarra and T. Jiang. The power of alternating one-reversal counters and stacks. *SIAM Journal on Computing*, 20(2):278–290, 1991.

[Min61] M. Minsky. Recursive unsolvability of Post's problem of tag and other topics in the theory of Turing machines. *Ann. of Math.*, 74:437–455, 1961.

[Mon84] B. Monien. Deterministic two-way one-head pushdown automata are very powerful. *Info. Proc. Letters*, 18:239–242, 1984.

[Val74] L. Valiant. The equivalence problem for deterministic finite-turn pushdown automata. *Inform. and Contr.*, 25:123–133, 1974.

Computability Properties of Low-dimensional Dynamical Systems *

Michel Cosnard, Max Garzon and Pascal Koiran

LIP – IMAG
Unité de Recherche Associée 1398 du CNRS
Ecole Normale Supérieure de Lyon
46, Allée d'Italie
69364 Lyon Cedex 07
France

Abstract. It has been known for a short time that a class of recurrent neural networks has universal computational abilities. These networks can be viewed as iterated piecewise-linear maps in a high-dimensional space. In this paper, we show that similar systems in dimension two are also capable of universal computations. On the contrary, it is necessary to resort to more complex systems (e.g., iterated piecewise-monotone maps) in order to retain this capability in dimension one.

1 Introduction

First-order recurrent neural networks using the saturated-linear output function σ can simulate universal Turing machines [9] in linear time [10] (i.e., the transition function of a Turing machine can be computed in constant time). The global transition function of such a network of d analog units is a piecewise-linear function $F : [0,1]^d \longrightarrow [0,1]^d$ ($d = 1058$ units are sufficient [10]). This result raises the problem of finding the minimum dimension d for which Turing machine simulation by iteration of piecewise-linear functions is possible. In this paper, we show that $d = 2$ is sufficient. Our construction can be used to give another proof of the existence of universal neural networks.

Simulation of cellular automata is also compared to simulation of Turing machines, and the computational capabilities of piecewise-linear functions and other natural classes of functions in dimension 1 are investigated. Here, our main results are that one-dimensional piecewise-linear maps cannot perform universal computations, and that two-dimensional piecewise-linear maps cannot simulate arbitrary cellular automata. These negative results are proved using natural, although somewhat restrictive models of universality. Our positive results are all constructive.

Iterations of piecewise-linear and piecewise-monotone functions on an interval have been extensively studied in the dynamical systems literature, and have exhibited very rich behavior (see for instance [2] and [6]). Whether this assertion remains true for their computational behavior seems to us an important open problem. In [5],

* This work was partially supported by the Programme de Recherches Coordonnées C³ of the CNRS and the Ministère de la Recherche et de la Technologie.

C. Moore studies computation-universal dynamical systems. His main results are similar to our Theorem 2: a universal Turing machine can be simulated by a "generalized shift" on a two-dimensional Cantor set, this map can embedded in a smooth map in R^2, and in a smooth flow in R^3.

2 Preliminaries

The definitions and notations used throughout the paper are listed below. I is the unit interval $[0, 1]$. PL_d is the set of piecewise-linear continuous functions on I^d. More precisely, $f : I^d \rightarrow I^d$ belongs to PL_d if

- f is continuous;
- there is a sequence $(P_i)_{1 \leq i \leq p}$ of convex closed polyhedra (of non-empty interior) such that $f_i = f_{|P_i}$ is affine, $I^d = \bigcup_{i=1}^{p} P_i$ and $\overset{\circ}{P_i} \cap \overset{\circ}{P_j} = \emptyset$ for $i \neq j$.

In the case $d = 1$, we also use the notation $I_i = [c_i, c_{i+1}] = P_i$. Let $(a_i, b_i)_{1 \leq i \leq p}$ be the parameters such that $f_i(x) = a_i x + b_i$ for $x \in [c_i, c_{i+1}]$. $RPL_1 \subset PL_1$ is the set of functions such that the a_i's, b_i's and c_i's are all rational. Piecewise-analytic and piecewise-monotone functions are defined in the same obvious way. If the set of the I_i's is countably infinite rather than finite, we will speak of *countably piecewise*-linear (or analytic, monotone, etc.) functions. In this case, some of the I_i's may be reduced to a single point.

Given a function $f : I^d \rightarrow I^d$, a sequence $(x_i)_{0 \leq i \leq k-1}$ of distinct points is a period-k cycle if $f(x_i) = x_{i+1 \pmod{k}}$. A point is said to be of period k if it belongs to a period-k cycle.

We consider one-tape one-head Turing machines, with an alphabet A containing a "blank symbol" B, and a finite state set Q. The space of valid tape configurations is the subset $R \subset A^Z$ of configurations with a finite number of non-blank cells. A configuration of the machine is an element of $C = R \times Q \times Z$ (the third component stands for the position of the read-write head on the tape). $T : C \rightarrow C$ is the usual transition function of a Turing machine.

A one-dimensional cellular automata is also defined by a finite state set Q, and a local transition function $\delta : Q^3 \rightarrow Q$. Its configuration space is $C = Q^Z$, and its global transition function $T : C \rightarrow C$ is defined by:

$$(T(x))_i = \delta(x_{i-1}, x_i, x_{i+1}) .$$

C is endowed with the standard "Cantor" topology [7], which is the product topology of the discrete topology on Q. Intuitively, this means that a configuration $c' \in C$ is close to $c \in C$ if there is a large $r > 0$ such that $c'(i) = c(i)$ for $i \in [-r, r]$. T is continuous for this topology, and C is homeomorphic to the middle-third Cantor set of I.

This paper deals only with real time simulations, precisely defined as follows.

Definition 1. Let T be the transition function of a machine $\mathcal{M}$ (which may be a Turing machine, a cellular automaton, a pushdown automaton, ...). A function

$f : I^d \to I^d$ simulates $\mathcal{M}$ if there is an f-stable subset $D \subset I^d$ and a bijective function $\phi : C \to D$ such that

$$T = \phi^{-1} \circ f \circ \phi .$$

Intuitively, this means that in order to apply T, one can encode the configuration with ϕ, apply f, and then decode the result with ϕ^{-1}. For cellular automata, we shall make the additional assumption that ϕ is a homeomorphism (ϕ is a homeomorphism if and only if it is continuous, since C is compact). With this assumption, f simulates a cellular automaton if there is a conjugacy between $f_{|D}$ and T. Conjugacy is a natural tool for studying the dynamical properties of cellular automata and neural networks (see for example [1]).

A machine $\mathcal{M}_1$ is usually said to simulate another machine $\mathcal{M}_2$ in real time (resp. linear time, quadratic time,...) if a computation of $\mathcal{M}_2$ for t time units can be performed by $\mathcal{M}_1$ in time t (resp. $O(t)$, $O(t^2)$,...). Since the class of piecewise-linear (resp. piecewise-analytic, piecewise-monotone) functions is closed under composition, linear time simulation is equivalent to real time simulation.

3 Universality in Dimension 2

In this section, we show that two-dimensional piecewise-linear functions are universal. In the following, we prove that unlike Turing machines, cellular automata cannot be simulated by these functions.

Theorem 2. *An arbitrary one-tape Turing machine can be simulated in linear time by a function of PL_2.*

Proof. We simulate pushdown automata with two binary stacks on the alphabet $\{1,3\}$. It is well known that these automata can simulate one-tape Turing machines in linear time. The state of an automaton $\mathcal{M}$ and the content of its stacks are encoded in the radix-4 expansion of a point $(x_1, x_2) \in I^2$. The p_1 first digits of x_1 and p_2 first digits of x_2 can encode the state of $\mathcal{M}$ if it has less than $2^{p_1+p_2}$ states (one could take $p_2 = 0$ but this form is more symmetric). In the following, we assume that the set of states of $\mathcal{M}$ is $Q = \{1,3\}^{p_1} \times \{1,3\}^{p_2}$. A state $(q_{i,j})_{1 \le j \le p_i}$ and a stack $(s_{i,j})_{1 \le j \le n_i}$ ($i = 1,2$ and $s_{i,j} \in \{1,3\}$) are thus encoded in the real number

$$x_i = \sum_{j=1}^{p_i} \frac{q_{i,j}}{4^j} + \sum_{j=1}^{n_i} \frac{s_{i,j}}{4^{p+j}} .$$

Note that x_i belongs to a kind of "Cantor-like set" (already used in [10]), since the digits 0 and 2 are forbidden. In the following, $\overline{0.a_1 a_2 \cdots a_n}$ denotes a finite radix-4 expansion. Unless otherwise specified, $a_i \in \{1,3\}$.

The function f simulating $\mathcal{M}$ is affine on each of the $3|Q|$ products $I_{1,l_1} \times I_{2,l_2}$ with

$$I_{i,l_i} = [l_i, l_i + 1/4^{p_i+1}[\quad \text{and} \quad l_i = \overline{0.q_{i,1} \cdots q_{i,p_i} s_{i,1}}$$

or

$$I_{i,l_i} = \{l_i\} \quad \text{and} \quad l_i = \overline{0.q_{i,1} \cdots q_{i,p_i}} .$$

The stack is nonempty in the first case, and empty in the second one. For $x_i \in I_{i,l_i}$, we denote $\Delta x_i = x_i - l_i$. Let us assume that (x_1, x_2) encodes the state and stacks of $\mathcal{M}$ at time t. Let (q_1', q_2') be the next state of $\mathcal{M}$ (determined by the current state (q_1, q_2) and the top-of-stack letters $s_{i,1}$ and $s_{i,2}$). On $I_{1,l_1} \times I_{2,l_2}$, f is such that $f(x_1, x_2) = (x_1', x_2')$ with

$$x_i' = \overline{0.q_{i,1}' \cdots q_{i,p_i}'} + \Delta x_i'$$

and $\Delta x_i'$ defined as follows:

- $\Delta x_i' = 4\Delta x_i$ if stack i is popped;
- $\Delta x_i' = \frac{s_{i,1}}{4^{p_i+1}} + \Delta x_i$ if stack i is unchanged;
- $\Delta x_i' = \frac{a_i}{4^{p_i+1}} + \frac{s_{i,1}}{4^{p_i+2}} + \frac{\Delta x_i}{4}$ if a_i is pushed on stack i.

The two last operations can apply to empty stacks, with the convention $s_{i,1} = 0$. It is clear that (x_1', x_2') encodes the state and stacks of $\mathcal{M}$ at time $t+1$. f is piecewise-linear since the operations applied to the stacks are the same for all the points of a given product $I_{1,l_1} \times I_{2,l_2}$.

In order to complete the proof, we have to extend f outside

$$\mathcal{C} = \bigcup_{l_1,l_2} (I_{1,l_1} \times I_{2,l_2}) \ ,$$

to the whole of I^2. This extension cannot interfere with the simulation of $\mathcal{M}$, since only points of $\mathcal{C}$ are used in a computation. There are continuous piecewise-linear extensions of f, since the distance between two distinct products is greater than zero. As a matter of fact, the max distance is bounded below by $\max(1/4^{p_1+1}, 1/4^{p_2+1})$.

This proof can be easily modified to show that a Turing machine with d tapes can be simulated in linear time by $f \in PL_{2d}$ (and of course by $f \in PL_2$ in polynomial time).

The simulation above is naive in the sense that no attempt was made to follow precisely definition 1. This can be done with a few modifications, outlined below. The usual way of simulating a Turing machine T by a pushdown automaton is to encode the part of the tape on the left of the read-write head in the first stack, and the part on the right in the second stack. The problem with this encoding is that $\phi(c)$ is unchanged if the read-write head and the content of the tape of a configuration c are submitted to the same translation. This is unacceptable since ϕ is supposed to be injective. Let us consider Turing machines on the alphabet $\{1, 3\}$ with the blank symbol $B \equiv 1$. The idea is to use a marker differentiating cell 0 from the other cells. One might for example work with a two-tape machine, and leave the read-write head of the second tape on cell 0. We decided instead to encode a tape configuration τ_1 in a new configuration τ_2 in which $\tau_1(i)$ is coded by the 2 symbols $\tau_2(2i)\tau_2(2i+1)$. One may for instance encode 1 by 11, 3 by 33 if $i \neq 0$, and 1 by 13, 3 by 31 if $i = 0$. A machine configuration $c \in C$ with the read-write head on cell h is encoded in the point $\phi(c) = (x_1, x_2)$ with

$$x_i = q_i + y_i \tag{1}$$

$$q_i = \sum_{j=1}^{p_i} \frac{q_{i,j}}{4^j} \tag{2}$$

$$y_1 = \sum_{j=1}^{+\infty} \frac{\tau_2(2h-j)}{4^{j+p_1}} \tag{3}$$

$$y_2 = \sum_{j=1}^{+\infty} \frac{\tau_2(2h+j-1)}{4^{j+p_2}} \tag{4}$$

(the $q_{i,j}$'s and p_i's are defined in the proof of theorem 2). With this injective encoding, the simulation is very similar to the one of the theorem.

A simple radix-2 encoding could be used instead of the Cantor set encoding, but f would not be continuous. f would still be continuous with a unary encoding, but then the simulation would not be feasible in linear time.

A rather crude estimate of the complexity of the construction (i.e., the number S of polygons on which f is affine) is as follows. With q states and l letters ($l = 2$ up to now), the number of products $I_{1,l_1} \times I_{2,l_2}$ is $q(l+1)$. Encode the state in the first variable only (i.e., take $p_2 = 0$). The rectangular gap between two consecutive products can be divided in two triangles, and each triangle can be filled by an affine function. Hence we end up with $S = 3q(l+1)$. In the proof of Theorem 2, one may in fact use an arbitrary alphabet (for $l = 3$, take a radix-6 encoding using the digits 1, 3 and 5 only). One may also work with downward infinite tapes (such as those defined by equations (3) and (4)), in order to suppress the empty stack test. Hence the complexity is reduced to $S = 3ql$, and moreover a Turing machine can be simulated without increasing the number of states or symbols. Minsky constructed a universal Turing machine with seven states and four letters [4], which yields $S = 84$. In 1982, Rogozhin [8] obtained an even smaller machine, with four states and six letters. This gives $S = 72$.

Our construction can be extended so as to give another proof of the result of [10] on the computational universality of analog networks with saturated-linear outputs. The idea is to construct a neural net computing our universal function $f : I^2 \to I^2$. This can be done easily because we need to compute f on C only. If $\mathcal{R}$ is the set of products $I_{1,l_1} \times I_{2,l_2}$, the transition function of x_i is given by the formula

$$x_i' = \sigma \left[\sum_{\mathcal{P} \in \mathcal{R}} \sigma(a_{i,\mathcal{P}} x_i + b_{i,\mathcal{P}} + \theta_\mathcal{P}(x_1, x_2)) \right] ,$$

with $\sigma(x) = x$ if $x \in I$, $\sigma(x) = 0$ if $x \leq 0$, $\sigma(x) = 1$ if $x \geq 1$. On each $\mathcal{P}$, $x_i \mapsto a_{i,\mathcal{P}} x_i + b_{i,\mathcal{P}}$ is the affine function defined in the proof above. $\theta_\mathcal{P}(x_1, x_2) = 0$ if $(x_1, x_2) \in \mathcal{P}$; if (x_1, x_2) belongs to another product $\mathcal{P}'$, $\theta_\mathcal{P}(x_1, x_2)$ is equal to a "large" negative value, in order to ensure $\sigma(a_{i,\mathcal{P}} x + b_{i,\mathcal{P}} + \theta_\mathcal{P}(x_1, x_2)) = 0$. This can be done by a net using σ as a "hardlimiter" (i.e., an input fed to σ should always be smaller than 0 or larger than 1), since the distance between two products in $\mathcal{R}$ is greater than zero.

As mentioned in the introduction, the universal neural network construction of [10] can be viewed as a universality result for piecewise-linear functions in dimension d with $d = 1058$. This section shows how to reduce d from 1058 to 2. It may be interesting to notice that d can be reduced from 1058 to 92 with little effort as follows. The universal network of [10] is composed of 4 layers, each layer feeding into the next one and the last back into the first. Since the configuration of the machine simulated by the net is encoded in the first layer of 92 neurons, a universal function with $d = 92$ can be obtained by composing the functions computed by the four layers.

Let us show now that cellular automata cannot be simulated by two-dimensional piecewise-linear functions (it is conjectured that the same is true in any dimension). In order to do this, we need further assume that the encoding function is continuous. This difference between cellular automata and Turing machines is not a mere artifact due to this additional requirement: as shown at the end of this section, the encoding defined by equations (1)–(4) is actually a homeomorphism.

A few notations: configurations are identified with bi-infinite words on the alphabet Q; uv denotes the concatenation of the (finite or infinite) words u and v whenever it is possible; $0^{-\infty}$ is the word $(u_i)_{i \leq 0}$ such that $\forall i, u_i = 0$; $Q^{+\infty}$ is the set of right-infinite words $(u_i)_{i>0}$.

Theorem 3. *There exist cellular automata that cannot be simulated by a function of PL_2 with a continuous encoding.*

Proof. Let $\mathcal{A}$ be a cellular automaton with two distinguished "stable" states, 0 and 1, such that $\forall (q_l, q) \in \{0, 1\}^2, \forall q_r \in Q, \delta(q_l, q, q_r) = q$. The other states are said to be "non-stable". Let $f \in PL_2$ be a function capable of simulating $\mathcal{A}$.

Assume first that

$$\exists i, k \in N, \phi(0^{-\infty}1^k 0^\infty) \in \overset{\circ}{P_i} . \tag{5}$$

Since ϕ is continuous, $\exists l \in N, \forall x \in Q^{+\infty}, \phi(0^{-\infty}1^k 0^l x) \in P_i$. In the remainder of the proof, we always denote: $a = 0^{-\infty}1^k 0^l$. Since $f_i \circ \phi(ax) = \phi \circ T(ax)$ and $T(ax) \in aQ^{+\infty}$ (by definition of the stable states), $\phi(aQ^{+\infty})$ is stable by f_i. Hence

$$\forall n \geq 0, \forall x \in Q^{+\infty}, T^n(ax) = \phi^{-1} \circ f_i^n \circ \phi(ax).$$

The sequence $(f_i^n(\phi(ax)))_n$ has a finite number of accumulation points because f_i is affine. ϕ^{-1} is continuous, therefore $(T^n(ax))_n$ also has a finite number of accumulation points.

Assume now that (5) does not hold. Since ϕ is injective, there must be an edge E with at least 3 distinct configurations of the form $0^{-\infty}1^p 0^{+\infty}$ mapped to E by ϕ. At least one of these configurations (say, $0^{-\infty}1^k 0^{+\infty}$) is not mapped to an endpoint of E. If E is the edge of a single polygon P_i (i.e., if E lies on one of the sides of I^2), $\phi(aQ^{+\infty}) \subset P_i$ for l large enough. It follows from the same argument as in the first case that any sequence of iterates $(T^n(ax))_n$ has a finite number of accumulation points. Let us finally consider the case $E = P_i \cap P_j$ with $i \neq j$. By continuity, $\exists l, \phi(aQ^{+\infty}) \in P_i \cup P_j$, and $\phi(aQ^{+\infty})$ is stable by f. E is invariant by f_i and f_j since there are more than 2 fixed points on E. Let H_i (resp. H_j) be the half-plane delimited by E containing P_i (resp. P_j). Consider for instance a configuration $ax \in \phi^{-1}(P_i)$. Several cases can be distinguished.

1. $f_i(H_i) \subset H_i$. In this case, $T^n(ax) = \phi^{-1} \circ f_i^n \circ \phi(ax)$.
2. $f_i(H_i) = H_j$. In this case, 2 subcases can be distinguished.

(a) $f_j(H_j) \subset H_j$, and $T^{n+1}(ax) = \phi^{-1} \circ f_j^n \circ f_i \circ \phi(ax)$.

(b) $f_j(H_j) = H_i$, and $T^{2n}(ax) = \phi^{-1} \circ (f_j \circ f_i)^n \circ \phi(ax)$.

$f_j \circ f_i$ is also affine, therefore in all cases $T^n(ax)$ has a finite number of accumulation points. Let $\mathcal{A}$ be a cellular automaton such that there exists $x_0 \in Q^{+\infty}$ such that $\forall k, l, T^n(0^{-\infty} 1^k 0^l x_0)$ has an infinite number of accumulation points (for instance, the left shift on the non-stable states: $\delta(q_l, q, q_r) = q_r$ if $q \notin \{0, 1\}$). $\mathcal{A}$ cannot be simulated by a function of PL_2.

The "next configuration" of a cellular automaton with N consecutive active cells can be computed in time $O(N)$ by a Turing machine. Hence it follows from Theorem 2 that a cellular automaton with a finite initial configuration can be simulated in quadratic time by a function of PL_2 (a configuration is finite if only a finite number of cells are in a non-stable state). Definition 1 is maybe more relevant for cellular automata working on infinite configurations. Such automata may be viewed as models of massively parallel machines, and are strictly more powerful than Turing machines (since they can deal with infinite inputs such as binary expansions of real numbers [3]). For automata working on finite configurations, theorem 3 should be regarded more as a complexity result than a computability result: cellular automata cannot be simulated in linear time by piecewise-linear functions. It is not surprising that cellular automata simulation is slower than Turing machine simulation, since the former model is intrinsically parallel. Note that Theorem 3 actually applies if finite configurations only are considered.

Let us now show that equations (1)–(4) define an homeomorphism. In order to have a topology to work with, a Turing machine $\mathcal{T}$ is viewed as a cellular automaton with a new state set

$$Q' = \{1, 3\} \cup (\{1, 3\} \times Q).$$

The configuration space of $\mathcal{T}$ is a proper subset $C' \subset C$: at any given time, there must be exactly one cell in a state of the form (a, q). $c(i) = (a, q)$ if and only if the read-write head of $\mathcal{T}$ is on cell i, and $\mathcal{T}$ is in state q. Otherwise, $c(i) \in \{1, 3\}$. Let $c, c' \in C'$ be two configurations such that $c(h) = (a, q)$ and $c'(i) = c(i)$ if $i \in [-|h| - r, |h| + r]$, for some $r \geq 0$. Set $\phi(c') = (x'_1, x'_2)$. It holds that $|x'_1 - x_1| \leq \frac{1}{4^{p_1 + 2r}}$ and $|x'_2 - x_2| \leq \frac{1}{4^{p_2 + 2r + 2}}$. ϕ is thus continuous in c since $\|\phi(c') - \phi(c)\|$ can be made as small as desired by taking r large enough. Conversely, for a given (x_1, x_2), set $c = \phi^{-1}(x_1, x_2)$ and $c(h) = (a, q)$. If $|x'_1 - x_1| \leq \frac{1}{4^{p_1 + 2r}}$ and $|x'_2 - x_2| \leq \frac{1}{4^{p_2 + 2r + 2}}$, then $c'(i) = c(i)$ for $i \in [h - r, h + r]$. Hence ϕ^{-1} is also continuous.

4 One-dimensional Universality

The main result of this section is that Turing machines cannot be simulated by one-dimensional piecewise-linear functions with the model of Definition 1 (one-stack pushdown automata can be simulated by these functions using a straightforward adaptation of Theorem 2). However, it is shown that more complicated functions are universal. Cellular automata are again compared to Turing machines. The complete proofs of these results are omitted.

Theorem 4. *1) There exist Turing machines that cannot be simulated by a function of PL_1 .*

2) An arbitrary Turing machine can be simulated in linear time by a countably piecewise-linear function.

3) An arbitrary cellular automaton cannot be simulated with a continuous encoding by a countably piecewise-monotone function.

4) An arbitrary Turing machine can be simulated in linear time by a continuous piecewise-monotone function.

Proof sketch of theorem 4. 1) Let T be a Turing machine having infinitely many period-k cycles for infinitely many values of k. Assume that T can be simulated by $f : I \to I$. It follows immediately from definition 1 that distinct period-k cycles of T are mapped by ϕ to distinct period-k cycles of f. Hence f cannot be piecewise-linear since it can be shown that such functions cannot have infinitely many period-k cycles for infinitely many values of k.

T can be easily constructed as follows. Starting on a blank cell, the read-write head goes to the right until it arrives on another blank symbol. It then goes back to the left, to the first blank symbol, then again on the right, and so on. If there are $k - 1$ cells between the two blanks, T has a period-k cycle. It actually has infinitely many period-k cycles (provided that $|A| \geq 2$), since all cells can be assigned arbitrary symbols, except those located between the two blanks.

2) Let T be a Turing machine, and q, h, r and s integer encodings of its state, the position of its read-write head, the parts of the tape on the left and on the right of its head, respectively. A configuration of T is encoded in the rational number $x_{q,h,r,s} = 1/(2^q 3^h 5^r 7^s)$. Since all these numbers are distinct, they form a decreasing sequence $(y_i)_{i \in N}$. Let f be a function affine on $[y_0, 1]$, on each interval $[y_{i+1}, y_i]$, and mapping each y_i to the encoding of the "next configuration". f is piecewise-linear continuous on $]0, 1]$, and simulates T by definition. f can be extended continuously in 0 by setting $f(0) = 0$, since a configuration with a "large" value of h, r or s has a successor with a large value of h, r or s.

3) Let f be a piecewise-monotone function simulating a cellular automaton with two stable states 0 and 1, like in the proof of theorem 3. The set of configurations for which all cells are in a stable state is not countable, therefore one of these configu-rations is mapped by ϕ to the interior $\overset{\circ}{J}$ of an interval J on which f is monotone. A half-line of automata can thus be simulated by iterating the monotone function f_J (same argument as for theorem 3). This is not possible for all cellular automata, because a sequence of iterates of f_J has at most one accumulation point.

4) We simulate a Turing machine T on an alphabet A endowed with an arbitrary total order having B as smallest element, and assume without loss of generality that T never writes a blank character. All the configurations in which T is in a given state q and its read-write head reads a given letter l are encoded in a point of the same interval $I_{q,l} = [a_{q,l}, b_{q,l}]$. All these intervals are disjoint, and $I_{q,l} < I_{q,l'}$ (i.e., $b_{q,l} < a_{q,l'}$) if $l < l'$. It can be shown that T can be simulated by a function f increasing on each $I_{q,l}$. A piecewise-monotone extension of f on I can then be obtained by just "filling the gaps" between the $I_{q,l}$'s.

5 Discussion

The only positive result for cellular automata is that they can be simulated by continuous function on I as follows. It was remarked in Section 2 that the space of configurations C is homeomorphic to the standard Cantor set K. A cellular automaton can therefore be simulated by a continuous function on K. Since K is compact, this function can be continuously extended on I, whence the result.

In the future, we hope to prove (or maybe disprove) negative results for more general models of universality. A first step in this direction was made in this paper. Instead of attacking this problem directly, it might be useful to first tackle the following related problem, which is more precisely defined, and maybe simpler:

Problem 5. Is it decidable to find, given $f \in RPL_1$ and $x \in Q$, whether there exists $t \in N$ such that $f^t(x) = f^{t+1}(x)$?

If this problem is undecidable, one could likely obtain a universality result for RPL_1, since most undecidability results are based on simulations of Turing machines (or other universal devices). Conversely, if this problem is decidable, RPL_1 is not likely to be universal, since in this case there would be an algorithm solving the halting problem for Turing machines (this latter heuristic argument is meaningful only if the end of the "computation" of f is defined by stabilization on a fixed point). Proving that a function is not universal with very general definitions of encodings and simulations is likely to be quite difficult (this problem is already difficult for discrete machines).

References

1. F. Bothelho and M. Garzon. On dynamical properties of neural networks. *Complex Systems*, 5(4):401–403, 1991.
2. P. Collet and J.P. Eckmann. *Iterated maps on the interval as dynamical systems*, volume I of *Progress in Physics*. Birkhäuser, Boston, 1980.
3. M. Garzon and S.P. Franklin. Neural computability II. In *Proc. 3rd Int. Joint Conf. on Neural Networks, Wash. D.C.*, volume 1, pages 631–637, 1989.
4. M. L. Minsky. *Computation: Finite and Infinite Machines*. Prentice Hall, Engelwood Cliffs, 1967.
5. C. Moore. Generalized shifts: unpredictability and undecidability in dynamical systems. *Nonlinearity*, 4:199–230, 1991.
6. C. Preston. *Iterates of piecewise monotone mappings on an interval*, volume 1347 of *Lecture Notes in Mathematics*. Springer-Verlag, 1988.
7. D. Richardson. Tessellation with local transformations. *Journal of Computer and System Sciences*, 6:373–388, 1972.
8. Y. V. Rogozhin. Seven universal Turing machines. *Mat. Issled.*, 69:76–90, 1982. (Russian).
9. H. T. Siegelman and E. D. Sontag. Neural nets are universal computing devices. SYCON Report 91-08, Rutgers University, May 1991.
10. H. T. Siegelman and E. D. Sontag. On the computational power of neural nets. In *Proc. Fifth ACM Workshop on Computational Learning Theory*, July 1992.

Fixed-Parameter Intractability II
(Extended Abstract)

Karl A. Abrahamson[1], Rodney G. Downey[2] *, Michael R. Fellows[3] **

[1] Washington State University, Department of E.E. & C.S., Pullman, Washington
99164-1210, U.S.A. (karl@eecs.wsu.edu)
[2] Victoria University of Wellington, Department of Mathematics, P.O. Box 600,
Wellington, New Zealand (downey@math.vuw.ac.nz)
[3] University of Victoria, Department of Computer Science, Victoria, British
Columbia V8W 3P6, Canada (mfellows@csr.uvic.ca)

Abstract. We describe new results in parameterized complexity theory,
including an analogue of Ladner's theorem, and natural problems concerning k-move games which are complete for parameterized problem
classes that are analogues of P-space.

1 Introduction

The theory of NP-completeness provides an excellent vehicle for explaining
the apparent asymptotic intractability of many algorithmic problems. Yet while
many natural problems do behave intractably *in the limit*, the manner *by which*
they arrive at this intractable behavior can vary considerably. The standard
NP and other completeness models are often far too coarse to give insight into
this variation. To be specific, many natural computational problems take input
consisting of two or more parts.

Example 1. The Vertex Cover problem takes as input a pair (G, k) consisting of
a graph G and integer k, and determines whether there is a set of k vertices in
G such that every edge in G has at least one endpoint in this set.

Example 2. The Graph Genus problem takes as input a pair (G, k) as above, and
determines whether the graph G embeds on the surface of genus k.

Example 3. The Planar Improvement problem takes as input a pair (G, k) and
determines if G is a subgraph of a planar graph G' of diameter at most k.

Example 4. The Graph Linking Number problem takes as input a pair (G, k) as
above, and determines whether G can be embedded in 3-space so that at most
k disjoint cycles in G are topologically linked.

---

* Research supported by Victoria University IGC, by the United States / New Zealand
Cooperative Science Foundation under grant INT 90-20558, by the University of
Victoria, and by the Mathematical Sciences Institute at Cornell University.
** Research supported by the National Science and Engineering Research Council of
Canada, and the U.S. National Science Foundation under grant MIP-8919312.

Example 5. The Dominating Set problem takes as input a pair (G, k) as above, and determines whether there is a set of k vertices in G having the property that every vertex of G either belongs to the set, or has a neighbor in the set.

With the exception of examples 3 and 4 for which this question is open, the above problems are known to be NP-complete. But what can be said when the parameter k is held fixed? For examples 1-4, there is a constant α such that for every fixed k the problem can be solved in time $O(n^\alpha)$. For examples 2 and 4 we may take $\alpha = 3$ by the deep results of Robertson and Seymour [17] [18]. Example 5 illustrates the contrasting situation where for fixed values of k we seem to be able to do no better than a brute force examination of all possible solutions. We are thus concerned with an issue that is very much akin to P *versus* NP. The previous papers of this series [7] [8] [9] [10], established a framework with which to address the apparent fixed-parameter intractability of problems such as example 5. We feel that our framework provides an important contribution to the analysis of complexity of combinatorial problems for the following reasons.

(i) Distinct from most other notions and classes introduced since the original clarification of NP and $PSPACE$ completeness, our framework is applicable to a *wide* class of *practical* problems.

(ii) Our framework provides a refined measure to that helps to explain the apparent diversity of *actual* behavior of many hard problems, as well as having numerous other applications.

2   Preliminaries

A *parameterized problem* is a set $L \subseteq \Sigma^* \times \Sigma^*$. Typically, the second component represents a parameter $k \in N$ in unary. For $k \in \Sigma^*$ we write $L_k = \{y | (y, k) \in L\}$. Consideration of examples 1-4 of §1 leads to three flavours of tractability and reduction.

Definition 1. We say that a parameterized problem L is
(1) *nonuniformly fixed-parameter tractable* if there is a constant α and a sequence of algorithms Φ_x such that, for each $x \in N$, Φ_x computes L_x in time $O(n^\alpha)$;
(2) *uniformly fixed-parameter tractable* if there is a constant α and an algorithm Φ such that Φ decides if $(x, k) \in L$ in time $f(k)|x|^\alpha$ where $f : N \to N$ is an arbitrary function;
(3) *strongly uniformly fixed-parameter tractable* if L is uniformly fixed-parameter tractable with the function f recursive.

Example 1 is strongly uniformly f.p. tractable (as are most examples of f. p. tractability obtained without essential use of the Graph Minor Theorem). Example 2 can be shown to be strongly uniformly f.p. tractable by the methods of [14] (the GMT alone gives only give nonuniform tractability). Example 3 can be shown to be uniformly f.p. tractable by the method of [13] (since the technique of [14] is not presently known to apply, we do not know a strongly uniform algorithm). Example 4 is at present only known to be nonuniformly f.p. tractable. If $P = NP$ then example 5 is also f.p. tractable.

Definition 2. Let A, B be parameterized problems. We say that A is *uniformly P-reducible* to B if there is an oracle algorithm Φ, a constant α, and an arbitrary function $f : N \to N$ such that
(a) the running time of $\Phi(B; \langle x, k \rangle)$ is at most $f(k)|x|^{\alpha}$,
(b) on input $\langle x, k \rangle$, Φ only asks oracle questions of $B^{(f(k))}$ where

$$B^{(f(k))} = \bigcup_{j \leq f(k)} B_j = \{\langle x, j \rangle : \langle x, j \rangle \in B\}$$

(c) $\Phi(B) = A$.

If A is uniformly P-reducible to B, write $A \leq_T^u B$. We may say that $A \leq_T^u B$ *via* f. If the reduction is many:1 (an *m-reduction*), write $A \leq_m^u B$.

Definition 3. We say that A is *strongly uniformly P-reducible* to B if $A \leq_T^u B$ via f where f is recursive. We write $A \leq_T^s B$ in this case.

Definition 4. We say that A is *nonuniformly P-reducible* to B if $\exists$ a constant α, a function $f : N \to N$, and a collection of procedures $\{\Phi_k : k \in N\}$ such that $\Phi_k(B^{(f(k))}) = A_k$ for $k \in N$, and the running time of Φ_k is $f(k)|x|^{\alpha}$. Here we write $A \leq_T^n B$.

Note that the above are good definitions since whenever $A < B$ with $<$ any of the reducibilities, if B is f.p. tractable so too is A. We will write $FPT(\leq)$ for the f.p. tractable class corresponding to the reducibility $\leq$.

Theorem 5. *[11] The ordering $\leq_T^s$ partitions $FPT(\leq_T^u)$ into infinitely many classes. Similarly $\leq_T^u$ partitions $FPT(\leq_T^n)$ into infinitely many classes.*

Fix attention on any of the above reducibilities, and call it *fp-reducibility*. We consider circuits (termed *mixed type*) in which some gates have bounded fan-in (*small gates*) and some have unrestricted fan-in (*large gates*).

Definition 6. The *depth* $d(C)$ of a circuit C is the maximum number of gates (small or large), on an input-output path in C. The *weft* $w(C)$ of a circuit C is the maximum number of large gates on an input-output path in C.

Definition 7. We say that a family of circuits F has *bounded depth* if $\exists$ a constant h such that $\forall C \in F$, $d(C) \leq h$. We say that F has *bounded weft* if $\exists$ a constant t such that $\forall C \in F$, $w(C) \leq t$. F is a *decision circuit family* if each circuit has a single output. A decision circuit C *accepts* an input vector x if the single output gate has value 1 on input x. The *weight* of a boolean vector x is the number of 1's in the vector.

Definition 8. Let F be a family of decision circuits. We allow that F may have many different circuits with a given number of inputs. To F we associate the parameterized circuit problem $L_F = \{(C, k) : C \in F \text{ and } C \text{ accepts an input vector of weight } k\}$. A parameterized problem L belongs to $W[t]$ if L reduces to the parameterized decision circuit problem $L_{F(t,h)}$ for the family $F(t,h)$ of mixed type decision circuits of weft at most t, and depth at most h, for some constant h. A parameterized problem L belongs to $W[P]$ if L reduces to the circuit problem L_F where F is the set of all circuits (no restrictions).

The above leads to an interesting hierarchy of parameterized problem classes

$$FPT \subseteq W[1] \subseteq W[2] \subseteq \ldots \subseteq W[P]$$

If $P = NP$ then the hierarchy collapses. We conjecture that each of the containments is proper. Many natural problems are complete for various levels. For example, Independent Set is complete for $W[1]$ and Dominating Set is complete for $W[2]$. Determining whether there are k vertices in a graph covering all subgraphs of minimum degree 3 is complete for $W[P]$. For a catalogue of problem classifications see [8], [10].

3   Fixed Parameter Analogs of PSPACE

Several game problems are known to be PSPACE-complete. Typically, such problems ask whether the first player to move has a winning strategy. A natural parameterized version of the problem is whether the first player has a strategy that wins within at most k moves.

Some hard parameterized game problems are f. p. tractable. An example is the Alternating Hitting Set game [15] [19] restricted to sets of size 2, which is PSPACE-complete. Some game problems appear not to be f. p. tractable. Generalized Geography is a game played on a directed graph G with a distinguished start vertex [15], [19]. Players alternate choosing vertices, starting at the start vertex, in such a way that the chosen vertices form, in sequence, a simple directed path in G. The first player who is unable to choose a vertex loses. Determining whether player 1 has a winning strategy in a Generalized Geography game is PSPACE-complete. A good candidate for a game problem that is not f. p. tractable is *Short Geography*, in which it is asked whether player 1 has a strategy that wins a given game of Generalized Geography in at most k moves.

In order to address such questions we introduce the class AW and $AW[*]$, which plausibly contain problems that are not in FPT. We show that Short Geography is $AW[*]$-complete.

Like W, AW is the closure under fp-reductions of a kernel problem of such a general nature that it appears not to be fixed parameter tractable. This problem is a parameterized version of Quantified Boolean Formulas, defined as follows.

Definition 9. *PQBF* is the parameterized problem specified
Instance: A sequence $s_1, \ldots, s_r$ of pairwise disjoint sets of boolean variables, and a boolean formula p involving the variables in $s_1 \cup \cdots \cup s_r$.
Parameters: $r, k_1, \ldots, k_r$.
Question: Is it the case that there exists a size k_1 subset t_1 of s_1 such that for every size k_2 subset t_2 of s_2 there exists a size k_3 subset t_3 of s_3 such that

...(alternating quantifiers) such that, when the variables in $t_1 \cup \cdots \cup t_r$ are made true, and all other variables are made false, formula p is true?

Definition 10. AW is the set of all problems that fp-reduce to $PQBF$.

AW appears to be too large a class for our purposes. Instead, we concentrate on the class $AW[*]$.

Definition 11. $PQBF_t$ is the restriction of $PQBF$ in which the formula part must consist of t alternating layers of conjunctions and disjunctions, with negations applied only to variables, and the main operator a conjunction. For example, if $t = 2$ then the formula must be in conjunctive normal form. $AW[t]$ is the set of all parameterized problems that fp-reduce to $PQBF_t$, and $AW[*] = \bigcup_t AW[t]$.

Definition 12. A parameterized problem X is $AW[t]$-*complete* iff X is in $AW[t]$ and every problem in $AW[t]$ fp-reduces to X. X is $AW[*]$-*complete* iff X is in $AW[*]$ and every problem in $AW[*]$ fp-reduces to X.

Short Geography can be shown to be in $AW[3]$. This section sketches of a proof that $PQBF_t$ fp-reduces to Short Geography for every t. The reduction is actually from a restricted form of $PQBF_t$.

Definition 13. *Unitary* $PQBF_t$ is the restriction of $PQBF_t$ in which the parameters $k_1, \ldots, k_r$ are all 1.

The proof of the following lemma can be found in [1].

Lemma 14. *For $t > 0$, Unitary $PQBF_{2t}$ is $AW[2t]$-complete.*

Theorem 15. *Short Geography is $AW[*]$-complete. Hence, $AW[*] = AW[3]$.*

Proof sketch. We reduce $PQBF_{2t}$ to Short Geography for an arbitrary $t > 0$. Let $I = (r, k_1, \ldots, k_r, s_1, \ldots, s_r, p)$ be an instance of $PQBF_{2t}$, and assume that r is odd. The reduction is a modification of Schaefer's polynomial time reduction from QBF to Generalized Geography [19]. The graph on which the geography game is played has three parts: the choice component, the formula testing component and the literal testing component.

The choice component is similar to Shaefer's, and is designed so that player 1 chooses a member of s_1, then player 2 chooses a member of s_2, then player 1 chooses a member of s_3, etc. A total of $3r$ moves are made through this component, and it is player 2's move at the end, where the game enters the formula testing component.

The formula testing component is also similar to Shaefer's, but has $2t$ levels. It uses player 1's moves to simulate disjunctions, and player 2's moves to simulate conjunctions. A total of $2t$ moves are made through this component. Play ends at a *literal vertex* v, corresponding to a literal in formula p, with the move being player 2's.

A literal vertex v corresponding to a positive literal x has an edge to the vertex v_x in the choice component that corresponds to x. If v_x was chosen (variable x is true), then player 2 has no move, and player 1 wins. If v_x was not chosen (so x is false), then player 2 moves to v_x and wins.

If literal vertex v corresponds to a negative literal $\bar{x}$, then the literal testing component has edges (v, u_x) and (u_x, v_x), where u_x is a new vertex and v_x is the vertex corresponding to x in the choice component. Vertex u_x switches the initiative, and causes player 1 to win if v_x was not chosen, and player 2 to win if v_x was chosen.

In summary, player 1 wins if and only if I is a *yes* instance of $PQBF_t$. The total number of moves is at most $3r + 2t + 2$. Since t is fixed, the conditions of an fp-reduction are met. $\qquad\qquad\Box$

4 Density and other Structural Results

We begin with an analogue of Ladner's density theorem. At present we can prove this only for strong uniform reducibility.

Theorem 16. *If A and B are recursive sets with $A < B$ and $<$ either of $<_T^s$ or $<_m^s$ then there is a recursive set C such that $A < A \oplus C < B$.*

Proof sketch. We begin by recalling the proof of Ladner's [16] density theorem for the polynomial time degrees. Recall that this works as follows. We are given recursive sets $A \not< B$ (working with $\leq_T^p$, say). Let $\{z_n : n \in N\}$ be a standard P-time length/lexicographic ordering of Σ^*. We can assume that A and B are given as the range of P-time functions with domain N in unary notation. We write $A_s = \{f(1^0), ..., f(1^s)\}$ if $f(N) = A$ in this sense. We can also ask that if $|f(1^y)| > |f(1^{y-1})|$ then for all $z > y$, $|f(z)| \geq |f(1^y)|$. We call this a *P-standard enumeration*. So we will assume that we have such enumerations of A and B. Recall also for a reduction Δ on a set E, $u(\Delta(E; x))$ denotes the length of the longest element used in the computation. Let $\{\Phi'_e : e \in N\}$ denote a standard enumeration of all P-time T-procedures.

We must build C to satisfy $C \leq_m^p B$ and the requirements:

$$R'_{2e} \ : \ \Phi'_e(A \oplus C) \neq B$$

$$R'_{2e+1} \ : \ \Phi'_e(A) \neq C$$

For the sake of the R'_j we define a polynomial time relation $R(n)$ on $N = \{1\}^*$. Then we declare that $x \in C$ iff $R(|x|) = 0$ and $x \in B$. Clearly this makes $C \leq_m^p B$.

Now we meet the R'_j *in order* by 'delayed' diagonalization. So we begin with R'_0. At each stage s, set $R(s) = 1$ until a stage t is found where (i) - (iv) below hold. (Here we consider s, t etc as being in N.)

(i) $\Phi'_{0,t}(A_t \oplus \emptyset; z_n) \downarrow$ in less than t steps.
(ii) $A_t[q] = A[q]$ if $|q| < u(\Phi'_0(A_t \oplus \emptyset; z_n))$.

(iii) $B_t[z_n] = B[z_n]$.

(iv) $\Phi'_{0,t}(A_t \oplus \emptyset; z_n)(= \Phi'_0(A \oplus \emptyset; z_n)) \neq B(z_n) = B_t(z_n)$.

At stage t we say that we have diagonalized R'_0 at z_n, this being found by *looking back for an A- and a B- certified disagreement*. The idea is then to move to R'_1 and then to R'_2 etc. For R'_1 we set $R(t+1) = 0$, causing C to look like B locally. So we keep $R(u)$ for $u > t$ equal to zero until a stage v is found with some $m \leq v$ and $\Phi'_{0,v}(A_v; z_m) \neq C_v(z_m)$, via A- and B- certified computations. We then move to R'_2 setting $R(v+1)$ to be 1 again. Thus the set C so constructed looks like B with 'holes' in it.

The above forms a sort of inner strategy for the full construction. The next step in the journey is to consider the strategy used by the first two authors to prove the density theorem for the strong uniform reducibility $\leq^s_T$ (and $\leq^s_m$) in [11]. Now imagine we are given $A < B$ with $\leq$ either $\leq^s_T$ or $\leq^s_m$. Again we must construct C, now to meet the following requirements:

$R_{2(e,n)}$: Either ϕ_e is not total,
    or $(\exists k)(B_k \neq \Phi_e(A \oplus C^{(\phi_e(k))}))$
    or $(\exists x, k)(\Phi_e(A \oplus C^{(\phi_e(k))}; \langle x, k \rangle))$
    does not run in time $\phi_e(k)|x|^n$.

$R_{2(e,n+1)}$: Either ϕ_e is not total,
    or $(\exists k)(C_k \neq \Phi_e(A^{(\phi_e(k))}))$
    or $(\exists x, k)(\Phi_e(A^{(\phi_e(k))}; \langle x, k \rangle))$
    does not run in time $\phi_e(k)|x|^n$).

To aid the discussion we will use several conventions. First, if $\phi_{e,s}(k) \downarrow$, then the computation $\Phi_e(E^{(\phi_e(k))}; \langle x, k \rangle)$ cannot call any y of the form (k', z) for $k' > \phi_e(k)$. Also since we get a win for free if $\phi_{e,s}(k) \downarrow$ and the running time of $\Phi_e(E^{(\phi_e(k))}; \langle x, k \rangle)$ exceeds $\phi_e(k)|x|^n$, we shall assume that in the above the third option does not pertain to R_j and concentrate on the first two. This is because if the running time exceeds the bounds during the construction, we can *cancel* the relevant requirement. The argument to follow is a priority one with the Ladner strategy embedded.

Without loss of generality we can take ϕ_e to be strictly increasing. Again there will be long intervals with $C(\langle x, k \rangle)$ equal to $\emptyset$ and long intervals where it looks like B, for 'many' k. We have problems, since, for instance, we cannot decide if ϕ_e is total. We first focus on the satisfaction of a single $R_0 = R_{2(e,n)}$. We then describe the basic module for an odd type requirement, and finally describe the coherence mechanism whereby we combine strategies.

The Basic R_0-Module.

To meet R_0 above, we perform the following cycle. We have a parameter $k(0, s)$ that is nondecreasing in s and such that $\lim_s k(0, s) = k(0)$ exists. This is meant to be the number of "rows" devoted to R_0. It remains constant until we change it.

1. (Initialization.) Pick $k(0, 0) = 1$.

2. Wait until a stage s occurs with one of the following holding:

2(a). (Win.) "Looking back" we see a disagreement. That is, as with the Ladner argument, we see an $n < s$ with $z_n \in \{\langle x, j \rangle : j < k(0, s)\}$.

$$\Phi_{e,s}(A \oplus C^{(\phi_e(k(0,s)-1))}; z_n) \neq B(z_n)$$

via A- and B-certified computations, or

2(b). Not (2a) and $\phi_{e,s}(k(0,s)) \downarrow$.

Comment If s does not occur then $\phi_e(k(0,s)) \uparrow$ and hence ϕ_e is not total. In this case we call $k(0,s)$ a *witness to the nontotality* of ϕ_e.

If 2(a) pertains, we declare R_0 to be *satisfied* (forever) and end its effect (forever). If 2(b) pertains, then we perform the following action.

3. R_0 *asserts control of* $C^{(\phi_e(k(0,s)))}$. That is, R_0 asks that for all $t \geq s$, until 2(b) pertains, we promise to set $C^{(\phi_e(k(0,s)))}(y) = 0$ for all y with $|y| = t$ and $y \in (\Sigma^*)^{(\phi_e(k(0,s)))}$. This can be achieved *via* a restraint $r(n,k)$.

4. Reset $k(0, s+1) = k(0,s) + 1$ and go to 2.

The Outcomes of the Basic R_0 Module.

We claim that 2(b) cannot occur infinitely often and hence $\lim_s k(0,s) = k(0)$ exists. Note that we have only reset $k(0,s)$ if 2(b) pertains in step 3. So suppose $k(0,s) \to \infty$ and hence $\phi_e(k(0,s)) \to \infty$. Then for each q and almost all y, we have $C(\langle q, y \rangle) = 0$. We write $A =^* B$ to denote that the symmetric difference of A and B is finite. So $C_q =^* \emptyset$ for all q. Furthermore, for all q, we can compute a stage $h(q)$ where

$$[\forall t > h(q)](C_q(\langle y, q \rangle) = 0 \quad \text{for all } y \text{ with } |y| > h(q))$$

where $h(q)$ is the stage where R_0 asserts control of row q. Finally, we know that for all k,

$$\Phi_e((A \oplus C)^{(\phi_e(k))}) = B_k$$

This allows us to get a reduction $\Delta(A) = B$. For each input $\langle y, k \rangle$, Δ simply computes $B(\langle y, k \rangle)$ for all y with $|y| \leq h(k)$, and $C(\langle z, k' \rangle)$ for all k', z with $k' \leq \phi_e(k)$ and $|z| \leq h(k)$. Then Δ simulates $\Phi_e(A^{(\phi_e(k))}; \langle y, k \rangle)$ if $|y| > h(k)$ with the exception that, if Φ_e calls some $\langle r, k' \rangle$ with $|r| \leq h(k)$ (and necessarily $k' \leq \phi_e(k)$), then Δ uses the table of values for C to provide the answer.

Note that the computations of $\Delta(A; \langle x, k \rangle)$ and $\Phi_e(C; \langle x, k \rangle)$ must agree and hence $\Delta(A) = B$, a contradiction. Thus 2(b) can pertain only finitely often. It follows that there are two outcomes.

Outcome $(0, f)$: 2(a) occurs for some t. Then we win R_0 with finite effect. (*Comment:* Once R_0 is met in this way, say at stage t, then we are completely free to do what we like with all y for which $|y| > t$ without injuring R_0.)

Outcome $(0, \infty)$: 2(a) does not occur. Then ϕ_e is not total. Note that the effect of R_0 is in this case infinite and for some $k = \lim_s k(0,s) - 1$, we will have

$$C^{(\phi_e(k))} =^* \emptyset$$

and furthermore, there is a reduction Δ_0 with time bound $\phi_e(k)|x|^n$ for which

$$\Delta_0(A^{(\phi_e(k))}) = B^{(k)}$$

Note that for the basic module, Δ_0 is simply Φ_e.

The Basic Module for R_1.

This is essentially the same as for R_0 except that for R_1 we wish to set $C(\langle x, k \rangle) = B(\langle x, k \rangle)$. Herein is the basic conflict: an even-indexed requirement R_j asks that lots of rows look like $\emptyset$ and an odd-indexed R_j asks for them to look like B.

Combining Strategies.

We cannot perform a delayed diagonalization as in the proof of Ladner's theorem, since we cannot know if $\phi_e(k)$ is defined. The combination of strategies needs the priority method. Let us consider a module for R_1 that works in the outcomes of R_0. We cannot know if this outcome is $(0, f)$ or $(0, \infty)$. Instead we have a strategy based on a guess as to R_0's behavior. Basically R_0 always believes that $k(0, s)$ is $k(0)$, that is, that the current value is the final one. Let $e = e(0)$, $n = n(0)$, $f = e(1)$ and $m = n(1)$.

Whilst R_1 believes that $\phi_e(k(0,0)) \uparrow$, R_1 acts as if R_0 is not there. So if $k(0,0) = k(0)$ and $\phi_e(k(0,0)) \uparrow$ then we win R_1 for the same reasons as we did for R_0. On the other hand, if $\phi_e(0) \downarrow$ for some least stage s, then R_0 will assert control of $C^{(\phi_e(k(0,0)))}$. For the sake of R_1 we have probably been setting $C(0, x) = B(0, x)$ for all x with $|x| < s$. Since R_0 has higher priority than R_1, R_1 must release its control of C_0 (and indeed of C_j for $j \le \phi_e(k(0))$) until a stage, if any, occurs where 2(a) pertains to R_0 so that R_0 is satisfied and releases control forever (or it becomes inactive because of a time bound being exceeded). Note that if 2(a) pertains at t, then R_1 is free to reassert control of C_0 for all y of the form $\langle y, 0 \rangle$ with $|y| > t$. Also, in this case, as R_1 is the requirement of highest overall priority remaining, its control cannot be violated and hence it will be met.

On the other hand, while R_0 can hope that 2(a) will pertain to R_1, R_0 may have outcome $(0, \infty)$ and R_0 will never release control of C_0. The key idea at this point is that we begin anew with a version of R_1 believing that $k(0, s+1) = k(0)$. That is, R_0 will *never again act*.

This version of R_1 can only work with C_q for $q > \phi_e(k(0, s)) = \phi_e(k(0, 0))$. Some care is needed since potentially we need all of B to meet R_1.

An elegant solution to this difficulty is to *shift* B into C above $\phi_e(k(0, s))$. Thus R_1 will ask that

$$C(\langle x, q \rangle) = B(\langle x, q - \phi_e(k(0, s)) - 1 \rangle)$$

for $q > \phi_e(k(0, s))$. It does so until either $k(0, t)$ is reset again, or 2(a) pertains, or the time bounds are exceeded. In the latter cases, it reverts to the $(0, f)$-strategy. In the first case it begins anew on $q > \phi_e(k(0, t))$. Since this restart process only occurs finitely often, it follows that we eventually get a *final* version of R_1 whose actions will not be disturbed.

Thus there is a final version of R_1 that is met as follows. As $\lim_s k(0, s) = k(0)$ exists, there is a value r and a stage s_0 so that for $q \geq r$ and $s > s_0$, R_1 is not initialized at stage s and can assert control on C_q if it so desires. If R_0 has outcome $(0, f)$, then $r = 0$, otherwise $r = \phi_e(k(0) - 1) + 1$. So we know that if R_1 fails then for all j there is a stage $h(j)$ (computable from the parameters r and s_0) where for y with $|y| > h(j)$

$$C(\langle y, r + j \rangle) = B(\langle y, j \rangle) \text{ and}$$

$$\Phi_f(A; \langle y, r + j \rangle) = C(\langle y, r + j \rangle).$$

Thus if R_1 fails again we can prove there is a reduction $\Delta(A) = B$ with running time $O(|z|^m)$ and computable constants. This is a contradiction.

The outcomes for R_1 are thus either $(1, \infty)$ and $(1, f)$. In the former case we know that for a finite number of rows j and for almost all y, $C(\langle y, j \rangle) = B(\langle y, j \rangle)$. But we also know that for such rows there is a reduction Δ_f such that

$$\Delta_f(A; \langle y, j \rangle) = C(\langle y, j \rangle) \text{ in time } O(|y|^m)$$
$$\text{and computable constants.}$$

We continue in the obvious way with the inductive strategies. Consider e.g. R_2. It is confronted with at worst a finite number of rows permanently controlled by R_0 and a finite number by R_1. However, in each case we know that there is a reduction from a computable number of rows af A to these rows, and hence a reduction

$$\Psi_2(A; \langle y, j \rangle) = C(\langle y, j \rangle)$$

for all j cofinally under the control of either R_0 or R_1. Therefore to argue that R_2 is met, we get to use Ψ_2 to help construct a reduction from A to B. That is, for R_i, let $e = e(i)$ and $n = n(i)$. Then inductively we have a reduction and constants $p(2), m(2)$ and $r(2)$ with

$$\Psi_2(A^{m(2)}; \langle x, j \rangle) = C(\langle x, j \rangle)$$

for all $j \leq p(q)$ running in time $m(2)|x|^{r(2)}$. Futhermore, we have a stage s_2 such that for all $k < 3$, R_k ceases further activity.

Thereafter R_2 is free to assert control over any row q of C for $q > p(2)$. If we suppose that R_2 fails, then for each such q, R_2 will eventually assert control of C_q at some stage $h(q)$ to make $C(\langle x, q \rangle) = 0$ for all x with $|x| > h_2(q)$ and we have $\Phi_{e(2)}(C) = B$.

Now to get a reduction Δ from A to B we go as for R_0 except that now if $\Phi_{e(2)}$ makes an oracle question of $\langle y, j \rangle$ for $j \leq p(2)$,we use Ψ_2 to answer this question.Thus we get a reduction Δ_2 that runs in time $O(|x|^{r(2)+n(2)})$, with computable constants and correct use. Thus again $B \leq A$, a contradiction. Further details can be found in [11]. $\qquad\square$

Remark. The Ladner paper not only proved density and other theorems for polynomial time reducibilities but additionally introduced the technique of delayed diagonalization ("looking back") which has been central to most structural analyses of polynomial-time degree structure. In our case we similarly introduce new techniques that would seem to be central to any analyses of the local degree structure for these parameterized reducibilities.

While we can only prove the general density theorem for the strongly uniform reducibilities, we have been able to prove some weaker versions of the density theorem for the other less uniform reducibilities. For instance we have been able to show that if there is a row k such that $B_k \not\leq_T^u A$ but $A \leq_T^u B$ then there is a C with $A <_T^u A \oplus C <_T^u B$. This again uses an infinite injury priority argument.

Ladner's Theorem holds much more generally than simply for the polynomial time degrees of *recursive* sets. Shinoda (see [11] [20] [4] observed that for $q = T$ the theorem holds for *any* sets $A <_T^p B$. This is not true for our reducibilities.

Theorem 17. *There exist sets A, B such that $A >_T^s B$ and for all D it is not the case that $A >_T^s D >_T^s B$. (Similarly for the other reducibilities.)*

The proof of this result uses a tree of strategies priority argument, and can be found in [11]. With Peter Cholak, the second author has also analysed the complexity of the reducibility orderings. Using a coding similar to that used by Ambos-Spies and Nies [2], for the P-time m-degrees, and a coding similar to that used by Ambos-Spies, Nies, and Shore [3], for the r.e. *wtt*-degrees. Cholak and Downey have proven the undecidability of the recursive sets under any of the m-reductions of section 2. The proofs are technically rather more difficult since the orderings are Σ_4 in the non-strongly uniform case. These proofs use $0^{(4)}$ priority techniques together with the speedup technique of [6]. For the reader familiar with [3] or [2] things are also hampered by the lack of an exact pair theorem for the relevant structures. In [5] it is also shown that one cannot just hope to lift the P-time result by, say, taking as a representative of a set A for this purpose the set which is empty on all rows except the first where is copies A. For instance, it is shown that this process can take a minimal pair for $\leq_T^p$ and turn the pair into a pair without infimum for $\leq_T^u$. This uses new techniques to analyse the normal polynomial degrees and shows how the study of these new structures and reducibilities can shed real light on the structure of the classic Karp and Cook reducibilities.

Many problems remain to be resolved. Aside from the general density question, one of great interest is whether collapse at the k-th level propogates upward in the W hierarchy. We conclude this section by mentioning some related oracle results. In [11], we proved:

Theorem 18. *There exist recursive oracles A, B, and C such that $P^A = NP^A$, $P^B \neq NP^B$, yet $W[P]^A = W[P]^B = FPT^A = FPT^B$, and $W[1]^C \neq W[P]^C$.*

These results would seem to support the thesis that the W hierarchy is distinct from NP.

References

1. K. Abrahamson, R. Downey, and M. Fellows, "Fixed Parameter Tractability and Completeness IV: $W[P]$ and $PSPACE$," to appear.
2. K. Ambos-Spies and A. Nies, "The Theory of The Polynomial Time Many-One Degrees is Undecidable," to appear.
3. K. Ambos-Spies, A. Nies, and R.A. Shore, "The Theory of the Recursively Enumerable Weak Truth Table Degrees is Undecidable," to appear.
4. K. Aoki, J. Shinoda, and T. Tsuda, "On Π_2 Theories of hp-T Degrees of Low Sets," to appear.
5. P. Cholak and R. Downey, "Undecidability and Definability for Parameterized Polynomial Time Reducibilities," in preparation.
6. R. Downey, "Nondiamond Theorems for Polymomial Time Reducibility," to appear, J.C.S.S.
7. R. Downey and M. Fellows, "Fixed Parameter Tractability and Completeness," Congr. Num., 87 (1992) 161-187.
8. R. Downey and M. Fellows, "Fixed Parameter Tractability and Completeness I: Basic Results," to appear.
9. R. Downey and M. Fellows, "Fixed Parameter Tractability and Completeness II: On Completeness for $W[1]$," to appear.
10. R. Downey and M. Fellows, "Fixed Parameter Intractability (Extended Abstract)," Proc. 7th Conf. on Structure in Complexity Theory (1992), 36-49.
11. R. Downey and M. Fellows, "Fixed Parameter Tractability and Completeness III: Some Structural Aspects of the W-Hierarchy," in preparation.
12. R. Downey and M. Fellows, "Fixed Parameter Tractability," monograph in preparation.
13. M. R. Fellows and M. A. Langston, "On Search, Decision and the Efficiency of Polynomial-Time Algorithms." In Proc. Symp. on Theory of Computing (STOC) (1989), 501-512.
14. M. R. Fellows and M. A. Langston, "An Analogue of the Myhill-Nerode Theorem and Its Use in Computing Finite Basis Characterizations." In Proc. Symp. Foundations of Comp. Sci. (FOCS) (1989), 520-525.
15. M. R. Garey and D. S. Johnson, Computers and Intractability: A Guide to the Theory of NP-Completeness (Freeman, San Francisco, 1979).
16. R. Ladner, "On the Structure of Polynomial Time Reducibility," J.A.C.M. 22 (1975), 155-171.
17. N. Robertson and P. D. Seymour, "Graph Minors XIII. The Disjoint Paths Problem," to appear.
18. N. Robertson and P. D. Seymour, "Graph Minors XV. Wagner's Conjecture," to appear.
19. T. J. Schaefer, "Complexity of Some Two-person Perfect Information Games," J. Comput. Sys. Sci. 16 (1978), 185-225.
20. J. Shinoda, Personal Communication, 1991.

Limits on the Power of Parallel Random Access Machines with Weak Forms of Write Conflict Resolution

Faith E. Fich[1], Russell Impagliazzo[2], Bruce Kapron[3], Valerie King[3], and Miroslaw Kutylowski[4]

[1] University of Toronto
[2] University of Toronto, present address: University of California, San Diego
[3] University of Toronto, present address: University of Victoria
[4] Heinz Nixdorf Institut, Universität Paderborn, present address: Uniwersytet Wroclaw

1 Introduction

A parallel random access machine (PRAM) that allows concurrent writes must specify how to resolve write conflicts when they occur. One method is to let an adversary determine what value appears [1]. In other words, an algorithm must compute the correct answer no matter what values appear when write conflicts occur. Hagerup and Radzik [12] call this model the ROBUST PRAM. Such a model is very weak, since the way an adversary resolves write conflicts may depend on the entire algorithm and the values of all the inputs.

We define a *fixed adversary* PRAM to be a concurrent-read concurrent-write PRAM in which the value that appears in a given cell after a given time step can be expressed as a function of only the value already in the cell, the processors attempting to write to the cell, and the values they are attempting to write. The method for determining the outcome of write conflicts for different memory cells or different time steps may be different. However, the choice of methods cannot depend on what algorithm will be run. Essentially, the write conflict resolution mechanism is algorithm oblivious. By definition, any fixed adversary PRAM is at least as powerful as the ROBUST PRAM.

Many different write conflict resolution schemes for the PRAM have been studied. In the PRIORITY PRAM [5, 8], the processor of lowest index that attempts to write into a given cell at a given time step succeeds. When two or more processors simultaneously attempt to write into the same cell in the COLLISION PRAM [5], a special collision symbol appears. In the TOLERANT PRAM [9], the value of the cell remains unchanged in case of a write conflict. Another example is the MAXIMUM PRAM [4], in which the largest value written to a memory cell at a given time step is the value that appears there. These are all examples of fixed adversary PRAMs.

In the ARBITRARY PRAM [5, 7], an adversary is allowed to determine which one of the values that is written to a given cell will appear. Unlike the ROBUST PRAM, the adversary cannot leave the cell contents unchanged nor write some unrelated value when a write conflict occurs. The ARBITRARY PRAM is at least as powerful as the ROBUST PRAM. However, it is not an example of a fixed adversary PRAM.

The COMMON PRAM [5, 13] is a fixed adversary PRAM that can only run a restricted class of algorithms. In this model, many processors may simultaneously attempt to write to the same cell, provided they all attempt to write the same value. This value appears as the result of the write. The relationship between the computational powers of the COMMON and ROBUST PRAMs is not well understood. Specifically, it is unknown whether there are problems that can be solved substantially faster by the ROBUST PRAM than by the COMMON PRAM or vice versa.

Except for the ROBUST PRAM, every previously studied concurrent-read concurrent-write (CRCW) PRAM can easily compute the OR of n Boolean variables in constant time using n processors, whereas $\Omega(\log n)$ steps are necessary for the concurrent-read exclusive-write (CREW) PRAM, even with an unbounded number of processors [2, 3]. It is unknown whether the ROBUST PRAM can compute OR any faster than the CREW PRAM. More generally, it is not known whether this very weak form of concurrent-write is useful for deterministically computing any function over a complete domain.

We address the question of the relative power of the ROBUST PRAM and the CREW PRAM. In Section 2, we prove a lower bound of $\Omega(\log(d)/\log(kq))$ on the time required by the ROBUST PRAM to compute Boolean functions in terms of q^k, the number of different values each memory cell of the PRAM can contain, and the degree d of the function when expressed as a polynomial over the finite field of q elements. For almost all Boolean functions, including OR, this implies that the ROBUST PRAM with 1-bit memory cells requires $\Omega(\log n)$ steps. This is significant, since every function can be computed by the CREW PRAM with 1-bit memory cells in $O(\log n)$ steps [2]. We also derive a lower bound of $\Omega\left(\min\left\{\sqrt{\log(d)}, \log(d)/\log\log_q(p)\right\}\right)$ steps for computing any Boolean function of degree d over $\mathbb{F}_q$ by the ROBUST PRAM with p processors, even if memory cells can contain arbitrarily large values. In particular, the ROBUST PRAM with $2^{2^{O(\sqrt{\log n})}}$ processors requires $\Omega(\sqrt{\log n})$ steps to compute OR. These lower bounds are obtained using carefully chosen fixed adversary PRAMs.

In Section 3, we show the limitations of these techniques, by describing how any fixed adversary PRAM with p processors and $O(\log(p/n))$-bit memory cells can compute OR in $O(\log n/\log\log(p/n))$ steps. In particular, with $2^{2^{\Omega(\sqrt{\log n})}}$ processors, $O(\sqrt{\log n})$ steps are needed. With $2^n - 1$ processors, only 2 steps and one n-bit memory cell are needed. This result gives rise to a simulation of the p-processor PRIORITY PRAM by any fixed adversary PRAM using only a constant factor more time and a factor of p more memory cells, but with an exponential increase in the number of processors.

Adding randomization to the ROBUST PRAM increases its computational power. Borodin, Hopcroft, Paterson, Ruzzo, and Tompa [1] showed that the randomized ROBUST PRAM can compute OR in $O(\log\log n)$ time, with any constant probability of error. Hagerup and Radzik [12] also showed that $O(\log\log n)$ time is sufficient to compute OR, using only n processors and with error probability $2^{-(\log n)^{O(1)}}$. In Section 4, we present a new randomized ROBUST PRAM algorithm that uses only $O(\log^* n)$ time and $n/(\log^* n)$ processors and has error probability $2^{-O(2^{(\log^* n)/4})}$.

In contrast, even with an unlimited number of processors, the randomized CREW PRAM requires $\Omega(\log n)$ steps [3]. Together with our lower bounds, these results prove a separation between the deterministic and randomized ROBUST PRAM. For the CREW PRAM, no such separation exists, since randomization provides no more than a factor of 8 in speedup over the deterministic model [3].

Throughout this paper, we use $P_1, \ldots, P_p$ to denote the p processors of a PRAM and $M_1, \ldots, M_m$ to denote its m memory cells. If the input consists of n variables, $x_1, \ldots, x_n$, we assume that they are initially located in memory cells $M_1, \ldots, M_n$, respectively. The other memory cells are initialized to 0. Each step of a PRAM computation is assumed to consist of three phases. In the first phase, each processor can read from a cell of shared memory; in the second phase, processors are allowed to do an arbitrary amount of local computation; and in the third phase, each processor can attempt to write to a cell of shared memory. Formal definitions of the PRAM model can be found in [2, 3].

2 Lower Bounds

Given any field F and any function $f : D \to R$, where $D \subseteq F^n$ and $R \subseteq F$, the polynomial $g : F^n \to F$ *represents* f *over* F if $g(x) = f(x)$ for all $x \in D$. In particular, every Boolean function can be uniquely expressed as a multilinear polynomial (i.e. as a sum of monomials) over any field [14]. The *degree* of f over F is defined to be the minimum degree of any polynomial that represents f over F. The degree of f over F is undefined if there is no polynomial that represents f over F.

In [3], it was shown that the time complexity of computing any Boolean function of degree d over the field of real numbers is $\Theta(\log d)$. Here, using a similar approach, we derive lower bounds for the time to compute a Boolean function on a particular fixed adversary PRAM (and hence the ROBUST PRAM) in terms of its degree deg_q over the finite field $\mathbb{F}_q$ of q elements.

Theorem 1. *On the ROBUST PRAM with memory cells that can hold at most* q^k *different values,* $\Omega(\log(d)/\log(kq))$ *steps are required to compute any Boolean function of degree d over $\mathbb{F}_q$.*

To prove this result, it suffices to prove the lower bound on any fixed adversary PRAM, each of whose memory cells holds a k-tuple of elements in $\mathbb{F}_q$. The key is to choose a fixed adversary PRAM with nice properties.

When memory cells can contain only single bits (i.e. when $q = 2$ and $k = 1$), we use the $\mathbb{F}_2$-*adversary PRAM*. In this model, the value of a shared memory cell changes exactly when an odd number of processors simultaneously attempt to write the negated value. In other words, if a memory cell contains the value 0 (1) before a given step, then it will contain the value 1 (0) after the step, if there are an odd number of processors that attempt to write the value 1 (0) there during the step, and it will remain 0 (1) otherwise.

For larger values of q, the write conflict resolution rule can be generalized. Specifically, in the $\mathbb{F}_q$-*adversary PRAM*, if a memory cell M contains the value $v \in \mathbb{F}_q$

before a given step, then, after that step, M will contain the value

$$v + \sum_{u \in \mathbb{F}_q} (u-v) \cdot (\text{the number of processors that attempt to write the value } u \text{ to } M),$$

where all operations are performed in the field $\mathbb{F}_q$. Note that, if no processors write to M, then the sum is empty and M will retain its old value v. If all the processors that write to M attempt to write v, M also retains the value v. However, if exactly one processor writes to M, then M will contain the value that processor wrote.

The $\mathbb{F}_q$-adversary PRAM works component-wise for $k > 1$, treating each component of each memory cell separately. Short tuples can be padded with leading zeros when necessary, so the actual number of components k does not need to be specified. However, when k is bounded, it is possible to derive lower bounds for the time to compute Boolean functions on the $\mathbb{F}_q$-adversary PRAM.

Lemma 2. *On the $\mathbb{F}_q$-adversary PRAM with memory cells that hold k-tuples of elements in $\mathbb{F}_q$, $\Omega(\log(d)/\log(kq))$ steps are required to compute any Boolean function of degree d over $\mathbb{F}_q$.*

Proof. Consider any $\mathbb{F}_q$-adversary PRAM algorithm for memory cells that hold k-tuples of elements in $\mathbb{F}_q$. Without loss of generality, we may assume that a processor's state is merely (an encoding of) the sequence of values it has read at each step (so a processor never forgets information). Given an input $x = (x_1, \ldots, x_n) \in \{0,1\}^n$, let

$$S_{P,t,w}(x) = \begin{cases} 1 & \text{if processor } P \text{ is in state } w \text{ immediately after step } t, \\ 0 & \text{otherwise.} \end{cases}$$

Then $S_{P,t,w}(x)$ is the characteristic function describing those inputs x for which processor P is in state w at time t. Note that for different states w and w', the set of inputs for which processor P is in state w at time t is disjoint from the set of inputs for which processor P is in state w' at time t. Thus for any set of states W, $\sum_{w \in W} S_{P,t,w}(x)$ is the characteristic function of the set of inputs for which processor P is in a state of W at time t.

Let $C_{M,t,i}(x)$ denote the contents of the ith component of memory cell M immediately after step t on input x and let

$$B_{M,t,i,u}(x) = \begin{cases} 1 & \text{if } C_{M,t,i}(x) = u, \\ 0 & \text{otherwise} \end{cases}$$

be the characteristic function of the set of inputs for which the ith component of memory cell M has value u at time t. Define

$$s(t) = \max_{P,w} deg_q(S_{P,t,w}),$$
$$c(t) = \max_{M,i} deg_q(C_{M,t,i}), \text{ and}$$
$$b(t) = \max_{M,i,u} deg_q(B_{M,t,i,u})$$

to be the maximum degrees of these functions over $\mathbb{F}_q$.

Since each processor is in its initial state at time 0 for all inputs, the associated characteristic functions are all constant, so $s(0) = 0$. The initial contents of the least significant components of the memory cells $M_1, \ldots, M_n$ are described by the linear functions $x_1, \ldots, x_n$, respectively. The other components of memory cells $M_1, \ldots, M_n$ and all k components of any other memory cells are all initially 0 and their contents are described by the constant 0 function. Furthermore, for $i = 1, \ldots, k$, $\mathcal{B}_{M,0,i,1}(x) = \mathcal{C}_{M,0,i}(x)$, $\mathcal{B}_{M,0,i,0}(x) = 1 - \mathcal{C}_{M,0,i}(x)$, and $\mathcal{B}_{M,0,i,u}(x) = 0$ if $u \in \mathbb{F}_q - \{0, 1\}$. Therefore $c(0) = b(0) = 1$.

Processor P is in state $\langle v^{(1)}, \ldots, v^{(t-1)}, v \rangle$ immediately after step t if and only if it is in state $\langle v^{(1)}, \ldots, v^{(t-1)} \rangle$ immediately after step $t - 1$ and the memory cell M that it reads during step t contains value $v = (v_k, \ldots, v_1)$. Hence

$$S_{P,t,\langle v^{(1)}, \ldots, v^{(t-1)}, v \rangle}(x) = S_{P,t-1,\langle v^{(1)}, \ldots, v^{(t-1)} \rangle}(x) \cdot \prod_{i=1}^{k} \mathcal{B}_{M,t-1,i,v_i}(x)$$

and $s(t) \le s(t-1) + kb(t-1)$ for $t > 0$.

Now consider the writing phase of step t. Let $W(P, M, t, i, u)$ denote the set of states in which processor P writes the value u to the ith component of memory cell M at step t. Then $\displaystyle\sum_{w \in W(P,M,t,i,u)} S_{P,t,w}(x)$ has value 1, if processor P attempts to write the value u to the ith component of memory cell M at step t on input x, and has value 0, otherwise. It follows from the definition of the write conflict resolution rule that the ith component of the contents of memory cell M at the end of step t can be expressed as

$$\mathcal{C}_{M,t,i}(x) = \mathcal{C}_{M,t-1,i}(x) + \sum_{u \in \mathbb{F}_q} (u - \mathcal{C}_{M,t-1,i}(x)) \sum_P \left(\sum_{w \in W(P,M,t,i,u)} S_{P,t,w}(x) \right),$$

when viewed as a polynomial over $\mathbb{F}_q$. Thus $c(t) \le c(t-1) + s(t)$ for $t > 0$.

Finally, over $\mathbb{F}_q$,

$$\mathcal{B}_{M,t,i,u}(x) = 1 - (\mathcal{C}_{M,t,i}(x) - u)^{q-1} = \begin{cases} 1 & \text{if } \mathcal{C}_{M,t,i}(x) = u \\ 0 & \text{otherwise,} \end{cases}$$

so $b(t) \le (q-1)c(t)$.

It is easily shown by induction that

$$s(t) \le \frac{k(q-1)}{\Delta} \left[\left(\frac{k(q-1)+2+\Delta}{2} \right)^t + \left(\frac{k(q-1)+2-\Delta}{2} \right)^t \right] \quad \text{and}$$

$$c(t) \le \frac{k(q-1)+\Delta}{2\Delta} \left(\frac{k(q-1)+2+\Delta}{2} \right)^t - \frac{k(q-1)-\Delta}{2\Delta} \left(\frac{k(q-1)+2-\Delta}{2} \right)^t$$

where $\Delta = \sqrt{k(q-1)[k(q-1)+4]}$.

If an algorithm computes a Boolean function f, then the contents of the least significant component of the output cell at the end of the computation is described by the function f. Hence the number of steps t taken by the algorithm satisfies $c(t) \ge \deg_q(f)$, which implies that $t \ge \log\left(\frac{2\Delta \deg_q(f)}{k(q-1)+\Delta}\right) / \log\left(\frac{k(q-1)+2+\Delta}{2}\right) \in \Omega(\log(\deg_q(f))/\log(kq))$. $\quad\square$

In the special case when the memory cells can contain only single bits, it follows from the bound derived in the proof of Lemma 2 that at least $\varphi(deg_2(f))$ steps are required to compute the Boolean function f. Here $\varphi(d) = \min\{j|F_{2j+1} \geq d\}$ and $F_0, F_1, F_2, \ldots$ is the Fibonacci sequence defined by the recurrence $F_0 = 1$, $F_1 = 1$, and $F_j = F_{j-1} + F_{j-2}$ for $j \geq 2$. In particular, since the OR of n Boolean variables has degree n over $\mathbb{F}_2$, the $\mathbb{F}_2$-adversary PRAM and the ROBUST PRAM both require $\varphi(n)$ steps to compute this function with single bit memory cells. This lower bound exactly matches the upper bound for computing OR on the CREW PRAM with single bit memory cells [2].

The threshold k function of n Boolean variables and the exactly k out of n function both have degree at least $n/2$ over $\mathbb{F}_2$. In fact, over $\mathbb{F}_2$, only a very tiny fraction (at most $1/2^{2^{n-1}}$) of all polynomials of n variables have degree less than $n/2$. Hence, most Boolean functions of n arguments require at least $\varphi(n) - 1$ steps to be computed by the ROBUST PRAM with single bit memory cells.

Any nonconstant Boolean function f satisfies $|f^{-1}(0)|, |f^{-1}(1)| \geq 2^{n-deg_2(f)}$ [6]. Thus, if $0 < |f^{-1}(0)| \leq 2^{n-d}$ or $0 < |f^{-1}(1)| \leq 2^{n-d}$, then $deg_2(f) \geq d$, so the ROBUST PRAM with 1-bit memory cells requires at least $\varphi(d)$ steps to compute f.

The PARITY function of n variables has degree 1 over $\mathbb{F}_2$. However, over $\mathbb{F}_3$, it has degree n. It follows from the bound derived in the proof of Lemma 2 that a ROBUST PRAM whose memory cells can hold at most 3 different values requires at least $0.45 \log_2 n$ steps to compute PARITY.

For the ROBUST PRAM, the actual values written to and read from shared memory are not important. They can be renamed essentially arbitrarily without affecting the number of steps performed. Specifically, let A be any ROBUST PRAM algorithm and let $h : \mathbb{N} \rightarrow \mathbb{N}$ be any bijection of the natural numbers that maps each possible input or output value to itself. Then, construct a new algorithm $h(A)$ in which every processor applies the function h to each value it attempts to write into shared memory and applies the function h^{-1} to each value it reads from shared memory. Because the input and output values are not affected by the renaming, the algorithms A and $h(A)$ compute the same function. Furthermore, since processors are allowed to perform an arbitrary amount of local computation at each step, $h(A)$ uses no more steps than A.

Lemma 3. *Consider any ROBUST PRAM algorithm A computing a Boolean function using p processors. There is a renaming function h such that, during the first t steps of $h(A)$ on the $\mathbb{F}_q$-adversary PRAM, all except the $\lfloor 2^t \log_q(2pq) \rfloor$ least significant components of every memory cell are 0 (when integers are represented in q-ary notation) and, after step t, every processor is in at most $(2pq)^{2^t-1}$ different states.*

Proof. The proof is by induction on n. Initially, the only values in shared memory are 0 and 1 and every processor is in its one initial state. Since $1 \leq \lfloor 2^0 \log_q(2pq) \rfloor$ and $1 = (2pq)^{2^0-1}$, the claim is true for $t = 0$ with h as the identity function.

Let $t \geq 0$ and assume the claim is true for t with renaming function h. Consider step $t + 1$ of $h(A)$ on the $\mathbb{F}_q$-adversary PRAM. At the beginning of this step, each processor is in at most $(2pq)^{2^t-1}$ states and, in each state, it can read one of at most q^e different values, where $e = \lfloor 2^t \log_q(2pq) \rfloor$. Therefore, at the end of step $t + 1$, every processor is in at most $(2pq)^{2^t-1} \cdot q^e \leq (2pq)^{2^t-1} \cdot (2pq)^{2^t} = (2pq)^{2^{t+1}-1}$ states.

Let V denote the set of those values greater than or equal to q^e that processors attempt to write to shared memory during this step. Since each processor can write at most $(2pq)^{2^t-1} \cdot q^e$ different values during time step $t + 1$, it follows that $|V| \le p \cdot q^e \cdot (2pq)^{2^t-1}$. Let h' be any bijection that maps the same element as h does to each of $0, \ldots, q^e - 1$ and maps each element in V to the range $\{q^e, \ldots, q^e + |V| - 1\}$.

Note that every execution of $h'(A)$ on the $\mathbb{F}_q$-adversary PRAM is identical to an execution of $h(A)$ on the $\mathbb{F}_q$-adversary PRAM for the first t steps. Furthermore, each value a processor attempts to write during step $t + 1$ of $h'(A)$ on the $\mathbb{F}_q$-adversary PRAM has value less than $q^e + |V|$, so all except its $\lceil \log_q (q^e + |V|) \rceil \le e + 1 + \left\lfloor \log_q \left(p(2pq)^{2^t-1} \right) \right\rfloor \le \lfloor 2^{t+1} \log_q(2pq) \rfloor$ least significant q-ary digits are 0. It follows from the definition of the $\mathbb{F}_q$-adversary PRAM that all except the $\lfloor 2^{t+1} \log_q(2pq) \rfloor$ least significant components of every memory cell are 0 at the end of step $t+1$. Thus the claim is true for $t + 1$ with renaming function h'. $\qquad\square$

Theorem 4. *With p processors (and memory cells that can contain arbitrarily large values), the ROBUST PRAM requires $\Omega \left(\min \left\{ \sqrt{\log(d)}, \log(d)/\log\log_q(p) \right\} \right)$ steps to compute any Boolean function of degree d over $\mathbb{F}_q$.*

Proof. Let f be a Boolean function of degree d over $\mathbb{F}_q$ that can be computed by a ROBUST PRAM algorithm A in T steps. By Lemma 3, there is a renaming function h such that when $h(A)$ is run on the $\mathbb{F}_q$-adversary PRAM, all except the $\lfloor 2^T \log_q(2pq) \rfloor$ least significant components of every memory cell are 0. Since $h(A)$ computes f, it follows from Lemma 2 that $T \in \Omega \left(\frac{\log(d)}{\log(2^T \log_q(2pq))} \right)$ or, equivalently, $T^2 + T \log\log_q(2pq) \in \Omega(\log(d))$. Hence $T \in \Omega \left(\min \left\{ \sqrt{\log(d)}, \frac{\log(d)}{\log\log_q(p)} \right\} \right)$. $\qquad\square$

In particular, since $deg_2(\mathrm{OR}) = n$, the ROBUST PRAM with $2^{2^{O(\sqrt{\log n})}}$ processors requires $\Omega(\sqrt{\log n})$ steps to compute the OR of n bits. Moreover, to compute OR in constant time, the ROBUST PRAM requires at least $2^{n^{\Omega(1)}}$ processors and shared memory cells with wordsize at least $n^{\Omega(1)}$.

3 Constant Time Upper Bounds for Fixed Adversary PRAMs

It is not known whether the ROBUST PRAM can compute the OR of n bits faster than the CREW PRAM, even if it is allowed an unlimited number of processors and an unlimited number of memory cells of unlimited wordsize. (The *wordsize* of a memory cell is the number of bits needed to represent the values it can contain.) In this section, we show that any fixed adversary PRAM can even simulate the PRIORITY PRAM with only a constant factor increase in time, given sufficient resources. In particular, this indicates that new proof techniques will be needed to prove that the ROBUST PRAM is no more powerful than the CREW PRAM.

The key to the simulation is an algorithm for computing OR.

Theorem 5. *The OR of n bits can be computed in 2 steps on any fixed adversary PRAM with $2^n - 1$ processors and one memory cell of wordsize n.*

Proof. Let $p = 2^n - 1$. For any subset $W \subseteq \{1, 2, ..., p\}$, let $v(W)$ denote the value that appears in the memory cell after step 1 when each processor whose number is in W attempts to write its number to the memory cell and the remaining processors do not attempt to write. The memory cell is assumed to be initialized to 0.

If no processors attempt to write, the contents of the memory cell remains unchanged and if exactly one processor attempts to write, the memory cell will contain the number of that processor. Thus the range of the function v has size at least $p+1$.

We will partition the processors into three sets, A, N, and D, with $|D| = n$, and show that there exists a subset $S \subseteq D$ such that $v(A \cup S) \neq v(A \cup S')$ for all subsets $S' \subseteq D$ that differ from S. Using these sets, the following algorithm computes the OR of n Boolean variables. In the read phase of the first step, each processor in D is assigned a different bit of input to read. Processors in A will *always* attempt to write their numbers, processors in N will *never* write, and each processor in D will write its number *depending* on the value of the input bit it read. A processor in S attempts to write its number if it reads the value 0 and a processor in $D - S$ attempts to write its number if it reads the value 1.

If the input bits are all 0, then the processors in $A \cup S$ are exactly those that attempt to write and, as a result, the memory cell will contain the value $v(A \cup S)$. Otherwise, the set of processors attempting to write is $A \cup S'$ for some subset $S' \subseteq D$ that differs from S. In this case, the memory cell will contain a value other than $v(A \cup S)$.

Therefore, in the next step, any predetermined processor can complete the computation by reading the contents of the memory cell and writing the value 0 if it saw the value $v(A \cup S)$ and writing the value 1 if it saw anything else.

Now we show how to construct sets A, N, and S satisfying the desired properties. Since the function v has a range of size at least $p + 1$, there is at least one value r in the range that is the image of at most $2^p/(p+1)$ different subsets in the domain. Let C initially be the collection of subsets that map to r (i.e. $C = v^{-1}(r)$).

While there are at least two subsets remaining in C, choose a processor P that occurs in some but not all of the subsets in C. If the majority of subsets in C contain P, add P to N and remove any subset that contains P from C. Otherwise, add P to A, and remove any subset that does not contain P from C.

At each step, C is reduced in size by at least a factor of 2. After no more than $\log(2^p/(p+1)) = p - \log(p+1) = p - n$ iterations, only one subset remains and $|A \cup N| \leq p - n$. The subsets remaining in C are those that map to r, contain A, and are disjoint from N.

Let L be the last subset of processors in C. Let $S = L - A$. If S contains at most n processors, let D be any set of n processors that contains S and is disjoint from $A \cup N$. Otherwise move processors from S to A until S has size n and then let $D = S$. Since $A \cup S = L \in C$, $v(A \cup S) = r$.

Now suppose $S' \subseteq D$ and $v(A \cup S') = r$. Then $A \cup S'$ was originally in C. But $A \cup S'$ contains no processors in N and every processor in A; therefore it was never removed from C. Since L is the only subset in C at the end of the construction, $A \cup S' = L$ and, hence, $S' = S$. Therefore $v(A \cup S') \neq r$ for all $S' \subseteq D$ such that $S' \neq S$. □

Corollary 6. *The OR of n bits can be computed in $O(\log n / \log \log(p/n))$ steps on* *any fixed adversary PRAM with p processors and wordsize* $\log(p/n) + \log\log(p/n)$.

Proof. Divide the bits into groups of size $s = \log(p/n) + \log\log(p/n)$ and assign $2^s - 1$ processors to each group. Since there are at most n/s groups and $(2^s - 1)n/s < n(p/n)\log(p/n)/(\log(p/n) + \log\log(p/n)) < p$, there is a sufficient number of processors available. By Theorem 5, the OR of each group can be computed in $O(1)$ steps, leaving a problem of size n/s.

If this process is repeated $t = \log(n)/\log\log(p/n)$ times, a problem of size $n/s^t = 1$ remains, which is the solution to the original problem. $\square$

In particular, the OR of n bits can be computed in $O(\sqrt{\log n})$ steps using $2^{2^{\Omega(\sqrt{\log n})}}$ processors.

Theorem 7. *The PRIORITY PRAM with p processors and m memory cells can be simulated for t steps by any fixed adversary PRAM with $2^p - 1$ processors and $m(p+1)$ memory cells in $O(t)$ steps.*

Proof. Processor P_i is simulated by a team of 2^{i-1} processors, one of which is designated P_i'. Each memory cell M_j is simulated using one memory cell M_j' and p auxiliary memory cells $M_{j,1}', \ldots, M_{j,p}'$ that are initialized to 0.

When processor P_i reads M_j, the ith team of processors all read M_j' and they all perform the same local computations. When processor P_i attempts to write to M_j, processor P_i' writes the value 1 in location $M_{j,i}'$. Then the ith team computes the OR of the values in locations $M_{j,1}', \ldots, M_{j,i-1}'$ (using the algorithm in Theorem 5) and writes the answer in $M_{j,i}'$. Processor P_i' reads $M_{j,i}'$ and, if it contains the value 0, writes the value P_i attempted to write to location M_j'. Otherwise P_i' writes 0 to M_j'. $\square$

4 Randomized Algorithms for Computing OR on the ROBUST PRAM

In this section, we describe a randomized algorithm for computing OR in $O(\log^* n)$ time on the ROBUST PRAM with single bit shared memory cells. The algorithm has one-sided error: when the value 1 is output, it is always correct; when 0 is output, it errs with probability $o(1)$. Virtually the same algorithm may be used to simulate a step of the ARBITRARY PRAM with the same error and time bounds, provided memory cells can contain at least p different values.

Hagerup and Radzik [12] describe a randomized algorithm to simulate a step of the ARBITRARY PRAM in time $O(\log\log n)$ with error at most $1/n$, using $O(n\log n/\log\log n)$ processors. Our algorithm uses a routine REDUCE which is similar to theirs, but replaces their randomized "scattering" technique with a simple deterministic method. To achieve the better time bounds, our algorithm involves the repeated application of REDUCE, which compounds the error.

The idea of our algorithm is to sample varying amounts of the input in parallel, in such a way that, when the input contains a 1, we find a sample in which a small number of input bits are 1.

Let $X = \{x_1, x_2, ..., x_n\}$ be the set of input bits. Using at most $n(1 + \log_2 n)^4$ processors and a constant number of parallel steps, REDUCE(X) reduces the input set to a set Y containing at most $4(1 + \log_2 n)^4$ bits, so that if OR(X)=0 then OR(Y)=0, and if OR(X)=1 then, with probability less than $1/n$, OR(Y)=0.

REDUCE (X)

Perform the following $\lceil \log_2 n \rceil$ times, independently and in·parallel:

1. For each of the n input bits x_i, associate a group of $(\lfloor \log_2 n \rfloor + 1)^3$ processors $\{P_{i,j,k,l} \mid 0 \leq j, k, l \leq \lfloor \log_2 n \rfloor\}$, all of which read x_i.
2. Consider a matrix A with n rows and $\lfloor \log_2 n \rfloor + 1$ columns. For each input bit x_i, one processor in its group, say $P_{i,j,1,1}$, writes the value 1 to $A(i,j)$ with probability $1/2^j$, provided $x_i = 1$; otherwise, it writes the value 0. Note that if $x_i = 0$, then the entire ith row of A is 0.
3. For each column j, initialize a $(\lfloor \log_2 n \rfloor + 1) \times 2 \times (\lfloor \log_2 n \rfloor + 1) \times 2$ array B_j to 0. This can be accomplished by having processors $P_{1,j,k,l}$, $P_{2,j,k,l}$, $P_{3,j,k,l}$, and $P_{4,j,k,l}$, write the value 0 to $B_j(k,0,l,0)$, $B_j(k,0,l,1)$, $B_j(k,1,l,0)$, and $B_j(k,1,l,1)$, respectively.
4. Each processor $P_{i,j,k,l}$ reads $A(i,j)$ and, if $A(i,j) = 1$, writes the value 1 to $B_j(k, i_k, l, i_l)$, where $i_{\lfloor \log_2 n \rfloor + 1} \cdots i_0$ is the binary representation of i.

The $4(\lfloor \log_2 n \rfloor + 1)^3 \lceil \log_2 n \rceil$ element output array Y is created by concatenating the entries in all the B arrays created during all of the parallel executions.

If $OR(X) = 0$, then the value 1 is never written and the output Y is entirely 0. If $OR(X) = 1$, the output Y should contain at least one 1. We show that this happens with probability at least $1 - 1/n$.

Lemma 8. *If OR(X) = 1, then Y fails to contain a 1 with probability at most $1/n$.*

Proof. Assume $OR(X) = 1$. Let r be the number of ones contained in X. Consider any one of the parallel executions and let z be the number of ones in the $\lfloor \log_2 r \rfloor$'th column of A.

The probability that $z = 0$ is $(1 - 1/2^{\lfloor \log_2 r \rfloor})^r \leq 1/e$. The expected value of z is $r(1/2^{\lfloor \log_2 r \rfloor}) < 2$. Chernoff bounds show that the probability of z being at least three times its expected value is less than $1/e^4$. Hence $Pr[1 \leq z \leq 5] > 1 - 1/e - 1/e^4 > 1/2$.

Suppose that $1 \leq z \leq 5$. In this case, some cell of $B_{\lfloor \log_2 r \rfloor}$ will have the value 1 written to it by exactly one processor. To see this, consider the indices i such that $A(i, \lfloor \log_2 r \rfloor) = 1$. Then there exist two bits which distinguish one of these indices from the others.

The output Y fails to contain a 1 only when all the $\lceil \log_2 n \rceil$ parallel executions fail to produce z within the required range. If $OR(X) = 1$, the probability of these $\lceil \log_2 n \rceil$ independent events all occurring is less than $1/n$. □

Independently, Hagerup [10] developed a similar technique, *graduated conditional scattering*, that can be used to reduce the problem of computing the OR from n bits to $O((\log n)^2)$ bits with n processors and error probability $O(1/\log n)$.

After a sufficient number of applications of REDUCE, the original problem is reduced to computing the OR of a very small number of bits, which may be done deterministically. The resulting algorithm is always correct when it outputs 1, although it may err when it outputs 0.

Lemma 9. *The OR of n bits can be computed by a ROBUST PRAM with $O(n(\log n)^4)$ processors and 1-bit shared memory cells in $O(\log^* n)$ steps using a randomized algorithm that errs with probability $O(1/2^{4(\log^* n)})$.*

Proof. Let $h(n)$ denote the minimum integer h such that $\log^{(h)} n \leq 2^{\log^* n}$. Then $h(n) \leq \log^* n$. Iterate REDUCE $h(n)$ times. The size of the remaining problem is in $\Theta((\log^{(h(n))} n)^4) \subseteq O(2^{4\log^* n})$. Solve this problem using a deterministic CREW PRAM algorithm in $O(\log^* n)$ steps [2]. The failure probability of this algorithm is at most $1/n + \sum_{h=1}^{h(n)-1} 1/\Omega((\log^{(h)} n)^4) = O(1/(\log^{(h(n)-1)} n)^4) \subseteq O(1/2^{4\log^* n})$. $\square$

Using the standard technique of partitioning a problem into successively larger subproblems, the number of processors can be reduced to n and the error probability can be improved.

Lemma 10. *The OR of n bits can be computed by a ROBUST PRAM with n processors and 1-bit shared memory cells in $O(\log^* n)$ steps using a randomized algorithm that errs with probability $O(1/2^{2^{(\log^* n)/4}})$.*

Proof. First partition the bits into $n/2^{\log^* n}$ sets of size $2^{\log^* n}$ and use a deterministic CREW PRAM algorithm to compute the OR of each set in $O(\log^* n)$ steps. This leaves a subproblem of size $n/2^{\log^* n}$.

Let $z_0 = 2^{\log^* n}$, and for $i \geq 0$, let $z_{i+1} = 2^{z_i^{1/4} - 3}$. In the $(i+1)$st iteration, divide the remaining n/z_i bits into $n/z_i s_i$ subproblems each of size $s_i = 2^{z_i^{1/4} - 1}$ and allocate $s_i(1 + \log_2 s_i)^4 = s_i z_i$ processors to each. Apply REDUCE to each subproblem in parallel. This reduces each subproblem from size s_i to size $4(1 + \log_2 s_i)^4 = 4z_i$. Therefore, at the end of the ith iteration, $4n/s_i = n/z_{i+1}$ bits remain. After $t = \min\{i|z_i \geq n\}$ iterations, the algorithm terminates.

Provided n is sufficiently large, $z_{i+2} \geq 2^{2^i}$ for all $i \geq 0$. Therefore $t \in O(\log^* n)$. Each iteration takes constant time. Hence, the time complexity of this algorithm is in $O(\log^* n)$.

The probability of error is the probability that some 1 in the input fails to appear in any of the reductions. From the Lemma 8, it follows that the total probability of error is at most $\sum_{i=1}^{k} 1/s_{i-1} \in O(1/2^{z_0^{1/4}}) = O(1/2^{2^{(\log^* n)/4}})$. $\square$

There is another way to obtain an algorithm for computing OR that runs in $O(\log^* n)$ time and uses n processors: repeatedly apply graduated conditional scattering until the problem size is $2^{\Theta(\log^* n)}$ and then solve the remaining problem deterministically, as in the proof of Lemma 9 [11]. The resulting algorithm has error probability $2^{-O(\log^* n)}$.

By first partitioning the bits into groups of size $\Theta(\log^* n)$ and computing the OR of each group sequentially, the number of processors can be reduced from n to $O(n/\log^* n)$ without increasing the time by more than a constant factor. The two resulting algorithms are efficient in the sense that their time-processor products are $\Theta(n)$, the sequential complexity of computing OR.

Theorem 11. *The OR of n bits can be computed by a ROBUST PRAM with $O(n/\log^* n)$ processors and 1-bit shared memory cells in $O(\log^* n)$ steps using a randomized algorithm that errs with probability $2^{-O(2^{(\log^* n)/4})}$.*

Acknowledgements

We would like to thank Torben Hagerup and Charlie Rackoff for helpful discussion. This work was supported by the Natural Sciences and Engineering Research Council of Canada, the Information Technology Research Centre of Ontario, the Defense Advanced Research Projects Agency of the United States, NEC, and the Deutsche Forschungsgemeinschaft.

References

1. A. Borodin, J. Hopcroft, M. Paterson, L. Ruzzo, and M. Tompa, "Observations Concerning Synchronous Parallel Models of Computation", manuscript, 1980.
2. S. Cook, C. Dwork, and R. Reischuk, "Upper and Lower Time Bounds for Parallel Random Access Machines without Simultaneous Writes", *SIAM J. Comput.*, volume 15, 1986, pages 87-97.
3. M. Dietzfelbinger, M. Kutylowski, and R. Reischuk, "Exact Time Bounds for Computing Boolean Functions without Simultaneous Writes", *Proc. Second Annual ACM Symposium on Parallel Algorithms and Architectures*, 1990, pages 125-135.
4. D. Eppstein and Z. Galil, "Parallel Algorithmic Techniques for Combinatorial Computing", *Ann. Rev. Comput. Sci.*, volume 3, 1988, pages 233-283.
5. F. Fich, P. Ragde, and A. Wigderson, "Relations Between Concurrent-Write Models of Parallel Computation", *SIAM J. Comput.*, volume 17, 1988, pages 606-627.
6. P. Fischer, and H. U. Simon, "On Learning Ring-Sum-Expansions", *Proc. Third Workshop on Computational Learning Theory*, 1990, to appear in *SIAM J. Comput.*
7. S. Fortune and J. Wyllie, "Parallelism in Random Access Machines", *Proc. 10th Annual Symposium on Theory of Computing*, 1978, pages 114-118.
8. L. Goldschlager, "A Unified Approach to Models of Synchronous Parallel Machines", *JACM*, volume 29, 1982, pages 1073-1086.
9. V. Grolmusz and P. Ragde, "Incomparability in Parallel Computation", *Discrete Applied Mathematics*, volume 29, no. 1, 1990, pages 63-78.
10. T. Hagerup, "Fast and Optimal Simulations between CRCW PRAMs", *Proc. 9th Annual Symposium on Theoretical Aspects of Computer Science*, 1992, pages 45-48.
11. T. Hagerup, personal communication.
12. T. Hagerup and T. Radzik, "Every Robust CRCW PRAM can Efficiently Simulate a PRIORITY PRAM", *Proc. Second Annual ACM Symposium on Parallel Algorithms and Architectures*, 1990, pages 117-124.
13. L. Kucera, "Parallel Computation and Conflicts in Memory Access", *Information Processing Letters*, volume 14, 1982, pages 93-96.
14. R. Smolensky, "Algebraic methods in the theory of lower bounds for Boolean circuit complexity", *Proc. 19th Annual ACM Symposium on Theory of Computing*, 1987, pages 77-82.

On Using Oracles That Compute Values

Stephen Fenner[1] and Steve Homer[2] and Mitsunori Ogiwara[3] and Alan L. Selman[4]

[1] University of Southern Maine[†]
[2] Boston University[§]
[3] University of Electro-Communications[¶]
[4] SUNY at Buffalo[‖]

Abstract. This paper focuses on complexity classes of partial functions that are computed in polynomial time with oracles in NPMV, the class of all multivalued partial functions that are computable nondeterministically in polynomial time. Concerning deterministic polynomial-time reducibilities, it is shown that

1. A multivalued partial function is polynomial-time computable with k adaptive queries to NPMV if and only if it is polynomial-time computable via $2^k - 1$ nonadaptive queries to NPMV.
2. A characteristic function is polynomial-time computable with k adaptive queries to NPMV if and only if it is polynomial-time computable with k adaptive queries to NP.
3. Unless the Boolean hierarchy collapses, k adaptive (nonadaptive) queries to NPMV is different than $k+1$ adaptive (nonadaptive) queries to NPMV for every k.

Nondeterministic reducibilities, lowness and the difference hierarchy over NPMV are also studied. The difference hierarchy for partial functions does not collapse unless the Boolean hierarchy collapses, but, surprisingly, the levels of the difference and bounded query hierarchies do not interleave (as is the case for sets) unless the polynomial hierarchy collapses.

1 Introduction

In this paper we study classes of partial functions that can be computed in polynomial time with oracles in NPMV and NPSV; namely, we study the classes $\mathrm{PF}^{\mathrm{NPMV}}$ and $\mathrm{PF}^{\mathrm{NPSV}}$.

NPMV is the set of all partial multivalued functions that are computed nondeterministically in polynomial time, and NPSV is the set of all partial functions

[†] Dept. of Computer Science, Portland, ME 04103. Research partially supported by the National Science Foundation under grant no. CCR-9209833.

[§] Dept. of Computer Science, Boston, MA 01003. Research partially supported by the National Science Foundation under grant no. CCR-9103055

[¶] Dept. of Computer Science, University of Electro-Communications, Chofu-shi, Tokyo 182, Japan. Research performed while visiting at: Dept. of Computer Science, SUNY at Buffalo, Buffalo, NY 14260. Research partially supported by the National Science Foundation under grant no. CCR-9002292.

[‖] Dept. of Computer Science, SUNY at Buffalo, Buffalo, NY 14260. Research partially supported by the National Science Foundation under grant no. CCR-9002292.

in this class that are single-valued. NPMV captures the complexity of computing witnesses to problems in NP. For example, let sat denote the partial multivalued function defined by $sat(x)$ maps to a value y if and only if x encodes a formula of propositional logic and y encodes a satisfying assignment of x. Then, sat belongs to NPMV, and the domain of sat (i.e., the set of all words x for which the output of $sat(x)$ is non-empty) is the NP-complete satisfiability problem, SAT. Also, NPMV captures the complexity of inverting polynomial time honest functions. To wit, the inverse of every polynomial time honest function belongs to NPMV, and the inverse of every one-one polynomial time honest function belongs to NPSV.

The class of partial functions with oracles in NP, namely, PF^{NP} has been well-studied [Kre88, Bei88], as have been the corresponding class of partial functions that can be computed nonadaptively with oracles in NP, viz. PF_{tt}^{NP} [Sel92], and the classes of partial functions that are obtained by limiting the number of queries to some value $k \geq 1$, namely, $PF^{NP[k]}$ and $PF_{tt}^{NP[k]}$ [Bei91]. A rich body of results is known about these classes.

Here we raise the question, "What is the difference between computing with an oracle in NPMV versus an oracle in NP?" The answer is not obvious. If the partial function sat is provided as an oracle to some polynomial-time computation M, then on a query x, where x encodes a satisfiable formula of propositional logic, the oracle will return some satisfying assignment y. However, if the oracle to M is the NP-compete set SAT, then to this query x, the oracle will only return a Boolean value "yes." On the other hand, by the well-known self-reducibility of SAT, M could compute y for itself by judicious application of a series of adaptive queries to SAT. Indeed Theorem 2 states that unbounded access to an oracle in NPMV is no more powerful than such an access to an oracle in NP. However, in Section 3 we will see that the situation for bounded query classes is much more subtle. In general, function oracles cannot be replaced by set oracles—but set oracles are still useful. We will show that every partial multivalued function in $PF^{NPMV[k]}$ can be computed by a partial multivalued function of the form $f \circ g$, where f is in NPMV and g is a single-valued function belonging to $PF^{NP[k]}$. Moreover, most surprisingly, the relationship between access to an oracle in NPMV and access to an oracle in NP is tight regarding set recognition; that is, $P^{NPMV[k]} = P^{NP[k]}$. This means that when we are computing characteristic functions, k bounded queries to an oracle in NPMV give no more information than the same number of queries to an oracle in NP.

We will show that the levels of the nonadaptive and adaptive bounded query hierarchies interleave (for example, k adaptive queries to a partial function in NPMV is equivalent to $2^k - 1$ nonadaptive queries to a partial function in NPMV), and we will show that these bounded query hierarchies collapse only if the Boolean hierarchy collapses.

In Section 4 we study nondeterministic polynomial time reductions to partial functions in NPMV. Unlike the case for deterministic functions, we will see that just one query to an NP oracle can substitute for an unbounded number of queries to any partial function in NPMV. The hierarchy that is formed by iteratively applying NP reductions is an analogue of the polynomial hierarchy, and we will show that this hierarchy collapses if and only if the polynomial hierarchy collapses.

In Section 5 we will study the difference hierarchy over NPMV. We define $f - g$ to be a partial multivalued function that maps x to y if and only if f maps x to y and g does *not* map x to y, and we define $NPMV(k) = \{f_1 - (f_2 - (\cdots - f_k))$: $f_1, \cdots, f_k \in NPMV\}$. Since the properties of the bounded query hierarchies over NPMV are largely similar to those over NP, one might hope that the same thing happens here—that the difference hierarchy over NPMV and the difference hierarchy over NP are similar. However, the contour of this hierarchy is, to our astonishment, totally different than its analogy for NP. Although BH $= \bigcup_k NP(k) \subseteq P^{NP}$, with no assumption, we will show that NPMV(2) is included in PF^{NPMV} if and only if PH $= \Delta_2^P$. Also, in this section we will introduce the notion of NPMV-lowness, and we will give a complete characterization of NPMV-lowness.

Consideration of reduction classes with oracles in NPSV, to be studied in Section 6, is motivated in part by a desire to understand how difficult it is to compute satisfying assignments for satisfiable formulas. We take the point of view that a partial multivalued function is easy to compute if for each input string in the domain of the function, some value of the function is easy to compute. For this reason, we define the following technical notions. Given partial multivalued functions f and g, define g to be a *refinement* of f if $dom(g) = dom(f)$ and for all $x \in dom(g)$ and all y, if y is a value of $g(x)$, then y is a value of $f(x)$. Let $\mathcal{F}$ and $\mathcal{G}$ be classes of partial multivalued functions. Purely as a convention, if f is a partial multivalued function, we define $f \in_c \mathcal{G}$ if $\mathcal{G}$ contains a refinement g of f, and we define $\mathcal{F} \subseteq_c \mathcal{G}$ if for every $f \in \mathcal{F}$, $f \in_c \mathcal{G}$. This notation is consistent with our intuition that $\mathcal{F} \subseteq_c \mathcal{G}$ should entail that the complexity $\mathcal{F}$ is not greater than the complexity of $\mathcal{G}$. Let PF denote the class of partial functions that are computable deterministically in polynomial time. The assertion "NPMV $\subseteq_c$ PF" means that every partial multivalued function in NPMV has a refinement that can be computed efficiently by some deterministic polynomial time transducer. It is well-known that $sat \in_c$ PF if and only if NPMV $\subseteq_c$ PF if and only if P $=$ NP [Sel92]. Thus, one does not expect that $sat \in_c$ PF. Is sat computable in some larger single-valued class of partial functions? It is shown in [Sel92] that PF $\subseteq$ NPSV $\subseteq$ PF$_{tt}^{NP}$, and it is an open question whether $sat \in_c$ NPSV or whether $sat \in_c$ PF$_{tt}^{NP}$. (Watanabe and Toda [WT91] have shown that $sat \in_c$ PF$_{tt}^{NP}$ relative to a random oracle, and Naik, Ogiwara, and Selman [NOS92] have obtained an oracle relative to which $sat \notin_c$ PF$_{tt}^{NP}$.) We will consider classes of the form $PF^{NPSV[k]}$ and $PF_{tt}^{NPSV[k]}$, where $k \geq 1$, and we will show that the adaptive and the nonadaptive classes form proper hierarchies unless the Boolean hierarchy collapses. Thus, these classes form a finer classification in which to study the central question of whether sat has a refinement in some interesting class of single-valued partial functions.

Finally, we note in passing that the complexity theory of decision problems, i.e., of sets, is extremely well developed. Although the computational problems in which we are most interested are naturally thought of as partial multivalued functions, the structural theory to support classification of these problems has been slight. By introducing several natural hierarchies of complexity classes of partial multivalued functions, with strong evidence supporting these claims, we intend this paper to make significant steps in correcting this situation.

2 Preliminaries

We fix Σ to be the finite alphabet $\{0, 1\}$. Let $f : \Sigma^* \mapsto \Sigma^*$ be a partial multivalued function. We write $f(x) \mapsto y$ (or, $f(x)$ maps to y), if y is a value of f on input string x. Define $graph(f) = \{\langle x, y \rangle \mid f(x) \mapsto y\}$, $dom(f) = \{x \mid \exists y(f(x) \mapsto y)\}$, and $range(f) = \{y \mid \exists x(f(x) \mapsto y)\}$. We will say that f is undefined at x if $x \notin dom(f)$.

A transducer T is a nondeterministic Turing machine with a read-only input tape, a write-only output tape, and accepting states in the usual manner. T computes a value y on an input string x if there is an accepting computation of T on x for which y is the final content of T's output tape. (In this case, we will write $T(x) \mapsto y$.) Such transducers compute partial, multivalued functions. (As transducers do not typically accept all input strings, when we write "function", "partial function" is always intended. If a function f is total, it will always be explicitly noted.)

- NPMV is the set of all partial, multivalued functions computed by nondeterministic polynomial time-bounded transducers;
- NPSV is the set of all $f \in$ NPMV that are single-valued;
- PF is the set of all partial functions computed by deterministic polynomial time-bounded transducers.

Now we describe oracle Turing machines with oracles that compute partial functions. For the moment, we assume that the oracle is a single-valued partial function. Let $\perp$ be a symbol not belonging to the finite alphabet Σ. In order for M to access a partial function oracle, M contains a write-only input oracle tape, a separate read-only output tape, and a special oracle call state q. When M enters state q, if the string currently on the oracle input tape belongs to the domain of the oracle partial function, then the result of applying the oracle appears on the oracle output tape, and if the string currently on the oracle input tape does not belong to the domain of the oracle partial function, then the symbol $\perp$ appears on the oracle output tape. Thus, if the oracle is some partial function g, given an input x to the oracle, the oracle, if called, returns a value $g(x)$ if one exists, and returns $\perp$ otherwise. (It is possible that M may read only a portion of the oracle's output if the oracle's output is too long to read with the resources of M.)

If g is a single-valued partial function and M is a deterministic oracle transducer as just described, then we let $M[g]$ denote the single-valued partial function computed by M with oracle g.

Definition 1. Let f and g be multivalued partial functions. f *is Turing reducible to g in polynomial time*, $f \leq_T^P g$, if for some deterministic oracle transducer M, for every single-valued refinement g' of g, $M[g']$ is a single-valued refinement of f.[9]

---

[9] A notion of polynomial-time Turing reducibility between partial functions is defined in [Sel92]. It is important to note that the definition given here is *different* than the one in [Sel92]. Here the oracle "knows" when a query is not in its domain. In the earlier definition, this is not the case. The authors recommend that the reducibility defined in [Sel92] should in the future be denoted as $\leq_T^{PP}$, which is the common notation for reductions between promise problems. We make this recommendation because conceptually and technically this reducibility between functions is equivalent to a promise problem

Let $\mathcal{F}$ be a class of partial multivalued functions. $\mathrm{PF}^{\mathcal{F}}$ denotes the class of partial multivalued functions f that are $\leq_{T}^{P}$-reducible to some $g \in \mathcal{F}$. $\mathrm{PF}^{\mathcal{F}[k]}$ (respectively, $\mathrm{PF}^{\mathcal{F}[\log]}$) denotes the class of partial multivalued functions f that are $\leq_{T}^{P}$-reducible to some $g \in \mathcal{F}$ via a machine that, on input x, makes k adaptive queries (respectively, $\mathcal{O}(\log |x|)$ adaptive queries) to its oracle.

$\mathrm{PF}_{tt}^{\mathcal{F}}$ denotes the class of partial multivalued functions f that are $\leq_{T}^{P}$-reducible to some $g \in \mathcal{F}$ via an oracle Turing machine transducer that queries its oracle nonadaptively. That is, a partial multivalued function f is in $\mathrm{PF}_{tt}^{\mathcal{F}}$ if there is an oracle Turing machine transducer T such that $f \in \mathrm{PF}^{\mathcal{F}}$ via T with an oracle g in $\mathcal{F}$ and a polynomial time computable function $h : \{0,1\}^* \mapsto (c\{0,1\}^*)^*$ such that, for each input x to T, T only calls the oracle g on strings in the list $h(x)$.

$\mathrm{PF}_{tt}^{\mathcal{F}[k]}$ denotes the class of partial multivalued functions f that are $\leq_{T}^{P}$-reducible to some $g \in \mathcal{F}$ via a machine that makes k nonadaptive queries to its oracle.

$\mathrm{P}^{\mathcal{F}}$, $\mathrm{P}^{\mathcal{F}[k]}$, $\mathrm{P}^{\mathcal{F}[\log]}$, $\mathrm{P}_{tt}^{\mathcal{F}}$ and $\mathrm{P}_{tt}^{\mathcal{F}[k]}$, respectively, denote the classes of all characteristic functions contained in $\mathrm{PF}^{\mathcal{F}}$, $\mathrm{PF}^{\mathcal{F}[k]}$, $\mathrm{PF}^{\mathcal{F}[\log]}$, $\mathrm{PF}_{tt}^{\mathcal{F}}$ and $\mathrm{PF}_{tt}^{\mathcal{F}[k]}$.

For a class of sets $\mathcal{C}$, we may say that $\mathrm{PF}^{\mathcal{C}}$ denotes the class of partial multivalued functions that are $\leq_{T}^{P}$-reducible to the characteristic function of some set in $\mathcal{C}$. $\mathrm{PF}^{\mathcal{C}[k]}$, $\mathrm{PF}^{\mathcal{C}[\log]}$, $\mathrm{PF}_{tt}^{\mathcal{C}}$, $\mathrm{PF}_{tt}^{\mathcal{C}[k]}$, $\mathrm{P}^{\mathcal{C}}$, $\mathrm{P}^{\mathcal{C}[k]}$, $\mathrm{P}^{\mathcal{C}[\log]}$, $\mathrm{P}_{tt}^{\mathcal{C}}$, and $\mathrm{P}_{tt}^{\mathcal{C}[k]}$ are defined similarly. In particular, $\mathrm{PF}^{\mathrm{NP}}$ is the class of partial multivalued functions computed in polynomial time with oracles in NP, and $\mathrm{PF}_{tt}^{\mathrm{NP}}$ is the class of partial multivalued functions that can be computed nonadaptively with oracles in NP. In the current literature, these classes contain single-valued functions only. The reason is that heretofore, polynomial time polynomial Turing reducibility, $\leq_{T}^{P}$, has been defined as a binary relation over single-valued objects. To see that $\mathrm{PF}^{\mathrm{NP}}$ contains partial functions that are not single-valued, consider the partial single-valued function $maxsat$ that on an input x where x encodes a formula of propositional logic, maps to the encoding of the lexicographically largest satisfying assignment of x, if $x \in \mathrm{SAT}$. Clearly, $maxsat \in \mathrm{PF}^{\mathrm{NP}}$, and $sat \leq_{T}^{P} maxsat$ by Definition 1, so the partial multivalued function sat belongs to $\mathrm{PF}^{\mathrm{NP}}$. Readers are free to interpret references to $\mathrm{PF}^{\mathrm{NP}}$ and $\mathrm{PF}_{tt}^{\mathrm{NP}}$ with their familiar meaning because the results that we will state for these classes, and for the corresponding bounded query classes, remain correct if they are replaced with the result of including only the single-valued partial functions that they contain.

Obviously $\mathrm{PF}^{\mathrm{NP}} \subseteq \mathrm{PF}^{\mathrm{NPMV}}$. Conversely, for a function $f \in \mathrm{NPMV}$, define f' to be a function such that $f'(x) = \min\{y : f(x) \mapsto y\}$. f' is a single-valued refinement of f and in $\mathrm{PF}^{\mathrm{NP}}$. Therefore, the following theorem holds.

Theorem 2. $\mathrm{PF}^{\mathrm{NPMV}} = \mathrm{PF}^{\mathrm{NP}}$.

Theorem 2 states that unbounded access to an oracle in NPMV is no more powerful than such an access to an oracle in NP.

The following examples illustrate the power of $\mathrm{PF}^{\mathrm{NPMV}}$ and $\mathrm{PF}_{tt}^{\mathrm{NPMV}}$. Consider the partial multivalued function $maxTsat$ defined as follows:

---

reduction. Also, we note that the reducibility defined in [Sel92] is not useful for our purposes here. In particular, it is easy to see that iterating reductions between functions in NPMV does not gain anything new unless the oracle is endowed with the ability to know its domain.

$maxTsat(x) \mapsto y$, if y is a satisfying assignment of x with the maximum number of $true$'s.

Obviously, $maxTsat$ belongs to $\mathrm{PF}^{\mathrm{NPMV}}$. Let f be a function that maps a pair (x, n) to y if and only if y is a satisfying assignment of x with n $true$'s. Since the number of variables in a formula is bounded by its length, it holds that $maxTsat(x) = f(x, n_x)$, where n_x is the largest $n, 1 \leq n \leq |x|$ such that $(x, n) \in dom(f)$. This implies that $maxTsat \in \mathrm{PF}_{tt}^{\mathrm{NPMV}}$.

Similarly, the partial multivalued function $maxclique$ that on input a graph G outputs a clique of maximum size, if G has a clique, belongs to $\mathrm{PF}_{tt}^{\mathrm{NPMV}}$. The function $maxedgewieightedclique$ that is defined over edge-weighted graphs and that outputs a clique of maximum weight, if G has a clique, belongs to $\mathrm{PF}^{\mathrm{NPMV}}$, but may not belong to $\mathrm{PF}_{tt}^{\mathrm{NPMV}}$ because weights may grow exponentially.

We should note that several of the classes we investigate here seem to capture the complexity of finding witnesses to NP-optimization problems. This observation is explored by Chen and Toda [CT92] and by Wareham [War92].

3 Bounded Query Classes

Now we state our main results; proofs are given in the full draft paper.

Let f and g be partial multivalued functions. $f \circ g$ denotes the function h such that for every x,

– $h(x)$ maps to y if and only if there exists some z such that $g(x)$ maps to z and $f(z)$ maps to y.

Let $\mathcal{F}$ and $\mathcal{G}$ be classes of partial multivalued functions. $\mathcal{F} \circ \mathcal{G}$ denotes $\{f \circ g \mid f \in \mathcal{F}$ and $g \in \mathcal{G}\}$.

Theorem 3. *For every* $k \geq 1$, $\mathrm{PF}^{\mathrm{NPMV}[k]} = \mathrm{PF}_{tt}^{\mathrm{NPMV}[2^k-1]} \subseteq_c \mathrm{NPMV} \circ \mathrm{PF}^{\mathrm{NP}[k]} \subseteq \mathrm{NPMV} \circ \mathrm{PF}_{tt}^{\mathrm{NP}[2^k-1]} \subseteq \mathrm{PF}^{\mathrm{NPMV}[k+1]} = \mathrm{PF}_{tt}^{\mathrm{NPMV}[2^{k+1}-1]}$. *Also,* $\mathrm{NPMV} \circ \mathrm{PF}_{tt}^{\mathrm{NP}[2^k-1]} \subseteq_c \mathrm{NPMV} \circ \mathrm{PF}^{\mathrm{NP}[k]}$.

For general bounded query classes, it is not known whether $\mathrm{PF}^{\mathrm{NPMV}[k]} \subseteq_c \mathrm{PF}^{\mathrm{NP}[k]}$. But, for reduction classes of sets, this type of equivalence holds.

Theorem 4. *For every* $k \geq 1$, $\mathrm{P}^{\mathrm{NPMV}[k]} = \mathrm{P}^{\mathrm{NP}[k]}$.

Theorem 5. *For every* $k \geq 1$, $\mathrm{P}_{tt}^{\mathrm{NPMV}[k]} = \mathrm{P}_{tt}^{\mathrm{NP}[k]}$.

The following theorems give evidence to show that bounded query hierarchies do not collapse.

Lemma 6. *Let* $k \geq 1$. *If* $\mathrm{PF}^{\mathrm{NPMV}[k+1]} = \mathrm{PF}^{\mathrm{NPMV}[k]}$, *then for every* $l \geq k$, $\mathrm{PF}^{\mathrm{NPMV}[l]} = \mathrm{PF}^{\mathrm{NPMV}[k]}$.

Lemma 7. *Let* $k \geq 1$. *If* $\mathrm{PF}_{tt}^{\mathrm{NPMV}[k+1]} = \mathrm{PF}_{tt}^{\mathrm{NPMV}[k]}$, *then for every* $l \geq k$, $\mathrm{PF}_{tt}^{\mathrm{NPMV}[l]} = \mathrm{PF}_{tt}^{\mathrm{NPMV}[k]}$.

We denote the k-th level of the Boolean hierarchy as $NP(k)$. By definition,

1. $NP(1) = NP$, and
2. for every $k \geq 2$, $NP(k) = NP - NP(k-1)$.

The Boolean hierarchy over NP, denoted by BH, is the union of all $NP(k)$, $k \geq 1$.

Theorem 8. *Let* $k \geq 1$. *If* $PF^{NPMV[k+1]} = PF^{NPMV[k]}$, *then* BH *collapses to its* 2^k-*th level.*

Proof. Suppose that $PF^{NPMV[k+1]} = PF^{NPMV[k]}$. By Lemma 6 and Theorem 3, for every $m > k$, $PF^{NPMV[m]} \subseteq PF^{NPMV[k]} = PF_{tt}^{NPMV[2^k-1]}$. So, by Theorem 4 and results of Köbler, Schöning, and Wagner [KSW87], we have, for every $m > k$, $P^{NP[m]} = P_{tt}^{NP[2^k-1]} \subseteq NP(2^k)$. Thus, BH $= NP(2^k)$. □

The following theorem is proved in a similar manner.

Theorem 9. *Let* $k \geq 1$. *If* $PF_{tt}^{NPMV[k+1]} = PF_{tt}^{NPMV[k]}$, *then* BH *collapses to its* $(k+1)$-*st level.*

Analogous to the theorems stated so far, the following theorems hold for reduction classes that make logarithmic many queries to partial functions in NPMV.

Theorem 10. *1.* $PF^{NPMV[\log]} = PF_{tt}^{NPMV}$.
2. $NPMV \circ PF^{NP[\log]} \subseteq NPMV \circ PF_{tt}^{NP}$.
3. $NPMV \circ PF_{tt}^{NP} \subseteq_c NPMV \circ PF^{NP[\log]}$.
4. $PF^{NPMV[\log]} \subseteq_c NPMV \circ PF^{NP[\log]}$.
5. $NPMV \circ PF^{\overline{NP}[\log]} \subseteq PF^{NPMV[\log]}$.

Theorem 11. $P^{NPMV[\log]} = P_{tt}^{NPMV} = P^{NP[\log]} = P_{tt}^{NP}$.

4 Nondeterministic Polynomial-Time Reductions

We define nondeterministic reductions between partial functions so that the access mechanism is identical to that for deterministic reductions. Namely, let f be a single-valued partial function and N be a polynomial-time nondeterministic oracle Turing machine. $N[f]$ denotes a multivalued partial function computed by N with oracle f in accordance with the following mechanism:

- when N asks about $y \in dom(f)$, f returns $f(y)$ and
- when N asks about $y \notin dom(f)$, f answers a special symbol $\perp$.

Let f and g be multivalued partial functions. We say that f is nondeterministic polynomial-time Turing reducible to g, denoted by $f \leq_T^{NP} g$ if there is a polynomial-time nondeterministic Turing machine N satisfying the following conditions: for every x and for every single-valued refinement g' of g,

− $x \in dom(f)$ if and only if $x \in dom(N[g'])$ and
− if $N[g']$ maps x to y, then f maps x to y.

In other words, $N[g']$ is a refinement of f.

Let $\mathcal{F}$ be a class of partial multivalued functions. NPMV$^{\mathcal{F}}$ denotes the class of partial multivalued functions that are $\leq_T^{NP}$-reducible to some $g \in \mathcal{F}$. NPMV$^{\mathcal{F}[k]}$ denotes the class of partial multivalued functions that are $\leq_T^{NP}$-reducible to some $g \in \mathcal{F}$ via a machine that makes k adaptive queries to its oracle.

NPMV$_{tt}^{\mathcal{F}}$ denotes the class of partial multivalued functions that are $\leq_T^{NP}$-reducible to some $g \in \mathcal{F}$ via a machine that makes nonadaptive queries to its oracle. NPMV$_{tt}^{\mathcal{F}[k]}$ denotes the class of partial multivalued functions that are $\leq_T^{NP}$-reducible to some $g \in \mathcal{F}$ via a machine that makes k nonadaptive queries to its oracle.

For a class of sets $\mathcal{C}$, we write NPMV$^{\mathcal{C}}$ to denote the class of multivalued partial functions that are computed by an nondeterministic Turing machine relative to an oracle in $\mathcal{C}$. NPMV$^{\mathcal{C}[k]}$, NPMV$_{tt}^{\mathcal{C}}$ and NPMV$_{tt}^{\mathcal{C}[k]}$ are defined similarly.

For $k \geq 1$, $\mathit{\Sigma}MV_k$ denotes $\underbrace{\text{NPMV}^{\cdot^{\cdot^{\text{NPMV}}}}}_{k}$.

Lemma 12. *For every $k \geq 1$, $\mathit{\Sigma}MV_k = \text{NPMV}^{\Sigma_{k-1}^p[1]}$ and for every $f \in \mathit{\Sigma}MV_k$, $dom(f) \in \Sigma_k^p$.*

This lemma yields the following theorem.

Theorem 13. *Let f be a partial multivalued function. For every $k \geq 1$, the following statements are equivalent:*

(i) *f is in $\mathit{\Sigma}MV_k$;*
(ii) *f is polynomially length-bounded, $dom(f) \in \Sigma_k^p$, and $graph(f) \in \Sigma_k^p$;*
(iii) *f is polynomially length-bounded and $graph(f) \in \Sigma_k^p$.*

Theorem 14. *For every $k \geq 1$, $\mathit{\Sigma}MV_{k+1} = \mathit{\Sigma}MV_k$ if and only if $\Sigma_{k+1}^p = \Sigma_k^p$.*

Thus, these classes form function analogues of the polynomial hierarchy, and, unless the polynomial hierarchy collapses, they form a proper hierarchy.

5   The Difference Hierarchy

Let $\mathcal{F}$ be a class of partial multivalued functions. A partial multivalued function f is in co$\mathcal{F}$ if there exist $g \in \mathcal{F}$ and a polynomial p such that for every x and y

− $f(x)$ maps to y if and only if $|y| \leq p(|x|)$ and $g(x)$ does not map to y.

Let $\mathcal{F}$ and $\mathcal{G}$ be two classes of partial multivalued functions. A partial multivalued function h is in $\mathcal{F} \wedge \mathcal{G}$ if there exist partial multivalued functions $f \in \mathcal{F}$ and $g \in \mathcal{G}$ such that for every x and y,

− $h(x)$ maps to y if and only if $f(x)$ maps to y and $g(x)$ maps to y.

A partial multivalued function h is in $\mathcal{F} \vee \mathcal{G}$ if there exist partial multivalued functions $f \in \mathcal{F}$ and $g \in \mathcal{G}$ such that for every x and y,

– $h(x)$ maps to y if and only if $f(x)$ maps to y or $g(x)$ maps to y.

$\mathcal{F} - \mathcal{G}$ denotes $\mathcal{F} \wedge \mathrm{co}\mathcal{G}$.

NPMV(k) is the class of partial multivalued functions defined in the following way:

1. NPMV(1) = NPMV, and
2. for $k \geq 2$, NPMV(k) = NPMV − NPMV($k - 1$).

Lemma 15. *For every $k \geq 1$, $f \in$ NPMV(k) if and only if f is polynomially length-bounded and $\mathrm{graph}(f) \in$ NP(k).*

This lemma is proved by induction. We use it to obtain the following theorem.

Theorem 16. *For every $k \geq 1$, NPMV($k+1$) = NPMV(k) if and only if NP($k+1$) = NP(k).*

Theorem 17. NP = co-NP *if and only if* NPMV $\subseteq$ coNPMV *if and only if* coNPMV $\subseteq$ NPMV.

A function f is said to be NPMV-low if $\mathrm{NPMV}^f = \mathrm{NPMV}$.

Theorem 18. *A function f is NPMV-low if and only if $f \in$ NPMV with $\mathrm{dom}(f) \in$ NP $\cap$ co-NP.*

Theorem 19. NPMV(2) $\subseteq_c \mathrm{PF}^{\mathrm{NPMV}}$ *if and only if* $\Sigma_2^p = \Delta_2^p$.

Theorem 20. $\mathrm{PF}^{\mathrm{NPMV}[k]} \subseteq_c \mathrm{NPMV}(2^{k+1} - 1)$.

By Theorem 16, the levels of the difference hierarchy of partial functions are distinct if and only if the same levels of the Boolean hierarchy are distinct. Yet, whereas the Boolean hierarchy resides entirely within P^{NP}, by Theorem 19, this is unlikely to be true of the difference hierarchy of partial functions.

6 Reduction classes to NPSV

In this section, we set down some results about reduction classes to NPSV. All of our results are corollaries of theorems that we already proved, and our interest is primarily in Corollaries 23 and 24 which demonstrate that bounded query hierarchies with oracles in NPSV do not collapse unless the Boolean hierarchy collapses.

Corollary 21. *For every $k \geq 1$, $\mathrm{P}^{\mathrm{NPSV}[k]} = \mathrm{P}^{\mathrm{NP}[k]}$.*

Corollary 22. *For every $k \geq 1$, $\mathrm{P}^{\mathrm{NPSV}[k]}_{tt} = \mathrm{P}^{\mathrm{NP}[k]}_{tt}$.*

Corollary 23. *If* $\mathrm{PF}_{tt}^{\mathrm{NPSV}[k+1]} = \mathrm{PF}_{tt}^{\mathrm{NPSV}[k]}$ *for some* $k \geq 1$, *then* BH *collapses to its* $(k+1)$-*st level.*

Corollary 24. *If* $\mathrm{PF}^{\mathrm{NPSV}[k+1]} = \mathrm{PF}^{\mathrm{NPSV}[k]}$ *for some* $k \geq 1$, *then* BH *collapses to its* 2^k-*th level.*

Recall from the Inroduction that it is not known whether *sat* belongs to $\mathrm{PF}^{\mathrm{NPSV}[k]}$ for any k. It is well known that *maxsat* is complete for $\mathrm{PF}^{\mathrm{NPMV}}$ [Kre88]. Thus, by Corollary 24, if, for any $k \geq 1$, $maxsat \in \mathrm{PF}^{\mathrm{NPSV}[k]}$, then the Boolean and polynomial hierarchies collapse.

References

[Bei88] R. Beigel. NP-hard sets are P-superterse unless R = NP. Technical Report 88-04, Department of Computer Science, The Johns Hopkins University, 1988.

[Bei91] R. Beigel. Bounded queries to SAT and the Boolean hierarchy. *Theor. Computer Science*, 84(2):199–223, 1991.

[CT92] Z. Chen and S. Toda. On the complexity of computing optimal solutions. Department of Computer Science and Information Mathematics, University of Electro-Communications, Chufo-shi, Tokyo 182, Japan, 1992.

[Kre88] M. Krentel. The complexity of optimization problems. *J. Computer Systems Sci.*, 36:490–509, 1988.

[KSW87] J. Köbler, U. Schöning, and K. Wagner. The difference and truth-table hierarchies for NP. *Theoretical Informatics and Applications (RAIRO)*, 21:419–435, 1987.

[NOS92] A. Naik, M. Ogiwara, and A. Selman. P-selective sets, and reducing search to decision vs. self-reducibility. manuscript, 1992.

[Sel92] A. Selman. A taxonomy of complexity classes of functions. *J. Comput. Systems Sci.*, 1992. In press.

[War92] H. Wareham. On the comptutational complexity of inferring evolutionary trees. Master's thesis, Department of Computer Science, Memorial University of Newfoundland, 1992.

[WT91] O. Watanabe and S. Toda. Structural analysis of the complexity of inverse functions. *Math. Systems Theory*, 1991. In Press.

Multicounter Automata with Sublogarithmic Reversal Bounds

Romain Gengler

Institut für Informatik I, Universität Bonn
Römerstrasse 164, D-5300 Bonn 1

Abstract. No two-way nondeterministic multicounter automaton has reversal cost lying between $O(1)$ and $o(\sqrt{\log})$ and no two-way deterministic multicounter automaton has reversal cost lying between $O(1)$ and $o(\log / \log\log)$. Reversals are counted not only on the counter tapes but also on the input tape.

Topic: Computational Complexity

1 Introduction

Reversal complexity is closely associated with space and time complexity. Reversal complexity of deterministic multitape Turing machines is polynomially associated with space complexity of Turing machines if the cost is at least logarithmic [CY87]. A similar result does not hold in the nondeterministic case since every recursively enumerable language can be accepted by a nondeterministic automaton with two pushdown tapes and reversal cost two [BB74]. Reversal complexity of multicounter automata is polynomially associated with time complexity of Turing machines if the cost is at least linear [Cha81, Cha88]. This result holds as well in the deterministic case as in the nondeterministic case. Thus the space and time hierarchies induce reversal hierarchies (for multitape Turing machines see [CY87], for multicounter automata see [Cha81]). It remains to investigate sublogarithmic and sublinear reversal costs respectively. Costs in $O(1)$ have been studied several times (see [Iba74], [Iba78], [GI81]). Chan noted that the costs 0, 1, log and id define distinct complexity classes of deterministic two-way multicounter automata. Duris and Galil refined this result by proving a dense hierarchy between log and id [DG82]. In this paper we prove that there is a gap between $O(1)$ and $\sqrt{\log}$ for two-way nondeterministic multicounter automata. Moreover no such machine has reversal cost in $o(\sqrt{\log})$ but not in $O(1)$. In the case of deterministic counter automata we can improve the upper boundary of the gap to $\log / \log\log$. In both cases we count the reversals on all tapes (the input tape included).

The essential idea in the paper is the following. We decompose the computation of the multi-counter automaton in parts called cycles and sweeps of periods. If we find a decomposition with dertain properties we count the number of occurrences of such periodical parts and call them the index of the decomposition. Then we describe the counter heights at the moments of reversal by an affine transformation of the index. We show an invariance property with respect to these transformations: every index (if large enough) can be modified (not to much) such that the transformation of both of the index and of its modification have the same sign $(-, 0, +)$. This sign equality guarantees that the corresponding modified computation is valuable, i.e. that a modified word is accepted although it is to be distinguished from the original word. A certain amount of formalism cannot be avoided.

2 Definitions

A *deterministic (nondeterministic) k-counter automaton*, for short $2DC^k$-automaton ($2NC^k$-automaton), is a deterministic (nondeterministic) Turing machine with a two-way read-only input tape and k counter tapes (for short *counters*). Let Q be the set of *states* and Σ the *input alphabet*. The instructions have the form $(q, a, c_1, \ldots, c_k, q', d_0, d_1, \ldots, d_k) \in Q \times \Sigma \times \{\square, \perp\}^k \times Q \times \{-1, 0, +1\}^{k+1}$ where q is the *source state*, a the *input symbol*, c_i the i-th *counter symbol* $(i = 1, \ldots, k)$, q' the *target state*, and d_i the *move* of the i-th head $(i = 0, \ldots, k)$ where head 0 is the input head. W.l.o.g. the instructions satisfy the condition $c_i = \perp \implies d_i = 1$ $(i = 1, \ldots, k)$.

An *instantaneous description (ID)* is a tuple $(q, w, \mu, h_1, \ldots, h_k) \in Q \times \Sigma^* \times \mathbb{N}^{k+1}$ where q is the *current state*, w the *input word*, μ the *position* of the input head, and h_i the *height* of the i-th counter $(i = 1, \ldots, k)$. Let $S = s_1, s_2, s_3, \ldots$ be a sequence of ID's and $\pi = b_1, b_2, b_3, \ldots$ a sequence of instructions such that b_i leads from s_i to s_{i+1} for $i = 1, 2, 3, \ldots$. Then we call S a *computation* and π an *(instruction) path* with respect to S. We call π a *w-path* if in addition S and π are finite, $s_1 = (q_0, w, 1, 0, \ldots, 0)$ and the last element of S is a halting ID with an accepting current state. A $(k+1)$-vector $D_i = (D_i^0, \ldots, D_i^k)$ is related to each instruction b_i in $\pi = (b_1, \ldots, b_t)$ where

$$D_i^\nu := \begin{cases} \text{headmove}_\nu(b_j) & \text{where } b_j \text{ is the last instruction before } b_i \\ & \text{with headmove}_\nu(b_j) \neq 0 \text{ if it exists} \\ 1 & \text{else} \end{cases}$$

We call D_i the *status* and components D_i^ν the *move directions* of the instruction b_i with respect to π. W.l.o.g. we assume that the source state of an instruction indicates its status. The instruction b_i is called a *reversal* with respect to π if the statuses of the instructions b_{i-1} and b_i are different or if b_i is the first instruction. It is called a *reversal* of the ν-th head if the move directions of the ν-th head are different. The reversal cost $r(\pi)$ of a w-path π is the number of reversals in π. $r_M(n)$ denotes the maximal reversal cost of any w-path of M for any $w \in L(M)$ with length $|w| = n$. We call r_M the reversal cost of M.

Given an integer $n \times m$-matrix $A = (a_{i,j})_{\substack{i=1\ldots,n \\ j=1,\ldots,m}}$ and an integer vector $C = (c_1, \ldots, c_n)$ we define $\|A\| := \max\{|a_{i,j}| \mid i = 1, \ldots, n, j = 1, \ldots, m\}$ and $\|C\| := \max\{c_1, \ldots, c_n\}$. By section of a sequence we understand a subsequence of consecutive entries.

3 Good Descriptions

In this section we decompose paths in cycles (on one cell), and periodic parts (on a section of the input), and unperiodical parts of the path. Such a decomposition is called a good description if it has certain properties. We will see, that for every accepted word there is a word w of the same length which has a good path.

Consider a $2NC^k$-automaton M, a word $w \in L(M)$ of length n, and a w-path π with r reversals. The reversals decompose the w-path π into r *phases* $\pi_1, \ldots, \pi_r$: The i-th phase π_i begins with the i-th reversal of π and contains no other reversal of π. A *cycle* σ of π is a section of π satisfying:

- σ contains no reversal,
- no instruction of σ moves the input head,
- the source state of the first instruction of σ and the target state of the last instruction of σ are equal,
- the source states of the instructions in σ are different.

Every cycle is contained in one phase. A cell scanned by the input head during a cycle is called a *cycle cell*. We denote the number of all possible cycles by e. It is a machine constant ($e \leq \psi^q$ where ψ is the number of distinct instructions and q the number of states of M). In the following let $z_0, \ldots, z_{e-1}$ be a fixed standard enumeration of all possible cycles.

We call $\overline{\pi} = ((u_0, v_1, u_1, \ldots, u_{s-1}, v_s, u_s), (j_1, \ldots, j_s))$ a *good description* of π ($s \in \mathbb{N}$) if

- $\pi = u_0 v_1^{j_1} u_1 \cdots u_{s-1} v_s^{j_s} u_s$,
- v_i is a cycle of π ($i = 1, \ldots, s$),
- u_i contains no cycle of π ($i = 0, \ldots, s$),
- v_i and v_j belong to different phases if $v_i = v_j$ and $i \neq j$.

We call the cycles v_i the *description cycles* of $\overline{\pi}$. Let

$$\beta_{\rho,\lambda} := \begin{cases} j_i & \text{if } v_i \text{ is the cycle } z_\lambda \text{ of the standard enumeration} \\ & \text{and belongs to the } \rho\text{-th phase} \\ 0 & \text{else} \end{cases}$$

We call $\beta := (\beta_{1,0}, \ldots, \beta_{1,e-1}, \beta_{2,0}, \ldots, \beta_{2,e-1} \ldots, \beta_{r,0}, \ldots, \beta_{r,e-1})$ the *cycle index* of the description $\overline{\pi}$. A w-path π is *good* if there is a good description of π. Note that a good w-path has at most er cycle cells.

Lemma 1. *Every w-path of a $2DC^k$-automaton M is good.*

Proof: If M enters a cycle M repeats this cycle until some counter gets empty (M is deterministic). The subsequent instruction is a reversal since empty counters are incremented immediately. Thus every w-path has a good description. □

The situation is different in the nondeterministic case since not every w-path is good. But:

Lemma 2. *Let M be a $2NC^k$-automaton and $w \in L(M)$. Then there exists a good w-path.*

Proof: Let π be an accepting w-path. We transform π in a path π' by applying the following procedure GATHER:

procedure CYCLE_GATHER
for every phase π_l in π *do* (* all instructions of π_l are unmarked *)
while there is an unmarked cycle in π_l (no instruction is marked) *do*
choose an unmarked cycle σ in π_l (let i be its beginning position);
if σ occurs in π_l in a marked form (all instructions are marked) at positions j
then remove σ at position i from π_l and reinsert a copy of σ before position j
in marked form
else mark all instructions in σ at positions i *fi endwhile endfor endproc*

In every phase this procedure gathers occurences of a cycle σ in one chain of copies of σ. The resulting path is a good w-path. □

The i-th *crossing sequence* ξ_i of π is the sequence of all target states of the instructions of π which force the input head to cross the boundary between cell $i-1$ and cell i $(i=0,\ldots,n+1)$. Note that ξ_0 and ξ_{n+1} are empty.

The *cell cut* C_i of cell i in π is the subsequence of π consisting of all instructions executed while the input head is scanning the i-th cell $(i=1,\ldots,n)$. Note that the cut of cell i determines the crossing sequences ξ_i (its *left crossing sequence*) and ξ_{i+1} (its *right crossing sequence*). $\Gamma := (C_1,\ldots,C_n)$ is the *cut sequence* of π.

A cell scanned by the input head during a reversal is called a *reversal cell*. A *segment* of Γ is a maximal section of the cut sequence Γ containing no reversal cell cut. Thus Γ consists of its segments and the reversal cell cuts. Note that there are at most r segments. We denote the maximal number of distinct cycle free cell cuts in one segment Γ by $d(\pi)$. We define $d_M(n)$ by:

$$d_M(n) := \max\{d(\pi) \mid \pi \text{ is a good } w\text{-path of } M \text{ for some } w \in \Sigma^n\} \qquad (n \in \mathbb{N})$$

The ρ-th *sweep* of a segment or a section of a segment is the (possibly empty) maximal section of phase π_ρ which is part of the segment or the section of the segment respectively. $(\rho = 1,\ldots,r)$. The sweep of a cell cut is called a *cell sweep*.

Lemma 3. *Let M be a k-counter automaton with reversal costs r.*
(i) *If M is nondeterministic $d_M(n)$ is bounded by $2^{cr(n)}$ for some constant $c \in \mathbb{N}$.*
(ii) *If M is deterministic $d_M(n)$ is bounded by some constant $c \in \mathbb{N}$.*

Proof: Let M be $2NC^k$-automaton with q states and ψ instructions, $w \in \Sigma^*$, π a good w-path of M, and Φ a segment of the sequence $\Gamma(\pi)$ of cell cuts.

ad (i): We consider only the cycle free cell cuts. The length of the cell sweeps is bounded by q (since there are no cycles). Thus the number of cell sweeps is bounded by ψ^q and the number of distinct cycle free cell cuts is bounded by $\psi^{q(r(n))}$ (since a cell cut contains at most $r(n)$ cell-sweeps). Thus $d_M(n) \leq 2^{\text{const}\cdot r(n)}$ for an appropriate constant.

ad (ii): We consider a segment Φ. Since M is deterministic M repeats any cycle until a counter gets empty thereby causing a reversal. Thus every cycle cell is a reversal cell. Since a segment contains no cell cut of a reversal cell, Φ contains only cycle free cell cuts. If the i-th sweep and the j-th sweep of segment Φ start on the same side and begin with instructions having same source states then they are equal since M is deterministic. Therefore the number s of distinct sweeps is bounded by $2q$. Let sweeps $i_1,\ldots,i_s$ be the s first distinct sweeps of Φ. If two cell cuts in Φ are different then they differ in their i-th cell sweep for some $i \in \{i_1, \ldots, i_s\}$. Thus the number of distinct cell cuts in segment Φ is bounded by $(\psi^q)^s \leq (\psi^q)^{2q}$ (since the length of sweeps of cycle free cells cuts is bounded by q their number is bounded by ψ^q). Therefore $d_M(n)$ is bounded by an appropriate machine constant. $\square$

A section $P = (C_i, \ldots, C_j)$ of the cut sequence Γ is called *(cut) period* of Γ if the following holds:

- P contains no reversal cell cut,
- P contains no cycle cell cut,
- the left crossing sequence of cell i and the right crossing sequence of cell j are equal,
- the left crossing sequences of the cells i up to j are different.

Every period is contained in one segment. The crossing sequences lying left and right of a period are called the *borders* of the period, the number of cell cuts in a period is called the *length* of the period. Note that the length of a period is less than $d_M(n)$ and that a sweep of a period contains at most $q \cdot d_M(n)$ instructions.

For a sequence γ of instructions of π we can consider the alterations made by the instructions of γ on the ν-th counter. We define: the *alteration* $\delta^\nu(\gamma)$ is the sum of the moves ($\in \{-1, 0, +1\}$) of the ν-th counter head during the instructions of γ. The *alteration* $\delta(P)$ *of a period* P with sweeps $\sigma_1, \ldots, \sigma_r$ (σ_i is the sweep during phase i) is the tuple $\left(\delta^1(\sigma_1), \ldots, \delta^k(\sigma_1), \ldots, \delta^1(\sigma_r), \ldots, \delta^k(\sigma_r)\right)$. Note that $\|\delta(P)\| \leq q \cdot d_M(n)$.

Two periods occuring in the same segment are called *similar* if they have same length, same alteration and same borders. The number of similarity classes in the set of periods occuring in one segment is bounded by

$$d_M(n) \cdot \left(2q \cdot d_M(n)\right)^{kr} \cdot d_M(n) \leq \left(2q \cdot d_M(n)\right)^{kr+2}$$

We call $\overline{\Gamma} = \left((U_0, P_1, U_1, \ldots, U_{g-1}, P_g, U_g), (\alpha_1, \ldots, \alpha_g)\right)$ a *good description* of the cut sequence Γ ($g \in \mathbb{N}$) if

- $\Gamma = U_0 P_1^{\alpha_1} U_1 \ldots U_{g-1} P_g^{\alpha_g} U_g$,
- P_i is period in Γ ($i = 1, \ldots, g$),
- U_i contains no period of Γ ($i = 0, \ldots, g$),
- P_i and P_j belong to different segments if $P_i = P_j$ and $i \neq j$.

$P_1, \ldots, P_g$ are called the *description periods*, $\alpha := (\alpha_1, \ldots, \alpha_g)$ the *period index*, g the *degree* (noted as $\deg(\overline{\Gamma})$), and $U_0, \ldots, U_g$ the *unperiodic parts* of $\overline{\Gamma}$. Note that the length of an unperiodic parts is bounded by $e \cdot r \cdot d_M(n)$.

A cut sequence is called *good* if it has a good description. A word w is called *good* if it has a good w-path with a good cut sequence.

Lemma 4. *Let M be a $2NC^k$-automaton, $w \in L(M)$ of length n, and π an accepting w-path with r reversals. Then there exists a word $w' \in L(M)$, an accepting w'-computation π' with sequence $\Gamma'(\pi')$ of cell cuts satisfying:*

(1) π' *and* $\Gamma'(\pi')$ *have good descriptions* $\overline{\pi'}$ *and* $\overline{\Gamma'}$

(2) $|w| = |w'|$, π *and* π' *have the same reversal cost*

(3a) $\deg(\overline{\Gamma'}) \leq r \cdot \left(d_M(n)\right)^{d_M(n)}$

(3b) $\deg(\overline{\Gamma'}) \le r \cdot \left(q \cdot d_M(n)\right)^{kr+2}$

Proof: By lemma 2 we can assume w.l.o.g. that π has a good description $\overline{\pi}$. Let Γ be the sequence of cell cuts of π. To get w', π', $\overline{\pi'}$, Γ' and $\overline{\Gamma'}$ satisfying (1), (2) and (3a) we apply the following procedure PERIOD_GATHER which is similar to the procedure CYCLE_GATHER.

procedure PERIOD_GATHER
for every segment Φ in Γ *do* (* all cell cuts of Φ are unmarked *)
while there is an unmarked period in Φ (no cell cut in P is marked) *do*
choose an unmarked period P in Φ (let i be its beginning position)
if P occurs in Φ in a marked form (all cell cuts are marked) at position j
then remove P at position i from Φ and reinsert a copy of P before position j in marked form
else mark all cell cuts in P at position i *fi endwhile endfor endproc*

In every segment this procedure gathers occurences of a period P in one chain of copies of P. (3a) is satisfied since at most $\left(d_M(n)\right)^{d_M(n)}$ distinct periods occur in one segment.

To satisfy (1),(2) and (3b) we modify the procedure PERIOD_GATHER to a procedure EXCHANGE:

procedure EXCHANGE
for every segment Φ in Γ *do* (* all cell cuts of Φ are unmarked *)
while there is an unmarked period in Φ (no cell cut in P is marked) *do*
choose an unmarked period P in Φ (let i be its beginning position)
if a similar period P' occurs in Φ in a marked form (all cell cuts are marked) at position j
then remove P at position i from Φ and reinsert a copy of P' before position j in marked form
else mark all cell cuts in P at position i *fi endwhile endfor endproc*

In every segment this procedure replaces occurences of a period P and occurences of the periods similar to P by copies of P. As similar periods have same border and alteration, the result is again a sequence of cell cuts. We call the corresponding path π'' and the corresponding input word w''. Now, w'', π'' Γ'' and $\overline{\Gamma''}$ satysfy the conditions (1), (2) and (3b):

ad 1,2: By construction ($|w| = |w''|$ since similar periods have same length).

ad 3b: In one segment there at most as many chains of identical periods as there are similarity classes in the set of periods occuring in this segment. This number is bounded by $\left(2q \cdot d_M(n)\right)^{kr+2}$. Note that the bound of (3a) is satisfied, too. □

4 The Induced Affine Mapping

In this section we will see that the counter heigths after the phases of a good path depend linearly on the cycle index and the period index of the good descriptions of the path and the cut sequence. We will give an affine mapping which relates these indices to the vector of counter heigths. In certain circumstances we can modify the indices slightly to get an accepting path with same number of reversals for another word. We will use this fact to prove our main result, the gap theorem for reversal cost below loglog and $\sqrt{(\log)}$ respectively.

Let $w \in L(M)$ a good word with a good w-path π and a good cut sequence Γ, r the number of reversals in π, $\overline{\pi} = ((u_0, v_1, u_1, \ldots, u_{g-1}, v_s, u_s), (j_1, \ldots, j_s))$ a good description of π with cycle index $\beta = (\beta_{1,0}, \ldots, \beta_{1,e-1}, \ldots, \beta_{r,0}, \ldots, \beta_{r,e-1})$ and $\overline{\Gamma} = ((U_0, P_1, U_1, \ldots, U_{g-1}, P_g, U_g), (\alpha_1, \ldots, \alpha_g))$ a good description of Γ with period index $\alpha = (\alpha_1, \ldots, \alpha_g)$. Let $\sigma_{\rho,j}$ be the ρ-th sweep of period P_i ($\rho = 1, \ldots, r, j = 1, \ldots, g$), z_i the i-th cycle in the standard enumeration ($i = 0, \ldots, e-1$), and ω_ρ the subsequence of instructions of the ρ-th phase π_ρ neither belonging to a description period P_i ($i = 1, \ldots, g$) nor to a description cycle v_i ($i = 1, \ldots, s$).

The alteration of a phase π_ρ on counter ν is the sum of the alterations of the periods in π_ρ, of the description cycles in π_ρ, and of the remaining instructions in π_ρ ($\nu = 1, \ldots, k, \rho = 1, \ldots, r$) i.e.

$$\delta^\nu(\pi_\rho) = \sum_{i=1}^{g} \delta^\nu(\sigma_{\rho,i}) \cdot \alpha_i + \sum_{j=0}^{e-1} \delta^\nu(z_j) \cdot \beta_{\rho,j} + \delta^\nu(\omega_\rho)$$

Let h_ρ^ν be the height of the ν-th counter after the ρ-th phase π_ρ. Since the height h_ρ^ν is the result of the alterations in the phases π_1 up to π_ρ we have

$$h_\rho^\nu = \sum_{l=1}^{\rho} \delta^\nu(\pi_l)$$

$$= \sum_{i=1}^{g} \sum_{l=1}^{\rho} \delta^\nu(\sigma_{\rho,i}) \cdot \alpha_i + \sum_{j=0}^{e-1} \sum_{l=1}^{\rho} \delta^\nu(z_j) \cdot \beta_{l,j} + \delta^\nu \sum_{l=1}^{\rho}(\omega_\rho)$$

$$= \sum_{i=1}^{g} a_{\rho,i} \cdot \alpha_i + \sum_{j=1}^{re} b_{\rho,i} \cdot \beta_j + c_\rho$$

where $a_{\rho,j} = \sum_{l=1}^{\rho} \delta^\nu(\sigma_{l,i})$ $b_{\rho,j} = \begin{cases} \delta(z_i) & \text{with } i = j \bmod e \text{ if } j < e \cdot \rho \\ 0 & \text{else} \end{cases}$ $c_\rho = \sum_{l=1}^{\rho} \delta^\nu(\omega_l)$

(Let $\beta_{i \cdot (j+1)} := \beta_{i,j}$. Then we can write $\beta = (\beta_1, \ldots, \beta_{re})$, too)

We combine these equations in matrix notation and we get ($\nu = 1, \ldots, k$):

$$H^\nu = A^\nu \cdot \alpha + B^\nu \cdot \beta + C^\nu$$

where

$$H^\nu := (h_1^\nu, \ldots, h_r^\nu) \quad A^\nu := \begin{pmatrix} a_{1,1}^\nu \cdots a_{1,g}^\nu \\ \vdots \quad \vdots \\ a_{r,1}^\nu \cdots a_{r,g}^\nu \end{pmatrix} \quad B^\nu := \begin{pmatrix} b_{1,1}^\nu \cdots b_{1,re}^\nu \\ \vdots \quad \vdots \\ b_{r,1}^\nu \cdots b_{r,re}^\nu \end{pmatrix} \quad C^\nu := (c_1^\nu, \ldots, c_r^\nu)$$

By putting together these equation systems we get

$$H^\nu = A \cdot \alpha + B^\nu \cdot \beta + C^\nu = [AB] \cdot \begin{bmatrix} \alpha \\ \beta \end{bmatrix} + C$$

where $\quad H := \begin{bmatrix} H^1 \\ \vdots \\ H^k \end{bmatrix} \quad A := \begin{bmatrix} A^1 \\ \vdots \\ A^k \end{bmatrix} \quad B := \begin{bmatrix} B^1 \\ \vdots \\ B^k \end{bmatrix} \quad C := \begin{bmatrix} C^1 \\ \vdots \\ C^k \end{bmatrix}$

Now, the heigths of the counters after the different phases are described by an affine mapping $\Theta(X) := [AB] \cdot X + C$ in dependance on the indices α and β. We call $\Theta: Z^{g+er} \longrightarrow Z^{rk}$ the affine mapping induced by $\overline{\pi}$ and $\overline{\Gamma}$.

Note that whenever a counter gets empty a reversal follows immediately. Therefore the height of a counter can be zero only at the end of a phase.

Assume that we modify the indices α and β to α' and β' such that a component of α' or β' is greater than zero if and only if the corresponding component of α or β is greater than zero as well. This means that we cut or insert cycles and sweeps of periods in π, but never all occurences of a cycle or a period, and only cycles or periods which occur already. Therefore we get a new instruction sequence π' having the same cycles and periods but working on a new input w'. The instructions corresponding to the reversals in π are reversals in π, too, and they decompose π' in r parts. It can be shown by induction that π' is a w'-path if counters get empty only at the ends of parts and if exactly the same counters get empty at the end of the corresponding phases of π. Again by induction it can be seen that the counter heigths after the parts of π' are given by $\Theta\left(\left[\begin{smallmatrix}\alpha'\\\beta'\end{smallmatrix}\right]\right)$. Therefore the last condition can be expressed by: a component of $\Theta\left(\left[\begin{smallmatrix}\alpha'\\\beta'\end{smallmatrix}\right]\right)$ is greater than zero if and only if the corresponding component of $\Theta\left(\left[\begin{smallmatrix}\alpha\\\beta\end{smallmatrix}\right]\right)$ is greater than zero as well. Note that both modified descriptions are good descriptions as well.

We call such a modification a sign invariant modification because it preserves the "sign" ($\in \{-, 0, +\}$) of the components of α or β and of the counter heigths after the phases. Therefore we define: $X = (x_1, \ldots, x_n)$ and $Y = (y_1, \ldots, y_n)$ in $\mathbf{Z}^n$ are called *sign equal* (we write $X \overset{\text{sig}}{=} Y$) if:

(i) $x_i \in \mathbb{N}$ iff $y_i \in \mathbb{N}$ $(i = 1, \ldots, n)$

(ii) $x_i = 0$ iff $y_i = 0$ $(i = 1, \ldots, n)$

Let Θ be an affine mapping from $\mathbb{N}^n$ into $\mathbf{Z}^n$, $K \in \mathbf{Z}^n$ and $\Delta \in \mathbf{Z}^n$. We say that Δ is a *sign invariant modification* of K with respect to Θ if:

(i) $K + \Delta \overset{\text{sig}}{=} K - \Delta \overset{\text{sig}}{=} K$

(ii) $\Theta(K + \Delta) \overset{\text{sig}}{=} \Theta(K - \Delta) \overset{\text{sig}}{=} \Theta(K)$

Remark: If Δ is a sign invariant modification of K with respect to Θ then $-\Delta$ is a sign invariant modification of K as well.

Using methods of linear algebra we can find conditions for the existence of sign invariant modifications of an affine mapping Θ. Moreover we can give a bound on the size of the modification.

Theorem 5 modification theorem. *Let* $\Theta : \mathbf{Z}^n \to \mathbf{Z}^m$ *be an affine mapping with* $\Theta(X) = A \cdot X + C$ *where* $A \in \mathbf{Z}^{m \times n}$ *and* $C \in \mathbf{Z}^m$. *Let* $K \in \mathbf{Z}^n$ *satisfy* $\|K\| \geq n \cdot \|C\| \cdot \|A\|^{2 \cdot \mathrm{rank} A + 2} \cdot \left((\mathrm{rank} A + 1)!\right)^2$.
Then there is a sign invariant modification $\Delta \in \mathbb{N}^n \setminus \{0\}$ *of* K *with respect to* Θ *satisfying* $\|\Delta\| \leq (\mathrm{rank} A + 1)!) \cdot \|A\|^{\mathrm{rank} A + 1}$.

Proof: see [Gen92]. □

Now we are ready to prove our main theorem.

Theorem 6 gap theorem.

(1) *If M is a two-way deterministic multicounter automaton with unbounded reversal cost r_M then $r_M \notin o(\log / \log\log)$.*

(2) *If M is a two-way nondeterministic multicounter automaton with unbounded reversal cost r_M then $r_M \notin o(\sqrt{\log})$.*

Proof: Assume r_M is unbounded. Let $r \in r_M(\mathbb{N})$. We arrange the period indices first according to the number of their components, then according to the sum of their components and finally lexicographically. We arrange the cycle indices analogously. Let n be the minimal length of accepted words having an accepting path with r reversals. According to lemma 4 there are good words having a good path with r reversals, too. We choose a good cut sequence description $\overline{\Gamma}$ with minimal period index α such that the corresponding path π has r reversals and an input w of length n. Then we choose a good description $\overline{\pi}$ of π with minimal cycle index β.

Let $\Theta : \mathbf{Z}^{g+er} \longrightarrow \mathbf{Z}^{rk}$ with $\Theta(X) := [AB] \cdot X + C$ be the affine mapping induced by $\overline{\pi}$ and $\overline{\Gamma}$.

Assume that there exists a sign invariant modification $\Delta \in \mathbf{Z}^{g+er} \setminus \{0\}$ of $\begin{bmatrix} \alpha \\ \beta \end{bmatrix}$ with respect to Θ. Then there is a path π_+ with description $\overline{\pi}_+$ and $\overline{\Gamma}_+$ and indices $\begin{bmatrix} \alpha_+ \\ \beta_+ \end{bmatrix} = \begin{bmatrix} \alpha \\ \beta \end{bmatrix} + \Delta$ which is an accepting path for a word w_+ with r reversals. We arrange triples consisting of an input length, a period index and a cycle index lexicographically. If $(|w_+|, \alpha_+, \beta_+)$ precedes $(|w|, \alpha, \beta)$, we have a contradiction to our minimal choice. Otherwise we use $\begin{bmatrix} \alpha_- \\ \beta_- \end{bmatrix} = \begin{bmatrix} \alpha \\ \beta \end{bmatrix} - \Delta$. Since $-\Delta$ is a sign invariant modification as well, we get again an accepted word w_- with $(|w_-|, \alpha_-, \beta_-)$ preceding $(|w|, \alpha, \beta)$ which is contradictory again. Note that one of the tuples $(|w_+|, \alpha_+, \beta_+)$, $(|w_-|, \alpha_-, \beta_-)$ precedes $(|w|, \alpha, \beta)$.

Thus we know that there is no sign invariant modification of $\begin{bmatrix} \alpha \\ \beta \end{bmatrix}$ with respect to Θ. According to the modification theorem it follows that

$$\left\| \begin{bmatrix} \alpha\beta \end{bmatrix} \right\| \leq (g+er) \cdot \|C\| \cdot \left\| [AB] \right\|^{2\mathrm{rank}[AB]+2} \cdot \left((\mathrm{rank}[AB]+1)! \right)^2 \qquad (\dagger)$$

On the other side we know about the input length $n := |w|$ that

$$|w| = n \leq g \cdot \|P\| \cdot \|\alpha\| + (g+1) \cdot \|U\| \qquad (\dagger\dagger)$$

where $\|P\|$ and $\|U\|$ denote the maximum length of the description periods P_i and of the unperiodic parts U_i of $\overline{\Gamma}$ respectively. Let $d := d_M(n)$. To reduce the numbers of parameters we note:

$$\mathrm{rank}[AB] \leq kr \leq const \cdot r \quad \text{(there are only } kr \text{ rows in } [AB])$$

$$\|P\| \leq d \leq const \cdot d \quad \text{(period lengths bounded by } d_M(n))$$

$$\|U\| \leq red \leq const \cdot dr$$

$$\|[AB]\| \leq qrd \leq const \cdot dr$$

(the alteration in a sweep of a period or in a cycle is bounded by $q \cdot \|P\|$)

$$\|C\| \leq r(g+1) \cdot \|U\| \leq const \cdot dr^2 \quad \text{(there are } g+1 \text{ unperiodic parts)}$$

By combining with ($\dagger$), ($\dagger\dagger$) and the fact " $\|\alpha\| < \|[\alpha\beta]\|$" we get:

$$n \leq g \cdot \|P\| \cdot (g+er) \cdot \|C\| \cdot \|[AB]\|^{2 \cdot \mathrm{rank}[AB]+2} \cdot \left((\mathrm{rank}[AB]+1)! \right)^2 + (g+1) \cdot \|U\|$$

$$\leq g^3 \cdot d^{const \cdot r} \cdot 2^{const \cdot r \cdot \log(r)} \qquad \text{for appropriate constants.} \qquad (\ddagger)$$

ad (1) *M is a deterministic automaton:*
In this case we can bound d by some constant (see lemma 3) and g by $g < rd^d$ (see lemma 4). Thus $g < const \cdot r$ for an appropriate constant. By substituting in ($\ddagger$) we get:

$$n \leq 2^{const \cdot r \cdot \log(r)}$$

or

$$\log(n) \leq const \cdot r(n) \cdot \log\big(r(n)\big)$$

hence

$$r(n) > const \cdot \log(n)/\log\log(n) \qquad (*)$$

Since r is unbounded $r(\mathbb{N})$ is infinite, and we can find infinitely many n such that $(*)$ is satified and therefore $r \notin o(\log/\log\log)$.

ad (2) *M is a nondeterministic automaton:*
In this case we can bound d by $2^{const \cdot r}$ (see lemma 3) and g by $g < r \cdot (qd)^{kr+k+3}$ (see lemma 4). Thus $g < d^{const \cdot r^2}$ for an appropriate constant. By substituting in ($\ddagger$) we get:

$$n \leq d^{const \cdot r} \cdot 2^{const \cdot r \cdot \log(r)} \leq 2^{const \cdot r^2}$$

or

$$\log(n) \leq const \cdot \big(r(n)\big)^2$$

hence

$$r(n) \geq const \cdot \sqrt{\log(n)} \qquad (**)$$

Since r is unbounded $r(\mathbb{N})$ is infinite, and we can find infinitely many n such that $(**)$ is satified and therefore $r \notin o(\sqrt{\log(n)})$. $\quad\square$

References

[BB74] B. S. Baker and R. V. Book. Reversal-bounded multipushdown machines. *Journal of Computer and Systems Sciences*, 8:315–322, 1974.

[Cha81] T.-H. Chan. Reversal complexity of counter machines. In *Proc 13. Ann. ACM Symp. on Theory of Computing*, pages 146–157, Milwaukee, Wisconsin, 1981.

[Cha88] T.-H. Chan. Pushdown automata with reversalbounded counters. *Journal of Computer and Systems Sciences*, 37:269–291, 1988.

[CY87] J. Chen and C. Yap. Reversal complexity. In *Proc. 2nd Structure in Complexity Theory*, pages 14–19, 1987.

[DG82] P. Duris and Z. Galil. On reversal-bounded counter machines and on pushdown automata with a bound on the size of the pushdown store. *Information and Control*, 54:217–227, 1982.

[Gen92] R. Gengler. Multicounter automata with sublogrithmic reversal bounds. research report 8585CS, Institut für Informatik der Universität Bonn, Römerstr. 164 D-W5300 Bonn 1, Germany, 1992.

[GI81] E. M. Gurari and O.H. Ibarra. The complexity of decision problems for finite-turn multicounter machines. *Journal of Computer and Systems Sciences*, 22:220–229, 1981.

[Iba74] O. H. Ibarra. A note on semilinear sets and bounded-reversal multihead pushdown automata. *Information Processing Letters*, 3:25–28, 1974.

[Iba78] O. H. Ibarra. Bounded multicounter machines and their decision problem. *J. Assoc. Comput. Mach.*, 25:116–133, 1978.

Structured Operational Semantics for Concurrency and Hierarchy

Andrew C. Uselton

uselton@cs.sunysb.edu

Abstract

This paper presents a language, CHA, and semantics for studying **Statecharts**-like drawings. CHA is a process algebra. CHA terms are interpreted as programs that extend *Mealy*-style finite automata with concurrent execution and hierarchical structure. Transitions in CHA can cross hierarchy boundaries, and it is this fact that makes giving a semantics to CHA (and to **Statecharts**) an interesting problem. In the terminology of [Mil89] all of the function symbols in CHA except the constants are *static combinators*.

CHA is given an operational semantics in the *Structural Operational Semantics* (SOS) style of Plotkin [Plo81]. The *Transition System Specification* (TSS) methodology of [GV88] is employed, and the TSS presented is in the *tyft/tyxt* format from that paper. Conformance to the *tyft/tyxt* format has several benefits for analyzing CHA, the most important of which is that bisimulation is a congruence in the Labeled Transition System (LTS) $\mathcal{C}$ of the language.

1 Introduction

Important considerations in developing a graphical design environment include allowing *hierarchy, concurrency*, and *modularity*. Hierarchy allows a design to be viewed abstractly with details of the implementation suppressed. Modularity allows a design to be viewed a piece at a time. Concurrency allows otherwise complex components to be viewed as simpler independent components working together.

The **Statecharts** graphical language includes both hierarchical and concurrent extensions to **Mealy** style *finite state automata* (FSA's)[Har87]. A simple example of such a design is the *coffee_machine* on the following the page.

The design is quite modular and one would expect that there would be a variety of implementations of the details of the *service* box that could be used interchangeably above. A problem arises, though, should an implementation include some transition that not only violates the specification, but also requires a transition from deep inside the inner box to some other component, as in the sketch beneath the example. It is not clear how to add this transition to the original drawing, or how such a modification would affect the modularity of the design. The **Statecharts** language allows just such transitions.

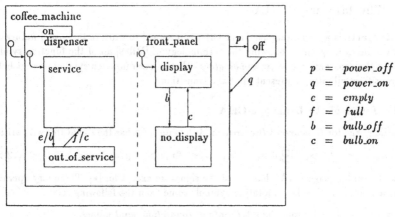

A transition violating the hierarchy:

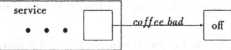

It is the goal of formal semantics to give a precise meaning to the terms of a language. Previous work on the semantics of **Statecharts** includes [HPSS87] in which single transitions called *micro-steps* are carefully defined, and then a state transition or *macro-step* is defined as a *maximal sequence* of micro-steps. In [HGdR88] a denotational approach is used to formulate a compositional semantics for **Statecharts** program fragments called *Unvollendetes*. Unvollendetes differ from **Statecharts** in that some of the transitions may be incompletely specified. Each term in the Unvollendetes language computes a function from histories of computation to histories of computation.

This paper presents an algebraic language CHA for describing a restricted version of **Statecharts**-like drawings. In CHA there are no labels on states and no interpretation is given to the labels on the transitions. The operators of the language allow the construction of automata with hierarchy and concurrency.

CHA is given an operational semantics in the *Structural Operational Semantics* (SOS) style of Plotkin [Plo81]. The *Transition System Specification* (TSS) methodology of [GV88] is employed, and the TSS presented is in the *tyft/tyxt* format from that paper. Conformance to the *tyft/tyxt* format has several benefits for analyzing CHA, the most important of which is that bisimulation is a congruence in the Labeled Transition System (LTS) $\mathcal{C}$ of the language.

The next section introduces the language CHA for *Concurrent Hierarchical Automata*. CHA is a textual representation of boxes and arrows joined sequentially, concurrently, or hierarchically. Section 3 presents an SOS rule system for deriving the behaviors of CHA terms, and gives some of the important properties of the language. The conclusion summarizes what CHA contributes to our understanding of concurrent and hierarchical automata and discusses the problems in, and approaches to, extending CHA to include the full range of **Statecharts** behaviors.

2 The language CHA

Statecharts is a visual language and CHA is designed to capture the visual nature of a Statecharts program. Following the terminology of [Mil89] all of the function symbols except the constants are *static combinators* - that is, each function symbol present before a transition will also be present after the transition.

2.1 Terms of the Language CHA

The language for *Concurrent Hierarchical Automata* CHA has the signature (with arities):

$$\Sigma_{CHA} = \{< \square, 0 >, < \boxed{*}, 0 >, < \overset{x}{\mapsto}, 1 >, < \overset{a}{\hookrightarrow}, 1 >, < [l/a], 1 >, < +, 2 >, < \times, 2 >\}$$

and the sublanguage CHA$^-$ has the above signature except for $\boxed{*}$. The unary operators are each annotated. The annotating symbols come from the following sets:

- In $\overset{a}{\hookrightarrow}$ the a is from the set *Points* of *connection point names*,

- In $\overset{x}{\mapsto}$ the x is from *Points* $\cup \overline{Points}$, where $\overline{Points} = \{\bar{a} : a \in Points\}$ is the set of connection point *co-names*.

- In $[l/a]$ the a is from *Points* and the l is from the set *Labels*, which is generated from a primitive set *Lab* and a composition operator. Thus $l \in Lab \Rightarrow l \in Labels$ and $l_1, l_2 \in Labels \Rightarrow l_1 \circ l_2 \in Labels$.

The language CHA (and CHA$^-$) is the set of terms over the signature Σ_{CHA} (respectively Σ_{CHA^-}).

$$f \in \Sigma_{CHA} \text{ and } \underline{M} \in CHA \Rightarrow f(\underline{M}) \in CHA$$

where $\underline{M}$ is a vector of terms whose length matches the arity of f (0, 1, or 2). Introducing the constant $\boxed{*}$ provides the ability to explicitly mark the *active* primitive boxes of a term. The term and drawing on the left are in a state in which the lower box is active, and on the right they are *concurrently* active in both the lower left and the upper right primitive boxes.

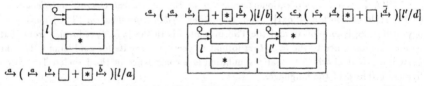

A term in CHA$^-$ will (in general) have many $\square$ primitives, each of which could have been written $\boxed{*}$ thereby making the term an element of CHA (but not CHA$^-$). Each choice of $\square$ versus $\boxed{*}$ is independent of the other choices, so for a term in CHA$^-$ with n $\square$ primitives there are 2^n terms in CHA.

Definition 2.1 *(Activation).* A term $M' \in$ CHA that is otherwise identical to a term $M \in$ CHA$^-$ except that some of the $\square$ primitives of M have been changed to $\boxed{*}$ primitives is called an *activation* of M. Any subterm of M' containing a $\boxed{*}$ is said to be *active* as is the term itself.

Definition 2.2 *(Program)*.   A CHA *program* M is an element of CHA$^-$, and the *execution* of M is a sequence of terms drawn from the set $Actv(M)$ of activations of M.

Definition 2.3 *(State)*.   The *state* of a CHA program M is given by the choice from amongst its activations.

The foregoing definitions capture the idea that the structure of a program (the picture one would draw of it) does not change during execution, and this is indeed how **Statecharts** behaves. The next section introduces the idea of transitions. It is one goal of the semantics to insure that all of the transitions occur between activations of the same program.

2.2   Transitions Between CHA Terms

A *transition* of a term $M \in$ CHA to another term $M' \in$ CHA reflects a change in the choice of which primitive boxes are active. The term M becomes M':

In doing so the term has "carried out" the action l while "going from M to M'." Symbolically:

$$M \xrightarrow{l} M'$$

The above *transition formula* may be thought of as an assertion about M, M', and their relationship. In particular M and M' differ only in the choice of $\square$ versus $\boxed{*}$. Furthermore, in the above example one should not be able to conclude $M' \xrightarrow{l'} M''$ for any l' and M'', since (referring to the diagram) there is no such arrow.

It is the purpose of a *Transition System Specification* (TSS) to give a formal (structural) operational semantics to a language and thereby provide a formal meaning capturing (or defining) the above intuition. A TSS Γ is a structure (Σ, Act, R) consisting of a signature Σ, a set of labels Act^1, and a set of inference rules R for proving transition formulas over the terms of the algebra.

A transition formula for terms M and $M' \in CHA$ is written:

$$M \xrightarrow{act} M'$$

and $act \in Act = Points \cup \overline{Points} \cup Labels \cup \{*,\_\} \cup Extra$. (The five portions of ACT are pairwise disjoint.) The ACT element $\_$ is meant to signify that no explicit symbol is present. Thus

$$M \longrightarrow M'$$

---

[1]The labels of a TSS should not be confused with the set *Labels*.

is a transition formula with the special *blank action*. The *ACT* element ∗ is also a special symbol whose use will be explained below. The set *Extra* is introduced for technical reasons, and the full version of the paper explains their use in greater detail.

Below is a diagram of the simple Coffee Machine translated from the Statecharts formalism into the sort of object modeled by CHA. There is a simple hierarchy of boxes in the diagram, and one box has a pair of concurrently executing automata within it.

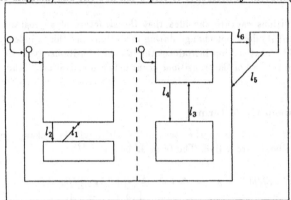

The language CHA ignores the labels on the boxes and does not give a detailed interpretation to the labels on the arrows, so in the inactive CHA term below the labels are simple objects:

$$M = \; \overset{c}{\mapsto} (\; \overset{c}{\mapsto} \; \overset{a}{\mapsto}$$
$$(\; \overset{c}{\mapsto} (\; \overset{c}{\mapsto} \; \overset{a}{\mapsto} \Box \overset{\bar{b}}{\mapsto} + \overset{b}{\mapsto} \Box \overset{\bar{a}}{\mapsto})[l_1/a][l_2/b] \times$$
$$\overset{c}{\mapsto} (\; \overset{c}{\mapsto} \; \overset{a}{\mapsto} \Box \overset{\bar{b}}{\mapsto} + \overset{b}{\mapsto} \Box \overset{\bar{a}}{\mapsto})[l_3/a][l_4/b]) \overset{\bar{b}}{\mapsto}$$
$$+ \overset{b}{\mapsto} \Box \overset{\bar{a}}{\mapsto})[l_5/a][l_6/b]$$

There are 2^5 possible activations of the coffee machine, however many (most) of them do not correspond to the sort of states one encounters in **Statecharts**. Specifically, there should never be a context $M_1 + M_2$ in which both M_1 and M_2 are active, and in every context $M_1 \times M_2$ both M_1 and M_2 should agree on being active or not. In the coffee machine, instead of 32 possible states, **Statecharts** allows only 5.

Definition 2.4 *(Active)*. The set *Active* is the set of terms from CHA that are active and formed as above.

- $\boxed{*} \in Active$,
- if $M \in Active$ and $f \in \{\; \overset{a}{\mapsto}, \; \overset{c}{\mapsto}, [l/a]\}$ then $f(M) \in Active$,
- if $M_1 \in Active$ and $M_2 \in \text{CHA}^-$ then $M_1 + M_2, M_2 + M_1 \in Active$, and
- if $M_1, M_2 \in Active$ then $M_1 \times M_2 \in Active$.

The next section introduces a TSS Γ_{CHA} for CHA. It will be the burden of this TSS to insure that all the provable transitions between terms in CHA involve only terms from $Active \cup \text{CHA}^-$. Thus every term that is not in $Active \cup \text{CHA}^-$ will be like the $\emptyset$ or *Null* processes from other Process Algebras. In this way we insure that CHA only exhibits Statecharts-like behaviours.

3   A Transition System Specification for CHA

A Transition System Specification (TSS) is a set of inference rules for proving transition formulas $M \xrightarrow{act} M'$ [GV88]. Each inference rule is presented in the form:

$$\frac{premise_1, ..., premise_n}{conclusion}$$

The conclusion and each premise is a transition formula $M \xrightarrow{act} M'$ in which M and M' may have free variables. Some rules will use the premises $inactive(M)$ and $\alpha \notin free(M)$. Though neither of these assertions looks like a transition formula, they are included for readability. $inactive(M)$ should be read as a transition formula $M \xrightarrow{ok} M'$ where ok and M' are of no consequence (they do not appear in the conclusion). $\alpha \notin free(M)$ should be viewed similarly. Since the details of justifying their use are a distraction to the main results of this paper, the formal justification of their use has been left out. Informally, the idea is to introduce a collection of additional rules that derive some special transition that amounts to the above assertions while not actually changing what the programs themselves do. It is with the set $Extra$ that this is accomplished.

3.1   Variables, Open Terms, and Substitution

The language CHA is extended to include some countable set of variables Var with typical elements $X, Y, Z, X_1, \ldots$ The new language $CHA(Var)$ is inductively defined as before except that terms may have variables:

$$X \in Var \Rightarrow X \in CHA(Var)$$

as well as

$$f \in \Sigma_{CHA}, \underline{M} \in CHA(Var) \Rightarrow f(\underline{M}) \in CHA(Var)$$

$CHA(Var)$ is the set of *open terms* over the signature Σ_{CHA} and the variables of Var. The *closed terms* of $CHA(Var)$ are the terms in CHA.

A substitution σ is a (partial) map from variables to terms

$$\sigma : Var \rightsquigarrow CHA(Var)$$

and may be extended to arbitrary terms $\sigma : CHA(Var) \rightsquigarrow CHA(Var)$ while a *closed substitution* maps terms to closed terms $\sigma_{closed} : CHA(Var) \rightsquigarrow CHA$.

The rules will sometimes mention action variables $\alpha, \beta, \ldots$ rather than particular actions, and a signature variable f rather than a particular signature element. Any *application* of a rule will require a particular choice of action and signature element as given by the side conditions as well as a closed substitution σ for the variables from Var. Thus each rule presented should be understood as shorthand for a collection of rules, one for each particular choice of allowable action and signature element.

In order to insure that all the provable transitions involve only terms from *active* and CHA$^-$ there will be occasion to check that one or the other of the terms being placed in a + context is not active. In those rules the premise $inactive(M)$ stands in place of a proof tree as described in the extended version of the paper[2]. Similarly, it will be convenient

[2]The extended version of this paper is available as a technical report - contact uselton@cs.sunysb.edu

to use $a \notin free(M)$ to mean that there is not a connection point name in a term that matches the one being used in the rule. That premise should also be seen as standing in for a proof sub-tree.

3.2 Rules

The following chart lists the rules for the TSS for CHA:

1 $$\dfrac{}{\square \xrightarrow{\;\cdot\;} \boxed{*}}$$	**2** $$\dfrac{}{\boxed{*} \longrightarrow \square}$$
3 $$\dfrac{X \xrightarrow{\;\cdot\;} Y}{\,_{\circ}X \xrightarrow{\;\alpha\;} \,_{\circ}Y}$$	**4** $$\dfrac{X \longrightarrow Y}{X\,_{\bar{\alpha}} \xrightarrow{\;\bar{\alpha}\;} Y\,_{\bar{\alpha}}}$$
5 $$\dfrac{X \xrightarrow{\;\alpha\;} Y}{\,_{\circ}X \xrightarrow{\;\cdot\;} \,_{\circ}Y}$$	**6** $$\dfrac{X_i \longrightarrow Y_i, \; inactive(X_j)}{+(\underline{X}) \longrightarrow +(\underline{X}[Y_i/X_i])}$$
7 $$\dfrac{\{X_i \xrightarrow{\;\cdot\;} Y_i\}}{f(\underline{X}) \xrightarrow{\;\cdot\;} f(\underline{Y})}$$ $f \in \{\,_{\circ}\!\!\rightarrow, \,_{\bar{\circ}}\!\!\rightarrow, [l/\alpha], \times\}$	**8** $$\dfrac{\{X_i \longrightarrow Y_i\}}{f(\underline{X}) \longrightarrow f(\underline{Y})}$$ $f \in \{\,_{\circ}\!\!\rightarrow, \,_{\bar{\circ}}\!\!\rightarrow, \,_{\circ}\!\!\rightarrow, [l/\alpha], \times\}$
9 $$\dfrac{X_i \xrightarrow{\;\alpha\;} Y_i, \; X_j \xrightarrow{\;\cdot\;} Y_j, \; \alpha \notin free(X_j)}{\times(\underline{X}) \xrightarrow{\;\alpha\;} \times(\underline{Y})}$$	**10** $$\dfrac{X_i \xrightarrow{\;\bar{\alpha}\;} Y_i, \; X_j \longrightarrow Y_j}{\times(\underline{X}) \xrightarrow{\;\bar{\alpha}\;} \times(\underline{Y})}$$
11 $$\dfrac{\{X_i \xrightarrow{\;\alpha\;} Y_i\}}{f(\underline{X}) \xrightarrow{\;\alpha\;} f(\underline{Y})}$$ for $f \in \{\,_{\bar{\beta}}\!\!\rightarrow, \times\}$ or if $\alpha \neq \beta$ then $f \in \{\,_{\beta}\!\!\rightarrow, \,_{\beta}\!\!\rightarrow, [l/\beta]\}$	**12** $$\dfrac{X \xrightarrow{\;\bar{\alpha}\;} Y}{f(\underline{X}) \xrightarrow{\;\bar{\alpha}\;} f(\underline{Y})}$$ if $f \in \{\,_{\beta}\!\!\rightarrow, \,_{\beta}\!\!\rightarrow\}$ or if $\alpha \neq \beta$ and $f \in \{\,_{\beta}\!\!\rightarrow, [l/\beta]\}$
13 $$\dfrac{X_i \xrightarrow{\;\alpha\;} Y_i, \; inactive(X_j)}{+(\underline{X}) \xrightarrow{\;\alpha\;} +(\underline{X}[Y_i/X_i])}$$	**14** $$\dfrac{X_i \xrightarrow{\;\bar{\alpha}\;} Y_i, \; inactive(X_j)}{+(\underline{X}) \xrightarrow{\;\bar{\alpha}\;} +(\underline{X}[Y_i/X_i])}$$
15 $$\dfrac{X \xrightarrow{\;\bar{\alpha}\;} Y, \; Y \xrightarrow{\;\alpha\;} Z}{X[l/\alpha] \xrightarrow{\;l\;} Z[l/\alpha]}$$	
16 $$\dfrac{\{X_i \xrightarrow{\;l_i\;} Y_i \mid i \in 1\ldots arity(f)\}}{f(\underline{X}) \xrightarrow{\;\circ,l_i\;} f(\underline{Y})}$$ $f \in \{\,_{\circ}\!\!\rightarrow, \,_{\bar{\circ}}\!\!\rightarrow, \,_{\circ}\!\!\rightarrow, [l'/\alpha], \times\}$	**17** $$\dfrac{X_i \xrightarrow{\;l\;} Y_i, \; inactive(X_j)}{+(\underline{X}) \xrightarrow{\;l\;} +(\underline{X}[Y_i/X_i])}$$

The "real" behaviors of a **Statecharts** program are those involving the actions from the set *Labels* as in the conclusion of rule 15. This rule provides the only way of inferring a new transition $\xrightarrow{\;l\;}$ for a term when that capability was not present in one of the subterms. Rules 16 and 17 show that the other operators besides $[l/a]$ neither add nor remove the $\xrightarrow{\;l\;}$ capability to a term. The premise $inactive(X_j)$ on the rule for $+$ is necessary, since an ill-formed term could otherwise be introduced. Notice that in the rule for $\times$ both subterms must be able to perform some step. The result is that the term in the conclusion performs the composite step. The following additional notes should help the reader in following how the rules determine the behaviors of a program:

- In the rules the set braces in the premise are to be understood to mean the i ranges over the integers from 1 to the arity of f, the indices i, j are to be read as "one and the other of $\{1, 2\}$," and the notation $(\underline{X}[Y_i/X_i])$ just means put Y_i in place of X_i in the vector $\underline{X}$.

- The intuition behind the transition formula $M \xrightarrow{a} M'$ is that M is inactive and has a (free) incoming connection point named a. Upon doing the a action the term M' is an active version of M and the active state of M' is the one with the connection point a. Rules 3, 9, 11, and 13 govern this capability.

- Default activation $\xrightarrow{\;\;}$ is a capability of any term which "knows how to become active" without any explicit mention of the actual state being activated. Rules 1, 5, and 7 govern this capability.

- The rules for $\xrightarrow{a}$ and $\xrightarrow{\;\;}$ interact to allow the inference, in inactive terms, of exactly how activation is carried out. Thus proving that $M \xrightarrow{a} M'$ not only means that M is inactive and M' well-formed and active, but also means that M' is the term in which the active state is exactly the one labeled by a.

- The $\xrightarrow{\bar{a}}$ operator provides the $\xrightarrow{\bar{a}}$ capability to a term. Rules 8, 10, 12, and 14 govern this capability.

- The base case for inferring how to become inactive is given by rule 2. Rules 4 and 6 support $\longrightarrow$ trivially:

4 Results

4.1 The Properties of Provable Formulas

Theorem 4.1. If $R_{CHA} \vdash M \xrightarrow{act} M'$ then M and M' are states of the same program.
Proof. This follows directly from the fact that all the function symbols (except the constants) are all static combinators. $\square$

Theorem 4.2. If $R_{CHA} \vdash M \xrightarrow{act} M'$ then

- if $act \in Labels$ then $M, M' \in Active$,

- if $act \in Points \cup \{*\}$ then $M \in CHA^-$ and $M' \in Active$, and

- if $act \in \overline{Points} \cup \{\_\}$ then $M \in Active$ and $M' \in CHA^-$.

Proof. (Sketch) Use a structural induction on terms with a case analysis on rules. The axioms support the above assertion and each rule preserves its truth. $\square$

Theorem 4.3 *(Removing extraneous operators).*
  Part 1 If $\xrightarrow{a}$ (or $[l/a]$) is applied to a term in which a (respectively $< a, \bar{a} >$) is not free then the term may be rewritten without the operator without changing its provable transition formulas.
  Part 2 If a (or $\bar{a}$) if free in a term M then the occurrences of $\xrightarrow{a}$ (resp. $\xrightarrow{\bar{a}}$) leading to that free occurrence may be removed without changing M's provable labeled transitions $M \xrightarrow{l}$.

Proof. Rules for $\xrightarrow{a}$ (and $[l/a]$) explicitly test for the $\xrightarrow{a}$ (and $\xrightarrow{\bar{a}}$) capabilities thus requiring the connection points to be free. Conversely, a free connection point will not contribute to any labeled transitions, since if it did it would be bound and not free. □

The function $clean(M)$ removes all the extraneous operators from M.

4.2 The Operational Semantics of CHA

A Labelled Transition System (LTS) is a structure $(S, A, \rightarrow)$ with S a set of states, A a set of actions, and the transition relation $\rightarrow \subseteq S \times A \times S$.

The LTS $\mathcal{C} = (CHA, Act, \rightarrow)$ is a labelled transition system with a state for each term of the language CHA. The actions set has all the actions from $Points \cup \overline{Points} \cup Labels \cup \{*, \_\} \cup Extra$. The transition relation consists of all provable transition formulas under R_{CHA}. Theorem 4.2 garantees us that no transition mentions ill-formed terms - those with multiple active terms in a $+$ context or some, but not all, active terms in a $\times$ context. Finally we get the following result:

Theorem 4.4. *Let $\mathcal{C}$ be the LTS for CHA resulting from the TSS Γ_{CHA}. Bisimulation $\overset{\longleftrightarrow}{\rightarrow}_{\Gamma_{CHA}}$ is a congruence in $\mathcal{C}$ for the function symbols of CHA.*
Proof. All of the rules are in the $tyft/tyxt$ format of [GV88][3], so it is sufficient to appeal to Theorem 5.10 of [GV88] where it is demonstrated that any TSS in $tyft/tyxt$ format (with non-cirular rules) will have bisimulation be a congruence. □

5 Conclusion

The language CHA gives a means of analyzing state machine drawings that incorporate hierarchy and concurrency. Since the rules of the TSS are in the $tyft/tyxt$ format there are some general properties that make the language useful. Foremost of these is that bisimulation is a congruence in $\mathcal{C}$. Thus a modular design strategy is possible. If two components are bisimilar then any context may use either component without changing the behavior of the composite machine.

5.1 Future Work

The original impetus for this research was the Statecharts graphical programming environment. In that system each label is interpreted as an input/output pair written as *event/action* as in a Mealy machine. A transition in that framework is possible only if the environment provides the *event*. Should that happen the program contributes the *action* to the environment allowing further *events* to be triggered. The events and actions are broadcast to the whole of the program, and a step of computation consists of a *maximal* collection of single steps. In order to make CHA consistent with the Mealy interpretation several modifications would have to be made. In order to get I/O behavior the proof system would have to be extended to include events as premises to the rule for proving $\xrightarrow{l}$ transitions. To get broadcast behavior the rule for $\times$ would have to be changed. In order to model the *maximal* steps idea there would need to be a negative premise in the

---

[3]The technical details of showing that proof trees for actions from *Extra* are in $tyft/tyxt$ format are in the extended version of the paper.

$\times$ rule, and the resulting TSS would have to be compared with the $ntyft/ntyxt$ format from [Gro89, BG90]. All of these considerations present interesting challenges, and the author is confident that in some form CHA will be able to handle all these modifications.

References

[BG90]   R. Bol and J. F. Groote. *The Meaning of Negative Premises in Transition System Specifications*. Technical Report CS-R8950, Centre for Mathematics and Computer Science, Amsterdam, The Netherlands, 1990.

[Gro89]   J. F. Groote. *Transition System Specifications with Negative Premises*. Technical Report CS-R8950, Centre for Mathematics and Computer Science, Amsterdam, The Netherlands, 1989. An extended abstract appeared in J.C.M. Baeten and J. W. Klop, editors, *Proceedings of Concur90*, LNCS 458, Amsterdam, 1990, Springer-Verlag.

[GV88]   J. F. Groote and F. W. Vaandrager. *Structured Operational Semantics and Bisimulation as a Congruence*. Technical Report CS-R8845, Centre for Mathematics and Computer Science, Amsterdam, The Netherlands, 1988. An extended abstract appeared in G. Ausiello, M. Dezani-Ciancaglini and S. Ronchi Del, editors, *Proceedings of ICALP 89*, LNCS 372, Stresa, 1990, Springer-Verlag.

[Har87]   D. Harel. Statecharts: a visual formalism for complex systems. In *Science of Computer Programing*, 1987.

[HGdR88] C. Huzing, R. Gerth, and W. P. de Roever. Modeling statecharts behavior in a fully abstract way. In *13th CAAP, Lecture notes in Computer Science 299*, Springer, Berlin, 1988.

[HPSS87] D. Harel, A. Pnueli, J. P. Schmidt, and R. Sherman. On the formal semantics of statecharts. In *Proc. 2nd IEEE Symposium on Logic in Computer Science*, 1987.

[Mil89]   R. Milner. *Communication and Concurrency*. Series in Computer Science, Prentice-Hall, 1989.

[Plo81]   G. D. Plotkin. *A Structural Approach To Operational Semantics*. Technical Report DAIMI FN-19, Computer Science Department, Aarhus University, 1981.

The Complexity of Verifying Functional Programs

Hardi Hungar

Computer Science Department
University Oldenburg
D-2900 Oldenburg, Germany
hardi.hungar@arbi.informatik.uni-oldenburg.de

Abstract. The set of finite interpretations in which a formula is valid is called the spectrum of the formula. For some program logics, the classes of spectra form complete subclasses of well known complexity classes. For various imperative and functional programming languages we know the complexity classes corresponding to the classes of spectra of partial correctness formulae. This means that for those formulae we know how hard it is to *decide* the sets of finite models.

For some imperative languages it has already been shown that *constructing formal proofs* for valid formulae is of the same order of complexity. In this paper we prove the same result, i.e. that proofs can be constructed efficiently, for functional languages where recursive functions of arbitrary finite type are allowed.

Since denotational semantics translates imperative programs into functional terms, the proof system for functional programs gives one for imperative programs as well. Choosing the right denotational semantics, we can show the effiency of the resulting verification method for Clarke's language L4.

1 Introduction

In analyzing the power of different logics, the notion of the *spectrum* of a formula has proved to be useful. If p is a formula over some first-order signature Σ, then $spec(p)$ is the set of those finite interpretations of Σ where p is valid. Collecting the spectra of all formulae of a logic we get a class of languages, the *spectrum class* of the logic.

Depending on the logic, this class may be related to some complexity class. In particular, the partial correctness logics of various programming languages can be characterized by appropriate complexity classes. Their spectrum classes form *complete subclasses* of well-known complexity classes. The term complete subclass means that any spectrum is accepted by some Turing machine within the given bounds (the spectrum class is a subclass) and that any problem of the complexity class can be reduced to some spectrum (complete).

For example, the spectrum class of (non)deterministic while-programs is characterized by (N)LOGSPACE, whereas $DTIME(\exp^k(O(\log n)))$ corresponds to the spectrum class of functional or procedural programs with type depth of functions or procedures limited by k.

This observation – that the complexity of *deciding* the spectra of partial correctness formulae can be fixed for various programming languages – leads to a new question related to proof systems for those logics, i.e. whether they are "good" in the sense that *constructing* formal proofs for valid formulae is a problem of the same complexity.

In [11] a partial answer has been given: For several imperative programming languages these complexities are the same. But functional programming languages have not been considered there. For functional languages, the assertion language and the proof system are quite different from those for imperative programs. E.g. a proof is not simply an annotation of the syntax tree of the program as it is the case for most imperative languages.

The functional languages we consider here are sublangauges of the finitely typed lambda calculus with recursion. A program is a function of first-order type (i.e. it maps a number of elements of ground type to another ground type element), but it may contain function definitions of higher type. The maximal type depth of a function occuring in a program gives the *level* of the program. Let L^k be the set of programs with maximal level k.

For those programs a partial correctness logic can be defined [5] which allows to specify programs much like imperative programs can be specified by usual partial correctness formulae. For each L^k, the spectral complexity is known (it is $DTIME(\exp^k(O(\log n)))$, see above). Moreover, the logic can be axiomatized: There is a sound and relatively complete (in the sense of [2]) proof system. Thus, for any formula and any finite interpretation where the formula is valid, there exists a formal proof of the formula from the first-order theory of the interpretation.

Hence it makes sense to ask whether proof construction for formulae involving L^k-programs is of the same degree of complexity as deciding them, i.e whether proof construction can be done efficiently. Our main theorem is the affirmative answer to this question.

Theorem 8. *For every $k \geq 1$ and every formula $t\,q$ with $t \in L^k$ there is a proof constructor working in time $\exp^k(O(\log |I|))$.*

A *proof constructor* is a Turing machine which, given the code of an interpretation as input, decides the validity of the formula and outputs (correctly) either that the formula is not valid or a formal proof for it.

This result means that constructing a proof is not unnecessarily hard. In other words: It implies that Hoare-style proof systems are adequate tools to prove the correctness of functional programs.

Then we go on to examine proof systems for imperative language which can be generated from the proof system for L^k. Goerdt [7] has extended the proof system for lambda-terms to the many-sorted case. Those many-sorted terms can express a set of semantic objects useful for giving a denotational semantics to imperative programs. For example, the meanings for programs from Clarke's language L4 [1] can be expressed in this way. And partial correctness formulae correspond to formulae of the logic for finitely typed lambda-terms. Thus, the proof system for lambda-terms gives a system for the verification of imperative languages (including L4) as well.

But do the generated proof systems allow efficient proof construction? We show that they do (for L4), provided that the denotational semantics is chosen carefully.

So Goerdt's system gives rise to an alternative proof system for L4 to the one from [4] which is equally good in terms of the complexity of proof construction.[1]

Related Work. Complexity questions related to program correctness have already been studied by many researchers. For example, Jones and Muchnik [12, 13] fixed the interpretation and derived complexities of correctness problems, measured in the size of the programs. Others, which is close to our approach, fixed formulae from program logics and derived complexities of the sets of finite models (of specific kind: Herbrand definability was an assumption in most cases). Harel and Peleg [10], Kfoury, Tiuryn and Urzyczyn [14, 18] and Goerdt [8] did so. In [11] those results were extended and applied to the question whether proof construction can be done efficiently for imperative languages.

Structure of the Paper. Section 2 contains definitions of the syntax and semantics of all involved languages and the proof system (complete for the treatment of lambda-terms). In Section 3 the key notions (spectrum of a formula, spectral complexitiy) are given. Section 4 contains the main result, Section 5 the application to L4.

2 Definitions

Finite Types. The set of *finite types* T is given by the production rules

$$\tau ::= \delta \mid \beta \mid (\tau \to \tau).$$

δ is the type of domain elements, β is the type for booleans. A type $(\tau_1 \to (\tau_2 \to (\ldots(\tau_n \to \tau_0)\ldots)))$ is abbreviated by $(\tau_1, \tau_2, \ldots, \tau_n, \tau_0)$.

The *level* of a type is inductively defined by:

$$\text{lev}(\delta) = \text{lev}(\beta) = 0, \quad \text{lev}(\tau \to \rho) = max(\text{lev}(\tau) + 1, \text{lev}(\rho)).$$

Thus, types of level 1 are of the form $(\tau_1, \tau_2, \ldots, \tau_n, \tau_0)$ with $\tau_i \in \{\delta, \beta\}$ and $n \geq 1$.

Any set D can be chosen to be the basis of a *type structure* $\{D^\tau \mid \tau \in T\}$. D^δ is the flat cpo with elements $D \cup \{\perp_\delta\}$, D^β is $\{tt, ff, \perp_\beta\}$ and $D^{\rho \to \tau}$ is the cpo of continuous functions from D^ρ to D^τ. Type structures will provide the semantic domains for the meanings of functional programs.

Signatures and Interpretations. A *signature* is a finite set of symbols for constants (of type δ), functions (of type $(\delta, \ldots, \delta)$) and relations (of type $(\delta, \ldots, \delta, \beta)$).

We assume that a signature contains at least one function symbol. If there is just one function symbol, which in addition is unary, we need at least one relation symbol. These restrictions save us from considering exceptional cases in definitions and results concerning the spectral complexity (cf. [10, 18]).

An *interpretation* of a signature consists of a *domain* D, which is simply a set, and an assignment of an object of appropriate type to each symbol (i.e. $I(c^\tau) \in D^\tau$), with the restriction that no constant must be interpreted by $\perp_\delta$ and functions and relations are strict extensions of total functions and relations. Thus, interpretations according to this definition can be thought of as usual first-order structures.

---

[1] The system from [4] has been specifically designed for L4. In [11] it has been shown to allow efficient proof construction. Giving a denotational semantics and using Goerdt's system for functional terms is a more flexible approach.

First-Order Logic. First-order formulae, which will be the basis for the assertion languages, are defined (almost) as usual: We fix infinite sets $Ivar = \{x, \ldots\}$ and $Bvar = \{b, \ldots\}$ of individual variables and boolean variables. *Terms* and *first-order formulae* are generated by the following production rules.

$$t ::= x \mid c^\delta \mid f^{(\delta, \ldots, \delta)}(t) \ldots (t)$$
$$p ::= b \mid \mathbf{true} \mid R^{(\delta, \ldots, \delta, \beta)}(t) \ldots (t) \mid t \simeq t \mid \neg p \mid (p \wedge p) \mid (\forall x.p) \mid (\forall b.p)$$

where x is a variable, b a boolean variable, c is a constant symbol and f and R are function resp. relation symbols of appropriate types.

Given an interpretation I and a valuation σ of $Ivar$ in I and $Bvar$ in $B = \{tt, ff\}$, every formula evaluates to either *true* or *false*. (Quantifiers range over I resp. B only, not including $\bot$.) We adopt the usual notion of validity ($I \models p$) and denote the theory of an interpretation by $Th(I)$. Note that the bottom elements which are added to the domains do not affect the semantics of first-order formulae.

Typed Terms and Programs. Next we introduce the sets T^τ of *applicative terms* of type τ. For every type τ let $Tvar^\tau$ be an infinite set of variables $\{y^\tau, \ldots\}$, all being pairwise disjoint (and disjoint to $Ivar$ and $Bvar$). Then

$$t^\tau \quad ::= \quad y^\tau \mid c^\tau \mid t^{(\rho \to \tau)}(t^\rho) \quad \text{(for all } \tau)$$
$$t^\delta \quad ::= \quad \mathbf{if} \ t^\beta \ \mathbf{then} \ t^\delta \ \mathbf{else} \ t^\delta$$
$$t^\beta \quad ::= \quad (t^\delta \simeq t^\delta) \mid (t^\beta \simeq t^\beta) \mid (t^\beta \wedge t^\beta) \mid \neg t^\beta \mid \mathbf{if} \ t^\beta \ \mathbf{then} \ t^\beta \ \mathbf{else} \ t^\beta$$
$$t^{\rho \to \tau} ::= \quad \lambda y^\rho.t^\tau$$

A valuation μ of $Tvar$ assigns to each typed variable an element of the appropriate I^τ. Other than a valuation σ of $Ivar \cup Bvar$, μ may assign $\bot$. The semantics of an applicative term $t \in T^\tau$, given a valuation μ, is an object in the cpo I^τ. We take standard call-by-name semantics. $\simeq$, $\wedge$ and $\neg$ are given their obvious strict meaning. if is strict only in its first component.

For our programming language we choose a notation similar to that in [14]. Alternatively, we could have taken one of the (equivalent) formalisms from [8].

The constituent parts of a program are *function definitions*. A function definition has the form

$$F^\tau \leftarrow \lambda y_1^{\tau_1} \ldots y_n^{\tau_n}.t^{\tau_0},$$

where $F^\tau, y_1^{\tau_1}, \ldots, y_n^{\tau_n}$ are variables, $\tau = (\tau_1, \ldots, \tau_n, \tau_0)$ and t^{τ_0} is an applicative term containing no λ. τ is the *type* of the function, F^τ is its *name*, the level of τ is its *level*, $y_i^{\tau_i}$ are its *parameters* and t^τ is its *body*.

A *program* is a set of function definitions with the following additional restrictions. No function may be defined twice. Within the body of a function the only variables which may occur are its parameters and names of other functions. The first function definition in a program is the main function. Its type has to be first-order.

L is the set of all programs. The *level* of a program is the maximum of the levels of its functions. L^k is the set of all programs of level k.

The semantics of a program

$$F_1 \leftarrow \lambda y_1.t_1, \ldots, F_n \leftarrow \lambda y_n.t_n$$

is the projection to the first component of the minimal fixpoint of

$$(d_1, \ldots, d_n) \mapsto (I[\lambda \mathbf{y_1}.t_1](\mu[d/\mathbf{F}]), \ldots, I[\lambda \mathbf{y_n}.t_n](\mu[d/\mathbf{F}]))$$

with arbitrary μ (arbitrary because programs are closed).

Program Logic. Assertions (taken from [5]) are typed formulae describing sets of typed objects. Their syntax and semantics is as follows.

$$q^\tau \quad ::= \quad (p)_x, \quad \text{for } p \text{ first-order and either } \tau = \delta,\ x \in Ivar \text{ or } \tau = \beta,\ x \in Bvar$$
$$q^{\rho \to \tau} ::= \quad (q^\rho, q^\tau) \mid q^{\rho \to \tau} \wedge q^{\rho \to \tau} \mid \forall x.q^{\rho \to \tau}$$

If σ is a valuation of $Ivar$ and $Bvar$ in I and B (note: $\sigma(x) \neq \bot$), then

$$I[(p)_x]\sigma = \{\, d \in I^\tau \mid d = \bot \text{ or } I, \sigma[d/x] \models p \,\}$$
$$I[(q^\tau, r^\rho)]\sigma = \{\, d \in I^{\tau \to \rho} \mid d(I[q^\tau]\sigma) \subset I[r^\rho]\sigma \,\}$$
$$I[q^\tau \wedge r^\tau]\sigma = I[q^\tau]\sigma \cap I[r^\tau]\sigma$$
$$I[\forall x.q^\tau]\sigma = \bigcap \{\, I[q^\tau]\sigma[d/x] \mid d \neq \bot \,\}$$

It is easy to see that each $I[q^\tau]\sigma$ is a downward closed subset of I^τ. Furthermore, it is closed w.r.t. limits of ascending chains [5]. The latter property is needed for the soundness of the fixpoint rule.

Formulae of the program logic are of the form

$$y_1^{\tau_1} q_1^{\tau_1}, \ldots, y_n^{\tau_n} q_n^{\tau_n} \; \to \; t^\tau q^\tau$$

where the $y_i^{\tau_i}$ are typed variables, $q_i^{\tau_i}$ and q^τ are assertions and t^τ is an applicative term or a program.

Semantically, the pairs $y_i^{\tau_i} q_i^{\tau_i}$ are assumptions. They are used to restrict valuations of the typed variables y_i to values satisfying the τ_i. Formally, if σ is a valuation of $Ivar \cup Bvar$ and μ a valuation of $Tvar$, a formula $f = y_1^{\tau_1} q_1^{\tau_1}, \ldots, y_n^{\tau_n} q_n^{\tau_n} \to t^\tau q^\tau$ is valid at σ and μ ($I, \sigma, \mu \models f$) iff

$$\mu(y_i) \in I[q_i]\sigma \text{ for } 1 \leq n \Rightarrow I[t]\mu \in I[q]\sigma.$$

It is valid in I ($I \models f$) iff it is valid for all σ and μ.

Proof System. The rules of the calculus (mostly quoted from [5]) are as follows.

Application Rule

$$\frac{A \to t(q, r) \quad B \to s\,q}{A \cup B \to t(s)\,r}$$

If Rule

$$\frac{A \to s(p_1)_b, \quad B \to t(p_2)_x, \quad C \to u(p_3)_x}{A \cup B \cup C \to \text{if } s \text{ then } t \text{ else } u\,((p_1[\text{true}/b] \wedge p_2) \vee (p_1[\neg\text{true}/b] \wedge p_3))_x}$$

Abstraction Rule

$$\frac{A, y\,q \to t\,r}{A \to \lambda y.t\,(q, r)}, \text{ if } y \text{ not in } A$$

Program Rule

$$\frac{F_1 q_1, \ldots, F_n q_n \to \lambda \mathbf{y_1}.t_1 q_1, \ \ldots, \ F_1 q_1, \ldots, F_n q_n \to \lambda \mathbf{yn}.t_n q_n}{F_1 \leftarrow \lambda \mathbf{y_1}.t_1, \ldots, F_n \leftarrow \lambda \mathbf{yn}.t_n \ q_1}$$

And Rule

$$\frac{A \to t\,q, \ B \to t\,r}{A \cup B \to t\,q \wedge r}$$

Quantifier Rule

$$\frac{A \to t\,q}{A \to t\,\forall x.q}, \ \text{if } x \text{ not free in } A$$

Implication Rule

$$\frac{A \to t\,q, \ impl(q,r)}{A \to t\,r}$$

Oracle Axiom

$$p, \ \text{for } p \in Th(I)$$

Assumption Introduction

$$A \to y\,q, \ \text{for } y\,q \in A$$

Signature Symbol Axiom (for a unary function symbol)

$$A \to ((false)_x, (false)_x) \wedge \forall z.((z \simeq x)_x, (f(z) \simeq x)_x)$$

The first conjunct of the last axiom expresses that the function is strict in its argument, the second conjunct describes the effect of the function when applied to ordinary elements. The discussion of *strongest assertions* in Section 4 will further explain its formulation.

$impl(q, r)$ in the Implication Rule is a first-order formula which is (syntactically) computed from q and r. If $impl(q, r)$ is valid in I, then $I[q]\sigma \subset I[r]\sigma$ for all σ. (in general, the converse is false.) The definition of $impl$ is as follows.

$$impl((p)_x, (p\prime)_x) = \forall x.p \to p\prime$$
$$impl(q^\tau, r^\tau) = impl_r(q^\tau, r^\tau), \ \text{if } lev(\tau) \geq 1$$
$$impl_r(q, r_1 \wedge r_2) = impl_r(q, r_1) \wedge impl_r(q, r_1)$$
$$impl_r(q, \forall x.r) = \forall x.impl_r(q, r) \text{ with } x \notin free(q)$$
$$impl_r(q, (r_1, r_2)) = \begin{cases} \forall x\prime.impl_l(q, ((r_1\prime \wedge x\prime \simeq x)_x, r_2)) & \text{if } r_1 = (r_1\prime)_x \text{ for some } x \\ impl_l(q, (r_1, r_2)) & \text{otherwise} \end{cases}$$
$$impl_l(q_1 \wedge q_2, r) = impl_l(q_1, r) \vee impl_l(q_2, r)$$
$$impl_l(\forall x.q, r) = \exists x.impl_l(q, r) \text{ where } x \notin free(r)$$
$$impl_l((q_1, q_2), r) = impl_l((q_1, q_2), (r_1, r_2))$$
$$= impl(r_1, q_1) \wedge impl(q_2, r_2)$$

The last equation of the definition of $impl$ corresponds to the well-known rule of consequence of proof systems for imperative languages.

From [5, 6] we get that these rules indeed are an axiomatization.

Theorem 1. *The proof system is sound and relatively complete for the program logic over* **L**.

Proof. The only rule which does not appear in Goerdt's system is the Program Rule. But if we replace the recursive function definitions by a (semantically equivalent) iterated fixpoint, the Program Rule can be shown to be a derived rule. On the other hand can all derivations for an iterated fixpoint be transformed into a derivation about mutually recursive function definitions. □

3 Spectra and Spectral Complexities

The notions *spectrum* of a formula and *spectral complexity* of a programming language, which were used in [11] for imperative programming languages, are meaningful also in the context of functional programming languages. They both are based on a simple encoding function Φ_Σ which codes finite interpretations of Σ by strings (essentially by giving tables for functions and relations). For any Σ, $|\Phi_\Sigma(I)|$ is polynomially related to $|I|$.

Definition 2. Let the *spectrum* of a first-order formula or a formula of the form $t\,q$ be the set of codes of finite interpretations where it is valid. The *spectrum class* of a programming language is the set of spectra of all formulae $t\,q$ with t in the language. I.e.:

$$spec(t\,q) = \{\Phi_\Sigma(I) \mid I \models t\,q\}, \; spec(L) = \{spec(t\,q) \mid t \in L\}.$$

Using a function Ψ_Σ which codes strings in finite interpretations of Σ (it is not an inverse to Φ_Σ), we are able to show *completeness* of spectrum classes.

Definition 3 [11]. The spectrum class S of a programming language is *complete* for a complexity class C if S is contained in C and every problem of C is reduced by $\Phi_\Sigma \circ \Psi_\Sigma$ to an element of S.

Since $\Phi_\Sigma \circ \Psi_\Sigma$ is log-space computable, completeness characterizes how hard it is to decide spectra of formulae, as the following proposition illustrates.

Proposition 4 [11]. *If the spectrum class of a programming language L is complete for a complexity class, then for every problem P of the complexity class there is a formula $t\,q$ with $t \in L$ s.t. P is log-space reducible to the spectrum of $t\,q$.*

In [8] complexity results (extending earlier results from [14]) for $\mathbf{L}^k$ were established which are very close to our notion of spectral complexity. They relate $\mathbf{L}^k$ to $DTIME(\exp^k(O(\log|I|)))$. Taking those proofs as a basis, the spectral complexity of $\mathbf{L}^k$ can be derived. We defer the proof to the full version of the paper.

Theorem 5. *The spectral complexity of $\mathbf{L}^k$ is $DTIME(\exp^k(O(\log|I|)))$.*

The spectral complexity of $\mathbf{L}^k$ will be contrasted with the complexity of proof construction.

Definition 6. A *proof constructor* for a formula is a Turing machine which, given the code of a finite interpretation as input, decides the validity of the formula and outputs correctly either that the formula is not valid or a formal proof for the formula from $Th(I)$.

If for every formula from some logic there is a proof constructor in some complexity class C, it is said that proof construction is of complexity at most C.

4 Efficient Proof Construction in Finite Interpretations

If t is an applicative term without free variables or a program, a *strongest assertion* for t in I [5] is an assertion q s.t. for all σ, $I[\![q]\!]\sigma$ consists of all elements in I^τ which are less or equal to the semantics of t. Then q is the strongest assertion s.t. $t\,q$ is valid. Strongest assertions play an important role in the relative completeness proof of [6] and will be important for our proof constructing procedure.

For a term of first-order type one would expect a strongest assumption to look like

$$\forall x_1.((x \simeq x_1)_x(\ldots \forall x_n.((x \simeq x_n)_x, (p(x_1, \ldots, x_n, x))_x)\ldots)),$$

where $p(x_1, \ldots, x_n, x)$ expresses the output in terms of the input. However, since $\forall$ ranges over proper values only, subassertions of the form $\wedge((false)_x(\ldots))$ have to be inserted at appropriate places to include $\perp$ as argument.

When constructing proofs we will have to compute such strongest assertions. We will first compute (a representation of) the semantics of the term and afterwards the formulae $p(x_1, \ldots, x_n, x)$. These formulae will be constructed with the same technique as in [11].

For closed terms $t^{\tau \to \rho}$ of higher type strongest assertions are as follows. If the level of τ is 0 they are very similar to the assertions above:

$$(\forall x_1.((x \simeq x_1)_x, q_1^\rho)) \wedge ((false)_x, q_2^\rho).$$

There, q_1 is an assertion with free variable x_1.

If τ is of higher type, they are conjunctions of formulae $(q_i^\tau, r_{q_i}^\rho)$, where the q_i vary over all strongest assertion for the argument type.[2]

This roughly explains how strongest assertions for programs and *closed* terms look like and how they can be constructed once the semantics of the term or program is known.

But in the derivation, intermediate correctness formulae will involve terms with *free variables*. For a term t^τ with free variables $y_1^{\tau_1}, \ldots, y_n^{\tau_n}$, a strongest assertion depends on a set of strongest assertions for the y_i: If $q_1^{\tau_1}, \ldots, q_n^{\tau_n}$ are strongest assertions for closed terms of types $\tau_1, \ldots, \tau_n$, q^τ is a strongest assertion for t^τ *relative to the assumptions* if it is (semantically) the strongest assertion s.t.

$$y_1^{\tau_1}\, q_1^{\tau_1}, \ldots, y_n^{\tau_n}\, q_n^{\tau_n} \;\to\; t^\tau\, q^\tau$$

is valid in I. Again, for those τ_i of type level 0, q_i just introduces a free variable.

---

[2] Types of level 0 have to be treated differently, since not every element need to be denotable by a constant term.

Those relative assertions can be constructed in a way similar to the one sketched above. Note however that they may contain free variables which are related to typed variables in the assumptions.

For us it is important that we can construct all those formulae within the given complexity bounds. In the following, n-exponential means less or equal to $\exp^n(pol(|I|))$ for some polynomial pol.

Lemma 7. (a) *Let t^τ be a term with no free variables or a program. Let $k \geq 1$ be the level of its type. Then there exists a strongest assertion for t^τ whose length is $(k-1)$-exponential. It can be computed in $(m-1)$-exponential time, if m is the highest occurring type level.*

(b) *Let t^τ be a term with free typed variables $y_1^{\tau_1}, \ldots, y_n^{\tau_n}$. Let k be the highest type level occurring. If the level τ_i is at least 1, let a representation of a program- or term-definable element $d_i \in I^{\tau_i}$ be given. Otherwise, let $q_i^{\tau_i}$ be of the form $(x_i \simeq x)_x$ or $(false)_x$.*

Then we can construct assertions q^τ and $q_i^{\tau_i}$ in $(k-1)$-exponential time s.t. for $\mathrm{lev}(\tau_i) \geq 1$, $q_i^{\tau_i}$ is a strongest assertion for $d_i^{\tau_i}$, and q^τ is a strongest assertion for t^τ relative to the given assumptions.

(c) *Let q_1^τ and q_2^τ be two assertions (of the same type τ). Then $|Impl(q_1, q_2)|$ is bounded by a polynomial in $|q_1|$ and $|q_2|$ and can be computed in according time.*

Proof. For first-order types we proceed as in [11]. Strongest assertion can be constructed in polynomial time, which gives (a) and (b) for first-order types.

For types $\rho \to \tau$ with $\mathrm{lev}(\rho) \geq 1$ the formula q is a conjunction with $|I^\rho|$ (which is, according to [8], $(\mathrm{lev}(\rho))$-exponential) conjuncts (r_1^ρ, r_2^τ). If $\mathrm{lev}(\rho) \geq \mathrm{lev}(\tau)$, then its length is $\mathrm{lev}(\rho)$-exponential, otherwise $(\mathrm{lev}(\tau)-1)$-exponential.

For types $\rho \to \tau$ with $\mathrm{lev}(\rho) = 0$ (and $\mathrm{lev}(\tau) > 1$), q is an assertion of $(\mathrm{lev}(\tau)-1)$-exponential length constructed from two assertions of type τ with a free variable for the additional parameter.

Since the computation of the assertions from a semantic description is simple, (a) and (b) follow.

To get (c), we note that $Impl(q_1, q_2)$ is essentially a formula made up from all pairs of atomic subassertions of q_1 and q_2. Therefore, $|Impl(q_1, q_2)|$ is bounded by $c \times |q_1| \times |q_2|$ for some constant c as an induction shows. Again, the time needed to construct it is dominated by the length of the formula. $\square$

In short this lemma says that within the given time bounds we can compute all formulae which we need to construct the proof. This allows us to prove our main theorem.

Theorem 8. *For every $k \geq 1$ and every $t q$ with $t \in \mathbf{L}^k$ there is a proof constructor of complexity $DTIME(\exp^k(O(\log |I|)))$.*

Proof. By analyzing the structure of the derivations to be constructed (bearing in mind the form of the strongest assertions), the number of rule applications can be computed to be at most $(k-1)$-exponential for a program from $\mathbf{L}^k$. Lemma 7 tells us that all assertions to be filled in can be computed in $(k-1)$-exponential time from representations of the semantics of the objects. And representations of the semantics can be computed efficiently as in the proof of Theorem 5. $\square$

5 Proving L4-Programs Correct

The language of finitely typed lambda-terms is rather powerful. As a denotational semantics is a translation of programs into lambda-terms, it is natural to ask: which programming languages can be translated into finitely typed terms? For those terms, we have the proof system from Section 2. And if we can translate not only the programs but also correctness formula (into the logic for lambda-terms), we can use the proof system to verify them.

This idea has been applied by Goerdt in [7] to indicate how a proof system for Clarke's language L4 can be derived. L4 is a very powerful imperative programming language. Just as L, it can be split into an infinite hierarchie of sublanguages $L4^k$. For each k, the spectral complexity of $L4^k$ is the same as the one of L^k.

Goerdt claims that by such translations a major part of Hoare logics can be unified. In view of our considerations, additionally the question arises whether efficiency might be lost in the process. The following investigations show that this does not happen if the denotational semantics is chosen carefully.

For a precise definition of the language L4, we refer the reader to [4] (or [11]). In short, it is an ALGOL-like programming language. Input and output is handled by free individual variables. There are also declarations of individual variables and of procedures. Procedures are finitely typed and (very important to make spectra decidable) do not refer to nonlocal (individual) variables.

To translate L4-programs into lambda-terms, we need two new base types in the typed lambda calculus: A type $vidf$ consisting of all individual variables occuring in the program under investigation and a finite set loc of *locations* ($|loc|$ should equal the number of different individual variables of the program). Then we need a type env of *environments* which map $vidf$ to loc and a type st for *storages* which assign domain elements to locations. Both env and st consist of total functions only. Signatures for the translated programs will include a constant $empty$ (of type env) and functions $addvar$ (of type $(vidf, loc, env, env)$, which extends an environment), $firstfree$ (of type (env, loc), which gives an unused location) and $update$ (of type (loc, st, δ, st), which updates the store). The proof system can be extended to cope with this enlarged set of lambda-terms as well, cf. [7].

We have to define the translation function Λ from L4 to L in such a way that $\Lambda(L4^k) \subseteq L^k$. For this purpose, a denotational semantics like the one in [17] is not adequate. There, a procedure of type τ would cause a term of type $\tau \rightarrow \tau$ to occur, the latter term representing the semantics of the body of the declaration as a function of the semantics of the procedure. Note that $lev(\tau \rightarrow \tau) = lev(\tau) + 1$. Speaking in terms of computing the semantics of a program, one would have to determine for all possible procedure meanings the meaning of the procedure body. But one only needs the least fixpoint of the body meaning, and to compute it, exponentially less procedure meanings (i.e. $\log(|D^\tau|)$) have to be considered.

We avoid this increase of type depth by translating into the language from Section 2 where function bodies are *not* explicitly functions of the function identifier.[3]

A program will be translated into an object of type (env, st, st). Some of the

---

[3] Also in [7], explicit functions were used.

most important clauses of the definition of Λ are as follows.

$$\Lambda(\{p_1\}\,\pi\,\{p_2\}) = (\Lambda\,\pi)\,senv\,((p_1[(s\,(senv\,x_1))/x_1,\ldots,(s\,(senv\,x_n))/x_n]),$$
$$(p_2[(s\,(senv\,x_1))/x_1,\ldots,(s\,(senv\,x_n))/x_n]),)$$

$$\Lambda(x := t)\,e\,s = update\,(e\,x)\,s\,((\Lambda\,t)\,e\,s)$$

$$\Lambda(\text{var }x;\pi)\,e\,s = update\,(e\,x)$$
$$((\Lambda\,\pi)\,(addvar\,x\,(firstfree\,e))\,(update\,(firstfree\,e)\,s\,c))$$
$$(s\,(e\,x))$$

$$\Lambda(g(x,h))\,e\,s = g\,(e\,x)\,h\,s$$

$$\Lambda(\text{proc }g(x,h) \leftarrow \pi) = g \leftarrow \lambda l : loc, h : loc \rightarrow st \rightarrow st.\,(\Lambda\,\pi)\,(addvar\,x\,empty)$$

In the above, $senv$ is a start environment (built up from $empty$ using $firstfree$), c is a constant to initialize local variables and h is a procedure with one variable parameter.

Formally, the translation as sketched above increases the level of the program: $lev(env, st, st) = 2$. But $|(env, st, st)|$ is only 1-exponential in $|I|$, as if it were a first-order type. So this increase of the type level is not harmful.

6 Conclusion

Let us end with a discussion of implications, limitations and possible extensions of our results.

They seem to indicate that the use of higher-order functions results in programs whose correctness problems are too hard to handle: We can certainly not cope with problems of exponential or double exponential time complexity. But to look at it this way is an oversimplification. We have not proved that the spectrum of every assertion $t\,q$ with $t \in \mathbf{L}^k \setminus \mathbf{L}^{k-1}$ is hard for $(k-1)$-exponential time. We have proved this as a worst case complexity only.

In practice, correctness formulae might be much easier to check and easier to prove than with our procedures which work for all programs. Certainly some nice formulae have nice, short correctness proofs. But to find such classes of programs will be very difficult. The only class which we can determine is $\mathbf{L}^1$.

That we were able to show the effiency (even w.r.t. a very rough measure) of proof constructing procedures indicates that for any class of programs with a feasible correctness problem, proof construction is feasible, too. The results for L4 further substantiate this hope.

On the other hand, our results are limited in another respect. Specifying a finite interpretation by giving tables for functions and relations (as we did) is a very natural thing to do. Note that we have exploited the fact that the number of elements of the interpretation and the length of its specification are polynomially related. But there are other natural ways to specify (finite) interpretations where this does not hold. For example, take first-order formulae to define them. There are interpretations with $Ack(n,n)$ (the well-known Ackermann function) elements and a first-order specification of length $O(n)$. In view of this it seems very likely that deciding the validity of correctness formulae is not of elementary recursive time complexity (in the length of the first-order specification), although the spectral complexity of first-order logic is at most LOGSPACE. What proof constructing procedures would look like in such a framework is a question which is hard to answer.

Another question which should be easier to answer is the following. Can Goerdt's system be used to derive a proof system (with efficient proof constructor, of course) for L4-like programs where procedures are allowed to *read* (not write) nonlocal variables? According to [15], the spectra of these programs are decidable. Thus an axiomatization might exist, but no one has been given up to now.

References

1. Clarke, E. M. *Programming languages for which it is impossible to obtain good Hoare axiom systems*, JACM 26 (1979) 129–147.
2. Cook, S. A. *Soundness and completeness of an axiom system for program verification*, SIAM J. Comp. 7 (1978) 70–90.
3. Clarke, E. M., German, S. M. and Halpern, J. Y. *Effective axiomatizations of Hoare logics*, JACM 30 (1983) 612–636.
4. German, S. M., Clarke, E. M. and Halpern, J. Y. *Reasoning about procedures as parameters in the language L4*, Inf. and Comp. 83 (1989) 265–359. (Earlier version: 1st LiCS (1986) 11–25)
5. Goerdt, A. *A Hoare calculus for functions defined by recursion on higher types*, In: Proc. Logics of Programs 1985, LNCS 193, 106–117.
6. Goerdt, A. *Hoare calculi for higher type control structures and their completeness in the sense of Cook*, MFCS 88, LNCS 324 (1988) 329–338.
7. Goerdt, A. *Hoare logic for lambda-terms as basis of Hoare logic for imperative languages*, Proc. 2nd LiCS (1987) 293–299.
8. Goerdt, A. *Characterizing complexity classes by general recursive definitions in higher types*, in: E. Börger and H. Kleine-Büning, CSL '88, Proceedings, LNCS 385 (1988).
9. Grabowski, M. und Hungar, H. *On the existence of effective Hoare logics*, Proc. 3rd LiCS (1988) 428–435.
10. Harel, D. and Peleg, D. *On static logics, dynamic logics, and complexity classes*, Inf. and Contr. 60 (1984) 86–102.
11. Hungar, H. *Complexity of proving program correctness*, Proc. Theoretical Aspects of Computer Software 1991, LNCS 526, 459–474.
12. Jones, N. D. and Muchnik, S. S. *Even simple programs are hard to analyze*, JACM 24 (1977) 338–350.
13. Jones, N. D. and Muchnik, S. S. *The complexity of finite memory programs with recursion*, JACM 25 (1978) 312–321.
14. Kfoury, A. J., Tiuryn, J. and Urzyczyn, P. *The hierarchie of finitely typed functions*, 2nd LiCS (1987) 225–235.
15. Langmaack, H. *On correct procedure parameter transmission in higher programming languages*, Acta Inf. 2 (1973) 110–142.
16. Olderog, E.-R. *A characterization of Hoare's logic for programs with PASCAL-like procedures*, 15th SToC (1983) 320–329.
17. Plotkin, G. D. *LCF considered as a programming language*, TCS 5 (1977) 223–255.
18. Tiuryn, J. and Urzyczyn, P. *Some relationships between logics of programs and complexity theory*, TCS 60 (1988) 83–108. (Earlier version: 24th FoCS (1983) 180–184)

Towards the Formal Design of Self-Stabilizing Distributed Algorithms

P.J.A. Lentfert and S.D. Swierstra

Department of Computer Science, Utrecht University, P.O. Box 80.089, 3508 TB Utrecht, The Netherlands.

Abstract. This article introduces two new logical operators in UNITY. These operators are used to present a general scheme to specify the problem a self-stabilizing algorithm is assumed to solve. Furthermore, a general solution strategy is specified for a class of problems. The theory is illustrated by an example.

1 Introduction

The concept of *self-stabilization* was first conceived by Dijkstra [4]. Since then a lot of work is published about the subject [1, 2, 5, 6]. Informally, a distributed algorithm is said to be self-stabilizing if its specification does not depend on a specific initial state of the system. Such a self-stabilizing system, once started, is guaranteed to reach a correct ("legitimate") state without any intervention from outside.

An interesting property of a self-stabilizing system is that it is tolerant to certain faults, such as the crashing of processors and the subsequent recovery in arbitrary states. When the period between two faults is sufficiently long, the system is able to reach a legitimate (stable) state and to remain in such a state until the next faults occurs.

Self-stabilizing algorithms have been proposed for resetting [1, 2, 5], taking snapshots [5] and routing in dynamic networks [9, 11, 14].

Because distributed algorithms, especially self-stabilizing distributed algorithms, are usually highly complex, the design and verification of these algorithms are error-prone. It is our experience that, especially when using informal arguments to design and verify distributed algorithms, errors are easily made. To ensure correctness, a formal proof must be given. In another paper [7] we use the formalism UNITY [3] in the design and verification of a distributed self-stabilizing algorithm to maintain the maximum value of a bag of integers. Every node in the network has associated with it a single element of this bag of inputs, and each input value may change spontaneously. The algorithm, executed by each node, makes the system reach legitimate states. When the system reaches a legitimate state, the maximum value of the inputs is determined.

In this article, we introduce two new logical operators into UNITY, which may be helpful in the formal design and verification of distributed self-stabilizing algorithms. Section 3, after a short introduction to UNITY in Section 2, defines the new operators using basic UNITY operators. Section 4 explains how these operators can be used to formally specify the problem which a self-stabilizing algorithm is assumed to solve. Moreover, it describes how to specify self-stabilizing distributed algorithms, provided that there are no circular dependencies between different variables.

Section 5 illustrates this by designing and verifying, using the new operators, a distributed algorithm for maintaining the maximum value of a possibly changing bag of integers. In this example the aforementioned circular dependency is avoided by imposing a spanning tree upon the network and letting each node maintain the maximum value of the inputs from its descendants in the spanning tree. The resulting specification consists of only two rules. In an earlier article [7], a specification of a similar algorithm (however not exactly the same) needed considerably more rules.

2 UNITY

UNITY is a formalism for the development of parallel and distributed programs which was developed by Chandy and Misra [3]. Presently, research on UNITY is going on [12, 13]. In UNITY, after stating a problem specification, a solution strategy is specified to solve the problem (as stated in the problem specification). Next, a program is developed by stepwise refinement of specifications of the solution strategy, until the specification is restrictive enough to be translated into UNITY code. Examples of this approach can be found in [3, 13, 7]. This section presents the aspects of UNITY that are relevant to our discussion. For more information and many examples, see [3] and [12].

2.1 Programs in UNITY

The execution of a UNITY program starts in a state in which all variables have the values specified in the **initially**-section. Uninitialised variables have arbitrary initial values.

In a step of a program execution, any statement from the **assign**-section is selected and executed. The execution of each statement always terminates. A program execution consists of an infinite number of steps. During program execution each statement is selected and executed infinitely often. A UNITY program can reach a fixed point, i.e. a state where the execution of any statement leaves the state unchanged.

Every statement is of the form

$$x_1, x_2, \ldots, x_n := e_1, e_2, \ldots, e_n \qquad \text{if } B$$

where each x_i is a variable, e_i an expression that may depend on all x_j's and B a boolean expression.

To denote quantified statements, the following notation is used

⟨|*variable-list* : *boolean-expression* :: *statement-list*⟩

To denote quantified expressions, a similar notation is used. For example, ⟨∀i :: $X[i] > 0$⟩ holds if and only if all elements of X are positive. In this case, the range of i is understood from the given context. If there is no instance of the quantification, the value of the quantified expression is the unit element of the operator. Moreover, any expression having a free variable, i.e. a variable that is neither bound nor a program variable, is assumed to be universally quantified over all possible values of the variable.

2.2 UNITY Logic

In this section the definitions of the UNITY operators are given. For of simplicity we have chosen to state the definitions as proposed by Chandy and Misra [3] (instead of the definitions as given by Sanders [12, 13]). The symbols p, q, r denote predicates. For a given program F, $F.INIT$ denotes a predicate that characterises the permitted initial states of F and $F.ASSIGN$ denotes the set of assignment statements of F.

unless:

For a given program F, p *unless* q is formally defined as

$$p \text{ unless } q \text{ in } F = \langle \forall s : s \in F.ASSIGN :: \{p \wedge \neg q\} \, s \, \{p \vee q\} \rangle$$

The operational interpretation of p *unless* q is that if p is true at some point in the execution of the program and q is not, in the next step of the execution p remains true or q becomes true.

Two important special cases of *unless*, *stable* and *invariant*, are given next.

$$\text{stable } p = p \text{ unless false}$$

Once p becomes true during the program execution, it remains true. Note, however, that p is not guaranteed to become true ever.

The definition of the *invariant* property, given some program F, is

$$\text{invariant } p = ((F.INIT \Rightarrow p) \wedge \text{stable } p)$$

That is, an invariant holds in every state during any execution.

ensures

The logical operator *ensures* is, for a given program F, defined as

$$p \text{ ensures } q \text{ in } F = (p \text{ unless } q \text{ in } F) \wedge \langle \exists s : s \in F.ASSIGN :: \{p \wedge \neg q\} \, s \, \{q\} \rangle$$

The operational interpretation of p *ensures* q is that once p is true during the execution of the program, it remains true as long as q is false, and q is guaranteed to become true eventually by the fact that there exists at least one statement which guarantees this progress.

leads-to

For a given program, $p \mapsto q$, is defined as

$p \mapsto q$ in F holds if and only if it can be derived using a finite number of applications of the following rules:

ensures promotion:

$$\frac{p \text{ ensures } q}{p \mapsto q}$$

Transitivity:

$$\frac{(p \mapsto q) , (q \mapsto r)}{p \mapsto r}$$

Disjunction: For any set W,

$$\frac{\langle \forall m : m \in W :: p(m) \mapsto q \rangle}{\langle \exists m : m \in W :: p(m) \rangle \mapsto q}$$

In other words, if $p \mapsto q$ holds, then once p becomes true during the program execution, q is true or will become true eventually.

3 Additional Operators

This section defines two additional logical operators in UNITY, and gives some theorems about them. For simplicity the operators are defined in terms of the standard operators as defined by Chandy and Misra. In [8] the operators are defined in terms of the standard operators as defined by Sanders [12, 13]. As will be shown in the next section, these operators are useful in the formal design and verification of (distributed) self-stabilizing algorithms.

3.1 Assures

For a given program F the logical operator *assures* is defined as
$$r\ assures_p\ q\ in\ F = ((r\ ensures\ q\ in\ F)\ \wedge\ (p \wedge q \wedge r\ unless\ \neg p\ in\ F))$$
The operational interpretation of $r\ assures_p\ q$ is that once r is true during the execution of the program, it remains true as long as q is false, and q is guaranteed to become true eventually by the fact that there exists at least one statement which is guaranteed to cause this progress. And during the execution when p, q and r hold, these continue to hold until p does not hold anymore.

3.2 Eventually-implies

For a program F the logical operator $\mapsto$, read as *eventually-implies*, is defined as
$$p \mapsto q\ in\ F = ((p \mapsto (q \vee \neg p)\ in\ F)\ \wedge\ (p \wedge q\ unless\ \neg p\ in\ F))$$
The operational interpretation of $p \mapsto q$ is that once p holds, q is or will be true or eventually p will not hold anymore, and when p and q both hold, these continue to hold until p does not hold anymore. In other words, when p holds, within finite time $p \Rightarrow q$ and this remains to hold until p is falsified.

3.3 Theorems

In this section some theorems are stated for combining the newly introduced operators. Proofs of these theorems can be found in [8].

assures promotion:
$$\frac{r\ assures_p\ q}{(p \wedge r) \mapsto q}$$

Reflexivity:
$$p \mapsto p$$

Restricted Consequence Weakening:
$$\frac{(p \mapsto (q \wedge r))\ ,\ (p \Rightarrow r)}{p \mapsto q}$$

Stability:
$$\frac{(p \mapsto q)\ ,\ (stable\ p)}{(p \mapsto q), (stable\ (p \wedge q))}$$

Implication:
$$\frac{p \Rightarrow q}{p \mapsto q}$$

Weak Transitivity:
$$\frac{(p \mapsto q)\ ,\ (q \mapsto r)}{p \mapsto (q \wedge r)}$$

Precondition Strengthening:
$$\frac{(p \Rightarrow q)\ ,\ (q \mapsto r)}{p \mapsto r}$$

Conjunction:
For any finite set of predicates p_i, q_i:
$$\frac{\langle \forall i\ ::\ p_i \mapsto q_i \rangle}{\langle \forall i\ ::\ p_i \rangle \mapsto \langle \forall i\ ::\ q_i \rangle}$$

4 Specifications of Self-Stabilizing Algorithms in UNITY

This section describes how self-stabilizing algorithms can be specified in UNITY, using the operators as defined in Section 3. Section 4.1 describes how the problem specifications of self-stabilizing algorithms can be formulated.

Section 4.2 gives a general scheme for specifying solution strategies in UNITY which assume (a network of) nodes with the following property:

If the state of node a depends on the state of node b ($b \neq a$), the state of b does not depend on the state of a.

4.1 Problem Specifications

In the following, the environment (env) is defined as that part of the system's state upon which the algorithm depends but which cannot be influenced (by the algorithm). For example, in the case of a routing algorithm, env denotes the (possibly changing) topology of the system, which can be expressed as the weights of the links between every two nodes.

LS is a predicate to denote that the program state is legitimate. For example, in case of the routing algorithm, LS may describe that all nodes have correct routing tables.

An obvious way to specify a self-stabilizing algorithm, in terms of temporal logic [10], is:

$$(\Diamond\Box(env = v)) \Rightarrow (\Diamond\Box LS).$$

In other words, if eventually the environment is stable (does not change anymore) and has some value v, within finite time the system reaches a legitimate state, and from then on every successor of a legitimate state is legitimate.

Until now it has not been possible to directly translate the displayed formula (in temporal logic) into UNITY properties. An alternative in UNITY is to use $\mapsto$ (*eventually-implies*). Suppose $((env = v) \mapsto LS)$ and *stable* $(env = v)$ hold, then the stability theorem states that within finite time after env has obtained the value v, $((env = v) \wedge LS)$ will hold forever.

A disadvantage, compared to the rules given in temporal logic, is that generally the resulting rules are more complex. The following specification is used to specify a self-stabilizing algorithm:

$$(env = v) \mapsto LS.$$

This specification states that always within finite time a legitimate state is reached or the environment changes, and once a legitimate state has been reached, the successor states remain legitimate until the environment changes.

Opposed to the specification given in temporal logic (and opposed to our informal requirements) the following scenario is not allowed given this specification. When the environment is stable, during the computation *temporarily* a legitimate state is reached (more or less accidentally) but the system is not stable yet. Within finite time, however, after the environment has become stable the system will stabilize, i.e. a legitimate state will be reached and the state will remain legitimate. To allow for this behaviour, the following (general) specification can be used:

$$(env = v) \mapsto term$$
$$term \Rightarrow LS$$

where *term* is a predicate describing that the system is stable until the environment changes. Moreover, *term* describes a set of states of the system such that each state in the set is legitimate and successor states of a state in the set are also in the set until the environment changes. Note that at this point of program design, a full definition of *term* need not to be known. A full definition may be obtained during program design.

4.2 Specifications of Solution Strategies

After the problem specification is formulated, a solution strategy to solve the problem must be specified. Next, the solution strategy must be refined until it is restrictive enough to be directly translated into UNITY code. *Leads-to* properties can be refined to *ensures* properties in order to directly obtain the program text satisfying the *leads-to* properties. Similarly, *eventually-implies* properties can be refined to *assures* properties in order to directly obtain the program text satisfying the *eventually-implies* properties. This section describes how the solution strategies can be formulated for a special class of distributed self-stabilizing algorithms.

Define relation $\lhd$ on states by: $a \lhd b$ iff the state of node b is dependent upon the state of node a. The relation $\lhd^*$ is defined as the reflexive transitive closure of $\lhd$. Then a solution strategy has the *non-circularity* property iff $\lhd^*$ is antisymmetric, that is $\lhd^*$ is a partial order relation.

Let $env(b)$ denote the local environment of b, that is that part of the environment the state of node b depends upon. All local environments together define the (global) environment. Define $term(b)$ to be a predicate to denote that every node $a \lhd^* b$ has stabilized (and is in a legitimate state). Then a solution strategy having the non-circularity property, thus $\lhd^*$ is antisymmetric, can generally be specified as follows:

$$((\forall a : a \lhd b :: term(a)) \land (env(b) = v_b)) \mapsto term(b)$$

In the next section, after the problem specification is presented, a non-circular solution strategy is specified and proven correct, i.e. every algorithm satisfying this solution strategy solves the problem as specified in the problem specification. Next, the specification is refined to *assures* properties from which a program text directly follows.

5 Example

Assume that every node in a network has a data-item, called its *input*. Inputs are (not necessarily unique) elements taken from a totally ordered set. The input of a node may change spontaneously. This section formally derives and verifies a distributed algorithm to maintain the maximum of all inputs in the network.

Section 5.1 formally presents the problem, using the (general) specification from Section 4.1. The environment corresponds to the bag of inputs and in a legitimate state a dedicated variable has as value the maximum of the inputs.

Next, Section 5.2 formally presents a solution strategy, using the general specification from Section 4.2, on a graph upon which a spanning tree is imposed. The local environment of a node corresponds to the input associated with the node. The state of every node in the spanning tree depends upon its local environment and the states of its sons.

Section 5.3 refines this strategy to a specification sufficiently restrictive for the program text to be directly obtainable from it.

In Section 5.4 some concluding remarks are given.

Note that due to space limitations just one proof is included. The rest of the proofs can be found in [8].

5.1 Maximum Maintenance on a Graph: Problem Specification

This section formally specifies the problem. Before this specification is given, some notation is introduced.

Notation Here is some notation and some variables (with their intended use).

$G = (N, E)$ denotes the finite graph corresponding to a network. Every node $a \in N$ corresponds to a processor in the network. Moreover, every node can be uniquely identified and will be denoted by small letters. Every edge $\{a, b\} \in E$ corresponds to a (bidirectional) link between processors a and b. These links are assumed to be fault-free and have a FIFO behaviour. Furthermore, it is assumed that the graph is *connected*.

For each node a, there is a variable $inp(a)$; $inp(a)$ contains the input of node a.

There is a variable $m(G)$; it is intended to hold the maximum of the inputs.

Expression $nodesval(G)$ is short for the set of $(a, inp(a))$ where a ranges over the nodes; i.e.,

$$nodesval(G) = \langle \cup a \ : a \in N \ :: (a, inp(a)) \rangle.$$

$\vec{M}$ denotes an arbitrary value of the type of $nodesval(G)$; we use it as a free variable in a specification.

There is a predicate *term*; $term(G)$ denotes that the system has *terminated*. For the time being we do not define this predicate in full, but only partially define it by requiring it to satisfy the following:

$$term(G) \Rightarrow (m(G) = \langle \max a \ : a \in N \ :: inp(a) \rangle).$$

Specification An obvious way of specifying the problem (in temporal logic) of maintaining the maximum value of the inputs in a network G is:

$$(\Diamond \Box (nodesval(G) = \vec{M})) \Rightarrow (\Diamond \Box (m(G) = \langle \max a \ : a \in N \ :: inp(a) \rangle)).$$

Section 4 gives a general UNITY specification to specify a problem which is formally presented with the above displayed temporal logic specification. This results in the following specification:

SP1: $(nodesval(G) = \vec{M}) \mapsto term(G)$

In other words, given an indexed set of inputs, eventually the algorithm terminates (and thus "delivers" the maximum input) or the indexed set of inputs changes. And once the algorithm terminates, this remains to hold until at least one input changes.

5.2 Solution Strategy: Maximum Maintenance on a Graph using a Spanning Tree

Before the solution strategy to solve the problem is presented, some more notation and assumptions are introduced.

Notation and Assumptions Upon the graph $G = (N, E)$, a *spanning tree* is imposed. $R(G)$ denotes the root of the spanning tree. We define that $a \lhd b$ holds if and only if (in the spanning tree) a is a son of b, and thus b is a father of a. If $a \lhd^* b$, we call a a *descendant of* b, and b an *ancestor of* a. Note that $\lhd^*$ is antisymmetric.

The inputs of descendants of node a are represented by $descval(a)$; i.e.,

$descval(a) = \langle \cup b \; : \; b \lhd^* a \; :: \; (b, inp(b)) \rangle$

Variable $m^a(a)$, which is called the *value of* a, is a's current view of the maximum of the inputs of the descendants of a. Moreover, $m^b(a)$ is b's view of $m^a(a)$ for every $a \lhd b$. (Think of $m^b(c)$ as located in node b, containing information about node c.)

The predicate *fatherknows*(a) is defined by:

$fatherknows(a) = \langle \forall a \; : \; a \lhd b \; :: \; m^b(a) = m^a(a) \rangle$

Informally, *fatherknows*(a) expresses that the value of a is known to its father.

The algorithm *has finished* for node a if and only if the variable $m^a(a)$ is the maximum of its input and all the values of its sons, and the algorithm has terminated (which is defined next) for these sons.

$hfinished(a) = (m^a(a) = \max \{inp(a), \langle \max b \; : \; b \lhd a \; :: \; m^a(b) \rangle\} \wedge$
$\langle \forall b \; : \; b \lhd a \; :: \; hterm(b) \rangle)$

The algorithm *has terminated* for node a if and only if the algorithm has finished for a and this value of a is known to the father of a.

$hterm(a) = (hfinished(a) \wedge fatherknows(a))$.

Because of the connectedness of G, there exists a spanning tree on G. The definitions imply the following: $(a \lhd^* R(G)) = (a \in N)$, $nodesval(G) = descval(R(G))$ and $hfinished(R(G)) = hterm(R(G))$.

Specification To maintain the maximum of all inputs in a graph (upon which a spanning tree is imposed), it is sufficient that each node in the graph maintains the maximum of all inputs at its descendants. The root of the graph then maintains the maximum of all inputs in the graph. In turn, this can be accomplished by maintaining at each node the maximum of its input and the values at its sons.

This observation suggests the following specification, consisting of two rules, SP2 and SP3.

SP2: $(\langle \forall b \; : \; b \lhd a \; :: \; hterm(b) \rangle \wedge (inp(a) = k)) \mapsto hfinished(a)$

In words, this rule formalises the following two properties.

1. After every descendant of each son of a has successfully computed its value (i.e. has computed the maximum of the inputs at its descendants) and a is aware of the value of each son $(\langle \forall b \; : \; b \lhd a \; :: \; hterm(b) \rangle$ holds), then within finite time node a computes the maximum of the inputs at its descendants such that $hfinished(a)$ holds, the value of the input at a changes or at least one descendant of a son of a must recompute its value $(\neg \langle \forall b \; : \; b \lhd a \; :: \; hterm(b) \rangle$ holds).

2. When every descendant of node a has successfully computed its value ($hfinished(a)$ holds), then this continues to hold until the value of the input at a changes or at least one descendant of a son of a must recompute its value ($\neg\langle\forall b : b \lhd a :: hterm(b)\rangle$ holds).

SP3: $hfinished(a) \mapsto hterm(a)$

In words, this rule formalises the following two properties.

1. When every descendant of node a has successfully computed its value ($hfinished(a)$ holds), then within finite time the father of a is notified of the maximum value of the inputs at the descendants of a such that $hterm(a)$ holds or at least one descendant of a must recompute its value ($\neg hfinished(a)$ holds).
2. And when every descendant of a has successfully computed its value and the father of a is aware of the value of a ($hterm(a)$ holds), then this continues to hold until at least one descendant of a must recompute its value ($\neg hfinished(a)$ holds).

Proof of Correctness We prove that the problem specification (SP1) is met by any solution strategy satisfying SP2 and SP3, that is, $SP1 \Leftarrow SP2 \land SP3$.

Lemma 1. $hfinished(a) = [(m^a(a) = \langle \max c : c \lhd^* a :: inp(c)\rangle) \land \langle\forall b : b \lhd a :: hterm(b)\rangle]$.

Section 5.1 required that $term(G) \Rightarrow (m(G) = \langle \max a : a \in N :: inp(a)\rangle)$. By defining $m(G) = m^{R(G)}(R(G))$, from Lemma 1 we conclude that if $term(G) = hfinished(R(G))$, this requirement is fulfilled. Hence, we have the following definitions: $m(G) = m^{R(G)}(R(G))$ and $term(G) = hfinished(R(G))$.

Theorem 2. *SP1 is met by SP2 and SP3.*

5.3 Refinement Step: Towards the Implementation

Opposed to the *ensures* (and therefore also to *assures* relations), a *leads-to* and *eventually-implies* relation cannot be translated directly into a program statement. Thus, the solution strategy given above is not yet in a form that can be directly translated into a program text. In order to obtain such a specification, conditions SP2 and SP3 must be refined. Furthermore, to be able to implement the resulting program on a distributed system, a statement within a process may only depend on its local state, i.e. information present within the process. For example, the execution of a statement may not depend on the state of other nodes, such as the condition that the algorithm has terminated in some node. In this section a specification will be given that satisfies these constraints.

Specification As stated in Section 5.2, specification rule SP2 formalises two properties. The first property of SP2 can be satisfied by ensuring that at any time each node eventually computes the maximum of its input and the values at its sons. Then, after every descendant of each son of node a has successfully computed its value, it is assured that a will recompute its value. After this recomputation, node a has successfully computed its value or at least one descendant of a son of a has an incorrect value and thus must recompute its value.

The second property of SP2 can be satisfied by assuring that once a node has computed the maximum of its input and the values of its sons, this must continue to hold until its input or a value of a son has changed.

These observations suggest the following specification rule:

SP4: true $assures_p$ $(m^a(a) = \max \{inp(a), \langle \max b \ : \ b \lhd a \ :: \ m^a(b)\rangle\})$
where $p = ((inp(a) = k) \wedge \langle \forall b \ : \ b \lhd a \ :: \ m^a(b) = m_b\rangle)$

Also specification rule SP3, as given in Section 5.2, formalises two properties. The first property can be satisfied by ensuring that at any time the father of each node a is eventually notified of the value of a. Then, it is guaranteed that if a has successfully computed its value, within finite time the father of a is notified of the value of a. After the notification, the father of a is aware of the maximum value of the inputs at the descendants of a or at least one descendant of a must recompute its value.

The second property of SP3 can be satisfied by assuring that once the father of node a is aware of the value of a, this father may not change its view of the value of a until the value of a changes.

These observations suggest the following relation:

SP5: true $assures_{(m^\bullet(a)=m_\bullet)}$ $fatherknows(a)$

Proof of Correctness We prove that the solution strategy, given by SP2 and SP3 is satisfied by any strategy satisfying SP4 and SP5.

Theorem 3. *SP2 is met by SP4 and SP5.*

Theorem 4. *SP3 is met by SP4 and SP5.*
Proof.

$\quad$ SP5
$=\quad$ {Definition of SP5}
$\quad$ true $assures_{(m^\bullet(a)=m_\bullet)}$ $fatherknows(a)$
$\Rightarrow\quad$ {$assures$ promotion}
$\quad (m^a(a) = m_a) \mapsto fatherknows(a)$
$=\quad$ {Reflexivity}
$\quad ((m^a(a) = m_a) \mapsto fatherknows(a)) \wedge (hfinished(a) \mapsto hfinished(a))$
$\Rightarrow\quad$ {Conjunction theorem}
$\quad ((m^a(a) = m_a) \wedge hfinished(a)) \mapsto (hfinished(a) \wedge fatherknows(a))$

$=$ {Rewriting the right side}

$\quad ((m^a(a) = m_a) \wedge hfinished(a)) \mapsto hterm(a)$

$=$ {Lemma 1}

$\quad hfinished(a) \mapsto hterm(a)$

                                                               □

Derivation of a Program from the Specification A program follows directly from the specification of the solution strategy. The function $inp(a)$ delivers the input of some node a.

SP4 suggests the recomputation of $m^a(a)$:

$\langle \mathbf{la} :: m^a(a) := \max \{inp(a), \langle \max b : b \lhd a :: m^a(b) \rangle\} \rangle$

SP5 suggests that every node is aware of the value of each of its sons:

$\langle \mathbf{la}, f : a \lhd f :: m^f(a) := m^a(a) \rangle.$

To show that these statements do not violate the safety properties (unless-parts of SP4 and SP5) is rather straightforward and left to the reader. The complete program follows.

Program {maximum computation on a spanning tree}
  assign
    $\langle \mathbf{la}, f : a \lhd f ::$
        $m^f(a) := m^a(a)$
        $\mathbf{I}$
        $m^a(a) := \max \{inp(a), \langle \max b : b \lhd a :: m^a(b) \rangle\}$
    $\rangle$
end {maximum computation on a spanning tree}

The program can be implemented on a distributed system in an obvious way. The variables $m^a(b)$ and $m^a(a)$ are local to a. The assignment $m^f(a) := m^a(a)$ is done by communicating the value of $m^a(a)$ over the channel between a and f. How channels are represented in UNITY, has been described in [3, 7].

5.4 Concluding Remarks

The problem of maintaining the maximum value of a bag of inputs as such does not seem to be of great interest. However, it is our hope that the techniques used in the formal design and verification of this algorithm will be helpful in the formal design of more self-stabilizing algorithms, especially routing algorithms. The problem of maintaining the maximum value of a (possibly changing) bag of inputs and the problem of keeping topological information about a (dynamical) network bear some similarities. The network can be considered as a set of nodes. To each node in this set corresponds a (possibly changing) set of paths from a source node to that node. Every node must, for every other destination node in the set, maintain the optimal (i.e. minimum length) path.

At first sight, routing algorithms do not satisfy the non-circularity property. In the routing algorithm as proposed by Tajibnapis [14] every node maintains a copy of the routing table of each neighbouring node. For each node, these copies are used to calculate its routing table. The data maintained by a node depends upon the data at its neighbours, and vice versa. However, by studying the algorithm more carefully, the following non-circularity property can be discovered. The algorithm computes successively the shortest paths of increasing length. Consequently, the *correct* routing information for some destination node d at node a does not depend upon the routing information for d at a neighbour node b of a if the distance from a to d is at most the distance from b to d.

6 Acknowledgement

The authors thank Arjen Uittenbogaard, Kaisa Sere, Rob Udink, Frans Rietman and Nico Verwer for their help during the course of this research.

References

1. A. Arora and M.G. Gouda. Distributed reset (extended abstract). In *Proc. of 10th Conf. on Foundations of Software Technology and Theoretical Computer Science*, pages 316–331. Springer-Verlag, 1990.
2. B. Awerbuch, B. Patt-Shamir, and G. Varghese. Self-stabilization by local checking and correction. In *Proc. of 32'nd IEEE Symp. on Foundations on Computer Science*, October 1991.
3. K.M. Chandy and J. Misra. *Parallel Program Design – A Foundation*. Addison-Wesley Publishing Company, Inc., 1988.
4. E.W. Dijkstra. Self-stabilizing systems in spite of distributed control. *Communications of the ACM*, 17(11):643–644, 1974.
5. S. Katz and K.J. Perry. Self-stabilizing extensions for message-passing systems. In *Proc. of the Ninth Annual ACM Symp. on Principles of Distributed Computing*, pages 91–101, Quebec City, August 1990.
6. H.S.M. Kruijer. Self-stabilization (in spite of distributed control) in tree structured systems. *Information Processing Letters*, 8(2):91–95, 1979.
7. P.J.A. Lentfert and S.D. Swierstra. Distributed maximum maintenance on hierarchically divided graphs. *Formal Aspects of Computing*, 1992.
8. P.J.A. Lentfert and S.D. Swierstra. Towards the formal design of self-stabilizing distributed algorithms. Technical Report RUU-CS-92-25, Utrecht University, July 1992.
9. P.J.A. Lentfert, A.H. Uittenbogaard, S.D. Swierstra, and G. Tel. Distributed hierarchical routing. Technical Report RUU-CS-89-5, Utrecht University, March 1989. Also in: P.M.G. Apers et al. (Eds.). *Proc. CSN89*. Utrecht, November 9–10, 1989.
10. Z. Manna and A. Pnueli. *The Temporal Logic of Reactive and Concurrent Systems*, volume 1. Springer Verlag, to appear.
11. J.M. McQuillan, I. Richer, and E.C. Rosen. The new routing algorithm for the arpanet. *IEEE Trans. on Communications*, com-28(5):711–719, May 1980.
12. B.A. Sanders. Stepwise refinement of mixed specifications of concurrent programs. In M. Broy and C.B. Jones, editors, *Proceedings IFIP Working Conf. on Programming and Methods*, pages 1–25. Elsevier Science Publishers B.V. (North Holland), May 1990.
13. B.A. Sanders. Eliminating the substitution axiom from UNITY logic. *Formal Aspects of Computing*, 3(2):189–205, 1991.
14. W.D. Tajibnapis. A correctness proof of a topology information maintenance protocol for a distributed computer network. *Computer Systems*, 20(7):477–485, July 1977.

Axiomatizations of Temporal Logics on Trace Systems

Wojciech Penczek[1]

Institute of Computer Science, Polish Academy of Sciences
Warsaw, ul. Ordona 21, Poland

Abstract

Partial order temporal logics interpreted on trace systems have been shown not to have finitary complete axiomatizations. The paper gives infinitary complete proof systems for several temporal logics on trace systems e.g. Partial Order Logic (POL), Computation Tree Logic with backward modalities, and an essential subset of Interleaving Set Temporal Logic (ISTL).

Keywords: Partial Order Temporal Logics; Concurrency; Trace Systems.
Classification: Theory of Parallel and Distributed Computation, Logic in Computer Science, Semantics and Logics of Programming Languages.

1 Introduction

Partial order temporal logics are becoming an important formalism used for specification and verification of concurrent systems [KP87, PP90, Pe90, Pe91, PKP91, Re89, Si90]. These logics are more expressive than linear and branching time temporal logics. They allow for expressing and proving important properties of concurrent systems like serializability of database transactions [PP90, PKP91], inevitability under concurrency fairness assumption [Pe90, Pe92a], causal successor [Re89], layering of a program [PP90], snapshots or the concurrency of program segments [PP90, Pe92a, Si90].

Mazurkiewicz's trace systems [Ma88] are frequently used partial order structures giving semantics to concurrent programs and interpreting temporal logics [GW91, PP90, Pe92a]. In [Pe92b] it was shown that propositional versions of Partial Order Logic [Si90] and Interleaving Set Temporal Logic [PP90] interpreted over trace systems are not decidable. Moreover, that the validity problem is Π_1^1-hard. Therefore, finitary complete axiomatizations for these logics do not exist. This explains why no axiomatizations for the logics on trace systems have existed so far. The lack of finitary axiomatizations is rather unusual for propositional logics. However, several examples of such logics are already known in the literature (see [Pe87, Pa91, LPRT92]).

In this paper we give infinitary complete proof systems for several temporal logics interpreted on trace systems like Partial Order Logic, the propositional version of the logic defined in [PKP91], and an essential subset of Interleaving

[1]Partly supported by the Polish grant No. 2 2047 9203

Set Temporal Logic. The proof systems we give, although they are infinitary, can have some important practical applications. For instance, one can use them in the formal justification of any derivation rules that are useful in proving partial order properties of concurrent programs or systems.

The method of proving completeness is strongly based on the technique of Q-filters [RS70] tuned to our logics. This technique is traditional in Algorithmic Logic [MS87] and it has been also used for proving completeness of an infinitary axiomatization of first-order linear time temporal logic [Sz87].

The rest of the paper is organized as follows. In Section 2, trace systems are defined. Section 3 contains the definition of Trace Logic (TL). A proof system is given in Section 4. A proof of its soundness and completeness is shown in Section 5. Proof systems for POL and ISTL are discussed in Section 6. Section 7 contains final remarks.

2 Trace Systems

By an *independence alphabet* we mean any ordered pair (Σ, I), where Σ is a finite set of symbols (*action names*) and $I \subseteq \Sigma \times \Sigma$ is a symmetric and irreflexive binary relation in Σ (the *independence* relation). Let (Σ, I) be an independence alphabet. Define $\equiv$ as the least congruence in the (standard) string monoid $(\Sigma^*, \circ, \epsilon)$ such that $(a, b) \in I \Rightarrow ab \equiv ba$, for all $a, b \in \Sigma$ i.e., $w \equiv w'$, if there is a finite sequence of strings $w_1, \ldots, w_n$ such that $w_1 = w$, $w_n = w'$, and for each $i < n$, $w_i = uabv$, $w_{i+1} = ubav$, for some $(a, b) \in I$ and $u, v \in \Sigma^*$. Equivalence classes of $\equiv$ are called *traces* over (Σ, I). The trace generated by a string w is denoted by $[w]$. Concatenation of traces $[w], [v]$, denoted $[w][v]$, is defined as $[wv]$.

Now, let T be the set of all traces over (Σ, I). The *labelled successor* relation $\rightarrow \subseteq T \times \Sigma \times T$ is defined as follows: $\tau \xrightarrow{a} \tau'$ iff $\tau[a] = \tau'$. The *prefix* relation $\leq$ in T is defined in the following way: $\tau \leq \tau'$ iff $\exists \sigma \in T : \tau\sigma = \tau'$. Let $\tau \in T$ and $Q \subseteq T$. We use the following notations:

- $\downarrow \tau = \{\tau' \in T \mid \tau' \leq \tau\}$, $\downarrow Q = \bigcup_{\tau \in Q} \downarrow \tau$.

We say that a subset Q of T *dominates* another subset R of T, if $R \subseteq \downarrow Q$. Two traces are *consistent*, if there is a trace in T dominating both of them and *inconsistent* otherwise. A set R of traces is said to be *proper*, if any two of its consistent traces are dominated by a trace in R, and *directed*, if arbitrary two traces in R are dominated by a trace in R. A set of traces Q is said to be *prefix-closed*, if $Q = \downarrow Q$.

By a *trace system* T over (Σ, I) we mean any prefix-closed and proper trace language over (Σ, I). Maximal (w.r.t. the inclusion ordering) directed subsets R of T are called *runs* of T. A run represents a single maximal execution of the system T. By a *path* in $R \subseteq T$ we mean a maximal sequence $x = \tau_0 a_0 \tau_1 a_1 \ldots$ in R such that $\tau_i[a_i] = \tau_{i+1}$ for all $i \geq 0$ (by maximal we mean that it cannot be extended in R). For convenience, we write also $x = \tau_0 \tau_1 \ldots$.

Let $\downarrow x = \{\tau \in T \mid \tau \leq \tau_i, \text{ for } i \geq 0\}$ be the set of traces dominated by the path x. By an *observation* of a run R in T we mean any path x in R such that $R = \downarrow x$; we say also that x is an observation (of T). Notice that an observation is a path which is cofinal with some run. Thus, it carries the information about all actions executed in the run.

Example 2.1 *An example of a trace system T_1 is presented below.*

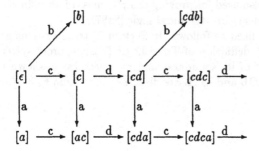

Figure 1: Trace system T_1 with the successor relation

The independence alphabet (Σ, I) is defined as follows:

- $\Sigma = \{a, b, c, d\}$, $I = \{(a, c), (c, a), (a, d), (d, a)\}$.

There are infinitely many finite runs R_i and one infinite run R in the trace system T_1: $R_i = \downarrow [(cd)^i b]$, for $i \geq 0$; $R = \bigcup_{i=1}^{\omega} \downarrow [(cd)^i a]$.
Every path in T_1 except for $x = [\epsilon][c][cd][cdc]...$ is an observation of some run. Trace systems are commonly used for giving semantics to Elementary Net Systems [Ma88], concurrent programs [PP90], and finite state programs [GW91].

3 Trace Logic

Firstly, we show how a trace system is turned into a model for a temporal logic. For technical reasons we assume that we deal with trace systems with infinite runs, only.

Let PV be a set of propositional variables.

Definition 3.1 *A frame is a 4-tuple $F_{v_0} = (W, \Sigma, \rightarrow, v_0)$, where W is a set of states, $\rightarrow \subseteq W \times \Sigma \times W$ is a labelled successor relation, and $v_0 \in W$ satisfying the following conditions:*

C0. $W = \{w \mid v_0 \rightarrow'^* w\}$, *where* $\rightarrow' = \{(v, v') \mid (\exists a \in \Sigma)\ v \xrightarrow{a} v'\}$,

$\quad\quad (\forall w \in W)\{v \mid w \rightarrow' v\} \neq \emptyset$ *(infiniteness of runs)*,

C1. $\{w \mid w \rightarrow' v_0\} = \emptyset$ *(beginning)*,

C2. $(\forall w, w', w'' \in W)\ w \xrightarrow{a} w'$ *and* $w \xrightarrow{a} w''$ *implies* $w' = w''$ *(determinism)*,

C3. $(\forall w, w', w'' \in W)\ w' \overset{a}{\to} w$ and $w'' \overset{a}{\to} w$ implies $w' = w''$ (no auto-concurrency),

C4. $(\forall w, w', w'' \in W)(\exists v \in W)$: if $w' \overset{a}{\to} w$ and $w'' \overset{b}{\to} w$ and $a \neq b$, then $v \overset{a}{\to} w''$ and $v \overset{b}{\to} w'$, (backward-diamond property),

C5. Let $I = \{(a,b) \mid (\exists w, w', w'' \in W) : w' \overset{a}{\to} w,\ w'' \overset{b}{\to} w$ and $a \neq b\}$,

$(\forall w, w', w'' \in W)(\exists v \in W)$: if $w \overset{a}{\to} w'$ and $w \overset{b}{\to} w''$ and $(a,b) \in I$, then $w' \overset{b}{\to} v$ and $w'' \overset{a}{\to} v$ (forward-diamond property),

C6. $(\forall w, w', w'' \in W)(\exists v \in W)$: if $w \overset{a}{\to} w' \overset{b}{\to} w''$ and $(a,b) \in I$, then $w \overset{b}{\to} v \overset{a}{\to} w''$ (concurrency closure property).$\square$

The conditions $C0-C6$ are slightly simpler than the axioms of general occurrence transition systems from [NRT91] or [Ro90].

One can see that each frame corresponds to a trace system and vice versa.

Theorem 3.1 Let $F_{v_0} = (W, \Sigma, \to, v_0)$ be a frame. Then, $T = \{[a_1 \ldots a_n] \mid v_0 \overset{a_1}{\to} \ldots \overset{a_n}{\to} v_n,$ for $a_i \in \Sigma$, $v_i \in W$ with $0 \leq i \leq n$, and $n \geq 0\}$ over (Σ, I) is a trace system, where $I = \{(a,b) \mid (\exists w, w', w'' \in W) : w' \overset{a}{\to} w,\ w'' \overset{b}{\to} w$ and $a \neq b\}$.
Let T be a trace system over (Σ, I). Then, $(T, \Sigma, \to, [\epsilon])$ is a frame, where $\to$ is the labelled successor relation in T.$\square$

Definition 3.2 A model is an ordered pair $M = (F_{v_0}, V)$, where $F_{v_0} = (W, \Sigma, \to, v_0)$ is a frame and $V : W \longrightarrow 2^{PV}$ is a valuation function.
Let $w_0 \in W$. By a forward path x starting at w_0 we mean a maximal sequence of states and actions $x = w_0 a_0 w_1 a_1 \ldots$ s.t. $w_i \overset{a_i}{\to} w_{i+1}$, for all $i \geq 0$. Let FP_{w_0} denote the set of all forward paths starting at w_0.
By a backward path x starting at w_0 we mean a sequence of states and actions $x = w_0 a_0 w_1 a_1 \ldots w_k$ s.t. $w_{i+1} \overset{a_i}{\to} w_i$, for all $i \geq k$ and $w_k = v_0$. Let BP_{w_0} denote the set of all backward paths starting at w_0.
When convenient, we refer to paths by giving sequences of its actions, only. $\square$

Next, it is given the definition of a very powerful temporal logic, called Trace Logic (TL), which is syntactically equal to POTL [PW84] and semantically to the propositional subset of the logic defined in [PKP91]. The proof system for TL will be used for defining proof systems for POL and ISTL.

3.1 Syntax of Trace Logic

The set *Form* of formulas is the maximal one generated by the rules:

S1. every member of PV is a formula,

S2. if φ and ψ are formulas, then so are $\neg\varphi$ and $\varphi \wedge \psi$,

S3. if φ and ψ are formulas, then so are $E(\varphi U \psi)$, $EG\varphi$ and $EX_a\varphi$ (for $a \in \Sigma$),

S4. if φ and ψ are formulas, then so are $E(\varphi S\psi)$, $EH\varphi$ and $EY_a\varphi$ (for $a \in \Sigma$).

The intuitive meaning of future formulas is as follows: $EG\varphi$ - there is a forward path s.t. φ holds along it, $E(\varphi U\psi)$ - there is a forward path s.t. eventually ψ holds and always before φ holds, and $EX_a\varphi$ - φ holds in a next moment in the future after executing a. For past formulas, the intuitive meaning is similar, but it concerns backward paths.

The following connectives and modalities will be used as abbreviations:

- $\varphi \vee \psi \overset{def}{=} \neg(\neg\varphi \wedge \neg\psi)$, $\varphi \Rightarrow \psi \overset{def}{=} \neg\varphi \vee \psi$, $tt \overset{def}{=} \varphi \vee \neg\varphi$, $ff \overset{def}{=} \neg tt$,

- $\varphi \oplus \psi \overset{def}{=} (\varphi \wedge \neg\psi) \vee (\neg\varphi \wedge \psi)$, $\varphi \equiv \psi \overset{def}{=} (\varphi \Rightarrow \psi) \wedge (\psi \Rightarrow \varphi)$,

- $EF\varphi \overset{def}{=} E(ttU\varphi)$, $AG\varphi \overset{def}{=} \neg EF\neg\varphi$, $AF\varphi \overset{def}{=} \neg EG\neg\varphi$,

- $EP\varphi \overset{def}{=} E(ttS\varphi)$, $AH\varphi \overset{def}{=} \neg EP\neg\varphi$. $AP\varphi \overset{def}{=} \neg EH\neg\varphi$.

- $A(\varphi U\psi) \overset{def}{=} \neg(E(\neg\psi U(\neg\varphi \wedge \neg\psi)) \vee EG(\neg\psi))$, $AX_a\varphi \overset{def}{=} \neg EX_a\varphi$,

- $A(\varphi S\psi) \overset{def}{=} \neg(E(\neg\psi S(\neg\varphi \wedge \neg\psi)) \vee EH(\neg\psi))$, $AY_a\varphi \overset{def}{=} \neg EY_a\varphi$,

- $EX\varphi \overset{def}{=} \bigvee_{a\in\Sigma} EX_a\varphi$, $EY\varphi \overset{def}{=} \bigvee_{a\in\Sigma} EY_a\varphi$, $AX\varphi \overset{def}{=} \neg EX\neg\varphi$, $AY\varphi \overset{def}{=} \neg EY\neg\varphi$.

3.2 Semantics of Trace Logic

Let $M = ((W, \Sigma, \rightarrow, v_0), V)$ be a model and $w \in W$. The notion of *truth* in M at w is defined by the relation $\models$ as follows:

S1. $w \models p$ iff $p \in V(w)$, for $p \in PV$,

S2. $w \models \neg\varphi$ iff not $w \models \varphi$,

    $w \models \varphi \wedge \psi$ iff $w \models \varphi$ and $w \models \psi$,

S3. $w_0 \models E(\varphi U\psi)$ iff there is a forward path $x \in FP_{w_0}$ s.t. there is $k \geq 0$ s.t. $w_k \models \psi$, and for all $0 \leq i < k$: $w_i \models \varphi$,

    $w_0 \models EG\varphi$ iff there is a forward path $x \in FP_{w_0}$ s.t. for all $i \geq 0$: $w_i \models \varphi$,

    $w_0 \models EX_a\varphi$ iff $(\exists w \in W)(w_0 \overset{a}{\rightarrow} w$ and $w \models \varphi)$,

S4. $w_0 \models E(\varphi S\psi)$ iff there is a backward path $x \in BP_{w_0}$ s.t. there is $k \geq 0$ s.t. $w_k \models \psi$, and for all $0 \leq i < k$: $w_i \models \varphi$,

    $w_0 \models EH\varphi$ iff there is a backward path $x \in BP_{w_0}$ s.t. for all $i \geq 0$: $w_i \models \varphi$,

$w_0 \models EY_a\varphi$ iff $(\exists w \in W)(w \xrightarrow{a} w_0$ and $w \models \varphi)$.

A formula φ is said to be *valid in a model M* (written $M \models \varphi$) iff $M, w \models \varphi$, for all $w \in W$. A formula φ is *valid* (written $\models \varphi$) iff $M \models \varphi$, for all models M. We adopt here the unanchored version of validity in order to get a neater proof system. One can easily notice that the undecidability results shown in [Pe92b], hold also for the unanchored version of validity of the logics. Note that if $\models_A$ denotes the anchored validity, then: $\models_A \varphi \Leftrightarrow \models AYff \to \varphi$.

Examples of expressiveness of TL can be found in [PKP91] and [Pe92a]. We show here only that concurrency of two actions a and b can be specified by the formula $EPEF(EY_att \wedge EY_btt)$. Now, a proof system for TL is given.

4 Proof System for Trace Logic

Denote by:

- $EX^i(\varphi) \overset{def}{=} \varphi \wedge EX(\varphi \wedge EX(\varphi \wedge ...EX(\varphi)...)$
  (the operator EX occurs i times, for $i \geq 0$),

- $EX^0(\varphi, \psi) \overset{def}{=} \psi$, $EX^i(\varphi, \psi) \overset{def}{=} \varphi \wedge EX(\varphi \wedge EX(\varphi \wedge ...EX(\psi)...)$
  (the operator EX occurs i times, for $i \geq 1$),

- $I(a, b) \overset{def}{=} EPEF(EY_att \wedge EY_btt)$, for $a, b \in \Sigma$.

Axioms

A1. all formulas of the form of tautologies of the classical prop. calculus

A2. $EX_a(\varphi \wedge \psi) \equiv EX_a(\varphi) \wedge EX_a(\psi)$, for $a \in \Sigma$ (determinism)

A3. $EG\varphi \equiv \varphi \wedge EX(EG\varphi)$

A4. $E(\varphi U\psi) \equiv \psi \vee (\varphi \wedge EX(E(\varphi U\psi)))$

A5. $EY_a(\varphi \wedge \psi) \equiv EY_a(\varphi) \wedge EY_a(\psi)$, for $a \in \Sigma$ (no auto-concurrency)

A6. $EH\varphi \equiv \varphi \wedge (AYff \vee EY(EH\varphi))$

A7. $E(\varphi S\psi) \equiv \psi \vee (\varphi \wedge EY(E(\varphi S\psi)))$

A8. $\varphi \Rightarrow AX_a EY_a\varphi$ for $a \in \Sigma$ (relating past and future)

A9. $\varphi \Rightarrow AY_a EX_a\varphi$ for $a \in \Sigma$ (relating past and future)

A10. $EXtt$ (infiniteness of runs)

A11. $EP(AYff)$ (beginning)

A12 $EY_a AY_b\varphi \Rightarrow AY_b EY_a\varphi$, for $a \neq b$ (backward-diamond property)

A13 $(I(a,b) \wedge EX_a AX_b \varphi) \Rightarrow AX_b EX_a \varphi$, for $a \neq b$ (forward-diamond property)

A14 $(I(a,b) \wedge EX_a EX_b \varphi) \Rightarrow EX_b EX_a \varphi$ (concurrency closure property)

Proof Rules

MP. $\varphi, \varphi \Rightarrow \psi \vdash \psi$

R1. $\varphi \Rightarrow \psi \vdash EX_a \varphi \Rightarrow EX_a \psi$

R2. $\varphi \Rightarrow \psi \vdash EY_a \varphi \Rightarrow EY_a \psi$

R3. $\{\phi \Rightarrow EX^i(\varphi)\}_{i \in \omega} \vdash \phi \Rightarrow EG\varphi$

R4. $\{EX^i(\varphi, \psi) \Rightarrow \phi\}_{i \in \omega} \vdash E(\varphi U \psi) \Rightarrow \phi$

R5. $\phi \Rightarrow (\varphi \wedge (AY ff \vee EY \phi) \vdash \phi \Rightarrow EH\varphi$

Lemma 4.1 *For every model M and each state w,*

(a). $M, w \models EG\varphi$ *iff* $M, w \models EX^i(\varphi)$, *for each* $i \in \omega$,

(b). $M, w \models E(\varphi U \psi)$ *iff* $M, w \models EX^i(\varphi, \psi)$, *for some* $i \in \omega$.$\Box$

Theorem 4.1 *The proof system is sound (i.e.,* $\vdash \varphi \Rightarrow \models \varphi$*).*$\Box$

5   Completeness of the proof system

Let $\sim \subseteq Form \times Form$ be the following relation: $\varphi \sim \psi$ *iff* $\vdash \varphi \equiv \psi$.
Note that $\sim$ is a congruence w.r.t. all the logical and modal operators. Let $Form/\sim$ denote the set of all equivalence classes of $\sim$. Elements of $Form/\sim$ are denoted as follows $[\varphi], [\psi], \dots$

Theorem 5.1 *The following conditions are satisfied:*

1. *The* Lindenbaum-Tarski algebra $LTA = (Form/\sim, \cup, \cap, -, [tt], [ff])$, *where*

   - $[\varphi] \cup [\psi] = [\varphi \vee \psi]$,
   - $[\varphi] \cap [\psi] = [\varphi \wedge \psi]$,
   - $-[\varphi] = [\neg \varphi]$,

   is a non-degenerate Boolean algebra,

2. $\vdash \varphi$ *iff* $[\varphi] = [tt]$,

3. $\nvdash \varphi$ *iff* $[\neg \varphi] \neq [ff]$.$\Box$

The proof of the above theorem is standard and can be found in [RS70] (p. 257).

Let $\leq$ be a partial ordering in $Form/\sim \times Form/\sim$, defined as follows: $[\varphi] \leq [\psi]$ iff $\vdash \varphi \Rightarrow \psi$.

Lemma 5.1 *In the algebra LTA the following conditions hold:*

(a). $[EG\varphi] = inf_{i\in\omega}\{[EX^i\varphi]\}$,

(b). $[E(\varphi U\psi)] = sup_{i\in\omega}\{[EX^i(\varphi,\psi)]\}$.$\square$

Let Q denote the following infinite operations in the algebra LTA:

1. $[EG\varphi] = inf_{i\in\omega}\{[EX^i(\varphi)]\}$,

2. $[E(\varphi U\psi)] = sup_{i\in\omega}\{[EX^i(\varphi,\psi)]\}$.

By a *Q-filter* in LTA we mean a maximal proper filter A which satisfies the following conditions:

- if $[E(\varphi U\psi)] \in A$, then there is $i \in \omega$ s.t. $[EX^i(\varphi,\psi)] \in A$,

- if $[EG\varphi] \notin A$, then there is $i \in \omega$ s.t. $[EX^i\varphi] \notin A$.

We assume the following result of [RS70].

Lemma 5.2 *If a set Q of infinite operations in a Boolean algebra is at most denumerable, then every non-zero element of the Boolean algebra belongs to a Q-filter.*$\square$

Theorem 5.2 *The proof system is complete (i.e., $\models \phi \Rightarrow \vdash \phi$).*

Proof. (sketch) We show that if $\nvdash \phi$, then there is a model for $\neg\phi$, which by contraposition implies that the theorem holds. Let QF be the family of all Q-filters in the algebra LTA. Define the following relations in QF:

- $\leq_{QF} = \{(B,C) \in QF \times QF \mid \{\varphi \mid [AG\varphi] \in B\} \subseteq C\}$,

- $\rightarrow_{QF} = \{(B,a,C) \in QF \times \Sigma \times QF \mid \{\varphi \mid [AX_a\varphi] \in B\} \subseteq C\}$,

- $\rightarrow'_{QF} = \{(B,C) \mid (\exists a \in \Sigma)B \rightarrow^a_{QF} C\}$,

- $\rightarrow'^*_{QF} = \bigcup_{i=0}^\omega \rightarrow'^i_{QF}$, where $\rightarrow'^0_{QF} = id_{QF}$.

We assume also the following result of [RS70].

Lemma 5.3 *Let B be a Q-filter. For any formulas $\varphi, \psi \in Form$, the following condition holds:*

If $[\psi \wedge EP\varphi] \in B$, then there is a Q-filter C s.t. $[\varphi \wedge EF\psi] \in C$ and $C \leq_{QF} B$.$\square$

Now, let ϕ be any formula s.t. $\not\vdash \phi$. Then, by Theorem 5.1, $[\neg\phi] \neq [ff]$. Therefore, by Lemma 5.2, there is a Q-filter B s.t. $[\neg\phi] \in B$. By the axiom A11, $[EP(AY(ff))] \in B$. Therefore, by Lemma 5.3, there is a Q-filter $C \in QF$ s.t. $C \leq_{QF} B$, $[AY(ff)] \in C$, and $[EF(\neg\phi)] \in C$. Next, we can define the frame $F_{v_0} = (W, \Sigma, \rightarrow, v_0)$ and the model $M = (F_{v_0}, V)$ as follows:

- $W = \{D \in QF \mid C \rightarrow_{QF}^{'*} D\}$, $\rightarrow = \rightarrow_{QF} \cap (W \times \Sigma \times W)$, $v_0 = C$,

- $p \in V(D)$ iff $[p] \in D$, where $p \in PV$ and $D \in W$.

In order to complete the proof we have to show that:

Lemma 5.4 *The following conditions hold:*

- *F_{v_0} is a frame,*

- *For each $\varphi \in Form$, $D \in W$: $M, D \models \varphi$ iff $[\varphi] \in D$.* $\square$

6 Logics POL and ISTL

The definitions of propositional versions of POL [Si90] and ISTL [KP87, PP90], we give below, differ slightly from their original versions. We label next step operators and backward step operators with action names $a \in \Sigma$. This is necessary if the logics are to be able to speak about actions, and therefore to express their concurrency. The alternative way of reaching the same aim would be to require that the valuation function encodes names of actions executed between adjacent states (see [GKP92, Pe92a]).

6.1 POL

The language of POL is a restriction of the set $Form$ s.t. only the following modalities are allowed: EF, EX_a, EP, and EY_a. The semantics of POL is the subset of the semantics of TL concerning POL formulas.

6.2 ISTL

We will consider here an extension of ISTL by backward modalities (see [PP90]), i.e., the language is equal to the set $Form$.

The semantics of ISTL differs of the semantics of TL in the following:

- ISTL formulas are interpreted over models corresponding to directed trace systems, (in fact models for ISTL are runs, but each directed trace system is the run of itself),

- the quantifiers $\forall$ and $\exists$ range over observations rather than over forward paths.

6.3 Proof systems for POL and ISTL

One can easily see that all the valid formulas of POL can be derived from the given proof system since POL is contained in TL. However, a difficult question is whether our proof system allows for deriving ISTL theorems. Now, we show that a little modification of the proof system leads to a complete proof system for a subset of ISTL without formulas of the form $EG\varphi$, but with formulas of the form $A(\varphi U\phi)$.

Since ISTL formulas are interpreted over directed trace systems the axiom A13 should be changed to: A13'. $EX_a AX_b\varphi \Rightarrow AX_b EX_a\varphi$, for $a \neq b$.

The main problem, however, stems from the fact that in the semantics of ISTL, the quantifiers range over observations rather than over forward paths. Let $\forall_o$ and $\exists_o$ denote the quantifiers ranging over observations, i.e., in the semantical rule $S3$ maximal paths are replaced by observations. We show that formulas of the form $E_o(\varphi U\phi)$ and $A_o(\varphi U\phi)$ can be expressed in the language of TL and therefore derived using the proof system.

Firstly, observe that $M, w \models E_o(\varphi U\phi)$ iff $M, w \models E(\varphi U\phi)$. But, the analogous property wouldn't hold for $A_o(\varphi U\psi)$. Let select a proposition $\sigma \in PV$ for which the three new axioms will be added to the proof system:

$A\sigma1.$ $AYff \Rightarrow \sigma$,

$A\sigma2.$ $\sigma \Rightarrow EX_!\sigma \wedge (AYff \vee EY_!\sigma)$,

    where $EX_!\sigma \overset{def}{=} \bigoplus_{a\in\Sigma} EX_a\sigma$, $EY_!\sigma \overset{def}{=} \bigoplus_{a\in\Sigma} EY_a\sigma$.

$A\sigma3.$ $EF\sigma$.

The above axioms specify that σ holds in exactly one observation in each model. Now, with the use of σ we show that formulas of the form $A_o(\varphi U\phi)$ can be expressed in the language of TL:

Theorem 6.1 *The following equivalence holds:*

$$\models \psi \Rightarrow A_o(\varphi U\phi) \quad iff \quad \models (\psi \wedge \sigma) \Rightarrow E((\varphi \wedge \sigma)U(\phi \wedge \sigma)),$$

where ψ, φ and ϕ do not contain σ.$\square$

In order to express formulas containing several subformulas of the form $A_o(\varphi_i U\phi_i)$, for each of them we have to select a special proposition σ_i and to add three new axioms for σ_i, as above.

Therefore, our extended proof system contains a complete axiomatization of ISTL without formulas of the form $E_o G\varphi$. Suprisingly, this is exactly the same subset of ISTL for which derivation rules were given in [PP90].

7 Final remarks

We have given infinitary complete proof systems for several temporal logics on trace systems. It follows from the completeness theorem that the set of all theorems of TL is at most Π_1^1 set. On the other hand as shown in [Pe92b] the validity problem for TL is Π_1^1-hard. Therefore, the validity problem is Π_1^1-complete.

One can easily notice that the same results hold for temporal logics interpreted on extended trace systems with conditional independence relation [KP90]. It would be interesting to see whether the results can be extended to occurrence transition systems [GKP92], where non-determinism of two actions a is also allowed.

8 References

[GW91]: Godefroid, P., Wolper, P., A Partial Approach to Model Checking, Proc. of LICS, 1991.

[GKP92]: Goltz, U., Kuiper, R., and Penczek, W., Propositional temporal logics and equivalences, Proc. of CONCUR'92, LNCS 630, pp. 222-236, 1992.

[KP87]: Katz, S., Peled, D., Interleaving Set Temporal Logic, 6th ACM Symposium on Principles of Distributed Computing, Vancouver Canada, pp. 178-190, 1987.

[LPRT92]: Lodaya, K., Parikh, R., Ramanujam, R., and Thiagarajan, P.S., A Logical Study of Distributed Transition Systems, submitted to publication.

[Ma88]: Mazurkiewicz, A., Basic Notions of Trace Theory, LNCS 354, pp. 285-363, 1988.

[MS87]: Mirkowska, G., and Salwicki, A., Algorithmic Logic, Reidel, Dordrecht and PWN, Warsaw 1987.

[NRT91]: Nielsen, M., Rozenberg, G., and Thiagarajan, Transition Systems, Event Structures and Unfoldings, in preparation, 1991.

[Pa91]: Paech, B., Concurrency as a Modality, PhD thesis, Munchen University, 1991.

[Pe87]: Peleg, D., Concurrent Dynamic Logic, Journal of ACM 34 (2), pp. 450-479, 1987.

[Pe90]: Penczek, W., A Concurrent Branching Time Temporal Logic, Proceedings of the Workshop on Computer Science Logic, Kaiserslautern, LNCS 440, pp. 337-354, 1990.

[Pe92a]: Penczek, W., Temporal Logics on Trace Systems, Proc. of the Workshop on Infinite Traces, Tubingen, 1992, also to appear in IJFCS.

[Pe92b]: Penczek, W., On Undecidability of Temporal Logics on Trace Systems, IPL 43, pp. 147-153, 1992.

[PKP91]: Peled, D., Katz, S., and Pnueli, A., Specifying and Proving Serializability in Temporal Logic, Proc. of LICS, 1991.

[PP90]: Peled, D., Pnueli, A., Proving Partial Order Liveness Properties, Proc. of ICALP, pp. 553-571, 1990.

[PW84]: Pinter, S.S., Wolper, P., A Temporal Logic for Reasoning about Partially Ordered Computations, Proc. 3rd Symp. on Principles of Distributed Computing, pp. 28-37, Vancouver 1984.

[Re89]: Reisig, W., Towards a Temporal Logic of Causality and Choice in Distributed Systems, LNCS 354, pp. 606-627, 1989.

[Ro90]: Rozoy, B., On Distributed Languages and Models for Distributed Computation, Technical Report 563, L.R.I., 1990.

[RS70]: Rasiowa, H., and Sikorski, R., The Mathematics of Metamathematics, PWN, Warsawa, 1970,

[Si90]: Sinachopoulos A, Partial Order Logics for Elementary Net Systems: State- and Event - approches, Proc. of CONCUR'90, 1990.

[Sz87]: Szalas, A., A complete axiomatic characterization of first-order temporal logic of linear time, TCS 54, pp. 199 - 214, 1987.

Capabilities and Complexity of Computations with Integer Division

(extended abstract)

Katharina Lürwer-Brüggemeier and Friedhelm Meyer auf der Heide*

Department for Mathematics and Computer Science
and Heinz Nixdorf Institute, University of Paderborn,
4790 Paderborn, Germany

Abstract. Computation trees with operation set $S \subseteq \{+, -, *, \mathrm{DIV}, \mathrm{DIV}_c\}$ (S-CTs) are considered. DIV denotes integer division, DIV_c integer division by constants. We characterize the families of languages $L \subseteq \mathbf{Z}^n$ that can be recognized by S-CTs, separate the computational capabilities of S-CTs for different operation sets S, and prove lower bounds for the depth of such trees.

Let $CC_n(S)$ denote the family of languages $L \subseteq \mathbf{Z}^n$ that can be recognized by an S-CT. In [7], $CC_1\{S\}$ is characterized for all $S \subseteq \{+, -, *, \mathrm{DIV}, \mathrm{DIV}_c\}$. It turns out that $CC_1(\{+, -, \mathrm{DIV}_c\}) = CC_1\{+, -, *, \mathrm{DIV}\}$.

In this paper we shed some more light on the computational power of integer division:

- We characterize $CC_n(S)$, $n > 1$, for $S = \{+, -, \mathrm{DIV}_c\}$ and $S = \{+, -, *, \mathrm{DIV}_c\}$, and partially characterize $CC_n(S)$, $n \geq 1$, for $S = \{+, -, \mathrm{DIV}\}$ and $S = \{+, -, *, \mathrm{DIV}\}$.
- We completely determine the relations among the classes $CC_n(S)$.

We further prove lower bounds:

- The component counting lower bound (e.g. $\Omega(n^2)$ for the knapsack problem) proven for $S = \{+, -, *\}$ by Ben Or and Yao also holds for $\{+, -, *, \mathrm{DIV}_c\}$.
- The GCD-algorithm due to Brent and Kung for $\{+, -, \mathrm{DIV}_c\}$-CTs is optimal even for $\{+, -, \mathrm{DIV}\}$-CTs.
- Testing whether $q(y) > x$ for an irreducible polynomial q of degree d takes time $\Omega(\mathrm{loglog}(d))$ for $\{+, -, *, \mathrm{DIV}\}$-CTs, even if arbitrary rational constants can be used at unit cost. This is the first nontrivial lower bound in this strong model (in which e. g. every finite language can be recognized in constant time, independent of the size of the language).

1 Introduction

The most common operations on integers supported by classical programming languages are $+, -, *, \mathrm{DIV}$, where DIV denotes integer division. In this paper we examine the computational capability (i.e.: what can be computed at all) and the complexity (i. e. how fast can computations be done) of computation trees in which the above operations and conditional branchings are allowed.

* Supported in part by DFG Grant Di 412/2-1

Computation Models

A computation tree with operation set $S \subseteq \{+, -, *, *_c, \mathrm{DIV}_c, \mathrm{DIV}\}$ and constants from C, $\{1\} \subseteq C \subseteq \mathbb{Q}$, for inputs $x_1, \ldots, x_n$ is a finite binary tree, a (S, C)-CT for short. $*_c, \mathrm{DIV}_c$ denote multiplication and integer division where one factor or the divisor is a constant, i.e. does not depend on the input values. Nodes v with degree 1 compute a function $g_v : \mathbb{Z}^n \to \mathbb{Q}$. g_v is either identical x_i for some $i \in \{1, \ldots, n\}$, or g_v is identical c for some $c \in C$, or g_v is of the form $g_{v_1} \, op \, g_{v_2}$ where v_1, v_2 are nodes on the path from the root to v, and $op \in S$. Nodes v with degree 2, the branchings, perform a test "$g(x_1, \ldots, x_n) > 0$" for some function g computed on the path to v. Each leaf is accepting or rejecting. An input $\bar{x} = (x_1, \ldots, x_n) \in \mathbb{Z}^n$ follows a path from the root to a leaf, at a branching v it follows the left or right branch according to whether it fulfills the test at that node, or not. $\bar{x}$ is accepted if it arrives at an accepting leaf. The language $L \subseteq \mathbb{Z}^n$ recognized by the CT is the set of inputs arriving at accepting leaves. The *complexity of the CT* is its depth.

If we only count the branching nodes for the depth, we talk about the *branching depth* of the tree. The *degree of a* $(\{+, -, *\}, C)$-*CT* is the maximum degree of the polynomials computed at its nodes.

The *computational capability* for inputs of dimension n of an operation set S is described by the family $CC_n(S)$ of languages $L \subseteq \mathbb{Z}^n$ that can be recognized by a CT with operation set S. Note: We assume that $\{+, -\} \subseteq S$. In this case the choice of C, $\{1\} \subseteq C \subseteq \mathbb{Q}$ does not affect $CC_n(S)$. We therefore refer to S-CTs instead of (S, C)-CTs, if the choice of C is not important.

Known Results

Let S be an operation set. We denote a function $f : \mathbb{Z}^n \to \mathbb{Z}$ as an S-*function*, if it can be computed by a straight line program (i.e. without branchings) using operations from S and constants from $\mathbb{Q}$. It can easily be checked that $L \subseteq \mathbb{Z}^n$ can be recognized by an S-CT, if and only if L is a Boolean combination of finitely many sets $\{\bar{x} \in \mathbb{Z}^n, f(\bar{x}) > 0\}$, for S-functions f. This is a satisfying characterization as long as S-functions are well understood. This is the case for e.g. $S = \{+, -, *_c\}$, $S = \{+, -, *\}$, $S = \{+, -, *, /\}$ (S-function are linear functions, polynomials, rational functions).

In [6] and [2], arguments from Algebraic Geometry are used to prove a lower bound for $\{+, -, *, /\}$-CTs with rational or real inputs based on the number of connected components of the language to be recognized, yielding e.g. an $\Omega(n^2)$ lower bound for the knapsack problem. In [13], these bounds are extended for a wide class of languages to integer inputs, in [12], [8] and [11] they are generalized to random access machines (in which also indirect addressing is allowed), for the case $S = \{+, -\}$.

If DIV or DIV_c is in S then S-functions are much less understood, thus good characterizations of computational capabilities and complexity results are much harder to achieve.

In [1] a very general result for an even stronger model where DIV and arbitrary analytic functions can be executed at unit cost is achieved. It shows that e.g. Linear Integer Programming with n variables and m restrictions cannot be done in time only dependent on n and m, (but not on its binary length) in this model. The same is shown for the GCD computation with operation set $\{+, -, *, \text{DIV}\}$ in [9].

If only one input variable is allowed, a complete characterization of the computational capabilities of S-CTs is shown in [7]. These capabilities are equivalent for operation sets $\{+, -, \text{DIV}_c\}$ and $\{+, -, *, \text{DIV}\}$; exactly those languages $L \subseteq \mathbb{Z}$ can be recognized which consist of a finite set and finitely many arithmetic progressions.

The complexities are different: If constants from $\mathbb{Q}$ are allowed, each $L \subseteq \mathbb{Z}$ that can be recognized at all can be recognized in constant time. This follows from techniques in [9] and [5] and the above characterization from [7]. On the other hand, [7] contains lower bounds $\Omega(\log(n)/\log\log(n))$ for some languages of size n, if only $\{+, -, \text{DIV}_c\}$ (but still arbitrary constants from $\mathbb{Q}$) are allowed. This is improved to $\Omega(\log(n))$[10].

Further lower bounds only hold if the allowed set of constants is restricted. If only constants from $\{0, 1\}$ are allowed, then computing the GCD of two n-bit numbers with operations $\{+, -, *, \text{DIV}\}$ needs time $\Omega(\log\log(n))$, as shown in [9], and time $\Omega(n)$ with operations $\{+, -, *_c, \text{DIV}_c\}$, see [4].

New Results

We shed some more light on the computational capabilities of CTs which use DIV or DIV_c, and prove lower bounds.

First consider the operation sets $\{+, -, *, \text{DIV}_c\}$ and $\{+, -, *_c, \text{DIV}_c\}$. Note that with $\{+, -, *\}$ polynomials can be computed, with $\{+, -, *_c\}$ only linear functions.

For $a \in \mathbb{N}$, $\overline{b} \in \mathbb{Z}^n$ we call a set $a\mathbb{Z}^n + \overline{b} = \{a\overline{x} + \overline{b},\ x \in \mathbb{Z}^n\}$ an a-lattice. The a-lattices $a\mathbb{Z}^n + \overline{b}$ for $\overline{b} \in \{0, \ldots, a-1\}^n$ form a partition of $\mathbb{Z}^n$ into a-lattices of edge length a.

Theorem 1. Let $S = \{+, -, *, \text{DIV}_c\}$ or $S = \{+, -, *_c, \text{DIV}_c\}$.

a) $L \subseteq \mathbb{Z}^n$ can be recognized by an S-CT D if and only if there is $a \in \mathbb{N}$ such that $\mathbb{Z}^n$ can be partitioned into a-lattices, such that L restricted to any of the lattices can be recognized by an $(S - \{\text{DIV}_c\})$-CT.

b) If D is an $(S, \mathbb{Q})$-CT with depth T, then the above $((S - \{\text{DIV}_c\}), \mathbb{Q})$-CTs have depth $O(T)$.

c) If D is an $(S, \{0, 1\})$-CT of depth T, then the above $(S - \{\text{DIV}_c\}, \mathbb{Q})$-CTs have depth $O(T)$, and the edge-length a of the lattices is at most $2^{2^{2^T}}$.

The above result includes a "normal form" for CTs with DIV_c: First use DIV_c to determine on which of the lattices the input lies, then determine membership in L using a CT without DIV_c. The lower bound in b) shows that there is only a constant loss in depth if this normal form is used.

As a corollary of Theorem 1b), we can show that the component counting lower bound for $\{+, -, *\}$-CTs from [2], extended to integer inputs in [13], even holds for integer inputs and $\{+, -, *, \text{DIV}_c\}$-CTs, for a wide class of languages. We quote some examples:

Corollary 1. *The following lower bounds hold for the depth of $(\{+,-,*,\mathrm{DIV}_c\},\mathbb{Q})$ CTs:*

- $\Omega(n\log(n))$ *for element distinctness (test whether all inputs $x_1,\ldots,x_n$ are distinct), (compare [2]).*
- $\Omega(n^2)$ *for the knapsack problem (input $a_1,\ldots,a_n,b$; test whether $y_1,\ldots,y_n \in \{0,1\}$ exist with $\sum_{i=1}^n a_i y_i = b$, compare [6]).*
- $\Omega(n^2\log(k+1))$ *for linear diophantine equations with k-bounded solutions (input $a_1,\ldots,a_n,b$, test whether $y_1,\ldots,y_n \in \{0,\ldots,k\}$ exist with $\sum_{i=1}^n a_i y_i = b$, compare [11]).*

Now we turn to computations with the unrestricted integer division. In this case we cannot present characterizations of the computational capabilities; we only get partial characterizations. For ease of description we only state them for 2 input variables.

Theorem 2.

a) *If $L \subseteq \mathbb{Z}^2$ can be recognized by a $\{+,-,*_c,\mathrm{DIV}\}$-CT D then the following holds: For each irrational β there is a pyramid $P := \{(x,y) \in \mathbb{Z}^2,\ c_1 < \frac{x}{y} < c_2\}$ for $c_1,c_2 \in \mathbb{Q},\ c_1 < \beta < c_2$, and $a \in \mathbb{N}$ such that, for each $\bar{b} \in \{0,\ldots,a-1\}^2$, L can be recognized by a $\{+,-,*_c\}$-CT for inputs from $(a\mathbb{Z}^2 + \bar{b}) \cap P$.*

b) *If D is a $(\{+,-,*_c,\mathrm{DIV}\},\{0,1\})$-CT of depth T, then there is $a \in \mathbb{N}$, $a \le 2^{2^{3T}}$, and a pyramid $P = \{(x,y) \in \mathbb{Z}^2,\ c_1 < \frac{x}{y} < c_2\}$ for $c_1,c_2 \in \mathbb{Q},\ c_1 < c_2, c_2 - c_1 \ge \frac{1}{2^{2^{3T}}}$ such that, for each $\bar{b} \in \{0,\ldots,a-1\}^2$, for inputs from $(a\mathbb{Z}^2 + \bar{b}) \cap P$, L can be recognized by a $(\{+,-,*_c\},\mathbb{Q}))$-CT of depth $O(T)$.*

In [3] an algorithm for computing the GCD of two n-bit numbers in time $O(n)$ is shown. It only uses operations $\{+,-,\mathrm{DIV}_c\}$. From results in [4] (based on the lower bound from [7]) a matching lower bound can be shown if only operations $\{+,-,\mathrm{DIV}_c\}$ are allowed. From Theorem 2b) we can conclude that the algorithm from [3] is optimal, even if $\{+,-,\mathrm{DIV}\}$ are allowed.

Corollary 2. *Testing whether two n-bit numbers x,y are relatively prime requires depth $\Omega(n)$ for a $(\{+,-,\mathrm{DIV}\},\{0,1\})$-CT.*

Now let us deal with the most powerful operation set under consideration, namely $\{+,-,*,\mathrm{DIV}\}$.

As noted earlier, achieving lower bounds in this case is hard; in particular, there are no lower bounds known if arbitrary rational constants are allowed. We will present the first such bounds. For ease of description we again restrict ourselves to the case $n = 2$.

Theorem 3.

a) *If $L \subseteq \mathbb{Z}^2$ can be recognized by a $\{+,-,*,\mathrm{DIV}\}$-CT D, then for each $c_1,c_2 \in \mathbb{N}$ there is a polynomial $q : \mathbb{Z} \to \mathbb{Q}$ and $k_1,k_2,z \in \mathbb{N}$ such that the following holds. Restricted to $\{(x,y) \in \mathbb{N},\ x \ge y^{k_1},\ x \equiv c_1 \bmod q(y),\ y \equiv c_2 \bmod k_2, y > z\}$, L can be recognized by a $\{+,-,*\}$-CT.*

b) *If D is a $(\{+,-,*,\mathrm{DIV}\},\mathbb{Q})$-CT of depth T, then we can achieve that q has degree $\le 2^{2^T}$, $k_1 \le 2^{2^T}$ and the $(\{+,-,*\},\mathbb{Q})$-CT has branching depth $O(T)$ and degree $O(2^{2^T})$.*

From part b) we can conclude the first nontrivial lower bounds for the depths of $(\{+,-,*,\text{DIV}\}, \mathbb{Q})$-CTs. Recall that this is a very powerful model, every finite language can be recognized in constant time (i. e. in time independent of the size of the language).

Corollary 3. *Let* $r : \mathbb{Z} \to \mathbb{Z}$ *be an irreducible polynomial of degree* d *with positive leading coefficient. Then each* $(\{+,-,*,\text{DIV}\}, \mathbb{Q})$-CT *that recognizes* $L_r = \{(x,y) \in \mathbb{N}^2, r(y) > x\}$ *has depth* $\Omega(\log\log(d))$.

The results about the computational capabilities (parts a) of the above three theorems) allow complete determination of the relative strengths of the different operation sets. In the following theorem, an arrow $S \to S'$ for operation sets S, S' means $CC_n(S') \subsetneq CC_n(S)$ for $n \geq 2$. $S --- S'$ means $CC_n(S)$ and $CC_n(S')$ are incomparable.

Theorem 4.

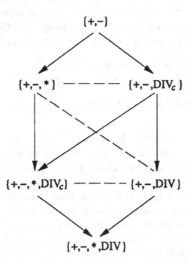

Note that the above diagram collapses to two classes, those without DIV or DIV_c and those with DIV or DIV_c, if we consider the case $n = 1$, see [7].

The rest of the paper is organized as follows: Theorem i and Corollary i is proven in Section $i + 1$, $i = 1, 2, 3$. Theorem 4 is proven in Section 5.

2 Results for Operation Sets Including DIV_c

In this chapter we sketch proofs for the characterization results and the general lower bounds stated in Theorem 1, and for the specific lower bound from Corollary 1.

Proof of Theorem 1 a).

"$\Leftarrow$" Let $\mathbb{Z}^n$ be partitioned into finitely many a-lattices $a\mathbb{Z}^n + \bar{b}, \bar{b} \in \{0, \dots, a-1\}^n$. Restricted to a fixed such lattice, L can be recognized by a $\{+,-\}$ resp. $\{+,-,*\}$-CT. The following algorithm with operation set $\{+,-,\text{DIV}_c\}$ resp. $\{+,-,*,\text{DIV}_c\}$ recognizes L.

1. Decide in which lattice $a\mathbb{Z}^n + \bar{b}$ the input $\bar{x}$ lies.
2. If $\bar{x} \in a\mathbb{Z}^n + \bar{b}$ decide with a $\{+,-\}$-CT resp. $\{+,-,*\}$-CT whether $\bar{x} \in L \cap (a\mathbb{Z}^n + \bar{b})$.

In Step 1, one can determine $\bar{b}$ by computing $b_i = x_i - (x_i \mathrm{DIV}_c a) \cdot a$ for $i = 1, \ldots, n$. This is possible without multiplication because a is a constant.

"$\Rightarrow$" We show this for $S = \{+,-,*,\mathrm{DIV}_c\}$. The proof for $S = \{+,-,\mathrm{DIV}_c\}$ is analogous. Let D be a $\{+,-,*,\mathrm{DIV}_c\}$-CT recognizing L. The basic idea is to replace, from the root to the leaves, each node v with a DIV_c operation by a multiway branching where we branch according to all possible results of $(x_1 \bmod a, \ldots, x_n \bmod a) \in \{0, \ldots, a-1\}^n$ for a constant $a \in \mathbb{N}$. We refer to such nodes as modulo-branching nodes, MB-nodes. This concept was introduced in [7].

Let v be a first node on a path from the root to a leaf where DIV_c is performed. Assume that $f(\bar{x})\mathrm{DIV}_c \frac{a}{b}$ is computed, for f previously computed on the path to v. As v is the first node with DIV_c on this path, f is a polynomial with rational coefficients. Let $k \in \mathbb{N}$ be such that $k \cdot f$ has integer coefficients. Replace v by a MB-node that branches according to the result of $(x_1 \bmod ka, \ldots x_n \bmod ka)$.

Lemma 5. *Restricted to inputs from the lattice* $ka\mathbb{Z}^n + \bar{c}$ *for* $\bar{c} \in \{0, \ldots, ka-1\}^n$, *we can express* $f(\bar{x})\mathrm{DIV}_c \frac{a}{b}$ *as* $\frac{b}{a}f(\bar{x}) - \frac{l}{ka}$, *for a constant* l *dependent on* $\bar{c}$.

The result is shown in [7] for $n = 1$. The proof for $n > 1$ is similar and is omitted here. □

Thus we can replace $f(\bar{x})\mathrm{DIV}_c \frac{a}{b}$ by an MB-node with degree $(ka)^n$, whose branches are copies of the subtree of D with root v, where the DIV_c computation at v is replaced by the computation $\frac{b}{a}f(\bar{x}) - \frac{l}{ka}$ as above. If we execute the above replacement from top to bottom at all DIV_c operations in the tree, we finally get a CT without DIV_c, but with MB-nodes, that recognizes L.

In order to achieve the desired characterization, notice that we obtain a $\{+,-,*\}$-CT if we fix the outcomes of all multiway branchings, i.e. if we restrict the input set to the intersection of the corresponding lattices. As this intersection is again a lattice, and we can get a refinement of this partition into lattices with common edge length, Theorem 1 a) follows. □

The *proofs of Theorem 1 b) and c)* are easy, careful analyses of the construction above. □

Corollary 1 follows from Theorem 1 b) and a result from [13] due to A. Yao. He shows that Ben Or's component counting lower bound from [2] for $\{+,-,*,/\}$-CTs also holds for certain languages if only integer inputs are allowed. A careful analysis of the proof shows that the result is even true if only inputs from a lattice $a\mathbb{Z}^n$, for arbitrary $a \in \mathbb{N}$ are considered. This allows to get lower bounds as described in Corollary 1, by applying Theorem 1 b). □

3   Results for Operation Set $\{+,-,*_c,\mathrm{DIV}\}$

Proof of Theorem 2 a). Let β be irrational. Consider a first node v with a DIV-operation on the path from the root to a leaf in a $\{+,-,*_c,\mathrm{DIV}\}$-CT D. At v,

$f(x,y) \text{ DIV } g(x,y)$ is computed, $f(x,y) = ax + by + c$, $g(x,y) = dx + ey + h$, $a, b, c, d, e, h \in \mathbb{Q}$.

If $d = e = 0$, then $f(x,y) \text{ DIV } h$ is computed, i.e. DIV_c is sufficient.

Otherwise, the following lemma tells us that we can replace the computation at v by finitely many branchings.

Lemma 6. *Let β be irrational. Let $f, g : \mathbb{Z}^2 \to \mathbb{Z}$ be linear functions with rational coefficients, g not constant. Then there are $c_1 < \beta < c_2$ such that $f(x,y)\text{DIV}g(x,y)$ only takes finitely many values for inputs from $P = \{(x,y) \in \mathbb{Z}^2, c_1 \leq \frac{x}{y} \leq c_2\}$.*

Proof of Lemma 6. Let $c_1, c_2, c_1 < \beta < c_2$ be chosen such that $d\gamma + e \neq 0$ for each $\gamma \in [c_1, c_2]$. This choice is possible as β is irrational. Then, for inputs from P, $f(x,y)\text{DIV}g(x,y) = ((a\gamma + b)y + c)\text{DIV}((d\gamma + e)y + h)$, if we substitute y by $\gamma x, \gamma \in [c_1, c_2]$. By the above choice of c_1, c_2, the above divisor is bounded away from 0, and both divident and divisor are bounded. Thus $f(x,y)\text{DIV}g(x,y)$ only takes finitely many values for inputs from P. □

We now can replace, from top to bottom, each DIV-operation as shown above, and each DIV_c operation as shown in Lemma 5. This yields Theorem 2 a). □

The proof of Theorem 2 b) is similar to the above, and is omitted here.

4 Results for Operation Set $\{+, -, *, \text{DIV}\}$

Proof of Theorem 3 a). Let D be a $\{+, -, *, \text{DIV}\}$-CT recognizing $L \subseteq \mathbb{Z}^2$. Again we shall substitute, from top to bottom, the functions computed at nodes v using DIV by computations without DIV, in this case by rational functions. The following lemma shows how to do the substitution.

Lemma 7. *Let $P, Q : \mathbb{Z}^2 \to \mathbb{Z}$ be polynomials with integer coefficients, $Q(x,y) = \Sigma_{i=0}^d f_i(y)x^i$. Let $\delta := \max\{-1, (\text{maximum degree of } x \text{ in } P)-(\text{maximum degree of } x \text{ in } Q)\}$, $p(y) = (f_d(y))^{\delta+1}$.*
There is a polynomial $B : \mathbb{Z}^2 \to \mathbb{Z}$ with rational coefficients and $k_1, k_2, c_1, c_2, z \in \mathbb{N}$, such that, for inputs from $I = \{(x,y) \in \mathbb{Z}^2, x > y^{k_1}, x \equiv c_1 \bmod p(y), y \equiv c_2 \bmod k_2, y \geq z\}$, $P(x,y)\text{DIV}Q(x,y) = \frac{B(x,y)}{p(y)}$.

Proof of Lemma 7. For a polynomial $q : \mathbb{Z}^2 \to \mathbb{Z}$ with variables x, y let $\deg_x(q)$ denote the maximum degree of x in q. Let P, Q, p, δ be as in Lemma 7.

Claim 1. *There are polynomials $A(x,y), R(x,y)$ with integer coefficients, $\deg_x R < \deg_x Q$, and $\deg_x A \leq \max\{0, \delta\}$, $\deg_y A \leq \deg_y P + \delta \deg_y Q$ such that*

$$P(x,y) = \frac{A(x,y) \cdot Q(x,y) + R(x,y)}{p(y)}.$$

Proof. We proceed by induction on δ. For $\delta = -1$ the hypothesis holds with $A(x,y) \equiv 0$, $R(x,y) = P(x,y)$. Let $\delta > -1$. Let $P(x,y) = \sum_{i=0}^e g_i(y)x^i$. Then $\delta = e - d$. Consider the polynomial

$$S(x,y) := f_d(y) \cdot P(x,y) - x^\delta \cdot g_e(y) \cdot Q(x,y). \tag{1}$$

Since $\deg_x S < \deg_x P$, the induction hypothesis holds for the pair $S(x,y)$ and $Q(x,y)$. This yields

$$S(x,y) = \frac{1}{f_d(y)^\delta} \tilde{A}(x,y) \cdot Q(x,y) + \frac{1}{f_d(y)^\delta} \tilde{R}(x,y) \tag{2}$$

for suitable $\tilde{A}, \tilde{R}$ with integer coefficients, $\deg_x(\tilde{R}) < \deg_x(Q)$.
(1) and (2) imply

$$P(x,y) = \frac{1}{f_d(y)^{\delta+1}} (\tilde{A}(x,y) + f_d(y)^\delta \cdot x^\delta \cdot p_e(y)) Q(x,y) + \frac{\tilde{R}(x,y)}{f_d(y)^{\delta+1}}.$$

Since $\deg_y S \le \deg_y P + \deg_y Q$ and $\deg_y \tilde{A} \le \deg_y S + (\delta - 1) \deg_y Q$ we get that $\deg_y A = \max\{\deg_y \tilde{A}; \delta \deg_y Q - \deg_y P\} \le \deg_y P + \delta \deg_y Q$. $\qquad\square$

From this claim we conclude

$$P(x,y) DIV Q(x,y) = \left\lfloor \frac{A(x,y)}{p(y)} + \frac{R(x,y)}{p(y) \cdot Q(x,y)} \right\rfloor.$$

Now we observe the following.

(i) Let $k_1 = \deg_x(Q) + 1$.
  For $x > y^{k_1}$, $\frac{R(x,y)}{p(y) \cdot Q(x,y)}$ tends to 0 when $\| (x,y) \|$ tends to infinity.
(ii) Let $c_1, c_2 \in \mathbf{Z}$ be fixed, $k_2 \in \mathbf{Z}$ be suitably chosen. For $x \equiv c_1 \bmod p(y)$, $y \equiv c_2 \bmod k_2$, it holds that $\frac{A(x,y)}{p(y)} \in \frac{1}{k_2}\mathbf{Z}$.

(i) follows directly from the definitions of R, p, and k_1.
(ii) can be seen as follows:
Let $x \equiv c_1 \bmod p(y)$, i. e. $x = l \cdot p(y) + c_1$ for some $l \in \mathbb{N}$. Then

$$\frac{A(x,y)}{p(y)} = \frac{\sum_{i=0}^n \sum_{j=0}^m a_{ij}(x - c_1)^i y^j}{p(y)}$$

$$= \sum_{i=1}^n \sum_{j=0}^m a_{ij}(l^i (p(y))^{i-1} \cdot y^j + \frac{\sum_{j=0}^m a_{0j} y^j}{p(y)}$$

$$=: \frac{\tilde{A}(x,y)}{p(y)} + \frac{s(y)}{p(y)}$$

The first summand has integer values, the second one has values from $\frac{1}{k_2}\mathbf{Z}$, for suitable k_2, as shown in [7].

Let $z > 0$ be sufficiently large. (i) and (ii) imply that, for inputs from I (compare Lemma 7),

$$P(x,y)\mathrm{DIV}Q(x,y) = A(x,y)\mathrm{DIV}p(y).$$

The proof of (ii) shows that

$$A(x,y)\mathrm{DIV}p(y) = \frac{\bar{A}(x,y)}{p(y)} + s(y)\mathrm{DIV}p(y).$$

In [7] it is shown that $s(y)\mathrm{DIV}p(y)$ can be represented as a polynomial $t(y)$ for inputs $y \equiv c_2 \bmod k_2$, $y > z$, for z sufficiently large. Thus the lemma holds if we choose $B(x,y) = \bar{A}(x,y) + t(y) \cdot p(y)$. $\square$

Now we can replace each DIV-operation in the CT D by the computation of a rational function as shown in Lemma 7.

This yields a $\{+, -, *, /\}$-CT that recognizes L for inputs from a set as described in Theorem 3. The polynomial $q(y)$ is the product of all polynomials p appearing as divisors when replacing DIV-operations as described in Lemma 7. It is easy to see how to get rid of the division in such a CT. $\square$

Proof of Theorem 3 b). We only have to analyze, by induction on the depth of the CT, the degrees of the rational functions $\frac{B(x,y)}{p(y)}$, and the size of k_1.

Claim 2. *After substituting the DIV-operations in the upper t levels of D the degrees of the nominator and denominator polynomials of the rational functions defined in Lemma 7 is $\leq 2^{2^{t-1}}$.*

Proof. For $t = 1$ the hypothesis is obvious.

Let the hypothesis hold for all $k < t$. Then at the tth-level for the DIV-computation labelled with $P(x,y)$ DIV $Q(x,y) = \frac{B(x,y)}{p(y)}$ we know that $\deg P \leq 2^{2^{t-2}}$ and $\deg Q \leq 2^{2^{t-2}}$ and $\deg_x B(x,y) \leq \deg_x Q \leq 2^{2^{t-2}}$. Therefore $\deg_y B(x,y) \leq \deg_y P + \delta \deg_y Q \leq 2^{2^{t-1}}$ and $\deg_y p \leq \delta \deg_y Q \leq 2^{2^{t-1}}$. $\square$

Since there are at most 2^t nodes the degree of the product of these polynomials is at most 2^{2^t}.

$k_1 \leq 2^{2^t}$ follows immediately from Lemma 3 of [9] and the above induction. $\square$

Proof of Corollary 3. Assume that a $(\{+, -, *, DIV\}, \mathbb{Q})$-CT M of depth T recognizes L_r. Theorem 3 b) shows that there is k_2 and a polynomial $p(y)$ with degree $\leq 2^{2^T}$ such that, for $y \in k_2\mathbb{Z}$, there are $x_1(y) < x_2(y), x_2(y) - x_1(y) \leq p(y), x_1(y) < r(y) < x_2(y)$ such that M accepts $A = \{x_1(y), y \in k_2\mathbb{Z}\}$ and rejects $B = \{x_2(y), y \in k_2\mathbb{Z}\}$. Thus $r(y)$ separates A from B.

If $d \leq \max\{k_1, \deg(p(y))\}$ the lower bound follows directly from Theorem 3 b).

Otherwise the $(\{+, -, *\}, \mathbb{Q})$-CT D' from Theorem 3 b) recognizes L also for inputs from $A \cup B$. Thus D' computes a polynomial $s(y)$ that separates A from B. As $s(y) \in \{x_1(y), \ldots, x_2(y)\} \subseteq \{r(y) - p(y), \ldots, r(y) + p(y)\}$, and $d > \deg(p(y))$, $s(y)$ has degree d. As D' only computes polynomials with degree $O(2^{2^T})$, we get $d = O(2^{2^T})$, which implies the Corollary. $\square$

5 Separation Results

We sketch a *proof of Theorem 4*. $CC_2\{+,-\} \subsetneq CC_2\{+,-,*\}$ is obvious, as e.g.
$L = \{(x,y), x^2 > y\} \in CC_2\{+,-,*\} - CC_2\{+,-\}$.
The following separations follow easily from [7], they already hold for $n = 1$.

- $CC_n(\{+,-\}) \subsetneq CC_n\{+,-,\text{DIV}_c\}$
- $CC_n\{+,-,\text{DIV}_c\} - CC_n\{+,-,*\} \neq \emptyset$
- $CC_n\{+,-,*\} \subsetneq CC_n\{+,-,*,\text{DIV}_c\}$

It is easy to conclude from Theorem 1:

- $CC_n\{+,-,\text{DIV}_c\} \subsetneq CC_n\{+,-,*,\text{DIV}_c\}$.

The remaining relations are implicit in the following corollary of Theorems 1 and 2.

Corollary 4.
a) $\{(x,y) \in \mathbb{Z}^2, x^2 > 2y^2\} \in CC_2(\{+,-,*\}) - CC_2(\{+,-,\text{DIV}\})$
b) $\{(x,y) \in \mathbb{Z}^2, (y-1)\text{DIV}x - y\text{DIV}x < 0\} \in CC_2(\{+,-,\text{DIV}\}) - CC_2(\{+,-,*,\text{DIV}_c\})$

The proofs are easy applications of Theorem 2 b) and Theorem 1 b). □

References

1. L. Babai, B. Just, F. Meyer auf der Heide, On the limits of computations with the floor function, Information and Computation 78(2), 99–107, 1988.
2. M. Ben-Or, Lower bounds for algebraic computation trees, 15th ACM-STOC, 80–86, 1983.
3. R. Brent, H. Kung, Systolic VLSI-arrays for linear time GCD-computation, Proc. Int. Conf. on Very Large Scale Integration. (VLSI 83, IFIP), F. Anceau and E. J. Aas (eds.), 145–154, 1983.
4. N. Bshouty, Euclidean GCD algorithm is not optimal, preprint 1989.
5. N. Bshouty, private communication, 1992.
6. D. Dobkin, R. L. Lipton, A lower bound of $\frac{1}{2}n^2$ on linear search programs for the knapsack problem, JCSS 16, 417–421, 1975.
7. B. Just, F. Meyer auf der Heide, A. Wigderson, On computations with integer division, RAIRO Informatique Theoretique 23(1), 101–111, 1989.
8. P. Klein, F. Meyer auf der Heide, A lower bound for the knapsack problem on random access machines, Acta Informatica 19(3), 385–396, 1983.
9. Y. Mansur, B. Schieber, P. Tiwari, Lower bounds for integer greatest common divisor computation, 29 IEEE FOCS, 54–63, 1988.
10. J. Meidanis, private communication, 1992.
11. F. Meyer auf der Heide, Lower bounds for solving linear Diophantine equations on random access machines, J. ACM 32(4), 929–937, 1985.
12. W. J. Paul, J. Simon, Decision trees and random access machines, Monographie 30, L'Enseignement Mathematique, Logique et Algorithmique, Univ. Geneva, Switzerland, 331-340, 1992.
13. A. Yao, Lower bounds for algebraic computation trees with integer inputs, 30th IEEE FOCS, 308–313, 1989.

Extended Locally Definable Acceptance Types*
(Extended Abstract)

Rolf Niedermeier and Peter Rossmanith

Fakultät für Informatik, Technische Universität München, Arcisstr. 21
D-8000 München 2, Fed. Rep. of Germany

Abstract. Hertrampf's locally definable acceptance types showed that many complexity classes can be defined in terms of polynomially time bounded NTM's with simple local conditions on the nodes of its computation tree, rather than global concepts like number of accepting paths etc. We introduce extended locally definable acceptance types as an extension of Hertrampf's work with respect to the number of characterizable complexity classes. Among the new characterizable classes are UP and $MODZ_kP$. It is shown how different types of oracle access, e.g. guarded access, can be characterized by this model. This sheds new light on the discussion on how to access unambiguous computation. We present simple functions that describe precisely objects of current research as the unambiguous oracle, alternation, and promise hierarchies. We exhibit the new class UAP which seems to be an unambiguous analogue of Wagner's ∇P.

1 Introduction

Many classes of central interest in structural complexity theory are defined via polynomially time bounded Turing machines (TM's). A word w, for example, belongs to the language of a nondeterministic TM M, if M has at least one accepting path on input w. Many other acceptance mechanisms exist that are defined via numbers of accepting paths. Recently Hertrampf introduced an evaluation scheme for nondeterministic TM's (NTM's) which relies on evaluation of simple functions to be done locally in the nodes of a computation tree rather than to demand global conditions on it [9]. Using only OR as local functions yields NP, while AND yields *Co*NP. Allowing both OR and AND results in the class PSPACE. This concept, called *locally definable acceptance type*, is capable to characterize many more important complexity classes, among them $\oplus P$, 1-NP, all levels of the polynomial hierarchy as well as all levels of the boolean hierarchy over NP (see [8, 9]).

There exist, however, many interesting classes which do not seem to be characterizable in terms of locally definable acceptance types, though they can intuitively be described by simple local conditions, among them the class UP defined via unambiguous TM's [14]. Unambiguous complexity classes are closely connected to the existence of one-way functions and public-key crypto systems [7, 13]. Though they were always objects of central interest, just now there are attempts to examine them even more closely by analyzing different types of oracle and alternation hierarchies built on unambiguous classes, as well as negative and positive relativization results

* Research supported by DFG-SFB 0342 TP A4 "KLARA"

(see e.g. [3]). The approach to build hierarchies has proven to be very fruitful in the case of NP. It is one aim of this paper to fully characterize all in an intuitive sense locally definable complexity classes. In order to do so, we extend Hertrampf's definition of locally definable acceptance types to capture also UP and related classes, as well as classes derived by different kinds of relativized unambiguous classes. In contrast to the classes of the polynomial time hierarchy there are a lot of reasonable possibilities for oracle access to unambiguous computations. Cai, Hemachandra, and Vyskoč [3] regard guarded and fault-tolerant access. It is our aim to apply Hertrampf's ideas to the realm of unambiguous computations. In order to do so we have to extend his definition a little bit. We show that *extended locally definable acceptance types* can characterize at least as many classes as locally definable acceptance types. Moreover, the class of characterizable classes is closed under complement, polynomially length bounded existential and universal quantifications and all other closure properties of [9]. In addition it is also closed under some closure properties which were introduced by Hemachandra. These include the unambiguous versions $\exists!$ and $\forall!$ of existential and universal quantification. The new characterizable classes include UP, CoUP, $UP_{\leq k}$, $MODZ_k P$ and all levels of the unambiguous alternation, oracle, and promise hierarchies. Please note that our concept is only a little bit more complicated than Hertrampf's one and that proofs are not harder. We claim that extended locally definable acceptance types capture exactly the intuitive notion of "being definable by simple local conditions".

The remainder of the paper is organized as follows: In the next section we start defining extended locally definable acceptance types and explain the difference to Hertrampf's original definition. In the third section we provide characterizations of UP, $MODZ_k P$, UAP and demonstrate the closure of extended locally definable acceptance types under several complexity theoretic operators and relativization. Finally, in Section 4 we investigate access to unambiguous computations within the framework of extended locally definable acceptance types and, in particular, study guarded access to unambiguous computations.

We assume the reader to be familiar with standard notations of computational complexity theory. In particular, we denote by $L(M)$ the language accepted by a TM M and by $L(M, A)$ the language accepted by an oracle TM with access to oracle A. $\|M(w)\|$ denotes the number of accepting paths of machine M on input w. All further special notations will be introduced before they are used. Due to lack of space some results appear without proof. Mainly proofs are omitted for results where similar techniques as in Hertrampf's work [9] apply. A full paper containing all proofs is available.

2 Extended locally definable acceptance types

Goldschlager and Parberry [6] introduced so-called *extended Turing machines* in order to generalize the concept of alternating Turing machines. They studied the power of nondeterministic, time-bounded Turing machines with an altered manner of acceptance. Instead of only labeling the states (and thus also the configurations) of the machine just with AND (universal), OR (existential), NOT (negating), ACCEPT or REJECT, as it is done in alternating Turing machines, they allowed states to be labelled with a larger range of functions, in particular, any set of Boolean functions. Recently, Hertrampf [9] further generalized this concept by permitting any functions from m-*valued logic* for some fixed integer m rather than only from Boolean logic as Goldschlager and Parberry did. In [8], Hertrampf gives a complete case analysis when three-valued logic is allowed. He completely classified all complexity classes which can be defined by locally definable acceptance types restricted to three-valued logic. Among them he found the complete second level of the polynomial time hierarchy and ∇P [15].

In this paper we further extend Hertrampf's definition [9] of locally definable acceptance types for polynomial time machines in order to characterize complexity classes without (known) complete problems (e.g. UP [14] as a simple case). We begin with defining the basic notions common to our and Hertrampf's work.

Definition 1. Let m be an integer, $m \geq 2$. A *function f from m-valued logic* is a function $\{0,\ldots,m-1\}^r \to \{0,\ldots,m-1\}$ for $r \geq 0$.

The set $\{0,\ldots,m-1\}$ is called the *base set* for the domain and codomain of f. Clearly, the restriction to natural numbers in the above definition only has been done for reasons of convenience. Subsequently we will make extensive use of the fact that arbitrary symbols can be encoded as numbers. In addition, we assume that always an extra value $\perp$ is available for m-valued functions, which is not explicitly mentioned as a member of the base set. Whenever a function of m-valued logic has $\perp$ as an argument, the function evaluates to $\perp$. The meaning of $\perp$ can be understood as "undefined". We say that all functions from m-valued logic are "strict" with respect to $\perp$.

Definition 2. An *(extended) m-valued locally definable acceptance type* is a set F of functions from m-valued logic. The base set of F is the union of the base sets of its functions. An (extended) locally definable acceptance type is called *finite* if F is a finite set. An *F-machine M* is a polynomially time bounded NTM, where each configuration with r successors is labeled by a function $f \in F \cup \{id\}$ with arity r, dependent only on the state of M. (Here id denotes the identity on the base set of F.) Leaves in the computation tree are labeled with an integer from $\{0,\ldots,m-1\}$ dependent on the state. On input w *values* are assigned to nodes in the computation tree as follows: The value of a leaf is the integer, the leaf is labeled with. An inner node c, labeled with f and having successors $c_1,\ldots,c_r$ with values $v_1,\ldots,v_r$, has value $f(v_1,\ldots,v_r)$. The value of the root of the computation tree is the *result* of M.

Definition 3. A language L is a member of the complexity class $[F]P$, iff there is an F-machine M such that the result of M on input w is 1 if $w \in L$ and 0 if $w \notin L$.

For the ease of notation we call a class of languages C *locally definable* iff $C = [F]P$ for some extended locally definable acceptance type F. To compare this to Hertrampf's locally definable acceptance types, we now give his definition.

Definition 4. [9] A language L is a member of $(F)P$, iff there is an F-machine M such that the result of M on input w is 1 if $w \in L$ and the result is different from 1 if $w \notin L$.

In order to simplify the presentation of our results we make several agreements for the rest of the paper. We will use extended locally definable acceptance types whose different functions may have different base sets. For example, let $F = \{f_1, f_2\}$ and $f_1 : X_1^{k_1} \to X_1$ and $f_2 : X_2^{k_2} \to X_2$ with $X_1 \neq X_2$. Then we settle that in fact f_1 and f_2 are extended to $\hat{f}_1, \hat{f}_2$ with base set $X := X_1 \cup X_2$ as follows: $\hat{f}_i : X^{k_i} \to X, \hat{f}_i(\vec{x}) := f_i(\vec{x})$ if $\vec{x} \in X_i^{k_i}$ and $\hat{f}_i(\vec{x}) := \bot$, otherwise $(1 \leq i \leq 2)$. We will also use underlined and overlined functions and numbers (e.g. we have $\overline{f}, \underline{f}$ or $\overline{0}, \underline{0}, \overline{x}, \underline{x}$ etc.). Let $f : \{0, \ldots, m-1\}^k \to \{0, \ldots, m-1\}$. Writing $\overline{f}$ means the function $\overline{f} : \{\overline{0}, \ldots, \overline{m-1}\}^k \to \{\overline{0}, \ldots, \overline{m-1}\}$ with $\overline{f}(\overline{x_1}, \ldots, \overline{x_k}) := f(x_1, \ldots, x_k)$ and $\overline{f}$ is undefined, otherwise. (Underlining is handled analogously.)

In Definition 5 we summarize several functions which will be used in the context with extended locally definable acceptance types. Most of the proofs in the paper can be done by making use of these "standard" functions.

Definition 5. Let $m \geq 2$ be a positive integer, let $a, b \in \{0, \ldots, m-1\}$ and let $A, B \subseteq \{0, \ldots, m-1\}$. We use the following functions from m-valued (resp. $2m$-valued) logic. If a value for some argument is not explicitly defined, it is $\bot$. (E.g. $\text{OR}!(1,1) = \text{AND}(0,2) = \bot$.)

1. Transformation functions: $\text{TRANS}_{B \to b}^{A \to a} : \{0, \ldots, m-1\} \to \{0, \ldots, m-1\}$, where

$$\text{TRANS}_{B \to b}^{A \to a}(x) := \begin{cases} a \text{ if } x \in A, \\ b \text{ if } x \in B. \end{cases}$$

2. Boolean functions: $\text{OR}, \text{OR}!, \text{AND}$, and $\text{AND}! : \{0, \ldots, m-1\}^2 \to \{0, \ldots, m-1\}$, where

$$\text{OR}(x,y) := \begin{cases} 0 \text{ if } x = y = 0, \\ 1 \text{ if } (x,y) \in \{(0,1), (1,0), (1,1)\}. \end{cases}$$
$$\text{AND}(x,y) := \begin{cases} 0 \text{ if } (x,y) \in \{(0,0), (0,1), (1,0)\}, \\ 1 \text{ if } x = y = 1. \end{cases}$$
$$\text{OR}!(x,y) := \begin{cases} 0 \text{ if } x = y = 0, \\ 1 \text{ if } (x,y) \in \{(0,1), (1,0)\}. \end{cases}$$
$$\text{AND}!(x,y) := \begin{cases} 0 \text{ if } (x,y) \in \{(0,1), (1,0)\}, \\ 1 \text{ if } x = y = 1. \end{cases}$$

3. Counting functions: $\text{ADD}_{\leq k}, \text{MOD}_k : \{0, \ldots, k\}^2 \to \{0, \ldots, k\}$, where

$$\text{ADD}_{\leq k}(x,y) := \begin{cases} x + y \text{ if } x + y \leq k, \\ \bot \quad\quad \text{otherwise} \end{cases}$$
$$\text{MOD}_k(x,y) := \begin{cases} 0 \quad\quad\quad\quad\quad\quad\quad \text{if } x = y = 0, \\ 1 + (x + y - 1) \bmod k \text{ otherwise.} \end{cases}$$

4. Function for modelling oracle access:
$\text{SELECT} : \{0, \ldots, m-1\}^2 \times \{\overline{0}, \ldots, \overline{m-1}\} \to \{0, \ldots, m-1\}$, where

$$\text{SELECT}(x,y,z) := \begin{cases} x \text{ if } z = \overline{1}, y \neq \bot, \\ y \text{ if } z = \overline{0}, x \neq \bot. \end{cases}$$

Before we come to our first results, we present a principle to be applied to F-TM's, playing a central role in the whole work. Due to Definition 3 each root node of a computation tree of an F-TM must evaluate to 0 or 1 (and nothing else is allowed). In this way, the functions which are contained in F force the computation tree to be of a special structure in order to avoid values different from 0 or 1 at its root. This is illustrated in the following two examples. First, consider the case where $F = \{\text{OR}!\}$. To keep away value $\perp$ from the root, it is necessary that at most one leaf node of the tree has value 1 and all the other leaves are 0. Second, if it holds $F = \{\overline{f}, \text{TRANS}_{A\mapsto 1}^{\overline{1}\mapsto 0}\}$, where $A = \{\overline{0}, \overline{2}, \ldots, \overline{m-1}\}$ and f is some function from $\{0, \ldots, m-1\}^k$ into $\{0, \ldots, m-1\}$, then the following tree structure (and node labelling) is imperative: The root node of the computation tree of the F-TM is labelled with the transformation function and is connected (by a deterministic step) to a computation tree where all inner nodes are labelled $\overline{f}$ (and the leaf nodes are labelled by a constant from A). Otherwise, the root clearly wouldn't evaluate to 0 or 1. The above observation will be called the *propagation principle* in the following. This name is motivated by the fact that e.g. the "undefined value" $\perp$ propagates through the whole computation tree to the root. Creation of value $\perp$ is always forbidden in a computation of a F-TM.

We start with stating (without proof due to the lack of space) that for extended acceptance types the same normal form theorem as for Hertrampf's acceptance types holds.

Theorem 6. *Let F be a finite, extended locally definable acceptance type. Then there exists one binary function g such that $[F]P = [\{g\}]P$.*

Extended locally definable acceptance types are at least as powerful as their counterparts of Hertrampf. In addition, we indicate the closure under complementation and under the Boolean operations. Note that these results already have been established for locally definable acceptance types by Hertrampf [9] and that the proofs are quite similar for our extended version.

Theorem 7. *For all locally definable acceptance types F there exists an extended locally definable acceptance type F' such that it holds $(F)P = [F']P$.*

Proof. (Sketch) Let C be a class characterizable by some locally definable acceptance type F. Then there exists a binary function $f : \{0, \ldots, m-1\}^2 \rightarrow \{0, \ldots, m-1\}$ such that $C = (\{f\})P$ [9]. We claim that $F' = \{\overline{f}, \text{TRANS}_{\overline{0,2},\ldots,\overline{m-1}\mapsto 0}^{\overline{1}\mapsto 1}\}$ serves the purpose.

Lemma 8. *Let C_1 and C_2 be locally definable. Then the classes $CoC_1, C_1 \wedge C_2 := \{A \cap B \mid A \in C_1, B \in C_2\}$, and $C_1 \vee C_2 := \{A \cup B \mid A \in C_1, B \in C_2\}$ are also locally definable.*

Proof. W.l.o.g. (Theorem 6) let $C = [\{f\}]P$, $C_1 = [\{f_1\}]P$, and $C_2 = [\{f_2\}]P$. We claim that $CoC = [\{\overline{f}, \text{TRANS}_{\overline{0}\mapsto 1}^{\overline{1}\mapsto 0}\}]P$ and $C_1 \vee C_2 = [\{\text{OR}(\ddot{\cdot}, \ddot{\cdot}), \overline{f_1}, \underline{f_2}\}]P$ hold. Herein, $\text{OR}(\ddot{\cdot}, \ddot{\cdot})$ is defined according to

$$\text{OR}(\ddot{\cdot}, \ddot{\cdot})(x, y) = \begin{cases} \text{OR}(u, v) & \text{if } \overline{u} = x, \underline{v} = y, u, v \in \{0, 1\}, \\ \perp & \text{otherwise.} \end{cases}$$

The claim for $C_1 \wedge C_2$ then follows by the closure under complementation and De Morgan's laws. (See the full paper for details.)

3 New Characterizations

We start with showing that UP, $\text{UP}_{\leq k}$, MODZ_kP, and UAP are all locally definable. Note that for all these classes it does not seem to be possible to get a characterization in terms of a plain locally definable acceptance type. For a TM M we denote by $\text{ACCEPT}(M, x)$ the number of accepting paths of M on input x. The class UP was defined by Valiant [14] via unambiguous polynomially time bounded TM's. Formally, a language L is a member of UP, if there exists a polynomially time bounded NTM M such that $\text{ACCEPT}(M, x) = 1$, if $x \in L$ and $\text{ACCEPT}(M, x) = 0$, if $x \notin L$.

Unambiguity plays an important role in complexity theory (e.g. cf. [2, 10, 11, 12] for some recent results) and, in particular, in cryptography where the question for existence of one-way functions is shown to be equivalent with the question whether $\text{P} = \text{UP}$ holds [7, 13]. $\text{UP}_{\leq k}$ is a generalization of UP defined by Cai, Hemachandra, and Vyskoč [3]. Here up to k (for some constant k) accepting paths are allowed rather than only one.

Theorem 9. UP and $\text{UP}_{\leq k}$ are locally definable.

Proof. We give the characterization for $\text{UP}_{\leq k}$. From this we also have a characterization for UP since $\text{UP}_{\leq 1} = \text{UP}$. We show that $\text{UP}_{\leq k} = [\{\overline{\text{ADD}_{\leq k}}, \text{TRANS}_{\overline{1}, \ldots, \overline{k-1} \mapsto 1}^{\overline{0} \mapsto 0}\}]\text{P}$ holds.

For the inclusion "$\subseteq$" analogous to previous proofs we augment the computation tree of the $\text{UP}_{\leq k}$-machine with a new root and a deterministic step to the root of the original tree. The new root is labeled with the transformation function all inner nodes of the original tree are labeled with $\overline{\text{ADD}_{\leq k}}$, and its leaves are labeled with values $\overline{0}$ or $\overline{1}$. Due to the definition of $\overline{\text{ADD}_{\leq k}}$ the claim immediately follows.

To prove "$\supseteq$" we again apply the propagation principle. From this we have that the computation tree of an $\{\overline{\text{ADD}_{\leq k}}, \text{TRANS}_{\overline{1}, \ldots, \overline{k-1} \mapsto 1}^{\overline{0} \mapsto 0}\}$-machine has to be of the above discussed form (that is the root is labeled with the transformation function and the remaining inner nodes have label $\overline{\text{ADD}_{\leq k}}$). Obviously, such a tree can be simulated by a $\text{UP}_{\leq k}$-machine.

MODZ_kP was introduced by Beigel, Gill, and Hertrampf [1]. $L \in \text{MODZ}_k\text{P}$, if there is a polynomially time bounded NTM M, such that

$$\begin{aligned} \text{ACCEPT}(M, x) &\not\equiv 0 \pmod{k} && \text{if } x \in L, \\ \text{ACCEPT}(M, x) &= 0 && \text{if } x \notin L. \end{aligned}$$

Theorem 10. MODZ_kP is locally definable.

Proof. The proof is similar to the proof for the characterization of $\text{UP}_{\leq k}$. Like there the number of accepting computations has to be counted (but now modulo k). It can be shown that $\text{MODZ}_k\text{P} = [\{\overline{\text{MOD}_k}, \text{TRANS}_{\overline{1}, \ldots, \overline{k-1} \mapsto 1}^{\overline{0} \mapsto 0}\}]\text{P}$.

Combining the concepts of unambiguity and alternation yields the class UAP. We call an alternating TM *unambiguous*, if for all inputs the computation tree does contain neither existential nodes with more than one accepting successor nor universal nodes with more than one rejecting successor. We call the class of languages accepted by this type of TM's UAP. UAP has some interesting properties, which we list without proof: $UP_{\leq k} \subseteq UAP$, $UAP \subseteq SPP \subseteq \oplus P$, and $UAP \subseteq \nabla P \cap Co\nabla P$. For a definition of Wagner's class ∇P see [9] or [15], for a definition of SPP see [5]. The next theorem shows another surprising property of UAP.

Theorem 11. $FewP \subseteq UAP$.

Proof. Let M be an NTM with at most $p(n)$ accepting paths, where p is some polynomial. Let $L_m := \{ w \mid \|N_M(w)\| \geq m \}$. Clearly, $L_{p(n)+1} = \emptyset$ and $L_1 = L(M)$.

For $1 \leq m \leq p(n)$ an unambiguous, alternating TM can compute L_m as follows: Nondeterministically choose method (i) or (ii).

(i) First guess m different computation paths $(p_1, \ldots, p_m)$ of M. If all of them are accepting paths, then accept iff $w \notin L_{m+1}$. If there are rejecting paths among $p_1, \ldots, p_m$ then reject.

(ii) Accept iff $w \in L_{m+1}$.

$w \in L_{m+1}$ or $w \notin L_{m+1}$ is determined by the same method. A simple induction shows that this computation is correct and unambiguous (including the choice (i) and (ii)). Since the computation ends, when m reaches $p(n) + 1$, it is also polynomially time bounded.

From Theorem 11 we also get the new inclusion $FewP \in \nabla P$. UAP is in some way an "unambiguous analogue" of ∇P. A simple variation of above proof shows that $Few \subseteq UAP$. To our best knowledge UAP is the smallest class containing Few, though our proof seems to be substantially easier than the proof of $Few \subseteq SPP$ [5].

Theorem 12. UAP *is locally definable*.

Proof. Again the proof is essentially a variation of the proof method used in Theorem 9. We claim that $UAP = [\{AND!, OR!\}]P$ holds.

By Theorem 7 all classes characterizable by locally definable acceptance types are also characterizable by extended locally definable acceptance types. Hertrampf showed that if a class $\mathcal{C}$ is characterizable, also $\exists \mathcal{C}$, $\forall \mathcal{C}$, $\oplus \mathcal{C}$, and $MOD_k \mathcal{C}$ are characterizable. We will now prove that extended locally definable acceptance types are also closed under these operations. Theorem 7 is not sufficient for this purpose, see for example $\forall UP$. Moreover, we show closure of extended locally definable acceptance types also under the operations $\exists !$ and $\forall !$ introduced by Hemachandra, as well as under $MODZ_k$ which is defined analogously to the MOD_k operator in [9].

Definition 13. 1. $L \in \exists! \mathcal{C}$ iff there exists a language $A \in \mathcal{C}$ and a polynomial p such that for all x, y, z such that $|y|, |z| \leq p(|x|)$, $\langle x, y \rangle, \langle x, z \rangle \in A$ we have $y = z$, and $x \in L \iff \exists y : |y| \leq p(|x|) \wedge \langle x, y \rangle \in A$,

2. $\forall! \mathcal{C} = Co \exists! Co\mathcal{C}$.

Theorem 14. $\exists C$, $\forall C$, $\exists! C$, $\forall! C$, $\text{MOD}_k C$, and $\text{MODZ}_k C$ are locally definable, if C is locally definable.

Proof. Let $C = [\{f\}]P$. We establish the following equalities:

1. $\exists C = [\{\overline{f}, \text{TRANS}_{\overline{1}\mapsto 1}^{\overline{0}\mapsto 0}, \text{OR}\}]P$,

2. $\forall C = [\{\overline{f}, \text{TRANS}_{\overline{1}\mapsto 1}^{\overline{0}\mapsto 0}, \text{AND}\}]P$,

3. $\exists! C = [\{\overline{f}, \text{TRANS}_{\overline{1}\mapsto 1}^{\overline{0}\mapsto 0}, \text{OR!}\}]P$,

4. $\forall! C = [\{\overline{f}, \text{TRANS}_{\overline{1}\mapsto 1}^{\overline{0}\mapsto 0}, \text{AND!}\}]P$,

5. $\text{MOD}_k C = [\{\overline{f}, \text{TRANS}_{\overline{1}\mapsto 1}^{\overline{0}\mapsto 0}, \underline{\text{MOD}_k}, \text{TRANS}_{1,\ldots,k-1\mapsto 1}^{0,k\mapsto 0}\}]P$,

6. $\text{MODZ}_k C = [\{\overline{f}, \text{TRANS}_{\overline{1}\mapsto 1}^{\overline{0}\mapsto 0}, \underline{\text{MOD}_k}, \text{TRANS}_{1,\ldots,k-1\mapsto 1}^{0\mapsto 0}\}]P$.

The first four points all lead to computation trees of the same form: First we have a tree (including the root node) where nodes are labeled with OR (AND, OR!, AND!, respectively), then each leaf of this tree is connected to some node labeled with the transformation function, and finally each of these nodes has a subtree where all inner nodes are labeled with $\overline{f}$.

Now we take a closer look at the characterization of $\exists C$. The inclusion "$\subseteq$" can be seen in the following way. By definition of the $\exists$ operator it holds that $L \in C$ iff there exists a language $A \in C$ and a polynomial p such that $x \in L \iff \exists y : |y| \leq p(|x|) \land \langle x, y \rangle \in A$. This mechanism can be simulated by an $\{\overline{f}, \text{TRANS}_{\overline{1}\mapsto 1}^{\overline{0}\mapsto 0}, \text{OR}\}$-machine as follows. We use a computation tree as described above. The OR-part is used to guess the string y and the $\overline{f}$-part is used to simulate the $\{f\}$-machine for C on input $\langle x, y \rangle$. Here we check whether it holds $\langle x, y \rangle \in A$. The transformation function in the above tree is just needed to have a clear separation between the (existential) guessing of y and the simulation of the machine for C by $\overline{f}$.

For the reverse direction we show that an $\{\overline{f}, \text{TRANS}_{\overline{1}\mapsto 1}^{\overline{0}\mapsto 0}, \text{OR}\}$-machine with computation tree of the above desc.ibed shape (which is the only one possible due to the propagation principle) can be simulated by $\exists C$. First, we have to existentially guess a path y through the OR-part of the above tree. Then this y is used to check whether $\langle x, y \rangle \in C$ holds (where x denotes the input word). This obviously is the analogue to the $\overline{f}$-part of the above tree. Then the simulation leads to an acceptance iff the root of an $\overline{f}$-part evaluates to $\overline{1}$, which again has the consequence that the root (which is labeled OR) of the whole computation tree evaluates to 1. (Note that $\overline{1}$ will be mapped to 1 by the transformation function.)

Thus the claim for the first characterization follows. The claims for $\forall C$, $\exists! C$, and $\forall! C$ are proven in a similar way and, therefore, are omitted. The proofs for $\text{MOD}_k C$ and MODZ_k are contained in the full paper.

UAP is defined by unambiguous, alternating TM's. If we restrict the maximum number of alternations to some constant we get the levels of the so-called unambiguous alternation hierarchy. Hemachandra showed that these levels coincide with classes obtained from UP by iteratively applying unambiguous existential and universal polynomially length bounded quantification, so e.g. $A\Sigma_2^{\text{UP}} = \forall! \exists! P = \forall! \text{UP}$, $A\Pi_2^{\text{UP}} = \exists! \forall! P$.

In the case of normal existential and universal polynomially length bounded quantifiers we get the levels of the polynomial time hierarchy which coincide with the levels of the alternation hierarchy. For unambiguous computation, however, the oracle and alternation hierarchies do *not* seem to coincide. Hemachandra could prove that all levels of the unambiguous alternation hierarchy coincide with levels of the unambiguous one-query oracle hierarchy. As a corollary of the last theorem we therefore can characterize all levels of the unambiguous one-query hierarchy in terms of extended locally definable acceptance types.

Theorem 15. *If C is locally definable, then* P^C, UP^C, *and* NP^C *are locally definable.*

Proof. We claim that $P^C = [\{\overline{f}, \text{SELECT}\}]P$, $UP^C = [\{\overline{f}, \text{SELECT}, \text{OR}*\}]P$, and $NP^C = [\{\overline{f}, \text{SELECT}, \text{OR}\}]P$, where $C = [\{f\}]P$. Herein, $\text{OR}*$ is defined as follows:

$$\text{OR}*(x,y) := \begin{cases} * & \text{if } x = y = 1 \text{ or } x = * \text{ and } y \neq \bot \text{ or } y = * \text{ and } x \neq \bot, \\ \text{OR}(x,y) & \text{otherwise.} \end{cases}$$

Observe that by Theorem 15 we are able to characterize all levels of the UP oracle hierarchy. Thus both unambiguous hierarchies are locally definable.

4 Access to unambiguous computations

The computation of a TM with access to an oracle can be interpreted in different ways. One possibility is to interpret the oracle as a database, a second one to see accesses to the oracle as subroutine calls or even remote procedure calls on some different computer. In the database case, all answers "are there", while in the subroutine view answers are computed if and only if they are queried.

The class P^{UP}, for example, is obtained in a database like way. For each language $L \in P^{UP}$, there is an oracle TM (OTM) M and an oracle $A \in UP$, such that $L = L(M, A)$. A is the database and $A \in UP$ means that all entries in the database are computed by an unambiguous polynomially time bounded NTM.

Cai, Hemachandra, and Vyskoč [3] introduced the class $P^{\mathcal{U}\mathcal{P}}$ which can be interpreted in a subroutine access way. Here $L \in P^{\mathcal{U}\mathcal{P}}$ iff $L = L(M, A)$, $A \in \mathcal{U}\mathcal{P}$, but A needs not necessarily be accepted by an unambiguous TM M_A. It suffices that M_A is unambiguous *only on all queries posted by* M. The overall computation (computation of M together with subroutine computations of M_A) remains unambiguous. Cai, Hemachandra, and Vyskoč claim that this notion of access to unambiguous computation (called *guarded access*), is more natural than the database view.

In this section we will show that guarded access is characterizable by extended locally definable acceptance types. Our contribution, however, goes deeper than this. We provide new insight into the problem of how to access unambiguous computations. Since extended locally definable acceptance types do not use oracles or other global concepts like number of accepting paths, they are a good means for an "overall computation" model. Extended locally definable acceptance types show which concepts can be realized by local conditions in a computation model. The characterization of guarded oracle access supports the conjecture of Cai, Hemachandra, and Vyskoč that guarded access to unambiguous computation is a natural notion.

Surprisingly, however, the unrestricted ("database") access is characterizable by extended locally definable acceptance types, too.

In the remainder of this section we will formalize these ideas and state the results. To formalize guarded access, Cai, Hemachandra, and Vyskoč used the notion of *promise problems* introduced by Even, Selman, and Yacobi.

Definition 16. [4] A *promise problem* is a pair of predicates (Q, R). Q is called the *promise* and R the *property*.

Definition 17. [3] We define $\mathcal{UP}$ ("promise UP") as the following class of promise problems: $\{(Q_i, R_i) \mid i \geq 1\}$, where $N_1, N_2, \ldots$ is a standard enumeration of nondeterministic polynomial-time Turing machines with $Q_i = \{w \mid \|N_i(w)\| \leq 1\}$, and $R_i = \{w \mid \|N_i(w)\| \geq 1\}$.

Definition 18. Let $A = (Q, R)$ be a promise problem. We say that $L \in P^A$ if there is a deterministic polynomial-time Turing machine M such that $L = L(M, R)$, and for every string x, in the computation of M every query z made to the oracle satisfies $z \in Q$. UP^A and NP^A are defined analogously.

For the proofs in this section we need the following technical notion:

Definition 19. Let F be an extended locally definable acceptance type. $(A, B) \in \langle F \rangle P$ iff there is an NTM M and an evaluation scheme as in Definition 2, but

- the root of M evaluates to one of $(0,0)$, $(0,1)$, $(1,0)$, or $(1,1)$ for all possible inputs,
- $w \in A$ iff the root of M evaluates either to $(1,0)$ or $(1,1)$ on input w,
- $w \in B$ iff the root of M evaluates either to $(0,1)$ or $(1,1)$ on input w.

By $(0,0)$, $(0,1)$, $(1,0)$, $(1,1)$ we understand comfortable names of integers, e.g., 0, 1, 2, and 3. For $\mathcal{UP}$ we have the following characterization which is stated without proof.

Lemma 20. $\mathcal{UP} = \langle \{h\} \rangle P$, where $h : \{(0,1), (1,0), (1,1)\}^2 \rightarrow \{(0,1), (1,0), (1,1)\}$ *is defined as*

h	$(0,1)$	$(1,0)$	$(1,1)$
$(0,1)$	$(0,1)$	$(0,1)$	$(0,1)$
$(1,0)$	$(0,1)$	$(1,0)$	$(1,1)$
$(1,1)$	$(0,1)$	$(1,1)$	$(0,1)$

Theorem 21. *Let F be an extended locally definable acceptance type. Then* $P^{\langle F \rangle P}$, $UP^{\langle F \rangle P}$, *and* $NP^{\langle F \rangle P}$ *are locally definable.*

Proof. (Sketch) We claim without proof that there is a single boolean function f such that $\langle F \rangle P = \langle \{f\} \rangle P$. (It can be shown by the same techniques as in Theorem 6.) Let $F_1 = \{\bar{f}, \text{CHOOSE}\}$, $F_2 = \{\bar{f}, \text{CHOOSE}, \text{OR*}\}$, and $F_3 = \{\bar{f}, \text{CHOOSE}, \text{OR}\}$. It can be shown $[F_1]P = P^{\langle F \rangle P}$, $[F_2]P = UP^{\langle F \rangle P}$, and $[F_3]P = NP^{\langle F \rangle P}$. CHOOSE is defined as

$$
\text{CHOOSE}(x, y, z) := \begin{cases} x \text{ if } z = \overline{(1,1)}, \, y \neq \perp, \\ y \text{ if } z = \overline{(1,0)}, \, x \neq \perp, \\ * \text{ if } z = \overline{(0,0)} \text{ or } z = \overline{(0,1)}, \, x \neq \perp, \, y \neq \perp, \\ \perp \text{ otherwise.} \end{cases}
$$

Corollary 22. *All levels of the unambiguous promise hierarchy and especially* P^{UP}, UP^{UP}, *and* NP^{UP} *are locally definable.*

Acknowledgment We are grateful to Uli Hertrampf for several fruitful remarks.

References

1. R. Beigel, J. Gill, and U. Hertrampf. Counting classes: Threshold, parity, mods, and fewness. In *Proc. of 7th STACS*, number 415 in LNCS, pages 49–57. Springer, 1990.
2. G. Buntrock, L. A. Hemachandra, and D. Siefkes. Using inductive counting to simulate nondeterministic computation. In *Proc. of 15th MFCS*, number 452 in LNCS, pages 187–194. Springer, 1990. (to appear in *Information and Computation*).
3. J.-Y. Cai, L. Hemachandra, and J. Vyskoč. Promise problems and access to unambiguous computation. In *Proc. of 17th MFCS*, number 629 in LNCS, pages 162–171. Springer, 1992.
4. S. Even, A. Selman, and Y. Yacobi. The complexity of promise problems with applications to public-key cryptography. *Inform. and Control*, 61(2):159–173, 1984.
5. S. A. Fenner, L. J. Fortnow, and S. A. Kurtz. Gap-definable counting classes. In *Proc. of 6th Conference on Structure in Complexity Theory*, pages 30–42, 1991.
6. L. Goldschlager and I. Parberry. On the construction of parallel computers from various bases of boolean functions. *Theoretical Comput. Sci.*, 43:43–58, 1986.
7. J. Grollmann and A. Selman. Complexity measures for public-key cryptosystems. *SIAM J. Comput.*, 17:309–335, 1988.
8. U. Hertrampf. Locally definable acceptance types—the three valued case. In *Proc. of LATIN'92*, number 583 in LNCS, pages 262–271. Springer, 1992.
9. U. Hertrampf. Locally definable acceptance types for polynomial time machines. In *Proc. of 9th STACS*, number 577 in LNCS, pages 199–207. Springer, 1992.
10. K.-J. Lange. Unambiguity of circuits. In *Proc. of 5th Conference on Structure in Complexity Theory*, pages 130–137, 1990. (to appear in TCS).
11. K.-J. Lange and P. Rossmanith. Characterizing unambiguous augmented pushdown automata by circuits. In *Proc. of 15th MFCS*, number 452 in LNCS, pages 399–406. Springer, 1990.
12. R. Niedermeier and P. Rossmanith. Unambiguous simulations of auxiliary pushdown automata and circuits. In *Proc. of LATIN'92*, number 583 in LNCS, pages 387–400. Springer, 1992.
13. A. L. Selman. A survey of one-way functions in complexity theory. *Mathematical Systems Theory*, 25(3):203–221, 1992.
14. L. Valiant. The relative complexity of checking and evaluating. *Inform. Proc. Letters*, 5:20–23, 1976.
15. K. W. Wagner. Alternating machines using partially defined "AND" and "OR". Technical Report 39, Institut für Informatik, Universität Würzburg, Jan. 1992.

Gap-Definability as a Closure Property[*]

Stephen Fenner[1][**], Lance Fortnow[2][***] and Lide Li[2][†]

[1] University of Southern Maine, Computer Science Department, 96 Falmouth St.,
Portland, ME 04103, USA
[2] University of Chicago, Department of Computer Science, 1100 E. 58th St.,
Chicago, IL 60637, USA

Abstract. Gap-definability and the gap-closure operator were defined
in [FFK91]. Few complexity classes were known at that time to be gap-
definable. In this paper, we give simple characterizations of both gap-
definability and the gap-closure operator, and we show that many com-
plexity classes are gap-definable, including $\mathbf{P^{\#P}}$, $\mathbf{P^{\#P[1]}}$, **PSPACE**,
EXP, **NEXP**, **MP**, and $\mathbf{BP \cdot \oplus P}$. If a class is closed under union, intersection and contains $\emptyset$ and Σ^*, then it is gap-definable if and only if
it contains **SPP**; its gap-closure is the closure of this class together with
SPP under union and intersection. On the other hand, we give some
examples of classes which are reasonable gap-definable but not closed
under union (resp. intersection, complement). Finally, we show that a
complexity class such as **PP** or **PSPACE**, if it is not equal to **SPP**,
contains a maximal proper gap-definable subclass which is closed under
many-one reductions.

1 Introduction

In 1979, Valiant [Val79] defined the class #**P**, the class of functions definable as
the number of accepting computations of some polynomial-time nondeterministic
Turing machine. Valiant showed many natural problems complete for this class,
including the permanent of a zero-one matrix. Toda [Tod91] showed that these
functions have more power than previously believed; he showed how to reduce
any problem in the polynomial-time hierarchy to a single value of a #**P** function.

The class #**P** has its shortcomings, however. In particular, #**P** functions
cannot take on negative values and thus #**P** is not closed under subtraction.
Also, one cannot express as a #**P** function the permanent of a matrix with
arbitrary (possibly negative) integer entries, or even a simple polynomial-time
function which outputs negative values.

Fenner, Fortnow and Kurtz [FFK91] analyzed the class GapP, a function
class consisting of differences—"gaps"—between the number of accepting and

---

[*] A full version of the paper is available from lilide@cs.uchicago.edu

[**] Partially Supported by NSF Grant CCR-9209833. Email: fenner@usm.maine.edu

[***] Partially Supported by NSF Grant CCR-9009936 and CCR-9253582. E-mail:
fortnow@cs.uchicago.edu

[†] Partially Supported by NSF Grant CCR-9253582. E-mail: lilide@cs.uchicago.edu

rejecting paths of **NP** Turing machines. This class is exactly the closure of #**P** under subtraction. Gap**P** also has all the other nice closure properties of #**P**, such as addition, multiplication, and binomial coefficients. Beigel, Reingold, & Spielman first used gaps to great advantage in [BRS91] to show that **PP** is closed under intersection. Toda and Ogiwara have also formulated their results in [TO92] using Gap**P** instead of #**P**.

Fenner, Fortnow and Kurtz looked at classes such as **PP**, C$_=$**P**, $\oplus$**P** and **SPP** that can be defined in terms of Gap**P** functions. They defined a natural general notion of gap-definability and also defined GapCl, a nonconstructive closure operation on sets (the 'gap-closure'). They showed that any countable set of languages $\mathcal{C}$ has a unique minimum gap-definable class GapCl($\mathcal{C}$) containing it. However, their definition does not yield an easy way to determine properties of gap definable classes or to determine which classes may be gap-definable.

In this paper we will take some of the mystery out of gap-definability. In Section 3 we give a simple characterization of when classes are gap-definable. Using this characterization we show many common classes, such as **P**$^{\#\mathbf{P}}$, **P**$^{\#\mathbf{P}[1]}$, **PSPACE**, **EXP**, **NEXP**, **MP** and **BP** $\cdot \oplus$**P**, are gap-definable. In general, for complexity classes with some reasonable restrictions, we give simple necessary and sufficient conditions for whether they are gap-definable. In Section 4 we give a simple characterization of gap-closure. By the definition of gap-definability, there is no restriction on the accepting set A and the rejecting set R. We show that A and R can be chosen to be recursive under reasonable circumstances. In Section 5 we use the results of the previous sections to describe some properties of the gap-closure and gap-definablility. We show that Boolean closure properties such as closure under union or intersection are not necessary for gap-definability. We also show that a complexity class such as **PP** or **PSPACE**, if it is not equal to **SPP**, contains a maximal proper gap-definable subclass which is closed under many-one reductions.

2 Preliminaries

Definition 1. Let M be a CM (i.e. *counting machine* or *NP machine*). We define the function #$M: \Sigma^* \to \mathbf{N}$ to be such that for all $x \in \Sigma^*$, #$M(x)$ is the number of *accepting* computation paths of M on input x. The CM $\overline{M}$ is the machine identical to M but with the accepting and rejecting states interchanged.

We assume that the reader is familiar with the common complexity classes such as **P**, **NP**, **BPP**, **PH**, **PSPACE**, **EXP** and **NEXP**.

Definition 2. – [Val79] #**P** $\overset{\text{df}}{=}$ {#M | M is a CM}.

– [FFK91] Gap**P** $\overset{\text{df}}{=}$ {gap$_M$ | M is a CM} where gap$_M$ $\overset{\text{df}}{=}$ #M $-$ #$\overline{M}$.

– We use **FP** to denote the classes of all poly-time computable functions.

– [Gil77] [Sim75] **PP** is the class of all languages L such that there exists a CM M and an **FP** function f such that, for all x, $x \in L \iff$ #$M(x) > f(x)$. An equivalent condition is, there exists a CM M such that for all x, $x \in L \iff$ gap$_M(x) > 0$.

– [RS92] [GKT92] **MP**, or **MidBitP**, is the class of all languages L such that there exists a function f in $\#\mathbf{P}$ and a function g in $\mathbf{FP}$ such that for all x, $x \in L$ iff there is a 1 at position $g(x)$ in the binary representation of $f(x)$.

It has been shown that $\#\mathbf{P}$ is closed under addition, multiplication and binomial coefficients [BGH90]. GapP has all these closure properties and it is also closed under subtraction [FFK91].

Definition 3. [FFK91] A class $\mathcal{C}$ of languages is *gap-definable* if there exist disjoint sets $A, R \subseteq \Sigma^* \times \mathbf{Z}$ such that, $\forall L$, $L \in \mathcal{C}$ if and only if there exists a GapP function g with $x \in L \implies (x, g(x)) \in A$, and $x \notin L \implies (x, g(x)) \in R$, for all $x \in \Sigma^*$. We let $\mathrm{Gap}(A, R)$ denote the class $\mathcal{C}$. A function $g \in \mathrm{GapP}$ is called *(A,R)-proper* if $\forall x, (x, g(x)) \in A \cup R$. A gap-definable class $\mathcal{C}$ is called *reasonable* if $\mathcal{C}$ contains $\emptyset$ and Σ^*.

It has been shown in [FFK91] that if $\mathcal{C}$ is gap-definable, then $\mathcal{C}$ is reasonable if and only if $\mathbf{SPP} \subseteq \mathcal{C}$. $\mathbf{SPP}$ is defined in Section 3 below.

Definition 4. [FFK91] Let $\mathcal{D} = \{L_1, L_2, L_3, \ldots\}$ be a countable collection of languages and $W = \{w_1, w_2, \ldots,\}$ be an immune set, i.e., W is infinite with no infinite recursively enumerable subset. Define $A_{\mathcal{D}} \overset{\mathrm{df}}{=} \{(x, w_i) \mid x \in L_i\}$ and $R_{\mathcal{D}} \overset{\mathrm{df}}{=} \{(x, w_i) \mid x \notin L_i\}$, and define $\mathrm{GapCl}(\mathcal{D}) \overset{\mathrm{df}}{=} \mathrm{Gap}(A_{\mathcal{D}}, R_{\mathcal{D}})$.

It has been shown that $\mathrm{GapCl}(\mathcal{D})$ is the unique minimum gap-definable class containing $\mathcal{D}$, we call it the gap-closure of $\mathcal{D}$. In Theorem 20 and Corollary 21 we show that immune sets are not required to represent $\mathrm{GapCl}(\mathcal{C})$ as a gap-definable class.

Certain functions δ_k^B were defined in [FFK91]. They have the property that for integers k and B with $0 \le k \le B$, we have $\delta_k^B(x) = 1$ if $x = k$; and $\delta_k^B(x) = 0$ if $x \ne k$ and $0 \le x \le B$. Also, if $f \in \mathrm{GapP}$, then $\delta_k^B(f(x)) \in \mathrm{GapP}$.

3 Gap-definability

We will first prove a theorem which characterizes gap-definability by a certain Boolean closure property with **SPP**. It will play an important role in the paper.

Definition 5. [FFK91] $\mathbf{SPP}$ is the class of all languages L such that there exists $g \in \mathrm{GapP}$ such that, for all x, $x \in L \implies g(x) = 1$, and $x \notin L \implies g(x) = 0$.

Theorem 6. *Let $\mathcal{C}$ be a countable class of languages containing $\emptyset$. The following are equivalent:*

1. $\mathcal{C}$ is gap-definable;

2. For all $L_1, L_2 \in \mathcal{C}$ and disjoint $S_1, S_2 \in \mathbf{SPP}$, $(L_1 \cap S_1) \cup (L_2 \cap S_2) \in \mathcal{C}$.

Proof. $(1 \implies 2)$: Let $\mathcal{C}$ be gap-definable, $L_1, L_2 \in \mathcal{C}$ and $S_1, S_2 \in \mathbf{SPP}$ with $S_1 \cap S_2 = \emptyset$. We want to show that $L = (L_1 \cap S_1) \cup (L_2 \cap S_2) \in \mathcal{C}$. There exist $A, R \subseteq \Sigma^* \times \mathbf{Z}$ and $g_1, g_2 \in \mathrm{GapP}$ such that for $i = 1, 2$, $x \in L_i \implies (x, g_i(x)) \in$

A, and $x \notin L_i \implies (x, g_i(x)) \in R$; there exist $f_1, f_2 \in \text{GapP}$ such that for $i = 1, 2$, $x \in S_i \implies f_i(x) = 1$, and $x \notin S_i \implies f_i(x) = 0$. Since $\emptyset \in \mathcal{C}, \exists g_3 \in \text{GapP}$ such that for all x, $(x, g_3(x)) \in R$. We define a function $h = g_1 f_1 + g_2 f_2 + g_3(1 - f_1)(1 - f_2)$. Clearly $h \in \text{GapP}$, and

$$x \in L \implies \exists i \in \{1, 2\}, x \in L_i \cap S_i \implies h(x) = g_i(x) \implies (x, h(x)) \in A$$
$$x \notin L \implies (x \notin S_1 \cup S_2) \text{ or } (x \in S_i \text{ but } x \notin L_i)$$
$$\implies (h(x) = g_3(x)) \text{ or } (h(x) = g_i(x), \text{but } (x, g_i(x)) \in R) \implies (x, h(x)) \in R$$

This shows that $L \in \mathcal{C}$, as witnessed by h.

$(2 \implies 1)$: We show that $\text{GapCl}(\mathcal{C}) = \mathcal{C}$. Let $\mathcal{C} = \{L_1, L_2, \cdots\}, L \in \text{GapCl}(\mathcal{C})$. We will show later that there exist pairwise disjoint $S_1, S_2, \cdots, S_r \in \textbf{SPP}$ such that $L = \bigcup_{i=1}^r (S_i \cap L_i)$ (Theorem 18). Now we show that condition 2 in the theorem implies that $L \in \mathcal{C}$ by induction on r. If $r = 1$, then $L = S_1 \cap L_1 \in \mathcal{C}$ by letting $L_2 = \emptyset$. Suppose $r > 1$. Let $L' = \bigcup_{i=2}^r (S_i \cap L_i)$, $S' = \bigcup_{i=2}^r S_i$. We have $L = (S_1 \cap L_1) \cup (\bigcup_{i=2}^r (S_i \cap L_i)) = (S_1 \cap L_1) \cup (S' \cap L')$. By the induction hypothesis, $L' \in \mathcal{C}$, and clearly $S_1 \cap S' = \emptyset$. Again, by condition 2 , we have $L \in \mathcal{C}$. $\quad\square$

Many interesting complexity classes are closed under union and intersection, and contain $\{\emptyset, \Sigma^*\}$. For them, the question of gap-definability is just a matter of whether or not they contain $\textbf{SPP}$.

Corollary 7. *If $\mathcal{C}$ is closed under union and intersection, and $\{\emptyset, \Sigma^*\} \subseteq \mathcal{C}$, then $\mathcal{C}$ is gap-definable if and only if $\textbf{SPP} \subseteq \mathcal{C}$.*

Proof. If $\mathcal{C}$ is gap-definable and $\{\emptyset, \Sigma^*\} \subseteq \mathcal{C}$, then $\textbf{SPP} \subseteq \mathcal{C}$ [FFK91]. Conversely, if $\mathcal{C}$ is closed under union and intersection, and $\textbf{SPP} \subseteq \mathcal{C}$, then clearly we have condition 2 in Theorem 6. So $\mathcal{C}$ is gap-definable. $\quad\square$

Corollary 8. *If $\mathcal{C} \subseteq \mathcal{D}$, $\mathcal{D}$ is closed under union and intersection, and $\mathcal{C}$ contains $\{\emptyset, \Sigma^*\}$, then $\mathcal{C}$ is gap-definable implies that $\mathcal{D}$ is gap-definable.* $\quad\square$

This corollary says that for many classes, each would be gap-definable if one of its subclass is gap-definable. For example, if we can show $\textbf{BPP}$, or Σ_k for some k is gap-definable, then $\textbf{PH}$ is gap-definable.

Definition 9. Let A be an oracle set or an oracle function. $\textbf{P}^A$ denotes the class of languages accepted by an deterministic polynomial-time oracle machine with oracle A. Let $\textbf{P}^{\mathcal{C}} = \bigcup_{A \in \mathcal{C}} \textbf{P}^A$. $\textbf{P}^{\mathcal{C}[1]}$ is defined in the same way but the machine is allowed to ask only one oracle question in each computation. The class $\textbf{NP}^{\mathcal{C}}$ is defined similarly.

Corollary 10. *If $\mathcal{C}$ is a gap-definable class containing $\{\emptyset, \Sigma^*\}$, and closed under join, then $\textbf{P}^{\mathcal{C}}$ and $\textbf{NP}^{\mathcal{C}}$ are also gap-definable.*

Proof. If $\mathcal{C}$ is closed under join, then it is not difficult to see that $\textbf{P}^{\mathcal{C}}$ and $\textbf{NP}^{\mathcal{C}}$ are closed under union and intersection. By the previous corollary, we get the conclusion. $\quad\square$

We are now able to prove that a number of well-known complexity classes are gap-definable.

Corollary 11. *1.* $\mathbf{P}^{\#\mathbf{P}}$, **PSPACE**, **EXP**, **NEXP** *are gap-definable;*
2. $\mathbf{P}^{\#\mathbf{P}[1]}$ *is gap-definable;   3.* **MP** *is gap-definable.*

Proof. 1. All these classes are clearly closed under union and intersection, and all contain **SPP**. So they are gap-definable by Corollary 7.

2. Since $\mathbf{SPP} \subseteq \mathbf{P}^{\#\mathbf{P}[1]}$, it suffices to show that $\mathbf{P}^{\#\mathbf{P}[1]}$ is closed under union and intersection. We omit the details of the proof.

3. **MP** was originally defined via $\#\mathbf{P}$ functions. It is easy to show that there is an alternative definition for **MP**: $L \in \mathbf{MP}$ if and only if $\exists g \in \mathbf{GapP}$, and $h \in \mathbf{FP}$ s.t. $x \in L$ iff the bit at position $h(x)$ in the binary representation of $g(x)$, which is called *midbit*, is 1. Let $L_1, L_2 \in \mathbf{MP}$ witnessed by g_1, g_2. It is not difficult to see that we may choose g_1, g_2 such that the same $h \in \mathbf{FP}$ could be used in defining both L_1 and L_2. Also let $S_1, S_2 \in \mathbf{SPP}$ with $S_1 \cap S_2 = \emptyset$, witnessed by f_1, f_2. Define function $g = g_1 f_1 + g_2 f_2$. Then it is not difficult to check that $x \in (L_1 \cap S_1) \cup (L_2 \cap S_2)$ if and only if the "midbit" of $g(x)$ is 1. This proves that $(L_1 \cap S_1) \cup (L_2 \cap S_2) \in \mathbf{MP}$. $\square$

Definition 12. 1. $L \in \exists \cdot B$ for some set B if there is a polynomial p s.t. $x \in L$ iff $\exists y \in \{0,1\}^{p(|x|)}, x\#y \in B$. For a class $\mathcal{C}$, we define $\exists \cdot \mathcal{C} = \bigcup_{B \in \mathcal{C}} \exists \cdot B$.
2. $L \in \mathbf{BP} \cdot \mathcal{C}$ if there is $C \in \mathcal{C}$, a polynomial p s.t.
$$x \in L \Longrightarrow Pr\{y \in \{0,1\}^{p(|x|)} \mid x\#y \in C\} > 2/3$$
$$x \notin L \Longrightarrow Pr\{y \in \{0,1\}^{p(|x|)} \mid x\#y \in C\} < 1/3$$
The class $\mathbf{P} \cdot \mathcal{C}$ is defined in the same way except we use $1/2$ instead of $2/3$ and $1/3$.

Definition 13. A class $\mathcal{C}$ of languages is *simply gap-definable* if there exist disjoint sets $A, R \subseteq \mathbf{Z}$ such that, for any language L, $L \in \mathcal{C}$ if and only if there exists a $g \in \mathbf{GapP}$ with $x \in L \Longrightarrow g(x) \in A$ and $x \notin L \Longrightarrow g(x) \in R$.

Clearly, the classes $\mathbf{PP}, \mathbf{C_=P}, \oplus \mathbf{P}$ and **SPP** are all simply gap-definable.

Theorem 14. *If $\mathcal{C}$ is simply gap-definable, then $\exists \cdot \mathcal{C}$, $\mathbf{BP} \cdot \mathcal{C}$, and $\mathbf{P} \cdot \mathcal{C}$ are gap-definable.*

Proof. The proof will apear in the full paper.

Corollary 15. $\mathbf{BP} \cdot \oplus \mathbf{P}$ *is gap-definable.* $\square$

So far in this paper we have given simple characterizations of gap-definability in a broad range of circumstances, and showed that many classes not previously known to be gap-definable are indeed so. We have yet to give any result stating that gap-definability has structural consequences not related to the class **SPP** or other gap-definable classes. The following proposition is a step in that direction.

Proposition 16. *If C is a reasonable gap-definable class which is closed under m-reductions and complements, then C is closed under 1-tt-reductions.*

Proof. Suppose $L \in C$ and $A \leq_{1-tt} L$ via the polynomial-time function f. ($f(x) = \langle \alpha, y \rangle$ where $y \in \Sigma^*$, $\alpha \in \{T, F, id, \neg\}$ is one of the unary Boolean functions, and $x \in A$ iff $\alpha(y \in L)$.) For each $b \in \{T, F, id, \neg\}$, let $S_b \stackrel{df}{=} \{x \mid (\exists y)f(x) = \langle b, y \rangle\}$. Clearly, $S_b \in \mathbf{P} \subseteq \mathbf{SPP}$ for each b, and the four sets are pairwise disjoint. Let $B \stackrel{df}{=} \{x \mid (\exists \alpha)(\exists y \in L)f(x) = \langle \alpha, y \rangle\}$. Since $B \leq_m L$, we have $B \in C$, and $\overline{B} \in C$ since C is closed under complements. It follows from the definition of 1-tt-reductions that $A = (\Sigma^* \cap S_T) \cup (\emptyset \cap S_F) \cup (B \cap S_{id}) \cup (\overline{B} \cap S_\neg)$, and thus $A \in C$ by Theorem 6. $\quad\square$

The result is nontrivial: for example, the class $\mathbf{NP} \cup \text{co-}\mathbf{NP}$ is closed under m-reductions and complements but is not closed under 1-tt-reductions unless $\mathbf{NP} = \text{co-}\mathbf{NP}$. Proposition 16 then implies that $\mathbf{NP} \cup \text{co-}\mathbf{NP}$ is unlikely to be gap-definable.

Corollary 17. *If $\{\emptyset, \Sigma^*\} \subseteq C$ and C is closed under m-reductions and complements, then $\mathrm{GapCl}(C)$ is closed under 1-tt-reductions.*

Proof. It was shown in [FFK91] that the GapCl operator preserves closure under m-reductions and closure under complements. $\quad\square$

4 The Gap Closure Operator, GapCl

The following theorem provides a simplified characterization of the gap-closure operator, GapCl.

Theorem 18. *Let C be a countable class of languages and L an arbitrary language. $L \in \mathrm{GapCl}(C)$ if and only if there exist $L_1, \ldots, L_k \in C$ and $S_1, \ldots, S_k \in \mathbf{SPP}$ such that 1. $S_i \cap S_j = \emptyset$ for all $i \neq j$, 2. $\bigcup_{i=1}^{k} S_i = \Sigma^*$, and 3. $L = \bigcup_{i=1}^{k}(L_i \cap S_i)$.*

Proof. Fix an immune set $W = \{w_1, w_2, w_3, \ldots\}$ and an enumeration $L_1, L_2, L_3, \ldots$ of the languages in C. As in definition 4, we define $A \stackrel{df}{=} \{\langle x, w_i \rangle \mid x \in L_i\}$, and $R \stackrel{df}{=} \{\langle x, w_i \rangle \mid x \notin L_i\}$. By definition, $\mathrm{GapCl}(C) = \mathrm{Gap}(A, R)$. First, suppose $L \in \mathrm{Gap}(A, R)$. Then there is an $f \in \mathrm{GapP}$ such that $\mathrm{range}(f) \subseteq W$ and for all $x \in \Sigma^*$, $x \in L \iff (x, f(x)) \in A$. Note that $(x, f(x)) \in R$ if $x \notin L$. Since W is immune, there is a k such that $\mathrm{range}(f) \subseteq \{w_1, \ldots, w_k\}$. For $1 \leq i \leq k$ we define $S_i \stackrel{df}{=} \{x \mid f(x) = w_i\}$. The sets $S_1, \ldots, S_k$ clearly satisfy the first two conditions of the theorem. To show that the third condition is satisfied, we note that for all x, $x \in L \iff (x, f(x)) \in A \iff (\exists i, 1 \leq i \leq k)[f(x) = w_i \ \& \ x \in L_i]$ $\iff x \in \bigcup_{i=1}^{k}(L_i \cap S_i)$. It remains to show that each S_i is in $\mathbf{SPP}$. Let $B \stackrel{df}{=} \max(w_1, \ldots, w_k)$ and let $f_i \stackrel{df}{=} \delta_{w_i}^{B} \circ f$ for $1 \leq i \leq k$. By the remarks made in section 2, each f_i is in GapP. For all $x \in \Sigma^*$, we have $f_i(x) = \delta^B_{w_i}(f(x)) = 1$ if $f(x) = w_i$, and 0 otherwise. Thus f_i witnesses that $S_i \in$ **SPP**.

Conversely, suppose there exist $S_1, \ldots, S_k \in$ **SPP** such that L satisfies the three conditions of the theorem. For $1 \leq i \leq k$, let $f_i(x)$ be the characteristic function of S_i, and define $f(x) \stackrel{\text{df}}{=} \sum_{i=1}^{k} f_i(x) \cdot w_i$. Clearly $f_i \in$ GapP and $f \in$ GapP. By the first two conditions, we see that for any given x, $f(x) = w_{i(x)}$ where $i(x)$ is the unique i such that $x \in S_i$. Thus the graph of f is contained in $A \cup R$. By the third condition, we have: $x \in L \iff (\exists i,\ 1 \leq i \leq k)[x \in L_i \cap S_i] \iff x \in L_{i(x)} \cap S_{i(x)} \iff x \in L_{i(x)} \iff (x, w_{i(x)}) \in A \iff (x, f(x)) \in A$. Therefore, f witnesses that $L \in$ Gap(A, R). This completes the proof. $\square$

In the definition of gap-definability (definition 3), there is no restriction on the accepting set A and rejecting set R. We will show that A and R can always be chosen such that $A \cup R$ is recursive, and under reasonable circumstances, both A and R themselves are recursive.

We say that a function f is *covered* by g if $(\forall x)(\exists i)[f(x) = g(x, i)]$.

Lemma 19. *There is a recursive function* $g : \Sigma^* \times \mathbf{N} \to \mathbf{N}$ *such that*
1. $\forall x, i,\ g(x, i) \in \{2i, 2i + 1\}$.
2. *For any fixed i, $g(x, i) = 2i$ for all but finitely many x.*
3. *If $f \in$ GapP is covered by g, then range(f) is finite.*

Proof. Let $h(i, x) = f_i(x)$ be a universal function for GapP, i.e., GapP $= \{f_0, f_1, f_2, \ldots\}$. There is a canonical linear ordering on $\Sigma^* \times \mathbf{N}$. We define g in stages: Initially all the f_i are unmarked. At stage (x, i), if there exists $j \leq i$ such that f_j is unmarked and $f_j(x) \in \{2i, 2i + 1\}$, choose the smallest such j, mark function f_j, and set $g(x, i) = 4i + 1 - f_j(x)$; otherwise set $g(x, i) = 2i$. Clearly g is recursive, and for all $x, g(x, i) \in \{2i, 2i + 1\}$. Now we fix i. Since $g(x, i) = 2i + 1$ only if there is a $j \leq i$ such that f_j is marked at stage (x, i), $g(x, i) = 2i$ for all but finitely many x. It remains to show the last part.

Suppose $f = f_i$ has no upper-bound. There is a stage s after which no more GapP functions prior to f will be marked. Since f is unbounded, we can find x such that $f(x) \in \{2j, 2j+1\}$ with $(x, j) > s$ and $j \geq i$. Then f must be marked at stage (x, j) if it has not already been marked. Suppose f is marked at stage (y, k), then $f(y) \neq g(y, k)$ by the definition of g. Note also that $f(y) \in \{2k, 2k + 1\}$ but $g(y, k') \notin \{2k, 2k + 1\}$ for any $k' \neq k$. Thus f is not covered by g. In other words, if f is covered by g, then f is upper-bounded, and therefore range(f) is finite since we also have $f(x) \geq 0$ for all x. $\square$

Theorem 20. *For any countable class C, there are sets A, R such that $A \cup R$ is recursive and* GapCl(C) = Gap(A, R).

Proof. Let $C = \{L_1, L_2, \ldots\}$ and g be the function defined in the lemma. Set $A = \{(x, g(x, i)) | x \in L_i\}$ and $R = \{(x, g(x, i)) | x \notin L_i\}$. Given (x, m), $(x, m) \in A \cup R$ iff there is i such that $g(x, i) = m$. Since $g(x, i) \in \{2i, 2i + 1\}$ and g is recursive, we have that $A \cup R$ is recursive.

Now we show that $\mathcal{C} \subseteq \text{Gap}(A, R)$. Let $L_i \in \mathcal{C}$. Define a function h s.t. $\forall x, h(x) = g(x, i)$. Since $g(x, i) = 2i$ for all but finitely many x, we have $h(x) \in$ **FP** $\subseteq$ **GapP**. Clearly $x \in L_i \implies (x, h(x)) = (x, g(x, i)) \in A$ and $x \notin L_i \implies (x, h(x)) = (x, g(x, i)) \in R$. So $L_i \in \text{Gap}(A, R)$. Thus $\mathcal{C} \subseteq \text{Gap}(A, R)$. Since $\text{Gap}(A, R)$ is gap-definable, we have $\text{GapCl}(\mathcal{C}) \subseteq \text{Gap}(A, R)$.

Conversely, let $L \in \text{Gap}(A, R)$. That is, there is $f \in$ **GapP** such that
$$x \in L \implies (x, f(x)) \in A \implies f(x) = g(x, i) \text{ for some } i \text{ and } x \in L_i$$
$$x \notin L \implies (x, f(x)) \in R \implies f(x) = g(x, i) \text{ for some } i \text{ and } x \notin L_i$$

Clearly f is covered by g, so $range(f)$ is finite by the lemma. Let $range(f) = \{n_1, n_2, ..., n_r\}$. By arguments similar to those in Theorem 18, it is not hard to see that $S_i \stackrel{\text{df}}{=} \{x | f(x) = n_i\} \in$ **SPP**, and $L = \bigcup_{i=1}^{r}(S_i \cap L_{\lfloor n_i/2 \rfloor})$. Also note that $\{S_1, S_2, ..., S_r\}$ is a partition of Σ^*, so we have $L \in \text{GapCl}(\mathcal{C})$ by Theorem 18. This completes the proof. $\quad\square$

Corollary 21. *If there is a universal recursive enumeration of $\mathcal{C}$, then there are recursive sets A and R such that $\text{GapCl}(\mathcal{C}) = \text{Gap}(A, R)$. (For example, $\text{GapCl}(\mathbf{NP}) = \text{Gap}(A, R)$ for some recursive sets A and R.)* $\quad\square$

It was shown in [FFK91] that $\text{GapCl}(\mathcal{C})$ inherits many closure properties of $\mathcal{C}$. Here we add to that list, and obtain as a corollary a simple characterization of $\text{GapCl}(\mathcal{C})$ for many common classes $\mathcal{C}$.

Lemma 22. *1. If class $\mathcal{C}$ is closed under union, then so is $\text{GapCl}(\mathcal{C})$.*
2. If class $\mathcal{C}$ is closed under intersection, then so is $\text{GapCl}(\mathcal{C})$.

Proof. 1. Let $\mathcal{C} = \{L_1, L_2, ...\}$ and $L_a, L_b \in \text{GapCl}(\mathcal{C})$. $\exists S_1, ..., S_m, T_1, ..., T_n \in$ **SPP** where $S_i \cap S_j = T_i \cap T_j = \emptyset$ for $i \neq j$ and $\bigcup_{i=1}^{m} S_i = \bigcup_{i=1}^{n} T_i = \Sigma^*$ s.t. $L_a = \bigcup_{i=1}^{m}(L_i \cap S_i), L_b = \bigcup_{j=1}^{m}(L_j \cap T_j)$, (Theorem 18). For $i, j, 1 \leq i \leq m, 1 \leq j \leq n$, let $Q_{ij} = S_i \cap T_j$. Then $S_i = \bigcup_{j=1}^{n} Q_{ij}, T_j = \bigcup_{i=1}^{n} Q_{ij}$. $L_a = \bigcup_{i=1}^{m}[L_i \cap (\bigcup_{j=1}^{n} Q_{ij})] = \bigcup_{i=1}^{m} \bigcup_{j=1}^{n}(L_i \cap Q_{ij}), \quad L_b = \bigcup_{j=1}^{n}[L_j \cap (\bigcup_{i=1}^{m} Q_{ij})] = \bigcup_{j=1}^{n} \bigcup_{i=1}^{n}(L_j \cap Q_{ij})$ Since $(L_i \cap Q_{ij}) \cup (L_j \cap Q_{ij}) = (L_i \cup L_j) \cap Q_{ij}, L_a \cup L_b = \bigcup_{i=1}^{m} \bigcup_{j=1}^{n}[(L_i \cup L_j) \cap Q_{ij}]$. Note that $L_i \cup L_j \in \mathcal{C}$, and $\{Q_{ij}\}_{1 \leq i \leq m, 1 \leq j \leq n}$ is a partition of Σ^*, we thus have $L_a \cup L_b \in \text{GapCl}(\mathcal{C})$.

2. Similarly, since $(L_i \cap Q_{ij}) \cap (L_j \cap Q_{ij}) = (L_i \cap L_j) \cap Q_{ij}$, and $(L_i \cap Q_{ij}) \cap (L_k \cap Q_{kl}) = \emptyset$ for $(i, j) \neq (k, l)$, applying distributive law, we have $L_a \cap L_b = \bigcup_{i=1}^{m} \bigcup_{j=1}^{n}[(L_i \cap L_j) \cap Q_{ij}]$. Again, since $L_i \cap L_j \in \mathcal{C}$ and $\{Q_{ij}\}_{1 \leq i \leq m, 1 \leq j \leq n}$ is a partition of Σ^*, we have $L_a \cap L_b \in \text{GapCl}(\mathcal{C})$. $\quad\square$

For some classes which seem unlikely to be gap-definable, such as **NP** and **BPP**, we want to know what their gap-closures are. The following corollary gives us a simple way to describe them. For example, $\text{GapCl}(\mathbf{NP})$ is exactly the closure of $\mathbf{NP} \cup \mathbf{SPP}$ under union and intersection.

Corollary 23. *If $\mathcal{C}$ is closed under union and intersection, and $\{\emptyset, \Sigma^*\} \subseteq \mathcal{C}$, then $\text{GapCl}(\mathcal{C})$ is the closure under union and intersection of $\mathcal{C} \cup \mathbf{SPP}$.*

Proof. Since $\{\emptyset, \Sigma^*\} \subseteq \mathcal{C} \subseteq \mathrm{GapCl}(\mathcal{C}), \mathbf{SPP} \subseteq \mathrm{GapCl}(\mathcal{C})$. Let $\mathcal{D}$ be the closure of $\mathcal{C} \cup \mathbf{SPP}$ under union and intersection. By Lemma 22, $\mathrm{GapCl}(\mathcal{C})$ is closed under union and intersection, and $\mathcal{C} \cup \mathbf{SPP} \subseteq \mathrm{GapCl}(\mathcal{C})$, so we have $\mathcal{D} \subseteq \mathrm{GapCl}(\mathcal{C})$. Conversely, since $\mathbf{SPP} \subseteq \mathcal{D}, \mathcal{D}$ is gap-definable by Corollary 7. Since $\mathcal{C} \subseteq \mathcal{D}, \mathrm{GapCl}(\mathcal{C}) \subseteq \mathcal{D}$. $\quad\square$

5 Other results

We have seen that for many classes, having certain Boolean closure properties implies gap-definability. One may ask whether these Boolean closure properties are necessary. We will show, however, that not all gap-definable classes, not even all reasonable gap-definable classes, are closed under union (resp. intersection, complement).

Theorem 24. *There exist*
  1. *a reasonable gap-definable class which is not closed under union.*
  2. *a reasonable gap-definable class which is not closed under intersection.*
  3. *a reasonable gap-definable class which is not closed under complement.*

Proof. 1. We want to find L_1, L_2 s.t. $L_1 \cup L_2 \notin \mathrm{GapCl}(\{L_1, L_2, \emptyset, \Sigma^*\})$, i.e. $L_1 \cup L_2 \neq (L_1 \cap S_i) \cup (L_2 \cap S_j) \cup S_k$ for all disjoint $S_i, S_j, S_k \in \mathbf{SPP}$ (Theorem 18). Let $\mathbf{SPP} = \{S_1, S_2, ...\}$. Construct L_1 and L_2 as follows. For each pairwise disjoint triple $S_i, S_j, S_k \in \mathbf{SPP}$ pick $x = 0^{i+1}1^{j+1}0^{k+1}$. If $x \in S_k$ put $x \notin L_1 \cup L_2$; If $x \in S_i$ put $x \in L_2 - L_1$; If $x \in S_j$ put $x \in L_1 - L_2$; If $x \notin S_i \cup S_j \cup S_k$ put $x \in L_1 - L_2$. It is easy to see that $L_1 \cup L_2$ is neither empty nor Σ^*. And $L_1 \cup L_2$ is not contained in $\mathrm{GapCl}(\{L_1, L_2, \emptyset, \Sigma^*\})$. In fact, if we fix i, j, k, then $x = 0^{i+1}1^{j+1}0^{k+1}$ is either in $L_1 \cup L_2$ but not in $(L_1 \cap S_i) \cup (L_2 \cap S_j) \cup S_k$, or in S_k but not in $L_1 \cup L_2$.

2. A similar argument will show that $L_1 \cap L_2 \notin \mathrm{GapCl}(\{L_1, L_2, \emptyset, \Sigma^*\})$.

3. Let $L \notin \mathbf{SPP}$, then $\overline{L} \notin \mathbf{SPP}$, where $\overline{L}$ is the complement of L. Then $\overline{L} \notin \mathrm{GapCl}(\{L, \emptyset, \Sigma^*\})$ for otherwise, $\overline{L} = (L \cap S_1) \cup S_2$ for some disjoint $S_1, S_2 \in \mathbf{SPP}$ by Theorem 18. So we would have $\overline{L} = S_2$, a contradiction. $\quad\square$

Another interesting phenomenon is that we have a "gap" between gap-definable classes. More precisely, classes like $\mathbf{PP}$ and $\mathbf{PSPACE}$ contain maximal proper gap-definable subclasses which are closed under many-one reductions, unless they equal $\mathbf{SPP}$.

Theorem 25. *Let $\mathbf{SPP}$ be properly contained in a class $\mathcal{D}$ which has a many-one complete set. Then there exists a maximal m-closed gap-definable class $\mathcal{M}$ such that $\mathbf{SPP} \subseteq \mathcal{M} \subset \mathcal{D}$. (m-closed means closed under many-one reductions.)*

Proof. Let $\mathcal{P}$ be the set of all classes $\mathcal{E}$ s.t. 1. $\mathbf{SPP} \subseteq \mathcal{E} \subset \mathcal{D}$, 2. $\mathcal{E}$ is m-closed, 3. $\mathcal{E}$ is gap-definable. Clearly $(\mathcal{P}, \subseteq)$ is a Poset. $\mathcal{P}$ is not empty since $\mathbf{SPP} \in \mathcal{P}$. Let $\mathcal{C}_1 \subseteq \mathcal{C}_2 \subseteq ...$, where $\mathcal{C}_i \in \mathcal{P}$. We want to show that this chain has an upper bound in $\mathcal{P}$. Let $\mathcal{B} = \bigcup(\mathcal{C}_i)$. It is clear that $\mathcal{B}$ is an upper bound of this chain. Now we show that $\mathcal{B}$ is in $\mathcal{P}$:

1. Clearly $\mathbf{SPP} \subseteq \mathcal{B}$. Since $\mathcal{C}_i \subseteq \mathcal{D}$ for all i, we have $\mathcal{B} \subseteq \mathcal{D}$. None of the $\mathcal{C}_i$'s contains a $\mathcal{D}$-complete set, for otherwise $\mathcal{C}_i = \mathcal{D}$ since $\mathcal{C}_i$ is m-closed. Thus $\mathcal{B} \neq \mathcal{D}$

2. $\mathcal{B}$ is m-closed: A language L many-one reduces to $\mathcal{B}$ implies that L many-one reduces to $\mathcal{C}_i$ for some i. Since $\mathcal{C}_i$ is m-closed, we have $L \in \mathcal{C}_i \subseteq \mathcal{B}$

3. $\mathcal{B}$ is gap-definable: $L_1, L_2 \in \mathcal{B} \Longrightarrow L_1, L_2 \in \mathcal{C}_i$ for some i
$\Longrightarrow (L_1 \cap S_1) \cup (L_2 \cap S_2) \in \mathcal{C}_i$ for all disjoint $S_1, S_2 \in \mathbf{SPP}$ (Theorem 6)
$\Longrightarrow (L_1 \cap S_1) \cup (L_2 \cap S_2) \in \mathcal{B} \Longrightarrow \mathcal{B}$ is gap-definable (Theorem 6) .

Now applying Zorn's Lemma, $\mathcal{P}$ has a maximal element. $\quad\square$

Corollary 26. *There exists a maximal m-closed gap-definable proper subclass of* $\mathbf{PP}$ *unless* $\mathbf{SPP} = \mathbf{PP}$. $\quad\square$

6 Open Problems

1. Are $\mathbf{NP}$, $\mathbf{BPP}$ and $\mathbf{PH}$ gap-definable?
2. Is there a notion of gap-closure for simply gap-definable classes?
3. Is there any reasonable gap-definable class which is not closed under union, intersection and complementation simultaneously?

References

[BGH90] R. Beigel, J. Gill, and U. Hertrampf. Counting classes: Thresholds, parity, mods, and fewness. In *Proceedings of the 7th Symposium on Theoretical Aspects of Computer Science*, pages 49–57, 1990.

[BRS91] R. Beigel, N. Reingold, and D. Spielman. PP is closed under intersection. In *Proc. of the 23rd ACM Symp. on the Theory of Computing*, pages 1–9, 1991.

[FFK91] S. Fenner, L. Fortnow, and S. Kurtz. Gap-definable counting classes. In *Proc. of the 6th Structure in Complexity Theory Conf.*, pages 30–42, 1991.

[Gil77] J. Gill. Computational complexity of probabilistic complexity classes. *SIAM Journal on Computing*, 6:675–695, 1977.

[GKT92] F. Green, J. Köbler, and J. Torán. The power of the middle bit. In *Proceedings of the 7th Structure in Complexity Theory Conf.*, pages 111–117, 1992.

[KST92] J. Köbler, U. Schöning, and J. Torán. Graph isomorphism is low for PP. In *Proc. of the 9th Symp. on Theoretical Aspects of Computer Science*, 1992.

[RS92] K. Regan and T. Schwentick On the power of one bit of a #P function. To appear in *Proc. of the 4th Italian Conf. in Theoretical Comp. Sci.*, 1992.

[Sim75] J. Simon. On some central problems in computational complexity. Technical Report TR75-224, Cornell University Department of Computer Science, 1975.

[Tod91] S. Toda. PP is as hard as the polynomial-time hierarchy. *SIAM J. on Computing*, 20(5):865–877, 1991.

[TO92] S. Toda and M. Ogiwara. Counting classes are at least as hard as the polynomial-time hierarchy. *SIAM J. on Computing*, 21(2):316–328, 1992.

[Val79] L. Valiant. The complexity of computing the permanent. *Theoretical Computer Science*, 8:189–201, 1979.

[Wag86] K. Wagner. The complexity of combinatorial problems with succinct input representation. *Acta Informatica*, 23:325–356, 1986.

On the Logical Definability of Some Rational Trace Languages (*)

C. Choffrut and L. Guerra

Université Paris 7, LITP
Tour 55-56, 1er étage, 75 251 Paris Cedex
cc@litp.ibp.fr

Abstract.— Trace monoids are obtained from free monoids by defining a subset I of pairs of letters that are allowed to commute. Most of the work of this theory is an attempt to relate the properties of these monoids to the properties of I. Following the work initiated by Büchi we show that when I is an equivalence relation (the trace monoid is then a free product of free commutative monoids) it is possible to define a second order logic whose models are the traces viewed as dependence graphs and which characterizes exactly the sets of traces that are rational. This logic essentially utilizes a predicate based on the ordering defined by the dependence graph and a predicate related to a restricted use of the comparison of cardinality.

Résumé.— Les monoïdes de traces sont obtenus à partir des monoïdes libres en définissant un sous-ensemble I de paires de lettres autorisées à commuter. La plupart des efforts de cette théorie consiste à relier les propriétés de ces monoïdes à celles de I. Poursuivant les travaux de Büchi nous montrons que, dans le cas où I est une relation d'équivalence, (le monoïde est alors un produit libre de monoïdes commutatifs libres), l'on peut définir une logique du second ordre dont les modèles sont les graphes de dépendance des traces et qui caractérise exactement les langages rationnels de traces. Cette logique utilise essentiellement un prédicat basé sur l'ordre partiel dans les graphes de dépendance et un prédicat de comparaison restreinte de cardinalité.

1 Introduction

Given a finite set Σ (an *alphabet*) we denote by Σ^* the free monoid it generates and we call *words* its elements. A relation of *partial commutation* or *independence* is a symmetric and reflexive relation $I \subseteq \Sigma \times \Sigma$. The *trace monoid* defined by this relation is the monoid $M(\Sigma, I)$ presented by $< \Sigma; \ ab = ba \text{ for all } (a,b) \in I >$, i.e., the quotient $M(\Sigma, I) = \Sigma^*/\underset{I}{\sim}$, where $\underset{I}{\sim}$ is the congruence over Σ^* generated by the relation $\{ab = ba \mid (a,b) \in I\}$.

Given an arbitrary monoid M, two basic families of subsets of M are usually defined, namely the family $\mathrm{Rat}M$ of *rational* subsets obtained from the singletons by using the rational operations of set union, product and star only, and the family $\mathrm{Rec}M$ of *recognizable* subsets defined as the subsets that are unions of classes of a congruence of finite index. It is well-known that $\mathrm{Rec}M$ is included in $\mathrm{Rat}M$ whenever M is finitely generated. In the case of trace monoids this inclusion is strict as soon

---

(*) this research was supported by the PRC Mathématiques et Informatique

as some pair of letters commute, e.g., for the presentation $M = < a, b; ab = ba >$ the subset $(ab)^*$ is not recognizable since its inverse image in the free monoid $\{a, b\}^*$ is the so-called Dyck language which is known not to be rational.

The connection between logic and finite automata is due to Büchi (and later to Elgot) who was concerned with deciding certain second order monadic theories and who showed how automata naturally come up when defining a normal form for their closed formulas ([5] and [6]). This enabled him to reduce the decidability of the logic to the decidability of the emptiness problem for finite automata. Originally, these automata recognized infinite words and were only considered as a tool for solving problems in mathematical logic. The other direction, namely using logic to classify languages of (actually finite) words or equivalently considering words as models of a certain theory, can be credited to McNaughton and Papert with their characterization of the "star-free" events by means of first order logic ([10]). Further refinements of this class of languages (the "dot-depth" hierarchy) as well as an extension of the notion of "star-freeness" to infinite words followed (cf., e.g., [13] and [11]).

Perhaps the most natural introduction of partial commutation in free monoids is obtained by considering pairs (or more generally tuples) of words, whether finite or infinite (cf., e.g., [8] and [15]). Indeed, if say, the two words are written over two disjoint alphabets, which can be assumed without loss of generality, this situation reduces to having the letters of the first alphabet commute with those of the second alphabet. Equivalently, the trace monoids thus obtained are simply the direct products of free monoids and we briefly discuss in the next paragraph the difficulties encountered while trying to characterize their rational subsets. For the subfamily of recognizable subsets the situation is more amenable and the characterization can be achieved with no restriction on the relation of partial commutation. More precisely, Thomas has considered the elements of an arbitrary trace monoid as "dependence graphs" (which in a sense is the extension of the linear structure of words), and has showed the logical definability of the family of recognizable subsets ([14]).

Our result is a continuation of the latter but is concerned with rational rather than recognizable subsets. As suggested by our previous remarks some extra restrictions are necessary, and we focus our attention on trace monoids where I is a relation of equivalence (cf. Example 2.2). In this case, the monoid $M(\Sigma, I)$ is a free product of free commutative monoids and we show that the family of rational trace subsets can be characterized by what we call the *restricted cardinality logic*, abbreviated $\mathcal{RCL}$, cf. Theorem section 2.3. More specifically, we view the elements of $M(\Sigma, I)$ as dependence graphs and consider those as models of a second order language. The dependence graph of a trace t is a finite acyclic graph labelled by the letters of the alphabet where each node is associated with exactly one occurrence of a letter in t. Roughly speaking, the edges between the nodes record the non-commutations between the corresponding occurrences of the letters (cf. next section for a more precise definition). We enrich the second order logic of Thomas with a second order predicate that says, with a restriction, that two subsets have the same cardinality (the necessity of such a restriction is clear from the monoid M in the above example). A related result, with the hypothesis that all letters commute, i.e., when $I = \Sigma \times \Sigma$, may be found in the literature. Indeed, using Presburger arithmetic, i.e., first order theory of addition, Ginsburg and Spanier were able to logically characterize the rational trace languages in the commutative case (cf. [7], Theorem 1.3). It is a different approach from ours since traces are identified with n-uples of integers. The language of traces associated with a formula having free individual variables $x_1, x_2, \ldots, x_n$ is defined as the set of n-uples for which the formula holds true.

Now we want to argue that our result is the most general possible if we do not restrict the use of connectives. Indeed, when our hypothesis on I is violated, then Σ contains 3 different letters a, b, c where a commutes with b and c and no other commutation between them holds. Then the set of rational subsets is not closed under intersection $((ab)^*c^* \cap b^*(ac)^*$ is not rational). Worse, when Σ contains 4 different letters a, b, c, d where a and b commute with c and d and no other commutation between them holds, then the emptiness problem for the intersection is not decidable, since the Post Correspondence Problem can be reduced to it (cf., e.g., [3], Theorem III 8.4). This does not rule out a possibility for a logical characterization but it is an indication that if such a characterization exists it is probably more involved.

Section 2 presents the preliminaries, i.e., it recalls the basic notions on trace monoids, rational and recognizable subsets, free commutative monoids etc.., and exposes our second order logic. In section 3 we show how to assign a closed formula of the restricted cardinality logic to each rational language by first considering the special case of the free commutative monoids. The converse, i.e., how to associate a rational language to each closed formula is done in the last section. It uses a structural induction on the formulas and takes crucial advantage of the specific properties of the rational subsets in the present case.

2 Preliminaries

2.1. Trace monoids

The theory of trace monoids has been given much attention in these last ten years as witnessed by the lenghty bibliography of the survey article [1]. We content ourselves with recalling what is essential to our purpose.

Given a finite set Σ (an *alphabet*) we denote by Σ^* the free monoid it generates. The elements of Σ^* are called *words* and the *empty* word is denoted by 1. Intuitively a trace is a word that is defined up to the commutations of certain pairs of letters. More precisely, we define a relation of *partial commutation* or *independence* as a symmetric and reflexive relation $I \subseteq \Sigma \times \Sigma$. The *trace monoid* defined by this relation is the monoid $M(\Sigma, I)$, or simply $M(\Sigma)$ when I is understood, presented by $< \Sigma; \; ab = ba$ for all $(a, b) \in I >$, i.e., the quotient $M(\Sigma, I) = \Sigma^*/\underset{I}{\sim}$, where $\underset{I}{\sim}$ is the congruence generated by the relation $\{ab = ba \mid$ for all $(a, b) \in I\}$. When no confusion may arise, we drop the subscript I and write $\sim$ instead of $\underset{I}{\sim}$. The *empty* trace, denoted by 1, is the class of the empty word.

EXAMPLE 2.1. — Consider $\Sigma = \{a, b, c\}$ and assume $I = \{(a, b), (b, a), (c, b), (b, c)\}$. Then $a\underline{ba}cbc \sim aabcbc \sim aabbcc$ etc...

In particular when $I = \{(a,a) \mid a \in \Sigma\}$, then we obtain the free monoid and when $I = \Sigma \times \Sigma$ then all letters commute and we get the free commutative monoid generated by Σ, also denoted by $\Sigma^{\oplus}$. We are concerned here with a composition of these two cases where I is an equivalence relation, i.e., when $M(\Sigma, I)$ is a free product of free commutative monoids. Then there exists a natural decomposition of the alphabet Σ into maximal subalphabets $\Sigma_i, i = 1, \cdots, n$ of pairwise commuting letters. In other words, for a given word in Σ^*, the commutations may only occur inside the maximal factors that are written over some fixed subalphabet Σ_i.

EXAMPLE 2.2. — Consider $\Sigma = \{a,b,c,d\}$ and let $I = \{(a,b),(b,a),(c,d),(d,c)\}$. The relation of independence determines the two subalphabets $\Sigma_1 = \{a,b\}, \Sigma_2 = \{c,d\}$. If we start with the word $w = abadcbacd$ then the unique commutations occur inside the maximal factors $w_1 = aba, w_2 = dc, w_3 = ba, w_4 = cd$. E.g., $ab\underline{a}dcbacd \sim aabdcb\underline{acd} \sim aabd\underline{cb}adc \sim aabcdbadc$ etc...

2.2 Rational and recognizable subsets

Given an arbitrary monoid M, two basic families of subsets of M are usually defined, namely the family of *rational* and the family of *recognizable* subsets. The first one, denoted by Rat$M$, is the least family $\mathcal{F}$ of subsets of M containing the singletons and closed under *set union* $X \cup Y$ more usually denoted by $X + Y$, *product* $X.Y$ also denoted by XY and defined as $\{xy \in M \mid x \in X \text{ and } y \in Y\}$ and *star operation* X^* defined as the submonoid generated by X :
  (i) for all $m \in M$, $\{m\} \in \mathcal{F}$.
  (ii) for all $X, Y \in \mathcal{F}$, we have $X + Y, XY, X^* \in \mathcal{F}$.

This family enjoys important properties such as being closed under morphisms or more generally finite (actually rational cf., e.g., [3] Proposition I.4.2) substitutions but is not necessarily closed under the Boolean operations. However, what concerns trace monoids, we know that they are closed under Boolean operations if and only if the relation of independence is an equivalence relation (cf., e.g., [4], [2] Theorem 3.6 and [12]).

The second family of subsets of M, denoted by Rec$M$ contains all subsets that are saturated by a congruence of finite index on M. It is well-known that Rec$M$ is included in Rat$M$ whenever M is finitely generated (cf., [9] or [3], Proposition III.2.4). In the case of trace monoids this inclusion is strict as soon as some pair of letters commute, e.g., for the presentation $M = < a,b; ab = ba >$ the subset $(ab)^*$ is not recognizable since its inverse image in the free monoid $\{a,b\}^*$ is not rational. In [14] the family of recognizable trace languages is characterized by means of a second order logic. Due to the non closure of rational trace languages under intersection there is no hope we can extend this result by just adding some new predicate. Rather, we will restrict ourselves to the case where this family is a Boolean algebra, i.e., where the independence relation is an equivalence relation.

2.3 The restricted cardinality logic

The second order language that we are interested in will be interpreted on traces considered as *dependence graphs*. We thus start with recalling this notion (cf. [1]).

With a given independence relation I on the alphabet Σ it is customary to associate the dependence relation $D = \{(a, b) \mid \in I \text{ or } a = b\}$. Let $w = a_1 a_2 \cdots a_n \in \Sigma^*$ (with $a_i \in \Sigma$ for $i = 1, \cdots, n$) be a word and let t be the trace it represents. The *dependence graph* associated with t is a finite directed acyclic graph whose nodes are labelled by the letters of the alphabet and which records the "essential" non-commutations between the letters, i.e., those that imply all the others by transitivity. Formally, it is a triple (V, E, β) where each vertex $v_i \in V$ is identified with the i-th letter position in w, where the label of v_i is a_i and where (v_i, v_j) is an edge of E if $i < j$, $(a_i, a_j) \in D$ and for no $i < k < j$, the condition $(a_i, a_k), (a_k, a_j) \in D$ holds (cf. [1], p. 13). It is not difficult to see that this definition only depends on the equivalence class of w, i.e., on the trace t. We also write $v \le v'$ (resp. and $v < v'$) when there is a path (resp. a non trivial path) from v to v' in the dependence graph. This relation defines an ordering of the vertices.

EXAMPLE 2.3 — Consider the word *abadcbacd* of example 2.2 and mark the positions of each occurrence of some letter: $a_1 b_2 a_3 d_4 c_5 b_6 a_7 c_8 d_9$. Then the dependence graph has 9 vertices and e.g., there is an edge between 4 and 7 because d_4 and a_7 do not commute and the occurrences c_5 and b_6 inbetween commute with d_4 or a_7. The reader may check that the 3 equivalent words have the same graph.

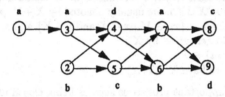

Fig. 1. The dependence graph associated with the trace of Example 2.2

The logic that we introduce to characterize the rational trace languages, has individual variables $x, y, \cdots$, set variables $X, Y, \cdots$, a monadic predicate Q_a for each letter $a \in \Sigma$, where $Q_a(x)$ is interpreted as meaning that the node x of the graph is labelled by a, a relation symbol $\prec$ between individual variables interpreted as follows: $x \prec z$ is true if and only if there exits a node y, $x \le y \le z$ and two letters $a \ne b$ in Σ such that $Q_b(y)$ and either $Q_a(x)$ or $Q_a(z)$, and a binary relation $\text{Card}_r(X, Y)$ of *restricted cardinality* between set variables interpreted as follows:

the predicate $\text{Card}_r(X, Y)$ is true if and only if X and Y have the same cardinality and all $x, y \in X \cup Y$ are incomparable in the strict ordering $\prec$

There are five *atomic formulas*:

(i) $x = y$ (ii) $x \prec y$ (iii) $Q_a(x)$ (iv) $\text{Card}_r(X, Y)$ and (v) $x \in X$

E.g., in the previous example, $2 \prec 9$ and $1 \prec 7$ hold but $1 \prec 3$ and $4 \prec 5$ do not. Also, $\text{Card}_r(\{7\}, \{6\})$ holds, but $\text{Card}_r(\{1, 3\}, \{2\})$ and $\text{Card}_r(\{4\}, \{9\})$ do not. Finally, we have $Q_c(5)$ is true but $Q_a(6)$ is false. The *formulas* are built up of atomic formulas by the Boolean connectives $\neg$, $\wedge$ and the quantifier $\exists$ for individual and subset variables.

The *restricted cardinality logic, RCL* for short, is the set of all sentences (the closed formulas), i.e., of all formulas with no free variables. With every sentence ϕ, we associate the set L_ϕ of all traces $t \in M(\Sigma, I)$ that satisfy ϕ:

$$L_\phi = \{t \in M(\Sigma, I) \mid t \models \phi\}$$

Our main result is the following logical characterization of the rational trace languages:

THEOREM Let $M(\Sigma, I)$ be a trace monoid such that $I \subseteq \Sigma \times \Sigma$ is an equivalence relation. Then a subset R of $M(\Sigma, I)$ is rational if and only if there exists a closed formula ϕ of the restricted cardinality logic such that $R = L_\phi$ holds

EXAMPLE 2.4 — Consider $\Sigma = \{a, b, c\}$ where all letters commute. We want to define the subset of all traces of the form $a^n b^n c^n$ for all $n \geq 0$. We use 3 set variables X_a, X_b, X_c standing for the positions of the occurrences of a, b and c respectively. We need to say (i) that the 3 subsets are disjoint, (ii) that all occurrences belong to the union of these 3 subsets, (iii) that the 3 subsets are of the same cardinality and (iv) that all elements of X_a (resp. X_b, X_c) are labelled by a (resp. b, c). Actually, because of the interpretation of Q_a this last condition implies the first one. This leads to the following sentence that is not strictly speaking consistent with the previous definition because of the use of the standard shorthands, but that can easily be seen to be equivalent:

$$\exists X_a \exists X_b \exists X_c \quad \forall x (x \in X_a \vee x \in X_b \vee x \in X_c)$$
$$\wedge (\mathrm{Card}_r(X_a, X_b) \wedge \mathrm{Card}_r(X_b, X_c) \wedge \mathrm{Card}_r(X_c, X_a))$$
$$\wedge \forall x ((\neg(x \in X_a) \vee Q_a(x)) \wedge (\neg(x \in X_b) \vee Q_b(x)) \wedge (\neg(x \in X_c) \vee Q_c(x)))$$

3 From trace languages to sentences

The purpose of this section is to sketch the proof asserting that a sentence of the restricted cardinality logic may be assigned to each rational trace language, provided the relation I is an equivalence relation. Here we treat the particular case where all letters commute entirely and explain somewhat more loosely how the general case (i.e., I an arbitrary equivalence relation) can be established.

3.1 Associating a sentence with a rational subset: the commutative case

In this section all letters commute, i.e., the relation I is universal and the trace monoid is the free commutative monoid $\Sigma^\oplus$. Then it is an elementary result that the rational languages are *semilinear*, i.e., they are finite unions of *linear* sets, each of which is of the form (cf., e.g., [7]):

(3.1) $\qquad uv_1^* v_2^* \cdots v_n^*$ for some integer $n \geq 0$ and for some $u, v_1, \cdots v_n \in \Sigma^\oplus$

We will freely use the ordinary abbreviations, $\forall x$, $\forall X$, $X = Y$, $X = \emptyset$, $X \cap Y = \emptyset$, $X \subseteq Y$, $X = \bigcup_{1 \le i \le k} X_i$ etc... We also introduce some other abbreviations that help reading the formulas. The first one $|X| = k$ expresses the fact that, for a fixed integer k, a subset has cardinality k:

$$(\exists x_1 \cdots \exists x_k \in X \bigwedge_{1 \le i < j \le k} x_i \ne x_j) \bigwedge (\forall x_1 \cdots \forall x_{k+1} \in X \bigvee_{1 \le i < j \le k+1} x_i = x_j)$$

The second $|X| = k|Y|$ says that for a fixed integer k, the set X has k times as many elements as the set Y. This is translated by saying that there exist k disjoint subsets $X_1, \cdots, X_k$ of the same cardinality as Y, the union of which equals X:

$$\exists X_1 \cdots \exists X_k (X = \bigcup_{1 \le i \le k} X_i) \bigwedge (\bigwedge_{1 \le i < j \le k} X_i \cap X_j = \emptyset) \bigwedge (\bigwedge_{1 \le i \le k} \mathrm{Card}_r(X_i, Y))$$

Let us verify that all rational trace languages in the free commutative monoid can be defined by some closed formula of the language $\mathcal{RCL}$. Observe first that it clearly suffices to show that linear sets as (3.1) are definable. We start with the two special cases where $R = a^r$ for some $a \in \Sigma$ and $R = v^*$ for some $v \in \Sigma^{\oplus}$ and then we prove that the products of languages of this type are still definable.

If $R = a^r$ for some $a \in \Sigma$ and some integer r, then we have: $R = L_\phi$ where ϕ is the sentence

$$\exists X(|X| = r) \wedge \neg \exists X(|X| = r + 1) \wedge \forall x Q_a(x)$$

Now assume $v = a_1^{r_1} a_2^{r_2} \cdots a_p^{r_p}$ and $R = v^*$. Then $R = L_\phi$ where ϕ is the sentence

$$\exists X, X_1 \cdots X_p (\forall x(x \in \bigcup_{1 \le i \le p} X_i)) \bigwedge (\bigwedge_{1 \le i \le p} |X_i| = r_i|X|) \bigwedge (\forall x \bigwedge_{1 \le i \le p} (x \in X_i \Rightarrow Q_{a_i}(x)))$$

Now assume we have $R_1 = L_{\phi_1}$ and $R_2 = L_{\phi_2}$. Consider two different variables X_1 and X_2 and transform ϕ_1 into ϕ_1' by replacing all occurrences of the quantifiers $\exists X$ and $\exists x$ by $\exists X(X \subseteq X_1)$ and $\exists x(x \in X_1)$ respectively. Formally, for all formulas ψ we define recursively the formula ψ' as follows: if $\psi = \chi \wedge \sigma$ then $\psi' = \chi' \wedge \sigma'$, if $\psi = \neg \chi$ then $\psi' = \neg \chi'$, if $\psi = \exists X \chi$ then $\psi' = \exists X(X \subseteq X_1 \wedge \chi')$ and finally if $\psi = \exists x \chi$ then $\psi' = \exists x(x \in X_1 \wedge \chi')$. Similarly, transform ϕ_2 into ϕ_2'' by replacing all occurrences of the quantifiers $\exists X$ and $\exists x$ by $\exists X(X \subseteq X_2)$ and $\exists x(x \in X_2)$ respectively. Then the product $R_1 R_2$ is defined by the formula ϕ where:

$$\phi \equiv \exists X_1 \exists X_2 (X_1 \cap X_2 = \emptyset) \wedge (\forall x(x \in X_1 \cup X_2)) \wedge (\phi_1' \wedge \phi_2'')$$

3.2 Associating a sentence with a rational subset: the general case

Given the equivalence relation I, we denote by $\Sigma_1, \ldots, \Sigma_n$ the maximal subalphabets of Σ for which two arbitrary letters commute. E.g., in Example 2.2 we have $\Sigma = \{a, b, c, d\}$ and $\Sigma_1 = \{a, b\}, \Sigma_2 = \{c, d\}$. It is not difficult to verify that all traces

$t \in M(\Sigma, I)$ can be factored into maximal factors (in terms of number of occurrences of letters in Σ) belonging to some submonoid $\Sigma_i^{\oplus}$ generated by the subalphabet Σ_i for $i = 1, \ldots, n$, two consecutive factors belonging to two different such submonoids.

EXAMPLE 3.1 — With I as in Example 2.2, the trace $t = abadcbacd$ is factored into $t = t_1 t_2 t_3 t_4$ where $t_1 = a^2 b \in \Sigma_1^{\oplus}$, $t_2 = t_4 = cd \in \Sigma_2^{\oplus}$ and $t_3 = ab \in \Sigma_1^{\oplus}$.

Now, consider a rational trace language R and an automaton $\mathcal{A}$ accepting it. In a path labelled by the trace t in the automaton $\mathcal{A}$, we may group all the transitions that envolve a specific subalphabet. This naturally leads to extend the ordinary definition of finite automaton by allowing transitions to be defined by arbitrary rational subsets (not just letters) in a specific subalphabet. The following more or less trivial technical Lemma that we state without proof allows to express logically the fact that a trace is recognized by some finite automaton.

LEMMA Let R be a rational subset of $M(\Sigma, I)$. Then there exists a finite set Q, two specific elements $q_-, q_+ \in Q$ and for each $q, q' \in Q$ and each $i = 1, \ldots, n$, a rational subset $X_{q,q'}^i \in \mathrm{Rat}\Sigma_i^{\oplus}$ such that the following holds:
for all $t \in M - \{1\}$ we have $t \in R$ if and only if there exists a factorization of t into maximal factors whose letters belong to some subalphabet $t = t_1 \cdots t_p$ and a sequence $q_0, q_1, \ldots, q_p$ of elements such that:

$$q_0 = q_-, q_p = q_+, \text{ and for each } i = 1, \ldots, p \text{ there exists } j \in \{1, \ldots, n\}$$
$$\text{such that } t_i \in X_{q_{i-1}, q_i}^j$$

With the help of the previous result we may now enquire how to logically translate the fact that a trace t belongs to a certain rational subset. It is not hard to show that we may assume without loss of generality that the empty trace does not belong to the rational subset. Now let $\mathcal{A}$ be an automaton accepting R and let $t = t_1 \cdots t_p$ be the factorization of a trace t into the maximal factors in the subalphabets $\Sigma_1, \cdots, \Sigma_n$. Then t is accepted by $\mathcal{A}$ if and only if for each factor t_i the following holds:

either t_i is the unique maximal factor of t, its alphabet is Σ_j, it takes the initial state q_- to the final state q_+ and it belongs to X_{q_-, q_+}^j

or t_i is the first factor but not the last factor, its alphabet is Σ_j, it takes the initial state to the state q and it belongs to $X_{q_-, q}^j$

or t_i is the last factor but not the first factor, its alphabet is Σ_j, it takes the state q to the final state q_+ and it belongs to X_{q, q_+}^j

or t_i is not the first or the last factor, its alphabet is Σ_j, it takes the state q to the state q' and it belongs to $X_{q, q'}^j$

The formal proof is an elaboration on the previous statement, e.g., we may express the fact that a subgraph represents a maximal factor, that a maximal factor follows another maximal factor, etc...

4 From sentences to trace languages

In this section we sketch the proof that asserts that the set of traces associated with a given sentence of the restricted cardinality logic, is rational.

The first step is quite standard and asserts that we may deal with set variables only, i.e., we may eliminate the individual variables. In other words we obtain the same expressive power by introducing the monadic relation Singleton(X) on set variables and by using as atomic formulas the following:

(i) $X \subseteq Y$ (ii) Singleton(X) (iii) $X \subseteq Q_a$ (iv) Card$_r(X,Y)$ and (v) $X \prec Y$

where $X \subseteq Q_a$ stands for: $\forall x(\neg(x \in X) \vee Q_a(x))$ and where $X \prec Y$ stands for

$$\forall x \forall y (x \in X \wedge y \in Y) \Rightarrow x \prec y$$

Let us briefly comment on the proof technique. We establish the result by induction on the number of operations involved in the definition of a given formula. However, this requires to assign a truth value to all subformulas, and those are not closed in general. We thus need to extend the induction hypothesis to all formulas, as indicated now. Let ϕ be a formula whose free variables are $X_{i_1}, \ldots, X_{i_p}$ and assume $i_1 < \ldots < i_p$. The idea is to encode the free variables of the formula into the label of each node by augmenting the label with as many new components as there are free variables. The induction hypothesis involves both intermediate and augmented languages as we will see. The k-th new component corresponding to the k-th free variable X_{i_k} in the formula, records whether or not the node is in X_{i_k}. Formally, we proceed in two steps, one yielding the notion of intermediate language and the second one the notion of augmented language. For a given formula ϕ let

$$\Delta = \{(a, \alpha_1, \cdots, \alpha_p) \mid a \in \Sigma, \alpha_i \in \{0,1\} \text{ for } i = 1, \cdots, p\}$$

be its *augmented* alphabet and let $\pi : \Delta \to \Sigma$ be the application that ignores all but the first component

$$\pi(a, \alpha_1, \cdots, \alpha_p) = a$$

Consider the independence relation on Δ

$$J = \{((a, \alpha_1, \cdots, \alpha_p), (b, \beta_1, \cdots, \beta_p)) \mid$$
$$(a, \alpha_1, \cdots, \alpha_p) = (b, \beta_1, \cdots, \beta_p) \text{ or } a \neq b \text{ and } (a, b) \in I\}$$

Observe that J is no longer an equivalence relation, i.e., $M(\Delta, J)$ is not a free product of free commutative monoids when $p > 0$. E.g., if $p = 1$ and $a \neq b$ then $(a, 1)$ and $(b, 0)$ commute and so do $(b, 0)$ and $(a, 0)$ but $(a, 1)$ and $(a, 0)$ do not. (However it is still a free product of direct products of free monoids). As a consequence, in any dependence graph, the set of maximal subgraphs all the nodes of which are labelled by a given subalphabet is linearly ordered. So for all $t \in M(\Delta, J)$ there is a unique decomposition $t = t_1 \cdots t_p$ where for each $i = 1, \cdots, p$ all the nodes of t_i are labelled by the letters of Σ_j for some $j = 1, \cdots, n$, two consecutive factors corresponding to two different subalphabets. By abuse of language we still denote by π the morphism that extends uniquely to $M(\Delta, J)$

$$\pi : M(\Delta, J) \to M(\Sigma, I)$$

The *intermediate language* associated with ϕ is the subset $F_\phi \subseteq M(\Delta, J)$ consisting of all traces $t \in M(\Delta, J)$ such that $\pi(t)$ satisfies ϕ when each subset variable $X_{i_k}, k = 1, \cdots, p$ is interpreted as being the subset of nodes such that $\alpha_k = 1$ holds. Finally let K be the independence relation on Δ that let two elements commute whenever their first components do

$$K = \{((a, \alpha_1, \cdots, \alpha_p), (b, \beta_1, \cdots, \beta_p)) \mid (a, b) \in I\}$$

Observe that K is an equivalence relation, i.e., $M(\Delta, K)$ is a free product of free commutative monoids. Furthermore, $J \subseteq K$ holds and therefore there exists a canonical morphism

$$\gamma : M(\Delta, J) \to M(\Delta, K)$$

Then the *augmented language* associated with ϕ is $L_\phi = \gamma(F_\phi)$.

We end up with a precise statement of the induction hypothesis:
(i) F_ϕ is saturated by the congruence $\underset{\gamma}{\sim}$, i.e., $F_\phi = \gamma^{-1}\gamma(F_\phi) = \gamma^{-1}(L_\phi)$ holds
   and
(ii) the augmented language L_ϕ is rational in $M(\Delta, J)$

We have no room for going through the verification of this statement. Suffice it to say that it consists essentially of verifying that the languages associated with the 5 atomic formulas are rational, and that if L_ϕ, L_{ϕ_1} and L_{ϕ_2} are rational trace languages, so are $L_{\exists\phi}, L_{\neg\phi}$ and $L_{\phi_1 \wedge \phi_2}$.

References

[1] IJ.J. AALBERSBERG, G. ROZENBERG, Theory of traces, *Theoret. Comput. Sci.* 60, 1988, 1-82

[2] IJ.J. AALBERSBERG, E. WELZL, Trace languages defined by regular string languages, *RAIRO Inform. Théor. Applic.* 20, 1986, 103-119

[3] J. BERSTEL, *Transductions and Context-Free Languages*, Teubner, 1979

[4] A. BERTONI, G. MAURI, N. SABADINI, Unambiguous regular trace languages, in *Algebra, Combinatorics and Logic*, (J. Demetrovics, G. Katona and A. Salomaa, eds), Col. Math. Soc. Janos Bolyay 42, North Holland, 1985

[5] J.R. BÜCHI, Weak Second Order Logic and Finite Automata, *Z. Math. Logik Grundlagen Math.* 6, 1960, 66-92

[6] C.C. ELGOT, Decision problems of finite automata design and related arithmetics, *Trans. Amer. Math. Soc.* 98, 1961, 21-52

[7] S. GINSBURG, E.H. SPANIER, Semigroups, Presburber Formulas, and Languages, *Pacific J. Math* **16**, 1966, 285-296

[8] H. LÄUCHLI, C. SAVIOZ, Monadic second order definable relations on the binary tree, *J. of Symbolic Logic* **52**, 1987, 219-226

[9] J.D. Jr. Mac KNIGHT, A.J STOREY, Equidivisible semigroups, *J. of Algebra* **12**, 1969, 24-48

[10] R. McNAUGHTON, S. PAPERT, *Counter-free-Automata* MIT Press, Cambridge Massachussets 1971

[11] D. PERRIN , J.-E. PIN , First order Logic and Star-Free Sets, *J. Comput. System Sci.* **32**, 1986, 393-406

[12] J. SAKAROVITCH, The "Last" Decision Problem, *Proceedings of LATIN'92*, *I. Simon (Ed.)* **LNCS 583**, 460-473

[13] W. THOMAS, Classifying Regular Events in Symbolic Logic, *J. Comput. System Sci.* **25**, 1982, 360-376

[14] W. THOMAS, On logical definability of trace languages, *Proceedings of the Workshop of the ASMICS Group held in Kochel am See*, Tech. Report TUM I9002, Universität München, 1990

[15] W. THOMAS, Infinite trees and automaton definable relations over ω-words, Proceedings of the 7-th STACS Conference held in Rouen, Lecture Notes in Computer Science 415, 1990, 263-279

Solving Systems of Set Constraints using Tree Automata*

Rémi Gilleron, Sophie Tison, Marc Tommasi

LIFL, URA 369 CNRS, IEEA Université de Lille I,
59655 Villeneuve d'Ascq Cedex France.
e-mail : {gilleron,tison,tommasi}@lifl.lifl.fr

Abstract. A set constraint is of the form $exp_1 \subseteq exp_2$ where exp_1 and exp_2 are set expressions constructed using variables, function symbols, and the set union, intersection and complement symbols. An algorithm for solving such systems of set constraints was proposed by Aiken and Wimmers [1]. We present a new algorithm for solving this problem. Indeed, we define a new class of tree automata called Tree Set Automata. We prove that, given a system of set constraints, we can associate a tree set automaton such that the set of tuples of tree languages recognized by this automaton is the set of tuples of solutions of the system. We also prove the converse property. Furthermore, if the system has a solution, we prove, in a constructive way, that there is a regular solution (i.e. a tuple of regular tree languages) and a minimal solution and a maximal solution which are actually regular.

1 Introduction

Set constraints are a natural formalism for describing properties of programs whose underlying domain of computation is a Herbrand universe. Given a set of function symbols Σ and a set of variables $\mathcal{X}$, a *set constraint* is of the form $exp_1 \subseteq exp_2$ where exp_1 and exp_2 are set expressions constructed using variables, function symbols, and the set union, intersection and complement symbols. Set constraints have been used in program analysis and type inference algorithms for functional languages (Reynolds [11], Jones and Muchnick [8], Aiken and Wimmers [1]), logic programming languages (Mishra [9], Heintze and Jaffar [7]), imperative languages, and recently for sorted unification (Uribe [13]).

Algorithms are known for a number of special cases of solving a system of set constraints. There are decidability results which deal with cases where the symbols are unary. Indeed, when restricted to unary symbols, the result is a consequence of Rabin's Tree Theorem which states that the monadic second-order theory of k successors is decidable ([10]). In the rest of the introduction, we will emphasize this remark in order to introduce our new class of tree automata.

---

* This research was partially supported by "GDR Mathématiques et Informatique" and ESPRIT Basic Research Action 6317 ASMICS2.

For set constraints involving function symbols of arbitrary arity, Heintze and Jaffar [6] give an algorithm for the class of definite set constraints. A definite set constraint is of the form $exp_1 \subseteq exp_2$ where exp_1 contains no complement operations and exp_2 contains no set operations. Heintze and Jaffar also use projection functions. They give a decision procedure for systems of definite set constraints. When restricted to definite set constraints, we can note that if there exists a solution, there is a least solution which is a regular solution (i.e. a tuple of regular tree languages). Früwirth, Shapiro, Vardi, Yardeni [3] consider the same class. They present a proof method and provide exact complexity bounds for the problem.

In the general case (even without projection functions) systems of set constraints do not necessarily have a least solution even when a solution exists. The general case (without projection functions) was solved by Aiken and Wimmers [1] and recently by Bachmair et al [2]. Here, we present a new proof using tree automata.

With our method we obtain some properties of set of solutions. We prove that if the set of solutions is non empty there exists a regular solution. Moreover, we can exhibit a minimal solution and a maximal solution which are regular (i.e. a tuple of regular tree languages). Thus our algorithm is an improvement of the algorithm proposed in [1]. Furthermore, for future work the definition of our automata could be enriched with acceptance conditions in order to solve more complex systems of set constraints (e.g. $exp_1 \not\subseteq exp_2$). Finally, this approach can be replaced in a more general context : the study of relations between logic and automata.

We first introduce our new class of tree automata. For this aim, we first consider the case of unary symbols and consider the following example. Our notations for monadic second-order theories are consistent with those in Thomas [12].

Example. [1] Let $\Sigma = \{f, a\}$ where f is a unary symbol and a is a constant. Let us consider the following system SSC of set constraints:
$$X \subseteq Y \quad ; \quad f(Y) \subseteq \overline{Y} \quad ; \quad f(\overline{Y}) \subseteq Y$$
The Herbrand universe $T(\Sigma)$ is in one to one correspondence with the set of the natural numbers and we can associate with SSC the following S1S-formula:
$$\phi(X, Y) \equiv \forall x (x \in X \to x \in Y) \wedge (x \in Y \to \neg(x+1 \in Y)) \wedge (\neg(x \in Y) \to x+1 \in Y)$$
Let $\alpha = ((0, 1).(0, 0))^\omega$, α satisfies ϕ for the canonical interpretation. The ω-language $L(\phi)$ of words in $(\{0, 1\}^2)^\omega$ satisfying ϕ is regular and we can associate with each word in this language a solution of SSC. For instance the corresponding solution of SSC for α is $X = \emptyset, Y = \{f^{2i}(a) \mid i \geq 0\}$.

Dealing with a set Σ of k unary symbols and one constant, in the same way, given a system SSC of set constraints with variables $X_1, \ldots, X_n$, we can associate with this system a first-order formula $\phi(X_1, \ldots, X_n)$ of SkS. The tree language $T(\phi)$ of infinite $\{0, 1\}^n$-valued k-ary trees is recognizable (Rabin recognizable and even Büchi recognizable) and with each tree in this language we can associate a solution of SSC. In this sense the set of (codes of) solutions is recognizable and the existence of a solution is decidable as emptiness is decidable for Rabin recognizable tree languages. We notice that we associate with a system of set constraints a simple first-order formula and that we can directly build a Rabin tree automaton from this system. Infinite tree automata can be viewed as word languages acceptors. We want now to deal with function symbols of arbitrary arity. For this aim, we define tree set automata which can be viewed as tree languages acceptors. We introduce the definition of such objects on the following example.

Example. We consider the same system of set constraints as in the previous example.

We define a tree set automaton $A = (\Sigma, Q, \mathcal{F}, S)$ where $Q = \{q_{\bar{X}\bar{Y}}, q_{\bar{X}Y}, q_{XY}\}$ is a set of states, $\mathcal{F} = (F_1, F_2)$ with $F_1 = \{q_{XY}\}$, $F_2 = \{q_{\bar{X}Y}, q_{XY}\}$ is a 2-tuple of sets of final states, and R is a set of rules defined as follows:

$$a \rightarrow q_{\bar{X}\bar{Y}} \mid q_{\bar{X}Y} \mid q_{XY} \qquad f(q_{\bar{X}\bar{Y}}) \rightarrow q_{\bar{X}Y} \mid q_{XY}$$
$$f(q_{\bar{X}Y}) \rightarrow q_{XY} \qquad f(q_{XY}) \rightarrow q_{\bar{X}\bar{Y}}$$

A run r is a mapping from $T(\Sigma)$ into Q compatible with the rules. For instance let us consider the run r_1 defined by $r_1(a) = q_{\bar{X}\bar{Y}}$, $r_1(f(a)) = q_{\bar{X}Y}$, $r_1(f(f(a))) = q_{\bar{X}\bar{Y}}$, ...(we alternatively apply the rules $f(q_{\bar{X}\bar{Y}}) \rightarrow q_{\bar{X}Y}$ and $f(q_{\bar{X}Y}) \rightarrow q_{\bar{X}\bar{Y}}$). We define $\mathcal{L}(A, r_1)$ the 2-tuple of tree languages accepted by A and r_1 with the following equations:

$$\mathcal{L}(A, r_1) = (L_1(A, r_1), L_2(A, r_1)) \text{ where } L_1(A, r_1) = \{t \in T(\Sigma) \mid r_1(t) \in F_1\} = \emptyset$$
$$\text{and } L_2(A, r_1) = \{t \in T(\Sigma) \mid r_1(t) \in F_2\} = \{f^{2i+1}(a) \mid i \geq 0\}.$$

The corresponding solution of SSC is $X = L_1(A, r_1)$, $Y = L_2(A, r_1)$. The run r_1 is a regular run and the 2-tuple of tree languages accepted by A and r_1 is a 2-tuple of regular tree languages. There exist non regular runs. For instance we can consider a run r_2 such that

$$\mathcal{L}(A, r_2) = (L_1(A, r_2), L_2(A, r_2)) \text{ with } L_1(A, r_2) = \{f^{2p}(a) \mid p \text{ is a prime number}\}$$
$$\text{and } L_2(A, r_2) = \{f^{2i}(a) \mid i \geq 0\}.$$

$\mathcal{L}(A)$ the set of tuples of tree languages recognized by A is the set of tuples of tree languages accepted by A and r for all the possible runs r

We define in Section 2 *Tree Set Automata* (TSA for short). TSA are nearly defined as classical bottom-up tree automata. A first difference is that we consider tuples of sets of final states in order to recognize tuples of tree languages. The main difference is in the behaviour of the tree automata. A run r is a mapping from $T(\Sigma)$ into Q compatible with the rules. For a given run r, we define $\mathcal{L}(A, r)$ the tuple of tree languages accepted by A and r. Hence we define $\mathcal{L}(A)$ the set of tuples of tree languages recognized by A as the set of all $\mathcal{L}(A, r)$ for all the possible runs r. We prove that emptiness is decidable, i.e. it is decidable whether or not $\mathcal{L}(A)$ is empty. Moreover, we define regular runs, we prove that for a regular run ρ $\mathcal{L}(A, \rho)$ is a tuple of regular tree languages, and we prove that $\mathcal{L}(A)$ is non empty if and only if there exists a regular run ρ. We define cylindrification for sets of tuples of tree languages and prove that the class of Tree Set Automata is closed under intersection, union, and cylindrification.

In Section 3, with input a system SSC of set constraints we give the construction of a TSA A such that $\mathcal{L}(A)$ is equal to $SOL(SSC)$ the set of solutions of SSC. We deduce from this result and from the results of Section 2 the following results. Satisfiability of systems of set constraints is decidable, if a system of set constraints is satisfiable there is a regular solution (i.e. a tuple of regular tree languages), a minimal and a maximal solution which are actually regular.

We assume that the reader is familiar with regular tree languages. Nevertheless, it is sufficient to notice the followings. Regular tree languages are a natural generalization to the tree case of regular languages of words over finite alphabet. All basic results about regular languages have their counterparts in the tree case (see Gecseg and Steinby [4]). The reader is also refered to Thomas [12] which contains all the basic results on regular (finite) tree languages, on automata on infinite trees, and on monadic second-order theories.

In this extended abstract many proofs are omitted or not detailed. The reader is referred to [5] for a full version of the paper.

2 Tree Set automata

2.1 Definitions

Definition 1. A tree set automaton (TSA for short) is a 4-tuple $\mathcal{A} = (\Sigma, \mathcal{Q}, \mathcal{F}, \mathcal{S})$. Σ is a finite *ranked alphabet*, $\mathcal{Q}$ is a finite set of *states*, $\mathcal{F}$ a tuple of sets of *final states* and $\mathcal{S}$ is a finite set of *rules* of the following form :
$$b(\mathbf{q_1}, \ldots, \mathbf{q_p}) \to \mathbf{q} \text{ with } b \in \Sigma_p \text{ and } \mathbf{q}, \mathbf{q_1}, \ldots \mathbf{q_p} \in \mathcal{Q}.$$

In the rest of the section we consider a TSA $\mathcal{A} = (\Sigma, \mathcal{Q}, \mathcal{F}, \mathcal{S})$. If $\mathcal{F} = (F_1, \ldots, F_n)$, where $F_i \subseteq \mathcal{Q}$, $1 \leq i \leq n$, n is called the *rank* of the automaton $\mathcal{A}$. Moreover, if there is no two rules in $\mathcal{A}$ with the same left hand side, $\mathcal{A}$ is said to be *deterministic*.

A run in an infinite tree automaton can be viewed as a mapping from Σ^* into a set of states, thus we give the following definition.

Definition 2. An $\mathcal{A}$-*run* r in a tree set automaton $\mathcal{A}$ is a mapping $r : T(\Sigma) \to \mathcal{Q}$ such that :
$$r(t_1) = \mathbf{q_1}, \ldots, r(t_p) = \mathbf{q_p}, r(b(t_1, \ldots, t_p)) = \mathbf{q} \Rightarrow b(\mathbf{q_1}, \ldots, \mathbf{q_p}) \to \mathbf{q} \in \mathcal{S} \ .$$

When $\mathcal{A}$ is clear from the context, we simply say a *run* for an $\mathcal{A}$-*run*. The set of all $\mathcal{A}$-runs is denoted by $\mathcal{R}$.

Definition 3. Let $\mathcal{A}$ be a TSA of rank n, the set $\mathcal{L}(\mathcal{A})$ of n-tuples of tree languages recognized by $\mathcal{A}$ is the set $\mathcal{L}(\mathcal{A}) = \{\mathcal{L}(\mathcal{A}, r) \mid r \in \mathcal{R}\}$ where $\mathcal{L}(\mathcal{A}, r) = (L_1(\mathcal{A}, r), \ldots, L_n(\mathcal{A}, r))$ and $\forall i \in [1, n]$, $L_i(\mathcal{A}, r) = \{t \in T(\Sigma) \mid r(t) \in F_i\}$.

We argue now that our tree set automata differ from classical bottom-up tree automata. Indeed, the first difference is that we consider tuples of sets of final states in order to recognize tuples of tree languages. The second difference is in the behaviour of the tree automata. Let us consider the following example:

Example 1. Let $\mathcal{A} = (\Sigma, \mathcal{Q}, \mathcal{F}, \mathcal{S})$ where $\Sigma = \{a, b\}$ (a is a constant and b is of arity 2); $\mathcal{Q} = \{q_0, q_1\}$; $\mathcal{F} = F = \{q_1\}$; $\mathcal{S} = \{a \rightarrow q_0 \mid q_1, \; b(q_1, q_1) \rightarrow q_0 \mid q_1, \; b(q_0, q_0) \rightarrow q_0, \; b(q_0, q_1) \rightarrow q_0, \; b(q_1, q_0) \rightarrow q_0\}$

With classical tree automata $L(A) = T(\Sigma)$. With our definition the set $\mathcal{L}(\mathcal{A})$ is all the tree languages L such that if $b(t_1, t_2) \in L$ then $t_1 \in L$ and $t_2 \in L$. We describe for instance, three runs r_1, r_2 and r_3.

Let $r_1 \in \mathcal{R}$ defined by $\forall t \in T(\Sigma)$ $r_1(t) = q_1$. Then, $\mathcal{L}(\mathcal{A}, r_1) = T(\Sigma)$.

Let $r_2 \in \mathcal{R}$ defined by $r_2(a) = q_1$, $r_2(b(a, a)) = q_1$, $r_2(b(a, b(a, a))) = q_1$ and $\forall t \in T(\Sigma) \backslash \{a, b(a, a), b(a, b(a, a))\}, r_2(t) = q_0$

Then, $\mathcal{L}(\mathcal{A}, r_2) = \{a, b(a, a), b(a, b(a, a))\}$.

Note that the tree languages $\mathcal{L}(\mathcal{A}, r_1)$ and $\mathcal{L}(\mathcal{A}, r_2)$ are regular but there exists non regular tree languages in $\mathcal{L}(\mathcal{A})$, for instance let $r_3 \in \mathcal{R}$ defined by $r_3(a) = q_1$, $r_3(b(t, t')) = q_1 \Leftrightarrow t = t' \; \forall t \in T(\Sigma)$. We easily verify that r_3 is really a run and $\mathcal{L}(\mathcal{A})$ is the set of all well-balanced trees over Σ.

With a TSA $\mathcal{A}$ we may associate for each i a bottom-up tree automaton $A_i = (\Sigma, \mathcal{Q}, F_i, \mathcal{S})$. Clearly, for any $\mathcal{A}$-run r $L_i(\mathcal{A}, r) \subseteq L(A_i)$. Furthermore, when all the A_i are deterministic and complete there is one and only one $\mathcal{A}$-run and $\mathcal{L}(\mathcal{A}) = (L(A_1), \ldots, L(A_n))$. When all the A_i are deterministic, connected but not complete $\mathcal{L}(\mathcal{A})$ is empty. So, when $\mathcal{A}$ is deterministic and connected either $\mathcal{L}(\mathcal{A})$ is a singleton set which contains a tuple of regular tree languages or $\mathcal{L}(\mathcal{A})$ is empty.

2.2 Emptiness Is Decidable

Theorem 4. *Let* $\mathcal{A} = (\Sigma, \mathcal{Q}, \mathcal{F}, \mathcal{S})$ *be a TSA, the existence of an $\mathcal{A}$-run is decidable, i.e. emptiness of $\mathcal{L}(\mathcal{A})$ is decidable.*

Proof. We construct the set Ω of all elements $\omega \subseteq Q$ verifying $COND_\omega$ defined as follows : $COND_\omega \equiv \forall b \in \Sigma_p \; \forall \mathbf{q_1}, \ldots, \mathbf{q_p} \in \omega \;\; \exists (b(\mathbf{q_1}, \ldots, \mathbf{q_p}) \rightarrow q) \in \mathcal{S}$ where $\mathbf{q} \in \omega$.

The elements in Ω satisfy the property : $\forall \omega \in \Omega \; \exists r \in \mathcal{R}$ such that $r(T(\Sigma)) \subseteq \omega$ and there exists an $\mathcal{A}$-run if and only if Ω is non empty. $\qquad \square$

Example 2. Let $\mathcal{A} = (\Sigma, \mathcal{Q}, \mathcal{F}, \mathcal{S})$ where $\Sigma = \{a, b\}$ (a is a constant and b is of arity 2); $\mathcal{Q} = \{q_{00}, q_{01}, q_{10}, q_{11}\}$; $\mathcal{F} = (\{q_{11}, q_{10}\}, \{q_{11}, q_{01}\})$ and $\mathcal{S} = \{a \rightarrow q_{00} \mid q_{01} \mid q_{11} \mid q_{10}, \; b(q, q') \rightarrow q_{00} \mid q_{01} \mid q_{11} \mid q_{10}\}$; where $(q, q') \in \mathcal{Q} \times \mathcal{Q} \backslash \{(q_{10}, q_{01}), (q_{10}, q_{11}), (q_{11}, q_{01}), (q_{11}, q_{11})\}$.

There is no run such that $r(t) = q_{10}$ and $r(t') = q_{01}$ because $r(b(t, t'))$ would not be defined. The construction of the previous proof leads to the following set $\Omega = \{\{q_{00}\}, \{q_{01}\}, \{q_{10}\}, \{q_{00}, q_{01}\}, \{q_{00}, q_{10}\}\}$.

When restricted to, for instance, $\omega = \{q_{00}, q_{01}\}$, if $r(t)$ and $r(t')$ are defined, $r(b(t, t'))$ can always be defined.

2.3 Regular Runs in a TSA

In this Section we define regular runs. Roughly speaking a run is regular if it can be finitely defined. We prove that there exists a regular run if there exists a run. This property could be related to the existence of a regular tree in any non empty Rabin recognizable set of infinite trees. We prove that if ρ is a regular run then $\mathcal{L}(\mathcal{A}, \rho)$ is a tuple of regular tree languages.

Definition 5. Let $\mathcal{A} = (\Sigma, \mathcal{Q}, \mathcal{F}, \mathcal{S})$ be a TSA and ρ a run in $\mathcal{R}$. ρ is a regular run if there exists a finite set F, a mapping $f : T(\Sigma) \rightarrow F$ and a mapping $g : F \rightarrow \mathcal{Q}$ such that :

- $\rho = g \circ f$;
- $f(t_1) = f(t_2) \Rightarrow f(u(t_1)) = f(u(t_2))$ for every context u . (1)

For instance, the previous run r_2 could be rationally defined by:
$F = \{s_1, s_2, s_3, s_4\}$; $f(a) = s_1$, $f(b(a,a)) = s_2$, $f(b(a, b(a,a))) = s_3$, $\forall t \in T(\Sigma) \backslash \{a, b(a,a), b(a, b(a,a))\}$, $f(t) = s_4$; and $g(s_1) = g(s_2) = g(s_3) = q_1$, $g(s_4) = q_0$.

The set of all regular runs of a TSA $\mathcal{A}$ is denoted by $\mathcal{RR}$. The following two propositions give another characterization of regular runs. The proofs are omitted.

Proposition 6. Let $\mathcal{A} = (\Sigma, \mathcal{Q}, \mathcal{F}, \mathcal{S})$ be a TSA. Let $A = (\Sigma, Q, Q_f, S)$ be a complete and deterministic bottom-up tree automaton. Let $h : Q \rightarrow \mathcal{Q}$ be a mapping verifying :

$$\forall b \in \Sigma_p \ b(q_1, \ldots, q_p) \rightarrow q \in S \Rightarrow b(h(q_1), \ldots, h(q_p)) \rightarrow h(q) \in \mathcal{S}. \quad (2)$$

We denote by q_t the state such that $t \xrightarrow{*}_S q_t$.

The mapping ρ from $T(\Sigma)$ into $\mathcal{Q}$ defined with $\rho(t) = h(q_t)$, for every t in $T(\Sigma)$ is a regular run.

Proposition 7. Let $\mathcal{A} = (\Sigma, \mathcal{Q}, \mathcal{F}, \mathcal{S})$ be a TSA and ρ be a regular run in $\mathcal{RR}$. There exist a complete and deterministic bottom-up tree automaton $A = (\Sigma, Q, Q_f, S)$ and a mapping $h : Q \rightarrow \mathcal{Q}$ verifying the property (2) such that $\forall t \in T(\Sigma) \quad \rho(t) = h(q_t)$ where q_t is the state verifying $t \xrightarrow{*}_S q_t$.

Theorem 8. Let $\mathcal{A}$ be a TSA and r be an $\mathcal{A}$-run,

1. if ρ is a regular run, then $\mathcal{L}(\mathcal{A}, \rho)$ is a tuple of regular tree languages.
2. if $\mathcal{L}(\mathcal{A}, r)$ is a tuple of regular tree languages, then there exists a regular run ρ such that $\mathcal{L}(\mathcal{A}, r) = \mathcal{L}(\mathcal{A}, \rho)$.

Sketch of proof. To prove the first point, we define for each i a bottom-up tree automaton recognizing each $L_i(\mathcal{A}, \rho)$ from the bottom-up tree automaton A and the mapping h of the Proposition 7.

To prove the second point, we define according to Proposition 6 a regular run ρ with a complete and deterministic bottom-up tree automaton A and a mapping h satisfying the property 2 such that $\mathcal{L}(\mathcal{A}, \rho) = \mathcal{L}(\mathcal{A}, r)$. We have to consider in the proof the minimal deterministic and complete tree automaton recognizing $L_i(\mathcal{A}, r)$. □

We deduce from the proof of Proposition 8 the following result :

Corollary 9. *Let $\mathcal{A}$ be a TSA and $(L_1, \ldots, L_n)$ be a tuple of regular languages, it is decidable whether $(L_1, \ldots, L_n) \in \mathcal{L}(\mathcal{A})$.*

Proposition 10. *A TSA admits a regular run whenever it admits a run, i.e., $\mathcal{R} \neq \emptyset \Rightarrow \mathcal{RR} \neq \emptyset$.*

Sketch of proof. We use the set Ω defined in the proof of Theorem 4. There exists ω in Ω since $\mathcal{R} \neq \emptyset$ and we construct a regular run from $T(\Sigma)$ into ω. □

Corollary 11. *Let $\mathcal{A}$ be a TSA. If $\mathcal{L}(\mathcal{A})$ is non empty then there exists a tuple of regular tree languages in $\mathcal{L}(\mathcal{A})$.*

2.4 Minimal and Maximal Runs

This section is devoted to the study of minimal and maximal runs ; the results will be used in Section 3 to prove the existence of minimal solution and maximal solution which are actually regular to a system of set constraints whenever it admits a solution.

Let $\leq$ be the partial order defined on n-tuples of languages by: $(L_1, \ldots, L_n) \leq (L'_1, \ldots, L'_n) \Leftrightarrow \forall i \quad L_i \subseteq L'_i$. Then $\leq$ induces notions of minimal and maximal, greatest and least n-tuples of languages.

Definition 12. A minimal (respectively maximal) run ρ in a TSA $\mathcal{A}$ is such that the tuple of languages accepted by ρ is minimal (respectively maximal) w.r.t. $\mathcal{L}(\mathcal{A})$.

Example 3. Let $\mathcal{A} = (\Sigma, \mathcal{Q}, \mathcal{F}, \mathcal{S})$ where $\Sigma = \{a, b\}$ (a is a constant and b is of arity 1); $\mathcal{Q} = \{q_{110}, q_{011}, q_{001}, q_{010}\}$; $\mathcal{F} = F_1 = \{q_{110}, q_{011}, q_{010}\}$; $\mathcal{S} = \{a \rightarrow q_{110}, b(q_{110}) \rightarrow q_{011}, b(q_{011}) \rightarrow q_{011} \mid q_{001}, b(q_{001}) \rightarrow q_{010}, b(q_{010}) \rightarrow q_{011} \mid q_{001}\}$
$\mathcal{L}(\mathcal{A}) = \{L \subseteq T(\Sigma) \mid a \in L, b(a) \in L, (t \notin L) \Rightarrow (b(t) \in L \text{ and } b(b(t)) \in L)\}$. One can easily prove there exists in $\mathcal{L}(\mathcal{A})$ an infinite number of minimal regular tree languages and an infinite number of minimal non regular tree languages.

Proposition 13. *A TSA admits a minimal run and a maximal run which are regular whenever it admits a run.*

Sketch of proof. As in the proof of Proposition 10 we construct a minimal and a maximal regular run from $T(\Sigma)$ into ω for some ω in Ω. □

Example 4 (3 continued). The construction of a minimal regular run leads to the set of rules $\{a \rightarrow q_{110}, b(q_{110}) \rightarrow q_{011}, b(q_{011}) \rightarrow q_{001}, b(q_{001}) \rightarrow q_{010}, b(q_{010}) \rightarrow q_{001}\}$ and to the language $\{b^{3i}(a), b^{3i+1}(a) \mid i \in \mathbb{N}\}$.

2.5 Operations on TSAs

In the following we prove that the class of tree set automata is closed under union, intersection and cylindrification. Cylindrification is mainly used to extend intersection and union on tree set automata of different rank and is defined by the following equation: Let $\mathcal{D}$ be a set of n-tuples of tree languages. Let x be a natural number, $1 \leq x \leq n$. We define $\mathcal{C}_x(\mathcal{D})$

$$(L_1, \ldots, L_{n+1}) \in \mathcal{C}_x(\mathcal{D}) \Leftrightarrow (L_1, \ldots, L_{x-1}, L_{x+1}, \ldots, L_{n+1}) \in \mathcal{D} \text{ and } L_x \subseteq T(\Sigma)$$

Proposition 14. *The class of tuple of tree languages acceptable by a TSA is closed under union, intersection and cylindrification. Given two TSA's $\mathcal{A}_1$ and $\mathcal{A}_2$, we can construct $\mathcal{A}$ verifying $\mathcal{L}(\mathcal{A}) = \mathcal{L}(\mathcal{A}_1) \cap \mathcal{L}(\mathcal{A}_2)$, $\mathcal{A}'$ verifying $\mathcal{L}(\mathcal{A}') = \mathcal{L}(\mathcal{A}_1) \cup \mathcal{L}(\mathcal{A}_2)$ and given a TSA $\mathcal{A}_3$ of rank n and x $1 \leq x \leq n$ we can construct $\mathcal{A}''$ verifying $\mathcal{L}(\mathcal{A}'') = \mathcal{C}_x(\mathcal{L}(\mathcal{A}_3))$.*

3 Set Constraints

3.1 Definitions

Let Σ be a finite set of function symbols and let $\mathcal{X}$ be a set of variables. Then $T(\Sigma, \mathcal{X})$ is the set of terms over the alphabet Σ and the set $\mathcal{X}$. Let $\bot$ and $\top$ be special symbols.

A *set expression* is defined to be either a variable, a constant, the special symbol $\top$ or $\bot$ or of the form $b(e_1, \ldots, e_p)$, $\overline{e}$, $e_1 \cap e_2$, $e_1 \cup e_2$ where $e, e_1, \ldots, e_p$ are set expressions. A set constraint is of the form $e \subseteq e'$ where e and e' are set expressions, and a system of set constraints is defined by $\bigwedge_{i=1}^{k} SC_i$ where SC_i $1 \leq i \leq k$ are set constraints.

An interpretation $\mathcal{I}$ is a mapping from $\mathcal{X}$ into $2^{T(\Sigma)}$. It can immediately be extended to each expression in the following way: $\mathcal{I}(\top) = T(\Sigma)$; $\mathcal{I}(\bot) = \emptyset$; $\mathcal{I}(t) = \{t\}$; $\mathcal{I}(b(e_1, \ldots, e_p)) = b(\mathcal{I}(e_1), \ldots, \mathcal{I}(e_p))$; $\mathcal{I}(\overline{e}) = T(\Sigma) \setminus \mathcal{I}(e)$; $\mathcal{I}(e \cup e') = \mathcal{I}(e) \cup \mathcal{I}(e')$ and finally $\mathcal{I}(e \cap e') = \mathcal{I}(e) \cap \mathcal{I}(e')$.

We deduce an interpretation of set constraints in $\mathcal{B} = \{0, 1\}$, the Boolean values. For a system of set constraints SSC, all the interpretations $\mathcal{I}$ such that $\mathcal{I}(SSC) = 1$ are called *solutions* of SSC. We denote by SOL(SSC) the set of all solutions of the system of set constraints SSC.

In the remainder, we will consider systems of set constraints of n variables $X_1, \ldots, X_n$. We will confuse a *solution* of a system of set constraints and a *n-tuple of tree languages*. Moreover, maximal, minimal, least and greatest solutions will stand for maximal, minimal, least and greatest n-tuple of tree languages with respect to the set of solutions.

3.2 Solving a System of Set Constraints

Theorem 15. *Let SSC be a system of set constraints. There exists a TSA $\mathcal{A}$ such that $\mathcal{L}(\mathcal{A}) = $ SOL(SSC).*

Sketch of proof. Let $SSC = \cap_{i=1}^{k} SC_i$ be a system of set constraints and let us suppose there exist $\mathcal{A}_1, \ldots, \mathcal{A}_k$, k TSA's verifying $\mathcal{L}(\mathcal{A}_i) = SOL(SC_i)$. Then we can construct a TSA $\mathcal{A}$ such that $\mathcal{L}(\mathcal{A}) = SOL(SSC)$ using cylindrification and intersection, (See Proposition 14). Hence it is sufficient to prove the result for a set constraint SC of n variables $X_1, \ldots, X_n$.

Notations and definitions. Let $E(exp)$ be the set of expressions occurring in a set expression exp: $E(\perp) = \emptyset$; $E(\top) = \emptyset$; $E(X) = \{X\}$; $E(b(e_1, \ldots, e_p)) = b(e_1, \ldots, e_p)$; $E(\cup_i e_i) = E(\cap_i e_i) = \cup_i E(e_i)$; $E(\bar{e}) = E(e)$; $E(SC) = E(exp) \cup E(exp')$

Let φ be a Boolean valuation, i.e. a mapping φ from $E(SC)$ into $\mathcal{B}$. This valuation can easily be extended to any set constraint SC (respectively set expression exp) built with elements of $E(SC)$ (respectively $E(exp)$) and some set operators. The connectives $\cup$, $\cap$, $^-$ and $\subseteq$ are respectively interpreted as $\wedge$, $\vee$, $\neg$ and $\Rightarrow$ and the two special symbols $\top$ and $\perp$ are interpreted as 0 and 1.

Definition of $\mathcal{A}$. Given a set constraint SC of n variables $X_1, \ldots, X_n$, we first give the definition of a TSA. Let $\mathcal{A} = (\Sigma, Q, \mathcal{F}, \mathcal{S})$ be the tree set automaton where :
$Q = \{\varphi \mid \varphi(SC) = 1\}$; $\mathcal{F} = (F_1, \ldots, F_n)$ with $F_i = \{\varphi \in Q \mid \varphi(X_i) = 1\}$. $\mathcal{S}$ is the following set of rules :

Initial Rules : $a \longrightarrow \varphi$ where $a \in \Sigma_0$ and φ satisfies :
$$\forall e \in E(SC) \quad (e \notin \mathcal{X}) \Rightarrow ((e = a) \Leftrightarrow (\varphi(e) = 1)) \ .$$

Progression Rules : $b(\varphi_1, \ldots, \varphi_p) \longrightarrow \varphi$ where $b \in \Sigma_p$ and φ, φ_i satisfy $\forall e \in E(SC)$

$$(e \notin \mathcal{X}) \Rightarrow \left((\varphi(e) = 1) \Leftrightarrow \left(\begin{array}{l} e = b(e_1, \ldots, e_p) \\ \forall i \ 1 \leq i \leq p \ \varphi_i(e_i) = 1 \end{array} \right) \right) \ .$$

For a lack of space we will omit the proof of correctness. $\square$

Example 5. If SC is the following set constraint: $b(X, Y) \subseteq \perp$, then the set $E(SC) = \{X, Y, b(X, Y)\}$. Let us apply the construction.
$Q = \{\varphi \mid \varphi(SC) = 1\} = \{\varphi \mid \varphi(b(X, Y)) = 0\}$. Hence, $Q = \{\varphi_1, \varphi_2, \varphi_3, \varphi_4\}$ where $\varphi_1(X) = 0$, $\varphi_1(Y) = 0$, $\varphi_2(X) = 1$, $\varphi_2(Y) = 0$, $\varphi_3(X) = 0$, $\varphi_3(Y) = 1$, $\varphi_4(X) = 1$, $\varphi_4(Y) = 1$, $\mathcal{F} = (F_1, F_2)$ where $F_1 = \{\varphi_2, \varphi_4\}$ and $F_2 = \{\varphi_3, \varphi_4\}$; $\mathcal{S} = \{a \to \varphi_1 \mid \varphi_2 \mid \varphi_3 \mid \varphi_4, \ b(\varphi, \varphi') \to \varphi_1 \mid \varphi_2 \mid \varphi_3 \mid \varphi_4\}$ where $(\varphi, \varphi') \in Q \times Q \backslash \{(\varphi_2, \varphi_3), (\varphi_2, \varphi_4), (\varphi_4, \varphi_3), (\varphi_4, \varphi_4)\}$.

Up to renaming the states, it is the same TSA as in Example 2.

We also prove the converse of the Theorem 15. Let $\mathcal{X}$ be a set of variables. We will denote by $SOL(SSC)_{|E}$ with $E \subseteq \mathcal{X}$ the solutions of the system of set constraints SSC restricted to the variables in E.

Theorem 16. *Let $\mathcal{A}$ be a TSA of rank n there exists a system of set constraints SSC such that $SOL(SSC)_{|E} = \mathcal{L}(\mathcal{A})$ with $E = (X_1, \ldots, X_n)$.*

We now give the main theorem of this section. This theorem is a consequence of Theorem 15 and of the results on tree set automata obtained in Section 2.

Theorem 17. *Let SSC be a system of set constraints. It is decidable whether SOL(SSC) is empty or not. If SOL(SSC) is non empty then there exist a regular solution, a minimal solution and a maximal solution which are actually regular. These regular solutions can be exhibited in an effective way.*

4 Conclusion

We have introduced an acceptor model (TSA) which corresponds to the specification power of systems of set constraints. By this way, we have got a new algorithm for solving systems of set constraints and we obtain certain properties of set of solutions. Moreover, TSA can be viewed as a draft of acceptor model for tuples of tree languages. Further work could lead, at first, to solve some more complex systems of set constraints, and perhaps to obtain decision results in other areas.

References

1. A. Aiken and E.L. Wimmers. Solving System of Set Constraints. In 7th *Symposium on LICS*, pages 329–340, 1992.
2. L. Bachmair, H. Ganzinger, and U. Waldmann. Solving Set Constraints by Ordered Resolution with Simplification. Draft manuscript, September 92.
3. T. Früwirth, E.Shapiro, M.Y. Vardi, and E.Yardeni. Logic Programs as Types for Logic Programs. In 6th *Symposium on LICS*, 1991.
4. F. Gecseg and M. Steinby. *Tree Automata*. Akademiai Kiado, 1984.
5. R. Gilleron, S. Tison, and M. Tommasi. Solving System of Set Constraints using Tree Automata. Technical Report IT-92-235, Laboratoire d'Informatique Fondamentale de Lille, Université des Sciences et Technologies de Lille, Villeneuve d'Ascq, France, July 1992.
6. N. Heintze and J. Jaffar. A Decision Procedure for a Class of Set Constraints. In 5th *Symposium on LICS*, 1990.
7. N. Heintze and J. Jaffar. A Finite Presentation Theorem for Approximating Logic Programs. IBM technical report RC 16089 (#71415), IBM, August 1990.
8. N.D. Jones and S.S. Muchnick. Flow Analysis and Optimization of LISP-like Structures. In *Proceedings 6th ACM Symposium on Principles of Programming Languages*, pages 244–246, 1979.
9. P. Mishra. Towards a Theory of Types in PROLOG. In *Proceedings 1st IEEE Symposium on Logic Programming*, pages 456–461, Atlantic City, 1984.
10. M.O. Rabin. Decidability of Second-Order Theories and Automata on Infinite Trees. *Trans. Amer. Math. Soc.*, 141:1–35, 1969.
11. J.C. Reynolds. Automatic Computation of Data Set Definition. *Information Processing*, 68:456–461, 1969.
12. W. Thomas. *Handbook of Theoretical Computer Science*, volume B, chapter Automata on Infinite Objects, pages 134–191. Elsevier, 1990.
13. T. E. Uribe. Sorted Unification Using Set Constraints. In D. Kapur, editor, *Lecture Notes in Computer Science*, New York, 1992. $11^{t}h$ International Conference on Automated Deduction.

Complement Problems and Tree Automata in AC-like theories (Extended Abstract)

D.Lugiez, J.L. Moysset [*]

CRIN-INRIA Nancy FRANCE

Introduction

Many problems arising in Computer Science involve formulae built on the equality predicate and terms. But terms are merely denotations for complex objects and a purely syntactical approach lacks any insight on the semantics of these objects. To avoid this drawback, a classical solution is to add axioms on terms which model the semantic behavior of the real objects. The most useful axioms are the *commutativity* axiom (C) $f(x,y) = f(y,x)$, the *associativity* axiom (A) $f(x, f(y, z)) = f(f(x, y), z)$, the *idempotency* axiom (I) $f(x, x) = x$ and the *unit element* axiom (1) $f(x, e) = e$. Many operators studied in Computer Science satisfy one or more of these axioms, for example the parallel operator in parallelism is associative-commutative (AC in short), the boolean connectives are associative-commutative and idempotent (ACI in short), and many algebraic functions are associative-commutative and have a unit element (AC1 in short). Usually the theory of equality modulo these axioms is not decidable, for instance the subclass of Σ_3 formulae modulo AC is undecidable [Tre90]). However in practice, the formulae we are interested in, are very specialized. Apart from the well-known unification question, the most interesting problem is that of *complement problem*, i.e to solve $t \neq_E t_1 \wedge \ldots \wedge t \neq_E t_n$ where E is the theory we are interested in. These formulae arise in the algebraic specification field when dealing with sufficient completeness, in logic programming, in the compilation of functional programs and in the paradigm of learning by example and counter-example.

This paper is devoted to solutions of the complement problem modulo AC-like axioms. More precisely, to solve $t \neq_E t_1 \wedge \ldots \wedge t \neq_E t_n$ is to decide if there is a ground instance of t which is not a ground instance of any t_i modulo E. First, we propose a new method which relies on tree automata. Since the set of ground instances modulo AC of a linear term is a regular tree language, we get an easy solution of the complement problem modulo AC when the $t_i's$ are linear. This approach is extended in various ways. Another method, based on instantiation techniques similar to that of [KLP91], provides solutions to some non-linear complement problems in the AC theory.

---

[*] author's address: e-mail lugiez,moyssetj@loria.fr, surface-mail CRIN-INRIA, BP239 54506 Vandoeuvres-les-Nancy, FRANCE

The paper is organized as follows: the basic notions on terms, equational theories, tree automata are gathered in section 1. Then the solution to the linear complement problems using tree automata is presented in section 2 and section 3 extends these results to other theories and to some non-linear cases. Section 4 presents a solution to the complement problem modulo AC in a non-linear case using instantiation techniques. Proofs and some applications of this work can be found in [LM92].

1 Definitions and notations

We need some definitions and notations, let us start with terms.

1.1 Terms

Terms, denoted by $s, t, r, \ldots$ are labelled trees constructed from a finite set F of function symbols denoted by $f, g, h, \ldots$, and a denumerable set X of variables, denoted $x, y, z, \ldots$. Functions of arity 0 are constants. We suppose that F contains at least one constant, therefore the set of ground terms, i.e. terms without variables is not empty. A term t is *linear* if each variable occurring in t occurs only once in t. $Var(t)$ is the set of variables occurring in t. The *size* of a term is its number of symbols. The depth of a term s is defined by $depth(x) = depth(a) = 0$ if $x \in X$ and $arity(a) = 0$ and $depth(f(s_1, \ldots, s_n)) = 1 + Max_i(depth(s_i))$. The width of a term is defined by $width(x) = width(a) = 0$ if $x \in X$ and $arity(a) = 0$, and $width(f(s_1, \ldots, s_n)) = Max(n, Max_i(width(s_i)))$.

A *position* is a sequence of integers, the empty sequence is denoted by ϵ, and a non-empty sequence is written as $p.i$ with i an integer and p a sequence. The subterm of a term s at position p, denoted by $s_{|p}$, is defined by $s_{|\epsilon} = s$ and $s_{|p.i} = s_i$ if $s_{|p} = f(s_1, \ldots, s_n)$ and $1 \leq i \leq n$. The *arguments* of a term $s = f(s_1, \ldots, s_n)$ are the s_i's. A *context* $C[.]$ is a term with one (or more) hole and $C[s]$ is the term obtained by putting the term s in the hole(s) of the context $C[.]$. The result of replacing the subterm of t at position p by a term s is denoted $t[s]_p$.

An equation (i.e. an axiom) is a pair of terms written $s = t$. A finite set E of equations defines an equational theory and induces a congruence relation on terms denoted by $=_E$. The class of a term t is the set of terms equal to t modulo E. We are mainly interested in the following equations: commutativity $f(x, y) = f(y, x)$, associativity $f(x, f(y, z)) = f(f(x, y), z)$, idempotency $f(x, x) = x$ and unit element $f(x, e) = e$. More precisely we shall consider the congruence $=_{AC}$ (resp. $=_{ACI}, \ldots$) i.e $F = F_{AC} \cup F_{NAC}$ (resp. $F = F_{ACI} \cup F_{NACI}, \ldots$) where all function symbols in F_{AC} are commutative and associative (resp. and idempotent...) and the function symbols in F_{NAC} are free. A term rewrite system R is a finite set of rewrite rules $l \rightarrow r$ which defines a rewrite relation $\rightarrow_R$ on terms. The system is left-linear if for each rule $l \rightarrow r$ of R, l is linear. A key property in inductionless induction is that of *inductive reducibility*: given a set E of equations and a set R of rewrite rules, a term t is inductively reducible iff each ground instance of t is reducible. This property is undecidable for the AC theory, but our solution to linear complement problems provides an algorithm to decide this property in for linear terms and left-linear rules.

Substitutions, denoted by $\sigma, \theta, \rho \ldots$, are the morphisms on terms and the application of σ to t is denoted by $t\sigma$. The domain of a substitution σ is the set $Dom(\sigma) = \{x \in X; x\sigma \neq x\}$. A term s is an E-instance of a term t iff $s =_E t\sigma$. It is an ground E-instance if s is ground.

To solve the **complement problem** $t \neq_E t_1 \wedge \ldots \wedge t \neq_E t_n$ modulo E with $Var(t) \cap Var(t_i) = \emptyset$ and $Var(t_i) \cap Var(t_j) = \emptyset$, is to find a ground instance of t which is not an E-instance of any t_i.

1.2 Tree automata

Tree automata are finite state automata which recognize languages of trees called regular tree languages. We recall some definitions and results, and we refer the reader to [GS84] for details.

Definition 1 *A bottom-up tree automaton $\mathcal{A}$ is a triple (Q, Q_{Final}, R) where Q is a finite set of states, $Q_{Final} \subseteq Q$ is a set of final states, and R is a set of transition rules of the form $f(q_1, \ldots q_n) \to q_{n+1}$ with $arity(f) = n$ and $q_i \in Q$.*

The transition relation $\to$ is defined by $t \to t'$ iff $t = C[f(q_1(t_1), \ldots, q_n(t_n))]$ and $t' = C[q_{n+1}(f(t_1, \ldots, t_n))]$. The language accepted by $\mathcal{A}$ is the set of ground terms t such that $t \xrightarrow{*} q[t]$ where $q \in Q_{Final}$ and $\xrightarrow{*}$ is the reflexive transitive closure of $\to$. A set of ground terms is a regular tree language iff it is accepted by a tree automaton.

Example If $F = \{0, s, f\}$, the automaton $\mathcal{A} = (\{q_0, q_s, q_F\}, \{q_F\}, R)$ with R being $\{0 \to q_0, s(q) \to q_s$ for any $q \in Q, f(q_0, q) \to q_F$ for any $q \in Q, f(q, q') \to q_s$ for any $q \in Q - \{q_0\}, q' \in Q\}$, recognizes the language composed of the ground instances of $f(0, x)$ ◀

A automaton is completely specified if each tree reaches some state, and it is deterministic when a tree can reach only one state. Tree automata enjoy good properties: the emptiness of the accepted language is decidable, there exists a determinization algorithm as well as a minimization algorithm. Moreover regular tree languages are closed under union, intersection and complementation.

1.3 Flattened terms

A function symbol which is AC can be seen as having an arbitrary arity, and we can *flatten* terms by erasing all useless occurrences of AC-symbol using the simplification $f(\ldots, f(s_1, \ldots, s_m), \ldots) \to f(\ldots, s_1, \ldots, s_m, \ldots)$. When no rewriting is possible, one has a *flattened* term which is unique up to commutativity. If t is a term, $flat(t)$ is one of its flattened versions. For simplicity, $f(n_1.s_1, \ldots, n_p.s_p)$

stands for $f(\underbrace{s_1, \ldots, s_1}_{n_1 occurrences}, \ldots, \underbrace{s_p, \ldots, s_p}_{n_p occurrences})$. All previous definitions on terms are still valid on flattened terms. We shall use flattened terms mainly in section 4.

2 Tree automata solution for linear AC-problems

In this section we give a tree automata solution to the complement problem modulo AC when the $t_i's$ are linear.

2.1 Tree automata solve linear AC-problems

The following result lays the foundation of our decidability result.

Proposition 1 *Let t be a linear term, then the set of ground AC-instances of t is a regular tree language.*

Example : Let $t = f(0, x)$ where $F_{AC} = \{f\}$ and $F_{NAC} = \{0, s\}$. An automaton recognizing 0 is $A_1 = (\{q_0\}, \{q_0\}, \{0 \rightarrow q_0\}$ and an automaton recognizing the instances of x is $A_2 = (\{q\}, \{q\}, \{0 \rightarrow q, s(q) \rightarrow q, f(q, q) \rightarrow q\})$. From that, we can build a non-deterministic automaton recognizing the ground AC-instances of $f(0, x)$. Let $A = (\{q, q_0, q_S\}, \{q_S\}, R)$ with R including the rules of A_1 and A_2 and new rules: $f(q_0, q) \rightarrow q_S, f(q, q_0) \rightarrow q_S, f(q, q_S) \rightarrow q_S, f(q_S, q) \rightarrow q_S$. ◀

We can now state our decidability results:

Theorem 1 *The complement problem $t \neq_{AC} t_1 \wedge \ldots \wedge t \neq_{AC} t_n$ where the t_i's are linear terms is decidable. The inductive reducibility modulo AC of a linear term t for a left-linear term rewriting system is decidable.*

Proof. If the term t is linear, its ground instances modulo AC are recognized by some tree automaton and we are done. If t is not linear then there is a ground AC-instance of t solution of the complement, which implies that there is a ground syntactic instance of t which is a solution too. Therefore it is sufficient to decide the emptiness of the intersection of the complementary of the union of ground AC-instances of the t_i's and of the ground syntactic instances of t. Let A be a deterministic automaton recognizing the complement. For each variable $x \in Var(t)$, allow the transition $x \rightarrow q$, if $t \xrightarrow{*} q_F[t]$ for $q_F \in Q_{Final}$ for some combination of x and q then there is a solution, otherwise there is none.

Moreover, the set of terms reducible by a linear term is also a regular tree language (use rules $f(\ldots, q, \ldots) \rightarrow q$ for any final state q) which proves the result concerning the inductive reducibility modulo AC. □

2.2 What's the trouble with non-linearity

Before giving extensions of the previous result, we show which problem arises when we consider non-linear terms. Let F_{AC} consist of one symbol f, and let F_{NAC} consist of two constants 0 and 1 and let t be $f(x,x)$. Then the ground AC-instances of $f(x,x)$ are extremely to characterize, some of these instances are trees such that the first son and its brother are not equal, even modulo AC. For instance $f(0, f(1, f(1,0)))$ and $f(0, f(1, f(1,0)))$ are ground AC-instances of $f(x,x)$. To know that a ground term (with root f) is an instance of $f(x,x)$, one must count $0's$ and $1's$ and there is no way to conclude before all $0's$ and $1's$ have been counted: a ground term is an AC-instance of $f(x,x)$ if there is an even number of $0's$ and an even number of $1's$. Classical tree automata cannot manage this. Moreover, a theoretical result proves that tree automata cannot recognize ground AC-instances of non-linear terms: the inductive reducibility modulo AC property would be decidable, and this property is undecidable [KNRZ87].

3 Extending the results

The tree automata approach can be extended in several ways.

3.1 To some non-linear cases

In this section, we extend the work of [BT92] on automata with equality tests between brothers to the AC case. This class of automata is used to solve non-linear complement problem cases when the non-linearity is strictly restricted, as defined by the next definition.

Definition 2 *The non-linearity of a term is strictly restricted iff for each non-linear variable x, there exists a position p such that all the occurrences of x occur at positions $p.i$ with i an integer, and the symbol at position p is not AC.*

Now we give the definition of automata with equality tests for the AC case.

Definition 3 *A automaton $\mathcal{A}$ with equality tests between brothers is a triple (Q, Q_F, R) where Q is a finite set of states, $Q_F \subseteq Q$ is a set of final states and R is a set of rules $< \varphi >: g(q_1, \ldots, q_n) \to q_{n+1}$ with $\varphi \in Form_n$ where $Form_n$ is inductively defined by:*

- *$\#i =_{AC} \#j \in Form_n$ (which means that the ith son is equal to the jth son modulo AC), $\top \in Form_n$ (meaning that no condition is required)*
- *if $\varphi \in Form_n$ and $\psi \in Form_n$ then $\neg\varphi \in Form_n$, $\psi \vee \varphi \in Form_n$, $\psi \wedge \varphi \in Form_n$.*

Moreover if $f \in F_{AC}$ and $< \varphi >: f(q_1, q_2) \to q_3 \in R$ we demand that φ is $\top$ (i.e there is no condition for rules with AC symbols). The transition function is defined by $t \to t'$ iff $t = C[g(q_1(t_1), \ldots, q_n(t_n))]$, $t' = C[q_{n+1}(f(t_1, \ldots, t_n))]$ and $(t_1, \ldots, t_n)$ satisfies φ. The reflexive transitive closure of $\to$ is denoted by $\xrightarrow{*}$. The accepted language $\mathcal{L}(\mathcal{A})$ is the set of trees t such that $t \xrightarrow{*} q[t]$ with $q \in Q_F$.

One should notice that equality tests are allowed under non-AC symbols only. Using the method of [BT92], we can compute a deterministic automaton from a non-deterministic one, and we can show that the class of accepted language is closed under union, intersection and complementation. Now, we show that we can use these conditional automata to recognize the set of ground AC-instances of a strictly restricted term.

Proposition 2 *Let t be a strictly restricted term, then there is a automaton with equality tests between brothers $\mathcal{A}$ which recognizes the set of ground AC-instances of t. Moreover, for each state q of $\mathcal{A}$ if $s \xrightarrow{*} q[s]$ then for all s' such that $s' =_{AC} s$, $s' \xrightarrow{*} q[s']$.*

The next step is to show that the emptiness of the language accepted by a deterministic automata with equality tests can be decided, provided that terms equivalent modulo AC reach the same state. In the sequel, we assume that this property holds. Let $< \varphi >: g(q_1, \ldots, q_n) \to q_{n+1}$ be a rule r, and suppose that α_i trees of distinct equivalence classes modulo AC reach the state q_i for $1 \leq i \leq n$. Let $N_r(\alpha_1 \ldots, \alpha_n)$ be the number of tree belonging to distinct equivalence classes modulo AC which reach q_{n+1} using this rule at the top and let *max-arity* be the maximal arity of function symbols, then:

Proposition 3
- $\exists i : \alpha_i \geq$ max-arity $\Rightarrow N_r(\alpha_1, \ldots, \alpha_n) = 0$ *or* $N_r(\alpha_1, \ldots, \alpha_n) \geq$ max-arity
- $\exists \alpha_i : N_r(\alpha_1, \ldots, \alpha_i, \ldots, \alpha_n) \geq$ max-arity $\Rightarrow N_r(\alpha_1, \ldots, \text{max-arity}, \ldots, \alpha_n) \geq$ max-arity.

The algorithm for deciding the emptiness of the language accepted by an automaton with equality tests modulo AC between brothers is a consequence of the previous result. In the algorithm, $N_{AC}(L)$ denotes the number of distinct equivalence classes of a finite set of ground terms L.

For each state q do set $\mathcal{L}_q^0 = \emptyset$.
i=1.
Repeat For each state q do
    $\mathcal{L}_q^i = \emptyset$
    For each rule r of the form $< \varphi >: h(q_1, \ldots, q_n) \to q$ do
    if $N_{AC}(\mathcal{L}_q^{i-1}) \geq$ max-arity then $\mathcal{L}_q^i = \mathcal{L}_q^{i-1}$
    else $\mathcal{L}_q^i = \mathcal{L}_q^{i-1} \cup \{h(t_1, \ldots, t_n) \; satisfying \; \varphi \; where \; t_j \in \mathcal{L}_{q_j}^{i-1}\}$
    i=i+1
until $\exists q \in Q_F$ s.t. $\mathcal{L}_q^i \neq \emptyset$ or $\forall q, \mathcal{L}_q^i = \mathcal{L}_q^{i-1}$

The correctness and termination of the algorithm rely on the previous proposition and on the fact that equivalence classes modulo AC are finite. The theorem on the decidability of complement problem and inductive reducibility is an immediate consequence of the previous results.

Theorem 2 *The complement problem* $t \neq_{AC} t_1 \wedge \ldots \wedge t \neq_{AC} t_n$ *(resp.* $\neq_A$*) where the* $t_i's$ *are strictly restricted, is decidable. The inductive reducibility modulo AC (resp. modulo A) of a strictly restricted term* t *for a term rewriting system with strictly restricted left-hand sides is decidable.*

3.2 To some other theories

The previous results can be easily extended to other theories. The first one is the AC1 theory, i.e AC with unity: for each AC-symbol f, there exists a constant e such that $f(x, e) = x$. To handle this new equation, we add the rules $e \rightarrow q_e$ and $f(q, q_e) \rightarrow q$ and $f(q_e, q) \rightarrow q$. The second one is the associativity theory: we simply drop the rules handling commutativity and we introduce the rules for associativity at the right place. Therefore we can state the next theorem [2]:

Theorem 3 *The complement problem* $t \neq_{AC1} t_1 \wedge \ldots \wedge t \neq_{AC1} t_n$ *(resp.* $\neq_A$*) where the* $t_i's$ *are linear terms is decidable. The inductive reducibility modulo AC1 (resp. modulo A) of a linear term* t *for a left-linear term rewriting system is decidable.*

Another interesting theory is ACI, i.e. each AC function f also satisfy the idempotency axiom $f(x, x) =_{ACI} x$. Instead of recognizing the set of all ground ACI-instances of a term, we shall recognize the set of ground ACI-instances once all possible applications of the idempotency axiom have been done. Indeed the relation defined on flattened terms by $f(\ldots, x, \ldots, x, \ldots) \rightarrow f(\ldots, x, \ldots)$ and $f(x, x) \rightarrow x$ is terminating and confluent up to commutativity-associativity. Therefore, we restrict ourselves to ground terms equal modulo AC to a normalized ground term, and we can assume that t and the t_i s are normalized too. To build an automaton recognizing the set of such instances of a term is similar to the AC-case, with one modification that we explain in the simplest case. Suppose that s_1 and s_2 are two non-variable terms such that their root are not ACI-symbols, and suppose that we have built $\mathcal{A}_1$ for s_1 and $\mathcal{A}_2$ for s_2. We proceed as in the AC-case, but we must take into account that an possible normalized ground ACI-instance of $f(s_1, s_2)$ is some $s_1\theta$ if $s_1\theta =_{ACI} s_2\theta$ when f is ACI. Therefore we must add the intersection of s_1 and s_2. But this intersection is also a regular tree language, which allows the overall construction.

3.3 Using a abstract criteria

Actually, the previous extensions follow from the general theorem:

Theorem 4 *Let* $\mathcal{L}$ *be a class of tree-automata closed under the boolean operations and such that the emptiness of the language accepted by an automaton of* $\mathcal{L}$ *is decidable, let E be a equational theory such that the set of ground E-instances of any term is the language accepted by some* $\mathcal{A} \in \mathcal{L}$*, then the complement problem and the inductive reducibility property in E are decidable.*

---

[2] in the associative case, this theorem shows a decidable subclass of the undecidable class Σ_2

Indeed we used a weaker form of this theorem, since we imposed conditions (linearity, strictly restricted non-linearity) on the set of terms which have a recognizable set of ground E-instances, and our decidability results hold for these restricted cases only.

This theorem reduces a difficult problem (complement modulo a theory) to a much simpler one (prove that the set of ground E-instances of some term are recognizable) and suggests two fruitful directions of research. The first one is to consider tree automata which are more general than bottom-up tree automata, the second one is to design syntactical criteria on the theory E which will ensure the property required on the ground E-instances of a term.

4 Solving some non-linear AC problems using test-sets

To conclude, we study the complement problem modulo AC in a particular case: all the occurrences of a non-linear variable are under the same node, as described in the next definition (from now we consider flattened terms only).

Definition 4 *A flattened term s is restricted iff all occurrences of a non-linear variable are under the same node and this node is labeled by a symbol in F_{AC} .*

For example $f(g(x, x, z), g(y, y))$ is restricted, and $f(g(x, z), g(y, z))$ is not since there are two occurrences of z under different nodes. *From now on, we consider the complement problem $t \neq_{AC} t_1 \wedge \ldots \wedge t \neq_{AC} t_n$ where t and all the t_i's are restricted flattened terms.* This section is devoted to the proof of the following theorem:

Theorem 5 *Let t and t_i's be restricted flattened terms, then the complement problem $t \neq_{AC} t_1 \wedge \ldots \wedge t \neq_{AC} t_n$ is decidable.*

The proof generalizes the proof given in [KLP91] in the case of one AC-symbol and constants and it relies on instantiation techniques. Tree automata provide nice and simple proofs and instantiation methods give tedious and difficult proofs. However, at the present time, we have stronger results with instantiation methods than with tree automata (but we are currently investigating some new classes of tree automata which may be as powerful as instantiation schemes). Let us introduce to our new proof method.

The key idea of the proof is to realize that there is a solution to the complement problem if and only if there is a solution in some finite set of instances of t, called a *test set*. Basically, to instantiate a flattened term makes the instantiated term become *deeper* or *wider* as in the following example: to instantiate $f(x, 0)$ by $x \leftarrow s(y)$ gives $f(s(y), 0)$ which is deeper, and to instantiate the same term by $x \leftarrow f(y, 0)$ gives $f(y, 0, 0)$ which is wider. Therefore we shall give two technical theorems, one dealing with deep terms, the second one with wide terms. The first theorem allows to bound the depth of terms occurring in the test set, the second one allows to bound the width of the terms occurring in the test set.

4.1 How to deal with deep terms

The first theorem on *deep* terms shows that when the variables of a term s are deep enough, the property *all ground instances of s are AC-instances of a set of terms R* is equivalent to *s is an AC-instance of one term of R*.

Theorem 6 *Let $R = \{t_1, \ldots, t_n\}$ be a set of flattened terms of maximal depth d and let s be a flattened term such that each variable of s occurs at depth greater than $d + 1$, then each ground AC-instance of s is an AC-instance of a t_i (depending of the given instance) iff s is an AC-instance of some t_i.*

4.2 How to deal with wide terms

Our goal is to put a bound on the width of the ground AC-instances of t that we must consider before finding a solution or knowing that there is none. Some technical notions and notations are required: let n_x be the number of occurrences of a non-linear variable $x \in Var(t_i)$, the number LCM is defined as the least common multiple of the n_x where x ranges over $\cup_{1 \leq i \leq n} Var(t_i)$. The number nvo is the number of occurrences of variables in t, and w is the maximal width of the $t_i's$. We can state the theorem concerning wide terms:

Theorem 7 *There is a solution to the complement problem $t \neq_{AC} t_1 \wedge \ldots \wedge t \neq_{AC} t_n$ iff there is a solution in the set of flattened terms r such that*

- *r is a ground AC-instance of t.*
- *the number of arguments of the subterms of r at depth d is bounded by $M(d)$ where $M(0) = 1 + w + (w + 1).nvo.LCM$ and $M(d) = 1 + (w + 1) + (w + 1 + \prod_{0 \leq i \leq d-1} M(i)).\prod_{0 \leq i \leq d-1} M(i).nvo.LCM$.*

4.3 Putting things together

From the two previous theorem, one gets a bound on the depth and a bound on the width of the AC-instances of t that we must consider to solve the complement problem $t \neq_{AC} t_1 \wedge \ldots \wedge t \neq_{AC} t_n$. The last thing is to combine these two results which yields the next proposition.

Proposition 4 *Let t be a flattened term of depth less than or equal to d. Let s be a flattened ground AC-instance of t such that the width of the subterms of s at depth i is less than $M(i)$ where $M(i)$ is the bound in theorem 7. Then,*

1. *either the depth of s is less than $2d$, hence s belongs to the finite set of terms of depth less than $2d$ and width less than $M(2d)$,*
2. *or else s is an AC-instance of a term belonging to the finite set $TS(t)$, the set of instances of t such that their variables occur at depth less than $2d + 1$ and greater than d, and such that their width is less than $M(2d + 1)$.*

Therefore, to decide the complement problem $t \neq_{AC} t_1 \wedge \ldots \wedge t \neq_{AC} t_n$ when t and the $t_i's$ are restricted, one computes the bound d on the depth of the $t_i's$ and t and the set of the instances of t of depth less than $2d$ and width less than $M(2d)$ and the set $TS(t)$ defined in the previous proposition. Then there is no solution to the complement problem if and only if each term in these sets is an AC-instance of the $t_i's$. A systematic way to construct these *test sets* can be used, for instance using pattern trees like in [KLP91].

Conclusion

We have presented a new approach to complement problem modulo a theory by reducing it to a simpler language problem: recognize the ground E-instances of a term by a automaton which belongs to a class closed under union and complementation and where the emptiness is decidable. Using tree automata, we could answer this question for linear terms in many theories including AC-like ones. Further developments can be expected from this method, especially concerning non-linear cases. Moreover we have presented a proof of a non-linear case in the AC-theory to illustrate the difficulties arising in instantiation-based methods. The question of solving this last case using a variant of conditional tree automata is under study and will probably give new interesting results.

References

[BT92]   B. Bogaert and S. Tison. Equality and disequality constraints on direct sub-terms in tree automata. In *Proceedings of the 9th Symposium on Theoretical Computer Science*, volume 577 of *Lecture Notes in Computer Science*, pages 161–172, 1992.

[GS84]   F. Gécseg and M. Steinby. *Tree automata*. Akadémiai Kiadó, Budapest, Hungary, 1984.

[KLP91]   E. Kounalis, D. Lugiez, and L. Pottier. A solution of the complement problem in associative commutative theories. In A.Tarlecki, editor, *16th International Symposium Mathematical Foundation of Computer Sciences*, volume 520 of *Lecture Notes in Computer Science*, pages 287–297. Springer-Verlag, 1991.

[KNRZ87]   D. Kapur, P. Narendran, D.J. Rosenkrantz, and H. Zhang. Sufficient-completeness, quasi-reducibility and their complexity. Technical report, State University of New York at Albany, 1987.

[LM92]   D. Lugiez and J.L. Moysset. Complement problems and tree automata in ac-like theories. Technical Report 92-R-175, CRIN, 1992.

[Tre90]   Ralf Treinen. A new method for undecidability proofs of first order theories. In K. V. Nori and C. E. Veni Madhavan, editors, *Proceedings of the Tenth Conference on Foundations of Software Technology and Theoretical Computer Science*, pages 48–62. Springer Lecture Notes in Computer Science, vol. 472, 1990.

Transparent (holographic) proofs

László Babai

Eötvös University, Budapest, Hungary H-1088
and
The University of Chicago, Chicago, IL 60637-1504

Abstract. Informally, a mathematical proof is *transparent* (or *holographic*) if it can be verified with large confidence by a small number of spotchecks. Recent work of a large group of researchers has shown that this seemingly paradoxical concept can be formalized and is feasible in a remarkably strong sense. This fact in turn has surprising implications toward the intractability of approximate solutions of a wide range of discrete optimization problems. Below we state some of the main results in the area, with pointers to the literature. David Johnson's excellent survey [Jo] of the same subject gives a different angle and greater detail, including many additional references.

1 Proof systems

1.1 Effective verification

A *proof system* is a computable predicate $A(T, P)$ where T and P are finite strings called "theorem candidate" and "proof-candidate", resp. A string P is a *proof* of T if the pair (T, P) is accepted ($A(T, P)$ holds). A string T is a *theorem* if it has a proof.

In some cases to be discussed below, we also require the string T to be a codeword in some *error-correcting code* which is capable of correcting (uniquely) say a string with up to 10% error. (Such a stipulation is necessary in order to allow results asserting the verifiability of proofs in time less than the length of the theorem-candidate.) We refer to this case as a *"proof system with encoded theorems"*, as opposed to *"ordinary proof systems"* (no encoding).

Since proof systems with encoded theorems may sound unusual, we should point out that given a proof system A and an error-correcting encoding function E, it is easy to define a proof system A' such that the theorems of A' are exactly the strings $E(T)$ for theorems T of A. Indeed, a proof in A' would simply start with inverting E and then appending an A-proof. Since E can be chosen to be easily computed and easily inverted, the difference between the complexities of computing A and A', resp., is insignificant.

1.2 Efficient verification

Our main goal is to replace reasonably efficiently computable predicates A with ultra-efficiently computable ones.

We say that two proof systems are *equivalent* if they have the same theorems (but not necessarily the same proofs). A *reduction* of a proof system to an equivalent one consists of a map f such that for each proof P of theorem T in the first system, $f(T, P)$ is a proof of T in the second system. The *cost* of the reduction is the complexity of the function f.

The standard measure of efficiency is the deterministic time complexity of the predicate $\mathcal{A}$ (in terms of the combined length of T and P). In this sense we talk about *polynomial time verifiable proofs*.

While in this definition we may use Turing machines as the model of computation, realistic proof systems actually allow verification in *nearly linear time* on a RAM. (A function f is *nearly linear* if it is of the form $f(n) \leq n(\log n)^c$ for some constant c and all $n > n_0$.) Furthermore, our aim is to reduce complexities well below linear in the input length. To achieve these objectives, random access is required, hence all the complexity statements below refer to RAMs.[1]

1.3 Randomized verifiers

A striking reduction of the complexity of verification is achieved via *randomization*.

A *randomized verifier* for an *ordinary proof system* is a randomized oracle machine which

- takes as input a theorem-candidate T and a random string R,
- generates a query set $Q(R, T) = \{w_1, \ldots, w_q\}$,
- reads the bits $P[w_1], \ldots, P[w_q]$ of the proof-candidate P,
- makes a computation based on the data R, T, and $P[w_1], \ldots, P[w_q]$.

A *randomized verifier* for an *proof system with encoded theorems* is a randomized oracle machine which

- takes as input a random string R,
- generates two query sets $Q(R) = \{w_1, \ldots, w_q\}$ and $Q'(R) = \{v_1, \ldots, v_{q'}\}$,
- reads the bits $P[w_1], \ldots, P[w_q]$ of the proof-candidate P and the bits $T[v_1], \ldots, T[v_{q'}]$ of the theorem-candidate T,
- makes a computation based on the data $R, P[w_1], \ldots, P[w_q]$, and $T[v_1], \ldots, T[v_{q'}]$.

(Note that in both cases, the queries are *oblivious*: they do not depend on the bits previously queried.)

We say that a randomized verifier *verifies proofs* of the proof system $\mathcal{A}$ if correct inputs (T, P) are always accepted by the verifier and any input with a reasonable chance of acceptance is *approximately correct* in the sense to be defined below.

---

[1] The choice of the deterministic RAM model for verification (equivalent to nondeterministic RAM acceptors) is supported by the *Kolmogorov–Uspenskiǐ thesis* which asserts that nondeterministic RAMs are the strongest model within nearly linear time, i.e. every conceivable nondeterministic model of computation, including any formal proof system, can be simulated, in nearly linear time, on a nondeterministic RAM. (Actually, the Kolomogorov-Uspenskiǐ thesis is stronger in that it operates with the cleaner model of *pointer machines* and asserts *linear time* simulations of any nondeterministic machine model on pointer-machines (cf. [BFLS]). Pointer-machines can in turn be simulated by nondeterministic RAMs in nearly linear time.) Of course, the Kolmogorov-Uspenskiǐ thesis is not a mathematical statement; its validity rests on the intellectual honesty of its authors and those who tried but did not succeed in constructing a plausibly arguable counterexample.

We say that two proof-candidates of equal length are *close* if their Hamming distance is less than say 5% of their common length. In the "encoded theorems" model we use the same definition for theorem-candidates. In the ordinary model, however, two theorem-candidates will be said to be *close* only if they are equal. (The motivation is that we don't care if the proof differs slightly from a correct proof (this still means the theorem is correct), but we do mind if the theorem is misstated (even by a single bit). On the other hand, a slight misstatement of the theorem in the "encoded theorems" model is uniquely correctable.)

The following definition covers both the ordinary and the "encoded theorems" models.

Definition 1. A randomized verifier is said to verify proofs of the proof system A if the following holds for every input (T, P):

(i) if $A(T, P)$ holds then the verifier accepts (T, P) (surely, regardless of the random bits);

(ii) if the verifier accepts the given input (T, P) with probability $\geq 1/2$ then there exists a pair (T', P') such that $A(T', P')$ holds, moreover T' is close to T and and P' is close to P.

Of course by k-fold repetition one can reduce the probability $1/2$ of one-way error to 2^{-k}.

For randomized verifiers we consider the following cost measures:

(a) t, the time (number of steps) required by the verifier;
(b) q, the number of bits of P queried by the verifier;
(c) r, the number of random bits used by the verifier.

Clearly $q \leq t$ and $r \leq t$.

Finally we have to consider the cost ℓ of reducing a given proof to another one (in an equivalent proof system) as defined at the end of the previous subsection. Note that this is not part of the verifier's expense: the proofs have to be written (and transformed) by a *prover*, who is presumably much more powerful (but less reliable) than the verifier.

2 The main results

2.1 Transparent (holographic) proofs

We use the informal terms "transparent proofs" and "holographic proofs" as synonyms. Both terms were coined by L. Levin; the first one was first used (in a technical sense) in [BFLS]. The second term appears to have a greater appeal.

We call a proof *transparent* (or *holographic*) if it can be verified by a randomized verifier within *reasonable* time t and by looking at a *small* number q of proof bits only. Informally, the main results state that *every proof can be transformed at a reasonable cost into a transparent proof* (for an equivalent proof system).

In one extremely strong version of this statement [ALMSS], the quantity q has been reduced to its extreme, $q = O(1)$ (only constant number of bits of the proof are queried), while $\ell = n^{O(1)}$ where n is the combined length of T and P. Moreover, in the "encoded theorems" model we have polylogarithmic verification: $t = (\log n)^{O(1)}$.

In an earlier version [BFLS], ℓ is kept close to linear: $\ell = O(n^{1+\epsilon})$ where $\epsilon > 0$ is an arbitrary positive constant. Moreover, in the "encoded theorems" model we have polylogarithmic verification (for fixed ϵ): $t = (\log n)^{2/\epsilon + O(1)}$.

In both cases, t has to be increased by $O(|T|)$ in the ordinary model (it becomes inevitable to read the theorem-candidate; this difficulty is avoided by the "encoded theorems" model).

Theorem 2 (Transparent proofs with bounded spotchecks) [ALMSS]. *Any polynomial time verifiable proof system $\mathcal{A}$ can be reduced at a polynomially bounded cost $\ell = n^{O(1)}$ to an equivalent proof system $\mathcal{A}'$ admitting randomized proof-verification with the following cost parameters: $r = O(\log n)$ random bits used, $q = O(1)$ proof-bits queried, and $t = O(n)$ time spent. In the "encoded theorems" model, t is poly-logarithmic: $t = (\log n)^{O(1)}$. Here n is the combined length of the theorem-candidate T and the proof-candidate P for the original proof system $\mathcal{A}$.*

Theorem 3 (Slightly superlinear transparent proofs) [BFLS]. *Given $\epsilon > 0$, any nearly linear time verifiable proof system $\mathcal{A}$ can be reduced at a slightly superlinear cost $\ell = O(n^{1+\epsilon})$ to an equivalent proof system $\mathcal{A}'$ admitting randomized proof-verification with the following cost parameters: $r \leq s$ random bits used and $q \leq s$ proof-bits queried, where the quantity s is polylogarithmic: $s = (\log n)^{2/\epsilon + O(1)}$. The time spent is $t = O(n)$. In the "encoded theorems" model, t is also polylogarithmic: $t \leq s$. Here, too, n is the combined length of the theorem-candidate T and the proof-candidate P.*

These two results are not comparable. While in Theorem 2, the number of query bits is constant, in Theorem 3 it is polylogarithmic. On the other hand, in Theorem 3, the length of the transparent proof is close to linear, while in Theorem 2, it is a polynomial with non-negligible exponent.

The proof of Theorem 2 is quite deep and builds substantially on a formidable arsenal of recent techniques, including [LFKN], [BFL], [BFLS], [FGLSS], [AS], [LS], [FL], [IZ], [Ru], [RS], [GLRSW]. All details of the proof, including proofs of the results used, can be found in a single volume in Madhu Sudan's thesis [Su].

There is some interest in the exact constant q in Theorem 2, i. e., the number of bits which need to be examined to reject faulty theorems with probability at least a half. A recent result of Carsten Lund shows that this is as small as 28 bits [Lu].

2.2 Cost of reliability reduced

The possibility of practical implications, advertised in the popular science press ([NYT], [SIAM], [SCI], even a comic strip [DISC]) are raised by the following interpretation of these results.

Suppose we have a complete formal specification of a system and a program is claimed to perform according to these specifications. While the correctness of the program cannot be verified in general (even the simplest questions regarding the performance of the program are undecidable), a step-by-step verification of each *instance* of computation by the program represents a mathematical proof of correctness of that instance. Now we ask the programmer (prover) to perform the additional job of turning this proof into a *transparent one*, verifiable by a much smaller machine.[2] (Observe that the logarithm of the number of atoms in the known Universe is less than 300, so a polylogarithmic verifier can be really tiny compared to the size of the proof.)

We stress that the transformation from proof to transparent proof does not need to be performed by a reliable machine; only the tiny verifier needs to be reliable. This opens the theoretical possibility of a considerable reduction of the cost of *reliability* of *any* (even nondeterministically specified) computation.

From this point of view, it is desirable to keep the amount of added workload of the prover (the quantity ℓ) as close to linear as possible. The term ε in the exponent in Theorem 3 constitutes a severe bottleneck. We *conjecture* that one can reduce ℓ to nearly linear and still retain polylogarithmic verification ($t = (\log n)^{O(1)}$).

2.3 Complexity classes: characterizations of NP

The only cost parameters considered by [BFLS] were ℓ (the cost of computing the transparent proof) and t (the time required for the verifier). The distinct roles played by the parameters q and r will be evident from Section 3. This role was first indicated in [FGLSS] and fully recognized and formalized by [AS]. The latter paper introduced the very useful and compact PCP-notation. (The letters stand for Probabilistically Checkable Proofs).

Definition 4 [AS]. Let $q(n)$ and $r(n)$ be positive functions. A language L is said to belong to the class $\mathrm{PCP}(r(n), q(n))$ if it has transparent membership proofs with the following parameters: polynomial verification time $t = n^{O(1)}$, and $q = O(q(n))$ queries, $r = O(r(n))$ random bits used. Here n is the length of the *input string* x (the theorem-candidate is the statement "$x \in L$").

For short, we write $\mathrm{PCP}(s(n))$ for $\mathrm{PCP}(s(n), s(n))$.

With this notation it is easy to see that $\mathrm{NP}=\mathrm{PCP}(0, n^{O(1)})$. Also, the class R of languages recognizable by polynomial time Monte Carlo algorithms with one-way error is clearly $\mathrm{R}=\mathrm{PCP}(n^{O(1)}, 0)$.

It should also be noted that

$$\mathrm{PCP}(r(n), q(n)) \subseteq \mathrm{NTIME}(n^{O(1)} + q(n) \cdot 2^{r(n)}). \qquad (1)$$

In particular,

$$\mathrm{PCP}(\log n, n^{O(1)}) \subseteq \mathrm{NP}. \qquad (2)$$

The class MIP of languages recognizable by "multiprover interactive proofs" [BGKW] can be equivalently defined [FRS] as $\mathrm{MIP}=\mathrm{PCP}(n^{O(1)})$. It then follows from observation (1) that $\mathrm{MIP} \subseteq \mathrm{NEXP}$ where $\mathrm{NEXP}= \bigcup_{k>0} \mathrm{NTIME}(2^{n^k})$. The first "transparent proofs" were found by [BFL] where the statement $\mathrm{MIP}=\mathrm{NEXP}$ was proved, hence $\mathrm{NEXP}=\mathrm{PCP}(n^{O(1)})$ is implicit.

---

[2] The approach of checking an instance of the computation (as opposed to trying to verify the program) was pioneered by Manuel Blum [BLR], [BK].

The next step was to scale this theorem down from exponential to polynomial time. This was achieved in [BFLS], with the corollary $NP \subseteq PCP((\log n)^{O(1)})$. (This corresponds to the weaker statement of Theorem 3, namely the ordinary case.) As pointed out by [ALMSS], the number of random bits used in [BFLS] can be reduced to $O(\log n)$ using a result of [IZ]. This, combined with the observation (2) yields the following characterization of NP:

$$NP = PCP(\log n, (\log n)^{O(1)}).$$

This result was improved in a sequence of papers to $NP = PCP(\log n, \log n \cdot \log \log n)$ [FGLSS], $NP = PCP(\log n, \sqrt{\log n})$ [AS], and the ultimate result [ALMSS]:

$$NP = PCP(\log n, 1) \tag{3}$$

corresponding to Theorem 2 (ordinary case).

It should be noted that these equalities do not relativize ([FRS], [Fo]). Their unrelativizability is in a sense inherited from one of their ingredients, the interactive LFKN protocol for verification of large sums ([LFKN]; cf. [BFL] for the format of the LFKN protocol used in subsequent work).

As pointed out by [AS], the fact that results like eqn. (3) do not relativize gives new hope to proving separation conjectures such as $NP \neq EXP$ by giving a relativizable proof (say by diagonalization) of the statement $PCP(\log n, 1) \neq EXP$. [AS] *conjecture* that this separation holds even if relativized, under any oracle.

3 Intractability of approximate discrete optimization

3.1 Maximum clique

It has been known for 20 years that determining the size $\omega(G)$ of a maximum clique in a graph G is NP-hard (Cook, cf. [GJ]). In a simple yet striking discovery, [FGLSS] recognized a direct link between the MIP=NEXP result and the hardness of obtaining a reasonable approximation to the maximum clique size. An ultimate extension of their result appears in [ALMSS] as a consequence of equation (3).

Let f, h be positive functions. We say that an algorithm (approximately) computes f within (error) h if it computes a function $g > 0$ such that for every sufficiently large input x,

$$\frac{1}{h(x)} \leq \frac{f(x)}{g(x)} \leq h(x).$$

Theorem 5 [ALMSS]. *There exists a constant $c > 0$ such that if some polynomial time algorithm is guaranteed to compute the maximum clique size $\omega(G)$ within a factor of ν^c where ν is the number of vertices of the graph G, then P=NP.*

To illustrate the idea of [FGLSS], we sketch the proof of the weaker statement that approximations within a factor of 10 are impossible, unless P=NP. We note that here and everywhere in this Section, references are always made to *ordinary proof systems*, there is no need for theorem-encoding.

Proof. (sketch). Assume a machine M computes an approximation of $\omega(G)$ within a factor of 10. Let L be any language in NP and x an input of length n. We show how to decide membership of x in L in polynomial time.

To this end, we construct a graph G as follows. First we note that if $x \in L$, this fact has a short proof and therefore it has a short *transparent proof* as well, of the type PCP($\log n, 1$). By repeating the verification 7 times, we reduce the error probability from $1/2$ to $1/128 < 1/100$.

As before, let q denote the number of bits of the proof queried by the verifier (number of spot-checks). (Now, q is a constant, e.g. $q = 7 \cdot 28 = 196$ by [Lu].) Let, moreover, r be the number of random bits used, so $r = O(\log n)$. To each string $R \in \{0,1\}^r$ of random bits there corresponds a query list $Q(R) = (w_1, \ldots, w_q)$ (we suppress the dependence on the theorem-candidate statement "$x \in L$" in the notation, having fixed x for now).

A *spot-check list* is a pair (R, S) where $R \in \{0,1\}^r$ and $S \in \{0,1\}^q$. We call the spot-check list (R, S) *accepting* if the verifier would accept a proof P based on the random string R and the outcome $P[w_j] = S[j]$ ($j = 1, \ldots, q$) of the queries.

Let the nodes of G correspond to all accepting spot-check lists. Therefore the number of nodes is $\leq 2^{r+q}$. (Note that this is bounded by $n^{O(1)}$.) We join two such nodes if they don't plainly contradict one another by asserting a different bit in the same position.

It is clear that no clique has size greater than 2^r in this graph. Indeed, otherwise two of the nodes in the clique would correspond to the same random string and therefore the same query list, yet the outcomes of the queries would differ, a contradiction.

If $x \in L$, the spot-check lists corresponding to a transparent proof yield a clique of size exactly 2^r. On the other hand, if $x \notin L$, then no clique of size greater than $2^r/128$ can exist (else, from this clique a proof-candidate could be pieced together with greater than $1/128$ chance of getting accepted).

Let us now use the machine M to compute $\omega(G)$ within a factor of 10. This is clearly sufficient to decide between the alternatives given, therefore it will decide whether or not $x \in L$ in polynomial time. □

In order to obtain the stronger result stated (Theorem 5), we need to reduce the probability of error further, to $n^{-\Omega(1)}$. This would seem to require $\Omega((\log n)^2)$ random bits; but by a result of [IZ], $O(\log n)$ random bits will actually suffice and essentially the same proof works.

Using a clever reduction from the clique problem, [LY] shows that Theorem 5 remains valid for the *chromatic number* in place of the clique number.

3.2 Polynomial-time approximation schemes

At the time [FGLSS] became known, it still seemed that the approximate clique problem was an isolated case, particularly well suited to capture the key facts about transparent proofs: that the verifier needs *very little information* about the proof; and there is a *large gap* between acceptance probabilities for correct and phony proofs.

The story took a further unexpected turn with the recognition that transparent proofs can be linked to the approximate solvability of a large class of discrete optimization problems [ALMSS]. The class of the optimization problems is question was introduced in [PY] and is denoted by MAX-SNP.

All problems in this class admit an approximate solution within a constant factor, computable in polynomial time. In such a case, one would wish to obtain approximations within $1 + \varepsilon$, for small values of $\varepsilon > 0$. If for every fixed $\varepsilon > 0$ such an approximation can be found in polynomial time, we say that the problem admits a *polynomial time approximation scheme* (PTAS).

The archetype of problems from MAX-SNP is the the MAX-3SAT problem, defined as follows. Given a list of disjunctive 3-clauses (of the form $x \vee y \vee z$ where x, y, z stand for Boolean variables and their negations), find the maximum number of simultaneously satisfiable clauses on the list.

Theorem 6 [ALMSS]. MAX-3SAT *does not admit a PTAS, unless* P=NP.

The proof of this result again follows from eqn. (3) through a fairly simple reduction.

This result in turn propagates to the large class of problems which are MAX-SNP-hard under "L-reductions" [PY]. L-reductions are defined so that they preserve approximability ratios within a constant factor. Consequently, a PTAS for a MAX-SNP-hard problem would imply a PTAS for all problems in MAX-SNP, including MAX-3SAT; therefore by Theorem 6 it would imply P=NP.

The class of known MAX-SNP-hard problems is large and growing. The dissertation [Ka] contains a [GJ]-style enumeration of the known problems in this class. Some of the most interesting ones are MAX-2SAT, maximum cut in a graph, maximum independent set in a graph of bounded degree [PY], the metric traveling salesman problem (with distances 1 and 2 only), shortest common superstring [BJLTY]. Consequently, none of these problems has a PTAS unless P=NP.

It is of interest to give explicit bounds on the degree of approximability in cases when a PTAS is known not to exist (unless P=NP). Again, [Lu] provides the best known bound showing that MAX-3SAT cannot be approximated within 112/111 unless P=NP.

The *longest path* problem is special in that it has the following self-improvement property (proved by a graph product construction): if one can compute the length of the longest path in graphs within some constant C, then one can compute it within *any* constant $c > 1$. In other words, a PTAS exists. However, the longest path problem is MAX-SNP-hard. Putting this all together, it follows that the longest path cannot be approximated in polynomial time *within any constant*, unless P=NP [KMR].

Acknowledgments

I am indebted to Katalin Friedl for clarifying many details of the paper [ALMSS] for me. I am grateful to Madhu Sudan for helpful comments on this manuscript.

References

[ALMSS] Arora, S., Lund, C., Motwani, R., Sudan, M., Szegedy, M.: Proof verification and hardness of approximation problems. In:*Proc. 33rd IEEE FOCS* (1992), pp. 14-23.

[AS] Arora, S., Safra, S.: Probabilistic checking of proofs. In: *Proc. 33rd IEEE FOCS* (1992), pp. 2-13.

[BFL] Babai, L., Fortnow, L., Lund, C.: Nondeterministic exponential time has two-prover interactive protocols. *Computational Complexity* 1 (1991) 3-40.

[BFLS] Babai, L., Fortnow, L., Levin, L.A., Szegedy, M.: Checking computations in polylogarithmic time. In: *Proc. 23rd ACM STOC* (1991), pp. 21-31.

[BGKW] Ben-Or, M., Goldwasser, S., Kilian, J., Wigderson, A.: Multi-prover interactive proofs: How to remove the intractability assumptions. In: *Proc. 20th ACM STOC* (1988), pp. 113-131.

[BJLTY] Blum, A., Jiang, T., Li, M., Tromp. J., Yannakakis, M.: Linear approximation of shortest superstrings. In: *Proc. 23rd ACM STOC* (1991), pp. 328-336.

[BK] Blum, M., Kannan, S.: Designing Programs that Check Their Work. In: *Proc. 21st ACM STOC* (1989), pp. 86-97.

[BLR] Blum, M., Luby, M., Rubinfeld, R.: Self-testing/correcting with Applications to Numerical Problems. In: *Proc. 22nd ACM Symp. on Theory of Computing* (1990), pp. 73-83.

[DISC] Gonick, Larry: Proof Positive? *Discover Magazine*, "Science classics" section, August 1992, pp. 26-27.

[FGLSS] Feige, U., Goldwasser, S., Lovász, L., Safra, S., Szegedy, M.: Approximating clique is almost NP-complete. In: *Proc. 32nd IEEE FOCS* (1991) 2-12.

[FL] Feige, U., Lovász, L.: Two-prover one-round proof systems: their power and their problems. In: *Proc. 24th ACM STOC* (1992), pp. 733-744.

[Fo] Fortnow, L.: private communication, 1992

[FRS] Fortnow, L., Rompel, J., Sipser, M.: On the power of multi-prover interactive protocols. In: *Proc. 3rd Structure in Complexity Theory Conf.* (1988), pp. 156-161.

[GJ] Garey, M. R., Johnson, D. S.: *Computers and Intractability, A Guide to the Theory of NP-Completeness*, Freeman, New York, 1979.

[GLRSW] Gemmell, P., Lipton, R., Rubinfeld, R., Sudan, M., Wigderson, A.: Self-testing/correcting for polynomials and for approximate functions. In: *Proc. 23rd ACM STOC* (1991) pp. 32-42.

[IZ] Impagliazzo, R., Zuckerman, D., How to recycle random bits. In: *Proc. 30th IEEE FOCS* (1989), pp. 248-253.

[Jo] Johnson, D. S.: The NP-Completeness Column: An Ongoing Guide. *J. of Algorithms* 13 (1992), 502-524.

[Ka] Kann, Viggo: On the approximability of NP-complete optimization problems. *Ph.D. Thesis*. Royal Institute of Technology, Stockholm, Sweden. May 1992.

[KMR] Karger, D., Motwani, R., Ramkumar, G. D. S.: On approximating the longest path in a graph. Manuscript, 1992.

[LS] Lapidot, D., Shamir, A.: Fully Parallelized Multi Prover Protocols for $NEXPTIME$. In: *Proc. 32nd IEEE FOCS*, 1991, pp. 13-18.

[Lu] Lund, Carsten: Efficient probabilistically checkable proofs. Manuscript, November 1992.

[LFKN] Lund, C., Fortnow, L., Karloff, H., Nisan, N.: Algebraic Methods for Interactive Proof Systems. In: *Proc. 31th IEEE FOCS* (1990), pp. 2-10.

[LY] Lund, C., Yannakakis, M.: On the hardness of approximating minimization problems. AT& T Technical Memorandum, 1992. Submitted to STOC'93.

[NYT] Kolata, Gina: New Short Cut Found for Long Math Proofs. *The New York Times*, April 7, 1992, Science Times section, p. B5.

[PY] Papadimitriou, C., Yannakakis, M.: Optimization, approximation, and complexity classes. In: *Proc. 20th ACM STOC* (1988), pp. 510-513.

[PS] Phillips, S., Safra, S.: *PCP* and tighter bounds for approximating $MAX - SNP$. Manuscript, Stanford University, April 1992.

[Ru] Rubinfeld, R.: A Mathematical Theory of Self-Checking, Self-Testing and Self-Correcting Programs. *Ph.D. Thesis*, Computer Science Dept., U.C. Berkeley (1990)

[RS] Rubinfeld, R., Sudan, M.: Testing polynomial functions efficiently and over rational domains. In:*Proc. 3rd ACM-SIAM SODA* (1992) 23-32

[SCI] Peterson, Ivars: Holographic proofs: keeping computers and mathematicians honest. *Science News*, vol. 141 (1992), 382-383.

[SIAM] Cipra, Barry A.: Theoretical Computer Scientists Develop Transparent Proof Technique. *SIAM News*, vol. 25, No. 3, May 1992.

[Su] Sudan, Madhu: Efficient checking of polynomials and proofs and the hardness of approximation problems. *Ph.D. Thesis*. U.C. Berkeley. October 1992.

Computing Symmetric Functions with AND/OR Circuits and a Single $MAJORITY$ Gate*

Zhi-Li Zhang[1], David A. Mix Barrington[1] and Jun Tarui[2]

[1] Computer Science Department, University of Massachusetts at Amherst,
Amherst, Massachusetts 01003, USA.
Email Addresses: zhzhang@cs.umass.edu, barrington@cs.umass.edu
[2] Department of Computer Science, University of Warwick,
Coventry, CV4 7AL, United Kingdom.
Email Address: jun@dcs.warwick.ac.uk

Abstract. Fagin et al. characterized those symmetric Boolean functions which can be computed by small AND/OR circuits of constant depth and unbounded fan-in. Here we provide a similar characterization for *d-perceptrons* — AND/OR circuits of constant depth and unbounded fan-in with a single $MAJORITY$ gate at the output. We show that a symmetric function has small (quasipolynomial, or $2^{\log^{O(1)} n}$ size) d-perceptrons *iff* it has only poly-log many *sign changes* (i.e., it changes value $\log^{O(1)} n$ times as the number of positive inputs varies from zero to n). A consequence of the lower bound is that a recent construction of Beigel is optimal. He showed how to convert a constant-depth unbounded fan-in AND/OR circuit with poly-log many $MAJORITY$ gates into an equivalent d-perceptron — we show that more than poly-log $MAJORITY$ gates cannot in general be converted to one.

1 Introduction

1.1 The d-Perceptron Model

The power of constant-depth circuits of unbounded fan-in AND and OR gates (e.g. the well-known AC^0 circuits) is by now fairly well understood [FSS, Aj, Hå, Ya]. One of the major open problems of complexity theory is to place any non-trivial bounds on the computing power of constant depth circuits of unbounded fan-in threshold or $MAJORITY$ gates. The class TC^0, of languages recognized by polynomial-size families of such circuits, might be equal to NP for all we can prove. A natural approach to bridging the gap between AND/OR circuits and threshold circuits is to consider models which combine the two kinds of gates.

* The first author was supported by grants CCR-8812567 and CCR-9008416. The second author was supported by NSF Computer and Computation Theory grants CCR-8922098 and CCR-9207829. The third author was supported in part by the ESPRIT II BRA Programme of the EC under contract 7141 (ALCOM II).

One very old example of such a model is the *perceptron* of Minsky and Papert [MP], which can be viewed as a $MAJORITY$ gate whose inputs are $ANDs$ of the input variables. These original perceptrons are rather limited and their computing power is well understood. But recently, perceptrons have been revived in a new form [BRS]. Along with a probabilistic version, there has emerged what we will call the d-perceptron, a constant-depth unbounded fan-in circuit which has AND and OR gates except for a single $MAJORITY$ gate at the output. It has been shown that such circuits require exponential size (exponentially many gates) to compute the MOD_2 function [Gr], to approximate the MOD_2 function [ABFR], or to compute or approximate the MOD_c function for any constant c [BS]. These d-perceptrons are closely linked to a model of computation which is interesting in its own right, where one evaluates a multilinear polynomial in the input variables, with coefficients in the integers or the reals, and outputs the sign of the result. (This can be extended to polynomials over the complex numbers, using an ad hoc notion of "sign" [BS].) Furthermore, the d-perceptron model is robust, in that other circuit models with a limited use of threshold gates can be mapped into it [BRS, ABFR, Be].

In the study of threshold computations, *harmonic analysis* has found many interesting applications (for some recent examples, see [Br, KKL, LMN]). Of particular interest to us is the work by Linial et al. [LMN], where they showed that any AC^0 function (any function computable by a poly-size constant-depth AND/OR circuit) can be closely approximated by a low-degree polynomial, a result which has consequences for the learnability of AC^0 functions. This work, together with [ABFR, BS], has been the chief inspiration for our work. However, our proof of the lower bound result is based on the *random restriction* technique [FSS, Hå, Ya].

1.2 Complexity of Symmetric Functions

The *symmetric* boolean functions are those which are invariant under any permutation of the inputs. We can describe a symmetric boolean function by giving its *spectrum*, which is the sequence $\langle f(0), \ldots, f(n) \rangle$, where each $f(i)$ is the value of the function when i of the n inputs are one. All symmetric functions are in TC^0, because they have linear-size depth-2 threshold circuits. In any model the complexity theory of the symmetric functions forms a subtheory of that of all boolean functions, and in some models this theory can be interesting and beautiful.

For example, consider the well-understood model of constant-depth circuits with unbounded fan-in AND/OR gates. A theorem of Fagin et al. [FKPS], using the exponential lower bound for $PARITY$ due to Yao [Ya, Hå], gives an elegant characterization of the symmetric functions which have polynomial size in this model (are in the class AC^0). These functions are those whose spectra are constant except for a poly-log section at either end. That is, there is some function $g(n) = \log^{O(1)} n$ such that for each n, $f(i)$ is constant in the range $g(n) \le i \le n - g(n)$. Our principal result is that a similar characterization holds in the d-perceptron model we consider.

1.3 The Main Result

In the d-perceptron model we add a single $MAJORITY$ gate to the AND/OR circuit, and thus we immediately allow new symmetric functions, such as $MAJ-ORITY$ itself, to be computed. In previous work in this model [ABFR], two key parameters of a boolean function have proven to be its *strong degree* and *weak degree*. These are based on a space of polynomials over the real numbers, where the boolean domain is taken to be $\{-1, 1\}$ rather than $\{0, 1\}$. The strong degree is the minimal degree of a polynomial whose sign always agrees with the target boolean function. The weak degree is the minimal degree of a polynomial, not identically zero, whose sign agrees with the target boolean function whenever the polynomial is nonzero. For symmetric functions, these two degrees are equal [ABFR], and furthermore they are equal to the number of *sign changes* of the spectrum (the number of i for which $f(i) \neq f(i + 1)$). It turns out that this parameter of symmetric functions give us an exact characterization of the symmetric boolean functions computable in the d-perceptron model as stated below.

Theorem 1 *A symmetric boolean function can be computed by a quasipolynomial size d-perceptron iff it has only poly-log many sign changes.*

The organization of the paper is as follows. In section 2 we define some notations and terminologies. In section 3 we give the easier part of the proof of Theorem 1 — the upper bound. In section 4 we give the harder part of the proof of Theorem 1 — the lower bound. Finally in section 5 we conclude our work and present some open problems.

2 Preliminaries

We will consider functions from $\{-1, 1\}^n$ to the reals R (with boolean functions being the special case with range $\{-1, 1\}$) as multilinear polynomials over R with input variables $\{x_1, \ldots, x_n\}$. The *size* of a polynomial is the number of nonzero coefficients, and the *degree* is the maximum number of variables appearing in any term with nonzero coefficient. We use $[n]$ to denote the set $\{0, 1, 2, \ldots, n\}$, and by $|\underline{x}|$ we mean the number of -1's in $\underline{x}$ (in general we think of -1 as "true" and 1 as "false").

A symmetric boolean function is a boolean function whose value only depends on $|\underline{x}|$. It can be proved that, over the reals, we can regard a symmetric boolean function as a function of $x = |\underline{x}|$. Hence, in this way, we convert a n-variable symmetric boolean function $f(\underline{x})$ (where $\underline{x} \in \{-1, 1\}^n$) into a univariate real function $f'(x)$ (where $x = |\underline{x}|$) such that $deg(f) = deg(f')$. In the sequel, we will use f to denote $f(\underline{x})$ and $f'(x)$ interchangeably. If $i \in [n]$, we say i is a *sign change* of a symmetric function f if $f(i) \neq f(i + 1)$. The number of sign changes of f is equal to the cardinality of the set $\{i|f(i) \neq f(i + 1)\}$. We will call $\langle f(0), f(1), \ldots, f(n) \rangle$ the *sign change spectrum* of f.

Following [ABFR], we define strong and weak representations of boolean functions as follows.

Definition 1 *We say a polynomial $F(\underline{x})$ over the reals R strongly represents a boolean function $f(\underline{x})$ if $sgn(F(\underline{x})) = f(\underline{x})$ for all $\underline{x} \in \{-1, 1\}^n$. Here $sgn(F(\underline{x})) = 1$ if $F(\underline{x}) > 0$ and $sgn(F(\underline{x})) = -1$ if $F(\underline{x}) < 0$.*

We say a polynomial $F(\underline{x})$ over the reals R weakly represents a boolean function $f(\underline{x})$ if $F(\underline{x})$ is not identically zero and for all $\underline{x} \in \{-1, 1\}^n$ such that $F(\underline{x}) \neq 0$, $sgn(F(\underline{x})) = f(\underline{x})$.

Definition 2 *Let $f(\underline{x})$ be a boolean function. The strong degree of $f(\underline{x})$ (denoted $d_s(f)$) is the minimum degree among all polynomials strongly representing $f(\underline{x})$, and the weak degree of $f(\underline{x})$ (denoted $d_s(f)$) is the minimum degree among all polynomials weakly representing $f(\underline{x})$.*

Notice that in general the weak degree of a boolean function may well be smaller than its strong degree. However, the following fact as first observed in [ABFR] says that this cannot happen for symmetric boolean functions.

Lemma 2 ([ABFR]) *Let $f(\underline{x})$ be a symmetric boolean function with k sign changes, then $d_s(f) = d_w(f) = k$.*

We call this quantity the *degree* of a symmetric boolean function.

The above lemma was proved in [ABFR] by exploring the duality relationship of certain function spaces. We note that it has a simpler proof using the symmetrization technique [MP]: Let $F(\underline{x})$ be a strong or weak representation of a symmetric boolean function $f(\underline{x})$. Note that $F(\underline{x})$ is not necessarily symmetric itself; however, we can easily use $F(\underline{x})$ to construct a symmetric function $G(\underline{x})$. Formally, $G(\underline{x}) = \sum_{\sigma \in S_n} F^\sigma(\underline{x})$, where S_n is the nth symmetric group and $F^\sigma(\underline{x}) = F(\underline{x}^\sigma) = F(x_{\sigma(1)}, \ldots, x_{\sigma(n)})$. Obviously $G(\underline{x})$ strongly (weakly) represents $f(\underline{x})$ if $F(\underline{x})$ strongly (weakly) represents $f(\underline{x})$, and $G(\underline{x})$ has the same degree as $F(\underline{x})$. Since $G(\underline{x})$ is symmetric, $G(\underline{x})$ can be written as a univariate real function of $|\underline{x}|$. Therefore the degree of $G(\underline{x})$ is at least the number of sign changes of $f(\underline{x})$, and thus that of $F(\underline{x})$. But it is easy to construct a real polynomial strongly representing $f(\underline{x})$ such that its degree equals the number of sign changes of $f(\underline{x})$.

3 The Upper Bound

We first define the d-perceptron model as introduced in [ABFR, BRS].

Definition 3 *A d-perceptron is a circuit with a $MAJORITY$ gate at the top and depth-d unbounded fan-in AND/OR subcircuits feeding into the top $MAJ-ORITY$ gate. The size of a d-perceptron is the number of gates in the circuit.*

We will be interested in d-perceptrons of polynomial and of *quasipolynomial* ($2^{\log^{O(1)} n}$) size. Note that by [FKPS], ordinary constant-depth AND/OR circuits of quasipolynomial size can compute no more symmetric functions than can circuits of polynomial size. For more on quasipolynomial size circuit classes, see [Ba].

Consider a polynomial strongly representing a boolean function on $\{0,1\}^n$ such that the coefficients are positive integers bounded by a quasipolynomial in n. It is easy to see that such a polynomial corresponds to a quasipolynomial size 1-perceptron whose gates on the first level are poly-log fan-in $ANDs$. In the following lemma we show that any symmetric boolean function with only poly-log degree (i.e. sign changes) has such a low degree polynomial representation, and hence can be computed by such 1-perceptrons.

Lemma 3 *Any symmetric boolean function with only poly-log degree can be computed by a quasipolynomial size 1-perceptron with $ANDs$ of poly-log fan-in.*

Proof. Let $0 \le c_1 < c_2 < \ldots < c_k < n$ be the positions of the sign changes of $f(\underline{x})$, where $k = \log^{O(1)} n$. Then the following function

$$F(\underline{x}) = (-1)^\delta \prod_{i=1}^{k} (c_i + \frac{1}{2} - \sum_{i=1}^{n} x_i), \text{ where } \delta = \begin{cases} 0 & \text{if } f(0) > 0 \\ 1 & \text{if } f(0) < 0 \end{cases}$$

agrees with $f(\underline{x})$ in sign (note here $\underline{x} \in \{0,1\}^n$).

$F(\underline{x})$ is a poly-log degree polynomial with rational coefficients, but we can easily make $F(\underline{x})$ a polynomial with integer coefficients (without changing its sign) by multiplying it by an appropriate positive constant.

The problem left now is to convert the polynomial into one with only positive coefficients. Reversing the procedure used in [MP] to prove the *Positive Normal Form Theorem*, we can eliminate all the negative coefficients without blowing up either the degree or the size of the coefficients.

4 The Lower Bound

In this section, we will prove that any symmetric boolean function with more than poly-log sign changes cannot be computed by any quasipolynomial size d-perceptron. The proof makes use of some key observations by Linial, et al [LMN], and uses the very technique of *random restriction*, first introduced in [FSS] and refined in [Ya, Hå], that gave the first exponential lower bound for AND/OR circuits.

A random restriction is a random mapping of the input variables to 0, 1 and $*$ according to some probability distribution. The function obtained from $f(x_1, \ldots, x_n)$ by applying a random restriction ρ is denoted by f^ρ, and its variables are those x_i for which $\rho(x_i) = *$. For our purpose, we will assume that ρ assigns values to each input variable independently and $Pr[0] = Pr[1] = \frac{1-Pr[*]}{2}$.

A simple observation is that any random restriction of a symmetric boolean function is still symmetric; furthermore, its sign change spectrum is a subinterval of that of the original function.

Recall that a *minterm* of a boolean function is a set of variables such that a partial assignment to the variables in the set makes the function identically 1, but no partial assignment to any subset of the set makes the function identically

1. Similarly, a *maxterm* is a set of variables such that a partial assignment to the variables in the set makes the function identically 0, but no partial assignment to a subset of the set makes the function identically 0.

A useful fact, which was independently discovered in [BI,HH, Ta], and explicitly stated in [LMN], states that if all the minterms and maxterms of a boolean function f have size at most s and t respectively, then f can be evaluated by a decision tree of depth at most st. Since each branch of the decision tree corresponds to a monomial over the reals, we see that f can be represented as a real polynomial of degree at most st. This observation will be used in the proof of lemma 5 below.

It is well-known that with high probability, a random restriction of an AC^0 function will have small minterm size and maxterm size. This can be proved by a repeated applications of Håstad's switching lemma [BoS, LMN]. We state this fact formally as follows.

Lemma 4 ([LMN]) *Let f be a boolean function computed by an AND/OR circuit of size M and depth d. Then*

$$Pr[f^\rho \text{ has a minterm or a maxterm of size } > t] \leq M2^{-t}$$

where ρ is a random restriction such that $Pr[*] = 1/(10t)^d$.

Lemma 5 *Let f be a symmetric boolean function on n variables. Suppose f can be computed by a d-perceptron such that the fan-in of the $MAJORITY$ gate is N, the size of each AND/OR subcircuit is at most M, and the depth is at most d, where $N, M \leq 2^{t-1}$. Then for a positive fraction of the random restrictions ρ in a distribution with $Pr[*] = p = \frac{n}{(10t)^d}$, f^ρ is a function of at least $np = \frac{n}{(10t)^d}$ variables, the number of sign changes of f^ρ is at most $O(t^2)$, and the sign change spectrum of f^ρ is a subinterval at most $O(\sqrt{n})$ off the center of the sign change spectrum of f.*

Proof. Let ρ be a random restriction with $Pr[*] = p = \frac{1}{(10t)^d}$. Denote by f_i, $1 \leq i \leq N$, the subfunctions computed by the AND/OR subcircuits, and by f_i^ρ, $1 \leq i \leq N$, the functions obtained by the random restriction. Applying Lemma 4 to each f_i, we have

$$Pr[f_i^\rho \text{ has a minterm or maxterm of size } > 2t] \leq M2^{-2t}.$$

Hence,

$$Pr[\bigwedge_{i=1}^{N} f_i^\rho \text{ has only minterms and maxterms of size } \leq 2t]$$

$$\geq 1 - \sum_{i=1}^{N} Pr[f_i^\rho \text{ has a minterm or maxterm of size } > 2t]$$

$$\geq 1 - NM2^{-2t} \geq 1 - 2^{2t-2}2^{-2t} \geq \frac{3}{4}$$

On the other hand, the expected number of variables assigned $*$ is $np = \frac{n}{(10t)^d}$. By the normal approximation to binomial distribution, for n large, we see that with probability at least $\frac{1}{4}$, ρ will assign $*$'s to at least np variables and an almost equal number of 0 and 1's to the rest of the input variables.

Therefore, there must be a ρ such that $f^\rho = MAJORITY(f_1^\rho, \ldots, f_N^\rho)$ is a function on at least np variables, and each f_i^ρ has both minterms and maxterms of size $\leq 2t$. It follows that f_i^ρ can be represented by a $(-1, 1)$-valued real function of degree at most $4t^2$, hence $g^\rho = \sum_{i=1}^N f_i^\rho - \frac{1}{2}$ is a strong representation of f^ρ. Since g^ρ has degree at most $4t^2$, f^ρ can have at most $4t^2$ sign changes.

Remark: If we choose $t = \log^{O(1)} n$, then f^ρ can have only poly-log many sign changes. Therefore for the original function f, there must exist a subinterval of length at least $\frac{n}{(10)^d} = \frac{n}{\log^{O(1)} n}$, near the center of the sign change spectrum of f, such that f has at most poly-log many sign changes in that interval.

To prove the result that any symmetric function of more than poly-log sign changes cannot be computed by any quasipolynomial size d-perceptron, we need to use a shifting technique to locate an interval in the sign change spectrum of the function such that we can apply the above lemma to obtain a contradiction.

Lemma 6 *If f is a symmetric boolean function of more than poly-log sign changes, then f cannot be computed by a quasipolynomial size d-perceptron for any constant d.*

Proof. Suppose the opposite is true: there exists a quasipolynomial size d-perceptron for some constant d. Let c be such that $N, M \leq 2^{\log^c n - 1}$ where N, M are as in lemma 5. Let $s(n)$ be the sign change function of f, by the hypothesis $s(n) = \log^{\omega(1)} n$.

Consider the interval $[s^{\frac{1}{2}}(n), n - s^{\frac{1}{2}}(n)]$ of the sign change spectrum of f, the number of sign changes in this interval is $\Omega(s(n))$. Without loss of generality, we assume that there are $\Omega(s(n))$ sign changes in $[s(n)^{\frac{1}{2}}, \frac{n}{2}]$. Partition this interval into k intervals of the form $[2^i s^{\frac{1}{2}}(n), 2^{i+1} s^{\frac{1}{2}}(n)]$, where $0 \leq i \leq k - 1$ and $k = \log n - \frac{1}{2} \log s(n) - 1 = O(\log n)$.

We further partition each of the intervals $[2^i s^{\frac{1}{2}}(n), 2^{i+1} s^{\frac{1}{2}}(n)]$ into δ subintervals of length $\frac{2^i s^{\frac{1}{2}}(n)}{\delta}$ where $\delta = (10t)^d$ and $t = \log^c n$, i.e. $\delta = (10 \log^c n)^d = O(\log^{dc} n)$. We contend that one of the subintervals must have $\omega(t^2)$ sign changes, since otherwise, the total number of sign changes in $[s^{\frac{1}{2}}(n), \frac{n}{2}]$ is at most $\sum_{i=0}^{k-1} \delta \cdot O(t^2) = O(t^2 \delta k) = \log^{O(1)} n$, a contradiction. Therefore for some i, $0 \leq i \leq k-1$, a subinterval of length $\frac{2^i s^{\frac{1}{2}}(n)}{\delta} = \log^{\omega(1)} n$ has $\omega(t^2)$ sign changes.

By an appropriate partial assignment to the input variables, we obtain from f a function f', of $2^i s^{\frac{1}{2}}(n)$ variables, whose sign change spectrum is identical to an interval of the sign change spectrum of f which contains the aforementioned subinterval at center. Note that the circuit for f induces a circuit for f' of size at most that for f and thus its N', M' are bounded by $2^{t-1} = 2^{\log^c n - 1}$. Therefore, applying lemma 5 to f', we have that there exists a random restriction

ρ such that f'^ρ contains the subinterval as its sign change spectrum. However, f'^ρ can have only $O(t^2) = \log^{O(1)} n$ many sign changes, hence we arrive at a contradiction.

We have now completed the proof of our main Theorem 1, by combining Lemma 3 and Lemma 6. We conclude by relating Lemma 6 to the optimality of a recent construction of Beigel [Be].

Beigel shows that d-perceptrons serve as a normal form for AND/OR circuit s augmented by a small number of $MAJORITY$ gates. In particular, a circuit of unbounded fan-in, quasipolynomially many AND, OR, and NOT gates, and poly-log many $MAJORITY$ gates can be converted into a d-perceptron of quasipolynomial size. (Applying this construction would provide an alternate proof of our Lemma 3.) One might ask whether there is a general method to eliminate more than poly-log many $MAJORITY$s in this way.

There is no such method, as can be seen from work prior to ours [ABFR] which shows that if $m = \log^{\omega(1)} n$, then the parity function on m variables requires $2^{\Omega(m)}$ size to be computed by a d-perceptron. Our Lemma 6 shows that *any* symmetric boolean function with m sign changes would do in place of the parity function.

5   Conclusion and Open Problems

In this paper, we proved an *if and only if* condition for a symmetric boolean function to be computable by a quasipolynomial size d-perceptron circuit. This work extends the line of an earlier work by Fagin, et al. [FKPS] where they gave an *if and only if* condition for a symmetric function to be computable by a polynomial size AND/OR circuit.

In an attempt to capture the complexity of symmetric functions in other models, in [ZB] we also studied the size complexity of symmetric functions in the parity-threshold model, i.e. circuits consisting of a $MAJORITY$ gate whose inputs are $PARITY$ gates. We conjectured that an analogous *if and only if* condition exists, but we were only able to partially resolve the problem under a certain technical condition. One particular case of interest is that for any constant $p > 2$, MOD_p is not computable by any quasipolynomial size parity-threshold circuit.

The analysis of threshold computation by algebra over fields of characteristic zero has proved somewhat fruitful. The computation of circuits of AND, OR, and MOD_p gates has been very well explained using algebra over fields of characteristic p ([Ra], [Sm]). Is it possible to combine the two methods, or otherwise place limits on the power of the following perceptron-like model: a $MAJORITY$ gate, whose inputs are constant-depth $AND/OR/MOD_p$ circuits?

References

[Aj]   M. Ajtai. $\sum_1^1$-formulae on finite structures. *Annals of Pure and Applied Logic*, 24 (1983), 1-48.

[ABFR] J. Aspnes, R. Beigel, M. Furst and S. Rudich. On the expressive power of voting polynomials. *Proceedings of the 23rd Annual Symposium on Theory of Computing* (1991), 402-409.

[Ba] D. A. M. Barrington. Quasipolynomial size circuit classes. *Proceedings: Structure in Complexity Theory, Seventh Annual Conference* (1992), 86-93.

[Be] R. Beigel. Do extra threshold gates help? *Proceedings of the 24th Annual Symposium on Theory of Computing* (1992), 450-454.

[BI] M. Blum and R. Impagliazzo. Generic oracles and oracle classes. *Proceedings of the 28th Annual Symposium on Foundations of Computer Science* (1987), 118-126.

[BoS] R. Boppana and M. Sipser. The complexity of finite functions. *Handbook of Theoretical Computer Science*, Vol. A, ed. by J. van Leeuwen (Elsevier and MIT Press, 1990).

[Br] J. Bruck. Harmonic analysis of polynomial threshold functions. *SIAM J. Disc. Math.* 3:2 (1990), 168-177.

[BRS] R. Beigel, N. Reingold and D. Spielman. The perceptron strikes back. *Proceedings of the 6th Annual Conference on Structrur in Complexity Theory* (1991), 286-291.

[BS] D. A. Mix Barrington and H. Straubing. Complex polynomials and circuit lower bounds for modular counting. *Proceedings of LATIN '92 (1st Latin American Symposium on Theoretical Informatics)* (1992), 24-31.

[FKPS] R. Fagin, M. M. Klawe, N. J. Pippenger, and L. Stockmeyer. Bounded depth, polynomial size circuits for symmetric functions. *Theoretical Computer Science* 36 (1985), 239-250.

[FSS] M. Furst, J. Saxe, and M. Sipser. Parity, circuits, and the polynomial time hierarchy. *Math. System Theory* 17 (1984), 13-27.

[Gr] F. Green. An oracle separating $\oplus P$ from PP^{PH}, *Proc. 5th Structure in Complexity Theory* (1990), 295-298.

[Hå] J. Håstad. *Computational Limitations of Small-Depth Circuits.* (Cambridge, MA, MIT Press, 1986).

[HH] J. Hartmanis and L. A. Hemachandra. One-way functions, robustness and non-isomorphism of NP-complete sets. Technical Report DCS TR86-796 (1987), Cornell University.

[KKL] J. Kahn, G. Kalai, and N. Linial. The influence of variables on boolean functions. *Proceedings of 29th Annual ACM Symposium on Theory of Computing* (1988), 68-80.

[LMN] N. Linial, Y. Mansour and N. Nisan. Constant depth circuit, fourier transform and learnability. *Proceedings of the 30th Annual IEEE Symposium on Foundations of Computer Science* (1989), 574-579.

[MP] M. L. Minsky and S. Papert. *Perceptrons* (Cambridge, MA, MIT Press, 1988). Original edition 1968.

[Ra] A. A. Razborov. Lower bounds for the the size of circuits of bounded depth with basis $\wedge$, $\oplus$. *Math. Zametki* 41:4 (1987), 598-607 (in Russian). English translation *Math. Notes Acad. Sci. USSR* 41:4 (1987), 333-338.

[Sm] R. Smolensky. Algebraic methods in the theory of lower bounds for boolean circuit complexity. *Proceedings of 19th Annual ACM Symposium on Theory of Computing* (1987), 77-82.

[Ta] G. Tardos. Query complexity, or why is it difficult to separate $NP^A \cap$ co-NP^A from P^A by a random oracle A? Manuscript (1988).

[Ya]   A. C.-C. Yao. Separating the polynomial-time hierarchy by oracles. *Proceedings 26th Annual IEEE Symposium on Foundations of Computer Science* (1985), 1-10.

[ZB]   Z.-L. Zhang and D. A. Mix Barrington. Lower bounds for symmetric functions in perceptron-like models. COINS Technical Report 91-81 (1991), University of Massachusetts at Amherst.

Threshold Circuits for Iterated Multiplication: Using AC^0 for Free

Alexis Maciel* and Denis Thérien**

McGill University, School of Computer Science,
Montréal (Québec), Canada, H3A 2A7

Abstract. We investigate small-depth threshold circuits for iterated multiplication and related problems. One result is that we can solve this problem with an AC^0-connection of TC_3^0-languages, i.e. an AC^0-connection of languages recognizable by depth-3 threshold circuits. This can be compared to the best known construction, which uses four levels of threshold gates (but no AC^0-circuitry). Similarly, we design small-depth circuits for powering, division and logarithm. Iterated multiplication is then considered in the context of finite fields. Finally, we look at circuits of quasipolynomial size and we establish various normal forms.

1 Introduction

In the last decade, much attention has been devoted to complexity classes defined by small depth circuits. One such class is AC^0, which consists of languages recognized by constant-depth polynomial-size circuits constructed with NOT gates and unbounded fan-in AND and OR gates. Powerful techniques have been introduced to understand the computing power of such circuits: it is for example known—by combining results of Fagin et al. [6] and Yao [17]—that the threshold function $(\Theta_{k_n,n})_{n>0}$ belongs to AC^0 iff the parameter k_n is polylogarithmic in n (here $\Theta_{k_n,n}(x_1,\ldots,x_n)$ returns 1 iff $\sum x_i \geq k_n$).

Another class that has been investigated is TC^0, which is obtained by considering constant-depth polynomial-size circuits constructed with arbitrary threshold gates, i.e. gates that compute arbitrary threshold functions. Since AND and OR gates are special cases of threshold gates we trivially have $AC^0 \subseteq TC^0$ and the remark in the previous paragraph implies that this inclusion is proper. The class TC^0 is poorly understood: it is not even known whether TC^0 contains all of NP. In fact, threshold circuits have been found to be surprisingly powerful [8]. For example, Beame, Cook and Hoover [2] gave algorithms to compute powering (given x, return x^n), iterated multiplication (given $x_1,\ldots,x_n$, return the product $x_1\cdots x_n$) and division (given x,y, return $\lfloor x/y \rfloor$) that are easily checked to be in TC^0, as was observed by Reif [14] and Immerman and Landau [11]. Note that throughout the paper, only non-uniform circuits are considered.

The natural parametrization of TC^0 takes into account the exact depth of the circuits. One thus defines TC_d^0 as the class of boolean functions computable in depth

---

* Supported by NSERC and FCAR scholarships. Electronic mail: alexis@cs.mcgill.ca
** Supported by NSERC grant A4546 and by FCAR grant 89-EQ-2933. Electronic mail: denis@cs.mcgill.ca

d by polynomial-size threshold circuits. Hajnal et al. [9] proved that the inclusions $TC_1^0 \subseteq TC_2^0 \subseteq TC_3^0$ are proper. Recently, Siu and Roychowdhury [15], building on work of Goldmann, Håstad and Razborov [7], and Goldmann and Karpinski [8], have produced circuits in TC_3^0 for powering and division, and in TC_4^0 for iterated multiplication.

In our paper, we study these problems in a different perspective. Considering that arbitrary threshold gates are much more powerful than AND and OR gates, we propose a parametrization of TC^0 which allows free use of AC^0-subcircuits: we define $\widehat{TC}^0$ to consist of constant-depth polynomial-size circuits constructed with NOT, AND, OR and threshold gates, and we declare that such a circuit is in $\widehat{TC}_d^0$ provided that no path traverses more than d threshold gates. Clearly $\widehat{TC}^0 = TC^0$ and $\widehat{TC}_0^0 = AC^0$.

A straightforward implementation of the algorithms of Beame, Cook and Hoover [2] gives $\widehat{TC}_4^0$, $\widehat{TC}_7^0$ and $\widehat{TC}_5^0$ circuits for powering, division and iterated multiplication, respectively. However, it is not hard to do better. For example, in the case of iterated multiplication, the algorithm of Immerman and Landau [11] can be easily implemented as a $\widehat{TC}_3^0$ circuit. On the other hand, analyzing the circuits of Siu and Roychowdhury [15] in light of our definition does not improve their results, i.e. we get $\widehat{TC}_3^0$ circuits for powering and division, and a $\widehat{TC}_4^0$ circuit for iterated multiplication. In this paper, we produce $\widehat{TC}_2^0$ circuits for powering and division, and a $\widehat{TC}_3^0$ circuit for iterated multiplication. Our constructions have the additional property of using AC^0-circuitry only at the top[3], so that, for example, iterated multiplication is shown to be realizable with an AC^0-connection of languages in TC_3^0. We also consider the logarithm function and show that it can be computed in $\widehat{TC}_2^0$ with accuracy 2^{-n} (in fact by an AC^0-connection of languages in TC_2^0).

In section 3, we study iterated multiplication over finite fields. The complexity of the problem can be seen to vary according to the growth rate of the cardinality of the field (constant, polynomial or exponential).

Finally we look at circuits of quasipolynomial size. We show that any function in $\widehat{TC}_d^0$ can be computed by a probabilistic TC_{d+2}^0 circuit of quasipolynomial size and by a (deterministic) TC_{d+3}^0 circuit of quasipolynomial size. We also prove that if a certain (natural) function can be realized by a constant-depth quasipolynomial-size circuit with only one level of threshold gates, then any circuit in TC^0 can be put in a simple normal form.

2 Problems on Integers

Let us start with ITERATED MULTIPLICATION, the problem of computing the n^2-bit binary representation of $\prod_{i=1}^n x_i$, given the n-bit binary representations of $x_1, \ldots, x_n$. Our strategy, following Beame, Cook and Hoover [2], is based on the Chinese Remainder Theorem whose standard constructive proof gives us the following lemma:

Lemma 1. *Suppose that $Q = \prod_{j=1}^m q_j$, the product of* poly(n) *pairwise relatively prime numbers bounded in* poly(n). *Then there exist $u_1, \ldots, u_m < Q$ such that for*

---

[3] The output gate is at the top, the input gates are at the bottom.

every n-bit number x, $x \equiv \sum_{j=1}^{m}(x \bmod q_j)u_j \pmod{Q}$. Moreover, if $x < Q$, then $x = \sum_{j=1}^{m}(x \bmod q_j)u_j - kQ$, for some k bounded in poly(n).

Let $x_1, \ldots, x_n$ be the input numbers of ITERATED MULTIPLICATION, let p_n be the nth prime number and $P = \prod_{j=1}^{n^2} p_j$. As a function of n, by the Prime Number Theorem, p_n is in $O(n \log n)$, so all the p_j are bounded in poly(n). Moreover $P \geq 2^{n^2} > \prod_{i=1}^{n} x_i$. By applying the lemma, we get that $\prod_{i=1}^{n} x_i = \sum_{j=1}^{n^2} b_j u_j - kP$, where $b_j = \prod_{i=1}^{n} x_i \bmod p_j$. Our goal now is to compute $\prod_{i=1}^{n} x_i \bmod p_j$.

Lemma 2. Let q be a number bounded in poly(n) and let x be an n-bit input number. Then $x \bmod q = h(\sum_{j=1}^{n} a_j x_j)$ with the a_j bounded in poly(n).

Lemma 3. Let x be an n-bit input number and suppose that $f(x) = h(s_1, \ldots, s_c)$, where c is a constant and $s_i = \sum_{j=1}^{n} a_{i,j} x_j$ with the $a_{i,j}$ bounded in poly(n). Then f can be computed with a symmetric gate.

Lemma 4. If f is computed by a symmetric gate, then f can be computed by a TC_2^0 circuit with the property that for some $t \in$ poly(n), (i) when $f(x) = 0$, then exactly t bottom threshold gates output 1, and (ii) when $f(x) = 1$, then exactly $t+1$ bottom threshold gates output 1.

Lemma 2 follows from the fact that $x \bmod q = (\sum_{j=1}^{n} x_j(2^{j-1} \bmod q)) \bmod q$. Lemma 3 is proved using a coding trick described by Hofmeister, Hohberg and Köhling [10]. One consequence of these two lemmas is that $x \bmod q$ can be computed with a symmetric gate, when q is bounded in poly(n). Lemma 4 was proved by Hajnal et al. [9]. If we let SYM denote the class of functions computed by symmetric gates, then this lemma allows us to transform a SYM of SYM circuit into a SYM of TC_1^0 circuit, and a TC_1^0 of SYM circuit into a TC_2^0 circuit.

We are now ready to compute $\prod_{i=1}^{n} x_i \bmod p_j$.

Lemma 5. Let $q = p^l$ be a prime power bounded in poly(n) and let $x_1, \ldots, x_n$ be n-bit input numbers. Then we can compute $\prod_{i=1}^{n} x_i \bmod q$ with a SYM of TC_1^0 circuit.

Proof. Let $\mathbb{Z}_{p^l}^* = \{0, 1, 2, \ldots, p^l - 1\} - \{0, p, 2p, \ldots, p^l - p\}$, i.e. the set of integers in $\mathbb{Z}_{p^l}$ that are not divisible by p. $\mathbb{Z}_{p^l}^*$ is a group with respect to multiplication modulo p^l. Moreover, $\mathbb{Z}_{p^l}^*$ is cyclic, unless $p = 2$ and $l > 2$; in that case, $\mathbb{Z}_{p^l}^*$ is generated by $2^l - 1$ and 5. (See [12, section 4.1] for more details.)

Suppose that $p \neq 2$ or $l \leq 2$. Let j_i be the largest power of p dividing $x_i \bmod p^l$ and let $j = \sum_{i=1}^{n} j_i$ thresh l, which means that $j = \sum_{i=1}^{n} j_i$ if $\sum_{i=1}^{n} j_i < l$, and $j = l$ otherwise. Then $y_i = (x_i \bmod p^l)/p^{j_i} \in \mathbb{Z}_{p^l}^*$ and, since $p^l \equiv 0 \pmod{p^l}$, we have that $\prod_{i=1}^{n} x_i \equiv p^j \prod_{i=1}^{n} y_i \pmod{p^l}$. Now let g be a multiplicative generator of $\mathbb{Z}_{p^l}^*$. Let $a_i < p^l - p^{l-1}$ be such that $g^{a_i} \bmod p^l = y_i$, and let $a = \sum_{i=1}^{n} a_i \bmod p^l - p^{l-1}$. Then $\prod_{i=1}^{n} x_i \equiv p^j g^a \pmod{p^l}$. By Lemma 3, since p, l and g are fixed, this implies that $\prod_{i=1}^{n} x_i \bmod p^l$ can be computed with a symmetric gate whose inputs are the bits of the j_i and of the a_i. Since, for any i, j_i and a_i depend only on $x_i \bmod p$, then, by Lemmas 2 and 3, they can be computed by a symmetric gate. This gives us a SYM of SYM circuit, hence the result.

The other case is handled similarly. □

Theorem 6. ITERATED MULTIPLICATION *can be computed by an* AC^0 *of* TC_3^0 *circuit.*

Proof. As noted earlier, there is a k bounded in poly(n) such that $\prod_{i=1}^{n} x_i = \sum_{j=1}^{n^2} b_j u_j - kP$, where $b_j = \prod_{i=1}^{n} x_i \bmod p_j$. Since u_j is fixed, $b_j u_j$ depends only on $\prod_{i=1}^{n} x_i \bmod p_j$. Therefore, by Lemma 5, $b_j u_j$ can be computed by a SYM of TC_1^0 circuit. Using the AC^0 of TC_1^0 circuit for ITERATED ADDITION of Chandra, Stockmeyer and Vishkin [5], we can thus compute $\sum_{j=1}^{n^2} b_j u_j - kP$ with an AC^0 of TC_3^0 circuit, for all the poly(n) possible values of k. Choosing the right answer can be done in AC^0 by testing $\sum_{j=1}^{n^2} b_j u_j - kP < P$. $\qquad\square$

POWERING is the problem of computing the n^2-bit binary representations of $x^2, \ldots, x^n$, given the n-bit binary representation of x. To compute x^t, for a fixed t, we use basically the same circuit that was used for ITERATED MULTIPLICATION, except that now we can compute $b_j u_j$ directly with a symmetric gate.

Theorem 7. POWERING *can be computed by an* AC^0 *of* TC_2^0 *circuit.*

DIVISION is the problem of computing the n-bit binary representation of $\lfloor x/y \rfloor$, given the n-bit binary representations of x and y.

Theorem 8. DIVISION *can be computed by an* AC^0 *of* TC_2^0 *circuit.*

Proof. The case when $y = 1$ is trivial, so we assume that $y \geq 2$. Let j be such that $2^{j-1} \leq y < 2^j$ and $u = 1 - y2^{-j}$. These definitions imply that $2 \leq j \leq n$, $0 < u \leq \frac{1}{2}$ and $y^{-1} = 2^{-j}(1 - u)^{-1} = 2^{-j} \sum_{i=0}^{\infty} u^i$. Let $\hat{y}^{-1} = 2^{-j} \sum_{i=0}^{n-1} u^i$. Then $0 \leq y^{-1} - \hat{y}^{-1} = 2^{-j} \sum_{i=n}^{\infty} u^i < 2^{-n}$. Let $t = x\hat{y}^{-1}$. Then $0 \leq xy^{-1} - t < x2^{-n} < 1$ and $0 \leq xy^{-1} - \lfloor t \rfloor < 2$. So if $xy^{-1} - \lfloor t \rfloor < 1$ then $\lfloor t \rfloor = \lfloor x/y \rfloor$; otherwise $\lfloor t \rfloor + 1 = \lfloor x/y \rfloor$. However, this test cannot be performed since we do not know the value of xy^{-1}. So instead we will test if $x - \lfloor t \rfloor y < y$.

Consider now the problem of computing $\lfloor t \rfloor z$, for a fixed value of j, where t is as defined above and z is an n-bit input number. Later, by restricting z to be either 1 or y, we will be able to compute both $\lfloor t \rfloor$ and $\lfloor t \rfloor y$. We have that $t = 2^{-jn} s$ where $s = \sum_{i=0}^{n-1} 2^{j(n-1-i)} x(2^j - y)^i$ is an integer. Choose $m \in$ poly(n) such that $P = \prod_{i=1}^{m} p_i > s$. Then there exists k bounded in poly(n) such that $s = \sum_{i=1}^{m} b_i u_i - kP$, where $b_i = s \bmod p_i$. Notice that s can be computed with a AC^0 of TC_2^0 circuit, since each b_i can be computed with a symmetric gate. Let $w_i = \lfloor 2^{-jn} b_i u_i \rfloor$, $w_0 = \lfloor 2^{-jn} kP \rfloor$, $v_i = b_i u_i \bmod 2^{jn}$, and $v_0 = (kP) \bmod 2^{jn}$. Then, a little bit of calculation shows that $\lfloor t \rfloor z = \sum_{i=0}^{m} w_i z + \lfloor 2^{-jn} \sum_{i=0}^{m} v_i \rfloor z$.

Before adding, we rearrange the products $w_i z$ as sums, by distributivity, so that each new term depends only on a b_i and on a bit of z; such a term can be computed with a symmetric gate. Similarly, each v_i can be computed with a symmetric gate. Both summations in the expression for $\lfloor t \rfloor z$ can now be computed with AC^0 of TC_2^0 circuits. Since $\lfloor 2^{-jn} \sum_{i=0}^{m} v_i \rfloor$ is bounded in poly(n), we can multiply it by z with an AC^0 circuit[4]. Therefore, computing $\lfloor t \rfloor z$ can be done with an AC^0 of TC_2^0 circuit.

---

[4] The fact that MULTIPLICATION of an n-bit number by a $O(\log n)$-bit number can be done in AC^0 is implicit in the work of Chandra, Stockmeyer and Vishkin [5]. First, reduce

Now, for all possible values of j and k, compute s, $\lfloor t \rfloor$ and $\lfloor t \rfloor y$ with AC^0 of TC_2^0 circuits. Then choose the right value for $\lfloor x/y \rfloor$ by testing $2^{j-1} \leq y < 2^j$, $0 \leq s < P$ and $x - \lfloor t \rfloor y < y$ in AC^0. $\square$

We now show how to compute $\log_b x$, with accuracy 2^{-n}, with an AC^0 of TC_2^0 circuit. Notice that b is not fixed, but given as input to the circuit.

Theorem 9. *Let b and x be n-bit input numbers such that $b > 1$. There is an AC^0 of TC_2^0 circuit that computes a number L such that $|L2^{-n} - (\log_b x)| < 2^{-n}$.*

Proof. As for DIVISION, we will use series. More precisely, we will use the fact that for all a and w, $\ln(a+w) = \ln a + \sum_{i=1}^{\infty}(-1)^{i+1}(1/i)(w/a)^i$, where the series converges if $|w/a| < 1$.

Let j be such that $2^j \leq x < 2^{j+1}$, i.e. let $j = \lfloor \log x \rfloor$. If $x < \frac{3}{2}2^j$ then let $a = 2^j$; otherwise let $a = \frac{2}{3}2^{j+1}$. In either case, we get that $1 \leq x/a < \frac{3}{2}$. Let $w = x - a$. Then $0 \leq w/a < \frac{1}{2}$ and $\ln x = \ln(a + w) = \ln a + \sum_{i=1}^{\infty}(-1)^{i+1}(1/i)(w/a)^i$.

Let $n' = n + 3 + \lceil \log n \rceil$, let A and C_i be the values of $(\ln a)2^{n'+2}$ and $(1/i)2^{n'+2}$ rounded to the nearest integer, and let $L(x) = 2^{-(n'+2)}(A + \sum_{i=1}^{n'}(-1)^{i+1}C_i(w/a)^i)$. Then, by bounding errors and by using the fact that the series alternates, we can show that $|L(x) - \ln x| < 2^{-n'-1}$. Notice that j, a and w depend on x and could have been written $j(x)$, $a(x)$ and $w(x)$, respectively. By substituting b for x, we get $|L(b) - \ln b| < 2^{-n'-1}$.

Now, consider $L(x)/L(b)$ as an approximation to $\log_b x = (\ln x)/(\ln b)$ and let $L_b(x) = \lfloor 2^{n+2}L(x)/L(b) \rfloor 2^{-n-2}$. Then, again by bounding errors, a little bit of calculation shows that $|L_b(x) - \log_b x| < 2^{-n-1}$. Let L be the value of $L_b(x)2^n$ rounded to the nearest integer. Then $|L2^{-n} - \log_b x| < 2^{-n}$.

We now have the problem of computing $L_b(x)$, for fixed values of $j(x)$ and $j(b)$. Let $v = (w/a)2^{j+2}$. We have that $L(x) = 2^{-(j+3)n'-2}s(x)$ where $s(x) = 2^{(j+2)n'}A + \sum_{i=1}^{n'}(-1)^{i+1}2^{(j+2)(n'-i)}C_iv^i$. Of course, the same holds for b. Notice that $s(x)$ and $s(b)$ are integers and that $L_b(x) = \lfloor \lfloor 2^{n+2+nn'}s(x)/s(b) \rfloor 2^{(j(b)-j(x)-n)n'} \rfloor 2^{-n-2}$. We compute $\lfloor 2^{n+2+nn'}s(x)/s(b) \rfloor$ by adapting the AC^0 of TC_2^0 circuit for DIVISION, with x replaced by $s(x)2^{n+2+nn'}$ and y replaced by $s(b)$.

This adaptation is straightforward, except maybe for the following two points. First, assuming the definitions of Theorem 8, consider the products w_iz: in the case of DIVISION, z is an input number; in our case, z is either 1 or $s(b)$. Therefore, we use Lemma 1 once more to obtain $s(b) = \sum_{k=1}^{m'} b'_k u'_k - t'P'$, where $b'_k = s(b) \bmod p_k$. Then $w_is(b) = \sum_{k=1}^{m'} w_i b'_k u'_k - w_i t'P'$, where each term can be computed with a symmetric gate. The second point concerns the multiplication of $\lfloor 2^{-jn} \sum_{i=0}^m v_i \rfloor$ by z, which, as we just mentioned, is either 1 or $s(b)$. Here, before multiplying, we simply compute $s(b)$ with an AC^0 of TC_2^0 circuit, by using Lemma 1.

The rest of the argument is similar to the one for DIVISION. $\square$

---

the multiplication to the ITERATED ADDITION of $O(\log n)$ n-bit numbers. Then, solve this new problem by using the AC^0 circuit that Chandra, Stockmeyer and Vishkin use at the top of their ITERATED ADDITION circuit.

3 Cyclic Groups and Finite Fields

In this section we generalize the problem of ITERATED MULTIPLICATION by replacing integers with elements of other multiplicative structures. In fact, we will be interested in sequences $(S_1, S_2, S_3, \ldots)$ of finite multiplicative structures where the size of S_n will be allowed to grow with n. For each of these, we get new ITERATED MULTIPLICATION and POWERING problems.

We start with sequences of cyclic groups, i.e. we let $S_n = \mathbb{Z}_q$, the cyclic group of order q, where q is a function of n. An element of $\mathbb{Z}_q$ will be given by the binary representation of a number in $\{0, \ldots, q-1\}$.

Let $ACC^0(q)$ be defined by constant-depth polynomial-size circuits constructed with NOT gates and unbounded fan-in AND, OR and MOD_q gates, i.e. gates that return 1 on input $x_1, \ldots, x_m$ iff $\sum_{i=1}^{m} x_i \equiv 0 \pmod{q}$. Then, let $ACC^0 = \bigcup_{q \geq 2} ACC^0(q)$ and let ACC_d^0 correspond to ACC^0 circuits of depth exactly d. The following lemma is similar to Lemma 5 and is proved in a similar way.

Lemma 10. *Let $p^l \leq q$ be a prime power and let $x_1, \ldots, x_n \leq q$ be input numbers. Then $\prod_{i=1}^{n} x_i \bmod p^l$ can be computed by an NC^0 of ACC_1^0 of NC^0 circuit, if $q \in O(1)$, and by a SYM of AND circuit where the bottom ANDs have $O(\log n)$ fan-in, if $q \in \text{poly}(n)$.*

Theorem 11. *Let $S_n = \mathbb{Z}_q$. Then ITERATED MULTIPLICATION can be computed*

1. *by an NC^0 of ACC_1^0 of NC^0 circuit, if $q \in O(1)$;*
2. *by an AC^0 of TC_1^0 of AND circuit where the bottom ANDs have $O(\log n)$ fan-in, if $q \in \text{poly}(n)$;*
3. *by an AC^0 of TC_3^0 circuit, if $q \in 2^{\text{poly}(n)}$.*

Also, POWERING can be computed by an AC^0 of TC_2^0 circuit, if $q \in 2^{\text{poly}(n)}$.

Proof. Case 1: $q \in O(1)$. Let $q = \prod_{i=1}^{r} q_i$ where the q_i are powers of distinct primes. Clearly, r and the q_i are bounded by a constant. By Lemma 1, we have that $(\prod_{i=1}^{n} x_i) \bmod q = (\sum_{j=1}^{r} b_j u_j) \bmod q$, where $b_j = (\prod_{i=1}^{n} x_i) \bmod q_j$. Therefore, $(\prod_{i=1}^{n} x_i) \bmod q$ can be computed in NC^0, given the bits of the b_j. The result now follows from the lemma.

Case 2: $q \in \text{poly}(n)$. We proceed in a similar fashion. Let $q = \prod_{i=1}^{r} q_i$ where the q_i are powers of distinct primes; r is bounded in $O(\log n)$ while the q_i are bounded in $\text{poly}(n)$. Again, we have that $(\prod_{i=1}^{n} x_i) \bmod q = (\sum_{j=1}^{r} b_j u_j) \bmod q$, where $b_j = (\prod_{i=1}^{n} x_i) \bmod q_j$. Given the bits of b_j, since their number is bounded in $O(\log n)$, we can compute $b_j u_j$ in AC^0. We can then sum these numbers in AC^0, since r is bounded in $O(\log n)$, by using an AC^0 circuit for the ITERATED ADDITION of $O(\log n)$ n-bit numbers. The result has only $O(\log n)$ bits, so it can be reduced modulo q in AC^0. Therefore, $(\prod_{i=1}^{n} x_i) \bmod q$ can be computed in AC^0, given the bits of the b_j. The result now follows from the lemma.

Case 3: $q \in 2^{\text{poly}(n)}$. As in the proof of Theorem 6, there is a k bounded in poly(n) such that $\prod_{i=1}^{n} x_i = \sum_{j=1}^{n^2} b_j u_j - kP$, where $b_j = \prod_{i=1}^{n} x_i \bmod p_j$. This implies that $\prod_{i=1}^{n} x_i \equiv \sum_{j=1}^{n^2} (b_j u_j \bmod q) - (kP \bmod q) \pmod{q}$, so that $\prod_{i=1}^{n} x_i \bmod q = \sum_{j=1}^{n^2} (b_j u_j \bmod q) - (kP \bmod q) - lq$, for some k and l both bounded in poly(n). Denote the right hand side of this last equation by $z_{k,l}$. In the proof of Theorem 6, it was shown that $\sum_{j=1}^{n^2} b_j u_j - kP$ can be computed by an AC^0 of TC$_3^0$ circuit, for all possible values of k. A similar argument shows that $z_{k,l}$ can be also be computed by an AC^0 of TC$_3^0$ circuit, for all the poly(n) possible values of k and l. Choosing the right answer can then be done in AC^0 by testing $0 \le \sum_{j=1}^{n^2} b_j u_j - kP < P$ and $0 \le z_{k,l} < q$.

The result for POWERING is obtained in the same way that Theorem 7 was obtained from Theorem 6. The main idea is to compute $b_j u_j$ and $(b_j u_j \bmod q)$ in SYM instead of SYM of TC$_1^0$. $\qquad\square$

We now consider sequences of finite fields: let $S_n = \mathbb{F}_{p^d}$, the finite field of order p^d, where p and d are functions of n. We will assume that when given such a sequence of finite fields we are also given a sequence of polynomials in one variable X; the nth polynomial F in this sequence has coefficients in $\mathbb{F}_p$, is of degree d and is irreducible over $\mathbb{F}_p$. Since $\mathbb{F}_{p^d}$ is isomorphic to $\mathbb{F}_p[x]/(F)$ [13], i.e. to the set of polynomials with coefficients in $\mathbb{F}_p$ modulo F, an element of $\mathbb{F}_{p^d}$ will be viewed as a congruence class of polynomials. Such a congruence class will be encoded by the unique polynomial of degree less than d that belongs to it. The encoding of this polynomial will simply be the list of its coefficients which, as before, will be encoded by the binary representation of a number in $\{0, \ldots, p-1\}$. Notice that the encoding of an element of $\mathbb{F}_{p^d}$ has length $d \log p = \log p^d$.

Theorem 12. *Let* $S_n = \mathbb{F}_{p^d}$. *Then* ITERATED MULTIPLICATION *can be computed*

1. *by an* NC^0 *of* ACC$_1^0$ *of* NC^0 *circuit, if* $p^d \in O(1)$;
2. *by a* SYM *of* AND *circuit where the bottom* ANDs *have* $O(\log n)$ *fan-in, if* $p^d \in$ poly(n);
3. *by an* AC^0 *of* TC$_3^0$ *circuit, if* $p^d \in 2^{\text{poly}(n)}$.

Also, POWERING *can be computed by an* AC^0 *of* TC$_2^0$ *circuit, if* $p^d \in 2^{\text{poly}(n)}$.

Proof. Case 1: $p^d \in O(1)$. We are given $F_1, \ldots, F_n \in \mathbb{F}_p[x]$ of degree less than d. Notice that these polynomials have encodings of length $\log p^d \in O(1)$. Since $\mathbb{F}_{p^d}$ is a field, $\mathbb{F}_{p^d}^*$, the set of non-zero elements of $\mathbb{F}_{p^d}$, is a cyclic group of order $p^d - 1$, with respect to multiplication modulo F. Let G be a generator of $\mathbb{F}_{p^d}^*$. Let $a_i < p^d - 1$ be such that $G^{a_i} \bmod F = F_i$, and let $a = (\sum_{i=1}^{n} a_i) \bmod (p^d - 1)$. Then, $(\prod_{i=1}^{n} F_i) \equiv G^a \pmod{F}$. The value of a is determined by $[\sum_{i=1}^{n} a_i - k \equiv 0 \pmod{p^d - 1}]$ for $k = 0, \ldots, p^d - 2$, which we can compute with a MOD$_{p^d-1}$ gate of ANDs of constant fan-in. This means that the value of $(\prod_{i=1}^{n} F_i) \bmod F$ depends on the output of a constant number of MOD$_{p^d-1}$ gates, hence the result.

Case 2: $p^d \in$ poly(n). Similar to the previous case.

Case 3: $p^d \in 2^{\text{poly}(n)}$. Let $F_i = \sum_{j=0}^{d-1} f_{ij} X^j$, where $f_{ij} \in \{0, \ldots, p-1\}$. Then $\prod_{i=1}^{n} F_i = \sum_{k=0}^{n(d-1)} h_k X^k$, with $h_k = \sum_{j_1 + \cdots + j_n = k} f_{1j_1} \cdots f_{nj_n}$, and $(\prod_{i=1}^{n} F_i) \bmod F = \sum_{k=0}^{n(d-1)} h_k (X^k \bmod F)$. For every k, let $X^k \bmod F = \sum_{l=0}^{d-1} g_{kl} X^l$, where $g_{kl} \in \{0, \ldots, p-1\}$. Then $(\prod_{i=1}^{n} F_i) \bmod F = \sum_{l=0}^{d-1} (g_l \bmod p) X^l$, where $g_l = \sum_{k=0}^{n(d-1)} h_k g_{kl}$.

Let s be the smallest power of 2 greater than $n(dp)^{n+1}$. Notice that $g_l < s$. For $i = 1, \ldots, n$, let $x_i = \sum_{j=0}^{d-1} f_{ij} s^j$ and let $y_l = \sum_{j=0}^{n(d-1)} g_{(n(d-1)-j)l} s^j$. These numbers can be computed without any gates since all the coefficients involved are less than s. We have that $(\prod_{i=1}^{n} x_i) y_l = (\sum_{k=0}^{n(d-1)} h_k s^k) \sum_{j=0}^{n(d-1)} g_{(n(d-1)-j)l} s^j = \sum_{i=0}^{2n(d-1)} (\sum_{k+j=i} h_k g_{(n(d-1)-j)l}) s^i$. Notice that the coefficient of $s^{n(d-1)}$ in the last expression is g_l. Since g_l is less than s, it can be simply read off the binary representation of $(\prod_{i=1}^{n} x_i) y_l$, which means that g_l can be computed with an AC^0 of TC_3^0 circuit.

To compute $g_l \bmod p$, let us take a closer look at the computation of $(\prod_{i=1}^{n} x_i) y_l$. As in the proof of Theorem 6, we have that $(\prod_{i=1}^{n} x_i) y_l = \sum_{j=1}^{(n+1)^2} b_j u_j - lP$, for some l bounded in $\text{poly}(n)$. Let $w_j = b_j u_j$, for $j = 1, \ldots, n$, and let $w_0 = -lP$; then $(\prod_{i=1}^{n} x_i) y_l = \sum_{j=0}^{(n+1)^2} w_j$. We know that w_j can be computed with a SYM of TC_1^0 circuit. Now, let $w_{j2} = w_j \text{ div } s^{n(d-1)+1}$, $w_{j1} = (w_j \text{ div } s^{n(d-1)}) \bmod s$ and $w_{j0} = w_j \bmod s^{n(d-1)}$, and let $z_k = \sum_{j=0}^{(n+1)^2} w_{jk}$, for $k = 0, 1, 2$. A little bit of calculation shows that $g_l \bmod p = (z_1 \bmod p + (z_0 \text{ div } s^{n(d-1)}) \bmod p - (((z_1 s^{n(d-1)} + z_0) \text{ div } s^{n(d-1)+1}) s) \bmod p) \bmod p$. The summations z_0 and z_1 in the second and third terms can be done in AC^0 of TC_3^0. On the other hand, we compute $z_1 \bmod p$ directly by using the idea in the proof of Lemma 2; this can also be done in AC^0 of TC_3^0. The remaining reductions can be done in AC^0 because of the small size of the numbers involved. Therefore, when computing $(\prod_{i=1}^{n} x_i) y_l$, compute, for every possible value of l, the value of $\sum_{j=1}^{(n+1)^2} b_j u_j - lP$, and the value of $g_l \bmod p$. All this can be done in AC^0 of TC_3^0. Choosing the right value for $g_l \bmod p$ is done in AC^0 by testing $\sum_{j=1}^{(n+1)^2} w_j < P$.

Once again, the result for POWERING is obtained in the same way that Theorem 7 was obtained from Theorem 6. This means that we compute w_j in SYM instead of SYM of TC_1^0. $\square$

4 Circuits of Quasipolynomial Size

In recent years, much work has been done to obtain characterizations of AC^0 and ACC^0 in terms of small depth threshold circuits of quasipolynomial size. For example, Beigel, Reingold and Spielman [3] and Tarui [16] have shown that every AC^0 function can be computed as the sum of $n^{\text{polylog}(n)}$ probabilistic ANDs of fan-in $\text{polylog}(n)$, and Beigel and Tarui [4] have shown that every ACC^0 function can be computed by a symmetric gate of $n^{\text{polylog}(n)}$ ANDs of $\text{polylog}(n)$ fan-in. In this section, we will show that similar results hold for $\widehat{TC}_d^0$. (For more on quasipolynomial size circuits, we refer the reader to the survey article of Barrington [1].)

First, some notation. If $\mathcal{C}$ is a circuit complexity class, we denote by $q\mathcal{C}$ the class defined by $\mathcal{C}$ circuits of quasipolynomial size, by $\mathcal{C}^+$ the class defined by circuits of the form $\mathcal{C}$ of ANDs of polylog(n) fan-in; and by prob $q\mathcal{C}$ the class defined by probabilistic $\mathcal{C}$ circuits of quasipolynomial size that use polylog(n) probabilistic bits and compute with error $1/n^{\text{polylog}(n)}$. The above mentioned results can now be stated as $\text{AC}^0 \subseteq \text{prob } q\Sigma^+$ and $\text{ACC}^0 \subseteq \text{qSYM}^+$. In fact, we also have that $\text{qAC}^0 \subseteq \text{prob } q\Sigma^+$ and $q(\text{SYM of ACC}^0) = \text{qSYM}^+$ [3, 16, 4].

We will need the following two extensions of earlier lemmas, which are proved with basically the same arguments.

Lemma 13. *Let x be an n-bit input and suppose that $f(x) = h(s_1, \ldots, s_m)$, where $m \in \text{polylog}(n)$ and $s_i = \sum_{j=1}^n a_{i,j} x_j$ with the $a_{i,j}$ bounded in $n^{\text{polylog}(n)}$. Then $f \in \text{qSYM}$.*

Lemma 14. *If $f \in \text{qSYM}$, then f can be computed by a qTC_2^0 circuit with the property that for some $t \in n^{\text{polylog}(n)}$, (i) when $f(x) = 0$, then exactly t bottom threshold gates output 1, and (ii) when $f(x) = 1$, then exactly $t+1$ bottom threshold gates output 1.*

Theorem 15. *For any d,*

$$\text{q}\widehat{\text{TC}}_d^0 \subseteq \text{prob } \text{q}(\Sigma \text{ of } \text{TC}_d^0)^+ \subseteq \text{q}(\text{SYM of } \text{TC}_d^0)^+ \subseteq \text{q}(\text{TC}_{d+2}^0)^+.$$

Proof. By definition, $\text{q}\widehat{\text{TC}}_d^0 \subseteq \text{qAC}^0$ of $(\text{qTC}_1^0$ of $\text{qAC}^0)^d$. Since $\text{qTC}_1^0 \subseteq \text{qSYM}$ and since $\text{q}(\text{SYM of ACC}^0) \subseteq \text{qSYM}^+$, we have that $\text{q}\widehat{\text{TC}}_d^0 \subseteq \text{qAC}^0$ of $(\text{qSYM}^+)^d$. By using the previous lemmas, we get $\text{q}\widehat{\text{TC}}_d^0 \subseteq \text{qAC}^0$ of $((\text{qSYM})^d)^+ \subseteq \text{q}(\text{AC}^0 \text{ of } \text{TC}_d^0)^+$. Now, using the fact that $\text{qAC}^0 \subseteq \text{prob } q\Sigma^+$, we get $\text{q}\widehat{\text{TC}}_d^0 \subseteq \text{prob } \text{q}(\Sigma^+ \text{ of } \text{TC}_d^0)^+ \subseteq \text{prob } \text{q}(\Sigma \text{ of } \text{TC}_d^0)^+$.

To make these circuits deterministic, we use the technique described by Beigel and Tarui in [4] to obtain $\text{q}\widehat{\text{TC}}_d^0 \subseteq \text{q}(\text{SYM of } \text{TC}_d^0)^+$. □

This characterization enables us to translate lower bounds for the usual TC_d^0 classes into lower bounds for $\text{q}\widehat{\text{TC}}_d^0$. For example, a lower bound for prob $(\text{qTC}_2^0)^+$ implies a lower bound for $\text{q}\widehat{\text{TC}}_1^0$. With the same kind of argument that was used in the proof of the theorem, we can also show the following:

Corollary 16. *For any $d \geq 1$.*

1. $\text{q}(\text{SYM of ACC}^0)^{d-1}$ of $\text{qSYM} = \text{q}(\text{SYM of } \text{TC}_{d-1}^0)$
2. $\text{q}(\text{TC}_1^0 \text{ of } \text{AC}^0 \text{ of } \text{TC}_{d-1}^0) \subseteq \text{prob } \text{qTC}_d^0$
3. $\text{q}(\text{AC}^0 \text{ of } \text{TC}_{d-1}^0) \subseteq \text{prob } \text{q}(\Sigma \text{ of } \text{TC}_{d-1}^0)$

Let $\text{MAJ}^{(2)}$ be the canonical TC_2^0 function[5]. In [4], Beigel and Tarui show that if $\text{MAJ}^{(2)} \in \text{qSYM}^+$, then $\text{qTC}^0 \subseteq \text{qSYM}^+$ ($\subseteq \text{qTC}_3^0$). By a similar argument, we can show that the same holds for $\text{q}\widehat{\text{TC}}_1^0$:

Theorem 17. *If $\text{MAJ}^{(2)} \in \text{q}\widehat{\text{TC}}_1^0$, then $\text{qTC}^0 \subseteq \text{q}\widehat{\text{TC}}_1^0$ ($\subseteq \text{qTC}_4^0$).*

---

[5] $\text{MAJ}^{(2)}(x_1, \ldots, x_n) = \text{MAJ}(M_1, \ldots, M_{\sqrt{n}})$, where $M_i = \text{MAJ}(x_{(i-1)\sqrt{n}+1}, \ldots, x_{i\sqrt{n}})$.

Proof. By induction on d, we prove that $qTC_d^0 \subseteq q\widehat{TC}_1^0$. If $d = 1$, there is nothing to prove, and if $d = 2$, the result is immediate. Assume that $d \geq 3$ and that $qTC_{d-1}^0 \subseteq q\widehat{TC}_1^0$, and consider a qTC_d^0 circuit. By replacing the top two levels of the circuit by a $q\widehat{TC}_1^0$ circuit, we obtain a $q(AC^0$ of TC_1^0 of AC^0 of $TC_{d-2}^0)$ circuit that we can transform into a $q(AC^0$ of $TC_{d-1}^0)$ circuit. The result now follows from the induction hypothesis. $\square$

References

1. Barrington, D.A.M.: Quasipolynomial size circuit classes. In *Proc. of the 7th Ann. Conf. on Structure in Complexity Theory*, 1992, 86–93
2. Beame, P.W., Cook, S.A., Hoover, H.J.: Log depth circuits for division and related problems. *SIAM J. on Computing* 15:4 (1986) 994–1003
3. Beigel, R., Reingold, N., Spielman, D.: The Perceptron strikes back. In *Proc. of the 6th Ann. Conf. on Structure in Complexity Theory*, 1991, 286–291
4. Beigel, R., Tarui, J.: On ACC. In *Proc. of the 32th Ann. IEEE Symp. on Foundations of Computer Sc.*, 1991, 783–792
5. Chandra, A.K., Stockmeyer, L., Vishkin, U.: Constant depth reducibility. *SIAM J. on Computing* 13:2 (1984) 423–439
6. Fagin, R., Klawe, M., Pippenger, N.J., Stockmeyer, L.: Bounded-depth polynomial-size circuits for symmetric functions. *Theoretical Computer Sc.* 36 (1985) 239–250
7. Goldmann, M., Håstad, J., Razborov, A.: Majority gates vs. general weighted threshold gates. In *Proc. of the 7th Ann. Conference on Structure in Complexity Theory*, 1992, 2–13. To appear in *Computational Complexity*.
8. Goldmann, M., Karpinski, M.: Simulating threshold circuits by majority circuits. Manuscript, 1992.
9. Hajnal, A., Maass, W., Pudlák, P., Szegedy, M., Turán, G.: Threshold circuits of bounded depth. In *Proc. of the 28th Ann. IEEE Symp. on Foundations of Computer Sc.*, 1987, 99–110
10. Hofmeister, T., Hohberg, W., Köhling, S.: Some notes on threshold circuits, and multiplication in depth 4. *Information Processing Letters* 39 (1991) 219–225
11. Immerman, N., Landau, S.: The complexity of iterated multiplication. In *Proc. of the 4th Ann. Conference on Structure in Complexity Theory*, 1989, 104–111
12. Ireland, K., Rosen, M.: *A Classical Introduction to Modern Number Theory*, 2nd ed., (Grad. Texts in Math., 84) Springer-Verlag, 1990
13. Lidl, R., Niederreiter, H.: *Finite Fields*, (Enc. of Math. and its App., 20) Addison-Wesley, 1983
14. Reif, J.H.: On threshold circuits and polynomial computation. In *Proc. of the 2nd Ann. Conference on Structure in Complexity Theory*, 1987, 118–123
15. Siu, K.-Y., Roychowdhury, V.: On optimal depth threshold circuits for multiplication and related problems. Manuscript, 1992. To appear in *SIAM J. on Discrete Math.*.
16. Tarui, J.: Randomized polynomials, threshold circuits, and the polynomial hierarchy. In *Proc. of the 8th Ann. Symp. on Theoretical Aspects of Computer Sc.*, (LNCS, 480) Springer-Verlag, 1991, 238–250. To appear in *Theoretical Computer Sc.* under the title: Probabilistic polynomials, AC^0 functions, and the polynomial-time hierarchy.
17. Yao, A.C.-C.: Separating the polynomial-time hierarchy by oracles. In *Proc. of the 26th Ann. IEEE Symp. on Foundations of Computer Sc.*, 1985, 1–10

Circuits with monoidal gates

(EXTENDED ABSTRACT)

Martin Beaudry [*]   Pierre McKenzie [†]   Pierre Péladeau [‡]
Univ. de Sherbrooke   Univ. de Montréal   Univ. Paris 6

Abstract. The problem of evaluating a circuit whose wires carry values from a fixed finite monoid M and whose non-input gates perform the monoid's operation is a natural extension to the well studied word problem over M, known to characterize NC^1 and most of its subclasses in terms of the algebraic properties of M [2, 5, 4, 18]. Here we investigate the circuit evaluation problem over M. We show that the case of any nonsolvable monoid is P-complete, while circuits over solvable monoids can be evaluated in $DET \subseteq NC^2$. We completely elucidate the case of the aperiodic monoids, which either lies in AC^0, or is L-complete, or is NL-complete. Finally, we show that the case of the cyclic group $\mathbb{Z}_q$, for fixed $q \geq 2$, is complete for the logspace counting class $co\text{-}MOD_q L$.

1 Introduction

Fix a finite monoid M, that is, a finite set with an associative binary operation for which an element of the set acts as an identity. Define a *circuit over M* as a circuit whose inputs are elements of M and whose gates perform the monoid's operation. What is the complexity of $CEP(M)$, i.e. the Circuit Evaluation Problem over the monoid M?

Problem $CEP(M)$ can be thought of as a generalization of the *word problem* over M; it is thus particularly interesting in view of the role played by word problems over monoids in the algebraic characterization of NC^1 and its subclasses [2, 5, 4, 18]. In this paper, we characterize the complexity of $CEP(M)$ as a function of the algebraic properties of M. Our results suggest that in a strong sense, circuit evaluation problems over monoids are to the complexity class P what word problems over monoids are to the complexity class NC^1.

---

[*]Dép. de mathématiques et d'informatique, Université de Sherbrooke, Sherbrooke (Québec), J1K 2R1 Canada. Work supported by NSERC grant OGP0089786 and FCAR grants 92-NC-0608 and 91-ER-0642.

[†]Dép. d'informatique et recherche opérationnelle, Université de Montréal, C.P. 6128, Succursale A, Montréal (Québec), H3C 3J7 Canada. Work supported by NSERC grant OGP0009979 and by FCAR grant 91-ER-0642.

[‡]Laboratoire Informatique Théorique et Programmation, Institut Blaise Pascal, Université Paris 6, 4, place Jussieu, 75253 Paris, France.

Our first observation is that having a single associative operator does not simplify the task of evaluating a circuit. More precisely, CEP(M) remains difficult, namely P-complete, whenever M is a nonsolvable monoid, i.e. includes a subset which forms a nonsolvable group. A similar situation had been encountered before: the word problem over a fixed monoid M is complete for the complexity class NC^1 if M is nonsolvable [2], and believed to be contained in a proper subclass of NC^1 otherwise [5].

What happens when M is solvable? The complexity of CEP(M) then apparently drops significantly. Indeed we prove that CEP(M) then belongs to DET, a subclass of NC^2 defined as the closure of the integer determinant problem under NC^1 (Turing) reducibility [12].

In the absence of groups altogether, we completely elucidate the complexity of CEP(M), assuming that the classes L and NL are distinct. Indeed let M be an aperiodic monoid, i.e. a monoid none of whose subsets forms a non-trivial group. If M is commutative and idempotent, then CEP(M) $\in AC^0$. Else, if the threshold of M exceeds 1 and if every idempotent of M commutes with each element of M, then CEP(M) is L-complete. Otherwise, CEP(M) is NL-complete. (Terms used in this paragraph are defined in a later section.)

Finally, write $\mathbb{Z}_q$ for the cyclic group of order $q \geq 2$. We prove that CEP($\mathbb{Z}_q$) is co-$MOD_q L$-complete, where $MOD_q L$ is the set of languages Y for which some nondeterministic logspace Turing machine N satisfies the property that $x \in Y$ iff the number of accepting paths of N on input x is not divisible by q [10].

Section 2 in this abstract gives preliminaries, including a result on relativized logspace counting classes which is used in the main section. Section 3 presents the minimal background on monoids required for the sequel. The main section is Section 4, which discusses the complexity of CEP(M). Section 5 concludes with a discussion and suggestions for further work.

Due to space limitation, some proofs are omitted from this abstract and others were trimmed down to a bare minimum. Details and expanded arguments will appear in the full paper.

2 Preliminaries and definitions

Unless otherwise specified, the input circuit in a CEP(M) instance is described solely by a variant of its direct connection language (see [11]). Since the operation performed at a gate is in general noncommutative, we add the condition that the tuples encoding the connections between a node and its inputs be numbered in a manner consistent with the order of evaluation at that node. Notice that we do not restrict the indegree of the nodes. Also, for nodes of indegree one, we take the convention that they output their input value, unmodified.

We assume familiarity with NP, P, NL, L, and with AC^0 and NC^k in their uniform settings. The precise choice of uniformity will not matter, but for definiteness we adopt $DLOGTIME$ uniformity for AC^0 [3] and U_{E^*} uniformity for

NC^k [20, 12]. The class DET is defined as the closure of the integer determinant problem under NC^1 (Turing) reducibility [12]:

$$AC^0 \subset NC^1 \subseteq L \subseteq NL \subseteq DET \subseteq NC^2 \subseteq P.$$

In general, we let the context distinguish between classes of languages and classes of functions, for example between L and the class FL of functions computed in logspace. Throughout this paper, we will say that language A "NC^1-reduces" to language B, written $A \leq_m^{NC^1} B$, iff A many-one reduces to B via an NC^1-computable function.

Let $t \geq 0$ and $q \geq 1$ be natural numbers. Define the $\theta_{t,q}$ relation on $\mathbb{N}$ as follows: $i \, \theta_{t,q} \, j$ iff $[(i = j) \vee ((i \geq t) \wedge (j \geq t))] \wedge [i \equiv j \pmod{q}]$. The $\theta_{t,q}$ relations have algebraic significance because they are the only equivalence relations on $\mathbb{N}$ which are in fact finite index congruences. Let $MOD_{t,q}L$ denote the set of languages Y such that, for some $i \in \mathbb{N}$ and some nondeterministic logspace Turing machine M, the following holds for each input x: $x \notin Y$ iff $i \, \theta_{t,q} \, |\text{ACCEPT}(M, x)|$, where $\text{ACCEPT}(M, x)$ denotes the set of accepting paths of M on input x. Observe that $MOD_{0,q}L$ is exactly the class MOD_qL as defined in [10]; this is because, as noted in [10, 7], for any i, a logspace nondeterministic machine M' can be constructed from a logspace nondeterministic machine M to satisfy, modulo q and for each x, $i \equiv |\text{ACCEPT}(M, x)|$ iff $0 \equiv |\text{ACCEPT}(M', x)|$. Observe further that $MOD_{1,1}L = NL \cup co\text{-}NL = NL$ [24, 15].

In order to analyze the complexity of problems $\text{CEP}(M)$ in the case of solvable monoids, it will be convenient to first obtain a structural complexity result which is of independent interest (Theorem 2.1 below). This result deals with relativized counting classes and requires a suitable definition of relativized space. Here we borrow the definition proposed by Ruzzo, Simon and Tompa [21]:

Definition. Space-bounded oracle machine model: Define M^A as the language recognized by a (possibly nondeterministic) machine M using oracle A in the following controlled manner: M has a write-only query tape not subject to a space bound, and operates deterministically from the time some symbol is written onto the tape until the time the next oracle query is made, after which the query tape is immediately erased. □

As pointed out in [21, Lemma 7], a language Y belongs to M^A for a logspace bounded machine M iff Y is logspace Turing reducible to some B (using queries which *are* subject to the space bound) and B is many-one reducible to A via a logspace transducer also having access to M's input.

When C is a complexity class and D is a set of languages, C^D represents the set of languages M^A such that M is a machine obeying the resource bounds associated with C and $A \in D$.

Theorem 2.1 $(MOD_{t,q}L)^{DET} \subseteq DET$ and $(co\text{-}MOD_{t,q}L)^{DET} \subseteq DET$, for any $t \geq 0$ and any $q \geq 1$.

Proof. We use an argument which is similar to the one used in [10] to prove that $L^{\#L} \subseteq DET$. Details are omitted here. □

3 Background on monoids and languages

Recall that a monoid is a set equipped with an associative binary operation and an identity for this operation. We will use M to denote both a finite monoid and its underlying set, and represent the monoid operation as a concatenation (i.e. the product of $a \in M$ and $b \in M$ will be denoted ab).

Let A be a finite set or *alphabet*. We write A^* for the *free monoid* over A with catenation as operation and the empty word as identity. Given a monoid M, let $\phi : M^* \to M$ be the canonical morphism. We will call a *word problem* of M any set or *language* of the form $Q\phi^{-1}$, where $Q \subseteq M$.

We write $\mathbb{Z}_q$ for the cyclic group modulo q and $C_{t,q}$ for the monoid performing addition modulo $\theta_{t,q}$ on the set $\{0, 1, \ldots, t + q - 1\}$. In particular, the operation of monoid $C_{1,1} = \{0, 1\}$ corresponds to the Boolean OR.

The *reverse* of a monoid M has the same underlying set as M but its operation is read in reverse order, i.e. evaluating abc in the reverse of M is equivalent to evaluating cba in M.

Except in the cases of $\mathbb{Z}_p$ and $C_{t,q}$ as above, we use 1 and 0 to denote the monoid identity and the universally absorbing element, when the latter is present.

It is extremely useful to classify monoids according to their algebraic complexity, and the tool to do this is the *variety*. A variety of monoids is a set of monoids which is closed under *division* (a monoid M divides a monoid T iff M is a homomorphic image of a submonoid of T) and finite direct products. See [14] and [19] for references on this subject.

Varieties of monoids explicitly mentioned in this paper are: the set of all *solvable* monoids, i.e. from which the only simple groups which can be obtained are cyclic; the set of all *aperiodic* (i.e. group-free) monoids, which is denoted by **A**; the smallest non-trivial aperiodic variety, denoted $\mathbf{J}_1$, which consists of all idempotent and commutative monoids; its superset the variety **J** of *J-trivial* monoids, and consisting of all monoids M such that for each $m, n \in M$ if $MmM = MnM$ then $m = n$ (see [19]); the variety $\mathbf{M_{nil}}$ of the *idempotent central* monoids, which contains $\mathbf{J}_1$ and is contained in **J**, and consists of those monoids M such that for all $e, m \in M$, if $e^2 = e$ then $em = me$ [23].

The above aperiodic varieties share the property that there is a finite set of *minimal monoids* outside them, namely a set of aperiodic monoids such that any monoid outside of the variety is divided by at least one of the monoids in the minimal set. For example $T_2 = \{1, a, a^2\}$ is the smallest J-trivial monoid outside of $\mathbf{J}_1$. The monoid $BA_2 = \{1, a, b, ab, ba, 0\}$ with operation satisfying $aa = bb = 0$, $aba = a$ and $bab = b$, along with monoid $R_1 = \{1, a, b\}$ with operation satisfying $aa = ba = a$ and $ab = bb = b$, and its reverse L_1 are the minimal aperiodic monoids which are not J-trivial. Also, $C_{1,1}$ is the minimal nontrivial aperiodic monoid. To our knowledge the minimal monoids outside of $\mathbf{M_{nil}}$ had not been identified until now.

Let $M_1 = \{1, a, b, 0\}$ be the monoid such that $aa = a$, $ba = bb = b$, and $ab = 0$; define also monoid $M_2 = \{1, a, b, 0\}$ to be such that $aa = a$, $ba = b$, and $ab = bb = 0$.

Lemma 3.1 R_1, M_1, M_2, and their reverses, along with BA_2 are the minimal aperiodic monoids outside of $\mathbf{M_{nil}}$.

Proof. Recall that $\mathbf{M_{nil}} \subset \mathbf{J}$. Our proof is based on the following property: any J-trivial monoid not in $\mathbf{M_{nil}}$ must contain a chain of the form $1 >_J a >_J b >_J 0$ (where $a >_J b$ iff $MaM \supset MbM$) with at least one of a or b being idempotent. We then only need to list all the four-element monoids satisfying this property and verify that only M_1, M_2 and their reverses are not in $\mathbf{M_{nil}}$. $\quad\square$

Another way to look at monoids is through the languages they recognize (via morphisms). A language $Y \subseteq A^*$ is *recognized* by a monoid M iff Y is the inverse image of a subset of M under some homomorphism from A^* to M. Straubing [23] identified the languages recognized by the idempotent central monoids.

Lemma 3.2 *A language* $Y \subseteq A^*$ *is recognized by a monoid in* $\mathbf{M_{nil}}$ *iff it is a Boolean combination of languages of the form* $B^* a_1 B^* a_2 \cdots B^* a_k B^*$ *where* $a_1, \ldots, a_k \in A$ *and* $B = A - \{a_1, \ldots, a_k\}$.

Note that in the above statement the a_i are not assumed to be distinct.

At the other end of the spectrum, Straubing [22] and Thérien [25] have developed a useful parametrization of the languages recognized by solvable monoids. We borrow verbatim from [5] the following description of this parametrization. Recall the $\theta_{t,q}$ congruences defined in Section 2. For any languages $L_0, L_1 \subseteq A^*$, define the languages $[L_0, a, L_1, i]_{t,q}$, $0 \le i < t+q$, to be all those words x having j distinct factorizations of the form $x = x_0 a x_1$ where $x_0 \in L_0$, $x_1 \in L_1$, and $i\,\theta_{t,q}\,j$.

If $\mathcal{L}$ is a family of languages over an alphabet A, let $\langle \mathcal{L} \rangle$ denote its Boolean closure. For each $t \ge 0$ and $q \ge 1$, define a hierarchy of families $\mathcal{M}_{t,q}^k$ by $\mathcal{M}_{t,q}^0 = \langle A^* \rangle$; and for $k > 0$, $\mathcal{M}_{t,q}^k = \langle \{[L_0, a, L_1, i]_{t,q} : L_0, L_1 \in \mathcal{M}_{t,q}^{k-1}, i \in \mathbb{N}\} \rangle$. The following results can be found in [25].

Lemma 3.3 *a) A language* Y *is recognizable by a finite aperiodic monoid iff* Y *is in* $\mathcal{M}_{t,1}^k$ *for some* $k, t \ge 0$ *iff* Y *is in* $\mathcal{M}_{1,1}^k$ *for some* $k \ge 0$.
b) A language Y *is recognizable by a finite solvable group iff* Y *is in* $\mathcal{M}_{0,q}^k$ *for some* $k \ge 0$, $q \ge 1$.
c) A language Y *is recognizable by a finite solvable monoid iff* Y *is in* $\mathcal{M}_{t,q}^k$ *for some* $k, t \ge 0$, $q \ge 1$ *iff* Y *is in* $\mathcal{M}_{1,q}^k$ *for some* $k \ge 0$, $q \ge 1$.

A byproduct of these properties is that given a finite solvable monoid M, one can find parameters k, t, and q such that every word problem of M lies in $\mathcal{M}_{t,q}^k$; in fact given any $Q \subseteq M$, one can actually compute an expression that represents $Q\phi^{-1}$ using A^* and the letters of A, with the operation $L_0, a, L_1, i \to [L_0, a, L_1, i]_{t,q}$ and the Boolean operations.

4 Complexity of circuit problems

This section contains all our upper bounds and hardness results on the complexity of CEP(M). For the purpose of our discussion, we also work in terms of the unconnected variant of this problem, where we lift the assumptions that the specified output node be the unique node of outdegree zero, and that it be accessible from all other nodes in the graph. We denote this variant by UCEP(M). As it will turn out, CEP(M) and UCEP(M) have identical complexities, except in the case of the aperiodic monoids, which is treated in subsection 4.2.

4.1 The impact of solvability

In this subsection we exhibit a significant gap in complexity for problem CEP(M), depending on whether the monoid is solvable or not (within the hypothesis that $NC^2 \neq P$), a pattern analogous to the one encountered with the word problem. We prove that CEP(M) and UCEP(M) are P-complete under $\leq_m^{NC^1}$ reducibility if M is nonsolvable, and belong to DET and hence to NC^2, otherwise.

Theorem 4.1 *If M contains a nonsolvable group, then* CEP(M) *is P-complete.*

Proof. Membership in P is obvious. To prove hardness we adapt Barrington's simulation of the Boolean operations AND, OR and NOT by products within the alternating group $\mathcal{A}_5$ [2, Theorem 1]. The generalization to the case of any nonsolvable group follows as in [2, Theorem 5]. (Alternatively, Y. Zalcstein pointed out that a construction related to Barrington's had been investigated independently by Bergman and others [9].) Details are omitted here. □

Extending the above to circuits with restricted depth, we obtain the following.

Corollary 4.2 *If M is any nonsolvable monoid, and $k \geq 0$, then problem* CEP(M) *restricted to depth-$O(\log^k n)$ circuits is complete for NC^{k+1}.* □

Theorem 4.3 *If M is a solvable monoid then* CEP(M) *belongs to DET.*

Proof. By Lemma 3.3 c), there exist $t \geq 0$, $q \geq 1$ and $k \geq 0$ such that $m\phi^{-1}$ belongs to $\mathcal{M}_{t,q}^k$ for each $m \in M$. We construct an algorithm by induction on k to solve in DET any instance of CEP(M) (we actually solve the more general problem UCEP(M)).

The case $k = 0$ is clear because then $x\phi^{-1} = M^*$ or $x\phi^{-1} = \emptyset$, for any $x \in M$.

Now for the induction step. Determining whether a given circuit evaluates to a target element x amounts to testing if the exponential size word W, obtained by "unravelling" the circuit, belongs to the language $x\phi^{-1}$. Recall that $x\phi^{-1}$ is expressible as a Boolean combination of languages $[L_0, a, L_1, i]_{t,q}$ with $L_0, L_1 \in \mathcal{M}_{t,q}^{k-1}$. Thus it suffices to give an algorithm for the language $[L_0, a, L_1, i]_{t,q}$.

Let M_0 and M_1 be the syntactic monoids of L_0 and L_1 with accepting sets $B_0 \subseteq M_0$ and $B_1 \subseteq M_1$. Denote the monoid operations by $*_0$ and $*_1$ respectively. The following algorithm tests for membership of W in $[L_0, a, L_1, i]_{t,q}$.

(Remark that the algorithm works on a circuit with indegree-two gates, which can be obtained from an arbitrary circuit through a logspace transduction.)

- Let w, u, and v be pointers to the output node and to its left and right children, respectively.
- Let $x_0 = 1$ and $x_1 = 1$.
- *Repeat* until w has indegree zero:
  - Nondeterministically pick a child of w.
  - *If* this is v (the right child), *then* do
    - Evaluate the subcircuit rooted at node u as if it were on monoid M_0. Denote by y the value thus obtained.
    - Let $x_0 = x_0 *_0 y$. Let $w = v$ and update u and v.
  - *If* this is u (the left child), *then* do
    - Evaluate the subcircuit rooted at node v as if it were on monoid M_1. Denote by y the value thus obtained.
    - Let $x_1 = y *_1 x_1$. Let $w = u$ and update u and v.
- *If* w carries input value a *and* $x_0 \in B_0$ *and* $x_1 \in B_1$, *then* accept; *else* reject.

If N is the number of accepting computations of the above algorithm, then $W \in [L_0, a, L_1, i]_{t,q}$ iff $i\, \theta_{t,q}\, N$. Since the subcircuit evaluations are instances of $\mathrm{UCEP}(M_0)$ and $\mathrm{UCEP}(M_1)$, by induction the algorithm puts the test for membership of W in $[L_0, a, L_1, i]_{t,q}$ in $(co\text{-}MOD_{t,q}L)^{DET} \subseteq DET$. $\qquad\square$

We now apply the algorithm to two special cases of solvable monoids.

Corollary 4.4 *If M is an aperiodic monoid then* $\mathrm{CEP}(M)$ *belongs to* NL.

Proof. By Lemma 3.3 a), the language $x\phi^{-1}$ to be tested for belongs to $\mathcal{M}_{1,1}^k$. Thus the analysis gives an inductive step complexity in NL^{NL}, and the result follows from the fact that $NL^{NL} = NL$ [15, 24]. $\qquad\square$

Corollary 4.5 *Let M be the cyclic group $\mathbb{Z}_q$. Then problem* $\mathrm{CEP}(M)$ *belongs to* $co\text{-}MOD_q L$.

Proof. This is a special case where the languages to be tested for with the above algorithm belong to $\mathcal{M}_{0,q}^1$, so that the recursive calls require no computation at all. Thus testing whether the circuit evaluates to a given target value reduces to testing whether the number of paths between two given nodes in an acyclic directed graph is congruent to 0 modulo q; this "zero mod-q accessibility problem" is $co\text{-}MOD_q L$-complete [10]. $\qquad\square$

Lemma 4.6 *Let $q \geq 2$. If M contains an element of period q, then $\mathrm{CEP}(M)$ is hard for co-$MOD_q L$ under $\leq_m^{NC^1}$ reducibility.*

Proof. It suffices to show that $\mathrm{CEP}(\mathbb{Z}_q)$ is hard for co-$MOD_q L$. We reduce the problem of determining whether the number of paths from u (of indegree zero) to v (of outdegree zero) in an acyclic directed graph is a multiple of q [10], to the evaluation of the circuit built from this graph by assigning 1 to u and 0 to any other indegree zero node, labeling the other nodes with the addition in $\mathbb{Z}_q$, and for each node $w \neq v$ of outdegree zero, adding a gadget connecting w to node v through exactly q distinct paths. Then the number of paths from u to v in the original graph is a multiple of q iff circuit node v outputs value 0. □

Theorem 4.7 *For $q \geq 2$ a fixed integer, problem $\mathrm{CEP}(\mathbb{Z}_q)$ is co-$MOD_q L$-complete under $\leq_m^{NC^1}$ reducibility.* □

4.2 The aperiodic case

In this section, we discuss the computational complexity of problems $\mathrm{CEP}(M)$ and $\mathrm{UCEP}(M)$ when M is aperiodic. This is the case in which the two variants have different complexities. We first discuss problem $\mathrm{CEP}(M)$, for which we obtain the following striking result:

Theorem 4.8 *Let M be an aperiodic monoid. Then exactly three cases arise:*
* *If M belongs to variety $\mathbf{J_1}$, then $\mathrm{CEP}(M)$ is in AC^0. (Lemma 4.9)*
* *If M belongs to variety $\mathbf{M_{nil}}$ and is of threshold 2 or more, then $\mathrm{CEP}(M)$ is L-complete. (Lemmas 4.10 and 4.11)*
* *If M does not belong to $\mathbf{M_{nil}}$, then $\mathrm{CEP}(M)$ is NL-complete. (Lemma 4.12 and Corollary 4.4)*

Corollary 4.4 was proved in subsection 4.1; we complete the proof of the theorem with the following lemmas.

Lemma 4.9 *If M belongs to $\mathbf{J_1}$, then $\mathrm{CEP}(M)$ can be solved in AC^0.*

Proof. When the expression for an element of an idempotent and commutative monoid is evaluated, each character involved contributes exactly once. Therefore by looking only at the content of the leaves, and ignoring the rest of the circuit (thus relying heavily on the hypothesis that the circuit is connected), we obtain for the output a fixed-length expression which can be evaluated using table look-up. □

Lemma 4.10 *The connected circuit problem on all non-idempotent aperiodic monoids is L-hard under $\leq_m^{NC^1}$ reducibility.*

Proof. Adapted from the method used in Lemma 4.6: we reduce from the accessibility problem in a directed forest [13] to problem CEP(T_2), where $T_2 = \{1, a, a^2\}$ is seen to divide any non-idempotent aperiodic monoid (see section 3). Details are omitted. □

Lemma 4.11 *The connected circuit problem on all monoids of variety* $\mathbf{M_{nil}}$ *is feasible in L.*

Proof. Let $M \in \mathbf{M_{nil}}$. From Lemma 3.2, for each $x \in M$ the language $x\phi^{-1}$ is a Boolean combination of languages $B^* a_1 B^* a_2 \cdots B^* a_k B^*$, with $a_1, \ldots, a_k \in A$ and $B = A - \{a_1, \ldots, a_k\}$ (the a_i not necessarily distinct). Given one such language $B^* a_1 B^* a_2 \cdots B^* a_k B^*$, let $A' = \{a'_1, \ldots, a'_{k'}\}$ be the set of letters in $S = \{a_1, \ldots, a_k\}$. It suffices to check if the sequence of leaves of all paths from the leaves labelled with the letters of A' to the root (in order) is a word in a language of the above form. For each letter a'_i, assume without loss of generality that there is exactly one leaf labelled a'_i. First we count the number of paths from this leaf to the root; if it differs from the number of occurrences of a'_i in S, we reject the instance. Otherwise we have the correct multiset of letters and it remains to verify that they appear in the correct order. This can be done with a set of registers, one for each pair of paths, where we record their relative ordering. We simply traverse the circuit from the leaves to the root, updating the value of the registers as we go along. Once we reach the root the setting of the registers tells us whether the inputs combine to give an element of $B^* a_1 B^* \cdots B^* a_k B^*$. Since the number of paths depends only on the monoid, and therefore is a constant, this algorithm can work in deterministic log space. □

Lemma 4.12 *If monoid M does not belong to* $\mathbf{M_{nil}}$, *then problem CEP(M) is NL-hard under* $\leq_m^{NC^1}$ *reducibility.*

Proof. By Lemma 3.1, at least one of monoids R_1, M_1, M_2, or their reverses, or BA_2 divides M. Thus it suffices to prove hardness for these seven minimal monoids. In all cases, we reduce from the accessibility problem in directed acyclic graphs. Details are omitted. □

Finally we state the computational complexity of UCEP(M) for the aperiodic monoids.

Proposition 4.13 *If M is a nontrivial aperiodic monoid, then problem UCEP(M) is NL-complete.*

Proof. Corollary 4.4 provides the upper bound. For NL-hardness, consider the minimal nontrivial aperiodic monoid, $C_{1,1}$. A reduction from the accessibility problem in a directed acyclic graph to UCEP(M) can be obtained by labelling the source node with value 1, all other indegree-zero nodes with value 0, and the remaining nodes with the monoid operation. □

5 Discussion

Assuming $L \neq NL \neq P$, we have completely determined the complexity of $CEP(M)$ when M is nonsolvable, or when M is aperiodic. In the remaining solvable cases, $CEP(M) \in DET \subseteq NC^2$.

As a first open problem, our analysis in the solvable case has to be refined in order to locate the complexity of $CEP(M)$ more precisely. Previous work on word and circuit problems on various types of algebras [5, 8, 18, 6, 16] has shown how such problems closely capture (through completeness results) complexity classes defined by the more "classical" means of Boolean circuits and resource-bounded Turing machines. Our NL and $co\text{-}MOD_q L$-completeness results, and our DET upper bound are but a first step toward obtaining a similar characterization. The classification of finite solvable groups will probably play a role, and it remains to be seen how closely it can be reexpressed in complexity-theoretic terms, through the analysis of $CEP(M)$. Consider in particular the well-understood nilpotent groups: is the barrier between nilpotent and non-nilpotent solvable groups relevant to the complexity of $CEP(M)$?

The complexity of $CEP(M)$ should also be contrasted with the complexity of the more restricted word problem over M, crucial to the analysis of NC^1. The same algebraic properties appear to be responsible for complexity jumps in each case. Thus a question may arise from the present work, namely to which extent can this similarity be exploited to better understand, for instance, the unresolved problem of the separation of ACC^0 from NC^1.

Acknowledgement

The authors thank Denis Thérien for helpful discussions and pointers to useful references.

References

[1] C. ÀLVAREZ AND B. JENNER, A very hard log space counting class, *Proc. of the 5th IEEE Structure in Complexity Theory Conference* (1990), pp. 154-168.

[2] D.A. BARRINGTON, Bounded-width polynomial-size branching programs recognize exactly those languages in NC^1, *J. Computer and Systems Science* **38** (1989), pp. 150-164.

[3] D.A.M. BARRINGTON, N. IMMERMAN AND H. STRAUBING, On uniformity within NC^1, *J. Computer and Systems Science* **41** (1990), pp. 274-306..

[4] D.A. BARRINGTON, H. STRAUBING AND D. THÉRIEN, Non-Uniform Automata Over Groups, *Information and Computation* **89, 2** (1990), pp. 109-132.

[5] D.A. BARRINGTON AND D. THÉRIEN, Finite Monoids and the Fine Structure of NC^1, *J. of the Association for Computing Machinery* **35** (1988), pp. 941-952.

[6] M. BEAUDRY AND P. MCKENZIE, Circuits, matrices, and nonassociative computation, *Proc. of the 7th IEEE Structure in Complexity Theory Conference* (1992), pp. 94-106.

[7] R. BEIGEL, J. GILL AND U. HERTRAMPF, Counting classes: thresholds, parity, mods, and fewness, Proc. of the 7th Symp. on Theoretical Aspects of Computer Science, *Springer Lecture Notes in Comp. Sci. 415* (1990), pp. 49-57.

[8] F. BÉDARD, F. LEMIEUX AND P. MCKENZIE, Extensions to Barrington's M-program model, *Proc. of the 5th IEEE Structure in Complexity Theory Conference* (1990), pp. 200-210. Extended version to appear in *Theoretical Computer Science*.

[9] G. BERGMAN, Embedding arbitrary algebras into groups, *Algebra Universalis 25* (1988), pp. 107-120.

[10] G. BUNTROCK, C. DAMM, U. HERTRAMPF AND C. MEINEL, Structure and importance of Logspace-MOD-classes *Math. Syst. Theory 25* (1992), pp. 223-237.

[11] S.R. BUSS, S. COOK, A. GUPTA AND V. RAMACHANDRAN, An optimal parallel algorithm for formula evaluation, (1989), to appear in *SIAM J. on Computing*.

[12] S.A. COOK, A taxonomy of problems with fast parallel solutions, *Information and Computation 64* (1985), pp. 2-22.

[13] S.A. COOK AND P. MCKENZIE, Problems Complete for Deterministic Logarithmic Space, *J. of Algorithms 8* (1987), pp. 385-394.

[14] S. EILENBERG, *Automata, Languages and Machines*, Vol. B, Academic Press (1976).

[15] N. IMMERMAN, Nondeterministic space is closed under complementation, *SIAM J. on Computing 17*, 5 (1988), pp. 935-938.

[16] N. IMMERMAN AND S. LANDAU, The complexity of iterated multiplication, *Proc. of the 3rd Structure in Complexity Conference* (1989), IEEE Computer Society Press, pp. 104-111.

[17] R.E. LADNER, The circuit value problem is log-space complete for P, *ACM SIGACT Newsletter 7* (1975), pp. 18-20.

[18] P. MCKENZIE, P. PÉLADEAU AND D. THÉRIEN, NC^1: the automata-theoretic viewpoint, *Computational Complexity 1* (1991), 330-359.

[19] J.-E. PIN, *Variétés de langages formels*, Masson (1984). *Varieties of Formal Langages*, Plenum Press (1986).

[20] W. RUZZO, On uniform circuit complexity, *J. Computer and Systems Science 22* (1981), pp. 365-383.

[21] W. RUZZO, J. SIMON AND M. TOMPA, Space-bounded hierarchies and probabilistic computations *J. Computer and Systems Science 28* (1984), pp. 216-230.

[22] H. STRAUBING *Varieties of recognizable sets whose syntactic monoids contain solvable groups*, Ph. D. Thesis, UC Berkely, 1978.

[23] H. STRAUBING The variety generated by finite nilpotent monoids, *Semigroup Forum 24* (1982), pp. 25-38.

[24] R. SZELEPCSÉNYI, The method of forcing for nondeterministic automata, *Bull. Europ. Assoc. Theor. Comp. Sci. 33* (1987), pp. 96-100.

[25] D. THÉRIEN, Classification of finite monoids: the language approach, *Theoretical Computer Science 14* (1981), pp. 195-208.

A Non-Probabilistic Switching Lemma for the Sipser Function

Sorin Istrail[*]   Dejan Zivkovic[†]

Department of Mathematics, Wesleyan University
Middletown, CT 06459, USA

Abstract. Valiant [12] showed that the clique function is structurally different than the majority function by establishing the following "switching lemma": Any function f whose set of prime implicants is a large enough subset of the set of cliques (and thus requiring big Σ_2-circuits), has a large set of prime clauses (i.e., big Π_2-circuits). As a corollary, an exponential lower bound was obtained for monotone $\Sigma\Pi\Sigma$-circuits computing the clique function. The proof technique is the only non-probabilistic super polynomial lower bound method from the literature. We prove, by a non-probabilistic argument as well, a similar switching lemma for the NC^1-complete Sipser function. Using this we then show that a monotone depth-3 (i.e., $\Sigma\Pi\Sigma$ or $\Pi\Sigma\Pi$) circuit computing the Sipser function must have super quasipolynomial size. Moreover, any depth-d quasipolynomial size non-monotone circuit computing the Sipser function has a depth-$(d-1)$ gate computing a function with exponentially many both prime implicants and (monotone) prime clauses. These results are obtained by a top-down analysis of the circuits.

1 Introduction

Proving lower bounds on the size or depth of Boolean circuits is a fundamental problem in complexity theory. It is quite remarkable that almost all methods used in deriving super polynomial lower bounds employ—in crucial parts of the argument—probabilistic reasoning. To appreciate the difficulty of obtaining non-probabilistic lower bound proofs, let us mention that there is only one such method in the literature due to Valiant [12]. It is used to show that any monotone $\Sigma\Pi\Sigma$-circuit computing the clique function requires exponential size.

Let us call *clique-like* a function whose prime implicants form a large enough subset of the set of cliques. Certainly such a function requires a big Σ_2-circuit.

---

[*]Supported in part by NSF grant CCR-8810074. The author's current address: Sandia National Laboratories, Dept. 1423, Algorithms and Discrete Math., Albuquerque, NM 87185-5800, USA. Email: scistra@cs.sandia.gov.

[†]The author's current address: Dept. of Math. and Comp. Science, Savannah State College, Savannah, GA 31404, USA. Email: dzivkov%uscn.bitnet@uga.cc.uga.edu.

The Valiant's result shows that any Π_2-circuit for the function is also big. This evidence was presented as a structural difference between the clique function and the majority function. Indeed, majority-like functions may have small Π_2-circuits.

In this paper we present results similar to those of Valiant's. They are stronger in the sense that they apply to a much easier function. Instead of the NP-complete clique function we show analogous results for the NC^1-complete Sipser function $S_{\log n}$, i.e., the alternating OR-AND complete binary tree of depth $\log n$. This means that the above type of structural difference, now between $S_{\log n}$ and majority, is present in NC^1 and therefore is not necessarily related to the fact that the clique function belongs to a higher complexity class.

Let us call *Sipser-like* a function whose set of prime implicants is a subset of at least $2^{\Theta(\sqrt{n}) - \log^{O(1)} n}$ prime implicants of $S_{\log n}$. We establish

1. A structural characterization of the self-reducibility of $S_{\log n}$;

2. *Switching Lemma*: Any Sipser-like function has an exponential size set of prime clauses.

3. Any Sipser-like function requires super quasipolynomial size monotone depth-3 circuits;

4. Every non-monotone depth-d circuit computing a Sipser-like function has a depth-$(d-1)$ gate computing a function whose both the number of prime implicants and the number of (monotone) prime clauses is exponential.

Our results are obtained through an extensive combinatorial analysis of the self-reducibility of the Sipser function. This is of an independent interest and, together with the NC^1-completeness, may speak in favor of the use of $S_{\log n}$ as a target function in other lower bound proofs (e.g., attacking the separation of TC^0 and ACC from NC^1).

The paper is organized as follows. After recalling basic definitions and notation we study the Sipser function in more detail. Section 4 contains our switching lemma, and section 5 its application to lower bounds on the size of circuits.

2 Basic definitions and notation

This section contains definitions and notation adopted throughout the paper. We first recall some of the basic notions of the theory of Boolean functions (for more details see, for example, [13]). A *literal* is a variable or a negated variable. A conjunction of literals, p, is an *implicant* of a Boolean function f if $p \leq f$ pointwise. If in addition, no conjunction of any proper subset of the literals comprising p is an implicant, then p is a *prime implicant* of f. By the same token, a disjunction of literals, s, such that $f \leq s$ is a *clause* of f. It is a *prime clause* if, in addition, no disjunction of any proper subset of the literals comprising s is a clause. A (prime) clause or implicant is *monotone* if it has no negated variables. In the case of monotone (prime) implicants and clauses, we will often regard them as sets of variables.

A Boolean formula $f(x_1, \ldots, x_n)$ determines the unique Boolean function $f : \{0,1\}^n \to \{0,1\}$ in a natural way. For a Boolean function f denote by $PI(f)$ and $PC(f)$, respectively, the set of prime implicants and the set of prime clauses. Likewise, the sets of all implicants and clauses of f are denoted by $I(f)$ and $C(f)$. By $\alpha(f)$ and $\beta(f)$ are meant the sizes of a smallest prime clause and prime implicant of f, i.e., $\alpha(f) = \min\{|s| \mid s \in PC(f)\}$ and $\beta(f) = \min\{|p| \mid p \in PI(f)\}$.

The set of variables that occur in a formula f is denoted by $V(f)$, and a mapping $\rho : V(f) \to \{0,1,*\}$ is referred to as a *restriction*. The function represented by the formula obtained by substituting $\rho(x)$ for each x in f for which $\rho(x) \neq *$ is denoted $f|\rho$. More generally, for a set F of formulas we write $F|\rho = \{f|\rho \mid f \in F\}$.

3 The Sipser function S_d

Definition 3.1 *The* Sipser function S_d *is defined for odd $d = 1, 3, \ldots$ such that if $n = 2^d$ then $S_d : \{0,1\}^n \to \{0,1\}$ as follows. Given the set $\{x_{i_1}, x_{i_2}, \ldots, x_{i_n}\}$ of n (distinct) variables, we form the complete binary tree of depth d with the root labelled $\vee$ and each level thereafter labelled with alternating $\wedge$ and $\vee$ nodes. If the leaves of the tree are now labelled with the variables $x_{i_1}, x_{i_2}, \ldots, x_{i_n}$, the tree represents the Boolean formula $S_d(x_{i_1}, x_{i_2}, \ldots, x_{i_n})$, which in turn defines the Sipser function S_d.*

In this section we study the Sipser function in more detail. Clearly S_d is a monotone function, hence prime implicants and clauses are made out of positive variables only. Moreover, every prime implicant and clause intersect in exactly one variable. (This is true in general for a monotone function iff it has a formula with no repeated variable [8].)

The number of all prime implicants $|PI(S_d)|$ and clauses $|PC(S_d)|$ of S_d is abbreviated, respectively, to $\Delta(S_d)$ and $\Gamma(S_d)$, as well as Δ_d and Γ_d. Lengths of prime implicants (clauses) of S_d are identical, and the length is denoted, respectively, by $\pi(S_d)$ and $\sigma(S_d)$, or π_d and σ_d for short. It is easy to see that $\Delta(S_d) = 2^{2^{(d+1)/2}-1}$, $\Gamma(S_d) = 2^{2(2^{(d-1)/2}-1)}$, $\pi(S_d) = 2^{(d-1)/2}$, and $\sigma(S_d) = 2^{(d+1)/2}$.

Lemma 3.2 *For $x \in V(S_d)$ denote by $\Delta_d(x)$ and $\Gamma_d(x)$ the number of prime implicants and prime clauses of S_d containing variable x. Then $\Delta_d(x) = \Delta_d/\sigma_d$ and $\Gamma_d(x) = \Gamma_d/\pi_d$.*

Proof: See [6]. ∎

Lemma 3.3 (Window Lemma) *Let S_d be the Sipser function given by the formula $S_d(x_{i_1}, \ldots, x_{i_n})$ and $X = \{x_{i_1}, \ldots, x_{i_n}\}$. If Y is a non-empty subset of X and $A_d(Y) = \{s \in PC(S_d) \mid Y \subseteq s\}$, then $|A_d(Y)| \leq \Gamma_d/2^{|Y|-2}$.*

Proof: See [6]. ∎

Let $\{L_r(S_d)\}_{r=1,2,\ldots}$ denote a sequence of subfunctions of S_d, called *layers*, which are defined as follows. Each layer will have the form $L_r(S_d) = T_0^r \wedge T_1^r \wedge \cdots \wedge T_{\tau_r}^r$, where $T_0^r, T_1^r, \ldots, T_{\tau_r}^r$ are subfunctions of S_d called *triangles*, each triangle being itself a Sipser function. Informally, the sequence is constructed iteratively so that next layer is obtained in the following way. First, we fix one variable from every triangle of the current layer. Let us call the fixed variables *pivots*. Secondly, we build a suitable restriction dependent on the choice of pivot variables. Finally, the next layer is defined to be the previous layer under the restriction.

Formally, to start with we think of S_d as a triangle in itself. Now, fixing a pivot $x \in V(S_d)$, the layer $L_1(S_d)$ is formed as follows. Take any $s \in PC(S_d)$ with $s = x \vee t$ and define the restriction ρ_x on $V(S_d)$ by

$$\rho_x(y) = \begin{cases} 0, & \text{if } y \in t \\ *, & \text{if } y \notin t \end{cases}.$$

Then we define $L_1(S_d) = S_d|\rho_x$. Observe that we can write $L_1(S_d) = T_0^1 \wedge T_1^1 \wedge T_2^1 \wedge \cdots \wedge T_{\tau_1}^1$, where $T_0^1, T_1^1, T_2^1, \ldots, T_{\tau_1}^1$ are the triangles of depth $0, 1, 3, \ldots, d-2$ respectively.

The next layer $L_2(S_d)$ is dependent on the choice of pivot variables $x_i^1 \in V(T_i^1)$, $(i = 0, 1, \ldots, \tau_1)$. Given such a choice, we define $L_2(S_d) = L_1(T_0^1) \wedge L_1(T_1^1) \wedge L_1(T_2^1) \wedge \cdots \wedge L_1(T_{\tau_1}^1)$. Put another way, we have $L_2(S_d) = T_0^2 \wedge T_1^2 \wedge \cdots \wedge T_{\tau_2}^2$, where $T_0^2, T_1^2, \ldots, T_{\tau_2}^2$ are all the triangles from $L_1(T_0^1), \ldots, L_1(T_{\tau_1}^1)$.

In general, each time choosing one pivot from every triangle of the current layer we proceed in the same way to get the next layer. Namely, for $r = 1, 2, \ldots$, $L_r(S_d) = T_0^r \wedge T_1^r \wedge T_2^r \wedge \cdots \wedge T_{\tau_r}^r$, and the choice of pivot variables $x_i^r \in V(T_i^r)$, $(i = 0, 1, \ldots, \tau_r)$, we define $L_{r+1}(S_d) = L_1(T_0^r) \wedge L_1(T_1^r) \wedge L_1(T_2^r) \wedge \cdots \wedge L_1(T_{\tau_r}^r)$, or equivalently $L_{r+1}(S_d) = T_0^{r+1} \wedge T_1^{r+1} \wedge \cdots \wedge T_{\tau_{r+1}}^{r+1}$, where $T_0^{r+1}, T_1^{r+1}, \ldots, T_{\tau_{r+1}}^{r+1}$ are all the triangles from $L_1(T_0^r), \ldots, L_1(T_{\tau_r}^r)$.

There are three aspects of the layer $L_r(S_d)$ which are of special interest to us: the number of prime implicants, the number of depth-non-zero triangles, and the product of the lengths of prime clauses of all triangles of the layer. They are denoted, respectively, $\ell_r(d)$, $\tau_r(d)$, $\lambda_r(d)$. Since their exact values are rather cumbersome, we compute only tight bounds for them which suffice for our purposes.

Theorem 3.4 *For every* $r = 1, 2, \ldots$, *if* $d = 1, 3, \ldots, 2r - 1$ *then* $\ell_r(d) = 1$, $\tau_r(d) = 0$, $\lambda_r(d) = 1$; *and if* $d \geq 2r + 1$ *then*

$$\frac{2^{2^{\frac{d+1}{2}} - 1}}{2^{\frac{4r}{r!}}} \leq \ell_r(d) \leq \frac{2^{2^{\frac{d+1}{2}} - 1}}{2^{(\frac{4}{3})^r \cdot \frac{1}{r!}}},$$

$$\tau_r(d) \leq \left(\frac{d}{2}\right)^r \cdot \frac{1}{r!},$$

$$2^{(\frac{d}{16})^{r+1}\cdot\frac{1}{(r+1)!}} \le \lambda_r(d) \le 2^{(\frac{d}{2})^{r+1}\cdot\frac{1}{(r+1)!}} .$$

Proof: See [6]. ∎

4 The switching lemma for S_d

It is well known that even a monotone Boolean function can have exponentially many prime implicants while only polynomially many prime clauses (or vice versa). In this section we deal with a similar problem of switching between prime implicants and clauses for the Sipser function S_d. More precisely, let F be a nonempty subset of the set of prime implicants of S_d and for $n = 2^d$ let $f : \{0,1\}^n \rightarrow \{0,1\}$ be the function defined by $f(x_1,\ldots,x_n) = \bigvee_{p\in F} p$. The question is: what is a lower bound on the size of $PC(f)$? We show that, roughly, if $|F|$ is big enough, then $|PC(f)|$ is also big. (Our argument can be easily modified for the corresponding dual case.) The proof's outline in major steps is as follows.

- first important observation is the relationship between $|PC(f)|$ and $\alpha(f)$, namely $|PC(f)| \ge 2^{\alpha(f)-2}$;

- since $\alpha(f)$ can be small, we show that if $|F|$ is big enough, then there is a restriction ρ such that $S_d|\rho = S_{d'}, f|\rho = f'$ where $f' = \bigvee_{q\in F'} q$ for some $F' \subseteq PI(S_{d'})$, and $\alpha(f')$ is amplified;

- using these and showing $|PC(f)| \ge |PC(f')|$ we get $|PC(f)|$ is big if $|F|$ is.

Lemma 4.1 *Let S_d be the Sipser function and $F \subseteq PI(S_d)$ be nonempty. If $f = \bigvee_{p\in F} p$, then $|PC(f)| \ge 2^{\alpha(f)-2}$.*

Proof: For each $t \in PC(f)$ thought of as the set of variables, we let $A_d(t) = \{s \in PC(S_d) \mid t \subseteq s\}$. (Note that $PC(f) \ne \emptyset$ since f is a non-constant function, hence it makes sense to talk about $A_d(t)$.) We claim that

$$PC(S_d) = \bigcup_{t\in PC(f)} A_d(t) . \tag{1}$$

The inclusion $\supseteq$ is trivial, and to see the other part take $s \in PC(S_d)$. Then s is a clause for f and so there is a $\hat{t} \in PC(f)$ such that $\hat{t} \subseteq s$, i.e., $s \in A_d(\hat{t})$.

Now, by Lemma 3.3 and definition of $\alpha(f)$ we have $|A_d(t)| \le \Gamma_d/2^{|t|-2} \le \Gamma_d/2^{\alpha(f)-2}$ for every $t \in PC(f)$, i.e.,

$$\max\{|A_d(t)| \mid t \in PC(f)\} \le \frac{\Gamma_d}{2^{\alpha(f)-2}} . \tag{2}$$

Combining (1) and (2), one obtains

$$\Gamma_d = |PC(S_d)| \le \sum_{t \in PC(f)} |A_d(t)| \le |PC(f)| \cdot \max\{|A_d(t)| \mid t \in PC(f)\}$$

$$\le |PC(f)| \cdot \frac{\Gamma_d}{2^{\alpha(f)-2}} \ .$$

Therefore, $|PC(f)| \ge 2^{\alpha(f)-2}$ as desired. ∎

Lemma 4.2 *Let S_d be the Sipser function and $F \subseteq PI(S_d)$ be nonempty. For each $x \in V(S_d)$ define the set $F(x) = \{p \in F \mid x \in p\}$. Then there is an $\hat{x} \in V(S_d)$ such that $|F(\hat{x})| \ge |F|/\sigma_d$.*

Proof: See [6]. ∎

Lemma 4.3 (Amplification Lemma) *Let S_d be the Sipser function and $F \subseteq PI(S_d)$ be nonempty. For $n = 2^d$ define $f : \{0,1\}^n \to \{0,1\}$ by $f(x_1, \ldots, x_n) = \bigvee_{p \in F} p$. If $|F| \ge \ell_r(d)$ and $d \ge 2^{5(r+1)}$ for some $r \ge 1$, then there is a restriction ρ on $V(S_d)$ such that*

a) $S_d|\rho = S_{d'}$ *with* $d' = \Omega(d)$,

b) $F|\rho = F'$ *where* $F' \subseteq PI(S_{d'})$, *and*

c) *if* $f' = f|\rho = \bigvee_{q \in F'} q$, *then* $\alpha(f') = 2^{\Omega(d)}$ *and* $\beta(f') = 2^{\Omega(d)}$.

Remark: The constants hidden in the Ω-notation depend on r.

Proof: Fix d and suppose $F \subseteq PI(S_d)$ is nonempty. For the sake of simplicity, in what follows we will usually omit notation for the depth d as a variable in quantities that depend upon it. Also, we put $\lambda_0 = \lambda_0(d) = \sigma_d$.

Now take $r \ge 1$ for which $|F| \ge \ell_r$ and $d \ge 2^{5(r+1)}$. We first construct a layer L_r, restriction η, and set $F_r \subseteq F \cap PI(L_r)$ such that $F_r = F|\eta$ and

$$|F_r| \ge \frac{|F|}{\lambda_0 \cdot \lambda_1 \cdots \lambda_{r-1}} \ .$$

To this end, for each $x \in V(S_d)$ define the set $F(x) = \{p \in F \mid x \in p\}$ and by Lemma 4.2 choose the pivot x_0^1 for L_1 such that $|F(x_0^1)| \ge |F|/\sigma_d = |F|/\lambda_0$. Building the layer L_1 in this way (i.e., using restriction $\eta_1 = \rho_{x_0^1}$), if $F_1 = F(x_0^1)$ we get $F_1 \subseteq F \cap PI(L_1)$, $F_1 = F|\eta_1$, and $|F_1| \ge |F|/\lambda_0$.

In order to obtain the layer L_2 let us introduce the following notation. For every variable $y_i \in V(T_i^1)$, where T_i^1, $(i = 0, 1, \ldots, \tau_1)$, are the triangles of the layer L_1, let

$$F_1(y_0) = \{p \in F_1 \mid y_0 \in p\},$$
$$F_1(y_0, y_1) = \{p \in F_1(y_0) \mid y_1 \in p\},$$
$$\vdots$$
$$F_1(y_0, y_1, \ldots, y_{\tau_1}) = \{p \in F_1(y_0, y_1, \ldots, y_{\tau_1-1}) \mid y_{\tau_1} \in p\}.$$

The pivots x_i^2, $(i = 0, 1, \ldots, \tau_1)$, for L_2 are now chosen as $x_0^2 = x_0^1$ (i.e., $F_1(x_0^2) = F_1$), and the others by repeated application of Lemma 4.2 such that for every $i = 1, \ldots, \tau_1$ we have $|F_1(x_0^2, x_1^2, \ldots, x_i^2)| \geq |F_1(x_0^2, x_1^2, \ldots, x_{i-1}^2)|/\sigma_i^1$, where $\sigma_i^1 = \sigma(T_i^1)$. It follows that

$$|F_1(x_0^2, x_1^2, \ldots, x_{\tau_1}^2)| \geq \frac{|F_1|}{\sigma_1^1 \cdot \sigma_2^1 \cdots \sigma_{\tau_1}^1} = \frac{|F_1|}{\lambda_1} \geq \frac{|F|}{\lambda_0 \cdot \lambda_1} .$$

Thus, if η_2 is the restriction yielding the layer L_2 and $F_2 = F_1(x_0^2, x_1^2, \ldots, x_{\tau_1}^2)$, then $F_2 \subseteq F \cap PI(L_2)$, $F_2 = F_1|\eta_2$, and $|F_2| \geq |F|/(\lambda_0 \cdot \lambda_1)$.

The reader should have no difficulty to see that, proceeding in this way for subsequent layers, we will eventually get the layer L_r with corresponding restriction η_r and the set $F_r = F_{r-1}(x_0^r, x_1^r, \ldots, x_{\tau_{r-1}}^r)$ such that $F_r \subseteq F \cap PI(L_r)$, $F_r = F_{r-1}|\eta_r$, and $|F_r| \geq |F|/(\lambda_0 \cdot \lambda_1 \cdots \lambda_{r-1})$. Therefore, for $\eta = \eta_1 \circ \eta_2 \circ \cdots \circ \eta_r$ we have $F|\eta = F_r$, and so our first goal is achieved.

Next, define the restrictions ξ_i, $(i = 0, 1, \ldots, \tau_r)$, on $V(L_r)$ by

$$\xi_i(y) = \begin{cases} * , & \text{if } y \in V(T_i^r) \\ 1 , & \text{if } y \notin V(T_i^r) \end{cases} ,$$

and let P_i, $(i = 0, 1, \ldots, \tau_r)$, be the sets given by $P_i = F_r|\xi_i$. If we define $\Delta_i^r = \Delta(T_i^r)$, $\mu_i = |P_i|/(\Delta_i^r/\sigma_i^r)$, and $\mu = \prod_{i=0}^{\tau_r} \mu_i$, then

$$|F_r| \leq |P_0| \cdot |P_1| \cdots |P_{\tau_r}| = \mu_0 \frac{\Delta_0^r}{\sigma_0^r} \cdot \mu_1 \frac{\Delta_1^r}{\sigma_1^r} \cdots \mu_{\tau_r} \frac{\Delta_{\tau_r}^r}{\sigma_{\tau_r}^r} = \mu \cdot \frac{\ell_r}{\lambda_r} .$$

On the other hand $|F_r| \geq |F|/(\lambda_0 \cdot \lambda_1 \cdots \lambda_{r-1}) \geq \ell_r/(\lambda_0 \cdot \lambda_1 \cdots \lambda_{r-1})$, and so $\mu \geq \lambda_r / \prod_{i=0}^{r-1} \lambda_i$. Since $\mu = \prod_{i=0}^{\tau_r} \mu_i$, it follows that there is a $k \in \{0, 1, \ldots, \tau_r\}$ such that

$$\mu_k \geq \left(\frac{\lambda_r}{\prod_{i=0}^{r-1} \lambda_i} \right)^{1/\tau_r} . \tag{3}$$

Using the assumption $d \geq 2^{5(r+1)}$ and Theorem 3.4, it requires straightforward algebra to check that the right-hand side of (3) is at least $2^{d/2^{5(r+1)}}$, which implies $\mu_k = 2^{\Omega(d)}$.

Clearly, if we take $F' = P_k$, $\rho = \eta \circ \xi_k$, and $S_{d'} = T_k^r$ where d' is the depth of T_k^r, then $F' = F|\rho$ and $F' \subseteq PI(S_{d'})$. Moreover, it is easy to see that $S_d|\rho = S_{d'}$ and $f|\rho = \bigvee_{q \in F'} q$. Thus, if $f' = f|\rho$ it remains to prove $\alpha(f')$ and d' are as claimed.

For that, for each $x \in V(S_{d'})$ define the set $F'(x) = \{q \in F' \mid x \in q\}$. Since one variable $x \in V(S_{d'})$ occurs by Lemma 3.2 in at most $\Delta_{d'}/\sigma_{d'}$ prime implicants of $S_{d'}$, we have $|F'(x)| \leq \Delta_{d'}/\sigma_{d'}$. Now, take any $s \in PC(f')$ and observe $F' = \bigcup_{x \in s} F'(x)$, hence $|F'| \leq \sum_{x \in s} |F'(x)| \leq |s| \cdot \Delta_{d'}/\sigma_{d'}$, i.e.,

$$|s| \geq \frac{|F'|}{\Delta_{d'}/\sigma_{d'}} = \frac{|P_k|}{\Delta_k^r/\sigma_k^r} = \mu_k .$$

Because $s \in PC(f')$ is arbitrary, this implies $\alpha(f') \geq \mu_k = 2^{\Omega(d)}$. Finally, $d' = \Omega(d)$ easily follows from $2^{\Omega(d)} = \alpha(f') \leq 2^{d'}$, and $\beta(f') = 2^{(d'-1)/2} = 2^{\Omega(d)}$. ∎

Lemma 4.4 *Let $f : \{0,1\}^n \to \{0,1\}$ be a monotone Boolean function represented by a formula $f(x_1,\ldots,x_n)$. If ρ is any restriction on $\{x_1,\ldots,x_n\}$, then $|PC(f)| \geq |PC(f|\rho)|$.*

Proof: Straightforward. ∎

Lemma 4.5 (Switching Lemma) *Let S_d be the Sipser function, and let $F \subseteq PI(S_d)$ be nonempty. For $n = 2^d$ define $f : \{0,1\}^n \to \{0,1\}$ by $f = \bigvee_{p \in F} p$. If $|F| \geq \ell_r(d)$ and $d \geq 2^{5(r+1)}$ for some $r \geq 1$, then $|PC(f)| = 2^{2^{\Omega(d)}}$.*

Remark: The constant hidden in the Ω-notation depends on r.

Proof: Let ρ be the restriction from Amplification Lemma such that $f' = f|\rho = \bigvee_{q \in F'} q$ for $F' \subseteq PI(S_{d'})$ and $\alpha(f') = 2^{\Omega(d)}$. Then

$$
\begin{aligned}
|PC(f)| &\geq |PC(f')| \text{ , by Lemma 4.4} \\
&\geq 2^{\alpha(f')-2} \text{ , by Lemma 4.1} \\
&= 2^{2^{\Omega(d)}} \text{ . } \blacksquare
\end{aligned}
$$

5 On depth-3 circuits computing S_d

In this section we use the previous results to easily obtain a lower bound on the size of depth-3 monotone circuits computing S_d. To this end we consider only $\Sigma\Pi\Sigma$-circuits since similar dual argument handles the case of $\Pi\Sigma\Pi$-circuits. Through the rest of the section we let $n = 2^d$.

Theorem 5.1 *Any monotone $\Sigma\Pi\Sigma$-circuit computing $S_{\log n}$ has super quasi-polynomial size.*

Proof: Let C be a monotone $\Sigma\Pi\Sigma$-circuit on n variables that computes $S_{\log n}$ and has size $2^{\log^k n}$, for some constant k. Then there is one AND gate on the middle level computing function, say, h with the following properties: $PI(h) = F \cup G$, where $F \subseteq PI(S_{\log n})$ and $|F| \geq \Delta_{\log n}/2^{\log^k n} = 2^{\Theta(\sqrt{n}) - \log^k n}$; moreover, every $q \in G$ has the form $q = q'q''$ with $q' \in PI(S_{\log n}) \backslash F$ and q'' a non-empty product of variables. Thus, we can apply the Switching Lemma to $f = \bigvee_{p \in F} p$ and conclude that there exists $\epsilon > 0$ such that $PC(h) \geq 2^{n^\epsilon}$. Now, it is not hard to see that $|PC(h)| \geq |PC(f)|$ and so $PC(h) \geq 2^{n^\epsilon}$. But then the monotone subcircuit rooted at the AND gate which computes the function h must have exponential size, a contradiction. ∎

At the end we note that we can prove a slightly stronger result. Namely, a non-monotone quasipolynomial size circuit computing the Sipser function still has a gate on the next-to-top level which computes a function with exponentially many monotone prime clauses. The details are omitted and can be found in [6].

Acknowledgments

We would like to thank Michael Sipser for insightful comments and discussions, and especially for pointing out an error in an earlier version of this paper. We also thank David Barrington for helpful suggestions about the results of our work.

References

[1] E. Allender, "A note on the power of threshold circuits", *Proceedings of the 30th IEEE Symposium on Foundations of Computer Science*, pp. 580–584, 1989.

[2] D. A. Barrington, "Bounded-width polynomial-size branching programs recognize exactly those languages in NC^1", *Journal of Computer and System Sciences*, Vol. 38, pp. 150–164, 1989.

[3] R. Beigel and J. Tarui, "On ACC", *Proceedings of the 32nd IEEE Symposium on Foundations of Computer Science*, pp. 783–792, 1991.

[4] R. B. Boppana and M. Sipser, "The Complexity of Finite Functions", *Handbook of Theoretical Computer Science, Vol. A* (J. van Leeuwen, ed., North-Holland, Amsterdam), pp. 757–804, 1990.

[5] J. Hastad, "Almost optimal lower bounds for small-depth circuits", *Proceedings of the 18th ACM Symposium on Theory of Computing*, pp. 6–20, 1986.

[6] S. Istrail and D. Zivkovic, "A non-probabilistic switching lemma for the Sipser function", *Wesleyan University, CS/TR-92-1*, 1992.

[7] M. Karchmer and A. Wigderson, "Monotone circuits for connectivity require super-logarithmic depth", *Proceedings of the 20th ACM Symposium on Theory of Computing*, pp. 539–550, 1988.

[8] D. Mundici, "Functions computed by monotone Boolean formulas with no repeated variables", *Theoretical Computer Science*, Vol. 66, pp. 113–114, 1989.

[9] A. A. Razborov, "Lower bounds on the monotone complexity of some Boolean functions", *Doklady Akademii Nauk SSSR*, Vol. 281(4), pp. 798–801, 1985 (in Russian). English translation in *Soviet Mathematics Doklady*, Vol. 31, pp. 354–357, 1985.

[10] A. A. Razborov, "Lower bounds on the size of bounded depth networks over a complete basis with logical addition", *Matematicheskie Zametki*, Vol. 41(4), pp. 598–607, 1987 (in Russian). English translation in *Mathematical Notes of the Academy of Sciences of the USSR*, Vol. 41(4), pp. 333–338, 1987.

[11] S. Skyum and L. G. Valiant, "A complexity theory based on Boolean algebra", *Journal of the ACM*, Vol. 22, pp. 484–504, 1985.

[12] L. G. Valiant, "Exponential lower bounds for restricted monotone circuits", *Proceedings of the 15th ACM Symposium on Theory of Computing*, pp. 110–117, 1983.

[13] I. Wegener, *The Complexity of Boolean Functions*, Wiley-Teubner, 1987.

Frontiers of Feasible and Probabilistic Feasible Boolean Manipulation with Branching Programs

Jordan Gergov and Christoph Meinel

FB IV – Informatik
Universität Trier
Postfach 3825
D-5500 Trier

Extended Abstract

Abstract. A central issue in the solution of many computer aided design problems is to find concise representations for circuit designs and their functional specification. Recently, a restricted type of branching programs (OBDDs) proved to be extremely useful for representing Boolean functions for various CAD applications [Bry92]. Unfortunately, many circuits of practical interest provably require OBDD-representations of exponential size. In the following we systematically study the question up to what extend more concise BP-representations can be successfully used in symbolic Boolean manipulation, too. We prove, in very general settings,

- The frontier of efficient (deterministic) symbolic Boolean manipulation on the basis of BP-representations are read-once-only branching programs (BP1).
- The frontier of efficient probabilistic manipulation with BP-based data structures are parity read-once-only branching programs ($\oplus$-BP1).

Since BP1s and $\oplus$-BP1s are generally more (sometimes even exponentially more) succinct than OBDD-representations our results make accessible more succinct types of BPs as data structures for practical purposes. (A BP1-package as well as a $\oplus$-BP1-package are in preparation.) On the other side, our results together with the results obtained in [GM92] show that the solution of basic tasks in Boolean manipulation for less restricted BP-types becomes NP-hard.

1 Introduction

Most of the problems in digital system design, combinatorial optimization, mathematical logic, or artificial intelligence can be formulated in terms of Boolean functions. Doing this the problems can be solved by means of algorithms that work with Boolean functions. The efficiency of such algorithms depends essentially on the data structures used for the representation of the involved Boolean functions. Hence, a central issue in the solution of many computer aided design problems is to find "efficient" data structures. Here "efficiency" means, on one hand, that the representation of the Boolean functions should be as succinct as possible, and, on the other hand, that the Boolean manipulation on the basis of this representation can be performed as efficient as possible. Since, usually, these requests are contradictory it is necessary to find good compromises.

Considering data structure based on branching programs, nowadays, the most popular representation that combines these requirements up to a certain degree are OBDDs (ordered binary decision diagrams). OBDDs introduced by Bryant [Bry86] provide a representation well suited for various CAD applications such as verification, synthesis, testing and simulation [e.g. BBR90, BCMD90, FFK88, MWBS88]. Most actual CAD-tools manipulate Boolean functions on the basis of such OBDDs. Unfortunately, the efficiency of OBDD-representations depends crucially on certain ordering constraints. Moreover, there are many functions of practical interest (e.g. integer multiplication, hidden weighted bit function, indirect storage function) which provably require exponential size OBDD-representations [Bry91, Bry92].

Since OBDDs have found such a great resonance in practice it would be most desirable to overcome the difficulties of the OBDD-model. Our approach is the following: On the basis of a systematical investigations of the complexity of the basic tasks of Boolean manipulation in terms of various restricted branching program models [GM92] we try to find out the most succinct BP-representations that allow feasible or at least probabilistically feasible Boolean manipulations.
In the following we prove:

1. One can work with read–once–only branching programs (BP1) similarly efficient as with OBDDs. (In the meantime similar results could be obtained in [SW92].)

2. Working with parity read–once–only branching programs ($\oplus$–BP1) similarly as with OBDDs Boolean manipulations are probabilistically feasible.

Both results are of great practical importance since BP1s as well as $\oplus$–BP1s are generally more (sometimes even exponential more) succinct than OBDDs [BHR91]. Moreover, while it is possible to prove exponential lower bounds on the size of BP1s and to show that $\oplus$–BP1s possess more (sometimes even exponential more) computational power than BP1s (and, hence OBDDs) [A&86,KMW91] up to now nobody was able to prove superpolynomial lower bounds on the size of $\oplus$–BP1s.

The paper is structured as follows. In Section 2 we introduce BP-representations for Boolean functions and mention the basic tasks of Boolean Manipulation. Shortly we cite some facts concerning OBDDs. Then, in Section 3 we show that Boolean Manipulation in terms of read–once–only branching programs is feasible. In order to obtain this result we introduce and investigate in detail consistent BP1s. In the final Section 4 we show that Boolean Manipulation in terms of parity read–once–only branching programs is probabilistically feasible. The key point in doing this is the development of a probabilistic equivalence test for $\oplus$–BP1s.

Almost all proofs have to be omitted in this extended abstract for the sake of limited space.

2 BP–Representations and Basic Tasks of Boolean Manipulation

2.1 Branching Programs and Ω-Branching Programs

One of the most important and interesting data structures for Boolean functions are branching programs. A *branching program (BP)* [e.g. Mei89] is a directed acyclic connected graph where each node has outdegree 2 or 0. There is a distinguished node, the *source*, which has indegree 0, and at most two nodes of outdegree 0, the *0-sink* and the *1-sink*, which are labelled by the Boolean constants 0 and 1, respectively. The remaining nodes are labelled by Boolean variables taken from a set $X_n = \{x_1, \ldots, x_n\}$. The two edges starting in a non-sink node are labelled by 0 and 1, respectively. The 0–successor and the 1–successor nodes of v are denoted by $v0$ and $v1$, respectively.

A branching program P over $X_n = \{x_1, \ldots, x_n\}$ can be used to *represent* or *compute* a Boolean function $f_P \in \mathbb{B}_n$ in the following way. Each input $w = w_1 \ldots w_n \in \{0,1\}^n$ defines a *computational path* through P that starts at the source. If this path reaches a node v which is labelled by the variable $x_i \in X_n$ then it follows the edge labelled by w_i. Since P is finite and acyclic finally a sink is reached whose label gives the value $f_P(w)$ on w. P is said to be a *BP-representation of f_P*. Two branching programs P, P' are called *computationally equivalent* if they represent the same function $f_P = f_{P'}$.

In order to increase the computational power of branching programs Ω–branching programs were introduced [Mei88]. An Ω–branching program P over X_n, $\Omega \subseteq \mathbb{B}_2$, is a branching program some of whose non–sink nodes are labelled by binary functions $\omega \in \Omega$ instead of Boolean variables . The Boolean values assigned to the sinks of P extend to Boolean values associated with all nodes of P in the following way: If both successor nodes v_0, v_1 of a node v of P carry the Boolean values δ_0 or δ_1, and if v is labelled by a Boolean variable x_i we associate with v the value δ_0 or δ_1 according to $x_i = 0$ or $x_i = 1$. If v is labelled by a function ω then we associate with v the value $\omega(\delta_0, \delta_1)$. P computes the value 1 (0) on an input $w \in \{0,1\}^n$ if the source of P associates with 1 (0) under w. For $\Omega = \{\vee\}, \{\wedge\}, \{\oplus\}, \{\vee, \wedge\}$ we speak of *disjunctive, conjunctive, parity* or *alternating branching programs*, respectively.

An Ω–branching program is said to be a *read–once–only Ω-branching program (Ω-BP1)* if each variable appears, on each source–to–sink path, at most once. A BP1 ($\Omega = \emptyset$) is called an *ordered binary decision diagram* (OBDD) if it tests the variables on all paths according to a predefined order. In [Mei88] it was proved that, within polynomial size, each Ω-BP (Ω-BP1), $\Omega \subseteq \mathbb{B}_2$, is computational equivalent to an Ω'–BP (Ω'-BP1) with $\Omega' \in \{\emptyset, \{\vee\}, \{\wedge\}, \{\oplus\}, \{\vee, \wedge\}\}$.

2.2 Basic tasks of Boolean Manipulation

Basic tasks of Boolean manipulation in CAD–systems that have to be performed frequently are
- equivalency test (in particular satisfiability test), and

- binary synthesis.

Other manipulation tasks for Boolean fucntions as their composition, the evaluation for given inputs, computing restrictions or the complement, are either trivial in the framework of BPs or can easily be reduced to the above mentioned basic tasks. Observe, that working with restricted Ω-BP-representations one has to maintain the restriction in the course of performing the synthesis.

Definition

Let X-Ω-BP denotes a class of restricted Ω-BPs. The *satisfiablility problem for* X-Ω-*BPs*, $SAT_{X-\Omega-BP}$, consists in the test whether a given X-Ω-BP represents a satisfiable Boolean function. The *equivalence problem for* X-Ω-*BPs*, $EQU_{X-\Omega-BP}$, consists in the test whether two given X-Ω-BPs represent the same function. If $*$ denotes a binary operator for Boolean functions then the $*$-*synthesis problem for* X-Ω-*BPs*, $*$-$SYN_{X-\Omega-BP}$, is the problem of constructing an X-Ω-BP-representation for the function $f = f' * f''$ from given X-Ω-BP-representations of f' and f''. Since $\{\wedge, \oplus, \neg\}$ is a complete basis for the set of Boolean operators it suffices to consider $\wedge$-$SYN_{X-\Omega-BP}$ and $\oplus$-$SYN_{X-\Omega-BP}$ (the complement is trivial for BPs).

2.3 OBDDs

Bryant has recognized that OBDD-representations [Bry86] for Boolean functions possess a variety of exceptional properties desirable for practical applications in CAD-systems. Among others, OBDD-representations with a fixed predefined variable ordering allow efficient satisfiability and equivalence tests as well as feasible synthesis algorithms. Hence, a number of CAD-tools uses OBDDs as data structure for Boolean functions [e.g. BBR90, BCMD90, FFK88, MWBS88].

Theorem 1.

1. Each function $f \in B_n$ can be canonically represented by means of a reduced OBDD w. r. t. a predefined variable ordering [Bry86] (see the next section for the Definition of reduced BP).
2. EQU_{OBDD} is feasible [FHS78].
3. Let $*$ be a binary operator for Boolean functions. $*$-SYN_{OBDD} is feasible for OBDDs that test variables in the same order[Bry86]. □

Unfortunately, there exist important Boolean functions such as integer multiplication, hidden weighted bit function, indirect storage function that, for no variable ordering, can be represented by polynomial size OBDDs [e.g. Bry91, BHR91].

3 Deterministic Feasible Boolean Manipulation in Terms of Read-once-only Branching Programs

3.1 Complexity of the Basic Tasks for BP1s

Investigating the complexity of the basic tasks of Boolean manipulation in terms of BP1s one obtains the following results:

Proposition 2.

1. SAT_{BP1} is feasible, $SAT_{BP1} \in \mathbf{P}$.
2. EQU_{BP1} is probabilistic feasible, $EQU_{BP1} \in \text{co} - \mathbf{R}$ [BCW80].
3. EQU_{BP2} is co-NP–complete [GM92] (BP2 are BPs where each variable appears at most two times on a source-to-sink path).
4. $\wedge$–SYN_{BP1} and $\wedge$–SYN_{OBDD} are NP–hard [GM92]. □

3.2 Feasible Boolean Manipulation within BP1–ideals

While the complexity of the satisfiability problem and the equivalence problem for BP1–representations is at least probabilistically feasible binary synthesis for such representations is, due to Proposition 2, NP–hard. At the first glance, this fact prohibits the use of BP1s as a data structure for CAD–tools. However, investigating the situation in more detail, we succeeded in realizing that also synthesis can be performed efficiently if one restricts oneself to BP1s of consistent types. For further details we refer to [GM92b].

Let v and v' be nodes of a BP P. v and v' are said to be *congruent* if the labels of v and v' are equal, and, if both v, v' are non–sinks, both 0–successor nodes $v0$ and $v'0$ as well as both 1–successor nodes $v1$ and $v'1$ are congruent. v is called *trivial* if it has only one successor in P, i.e. if $v0 = v1$. An *algebraical BP-reduction* applied to a BP P consists in the identification of the subprograms P_v and $P_{v'}$ for two congruent nodes v and v'. A BP P without different congruent nodes is said to be *algebraical reduced*. A *simple BP-reduction* applied to P consists in the deletion of the label of a trivial node and the identification of this node with its successor node. A BP P without simple nodes is said to be *simple reduced*. Undoing an algebraical (simple) BP-reduction is called an *algebraical (simple) BP-extension*.

Definition
A BP P is said to be *reduced* if it is algebraical and simple reduced.

Applying as many as possible reductions (algebraical, or, respectively, simple reductions) to a BP P we get a reduced (algebraical, or simple reduced) program, that is denoted by $red(P)$ ($red_a(P)$, or $red_s(P)$).

Proposition 3. (Efficient reductions of BP1s)
Let P be a BP1. $red(P)$, $red_a(P)$ and $red_s(P)$ are unique determined, and can be constructed efficiently. (In [SW92] a linear time bound was proved.) □

In order to identify certain similarities between different branching programs we have to compare their types.

Definition. (BP1–types, complete BP1–types)
A *BP1–type* is defined similar as a BP1 with the only exception that it possesses merely one sink. The BP1–type $typ(P)$ of a BP1 P is derived from P by identifying all sinks of P. A BP1–type over X_n is said to be *complete* if, on each source–to–sink path, each variable of X_n appears. A BP1–type τ is called a *subtype* of BP1–type τ', $\tau \leq \tau'$, if τ can be constructed from τ' be applying algebraical or simple type–reductions (BP-reductions can be applied in an obvious way to BP-types, too).

Definition. (BP1–ideals)
A set $\mathcal{K}$ of BP1s over X_n is called a *BP1–ideal* generated by a BP1–type τ, if
$$\mathcal{K} = \{Q : Q \text{ is a BP1 with } red_a(typ(red(Q))) \leq red_a(\tau)\}.$$

Let us only remark that, for a given BP1–type τ and two BP1s P, P', it can be tested efficiently whether P belongs the the BP1–ideal generated by τ, or whether P and P' belong to a common type–generated BP1–ideal (e. g. in time $O(n\; size(input))$).

In terms of BP1–ideals our results can be summarized as follows:

Theorem 4.
Let $\mathcal{K}$ be a BP1–ideal generated by a complete type τ over X_n.

1. Each function $f \in \mathbb{B}_n$ can be canonical represented within $\mathcal{K}$ by means of a reduced program.
2. $EQU_{\mathcal{K}}$ can be decided in linear time.
3. Let $*$ be a binary operator. The synthesis $*-SYN_{\mathcal{K}}$ can be performed in time $O(size(P')\; size(P'')\; size(\tau))$. If we drop the requirement to get a result in $\mathcal{K}$ then we can synthesize P' and P'' in time $O(size(P')\; size(P''))$.

Proof.
Let P' and P'' compute f' and f'', and let $* \in \mathbb{B}_2$ be any binary operator. Starting with P' and P'' the procedure *synthesis* given in the appendix of the paper constructs a BP1 P that computes $f' * f''$. After easy modification we can get a BP P in $\mathcal{K}$. $\square$

In [GM92b], combining methods and ideas for decision trees with the methods developed in the preceding section we are able to identify even larger BP1–ideals for which the manipulation remains feasible.

4 Probabilistic Feasible Boolean Manipulation in Terms of Parity Read-once-only Branching Programs

4.1 The Complexity of the Equivalence for Ω-BP1s

Since the equivalence problem for BPs (and, hence, for Ω–BPs) is intractable already for very restricted two–times–only BPs (Proposition 2) we concentrate ourself to Ω–BP1s. Further we have to consider only the following types of Ω–BP1s [Mei88].

Theorem 5.

1. Let $\Omega \in \{\{\wedge\}, \{\vee\}, \{\wedge, \vee\}\}$. Then $EQU_{\Omega-BP1}$ is co-NP-complete.
2. $EQU_{\oplus-BP1}$ is probabilistic feasible, $EQU_{\oplus-BP1} \in \text{co} - \text{R}$.

Proof.
To prove the second part of the theorem we extend a result of Blum, Chandra and Wegman [BCW80]. The function computed by a $\oplus$-BP1 can be characterized by a polynom over $GF(2^m)$. We can work in $GF(2^m)$ as in $\mathbb{F}_2[x]/p(x)$ where $p(x)$ is an irreducible polynomial of degree m. Such polynomials can be find quickly. For instance, $x^{2 \cdot 3^k} + x^{3^k} + 1$ is irreducible in $\mathbb{F}_2[x]$ for each $k \in \mathbb{N}$ [LN86]. It is easy to see that $k = \lceil log_3(\frac{\lceil log_2(2n)\rceil}{2})\rceil$ produces a field with sufficient many elements

(more than $2n$) and the multiplication in this field can be done efficiently (in time polynomial in n). To complete the proof see the corresponding algorithm given in the appendix. □

Since the proposition continues to hold also for type-restricted Ω-BP1s (see the next section), the only candidates for a manageable extension of BP1s in the settings of Ω-BPs are $\oplus$-BP1s. In the following we are going to show that $\oplus$-BP1s indeed provide a manageable extension at the price of giving up determinism.

4.2 Probabilistic Feasible Analysis and Manipulation of $\oplus$-BP1s

In order to make binary synthesis feasible, similar as in the case of BP1s, we consider type-restricted $\oplus$-BP1s.

Definition. (Type-restricted $\oplus$-BP1s)
A $\oplus$-BP1 P defines a $\oplus$-BP1-type $typ(P)$ in a similar way as BP1s do. P is called *type-restricted* if it is possible to transform $typ(P)$ into an ordinary BP1-type τ_P by means of a sequence of algebraical BP-type-reductions, simple type-reductions applied merely to $\oplus$-nodes, and (simple or algebraical) BP1-type-extensions.

In order to give an example of a type-restricted $\oplus$-BP1 consider $\oplus$-BP1s with the following property. The types of the BP1s rooting in the $\oplus$-nodes are comparable after eliminating $\oplus$-nodes. Indeed, starting in the sinks, all $\oplus$-nodes can be easily eliminated in such $\oplus$-BP1-types. One has only to extend one of the both types by means of certain BP-type-extensions before both types can be identified. Of course, the possibility of such an elimination of the $\oplus$-nodes does nothing say about the redundance of these nodes within the original $\oplus$-BP1s. For example, the $\oplus$-synthesis of BP1s (i.e. the elimination of one $\oplus$-node) can produce a quadratic blow-up.

Definition. (Consistent BP1s and $\oplus$-BP1s)
Two $\oplus$-BP1s (BP1s) P, P' are said to be *consistent* if they are type-restricted and if the corresponding BP1-types τ_P and $\tau_{P'}$ are subtypes of a common type.

Theorem 6.
Let P and P' are two consistent $\oplus$-BP1s.
1. The equivalence of P and P' can be tested probabilistically in polynomial time.
2. Let $*$ be a binary operator. The $*$-synthesis $*$-$SYN_{\oplus-BP1_c}$ of P and P' can be solved in polynomial time.

Proof.
Since the $\oplus$-synthesis can be trivially performed on $\oplus$-BP1s it suffices to consider $\wedge$-$SYN_{\oplus-BP1_c}$. Due to the distributivity of $\wedge$ and $\oplus$ a slight and straightforward extension of the synthesis algorithm for consistent BP1s given in the appendix yields the assertion of Theorem 7. Let us only remark, that, after this extension, the complexity of the algorithm remains moderate. □

5 Concluding Remarks

We have identified consistent BP1s and consistent $\oplus$-BP1s as those classes of branching programs where important CAD-tasks can be performed efficiently. Since $\oplus$-BP1 are often much more succinct than BP1s (e. g. $\oplus cl_{n,3}$ (odd number of triangles in a graph) can be computed with a polynomial size type–restricted $\oplus$-BP1 but requires exponential size BP1s [A&86]), and since BP1s are often much more succinct than OBDDs (e. g. [Bry91,Bry92]) we essentially contribute to the research of data structures suited for CAD applications. A BP1–package as well as a $\oplus$-BP1–package are in preparation.

References

[A&86] M. Ajtai, L. Babai, P. Hajnal, J. Komlos, P. Pudlak, V. Rödl, E. Szemeredi, G. Turan: Two Lower Bounds for Branching Programs, Proc. 18. ACM STOC, 1986, 30-38.

[BBR90] K. S. Brace, R. E. Bryant, R. L. Rudell: Efficient Implementation of a BDD package. Proc. of 27th Design Automation Conf., 1990, 40-45.

[BCW80] M. Blum, A. K. Chandra, M. N. Wegman: Equivalence of Free Boolean Graphs Can Be Decided Probabilistically in Polynomial Time, IPL 10, 2, 1980, 80-82.

[BHR91] Y. Breitbart, H. B. Hunt III, D. Rosenkrantz: The Size of Binary Decision Diagrams Representing Boolean Functions, submitted to Inf. and Comp. 1991.

[Bry86] R. E. Bryant: Graph-Based Algorithms for Boolean Function Manipulation, IEEE Trans. Computers, C-35, 8, 1986, 677-691.

[Bry92] R. E. Bryant: Symbolic Boolean Manipulation with Ordered Binary Decision Diagrams, to appear in IEEE Trans. Computers, 1992.

[BCMD90] J. R. Burch, E. M. Clarke, K. L. McMillan, D.L. Dill: Sequential Circuit Verification Using Symbolic Model Checking, Proc. 27th IEEE DAC'90, 1990, 46-51.

[CHS74] R. L. Constable, H. B. Hunt III, S. Sahni: On the Computational Complexity of Scheme Equivalence, Proc. 8th Princeton Conf. on Information Sciences and Systems, 1974.

[FHS78] S. Fortune, J. Hopcroft, E. M. Schmidt: The Complexity of Equivalence and Containment for Free Single Program Schemes. LNCS 62, 1978, 227-240.

[FFK88] M. Fuita, H. Fujisawa, N. Kawoto: Evaluation and Improvements of Boolean Comparison Method Based on Binary Decision Diagrams, Proc. IEEE ICCAD'88, 1988, 2-5.

[GM92] J. Gergov, Ch. Meinel: Analysis and Manipulation of Boolean Functions in Terms of Decision Graphs, Proc. WG'92, LNCS, 1992.

[GM92b] J. Gergov, Ch. Meinel: Efficient Analysis and Manipulation of OBDDs Can Be Extended to Read–once–only Branching Programs, Forschungsbericht Nr. 92-10, Univ. Trier, 1992.

[LN86] R. Lidl, H. Niederreiter: Introduction to Finite Fields and Their Applications. Cambridge University Press, 1986.

[KMW91] M. Krause, Ch. Meinel, S. Waack: Separating the Eraser Turing Machine Classes $L_e, NL_e, co-NL_e$ and P_e, TCS 86 (1991), 267-275.

[Mei88] Ch. Meinel: The Power of Polynomial Size Ω-Branching Programs, Proc. STACS'88 (Bourdeaux), LNCS 294, 81-90.

[Mei89] Ch. Meinel: Modified Branching Programs and Their Computational Power, Springer-Verlag, LNCS 370, 1989.

[Mei91] Ch. Meinel: Branching Programs - An Efficient Data Structure for Computer-Aided Circuit Design, Preprint UGH Paderborn, Nr. 93, 1991.

[MKLC89] S. Muroga, Y. Kambayashi, H. C. Lai, J. N. Culliney: The Transduction Method, IEEE Trans. Computers, C-38, 1989, 1404-1424.

[MWBS88] S. Malik, A. Wang, R. Bryant, A. Sangiovanni–Vincentelli: Logical Verification Using Binary Decision Diagrams in a Logical Synthesis Environment. Proc. IEEE Intern. Conf. on CAD, 1988, 6–9.

[SW92] D. Sieling, I. Wegener: Graph Driven BDDs - A New Data Structure for Boolean Functions, personal communications, manuscript.

6 Appendix

6.1 Feasible Algorithm for the Binary Synthesis of BP1s

We start with a procedure that, for each node v of a given BP1 P makes some information available about the variables to be tested in the successor nodes of v.

Definition. (Vectors s_v) Let P be a BP1 over $X_n = \{x_1, \ldots, x_n\}$, and let v be a node of P. The vector $s_v \in \{0,1\}^n$ is defined as follows:

$$s_v[x] = \begin{cases} 1 \text{ if } x \text{ has to be tested on any } v\text{-to-sink path in } P \\ 0 \text{ otherwise} \end{cases}$$

Lemma. The set of all vectors s_v, $v \in P$, can be computed in time $O(n * size(P))$. □

Presenting our algorithm we use the following denotations: Let v and v' are nodes of two BP1s P and P', respectively, and let $l(v)$ and $l(v')$ denote the variables tested in v and v'. We set

$$c(v, v') = \begin{cases} 0 \text{ if } l(v) \neq l(v') \text{ and if } s_v[l(v')] = s_{v'}[l(v)] = 1 \\ 1 \text{ otherwise,} \end{cases}$$

and

$$l(v, v') = \begin{cases} l(v) & \text{if } l(v) = l(v') \text{ or } s_{v'}[l(v)] = 0 \\ l(v') & \text{if } s_v[l(v')] = 0 \\ \text{undefined otherwise} \end{cases}$$

By $source(P)$ we denote the source of P. If $x \in X_n$ and x does not appear on any path in P then $P_{|x=0} = P_{|x=1} = P$. In the case $x = l(source(P))$ we denote by $P_{|x=\alpha}$, $\alpha \in \{0,1\}$, the BP1 that starts in the α-successor of $source(P)$.

Algorithm. (Synthesis of consistent BP1s)

Input:
A Boolean operator $* \in \mathbb{B}_2$, and two consistent reduced BP1s P' and P''.

Output:
A BP1 P consistent with P' and P'' that computes $f = f_{P'} * f_{P''}$.

Assumptions:
We assume that vectors s_v are computed for all nodes v of P' and P''.

$T[.,.]$ is a $size(P) \times size(P')$ table. Before the first call of $synthesis(*, P', P'', P)$ all entries of T are equal to zero.

procedure $synthesis(*, P', P'', P)$.

begin
  if
      One of P' and P'' is a α-sink, $\alpha \in \{0, 1\}$
  then
      {Generate P by modifying the sinks of the other BP1 according to α and $*$;
      (For instance, if $\alpha = 1$ and $* = \oplus$ a β-sink has to be changed to a $\bar{\beta}$-sink, $\beta \in \{0, 1\}$);
      $T[source(P'), source(P'')] :=$ a pointer to the result of the generated P};
  if
    $T[source(P'), source(P'')] \neq 0$)
  then
    $T[source(P'), source(P'')]$ is pointer to the already synthesized BP1 P
  else
      {We introduce a new node v and set $l(v) := l(source(P'), source(P''))$;
      $synthesis(*, P'_{l(v)=0}, P''_{l(v)=0}, P_0)$; $synthesis(*, P'_{l(v)=1}, P''_{l(v)=1}, P_1)$;
      We construct P by taking v as source and P_α, $\alpha \in \{0, 1\}$, as α-successor of v;
      $T[source(P'), source(P'')]$ is set to a pointer to P}; **end**;
begin /** main program **/
  $synthesis(*, P', P'', P)$;
  We compute $red(P)$;
  $return(red(P))$;
end.

6.2 Probabilistical Feasible Equivalence Test for $\oplus$-BP1s

Definition. Let P be a $\oplus$-BP1 and I an integral domain with $char(I) = 2$. Then we assign to each node v of P a polynom p_v in the following way:
1. $p_v = \alpha$ if v is an α-sink;
2. $p_v = (1 - x)p_{v_0} + xp_{v_1}$ if v is a inner node where v_α is the α-successor of v, $\alpha \in \{0, 1\}$, and $l(v) = x$;
3. $p_v = p_{v_0} + p_{v_1}$ if $l(v) = \oplus$ where v_0, v_1 denote the successors of v.
The polynom of P, $p(P)$, is the polynom of the source v_0 of P, $p_P = p_{v_0}$. p_P can be computed with $size(P)$ many additions and at most $2size(P)$ many multiplications.

Input:
Two $\oplus$-BP1s P' and P''.

Output:
If P' and P'' are equivalent the algorithm answers always with "yes" othercase the algorithm gives "no" with probability greater than $\frac{1}{2}$.

Assumptions:
F is a finite field of characteristic two with more than $2n$ elements.

procedure *equ(P',P'')*;
begin
choose independently and uniformly $a_1, a_2, \ldots, a_n$ *from* F;
compute $p_{P'}(a_1, \ldots, a_n)$ *in* F;
compute $p_{P''}(a_1, \ldots, a_n)$ *in* F;
if $(p_{P'}(a_1, \ldots, a_n) = p_{P''}(a_1, \ldots, a_n))$ **then** return("yes"); /*P' and P'' are equivalent */
else return("no"); /* P' and P'' are not equivalent */
end.

On Syntactic Congruences for $\omega-$languages

Oded Maler*
LGI-IMAG (Campus)
B.P. 53x
38041 Grenoble
France
maler@vercors.imag.fr

Ludwig Staiger**
Technische Universität Cottbus
Lehrstuhl für Theoretische Informatik
Karl-Marx-Str. 17
O-7500 Cottbus
Germany
staiger@tucs1.rz.tu-cottbus.de

Abstract. For $\omega-$languages several notions of syntactic congruence were defined. The present paper investigates relationships between the so-called simple (because it is a simple translation from the usual definition in the case of finitary languages) syntactic congruence and its infinitary refinements investigated by Arnold [Ar85]. We show that in both cases not every ω-language having a finite syntactic monoid is regular and we give a characterization of those ω-languages having finite syntactic monoids. As the main result we derive a condition which guarantees that the simple syntactic congruence and Arnold's syntactic congruence coincide and show that *all* ω-languages in the Borel class $F_\sigma \cap G_\delta$ satisfy this condition.

Finally we define an alternative canonical object for ω-languages, namely a family of right-congruence relations. Using this object we give a necessary and sufficient condition for a regular ω-language to be accepted by its minimal-state automaton.

---

* The results presented in this paper have been obtained while the author was with INRIA/IRISA, Rennes, France.

** The results presented in this paper have been obtained while the author was with Universität Siegen, Siegen, Germany.

1 Introduction

The well-known Kleene-Myhill-Nerode theorem for languages states that a language $U \subseteq \Sigma^*$ is regular (rational), iff its syntactic right-congruence $\sim_U$ defined by

$$x \sim_U y \text{ iff } \forall v \in \Sigma^* : xv \in U \leftrightarrow yv \in U$$

has a finite index. In that case the right-congruence classes correspond to the states of the unique minimal automaton that accepts U. An equivalent condition is that the finer two-sided syntactic congruence $\simeq_U$ defined by

$$x \simeq_U y \text{ iff } \forall u \in \Sigma^* : ux \sim_U uy$$

has a finite index. Here the congruence classes correspond to the elements of the transformation monoid associated with the minimal automaton accepting U.

As already observed by Trakhtenbrot [Tr62] these same observations are no longer true in the case of ω-languages (cf. also [JT83], [LS77] or [St83]). Here the class of ω-languages having a finite syntactic monoid (so-called finite-state ω-languages) is much larger than the class of ω-languages accepted by finite automata (regular or rational ω-languages) [St83].

Recently Arnold [Ar85] investigated a new concept of syntactic congruence for ω-languages. As his results show, this concept yields a characterization of regular ω-languages by finite monoids, but not in the same simple way as for finitary languages.

As we shall see below, despite the fact that Arnold's monoid is indeed more accurate (it is infinite for some ω-languages which are finite-state), yet there are even non-Borel ω-languages for which Arnold's monoid is finite. To this end we shall derive a necessary and sufficient condition for an ω-language for having a finite syntactic monoid in the sense of Arnold. As the main result we give a condition on ω-languages that guarantees that their Arnold's syntactic congruence coincides with the simple one. We show that this condition holds for all (including those which are not finite-state) ω-languages in the Borel-class $F_\sigma \cap G_\delta$ and thus extend the result in [St83].

Finally, we introduce an alternative notion of recognizability by a family of *right*-congruence relations, and give a necessary and sufficient condition for an ω-language to be acceptable by its "minimal-state" automaton, that is, an automaton isomorphic to its syntactic right-congruence.

2 Preliminaries

By Σ^* we denote the set (monoid) of finite words on a finite alphabet Σ, including the empty word e, let Σ^+ denote $\Sigma^* - \{e\}$ and Σ^ω the set of infinite words (ω-words). As usual we call subsets of Σ^* as *languages* and subsets of Σ^ω as ω-*languages*. For $u \in \Sigma^*$ and $\beta \in \Sigma^* \cup \Sigma^\omega$ let $u\beta$ be their concatenation and let u^ω be the ω-word formed by concatenating the word u infinitely often (provided $u \neq e$). The concatenation product extends in an obvious way to subsets $U \subseteq \Sigma^\omega$ and $B \subseteq \Sigma^* \cup \Sigma^\omega$. For a language $U \subseteq \Sigma^*$ let U^* and U^ω denote respectively the set of finite and infinite sequences formed by concatenating words in U. By $|u|_a$ we denote the number of occurrences of the letter $a \in \Sigma$ in the word $u \in \Sigma^*$. Finally $u \preceq v$ and $u \prec v$ denote the facts that u is a prefix and a proper prefix of v.

An equivalence relation $\simeq$ is a *congruence* on Σ^* if $u \simeq v$ implies $xuy \simeq xvy$ for every $u, v, x, y \in \Sigma^*$. We say that $\simeq$ is a *right-congruence* if $u \simeq v$ implies $uy \simeq vy$ for every $u, v, y \in \Sigma^*$. Clearly every congruence is also a right-congruence. We will denote by $[v] := \{w : w \in \Sigma^* \text{ and } w \simeq v\}$ the equivalence class containing the word v, and we shall use $\langle v \rangle$ instead of $[v]$ if the corresponding relation is a right-congruence. We will say that $\simeq$ is *finite* when it has a finite index (or alternatively, $\Sigma^* / \simeq$ is finite), and that it is *trivial* when $\simeq$ is $\Sigma^* \times \Sigma^*$.

As in [Ar85] we say that a congruence $\simeq$ *covers* an ω-language F provided $F = \bigcup\{[u][v]^\omega : uv^\omega \in F\}$ and we say that an ω-language F is *regular* provided there is a finite congruenc $\simeq$ which covers F.

The natural (*Cantor-*) topology on the space Σ^ω is defined as follows. A set $E \subseteq \Sigma^\omega$ is *open* iff it is of the form $U\Sigma^\omega$, where $U \subseteq \Sigma^*$ (in other words, $\beta \in E$ iff it has a prefix in U). A set is *closed* if its complement is open (or if its elements do not have any prefix in some $U' \subseteq \Sigma^*$). The class G_δ consists of all countable intersection of open sets. A set is in F_σ if its complement is in G_δ, or if it can be written as a countable union of closed sets. The rest of the Borel hierarchy is constructed similarly.

A deterministic Muller automaton is a quintuple $\mathcal{A} = (\Sigma, Q, \delta, q_0, \mathcal{F})$ where Σ is the input alphabet, Q is the state-space, $\delta : Q \times \Sigma \to Q$ is the transition function, q_0 the initial state and $\mathcal{F} \subseteq 2^Q$ is a family of accepting subsets. By $Inf(\mathcal{A}, \alpha)$ we denote the subset of Q which is visited infinitely many times while $\mathcal{A}$ is reading $\alpha \in \Sigma^\omega$. The ω-language accepted/recognized by $\mathcal{A}$ is $\{\alpha \in \Sigma^\omega : Inf(\mathcal{A}, \alpha) \in \mathcal{F}\}$. According to Büchi-McNaughton theorem an ω-language is regular iff it is recognized by some deterministic finite-state Muller automaton. Additional material on ω-languages appears in [Ei74, HR85, St87, Th90, PP91].

Definition 1 (Syntactic Congruences) *Let $E \subseteq \Sigma^\omega$ be an ω-language. We associate with E the following equivalence relations on Σ^*:*

– *Syntactic right-congruence:*

$$x \sim_E y \text{ iff } \forall \beta \in \Sigma^\omega : x\beta \in E \leftrightarrow y\beta \in E \tag{1}$$

– *Simple syntactic congruence:*

$$x \simeq_E y \text{ iff } \forall u \in \Sigma^* : ux \sim_E uy \tag{2}$$

– *Infinitary syntactic-congruence:*

$$x \approx_E y \text{ iff } \forall u, v \in \Sigma^* : u(xv)^\omega \in E \leftrightarrow u(yv)^\omega \in E \tag{3}$$

– *Arnold's syntactic-congruence:*

$$x \cong_E y \text{ iff } x \simeq y \land x \approx y \tag{4}$$

By definition $\simeq$ refines $\sim$ and $\cong$ refines both $\simeq$ and $\approx$. In the general case $\simeq$ and $\approx$ are not comparable, since they refer to two different kinds of interchangability of x and y. For example, for $E = \{a, b\}^* a^\omega$, $a \simeq_E b$ but $a \not\approx_E b$. On the other hand for $E = abc^\omega$, $a \not\simeq_E b$ but $a \approx_E b$. We shall see later that some conditions on E imply that $\simeq$ refines $\approx$. An ω-language E such that $\simeq_E$ (or equivalently, $\sim_E$) is finite is called *finite-state*.

3 Some observations on Arnold's congruence

In this section we show that despite the fact that $\cong_E$ provides additional information on E which is missing from $\simeq_E$, still it fails in characterizing regular ω-languages as does $\simeq$ for languages.

Fact 1 *There are ω-languages which are finite-state but their Arnold's syntactic monoid is infinite.*

Proof: Let the language $V \subseteq \{a,b\}^*$ be defined by the equation

$$V = a \cup bV^2$$

Alternatively, V may be defined as the language consisting of those words $v \in \Sigma^*$ satisfying $|v|_a = |v|_b + 1$ and $|u|_a \le |u|_b$ for every $u \prec v$. Let $E = V^\omega$. Then one easily verifies $E = VE = (a \cup bV^2)E = \{a,b\}E$. Thus $u \simeq_E v$ for every $u, v \in \{a,b\}^*$ and $\simeq_E$ is trivial. On the other hand we show that for every i, j such that $0 < i < j$, $b^i \not\cong_E b^j$, hence $\cong_E$ is infinite. To this end we show that $(b^i a^{i+1})^\omega \in E$ and $(b^j a^{i+1})^\omega \notin E$. Since $b^i a^{i+1} \in V$, we have $(b^i a^{i+1})^\omega \in E = V^\omega$. Since every word in V contains more occurrences of a than of b, $j > i$ implies that the ω-word $(b^j a^{i+1})^\omega$ has no prefix in V, and consequently $(b^j a^{i+1})^\omega \notin V^\omega = E$. $\square$

The second observation (as already noted in [Ar85]) is that, in general, the finiteness of $\cong_E$ does not guarantee regularity of E:

Fact 2 *The ω-language $Ult = \{uv^\omega : u \in \Sigma^*, v \in \Sigma^+\}$ of all ultimately periodic ω-words has a trivial syntactic monoid, that is $x \cong_{Ult} y$ for every $x, y \in \Sigma^*$, but Ult is not regular.*

Next we investigate the question which ω-languages have a finite syntactic monoid in the sense of Arnold. To this aim we show that with every ω-language E we can associate in a canonical way an ω-language F_E which is covered by $\cong_E$. Define

$$F_E = \bigcup \{[u][v]^\omega : uv^\omega \in E\}$$

where $[\cdot]$ denotes a congruence of $\cong_E$. It holds the following:

Lemma 3 $E \cap Ult = F_E \cap Ult$.

Proof: By definition $E \cap Ult \subseteq F_E \cap Ult$. Let $xy^\omega \in F_E$. Then there are u, v such that $uv^\omega \in E$ and $xy^\omega \in [u][v]^\omega$. From this we can obtain words y_1 and y_2 such that $y = y_1 y_2$, and natural numbers i, j, m and n such that $xy^i y_1 \in [u][v]^m$ and $y_2 y^j y_1 \in [v]^n$. Since $\cong_E$ is a congruence, it follows that $xy^i y_1 \cong_E uv^m$ and $y_2 y^j y_1 \cong_E v^n$, and because $uv^m (v^n)^\omega = uv^\omega \in E$, by the definition of $\cong_E$, also $xy^i y_1 (y_2 y^j y_1)^\omega = xy^\omega \in E$. $\square$

Theorem 4 *For every $E \subseteq \Sigma^\omega$, Arnold's syntactic congruence $\cong_E$ is finite iff E is finite-state and there is a regular ω-language F such that $E \cap Ult = F \cap Ult$.*

Proof: Let E be finite-state and let the regular ω-language F satisfy $E \cap Ult = F \cap Ult$. It can be easily verified that $x \simeq_E y$ and $x \cong_{F \cap Ult} y$ imply $x \cong_E y$ and thus $\simeq_E \cap \cong_F \subseteq \cong_E$. But the congruences $\simeq_E$ and $\cong_F$ are both finite and so is $\cong_E$. Conversely, let $\cong_E$ be finite. Then F_E is a regular ω-language satisfying $E \cap Ult = F_E \cap Ult$. $\square$

In [St83] it was shown that the cardinality of the set $\{E : \simeq_E \text{ is finite}\}$ is $2^{2^{\aleph_0}}$, in particular, there are already as many subsets of Σ^ω whose simple syntactic monoid is trivial. The following claim shows that the same is true in the case of $\cong_E$:

Claim 5 *There are $2^{2^{\aleph_0}}$ ω-languages having a trivial syntactic monoid in the sense of Arnold.*

Proof: Since the set $\{E : \simeq_E \text{ is trivial}\}$ is closed under Boolean operations, any such ω-language F splits in a unique way into a disjoint union $(F \cap Ult) \cup (F \setminus Ult)$ where for both parts $\simeq$ is trivial. As Ult is countable, there are at most $2^{\aleph_0}$ distinct parts of the form $F \cap Ult$. Consequently, there are $2^{2^{\aleph_0}}$ ω-languages $E \subseteq \Sigma^\omega \setminus Ult$ such that $\simeq_E$ is trivial. But for every such E $\approx_E$ is trivial and hence Arnold's syntactic congruence of E is trivial, what verifies our assertion. $\square$

Given that a a Borel class in Σ^ω contains only $2^{\aleph_0}$ sets and that there are only countably many Borel classes [Ku66], it follows that there are ω-languages E even beyond the Borel hierarchy for which $\approx_E$ is trivial. This is in sharp contrast with the Myhill-Nerode theorem where the finiteness of the syntactic monoid implies the regularity of the language.

4 The case when $\simeq$ and $\cong$ coincide

In Theorem 21 of [St83] it was proved that every finite-state ω-language E which is simultaneously in the Borel classes F_σ and in G_δ Σ^ω is regular. Our aim is to show that this very condition also guarantees that Arnold's syntactic congruence of E coincides with the simple syntactic congruence of E. It is remarkable that this condition holds for all ω-languages in $F_\sigma \cap G_\delta$ not only for those which are finite-state.

First let us mention the following simple properties of the congruences $\simeq_E$ and $\cong_E$:

Fact 6 *For every $u \in \Sigma^*$, $x, y \in \Sigma^+$: 1) If $x \simeq_E y$ then $u\{x,y\}^* x^\omega \cap E \neq \emptyset$ implies $u\{x,y\}^* x^\omega \subseteq E$ 2) If $x \cong_E y$ then $u\{x,y\}^* x^\omega \cap E \neq \emptyset$ implies $u\{x,y\}^* y^\omega \subseteq E$.*

Now we obtain the following necessary and sufficient condition under which the congruences $\simeq_E$ and $\cong_E$ coincide:

Lemma 7 *Let $E \subseteq \Sigma^\omega$. Then $\simeq_E = \cong_E$ if and only if the following condition holds*

$$\forall u \in \Sigma^* x, y \in \Sigma^+ : x \simeq_E y \to (u\{x,y\}^* x^\omega \subseteq E \to u\{x,y\}^* y^\omega \cap E \neq \emptyset)$$

Proof: Clearly, the condition is necessary. In order to show its sufficiency we assume $x \simeq y$, and we show that then

$$\forall u, v \in \Sigma^* : u(xv)^\omega \in E \to u(yv)^\omega \in E)$$

that is, the additional condition for $\cong_E$ is satisfied.

If $x \simeq y$ and $u(xv)^\omega \in E$ then $xv \simeq yv$, and by the above claim it holds also $u\{xv, yv\}^*(xv)^\omega \subseteq E$. Now our condition implies $u\{xv, yv\}^*(yv)^\omega \cap E \neq \emptyset$. Again the above claim shows that $u(xv)^\omega \in E$. □

As an immediate consequence we obtain the following:

Corollary 8 *If for every $u \in \Sigma^* x, y \in \Sigma^+$ the inclusion $u\{x, y\}^* x^\omega \subseteq E$ implies that $u\{x, y\}^* y^\omega \cap E \neq \emptyset$ then $\simeq_E = \cong_E$.*

In order to prove the announced statement for ω-languages in the Borel-class $F_\sigma \cap G_\delta$ we recall that for every ω-language $E \in G_\delta$ there exists a language $U \in \Sigma^*$ such that for every $\beta \in \Sigma^\omega$, $\beta \in E$ iff β has infinitely many prefixes in U.

Theorem 9 *For every ω-language $E \in F_\sigma \cap G_\delta$, and every $x, y \in \Sigma^*$ $x \simeq_E y$ iff $x \cong_E y$.*

Proof: It suffices to show that every ω-language E in the Borel-class $F_\sigma \cap G_\delta$ satisfies the premise of corollary 8.

Since both E and its complement are in G_δ, there exist two languages U and U' such that every ω-word in E has infinitely many prefixes in U and every ω-word not in E has infinitely many prefixes in U'. Suppose that for some $u, x, y \in \Sigma^*$, $u\{x, y\}^* x^\omega \subseteq E$ and $u\{x, y\}^* y^\omega \subseteq \Sigma^\omega \setminus E$.

Since $ux^\omega \in E$ there is a number k_1 such that ux^{k_1} has a prefix in U, and since $ux^{k_1} y^\omega \notin E$, the word $ux^{k_1} y^{l_1}$ has a prefix in U' for some l_1. Next we consider $ux^{k_1} y^{l_1} x^\omega \in E$: there must be some k_2 such that $ux^{k_1} y^{l_1} x^{k_2}$ has at least two prefixes in U, etc. Repeating this alternating argument, we construct an infinite sequence $ux^{k_1} y^{l_1} \ldots x^{k_i} y^{l_i} \ldots$ having infinitely many prefixes in U and infinitely many prefixes in U' and thus belonging simultaneously to E and to its complement. □

It is worth mentioning that this result does not hold for higher Borel classes, e.g., $\{a, b\}^* a^\omega$ which is in F_σ but not in G_δ. On the other hand, from claim 5 it follows that $\simeq_E$ and $\cong_E$ coincide for some non-Borel sets.

5 Acceptance by the minimal-state automaton

In this section we will give a necessary and sufficient condition for a regular ω-language E to be acceptable by its minimal-state automaton. We will start with a necessary condition which is based on a relation between $\approx_E$ and a refinement of $\simeq_E$. Then we introduce more subtle definitions in order to arrive to a condition which is also sufficient.

First we define a congruence relation based on $\sim_E$ which refines $\simeq_E$ by considering two words equivalent only if they have the same set of right-factors (modulo $\sim_E$).

Definition 2 (Factorized congruence) *The factorization of $\sim_E$ is a congruence $\sim_E^*$ defined as*

$$
\begin{aligned}
x \sim_E^* y \text{ iff } &\forall u \in \Sigma^* \ ux \sim_E uy \\
&\text{and} \quad (\forall v \prec x)(\exists v' \prec y) \ uv \sim_E uv' \\
&\text{and} \quad (\forall v' \prec y)(\exists v \prec x) \ uv \sim_E uv'
\end{aligned} \tag{5}
$$

It is more intuitive to see the meaning of this relation in terms the minimal-state automaton $\mathcal{A}$ isomorphic to $\sim_E$. Here $x \sim^* y$ iff from every state q both x and y lead to the same state while visiting the same set of states. One can see that $u \sim_E v$ and $x \sim^*_E y$ imply that for every z, $Inf(\mathcal{A}, u(xz)^\omega) = Inf(\mathcal{A}, v(yz)^\omega)$.

Claim 10 *An ω-regular set E can be accepted by its minimal-state automaton $\mathcal{A}$ using Muller condition only if for every $x, y \in \Sigma^*$, $x \sim^*_E y \to x \approx_E y$.*

Proof: Suppose $x \sim^*_E y \not\to x \approx_E y$, that is, for some $x \sim^*_E y$, there exist u, v such that $u(xv)^\omega \in E$ and $u(yv)^\omega \notin E$. But $xv \sim^*_E yv$, hence $Inf(\mathcal{A}, u(xv)^\omega) = Inf(\mathcal{A}, u(yv)^\omega)$ and $\mathcal{A}$ cannot accept E. □

The condition of the previous claim fails to be sufficient because two ω-words can have the same Inf in $\mathcal{A}$ without having the same $(\sim, \sim^*)$-factorization (for example, consider $E = \{ab^\omega\} \cup \{b, c\}^* c^\omega$ and the ω-words a^ω and ba^ω that reach their common Inf by different paths). For the sufficiency conditions we need different definitions. We consider $\sim_E$ as before and with *each* of its right-congruence classes $\langle u \rangle$ we associate two corresponding right-congruence relations: $\approx_u$ (syntactic) and $\sim^*_u$ (automatic).

Definition 3 (Syntactic induced right-congruence) *The syntactic right congruence induced by $\langle u \rangle$ is defined as:*

$$x \approx_u y \text{ iff } \quad ux \sim_E uy$$
$$\text{and } (\forall v \in \Sigma^*)(uxv \sim_E u) \to (u(xv)^\omega \in E \leftrightarrow u(yv)^\omega \in E) \tag{6}$$

One can see that $\approx_u$ is coarser than $\approx_E$ in two respects: 1) It does not quantify over all u (just those in $\langle u \rangle$), and 2) It does not quantify over all v, only over those for which v makes a cycle from $\langle u \rangle$. In fact $\sim_E$ and the induced family $\{\approx_u\}_{u \in \Sigma^*/\sim_E}$ can be considered as an alternative canonical object for E which satisfies the following saturation property:

Lemma 11 *For any regular ω-language E, let $\langle u \rangle$ be a class of $\sim_E$ and $[v]_u$ a class of $\approx_u$ satisfying $uv \sim u$. Then $\langle u \rangle([v]_u)^\omega \cap E \neq \emptyset$ implies $\langle u \rangle([v]_u)^\omega \subseteq E$*

Proof: We prove it similarly to lemma 2.2 in [Ar85]. Suppose the contrary, then by regularity there exists $uv^\omega \in E$ and $xy^\omega \in \langle u \rangle([v]_u)^\omega \setminus E$. By finiteness there exist some m, n such that $xy^\omega = zx_1 \ldots x_m(y_1 \ldots y_n)^\omega$ with $z \sim u$ and $x_i \approx_u y_j \approx_u v$ for every $i \leq m, j \leq n$. This implies that $zx_1 \ldots x_m \sim u$ and $y_1 \ldots y_n \approx_u v^n$ and thus by the definition of $\approx_u$, $zx_1 \ldots x_m(y_1 \ldots y_n)^\omega \in E$ if $u(v^n)^\omega \in E$ which means $xy^\omega \in E$ – a contradiction. □

Definition 4 (Automatic induced right-congruence) *The automatic right congruence induced by $\langle u \rangle$ is defined as:*

$$x \sim^*_u y \text{ iff } \quad ux \sim_E uy$$
$$\text{and } (\forall v \prec x)(((\exists z)uxz \sim_E uv) \to ((\exists v' \prec y)uv \sim_E uv'))$$
$$\text{and } (\forall v' \prec y)(((\exists z)uyz \sim_E uv') \to ((\exists v \prec x)uv \sim_E uv')) \tag{7}$$

Intuitively this means that in an automaton $\mathcal{A}$ isomorphic to $\sim_E$, $x \sim_u^* y$ iff $\delta(q_0, ux) = \delta(q_0, uy)$ and both ux and uy visit the same set of states in the strongly-connected component (SCC) of $\delta(q_0, ux)$. We do not care here if ux and uy visit different states outside that SCC.

Theorem 12 *Let E be a regular ω-language, let $\sim_E$ be its syntactic right-congruence (1) and let $\approx_u$ and $\sim_u^*$ be respectively the induced syntactic (6) and automatic (7) right congruences. E can be accepted by an automaton $\mathcal{A}$ isomorphic to its syntactic right-congruence $\sim_E$ if and only if for every $u, x, y \in \Sigma^*$, $x \sim_u^* y \rightarrow x \approx_u y$.*

Proof: It can be easily seen that all the ω-words having the same Inf in $\mathcal{A}$ admit the same factorization $\langle u \rangle ([v]_u)^\omega$ where $\langle u \rangle$ and $[v]_u$ are classes of $\sim$ and $\sim_u^*$ respectively and $uv \sim u$. Our condition implies that they have also the same factorization $\langle u \rangle ([v]_u)^\omega$ where $[v]_u$ is a class of $\approx_u$ and $uv \sim u$. According to lemma 11 all these ω-words are either in E or in $\Sigma^\omega \setminus E$ and thus $\mathcal{A}$ can accept E using Muller condition. Conversely, suppose $x \sim_u^* y \not\rightarrow x \approx_u y$, that is, for some $u, x, y \in \Sigma^*$ satisfying $x \sim_u^* y$, there exists v such that $uxv \sim u$, $u(xv)^\omega \in E$ and $u(yv)^\omega \notin E$. But in this case since $\delta(q_0, u)$ and $\delta(q_0, ux)$ share the same SCC, $x \sim_u^* y$ implies $Inf(\mathcal{A}, u(xv)^\omega) = Inf(\mathcal{A}, u(yv)^\omega)$ and thus $\mathcal{A}$ cannot accept E. □

As an illustration consider again $E = \{a, b\}^* a^\omega$. The relation $\sim_E$ is trivial, hence $\sim_u^*$ is trivial as well. On the other hand, $\approx_u$ has two classes a^+ and $(a^*b)^+$ and E cannot be accepted by its minimal-state automaton.

The introduction of the syntactic family of right-congruences $\{\approx_u\}_{u \in \Sigma^*/\sim_E}$ may have significance beyond the proof of the above theorem. Up to now the only syntactic characterization of ω-languages was by means of a two-sided congruence and the lack of the other half of a Myhill-Nerode theorem was believed to be an inherent feature of the theory of ω-languages. From a practical point of view, although Arnold's congruence $\cong_E$ (which is the intersection of $\{\approx_u\}$) has a simpler definition, its size might be exponentially larger, and there are situations[3] where *the right-congruences are the right congruences.*

Acknowledgement

We would like to thank A. Arnold for not believing a stronger version of claim 10 and E. Badouel for pointing out that an earlier version of theorem 12 was weaker than necessary.

References

[Ar85] A. Arnold, A syntactic congruence for rational ω-languages, *Theoret. Comput. Sci.* 39, 333-335, 1985.

[Ei74] S. Eilenberg, *Automata, Languages and Machines, Vol. A*, Academic Press, New-York, 1974.

[HR85] H.J. Hoogeboom and G. Rozenberg, Infinitary Languages - Basic Theory and Applications to Concurrent Systems, in J.W. de-Bakker et al. (Eds.), *Current Trends in Concurrency*, 266-342, LNCS 224, Springer, Berlin, 1985.

---

[3] For example, when we want to learn an ω-language from examples as in [MP91].

[JT83] H. Jürgensen and G. Thierrin, On ω-languages whose syntactic monoid is trivial, *Intern. J. Comput. Inform. Sci.* 12, 359-365, 1983.

[Ku66] K. Kuratowski, *Topology I*, Academic Press, New York, 1966.

[MP91] O. Maler and A. Pnueli, On the Learnability of Infinitary Regular Sets, in L.G. Valiant and M.K. Warmuth, Proc. of the 4th annual workshop on *Computational Learning Theory*, Morgan Kaufmann, San Mateo, 1991.

[PP91] D. Perrin and J.-E. Pin, *Mots Infinis*, Report LITP 91.06, Institut Blaise Pascal, Paris, 1991.

[LS77] R. Lindner und L. Staiger, *Algebraische Codierungstheorie – Theorie der sequentiellen Codierungen*, Akademie-Verlag, Berlin, 1977.

[St83] L. Staiger, Finite-state ω-languages, *J. Comput. System Sci.* 27, 434-448, 1983.

[St87] L. Staiger, Research in the Theory of ω-languages, *J. Inf. Process. Cybern. EIK* 23, 415-439, 1987.

[Th90] W. Thomas, Automata on Infinite Objects, in J. Van Leeuwen (Ed.), *Handbook of Theoretical Computer Science*, Vol. B, 133-191, Elsevier, Amsterdam, 1990.

[Tr62] B.A. Trakhtenbrot, Finite automata and monadic second order logic, *Siberian Math. J.* 3, 103-131, 1962. (Russian; English translation in: AMS Transl. 59, 23-55, 1969.)

A Polynomial Time Algorithm for the Equivalence of two Morphisms on ω-Regular Languages

Stefano Varricchio

Dipartimento di Matematica Università di Catania, Italy.

Abstract. Let $L \subseteq A^{\omega}$ be an ω-regular language given by means of a non-deterministic Büchi automaton M. Let $f, g : A^{\infty} \rightarrow B^{\infty}$ be two morphisms. We give an algorithm to decide whether f and g are equivalent (word by word) on L. This algorithm has time complexity $O(mn^3)$, where n is the number of arcs of M and m is the size of f and g. This result improves the only known algorithm for this problem which is exponential time [3].

1 Introduction and preliminaries

Infinite words and sets of them (ω-languages) played a central role in Computer Science and Formal Languages theory since the beginning. The theory of ω-regular languages, started with [2], studies the behavior of finite automata on infinite words. Morphisms of free monoids have always had great importance in this context, since they can express many undecidable problems. The following statement proved in [1] has been an open problem for many years (Ehrenfeucht's conjecture): Any language L of a finitely generated free monoid has a finite subset L' such that whenever two morphisms are equivalent on L' (word by word) they are equivalent on L (the set L' is also called a test set for L) . This property has been generalized to ω-languages in [7].

In principle the existence of finite test sets might assure the decidability of the equivalence of two morphism on a language L; unfortunately this is not the case, since the proof of Ehrenfeucht's conjecture is purely existential and in general no algorithm may be given to construct a finite test set. Any way for some families of formal languages (regular, context-free, DOL languages) an effective procedure can be given. In a recent paper [6] was proved that for a regular language L a finite test set can be found by an algorithm which is polynomial time with respect to the number of arcs of a non deterministic finite automaton which recognizes L. This also gives a polynomial time algorithm for the equivalence of two morphism on a regular language.

The equivalence problem for morphisms on ω-regular languages has been proved to be decidable in [3], anyway the algorithm proposed is exponential time. In this paper we give an algorithm to decide the equivalence of two morphism g, h on an ω-regular language L. The algorithm is polynomial time with respect to the size of g, h and the number of arcs of a Büchi automaton which recognizes L.

Let A be a finite non-empty set , or *alphabet*, and A^+ (resp. A^*) the *free semigroup* (resp. *free monoid*) over A. The elements of A are called *letters* and those of A^* *words* . The identity element of A^* is called *empty word* and denoted by Λ . For any word w, $|w|$ denotes its *length*. A word u is a *factor* (resp. *prefix*) of the word w if $w \in A^*uA^*$ (resp. $w \in uA^*$). For any $w \in A^*$, F(w) (resp. P(w)) denotes the set of all its factors (resp prefixes). A language L over the alphabet A is any subset of A^* . By F(L) (resp. P(L)) we denote the set of all factors (resp. prefixes) of the words of L. A word $w \in A^+$ is called *primitive* if $w \neq u^h$ with $h > 1$ and $u \neq \Lambda$. For any $w \in A^+$ the *primitive root* of w is defined as the unique primitive word z such that $w = z^h$ for some $h \geq 1$. Let $x, y \in$

A^+. We say that x, y are *conjugate* if there exist u, v $\in A^*$ such that x = uv and y = vu. For any x $\in A^*$, x = a_1 ....a_n , we call C(x) the cyclic permutation of x defined by C(x) = a_2 ....$a_n a_1$. For any integer p we will denote by C_p the cyclic permutation C^p. It is easy to see that p ≡ q (mod|x|) implies $C_p(x) = C_p(x)$ and if x is primitive the reverse holds, indeed any primitive word x has exactly |x| different conjugates (cf. [5]).

Let N_+ be the set of positive integers. A one-sided (from left to right) infinite word is any map w : $N_+ \to A$. For each n > 0 the factor w[1, n] = w_1 ....w_n of length n is called the *prefix* of w of length n and will be simply denoted by w[n] . The set of all infinite words w : $N_+ \to A$ will be denoted by A^ω, moreover we set $A^\infty = A^* \cup A^\omega$. An application f: $A^\infty \to B^\infty$ is a *morphism* if for any a $\in$ A, f(a) $\in B^*$ and for x = a_1 .... a_n (resp. x = a_1....a_n ...) one has f(x) = f(a_1) .... f(a_n) (resp. f(x) = f(a_1) .... f(a_n) ...). Given two morphisms f, g : $A^\infty \to B^\infty$, we set E^ω(f, g) = {γ $\in A^\omega$ | f(γ) = g(γ)} and size(f) = max{|f(x)| | x $\in$ A}. For any word u $\in A^+$ we denote by u^ω the infinite word uuu... obtained by the infinite concatenation of u with itself.

We write a (non deterministic) Büchi automaton M = (Q, A, δ, i , F), where Q is a finite set of states, A is the input alphabet, δ: Q × A $\to 2^Q$ is the transition function, i is the initial state and F is the set of final states. The set of the edges of M is defined by E_M = {(p,a,q) $\in$ Q × A × Q | q $\in$ δ(p,a)}. Let w = a_0 .... a_n ... , we say that an infinite sequence p = p_0 ....p_n ... of states is a run of w if p_0 = i and for any i ≥ 1 $p_i \in$ δ(q_{i-1}, a_i). We denote by Inf(p) the set of states that are infinitely many times repeated in p and we say that an infinite word w is accepted by M if there exists a run p of w such that Inf(p) contains at least an element of F. The set of all infinite words accepted by M is denoted by L^ω(M).

2 Preliminary results

We start this section with some technical lemmas that will be useful in the sequel.

Lemma 2.1. *Let* x $\in A^+$, w $\in A^\infty$. *If* w = xw *then* w = x^ω.
Proof. Since w = xw, by substituting one has w = xxw =xxxw = ... and by iteration one obtains w = x^ω. Q.E.D.

Lemma 2.2. *Let* γ $\in A^\infty$ *and* x, y $\in A^+$ *be primitive words such that* γ = $\lambda x^\omega = \mu y^\omega$ *for suitable* λ, μ $\in A^*$. *Then* x, y *are conjugate and moreover* x = y *if and only if* λ ≡ μ (mod|x|).

Proof. By hypothesis we can write γ = uγ' where γ' is an infinite word having periods |x| and |y|. By the Fine and Wilf theorem (cf. [5]) γ' has period M.C.D.(|x|, |y|). Since x and y are primitive, this implies that |x| = |y|. An easy computation shows that x, y are conjugate and x = $C_{|\lambda|-|\mu|}$(y). Since x, y are primitive , one has x = y if and only if |λ| ≡ |μ| (mod |x|). Q.E.D.

Let M = (Q, A, δ, i , F) be a Büchi automaton. A path of M is a sequence π = (p_0, a_1, p_1)(p_1, a_2, p_2) ... (p_{n-1}, a_n, p_n) such that (p_{i-1}, a_i, p_i) $\in E_M$ for 1 ≤ i ≤ n, and the label of π is the word |π| = $a_1 a_2$ ... a_n . Similarly an infinite path is an infinite sequence π

$= (p_0, a_1, p_1)(p_1, a_2, p_2) \ldots (p_{n-1}, a_n, p_n) \ldots$ such that $(p_{i-1}, a_i, p_i) \in E_M$ for for $i \geq 1$ and the label of π is defined by $|\pi| = a_1 a_2 \ldots a_n \ldots$. We denote by Π (resp. Π') the set of all finite paths (resp. infinite paths) of M and for any $p, q \in Q$ the symbols $\Pi_{p,q}, \Pi'_p$ denote respectively the set of the paths of M which go from p to q and the subset of Π' consisting of the infinite paths starting from p. We say that the Büchi automaton $M = (Q, A, \delta, i, F)$ is *trim* if for any $q \in Q$ one has that $\Pi_{i,p}$ is not empty and Π'_p contains at least a path which goes infinitely many times through an element of F. In what follows we will make a wide use of the concept of overflow introduced in [6].

Definition Let $f, g : A^\infty \to B^\infty$. For any $u \in A^*$ we define the *overflow* of f and g in u, denoted by Overf(f, g, u), as follows. If $f(u)$ is a prefix of $g(u)$ and $f(u)x = g(u)$ then Overf(f, g, u) = $(x, 2)$. If $g(u)$ is a prefix of $f(u)$ and $f(u) = g(u)x$ then Overf(f, g, u) = $(x, 1)$. In all the other cases Overf(f, g, u) is undefined. For any $\pi \in \Pi$ we define Overf(f, g, π) = Overf(f, g, $|\pi|$).

Remark We observe that Overf is a partial function . In the sequel we assume that any time we write Overf(f,g,u) or Overf(f, g, π), it means that for the given arguments the function Overf is defined; i.e. $f(u)$ is a prefix of $g(u)$ or viceversa. We observe that for a trim automaton M one has $L^\omega(M) \subseteq E^\omega(f,g)$ if and only if for any $p \in Q$ and $\pi \in \Pi_{i,p}$ Overf(f, g, π) is defined.

In the following we will write u pref v if u is a prefix of v or viceversa. The following lemma is proved in [6].

Lemma 2.3. *Let* $u, v \in A^*$, $a \in A$ *such that* $f(u)$ pref $g(u)$, $f(v)$ pref $g(v)$, $f(ua)$ pref $g(ua)$ *and* $f(va)$ pref $g(va)$. *Then* Overf(f, g, u) = Overf(f,g, v) *if and only if* Overf(f, g, ua) = Overf(f, g, va).

We introduce for any pair of conjugate primitive word $x, x' \in A^*$ a binary relation $\rho_{x,x'}$ in $A^* \times \{1, 2\}$ defined as follows. Let $(\lambda, i), (\mu, j) \in A^* \times \{1, 2\}$ we say that (λ, i) $\rho_{x,x'}(\mu,j)$ if there exists an integer $n \geq 0$ such that one of the following holds:

1) $i = 1, j = 2, \mu\lambda = x^n, \lambda\mu = x'^n$,

2) $i = 2, j = 1, \lambda\mu = x^n, \mu\lambda = x'^n$,

3) $i = 1, j = 1, \lambda = \mu x^n, x' = C_p(x)$, with $p \equiv -|\lambda| \equiv -|\mu| \bmod(|x|)$

4) $i = 1, j = 1, \mu = \lambda x^n, x' = C_p(x)$, with $p \equiv -|\lambda| \equiv -|\mu| \bmod(|x|)$

5) $i = 2, j = 2, \lambda = \mu x'^n, x' = C_p(x)$, with $p \equiv |\lambda| \equiv |\mu| \bmod(|x|)$

6) $i = 2, j = 2, \mu = \lambda x'^n, x' = C_p(x)$, with $p \equiv |\lambda| \equiv |\mu| \bmod(|x|)$

It is easy to prove, considering all the possible cases, that for any pair of conjugate primitive word $x, x' \in A^*$ $\rho_{x,x'}$ is an equivalence relation. The following lemma gives some useful information about the morphisms which are equivalent on an ω-regular language.

Lemma 2.4. *Let* f, g: $A^\infty \to B^\infty$ *be two morphisms and* $M = (Q, A, \delta, i, F)$ *a trim Büchi automaton such that* $L^\omega(M) \subseteq E^\omega(f,g)$. *For any* $q \in Q$ *one of the following holds:*
(i) for any $\pi_1, \pi_2 \in \Pi_{i,q}$ Overf(f, g, π_1) = Overf(f, g, π_2),
(ii) there exist two conjugate primitive words x, x' *such that for any* $\pi_1, \pi_2 \in \Pi_{i,q}$ Overf(f, g, π_1) $\rho_{x,x'}$ Overf(f, g, π_2) *and for any pair of conjugate primitive words* y, y' *if there exist two paths* $\pi_1, \pi_2 \in \Pi_{i,q}$ *with* Overf(f, g, π_1) $\rho_{y,y'}$ Overf(f, g, π_2) *and* Overf(f, g, π_1) ≠ Overf(f, g, π_2) *then* y = x *and* y' = x'.

Proof. Let us suppose that (i) does not hold. Then there exist two paths $\pi_1, \pi_2 \in \Pi_{i,q}$ such that Overf(f, g, π_1) ≠ Overf(f, g, π_2). Since M is supposed to be trim, there exists an infinite path $\pi \in \Pi'_q$ which contains infinitely many occurrences of an element of F. Thus the paths $\pi_1\pi$, $\pi_2\pi$ are accepting and their labels $|\pi_1\pi|$, $|\pi_2\pi|$ are in $L^\omega(M) \subseteq E^\omega(f,g)$. Set now u = $|\pi_1|$, v = $|\pi_2|$, $\gamma = |\pi|$ and consider the following subcases.

(a) Overf(f, g, π_1) = $(\lambda, 1)$, Overf(f, g, π_2) = $(\mu, 1)$, $|\lambda| < |\mu|$. In this case one has f(u) = g(u)λ, f(v) = g(v)μ. Since uγ, v$\gamma \in L^\omega(M) \subseteq E^\omega(f,g)$, one has also

$$f(u)f(\gamma) = g(u)g(\gamma), \quad f(v)f(\gamma) = g(v)g(\gamma),$$

therefore

$$g(u)\lambda f(\gamma) = g(u)g(\gamma), \ g(v)\mu f(\gamma) = g(v)g(\gamma),$$

by cancellation one obtains

$$\lambda f(\gamma) = g(\gamma), \quad \mu f(\gamma) = g(\gamma), \tag{2.1}$$

that implies

$$\lambda f(\gamma) = \mu f(\gamma).$$

Since $|\lambda| < |\mu|$, there exists w$\in$ B* such that λw = μ and f(γ) = wf(γ). Let x be the primitive root of w. One has then w = x^n, n > 0 and

$$\lambda x^n = \mu.$$

By Lemma 2.1 one derives f(γ) = x^ω and by (2.1) g(γ) = λx^ω. We set x' = $C_{-|\lambda|}(x)$ and we have

$$(\lambda, 1) \ \rho_{x,x'} \ (\mu, 1)$$

(b) Overf(f, g, π_1) = $(\lambda, 1)$, Overf(f, g, π_2) = $(\mu, 1)$, $|\mu| < |\lambda|$. As before one obtains for a suitable primitive word x and n > 0

$$\lambda = \mu x^n, \quad f(\gamma) = x^\omega \text{ and } g(\gamma) = \mu x^\omega$$

and for $x' = C_{-|\lambda|}(x)$ one has

$$(\lambda, 1) \rho_{x,x'} (\mu, 1).$$

(c) $\mathrm{Overf}(f, g, \pi_1) = (\lambda, 2)$, $\mathrm{Overf}(f, g, \pi_2) = (\mu, 2)$, $|\lambda| < |\mu|$. In this case , in a symmetric way, one derives the existence of a primitive word $x' \in B^*$ such that for a suitable $n > 0$

$$\mu = \lambda x'^n , \quad g(\gamma) = x'^\omega \text{ and } f(\gamma) = \lambda x'^\omega.$$

In this case if we set $x = C_{-|\lambda|}(x')$, one has $x' = C_{|\lambda|}(x)$ and

$$(\lambda, 2) \rho_{x,x'} (\mu, 2).$$

(d) $\mathrm{Overf}(f, g, \pi_1) = (\lambda, 2)$, $\mathrm{Overf}(f, g, \pi_2) = (\mu, 2)$, $|\mu| < |\lambda|$. In this case there exist a primitive word $x' \in B^*$ and an integer $n > 0$ such that

$$\lambda = \mu x'^n , \quad g(\gamma) = x'^\omega \text{ and } f(\gamma) = \mu x'^\omega.$$

As above if we set $x = C_{-|\lambda|}(x')$, one has $x' = C_{|\lambda|}(x)$ and

$$(\lambda, 2) \rho_{x,x'} (\mu, 2).$$

(e) $\mathrm{Overf}(f, g, \pi_1) = (\lambda, 1)$, $\mathrm{Overf}(f, g, \pi_2) = (\mu, 2)$. In this case $f(u) = g(u)\lambda$, $g(v) = f(v)\mu$. Since $u\gamma, v\gamma \in L^\omega(M) \subseteq E^\omega(f,g)$, one has also

$$f(u)f(\gamma) = g(u)g(\gamma), \quad f(v)f(\gamma) = g(v)g(\gamma),$$

therefore

$$g(u)\lambda f(\gamma) = g(u)g(\gamma), \quad f(v)f(\gamma) = f(v)\mu g(\gamma).$$

By cancellation one obtains

$$\lambda f(\gamma) = g(\gamma), \quad f(\gamma) = \mu g(\gamma),$$

that implies

$$f(\gamma) = \mu\lambda f(\gamma), \quad g(\gamma) = \lambda\mu g(\gamma).$$

Let x be the primitive root of $\mu\lambda$. There exists $n > 0$ such that $\mu\lambda = x^n$ and

$$f(\gamma) = x^n f(\gamma).$$

Thus by Lemma 2.1 one has

$$f(\gamma) = x^\omega.$$

Moreover, if x' is the primitive root $\lambda\mu$, it is easy to see that x' is a conjugate of x and $\lambda\mu = x'^n$ so

$$g(\gamma) = x'^\omega,$$

moreover

$$(\lambda, 1) \, \rho_{x,x'} \, (\mu,2).$$

(f) Overf(f, g, π_1) = (λ, 2), Overf(f, g, π_2) = (μ, 1). This case is symmetric to the previous one and one has for x primitive root of $\lambda\mu$ and x' primitive root $\mu\lambda$

$$f(\gamma) = x^\omega, \quad g(\gamma) = x'^\omega,$$

and

$$(\lambda, 2) \, \rho_{x,x'} \, (\mu,1).$$

Thus, in conclusion, in all the cases we have $(\lambda, i) \, \rho_{x,x'} \, (\mu,j)$ for some pair of primitive conjugate words x, x'. Moreover we remark that in any case for suitable s, t $\in$ B* one has

$$f(\gamma) = sx^\omega, \quad g(\gamma) = tx'^\omega, \quad |s| \equiv 0 \equiv |t| \pmod{|x|}.$$

Thus for any paths $\pi \in \Pi_{i,q}$, by a similar argument, one proves the existence of a pair of primitive conjugate words y, y' such that   Overf(f, g, π) $\rho_{y,y'}$ Overf(f, g, π_1) and choosing the same infinite word γ one obtains for suitable s', t' $\in$ B*

$$f(\gamma) = s'y^\omega, \quad g(\gamma) = t'y'^\omega, \quad |s'| \equiv 0 \equiv |t'| \pmod{|y|}.$$

Thus by Lemma 2.2 , the previous relations imply y = x, y' = x' and (ii) holds. This also proves the second part of (ii). Q.E.D.

Corollary 2.5. *Let f, g: A$^\infty$ $\to$ B$^\infty$ be two morphism and M = (Q, A, δ, i , F) a trim Büchi automaton such that L$^\omega$(M) $\subseteq$ E$^\omega$(f,g). Suppose that for some q $\in$ Q and π_1, π_2 $\in$ $\Pi_{i,q}$ Overf(f, g, π_1) = (λ, 1) $\neq$ Overf(f, g, π_2) (resp. Overf(f, g, π_1) = (λ, 2) $\neq$ Overf(f, g, π_2)) and there exist two conjugate primitive words x, x' such that Overf(f, g, π_1) $\rho_{x,x'}$ Overf(f, g, π_2). Then for any (q, a, p) $\in$ E$_M$ one has f(a) $\in$ Pref(x$^\omega$), g(a) $\in$ Pref(λx$^\omega$) (resp. f(a) $\in$ Pref(λx'$^\omega$), g(a) $\in$ Pref(x'$^\omega$))* .

Proof. Consider the case Overf(f, g, π_1) = (λ, 1) $\neq$ Overf(f, g, π_2) and choose, as in the proof of the previous lemma, an infinite path $\pi \in \Pi'_q$, with infinitely many occurrences of an element of F, and the further condition that the first edge of π is (q,a,p). Let $\gamma = |\pi|$ as before one obtains f(γ) = x$^\omega$, g(γ) = λx$^\omega$, and, since a is the first letter of γ, the statement follows. The case Overf(f, g, π_1) = (λ, 2) $\neq$ Overf(f, g, π_2) is symmetric. Q.E.D.

Lemma 2.6. *Let u $\in$ A* such that Overf(f, g, u) = (λ, 1), and x, x' $\in$ B* be two conjugate primitive words. Let a $\in$ A with f(a) = x^{m}z, x = zw, m $\geq$ 0, g(a) $\in$ Pref(λx$^\omega$). Then for any v $\in$ A* , Overf(f, g, u) $\rho_{x,x'}$ Overf(f, g , v) implies Overf(f, g, ua) $\rho_{y,y'}$*

Overf(f, g , va) *where* y,y' *are primitive conjugate words defined by* $y = wz$, $y' = C_p(y)$ *with* $p \equiv |g(a)| - |\lambda| - |f(a)| \pmod{|x|}$.

Proof. Let us set $\text{Overf}(f,g,v) = (\mu, j)$ and suppose $\text{Overf}(f, g, u) \, \rho_{x,x'} \, \text{Overf}(f, g , v)$. We consider the following cases:

(a) $j = 1$, $\mu = \lambda x^n$, $n \geq 0$. By definition $f(u) = g(u)\lambda$, $f(v) = g(v)\mu = g(v)\lambda x^n$. Let us first suppose that $g(a)$ is a prefix of $\lambda f(a)$. In this case we have $g(a)\xi = \lambda f(a)$ for some $\xi \in B^*$. Then we write $f(u)f(a) = g(u)\lambda f(a) = g(u)g(a)\xi$. From this it follows that

$$\text{Overf}(f, g, ua) = (\xi, 1).$$

On the other hand $f(v)f(a) = g(v)\mu x^m z = g(v)\lambda x^n x^m z = g(v)\lambda x^m z(wz)^n = g(v)g(a)\xi(wz)^n$ and so

$$\text{Overf}(f, g, va) = (\xi(wz)^n, 1).$$

If we pose $y = wz$, $y' = C_p(y)$, where $p \equiv -|\xi| \pmod{|x|}$ one has

$$\text{Overf}(f, g, ua) \, \rho_{y,y'} \, \text{Overf}(f, g, va).$$

Since $g(a)\xi = \lambda f(a)$, one obtains

$$p \equiv |g(a)| - |\lambda| - |f(a)| \pmod{|x|}.$$

Consider now the case in which $\lambda f(a)$ is a prefix of $g(a)$, i.e. $g(a) = \lambda f(a)\xi$ for some $\xi \in B^*$. Then we write $g(u)g(a) = g(u)\lambda f(a)\xi = f(u)f(a)\xi$. From this it follows that

$$\text{Overf}(f, g, ua) = (\xi, 2).$$

If $\lambda x^n f(a)$ is a prefix of $g(a)$ one has also $g(a) = \lambda x^n f(a)\xi'$ for some $\xi' \in B^*$ and then $g(v)g(a) = g(v)\lambda x^n f(a)\xi' = f(v)f(a)\xi'$ and so

$$\text{Overf}(f, g, va) = (\xi', 2).$$

From the equations $\lambda f(a)\xi = g(a) = \lambda x^n f(a)\xi' \in \text{Pref}(\lambda x^\omega)$ one derives $\xi = (wz)^s r$, $\xi' = (wz)^{s-n} r$, for some $s \geq n$ and $r \in \text{Pref}(wz)$. Let t be such that $wz = rt$ and let $y' = tr$, one has $\xi = \xi' y'^n$. Set $y = wz$, and observe that $y' = C_{|r|}(y) = C_{|\xi|}(y)$. From $g(a) = \lambda f(a)\xi$, by means of an easy computation, one obtains $y' = C_p(y)$ and

$$p \equiv |\xi| \equiv |g(a)| - |\lambda| - |f(a)| \pmod{|x|}.$$

Also in this case one has $\text{Overf}(f, g, ua) \, \rho_{y,y'} \, \text{Overf}(f, g, va)$.

It remains to consider the subcase $\lambda f(a)$ is a prefix of $g(a)$, and $g(a)$ is a prefix of $\lambda x^n f(a)$. As before $g(a) = \lambda f(a)\xi$ for some $\xi \in B^*$ and $g(u)g(a) = g(u)\lambda f(a)\xi = f(u)f(a)\xi$, so that

$$\text{Overf}(f, g, ua) = (\xi, 2).$$

If $g(a)$ is a prefix of $\lambda x^n f(a)$ one has also $g(a)\xi' = \lambda x^n f(a)$ for some $\xi' \in B^*$. Then $g(v)g(a)\xi' = g(v)\lambda x^n f(a) = f(v)f(a)$ and so

$$\text{Overf}(f, g, va) = (\xi', 1) .$$

From the equations $\lambda f(a)\xi = g(a)$ and $g(a)\xi' = \lambda x^n f(a) \in \text{Pref}(\lambda x^\omega)$ one derives $\lambda f(a)\xi\xi' \in \text{Pref}(\lambda x^\omega)$ and $|\xi\xi'| = |\xi'| + |\xi| = |\lambda x^n f(a)| - |g(a)| + |g(a)| - |\lambda f(a)| = |x^n|$. Since $f(a) = (zw)^m z$, one has $\xi\xi' = y^n$ with $y = wz$. On the other hand $\xi'\xi = y'^n$ where y' is chosen as $C_{|\xi|}(y)$ and also in this case $y' = C_p(y)$ with $p \equiv |\xi| \equiv |g(a)| - |\lambda| - |f(a)| \pmod{|x|}$ and $\text{Overf}(f, g, ua) \, \rho_{y,y'} \, \text{Overf}(f, g, va)$.

(b) $j = 1$, $\lambda = \mu x^n$, $n \geq 0$. This case is perfectly symmetric to the previous one and may be dealt by interchanging λ with μ.

(c) $j = 2$. In this case by definition one has $\mu\lambda = x^n$, $\lambda\mu = x'^n$, $n \geq 0$ and $f(u) = g(u)\lambda$, $f(v)\mu = g(v)$. Moreover $f(a) = x^m z$ and, since $g(a) \in \text{Pref}(\lambda x^\omega)$, $\mu g(a) \in \text{Pref}(x^\omega)$. One has to consider three subcases.

1) $g(a)$ is a prefix of $\lambda f(a)$ and $f(a)$ is a prefix of $\mu g(a)$. Then for suitable $\xi, \xi' \in B^*$ one has

$$g(a)\xi = \lambda f(a), \quad f(a)\xi' = \mu g(a) . \tag{2.2}$$

From $f(u) = g(u)\lambda$, it follows $f(u)f(a) = g(u)\lambda f(a) = g(u)g(a)\xi$, that implies $\text{Overf}(f,g,ua) = (\xi, 1)$. Similarly, by $f(v)\mu = g(v)$, one has $g(v)g(a) = f(v)\mu g(a) = f(v)f(a)\xi'$ and so $\text{Overf}(f,g,va) = (\xi', 2)$. By (2.2) one derives $\mu\lambda f(a) = \mu g(a)\xi = f(a)\xi'\xi = x^{n+m}z$. Since $f(a) = x^m z$, it follows $\xi'\xi = (wz)^n$. Moreover, posed $y = wz$, we have also $\xi\xi' = y'^n$ with $y' = C_{|\xi'|}(y)$. Let p be an integer such that $p \equiv |\xi'| \pmod{|x|}$. One has $y' = C_p(y)$ and by (2.2) one derives

$$p \equiv |\mu| + |g(a)| - |f(a)| \pmod{|x|}.$$

From $\mu\lambda = x^n$ one has $|\mu| \equiv -|\lambda| \pmod{|x|}$, and so

$$p \equiv |g(a)| - |\lambda| - |f(a)| \pmod{|x|}.$$

Also in this case one has $\text{Overf}(f, g, ua) \, \rho_{y,y'} \, \text{Overf}(f, g, va)$.

2) $g(a)$ is a prefix of $\lambda f(a)$ and $\mu g(a)$ is a prefix of $f(a)$. There exist $\xi, \xi' \in B^*$ such that

$$g(a)\xi = \lambda f(a), \quad f(a) = \mu g(a)\xi' . \tag{2.3}$$

From $f(u) = g(u)\lambda$, it follows $f(u)f(a) = g(u)\lambda f(a) = g(u)g(a)\xi$, that implies $\text{Overf}(f,g,ua) = (\xi, 1)$. Similarly by $f(v)\mu = g(v)$ one has $f(v)f(a) = f(v)\mu g(a)\xi' = g(v)g(a)\xi'$ and so $\text{Overf}(f,g,ua) = (\xi',1)$. By (2.3) one derives

$$g(a)\xi = \lambda\mu g(a)\xi'. \tag{2.4}$$

Since $\mu\lambda f(a) = x^{n+m}z = z(wz)^{n+m}$, by (2.4) and $g(a)\xi = \lambda f(a)$ one has that ξ, ξ' are both suffixes of $z(wz)^{n+m}$ and $|\xi| - |\xi'| = |\lambda\mu| = |x^n|$. Thus $\xi = \xi'(wz)^n$, so for $y = wz$ and $y' = C_{-|\xi|}(y)$ one has Overf(f, g, ua) $\rho_{y,y'}$ Overf(f, g, va) and $y' = C_p(y)$ with $p \equiv -|\xi|$ mod($|x|$). By (2.3) one derives $p \equiv |g(a)| - |\lambda| - |f(a)|$ (mod $|x|$).

3) $\lambda f(a)$ is a prefix of $g(a)$ and $f(a)$ is a prefix of $\mu g(a)$. Then for suitable $\xi, \xi' \in B^*$ one has

$$g(a) = \lambda f(a)\xi, \; f(a)\xi' = \mu g(a) . \tag{2.5}$$

From $f(u) = g(u)\lambda$, it follows $g(u)g(a) = g(u)\lambda f(a)\xi = f(u)f(a)\xi$, that implies Overf(f,g,ua) $= (\xi, 2)$. Similarly by $f(v)\mu = g(v)$ one has $g(v)g(a) = f(v)\mu g(a) = f(v)f(a)\xi'$ and so Overf(f,g,va) $= (\xi', 2)$. By (2.5) one derives $\mu\lambda f(a)\xi = \mu g(a) = f(a)\xi'$. Since $\mu g(a) \in$ Pref(x^ω), for a suitable y' conjugate of y one has $\mu g(a) = ty'^s$, $s > 0$ and $t \in$ Suff(y') and $\xi' = \xi y'^n$. On the other hand from $\mu g(a) = ty'^s$ and $\mu g(a) \in$ Pref(x^ω) it follows $y' = C_{|\mu g(a)|}(x)$. From $x = zw$, $y = wz$ one has $x = C_{-|z|}(y) = C_{-|f(a)|}(y)$. Thus $y' = C_{|\mu g(a)|-|f(a)|}(y)$ and for $p = |\mu g(a)|-|f(a)|$ one has $y' = C_p(y)$ and , as $\mu\lambda = x^n$ implies $\mu \equiv -|\lambda|$ (mod$|x|$), $p \equiv |g(a)| - |\lambda| - |f(a)|$ (mod $|x|$). By (2.5) one has also $|\xi| = |g(a)| - |\lambda| - |f(a)|$, therefore $y' = C_{|\xi|}(y)$ and so Overf(f, g, ua) $\rho_{y,y'}$ Overf(f, g, va). Q.E.D.

Lemma 2.7. *Let* $u \in A^*$ *such that* Overf(f, g, u) $= (\lambda, 2)$, *and* $x,x' \in B^*$ *be two conjugate primitive word. Let* $a \in A$ *with* $g(a) = x^m z$, $x' = zw$, $m \geq 0$, $f(a) \in$ Pref($\lambda x'^\omega$). *Then for any* $v \in A^*$, Overf(f, g, u) $\rho_{x,x'}$ Overf(f, g , v) *implies* Overf(f, g, ua) $\rho_{y,y'}$ Overf(f, g , va) *where* y,y' *are primitive conjugate words defined by* $y' = wz$, $y = C_p(y')$ *with* $p \equiv |f(a)| - |\lambda| - |g(a)|$ (mod $|x|$).

Proof. The proof is perfectly symmetric to the previous one. Q.E.D.

3 The algorithm

In this section we develop an algorithm to decide the equivalence of two morphisms on an ω-regular language L which works in $O(mn^3)$ where m is the size of the morphisms and n is the number of arcs of a non deterministic Büchi automaton recognizing L. In all this section we suppose that two morphisms f, g: $A^\infty \to B^\infty$ and a trim non deterministic Büchi automaton M = (Q,A, δ, i ,F) with L^ω(M) = L are given. We recall that this hypothesis is not restrictive, since for any non deterministic Büchi automaton M' one can construct in quadratic time another one M" such that M" is trim and L^ω(M') = L^ω(M"). In the sequel n will denote the number of arcs of M and m = max{size(f),size(g)}. We observe that card(Q) $\leq$ 2n and then all which is polynomial in the number of states is also polynomial in n with the same exponent.

Now we construct a subset of finite paths of M as follows. For any $q \in Q$ let π_q be a path of $\Pi_{i,q}$ of minimal length and for any $p, q \in Q$ let $\pi_{p,q}$ be a path of $\Pi_{p,q}$ of minimal length, if $\Pi_{p,q}$ is not empty. We observe that the set $S = \{\pi_q \mid q \in Q\}$ may be constructed so that it is prefix closed. Let us then consider the following sets of paths:

$$\Psi = \{\pi_q(q, a, p) \mid (q, a, p) \in E_M\},$$

$$\Sigma = \Psi \cup \{\pi\pi_{p,q} \mid p, q \in Q \text{ and } \pi \in \Pi_{i,p} \cap \Psi\}.$$

We observe that Ψ and Σ contain the set $S = \{\pi_q \mid q \in Q\}$, since S is prefix closed and for any $q \in Q$ π_q is of the kind $\pi_{q'}(q', a, q) \in \Psi$. Now we make a partition of Q in the two subsets

$$Q' = \{p \in Q \mid \text{Overf}(f, g, \pi) = \text{Overf}(f, g, \pi') \text{ for any } \pi,\pi' \in \Pi_{i,p} \cap \Sigma\}.$$

$$Q'' = Q \setminus Q'.$$

Let us suppose now that for any $p \in Q''$ there exists a pair of primitive conjugate words x,x' such that

$$\text{Overf}(f, g, \pi) \, \rho_{x,x'} \, \text{Overf}(f, g, \pi') \text{ for any } \pi,\pi' \in \Pi_{i,p} \cap \Sigma.$$

By Lemma 2.4 the previous condition is necessary in order to have $L^\omega(M) \subseteq E^\omega(f,g)$. In this way we associate to any $p \in Q''$ a pair of conjugate primitive words x, x' that will be also denoted by x(p), x'(p). The following lemma holds.

Lemma 3.1. *Suppose that* $L^\omega(M) \subseteq E^\omega(f,g)$ *and for any* $(p,a,q) \in E_M$ *, with* p, q $\in$ Q'' *let* $x = x(p)$, $x' = x'(p)$, $y = x(q)$, $y' = x'(q)$ *and let* $\text{Overf}(f, g, \pi_p) = (\lambda,1)$ *(resp.* $\text{Overf}(f, g, \pi_p) = (\lambda,2)$). *Then one has* $f(a) \in \text{Pref}(x^\omega)$, $f(a) = x^n z$, $x = zw$ $g(a) \in \text{Pref}(\lambda x^\omega)$ *(resp.* $g(a) \in \text{Pref}(x'^\omega)$, $g(a) = x'^n z$, $x' = zw$, $f(a) \in \text{Pref}(\lambda x'^\omega)$) *and* $y = wz$, $y' = C_p(y)$ *with* $p \equiv \lg(a) - |\lambda| - |f(a)| \pmod{|x|}$ *(resp.y' = wz, $y = C_p(y)$ with $p \equiv |f(a)| - |\lambda| - |g(a)| \pmod{|x|}$).*

Proof. Let us suppose $\text{Overf}(f, g, \pi_p) = (\lambda,1)$. By hypothesis there exists a path $\pi \in \Pi_{i,p} \cap \Sigma$ such that $\text{Overf}(f, g, \pi) \neq \text{Overf}(f, g, \pi_p)$ and $\text{Overf}(f, g, \pi) \, \rho_{x,x'} \, \text{Overf}(f, g, \pi_p)$. By Corollary 2.5 one has that $f(a) \in \text{Pref}(x^\omega)$, $f(a) = x^n z$, $x = zw$, $g(a) \in \text{Pref}(\lambda x^\omega)$. From $\text{Overf}(f, g, \pi) \neq \text{Overf}(f, g, \pi_p)$, by Lemma 2.2, it follows $\text{Overf}(f, g, \pi(p,a,q)) \neq \text{Overf}(f, g, \pi_p(p,a,q))$ and by Lemma 2.6 one has $\text{Overf}(f, g, \pi(p,a,q)) \, \rho_{u,u'} \, \text{Overf}(f,g,\pi_p(p,a,q))$ with $u = wz$, $u' = C_p(u)$ and $p \equiv \lg(a) - |\lambda| - |f(a)| \pmod{|x|}$. On the other hand by hypothesis there exist two paths $\pi', \pi'' \in \Pi_{i,q} \cap \Sigma$ such that $\text{Overf}(f, g, \pi') \neq \text{Overf}(f, g, \pi'')$, $\text{Overf}(f, g, \pi') \, \rho_{y,y'} \, \text{Overf}(f, g, \pi'')$ and by Lemma 2.4 one has $y = u$, $y' = u'$. The case $\text{Overf}(f, g, \pi_p) = (\lambda,2)$ can be proved taking in account of Lemma 2.7. Q.E.D.

Lemma 3.2. *For any* $p \in Q'$ *and for any* $\pi, \pi' \in \Pi_{i,p}$ *one has* $\text{Overf}(f, g, \pi) = \text{Overf}(f, g, \pi')$.

Proof. We will shown that for any $\pi \in \Pi_{i,p}$ one has $\text{Overf}(f, g, \pi) = \text{Overf}(f, g, \pi_p)$. The proof is by induction on the length of π. The case in which π is empty is trivial. Suppose then $\pi = \pi'(q,a,p)$ with $\pi' \in \Pi_{i,p}$, $(q,a,p) \in E_M$. Firstly we show that $q \in Q'$. In fact suppose by contradiction that there exists a path $\pi_1 \in \Pi_{i,q} \cap \Sigma$ such that $Overf(f, g, \pi_1) \neq Overf(f, g, \pi_q)$. Then there exists a prefix π_2 of π_1 such that

$$\pi_2 \in \Pi_{i,q'} \cap \Sigma \quad Overf(f, g, \pi_2) \neq Overf(f, g, \pi_{q'}), q' \in Q \qquad (3.1)$$

and π_2 is minimal in the set of prefixes of π_1 verifying (3.1). Now we can write $\pi_2 = \pi'_2(p',a',q')$, $\pi'_2 \in \Pi_{i,p'}$, $(p',a',q') \in E_M$. By the minimality of π_2 one has $Overf(f, g, \pi'_2) = Overf(f, g, \pi_{p'})$, and by Lemma 2.3

$$Overf(f, g, \pi_2) = Overf(f, g, \pi'_2(p',a',q')) = Overf(f, g, \pi_{p'}(p',a',q')). \qquad (3.2)$$

By (3.1) and (3.2) one obtains $Overf(f, g, \pi_{q'}) \neq Overf(f, g, \pi_{p'}(p',a',q'))$. By construction $\Pi_{q',p}$ is not empty and, by Lemma 2.3, one has

$$Overf(f, g, \pi_{q'}\pi_{q',p}) \neq Overf(f, g, \pi_{p'}(p',a',q')\pi_{q',p})$$

and $\pi_{q'}\pi_{q',p}$, $\pi_{p'}(p',a',q')\pi_{q',p} \in \Sigma$, which is in contradiction with $p \in Q'$.

So we have proved that $q \in Q'$ and by the inductive hypothesis one has $Overf(f, g, \pi') = Overf(f, g, \pi_q)$ and by Lemma 2.3 $Overf(f, g, \pi) = Overf(f, g, \pi'(q, a,p)) = Overf(f, g, \pi_q(q, a,p))$. The statement then follows from the fact that $\pi_q(q, a,p) \in \Sigma$ and $Overf(f, g, \pi_q(q, a,p)) = Overf(f, g, \pi_p)$. Q.E.D.

Lemma 3.3. *Suppose that for any* $(p,a,q) \in E_M$, *with* p, q $\in Q''$, *posed* $x = x(p)$, $x' = x'(p)$, $y = x(q)$, $y' = x'(q)$, $Overf(f, g, \pi_p) = (\lambda,1)$ (resp. $Overf(f, g, \pi_p) = (\lambda,2)$) *one has* $f(a) \in Pref(x^\omega)$, $f(a) = x^n z$, $x = zw$, $g(a) \in Pref(\lambda x^\omega)$ *(resp.* $g(a) = x'^n z$, $x' = zw$, $f(a) \in Pref(\lambda x'^\omega)$ *and* $y = wz$, $y' = C_p(y)$ *with* $p \equiv |g(a)| - |\lambda| - |f(a)| \pmod{|x|}$ *(resp.*y' $= wz$, $y = C_p(y')$ *with* $p \equiv |f(a)| - |\lambda| - |g(a)| \pmod{|x|}$). *Then for any* $p \in Q''$, $\pi \in \Pi_{i,p}$ *and* $\pi' \in \Pi_{i,p} \cap \Sigma$ *one has* $Overf(f, g, \pi) \, \rho_{x(p),x'(p)} \, Overf(f, g, \pi')$.

Proof. We prove that for any $p \in Q''$ and $\pi \in \Pi_{i,p}$ one has $Overf(f, g, \pi) \, \rho_{x(p),x'(p)} \, Overf(f, g, \pi_p)$. The proof is by induction on the length of π. If π is empty then there is nothing to prove. Suppose that $\pi = \sigma(q,a,p)$ with $\sigma \in \Pi_{i,q}$. If $q \in Q'$ then by Lemma 3.1 one has $Overf(f, g, \sigma) = Overf(f, g, \pi_q)$ and by Lemma 2.3 one has $Overf(f, g, \sigma(q,a,p))$ $= Overf(f, g, \pi_q(q,a,p))$ and, since $\pi_q(q,a,p) \in \Pi_{i,p} \cap \Sigma$, $Overf(f, g, \pi_q(q,a,p)) \, \rho_{x(p),x'(p)} \, Overf(f, g, \pi_p)$ and $Overf(f, g, \sigma(q,a,p)) \, \rho_{x(p),x'(p)} \, Overf(f, g, \pi_p)$.

Suppose now $q \in Q''$. In this case by the inductive hypothesis $Overf(f, g, \sigma) \, \rho_{x(q),x'(q)} \, Overf(f, g, \pi_q)$, we write $x = x(q)$, $x' = x'(q)$. Suppose that $Overf(f, g, \pi_q) = (\lambda,1)$, $\lambda \in A^*$. By hypothesis $f(a) \in Pref(x^\omega)$, $f(a) = x^n z$, $x = zw$, $g(a) \in Pref(\lambda x^\omega)$, and by Lemma 2.6 the conjugate word y, y' defined by $y = wz$, $y' = C_p(x)$ with $p \equiv |g(a)| - |\lambda| - |f(a)| \pmod{|x|}$ verify $Overf(f, g, \sigma(q,a,p)) \, \rho_{y,y'} \, Overf(f, g, \pi_q(q,a,p))$. By hypothesis one has $Overf(f, g, \pi_q(q,a,p)) \, \rho_{y,y'} \, Overf(f, g, \pi_p)$ and so $Overf(f, g, \pi) = $

Overf(f, g, σ(q,a,p)) $\rho_{y,y'}$ Overf(f, g, π_q). The case Overf(f, g, π_q) = (λ,2) can be proved in the same way taking in account of Lemma 2.7. Q.E.D.

Remark. The statements of Lemma 3.2 and Lemma 3.3, together imply, if the hypotheses are satisfied, that for any $p \in Q$ and $\pi \in \Pi_{i,p}$ one has that Overf(f, g, π) is not undefined. Since M is supposed to be trim, this implies $L^{\omega}(M) \subseteq E^{\omega}(f,g)$.

The algorithm consists then of the following steps.
1) Construct Σ.
2) Compute the sets Q' and Q".
3) Verify that that for any $p \in Q$" there exists a pair of primitive conjugate words x,x' such that Overf(f, g, π) $\rho_{x,x'}$ Overf(f, g, π') for any $\pi,\pi' \in \Pi_{i,p} \cap \Sigma$. If this is not the case then by Lemma 2.4 $L^{\omega}(M)$ is not contained in $E^{\omega}(f,g)$ and the algorithm terminates.
4) Control if the hypothesis of Lemma 3.3 are verified. If 'yes' then by Lemma 3.3 and Lemma 3.2 $L^{\omega}(M) \subseteq E^{\omega}(f,g)$ else by Lemma 3.1 $L^{\omega}(M)$ is not contained in $E^{\omega}(f,g)$.

We discuss now the time complexity of the proposed algorithm. We observe that the set S = $\{\pi_p \mid p \in Q \}$ may be constructed in quadratic time with respect to card(Q) and so in $O(n^2)$ time. Similarly the construction of the set T = $\{\pi_{p,q} \mid p, q \in Q$ and $\Pi_{p,q} \neq \varnothing\}$ may be performed in time $O(n^3)$.

It is easy to see that card(Σ) $\leq$ (n+1)card(Q) $\leq$ 2n(n + 1) and for any $\pi \in \Sigma$ length(π) $\leq$ 2card(Q) + 1 $\leq$ 4n +1 , therefore the total size of Σ is $O(n^3)$. We observe now Σ is easily obtained from S and T in time which is linear in the total size of Σ so Σ is obtained in time $O(n^3)$. Let now P = $\{|\pi| \mid \pi \in \Sigma\}$. The computation of the sets Q', Q" requires a test of the morphisms f,g on P and this may be performed in time $O(mn^3)$. The condition of the step 3) may be verified in the computation of the set Q', Q"; it suffices to store the pair x,x' any time we have Overf(f, g, π) $\rho_{x,x'}$ Overf(f, g, π') for some $\pi,\pi' \in \Pi_{i,p} \cap \Sigma$ (it must be observed that |x|, |x'| $\leq$ max $\{$max(|f(w)|, |g(w)|) w $\in$ P$\}$ $\leq$ 2mn) and to compare it with the pairs already stored for the same state $p \in Q$. The step 4) requires a control of the morphisms f, g on any (p,a,q) $\in E_M$ and this can be performed in time $O(mn)$. In conclusion the total time complexity of the algorithm is $O(mn^3)$.

References

1. M.H. Albert and J. Lawrence, A proof of Ehrenfeucht's conjecture, *Theoretical Computer Science*, 41 (1985) 121-123.

2. J.R. Büchi, Weak second-order arithmetic and finite automata, *Z. Math. Logik und Grundl. Math.*, 6 (1960) 66-92.

3. K. Culik II and J. K. Pachl, Equivalence problems for mappings on infinite strings, *Information and Control* , 49 (1981) 52-63.

4. Eilenberg, S., Automata, Languages and Machines, Vol A, Academic Press 1974.

5. Lothaire, M., Combinatorics on words, Cambridge University Press, 1982.

6. J. Karhumaki, W. Rytter and S. Jarominek, Efficient constructions of test sets for regular and context-free languages, preprint 1990.

7. A. de Luca, M. Pelagalli, S. Varricchio, Test set for languages of infinite words, Information Processing Letters, 29 (1988) 91-95.

Locally Threshold Testable Languages of Infinite Words

Thomas Wilke*

Christian-Albrechts-Universität zu Kiel, Institut für Informatik und Praktische Mathematik, D-W-2300 Kiel, Germany

Abstract. The class of finitely locally threshold testable ω-languages is proved to be decidable relatively to the class of all regular ω-languages. We apply this to the monadic second order theory of infinite word structures with successor function: it is decidable whether for a given monadic second-order formula there exists a first-order formula with the same set of infinite word models.

Introduction

A language L of infinite words is said to be finitely locally threshold testable if the answer to the question '$\alpha \in L$?' is determined by the prefix of α of a given fixed length and the number of occurrences of the factors of α of a bounded length counted up to a given fixed finite threshold. For (general) local threshold testability the answer may also depend on the set of the factors of α of a bounded length which occur infinitely often.

The present paper shows that the class of the finitely locally threshold testable ω-languages is decidable relatively to the class of all regular ω-languages. For (general) local threshold testability the corresponding result can be derived from [2]. As a consequence of our result, a result of [8], and the correspondence between regular ω-languages and monadic second-order definable classes of infinite word structures [4], we also obtain: It is decidable whether for a given monadic second-order formula over the signature of successor there exists a first-order formula which has the same set of infinite word models.

For the decidability of finite local threshold testability we show that a language is finitely locally threshold testable iff it is locally threshold testable and belongs to the class $\mathcal{F}_\sigma \cap \mathcal{G}_\delta$, in symbols: (*) $fin\text{-}\mathcal{L}tt = \mathcal{L}tt \cap \mathcal{F}_\sigma \cap \mathcal{G}_\delta$.— This yields the desired result since the classes $\mathcal{L}tt$, $\mathcal{F}_\sigma$, and $\mathcal{G}_\delta$ are decidable each relatively to the class of all regular ω-languages [5, 10].

The class $\mathcal{F}_\sigma \cap \mathcal{G}_\delta$ contains the regular ω-languages which are at the same time a countable union of closed sets (in $\mathcal{F}_\sigma$) and a countable intersection of open sets (in $\mathcal{G}_\delta$) or, equivalently (cf. [7]), which are a boolean combination of open (or closed) sets. The result (*) becomes clear from a further characterization

* Supported by ESPRIT Basic Research Action Working Group No. 3166 'Algebraic and Syntactic Methods in Computer Science' (ASMICS).

of $\mathcal{F}_\sigma \cap \mathcal{G}_\delta$: If L is a regular ω-language and $\mathfrak{A} = (Q, \delta, i,)$ is a semi automaton recognizing L with Muller acceptance, then $L \in \mathcal{F}_\sigma \cap \mathcal{G}_\delta$ if and only if $\mathfrak{A}$ recognizes L with weak acceptance, i.e., if there exists a set $\mathcal{F}$ of subsets of Q such that a word belongs to L if the set of states occurring in the run of $\mathfrak{A}$ on α belongs to $\mathcal{F}$. (Compare this to the Muller acceptance condition where the set of states occurring infinitely often is considered.)

The equation (∗) connects the syntactic and the topological approach to the theory of regular ω-languages, and supports the view that the regular $\mathcal{F}_\sigma \cap \mathcal{G}_\delta$-languages capture those ω-languages which are of 'finite' character.

Acknowledgement. I am very grateful to MANFRED SCHIMMLER who provided me with a lot of helpful counter examples and to DOMINIQUE PERRIN who explained the notion of De Bruijn graphs to me. I thank WOLFGANG THOMAS for his comments on several versions of this paper.

Notation, Basic Definitions, and Main Result

Let A be an *alphabet*, i.e., a finite set. A *finite word* over A is a sequence $n \rightarrow A$ where $n = \{0, \ldots, n-1\}$ is an initial segment of the set ω of natural numbers. An *infinite word* (ω-word) over A is a sequence $\omega \rightarrow A$. The domain of a word x is also called its *lengths* and is denoted by $|x|$.

We write A^* for the set of all finite words over A, use A^+ for the set of all finite and non-empty words over A, and A^ω for the set of all ω-words over A. The set of all words over A of length l is denoted by A^l. Similarly we write $A^{\geq l}$ for the set of all words of length greater than or equal to l.

Let x be an arbitrary word over A. For $i, j \in \omega \cup \{\omega\}$ the subsequence of x consisting of the items $x(k)$ with index $k \in \{l \mid i \leq l < j\}$ is denoted by $x(i, j)$; it is called a *factor* of x. The set of all *factors* of a fixed length $l \in \omega$ is defined by $\mathrm{fact}_l(x) = \{u \in A^l \mid (\exists i)\, x(i, i + l) = u\}$. The set of all factors of length l occurring infinitely often in an infinite word α is defined accordingly: $\inf_l(\alpha) = \{u \in A^l \mid (\forall i)(\exists j)(i < j \wedge \alpha(j, j + l) = u)\}$.

For $l \in \omega$ the *l-prefix* of a word x is defined by $\mathrm{pref}_l(x) = x(0, i)$. The l-suffix of a finite word u of length greater than or equal to l is given by $u(|u| - l, |u|)$. If the length of u is less than l then u itself is its l-suffix. If α is an infinite word, every factor of the form $\alpha(i, \omega)$ is called a *suffix* of α.

Let $\mathbb{N}_\infty$ denote the set $\mathbb{N}$ of natural numbers augmented by ∞. Throughout $\mathrm{card}(X)$ denotes the power of the set X if it is finite, and ∞ otherwise.

Let x be an arbitrary word. The number of occurrences of a finite word u in x as a factor is defined by $\|x\|_u = \mathrm{card}(\{i \mid x(i, i + l) = u\})$. The number of occurrences of a letter a in x is given by $|x|_a = \mathrm{card}(\{i \mid a = x(i)\})$. For a set B of letters, we use $|x|_B$ as an abbreviation for $\sum_{a \in B} |x|_a$.

Given a natural number $m > 0$, we define the threshold function $[.]_m \colon \mathbb{N}_\infty \rightarrow m + 1$ by $[n]_m = \begin{cases} n & \text{if } n < m, \\ m & \text{otherwise.} \end{cases}$ With $m, l > 0$ and a word x we associate the function $\mu_x^{l,m}: A^l \rightarrow m+1$, $u \mapsto [\|x\|_u]_m$, counting factors of length l up to the threshold m.

Infinite words α and β are *finitely l-locally m-threshold equivalent*, written $\alpha \approx^{l,m} \beta$, if $\mathrm{pref}_{l-1}(\alpha) = \mathrm{pref}_{l-1}(\beta)$ and $\mu_\alpha^{l,m} = \mu_\beta^{l,m}$. They are *l-locally m-threshold equivalent*, written $\alpha \approx_\omega^{l,m} \beta$, if in addition $\inf_l(\alpha) = \inf_l(\beta)$.

An ω-language is called *l-locally m-threshold testable* if it is a union of $\approx_\omega^{l,m}$-classes. It is *finitely l-locally m-threshold testable* if it is a union of $\approx^{l,m}$-classes. It is called *[finitely] l-locally threshold testable* if it is [finitely] l-locally m-threshold testable for some m, and it is called *[finitely] locally threshold testable* if it is [finitely] l-locally threshold testable for some l.

The corresponding classes of regular ω-languages are denoted by $\mathcal{L}tt_{l,m}$, $\mathcal{L}tt_l$, $\mathcal{L}tt$ and $\mathit{fin}\text{-}\mathcal{L}tt_{l,m}$, $\mathit{fin}\text{-}\mathcal{L}tt_l$, $\mathit{fin}\text{-}\mathcal{L}tt$.

Concerning topologically defined ω-languages we start at the lowest level of the Borel hierarchy. An ω-language is called *open* if it has the form UA^ω for a subset U of A^*. It is a countable intersection of open sets iff it has the form $\lim(U)$ for some subset U of A^* [5, p.378, Lemma 2.2], where $\alpha \in \lim(U)$ if for all i there is a $j > i$ such that $\alpha(0,j) \in U$. The corresponding set of ω-languages is denoted by $\mathcal{G}_\delta$. An ω-language is a countable union of closed sets iff it is a complement of a language in $\mathcal{G}_\delta$. The corresponding set of ω-languages is denoted by $\mathcal{F}_\sigma$. (For details see [9, pp. 152–156].)

In these terms we can state our main result.

Theorem 1. *We have*

(1) $\qquad \mathcal{L}tt_{l,m} \cap \mathcal{F}_\sigma \cap \mathcal{G}_\delta \subseteq \mathit{fin}\text{-}\mathcal{L}tt_{l,c}, \qquad$ *for $l, m > 0$ and $c = 2m \cdot \mathrm{card}(A)^{2l}$.*

(That means, every l-locally m-threshold testable ω-language which belongs to $\mathcal{F}_\sigma \cap \mathcal{G}_\delta$ is finitely l-locally c-threshold testable.)

The proof occupies Sections 1 to 6. A sketch of it is given at the end of this introduction.

Corollary 2.   (a) *We have*

$$\mathcal{L}tt \cap \mathcal{F}_\sigma \cap \mathcal{G}_\delta = \mathit{fin}\text{-}\mathcal{L}tt,$$
$$\mathcal{L}tt_l \cap \mathcal{F}_\sigma \cap \mathcal{G}_\delta = \mathit{fin}\text{-}\mathcal{L}tt_l, \qquad \text{for } l > 0.$$

(b) *It is decidable whether a regular ω-language is finitely locally threshold testable.*

Proof. (a) Both equations follow from Theorem 1 together with the inclusion $\mathit{fin}\text{-}\mathcal{L}tt \subseteq \mathcal{F}_\sigma \cap \mathcal{G}_\delta$ proved in [10, Lemma 7.5, p. 43].

(b) This is a consequence of (a) and the fact that the properties of a regular ω-language to belong to $\mathcal{F}_\sigma \cap \mathcal{G}_\delta$ and to be locally threshold testable are decidable [5, p. 279, Thm. 4.3],[10, Corollary 7.8, p. 44]. $\qquad \square$

To verify the inclusion (1) of Theorem 1 we proceed as follows. First (Sects. 1 and 2) we will investigate the properties of locally threshold testable languages which belong to $\mathcal{F}_\sigma \cap \mathcal{G}_\delta$. We will join $\approx_\omega^{l,m}$-classes into so-called l-m-blocks of largest possible size so that a given l-locally m-threshold testable language in $\mathcal{F}_\sigma \cap \mathcal{G}_\delta$ is a union of these blocks. This reduces the original problem to the claim that every l-m-block is finitely l-locally c-threshold testable. This will then be proven in Sects. 4, 5 and 6, after the presentation of an example (Sect. 3) illustrating the main ideas.

1 The $\mathcal{G}_\delta$-Lemma

Lemma 3. *Let $L \in \mathcal{L}tt_{l,m} \cap \mathcal{G}_\delta$, $\alpha \in L$ and $\beta \approx^{l,m} \alpha$. If $\inf_l(\alpha) \subseteq \inf_l(\beta)$, then $\beta \in L$.*

Proof. Assume that $L = \lim(U)$. We are going to construct a word $\gamma \in \lim(U)$ such that $\gamma \approx_\omega^{l,m} \beta$, which is enough.

First of all notice that for every element u of $\inf_l(\beta)$ there is a word $\gamma_u = uw_u\gamma_u'$ such that $\inf_l(\gamma_u) = \inf_l(\alpha)$ and $\mathrm{fact}_l(\gamma_u) = \inf_l(\beta) = \mathrm{fact}_l(w_u)$.

Take a finite prefix u_0 of β (or α) such that $\mathrm{pref}_{l-1}(u_0) = \mathrm{pref}_{l-1}(\beta)$, $\mu_{u_0}^{l,m} = \mu_\beta^{l,m}$ and $\mathrm{suff}_l(u_0) \in \inf_l(\beta)$. Let $v_0 = \mathrm{suff}_l(u_0)$. Since $u_0 w_{v_0} \gamma_{v_0} \in L$ by construction, there is a word u_1 belonging to U which is a prefix of $u_0 w_{v_0} \gamma_{v_0}$ such that $u_0 w_{v_0}$ in turn is a prefix of u_1. Let $v_1 = \mathrm{suff}_l(u_1)$. Then there is a word $u_2 \in U$ such that $u_1 < u_1 w_{v_1} < u_2$ by the same arguments as before. An iteration of this construction yields an increasing sequence

$$u_0 < u_0 w_{v_0} < u_1 < u_1 w_{v_1} < \ldots \quad \text{with } \mu_{u_i}^{l,m} = \mu_\beta^{l,m} \text{ and } u_i \in U \text{ for } i \in \omega.$$

Since $\mathrm{fact}_l(w_{v_i}) = \inf_l(\beta)$ for $i \in \omega$ by construction, the limit γ of the sequence is the desired word belonging to $\lim(U)$ such that $\beta \approx_\omega^{l,m} \gamma$. $\qquad\square$

Corollary 4. *Let $L \in \mathcal{L}tt_{l,m} \cap \mathcal{F}_\sigma$, $\alpha \in L$ and $\beta \approx^{l,m} \alpha$. If $\inf_l(\alpha) \supseteq \inf_l(\beta)$, then $\beta \in L$.*

Proof. Assume that β does not belong to L. Then Lemma 3 applied to the complement $A^\omega \setminus L$ of L implies $\alpha \in A^\omega \setminus L$, which is a contradiction. (Notice that $\mathcal{L}tt_{l,m}$ is closed under complementation.) $\qquad\square$

2 De Bruijn Graphs

By a *graph* $G = (V, E, i, t)$ we mean a set V of *vertices* and a set E of *edges* together with functions $i: E \to V$ and $t: E \to V$ determining *initial* and *terminal vertex*, respectively, of every edge.

The De Bruijn graph G_l of parameter $l > 0$ over the alphabet A is defined as follows (cf [1, p. 237]): The set A^{l-1} of all words of length $l-1$ forms the set V of *vertices* of G_l. The set A^l of all words of length l forms the set E of *edges* of G_l.

The *initial vertex* $i(e)$ of an edge e is its $l-1$-prefix. The *terminal vertex* $t(e)$ of an edge e is its $l-1$-suffix.

Every word x with length at least l gives us (exactly) one path (a word over E) through G_l: $\pi(x) = x(0,l), x(1,l+1), x(2,l+2), \ldots$, and conversely every non-empty path determines a word with length at least l. We have the equation $|\pi(x)|_u = \|x\|_u$ for $x \in A^{\geq l}$, $u \in A^l$, where on the left hand side u is taken as a 'letter', i.e., as an edge, whereas on the right hand side u denotes a word.

Next we need the concepts of 'induced subgraph' and 'connectedness'. As we are interested in the edge structure (rather than the vertex structure) of a given graph, we define these as follows.

Let G be a graph as above. If $E' \subseteq E$ is a set of edges of G, the *subgraph of G induced* by E' is the quadruple $G[E'] = (V', E', i|_{E'}, t|_{E'})$ where a vertex v belongs to V' if there is an edge $e \in E'$ such that $i(e) = v$ or $t(e) = v$.

A path in G is a non-empty word $p: n \to E$ such that $t(e_j) = i(e_{j+1})$ for every $j < n$ (where n may be ω). If p is finite we say that p *connects* e_0 with e_{n-1}. Edges e, e' are *connected* if there are paths p and p' connecting e with e' and e' with e, respectively. In this case we write $e \sim e'$. The *connectedness relation* $\sim$ is transitive and symmetric but need not to be reflexive (in contrast to the usual definition). A set $E' \subseteq E$ of edges in G is said to be *connected* in G if $E' \times E'$ is a subset of $\sim$.

We observe that for any connected subset E' of E the set $\{e \in E \mid (\exists e')e' \in E' \wedge e \sim e'\}$ is the largest connected subset including E'. Its induced subgraph is called the *connected component* of E'. Obviously, edge and vertex set of distinct connected components are pairwise disjoint.

For the rest of the paper we restrict our considerations to De Bruijn graphs. We assume that the De Bruijn graph $G = G_l$ of parameter l over the given alphabet A is given as (V, E, i, t). We are interested in the connected components $C_1, \ldots, C_n$ of the subgraph $G' = G[E']$ induced by some set of edges $E' \subset E$. We write E_i for the edge set of C_i and V_i for its vertex set. The union of all E_i is denoted by $\tilde{E}$, the set R is defined by $R = E' \setminus \tilde{E}$.

For a fixed E' we consider only ω-words α such that $\inf_l(\alpha) \subseteq E'$. With every such word we associate the connected component C_α of $\inf_l(\alpha)$ in G'. We write E_α for the edge set and V_α for the vertex set of C_α.

Often the set E' will be given by a $\approx^{l,m}$-class K: $E' = (\mu_\alpha^{l,m})^{-1}(m)$ for some $\alpha \in K$. This definition does not depend on α, so that we will simply write $E' = E_K$.

A first application of De Bruijn graphs is a reformulation of the $\mathcal{G}_\delta$-lemma. Let K be a fixed $\approx^{l,m}$-class and let $E' = E_K$ (see above).

Corollary 5. *If $L \in \mathcal{L}tt_{l,m} \cap \mathcal{F}_\sigma \cap \mathcal{G}_\delta$, $\alpha, \beta \in K$, and $E_\alpha = E_\beta$, then $\alpha \in L$ iff $\beta \in L$.*

Proof. By definition we have $E' = (\mu_\alpha^{l,m})^{-1}(m)$. Thus there is a word γ such that $\alpha \approx^{l,m} \beta \approx^{l,m} \gamma$ and $\inf_l(\gamma) = E_\alpha$. Consequently $\alpha \in L$ iff $\gamma \in L$ by Lemma 3 together with Corollary 4, and $\beta \in L$ iff $\gamma \in L$ by the same arguments. $\quad\square$

This result leads to the following definition: An *l-m-block* of a $\approx^{l,m}$-class K is a maximal subset of K of words with the same associated connected component, i.e., it is a set of the form $\{\beta \in K \mid E_\alpha = E_\beta\}$ for some $\alpha \in K$. (Notice that the blocks of K partition K.)

In these terms every *l*-locally *m*-threshold testable language in $\mathcal{F}_\sigma \cap \mathcal{G}_\delta$ is a union of *l-m*-blocks. Thus for the desired proof of Theorem 1 it suffices to show the following claim.

Claim 6. *Every l-m-block is finitely l-locally c-threshold testable.*

3 Demonstration

We present the promised example. Consider the following figure.

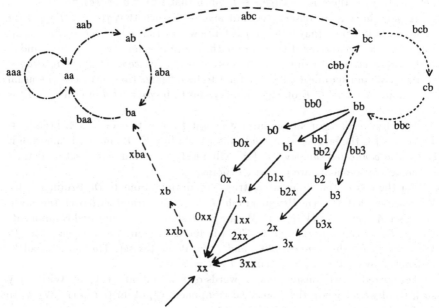

It shows a graph H which is a subgraph of the DE BRUIJN graph of parameter 3 over the alphabet $A = \{a, b, c, x, 0, 1, 2, 3\}$. We define K to be the language which contains an ω-words $\alpha \in A^\omega$ iff

- $\pi(\alpha)$ is a path through H,
- $\pi(\alpha)$ starts in xx,
- $|\pi(\alpha)|_e = 1$ iff the edge e is drawn as a connected arrow,
- $|\pi(\alpha)|_e \geq 2$ iff the edge e is drawn as a dotted arrow.

Then K is finitely 3-locally 2-threshold testable since it is a $\approx^{3,2}$-class.

There are exactly two connected components of $H' = H[E_K]$: one, C_l, in the upper left corner of H, the other, C_r, in the upper right corner. Thus we have two 3-2-blocks in K (B_l and B_r). Our aim is to show that they are finitely 3-locally threshold testable. Since they are obviously not finitely 3-locally 2-threshold testable, we see that we must increase the threshold.

We want to distinguish between the cases that a word of K eventually stays in C_l or C_r resp. Each path of a word of K passes exactly four times the space between the upper right circle of H and its origin xx, because every direct path from bb to xx must be used exactly once. Therefore, the edge abc is passed four or five times, and this depends just on which component the path finally stays in. This means: A word of K belongs to B_r iff its path has at least five occurrences of abc, otherwise it belongs to B_l. Thus B_l and B_r are finitely 3-locally 5-threshold testable. —

In the present example we can determine the block of a given word by threshold counting of edges coming in and going out of the connected components of the reduced graph G'. This illustrates a *general phenomenon*: As it turns out

- the number of incoming and outgoing edges of paths of a given $\approx^{l,m}$-class is bounded (Corollary 9); so counting them precisely can be done by counting them up to an appropriate threshold, and
- given a $\approx^{l,m}$-class K, the connected component to which a word of K belongs is determined by the number of incoming and outgoing edges in its path (Lemma 7).

4 IN-/OUT-Counting

In this section E' is an arbitrary set of edges in the graph $G = G_l$.

The set of *incoming* edges (in G_l) of a connected component C_i of G' is defined by $\text{IN}_i = \{e \in E \setminus E_i \mid t(e) \in V_i\}$. The set of *outgoing* edges of C_i is defined analogously: $\text{OUT}_i = \{e \in E \setminus E_i \mid i(e) \in V_i\}$. The union of all sets IN_i is denoted by IN, the union of all sets OUT_i is denoted by OUT, and IO is defined as to be $\text{IN} \cup \text{OUT}$.

Remark. (a) The sets IN_i are pairwise disjoint.
  (b) The sets OUT_i are pairwise disjoint.
  (c) $\text{IO} \cap E' \subseteq R$.

In the remainder of this section we will analyze how incoming and outgoing edges occur in a path through G_l.

Lemma 7. *Let p be an arbitrary finite path through G_l starting with e and ending with f. Set $u = \text{pref}(e)$ and $v = \text{suff}(f)$. Denote by χ_i the characteristic function of V_i. Then*

$$|p|_{\text{IN}_i} + \chi_i(u) = |p|_{\text{OUT}_i} + \chi_i(v), \quad \text{for } i \in \{1, \ldots n\}.$$

Proof. The proof proceeds by induction on the length of p. In the induction step we assume p' to be a path of length $j + 1$ and that the assertion is true for all pathvs p of length j. Write p' as pg with $|p| = j$ and $g \in E$. Let u and v as in the formulation of the lemma, and let $u' = \text{pref}(g)$ and $v' = \text{suff}(g)$. Then by induction hypothesis

$$|p|_{\text{IN}_i} + \chi_i(u) = |p|_{\text{OUT}_i} + \chi_i(v) \text{ and } |g|_{\text{IN}_i} + \chi_i(u') = |g|_{\text{IN}_i} + \chi_i(v').$$

Adding up both equations yields

$$|p'|_{\text{IN}_i} + \chi_i(u) + \chi_i(u') = |p'|_{\text{OUT}_i} + \chi_i(v') + \chi_i(v).$$

Thus it remains to show $\chi_i(v) = \chi_i(u')$, but this is true, for $u' = v$ by definition. $\square$

5 Bounding IN/OUT-Counting

Let $E' = E_K$ for some $\approx^{l,m}$-class K. We show that $|\pi(\alpha)|_{\text{IO}}$ is bounded for $\alpha \in K$.

Lemma 8. Let $\alpha \in K$.

(a) If $p \in E'^*$ is a factor of $\pi(\alpha)$, then $|w|_R \leq \text{card}(A)^l$.
(b) $|\pi(\alpha)|_{A^l \setminus E'} \leq (m-1)\text{card}(A)^l$.

Proof. (a) Assume that the first inequality does not hold. Then there is an edge e of R which occurs (at least) twice in p. Thus e belongs to a component of G'; hence $e \in \tilde{E}$ which contradicts $e \in R = E \setminus \tilde{E}$.

(b) Recall that every word of length l not belonging to E' occurs less than m times in α. $\square$

Corollary 9. Let $\alpha \in K$. Then $|\pi(\alpha)|_{\text{IO}} < 2m \cdot \text{card}(A)^l$.

Proof. Since $(\mu_\alpha^{l,m})^{-1}(m) = E'$, the path $\pi(\alpha)$ allows a decomposition $\pi(\alpha) = u_0 v_1 u_1 v_2 \ldots v_r \pi'$, where $u_i \in E'^+$, $v_i \in (A^l \setminus E')^+$ for $i > 0$, $u_0 \in E'^*$, $\pi' \in \bar{E}^\omega$. We split $|\pi(\alpha)|_{\text{IO}}$ into $|u_0 u_1 \ldots u_{r-1}|_{\text{IO}}$ and $|v_1 v_2 \ldots v_r \pi'|_{\text{IO}}$. Since $\text{IO} \cap \tilde{E} = \emptyset$, the latter term is equal to $|v_1 v_2 \ldots v_r|_{\text{IO}}$. From Lemma 8(b) we obtain (i) $r \leq (m-1)\text{card}(A)^l$. Then $|u_0 u_1 \ldots u_{r-1}|_{\text{IO}} \leq |u_0 u_1 \ldots u_{r-1}|_R = \sum_{i=0}^{r-1} |u_i|_R$ by Remark 4. Because of Lemma 8(a) the last term is $\leq r \cdot \text{card}(A)^l$, which is in turn $\leq (m-1)\text{card}(A)^l \text{card}(A)^l$ by (i). On the other hand we have $|v_1 v_2 \ldots v_r|_{\text{IO}} \leq |v_1 v_2 \ldots v_r|_{A^l \setminus E'}$ since $v_i \in A^l \setminus E'$ for $i \in \{1, \ldots, r\}$. The right hand side is bounded by $|\pi(\alpha)|_{A^l \setminus E'}$, which is $\leq (m-1)\text{card}(A)^l$ by Lemma 8(a). Adding up what we have yields

$$|\pi(\alpha)|_{\text{IO}} \leq (m-1)\text{card}(A)^l \text{card}(A)^l + (m-1)\text{card}(A)^l < 2m \cdot \text{card}(A)^{2l}.$$

$\square$

6 Proof of Theorem 1

We will prove that, for any $\approx^{l,c}$-equivalent words α and β, if α belongs to the l-m-block B, then β belongs to B. This shows Claim 6 (Sect. 2) and hence Theorem 1.

Let α belong to the $\approx^{l,m}$-class K. Consider $E' = E_K$. Since $\approx^{l,c}\subseteq\approx^{l,m}$, the word β belongs to an l-m-block B' in K. Then we are left with the proof of $B = B'$. This in turn is equivalent to $C_i = C_j$, when C_i is the component associated with α and C_j is the component associated with β.

Both paths $\pi(\alpha)$ and $\pi(\beta)$ allow decompositions $p\pi$ and $p'\pi'$ respectively such that p and p' are not empty and γ and γ' do not contain edges of IO. Furthermore we can assume that the last edge of p and every edge in π belong to E_i and, analogously, that the last edge of p' and every edge in π' belong to E_j.

Recall that c was defined just as to be the right hand side of the inequality in Corollary 9. Thus

(i) $|\alpha|_u = |\beta|_u$,   for $u \in$ IO.

Let u' denote the $l - 1$-prefix of the first edge of p' and v' the $l - 1$-suffix of the last edge of p'. We have $\chi_i(v) = 1$, thus Lemma 7 implies

(ii) $|p|_{\text{IN}_i} + \chi_i(u) = |p|_{\text{OUT}_i} + 1$ and $|p'|_{\text{IN}_i} + \chi_i(u') = |p'|_{\text{OUT}_i} + \chi_i(v')$.

From (i) we may conclude $|p|_{\text{IN}_i} = |p'|_{\text{IN}_i}$ and $|p|_{\text{OUT}_i} = |p'|_{\text{OUT}_i}$. Thus (ii) yields $\chi_i(u) = 1$ and $\chi_i(u') = \chi_i(v')$. Since $u = \text{pref}_{l-1}(\alpha) = \text{pref}(\beta) = u'$ we finally obtain $\chi_i(v') = 1$, hence $i = j$, whence $B = B'$, as was to be shown.   □

7 Application to Mathematical Logic

An *infinite k-word structure* is a tuple $(\omega, \text{succ}, P_1, \ldots, P_k)$ consisting of the set ω of natural numbers together with the successor function succ defined by $\text{succ}(n) = n + 1$ and k unary predicates $P_1, \ldots, P_k$.

The set of closed monadic second-order formulas using succ and $P_1, \ldots, P_k$ is denoted by S1S_k (second-order with 1 successor over $\mathbf{k}$ predicates). Each interpretation $\mathbf{M} = (M_1, \ldots, M_k)$ for the unary predicates of a formula belonging to S1S_k can be coded as an ω-word $\text{w}(\mathbf{M})$ over the alphabet 2^k in a natural way: the i-th component of the j-th letter of $\text{w}(\mathbf{M})$ is 1 iff $j \in M_i$. With $\phi \in \text{S1S}_k$ we associate the language $\text{L}(\phi)$ defined by $\text{L}(\phi) = \{\alpha \in \text{w}(\mathbf{M}) \mid n(\omega, \text{succ}, \mathbf{M}) \models \phi\}$.

Theorem 10 (BÜCHI, [4, pp. 5–7]).   (a) *An ω-language $L \subseteq (2^k)^\omega$ is regular iff there is a formula $\phi \in \text{S1S}_k$ such that $L = \text{L}(\phi)$.*
   (b) *There is an algorithm computing for every k and $\phi \in \text{S1S}_k$ a BÜCHI automaton recognizing $\text{L}(\phi)$.*

By F1S_k we denote the first-order formulas of S1S_k.

Theorem 11 (THOMAS, [8, Thm. 4.2, p. 373]).   *An ω-language $L \subseteq (2^k)^\omega$ is finitely locally threshold testable iff there is a formula $\phi \in \text{F1S}_k$ such that $L = \text{L}(\phi)$.*

Note that the less-than relation $<$ is not in the signature. If it is included, first-order formulas define exactly the star-free ω-languages.

Theorem 10, Theorem 11 and Corollary 2 jointly yield the desired decidability result.

Corollary 12. *It is decidable whether a given formula $\phi \in \text{S1S}_k$ is equivalent to a formula $\psi \in \text{F1S}_k$ (in the sense that $L(\phi) = L(\psi)$).* $\square$

Open Problems. In the special case $m = 1$ it was shown [10, Thm. 7.9, p. 45] that c can be chosen as 1. We leave open the question which is the optimal c in Theorem 1, and have as yet no results about the complexity of the involved decision procedures.

For biinfinite word structures JEAN ERIC PIN raised the decidability question solved here for the case of ω-words. So far it is not clear whether the methods used here could be helpful for the solution of this problem because they essentially refer to the fact that ω-words have a distinguished origin where counting can start.

References

1. Claude Berge, *Graphs*, second revised ed., North-Holland Mathematical Library, vol. 6, North-Holland, Amsterdam, 1985, part 1.

2. Daniele Beauquier and Jean Eric Pin, *Factors of words*, Automata, Languages and Programming: 16th Intern. Coll., Stresa, 1989, Proc. (G. Ausiello, M. Dezani-Ciancaglini, and S. Ronchi Della Rocca, eds.), Lecture Notes in Computer Science, vol. 372, Springer, 1989, pp 63–79.

3. Janus A. Brzozowski and Imre Simon, *Characterization of locally testable events*, Discrete Math. 4 (1973), 243–271.

4. J. Richard Büchi, *On a decision method in restricted second-order arithmetic*, Logic, Methodology, and Philosophy of Science: Proc of the 1960 International Congress (E. Nagel, P. Suppes, and A. Tarski, eds.), Stanford University Press, 1962, pp 1–11.

5. Laurence H. Landweber, *Decision problems for ω-automata*, Math. Systems Theory 3 (1969), 376–384.

6. Robert McNaughton, *Algebraic decision procedures for local testability*, Math. Systems Theory 8 (1974), 60–76.

7. Ludwig Staiger and Klaus Wagner, *Automatentheoretische Charakterisierungen topologischer Klassen regulärer Folgenmengen*, Elektron. Informationsverarb. Kybernet. 10 (1974), 379–392.

8. Wolfgang Thomas, *Classifying regular events in symbolic logic*, J. Comput. System Sci. 25 (1982), 360–376.

9. Wolfgang Thomas, *Automata on infinite objects*, Handbook of Theoretical Computer Science (Jan van Leeuwen, ed.), Elsevier Science Publishers B.V., 1990, pp 134–191.

10. Thomas Wilke, *An algebraic theory for regular languages of finite and infinite words*, Technical report 9202, Inst f. Inform. u. Prakt. Math., Univ. Kiel, Germany, 1992. To appear in Intern. J. Algebra Comput.

Deterministic asynchronous automata
for infinite traces[*]

EXTENDED ABSTRACT

Volker Diekert   Anca Muscholl

Universität Stuttgart
Institut für Informatik
Breitwiesenstr. 20-22
D-7000 Stuttgart 80

Abstract. This paper shows the equivalence between the family of recognizable languages over infinite traces and deterministic asynchronous cellular Muller automata. We thus give a proper generalization of McNaughton's Theorem from infinite words to infinite traces. Thereby we solve one of the main open problems in this field. As a special case we obtain that every closed (w.r.t. the independence relation) word language is accepted by some I-diamond deterministic Muller automaton. We also determine the complexity of deciding whether a deterministic I-diamond Muller automaton accepts a closed language.

1 Introduction

The main result of the present paper provides a positive answer to the open question of [GP92] and extends McNaughton's Theorem to recognizable real trace languages. Concretely, we show the equivalence between the family of recognizable real trace languages and the family of real trace languages which can be accepted by deterministic asynchronous cellular Muller automata. In fact, all our results have a natural extension to complex traces. This is not done here for sake of simplicity and will be done elsewhere.

The paper is organized as follows. Section 2 provides some basic notions. We also recall some facts about recognizable infinitary word and trace languages. Section 3 gives first a technical lemma which allows to follow the approach of Perrin/Pin [PP91]to McNaughton's Theorem. We define deterministic real trace languages and show as the main result of this section that the family of recognizable real trace languages is equivalent to the Boolean closure of deterministic languages. The results we obtain are a proper generalization of the analogous results in the word case. Based on the foregoing result, we show in Section 4 that the family of recognizable real trace languages coincides with the family of languages accepted by deterministic asynchronous cellular Muller automata. In fact, this kind of automaton is a special form of so-called I-diamond automata, which

---

[*] This research has been supported by the ESPRIT Basic Research Action No. 6317 ASMICS 2.

play an important role in the case of finite traces. In Section 5 we consider the complexity of deciding whether a Muller I-diamond automaton accepts a closed language or not. The complete characterization and decision procedure are left to a forthcoming paper.

2 Preliminaries

2.1 Basic Notions

We denote by (Σ, D) a finite *dependence alphabet*, with Σ being a finite alphabet and $D \subseteq \Sigma \times \Sigma$ a reflexive and symmetric relation called *dependence relation*. The complementary relation $I = (\Sigma \times \Sigma) \setminus D$ is called *independence relation*. Let also $D(a) = \{b \in \Sigma \mid (a, b) \in D\}$.

The monoid of *finite traces*, $\mathbb{M}(\Sigma, D)$, is defined as a quotient monoid with respect to the congruence relation induced by I, i.e., $\mathbb{M}(\Sigma, D) = \Sigma^* / \{ab = ba \mid (a, b) \in I\}$. Traces can be identified with their dependence graph, i.e., with (isomorphism classes of) labelled, acyclic, directed graphs $[V, E, \lambda]$, where V is a set of vertices labelled by $\lambda : V \to \Sigma$ and E is a set of edges with the property that $E \cup E^{-1} \cup \mathrm{id}_V = \lambda^{-1}(D)$. This notion can be extended to infinite dependence graphs. We denote by $\mathbb{G}(\Sigma, D)$ the set of infinite dependence graphs with a countable set of vertices V such that $\lambda^{-1}(a)$ is well-ordered for all $a \in \Sigma$. The requirement that any subset of vertices with the same label should be well-ordered, allows to represent the vertices as pairs (a, i), with $a \in \Sigma$ and i a countable ordinal. Note that $\mathbb{G}(\Sigma, D)$ is a monoid with respect to the operation $[V_1, E_1, \lambda_1][V_2, E_2, \lambda_2] = [V, E, \lambda]$, where $[V, E, \lambda]$ is the disjoint union of $[V_1, E_1, \lambda_1]$ and $[V_2, E_2, \lambda_2]$ together with new edges $(v_1, v_2) \in V_1 \times V_2$, whenever $(\lambda_1(v_1), \lambda_2(v_2)) \in D$ holds. The identity is the empty graph $[\emptyset, \emptyset, \emptyset]$. The concatenation is immediately extendable to infinite products. Let $(g_n)_{n \geq 0} \subseteq \mathbb{G}(\Sigma, D)$, then $g = g_0 g_1 \ldots \in \mathbb{G}(\Sigma, D)$ is defined as the disjoint union of the g_n, together with new edges from g_n to g_m for $n < m$ between vertices with dependent labels. Thus, we can now define for any $L \subseteq \mathbb{G}(\Sigma, D)$ the ω-iteration as $L^\omega = \{g_0 g_1 \ldots \mid g_n \in L, \forall n \geq 0\}$.

We denote by Σ^ω the set of infinite words over the alphabet Σ (i.e., mappings from $\mathbb{N}$ to Σ), and by Σ^∞ the set of all words $\Sigma^* \cup \Sigma^\omega$. The canonical mapping $\varphi : \Sigma^* \to \mathbb{M}(\Sigma, D)$ can be extended to Σ^∞, i.e., $\varphi : \Sigma^\infty \to \mathbb{G}(\Sigma, D)$. The image $\varphi(\Sigma^\infty) \subseteq \mathbb{G}(\Sigma, D)$ is called the set of *real traces* and is denoted by $\mathbb{R}(\Sigma, D)$. In other words, real traces can be identified with (in)finite graphs where every vertex has finitely many predecessors. Observe that $\mathbb{R}(\Sigma, D)$ is not a submonoid of $\mathbb{G}(\Sigma, D)$, since, in general, φ commutes neither with concatenation nor with ω-iteration (if $L, K \in \Sigma^\infty$, then $\varphi(LK) = \varphi(L)\varphi(K)$ and $\varphi(L^\omega) = (\varphi(L))^\omega$ hold if and only if L does not contain any infinite word). In the following we will denote $\mathbb{R}(\Sigma, D)$ ($\mathbb{M}(\Sigma, D)$ respectively) by $\mathbb{R}$ ($\mathbb{M}$ respectively). A word language $L \subseteq \Sigma^\infty$ is said to be *closed* (with respect to (Σ, D)) if $L = \varphi^{-1}\varphi(L)$ for the canonical mapping $\varphi : \Sigma^\infty \to \mathbb{R}$.

Let us give now some further basic notations related to finite traces. For $t \in \mathbb{M}$, we denote by $\mathrm{alph}(t)$ the set of letters occurring in t, and by $|t|_a$, $a \in \Sigma$, the number of a occurring in t. Moreover, $\text{alph}(L) = \bigcup_{t \in L} \text{alph}(t)$. We shall often use the abbreviation $(t, u) \in I$ for $\text{alph}(t) \times \text{alph}(u) \subseteq I$. The set of maximal elements of a finite trace $t \in M$, denoted by $\max(t)$, is defined as the set of labels corresponding to the maximal vertices of the dependence graph of t, i.e., $\max(t) = \{a \in \Sigma \mid \exists x \in \Sigma^* : \varphi(xa) = t\}$.

For (in)finite traces the prefix order $\leq$ is given by $u \leq t$ if and only if there exists a trace s with $t = us$. We shall often make use of intersections of prefixes of a given (in)finite trace in the following way: if $t \in \mathbb{R}$, $u \leq t$ and $v \leq t$, then $(u \cap v) \leq t$, too. Hereby is $u \cap v$ the trace obtained by intersecting the dependence graphs of u and v within the dependence graph of t, where the intersection is meant with respect to the labelled vertex sets of u, v. We use in the same sense the greatest lower (least upper) bound $\sqcap$ ($\sqcup$) of a set $X \subseteq \mathbb{R}$, whenever it exists.

2.2 Recognizable word languages

The family of *recognizable* infinitary word languages, denoted by $\text{Rec}(\Sigma^\infty)$, can be defined by means of finite state automata with suitable acceptance conditions for infinite words (see [Tho90]).

Let $\mathcal{A} = (Q, \Sigma, \delta, q_0, F)$ be a nondeterministic finite automaton where Q is the finite set of states, $\delta \subseteq Q \times \Sigma \times Q$ is the transition relation, q_0 is the initial state and F is the set of accepting states. If π denotes an infinite path in $\mathcal{A}$, then $\inf(\pi)$ is the set of states occurring infinitely often in π. An infinite word w is accepted by $\mathcal{A}$ as a Büchi automaton if there exists a transition path π of $\mathcal{A}$ labelled by w such that for some final state $f \in F$, $f \in \inf(\pi)$. For the Muller acceptance condition, we have additionally a state table $\mathcal{T} \subseteq \mathcal{P}(Q)$. An infinite word w is accepted by $\mathcal{A}$ as a Muller automaton if there is a path π labelled by w such that for some $T \in \mathcal{T}$, $\inf(\pi) = T$. Finite words are accepted by $\mathcal{A}$ in the usual way, by reaching a final state of F.

A language $L \subseteq \Sigma^\infty$ is called *recognizable* if it is accepted by some nondeterministic Büchi automaton. Furthermore, the well-known theorem of McNaughton [McN66] states that $\text{Rec}(\Sigma^\infty)$ coincides with the family of infinitary word languages accepted by deterministic Muller automata (see e.g. [Tho90]).

2.3 Recognizable Real Trace Languages

One possible way to define *recognizable* infinitary trace languages, denoted by $\text{Rec}(\mathbb{R})$, is by recognizing morphisms [Gas91]. Let $\eta : M \to S$ be a morphism to a finite monoid S. A real trace language $L \subseteq \mathbb{R}$ is *recognized* by η if for any sequence $(t_n)_{n \geq 0} \subseteq M$ the following holds:

$$t_0 t_1 t_2 \ldots \in L \implies \eta^{-1}\eta(t_0)\, \eta^{-1}\eta(t_1)\, \eta^{-1}\eta(t_2) \ldots \subseteq L$$

Moreover, in this case $L = \bigcup_{(s,e) \in P} \eta^{-1}(s)\, \eta^{-1}(e)^\omega$ with

$$P = \{(s, e) \in S^2 \mid se = s, e^2 = e \text{ and } \eta^{-1}(s)\, \eta^{-1}(e)^\omega \cap L \neq \emptyset\}.$$

From the point of view of automata, the family of recognizable real trace languages Rec($\mathbb{R}$) consists of those languages, which can be accepted by a nondeterministic Büchi asynchronous cellular automaton [GP92]. Hereto, we give the definition below.

For the family of finitary recognizable trace languages, Zielonka introduced asynchronous and asynchronous cellular automata ([Zie87], [Zie89]) and he showed the deep result of the equivalence between Rec($\mathbb{M}$) and the family of finitary trace languages accepted by some deterministic asynchronous cellular automaton (or deterministic asynchronous automaton).

An *asynchronous cellular automaton* is a tuple $\mathcal{A} = ((Q_a)_{a \in \Sigma}, (\delta_a)_{a \in \Sigma}, q_0, F)$ where for each $a \in \Sigma$, Q_a is a finite set of states, $q_0 \in \prod_{a \in \Sigma} Q_a$ is the initial state, $F \subseteq \prod_{a \in \Sigma} Q_a$ is the set of final states and $\delta_a \subseteq (\prod_{b \in D(a)} Q_b) \times Q_a$ is the local transition relation. We will denote in the following $\prod_{b \in A} Q_b$ (($q_b)_{b \in A}$, resp.) by Q_A (q_A, resp.), where $A \subseteq \Sigma$. In particular, for $a \in \Sigma$ we mean by $q_{D(a)}$ the local states tuple $(q_b)_{b \in D(a)}$.

The global transition relation $\Delta \subseteq Q_\Sigma \times \Sigma \times Q_\Sigma$ of $\mathcal{A}$ is defined by:

$$q' \in \Delta(q, a) \quad \Leftrightarrow \quad (\ q'_a \in \delta_a(q_{D(a)}) \quad \text{and} \quad q'_c = q_c, \text{ for all } c \neq a\ )$$

This means for a global state q and $a \in \Sigma$ that a next state $q' \in \Delta(q, a)$ exists if and only if $\delta_a(q_{D(a)})$ is not empty and in this case, the action of a changes merely the a-component of q and the new value q'_a depends only on the b components of q, for $b \in D(a)$. Thus, asynchronous cellular automata have the ability of parallel execution of independent actions. Note that this is a typical situation where common read is allowed, whereas writing operations are exclusive and every processor has his own writing domain (CROW).

In [GP92] acceptance conditions have been defined for infinite traces. If we consider an infinite path $\pi = (q_0, a_0, q_1, a_1, \dots)$ in $\mathcal{A}$, with $q_n \in Q_\Sigma$ and $a_n \in \Sigma$ for every $n \geq 0$, then let $\inf_a(\pi) = \{\ q_a \in Q_a \mid \exists^\infty n \text{ s.t. } q_{n,a} = q_a\ \}$ denote the set of local a-states which occur infinitely often in π. Then, an asynchronous cellular automaton viewed as a Büchi (Muller, resp.) automaton is given a table $\mathcal{T} \subseteq \prod_{a \in \Sigma} \mathcal{P}(Q_a)$ i.e., $\mathcal{A} = ((Q_a)_{a \in \Sigma}, (\delta_a)_{a \in \Sigma}, q_0, F, \mathcal{T})$. An infinite trace $t \in \mathbb{R}$ is accepted by the Büchi (Muller, respectively) automaton if there exists a path π labelled by t (i.e., by any $w \in \varphi^{-1}(t)$) and a set $T \in \mathcal{T}$ such that $\inf_a(\pi) \supseteq T_a$ ($\inf_a(\pi) = T_a$, respectively), for every $a \in \Sigma$. Note that the acceptance conditions are inherently local, thus being appropriate for this kind of automata with decentralized control. Finite traces are accepted in the usual way, by reaching a final state. Gastin/Petit showed the equivalence between Rec($\mathbb{R}$) and the family of real trace languages which are accepted by some nondeterministic Büchi asynchronous cellular automaton (an analogous result holds for Büchi asynchronous automata) [GP92]. However the construction of Gastin/Petit was inherently nondeterministic and so far there is no way to modify their approach (even considering different acceptance conditions) in order to obtain a deterministic automaton. The construction below is based on a totally different approach.

3 Algebraic Results on Recognizable Real Trace Languages

Let $L \in \text{Rec}(\mathbb{R})$ be recognized by a morphism $\eta : \mathbf{M} \to S$ to a finite monoid S. We define:

$$\mathbf{M}_s = \eta^{-1}(s), \quad \text{for } s \in S$$
$$\mathbf{P}_s = \mathbf{M}_s \setminus \mathbf{M}_s \mathbf{M}_+, \text{ with } \mathbf{M}_+ = \mathbf{M} \setminus \{1\}$$

Thus, $\mathbf{M}_s$ is the set of all finite traces mapped by η to $s \in S$ and $\mathbf{P}_s$ is the subset of $\mathbf{M}_s$ having no proper prefix in $\mathbf{M}_s$. Moreover, we may assume that $\text{alph}(t) = \text{alph}(t')$ for all $t, t' \in \mathbf{M}$ with $\eta(t) = \eta(t')$, since we may replace S by $S \times \mathcal{P}(\Sigma)$, with the multiplication defined by $(s, A)(s', A') = (ss', A \cup A')$ and $(1, \emptyset)$ as neutral element. Hence, $\text{alph}(s)$ for $s \in S$ is well-defined. It can also be viewed as an abbreviation for $\text{alph}(\mathbf{M}_s)$.

From the theory of finite monoids we will need only basic tools, such as the quasi-order relation $\leq_{\mathcal{R}}$ defined as $a \leq_{\mathcal{R}} b$ if and only if $aS \subseteq bS$ and the equivalence relation $\mathcal{R}$ defined as $a\mathcal{R}b$ if and only if $aS = bS$. Furthermore, let $E(S)$ denote the set of idempotent elements of S, $E(S) = \{ e \in S \mid e = e^2 \}$ and define the following partial order relation on $E(S)$: $f \leq e$ if and only if $ef = f$ (in fact, $f \leq e$ is equivalent to $f \leq_{\mathcal{R}} e$). By $f < e$ we mean $f \leq e$ and $e \not\leq f$.

Back to infinite traces, the following notation will be used frequently:

$$\text{Inf}(A) = \{ t \in \mathbb{R} \mid \text{alphinf}(t) = A \},$$
$$\mathbf{R}_A = \{ t \in \mathbb{R} \mid D(\text{alphinf}(t)) = D(A) \} \text{ for } A \subseteq \Sigma.$$

where for $t \in \mathbb{R}$, $\text{alphinf}(t)$ denotes the set of letters occurring infinitely often in t. In particular, we denote by $\text{Inf}(s)$ and $\mathbf{R}_s$ for $s \in S$ the sets $\text{Inf}(A)$ and $\mathbf{R}_A$ with $A = \text{alph}(s)$.

Remark 1. Note that in the word case (i.e., $D = \Sigma \times \Sigma$) we have $\mathbf{R}_A = \Sigma^\omega$, for every $\emptyset \neq A \subseteq \Sigma$ and $\mathbf{R}_\emptyset = \Sigma^*$. We prefer to use $\mathbf{R}_s$ instead of $\text{Inf}(s)$, since thereby we obtain the analogous results for infinite words as a special case of our results.

Definition 2. Let $L \subseteq \mathbf{M}$.
We define $\overrightarrow{L} := \{ t \in \mathbb{R} \mid t = \sqcup Y \text{ with } Y \text{ directed and } Y \subseteq L \}$.
(A set $Y \subseteq \mathbf{M}$ is called directed if for every $t, t' \in Y$, there exists an upper bound which also belongs to Y.)
In analogy to infinitary word languages, a *deterministic* real trace language is a language of type $\overrightarrow{L} \cap \mathbf{R}_A$, where $L \in \text{Rec}(\mathbf{M})$ and $A \subseteq \Sigma$.

Remark 3. i) Note that every deterministic language is recognizable. Clearly, $\mathbf{R}_A \in \text{Rec}(\mathbb{R})$, where $A \subseteq \Sigma$. Moreover, let $\eta : \mathbf{M} \to S$ be a morphism recognizing L. Then it is easy to check that $\overrightarrow{L} = \bigcup_{(s,e) \in P} \mathbf{M}_s \mathbf{M}_e^\omega$ holds, with P given by $P = \{ (s, e) \mid s \in \eta(L), se = s, e^2 = e \}$.
ii) The classical definition in the word case considers only infinite words. Here we have $L \subseteq \overrightarrow{L}$. According to our definition, we obtain the classical definition by the intersection $\overrightarrow{L} \cap \Sigma^\omega$. At least if one deals with traces our definition seems to

be more natural. In fact for word languages $L \subseteq \Sigma^\infty$ one usually intersects with Σ^* and with Σ^ω and investigates the finitary and infinitary part separately. For traces, these intersections are replaced by intersections with $\mathbf{R}_A$ for $A \subseteq \Sigma$. It is also via these intersections how one can easily extend the result to complex traces.

The following technical proposition is an important tool for all our results. It gives a characterization of infinite traces which belong to the set $\overrightarrow{LK}$, for $L, K \subseteq \mathbb{M}$. The proof is deferred to the full version of the paper.

Proposition 4. *Given* $(t_n)_{n \geq 0}, (w_n)_{n \geq 0} \subseteq \mathbb{M}$ *such that* $\{ t_n w_n \,|\, n \geq 0 \}$ *is an infinite, directed set and let* $x = \bigsqcup \{ t_n w_n \,|\, n \geq 0 \}$. *Then there exist a subsequence of indices* $(n_i)_{i \geq 0} \subseteq \mathbb{N}$ *and sequences of finite traces* $(s_i)_{i \geq 0}, (u_i)_{i \geq 0}, (v_i)_{i \geq 0} \subseteq \mathbb{M}$ *such that* $x = \bigsqcup \{ t_{n_i} w_{n_i} \,|\, i \geq 0 \}$ *satisfying for* $i \geq 0$ *the following conditions:*

$$t_{n_i} = s_0 u_0 \ldots s_{i-1} u_{i-1} s_i,$$
$$w_{n_i} = v_0 \ldots v_{i-1} u_i v_i$$
$$\text{and} \quad (v_i, s_j u_j) \in I, \quad \text{for } i < j.$$

Corollary 5. *Given* $L, K \subseteq \mathbb{M}$ *with* $K \in \text{Rec}(\mathbb{M})$ *such that* $K\mathbb{M}_+ \cap K = \emptyset$. *Let* $(t_n)_{n \geq 0} \subseteq L$, $(w_n)_{n \geq 0} \subseteq K$ *with* $\{ t_n w_n \,|\, n \geq 0 \}$ *be an infinite, directed set with* $x = \bigsqcup \{ t_n w_n \,|\, n \geq 0 \}$. *Let additionally* $D(\text{alphinf}(x)) = D(\text{alph}(K))$.
Then there exist a subsequence of indices $(n_i)_{i \geq 0} \subseteq \mathbb{N}$ *and sequences of finite traces* $(s_i)_{i \geq 0}, (u_i)_{i \geq 0} \subseteq \mathbb{M}$ *such that* $x = \bigsqcup \{ t_{n_i} w_{n_i} \,|\, i \geq 0 \}$ *and, for* $i \geq 0$:

$$t_{n_i} = s_0 u_0 \ldots s_{i-1} u_{i-1} s_i \qquad and \qquad w_{n_i} = u_i.$$

The next proposition generalizes the corresponding result for infinitary word languages (see also [PP91]) and will play a crucial role in the proof of the main result of this section. Apparently, the result differs from the analogous one for infinitary word languages, since we have an additional information about the alphabet at infinity. Nevertheless, observe that for $D = \Sigma \times \Sigma$, since $\mathbf{R}_e = \Sigma^\omega$ (if $e \neq 1$) we obtain indeed the result for Σ^ω as a special case of the next proposition (recall Rem. 1).

Proposition 6. *Let* S *be a finite monoid,* $\eta : \mathbb{M} \to S$ *a morphism and* $s, e \in S$ *such that* $se = s$ *and* $e \in E(S)$. *Then we have the following inclusions:*

$$\mathbb{M}_s \mathbb{M}_e^\omega \quad \subseteq \quad \overrightarrow{\mathbb{M}_s \mathbb{P}_e} \cap \mathbb{R}_e \quad \subseteq \quad \bigcup_{f \leq e} \mathbb{M}_s \mathbb{M}_f^\omega$$

Proof. We omit the proof, which is analogous to the word case ([PP91]). We note that it is an easy consequence of Cor. 5, together with the principle of Ramsey factorizations.

Corollary 7. *Let* S *be a finite monoid,* $\eta : \mathbb{M} \to S$ *a morphism and* $s, e \in S$ *such that* $se = s$ *and* $e \in E(S)$. *Then we have:*

1. $M_e^\omega = \overrightarrow{M_e P_e} \cap \mathbb{R}_e$

2. $\bigcup_{f \le e} M_s M_f^\omega = \bigcup_{f \le e} (\overrightarrow{M_s P_f} \cap \mathbb{R}_f)$.

The following lemma expresses a property of the set $P_L = \{(s,e) \in S^2 \mid e \in E(S), se = s \text{ and } M_s M_e^\omega \cap L \ne \emptyset\}$ belonging to $L \in \mathrm{Rec}(\mathbb{R})$. Two pairs $(s,e),(s',e') \in S^2$ are called *conjugated* ([PP91]) if for some $x, y \in S$ the equalities $s' = sx$, $e = xy$ and $e' = yx$ hold.

Lemma 8. *Let* $L = \bigcup_{(s,e) \in P_L} M_s M_e^\omega$ *be recognized by a morphism* $\eta : M \to S$, *with* P_L *as above. Then for every elements* $s, s' \in S$, $e, e' \in E(S)$ *with* $(s,e),(s',e') \in P_L$, $M_s M_e^\omega \cap M_{s'} M_{e'}^\omega \ne \emptyset$ *if and only if* (s,e) *and* (s',e') *are conjugated.*

Proof. Similar to [PP91].

The next theorem is the main result of this section. It shows that every recognizable real trace language belongs to the Boolean closure of the family of deterministic languages. We obtain the well-known result for words as a special case of this theorem.

Theorem 9. *Let* $L \in \mathrm{Rec}(\mathbb{R})$ *be recognized by the morphism* $\eta : M \to S$ *with* S *a finite monoid and* $P_L = \{(s,e) \in S^2 \mid se = s, e \in E(S), M_s M_e^\omega \cap L \ne \emptyset\}$. *Then we have:*

$$L = \bigcup_{(s,e) \in P_L} \left(\bigcup_{f \le e} (\overrightarrow{M_s P_f} \cap \mathbb{R}_f) \setminus \bigcup_{f < e} (\overrightarrow{M_s P_f} \cap \mathbb{R}_f) \right)$$

Proof. Consider $(s,e) \in P_L$ and $f\mathcal{R}e$ with $f \in E(S)$. Then, by Lemma 8, $(s,f) \in P_L$, since (s,e) and (s,f) are conjugated with $x = e$ and $y = f$ ($f = xy, e = yx, s = sx$). Hence, $L = \bigcup_{(s,e) \in P_L} M_s M_e^\omega \subseteq \bigcup_{(s,e) \in P_L} \bigcup_{f\mathcal{R}e} M_s M_f^\omega \subseteq L$, where the first inclusion is due to $e\mathcal{R}e$. We obtain $L = \bigcup_{(s,e) \in P_L} \bigcup_{f\mathcal{R}e} M_s M_f^\omega$. Furthermore, we have $f\mathcal{R}e$ if and only if $ef = f$ and $fe = e$, hence if and only if $f \le e$ and $f \not< e$.

Moreover, if $f < e$ holds, then $M_s M_e^\omega \cap M_s M_f^\omega = \emptyset$. $\qquad (*)$

Otherwise, (s,e) and (s,f) would be conjugated (by Lemma 8) and one can easily check that this implies $e \le f$, hence $f \not< e$.

We may now conclude the proof:

$$\bigcup_{f\mathcal{R}e} M_s M_f^\omega = \bigcup_{f \le e, f \not< e} M_s M_f^\omega \overset{(*)}{=} \bigcup_{f \le e} M_s M_f^\omega \setminus \bigcup_{f < e} M_s M_f^\omega =$$

$$= \bigcup_{f \le e} M_s M_f^\omega \setminus \bigcup_{f < e} \bigcup_{g \le f} M_s M_g^\omega \overset{\mathrm{Cor.7}}{=}$$

$$\bigcup_{f \le e} (\overrightarrow{M_s P_f} \cap \mathbb{R}_f) \setminus \bigcup_{f < e} \bigcup_{g \le f} (\overrightarrow{M_s P_g} \cap \mathbb{R}_g) =$$

$$= \bigcup_{f \le e} (\overrightarrow{M_s P_f} \cap \mathbb{R}_f) \setminus \bigcup_{f < e} (\overrightarrow{M_s P_f} \cap \mathbb{R}_f)$$

Corollary 10. $\mathrm{Rec}(\mathbb{R})$ *is equivalent to the Boolean closure of the family of deterministic real trace languages.*

4 Deterministic Asynchronous Automata for Rec(R)

In this section we will construct deterministic asynchronous cellular Muller automata for languages of the form $\overrightarrow{L}$ with $L \in \text{Rec}(\mathbb{M})$. Since for every $\mathbb{R}_A$ ($A \subseteq \Sigma$) one can clearly exhibit a deterministic asynchronous cellular Muller automaton, we will obtain at the end the equivalence between $\text{Rec}(\mathbb{R})$ and the family of languages accepted by deterministic asynchronous cellular Muller automata. Recall also from the definition of Muller automata that the accepted languages are closed under the Boolean operations.

We begin with a lemma which shows that we may restrict ourselves to a particular type of $\overrightarrow{L}$ with $L \in \text{Rec}(\mathbb{M})$. Roughly speaking, we are interested in $\overrightarrow{L}$ where the alphabet at infinity A is the same for all traces and where for every infinite trace in $\overrightarrow{L}$, its (infinitely many) L-prefixes have exactly one maximal element for each connected component of A.

Lemma 11. *Let $A = \bigcup_{i=1}^{k} A_i$ be a decomposition in connected components for $A \subseteq \Sigma$, i.e., $(A_i, A_j) \in I$ for $i \neq j$ and A_i is connected for every $i = 1, \ldots, k$. Choose a fixed $a_i \in A_i$ for each i and let $\mathbb{M}_{A,i}$ ($\mathbb{P}_{A,i}$ respectively) denote the following recognizable subsets of $\mathbb{M}$:*

$$\mathbb{M}_{A,i} = \{ t \mid \text{alph}(t) = A_i \text{ and } \max(t) = \{a_i\} \}$$
$$\mathbb{P}_{A,i} = \mathbb{M}_{A,i} \setminus \mathbb{M}_{A,i}\mathbb{M}_+$$

Then we have for $L \subseteq \mathbb{M}$:

$$\overrightarrow{L} \cap \text{Inf}(A) = \overrightarrow{L\mathbb{P}_{A,1}\ldots\mathbb{P}_{A,k}} \cap \text{Inf}(A).$$

Proof. The proof is similar to the proof of Proposition 6.

Before stating the main theorem of this section, let us recall some important concepts of Zielonka's construction of asynchronous cellular automata for $\text{Rec}(\mathbb{M})$, which we will need in our construction (see also [Die90], [CMZ89]).

The a-prefix (A-prefix, respectively) $\partial_a(t)$ ($\partial_A(t)$, respectively) of a finite trace t has been defined as the minimal prefix of t containing all a (all letters $a \in A$, respectively), which occur in t. More precisely, for every $a \in \Sigma$, $A \subseteq \Sigma$ and $t \in \mathbb{M}$,

$$\partial_a(t) = \sqcap\{ u \leq t \mid |t|_a = |u|_a \}, \quad \partial_A(t) = \bigsqcup_{a \in A} \partial_a(t) \quad \text{(in particular } \partial_\emptyset(t) = 1).$$

Zielonka's construction is based on the concept of *asynchronous mapping* (see e.g. [Die90], p. 49). It is a mapping $\varphi : \mathbb{M} \to Q$ to a set Q satisfying the following 2 conditions, for every $t \in \mathbb{M}$, $a \in \Sigma$ and $A, B \subseteq \Sigma$:

- The value of $\varphi(\partial_{A \cup B}(t))$ is uniquely determined by $\varphi(\partial_A(t))$ and $\varphi(\partial_B(t))$.
- The value of $\varphi(\partial_{D(a)}(ta))$ is uniquely determined by $\varphi(\partial_{D(a)}(t))$ and by a.

Given an asynchronous mapping $\varphi : \mathbb{M} \to Q$ and a set $R \subseteq Q$, then an asynchronous cellular automaton $\mathcal{A} = (Q^\Sigma, \delta, q_0, F)$ with the following partial transition function accepts $\varphi^{-1}(R)$:

$$\delta : Q^\Sigma \times \mathbb{M} \to Q^\Sigma,$$
$$\delta((\varphi(\partial_b(t)))_{b \in \Sigma}, a) = (\varphi(\partial_b(ta)))_{b \in \Sigma}$$

(It is easy to check that δ is well-defined and satisfies the requirement for the partially defined transition function of an asynchronous cellular automaton, see e.g. [Die90], Prop. 2.4.4). The initial state of $\mathcal{A}$ is $q_0 = (\varphi(1), \ldots, \varphi(1))$ and F is given by $F = \{ (\varphi(\partial_a(t)))_{a \in \Sigma} \mid \varphi(t) \in R \}$. Moreover, we have $\delta(q_0, t) = (\varphi(\partial_a(t)))_{a \in \Sigma}$.

Finally, suppose we are given a finitary recognizable language $K \subseteq \mathbb{M}$ recognized by a morphism $\eta : \mathbb{M} \to S$ onto a finite monoid S. Then, Zielonka's construction of an asynchronous cellular automaton accepting K provides an asynchronous mapping $\varphi : \mathbb{M} \to Q$ to a finite set Q and a mapping $\pi : Q \to S$ such that $\eta = \pi \circ \varphi$.

A crucial feature of the construction is the fact that the global state of the asynchronous cellular automaton based on φ which is reached after having read a finite trace t, can be reconstructed by using the local states corresponding to the maximal elements of t: since $t = \partial_{\max(t)}(t)$ holds, we have $\varphi(t) = \varphi(\partial_{\max(t)}(t))$, which means that $\varphi(t)$ is exactly determined by $\{ \varphi(\partial_a(t)) \mid a \in \max(t) \}$ (since φ is an asynchronous mapping).

Theorem 12. *Let $L \in \mathrm{Rec}(\mathbb{M})$ be a recognizable finitary trace language. Then $\overrightarrow{L}$ can be recognized by a deterministic asynchronous cellular Muller automaton.*

Proof. Since we have

$$\overrightarrow{L} \quad = \quad \bigcup_{A \subseteq \Sigma} (\overrightarrow{L} \cap \mathrm{Inf}(A)) \quad \overset{\text{Lemma 11}}{=} \quad \bigcup_{A \subseteq \Sigma} (\overrightarrow{L\mathbb{P}_{A,1} \ldots \mathbb{P}_{A,k}} \cap \mathrm{Inf}(A)),$$

with $\mathbb{P}_{A,1}, \ldots \mathbb{P}_{A,k}$ depending on A and defined as in the previous lemma, it will suffice to construct a deterministic Muller automaton accepting $\overrightarrow{L\mathbb{P}_{A,1} \ldots \mathbb{P}_{A,k}} \cap \mathrm{Inf}(A)$.

Let $\eta : \mathbb{M} \to S$ be a morphism to a finite monoid S recognizing $L\mathbb{P}_{A,1} \ldots \mathbb{P}_{A,k}$, and let $\varphi : \mathbb{M} \to Q$ be the asynchronous mapping to the finite set Q such that there exists a mapping π with $\eta = \pi \circ \varphi$. Finally, consider the deterministic asynchronous cellular automaton $\mathcal{A}' = ((Q'_a)_{a \in \Sigma}, (\delta'_a)_{a \in \Sigma}, q'_0, F)$ accepting $L\mathbb{P}_{A,1} \ldots \mathbb{P}_{A,k}$, which is obtained by Zielonka's construction. In particular, we have $\delta'(q'_0, t) = (\varphi(\partial_a(t)))_{a \in \Sigma}$, for every $t \in \mathbb{M}$, $a \in \Sigma$.

Furthermore, consider for every $f \in F$ the language

$$L_{A,f} = \{ t \in \mathbb{R} \mid \mathrm{alphinf}(t) = A, \ t = \bigsqcup \{ t_n \mid n \geq 0 \} \text{ with } t_0 \leq t_1 \leq \ldots \text{ infinite,}$$
$$t_n \in L\mathbb{P}_{A,1} \ldots \mathbb{P}_{A,k} \text{ and } \delta'(q'_0, t_n) = f, \text{ for every } n \geq 0 \}$$

Clearly $\overrightarrow{L\mathbb{P}_{A,1} \ldots \mathbb{P}_{A,k}} \cap \mathrm{Inf}(A) = \bigcup_{f \in F} L_{A,f}$ holds, since $\overrightarrow{K_1 \cup K_2} = \overrightarrow{K_1} \cup \overrightarrow{K_2}$, for $K_1, K_2 \subseteq \mathbb{M}$. Therefore, it suffices to construct a deterministic asynchronous cellular Muller automaton $\mathcal{A} = ((Q_a)_{a \in \Sigma}, (\delta_a)_{a \in \Sigma}, q_0, \mathcal{T})$ accepting $L_{A,f}$. Let us define for $a \in \Sigma$:

$$Q_a = Q_a' \times \mathbb{Z}/2\mathbb{Z}$$
$$\delta_a((q, i)_{D(a)}) = (\delta_a'(q_{D(a)}), i_a + 1)$$
$$q_0 = (q_{0a}', 0)_{a \in \Sigma}$$

Hence, we have $\delta_a(s_{D(a)}) \neq s_a$, for every $s_a \in Q_a$, $a \in \Sigma$. Thus, $|\inf_a(t)| \geq 2$ if and only if $a \in \text{alphinf}(t)$, for each $a \in \Sigma$. We now define the table $\mathcal{T}$:

$$T = (T_a)_{a \in \Sigma} \in \mathcal{T} \quad \text{if and only if} \quad \text{for some } i_a \in \mathbb{Z}/2\mathbb{Z}$$
$$T_a = \{(f_a, i_a)\} \text{ for } a \in \Sigma \setminus A,$$
$$(f_a, i_a) \in T_a \text{ and } |T_a| \geq 2, \text{ for } a \in A$$

The inclusion $L_{A,f} \subseteq L(\mathcal{A})$ is not hard to be seen. Conversely, let $t \in L(\mathcal{A})$ be accepted by $T \in \mathcal{T}$. Clearly, $\text{alphinf}(t) = \{a \in \Sigma \mid |T_a| \geq 2\} = A$, so let us factorize t as $t = t_0 t_1 \ldots$ such that for some $i_a \in \mathbb{Z}/2\mathbb{Z}$, $a \in \Sigma$:

$$\text{alph}(t_n) = A \qquad \text{for } n \geq 1,$$
$$\delta(q_0, t_0 t_1 \ldots t_n)_a = (f_a, i_a) \qquad \text{for } a \in (\Sigma \setminus A) \cup \{a_1, \ldots, a_k\} \text{ and } n \geq 0,$$
$$\max(t_0 \ldots t_n) \cap A = \{a_1, \ldots, a_k\} \quad \text{for } n \geq 0.$$

(such a factorization exists because of the definition of the table $\mathcal{T}$ together with $a_i \in A_i$, with $(A_i, A_j) \in I$, for $i \neq j$).

We show that $t_0 t_1 \ldots t_n \in L\mathbb{P}_{A,1} \ldots \mathbb{P}_{A,k}$, $n \geq 0$. Evidently, $\delta'(q_0', t_0 \ldots t_n)_a = f_a$, for $a \in (\Sigma \setminus A) \cup \{a_1, \ldots, a_k\}$, $n \geq 0$. From the definition of $\mathcal{A}'$, we know $f = (\varphi(\partial_a(u)))_{a \in \Sigma}$ for some $u \in L\mathbb{P}_{A,1} \ldots \mathbb{P}_{A,k}$. Note also that $\max(u) \cap A = \{a_1, \ldots, a_k\}$ and that for every $n \geq 0$, $a \in (\Sigma \setminus A) \cup \{a_1, \ldots, a_k\}$ the following holds:

$$(\delta'(q_0', t_0 \ldots t_n)_a =) \quad \varphi(\partial_a(t_0 \ldots t_n)) = \varphi(\partial_a(u)) \quad (= f_a)$$

Since $\max(u), \max(t_0 \ldots t_n) \subseteq (\Sigma \setminus A) \cup \{a_1, \ldots a_k\}$, the observation made before we stated the theorem yields $\varphi(t_0 \ldots t_n) = \varphi(u)$, hence $\eta(t_0 \ldots t_n) = \eta(u)$, thus implying $t_0 \ldots t_n \in L\mathbb{P}_{A,1} \ldots \mathbb{P}_{A,k}$.

Corollary 13. *The family of recognizable real trace languages is equivalent to the family of languages, which are accepted by deterministic asynchronous cellular Muller automata.*

5 Deterministic I-diamond Muller automata

The rest of the paper can be read independently of the first part. It can also be omitted if the reader is interested only in the existence of deterministic asynchronous automata. We have included this section in this paper since due to the previous section we know for the first time that every closed recognizable language of Σ^ω can be recognized by some deterministic I-diamond Muller automaton. We give in the following no proofs, complexity results being deferred to a forthcoming paper.

Let M be any monoid, then the classical definition [Eil74] defines a language $L \subseteq M$ to be recognizable if it is accepted by some deterministic M-automaton. In the case of $M = \mathbb{M} = \mathbb{M}(\Sigma, D)$ an $\mathbb{M}$-automaton $\mathcal{A}$ is the same as a deterministic finite automaton $\mathcal{A} = (Q, \delta, q_0, F)$ over Σ which satisfies the I-diamond property:

$$\forall q \in Q,\ (a, b) \in I : q \cdot ab = q \cdot ba$$

In some sense I-diamond finite automata do not accept traces directly, but they accept any representing word. So they accept closed languages.

Let us note that the I-diamond property does not ensure in the case of Muller automata that the accepted language is closed. We need some restriction of the tables in order to accept closed languages. We will give these restrictions for reduced tables, only. For this, consider a Muller automaton $\mathcal{A} = (Q, \delta, q_0, \mathcal{T})$. The table $\mathcal{T}$ is called reduced if for every $T \in \mathcal{T}$ there is some $u \in \Sigma^\omega$ such that T represents the set of states occurring infinitely often on the path starting with q_0 and labelled by u. Let us denote the set of states on the path starting by a state $q \in Q$ and labelled by $v \in \Sigma^*$ by $\tau(q, v)$, i.e., $\tau(q, v) = \{ qu \mid u \text{ is a prefix of } v \}$. The table $\mathcal{T}$ is called *closed* if for all $T \in \mathcal{T}, q \in T$ and $v \in \Sigma^*$ such that $qv = q$ and $T = \tau(q, v)$ we have $\tau(q, w) \in \mathcal{T}$, too, provided $w \in \Sigma^*$ denotes the same trace as v.

The next proposition is a special case of [GP91].

Proposition 14 Gastin/Petit. *Let $\mathcal{A} = (Q, \delta, q_0, \mathcal{T})$ be a deterministic I-diamond Muller automaton where $\mathcal{T}$ is reduced. Then $\mathcal{A}$ accepts a closed language if and only if the table $\mathcal{T}$ is closed.*

It is also stated in [GP91] that it is effectively decidable whether a reduced table is closed. However the decision procedure of [GP91] is based on the observation that the path length can be bounded. This does not yield any practical algorithm. However, giving an efficient decision procedure requires a subtler characterization of closed tables. Based on this characterization, we are able to show the NL completeness of the decision procedure. By NL we denote the class of problems decidable in non-deterministic logarithmic space, NSPACE (log(n)).

Proposition 15. *It is NL - complete to decide given a deterministic I-diamond Muller automaton $\mathcal{A} = (Q, \delta, q_0, \mathcal{T})$ over (Σ, D) whether the table $\mathcal{T}$ is reduced.*

The proposition above shows that the preprocessing used to check the hypothesis of Proposition 14 is already NL-complete. However, the interesting fact is that even if we get this preprocessing for free, the test whether the accepted language is closed is still NL-complete.

Proposition 16. *There is an NL-algorithm to decide given a deterministic I-diamond Muller automaton $\mathcal{A} = (Q, \delta, q_0, \mathcal{T})$ over (Σ, D), whether $L(\mathcal{A}) \subseteq \Sigma^\omega$ is closed.*

For the hardness we may even restrict us to a three letter alphabet.

Theorem 17. *Let $(\Sigma, D) = a - c - b$. It is NL-hard to decide given a deterministic I-diamond Muller automaton $\mathcal{A} = (Q, \delta, q_0, \mathcal{T})$ where $\mathcal{T}$ is reduced whether $L(\mathcal{A})$ is closed.*

6 Conclusion

In this paper we gave a characterization of recognizable real trace languages by deterministic asynchronous Muller automata, thus answering one of the main open problems about infinite traces, see e.g. [GP92]. We showed that classical results of the theory of recognizable infinitary word languages have a natural extension in the case of real traces. One open problem which arises is whether there exists a characterization of $\overrightarrow{L}$ with $L \in \text{Rec}(\mathbf{M})$ (i.e., without intersecting with sets $\mathbb{R}_A$) by means of deterministic asynchronous Büchi automata.

Acknowledgements: We thank Paul Gastin for fruitful discussions and Wieslaw Zielonka who told us that independently he has developed similar ideas. We also thank the anonymous referees from STACS for many valuable comments.

References

[CMZ89] R. Cori, Y. Métivier, and W. Zielonka. Asynchronous mappings and asynchronous cellular automata. Tech. rep. 89-97, LABRI, Univ. Bordeaux, 1989.

[Die90] V. Diekert. *Combinatorics on Traces*. Number 454 in Lecture Notes in Computer Science. Springer, Berlin-Heidelberg-New York, 1990.

[Eil74] S. Eilenberg. *Automata, Languages and Machines*, volume I. Academic Press, New York and London, 1974.

[Gas91] P. Gastin. Recognizable and rational trace languages of finite and infinite traces. In Choffrut C. et al., editors, *Proceedings of the 8th Annual Symposium on Theoretical Aspects of Computer Science (STACS'91), Hamburg 1991*, number 480 in Lecture Notes in Computer Science, pages 89–104. Springer, Berlin-Heidelberg-New York, 1991.

[GP91] P. Gastin and A. Petit. Büchi (asynchronous) automata for infinite traces. Tech. rep., LRI, Université Paris-Sud, 1991.

[GP92] P. Gastin and A. Petit. Asynchronous cellular automata for infinite traces. In W. Kuich, editor, *Proceedings of the 19th International Colloquium on Automata Languages and Programming (ICALP'92), Vienna (Austria) 1992*, Lecture Notes in Computer Science. Springer, Berlin-Heidelberg-New York, 1992. Also available as Tech. Rep. 91-68, LITP, Université Paris 6, France, 1991.

[McN66] R. McNaughton. Testing and generating infinite sequences by a finite automaton. *Information and Control*, 9:521–530, 1966.

[PP91] D. Perrin and J.E. Pin. Mots Infinis. Technical Report, LITP 91.06, Université de Paris 6, 1991. Book to appear.

[Tho90] W. Thomas. Automata on infinite objects. In Jan van Leeuwen, editor, *Handbook of theoretical computer science*, pages 133–191. Elsevier Science Publishers, 1990.

[Zie87] W. Zielonka. Notes on finite asynchronous automata. *R.A.I.R.O.-Informatique Théorique et Applications*, 21:99–135, 1987.

[Zie89] W. Zielonka. Safe executions of recognizable trace languages by asynchronous automata. In A. R. Mayer et al., editors, *Proceedings Symposium on Logical Foundations of Computer Science, Logic at Botik '89, Pereslavl-Zalessky (USSR) 1989*, number 363 in Lecture Notes in Computer Science, pages 278–289. Springer, Berlin-Heidelberg-New York, 1989.

Recursive Automata on Infinite Words

Ludwig Staiger

Universität Siegen, Fachbereich Elektrotechnik und Informatik, Hölderlinstr. 3,
W-5900 Siegen, Germany*

Abstract. The present paper gives a thorough charcterization classes of ω-languages defined by several classes of recursive automata and elementary acceptance conditions in terms of the arithmetical hierarchy. Here it is interesting to note that finitely branching nondeterministic *looping* or *Co-Büchi*-accepting automata are only as powerful as their deterministic counterparts whereas nondeterministic *Büchi*-accepting automata are more powerful than deterministic ones.

These results are used to estimate the complexity of verification problems for programs and specifications defining recursive automata.

This paper is concerned with sets of infinite sequences (so-called ω-languages) definable by recursive automata. It is motivated by the fact that the study of infinite computations has gained increasing interest in computer science, especially in the area of specification and verification of concurrent programs (cf. e.g. the brief surveys contained in [Kl90], [Th90] or [Va87]). A framework based on recursive automata that unifies a large number of trends in this area, such as temporal logic, model checking, automata theory, and fair termination, was presented by Vardi [Va87]. He suggests the use of effective not necessarily finite-state (so-called recursive) automata on infinite words. a similar approach is contained in Chap. 7 of [Kl90]. Earlier investigations on recursive devices on infinite words are contained in the papers [CG78] and [WS77] (cf. also [St86a]) dealing with infinite computations on Turing machines.

Regard a program P as defining an automaton $\mathcal{P}$ which describes the possible execution sequences (computations of the program) $T(\mathcal{P})$. Similarly, a specification S defines an automaton $\mathcal{S}$ describing the allowed computations $T(\mathcal{S})$. To verify that P satisfies S amounts to checking whether every computation of $\mathcal{P}$ is a computation of $\mathcal{S}$, that is, whether the behaviour $T(\mathcal{P})$ is contained in $T(\mathcal{S})$ (cf. [VW86]). Hence the verification problem reduces to the containment problem "$T(\mathcal{P}) \subseteq T(\mathcal{S})$?" This problem is intrinsically difficult for nondeterministic recursive automata, because the question "$T(\mathcal{P}) \subseteq T(\mathcal{S})$?" depends on the one hand on a universal quantifier over an infinite object, and on the other hand the description of the behaviour of a nondeterministic recursive automaton involves an existential quantifier over an infinite object (cf. [Va87] and [SW77]), therefore it is Π_2^1-complete, as observed e.g. in [DY92] or [Si89]. For some classes of recursive automata, e.g. for deterministic ones which do not involve this existential quantifier, however, the verification problem is simpler.

---

* The author is now with: Technische Universität Cottbus, Lehrstuhl für Theoretische Informatik, Karl-Marx-Str. 17, O-5700 Cottbus, Germany

In this paper we investigate in more detail which reasons lead to a simplification of the verification problem "$T(\mathcal{P}) \subseteq T(S)$?". In particular, we are interested in the question when the above mentioned quantifiers over infinite objects can be substituted by quantifiers over finite objects, and still more restrictive, can be removed at all. In particular, it is of interest when a program P can be verified according to a specification S using only quantifiers over finite objects and having at most one alternation in the prefix of quantifiers.

It turns out that the branching behaviours of the corresponding automata as well as of the underlying tree (set) of computations play a crucial rôle in this respect:

- We get several simplifications which allow for a removal of the existential quantifier over infinite objects in the description of the behaviour when the recursive automata $\mathcal{P}$ and S are restricted to be deterministic, or finitely branching instead of countably branching. It is interesting to note that these simplifications do also depend on the acceptance conditions.
- It is well-known that quantifiers over infinite objects are easier to remove if the object under consideration is a set variable (sequence over a finite alphabet) in contrast to, the general case when it is a function variable (sequence over N) [Ro67].

Utilizing this effect we show that in several instances verification problems for computations with only a finite number of possible executions, that is, when the underlying alphabet is finite, allow for an additional removal of the universal quantifier. Since this finiteness condition seems to be a severe restriction (unless we confine ourselves to the case of finite automata) we derive a condition on the branching behaviour of the automata $\mathcal{P}$ and S which guarantees that the respective sets of computations $T(\mathcal{P})$ and $T(S)$ can be simultaneously (one-to-one and recursively) encoded via a finite alphabet.

It should be noted, however, that in general there is no relationship between the branching behaviours of an automaton $\mathcal{A}$ and of the tree (set) of computations definable by $\mathcal{A}$, $T(\mathcal{A})$.

Although the usual verification techniques are based on local manipulations of the devices defining $T(\mathcal{P})$ and $T(S)$, we utilize here the global description in terms of the arithmetical hierarchy. To this end we have to relate the sets of sequences accepted (defined) by recursive automata under various acceptance conditions to the classes of the arithmetical hierarchy. This allows for a thorough characterization of the complexity of verification problems for several classes of recursive automata (deterministic, finitely branching and countably branching nondeterministic) and various acceptance conditions.

After some preparatory considerations on recursive automata we derive in Section 2 relationships between the behaviours of deterministic and nondeterministic recursive automata and derive their characterization in terms of classes of the arithmetical hierarchy. This leads to a concise presentation of our verification results which is given in Section 3. Here we also show the above mentioned embedding result.

1   Notation

By $N = \{0, 1, 2, \ldots\}$ we denote the set of natural numbers. As *alphabets* we consider nonempty initial segments of N containing at least $\{0, 1\}$. A *string* b is a function mapping an initial segment of $\omega = \{1, 2, \ldots\}$ to the alphabet X. Let $|b| = \sup b^{-1}(X)$ denote the *length* of the string b. If $|b|$ is finite we call b a *word*. As usual X^* is the set of all words over X, including the empty word e, and X^ω is the set of all infinite strings (sequences) over X. Subsets of X^* and X^ω will be referred to as *languages* or $\omega-$*languages*, respectively.

For $w \in X^*$ and $b \in X^* \cup X^\omega$ let $w \cdot b$ be their concatenation. This concatenation product extends in an obvious way to subsets $W \subseteq X^*$ and $B \subseteq X^* \cup X^\omega$.

$A(B) := \{w : w \in X^* \wedge \exists b(w \cdot b \in B)\}$ is the set of all *initial words (prefixes)* of the set $B \subseteq X^* \cup X^\omega$. Moreover, we shall abbreviate $w \in A(b)$ by $w \sqsubseteq b$ and the interval $b(n+1) \cdot \ldots \cdot b(\min\{m, |b|\})$ of the string b by $b(n, m]$.

An *automaton* $\mathcal{A}$ over X is a quadruple $[Z, z_0, R, Z_f]$ where Z is a nonempty set of states, $z_0 \in Z$ is the initial state, $Z_f \subseteq Z$ is the set of final states , and $R \subseteq Z \times X \times Z$ is the transition relation. An automaton $\mathcal{A}$ is said to be *recursive* provided Z is an initial segment of N, and Z_f and R are recursively enumerable.[2]

We consider the function $\theta_R : Z \times X \to N \cup \{\infty\}$ telling us the cardinality of the set $R(z, x) := \{z' : (z, x, z') \in R\}$, $\theta_R(z, x) := \operatorname{card} R(z, x)$, and we classify an automaton $\mathcal{A}$ as *finitely* or *countably branching* according to whether $\theta_R(Z \times X) \subseteq N$ or not.

An automaton $\mathcal{A}$ is called *deterministic* if $\theta_R(Z \times X) \subseteq \{0, 1\}$, that is, if R may be considered as a partial recursive function mapping $Z \times X$ to Z, and a finitely branching recursive automaton $\mathcal{A}$ is referred to as *strictly recursive* if Z_f is recursive and its branching behaviour is recursive, that is, θ_R is a recursive function.[3]

Let **(S)D**, **(S)N**, and **CN** denote the classes of deterministic (strictly) recursive, finitely branching nondeterministic (strictly) recursive, and countably branching recursive automata, respectively.

For a word $w = w(1)w(2) \ldots w(n) \in X^*$ we call a sequence of states $z_1, \ldots, z_n$ a *run* of $\mathcal{A}$ over w if $(z_0, w(1), z_1), (z_1, w(2), z_2), \ldots, (z_{n-1}, w(n), z_n) \in R$. The set of all words w having a run of $\mathcal{A}$ with $z_{|w|} \in Z_f$ is called the language *accepted* by the automaton $\mathcal{A}$, $\mathbf{T}(\mathcal{A})$.

For a sequence $\xi \in X^\omega$ a run of $\mathcal{A}$ over ξ is an infinite sequence $z_1, \ldots, z_n, \ldots$ of states such that $(z_0, \xi(1), z_1), (z_1, \xi(2), z_2), \ldots, (z_{n-1}, \xi(n), z_n), \ldots \in R$.

A run of $\mathcal{A}$ over ξ is called everywhere (e-), once (1-), almost everywhere (ae-) or infinitely often (io-)*successful* provided $\forall i \geq 1(z_i \in Z_f)$, $\exists i \geq 1(z_i \in Z_f)$, $\exists n \forall i \geq n(z_i \in Z_f)$, or $\forall n \exists i \geq n(z_i \in Z_f)$, respectively, and a sequence $\xi \in X^\omega$ is e-*accepted* (1-*accepted*, ae-*accepted*, io-*accepted*) if there is an e-successful (1-successful, ae-successful, or io-successful, respectively) run of $\mathcal{A}$ over ξ.

---

[2] We generally require that the set of states Z be an initial segment of N for recursive automata, though it is sometimes more convenient to use recursive subsets of N, X^* or Cartesian products thereof. If we do so, in the sequel we tacitly assume an obvious recursive one-to-one embedding into N.

[3] The latter fact readily implies that R itself is a recursive relation, but not vice versa.

Let for $\alpha \in \{e, 1, ae, io\}$ be $\mathbf{T}_\alpha(\mathcal{A}) := \{\xi : \xi \in X^\omega \wedge \xi \text{ is } \alpha\text{--accepted by } \mathcal{A}\}$ the ω-language of all sequences α-accepted by $\mathcal{A}$, and let for a class of automata, Ω, $\mathbf{T}_\alpha(\Omega) := \{\mathbf{T}_\alpha(\mathcal{A}) : \mathcal{A} \in \Omega\}$.

The relevance of our accepting conditions for the purposes of verification is supported by the facts that Vardi's [Va87] looping automata are particular cases of e-accepting automata and that ae-acceptance and io-acceptance (the latter is Büchi's [Bü62] acceptance) are the atomic parts as well of Rabin's [Ra69] as of Streett's [S-r82] accepting conditions investigated e.g. in [KK91] and [Va87] in more detail. We shall return to that question below.

As for deterministic automata their infinite behaviour is easily derived from their finite one, we introduce the following operators which map languages $W \subseteq X^*$ to ω-languages:

$$\lim W := \{\xi : \xi \in X^\omega \wedge A(\xi) \subseteq W\} = X^\omega \setminus (X^* \setminus W) \cdot X^\omega,$$
$$W^\sigma := \{\xi : \xi \in X^\omega \wedge A(\xi) \setminus W \text{ is finite}\}, \text{ and}$$
$$W^\delta := \{\xi : \xi \in X^\omega \wedge A(\xi) \cap W \text{ is infinite}\} = X^\omega \setminus (X^* \setminus W)^\sigma.$$

We extend this notation in an obvious way to classes of languages and ω-languages, e.g. $\lim \mathcal{K} = \{\lim W : W \in \mathcal{K}\}$, and $\mathcal{K} \cdot X^\omega = \{W \cdot X^\omega : W \in \mathcal{K}\}$.

The following connection between $\mathbf{T}(\mathcal{A})$ and $\mathbf{T}_e(\mathcal{A})$, $\mathbf{T}_{ae}(\mathcal{A})$, $\mathbf{T}_{io}(\mathcal{A})$, and $\mathbf{T}_1(\mathcal{A})$ is immediate:

Property 1. *If $\mathcal{A} := [Z, z_0, R, Z_f]$ is a completely specified automaton, that is, if $R(z, x) \neq \emptyset$ for all $z \in Z$ and $x \in X$, then $\mathbf{T}_1(\mathcal{A}) = \mathbf{T}(\mathcal{A}) \cdot X^\omega$, and if $\mathcal{A}$ is deterministic, but not necessarily completely specified, then $\mathbf{T}_e(\mathcal{A}) = \lim \mathbf{T}(\mathcal{A})$, $\mathbf{T}_{ae}(\mathcal{A}) = \mathbf{T}(\mathcal{A})^\sigma$, and $\mathbf{T}_{io}(\mathcal{A}) = \mathbf{T}(\mathcal{A})^\delta$.*

2 Arithmetical Hierarchy

In order to describe the classes of ω-languages accepted by deterministic recursive automata it is useful to introduce the arithmetical hierarchies of languages and ω-languages, respectively (cf. [Ro67], [WS77]):

We say that a language $W \subseteq X^*$ belongs to the class Σ_n iff $W = \{w : \exists a_1 \ldots Q a_n : P(a_1, \ldots, a_n, w)\}$, and $F \subseteq X^\omega$ belongs to the class $\Sigma_n^{(X)}$ iff $F = \{\xi : \exists a_1 \ldots Q a_n : P'(a_1, \ldots, a_{n-1}, \xi(0, a_n])\}$, where P and P' are recursive predicates. The classes Π_n and $\Pi_n^{(X)}$ are defined as $\Pi_n := \{X^* \setminus W : W \in \Sigma_n\}$ and $\Pi_n^{(X)} := \{X^\omega \setminus F : F \in \Sigma_n^{(X)}\}$. In particular, $\Pi_1 \cap \Sigma_1$ and Σ_1 are the classes of recursive and recursively enumerable languages, respectively.

Lemma 2.

$$\mathbf{T}_e(\mathrm{SD}) = \lim(\Pi_1 \cap \Sigma_1) = \lim \Pi_1 = \Pi_1^{(X)}$$
$$\mathbf{T}_e(\mathrm{D}) = \lim \Sigma_1$$
$$\mathbf{T}_{ae}(\mathrm{SD}) = (\Pi_1 \cap \Sigma_1)^\sigma = (\Pi_1)^\sigma = \Sigma_2^{(X)}$$
$$\mathbf{T}_{ae}(\mathrm{D}) = (\Sigma_1)^\sigma$$
$$\mathbf{T}_{io}(\mathrm{SD}) = (\Pi_1 \cap \Sigma_1)^\delta = \Pi_2^{(X)}$$
$$\mathbf{T}_{io}(\mathrm{D}) = (\Sigma_1)^\delta = \Pi_2^{(X)}$$

The first parts of each equation are immediate from Property 1, proofs of the other identities are found in [CG77] and [St86a]. In particular, we have $\mathbf{T}_{io}(\mathbf{SD}) = \mathbf{T}_{io}(\mathbf{D})$.

We mention still $(\Pi_1 \cap \Sigma_1) \cdot X^\omega = \Sigma_1 \cdot X^\omega = \Sigma_1^{(X)}$, and the following inclusion properties (All inclusions are proper, and other inclusions do not hold [St86a,b].):

$$\Pi_1^{(X)} \cup \Sigma_1^{(X)} \subset \Pi_2^{(X)} \cap \Sigma_2^{(X)}$$
$$\Pi_1^{(X)} \subset \lim \Sigma_1 \subset \Pi_2^{(X)} \cap (\Sigma_1)^\sigma$$
$$\Sigma_2^{(X)} \subset (\Sigma_1)^\sigma$$

In order to obtain relationships between the behaviour of deterministic and non-deterministic recursive automata we utilize the approach of [St84] via projections. To this end let $pr : (X \times Y)^\omega \to X^\omega$ be the mapping deleting the second coordinate from every letter (x, y) of a sequence $\beta \in (X \times Y)^\omega$.

Theorem 3. Let $\mathcal{A} := [Z, z_0, R, Z_f]$ be a finitely branching (strictly) recursive automaton. Then there is a deterministic (strictly) recursive automaton $\mathcal{A}'$ over $(X \times \{0, 1\})$ such that $\mathbf{T}_\alpha(\mathcal{A}) = pr\ \mathbf{T}_\alpha(\mathcal{A}')$ for $\alpha \in \{e, ae, io\}$.

Proof. Without loss of generality we may assume $\mathcal{A}$ to be deterministic in its first step, that is, for each $x \in X$ there is at most one $z \in Z$ satisfying $(z_0, x, z) \in R$.

Let $h : N \to R$ be a recursive one-to-one enumeration of R, and define $\mathcal{A}' := [S, s_0, f, S_f]$ as follows:

$$S := Z \times (X^* \setminus \{e\}) \times N \cup \{z_0\}, \text{ where } z_0 \notin Z \times (X^* \setminus \{e\}) \times N,$$

$$f(z_0, (x, y)) := (z, x, 0), \text{ where } (z_0, x, z) \in R \ . \text{ [initialize buffer]}$$

$$f((z, xv, n), (x', y)) := \begin{cases} (z', vx', 0) & , \text{ if } y = 1 \text{ and } h(n) = (z, x, z'), \\ & \text{ [apply transition } h(n) \text{ of } \mathcal{A}] \\ (z, xvx', n+1) & , \text{ otherwise } . \text{ [store to buffer]} \end{cases}$$

$$S_f := \{(z, xw, n) : z \in Z_f \wedge x \in X \wedge w \in X^* \wedge \exists m \geq n \exists z'(h(m) = (z, x, z'))\}.$$

This construction is an effective version of the queue-buffer construction (Lemma 4 of [St84]) with the only modification that the queues of [St84] containing the possibly applicable transitions are substituted by a single stack represented by the function h. $\mathcal{A}'$ simulates $\mathcal{A}$ during the steps when the second coordinate of the input letter is 1 and the transition $h(n) = (z, x, z')$ of the stack applies to the current situation [stored state = z, first letter of the buffer = x], otherwise $\mathcal{A}'$ stores the input letters to a buffer and moves to the next entry of the stack $h(n + 1)$.

Since $\mathcal{A}$ is finitely branching, the function h has for every pair (z, x) only finitely many values of the form (z, x, z'). Consequently, if from some moment on, due to the fact that the value of the counter, n, is larger than any value m such that $\exists z'(h(m) = (z, x, z'))$, $\mathcal{A}'$ cannot apply any transition of $\mathcal{A}$, the construction of S_f guarantees that $\mathcal{A}'$ will ultimately leave the set of final states. Therefore, the construction in general yields only a recursively enumerable set of final states S_f even if Z_f is recursive.

The condition $\exists m \geq n \exists z'(h(m) = (z, x, z'))$ in the definition of S_f can be effectively checked if our branching function θ_R is recursive. Thus the theorem holds also for strictly recursive automata.

□

This construction may be modified to work also in the case of countably branching recursive automata. To this end we fix the set $E := \left((X \times \{0,1\})^* \cdot (X \times \{1\}) \right)^{\omega}$ of all ω-words having infinitely many ones in the second coordinate. It is well-known that $E \in \mathbf{T}_{io}(\mathbf{SD})$ but $E \neq W^{\sigma}$ for every $W \subseteq (X \times \{0,1\})^*$ (cf [La69]).

Lemma 4. Let $\mathcal{A} = [Z, z_0, R, Z_f]$ be a countably branching recursive automaton over X. Then there is a deterministic recursive automaton $\mathcal{A}' = [S, s_0, f, S_f]$ over $X \times \{0,1\}$ such that $\mathbf{T}_{\alpha}(\mathcal{A}) = pr(\mathbf{T}_{\alpha}(\mathcal{A}') \cap E)$ for $\alpha \in \{e, ae, io\}$.

Proof. Without loss of generality we may assume that $\mathcal{A}$ has a dead sink $s \in Z \setminus Z_f$, that is, $(z, x, s) \in R$ for all $z \in Z$ and $x \in X$, and $(s, x, z) \notin R$ unless $z = s$.

We construct $\mathcal{A}'$ as follows: Let $h : N \rightarrow R$ be a recursive one-to-one enumeration of R. Define for $z \in Z$ and $x \in X$ the recursive sequences $\mu(z, x) \in Z^{\omega}$ via

$$\mu(z,x)(n) := \begin{cases} z' & \text{, if } h(n) = (z, x, z') \\ s & \text{, otherwise .} \end{cases}$$

Then the rest of the proof works in the same way as the nonrecursive queue-buffer construction (Lemma 5 of [St84]).

□

The importance of Theorem 3 and Lemma 4 consists, similar to the case of arbitrary automata [St84], in the close relations between the deterministic and nondeterministic classes of recursive automata via projections deleting a $\{0,1\}$-valued coordinate and involving only an additional intersection with the ω-language E in the case of countably branching automata.

Thus we turn to the consideration of projections of ω-languages in the above mentioned classes $\Pi_2^{(X)}$, $(\Sigma_1)^{\sigma}$, $\lim \Sigma_1$, $\Sigma_2^{(X)}$, $\Pi_1^{(X)}$.

Lemma 5. Let $F \subseteq (X \times \{0,1\})^{\omega}$. Then $F \in (\Sigma_1)^{\sigma}$ $(\lim \Sigma_1, \Sigma_2^{(X \times \{0,1\})}, \Pi_1^{(X \times \{0,1\})}$ or $\Sigma_1^{(X \times \{0,1\})})$ implies that $pr\, F$ is also in $(\Sigma_1)^{\sigma}$ $(\lim \Sigma_1, \Sigma_2^{(X)}, \Pi_1^{(X)}$ or $\Sigma_1^{(X)}$, respectively).

Proof. The proof makes use of the Tarski-Kuratowski-algorithm (cf. [Ro67]), and of König's infinity lemma which states that a finitely branching tree contains an infinite branch if and only if it is infinite [Kö36].

We derive the proof only for the most complicated case $(\Sigma_1)^{\sigma}$. The other cases are proved in [WS77] and [St86a].

Let $V \subseteq (X \times \{0,1\})^*$ be recursively enumerable. Then $pr\, V^{\sigma} = \{\beta : \exists \xi \exists m \forall n \geq m(\langle \beta, \xi \rangle(0, n] \in V)\}$, where $\langle b_1, b_2 \rangle$ denotes the string in $(X \times \{0,1\})^* \cup (X \times \{0,1\})^{\omega}$ whose first coordinates form the string b_1 and whose second coordinates form b_2, provided $|b_1| = |b_2|$. By König's infinity lemma the condition involved is equivalent to the following one:

$$\exists m \forall n \geq m \exists v \left(|v| = n \wedge \forall j \, (m \leq j \leq n \rightarrow \langle \beta(0, j], v(0, j] \rangle \in V) \right).$$

Let Q be the Σ_1-predicate defined as follows:

$$Q(w,m) \text{ iff } \exists v\,(|v| = |w| \wedge \forall j\,(m \le j \le |w| \rightarrow \langle w(0,j], v(0,j] \rangle \in V))$$

Q has the following properties

1. $prV^\sigma = \{\beta : \exists m \forall n Q(\beta(0,n], m)\}$,
2. $Q(w,m)$ and $(u \sqsubseteq w$ or $k \ge m)$ imply $Q(u,k)$, and
3. $Q(w,m)$ whenever $|w| < m$.
   Using a padding argument yields a Σ_1-predicate Q' such that
4. $Q(w,m)$ implies $Q'(w,m)$,
5. $prV^\sigma = \{\beta : \exists m \forall n Q'(\beta(0,n], m)\}$, and
6. for every m the language $L_m := \{w : \neg Q'(w,m)\}$ is prefix-free.

Then $X^\omega \setminus pr\, V^\sigma = \{\beta : \forall m \exists n \neg Q'(\beta(0,n], m)\}$ and, since the L_m are prefix-free languages, for every $\beta \in X^\omega$ the set $\psi_\beta := \{(m,w) : w \sqsubseteq \beta \wedge \neg Q'(w,m)\}$ defines a partial function assigning to each $m \in N$ the corresponding $w \sqsubseteq \beta$ such that $\neg Q'(w,m)$ (if w exists). By the above properties 2, 4 and 5 we have that the domain $\mathrm{dom}\,\psi_\beta$ is either finite or $\mathrm{dom}\,\psi_\beta = N$ according to whether $\beta \in X^\omega \setminus (prV^\sigma)$ or not.

Using a recursive Cantor pairing function $c : N \times N \to N$ with $c(m,n) \ge n$, we encode a pair (w,m) as a finite set $w \cdot X^{c(m,|w|)-|w|}$. Thus $\mathrm{dom}\,\psi_\beta = N$ iff $\beta \in X^\omega$ has infinitely many prefixes in the language $W := \{w \cdot v : w,v \in X^* \wedge \neg Q'(m,w) \wedge |w \cdot v| = c(m,|w|)\}$. Then it is easily verified that $X^* \setminus W$ is a recursively enumerable language such that $pr\, V^\sigma = (X^* \setminus W)^\sigma$.

$\square$

Thus we have shown that, similar to the case of finite automata (cf. [SW74] or [Wa79]) and arbitrary automata (cf. [Ar83] or [St84]), for finitely branching e- or ae-accepting (strictly) recursive automata nondeterminism can be removed.

Now we turn to the investigation of the behaviour of countably branching or io-accepting automata. To this end we introduce the first Σ-class of the analytical hierarchy, $\Sigma_1^{1(X)}$ of ω-languages (cf. [WS77]):

$$F \in \Sigma_1^{1(X)} \text{ iff } F = \{\beta : \exists \xi \in \{0,1\}^\omega \forall n \exists m(P(n, \beta(0,m], \xi(0,m]))\},$$

for some recursive predicate P, that is, $\Sigma_1^{1(X)} = \{pr\, F : F \in \Pi_2^{(X \times \{0,1\})}\}$. The following facts are known (cf. [Ro67]): $\Sigma_n^{(X)} \cup \Pi_n^{(X)} \subset \Sigma_1^{1(X)}$, and if $F \in \Sigma_1^{1(X \times Y)}$ then $pr\, F \in \Sigma_1^{1(X)}$.

Since the ω-language E is in $\Pi_2^{(X \times \{0,1\})} \subseteq \Sigma_1^{1(X \times \{0,1\})}$, and $\Sigma_1^{1(X \times \{0,1\})}$ is closed under intersection, Lemmas 2 and 4 yield that all classes $\mathbf{T}_e(\mathbf{CN})$, $\mathbf{T}_{ae}(\mathbf{CN})$, $\mathbf{T}_{io}(\mathbf{SN})$, $\mathbf{T}_{io}(\mathbf{N})$, and $\mathbf{T}_{io}(\mathbf{CN})$ are contained in $\Sigma_1^{1(X)}$.

On the other hand, from Lemma 2 and Theorem 3 we obtain $\Sigma_1^{1(X)} \subseteq \mathbf{T}_{io}(\mathbf{SN})$. Consequently, $\mathbf{T}_{io}(\mathbf{SN}) = \mathbf{T}_{io}(\mathbf{N}) = \mathbf{T}_{io}(\mathbf{CN}) = \Sigma_1^{1(X)}$ what proves that in the case of io-accepting automata nondeterminism strictly increases power.

In order to show the remaining identity $\mathbf{T}_e(\mathbf{CN}) = \mathbf{T}_{ae}(\mathbf{CN}) = \Sigma_1^{1(X)}$ it suffices to verify that $\Pi_2^{(X)} \subseteq \mathbf{T}_e(\mathbf{CN}) \cap \mathbf{T}_{ae}(\mathbf{CN})$.

To this end we use the guess-and-check-method given in Sect. 5 of [St84] which yields in the case of a recursive language V a recursive automaton $\mathcal{A}_V$.

Lemma 6. *Let $V \subseteq X^*$ be recursive. Then there is a (countably branching) recursive automaton $\mathcal{A}_V$ such that $\mathbf{T}_e(\mathcal{A}_V) = \mathbf{T}_{ae}(\mathcal{A}_V) = V^\delta$.*

We summarize our results on the classes of ω-languages accepted by recursive automata in the following figure.

	SD	SN	D	N	CN
e	$\Pi_1^{(X)}$	$\Pi_1^{(X)}$	$\lim \Sigma_1$	$\lim \Sigma_1$	$\Sigma_1^{1(X)}$
ae	$\Sigma_1^{(X)}$	$\Sigma_1^{(X)}$	$(\Sigma_1)^\sigma$	$(\Sigma_1)^\sigma$	$\Sigma_1^{1(X)}$
io	$\Pi_2^{(X)}$	$\Sigma_1^{1(X)}$	$\Pi_2^{(X)}$	$\Sigma_1^{1(X)}$	$\Sigma_1^{1(X)}$

3 Verification

Utilizing the results of the previous section we can now reformulate the question about the complexity of the verification problem "$\mathbf{T}(\mathcal{P}) \subseteq \mathbf{T}(\mathcal{S})$?" for several classes of automata in terms of the arithmetical hierarchy.

In terms of predicate logic "$F \subseteq F'$?" is equivalent to "$\forall \xi (\xi \in F \rightarrow \xi \in F')$?", thus involves a quantifier ranging over an infinite object. We can simplify our verification problem only in case when it is possible to eliminate this quantifier. Above in the proof of Lemma 5 we have seen that König's infinity lemma may serve for those purposes provided the infinite object is a sequence over a finite alphabet.

The results of the previous section do not depend on the size of the alphabet X but rather on the branching behaviour of the automata, on the other hand as just pointed out, now the finiteness of the alphabet plays a crucial role. As it seems not to be possible to generally bound the size of the alphabet of the execution sequences of a program or a specification, we derive a condition ensuring that the behaviours $\mathbf{T}(\mathcal{P})$ and $\mathbf{T}(\mathcal{S})$ can be recursively embedded into $\{0, 1\}^\omega$.

Lemma 7. *Let $W \subseteq X^*$ be recursively enumerable and let there be a recursive function $f : X^* \to N$ such that $f(w) \geq \text{card}\{x : x \in X \wedge w \cdot x \in W\}$ for all $w \in W$. Then there is a recursive one-to-one embedding $\Phi : \lim W \to \{0, 1\}^\omega$.*

Remark: We call here a mapping $\Phi : F \to \{0, 1\}^\omega$ where $F \subseteq X^\omega$ a recursive embedding if there is a partial recursive function $\phi : X^* \to \{0, 1\}^*$ monotone with respect to the initial word relation "$\sqsubseteq$" such that $\{\Phi(\xi)\} = \phi(A(\xi))^\delta$ (cf. [St87]).[4]

---

[4] Here $\{\Phi(\xi)\} = \phi(A(\xi))^\delta = \emptyset$ means that $\Phi(\xi)$ is not defined.

The above hypothesis on a recursive bounding of the *"branching"* of a language is satisfied, in particular, if $W = A(\mathbf{T}([Z, z_0, R, Z']))$ for a recursive automaton having a recursive bound $h : Z \to N$ such that $h(z) \geq \sum_{x \in X} \theta_R(z, x)$ for every $z \in Z$.

If both the program and the specification automata $\mathcal{P}$ and $\mathcal{S}$ satisfy this property then one can $\mathbf{T}(\mathcal{P})$ and $\mathbf{T}(\mathcal{S})$ simultaneously embed into $\{0, 1\}^\omega$, that is, one can find an one-to-one embedding $\Phi : \lim W \to \{0, 1\}^\omega$ such that $\lim W \supseteq \mathbf{T}(\mathcal{P}) \cup \mathbf{T}(\mathcal{S})$, and the verification problem "$\mathbf{T}(\mathcal{P}) \subseteq \mathbf{T}(\mathcal{S})$?" in X^ω reduces to the following one in $\{0, 1\}^\omega$: "$\Phi(\lim W) \subseteq \Phi(\mathbf{T}(\mathcal{S}) \cup (\lim W \setminus \mathbf{T}(\mathcal{P}))$?"

To state our verification problems precisely we assume a Gödel numbering of all recursively enumerable languages over an alphabet X, $(W_i)_{i \in N}$. This numbering yields via $(\lim(X^* \setminus W_i))_{i \in N}$, $(W_i \cdot X^\omega)_{i \in N}$, $(\lim W_i)_{i \in N}$, $((X^* \setminus W_i)^\sigma)_{i \in N}$, $(W_i^\delta)_{i \in N}$, and $(W_i^\sigma)_{i \in N}$ Gödel numberings of the classes $\Pi_1^{(X)}$, $\Sigma_1^{(X)}$, $\lim \Sigma_1$, $\Sigma_2^{(X)}$, $\Pi_2^{(X)}$, or $(\Sigma_1)^\sigma$ respectively. The verification problem for classes $(K_i)_{i \in N}$ and $(M_i)_{i \in N}$ can be formulated now as $VER((K_i)_{i \in N}, (M_j)_{j \in N}) = \{(i, j) : K_i \subseteq M_j\}$.

Klarlund [Kl90] has shown that for an infinite alphabet X:

1. $VER(\Sigma_1^{(X)}, \Pi_1^{(X)})$ is Π_1-complete, and
2. $VER(\Pi_1^{(X)}, \Sigma_1^{(X)})$, $VER(\Sigma_1^{(X)}, \Sigma_1^{(X)})$, $VER(\Pi_1^{(X)}, \Pi_1^{(X)})$ are Π_1^1-complete.

Since in this paper we are mainly interested in verification problems for which the quantification over an infinite object can be removed, this result bounds our range of search, in particular we confine the following considerations to ω-languages over a finite alphabet.

Theorem 8. *Let X be a finite alphabet. Then*
$VER(\Sigma_1^{(X)}, \Pi_1^{(X)})$ *is Π_1-complete,*
$VER(\Pi_1^{(X)}, \Sigma_1^{(X)})$ *is Σ_1-complete,*
$VER(\Pi_1^{(X)}, \Pi_1^{(X)})$ *and $VER(\Sigma_2^{(X)}, \Pi_2^{(X)})$ are Π_2-complete,*
$VER(\lim \Sigma_1, \Sigma_1^{(X)})$ *is Σ_2-complete,*
$VER(\lim \Sigma_1, \Pi_1^{(X)})$ *and $VER((\Sigma_1)^\sigma, \Pi_2^{(X)})$ are Π_3-complete, and*
$VER(\Pi_2^{(X)}, \Pi_1^{(X)})$ *and $VER(\Pi_2^{(X)}, \Sigma_1^{(X)})$ are Π_1^1-complete,*
and the complexity of the remaining verification problems can be determined from the given ones, the inclusion relations between the classes of the arithmetical hierarchy depicted after Lemma 2, and the complementation property

$$VER((K_i)_{i \in N}, (M_j)_{j \in N}) = VER((X^\omega \setminus M_j)_{j \in N}, (X^\omega \setminus K_i)_{i \in N}) \; .$$

Proof. First we show as an example that $VER((\Sigma_1)^\sigma, \Pi_2^{(X)}) \in \Pi_3$, for the other cases the proofs of the containment in the respective classes are similar.

We have

$$W_i^\sigma \subseteq W_j^\delta \Leftrightarrow X^\omega = (X^* \setminus W_i)^\delta \cup W_j^\delta = ((X^* \setminus W_i) \cup W_j)^\delta \; ,$$

which in turn can be transformed, using König's lemma to

$$\forall w \in X^* \; \exists n \in N \; \forall v \in X^n \; \exists k \leq n \; (w \cdot (v(0, k]) \in ((X^* \setminus W_i) \cup W_j)) \; .$$

Now, the assertion follows from $((X^* \backslash W_i) \cup W_j) \in \Sigma_2$ and because the quantifiers $\forall v$ and $\exists k$ are bounded.

To solve the completeness questions we derive several instances of the verification problems which are complete in the respective class.

$\{i : W_i^\delta = \emptyset\}$ is Π_1^1-complete,

$\{i : W_i^\sigma = \emptyset\}$ and $\{i : \lim W_i \subseteq \{0^\omega\}\}$ are Π_3-complete,

$\{i : W_i^\delta = X^\omega\}$ and $\{i : \lim(X^* \backslash W_i) \subseteq \{0^\omega\}\}$ are Π_2-complete,

$\{i : \lim W_i = \emptyset\}$ is Σ_2-complete,

$\{i : W_i \cdot X^\omega = \emptyset\} = \{i : W_i = \emptyset\}$ is Π_1-complete, and

$\{i : \lim(X^* \backslash W_i) = \emptyset\}$ is Σ_1-complete.

□

We conclude with a remark on Rabin's [Ra69] and Streett's [Sr82] acceptance conditions:

A Rabin or Streett accepting condition consists of a pair (U, V) of subsets $U, V \subseteq N \times Z$. A sequence $\xi \in X^\omega$ is *Rabin*-accepted (*Streett*-accepted) if and only if $\xi \in \mathbf{T}_{ae}(A_i) \cap \mathbf{T}_{io}(A'_i)$ for some $i \in N$ ($\xi \in \mathbf{T}_{ae}(A_i) \cup \mathbf{T}_{io}(A'_i)$ for all $i \in N$, respectively) where A_i is the automaton $[Z, z_0, R, Z_f]$ with $Z_f = \{z : (i, z) \in U\}$, A'_i is the automaton $[Z, z_0, R, Z'_f]$ with $Z'_f = \{z : (i, z) \in V\}$. Thus for recursive automata A (here U and V are also assumed to be recursive) the class of ω-languages Rabin-accepted by deterministic recursive automata is easily identified as $\Sigma_3^{(X)}$. Analogously, the class of ω-languages Streett-accepted by deterministic recursive automata is $\Pi_3^{(X)}$. Thus a verification problem involving the whole class of deterministically Rabin- or Street-definable ω-languages is necessarily Π_1^1-complete.

References

[Ar83]   Arnold, A.: Topological characterizations of infinite behaviours of transition systems. In: Automata, Languages and Programming (ed. J. Diaz), Lect. Notes Comput. Sci. **154**, Springer-Verlag, Berlin 1983, 28–38

[Bü62]   Büchi, J.R.: On a decision method in restricted second order arithmetic. In: "Logic, Method. and Philos. of Sci.", Proc. 1960 Intern. Congr." (eds. E. Nagel et al.), Stanford Univ. Press, 1962, 1–11

[CG78]   Cohen, R.S., Gold, A.Y.: ω-computations on Turing machines. Theoret. Comput. Sci. **6** (1978) 1–23

[DY92]   Darondeau, Ph., Yoccoz, S.: Proof systems for infinite behaviours. Inform. Comput. **99** (1992) 178–191

[Kl90]   Klarlund, N.: Progress measures and finite arguments for infinite computations. PhD thesis, TR-1153, Cornell Univ. 1990

[KK91]   Klarlund, N., Kozen, D.: Rabin measures and their applications to fairness and automata theory. In: Proc. 6th IEEE Symp. on Logic in Comput. Sci., 1991

[Kö36]   König, D.: Theorie der endlichen und unendlichen Graphen. Akadem. Verlagsgesellsch., Leipzig, 1936

[La69]   Landweber, L.H.: Decision problems for ω-automata. Math. Syst. Theory **3** (1969) 4, 376–384

[Ra69]   Rabin, M.O.: Decidability of second-order theories and automata on infinite trees. Trans. Amer. Math. Soc. **141** (1969), 1–35

[Ro67]   Rogers, Jr., H.: Theory of Recursive Functions and Effective Computability. Mac-Graw-Hill, New York, 1967

[Si89]   Sistla, A.P.: On verifying that a concurrent program satisfies a nondeterministic specification. Inform. Process. Lett. **32** (1989) 17–24

[St84]   Staiger, L.: Projection lemmas for ω-languages. Theoret. Comput. Sci. **32** (1984) 3, 331–337

[St86a] Staiger, L.: Hierarchies of recursive ω-languages. J. Inform. Process. Cybernetics EIK **22** (1986) 5/6, 219–241

[St86b] Staiger, L.: ω-computations on Turing machines and the accepted languages. In: Theory of Algorithms (eds. L. Lovász and E. Szemerédi), Coll. Math. Soc. János Bolyai No. **44**, North Holland, Amsterdam 1986, 393–403

[St87]   Staiger, L.: Sequential mappings of ω-languages. RAIRO Informatique thèor. et Appl. **21** (1987) 2, 147–173

[SW74]   Staiger, L., Wagner, K.: Automatentheoretische und automatenfreie Charakterisierungen topologischer Klassen regulärer Folgenmengen. Elektron. Inf.-verarbeitung u. Kybernetik EIK **10** (1974) 379–392

[Sr82]   Streett, R.S.: Propositional dynamic logic of looping and converse. Inform. Control **54** (1982) 121–141

[Th90]   Thomas, W.: Automata on infinite objects. In: Handbook of Theoretical Computer Science, Vol. B, (ed. J.v.Leeuwen), North-Holland, Amsterdam 1990, 133–191

[Va87]   Vardi, M.Y.: Automatic verification of concurrent programs: The automata-theoretic framework. In: Proc. 2nd IEEE Symp. on Logic in Comput. Sci., Ithaca, 1987, 167–176

[VW86]   M.Y. Vardi, M.Y., Wolper, P.: An automata theoretic approach to automatic program verification. In: Proc. 1st IEEE Symp. on Logic in Comput. Sci., Boston, 1986, 332–344

[Wa79]   Wagner, K.: On ω-regular sets. Inform. Control **43** (1979) 123–177

[WS77]   Wagner, K., Staiger, L.: Recursive ω-languages. In: Proc. Fundamentals of Computation Theory '77 (ed. M. Karpinski), Lect. Notes Comput. Sci. **56**, Springer-Verlag, Berlin 1977, 532–537 (see also:
Staiger, L., Wagner, K.: Rekursive Folgenmengen I. Zeitschr. Math. Logik Grundlag. Math. **24** (1978) 6, 523–538)

A Complexity Theoretic Approach
to Incremental Computation*

S. Sairam, Jeffrey Scott Vitter, and Roberto Tamassia

Department of Computer Science, Brown University, Providence, R. I. 02912, USA
{ss, jsv, rt}@cs.brown.edu

Abstract. We present a new complexity theoretic approach to incremental computation. We define complexity classes that capture the intuitive notion of incremental efficiency and study their relation to existing complexity classes. We give problems that are complete for P, NLOGSPACE, and LOGSPACE under incremental reductions. We introduce a restricted notion of completeness called NRP-completeness and show that problems which are NRP-complete for P are also incr-POLYLOGTIME-complete for P.

We also look at the incremental space-complexity of circuit value and network stability problems restricted to comparator gates. We show that the dynamic version of the comparator circuit value problem is in LOGSPACE while the dynamic version of the network stability problem can be solved in LOGSPACE given an NLOGSPACE oracle. This shows that problems like the Lex-First Maximal Matching problem and the Man-Optimal Stable Marriage problem can be quickly updated in parallel even though there are no known NC algorithms to solve them from scratch.

1 Introduction

What is the "best" algorithm for a given problem? There is obviously more than one answer, depending on what we mean by "best." If we consider worst-case time behavior, traditionally an algorithm is considered the best possible if it meets the information theoretic lower bound. There is another way of looking at the situation, wherein we are not worried about the time taken to evaluate every instance from scratch. We ask that once the algorithm has preprocessed an instance of the problem, it should handle any changes to the instance (up to a certain limit) very fast.

In Section 2 we formalize the notions of incremental efficiency in terms of the classes incr-POLYLOGTIME, the class of problems whose dynamic versions are solvable in poly-logarithmic time, and incr-POLYLOGSPACE, the class whose dynamic versions can be solved with poly-logarithmic work space. We also give a restricted notion of nondeterministic incremental computation. We then introduce the concept of an *incremental reduction* between problems, and show how to relate problems under such a reduction.

* Research supported in part by a National Science Foundation Presidential Young Investigator Award CCR–9047466 with matching funds from IBM, by NSF research grant CCR–9007851, by Army Research Office grant DAAL03–91–G–0035, and by the Office of Naval Research and the Defense Advanced Research Projects Agency under contract N00014–91–J–4052 and ARPA order 8225.

In Section 3 we show that all commonly known P-complete problems listed in [11] and [4] are *incr*-POLYLOGTIME-complete for the class P. We further prove that all *non-redundant* P-complete problems are *incr*-POLYLOGTIME-complete for P. We also give incrementally complete problems for NLOGSPACE, LOGSPACE, and NC¹. In Section 4 we demonstrate that under certain restrictions problems which have efficient dynamic solutions also have efficient parallel solutions.

In Section 5 we look at *incr*-LOGSPACE; the class of problems that can be "updated" using only logarithmic work space. We show that the circuit value problem for comparator gates, discussed in Mayr and Subramanian [8] is in *incr*-LOGSPACE while the network stability problem is in relativized *incr*-LOGSPACE with respect to an NLOGSPACE oracle. Since these problems have no known NC solutions, we get a new class of problems which seem to be somewhat more sequential in nature than the problems in NC but nonetheless exhibit a degree of parallelism absent in P-complete problems. In Section 6 we present the conclusions and some open problems.

2 Preliminaries

Informally, we want a decision problem π to belong to the class *incr*-TIME[$f(n)$] if we can "react" to the changes in a given instance of the problem in time proportional to $f(n)$. We formalize this notion as follows:

Definition 1. A decision problem π belongs to the class *incr*-TIME[$f(n)$] if there are RAM programs P_1 and P_2 such that for all $n \in \mathbb{N}$ we have

1. Given any initial instance I_0 of π ($|I_0| \le n$), P_1 efficiently precomputes some auxiliary data structure D_{I_0} associated with instance I_0.
2. Given the current input instance I, the incremental change Δ to I (where Δ changes I to another instance I' of π, for which $|I'| \le n$) and the current data structure D_I in the random access memory, P_2 determines $\pi(I')$, and modifies D_I into the new data structure $D_{I'}$ in $O(|\Delta|f(n))$ time.

Our notion of "efficient" in condition 1 is somewhat flexible; we could require that the precomputation be doable in polynomial time or logarithmic space, for example.

We denote by *incr*-POLYLOGTIME the class $\bigcup_{k \ge 0}$ *incr*-TIME[$\log^k n$]. It is easy to see that such a definition captures the intuitive notion of incremental computation; for example the problem of maintaining an ordered set through a set of updates and queries is in *incr*-TIME[$\log n$].

We can define the class *incr*-SPACE[$f(n)$] as above, except that P_2 is required instead to use $O(|\Delta|f(n))$ space. We use *incr*-LOGSPACE to denote *incr*-SPACE[$\log n$] and define *incr*-POLYLOGSPACE to be the class $\bigcup_{k \ge 0}$ *incr*-SPACE[$\log^k n$].

To extend these notions to nondeterminism seems to be hard since we can then have multiple copies of the data structure. We side step that issue by allowing nondeterminism only in the form of decision oracles. We say that a problem π is in *rincr*-LOGSPACE(NLOGSPACE) (read as π is in *incr*-LOGSPACE relative to the class NLOGSPACE) if the updating procedure P_2 works in $O(|\Delta|\log(n))$ work-space and is allowed to make calls to a nondeterministic decision procedure S that uses $O(|\Delta|\log(n))$ work-space.

To compare the "hardness" of solving two problems in this incremental sense, we need the notion of incremental reduction. The procedure does the reduction has to be incrementally map instances of the first problem into those of the second problem. We formalize this as follows:

Definition 2. A decision problem π_1 is *incrementally reducible* to another decision problem π_2 in time and size bounds $[f(n), g(n)]$, denoted $\pi_1 \leq_{incr[f(n), g(n)]} \pi_2$, if the following conditions are satisfied:

1. There is a mapping $T : \pi_1 \rightarrow \pi_2$ between instances of π_1 and π_2 such that I is a positive instance of π_1 if and only if $T(I)$ is a positive instance of π_2. Furthermore, if I and I' are two instances such that Δ is the incremental change required to transform I to I', then the size of the incremental change $\tilde{\Delta}$ required to transform the corresponding instance $T(I)$ to $T(I')$ is no more than $|\Delta| g(n)$.

2. The transformation T is incremental in the sense of definition 1 except for the following modification: Given the incremental change Δ to the current instance I and the current data structure D_I, P_2 computes the incremental change $\tilde{\Delta}$ to the mapping $T(I)$, and modifies D_I into the new data structure $D_{I'}$ in $O(|\Delta| f(n))$ time.

Note that $g(n) = O(f(n))$. We say that $\pi_1 \leq_{incr[f(n)]} \pi_2$ if $\pi_1 \leq_{incr[f(n), f(n)]} \pi_2$.

Theorem 3. *If π_1 is incrementally reducible to π_2 in time and size bounds $[f(n), g(n)]$, and if π_2 is in incr-TIME$[h(n)]$, then π_1 is in incr-TIME$[f(n) + h(n)g(n)]$.* □

3 Incrementally-Complete Problems

We now turn to the notion of incremental completeness. The idea is to find a problem which is as hard to solve incrementally as any other problem in a given class. In this section we use incremental reductions to get natural problems incrementally complete for P, NLOGSPACE, LOGSPACE, and NC^1.

Definition 4. A problem π is said to be *incr$[f(n), g(n)]$-complete* for a class C if π is in the class C and every other problem $\pi_1 \in C$ is incrementally reducible to π in time and size bounds $[f(n), g(n)]$.

We say that π is *incr$[f(n)]$-complete* for a class C if it is *incr$[f(n), f(n)]$-complete* for a class C. We call a problem π *incr-POLYLOGTIME-complete* for a class C if π is *incr$[f(n)]$-complete* for C, where $f(n)$ is $O(\log^k n)$ for some k. We define *incr-CONSTANTTIME-completeness* in an analogous fashion.

The obvious question is: How are the incremental time and space complexity classes related to the well known sequential complexity classes? Our first intriguing result is as follows:

Theorem 5. *All the P-complete problems in [11] and [4] are incr-POLYLOGTIME-complete for the class P.*

Proof Sketch: We present the proof for the case of circuit value problem. Given any problem π in P and an initial instance I^0 with $|I^0| \leq n$, we use the standard LOGSPACE reduction [7] to create a circuit that emulates a P-time turing machine M used to solve π. The input I_0 to M is also the input to the circuit. It is easy to see that a one-bit change to the current instance of π corresponds to a one-bit change to the input of the circuit, and thus the Circuit-Value problem is *incr*-POLYLOGTIME-complete for P.

We can provide similar proofs for the other problems listed in [11] and [4]. The reductions needed to show this are sometimes different from those given in the literature. □

Corollary 6. *If the P-complete problems in [11] and [4], like circuit value problem, are in incr-POLYLOGTIME then all of P is in incr-POLYLOGTIME. Similarly if there are NC algorithms to dynamically update these problems then we automatically get NC algorithms to dynamically update all of P.*

This suggests that it is highly unlikely that problems like the circuit value problem can be dynamized.

In related work Kasif and Delcher [3] define the incremental version of a function f (Inc-f) as the function that given inputs of the form $(X, f(X), X')$, computes $f(X')$. The instances X and X' are allowed to differ in at most $\log|X|$ bits. A function f is Inc-P-complete iff for every function g in P, Inc-g is LOGSPACE-reducible to Inc-f. They show that the "all-output monotone circuit value problem" is Inc-P-complete. The drawback in this approach is that it disallows the use of dynamic data structures.

Interesting notions of completeness are sketched by Reif [13]. He shows that some problems are unlikely to have efficient incremental solutions, but he does not develop a comprehensive theory or consider the necessary details of preprocessing. Similar notions of completeness are considered by Miltersen [10], but he ignores classes other than P and even for that he does not establish any formal relationship between P-completes and *incr*-POLYLOGTIME-completeness. Some interesting techniques are explored in [2] to derive lower bounds for incremental algorithms. Their main idea is to construct an algorithm for the batch version of the problem by using an incremental algorithm and applying repeated changes to some easy initial instance. The drawbacks of this approach are that it limits the amount of preprocessing available and is problem specific.

Theorem 5 would seem to suggest that any problem that is P-complete is also *incr*-POLYLOGTIME-complete for P. Unfortunately that is not the case. As the following Theorem demonstrates, there are P-complete problems that can be solved effectively incrementally.

Theorem 7. *There are P-complete problems that are in incr-POLYLOGTIME.*

Proof Sketch: Let L be some P-complete language over the alphabet $\sum = \{0,1\}$ such that it takes linear sequential time to determine whether a given word w is in L or not. Let us consider the language $L' = \{w^{|w|} | w \in L\}$. Obviously L' is also P-complete. Consider an initial n^n-bit instance $I^0 = w_0^{|w_0|}$ (instances which are not of the form n^n for some $n \in N$ can be handled without too much trouble). Initially we spend polynomial time to see if I^0 is in L'. This can be done by using a linear time routine S_L to check the membership of w in L. Assume that at any given time the current instance I is a concatenation of n-bit strings a_1 through a_n. Our dynamic algorithm works as follows:

As long as less than $n/2$ of the a_i's are equal (that is, less than $n/2$ of the strings are the copy of the same string w) we answer "no" for every instance. If at some point more than $n/2$ of the a_i's are all equal to the same w, we start a background process which executes the subroutine S_L on the string w. As long as more than half the a_i's are equal to w we spend a constant amount of time on the background computation for every update to the current instance. Therefore, by the time I becomes equal to $w^{|w|}$ we would have run S_L for a linear number of steps and thus will know whether w is in L or not. We can therefore answer the membership query of I in L' at that point. □

A more careful look shows us that the anomalous behavior of language L' is due to the large Hamming distance between any two "yes" instances. We achieved this sparseness by introducing many redundant copies of a string in L to create a string in L'. We now look at a much stricter definition of P-completeness due to Skyum and Valiant [14].

Definition 8. A decision problem π_1 is *projection reducible* to another decision problem π_2 ($\pi_1 \leq_{proj} \pi_2$) if there is a function $p(n)$ bounded above by a polynomial in n, and a family of polynomial time computable mappings $\sigma = \{\sigma_n\}_{n \geq 1}$ where

$$\sigma_n : \{y_1, \ldots, y_{p(n)}\} \to \{x_1, \overline{x_1}, \ldots, x_n, \overline{x_n}, 0, 1\},$$

and any n-bit instance I is a positive instance of π_1 if and only if the corresponding $p(n)$-bit instance I' (derived using the mapping σ_n) is a positive instance of π_2. To derive I' we give x_i the same value as the ith bit of I and use $\sigma_n(y_i)$ as the ith bit of I'. We say that σ is bounded above by p and π_1 is σ-reducible to π_2.

A problem π is said to be $<_{proj}$-*complete* for a class C if π is in C and there is a function $p(n)$ bounded above by a polynomial in n, such that every problem $\pi_1 \in C$ is σ-reducible to π by a projection $\sigma = \{\sigma_n\}_{n \geq 1}$ bounded above by p.

Problems like the circuit value problem are $\leq_{proj}$-complete for P. Even under this restricted setting it is possible to create problems which are $\leq_{proj}$-complete for Pbut are in *incr*-POLYLOGTIME. To remedy that we define the following notion of *non-redundancy*:

Definition 9. Let π_1 be a decision problem and π be another problem such that $\pi_1 \leq_{proj} \pi$. We say that π is *non-redundant with respect to* π_1 if there exists a polynomial time computable family $\sigma = \{\sigma_n\}_{n \geq 1}$ of mappings and a number $k \in N$ such that π_1 is σ-reducible to π (where σ_n is a mapping from the set $\{y_1, \ldots, y_{p(n)}\}$ to the set $\{x_1, \overline{x_1}, \ldots, x_n, \overline{x_n}, 0, 1\}$), and for all symbols x_i, $|\sigma_n^{-1}\{x_i, \overline{x_i}\}| = O(\log^k n)$.

We now define the notion of non-redundancy with respect to a class C.

Definition 10. Let π be a problem which is $\leq_{proj}$-complete for C. We say that π *is non-redundant with respect to* C if it is non-redundant with respect to every problem in C. We then call π a *non-redundant projection complete problem* (or a NRP-complete problem) for the class C.

Lemma 11. *Let* C *be a class of decision problems and let* π_1 *be a NRP-complete problem for* C. *If* π *is another decision problem in* C *such that* $\pi_1 \leq_{proj} \pi$ *and* π *is non-redundant with respect to* π_1 *then* π *is NRP-complete for* C

Proof: The proof follows from the definitions in a straightforward manner. □

The P-complete problems listed in [11] and [4] are all NRP-complete for P. The following theorem shows that this large class of P-complete problems are difficult to make efficient incrementally.

Theorem 12. *Let* C *be a class of decision problems and* π *be a NRP-complete problem for* C, *then* π *is incr-POLYLOGTIME-complete for* C.

Proof Sketch: The proof follows from noting the fact that given any problem $\pi_1 \in$ C, there is projection mapping from π to π_1 such that a one bit change in an input instance of π_1 causes at most polylog number of bits to change in the corresponding instance of π. □

We now look at the classes NLOGSPACE, LOGSPACE and NC^1.

Theorem 13. *The following variant of transitive closure is incr-CONSTANTTIME -complete for* NLOGSPACE:

   Input: A directed graph $G = (V, E)$ *such that each* $e \in E$ *is colored with* 0 *or* 1; *a pair of vertices* v_1 *and* v_2; *a partitioning of* V *into sets* $V_1, V_2, ..., V_k$; *and a color vector* C *of length* k.
   Output: Is there is a path p *from* v_1 *to* v_2 *such that all edges in* p *emanating from vertices in* V_i *have color* $C[i]$?

Proof: The reduction from any problem in NLOGSPACE to this variant is straightforward. The trick that makes the reduction go in constant time and constant storage is the use of the sets $V_1, V_2, ..., V_k$ and the color vector. We group all intermediate states that read the input bit i into the class V_i; $C[i]$ is assigned the same value as input bit i. Now a change in some input bit i changes $C[i]$. □

A restriction of this problem is *incr*-CONSTANTTIME-complete for LOGSPACE while a similar variant of bounded width polynomial size branching programs [1] gives us an *incr*-CONSTANTTIME-complete problem for non-uniform NC^1.

Surprisingly however there are problems which are NC^1-complete for LOGSPACE, but are nevertheless in *incr*-POLYLOGTIME, as demonstrated by the following theorem:

Theorem 14. *The problem of Undirected Forest accessibility is in incr-TIME[$\log n$], under additions, deletions, linking and cutting of trees.*

Proof Sketch: The dynamic maintenance is done by using balanced trees such as red-black trees to maintain ordered sets with insert, delete, split, and join [5]. It is easy to show that connectivity information in a forest of trees can be maintained in a fully-dynamic environment by maintaining their Euler tours in red-black trees. □

The interesting thing to note here is that even though this problem is not known to be in NC^1 it is in *incr*-TIME[$\log n$]. At the same time, all of NC^1 is not known to be in *incr*-TIME[$\log n$].

4 Incremental Computation in Restricted Realms

The class of *Z-stratified trees* was introduced by Overmars [12] in an effort to form a general theory of balancing in search trees. It subsumes a large portion of the search structures used to design dynamic algorithms. In this section we show that under reasonable assumptions problems which have incremental solutions based on these structures also have parallel solutions.

Theorem 15. *Let π be a problem in incr-TIME[$\log^k n$], for some $k \geq 1$. Then π is in NC^{k+2}, if the following constraints hold:*

1. *The data structure used is an augmented Z-stratified search tree. Each internal node contains the result of some function f computable in $O(\log^k n)$ time using the values stored at its children. The f-values are used for searching the tree and for determining the order between the elements in the search tree. Furthermore, there is a special initial instance I_0 whose corresponding tree can be built in LOGSPACE.*

2. *Any ℓ-bit change to the current input I $(1 \leq \ell \leq n)$ involves modifying the tree by inserting or removing some number of elements. The elements to be inserted or deleted are functions of the current input, the current data structure, and the change, and can be computed in LOGSPACE. After all the insertions and deletions some sort of search is conducted in the tree in time $O(\log^k n)$ to get the answer to the updated instance.*

Proof Sketch: Given instance I we proceed as follows: First we create the tree corresponding to I_0 in LOGSPACE. We then calculate all the additions and deletions needed to get the tree for I. Using this we determine the final set of elements and the order in which they are present in the final tree. Since the function f is computable in $O(\log^k n)$ time the elements corresponding to I can be sorted in $EREW^{k+1}$, and hence in NC^{k+2} (see [6]). Using this information we build the tree corresponding to I in parallel in a bottom-to-top sweep. This can be done in NC^{k+2} because Z-Stratified trees have logarithmic depth, and the value of f at any node depends only on the contents of its children. All we have to do now is to let one processor walk down the tree and get the answer to I in time $O(\log^k n)$. $\qquad\qquad\square$

This deceptively simple theorem demonstrates why most known problems with efficient dynamic solutions have optimal parallel solutions. For example we can use this theorem to parallelize dynamic algorithms using degree-balanced trees, height-balanced trees, path-balanced trees etc. We can derive similar results for other classes of trees as well.

One important technique in getting dynamic solutions for problems is the divide and conquer approach. To exploit this technique Mehlhorn and Overmars [9] consider an important class of problems called order-decomposable problems.

Definition 16. A set problem π is called $C(n)$-*order-decomposable* if and only if there exists an ordering ORD and a function $\square$ such that for each set of $n \geq 1$ points $V = \{p_1, p_2, \ldots, p_n\}$, ordered according to ORD, and for each $1 \leq i \leq n$, we have

$$\pi(\{p_1, p_2, \ldots, p_n\}) = \square(\pi(\{p_1, p_2, \ldots, p_i\}), \pi(\{p_{i+1}, p_{i+2}, \ldots, p_n\})),$$

where □ takes at most $C(n)$ time to compute when V contains n points. In other words a problem is order decomposable if after arranging it according to a specific ordering, the problem can be split at any point to give two smaller subproblems whose solutions can be glued together "efficiently" to get the solution for the original problem.

Mehlhorn and Overmars essentially prove that if π is an $O(\log^k n)$-order-decomposable set problem and it takes less than $O(\log^k n)$ time to compare two elements to determine their ordering with respect to ORD, then $\pi \in incr$-TIME$[\log^{k+1} n]$. We make the following rather simple extension.

Theorem 17. *If π is an $O(\log^k n)$-order-decomposable set problem and the ordering of two elements with respect to ORD takes time $O(\log^k n)$, then $\pi \in incr$-TIME $[\log^{k+1} n]$ and $\pi \in NC^{k+2}$.*

Proof Sketch: To solve the problem we first sort the input according to the ordering function ORD. To solve it in parallel we use a simple divide-and-conquer approach to split the problem into two roughly equal sized subproblems. We recursively solve the two subproblems in parallel by dividing the processor evenly and glue their solutions using □ to get the final answer. All of this can be easily done in NC^{k+2}. □

This theorem gives automatically generated parallel algorithms for problems such as: Calculating the convex hull of a set of points, finding the maximal element in two dimension, and calculating the Voronoi diagram of a set of points in two dimension.

5 Problems on Comparator Gates

In this section we consider the circuit value and network stability problems over comparator gates, introduced in [8] and show that they are in $incr$-LOGSPACE and in $rincr$-LOGSPACE(NLOGSPACE) respectively. The definitions of circuits and gates are taken from [8] and are given here for the sake of completeness.

Definition 18. A *circuit* is a directed acyclic graph, where each node represents a gate. The incoming edges are inputs while the outgoing ones are the outputs of the gate. A *network* is a circuit with feedback, in other words the underlying graph need not be acyclic. A gate preserves adjacency (is *adjacency preserving*) if it maps adjacent input words (binary words of the same length that differ in at most one bit) into adjacent output words. A gate is *monotone* if it cannot simulate the NOT gate. A *comparator* gate, takes as input a and b and gives as output $a \wedge b$ and $a \vee b$. The circuit value problem over comparator gates (C-CV) is the circuit value problem where all the gates are comparator gates.

Theorem 19. *The comparator circuit value problem is in $incr$-LOGSPACE.*

Proof: Initially the circuit is evaluated in linear time by propagating the inputs one by one. Comparator circuits are adjacency preserving; a one bit change at any place transmits only a one bit change to succeeding levels. Therefore, the result of a one bit change in the input is a change along a path in the circuit. Such a change can be easily made using only logarithmic work-space. □

A similar argument holds for any circuit that is adjacency preserving. This result is interesting because C-CV is not known to be in NC. Therefore, C-CV has the distinction of being a problem that can be updated fast in parallel, though it is not known whether it can be solved fast from scratch in parallel. This also means that problems like the "Lex-First Maximal Matching," problem which can be parsimoniously reduced to C-CV are in *incr*-LOGSPACE.

We now turn our attention to the network stability problem on comparator gates. A network is stable for a given input assignment if we can assign values to the edges which are consistent with the gate equations and the given input assignment. Given a network N on comparator gates and an input assignment S_{in} there always exists a stable configuration. The interesting question therefore, is the value of an edge in particular types of stable configurations. Given such a network we are interested in knowing the value of an edge in the "most-zero" stable configuration S_{min}. If an edge e is zero in S_{min} then it is zero in every stable configuration of N under the input S_{in}.

Theorem 20. *The problem of finding whether an edge e is 0 in the "most-zero" configuration of a comparator network N is in rincr-LOGSPACE(NLOGSPACE).*

The strategy for updating the network is similar to that of the circuit problem. The only difference is that we now need the use of nondeterminism to recognize and traverse cycles in the network. The details are omited in this abstract.

Subramanian [15] has shown that a number of problems concerning stable marriage are equivalent to the problem of network stability in comparator gates. Decision problems based on the "man-optimal stable marriage problem" and other problems parsimoniously reducible to the comparator network stability problem are therefore in *rincr*-LOGSPACE(NLOGSPACE). Like the Comparator Circuit Value problem, these too have no known NC algorithms to solve them from scratch.

6   Conclusions and Open Problems

We have provided a firm theoretical base to conduct the study of incremental computation. We have demonstrated the existence of problems that are incrementally complete for various natural complexity classes and shown some important special cases wherein dynamic solutions imply parallel ones. However, many questions remain open. For instance we would like to know if there are meaningful restrictions of P, LOGSPACE, NLOGSPACE, and NC[1] that are in the class *incr*-POLYLOGTIME? Is there any relationship between *incr*-POLYLOGTIME and the class of problems which have optimal parallel algorithms?

We believe that the classes *incr*-TIME and *incr*-SPACE are an important means for getting a better understanding of the relationship between incremental and parallel computation.

References

[1] D. Barrington, "Bounded Width Polynomial Size Programs Recognize Exactly Those Languages in NC^1," *Proc. 18th Symposium on Theory of Computing* (1986), 1–5.

[2] A. M. Berman, M. C. Paul, and B. G. Ryder, "Proving Relative Lower Bounds for Incremental Algorithms," *Acta Informatica* 27 (1990), 665–683.

[3] A. Delcher and S. Kasif, "Complexity Issues in Parallel Logic Programming," Johns Hopkins University, Ph.D Thesis, 1989.

[4] R. Greenlaw, H. J. Hoover, and W. L. Ruzzo, "A Compendium of Problems Complete for P," Department of Computer Science and Engineering, University of Washington, Technical Report TR-91-05-01, 1991.

[5] L.J. Guibas and R. Sedgewick, "A Dichromatic Framework for Balanced Trees," *Proc. 19th IEEE Symposium on Foundations of Computer Science* (1978), 8–21.

[6] R.M. Karp and V. Ramachandran, "A Survey of Parallel Algorithms for Shared Memory Machines," in *Handbook of Theoretical Computer Science*, North Holland, 1990, 871–941.

[7] R. E. Ladner, "The Circuit Value Problem is Log Space Complete for P," *SIGACT News* 7 (1975), 18–20.

[8] E. Mayr and A. Subramanian, "The Complexity of Circuit Value and Network Stability," *Proc. 4th Annual Conference on Structure in Complexity Theory* (1989), 114–123.

[9] K. Mehlhorn and M. Overmars, "Optimal Dynamization of Decomposable Searching Problems," *Information Processing Letters* 12 (1981), 93–98.

[10] P. B. Miltersen, "On-line reevaluation of functions," Computer Science Dept, Aarhus University, Aarhus DK., Technical Report ALCOM-91-63, May 1991.

[11] S. Miyano, S. Shiraishi, and T. Shoudai, "A List of P-Complete Problems," Research Institute of Fundamental Information Science, Kyushu , Research Report , 1989.

[12] M. Overmars, "The Design of Dynamic Data Structures," *Lecture Notes in Computer Science* 156 (1983).

[13] J.H. Reif, "A Topological Approach to Dynamic Graph Connectivity," *Information Processing Letters* 25 (1987), 65–70.

[14] S. Skyum and L. G. Valiant, "A Complexity Theory Based on Boolean Algebra," *Proc. 22nd IEEE Symposium on Foundations of Computer Science* (1981), 244–253.

[15] A. Subramanian, "A New Approach to Stable Matching Problems," Department of Computer Science, Stanford University, Technical Report STAN-CS-89-1275, 1989.

Precise Average Case Complexity

Rüdiger Reischuk and Christian Schindelhauer

Technische Hochschule Darmstadt[*]

Abstract. A new definition is given for the average growth of a function $f : \Sigma^* \to \mathbb{N}$ with respect to a probability measure μ on Σ^*. This allows us to define meaningful average case distributional complexity classes for arbitrary time bounds (previously, one could only distinguish between polynomial and superpolynomial growth). It is shown that basically only the ranking of the inputs by decreasing probabilities are of importance.

To compare the average and worst case complexity of problems we study average case complexity classes defined by a time bound and a bound on the complexity of possible distributions. Here, the complexity is measured by the time to compute the rank functions of the distributions. We obtain tight and optimal separation results between these average case classes. Also the worst case classes can be embedded into this hierarchy. They are shown to be identical to average case classes with respect to distributions of exponential complexity.

These ideas are finally applied to study the average case complexity of problems in $\mathcal{NP}$. A reduction between distributional problems is defined for this new approach. We study the average case complexity class $\mathcal{AvP}$ consisting of those problems that can be solved by DTMs on the average in polynomial time for all distributions with efficiently computable rank function. Fast algorithms are known for some $\mathcal{NP}$–complete problems under very simple distributions. For langugages in $\mathcal{NP}$ we consider the maximal allowable complexity of distributions such that the problem can still be solved efficiently by a DTM, at least on the average. As an example we can show that either the satisfiability problem remains hard, even for simple distributions, or $\mathcal{NP}$ is contained in $\mathcal{AvP}$, that means every problem in $\mathcal{NP}$ can be solved efficiently on the average for arbitrary not too complex distributions.

1 Introduction and Overview

Levin observed that a sound definition of average case complexity and complexity classes is not at all obvious ([Levi86]). The classical notion of average-case time complexity of a machine M with respect to given probability distributions μ_n on inputs x of length n takes the expectation

$$Time_M^\mu(n) := \sum_{|x|=n} \mu_n(x) \cdot time_M(x) \,,$$

* Institut für Theoretische Informatik, Alexanderstraße 10, 6100 Darmstadt, Germany
email: reischuk/schindel @iti.informatik.th-darmstadt.de

where $\text{time}_M(x)$ denotes the running time of M on x and $\mu := \mu_1, \mu_2, \dots$. The machine M is μ–**average T–time bounded** (in the expected sense) for a resource bound $T : \mathbb{N} \to \mathbb{N}$, if $Time_M^\mu \leq T$, that means for all n

$$\sum_{|x|=n} \mu_n(x) \cdot \frac{\text{time}_M(x)}{T(|x|)} \leq 1 \, .$$

The problem with this definition is that polynomial time simulations of polynomial average time machines can result in superpolynomial average time complexity. It was resolved by Levin by applying the inverse of T to the fraction, thus requiring

$$\sum_{|x|=n} \mu_n(x) \cdot \frac{T^{-1}(\text{time}_M(x))}{|x|} \leq 1 \, .$$

This definition does not take into account that the weights of different input length may be very unequal. Thus one considers only distributions μ defined over the whole set of inputs and requires

$$\sum_{x} \mu(x) \cdot \frac{T^{-1}(\text{time}_M(x))}{|x|} \leq 1 \, .$$

M is then called (Levin)–μ–**average T–time bounded**. For a discussion of this approach see the detailed exposition in [Gure91].

Still there remains an unpleasant property, the influence of the functional growth of $\mu(x)$ on the time bound T. If, for example, one takes the "standard" *uniform probability distribution*, which assigns probability $\mu_{\text{uniform}}(x) := 6/\pi^2 \cdot |x|^{-2} \cdot 2^{-|x|}$ to a string $x \in \{0,1\}^*$ a machine using n^2 steps on every input of length n would already be average $O(n^{1+\epsilon})$–time bounded for arbitrary $\epsilon > 0$. This problem can be resolved to a certain extent (see [Gure91]), but not completely.

Our first contribution to the average case analysis will be a new definition of average T–time bounded, which gets rid of this problem. It will allow us to differenciate between bounds T_1 and T_2 for any $T_1 \leq o(T_2)$. The idea is to bound the complexity of a machine not only with respect to the probability distribution μ, but with respect to all monotone transformations of μ. At first glance, it seems that this complicates the analysis even more. But we will show that this larger set of conditions is equivalent to a very simple property of the distribution μ, which does not involve probabilities explicitly anymore. The only thing that matters is the ranking of the inputs by μ, that is the sequence of inputs ordered by decreasing probabilities.

In practice, one often does not know the values of the distribution exactly, but for each pair of inputs at least one can decide which input is more likely. This way, the whole analysis is greatly simplified. Each ranking of the input space describes a whole equivalence class of distributions, and we get rid of the influence of the asymptotic growth of the probability measure.

A **distributional problem** is a pair (L, μ), consisting of a language $L \subseteq \{0,1\}^*$ and a probability distribution μ on $\{0,1\}^*$. We define *distributional complexity classes*

DistDTime(T) containing all pairs (L, μ), for which there exists a DTM accepting L that is μ-average T-time bounded in this generalized sense.

Given a language $L \in DTime(T)$ and a DTM M for L, it is easy to see that by cycling through all inputs of length n one can find an x, on which M spends the maximal time for inputs of length n. If a probability measure μ gives all its weight for inputs of length n to this x then the average time of M (in the expected sense) with respect to this μ equals the worst case complexity. $\mu(x)$ can be computed in time $O(2^{|x|} \cdot T(|x|))$. Using this idea, Miltersen has shown that allowing exponential time overhead a measure μ can be constructed that is *malign* for all expected T-time bounded machines ([Milt91]). That means their expected time complexity with respect to this μ is no more than a constant factor smaller than their worst case complexity.

On the other hand, restricting an average case analysis to some simple distributions may yield results with little practical value. The satisfiability problem, for example, has been shown quickly solvable for certain symmetric distributions, but the input space generated this way seems to be of not interest for applications in AI (see for example the discussion in [MiSeLe92]). These observation motivate to consider *average case complexity classes* $AvDTime(T, C)$ consisting of all languages L that can be recognized in μ-average time T for distributions μ of complexity at most C, for certain bounds C. That way, average case complexity classes are directly comparable to the standard worst case classes, because both contain only languages.

In this paper a notation different from the one in previous research on average case complexity will be used, because we feel that this new one is more appropriate and natural. There should be a clear distinction between distributional classes, where distributions appear explicitly, and average case classes the elements of which are languages in the usual sense. From a complexity theoretic point of view one is more interested in the second kind of classes.

The complexity of a distribution is taken w.r.t. its **rankability**, that is the effort to compute the rank of an input x. Previous approaches have bounded the complexity of distributions using the notion of **computable** and **sampleable**. A distribution is POL-computable if the sum of all weights of inputs lexicographically lower than x can be computed in polynomial time w.r.t. the length of x and the binary expansion ([Levi86],[Gure91]). A distribution μ is POL-samp<u>l</u>able, if there exists a randomized algorithm that outputs the string x with probability $\mu(x)$ in polynomial time w.r.t. $|x|$ ([BCGL92]). These concepts are not directly comparable to rankability, a discussion of their relation will be given in the full version of this paper.

As an analog to the worst case class $\mathcal{P}$ the average case complexity class
$$Av\mathcal{P} := AvDTime(\text{POL}, \text{POL-rankable})$$
seems to be the most natural candidate. Problems in this class are efficiently solvable in practice, because for all not too complex distributions their average time complexity is bounded by a polynomial. Our second main contribution is a tight separation and inclusion results for average case complexity classes within $Av\mathcal{P}$.

Finally, we consider reductions between distributional problems and relations between nondeterministic and average case complexity classes. Of particular interest are distributional problems (L, μ) such that $L \in \mathcal{NP}$ and the complexity of μ is polynomially bounded (again, we consider here the rankability). In Levin's model this class has been called distributional $\mathcal{NP}$ or randomized $\mathcal{NP}$, but both notions are somehow misleading (distributional $\mathcal{NP}$ should better be used for the class $DistNTime(\text{POL})$).

For a meaningful reduction between distributional problems one needs an additional property called *domination* (see [Levi86] or [Gure91]). In our model this becomes a simple condition on the transformation of the ranks between two probability distributions. Similar to the previous models one can show that the bounded halting problem for NTM together with a natural ranking is complete for distributional problems taken from $\mathcal{NP}$.

Finally, we discuss the relation between $\mathcal{NP}$ and $\mathcal{AvP}$. To analyse the average case behaviour of problems in $\mathcal{NP}$ we propose to classify them w.r.t. the largest amount of rankability one can allow such that the average time complexity stays polynomial. We call this the *nose* of a problem.

Some $\mathcal{NP}$–complete problems are known that can be solved very fast on the average for simple distributions. Examples are 3-colourability of graphs or Hamiltonian circuits (for a discussion and references see [John84] and [Gure91]). If a problem is complete in the sense above simple distributions, which might yield a polynomial time complexity on the average, probably do not exist. Otherwise, by a result of Ben-David and Luby (see [Gure91]) deterministic and nondeterministic exponential time would be identical. Our last result shows that satisfiability has no nose, that means it will require superpolynomial time for almost all distributions, unless $\mathcal{NP} \subseteq \mathcal{AvP}$.

Most of the proofs have to be omitted in this short report. For a complete version see [ReSc92], some of the results can already be bound in [Schi91].

2 Notations

Let $\mathcal{N}$ denote the identity function on the natural numbers $\mathbb{N}$. A complexity bound is a function $T : \mathbb{N} \to \mathbb{N}$. All complexity bounds in this paper are assumed to be monotone increasing and time-constructible. The following sets of complexity bounds will be of special interest: $\text{POL} := \bigcup_{k \in \mathbb{N}} O(\mathcal{N}^k)$, $\text{EXL} := \exp \Theta(\mathcal{N})$ and $\text{EEXL} := \exp \exp \Theta(\mathcal{N})$. For a complexity bound T, which does not necessarily have to be injective, we define the inverse T^{-1} by

$$T^{-1}(m) := \min\{n \mid T(n) \geq m\} .$$

Let $M_1, M_2, \ldots$ be an enumeration of all deterministic Turing machines (in some cases we also consider nondeterministic machines). We may assume that all machines have only 2 work tapes, implying that one can use a universal machine with only a constant factor slowdown.

When talking about an ordering of binary strings, $x \leq y$ we refer to the lexicographical ordering. We consider probability measures (density functions) $\mu : \Sigma^* \to [0, 1]$ over the input space. μ has to satisfy $\sum_x \mu(x) \leq 1$. bin $: \mathbb{N} \to \{0, 1\}^*$ denotes the standard correspondence between binary strings and natural numbers.

3 Refinement of Levin's Average Case Measure

In the introduction we have already discussed the problem to measure precisely the average complexity of a time bound T with respect to a probability distribution μ. Levin's solution essentially can only distinguish between polynomial and superpolynomial growth.

Definition 1 *The pair (f, μ) consisting of a function $f : \Sigma^* \to \mathbb{N}$ and a distribution μ belongs to the class $lAv(\text{POL})$ with respect to a distribution μ iff for some number k*

$$\sum_x \mu(x)\frac{f(x)^{1/k}}{|x|} < \infty .$$

The problem with the standard uniform distribution mentioned above can somehow be diminished, by giving $\{0, 1\}^n$ a total weight proportional to $n^{-1} \cdot \log^{-2} n$ or even less, instead of n^{-2}. Still, it can never be resolved completely. Below, we will present a precise average case measure. The idea is to consider simultaneously all distributions $\tilde{\mu}$ that yield the same ordering of inputs by decreasing probabilities as μ, that means if $\mu(10001) < \mu(11)$ then $\tilde{\mu}(10001) \leq \tilde{\mu}(11)$. Thus, only the ranking of the inputs by decreasing weights matters.

Definition 2 $\text{rank}_\mu(x) := |\{z \in \Sigma^* \mid \mu(z) \geq \mu(x)\}|$.

μ–average bounded by T will then defined to be $\tilde{\mu}$–average bounded by T in the sense above for all such $\tilde{\mu}$. The set of such $\tilde{\mu}$ can be generated by *monotone transformations* of μ.

Definition 3 *A real-valued monotone function $m : [0, 1] \to [0, 1]$ is called a **monotone transformation** of the distribution μ if $\sum_x m(\mu(x)) \leq 1$.*
The set $\text{Av}(T)$ contains all pairs (f, μ) consisting of a function $f : \Sigma^* \to \mathbb{N}$ and a distribution μ such that for all monotone transformations m of μ

$$\sum_x m(\mu(x))\frac{T^{-1}(f(x))}{|x|} \leq 1 .$$

Because of the universal quantifier over all monotone transformations the above definition for $\text{Av}(T)$ is even more complicated than the one given by Levin. But there exists an equivalent, very simple characterization of $\text{Av}(T)$. Consider the special case of *threshold functions* $\text{thr}_l : [0, 1] \to [0, 1]$ as monotone transformations, where for $l = \text{rank}_\mu(x)$ we define $\text{thr}_l(z) := 1/l$ if $z \geq \mu(x)$ and 0 else.

Lemma 1

$$(f, \mu) \in Av(T) \quad \Longleftrightarrow \quad \forall l \quad \sum_x \text{thr}_l(\mu(x)) \frac{T^{-1}(f(x))}{|x|} \leq 1 .$$

As an immediate consequence of this lemma we obtain the following fundamental result, which shows that an average bound can be computed without considering all possible transformations.

Proposition 1

$$(f, \mu) \in Av(T) \iff \forall l \sum_{\text{rank}_\mu(x) \le l} \frac{T^{-1}(f(x))}{|x|} \le l .$$

In the following we will only use this characterization to verify membership in $Av(T)$. This generalization keeps polynomial bounds, which are increased by a polynomial, in that class. Each rank function represents a whole set of distributions, namely those which are equivalent with respect to the definition of the sets $Av(T)$.

We are now ready to define the following **distributional complexity classes.**

Definition 4

$$DistDTime(\mathbf{T}) := \{(L, \mu) | \exists \, DTM \, M \text{ with } L(M) = L, \, (time_M, \mu) \in Av(T)\} ,$$
$$DistP := \bigcup_{T \in \text{POL}} DistDTime(T) .$$

Note that in this setting already for simple distributions like the uniform one there can only be an exponential difference between the distributional and the worst case complexity of a problem. That means, if $(L, \text{uniform}) \in DistP$ then $L \in DTime(\text{EXL})$. For Levin's model separation results between polynomial distributional complexity classes are given in [WaBe92], but the separating languages are in classes higher than exponential time. The technical trick to achieve this is to let the uniform probabilities for inputs of length n converge very fast to 0 with n. Such a separation result does not seem to yield much insight into average case complexity.

4 Hierarchies of Average Case Complexity Classes

Since for this new average case measure all essential information of a distribution is the rank function we will identify both in the following. Thus (L, μ) and (L, rank_μ) denote the same distributional problem. The straightforward way to restrict distributions is a time limit for computing the rank.

Definition 5 Let T−**rankable** be the set of all distributions μ for which there exists a DTM M that on input x computes $bin(\text{rank}_\mu(x))$ in time $T(|x|)$.

In order to compare the worst case and the average case complexity of problems we consider the distributional complexity of languages L with respect to a set C of distributions and define

Definition 6

$$AvDTime(T, C) := \{L \mid \forall \mu \in C \ (L, \mu) \in DistDTime(T)\} \ ,$$
$$Av\mathcal{P} := AvDTime(POL, POL\text{-}rankable) \ .$$

Let us first show that for complex distributions there is no difference between the average and the worst case complexity. We will construct a rank function that for any DTM M with $L(M) \notin DTime(T)$ gives small ranks ρ to inputs with long computations, thus (L, ρ) does not belong to $DistDTime(T)$. For this purpose, the following $\mathcal{NP}$-complete language is helpful.

Definition 7

$$\mathbf{H_T} := \{(w, 1^i) \mid M_i \text{ is a DTM and } \exists x \leq w \text{ with } time_{M_i}(x) > T(|x|)\} \ .$$

Let $\mathbf{h(T)} \geq \Omega(T^2)$ be a time bound such that $H_T \in DTime(h(T))$.

Obviously, $h(T)$ is of order at most $2^n \cdot T(n)$ (remember that all bounds were assumed to be monotone).

Theorem 1 *For all $T \geq \mathcal{N}$ and for all $\delta > 1$ holds*

$$AvDTime(T, h(T)\text{-}rankable) \subseteq DTime(T(\delta \mathcal{N})).$$

Since the rank functions of these distributions can be computed in time $T \cdot EXL$, compared to the worst case, no machine works significantly faster on the average with respect to this set of distributions.

Corollary 1 *For all $T \in POL$:*

$$AvDTime(T, (T \cdot EXL)\text{-}rankable) = DTime(T) \ .$$

Miltersen has shown that there exists a distribution μ malign for $DTime(\mathcal{N}^k)$, which can be computed in polynomial time with an $\Sigma_2^{\mathcal{P}}$-oracle ([Milt91]). The proof of this theorem yields that for the more general situation we consider here already an $\mathcal{NP}$-oracle suffices.

The equality above cannot be generalized to arbitrary large time bounds T. This has technical reasons when taking the inverse of a large bound (the price one has to pay for the closure under polynomial growth). Indeed, we can show

Theorem 2 *For $T \geq EEXL$ and the set of all distributions U holds:*

$$DTime(T) \subset AvDTime(T, U) \ .$$

For average case complexity classes with a fixed bound on the rankability of the distributions we can establish a tight hierarchy, comparable to the situation in the worst case.

Theorem 3 *For time bounds $T_1, T_2, V \geq (1 + \omega(1)) \cdot \mathcal{N}$ with $T_1 \leq o(T_2)$ holds:*

$$AvDTime(T_1, V\text{-}rankable) \subset AvDTime(T_2, V\text{-}rankable) .$$

Proof Sketch: First we show that even under the simplest distributions, the uniform ones, not all problems with worst case time bound T_2 can be solved in time T_1 on the average, that means

$$DTime(T_2) \setminus AvDTime(T_1, \{uniform\}) \neq \emptyset .$$

The idea is to diagonalizes slowly enough over the sequence of DTM $M_1, M_2, \ldots$ such that either an input can be found, on which M_i differs from the diagonal language L to be constructed, or M_i spends too much time on sufficiently many inputs. These inputs will have enough weight to contradict that L is accepted by M_i in average time T_1.

Now observe that if $V_1 \leq V_2$ then V_1-rankable $\subseteq V_2$-rankable. Therefore,

$$DTime(T) \subseteq AvDTime(T, V_1\text{-}rankable) \subseteq AvDTime(T, \{uniform\})$$ ∎

Furthermore, we can show an optimal separation of these averge case classes with respect to the complexity of the distributions.

Theorem 4 *For $\delta > 1$, $\mathcal{N} \leq V_2 \leq o(V_1)$ and $V_1(\delta\mathcal{N}) \leq O(T)$ holds:*

$$AvDTime(T, V_1\text{-}rankable) \subset AvDTime(T, V_2\text{-}rankable) .$$

The proof of this separation result with a fixed time bound is a rather complicated diagonal construction. We construct a distribution that is V_1- but not V_2-rankable with the property that some long inputs are assigned small ranks.

The left side of fig. 1 shows a pictorial description of the hierarchies implied by the last two theorems. Each point in the diagram represents a complexity class $AvDTime(T, V\text{-}rankable)$ defined by the two complexity bounds T and V.

5 Reductions and Completeness for Average Case Complexity Classes

A meaningful reduction between distributional problems (L_1, ρ_1) and (L_2, ρ_2) has to relate the distributions μ_i, resp. rank functions ρ_i in order to guarantee that a good average case behaviour of one problem is transferred to the other. For this prupose, Levin introduced the notion of *dominance*. Considering the ranking, this property can be expressed by a simple condition if the reduction is injective. This is not a real restriction for reductions between standard $\mathcal{NP}$-complete problems. For technical reasons we assume in the following that all distributions μ have the property that all ranks are unique, that means the corresponding rank function $\rho = rank_\mu$ is injective. By a slight perturbation of the probabilities, this can always be achieved.

Definition 8 *An injective function* $f : \Sigma^* \to \Sigma^*$ *is a* **distributional reduction** *from the distributional problem* (L_1, ρ_1) *to the distributional problem* (L_2, ρ_2) *if the following conditions hold:*

1. f *is a polynomial time reduction from* L_1 *to* L_2 *in the classical sense, that means* f *can be computed in deterministic polynomial time and* $x \in L_1 \Leftrightarrow f(x) \in L_2$.

2. Domination: *There exist constants* $c_0, c_1 > 0$ *such that for all* $x \in \Sigma^*$
$$\rho_2(f(x)) \leq c_0 \, |x|^{c_1} \, \rho_1(x) \ .$$

In order to analyse the average case complexity of problems in $\mathcal{NP}$ we first consider distributional problems.

Definition 9

$$\mathcal{NP}^{\text{dist}} := \mathcal{NP} \times POL\text{-}rankable = \{(L, \mu) | L \in \mathcal{NP} \text{ and } \mu \in POL\text{-}rankable\} \ .$$

A distributional problem (L, ρ) *is* $\mathcal{NP}$*–distributional complete if* $(L, \rho) \in \mathcal{NP}^{\text{dist}}$ *and if for all distributional problems in* $\mathcal{NP}^{\text{dist}}$ *there exists a distributional reduction to* (L, ρ).
A language L *is* $\mathcal{NP}$*–average complete if* $L \in \mathcal{NP}$ *and for all* $L' \in \mathcal{NP}$ *and* $\rho' \in POL\text{-}rankable$ *there exists a distribution (ranking)* $\rho \in POL\text{-}rankable$ *such that* (L', ρ') *has a distributional reduction to* (L, ρ).

Lemma 2 *If* $(L_1, \rho_1) \in \mathcal{NP}^{\text{dist}}$, $(L_2, \rho_2) \in Dist\mathcal{P}$, *and* (L_1, ρ_1) *has a distributional reduction to* (L_2, ρ_2) *then* $(L_1, \rho_1) \in Dist\mathcal{P}$.
If (L, ρ) *is* $\mathcal{NP}$*–distributional complete then* L *is* $\mathcal{NP}$*–average complete.*

Theorem 5 *If an* $\mathcal{NP}$*–average complete language belongs to* $\mathcal{AvP}$ *then* $\mathcal{NP} \subseteq \mathcal{AvP}$.

Definition 10 *The bounded halting problem* NBH *for NTM is the language*

$$\text{NBH} := \{(x01^t0^i) \mid time_{M_i}(x) \leq t\} \ .$$

Let $cod(n)$ *be a self-delimiting binary encoding of the natural number* n *of length* $O(\log n)$ *that can be computed in time* $O(n)$. *Define a distribution for* NBH *by*

$$rank_{\text{NBH}}(w) := \begin{cases} bin^{-1}(x \ cod(t) \ cod(i)) & \text{if } w = x01^t0^i, \\ \infty & else. \end{cases}$$

Observe that $rank_{\text{NBH}}$, resp. any distribution with this rank function, is linear rankable. The following reduction uses Levin's idea in case of computable distributions (see [Levi86] and [Gure91]).

Theorem 6 (NBH, rank_{NBH}) *is $\mathcal{NP}$-distributional complete.*

Proof: Let $(L,\mu) \in \mathcal{NP}^{\text{dist}}$ with rank function r and M_i be a NTM that accepts $x \in L$ in time $q(|x|)$, where q is a polynomial. For inputs not in L the machine M_i does not halt on any computation. Let M_j be a NTM that on input by, where b is a single bit and $y \in \Sigma^*$, does the following:
If $b = 0$ then find a string x such that $r(x) = \text{bin}(y)$, else set $x := y$.
Simulate M_i on input x. There exists a polynomial p such that M_j halts on input x in time $p(|x|)$ iff M_j accepts. We define a reduction f by

$$f(x) := \begin{cases} 1x01^{p(|x|)}0^j & \text{if } r(x) \geq \text{bin}^{-1}(x), \\ 0\text{bin}(r(x))01^{p(|x|)}0^j & \text{if } r(x) < \text{bin}^{-1}(x). \end{cases}$$

The reduction property is obvious for f. Domination is achieved because a string is coded by its rank in case the rank is smaller than its binary length. ∎

Corollary 2 NBH *is $\mathcal{NP}$-average complete.*

Let us consider a standard (worst-case) reduction f that is injective, invertible in polynomial time and honest, that means $|f^{-1}(y)| \leq R(|y|)$ for some polynomial R. Then the reduction can be translated into one for the average case.

Theorem 7 *Let f be an injective, polynomial time invertible and honest reduction from L_1 to L_2. If L_1 is $\mathcal{NP}$-average complete then the same holds for L_2.*

Proof: To get a distributional reduction from a distributional problem (L_1,ρ_1) to L_2 define the rank function for L_2 by $\rho_2(y) := \rho_1(f^{-1}(y))$. Thus the dominance property is trivially fulfilled and because of the invertibility and honesty of f the complexity of ρ_2 is polynomially bounded if this holds for ρ_1. ∎

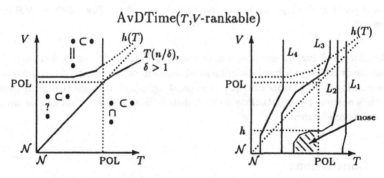

AvDTime(T,V-rankable)

Fig. 1. On the left: hierarchies between average case complexity classes; on the right: different average case behaviour of languages L_i

6 The Average Case Complexity of Problems in $\mathcal{NP}$

An interesting question is whether $\mathcal{NP}$ problems for certain bounds V can be solved efficiently on average, at least for V-rankable distributions. Therefore, for $L \in \mathcal{NP}$ we look at the set of all pairs $(T, V) \in (\text{POL}, \text{POL})$ such that $L \in AvDTime(T, V\text{-rankable})$ and call this the nose of L.

An $\mathcal{NP}$-problem that has a nontrivial nose can be considered feasible on average for most practical applications. The height of a nose is defined by the supremum V of all pairs (T, V) contained in the nose. If L has a nose of height h we know that there is a polynomial average time algorithm for L unless the inputs are supplied by an adversary that needs at least $O(h(|x|))$ steps (in the worst case) to compute the rank of x.

The right side of figure 1 visualizes the possible average case behaviour of languages in $\mathcal{NP}$. The right halfspace of a line corresponding to a language L_i contains all pairs (T, V) such that $L_i \in AvDTime(T, V\text{-rankable})$. L_1 is an example of a language that cannot be solved efficiently, even on the average with respect to very simple distributions. L_2 represents a feasible problem for all distributions that can be computed within the complexity bound h, but not for more complex distributions. If $\mathcal{NP}$ contains such a language with $h \in \text{POL}$ then $\mathcal{NP} \not\subseteq Av\mathcal{P}$. On the other hand, L_3 can be solved efficiently for all polynomially rankable distributions and if such a language were $\mathcal{NP}$-average complete then $\mathcal{NP} \subseteq Av\mathcal{P}$. If L_4 were $\mathcal{NP}$-complete then $\mathcal{NP}$ would collapse to $\mathcal{P}$ since, as we have shown, for ranking bounds above $h(T)$ the average case complexity equals the worst case complexity.

Using the completeness of the bounded halting problem and invertible distributional reductions, standard $\mathcal{NP}$-complete problems can be shown to be $\mathcal{NP}$-average complete for a linear rankable distribution. As an example, we can prove this for the satisfiability problem SAT.

Theorem 8 *There exists a ranking ρ of linear complexity such that the distributional problem (SAT, ρ) is $\mathcal{NP}$-distributional complete. Thus, SAT is $\mathcal{NP}$-average complete.*

Therefore SAT has no nontrivial nose unless $\mathcal{NP} \subseteq Av\mathcal{P}$. An explicit distribution that turns SAT into a hard distributional problem can efficiently be computed from the ranking ρ, for example as $\mu(x) := c/(\rho(x) \log^2 \rho(x))$. It seems that with respect to Levin's notion of computability no such distribution is known that can be computed in polynomial time.

7 Conclusions

We have shown that the average case time complexity of an algorithm can be estimated as precisely as in the worst case. Ranking the input space and measuring the complexity of a distribution with respect to its rankability has been proved to an appropriate and natural concept. Classical results like tight hierachies can be obtained this way, both for the time complexity and the complexity of the distributions. Based on these notions, starting with distributional complexity classes we have presented meaningful definitons of average case complexity classes the elements of which are languages in the standard sense. They are directly comparable to worst case classes.

Definitions for reductions and completeness have been given for distributional and average case classes. This way, one overcomes problems with flat distributions in Levin's approach as observed by Gurevich [Gure91]. In a natural way, standard $\mathcal{NP}$-completeness translates into a completeness for average case analysis. In contrast to computability, for many $\mathcal{NP}$-problems a hard polynomial time bounded rank function can be constructed, and in contrast to sampleability this function can be used to construct computable distributions efficiently. We have shown this for the basic complete problem SAT. The maximal complexity of distributions such that a problem can be solved in average polynomial time – the height of the nose – has been proposed as a measure for the average case complexity of problems above $\mathcal{P}$. It may be possible to prove the existence of problems with nontrivial noses by using one-way-functions as reductions (compare [VeLe88] and [ImLe90]).

These ideas can also be applied to other cases like the analysis of average space complexity.

References

[BCGL92] S. Ben-David, B. Chor, O. Goldreich, M. Luby, *On the Theory of Average Case Complexity*, J. CSS 44, 1992, 193-219; see also Proc. 21. STOC, 1989, 204-261.

[Gure91] Y. Gurevich, *Average Case Completeness*, J. CSS 42, 1991, 346-398.

[ImLe90] R. Impagliazzo, L. Levin, *No Better Ways to Generate Hard $\mathcal{NP}$ Instances than Picking Uniformly at Random*, Proc. 31. FoCS, 1990, 812-821.

[John84] D. Johnson, *The $\mathcal{NP}$-Completeness Column*, J. of Algorithms 5, 1984, 284-299.

[Levi86] L. Levin, *Average Case Complete Problems*, SIAM J. Computing 15, 1986, 285-286.

[Milt91] P. Miltersen, *The Complexity of Malign Ensembles*, Proc. 6. Structure in Complexity Theory, 1991, 164-171.

[MiSeLe92] D. Mitchell, B. Selman, H. Levesque *Hard and Easy Distributions of SAT Problems*, Proc. 10. Nat. Conf. on Artificial Intelligence, 1992, 459-465.

[ReSc92] R. Reischuk, Chr. Schindelhauer, *Precise Average Case Complexity Measures*, Technical Report, Technische Hochschule Darmstadt, 1992.

[Schi91] Chr. Schindelhauer, *Neue Average Case Komplexitätsklassen*, Diplomarbeit, Technische Hochschule Darmstadt, 1991.

[VeLe88] R. Venkatesan, L. Levin, *Random Instances of Graph Coloring Problems are Hard*, Proc. 20. SToC, 1988, 217-222.

[WaBe92] J. Wang, J. Belanger, *On Average $\mathcal{P}$ vs. Average $\mathcal{NP}$*, Proc. 7. Struc. Compl., 1992.

The bit probe complexity measure revisited *

Peter Bro Miltersen

Aarhus University, Computer Science Department, Ny Munkegade, Building 540,
DK-8000 Aarhus C, Denmark. E-mail: pbmiltersen@daimi.aau.dk

Abstract. A static data structure problem consists of a set of data D, a set of queries Q and a function f with domain $D \times Q$. Given a space bound b, a (good) solution to the problem is an encoding $e : D \rightarrow \{0,1\}^b$, so that for any y, $f(x,y)$ can be determined (quickly) by probing $e(x)$. The worst case number of probes needed is $C^b(f)$, the bit probe complexity of f. We study the properties of the complexity measure $C^b(\cdot)$.

1 Introduction and preliminaries

Elias and Flower [5] introduced the following model of retrieval problems: A set D, called the set of *data*, a set Q, called the set of *queries* and a set A, called the set of *answers* is given, along with a function $f : D \times Q \rightarrow A$. The problem is to devise a scheme for encoding elements of D into data structures in the memory of a random access machine. When an $x \in D$ has been encoded, it should be possible at a later point in time to come forward with any $y \in Q$ and efficiently compute $f(x,y)$ using random access to the data structure encoding x.

This model is a convenient model for any combinatorial static data structure problem.

A complexity measure considered by Elias and Flower was the *bit probe* measure, measuring only the number of bitwise accesses to the data structure. Computation is for free. The bit probe measure was later generalized to the *cell probe* measure by Yao [13], where memory cells, accessed in a single operation, may contain more than one bit. While these models do not necessarily provide realistic upper bounds, lower bounds derived in this model are certainly valid as lower bound for any realistic, sequential model of computation.

In order to be able to make some fine grained distinctions which could otherwise not be made, the version of the measure we adopt is the bit probe measure. We also consider this to be the most appealing combinatorial measure, architecture independent as it is.

In order to make a combinatorial theory we have to assume that the sets D and Q are finite. Given a problem, it is easy to convert it to a finite problem by making suitable restrictions on the size of the inputs. For convenience, we will restrict ourselves to decision problems and thus assume $A = \{0,1\}$.

Definition 1. Let $f : D \times Q \rightarrow \{0,1\}$. Let b be a natural number. Let $G : D \rightarrow \{0,1\}^b$ be a scheme for encoding elements of D into binary strings of length b. The

* Work partially supported by the ESPRIT II Basic Research Actions Program of the EC under contract No. 7141 (project ALCOM II).

bit probe complexity of f with respect to G, $C^G(f)$ is the number of bits one needs to probe in $G(x)$ in order to compute $f(x,y)$ knowing y for worst case x,y. If $f(x,y)$ can not be determined from probing $G(x)$, we put $C^G(f) = \infty$. The bit probe complexity of f is

$$C^b(f) = \min\{C^G(f)|G : D \rightarrow \{0,1\}^b\}$$

The object of this paper is the study of the properties of $C^b(\cdot)$ as a complexity measure in its own right, the motivation being to gain an understanding about which functions possess feasible data structure and which do not. Note that we restrict ourselves to worst case analysis. Elias and Flower considered, simultaneously, worst case complexity, average complexity and the computational complexity of performing the access operation. Later studies in cell probe complexity have, however, focused on worst case complexity.

Note that the limitation b on the space used by a static data structure is essential in order to get a non-trivial theory. Indeed, if the number of bits in the data structure is allowed to be as much as $|Q|$, it is possible to construct a data structure which make any query answerable in constant time, by simply letting the data structure consist of a table containing the answer to each possible query. When a query is made, the answer can be found by a single probe to the data structure, i.e.

Proposition 2. *For any* $f : D \times Q \rightarrow \{0,1\}$,

$$C^{|Q|}(f) \leq 1$$

Note that if the set of queries *separates* the set of data, i.e. $x \neq y \Rightarrow \exists q \in Q : f(x,q) \neq f(y,q)$, it is not possible to determine $f(x,y)$ from $G(x)$ unless any x gets a unique encoding, and we have

Proposition 3. *If* Q *separates* D *in* $f : D \times Q \rightarrow \{0,1\}$, *then for* $b < \lceil \log|D| \rceil$

$$C^b(f) = \infty$$

If we have probed sufficiently to identify x completely, the value of $f(x,y)$ can be determined, so

Proposition 4. *For any* $f : D \times Q \rightarrow \{0,1\}$ *and* $b \geq \lceil \log|D| \rceil$,

$$C^b(f) \leq \lceil \log|D| \rceil$$

We shall improve this bound slightly in Section 2.

Notation

All logarithms in this paper are base 2. When we in the future say a function $f : D \times Q \rightarrow \{0,1\}$ we more often than not mean an infinite family of functions $f_i : D_i \times Q_i \rightarrow \{0,1\}$ with $|D_i| \rightarrow \infty$ for $i \rightarrow \infty$. Let $\mathcal{ALL}$ be the family of all such functions. In that case, the size bound b is really an infinite family b_i with $b_i \geq \log|D_i|$ and $C^b(f)$ is the family $C^{b_i}(f)$.

2 Bounds for the full problem ε

We consider the problem $\varepsilon : D \times \mathcal{P}(D) \to \{0,1\}$ given by $\varepsilon(x,y) = 1$ iff $x \in y$. We call this problem the *full* problem, since there is a query for each predicate over the set of data. Thus, we should prepare ourselves for any question whatsoever about the input. The problem was investigated by Elias and Flower, but since they considered worst case complexity and average case complexity simultaneously, their upper and lower bounds do not directly apply for the bit probe complexity measure. We will determine the exact bit probe complexity of this problem, up to a small additive constant.

Theorem 5. *If* $(1 + \Omega(1)) \log|D| \leq b \leq 2^{|D|}$ *then*

$$C^b(\varepsilon) \leq \lceil \log|D| \rceil - \log\log b + 2 + o(1)$$

Proof. An $x \in D$ can be encoded in binary using $n = \lceil \log|D| \rceil$ bits. Fix any such encoding. By our assumptions on b, we can select a constant $k > 0$ so that $n + \frac{b}{k} \leq b$ for sufficiently large n. Let $r = \lfloor \log\log b - s \rfloor$, where $s = \log \frac{1}{1 - \frac{\log k}{\log b}}$. We consider a data structure for encoding $x \in D$ consisting of two parts.

- The $n - r$ first bits in the binary encoding of x
- For each predicate $p : \{0,1\}^r \to \{0,1\}$, the value of p on the final r bits in the encoding of x.

The number of bits used in this structure is

$$B = n - r + 2^{2^r} \leq n + 2^{2^{-s} \log b} = n + b^{1 - \frac{\log k}{\log b}} = n + \frac{b}{k} \leq b.$$

Thus, the data structure is legal. In order to answer a query $S \subseteq D$, we read the first $n - r$ bits of the data structure, i.e. the first $n - r$ bits of the input $x \in D$. Let these bits form the string x_1. Let p be the predicate over the last r bits in the input defined by

$$p(x_2) \Leftrightarrow x_1 x_2 \in S$$

We can identify the predicate p using our knowledge about x_1 and S only, i.e. without reading further in the structure. The answer to the query is the value of $p(x_2)$ which can be read directly in the structure. Thus $C^b(\varepsilon) \leq n - r + 1$. Since $s = o(1)$, we have the desired bound.

□

Since ε is the full problem, we have that for any set D, Q and any function $f : D \times Q \to \{0,1\}$, $C^b(f) \leq \lceil \log|D| \rceil - \log\log b + 2 + o(1)$ with b as in the theorem. For reasonable values of b, this is only a slight improvement on the naive upper bound $\lceil \log|D| \rceil$ which holds for all functions. However, the next theorem tells us that the bound is optimal up to a small, additive constant.

Theorem 6.

$$C^b(\varepsilon) \geq \log|D| - \log\log b - o(1)$$

Proof. Let $d = C^b(\varepsilon)$. Thus, any query can be answered by decision tree of depth d over the b bits in the optimal structure. The number of such trees is easily seen to be

$$t = b^{2^d-1} 2^{2^d} \le (2b)^{2^d} = 2^{(\log b + 1)2^d} = 2^{2^{d+\log\log b + o(1)}}$$

There has to be a different tree for each different query. The number of queries is $2^{|D|}$. Thus.

$$2^{2^{d+\log\log b + o(1)}} \ge 2^{|D|}$$

and

$$d \ge \log|D| - \log\log b - o(1).$$

□

Thus, we have determined the complexity of ε within $1.5 + o(1)$ probes for sufficiently large $|D|$ and exhibited an interesting trade off between b and $C^b(\varepsilon)$.

We can prove a similar trade off between b and $C^b(f)$ for any function f.

Theorem 7. *For any f, b, $k \le C^b(f)$,*

$$C^{(2b)^{2^k}-1}(f) \le C^b(f) - k + 1$$

Proof. Let $C^b(f) = d$ and let an optimal encoding G establishing this be given. Now consider a data structure for encoding $x \in D$ consisting of

- For each possible decision tree T of depth k over the b bits in the original structure, for which the answer in the leftmost leaf is 0, the answer to T in $G(x)$.

As in the proof of Theorem 6, there are $b^{2^k-1} 2^{2^k}$ decision trees of depth k over b bits, so the size of the structure is $(2b)^{2^k-1}$. Now consider answering any query $y \in Q$. Since the bits in $G(x)$ are present in the new structure, we can simulate the original algorithm for $d - k$ probes and arrive at a node in the decision tree for y which is the root of a tree of depth k. Either the answer to this tree or the answer to its negation is present in the structure, so we may now simply look up the answer to y or its negation, using one probe.

□

3 Functions with small query sets

The full function is not really typical when considered as a static data structure problem, since the cardinality of the set of queries vastly exceeds the cardinality of the set of data. In natural applications, we expect a query to be describable in much fewer bits than the data. Indeed, the point of making static data structures is to be able to answer queries in time comparable to the time it takes to make the query, rather than in time comparable to the size of the data. If the number of bits in a query is at least $\log|D|$, this is always possible, and the problem is therefore trivialized.

Therefore, we consider now situations where $|Q| << |D|$. Of course, if $|Q|$ gets as small as b, we know from the Introduction that one probe suffices. It turns out that if a single query is added, so that $|Q| = b+1$, the complexity may jump from constant to linear and if $|Q| = (1+\epsilon)b$, we may get the complexity of the full function, up to an additive constant. Furthermore, this happens for almost all functions.

Theorem 8. *For any* D, b, *a function* $f : D \times \{1, \ldots, b+1\} \to \{0, 1\}$ *exists with*

$$C^b(f) \geq \log |D| - \log b - \log \log b - o(1)$$

Almost all functions f *on this domain has*

$$C^b(f) \geq \log |D| - \log b - \log \log b - O(h),$$

where h *is any function with* $\lim_{i \to \infty} h(i) = \infty$. *Also, for any* $\epsilon > 0$, *almost all functions* $g : D \times \{1, \ldots \lceil (1+\epsilon)b \rceil\} \to \{0, 1\}$ *has*

$$C^b(g) \geq \log |D| - \log \log b - \log \frac{1+\epsilon}{\epsilon} - o(1).$$

Proof. A protocol for a problem $f : D \times Q \to \{0, 1\}$ is given by the encoding for each $x \in D$ and the decision tree for each $y \in Q$. Thus, there are at most $2^{|D|b} 2^{2^{d+\log \log b + \delta(b)}|Q|}$ protocols using b bits and d probes, where δ is $o(1)$. If $|Q| = b+1$ there are thus less than $2^{|D||Q|}$ functions having $C^b(f) \leq |D| - \log \log b - \delta(b) - \log(b+2)$, and the number of functions having $C^b(f) \leq |D| - \log \log b - \log b - \omega(1)$ vanishes against $2^{|D||Q|}$. If $|Q| \geq (1+\epsilon)b$, there are at most $2^{|D||Q| - \Omega(|D|)}$ functions having $C^b(f) \leq \log |D| - \log \log b - \delta(b) - \log \frac{1+\epsilon}{\epsilon} - \log \frac{|Q|}{|Q|-1}$. Again, this number vanishes against $2^{|D||Q|}$.

□

Note that in the case $|Q| = b+1$, there is an additive gap of $\log b$ between the lower bound and the complexity of the full function. We do not know if the upper bound can be improved for very small $|Q|$ or if better lower bounds are available. We consider this an interesting open problem.

4 The bit probe hierarchy

It seems natural to compare the number of bits b used by a static structure to the size of a non-redundant representation of the data, i.e. $\lceil \log |D| \rceil$ and to compare the number of probes used to the size of a Boolean representation of the query, i.e. $\lceil \log |Q| \rceil$. This leads to the following definition:

Definition 9. For functions $h, g : \mathcal{N} \to \mathcal{N}$, let $BP[h, g]$ be the subset of $\mathcal{ALC}$ defined by

$$BP[h, g] = \{ \{f_i\} \mid \forall i : C^{h(\lceil \log |D_i| \rceil)}(f_i) \leq g(\lceil \log |Q_i| \rceil) \}.$$

For convenience of notation, we will often use n as a free variable in the first argument of BP and m as a free variable in the second argument of BP and thus write $BP[h, g]$ as $BP[h(n), g(m)]$. If H and G are classes of functions, we define

$$BP[H, G] = \bigcup_{h \in H, g \in G} BP[h, g].$$

In this notation, we get from the results of the previous sections, the following two complementary theorems.

Theorem 10. *Let h, g be increasing functions with $h(i) \geq i$ and $h(g(i)) \geq 2^i$ for all i. Then $\mathrm{BP}[h(n), g(m)] = \mathcal{ALC}$.*

Theorem 11. *Let h, g be functions with $h(i) \geq i$ and $h(g(i)) \leq 2^i$ for all i and $g(i) = \omega(\log i)$. Then for any $\epsilon > 0$.*

$$(\mathrm{BP}[h(n), 1] \cap \mathrm{BP}[n, g(m)]) - \mathrm{BP}[(1 - \epsilon)h(n), (1 - \epsilon)g(m)] \neq \emptyset$$

We see that the classes $\mathrm{BP}[h, g]$ form a very tight hierarchy. For "reasonable" h and g, there are functions which can not be encoded using $h(n)$ bits and be answered in time $g(m)$, but if $(1 + \epsilon)h(n)$ bits are allowed in the encoding, the answer can be found in constant time, and if $(1 + \epsilon)g(m)$ probes are allowed, a non-redundant representation of the data is sufficient.

5 Lower bounds for explicitly defined functions

How large lower bounds can be proven for explicitly defined functions with a small query set? Yao [13] and Ajtai [2] proved lower bounds in the cell probe model for various dictionary problems. These lower bounds are however quite small, compared to the lower bounds we know most problems have. The best known lower bound in the bit probe model appears to be the one derived by Elias and Flower [5], showing in our notation that for the *equality* function $\delta : Q \times Q \to \{0, 1\}$ with $\delta(x, y) = 1$ iff $x = y$ has $2^{C^b(\delta)+1} \binom{b}{C^b(\delta)} \geq |Q|$, i.e. $C^b(\delta) = \Omega(\frac{\log |Q|}{\log b})$. In this section we show how this lower bound by Elias and Flower can be generalized using communication complexity, but we obtain no better lower bounds. A slightly different form of their lower bound is given as a corollary. For a function $f : D \times Q \to \{0, 1\}$, let $C_2(f)$ be the (two-way) communication complexity of f (for definitions and a survey on communication complexity, see e.g. Lovász [7]).

Theorem 12.

$$C^b(f) \geq C_2(f)/(\lceil \log b \rceil + 1)$$

Proof. Let an optimal static data structure for f be given. Let Alice be in possession of $x \in D$ and Bob in possession of $y \in Q$. A protocol for computing $f(x, y)$ is as follows.

- Alice computes the structure corresponding to her input x, but does not send anything yet.
- Bob simulates the query operation corresponding to his input y by sending Alice requests for the bits he wants to read in the structure. A request can be described in $\lceil \log b \rceil$ bits. Alice sends the value of the bit in question back. This is repeated until Bob has read what he needed in the data structure, i.e. for at most $C^b(f)$ rounds.
- After this, Bob knows $f(x, y)$.

Thus $C_2(f) \leq (\lceil \log b \rceil + 1)C^b(f)$

$\square$

Several interesting functions with $|D| = |Q|$ has linear communication complexity. A useful inequality for showing this is the rank lower bound by Mehlhorn and Schmidt [8]: Let M^f be the $|D| \times |Q|$ matrix defined by $M^f_{ij} = f(i,j)$. Then $C_2(f) \geq \lceil \log \text{rank}_F(M^f) \rceil$, where the rank of the matrix is taken over any field F. We thus get

Corollary 13.

$$C^b(f) \geq \frac{\lceil \log \text{rank}_F(M^f) \rceil}{\lceil \log b \rceil + 1}$$

For instance, the equality function δ has $\text{rank}_F(M^\delta) = |Q|$. We thus get:

$$C^b(\delta) \geq \frac{\lceil \log |Q| \rceil}{\lceil \log b \rceil + 1}$$

Let us briefly sketch another approach which may lead to larger lower bounds for explicitly defined functions.

Definition 14. Let D be a set, and let A be a set system on D, i.e. a subset of $\mathcal{P}(D)$. Let $\text{prod}_d(A)$ be the set system on D consisting of the sets which can be described as the intersection of at most d sets from A. Let $\text{span}_d(A)$ be the set system consisting of disjoint unions (of any size) of sets in $\text{prod}_d(A)$. Let B be a set system on D. Let $\text{rank}_d(B) = \min\{|A| \mid B \subseteq \text{span}_d(A)\}$.

Given a function f and a $q \in Q$, let S_f be the set system $\{s_q \mid q \in Q\}$, where $s_q = \{x \in D \mid f(x,q) = 1\}$. We omit the proof of the following theorem.

Theorem 15. *For any d,*

$$C^b(f) \geq d\left(\frac{\log \text{rank}_d(S_f)}{\log b + 1} - 1\right) + 1$$

Note that $\text{rank}_F(M^f)$ is a lower bound on $\text{rank}_1(S_f)$, where F is any field. Putting $d = 1$, this gives us a slightly different version of Corollary 13. We suggest that developing techniques for proving good lower bounds on rank_d-values for larger values of d may be a feasible approach to getting better lower bounds than $\Omega(\frac{\log |Q|}{\log b})$ on explicitly defined functions.

6 Feasible problems, reductions and completeness

There is a huge gap between the lower bounds we are able to obtain for explicitly defined functions and the complexity we know most functions must have. Still, we would like to be able to argue that certain natural problems are not likely to possess good data structures. A natural approach to this are the notions of reductions and completeness. Let us first give a reasonable definition of feasibility in the case of data structures.

Definition 16. Let the class of *access feasible* problems S be defined by

$$S = \{ \{f_i\} \in \mathrm{BP}[n^{O(1)}, m^{O(1)}] \mid \forall i |D_i| \geq |Q_i| \}$$

That is, for a problem to be access feasible, we require that a query can be answered with a polynomial (in the size of the query) amount of probing in a data structure of polynomial (in the size of the data) size. This definition seems to be the most reasonable, robust, definition of an access feasible static problem. The requirement that the set of data should be bigger than the set of queries is added for technical reasons in connection with the reductions considered below. It is a natural requirement anyway. Note that δ from section 5 is considered access feasible by the definition, but this is because of the size of the query set. Note also that if a problem has $|Q| = O(\log|D|)$, the problem is access feasible by the structure consisting of the answer to any possible query, and if $\log|Q| = \log^{\Omega(1)}|D|$, it is access feasible by the structure consisting of any non-redundant encoding of $x \in D$. The definition is therefore only interesting for intermediate values of $|Q|$.

If we want to prove that a problem is access infeasible we can not use Theorem 12, since $C_2(f) \leq \min\{\lceil \log|D| \rceil, \lceil \log|Q| \rceil\}$. However, we do know that access infeasible problems exist, by Theorem 11.

Let us next identify a class which is likely to contain all problems for which we want to make static data structures. We are not likely to make data structures for computationally infeasible problems, so the class $\mathcal{P}$ seems to be an obvious choice. To get around the technical inconvenience that this class consists of one argument functions, let us fix a polynomial time computable bijective pairing function $\pi : \{(x, y) \in (\{0,1\}^*)^2 \mid |x| \geq |y|\} \to \{0,1\}^*$ with polynomial time projections. By replacing f with $f \circ \pi$, we can consider $\mathcal{P}$ as a class of families of functions $f : D \times Q \to \{0,1\}$ with $|D| \geq |Q|$. If $\mathcal{P} \subseteq S$, we are able to make an access feasible implementation of any computationally feasible problem. We conjecture that this is not so, but have to leave the conjecture open, due to our inability to prove large lower bounds for explicitly defined functions. Under the assumption that $\mathcal{P} \not\subseteq S$, we are, however, able to point out hard problems.

Definition 17. A problem $f : D \times Q \to \{0,1\}$ with $|D| \geq |Q|$ *statically reduces* to a problem $\tilde{f} : \tilde{D} \times \tilde{Q} \to \{0,1\}$ with $|\tilde{D}| \geq |\tilde{Q}|$ if

- $\log|\tilde{D}| = \log^{O(1)}|D|$
- $\log|\tilde{Q}| = \log^{O(1)}|Q|$
- A function $r : D \to \tilde{D}$ and a function $q : Q \to \tilde{Q}$ exist, so that $f(x,y) = \tilde{f}(r(x), q(y))$.

Note that this reduction is actually a slight variation of the *rectangular reduction* suggested for communication problems by Babai, Frankl and Simon [3]. S is easily seen to be closed under static reductions and the following problem is easily seen to be $\mathcal{P}$-complete.

- D is the set of circuits of size n with m inputs.
- Q is the set of assignments to m inputs ($m \leq n$).
- $\mathrm{cv}(x, y)$ is the value of the circuit x when y is given as input.

Thus cv is not in $\mathcal{S}$ unless $\mathcal{P} \subseteq \mathcal{S}$.

Using the existence of access infeasible problems and the ability to search for them in exponential space, it is easy to see that there are functions in $\mathcal{EXPSPACE} - \mathcal{S}$. We can thus exhibit provably access infeasible problems.

- $D = \{0,1\}^n$.
- Q is the set of Turing machines describable in at most m bits using the standard enumeration, $m \leq n$.
- $t(x,y) = 1$ iff y accepts x using space at most 2^n.

Theorem 18. t *is complete for* $\mathcal{EXPSPACE}$ *with respect to static reductions and thus* $t \notin \mathcal{S}$.

Note however, that completeness with respect to classical reductions (e.g. logspace reductions) is not sufficient to ensure access infeasibility. This is because such reductions do not necessarily respect the distinction between data and query. For a natural example of this consider the following problem, equiv:

- Given a finite alphabet Σ and two expressions r_1, r_2 over Σ, $\cdot$ (concatenation), $\cup$ (union), $*$ (Kleene star) and ^{2} (squaring), tell whether they denote the same language.

It is known [9] that equiv is $\mathcal{EXPSPACE}$-complete in the usual sense. The domain of this problem has a natural factorization, i.e. we can consider it as a static data structure problem, where r_1 is the datum and r_2 the query. However, this problem has an access feasible solution, because we can encode r_1 as a prefix free encoding of $\min(r_1)$, the lexicographically least extended regular expression denoting the same language as r_1, padded with zeroes to make all data structures for expressions of length $|r_1|$ the same length. The number of bits required is $O(|r_1|)$. In order to find out if $r_2 = r_1$, one computes $\min(r_2)$ and checks if the encoding of this expression is a prefix of the data structure. The number of probes required is $O(|r_2|)$. We do unfortunately not know any natural problems, complete for $\mathcal{EXPSPACE}$ with respect to static reductions. We pose it as an open problem to find any such examples, and also non-trivial examples of $\mathcal{P}$-completeness.

7 An application to dynamic problems

Sairam, Vitter and Tamassia [11] proposed a complexity theory of dynamic problems, and defined the class $incr\text{-}\mathcal{POLYLOGTIME}$. Miltersen [10] independently defined the same class under the name $\mathcal{D}$. In both cases, the conjecture $P \neq incr\text{-}\mathcal{POLYLOGTIME}$ was made. We show a link between this question and the question considered in the previous section.

Theorem 19. $\mathcal{P} = incr\text{-}\mathcal{POLYLOGTIME} \Rightarrow \mathcal{P} \subseteq \mathrm{BP}[n \log^{O(1)} n, m^{O(1)}]$

Proof sketch. Given a polynomial time computable function $f : D \times Q \to \{0,1\}$, let $\bar{f} : \{0,1,\#\}^* \to \{0,1\}$ have $\bar{f}(x\#y) = f(x,y)$. Under the assumption $\mathcal{P} = incr\text{-}\mathcal{POLYLOGTIME}$, we can find an efficient dynamic data structure maintaining the value of $\tilde{f}(z)$ during changes of the letters in z. The static data structure for $x \in D$ consists of a sorted list of the addresses of the bits changed in the dynamic structure when z is changed from $0^{\log |D|} \# 0^{\log |Q|}$ to $x \# 0^{\log |Q|}$.

$\square$

Thus, if $\mathcal{P} = incr\text{-}\mathcal{POLYLOGTIME}$, we would not only have $\mathcal{P} \subseteq \mathcal{S}$, but quasi-linear sized structures would be sufficient. We consider this as strong evidence for $\mathcal{P} \neq incr\text{-}\mathcal{POLYLOGTIME}$.

References

1. L. Adleman, Two theorems on random polynomial time, 19th Symp. Found. of Comp. Sci. (1978), 75-83.
2. M. Ajtai, A lower bound for finding predecessors in Yao's cell probe model, Combinatorica 8 (1988) 235-247.
3. L. Babai, P. Frankl, J. Simon, Complexity classes in communication complexity theory, Proc. 27th IEEE FOCS (1986) 337-347.
4. H. Chernoff, A measure of asymptotic efficiency for tests based on the sum of observations, Ann. Math. Statist. 23 (1952), 493-509.
5. P. Elias, R.A. Flower, The complexity of some simple retrieval problems, J. Ass. Comp. Mach. 22 (1975), 367-379.
6. T. Hagerup, C. Rüb, A guided tour of Chernoff bounds, Inform. Proces. Lett. 33 (1990), 305-308.
7. L. Lovász, Communication complexity: A survey, in "Paths, Flows, and VLSI Layout", edited by B.H. Korte, Springer Verlag, Berlin New York (1990).
8. K. Mehlhorn, E.M. Schmidt, Las Vegas is better than determinism in VLSI and distributed computing, Proc. 14th ACM STOC (1982) 330-337.
9. A.R. Meyer, L. Stockmeyer, The equivalence problem for regular expressions with squaring requires exponential space, IEEE 13th Annual Symposium on Switching and Automata Theory (1972), 125-129.
10. P.B. Miltersen, On-line reevaluation of functions, Aarhus University Tech. Report DAIMI PB-380.
11. S. Sairam, J.S. Vitter, R. Tamassia, A complexity theoretic approach to incremental computation, these proceedings.
12. A. C.-C. Yao, Some complexity questions related to distributive computing, Proc. 11th ACM STOC (1979) 209-213.
13. A. C.-C. Yao, Should tables be sorted?, JACM 28 (1981), 615-628.

Language Learning With Some Negative Information[*]

Ganesh Baliga[1], John Case[1] and Sanjay Jain[2]

[1] Department of CIS, Univ. of Delaware, Newark, DE 19716, USA
[2] Inst. of Systems Science, Nat. Univ. of Singapore, Singapore 0511

1 Introduction

Gold-style formal language learning [Gol67] features the learning of generating procedures for formal languages from enumerations of positive information about the languages. Herein we consider Gold-style formal language learning augmented in various ways by some amount of negative information about the languages.

Chapter 6 of [Ful85] treats the case of augmentation with various powerful forms of nearly complete grammatical information for the complement of the language. In [Cas86] the report on this chapter is motivated by treating negative information as a more mathematically tractable substitute for semantic information. [MB72, MB73] present evidence that semantics in addition to positive information may be essential to human language learning. [JS91] examines language learning with varying *densities* of negative information provided.

Fulk's chapter, of necessity, is about learning recursive languages, but we would like to consider the learning of r.e. not recursive languages too, where the positive information is supplemented by some negative information. For example, some recursively axiomatizable theories such as first order group theory are r.e. not recursive [Men86], yet we might want to study the learning of recursive axiomatizations (i.e., generators) for them.

In the present paper we consider the effects on learning power obtained by augmenting the positive information by apparently small, finite, *core* amounts of negative information. We consider two cases, one (Section 3) where only the finite core is supplied and one (Section 4) where negative information in addition to the finite core is allowed. This latter case was motivated in part by [Mot92] which itself, in part, was motivated by [Ang80, Shi86]. We refer to the latter style of negative information presentation as *open*.

In Section 3 we present results to the effect that tremendous gains in learning power are obtained from adding apparently very small, suitable, finite sets of negative information.

In Section 4 we present results showing that, with respect to learning power, in some cases, allowing more mistakes in final generators learned can more than compensate information theoretically for open negative information. In other cases, we show that small additions of open negative information can more than

---

[*] Email addresses of the authors are baliga@cis.udel.edu, case@cis.udel.edu and sanjay@iss.nus.sg respectively.

compensate, also information theoretically, for mistakes in final grammars. It is noted that, in almost all cases, additional open negative information results in strictly more learning power. We discuss the relation of this to the hypothesis in [McN66] that increasing certain forms of language correction leads to increased speed in language development. In Section 4 it is also noted (Theorem 28) that, regarding learning power for languages, being given unbounded, finite cores of open negative information about languages is equivalent to being given their entire complements.

Finally in Section 5 we present a surprising preliminary result supportive of the hypothesis of [McN66] mentioned in the just previous paragraph. This result says that one does see a learning *speed* increase (as measured by mind-change complexity [CS83]) from a minimal, non-vacuous amount of open negative information. Throughout this paper, we will present our theorems without proof. The interested reader is invited to refer to [BCJ92] for details.

2   Preliminaries

2.1   Notation

Any unexplained recursion theoretic notation is from [Rog67]. N denotes the set of natural numbers, $\{0, 1, 2, 3, \ldots\}$. Unless otherwise specified, i, j, n, x, y, z, with or without decorations[3], range over N. $*$ denotes a non-member of N and is assumed to satisfy $(\forall n)[n < * < \infty]$. a, b and c, with or without decorations, range over $N \cup \{*\}$. $\emptyset$ denotes the empty set. $\subseteq$ denotes subset. $\subset$ denotes proper subset. $\supseteq$ denotes superset. $\supset$ denotes proper superset. S, with or without decorations, ranges over sets. $\mathcal{P}(S)$ denotes the power set of S. $\mathrm{card}(S)$ denotes the cardinality of S. $S_1 \oplus S_2 \stackrel{\text{def}}{=} \{2x \mid x \in S_1\} \cup \{2x + 1 \mid x \in S_2\}$. $S_1 \Delta S_2$ denotes the symmetric difference between S_1 and S_2. $S_1 =^n S_2$ denotes $\mathrm{card}(\{x \mid x \in S_1 \Delta S_2\}) \leq n$; $S_1 =^* S_2$ means that $\mathrm{card}(\{x \mid x \in S_1 \Delta S_2\})$ is finite. D_x denotes the finite set with canonical index x [Rog67]. We sometimes identify finite sets with their canonical indices. We do this when we consider functions or machines which operate on complete knowledge of a finite set (equivalently, an argument which is a canonical index of the finite set), but when we want to display the argument simply as the set itself.

$\uparrow$ denotes undefined. η ranges over *partial* functions with arguments and values from N. $\eta(x)\!\downarrow$ denotes that $\eta(x)$ is defined; $\eta(x)\!\uparrow$ denotes that $\eta(x)$ is undefined.

f, g and F with or without decorations range over *total* functions with arguments and values from N. $\mathrm{domain}(\eta)$ and $\mathrm{range}(\eta)$ denote the domain and range of the function η, respectively.

$\langle i, j \rangle$ stands for an arbitrary, computable, one-to-one encoding of all pairs of natural numbers onto N [Rog67]. Similarly we can define $\langle \cdot, \ldots, \cdot \rangle$ for encoding multiple natural numbers onto N.

The quantifiers '$\overset{\infty}{\forall}$', and '$\overset{\infty}{\exists}$' essentially from [Blu67], mean 'for all but finitely many' and 'there exist infinitely many', respectively. The quantifier '$\exists!$' means 'there exists a unique'.

---

[3] Decorations are subscripts, superscripts and the like.

φ denotes a fixed *acceptable* programming system for the partial computable functions: $N \rightarrow N$ [Rog58, Rog67, MY78]. φ_i denotes the partial computable function computed by program i in the φ-system. Φ denotes an arbitrary fixed Blum complexity measure [Blu67, HU79] for the φ-system.

W_i denotes domain(φ_i). W_i is, then, the r.e. set/language ($\subseteq N$) accepted (or equivalently, generated) by the φ-program i. $\mathcal{E}$ will denote the set of all r.e. languages. L, with or without decorations, ranges over $\mathcal{E}$. For language L, we use χ_L to denote the characteristic function of L. $\mathcal{L}$, with or without decorations, ranges over subsets of $\mathcal{E}$. $\mathcal{FIN} \stackrel{\text{def}}{=} \{L \mid \text{card}(L) < \infty\}$. $\mathcal{SVT} \stackrel{\text{def}}{=} \{L \mid (\forall x)(\exists! y)[\langle x, y \rangle \in L]\}$.

We sometimes consider partial computable functions with multiple arguments in the φ system. In such cases we implicitly assume that a $\langle \cdot, \ldots, \cdot \rangle$ is used to code the arguments, so, for example, $\varphi_i(x, y)$ stands for $\varphi_i(\langle x, y \rangle)$.

2.2 Learning Machines

We now consider language learning machines. Definition 1 below introduces a notion that facilitates discussion about elements of a language being fed to a learning machine.

Definition 1. A *sequence* σ is a mapping from an initial segment of N into $(N \cup \{\#\})$. The *content* of a sequence σ, denoted content(σ), is the set of natural numbers in the range of σ. The *length* of σ, denoted by $|\sigma|$, is the number of elements in σ.

Intuitively, #'s represent pauses in the presentation of data. We let σ and τ, with or without decorations, range over finite sequences. SEQ denotes the set of all finite sequences. The set of all finite sequences of natural numbers and #'s, SEQ, can be coded onto N.

Definition 2. A *language learning machine* is an algorithmic device which computes a mapping from SEQ into N.

Later in Definition 9 and, again in Definition 29, we present variants of the language learning machines from Definition 2 just above. For convenience of exposition we avoid introducing these variants until we need them.

We let **M**, with or without decorations, range over learning machines.

2.3 Fundamental Language Identification Paradigms

Definition 3. A *text* T for a language L is a mapping from N into $(N \cup \{\#\})$ such that L is the set of natural numbers in the range of T. The *content* of a text T, denoted content(T), is the set of natural numbers in the range of T.

Intuitively, a text for a language is an enumeration or sequential presentation of all the objects in the language with the #'s representing pauses in the listing or presentation of such objects. For example, the only text for the empty language is just an infinite sequence of #'s.

We let T, with or without superscripts, range over texts. $T[n]$ denotes the finite initial sequence of T with length n. Hence, domain($T[n]$) = $\{x \mid x < n\}$. For $n \leq |\sigma|$, $\sigma[n]$ denotes the finite initial sequence of σ with length n.

Explanatory Language Identification

In Definition 4 below we spell out what it means for a learning machine on a text to converge in the limit.

Definition 4. Suppose M is a learning machine and T is a text. $M(T){\downarrow}$ (read: $M(T)$ *converges*) $\Leftrightarrow (\exists i)(\overset{\infty}{\forall} n) [M(T[n]) = i]$. If $M(T){\downarrow}$, then $M(T)$ is defined $=$ the unique i such that $(\overset{\infty}{\forall} n)[M(T[n]) = i]$; otherwise, we say that $M(T)$ *diverges* (written: $M(T){\uparrow}$).

We now introduce criteria for a learning machine to be considered *successful* on languages.

Definition 5. [Gol67, CL82, OW82a] Recall that a ranges over $N \cup \{*\}$.

(a) M $\mathbf{TxtEx}^a$-*identifies* L (written: $L \in \mathbf{TxtEx}^a(M)$) $\Leftrightarrow (\forall$ texts T for $L)(\exists i \mid W_i =^a L)[M(T){\downarrow} = i]$.

(b) $\mathbf{TxtEx}^a = \{\mathcal{L} \mid (\exists M)[\mathcal{L} \subseteq \mathbf{TxtEx}^a(M)]\}$.

Gold [Gol67] introduced the criteria we call $\mathbf{TxtEx}^0$. The generalization to the $a > 0$ case in Definition 5 was motivated by the observation that humans rarely learn a language perfectly. The $a > 0$ case is from [CL82], but [OW82a], independently, introduced the $a = *$ case. The influence of Gold's paradigm [Gol67] to human language learning is discussed by Pinker [Pin79], Wexler and Culicover [WC80], Wexler [Wex82], and Osherson, Stob, and Weinstein [OSW82, OSW84, OSW86].

We sometimes write $\mathbf{TxtEx}$ for $\mathbf{TxtEx}^0$ including in the names of those learning classes introduced in later sections where '$\mathbf{TxtEx}^0$' is a proper substring of those names.

Behaviorally Correct Language Identification

Definition 6.

(a) M $\mathbf{TxtBc}^a$-*identifies* L (written: $L \in \mathbf{TxtBc}^a(M)$) $\Leftrightarrow (\forall$ texts T for $L)(\overset{\infty}{\forall} n)[W_{M(T[n])} =^a L]$.

(b) $\mathbf{TxtBc}^a = \{\mathcal{L} \mid (\exists M)[\mathcal{L} \subseteq \mathbf{TxtBc}^a(M)]\}$.

Definition 6 is from [CL82]. The $a \in \{0, *\}$ cases were independently introduced in [OW82a, OW82b].

We sometimes write $\mathbf{TxtBc}$ for $\mathbf{TxtBc}^0$ including in the names of those learning classes introduced in later sections where '$\mathbf{TxtBc}^0$' is a proper substring of those names.

Language Learning on Characteristic Function Input

Let $f[n]$ denote the sequence $(\langle 0, f(0)\rangle, \langle 1, f(1)\rangle, \ldots, \langle n-1, f(n-1)\rangle)$. We say that $M(f){\downarrow} = i \Leftrightarrow (\overset{\infty}{\forall} n)[M(f[n]) = i]$.

Definition 7. [CL82]

(a) M $\mathbf{ExGen}^a$-*identifies* L (written: $L \in \mathbf{ExGen}^a(M)$) $\Leftrightarrow M(\chi_L){\downarrow}$ and $W_{M(\chi_L)} =^a L$.

(b) $\mathbf{ExGen}^a = \{\mathcal{L} \mid (\exists M)[\mathcal{L} \subseteq \mathbf{ExGen}^a(M)]\}$.

Similarly one can define $\mathbf{BcGen}^a$, a $\mathbf{Bc}^a$ analog of $\mathbf{ExGen}^a$ [CL82].

Some Basic Results

Theorem 8. *For all n, the following hold.*

(a) $(\mathbf{TxtEx}^{n+1} \cap \mathcal{P}(\mathcal{SVT})) - \mathbf{TxtEx}^n \neq \emptyset$.

(b) $(\mathbf{TxtBc}^{n+1} \cap \mathcal{P}(\mathcal{SVT})) - \mathbf{TxtBc}^n \neq \emptyset$.

(c) $\mathbf{TxtEx}^{2n+1} - \mathbf{TxtBc}^n \neq \emptyset$.

(d) $(\mathbf{TxtEx}^* \cap \mathcal{P}(\mathcal{SVT})) - \bigcup_n \mathbf{TxtEx}^n \neq \emptyset$.

(e) $(\mathbf{TxtBc} \cap \mathcal{P}(\mathcal{SVT})) - \mathbf{TxtEx}^* \neq \emptyset$.

(f) $(\mathbf{TxtBc}^* \cap \mathcal{P}(\mathcal{SVT})) - (\bigcup_n \mathbf{TxtBc}^n \cup \mathbf{TxtEx}^*) \neq \emptyset$.

(g) $\mathbf{TxtEx}^{2n} \subset \mathbf{TxtBc}^n$.

(h) $\mathcal{E} \notin \mathbf{TxtBc}^*$.

Parts (a), (b), (d), (e) and (f) of the above theorem can be derived from theorems proved in [CL82] and [CS83]. Parts (c), (g) and (h) of the above theorem are directly from [CL82].

3 Identification with Finite Negative Information

In this section we consider the effects on learning if an apparently small finite set of negative information is given in addition to text. For this purpose, we introduce a variant of learning machine (called *type 2*).

Definition 9. A *type 2 language learning machine* is an algorithmic device which computes a mapping from $\mathrm{SEQ} \times N$ into N.

Intuitively the second argument is for a canonical index for a finite set of negative information about the language to be learned.[4] From now on we will drop the phrase *type 2*. Context will show which type of learning machine we have in mind. $\mathbf{M}$, with or without decorations, will range over both types of learning machine.

Definition 10. We say that $\mathbf{M}(T, i)$ *converges to* j (denoted $\mathbf{M}(T, i){\downarrow} = j$) $\Leftrightarrow$ $(\overset{\infty}{\forall} n)[\mathbf{M}(T[n], i) = j]$; we say that $\mathbf{M}(T, i){\uparrow} \Leftrightarrow (\overset{\infty}{\exists} n)[\mathbf{M}(T[n], i) \neq \mathbf{M}(T[n+1], i)]$.

3.1 Definitions

Recall from Section 2.1 that we sometimes identify finite sets with their canonical indices. In part (a) of both Definitions 11 and 12 just below, S is the *core* of negative information.

Definition 11.

(a) $\mathbf{M}\ \mathbf{NegF}^b\mathbf{TxtEx}^a$-*identifies* $L \in \mathcal{E}$ (written: $L \in \mathbf{NegF}^b\mathbf{TxtEx}^a(\mathbf{M})$) $\Leftrightarrow$ $(\exists S \subseteq \overline{L} \mid \mathrm{card}(S) \leq b)(\forall T \mid T$ is a text for $L)[\mathbf{M}(T, S){\downarrow}$ and $W_{\mathbf{M}(T,S)} =^a L]$.

---

[4] The canonical index is convenient but not essential; see Remark 13 in Section 3.1 below.

(b) $\mathbf{NegF}^b\mathbf{TxtEx}^a = \{\mathcal{L} \subseteq \mathcal{E} \mid (\exists \mathbf{M})[\mathcal{L} \subseteq \mathbf{NegF}^b\mathbf{TxtEx}^a(\mathbf{M})]\}$.

Definition 12.

(a) $\mathbf{M}$ $\mathbf{NegF}^b\mathbf{TxtBc}^a$-*identifies* $L \in \mathcal{E}$ (written: $L \in \mathbf{NegF}^b\mathbf{TxtBc}^a(\mathbf{M})) \Leftrightarrow$
$(\exists S \subseteq \overline{L} \mid \mathrm{card}(S) \leq b)(\forall T \mid T$ is a text for $L)(\overset{\infty}{\forall} n)[W_{\mathbf{M}(T[n],S)} =^a L]$.

(b) $\mathbf{NegF}^b\mathbf{TxtBc}^a = \{\mathcal{L} \subseteq \mathcal{E} \mid (\exists \mathbf{M})[\mathcal{L} \subseteq \mathbf{NegF}^b\mathbf{TxtBc}^a(\mathbf{M})]\}$.

Remark 13. In part (b) of Definitions 11 and 12 above the learning classes defined are extensionally equivalent to those we would obtain if, instead, we fed an r.e. index or a characteristic index of S to the learning device instead of a canonical index. Actually the classes would be extensionally invariant if we merely fed an enumeration of S marked as negative.

3.2 Results

Trivially, for all a, $\mathbf{NegF}^0\mathbf{TxtEx}^a = \mathbf{TxtEx}^a$ and $\mathbf{NegF}^0\mathbf{TxtBc}^a = \mathbf{TxtBc}^a$. We can also prove that $\mathcal{E}$ belongs to $\mathbf{NegF}^2\mathbf{TxtEx}$, $\mathbf{NegF}^1\mathbf{TxtEx}^1$ as well as $\mathbf{NegF}^1\mathbf{TxtBc}$. It can also be proved that $\mathbf{NegF}^1\mathbf{TxtEx} - \mathbf{TxtBc}^* \neq \emptyset$. Thus, it is clear that tremendous learning power is obtained already from sets of negative information with cardinality less than or equal two. By contrast, we can prove that $\mathcal{E} \notin \mathbf{NegF}^1\mathbf{TxtEx}$.

4 Identification with Open Negative Information

In this section we introduce a different way of presenting some negative information to learning machines. Here the negative information is supplied in a manner reminding one of the basic open sets for the topology with respect to which enumeration operators are continuous. This is the first topology described in [Rog67, Exercise 11-35, page 217]. The basic definitions in this section were suggested to us in part by those in [Mot92] and those in Section 3 above. Basically, in this section, we allow the possibility of more negative information being supplied in addition to the finite cores of negative information; whereas, in Section 3 we considered supplying only the finite cores.

4.1 Definitions

For a segment σ, let $\mathrm{PosInfo}(\sigma) = \{x \mid 2x \in \mathrm{content}(\sigma)\}$, and $\mathrm{NegInfo}(\sigma) = \{x \mid 2x + 1 \in \mathrm{content}(\sigma)\}$. For a text T, let $\mathrm{PosInfo}(T) = \{x \mid 2x \in \mathrm{content}(T)\}$, and $\mathrm{NegInfo}(T) = \{x \mid 2x + 1 \in \mathrm{content}(T)\}$.

Definition 14.

(a) $\mathbf{M}$ $\mathbf{NegO}^b\mathbf{TxtEx}^a$-*identifies* $L \in \mathcal{E}$ (written: $L \in \mathbf{NegO}^b\mathbf{TxtEx}^a(\mathbf{M})$)
$\Leftrightarrow (\exists S \subseteq \overline{L} \mid \mathrm{card}(S) \leq b)(\forall L' \mid S \subseteq L' \subseteq \overline{L})(\forall T \mid \mathrm{content}(T) = L \oplus L')[\mathbf{M}(T)\downarrow$ and $W_{\mathbf{M}(T)} =^a L]$.

(b) $\mathbf{NegO}^b\mathbf{TxtEx}^a = \{\mathcal{L} \subseteq \mathcal{E} \mid (\exists \mathbf{M})[\mathcal{L} \subseteq \mathbf{NegO}^b\mathbf{TxtEx}^a(\mathbf{M})]\}$.

Definition 15.

(a) M **NegO^{b}TxtBc^a**-*identifies* $L \in \mathcal{E}$ (written: $L \in$ **NegO^{b}TxtBc^a(M)**) $\Leftrightarrow$
$(\exists S \subseteq \overline{L} \mid \text{card}(S) \leq b)(\forall L' \mid S \subseteq L' \subseteq \overline{L})(\forall T \mid \text{content}(T) = L \oplus L')(\overset{\infty}{\forall} n)[W_{M(T[n])} =^a L]$.

(b) **NegO^{b}TxtBc^a** $= \{\mathcal{L} \subseteq \mathcal{E} \mid (\exists M)[\mathcal{L} \subseteq$ **NegO^{b}TxtBc^a(M)**$]\}$.

A quantificational variant of our **NegO^{b}TxtEx^0**-identification (from Definition 14 above) is quite close to **PP^b**-identification from Section 5.3 of [Shi86]: for **PP^b**-identification different finite sets can be used for different texts for the same language (and the finite sets are required to be of size at least b). We can show there are language classes **NegO^{b}TxtEx^0**-identifiable but not **PP^b**-identifiable with **PP^b**-identification generalized to the **TxtBc*** case (and even if the finite sets are required to be of size less than or equal to b). Trivially, for all a, **NegO^{0}TxtEx^a** = **TxtEx^a** and **NegO^{0}TxtBc^a** = **TxtBc^a**.

4.2 Results

Proposition 16. *For all a, **NegO*TxtEx^a** $\cap \mathcal{P}(\mathcal{SVT})$ = **TxtEx^a** $\cap \mathcal{P}(\mathcal{SVT})$.*

Proposition 17. *For all a, **NegO*TxtBc^a** $\cap \mathcal{P}(\mathcal{SVT})$ = **TxtBc^a** $\cap \mathcal{P}(\mathcal{SVT})$.*

The following two theorems provide classes of languages which can be learned with $n + 1$ mistakes, but not with n, no matter how much open negative information is provided in the n mistake case. The mechanism partly responsible is that the gap left by the possible extra anomaly can be greater in information content than the information provided by open negative information.

Theorem 18. *For all n, **TxtEx^{n+1}** $-$ **NegO*TxtEx^n** $\neq \emptyset$.*

Theorem 19. *For all n, **TxtBc^{n+1}** $-$ **NegO*TxtBc^n** $\neq \emptyset$.*

The language class witnessing Theorem 19 immediately above (in [BCJ92]) is also not in **NegO*TxtEx***. Additionally, we have the following.

Theorem 20. **TxtBc** $-$ **NegO*TxtEx*** $\neq \emptyset$.

Theorem 21. $\mathcal{E} \in$ **NegO*TxtBc***.

The next three theorems contrast nicely with Theorems 18 and 19 above. They provide classes of languages which can be learned with $n + 1$ pieces of open negative information, but not with n, no matter how many anomalies are permitted in the n piece case. The mechanism partly responsible is that the extra possible negative information can be greater in information content than the information that may be omitted by the anomalies.

Theorem 22. **NegO^{1}TxtEx** $-$ **NegO^{0}TxtBc*** $\neq \emptyset$.

Theorem 23. *For all n, **NegO^{n+1}TxtEx** $-$ **NegO^{n}TxtEx*** $\neq \emptyset$.*

The language class (in [BCJ92]) which witnesses the previous theorem also witnesses the theorem below.

Theorem 24. *For all n, $NegO^{n+1}TxtEx - \bigcup_j NegO^n TxtBc^j \neq \emptyset$.*

The previous three theorems have the following straightforward corollary.

Corollary 25. *For all a, j and n,*

(a) $NegO^{n+1}TxtEx^a - NegO^n TxtEx^a \neq \emptyset$ and
(b) $NegO^{n+1}TxtBc^j - NegO^n TxtBc^j \neq \emptyset$.

McNeill [McN66] posits that there is *faster* learning of language for children in homes in which more corrections (usually in the form of *possibly exemplary expansions*) are given. These corrections are, in part, a form of negative information. The previous corollary says with more core open negative information (bigger S), there is more *learning power*. It doesn't, however, directly inform us about more *speed* of learning, but is, nonetheless, quite interesting. In Section 5 below we present a preliminary result (Theorem 31) showing that an improvement in *speed* (measured by mind-changes) can result from the presence of minimal, non-vacuous, open negative information.

The proof of Theorem 27 is similar to the proof used by Case and Lynes [CL82] (see also [Cas88, Cas92]) to show that $TxtEx^{2j} \subseteq TxtBc^j$.

Theorem 26. $TxtEx^* \subseteq NegO^1 TxtBc$.

Theorem 27. *For all a and j, $[NegO^a TxtEx^{2j} \subseteq NegO^a TxtBc^j]$.*

We refer the reader to Section 2.3 for the definition of $ExGen^a$.

Theorem 28. *For all a,*

(a) $NegO^* TxtEx^a = ExGen^a$ and
(b) $NegO^* TxtBc^a = BcGen^a$.

The proof of Theorem 28 suggests interesting connections between open negative information, on one hand, and *locking sequences* [BB75, OW82a, OSW86, Ful85, Ful90] for the *complements* of languages, on the other.

5 Complexity Advantages of Open Negative Information

For this section it is convenient to change slightly the meaning of the first kind of learning machine (introduced in Definition 2) to the following.

Definition 29. A *language learning machine* is an algorithmic device which computes a mapping from SEQ into $N \cup \{?\}$.

Intuitively the outputted ?s represent the machine not yet committing to an output. The reason we want the ?s is so we can avoid biasing the number of program *mind changes* before a learning machine converges: if we allow initial outputs ?s before, if ever, the first program is output, then we can learn more things within n mind changes than if we had to begin with a program (numerical) output.

In the next definition, the subscript b represents a bound on the number of mind changes allowed before convergence.

Definition 30. We say that $\mathbf{M}\ \mathbf{TxtEx}_b^a\text{-}identifies\ L \Leftrightarrow [[L \in \mathbf{TxtEx}^a(\mathbf{M})] \wedge$
$(\forall\ \text{texts}\ T\ \text{for}\ L)[\mathrm{card}(\{x\ |\ [?\neq \mathbf{M}(T[x])] \wedge [\mathbf{M}(T[x]) \neq \mathbf{M}(T[x+1])]\}) \leq b]]$.

In a similar fashion, we can expand the definition of $\mathbf{NegO}^c\mathbf{TxtEx}^a$ into the obvious definition of $\mathbf{NegO}^c\mathbf{TxtEx}_b^a$.

Just below is the theorem we promised showing a speed advantage from minimal, non-vacuous open negative information.

Theorem 31. *There exists a class of language* $\mathcal{L}$ *such that,*

(a) $\mathcal{L} \in \mathbf{TxtEx}$,
(b) $\mathcal{L} \in \mathbf{NegO}^1\mathbf{TxtEx}_0$, *and*
(c) $\mathcal{L} \notin \bigcup_n \mathbf{TxtEx}_n^*$.

6 Open Problems

We list some of the open problems.

(a) For $i \geq 1$, $\mathcal{E} \in \mathbf{NegO}^i\mathbf{TxtBc}^*$? We draw the attention of the reader to Theorem 21.
(b) In [CL82], it was shown that $\mathbf{TxtEx}^{2j+1} - \mathbf{TxtBc}^j \neq \emptyset$. Similarly, can it be shown that, for $i \geq 1$, $\mathbf{NegO}^i\mathbf{TxtEx}^{2j+1} - \mathbf{NegO}^i\mathbf{TxtBc}^j \neq \emptyset$?
(c) For $i \geq 1$, $\mathbf{NegO}^i\mathbf{TxtEx}^* \subset \mathbf{NegO}^{i+1}\mathbf{TxtBc}$? So far we know that, for all i, $\mathbf{NegO}^i\mathbf{TxtEx}^* \subset \mathbf{NegO}^*\mathbf{TxtBc}$.

References

[Ang80] D. Angluin. Inductive inference of formal languages from positive data. *Information and Control*, 45:117–135, 1980.

[BB75] L. Blum and M. Blum. Toward a mathematical theory of inductive inference. *Information and Control*, 28:125–155, 1975.

[BCJ92] G. Baliga, J. Case, and S. Jain. Language learning with some negative information. Technical Report TR-92-27, University of Delaware, May 1992.

[Blu67] M. Blum. A machine independent theory of the complexity of recursive functions. *Journal of the ACM*, 14:322–336, 1967.

[Cas86] J. Case. Learning machines. In W. Demopoulos and A. Marras, editors, *Language Learning and Concept Acquisition*. Ablex Publishing Company, 1986.

[Cas88] J. Case. The power of vacillation. In D. Haussler and L. Pitt, editors, *Proceedings of the Workshop on Computational Learning Theory*, pages 133–142. Morgan Kaufmann Publishers, Inc., 1988. Expanded in [Cas92].

[Cas92]   J. Case. The power of vacillation in language learning. Technical Report 93-08, University of Delaware, 1992. Expands on [Cas88]; journal article under review.

[CL82]   J. Case and C. Lynes. Machine inductive inference and language identification. In M. Nielsen and E. M. Schmidt, editors, *Proceedings of the 9th International Colloquium on Automata, Languages and Programming*, volume 140, pages 107–115. Springer-Verlag, Berlin, 1982.

[CS83]   J. Case and C. Smith. Comparison of identification criteria for machine inductive inference. *Theoretical Computer Science*, 25:193–220, 1983.

[Ful85]   M. Fulk. *A Study of Inductive Inference machines*. PhD thesis, SUNY at Buffalo, 1985.

[Ful90]   M. Fulk. Prudence and other conditions on formal language learning. *Information and Computation*, 85:1–11, 1990.

[Gol67]   E. M. Gold. Language identification in the limit. *Information and Control*, 10:447–474, 1967.

[HU79]   J. Hopcroft and J. Ullman. *Introduction to Automata Theory Languages and Computation*. Addison-Wesley Publishing Company, 1979.

[JS91]   S. Jain and A. Sharma. Learning in the presence of partial explanations. *Information and Computation*, 95-2:162–191, 1991.

[MB72]   D. Moeser and A. Bregman. The role of reference in the acquisition of a miniature artificial language. *Journal of Verbal Learning and Verbal Behavior*, 11:759–769, 1972.

[MB73]   D. Moeser and A. Bregman. Imagery and language acquisition. *Journal of Verbal Learning and Verbal Behavior*, 12:91–98, 1973.

[McN66]   D. McNeill. Developmental psycholinguistics. In F. Smith and G. A. Miller, editors, *The Genesis of Language*, pages 15–84. MIT Press, 1966.

[Men86]   E. Mendelson. *Introduction to Mathematical Logic*. Brooks-Cole, San Francisco, 1986. 3rd Edition.

[Mot92]   T. Motoki. Inductive inference from all positive and some negative data. Unpublished, 1992.

[MY78]   M. Machtey and P. Young. *An Introduction to the General Theory of Algorithms*. North Holland, New York, 1978.

[OSW82]   D. Osherson, M. Stob, and S. Weinstein. Ideal learning machines. *Cognitive Science*, 6:277–290, 1982.

[OSW84]   D. Osherson, M. Stob, and S. Weinstein. Learning theory and natural language. *Cognition*, 17:1–28, 1984.

[OSW86]   D. Osherson, M. Stob, and S. Weinstein. *Systems that Learn, An Introduction to Learning Theory for Cognitive and Computer Scientists*. MIT Press, Cambridge, Mass., 1986.

[OW82a]   D. Osherson and S. Weinstein. Criteria of language learning. *Information and Control*, 52:123–138, 1982.

[OW82b]   D. Osherson and S. Weinstein. A note on formal learning theory. *Cognition*, 11:77–88, 1982.

[Pin79]   S. Pinker. Formal models of language learning. *Cognition*, 7:217–283, 1979.

[Rog58]   H. Rogers. Gödel numberings of partial recursive functions. *Journal of Symbolic Logic*, 23:331–341, 1958.

[Rog67]   H. Rogers. *Theory of Recursive Functions and Effective Computability*. McGraw Hill, New York, 1967. Reprinted, MIT Press 1987.

[Shi86]   T. Shinohara. *Studies on Inductive Inference from Positive Data*. PhD thesis, Kyushu University, Kyushu, Japan, 1986.

[WC80]   K. Wexler and P. Culicover. *Formal Principles of Language Acquisition*. MIT Press, Cambridge, Mass, 1980.

[Wex82]   K. Wexler. On extensional learnability. *Cognition*, 11:89–95, 1982.

Language Learning with a Bounded Number of Mind Changes

Steffen Lange

TH Leipzig

FB Mathematik und Informatik

PF 66

O–7030 Leipzig

steffen@informatik.th-leipzig.de

Thomas Zeugmann

TH Darmstadt

Institut für Theoretische Informatik

Alexanderstr. 10

W–6100 Darmstadt

zeugmann@iti.informatik.th-darmstadt.de

Abstract

We study the learnability of enumerable families $\mathcal{L}$ of uniformly recursive languages in dependence on the number of allowed mind changes, i.e., with respect to a well–studied measure of efficiency. We distinguish between *exact* learnability ($\mathcal{L}$ has to be inferred w.r.t. $\mathcal{L}$) and *class preserving* learning ($\mathcal{L}$ has to be inferred w.r.t. some suitable chosen enumeration of all the languages from $\mathcal{L}$) as well as between learning from *positive* and from both, *positive and negative* data.

The measure of efficiency is applied to prove the superiority of class preserving learning algorithms over exact learning. We considerably improve results obtained previously and establish two infinite hierarchies. Furthermore, we separate exact and class preserving learning from positive data that avoids *overgeneralization*. Finally, language learning with a bounded number of mind changes is completely characterized in terms of recursively generable finite sets. These characterizations offer a new method to handle overgeneralizations and resolve an open question of Mukouchi (1992).

1. Introduction

Inductive inference is the process of hypothesizing a general rule from eventually incomplete data. Within the last three decades it received much attention from computer scientists. Nowadays inductive inference can be considered as a form of machine learning with potential applications to artificial intelligence (cf. e.g. Angluin and Smith, 1987, Osherson, Stob and Weinstein, 1986).

The present paper deals with inductive inference of formal languages, a field in which many interesting and sometimes surprising results have been obtained (cf. e.g. Case and Lynes, 1982, Case, 1988, Fulk, 1990). Looking at potential applications it seemed reasonable to restrict ourselves to study language learning of families of uniformly recursive languages. Recently, this topic has attracted much attention (cf. e.g. Shinohara, 1990, Kapur and Bilardi, 1992, Lange and Zeugmann, 1992, Mukouchi, 1992). The general situation investigated in language learning can be described as follows: Given more and more information concerning the language to be learnt, the inference device has to produce, from time to time, a hypothesis about the phenomenon to be inferred. The set of all admissible hypotheses is called space of hypotheses. Furthermore, the information given may contain only *positive examples*, i.e., exactly all the strings contained in the language to be recognized, as well as both *positive and negative examples*, i.e., all strings over the underlying alphabet which are classified with respect to their containment to the unknown language. The sequence of hypotheses has to converge to a hypothesis correctly describing the object to be learnt. Consequently, the inference process is an ongoing one. If $d_1, d_2, \ldots$ denotes the sequence of data the inference machine M is successively fed with, then we use $h_1, h_2, \ldots$ to denote the corresponding hypotheses produced by M. We say that M changes its mind, or synonymously, M performs a mind change, iff $h_i \neq h_{i+1}$. The number of mind changes is a measure of efficiency and has been introduced by Barzdin and Freivalds (1972). Subsequently, this measure has been intensively studied. Barzdin and Freivalds (1972) proved the following remarkable result concerning inductive inference of enumerable classes of recursive functions. Gold's (1967) *identification by enumeration* technique yields successful inference *within the enumeration* but $n - 1$ mind changes may be necessary to learn the nth function. On the other hand, there are a learning algorithm and a space of hypotheses such that the nth function in enumeration can be learnt with at most $O(\log n) + o(\log n)$ mind changes. This bound is optimal. Their result impressively shows that a careful choice of the space of hypotheses may considerably influence the efficiency of learning. Moreover, Case and Smith (1983) established a hierarchy in terms of mind changes and anomalies. Wiehagen, Freivalds and Kinber (1984) used the number of mind changes to prove advantages of probabilistic learning algorithms over deterministic ones. Gasarch and Velauthapillai (1992) studied *active learning* in dependence on the number of mind changes.

Hence, it is only natural to ask whether or not this measure of efficiency is of equal importance in language learning. Answering this question is by no means trivial, since, in general, at least inductive inference from positive data may behave totally different than inductive inference of recursive functions does (cf. e.g. Case, 1988, Fulk, 1990). This is already caused by the fact that Gold's (1967) identification by enumeration technique does not necessarily succeed. The main new problem consists in detecting or avoiding overgeneralizations, i.e., hypotheses describing proper supersets of the target language. Mukouchi (1992) studied the power of mind changes for learning algorithms that infer indexed families of recursive languages *within the given enumeration*. Moreover, he characterized language learning with a bounded number of mind changes in case that equality of languages within the given enumeration is decidable.

What we present in the sequel is an almost complete investigation of the power of mind changes. For the sake of presentation we introduce some notations. An indexed family $\mathcal{L}$ is said to be *exactly* learnable if there is a learning algorithm inferring $\mathcal{L}$ with respect to $\mathcal{L}$ itself. Furthermore, $\mathcal{L}$ is learnable by a *class preserving* learning algorithm M, if there is a space $\mathcal{G} = (G_j)_{j \in \mathbb{N}^+}$ of hypotheses such that any G_j describes a language from $\mathcal{L}$, and M infers $\mathcal{L}$ with respect to $\mathcal{G}$. In other words, any produced hypothesis is required to describe a language contained in $\mathcal{L}$ but we have the freedom to use a possibly *different enumeration* of $\mathcal{L}$ and possibly *different descriptions* of any $L \in \mathcal{L}$.

We compare exact and class preserving language learning in dependence on the allowed number of mind changes as well as in dependence on the choice of the space of hypotheses and on information presentation. The strongest possible separation is established, i.e., we prove that there are indexed families $\mathcal{L}$ which are exactly learnable from positive data with at most $k + 1$ mind changes but that are not class preservingly learnable from *positive and negative* data with at most k mind changes. This result sheds considerably more light on the power of one additional mind change than Mukouchi's (1992) hierarchy of exact learning in terms of mind changes. Furthermore, we compare exact and class preserving language learning avoiding overgeneralization and separate them (cf. Corollary 10). Applying the proof technique developed we show that exact language learning from positive data with a bounded number of mind changes is always less powerful than class preserving inference restricted to the same number of mind changes (cf. Theorem 11). Finally, we completely characterize class preserving language learning in terms of recursively generable finite sets (cf. Theorem 14 and 15). In particular, we offer a different possibility to handle overgeneralization than Angluin (1980) did.

2. Preliminaries

By $\mathbb{N} = \{0, 1, 2, 3, ...\}$ we denote the set of all natural numbers. Moreover, we set $\mathbb{N}^+ = \mathbb{N} \setminus \{0\}$. In the sequel we assume familiarity with formal language theory. By Σ we denote any fixed finite alphabet of symbols. Let Σ^* be the free monoid over Σ. The length of a string $s \in \Sigma^*$ is denoted by $|s|$. Any subset $L \subseteq \Sigma^*$ is called a language. By $co - L$ we denote the complement of L. Let L be a language and $t = s_1, s_2, s_3, ...$ an infinite sequence of strings from Σ^* such that $range(t) = \{s_k \mid k \in \mathbb{N}^+\} = L$. Then t is said to be a *text* for L or, synonymously, a *positive presentation*. Furthermore, let $i = (s_1, b_1), (s_2, b_2), ...$ be a sequence of elements of $\Sigma^* \times \{+, -\}$ such that $range(i) = \{s_k \mid k \in \mathbb{N}^+\} = \Sigma^*$, $i^+ = \{s_k \mid (s_k, b_k) = (s_k, +), k \in \mathbb{N}^+\} = L$ and $i^- = \{s_k \mid (s_k, b_k) = (s_k, -), k \in \mathbb{N}^+\} = co - L$. Then we refer to i as an *informant*. If L is classified via an informant then we also say that L is represented by *positive and negative data*. Moreover, let t, i be a text and an informant, respectively, and let x be a number. Then t_x, i_x denote the initial segment of t and i of length x, respectively.

We restrict ourselves to deal exclusively with indexed families of recursive languages defined as follows (cf. Angluin, 1980):
A sequence $L_1, L_2, L_3, ...$ is said to be an *indexed family* $\mathcal{L}$ of recursive languages

provided all L_j are non–empty and there is a recursive function f such that for all numbers j and all strings $s \in \Sigma^*$ we have

$$f(j, s) = \begin{cases} 1 & , \quad if \quad s \in L_j \\ 0 & , \quad otherwise. \end{cases}$$

In the sequel we often denote an indexed family and its range by the same symbol $\mathcal{L}$. What is meant will be clear from the context.

As in Gold (1967) we define an *inductive inference machine* (abbr. IIM) to be an algorithmic device which works as follows: The IIM takes as its input larger and larger initial segments of a text t (an informant i) and it either requires the next input string, or it first outputs a hypothesis, i.e., a number encoding a certain computer program, and then it requires the next input string (cf. e.g. Angluin, 1980).

At this point we have to clarify what space of hypotheses we should choose. Gold (1967) and Wiehagen (1977) pointed out that there is a difference in what can be inferred in dependence on whether we want to synthesize in the limit grammars or decision procedures. Case and Lynes (1982) investigated this phenomenon in detail. As it turns out, IIMs synthesizing grammars can be more powerful than those ones which are requested to output decision procedures. However, in the context of identification of indexed families both concepts are of equal power as long as uniform decidability of membership is required. Nevertheless, we decided to require the IIMs to output grammars, since this learning goal fits better with the intuitive idea of language learning. Furthermore, since we exclusively deal with indexed families $\mathcal{L} = (L_j)_{j \in \mathbb{N}^+}$ of recursive languages we almost always take as space of hypotheses an enumerable family of grammars $G_1, G_2, G_3, \ldots$ over the terminal alphabet Σ satisfying $\mathcal{L} = \{L(G_j) \mid j \in \mathbb{N}^+\}$. Moreover, we require that membership in $L(G_j)$ is uniformly decidable for all $j \in \mathbb{N}^+$ and all strings $s \in \Sigma^*$. The IIM outputs numbers j which we interpret as G_j.

A sequence $(j_x)_{x \in \mathbb{N}^+}$ of numbers is said to be convergent in the limit iff there is a number j such that $j_x = j$ for almost all numbers x.

Definition 1. (Gold, 1967) *Let $\mathcal{L}$ be an indexed family of languages, $L \in \mathcal{L}$, and let $\mathcal{G} = (G_j)_{j \in \mathbb{N}^+}$ be a space of hypotheses. An IIM M LIM$-$TXT (LIM$-$INF)$-$identifies L on a text t (an informant i) with respect to $\mathcal{G}$ iff it almost always outputs a hypothesis and the sequence $(M(t_x))_{x \in \mathbb{N}^+}$ $((M(i_x))_{x \in \mathbb{N}^+})$ converges in the limit to a number j such that $L = L(G_j)$.*
Moreover, M LIM $-$ TXT (LIM $-$ INF)$-$identifies L, iff M LIM $-$ TXT (LIM $-$ INF)$-$identifies L on every text (informant) for L. We set:
LIM $-$ TXT(M) = \{L \in \mathcal{L} \mid M LIM $-$ TXT $-$ identifies L\} and define LIM $-$ INF(M) analogously.
Finally, let LIM $-$ TXT (LIM $-$ INF) denote the collection of all families $\mathcal{L}$ of indexed families of recursive languages for which there is an IIM M such that $\mathcal{L} \subseteq$ LIM $-$ TXT(M) ($\mathcal{L} \subseteq$ LIM $-$ INF(M)).

Definition 1 could be easily generalized to arbitrary families of recursively enumerable languages (cf. Osherson et al., 1986). Nevertheless, we exclusively consider the restricted case defined above, since our motivating examples are all indexed families of recursive languages. Moreover, it may be well conceivable that the weakening of $\mathcal{L} = \{L(G_j) \mid j \in \mathbb{N}^+\}$ to $\mathcal{L} \subseteq \{L(G_j) \mid j \in \mathbb{N}^+\}$ may increase the collection of inferable indexed families. However, it does not, as the following proposition shows.

Proposition 1. *Let $\mathcal{L}$ be an indexed family and let $\mathcal{G} = (G_j)_{j \in \mathbb{N}^+}$ be any space of hypotheses such that $\mathcal{L} \subseteq \{L(G_j) \mid j \in \mathbb{N}^+\}$ and membership in $L(G_j)$ is uniformly decidable. Then we have: If there is an IIM M inferring $\mathcal{L}$ on text (informant) with respect to $\mathcal{G}$, then there is also an IIM $\hat{M}$ that learns $\mathcal{L}$ on text (informant) with respect to $\mathcal{L}$.*

Nevertheless, the proof of Proposition 1 does not preserve the number of mind changes. As we shall see later, the efficiency of learning may be well influenced by the choice of the space of hypotheses.

Within the next definition we consider the case that the number of allowed mind changes is bounded by an a priorily fixed number.

Definition 2. (Barzdin and Freivalds, 1972) *Let $\mathcal{L}$ be an indexed family of languages, $\mathcal{G} = (G_j)_{j \in \mathbb{N}^+}$ a space of hypotheses, $k \in \mathbb{N} \cup \{*\}$, and $L \in \mathcal{L}$. An IIM M $LIM_k - TXT$ ($LIM_k - INF$)–identifies L on text t (informant i) with respect to $\mathcal{G}$ iff for every text t (informant i) the following conditions are fulfilled:*

(1) $L \in LIM - TXT(M)$ $(L \in LIM - INF(M))$

(2) For any $L \in \mathcal{L}$ and any text t (informant i) of L the IIM M performs, when fed with t (i), at most k ($k = *$ means at most finitely many) mind changes.

$LIM_k - TXT(M)$, $LIM_k - INF(M)$ as well as $LIM_k - TXT$ and $LIM_k - INF$ are defined in the same way as above.

Obviously, $LIM_* - TXT = LIM - TXT$ as well as $LIM_* - INF = LIM - INF$.

Next to we sharpen Definition 1 in additionally requiring that any mind change has to be caused by a "provable misclassification" of the hypothesis to be rejected.

Definition 3. (Angluin, 1980) *Let $\mathcal{L}$ be an indexed family, $L \in \mathcal{L}$, and let $\mathcal{G} = (G_j)_{j \in \mathbb{N}^+}$ be a space of hypotheses. An IIM M CONSERVATIVE-TXT identifies L on text t with respect to $\mathcal{G}$ iff for every text t the following conditions are satisfied:*

(1) $L \in LIM - TXT(M)$

(2) If M on input t_x makes the guess j_x and then makes the guess $j_{x+k} \neq j_x$ at some subsequent step, then $L(G_{j_x})$ must fail to contain some string from t_{x+k}

$CONSERVATIVE-TXT(M)$ as well as the collections of sets $CONSERVA-$
$TIVE-TXT$ are analogously defined as above.

For any mode of inference defined above we use the prefix E to denote exact learning, i.e., the fact that $\mathcal{L}$ has to be inferred with respect to $\mathcal{L}$ itself. For example, $ELIM_k - TXT$ denotes exact learnability with at most k mind changes from text. Despite the fact that $LIM - TXT = ELIM - TXT$, $LIM_0 - TXT = ELIM_0 - TXT$ as well as $LIM - INF = ELIM - INF$, $LIM_0 - INF = ELIM_0 - INF$ none of the analogous statements is true for the other modes of inference defined above, as we shall see.

3. Separations

The aim of the present chapter is to relate the different types of language learning defined above one to the other.

Theorem 1. (Mukouchi, 1992)

$ELIM_0 - TXT \subset ELIM_1 - TXT \subset ELIM_2 - TXT \subset ... \subset ELIM_* - TXT$

We want to strengthen the theorem above in two directions. Our first sharpening is a refinement of Theorem 1.

Theorem 2. $\bigcup_{k \in \mathbb{N}} LIM_k - TXT \subset LIM - TXT$

The proof of Theorem 2 allows the following corollary.

Corollary 3. $ECONSERVATIVE\text{-}TXT \setminus \bigcup_{k \in \mathbb{N}} LIM_k - TXT \neq \emptyset$

Our next theorem shows that, in general, one additional mind change can neither be traded versus information presentation nor versus an appropriate choice of the space of hypotheses.

Theorem 4. For all $k \geq 0$: $ELIM_{k+1} - TXT \setminus LIM_k - INF \neq \emptyset$

The following hierarchy is an immediate consequence of the latter theorems.

$LIM_0 - TXT \subset LIM_1 - TXT \subset ... \subset LIM_k - TXT \subset ... \subset \bigcup_{k \in \mathbb{N}} LIM_k - TXT \subset LIM - TXT$

We have shown that $LIM_0 - INF \subset CONSERVATIVE\text{-}TXT$ (cf. Lange, Zeugmann and Kapur, 1992). Surprisingly, it makes a real difference, if an IIM is allowed to change its mind at most one time.

Theorem 5. $ELIM_1 - INF \setminus LIM - TXT \neq \emptyset$

Moreover, $LIM_k - TXT \subseteq LIM_k - INF$. Since $LIM_0 - TXT \subset LIM_0 - INF$ Theorem 5 yields the following corollary.

Corollary 6.

(1) For all $k \geq 0$, $LIM_k - TXT \subset LIM_k - INF$

(2) $LIM_0 - INF \subset LIM_1 - INF \subset LIM_2 - INF \subset ... \subset LIM_* - INF$

As above, this result can be sharpened, too.

Lemma 7. $\bigcup_{k \in \mathbb{N}} LIM_k - INF \subset LIM - INF$

The latter result has the following consequence.

Corollary 8. $LIM - TXT \# \bigcup_{k \in \mathbb{N}} LIM_k - INF$.

Summarizing the results above we obtain the following hierarchy:

$LIM_0 - INF \subset LIM_1 - INF \subset ... \subset LIM_k - INF \subset ... \subset \bigcup_{k \in \mathbb{N}} LIM_k - INF \subset LIM - INF$

Finally, we want to compare exact and class preserving language learning with an a priori bounded number of mind changes. Moreover, we compare conservatively working IIMs with those ones performing a bounded number of mind changes. The next theorems and a corollary thereof relate these different modes of inference one to the other. In particular, we show class preserving learning with at most one mind change has to be performed by conservatively working IIMs. Moreover, one mind change is already sufficient to beat exact conservative learning.

Theorem 9.

(1) $LIM_1 - TXT \subset CONSERVATIVE\text{-}TXT$

(2) $LIM_1 - TXT \setminus ECONSERVATIVE\text{-}TXT \neq \emptyset$

The following corollary is an immediate consequence of the latter theorem.

Corollary 10.

(1) $ECONSERVATIVE\text{-}TXT \subset CONSERVATIVE\text{-}TXT$

(2) $ELIM_1 - TXT \subset LIM_1 - TXT$

Finally, a nontrivial modification of the proof technique above may be applied to obtain the desired separation of exact and class preserving language learning with a bounded number of mind changes.

Theorem 11. *For all $k \geq 1$:*

(1) $ELIM_k - TXT \subset LIM_k - TXT$

(2) $ELIM_k - INF \subset LIM_k - INF$

However, some problems remained open. The most intriguing question is whether $LIM_k - TXT \setminus CONSERVATIVE\text{-}TXT \neq \emptyset$. In Lange, Zeugmann and Kapur (1992) we have shown that there is an indexed family $\mathcal{L} \in LIM - TXT \setminus CONSERVATIVE\text{-}TXT$. Nevertheless, the proof given there does not yield any a priori bound for the number of allowed mind changes. On the other hand, a careful analysis of our proof showed that the IIM witnessing $\mathcal{L} \in LIM - TXT$ does not work *semantically finite*. An IIM is said to work *semantically finite* iff for all $L \in \mathcal{L}$, any text t of L the following condition is satisfied: Let j be the hypothesis the sequence $(M(t_x))_{x \in \mathbb{N}+}$ converges to and let z be the least number such that $M(t_z) = j$. Then $L(G_{M(t_y)}) \neq L(G_j)$ for all $y < z$. That means, a semantically finite working IIM is never allowed to reject a guess that is correct for the language to be learnt. As it turns out, this phenomenon is a general one.

Theorem 12. *Let $\mathcal{L}$ be an indexed family, and let $\mathcal{G} = (G_j)_{j \in \mathbb{N}+}$ be a space of hypotheses. If there is an IIM M working semantically finite such that $\mathcal{L} \in LIM - TXT(M)$, then $\mathcal{L} \in CONSERVATIVE\text{-}TXT$.*

Finally, we obtain the following characterization of conservatively working IIMs.

Theorem 13. *Let $\mathcal{L}$ be an indexed family. Then $\mathcal{L} \in$ CONSERVATIVE-TXT iff there is a space $\mathcal{G}$ of hypotheses and an IIM M inferring $\mathcal{L}$ semantically finite in the limit with respect to $\mathcal{G}$.*

4. Characterization Theorems

Characterizations play an important role in that they lead to a deeper insight into the problem how algorithms performing the inference process may work (cf. e.g. Blum and Blum, 1975, Wiehagen, 1977, Angluin, 1980, Zeugmann, 1983, Jain and Sharma, 1989). Moreover, characterizations may help gain a better understanding of the properties objects should have in order to be inferable in the desired sense. A very illustrative example is Angluin's (1980) characterization of those indexed families for which learning in the limit from positive data is possible. In particular, this theorem provides insight into the problem how to deal with overgeneralizations. Our next theorem offers an alternative way to resolve this question. We characterize $LIM_k - TXT$ in terms of recursively generable finite tell-tales. A family of finite sets $(T_j)_{j \in \mathbb{N}^+}$ is said to be recursively generable, iff there is a total effective procedure g which, on input j, generates all elements of T_j and stops. If the computation of $g(j)$ stops and there is no output, then T_j is considered to be empty. Finally, for notational convenience we use $L(\mathcal{G})$ to denote $\{L(G_j) \mid j \in \mathbb{N}^+\}$ for any space $\mathcal{G} = (G_j)_{j \in \mathbb{N}^+}$ of hypotheses.

Theorem 14. *Let $\mathcal{L}$ be an indexed family of recursive languages, and $k \in \mathbb{N}$. Then: $\mathcal{L} \in LIM_k - TXT$ if and only if there is a space of hypotheses $\hat{\mathcal{G}} = (\hat{G}_j)_{j \in \mathbb{N}^+}$, a computable relation $\prec$ over $\mathbb{N}^+$, and a recursively generable family $(\hat{T}_j)_{j \in \mathbb{N}^+}$ of finite and non-empty tell-tale sets such that*

(1) $range(\mathcal{L}) = L(\hat{\mathcal{G}})$.

(2) For all $z \in \mathbb{N}^+$, $\hat{T}_z \subseteq L(\hat{G}_z)$.

(3) For all $L \in \mathcal{L}$, any $z \in \mathbb{N}^+$, if $\hat{T}_z \subseteq L$, $L(\hat{G}_z) \neq L$, then there is a j such that $z \prec j$, $\hat{T}_z \subseteq \hat{T}_j$ and $L(\hat{G}_j) = L$.

(4) For all $L \in \mathcal{L}$, there is no sequence $(z_j)_{j=1,\ldots,m}$ with $m > k+1$ such that $z_j \prec z_{j+1}$ as well as $\hat{T}_{z_j} \subseteq \hat{T}_{z_{j+1}} \subseteq L$, for all $j < m$.

Next we give a characterization of $LIM_k - INF$. For that purpose we define a relation $\prec$ over pairs of sets as follows. Let A, B, C, D be sets. Then $(A, B) \prec (C, D)$ iff $A \subseteq C$, $B \subseteq D$ and $A \subset C$ or $B \subset D$. Note that $\prec$ is computable if A, B, C, D are finitely generable. Now we are ready to state the announced characterization.

Theorem 15. *Let $\mathcal{L}$ be an indexed family of recursive languages and $k \in \mathbb{N}$. Then: $\mathcal{L} \in LIM_k - INF$ iff there are a space of hypotheses $\hat{\mathcal{G}} = (\hat{G}_j)_{j \in \mathbb{N}^+}$ and recursively generable families $(\hat{P}_j)_{j \in \mathbb{N}^+}$ and $(\hat{N}_j)_{j \in \mathbb{N}^+}$ of finite sets such that*

(1) $range(\mathcal{L}) = L(\hat{\mathcal{G}})$

(2) For all $j \in \mathbb{N}^+$, $\emptyset \neq \hat{P}_j \subseteq L(\hat{G}_j)$ and $\hat{N}_j \subseteq co - L(\hat{G}_j)$

(3) For all $L \in \mathcal{L}$ and $z \in \mathbb{N}^+$, if $\hat{P}_z \subseteq L \neq L(\hat{G}_z)$ and $\hat{N}_z \subseteq co - L$, then there is a $j \in \mathbb{N}^+$ such that $(\hat{P}_z, \hat{N}_z) \prec (\hat{P}_j, \hat{N}_j)$ as well as $L = L(\hat{G}_j)$.

(4) For all $L \in \mathcal{L}$ there is no sequence $(\hat{P}_{z_j}, \hat{N}_{z_j})_{j=1,\ldots,m}$ with $m > k+1$ such that $(\hat{P}_{z_j}, \hat{N}_{z_j}) \prec (\hat{P}_{z_{j+1}}, \hat{N}_{z_{j+1}}) \prec (L, co - L)$, for all $j < m$.

5. Conclusions and Open Problems

We have dealt with the learnability of enumerable families $\mathcal{L}$ of uniformly recursive languages in dependence on the number of allowed mind changes. Applying this measure of efficiency we could prove that class preserving learning algorithms are superior to exact learnability. Moreover, in improving Mukouchi's (1992) results we established two new infinite hierarchies. On the other hand, we also proved that even a single additional mind change can neither be compensated by a suitable choice of the space of hypotheses nor by information presentation. Furthermore, we have separated exact and class preserving language learning that avoids overgeneralization. Finally, we presented a complete characterization of language learning in terms of recursively generable finite sets. These theorems resolved the problem that remained open in Mukouchi (1992). Additionally, they offer a new approach to handle overgeneralized hypotheses. However, some problems remained open. It would be very interesting to know how many mind changes are necessary to learn indexed families that cannot be inferred by class preserving conservatively working IIMs.

Acknowledgement

The first author has been supported by the German Ministry for Research and Technology (BMFT) under grant no. 01 IW 101.

We gratefully acknowledge many valuable comments on the preparation of the paper by Yasuhito Mukouchi.

6. References

ANGLUIN, D. (1980), Inductive inference of formal languages from positive data, *Inf. and Control* 45, 117 - 135.

ANGLUIN, D., AND SMITH, C.H. (1987), Formal inductive inference, *in* "Encyclopedia of Artificial Intelligence" (St.C. Shapiro, Ed.), Vol. 1, pp. 409 - 418, Wiley-Interscience Publication, New York.

BARZDIN, YA.M., AND FREIVALDS, R.V. (1972), On the prediction of general recursive functions, *Sov. Math. Dokl.* 13, 1224 - 1228.

BLUM, L., AND BLUM, M. (1975), Toward a mathematical theory of inductive inference, *Inf. and Control* 28, 122 - 155

CASE, J. (1988), The power of vacillation, *in* "Proc. 1st Workshop on Computational Learning Theory," (D. Haussler and L. Pitt, Eds.), pp. 196 -205, Morgan Kaufmann Publishers Inc.

CASE, J., AND LYNES, C. (1982), Machine inductive inference and language identification, in "Proc. Automata, Languages and Programming, 9th Colloquium," (M. Nielsen and E.M. Schmidt, Eds.), Lecture Notes in Computer Science Vol. 140, pp. 107 - 115, Springer-Verlag, Berlin.

CASE, J., AND SMITH, C. (1983), Comparison of identification criteria for machine inductive inference, *Theoretical Computer Science* 25, 193 - 220.

FULK, M.(1990), Prudence and other restrictions in formal language learning, *Inf. and Computation* 85, 1 - 11.

GASARCH, W.I., AND VELAUTHAPILLAI, M. (1992), Asking questions versus verifiability, in "Proc. 3rd International Workshop on Analogical and Inductive Inference," (K.P. Jantke, ed.) Lecture Notes in Artificial Intelligence Vol. 642, pp. 197 - 213, Springer-Verlag, Berlin.

GOLD, E.M. (1967), Language Identification in the Limit, *Inf. and Control* 10, 447 - 474.

JAIN, S., AND SHARMA, A. (1989), Recursion theoretic characterizations of language learning, Univ. of Rochester, Dept. of Comp. Sci., TR 281.

KAPUR, S., AND BILARDI, G. (1992), Language learning without overgeneralization, in "Proc. 9th Annual Symposium on Theoretical Aspects of Computer Science," (A. Finkel and M. Jantzen, Eds.), Lecture Notes in Computer Science Vol. 577, pp. 245 - 256, Springer-Verlag, Berlin.

LANGE, S., AND ZEUGMANN, T. (1992), Types of monotonic language learning and their characterization, in "Proc. 5th Annual ACM Workshop on Computational Learning Theory," pp. 377 - 390, ACM Press.

LANGE, S.,ZEUGMANN, T., AND KAPUR, S. (1992), Class preserving monotonic language learning, GOSLER–Report 14/92, FB Mathematik und Informatik, TH Leipzig.

MUKOUCHI, Y. (1992), Inductive Inference with Bounded Mind Changes, in Proc. "Algorithmic Learning Theory," October 1992, Tokyo, Japan, JSAI.

OSHERSON, D., STOB, M., AND WEINSTEIN, S. (1986), "Systems that Learn, An Introduction to Learning Theory for Cognitive and Computer Scientists," MIT-Press, Cambridge, Massachusetts.

SHINOHARA, T. (1990), Inductive Inference from Positive Data is Powerful, in "Proc. 3rd Annual Workshop on Computational Learning Theory," (M. Fulk and J. Case, Eds.), pp. 97 - 110, Morgan Kaufmann Publishers Inc.

WIEHAGEN, R. (1977), Identification of formal languages, in "Proc. Mathematical Foundations of Computer Science," (J. Gruska, Ed.), Lecture Notes in Computer Science Vol. 53, pp. 571 - 579, Springer-Verlag, Berlin.

WIEHAGEN, R., FREIVALDS, R., AND KINBER, B. (1984), On the power of probabilistic strategies in inductive inference, *Theoretical Computer Science* 28, 111 - 133.

ZEUGMANN, T. (1983), A–posteriori characterizations in inductive inference of recursive functions, *J. of Inf. Processing and Cybernetics (EIK)* 19, 559 - 594.

Efficient Sharing of Many Secrets

Carlo Blundo, Alfredo De Santis, and Ugo Vaccaro

Dipartimento di Informatica ed Applicazioni
Università di Salerno, 84081 Baronissi (SA), Italy

Abstract

A multi-secret sharing scheme is a protocol to distribute n secrets $s_1, \ldots, s_n$ among a set of participants $\mathcal{P}$ in such a way that: 1) any non-qualified subset of participants $A \subseteq \mathcal{P}$ has absolutely no information on the secrets; 2) any qualified subset can recover all the secrets, but 3) any non-qualified subset knowing the value of a number of secrets might have some information on other secrets.

In this paper we lay foundations for a general theory of multi-secret sharing schemes by using the entropy approach, as done in [4] and [6] to analyze single-secret sharing schemes. We prove lower bounds on the size of information held by each participant in any multi-secret sharing scheme. We provide an optimal protocol for multi-secret sharing schemes on a particular access structure, where the access structure specifies the subsets of participants qualified to reconstruct the secret.

1 Introduction

A secret sharing scheme is a technique to share a secret s among a set $\mathcal{P}$ of participants in such a way that only subsets qualified to know the secret, pooling together their information, can reconstruct the secret value; but subsets of participants that are not enabled to recover the secret have no information on it. Secret sharing schemes were introduced by Shamir [13] and Blakley [2]. They analyzed the case when only subsets A of $\mathcal{P}$ of cardinality $|A| \geq t$, for a fixed integer t, can reconstruct the secret. These schemes are called (t, w) threshold schemes, where $w = |\mathcal{P}|$. For a general description of secret sharing schemes the reader can consult the recent surveys by Stinson [15] and Simmons [14].

There are several situations in which more than one secret is to be shared among participants. As an example, consider the following situation, proposed by Simmons [14]: There is a missile battery and not all of the missiles have the same launch enable code. The problem is to devise a scheme which will allow any one, or any selected subset, of the launch enable codes to be activated in this scheme. What is needed is an algorithm such that the same pieces of private information could be used to recover different secrets. This problem could be trivially solved by realizing different secret sharing schemes, one for each of the launch enable codes, but this solution is clearly unacceptable since each participant should remember too much information since the size of shares distributed with this technique will be of relevant size. Moreover, the algorithms used to realize the scheme and to reconstruct the secrets will be inefficient.

Another scenario in which the sharing of many secrets is importants was considered by Franklin and Yung [9]. They investigated the communication complexity of unconditionally secure multi–party computation, and its relations with various fault–tolerance models. They presented a general technique for parallelizing non–cryptographic computation protocols, at a small cost in fault–tolerance. Their technique replaces polynomial–based (single) secret sharing with a technique allowing multiple secrets to be hidden in a single polynomial. The technique applies to all of the protocols for secure computation which use polynomial–based threshold schemes and applies to all fault–tolerance models. Franklin and Yung [9] considered also the case of dependent secrets so the size of information distributed to any participant is less than the information distributed with independent schemes.

Other papers that have considered the problem of sharing many secrets are [10] and [12].

Although many researchers have already considered the issue of sharing multiple secrets, it lacks a general theory that takes into account both the "level of security" and the degrees of dependence among the secrets to be shared.

Informally a multi-secret sharing scheme is a protocol to distribute n secrets $s_1, \ldots, s_n$ among a set of participants $\mathcal{P}$ in such a way that: 1) any non-qualified subset of participants $A \subseteq \mathcal{P}$ has absolutely no information on the secrets; 2) any qualified subset can recover all the secrets, but 3) any non-qualified subset knowing the value of a number of secrets might have some information on other secrets.

In this paper we lay foundations for a general theory of multi-secret sharing schemes by using the entropy approach, as done in [4] and [6] to analyze single-secret sharing schemes. We prove lower bounds on the size of information held by each participant in any multi-secret sharing scheme. We provide an optimal protocol for multi-secret sharing schemes on a particular access structure, where the access structure specifies the subsets of participants qualified to reconstruct the secret. Finally, we prove a lower bound on the size of information held by some participants in an access structure of particular relevance. This access structure $\mathcal{AS}$ is the closure of the set $\{P_1P_2, P_2P_3, P_3P_4\}$. Several researchers have studied this access structure, most notably Benaloh and Leichter [1] and Brickell and Stinson [5]. The relevance of such structure $\mathcal{AS}$ lies in the fact that it represents the first structure for which a "non-trivial" lower bound on the size of shares held by participants could be proved. The study of $\mathcal{AS}$ culminated in the paper [6] by Capocelli, De Santis, Gargano, and Vaccaro who found the optimal lower bound.

Another kind of multi-secret sharing schemes we will consider are (c, t, w) ramp schemes. A (c, t, w) ramp scheme is a protocol to distribute a secret s among a set $\mathcal{P}$ of w participants in such a way that sets of participants of cardinality greater than or equal to t can reconstruct the secret s; sets of participants of cardinality less than or equal to c have no information on s; whereas sets of participants of cardinality greater than c and less than t might have "some" information on s. Note that if $t = c + 1$ then a (c, t, w) ramp scheme is a (t, w) threshold scheme.

The (c, t, w) ramp schemes are useful in the protocols for secure computation in fault–tolerant models. In fact the protocol proposed by Franklin and Yung [9] can be viewed as a ramp scheme. (c, t, w) ramp schemes are also useful in those practical situations in which it is not possible to give to participants all the secret information required to preserve perfect security since they allow to achieve a certain amount of data compression at the cost of some degradation in the security (see [12]). Our approach allows to formally quantify this trade-off. In this paper we formally define the (c, t, w) ramp schemes by using the entropy approach and we give a lower bound on the size of information held by each participant. Our lower bound proves that the scheme proposed by Franklin and Yung [9] and McEliece and Sarwate [12] are optimal with respect to the information given to each participant.

The paper is organized as follows. In Section 2 we formally define multi-secret sharing schemes. In Subsection 2.2 we prove a general lower bound on the information distributed to any participant in multi–secret sharing schemes. In Subsection 2.3 we describe an optimal protocol for multi–secret sharing schemes for a particular access structure; in Section 3 we first formally define (c, t, w) ramp schemes, then we prove a general lower bound on the information distributed to each user.

2   Multi–Secret Sharing Schemes

A secret sharing scheme permits a secret to be shared among a set of participants in such a way that only qualified subsets of them can recover the secret, but any non-qualified subset has absolutely no information on the secret. An access structure $\mathcal{A}$ is the set of all subsets of $\mathcal{P}$ that can recover the secret. In this section we consider the case in which we want to share several secrets and not just one. A multi–secret sharing scheme permits some secrets to be shared among a set of participants in such a way that only qualified subsets of them can recover *all* the secrets; any non-qualified subset has absolutely no information on *any* secret, but any non-qualified subset knowing some secrets might have some information on other secrets.

Definition 2.1 *Let $\mathcal{P}$ be a set of participants, a monotone access structure $\mathcal{A}$ on $\mathcal{P}$ is a subset $\mathcal{A} \subseteq 2^{\mathcal{P}}$, such that*

$$A \in \mathcal{A}, A \subseteq A' \subseteq \mathcal{P} \Rightarrow A' \in \mathcal{A}.$$

Definition 2.2 *Let $\mathcal{P}$ a set of participants and $A \subseteq 2^{\mathcal{P}}$. The closure of $\mathcal{A}$, $cl(\mathcal{A})$, is the set*

$$cl(\mathcal{A}) = \{C | B \in \mathcal{A} \text{ and } B \subseteq C \subseteq \mathcal{P}\}.$$

For a monotone access structure $\mathcal{A}$ we have $\mathcal{A} = cl(\mathcal{A})$.

2.1   The Model

The first model of multi-secret sharing that one could naturally consider is the following. There are n access structures $\mathcal{A}_1, \ldots, \mathcal{A}_n \subseteq 2^{\mathcal{P}}$ and n secrets $s_1, \ldots s_n$;

the dealer has to distribute each s_i in the access structure $\mathcal{A}_i$ under the usual security conditions, that is, any qualified subset in $\mathcal{A}_i$ can recover s_i and any non-qualified subset has absolutely no information on s_i. It can be shown that if the secrets are statistically dependent, then no such sharing is possible. Indeed, if a set of participants $X \in \mathcal{A}_1$ reconstructs s_1, then it gains also some information on s_2 (being s_1 and s_2 related) even though $X \notin \mathcal{A}_2$. On the other hand, if the secrets are unrelated, a multi-secret sharing scheme for $s_1, \ldots s_n$ can be optimally realized (with respect to the size of the shares) by distributing each s_i by means of a single secret sharing scheme in $\mathcal{A}_i$. Therefore, in the rest of this paper we will consider the more intersting model of sharing different and arbitrarily related secrets in the same access structure.

Let $S_1, \ldots, S_n$ be the sets from which our secrets are chosen, let a secret sharing scheme for secrets in $S_1 \times \cdots \times S_n$ be fixed, and let $\{p(s_1, \ldots, s_n)\}_{(s_1, \ldots, s_n) \in S_1 \times \cdots \times S_n}$ be a probability distribution on $S_1 \times \cdots \times S_n$. For any participant $P \in \mathcal{P}$, let us denote by $K(P)$ the set of all possible shares given to participant P. Given a set of participants $A = \{P_{i_1}, \ldots, P_{i_r}\} \subset \mathcal{P}$, where $i_1 < i_2 < \ldots < i_r$, denote by $K(A)$ the set $K(P_{i_1}) \times \cdots \times K(P_{i_r})$. A secret sharing scheme for secrets in $S_1 \times \cdots \times S_n$ and the probability distribution $\{p(s_1, \ldots, s_n)\}_{(s_1, \ldots, s_n) \in S_1 \times \cdots \times S_n}$ naturally induce a probability distribution on S_i, for $i = 1, 2, \ldots, n$, denoted by $\{p_{S_i}(s)\}_{s \in S_i}$, and a probability distribution on $K(A)$, for any $A \subseteq \mathcal{P}$. Denote such probability distribution by $\{p_{K(A)}(a)\}_{a \in K(A)}$. Finally, denote by $H(S_i)$ the entropy of $\{p_{S_i}(s)\}_{s \in S_i}$, for $i = 1, 2, \ldots, n$, and by $H(A)$ the entropy of $\{p_{K(A)}(a)\}_{a \in K(A)}$, for any $A \subseteq \mathcal{P}$.

In terms of the probability distribution on the secrets and on the shares given to participants, we say that a multi–secret sharing scheme is a *perfect* multi–secret sharing scheme, or simply a multi–secret sharing scheme, for the monotone access structure $\mathcal{A} \subseteq 2^{\mathcal{P}}$ if

1. *Any subset $A \subseteq \mathcal{P}$ of participants not enabled to recover any secret has no information on any secret value:*
   Formally, if $A \notin \mathcal{A}$ then for all $s_i \in S_i$, $i = 1, \ldots, n$, and for all $a \in K(A)$ it holds $p(s_i|a) = p_{S_i}(s_i)$ for $i = 1, \ldots, n$.

2. *Any subset $A \subseteq \mathcal{P}$ of participants enabled to recover all secrets can compute all the secrets:*
   Formally, if $A \in \mathcal{A}$ then for all $a \in K(A)$ with $p_{K(A)}(a) > 0$ and for all $i = 1, \ldots, n$ a unique secret $s_i \in S_i$ exists such that $p(s_i|a) = 1$,

3. *Any subset $A \subseteq \mathcal{P}$ of participants not enabled to recover all secrets, knowing the value of a number of secrets might determine "some" information on other secrets.*
   We will formally define this property in the following.

Notice that property 1. means that the probability that the secret is equal to s_i, $i = 1, \ldots, n$, given that the shares held by $A \notin \mathcal{A}$ are a, is the same of the *a priori* probability that the secret is s_i. Therefore, no amount of knowledge of shares of participants not enabled to reconstruct the secrets enables a Bayesian opponent to modify an *a priori* guess regarding which the secrets are. Property 2. means that the value of the shares held by $A \in \mathcal{A}$ uniquely determines the secrets $s_i \in S_i$, $i = 1, \ldots, n$. Property 3. means that the value of the shares held by $A \notin \mathcal{A}$ and the value of some secrets can reveal "some" information on another secret.

Following the approach of [10], [11], [6], and [4] we can restate above conditions 1., 2. and formalize condition 3. using the *entropy* function (see [7] and [8] for all properties of the entropy). We define a multi–secret sharing scheme as follows.

Definition 2.3 *Let $\mathcal{A}$ be an access structure on a set $\mathcal{P}$ of participants. A multi–secret sharing scheme is a sharing of the secrets in $S_1, \ldots, S_n$ among participants in $\mathcal{P}$ such that*

1′. *Any non-qualified subset has absolutely no information on any secret.*
   Formally, for all $A \notin \mathcal{A}$ and for $i = 1, \ldots, n$ it holds $H(S_i|A) = H(S_i)$.

2′. *Any qualified subset can reconstruct all the secrets.*
   Formally, for all $A \in \mathcal{A}$ and for $i = 1, \ldots, n$ it holds $H(S_i|A) = 0$.

3′. *Any non-qualified subset knowing the value of a number of secrets might determine "some" information on other secrets.*
   Formally, there are $0 \le \alpha_{n-1} \le \alpha_{n-2} \cdots \le \alpha_1 \le 1$ such that for all $A \notin \mathcal{A}$ and $i_1, \ldots, i_j, i$ where $i \notin \{i_1, \ldots i_j\}$, it holds $H(S_i|S_{i_1} \ldots S_{i_j} A) = \alpha_j H(S_i)$.

Notice that $H(S_i|A) = 0$ means that each set of values of the shares in A corresponds to a unique value of the secret $s_i \in S_i$. In fact, by definition, $H(S_i|A) = 0$ is equivalent to the fact that for all $a \in K(A)$ with $p_{K(A)}(a) > 0$ exists $s_i \in S_i$ such that $p(s_i|a) = 1$. Moreover, $H(S_i|A) = H(S_i)$ is equivalent to state that the random variable S_i and A are statistically independent, i.e., for all $a \in K(A)$ for all $s_i \in S_i$, $p(s_i|a) = p_{S_i}(s_i)$ and therefore the knowledge of a gives no information about the secret. The property $H(S_i|S_{i_1} \ldots S_{i_j} A) = \alpha_j H(S_i)$ means that any not-qualified subset knowing some secret might reduce its uncertain on other secrets, that is, it can know part of other secrets.

To illustrate how to realize a multi–secret sharing scheme, consider the following example. Let $\mathcal{P} = \{P_1, P_2\}$ be the set of participants and $\mathcal{A} = \{P_1 P_2\}$ be the access structure. Suppose that we want to share two independent secrets s_1 and s_2, belonging to $GF(4)$, each consisting of two uniformly chosen bits, in such a way that

1. $H(S_1|P_1 P_2) = H(S_2|P_1 P_2) = 0$.

2. $H(S_1|P_1) = H(S_1|P_2) = H(S_1)$ and $H(S_2|P_1) = H(S_2|P_2) = H(S_2)$.

3. $H(S_1|S_2\ P_1) = H(S_1|S_2\ P_2) = 0.5H(S_1)$ and $H(S_2|S_1\ P_1) = H(S_2|S_1\ P_2) = 0.5H(S_2)$.

Let the operator $\otimes$ denote the bit-wise xor. A protocol realizing this multi–secret sharing is the following:

Dealer-Algorithm

Generation Phase

Uniformly choose a 3-bit string $\mathbf{x} = x_1 x_2 x_3$.

Compute the 3-bits string $\mathbf{y} = y_1 y_2 y_3$ in such a way that

$s_1 = x_1 x_2 \otimes y_1 y_3$ and $s_2 = x_1 x_3 \otimes y_2 y_3$.

Distribution Phase

Give the string $\mathbf{x}$ to participant P_1.

Give the string $\mathbf{y}$ to participant P_2.

Participant-Algorithm

Recovering Phase

Participants P_1, P_2 recover the secret s_1 by calculating $x_1 x_2 \otimes y_1 y_3$.

Participants P_1, P_2 recover the secret s_2 by calculating $x_1 x_3 \otimes y_2 y_3$.

It is easy to see that previous protocol realizes the scheme previously proposed. Properties 1 and 2 are immediately verified. If the participant P_1 knows the secret s_1 then it can compute the values y_2 and y_3. Since P_1 knows y_3 then it can compute one bit of the secret s_2 and, thus, its uncertainty on s_2 is one more bit and the Property 3 holds.

2.2 Lower Bounds on the Size of the Shares

A share is the information distributed to each participant in the scheme used to reconstruct the secret values. An important issue in the implementation of multi-secret sharing schemes as well as secret sharing schemes is the size of the shares. In fact the security of a system degrades as the amount of information that must keep secret grows. The size of the share given to participant $P \in \mathcal{P}$ is the number of bits needed to represent the elements of $K(P)$, therefore it is equal to $\log |K(P)|$. In this section we prove a lower bound on the size of shares for a multi-secret sharing scheme of n secrets, $s_1, \ldots, s_n$. Next theorem states a lower bound on the size of information held by each participant in the scheme.

Theorem 2.1 *Let $\mathcal{A}$ be an access structure. If $X \cup Y \in \mathcal{A}$ and $Y \notin \mathcal{A}$ then there exist n values $\alpha_0, \cdots, \alpha_{n-1}$, with $0 \leq \alpha_{n-1} \leq \alpha_{n-2} \cdots \leq \alpha_1 \leq \alpha_0 = 1$, such that*

$$H(X|Y) = \sum_{j=0}^{n-1} \alpha_j H(S_{j+1}) + H(X|Y \, S_1 \ldots S_n).$$

Next corollary is an immediate consequence of the previous theorem.

Corollary 2.1 *Let A be an access structure on a set P of participants. For any participant $P \in \mathcal{P}$ it holds*

$$H(P) \geq \sum_{j=0}^{n-1} \alpha_j H(S_{j+1})$$

where $0 \leq \alpha_{n-1} \leq \alpha_{n-2} \cdots \leq \alpha_1 \leq \alpha_0 = 1$.

If the secrets are uniformly chosen, that is, $H(S_i) = \log |S_i|$, for $i = 1, \ldots, n$, then we can bound the size of the shares distributed to participants.

Theorem 2.2 *If each secret s_i is uniformly chosen in S_i, for $i = 1, \ldots, n$ and there exist n values $0 \leq \alpha_{n-1} \leq \alpha_{n-2} \cdots \leq \alpha_1 \leq \alpha_0 = 1$ such that $H(S_i|S_{i_1} \ldots S_{i_j} P) = \alpha_j H(S_i)$ then*

$$\log |K(P)| \geq \sum_{j=0}^{n-1} \log |S_{j+1}|^{\alpha_j}$$

for any participant $P \in \mathcal{P}$.

Lemma 2.1 *Let consider an access structure A. If $X \cup Y \notin A$ then*

$$H(X|Y) = H(X|Y \ S_1 \ldots S_n).$$

Next two lemmas characterize the size of the sets where the secrets are chosen. If a number $\alpha_j < 1$ exists such that $H(S_i|S_{i_1} \ldots S_{i_j} X) = \alpha_j H(S_i)$ then all the secrets must be chosen from sets of equal cardinality; otherwise, if all α_j are equal to 1 then each secret can be chosen independently from each other, so all secrets can be chosen from sets of different size.

Lemma 2.2 *Let A be an access structure. If a set $X \notin A$ and a value $\alpha_j < 1$ exist, such that $H(S_i|S_{i_1} \ldots S_{i_j} X) = \alpha_j H(S_i)$, for all $i_1, \ldots, i_j$ and $i \notin \{i_1, \ldots, i_j\}$, then $H(S_i) = H(S_k)$ for $i \neq k$.*

Recalling that $H(X \ Y) = H(X) + H(Y)$ if and only if X and Y are statistically independent, next lemma states that if the knowledge of X and $S_{i_1} \ldots S_{i_j}$, for some j, gives no information whatsoever on S_i then secrets $s_1, \ldots, s_n$ must be statistically independent.

Lemma 2.3 *Let A be an access structure. If $H(S_i|S_{i_1} \ldots S_{i_j} X) = H(S_i)$, for all $i_1, \ldots, i_j$ and $i \notin \{i_1, \ldots, i_j\}$, then*

$$H(S_1 \ldots S_n) = \sum_{i=1}^{n} H(S_i).$$

Now we present a lower bound on the size of the information held by two participants, P_2 and P_3 in a well known access structure (see [1], [5], and [6]). Let $\mathcal{AS}$ be the access structure on the set of participants $\mathcal{P} = \{P_1, P_2, P_3, P_4\}$ defined as $\mathcal{AS} = cl\{P_1P_2, P_2P_3, P_3P_4\}$. Next theorem is a generalization of Theorem 4.1 [6] when we want to share n secrets for the access structure $\mathcal{AS}$.

Theorem 2.3 *Any multi–secret sharing scheme of n secrets in $S_1, \ldots, S_n$ for $\mathcal{AS}$ satisfies*

$$H(P_2P_3) \geq 3 \sum_{j=0}^{n-1} \alpha_j H(S_{j+1}).$$

2.3 An Optimal Protocol for Multi–Secret Sharing Schemes

In this subsection we present an optimal protocol for a simple access structure. This access structure $\mathcal{A}$ is based on two participants $\mathcal{P} = \{P_1, P_2\}$ and $\mathcal{A} = \{P_1P_2\}$.

Suppose we want to share three uniformly chosen 4-bit secrets s_1, s_2, and s_3 in such a way that

1. $H(S_i|P_1P_2) = 0$, for $i = 1, 2, 3$.

2. $H(S_i|P_1) = H(S_i|P_2) = H(S_i)$, for $i = 1, 2, 3$.

3.1 $H(S_i|S_j\ P_1) = H(S_i|S_j\ P_2) = 0.5H(S_i)$, for $i = 1, 2, 3$, and $j \in \{1, 2, 3\} \setminus \{i\}$.

3.2 $H(S_i|S_j\ S_l\ P_1) = H(S_i|S_j\ S_l\ P_2) = 0.25H(S_i)$, for $i = 1, 2, 3$, and $j, l \in \{1, 2, 3\} \setminus \{i\}$ with $j \neq l$.

From Corollary 2.1 and Lemma 2.2 it follows that $H(P_1) \geq 1.75H(S_i)$ and $H(P_2) \geq 1.75H(S_i)$, for $i = 1, 2, 3$. Next protocol distributes the minimum information possible, that is we have $H(P_1) = H(P_2) = 1.75H(S_i)$. The optimal protocol is the following:

Dealer-Algorithm

Generation Phase

Uniformly choose a 7-bit string $\mathbf{x} = x_1 x_2 \ldots x_7$.

Compute a 7-bit string $\mathbf{y} = y_1 y_2 \ldots y_7$ such that $s_1 = x_1 x_2 x_3 x_4 \otimes y_4 y_3 y_2 y_1$, $s_2 = x_1 x_2 x_5 x_6 \otimes y_1 y_2 y_5 y_6$, and $s_3 = x_2 x_3 x_6 x_7 \otimes y_7 y_6 y_2 y_3$.

Distribution Phase

Give the string $\mathbf{x}$ to participant P_1.

Give the string $\mathbf{y}$ to participant P_2.

Participant-Algorithm

Recovering Phase
    Participants P_1, P_2 recover the secret s_1 by calculating $x_1 x_2 x_3 x_4 \otimes y_4 y_3 y_2 y_1$.
    Participants P_1, P_2 recover the secret s_2 by calculating $x_1 x_2 x_5 x_6 \otimes y_1 y_2 y_5 y_6$.
    Participants P_1, P_2 recover the secret S_3 by calculating $x_2 x_3 x_6 x_7 \otimes y_7 y_6 y_2 y_3$.

It is easy to see that the previous protocol is optimal and that it realizes the scheme previously proposed.

3 (c, t, w) Ramp Schemes

In this section we present (c, t, w) ramp schemes. A (c, t, w) ramp scheme is a protocol to distribute a secret s among a set $\mathcal{P}$ of w participants in such a way that sets of participants of cardinality greater than or equal to t can reconstruct the secret s, sets of participants of cardinality less than or equal to c have no information on s, whereas sets of participants of cardinality greater than c and less than t might have "some" information on s. Note that if $t = c + 1$ then the (c, t, w) ramp scheme is a (t, w) threshold scheme. Formally, a (c, t, w) ramp scheme can be defined as follows.

A (c, t, w) ramp scheme, where $1 \leq c < t \leq w$, is a sharing of secrets among participants in $\mathcal{P}$, $|\mathcal{P}| = w$, such that

1. *Any set of at least t participants can reconstruct the secret.*
   Formally, for all $A \subseteq \mathcal{P}$ with $|A| \geq t$, it holds $H(S|A) = 0$.

2. *Any set of at most c participants has absolutely no information on the secret.*
   Formally, for all $A \subseteq \mathcal{P}$ with $|A| \leq c$, it holds $H(S|A) = H(S)$.

(c, t, w) ramp schemes are useful in distributed protocols for secure computation in the fault–tolerance model. Franklin and Yung [9] considered a multi-secret sharing scheme as the building block of a general compilation technique for parallelizing secure protocols. They introduced (c, t, k, w)-multi-secret sharing schemes, which are secret sharing schemes to distribute k secrets to w participants in such a way that: 1) any subset of at least t participants can recover all k secrets; 2) any subset of at most c participants can deduce anything about the k secrets. (c, t, k, w)-multi-secret sharing schemes can be viewed as (c, t, w) ramp schemes, by considering all the k secrets as a unique "super–secret". Franklin and Yung gives a construction of a multi-secret scheme by generalizing Shamir's scheme [13].

Another example of (c, t, w) ramp schemes can be found in [12]. More precisely, the authors of [12] considered the problem of sharing a given secret s by giving to participants share of size strictly smaller than the size of the secret. This requirement directly implies that absolute security is not possible, that is, sets of participants not enabled to reconstruct the secret still could gain some information on it. Their solution is based on Reed–Solomon codes and our next Theorem 3.4

shows that their algorithm is optimal with respect to the size of information given to participants.

Next theorems give lower bounds on the size of information held by any group of $t - c$ participants in a (c, t, w) ramp scheme.

Theorem 3.1 *In a (c, t, w) ramp scheme the entropy of any $t - c$ participants $P_{i_1} P_{i_2} \cdots P_{i_{t-c}}$ satisfies*

$$H(P_{i_1} P_{i_2} \cdots P_{i_{t-c}}) \geq H(S).$$

Proof: Let $X_A, X_B \subseteq \mathcal{P}$ be two disjoint sets of participants of size $|X_B| \leq c$ and $|X_A| \geq t - |X_B|$. The mutual information $I(X_A; S | X_B)$ can be written either as $H(X_A | X_B) - H(X_A | S X_B)$ or as $H(S | X_B) - H(S | X_A X_B)$. Since $H(S | X_A X_B) = 0$ and $H(S | X_B) = H(S)$, it follows

$$H(X_A | X_B) = H(S) + H(X_A | S X_B)$$

Since $|X_A| \geq t - c$, the theorem follows.   □

Next theorem specializes the lower bound on the size of shares held by participants, in case the secret is chosen under an uniform probability distribution.

Theorem 3.2 *In any (c, t, w) ramp scheme the sum of the size of the shares given to any group of $t - c$ participants is at least $\log |S|$.*

It is worth pointing out that one cannot prove a bound like $H(P) \geq H(S)/(t-c)$ for any $P \in \mathcal{P}$. Indeed, let T be a (c, t, w) ramp scheme for participants $P_1, P_2, \cdots, P_w$, and consider the $(c, t+1, w+1)$ ramp scheme obtained by adding an extra participant P_{w+1} giving him nothing as share. Then, the bound $H(P_{i_1} P_{i_2} \cdots P_{i_{t-c}} P_{w+1}) \geq H(S)$, where $1 \leq i_1, i_2, \cdots, i_{t-c} < w + 1$, holds but $H(P_{w+1}) = 0$. In general, we cannot prove a bound like $H(P_{i_1} P_{i_2} \cdots P_{i_{t-c-1}}) > 0$ for any set of participants $P_{i_1} P_{i_2} \cdots P_{i_{t-c-1}}$ in a (c, t, w) ramp scheme. Indeed, consider a $(c + 1, w - (t - c - 1))$ threshold scheme for participants $P_1, P_2, \cdots, P_{w-(t-c-1)}$ and add participants $P_{w-t+c}, \cdots, P_w$ giving them nothing as share. The resulting scheme is a (c, t, w) ramp scheme and $H(P_{w-t+c}, \cdots, P_w) = 0$. Therefore, the result stated by Theorem 3.1 is best possible for the number of participants: there can be a set of $t - c - 1$ participants with entropy 0. Essentially, this is due to the fact that the definition says nothing on sets of participants of size greater than c but less than t. They could reconstruct the entire secret or part of it. A natural requirement is that the information that sets of participants have on the secret grows linearly with the size of the set from c to t. Next, we analyze (c, t, w) *linear ramp schemes*, that is (c, t, w) ramp schemes which meets the following additional property:

3. *Any set of more than c and less than t participants might have "some" information on the secret S.*
   Formally, for all $A \subseteq \mathcal{P}$ with $c < |A| < t$, it holds $H(S|A) = \frac{t - |A|}{t - c} H(S)$.

Next theorem gives a bound on the entropy of the share held by any participant in a linear ramp scheme.

Theorem 3.3 *In any (c, t, w) linear ramp scheme the entropy of any participant $P \in \mathcal{P}$ satisfies*

$$H(P) \geq \frac{H(S)}{t - c}.$$

If the secret is uniformly distributed in S, Theorem 3.3 gives the following lower bound on the size of shares held by participants in the scheme.

Theorem 3.4 *If the secret is uniformly chosen in S, then in any (c, t, n) linear ramp scheme the size of the shares given to any participant $P \in \mathcal{P}$ satisfies*

$$\log |K(P)| \geq \frac{\log |S|}{t - c}.$$

From Theorem 3.4 it follows that the protocols of Franklin and Yung [9] and of McEliece and Sarwate [12] are optimal with respect to the size of the shares given to participants.

Acknowledgements.

We are grateful to Giuseppe Persiano for helpful discussions.

References

[1] J. Benaloh and J. Leichter, *Generalized Secret Sharing and Monotone Functions*, Lecture Notes in Computer Science, 403:27–35, 1990.

[2] G. R. Blakley, *Safeguarding Cryptographic Keys*, AFIPS Conference Proceedings, 48:313–317, 1979.

[3] C. Blundo, A. De Santis, D. R. Stinson, and U. Vaccaro, *Graph Decomposition and Secret Sharing Schemes*, in "Advances in Cryptology - EUROCRYPT 92", Ed. R. Rueppel, "Lecture Notes in Computer Science", Springer-Verlag, (to appear).

[4] C. Blundo, A. De Santis, L. Gargano, and U. Vaccaro, *On the Information Rate of Secret Sharing Schemes*, in "Advances in Cryptology - CRYPTO 92", Ed. E. Brickell, "Lecture Notes in Computer Science", Springer-Verlag, (to appear).

[5] E. F. Brickell and D. R. Stinson, *Some Improved Bounds on the Information Rate of Perfect Secret Sharing Schemes*, in "Advances in Cryptology - CRYPTO 90", "Lecture Notes in Computer Science", Springer-Verlag. To appear in J. Cryptology.

[6] R. M. Capocelli, A. De Santis, L. Gargano, and U. Vaccaro, *On the Size of Shares for Secret Sharing Schemes*, in "Advances in Cryptology - CRYPTO 91", Ed. J. Feigenbaum, vol. 576 of "Lecture Notes in Computer Science", Springer-Verlag, pp. 101–113. To appear in J. Cryptology.

[7] I. Csiszár and J. Körner, *Information Theory. Coding theorems for discrete memoryless systems*, Academic Press, 1981.

[8] R. G. Gallager, *Information Theory and Reliable Communications*, John Wiley & Sons, New York, NY, 1968.

[9] M. Franklin and M. Yung, *Communication Complexity of Secure Computation*, STOC 1992, pp. 699–710.

[10] E. D. Karnin, J. W. Greene, and M. E. Hellman, *On Secret Sharing Systems*, IEEE Trans. on Inform. Theory, vol. IT-29, no. 1, Jan. 1983, pp. 35-41.

[11] S. C. Kothari, *Generalized Linear Threshold Schemes*, in "Advances in Cryptology - CRYPTO 84", G. R. Blakley and D. Chaum Eds., vol. 196 of "Lecture Notes in Computer Science", Springer-Verlag, pp. 231–241.

[12] R. J. McEliece and D. Sarwate, *On Sharing Secrets and Reed–Solomon Codes*, Communications of the ACM, vol. 24, n. 9, pp. 583–584, September 1981.

[13] A. Shamir, *How to Share a Secret*, Commun. of the ACM, 22:612-613, 1979.

[14] G. J. Simmons, *An Introduction to Shared Secret and/or Shared Control Schemes and Their Application*, Contemporary Cryptology, IEEE Press, pp. 441–497, 1991.

[15] D. R. Stinson, *An Explication of Secret Sharing Schemes*, Technical Report UNL-CSE-92-004, Department of Computer Science and Engineering, University of Nebraska, February 1992. To appear in Codes, Design and Cryptography.

The KIV System
A Tool for Formal Program Development

Rainer Drexler, Wolfgang Reif, Gerhard Schellhorn, Kurt Stenzel, Werner Stephan,
Andreas Wolpers
Email: *surname*@ira.uka.de

Institut for Logic, Complexity and Deductive Systems
University of Karlsruhe
Postfach 6980
W–7500 Karlsruhe 1
Germany

1 Formal Program Development

In order to keep the tasks of specification, programming and verification in manageable orders of magnitude, a system for formal development should support the *structuring* of the development process.

This process starts with a horizontally structured (top-level) specification. While it is generally agreed that a formal specification has a significant value in itself, it is by no means a guarantee that the development process will end up with an implemented software system, let alone a correct one. A system for formal development must therefore also support the implementation process using a hierarchy of increasingly concrete intermediate specifications. Refinement steps may contain pieces of code of some suitable programmung language. The notion of correctness (of refinement steps) must be complemented by a program logic powerful enough to express the necessary proof obligations and by theorem proving support to actually prove these assertions.

In many aspects the techniques of "classical" theorem proving are not suitable for the deduction tasks that accompany the development process. The approach that has proven successful in this area is *Tactical Theorem Proving*, where a proof calculus is embedded into a (usually functional) *meta*-language. Proof search is then implemented by programs in this meta-language. Usually, a sequent calculus or Natural Deduction is used in such systems.

The availability of an entire programming language, rather than a mere set of axioms and rules, facilitates the sound *extension* of the basic logic, and in fact the construction of a complete *derived calculus*.

2 Current State of the KIV-System

In the case of the KIV system, the paradigm of Tactical Theorem Proving has been enhanced in several directions. First and most prominent, proofs in the KIV system are realized as *data structures*. The main advantage of this representation of proofs is that proofs can be stored, retrieved, inspected by the user, and inspected by the system itself. This last option makes a *re-use* of proofs possible, for example an old proof can be used as a guideline when minor changes have been made to a program and its specification and a new correctness proof is required.

Another enhancement is that for all objects there are *meta-variables*, so that schematic goals may be formulated. Since proof rules can be schematic as well, schematic proofs can be constructed with the system.

As a third improvement, the KIV system allows the definition of new proof rules. To guarantee soundness of the rule, the user must supply a *validation function*. When called with an instance of the premises and conclusion, this function must return a proof tree with the same premises and conclusion. Recursively calling all validations results in a proof in the basic calculus.

In its current version, KIV supports the specification of software systems as abstract data types, using full first order specifications and the usual specification structuring operations (actualization, union and enrichments). Specifications may be implemented by a set of procedures working on other, imported, abstract data types.

Assertions about the resulting *abstract* programs are formulated in an *uninterpreted* Dynamic Logic. The infinitary rules usually found in axiomatizations of such logics have been replaced by explicit bounded iterative and recursive programming constructs, auxiliary data structures to express the bounds, and induction principles.

Using this machinery, derived calculi tailored to the deduction problem at hand have been implemented, and strategies for the automation of the proof task have been built. For the implementation of abstract data types, the corresponding strategy can translate the correctness of an implementation into a set of DL formulas, and prove them with a high degree of automation, and some interactive help from the user.

Proof strategies for other kinds of deduction problems exist as well, for example for partial and total correctness assertions about programs (based on the calculi by Hoare and Burstall), or for program synthesis (based on a variety of approaches).

3 Project Activities and Applications

Currently, we participate in the BMFT Verbundprojekt Korrekte Software (KorSo) and in the construction of the verification support environment (VSE) for the Bundesanstalt für Sicherheit in der Informationstechnik (BSI).

Within these projects and in cooperation with industrial partners, the system is used for a variety of case studies, including scheduling software for a radio network, the heart plantation center in Berlin, and access control software for a federal nuclear power plant.

1x1 Grade — A System for Implementation, Testing and Animation of Graph Algorithms

Franz Höfting[1], Egon Wanke[2], Aurel Balmoŝan[1] and Curd Bergmann[1]

[1] Universität-Gesamthochschule Paderborn, Fachbereich 17, Warburger Str. 100,
4790 Paderborn, Germany, email: plexus@uni-paderborn.de
[2] Gesellschaft f'ur Mathematik und Datenverarbeitung, Institut f'ur
Grundlagenforschung, Schloß Birlinghoven, 5205 St. Augustin, Germany

Abstract. *1x1 Grade* is an integrated software system for the implementation, test and animation of graph algorithms. The system consists of a comfortable graphical editor for generating and manipulating graphs and a special programming language for the simple formulation of graph algorithms.

In some areas of computer science and related sciences, where the modeling of natural problems as problems in the concept of graphs is used, the task of a quick and simple realization of an algorithmic idea frequently appears. Undergraduate students, when learning basic classical algorithms, spend a lot of time implementing these algorithms in a common programming language. Hardly ever, a deep algorithmic understanding is a result of this work, because there is no adequate input or output to their implementations. It is not possible to observe what the algorithm is in fact doing. In other areas, a major interest lies in just demonstrating the progressing results of a certain procedure.

In all mentioned applications *1x1 Grade* promises to be a helpful tool. The implementation of well known or totally new algorithms turns out to be relatively simple. Input graphs, containing vertices and directed and/or undirected edges can be edited, placing arbitrary information at all graph objects for use in the algorithms. The algorithms can then be run directly on the user edited graphs and the program output can be shown in the graph editor. As an example, the application of the classical Kruskal algorithm for minimum spanning trees on a sample input graph is shown in Fig. 1.

The *1x1 Grade* system consists mainly out of two components: a graph editor and the *1x1 Grade* programming language. Following is a short description of the main characteristics of these components.

The **graph-editor** serves as a tool for generating and manipulating arbitrary graphs containing vertices and directed and/or undirected edges. Arbitrary information strings can be placed at all graph objects for use in the algorithms that are to be run on the graph. The appearance of the graph may be altered by moving the objects or by scaling. The visible part of a large graph may be shifted using the scrollbars. At the same time, the editor serves as the standard output for applications, as described later. Besides the graph editors there are graph buffers in which graphs can be shown but where they can not be altered. The contents of all these windows can easily be interchanged.

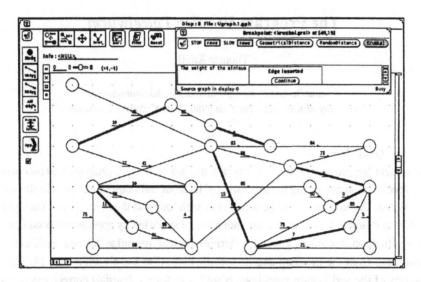

Fig. 1. The figure shows a screendump of a typical application of the *1+1 Grade*-system. In the graph editor window a graph is given, that is used as an input to the well known Kruskal-algorithm. The hilited edges are the spanning forest as the algorithm has calculated it so far. The small panel is the application control window for this algorithm. It contains buttons for two Boolean variables STOP and SLOW, two buttons for the automatical generation of edge weights, and the Kruskal start button. The algorithm has just been interrupted and can be continued on mouseclick.

The *1+1 Grade* **programming language** is a special purpose programming language with a syntax closely related to other languages like C, Oberon or Modula. It contains additional statements that are frequently used in textbooks for the abstract formulation of graph algorithms. For instance, the expression

```
FOR EACH DEDGE e FROM u DO something(e) END;
```

does **something** for any directed edge e starting at u. The language is easy to learn and since it is closely related to abstract graph algorithm languages, programming is simple. An editor is put to the users disposal and each program is compiled on mouseclick.

The **Integration of the components** graph editor and programming language makes up the particular power of the system: The user edited algorithm can be run on the user edited graphs and thereby the user has a lot of possibilities to observe the progressing algorithmic process. It is only this ensemble playing of the components that makes testing of algorithmic ideas easy and offers the opportunity of deep algorithmic understanding to students.

1+1 Grade was developed by the authors at the University of Paderborn, Germany. By now, the system (Version 2.0) is running under SUN-OS 4.1.1 with Open Windows 3.0. Version 3.0 will soon be available for other common configurations.

The Program Verifier *Tatzelwurm*

Thomas Käufl

Institut für Logik, Komplexität und Deduktionssysteme
University of Karlsruhe, Postfach 6980, 7500 Karlsruhe 1, Germany

1. An Overview

At present the program verifier works in a traditional way. A program together with the specification describing the properties of its input and output must be submitted to the system. An invariant must be attached to each loop and the behaviour of each procedure and function used in the program must be specified by appropriate conditions. A verification condition generator derives logical formulae termed verification conditions from the program and its specification. (For the algorithm see [4].) The validity of the verification conditions is sufficient for the (partial) correctness of the program. (Using the well founded sets method termination can also be proved in a partial correctness logic.) For the proof of the verification conditions a prover is available. It employs analytic tableaux and simplification procedures for theories.

2. The Programming Language Accepted by the System

A subset of Pascal comprising function and procedure calls, assignment, conditional, while and repeat statements is accepted as programming language. The data types treated are: Integer, real, scalar (enumerated) and subrange types. Also arrays and records are available. Pointers are not allowed. Each kind of declaration is permitted, provided the admissible data types are used. (For the programming language see [4, 5].) There are some restrictions on the calls of procedures. A variable must not occur twice or more as result parameter or as global variable and as result parameter. Function definitions may not contain global variables and result parameters.

The language used for the specifications and loop invariants is an order sorted first order logic with function symbols and equality.

The use of Pascal as programming language is not essential. The system is organized in such a way that the verification condition generator works independently of the parser. Thus the Pascal parser may be replaced by a parser for any other language compiling the program into the required format.

3. The Automated Theorem Prover

The automated theorem prover uses the analytic tableaux of Smullyan [7]. The set of rules is extended by rules for equivalences, for a restricted version of the analytic cut and for the equality. Rules for the modus ponens and its generalizations are simulated by the systematic tableau procedure. Equations are treated in three different ways. If an equation belongs to a theory a reduction procedure exists for which the equation is treated by this procedure. An equation declared as demodulator is used for rewriting each term occurring in literals inserted into a branch. Each equation not being a demodulator is used for updating a congruence relation on the ground terms appearing on the branch. Whenever the complementarity of two literals $L_1(t_1)$ and $\neg L_2(t_2)$ must be tested it is checked whether t_1 and t_2 are congruent. (Such a pair of complementary literals found $t_1 = t_2$ is proved using the substitutivity rules. The formulae necessary for this contradiction determined the needless formulae are removed.)

The prover uses reduction and decision procedures for theories. There are procedures for the linear inequalities and equations over the rationals and for the Presburger-Arithmetic, for the quantifier free theory of lists under cons, car and cdr, for the arrays under select and store and for a part of the theory of the enumerated types. (See [1].)

The prover can be used fully automatic or interactively.

4. Future Extensions
At present the parser and the verification condition generator is extended in such a way that it will be possible to develop programs by stepwise refinement. Also the treatment of the data type boolean will be implemented. An integration of the Knuth-Bendix-Completion into the prover is under way. The next major task will be the development of a language expressing proof tactics.

5. Conclusion
The program verifier is implemented in Common Lisp. It has been used in a project for the verification of a security sublayer in a communication network.

References
1. Th. Käufl: Reasoning about Theories with a Finite Model. 3. Österreichische Artificial Intelligence-Tagung 1987. Informatik-Fachberichte; Berlin, Heidelberg, New York: 1987; Springer
2. Th. Käufl: Reasoning about Systems of Linear Inequalities. 9th International Conference on Automated Deduction. Lecture Notes on Computer Science; Berlin, Heidelberg, New York: 1988; Springer
3. Th. Käufl: Simplification and Decision of Systems of Linear Inequalities over the Integers. Interner Bericht 9/88. Institut für Logik, Komplexität und Deduktionssysteme, Universität Karlsruhe: 1988
4. Th. Käufl: Program Verifier *Tatzelwurm*: The Correctness and Completeness of the Generation of the Verification Conditions. Interner Bericht 9/89. Institut für Logik, Komplexität und Deduktionssysteme, Universität Karlsruhe: 1989
5. Th. Käufl: The Program Verifier *Tatzelwurm*. in Sichere Software. Heinrich Kersten (Hrsg.). Heidelberg: 1990
6. Th. Käufl, N. Zabel: Coopeation of Decision Procedures in a Tableau-Based Theorem Prover. Revue d'Intelligence Artificielle, Vol. 4, no. 3: 1990, pp. 99 - 126
7. R.M. Smullyan: First Order Logic. Berlin, Heidelberg, New York: 1968

LEDA
A Library of Efficient Data Types and Algorithms *

Stefan Näher

Max-Planck-Institut für Informatik
D-6600 Saarbrücken, Germany

One of the major differences between combinatorial computing and other areas of computing such as statistics, numerical analysis and linear programming is the use of complex data types. Whilst the built-in types, such as integers, reals, vectors, and matrices, usually suffice in the other areas, combinatorial computing relies heavily on types like stacks, queues, dictionaries, sequences, sorted sequences, priority queues, graphs, points, segments, ... In the fall of 1988, we started a project (called **LEDA** for Library of Efficient Data types and Algorithms) to build a small, but growing library of data types and algorithms in a form which allows them to be used by non-experts. We hope that the system will narrow the gap between algorithms research, teaching, and implementation. The main features of LEDA are:

1. LEDA provides a sizable collection of data types and algorithms in a form which allows them to be used by non-experts. In the current version, this collection includes most of the data types and algorithms described in the text books of the area.

2. LEDA gives a precise and readable specification for each of the data types and algorithms mentioned above. The specifications are short (typically, not more than a page), general (so as to allow several implementations), and abstract (so as to hide all details of the implementation).

3. For many efficient data structures access by position is important. In LEDA, we use an item concept to cast positions into an abstract form.

---

*This work was supported by the ESPRIT II Basic Research Actions Program, under contract No. 3075 (project ALCOM).

We mention that most of the specifications given in the LEDA manual use this concept, i.e., the concept is adequate for the description of many data types.

4. LEDA contains efficient implementations for each of the data types, e.g., Fibonacci heaps for priority queues, skip lists and dynamic perfect hashing for dictionaries, ...

5. LEDA contains a comfortable data type graph. It offers the standard iterations such as "for all nodes v of a graph G do" or "for all neighbors w of v do", it allows to add and delete vertices and edges and it offers arrays and matrices indexed by nodes and edges,... The data type graph allows to write programs for graph problems in a form close to the typical text book presentation.

6. LEDA is implemented by a C++ class library. It can be used with allmost any C++ compiler (cfront, g++, bcc, ztc). LEDA is available by anonymous ftp from **ftp.cs.uni-sb.de** (/pub/LEDA), the Distribution contains all sources, installation instructions, a technical report, and the LEDA user manual. LEDA is not in the public domain, but can be used freely for research and teaching.

The main concepts and some implementation details of LEDA are described in [1] and [3]. The user manual ([2]) lists the specifications of all data types and algorithms contained in version 3.0 of the library and gives many example programs.

References

[1] K. Mehlhorn, S. Näher, *LEDA, a Library of Efficient Data Types and Algorithms*, Communications of the ACM, to appear

[2] S. Näher, *LEDA User Manual Version 3.0*, Technical Report, Max-Planck Institut für Informatik, Saarbrücken, 1992

[3] S. Näher, *Parameterized Data Types in LEDA*, in preparation

Defining λ-Typed λ-Calculi
by Axiomatizing the Typing Relation

Philippe de Groote

INRIA-Lorraine – CRIN – CNRS
Campus Scientifique - B.P. 239
54506 Vandœuvre-lès-Nancy Cedex – FRANCE

Abstract. We present a uniform framework for defining different λ-typed λ-calculi in terms of systems to derive typing judgements, akin to Barendregt's Pure Type Systems [3]. We first introduce a calculus called λ^λ and study its abstract properties. These are, among others, the property of Church-Rosser, the property of subject reduction, and the one of strong normalization. Then we show how to extend λ^λ to obtain an inferential definition. of Nederpelt's Λ [20]. One may also extend λ^λ to get inferential definitions of van Daalen Λ_β [24], and de Bruijn's $\Lambda\Delta$ [9] and we argue that these new inferential definitions are well suited for language-theoretic investigations.

1 Introduction

There is a growing interest in designing generic formal systems that can be used to specify various object logics [16, 18]. These systems, also known as *logical frameworks*, may be used to implement and automate many of the logics that are of interest in computer science. For this reason, they form the basis of generic theorem provers [23].

We think, as the author of [10] does, that λ-typed λ-calculi have an important role to play as the backbones of logical frameworks. λ-Typed λ-calculi are as elegant and simple than they are powerful. They correspond, at the implementation level, to a uniform data-structure allowing syntactic categories and formal languages, as well as logical rules and proofs to be represented. As pointed out in [17], systems such as LF [16] can be seen as higher-level languages that can be compiled into λ-typed λ-calculi. Nevertheless the notion of λ-type did not spread outside the AUTOMATH community.

In this paper, we define λ-typed λ-calculi in terms of systems to derive typing judgements, in the spirit of [3]. We consider, for instance, Nederpelt's Λ [20] whose original definition is strongly algorithmic. Indeed the notion of well-typed expressions is defined by means of an algorithm that tells whether an expression is well-typed or not. Such an algorithmic style of definition is better suited for implementation than it is for language-theoretic investigations. For a theoretical study, the inferential style of definition that we use here (called E-definition in [24]) presents further advantages:

1. it allows proofs to be conducted by induction on the derivations of judgements;
2. it provides a uniform framework to compare the different calculi with each other;
3. it makes easier the comparison between λ-typed λ-calculi and more usual typed λ-calculi such as the ones defined in [3].

The paper is organized as follows. In Section 2, we introduce and discuss the notion of λ-type from a general and somewhat intuitive point of view. In Section 3, and 4, we introduce the λ-typed λ-calculus λ^λ, which is equivalent to the variant of Nederpelt's Λ that we studied in [12]. The definition that we give is an adaptation of the one used by Barendregt in [3]. In Section 5, we studied the abstract properties of λ^λ and we show how the techniques used in [3, 4, 14, 15] may be adapted to the case of λ-typed λ-calculi. In Sections 6 we extend λ^λ by allowing for $\beta\eta$-conversion and we obtain a calculus equivalent to Nederpelt's Λ. In section 7, we suggest how to obtain inferential definitions of van Daalen's Λ_β [24] and de Bruijn's $\Lambda\Delta$ [9]. Finally, we conclude in Section 8.

2 The Notion of λ-Type

The notion of λ-type originated in the frame of the AUTOMATH project [8]. In the earliest versions of AUTOMATH, λ-types were already present, because a unique binding operator was used both for the terms and their types. Then, by a further unification of concepts, de Bruijn designed a language called AUT-SL (a shorthand for AUTOMATH *single line*), which permits

a whole AUTOMATH book to be expressed as a single λ-term [6]. This language gave rise to the calculus Λ that Nederpelt introduced in his dissertation and for which he proved strong normalization [20, 21]. Finally, a last achievement, due to de Bruijn again, was to provide the calculus $\Lambda\Delta$ [9] as a generalization of Λ.

The easiest way (but also maybe the most harmful) of understanding the notion of λ-type is based on the following simple observation: although the functional abstractor (λ) and the constructor of dependent types (Π) are usually distinguished, their syntactic features are basically the same; both are universal binding operators. Hence, it is consistent, at least syntactically, to identify them. This identification gives rise to calculi where the types that are assigned to λ-terms are themselves λ-terms.

To see λ-typed λ-calculi as the result of that syntactic identification between λ and Π is harmful for at least two reasons. First of all, it suggests that the λ-typed λ-calculi were designed after more usual typed λ-calculi. This is wrong. AUT-SL, for instance, is more than fifteen years older than LF. Second of all, it makes one feel that λ-typed λ-calculi are based on a syntactic confusion and amount, therefore, to a semantic absurdity. This is not true by any means since the consistency of a calculus like Nederpelt's Λ, for instance, can be established in a proof-theoretic way [20, 24] (see also Section 5, hereafter).

A better way of understanding λ-typed λ-calculi is to forget about other typed λ-calculi and to think of the untyped λ-calculus as a calculus of substitution. Then, λ-typed λ-calculi may be seen as calculi of substitution typed by substitution.[1] Actually, λ-typed λ-calculi are very natural in the sense that the only concepts

---

[1] It is worth noting that the notions of reduction considered in the AUTOMATH project (called mini-reductions by de Bruijn in [9]) do not amount to *global* substitutions, like β-reduction does, but to *local* ones. Recently, in [22], Nederpelt pursued further the study of these mini-reductions and provided a comparison with the explicit substitutions of Abadi, Cardelli, Curien, and Lévy [1].

needed to assign types to terms are the operations of abstraction and application, i.e. the central concepts of the (untyped) λ-calculus.

The terms and the types of a λ-typed λ-calculus obey the same syntax. This feature presents some technical advantages, notably when implementing the calculus. For example, the meta-operation of substituting a term for a variable into a type may be represented within the calculus by a β-redex. This, in turn, allows an explicit typing operator to be defined (see Section 5, Definition 10). We do not claim, however, that λ-typed λ-calculi must be preferred to other calculi. For instance, we do not think that Nederpelt's Λ must, in any case, be preferred to LF. Preference is often only a matter of style. What we believe is that λ-typed λ-calculi must not be forgotten or ignored.

3   Syntax of Raw λ-Expressions

λ-Expressions are built from a countably infinite set of variables $\mathcal{V}$ and a single constant τ.

Definition 1. The set $\mathcal{E}$ of λ-expressions is defined inductively as follows:

  i. $\tau \in \mathcal{E}$
  ii. $x \in \mathcal{V} \Rightarrow x \in \mathcal{E}$
  iii. $x \in \mathcal{V}$ and $A, B \in \mathcal{E} \Rightarrow (\lambda x : A. B) \in \mathcal{E}$
  iv. $A, B \in \mathcal{E} \Rightarrow (A B) \in \mathcal{E}$

The constant τ is akin to the constant Type of other calculi [5, 16] or to Barendregt's $*$ [3]. In Nederpelt's Λ, λ-expressions whose head is τ (i.e. expressions of the form $\lambda x_1 : A_1. \cdots \lambda x_n : A_n. \tau B_1 \cdots B_m$) are not assigned any type. Since we want to give to λ^λ a definition in the spirit of [3], contrary to Nederpelt, we will state the axiom

$$\vdash \tau : \kappa$$

where κ is another constant corresponding to Barendregt's $\square$. To this end, we introduce the set $\mathcal{K}$ of λ-kinds.

Definition 2. The set $\mathcal{K}$ of λ-kinds is defined inductively as follows:

  i. $\kappa \in \mathcal{K}$
  ii. $x \in \mathcal{V}$ and $A \in \mathcal{E}$ and $B \in \mathcal{K} \Rightarrow \lambda x : A. B \in \mathcal{K}$

For convenience, we also define the set of pseudo-expressions $\mathcal{P} = \mathcal{E} \cup \mathcal{K}$.

As customary, λ is a binding operator. The scoping rules are the usual ones. In particular, variables occurring free in a λ-expression A remain free in $\lambda x : A. B$. Pseudo-expressions that can be transformed into each other by renaming their bound variables are identified (see [7]).

The equality of λ^λ amounts to the relation of β-conversion ($\leftrightarrow_\beta$), which is defined as the reflexive, transitive, symmetric closure of the relation of β-contraction ($\rightarrow_\beta$). The latter is defined on raw pseudo-expressions, as usual.

4 Well-Typedness and Correctness

Type checking is defined according to typing contexts. A typing context is a sequence of declarations $x : A$, where $x \in \mathcal{V}$ and $A \in \mathcal{E}$. Any context $\Gamma, x : A$ is such that (i) the variable x is not declared in Γ, (ii) all the variables occurring free in the λ-expression A are declared in Γ. C is the set of typing contexts.

We define the notion of well-typed λ-expression by providing a proof system to derive typing judgements of the shape

$$\Gamma \vdash A : B \tag{1}$$

where Γ is a typing context and A and B are both λ-expressions. While A and B belong to the same syntactic category

(they are both in $\mathcal{E}$), we will sometimes, for convenience, refer to A as a term and to B as a type.

Another form of judgement is necessary. The judgements of this second form have also the shape of (1) with the difference that B is no longer a λ-expression but a λ-kind. Strictly speaking, the two forms of judgements are different. Nevertheless, by a slight abuse of language, we identify them and say that A is a well-typed λ-expression in both cases.

Definition 3. Let $\Gamma \in C$, $A \in \mathcal{E}$ and $B \in \mathcal{P}$. A typing judgment of λ^λ is an expression of the form

$$\Gamma \vdash A : B$$

derivable according to the following proof system:

$$\vdash \tau : \kappa \qquad\qquad (constant)$$

$$\frac{\Gamma \vdash A : B}{\Gamma, x : A \vdash x : A} \qquad\qquad (variable)$$

$$\frac{\Gamma, x : A \vdash B : C}{\Gamma \vdash \lambda x : A. B : \lambda x : A. C} \qquad\qquad (abstraction)$$

$$\frac{\Gamma \vdash A : \lambda x : C. D \quad \Gamma \vdash B : C}{\Gamma \vdash AB : D[x := B]} \qquad\qquad (application)$$

$$\frac{\Gamma \vdash A : B \quad \Gamma \vdash C : D}{\Gamma, x : C \vdash A : B} \qquad\qquad (weakening)$$

$$\frac{\Gamma \vdash A : B \quad \Gamma \vdash C : D}{\Gamma \vdash A : C} \quad \text{if } B \leftrightarrow_\beta C \qquad (type\ conversion)$$

Given some $A \in \mathcal{E}$ and some $\Gamma \in C$, one says that the λ-expression A is well-typed according to the context Γ if and only if there exists a pseudo-expression $B \in \mathcal{P}$ such that $\Gamma \vdash A : B$.

Given some $A \in \mathcal{E}$, A is called a correct λ-expression of λ^λ if and only if A is well-typed according to the empty context.

We may now compare the system given in Definition 3 with related systems such as LF [16] or Barendregt's λP [3]. Two rules of the present system seem to be unusual. The first one is the abstraction rule that introduces an abstractor λ in the right-hand side of the colon (instead of some specific type constructor such as Π). The second one is the weakening rule where no degree restriction is given on C. This means that any well-typed term may be used as a type or, in other words, that there may be chains $\Gamma \vdash A_1 : A_0$, $\Gamma \vdash A_2 : A_1$, ..., $\Gamma \vdash A_n : A_{n-1}$ of arbitrary lengths. This must be contrasted with the other (more usual) calculi where expressions of only three degrees are provided: the *kinds*, the *types*, and the *terms*.

5   The Language Theory of λ^λ

In this section, we review the main properties of λ^λ. Among others, we state the properties of Church-Rosser, of subject reduction, and of strong normalization. These properties, for Nederpelt's Λ, were first established by Nederpelt and van Daalen in their respective PhD theses [20, 24]. The proofs they give, however, are rather difficult because of the algorithmic nature of Nederpelt's original definition (see section 6 below). On the other hand, Definition 3 allows the same properties to be proven by induction on the derivations of the typing judgements. It is then a mere exercise to adapt the proofs that are given in [4, 15]

The first property that we state is the Church-Rosser Theorem for the set of pseudo-expressions.

Proposition 4. (Church-Rosser) *Let $A, B, C \in \mathcal{P}$ be such that $A \twoheadrightarrow_\beta B$ and $A \twoheadrightarrow_\beta C$. Then there exists $D \in \mathcal{P}$ such that $B \twoheadrightarrow_\beta D$ and $C \twoheadrightarrow_\beta D$.*

Proof. The usual Tait–Martin-Löf proof for type free λ-terms [2, pp. 61–62] generalizes easily to raw λ-expressions and λ-kinds. □

The next property of interest is subject reduction. This property turns out to be important in practice. If one sees β-reduction as the process of evaluating a λ-expression, a consequence of subject reduction is that there is no need for any kind of dynamic type checking.

Proposition 5. (Subject reduction) *For all $A, B \in \mathcal{E}$, $C \in \mathcal{P}$ and all $\Gamma \in \mathcal{C}$, if $A \twoheadrightarrow_\beta B$ and $\Gamma \vdash A : C$ then $\Gamma \vdash B : C$.*

Proof. The property can be established by induction on the derivation of $\Gamma \vdash A : C$. Some technical lemmas are needed. See [4] or [15] for details. □

The subject reduction and Church-Rosser properties allow one to give a simple characterization of the relation of β-equality between well-typed terms. β-equality is the least equivalence relation containing the relation of β-contraction between well-typed terms. It is defined, more explicitly, as follows.

Definition 6. Let $A, A' \in \mathcal{E}$ and $\Gamma \in \mathcal{C}$. We say that A and A' are β-equal with respect to Γ, and we write

$$\Gamma \vdash A =_\beta A'$$

if and only if there exist $A_1, \ldots, A_n \in \mathcal{E}$, $B_1, \ldots, B_n \in \mathcal{P}$ such that:

i. $A_1 \equiv A$ and $A_n \equiv A'$,

ii. for all $1 \leq i \leq n$, $\Gamma \vdash A_i : B_i$,

iii. for all $1 \leq i < n$, $A_i \rightarrow_\beta A_{i+1}$ or $A_{i+1} \rightarrow_\beta A_i$.

As a corollary of Propositions 4 and 5, we have that $\Gamma \vdash A =_\beta A'$ if and only if $A \twoheadleftrightarrow_\beta A'$, $\Gamma \vdash A : B$, and $\Gamma \vdash A' : B'$, for some $B, B' \in \mathcal{P}$. In connection with this (and with Proposition 8 below), it is worth noting that the type conversion rule of Definition 3 is equivalent to the following type equality rule:

$$\frac{\Gamma \vdash A : B \quad \Gamma \vdash B =_\beta C}{\Gamma \vdash A : C} \qquad (type\ equality)$$

Actually, the type equality rule is the intended meaning of the type conversion rule. Nevertheless if we replace the latter by the former, using Definition 6, we would introduce circularity into the definitions. It is possible to circumvent this problem by providing an axiomatization of the equality judgements, in the spirit of Martin-Löf's type theory [19]. This solution, however, would lengthen most of the proofs of the propositions.

Most of the typed λ-calculi that have been studied in the literature, among others the eight systems of Barendregt's λ-cube, are strongly normalizable. This property also holds for λ^λ.

Proposition 7. (Strong normalization) *Let $A, B \in \mathcal{P}$ and $\Gamma \in \mathcal{C}$ be such that $\Gamma \vdash A : B$. Then there is no infinite sequence of β-contraction starting in A.*

Proof. As in the case of LF or λP, strong normalization for λ^λ may be derived from strong normalization for the simply typed λ-calculus. See [15, 16]. □

Two other properties are related to the λ-expressions that are acting as types.

The peculiarity of λ-typed λ-calculi is that the set of terms is identical to the set of types. We know that this is certainly true at the context-free level of raw λ-expressions. To make sense, however, this identification must also exist for well-typed expressions. In other words, when a well-typed λ-expression is assigned another λ-expression as a type, we expect the latter λ-expression to be also well-typed. This is stated by the following result.

Proposition 8. (Well-typedness of types) *Let $A, B \in \mathcal{E}$ and $\Gamma \in \mathcal{C}$. If $\Gamma \vdash A : B$ then there exists $C \in \mathcal{P}$ such that $\Gamma \vdash B : C$.*

Proof. The proof is by induction on the derivation of $\Gamma \vdash A : B$. The only problematic case is the one of application for which a substitution lemma is needed. □

We also have that the type of an expression is unique up to β-conversion.

Proposition 9. (Unicity of types) *Let $A, B \in \mathcal{E}$, $C \in \mathcal{P}$ and $\Gamma \in \mathcal{C}$. If $\Gamma \vdash A : B$ and $\Gamma \vdash A : C$ then $B \twoheadleftrightarrow_\beta C$.*

Proof. A straightforward induction on the derivation of $\Gamma \vdash A : B$. □

One of the main consequences of the above metatheoretic properties is the decidability of the typing relation of λ^λ. Another application consists in designing other definitions of λ^λ that are more suited to implementation [12] and then proving their equivalence with definition 3. Let us illustrate partially this by introducing Nederpelt's typing operator.

Definition 10. Nederpelt's typing operator type: $\mathcal{C} \times \mathcal{E} \rightarrow \mathcal{P}$ is defined inductively according to the following clauses:

  i. $\text{type}_\Gamma[\tau] = \kappa$,
  ii. $\text{type}_\Gamma[x] = A$ if $x{:}A \in \Gamma$,
  iii. $\text{type}_\Gamma[\lambda x{:}A.\,B] = \lambda x{:}A.\,\text{type}_{\Gamma,x:A}[B]$,
  iv. $\text{type}_\Gamma[A\,B] = \text{type}_\Gamma[A]\,B$.

Except for the first clause, which is proper to our formalism, the above definition corresponds to the one given by Nederpelt's in his thesis.

The connection between this typing operator and the typing relation defined by Definition 3 is expressed by the following property.

Proposition 11. *Let* $A \in \mathcal{E}, B \in \mathcal{P}$ *and* $\Gamma \in \mathcal{C}$ *be such that* $\Gamma \vdash A : B$. *Then* $B \twoheadleftarrow\!\!\twoheadrightarrow_\beta \text{type}_\Gamma[A]$.

Proof. By induction on the derivation of $\Gamma \vdash A : B$.   □

It is remarkable that the operator type is defined on the raw expressions. This allows one to also define so-called applicability conditions on the raw expressions. Then the well-typedness of a λ-expression may be checked simply by structural induction except for the case of an application where, in addition, the applicability conditions must be satisfied. For λ^λ, we have that an application $(A\,B)$ is well typed according to a context Γ if and only if

  i. A and B are well-typed according to Γ,
  ii. there exist $C \in \mathcal{E}$ and $D \in \mathcal{P}$ such that $\text{type}_\Gamma[A] \twoheadrightarrow_\beta \lambda x{:}C.\,D$, and
  iii. $\text{type}_\Gamma[B] \downarrow_\beta C$ (where the relation $\downarrow_\beta$, by definition, indicates the existence of a common reduct).

Clauses ii and iii correspond to the applicability conditions.

6   Nederpelt's Λ

The main difference between λ^λ and Nederpelt's Λ [20, 21], besides the way in which they are defined, is that the equality of Λ is extensional in the sense that it is based on the notion of $\beta\eta$-reduction.

Let us look at the applicability conditions for Λ as defined by Nederpelt in [20]. First the degree of an expression is defined as follows.

Definition 12. The degree $\deg_\Gamma[A]$ of a λ-expression A according to a context Γ is defined inductively according to the following clauses:

i. $\deg_\Gamma[\tau] = 0$,

ii. $\deg_\Gamma[x] = \deg_\Gamma[A] + 1$ if $x{:}A \in \Gamma$,

iii. $\deg_\Gamma[\lambda x{:}A.\,B] = \deg_{\Gamma,x:A}[B]$,

iv. $\deg_\Gamma[A\,B] = \deg_\Gamma[A]$.

Then an iterated version of the typing operator is defined.

Definition 13. Let type^n be defined as follows:

i. $\text{type}^0_\Gamma[A] = A$,

ii. $\text{type}^{n+1}_\Gamma[A] = \text{type}^n_\Gamma[\text{type}_\Gamma[A]]$.

Then one defines $\text{type}^*_\Gamma[A] = \text{type}^d_\Gamma[A]$, where $d = \deg_\Gamma[A]$.

Finally, Nederpelt's applicability conditions are given by the following definition: a λ-expression A is applicable to a λ-expression B in the context γ if and only if there exist $C \in \mathcal{E}$ and $D \in \mathcal{P}$ such that

i. $\text{type}^*_\Gamma[A] \twoheadrightarrow_\beta \lambda x{:}C.\,D$,

ii. $\text{type}_\Gamma[B] \downarrow_{\beta\eta} C$.

The above applicability conditions might seem awkward. Nevertheless they may be explained in term of $\beta\eta$-conversion in a rather clean way. Roughly speaking, applicability conditions say that the *domain* of a functional expression must *match* the *type* of its argument. In the case of λ^λ, the *domain* and the *type* may be computed using the operator type, and the meaning of the word *"match"* is β-conversion.

In the case of Nederpelt's Λ, Clause (ii) above suggests that the meaning of the word *"match"* is $\beta\eta$-conversion. One also has that the *type* of the argument is computed using the same operator type. What is unclear is why an iterated version of the typing operator is used when computing the *domain*. In order to answer this question, let us first consider an example.

Example. Consider the context

$$\Gamma \equiv a : \lambda x{:}\tau.\,\tau,\, b : a,\, c : \tau$$

In this context, the expression b is applicable to the expression c according to Nederpelt's conditions (while, in λ^λ, $b\,c$ is not well-typed with respect to Γ). Indeed we have:

$$\text{type}^*_\Gamma[b] = \lambda x{:}\tau.\,\tau \quad \text{and} \quad \text{type}_\Gamma[c] = \tau.$$

Let us try now to extend λ^λ in order to derive $\Gamma \vdash b\,c : A$, for some λ-expression A. A possible derivation tree is the following:

$$
\cfrac{
  \Gamma \vdash b : a \qquad
  \cfrac{
    \cfrac{
      \cfrac{\vdots \qquad\qquad \vdots}{
        \cfrac{\Gamma, x:\tau \vdash a : \lambda x{:}\tau.\,\tau \quad \Gamma, x:\tau \vdash x : \tau}{\Gamma, x:\tau \vdash a\,x : \tau}
      }
    }{\Gamma \vdash \lambda x{:}\tau.\,a\,x : \lambda x{:}\tau.\,\tau}
  }{(\star)\ \Gamma \vdash b : \lambda x{:}\tau.\,a\,x} \qquad
  \cfrac{\vdots}{\Gamma \vdash c : \tau}
}{\Gamma \vdash b\,c : a\,x}
$$

The interesting step in the above derivation is $(\star)$. The expression b is assigned a functional type $\lambda x : \tau. a\, x$ thanks to the η-expansion $a \leftarrow_\eta \lambda x : \tau. a\, x$. This η-expansion is legitimate because the expanded expression, that is $\lambda x : \tau. a\, x$, is well-typed. Now, the reason why the latter expression is well-typed is because the type of a is functional or, in other words, because $type^\bullet_\Gamma [b]$ is functional.

This example demonstrates that the iterated version of the typing operator is simply related to η-conversion. Therefore, in order to get an inferential definition of Nederpelt's Λ, we must adapt Definition 3 to take η-conversion into account. The first idea consists of simply replacing the type conversion rule by the following one:

$$\frac{\Gamma \vdash A : B \quad \Gamma \vdash C : D}{\Gamma \vdash A : C} \quad \text{if } B \twoheadleftrightarrow_{\beta\eta} C \tag{2}$$

Unfortunately, this does not work. We have seen that, when dealing with β-conversion only, the type conversion rule is equivalent to a type equality rule. The problem, in the present case, is precisely that rule (2) is not equivalent to the corresponding type equality rule:

$$\frac{\Gamma \vdash A : B \quad \Gamma \vdash B =_{\beta\eta} C : D}{\Gamma \vdash A : C} \tag{3}$$

In fact, (2) and (3) are not equivalent because $\beta\eta$-reduction on pseudo-expressions is not Church-Rosser (see [14, 20, 24]). This was first pointed out by Nederpelt in his thesis [20]. The typical counterexample he gives is the following:

$$\lambda x : A. (\lambda x : B. C)\, x \rightarrow_\eta \lambda x : B. C \quad \text{and} \quad \lambda x : A. (\lambda x : B. C)\, x \rightarrow_\beta \lambda x : A. C$$

where A and B can be any λ-expressions. In particular, A and B could be such that the λ-expressions $\lambda x : B. C$ and $\lambda x : A. C$ would be well-typed. Therefore Rule (2) allows one to change arbitrarily the domain of a functional expression.

The problem can be circumvented by strengthening the type conversion rule as follows:

$$\frac{\Gamma \vdash A : B \quad \Gamma \vdash B : D \quad \Gamma \vdash C : D}{\Gamma \vdash A : C} \quad \text{if } B \twoheadleftrightarrow_{\beta\eta} C. \tag{4}$$

In Rule (4), the λ-expressions B and C are explicitly required to have the same type D. As a consequence, when B and C are functional expressions, they must have the same domain. This is clear for λ-expressions of degree 0 because type conversion is not allowed at the level of λ-kinds. Then, for λ-expressions of degree $n > 0$, it can be established by induction.

Definition 3 where the type conversion rule is replaced by Rule (4) corresponds to a new system that we will call $\lambda^\lambda_{\beta\eta}$. This system is equivalent to Nederpelt's Λ.

The system $\lambda^\lambda_{\beta\eta}$ is well suited for language-theoretic investigations. The metatheoretic results of Section 5 may be adapted. Nevertheless the adaptation is not straightforward. The problem, of course, is the failure of the Church-Rosser property on pseudo-expressions. $\beta\eta$-Reduction on well-typed expressions satisfies the Church-Rosser property, but to prove it is far from easy. In fact, the property was conjectured by Nederpelt in his thesis [20] and proven by van Daalen seven years later [24]. Recently, Geuvers has given a proof of the Church-Rosser property for a large class of Pure Type System with $\beta\eta$-reduction [14]. His techniques may be adapted to $\lambda^\lambda_{\beta\eta}$.

7 Van Daalen's Λ_β and de Bruijn's $\Lambda\Delta$

In his thesis [24], van Daalen investigates a subsystem of Nederpelt's Λ that he calls Λ_β. In [9] de Bruijn introduces the calculus $\Lambda\Delta$, which is a generalization of Nederpelt's Λ.

Definition 3 may be extended in order to get inferential definitions of van Daalen's and de Bruijn's calculi: by allowing for a weak form of η-expansion, one obtains a calculus equivalent to Λ_β; by adding a subject expansion rule, one obtains a calculus equivalent to $\Lambda\Delta$. We do not give the precise definitions for the sake of shortness.

8 Conclusions

While the idea of dealing with λ-types emerged more than twenty years ago, the concept of λ-typed λ-calculus has remained proper to the AUTOMATH project and appears to have been somewhat overlooked by the rest of the scientific community. There are two main reasons to this:

1. the identification between terms and types is felt to be purely syntactic and to carry little semantic content,
2. the original definitions of Λ and $\Lambda\Delta$ may be difficult to master because of their strong algorithmic flavor.

This first reason can be considered at the same time as a cause or as a consequence. It is true that no interesting model of λ-typed λ-calculi has been developed and that without such models it could be hard to have an intuition of what is a λ-type. However, properties such as Church-Rosser and normalization, which can be interpreted as consistency results, show that the notion of λ-type make sense and that, at least, we can construct a term model. Therefore, one may invert the argument. One may say that no interesting model of λ-typed λ-calculi has been developed not because the notion of λ-type is purely syntactic but because it has been overlooked.

The second reason is more pertinent. The first time one is confronted with the original definitions of Λ and $\Lambda\Delta$, which both consist in a type-checking algorithm, one has the feeling of being confronted with some complicated new system. This is because one has to face two problems at the same time. On the one hand, one has to understand the behavior of an algorithm while, on the other hand, one wants to understand abstractly the features of a new calculus. Moreover, to compare Λ and $\Lambda\Delta$ to other systems, with which one is possibly familiar, could be difficult. Hence, sooner or later, one is tempted to draw the wrong conclusion that λ-typed λ-calculi are artificially complicated because of the purely syntactic identification between abstractions and dependent types.

The inferential definitions that we have given in this paper should settle this misunderstanding. In particular, they enlighten the relation existing between λ-typed and other typed λ-calculi. They also explain unusual features of Λ and $\Lambda\Delta$ in terms of well-known notions. For instance, we have seen that the type-iteration that is used in [9, 20, 24] to compute the domain of a functional λ-expression may be explained in term of η-expansion.

References

1. M. Abadi, L. Cardelli, P.-L. Curien, and J.-J. Lévy. Explicit substitutions. *Journal of Functional Programming*, 1(4):375–416, 1991.
2. H.P. Barendregt. *The lambda calculus, its syntax and semantics*. North-Holland, revised edition, 1984.
3. H.P. Barendregt. Introduction to Generalised Type Systems. *Journal of Functional Programming*, 1(2):125–154, 1991.
4. H.P. Barendregt. Lambda calculi with types. In S. Abramsky, D. Gabbai, and T. Maibaum, editors, *Handbook of Logic in Computer Science*. Oxford University Press, 1992.
5. Th. Coquand. Metamathematical investigations of a calculus of constructions. In P. Odifreddi, editor, *Logic and Computer Science*, pages 91–122. Academic Press, 1990.
6. N.G. de Bruijn. AUT-SL, a single line version of AUTOMATH. Technical Report AUT 20, Department of Mathematics and Computing Science, Eindhoven University of Technology, 1971.
7. N.G. de Bruijn. Lambda calculus notations with nameless dummies, a tool for automatic formula manipulation, with an application to the Church-Rosser theorem. *Indigationes Mathematicae*, 34:381–392, 1972.
8. N.G. de Bruijn. A survey of the project Automath. In J.P. Seldin and J.R. Hindley, editors, *to H. B. Curry: Essays on Combinatory Logic, Lambda Calculus and Formalism*, pages 579–606. Academic Press, 1980.
9. N.G. de Bruijn. Generalizing automath by means of a lambda-typed lambda-calculus. In *Mathematical Logic and Theoretical Computer Science*, pages 71–92. Lecture Notes in pure and applied Mathematics, 106, Marcel Dekker, New York, 1987.
10. N.G. de Bruijn. A plea for weaker frameworks. In G. Huet and G. Plotkin, editors, *Logical Frameworks*, pages 40–67. Cambridge University Press, 1991.
11. N.G. de Bruijn. Algorithmic definition of λ-typed λ-calculus. In G. Huet and G. Plotkin, editors, *Logical Environments*. Cambridge University Press, 1992.
12. Ph. de Groote. *Définition et Propriétés d'un métacalcul de représentation de théories*. PhD thesis, Université Catholique de Louvain, Unité d'Informatique, 1991.
13. Ph. de Groote. Nederpelt's calculus extended with a notion of context as a logical framework. In G. Huet and G. Plotkin, editors, *Logical Frameworks*, pages 69–86. Cambridge University Press, 1991.
14. H. Geuvers. The Church-Rosser property for βη-reduction in typed λ-calculi. In *Proceedings of the seventh annual IEEE symposium on logic in computer science*, pages 453–460, 1992.
15. H. Geuvers and M.-J. Nederhof. Modular proof of strong normalization for the calculus of construction. *Journal of Functional Programming*, 1(2):155–189, 1991.
16. R. Harper, F. Honsel, and G. Plotkin. A framework for defining logics. In *Proceedings of the second annual IEEE symposium on logic in computer science*, pages 194–204, 1987.
17. R. Harper and F. Pfenning. A module systems for a programming language based on the lf logical framework. Submitted for publication, 1992.
18. G. Huet and G. Plotkin, editors. *Logical Frameworks*. Cambridge University Press, 1991.
19. P. Martin-Löf. An intuitionistic theory of types: Predicative part. In *Logic Colloquium '73*, pages 73–118. North-Holland, 1975.
20. R.P. Nederpelt. *Strong normalization in a typed lambda calculus with lambda structured types*. PhD thesis, Technische hogeschool Eindhoven, 1973.

21. R.P. Nederpelt. An approach to theorem proving on the basis of a typed lambda-calculus. In *Proceedings of the 5th international conference on automated deduction*, pages 182–194. Lecture Notes in Computer Science, 87, Springer Verlag, 1980.
22. R.P. Nederpelt. *The fine-structure of lambda calculus*. Computing Science Notes. Eindhoven University of Technology, 1992.
23. L.C. Paulson. Isabelle: The next 700 theorem provers. In P. Odifreddi, editor, *Logic and Computer Science*, pages 361–386. Academic Press, 1990.
24. D.T. van Daalen. *The language theory of Automath*. PhD thesis, Technische hogeschool Eindhoven, 1980.

Author Index

Lecture Notes in Computer Science

For information about Vols. 1–587
please contact your bookseller or Springer-Verlag

Vol. 624: A. Voronkov (Ed.), Logic Programming and Automated Reasoning. Proceedings, 1992. XIV, 509 pages. 1992. (Subseries LNAI).

Vol. 625: W. Vogler, Modular Construction and Partial Order Semantics of Petri Nets. IX, 252 pages. 1992.

Vol. 626: E. Börger, G. Jäger, H. Kleine Büning, M. M . Richter (Eds.), Computer Science Logic. Proceedings, 1991. VIII, 428 pages. 1992.

Vol. 628: G. Vosselman, Relational Matching. IX, 190 pages. 1992.

Vol. 629: I. M. Havel, V. Koubek (Eds.), Mathematical Foundations of Computer Science 1992. Proceedings. IX, 521 pages. 1992.

Vol. 630: W. R. Cleaveland (Ed.), CONCUR '92. Proceedings. X, 580 pages. 1992.

Vol. 631: M. Bruynooghe, M. Wirsing (Eds.), Programming Language Implementation and Logic Programming. Proceedings, 1992. XI, 492 pages. 1992.

Vol. 632: H. Kirchner, G. Levi (Eds.), Algebraic and Logic Programming. Proceedings, 1992. IX, 457 pages. 1992.

Vol. 633: D. Pearce, G. Wagner (Eds.), Logics in AI. Proceedings. VIII, 410 pages. 1992. (Subseries LNAI).

Vol. 634: L. Bougé, M. Cosnard, Y. Robert, D. Trystram (Eds.), Parallel Processing: CONPAR 92 – VAPP V. Proceedings. XVII, 853 pages. 1992.

Vol. 635: J. C. Derniame (Ed.), Software Process Technology. Proceedings, 1992. VIII, 253 pages. 1992.

Vol. 636: G. Comyn, N. E. Fuchs, M. J. Ratcliffe (Eds.), Logic Programming in Action. Proceedings, 1992. X, 324 pages. 1992. (Subseries LNAI).

Vol. 637: Y. Bekkers, J. Cohen (Eds.), Memory Management. Proceedings, 1992. XI, 525 pages. 1992.

Vol. 639: A. U. Frank, I. Campari, U. Formentini (Eds.), Theories and Methods of Spatio-Temporal Reasoning in Geographic Space. Proceedings, 1992. XI, 431 pages. 1992.

Vol. 640: C. Sledge (Ed.), Software Engineering Education. Proceedings, 1992. X, 451 pages. 1992.

Vol. 641: U. Kastens, P. Pfahler (Eds.), Compiler Construction. Proceedings, 1992. VIII, 320 pages. 1992.

Vol. 642: K. P. Jantke (Ed.), Analogical and Inductive Inference. Proceedings, 1992. VIII, 319 pages. 1992. (Subseries LNAI).

Vol. 643: A. Habel, Hyperedge Replacement: Grammars and Languages. X, 214 pages. 1992.

Vol. 644: A. Apostolico, M. Crochemore, Z. Galil, U. Manber (Eds.), Combinatorial Pattern Matching. Proceedings, 1992. X, 287 pages. 1992.

Vol. 645: G. Pernul, A M. Tjoa (Eds.), Entity-Relationship Approach – ER '92. Proceedings, 1992. XI, 439 pages, 1992.

Vol. 646: J. Biskup, R. Hull (Eds.), Database Theory – ICDT '92. Proceedings, 1992. IX, 449 pages. 1992.

Vol. 647: A. Segall, S. Zaks (Eds.), Distributed Algorithms. X, 380 pages. 1992.

Vol. 648: Y. Deswarte, G. Eizenberg, J.-J. Quisquater (Eds.), Computer Security – ESORICS 92. Proceedings. XI, 451 pages. 1992.

Vol. 649: A. Pettorossi (Ed.), Meta-Programming in Logic. Proceedings, 1992. XII, 535 pages. 1992.

Vol. 650: T. Ibaraki, Y. Inagaki, K. Iwama, T. Nishizeki, M. Yamashita (Eds.), Algorithms and Computation. Proceedings, 1992. XI, 510 pages. 1992.

Vol. 651: R. Koymans, Specifying Message Passing and Time-Critical Systems with Temporal Logic. IX, 164 pages. 1992.

Vol. 652: R. Shyamasundar (Ed.), Foundations of Software Technology and Theoretical Computer Science. Proceedings, 1992. XIII, 405 pages. 1992.

Vol. 653: A. Bensoussan, J.-P. Verjus (Eds.), Future Tendencies in Computer Science, Control and Applied Mathematics. Proceedings, 1992. XV, 371 pages. 1992.

Vol. 654: A. Nakamura, M. Nivat, A. Saoudi, P. S. P. Wang, K. Inoue (Eds.), Prallel Image Analysis. Proceedings, 1992. VIII, 312 pages. 1992.

Vol. 655: M. Bidoit, C. Choppy (Eds.), Recent Trends in Data Type Specification. X, 344 pages. 1993.

Vol. 656: M. Rusinowitch, J. L. Rémy (Eds.), Conditional Term Rewriting Systems. Proceedings, 1992. XI, 501 pages. 1993.

Vol. 657: E. W. Mayr (Ed.), Graph-Theoretic Concepts in Computer Science. Proceedings, 1992. VIII, 350 pages. 1993.

Vol. 658: R. A. Rueppel (Ed.), Advances in Cryptology – EUROCRYPT '92. Proceedings, 1992. X, 493 pages. 1993.

Vol. 659: G. Brewka, K. P. Jantke, P. H. Schmitt (Eds.), Nonmonotonic and Inductive Logic. Proceedings, 1991. VIII, 332 pages. 1993. (Subseries LNAI).

Vol. 660: E. Lamma, P. Mello (Eds.), Extensions of Logic Programming. Proceedings, 1992. VIII, 417 pages. 1993. (Subseries LNAI).

Vol. 661: S. J. Hanson, W. Remmele, R. L. Rivest (Eds.), Machine Learning: From Theory to Applications. VIII, 271 pages. 1993.

Vol. 662: M. Nitzberg, D. Mumford, T. Shiota, Filtering, Segmentation and Depth. VIII, 143 pages. 1993.

Vol. 663: G. v. Bochmann, D. K. Probst (Eds.), Computer Aided Verification. Proceedings, 1992. IX, 422 pages. 1993.

Vol. 664: M. Bezem, J. F. Groote (Eds.), Typed Lambda Calculi and Applications. Proceedings, 1993. VIII, 433 pages. 1993.

Vol. 665: P. Enjalbert, A. Finkel, K. W. Wagner (Eds.), STACS 93. Proceedings, 1993. XIV, 724 pages. 1993.